A-Z WEST YORK[illegible]E

CONTENTS

Key to Map Pages	2-3
Map Pages	4-169
Index to Str[illegible]ages and selected [illegible] of Interest	170-254
Index to Hospitals, Health Centres and Hospices	255-256

REFERENCE

Motorway	M1
Proposed	
A Road	A61
Under Construction	
Proposed	
B Road	B6157
Dual Carriageway	
One Way Street Traffic flow on A Roads is indicated by a heavy line on the driver's left.	
Restricted Access	
Pedestrianized Road	
City Centre Loop	
Residential Walkway	
Track / Footpath	
Local Authority Boundary	
Posttown Boundary	
Postcode Boundary	
National Park Boundary	
Railway	Station, Private Sta., Level Crossing, Tunnel
Built Up Area	ALMA ST.

Map Continuation	80
Car Park	P
Church or Chapel	†
Fire Station	■
House Numbers (A & B Roads only)	13 8
Hospital	H
Information Centre	i
National Grid Reference	430
Police Station	▲
Post Office	★
Toilet with facilities for the Disabled	
Viewpoint	
Educational Establishment	
Hospital or Health Centre	
Industrial Building	
Leisure or Recreational Facility	
Place of Interest	
Public Building	
Shopping Centre or Market	
Other Selected Buildings	

SCALE

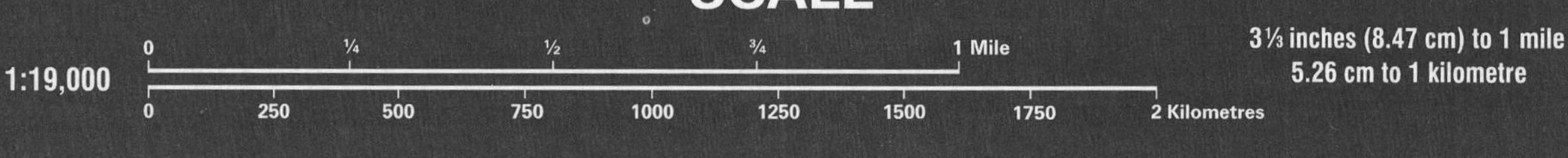

1:19,000
0
¼
½
¾
1 Mile
0
250
500
750
1000
1250
1500
1750
2 Kilometres
3⅓ inches (8.47 cm) to 1 mile
5.26 cm to 1 kilometre

Head Office:

Fairfield Road, Borough Green, Sevenoaks, Kent, TN15 8PP
Telephone 01732 781000

Showrooms:

44 Gray's Inn Road, London, WC1X 8HX
Telephone 020 7440 9500

Edition 1 2000

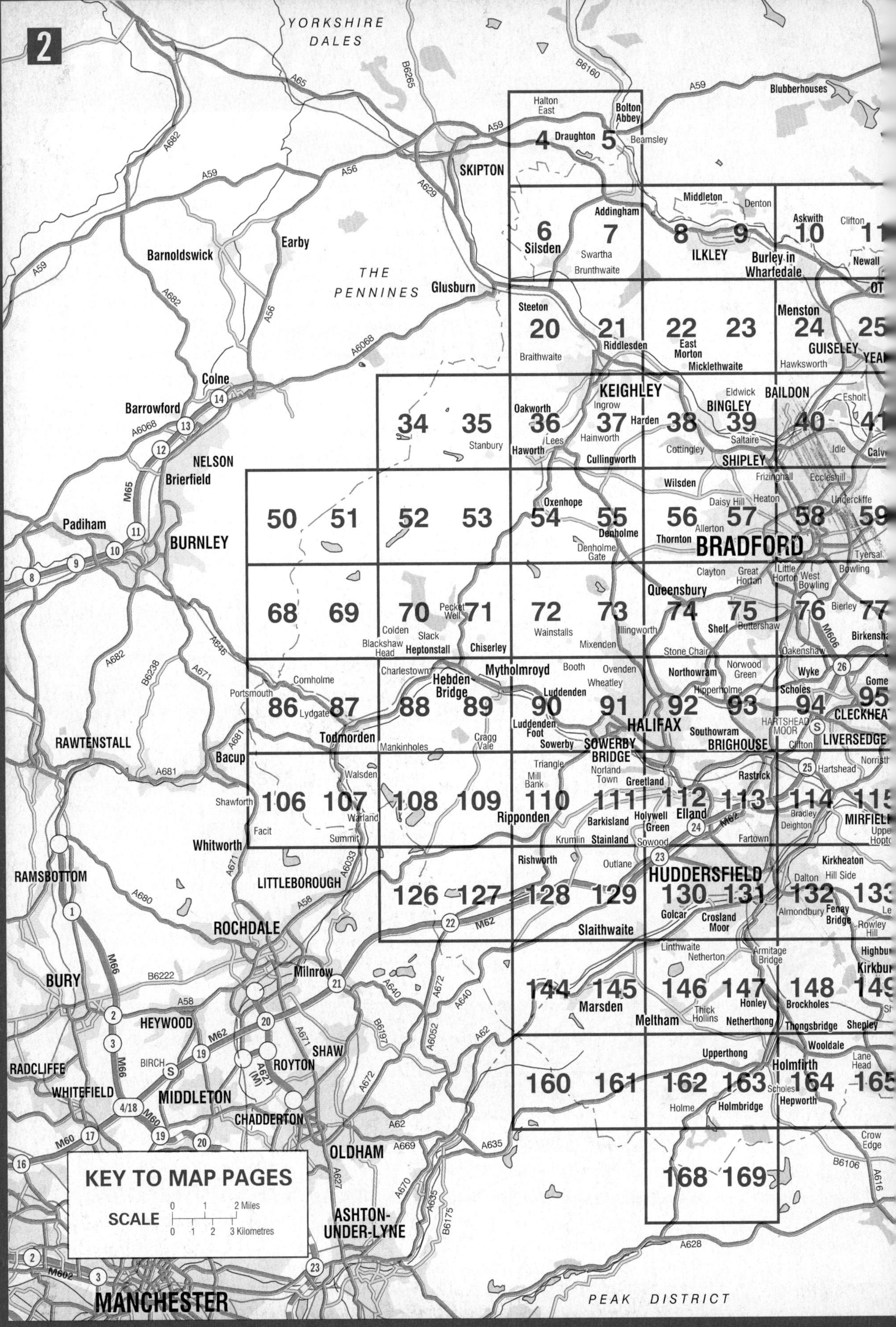
KEY TO MAP PAGES
SCALE
0 1 2 Miles
0 1 2 3 Kilometres
YORKSHIRE DALES
THE PENNINES
PEAK DISTRICT
Halton East
Bolton Abbey
4 Draughton 5
Beamsley
Blubberhouses
SKIPTON
Middleton
Denton
Addingham
6 Silsden
7 Swartha Brunthwaite
8 ILKLEY 9
Askwith 10
Clifton 11
Burley in Wharfedale
Newall
Barnoldswick
Earby
Glusburn
Steeton
20 Braithwaite
21 Riddlesden
22 East Morton
23 Micklethwaite
Menston 24 GUISELEY
25
Hawksworth
Colne
Barrowford
NELSON
Brierfield
KEIGHLEY
Ingrow
Oakworth
34 35 Stanbury
36 Haworth Lees
37 Hainworth
Harden 38 Cottingley
Eldwick BINGLEY 39 Saltaire
SHIPLEY
BAILDON
Esholt
40 Idle
41
Cullingworth
Padiham
BURNLEY
50 51 52 53
Oxenhope 54
55 Denholme
Denholme Gate
Wilsden
56 Thornton
Daisy Hill
Heaton
57 Allerton
BRADFORD
Frizinghall
Eccleshill
Undercliffe
58 59
Tyersal
Bowling
Clayton
Great Horton
Little Horton
West Bowling
Queensbury
68 69
70 Colden Slack
Pecket Well 71
Blackshaw Head
Heptonstall
Chiserley
72 Wainstalls
73 Mixenden
Illingworth
74 Stone Chair
75 Shelf Buttershaw
76 Bierley
77 Birkenshaw
Oakenshaw
RAWTENSTALL
Bacup
Portsmouth
Cornholme
86 Lydgate 87
Todmorden
Charlestown
88 Hebden-Bridge 89
Mytholmroyd
Cragg Vale
Mankinholes
Booth
Ovenden
Wheatley
Luddenden 90
Luddenden Foot
Sowerby
91 HALIFAX
SOWERBY BRIDGE
Northowram
Norwood Green
92 Hipperholme 93
Southowram
BRIGHOUSE
Wyke
Scholes
94
Gomersal
95
CLECKHEATON
HARTSHEAD MOOR
Clifton
LIVERSEDGE
Norristhorpe
Hartshead
Shawforth
106 Facit
107 Walsden Warland Summit
108 109
Triangle
Mill Bank
110 Ripponden
Norland Town
Greetland
111 Barkisland
Holywell Green
Stainland
112 Elland
Rastrick
113 Fartown
114 Bradley Deighton
MIRFIELD
Whitworth
RAMSBOTTOM
LITTLEBOROUGH
Krumlin
Sowood
Rishworth
Outlane
HUDDERSFIELD
Kirkheaton
Dalton
Hill Side
126 127 128 129
130 Golcar
131 Crosland Moor
132 Almondbury
Fenay Bridge
Rowley Hill
ROCHDALE
Slaithwaite
Linthwaite
Netherton
Armitage Bridge
Highburton
Kirkburton
BURY
Milnrow
144 145 Marsden
146 Meltham
Thick Hollins
147 Honley
Netherthong
148 Brockholes
Thongsbridge
Shepley
HEYWOOD
SHAW
ROYTON
BIRCH
Wooldale
Upperthong
Holmfirth
Lane Head
RADCLIFFE
WHITEFIELD
MIDDLETON
160 161
162 Holme
163 Scholes Holmbridge
164 Hepworth
165
CHADDERTON
OLDHAM
Crow Edge
168 169
ASHTON-UNDER-LYNE
MANCHESTER
A59
A65
A56
A629
A682
A6068
A646
A671
A681
A680
A6033
A58
A640
A672
A6052
A62
A627
A627(M)
A669
A670
A635
A628
A616
B6160
B6265
B6238
B6222
B6197
B6175
B6106
M65
M66
M62
M60
M602
M606

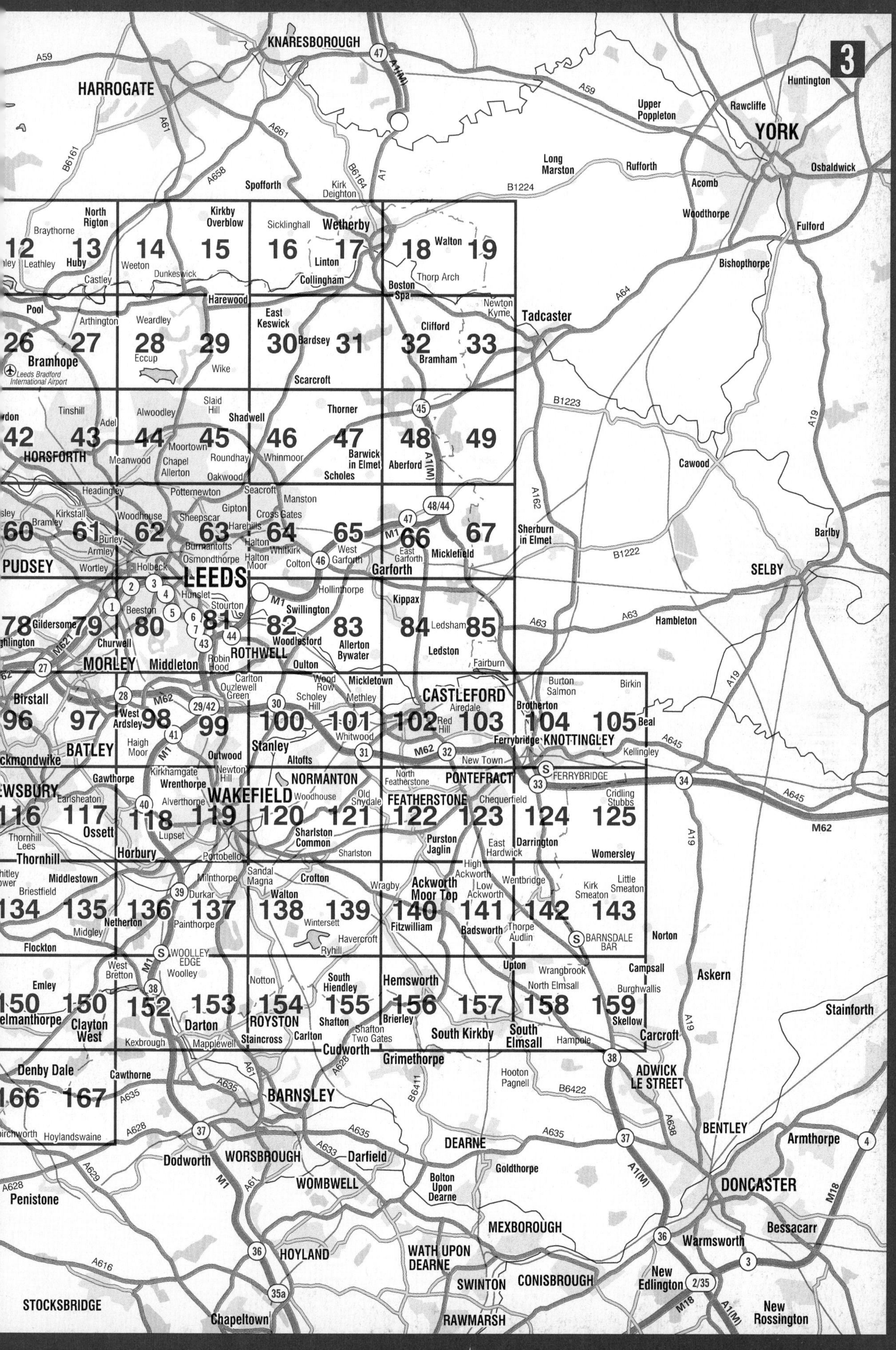
KNARESBOROUGH
HARROGATE
YORK
Huntington
Rawcliffe
Upper Poppleton
Long Marston
Rufforth
Acomb
Osbaldwick
Woodthorpe
Fulford
Bishopthorpe
Spofforth
Kirk Deighton
Wetherby
Sicklinghall
North Rigton
Braythorne
Kirkby Overblow
Leathley
Huby
Weeton
Dunkeswick
Castley
Linton
Collingham
Walton
Thorp Arch
Boston Spa
Harewood
Pool
Arthington
Weardley
East Keswick
Bardsey
Clifford
Newton Kyme
Tadcaster
Bramhope
Eccup
Wike
Scarcroft
Bramham
Leeds Bradford International Airport
Tinshill
Adel
Alwoodley
Slaid Hill
Shadwell
Thorner
HORSFORTH
Moortown
Roundhay
Whinmoor
Barwick in Elmet
Aberford
Scholes
Meanwood
Chapel Allerton
Oakwood
Cawood
Headingley
Potternewton
Seacroft
Manston
Kirkstall
Bramley
Woodhouse
Sheepscar
Gipton
Cross Gates
Harehills
Burley
Armley
Burmantofts
Osmondthorpe
Halton
Whitkirk
Halton Moor
Colton
West Garforth
East Garforth
Micklefield
Sherburn in Elmet
Barlby
PUDSEY
Wortley
Holbeck
LEEDS
Garforth
SELBY
Hunslet
Stourton
Hollinthorpe
Kippax
Beeston
Swillington
Ledsham
Hambleton
Gildersome
Churwell
Woodlesford
Allerton Bywater
Ledston
MORLEY
Middleton
Robin Hood
ROTHWELL
Oulton
Fairburn
Carlton
Ouzlewell Green
Wood Row
Mickletown
Burton Salmon
Birkin
Birstall
West Ardsley
Scholey Hill
Methley
CASTLEFORD
Airedale
Brotherton
Red Hill
Whitwood
Beal
BATLEY
Haigh Moor
Stanley
Outwood
Altofts
Ferrybridge
KNOTTINGLEY
Kellingley
New Town
Gawthorpe
Kirkhamgate
Wrenthorpe
Newton Hill
NORMANTON
North Featherstone
PONTEFRACT
FERRYBRIDGE
Earlsheaton
Alverthorpe
WAKEFIELD
Woodhouse
Old Snydale
FEATHERSTONE
Chequerfield
Cridling Stubbs
Ossett
Thornhill Lees
Lupset
Sharlston Common
Purston Jaglin
East Hardwick
Darrington
Thornhill
Horbury
Portobello
Sharlston
Womersley
Middlestown
Milnthorpe
Sandal Magna
Crofton
Wragby
High Ackworth
Ackworth Moor Top
Low Ackworth
Wentbridge
Kirk Smeaton
Little Smeaton
Briestfield
Durkar
Walton
Netherton
Painthorpe
Wintersett
Fitzwilliam
Badsworth
Thorpe Audlin
BARNSDALE BAR
Norton
Midgley
Havercroft
Ryhill
Flockton
WOOLLEY EDGE
Woolley
West Bretton
Upton
Wrangbrook
Campsall
Askern
Emley
Notton
South Hiendley
Hemsworth
North Elmsall
Burghwallis
Stainforth
Clayton West
Darton
ROYSTON
Shafton
Brierley
South Kirkby
South Elmsall
Skellow
Kexbrough
Mapplewell
Staincross
Carlton
Shafton Two Gates
Hampole
Carcroft
Cudworth
Grimethorpe
Denby Dale
Cawthorne
Hooton Pagnell
ADWICK LE STREET
BARNSLEY
Hoylandswaine
BENTLEY
Armthorpe
Dodworth
WORSBROUGH
Darfield
DEARNE
Goldthorpe
Bolton Upon Dearne
WOMBWELL
DONCASTER
Penistone
MEXBOROUGH
Bessacarr
Warmsworth
HOYLAND
WATH UPON DEARNE
SWINTON
CONISBROUGH
New Edlington
STOCKSBRIDGE
Chapeltown
RAWMARSH
New Rossington
A59
A61
A661
A658
B6161
B6164
A1
A1(M)
B1224
A64
B1223
A162
A19
B1222
A63
M1
M621
M62
A645
A628
A635
A633
A629
A616
B6411
B6422
A638
M18
12
13
14
15
16
17
18
19
26
27
28
29
30
31
32
33
42
43
44
45
46
47
48
49
60
61
62
63
64
65
66
67
78
79
80
81
82
83
84
85
96
97
98
99
100
101
102
103
104
105
116
117
118
119
120
121
122
123
124
125
134
135
136
137
138
139
140
141
142
143
150
150
152
153
154
155
156
157
158
159
166
167

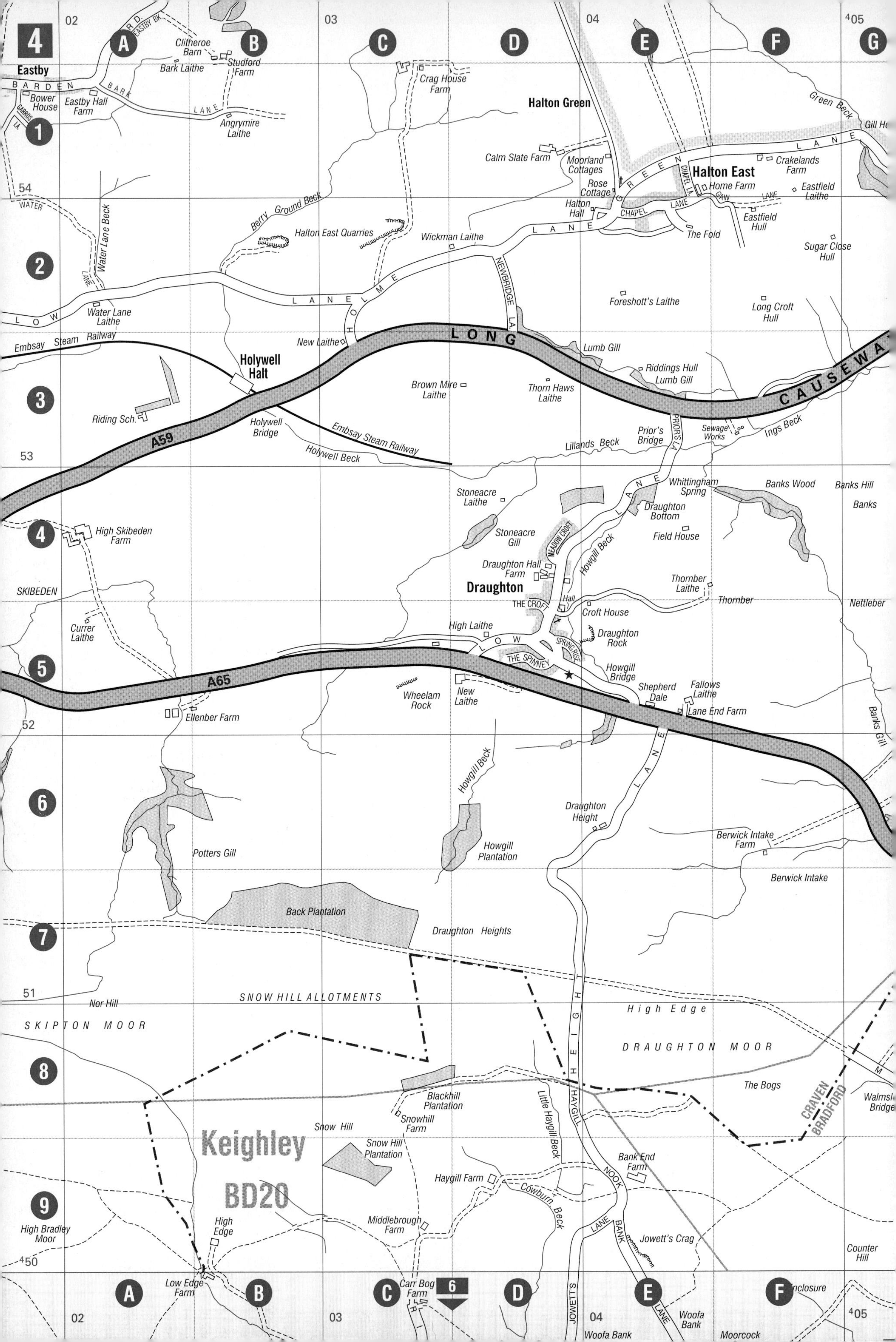

Eastby
Halton Green
Halton East
Holywell Halt
Draughton
Keighley
BD20
LONG CAUSEWAY
A59
A65
Embsay Steam Railway
Clitheroe Barn
Studford Farm
Bark Laithe
Bower House
Eastby Hall Farm
Angrymire Laithe
Crag House Farm
Calm Slate Farm
Moorland Cottages
Rose Cottage
Halton Hall
Crakelands Farm
Home Farm
Eastfield Laithe
Eastfield Hull
The Fold
Sugar Close Hull
Berry Ground Beck
Halton East Quarries
Wickman Laithe
Water Lane Beck
Water Lane Laithe
Foreshott's Laithe
Long Croft Hull
New Laithe
Lumb Gill
Riddings Hull
Brown Mire Laithe
Thorn Haws Laithe
Riding Sch.
Holywell Bridge
Holywell Beck
Lillands Beck
Prior's Bridge
Sewage Works
Ings Beck
Whittingham Spring
Banks Wood
Banks Hill
Banks
Stoneacre Laithe
Draughton Bottom
Field House
Stoneacre Gill
High Skibeden Farm
SKIBEDEN
Draughton Hall Farm
Howgill Beck
Thornber Laithe
Thornber
Nettleber
Croft House
Currer Laithe
High Laithe
Draughton Rock
Howgill Bridge
Shepherd Dale
Fallows Laithe
Lane End Farm
Wheelam Rock
New Laithe
Ellenber Farm
Banks Gill
Draughton Height
Berwick Intake Farm
Berwick Intake
Howgill Plantation
Potters Gill
Back Plantation
Draughton Heights
SNOW HILL ALLOTMENTS
Nor Hill
SKIPTON MOOR
High Edge
DRAUGHTON MOOR
The Bogs
CRAVEN
BRADFORD
Walmsley Bridge
Blackhill Plantation
Snowhill Farm
Snow Hill
Snow Hill Plantation
Little Haygill Beck
Bank End Farm
Haygill Farm
Cowburn Beck
Middlebrough Farm
Jowett's Crag
High Edge
High Bradley Moor
Counter Hill
Low Edge Farm
Carr Bog Farm
Enclosure
Woofa Bank
Moorcock

6

Skipton
BD23
Ilkley
LS29
Bolton Abbey
Bolton Bridge
Beamsley
Storiths
ADDINGHAM
YORKSHIRE DALES
NATIONAL PARK
A59
A65
B6160
BOLTON ROAD
WHARFEDALE ROAD
RIVER WHARFE
CHELKER RESERVOIR
BRACKEN GHYLL GOLF COURSE
HIGH PARK
LOW PARK
WARD HILL
CRIER HILL
ADDINGHAM LOW MOOR
Halton Gill Wood
Lythe Bank Bridge
Hambleton Cottages
Hambleton Farm
Railway Cottages
Hambleton Beck
Hesketh House
New Laithe
Catgill
Laverock Laithe
West Bank Wood
Stank House
Scar Top Seat
Bolton Hall
The Arches
Remains of Bolton Priory
Waterfall Bridge
Skiphouse Wheel Scar
Little Bridge
Tithe Barn
Cavendish Memorial
Ungain Deep
Dark Parlour
Dixon's Deep
Stepping Stones
Ungain Terrace
Cat Crags
Wandsworth Wood
Prior's Seat
Back o'th'Hill Farm
Banks Farm
Storiths Crag
Stoney Haw Spring
Hill Top Farm
Town End Farm
Storiths House Farm
Low House Farm
Raven's Gill
Raven's Gill Dike
Strawberry Bank Wood
Prior's Pool
The Strand
New Hall
Struff Wood
Holly Walk Seat
Tough Bank
Tough Bank Deep
Rocks Hill Plantation
Hospital Farm
Oakfield House
Lanehouse Farm
Oaks Hill
Deerstones Plantation
Bowers Hill
Hotel
Huffa Bri.
Cricket Ground
Flat Bri.
Bolton Bri.
Red Lion Farm
Scar Close Seat
The Boyle & Petyt School
The Lodge
Hardy Grange
Mill Race
Beamsley Hall
Beamsley Bridge
Caravan Park
Mill
Ford
Goose Hill
Resphill
Resphill Wood
Westhill Busks
Whitaker's Wood
Cargarth Wood
Harry Wall Gill
Waterfall
Haw Pike
Lob Wood
Lobwood Laithe
Eller Carr Wood
Berwick East
Berwick West
Weir
Lobwood House
Paradise Lathe
Strawberry Bank Wood
Thurstones Beck
Heald Wood
Farfield Hall
Little Round Plantation
Fulbrow Wood
Lowfield Farm
Heald Laithe
Heald Plain
Reservoir (Covered)
Hag Head Laithe
Newlands Gill
Hare Knoll
Pumping Sta.
Highfield Farm
Chelker House Farm
Syke House
Hag Laithe
Cunliffe Wood
Lathehouse Beck
Upper White Well
Low Sanfitt
Highfield House
Farfield House
Little Laithe
Stephen Bank Wood
Longlands
Low White Well
High Sanfitt
Hart House
Riddings Farm
Wine Beck
High Bank Cross
Cross Bank
Cross Bank Delf
Causeway Foot
Prospect House
Heathness Gill
Heathness Bridge
Club House
Vicar Wood
Back Beck
Chandler's Cote
Wine Beck Bridge
Addingham First Sch.
Addingham Mid. Sch.
High Mill
West Hall
Dales Way
Rec. Grd.
Hunterland
Saw Mill
Lib.
Chapel
WEST HALL LANE
LOW FIELD LANE
LANSHAW BANK
BEAMSLEY LANE
STORITHS LANE
HUFFA LANE
SKIPTON ROAD
CROSS BANK ROAD
MOOR LANE
SCHOOL LANE
MAIN ST.
BOLTON RD.
LONG RIDDINGS
HIGH MILL LA.
BARK LANE
SPRINGFIELD MT.
BACK BECK LA.
SUGAR HILL
CHAPEL ST.
BURNS HILL
TURNER LA.
PARSON'S LANE
HODGSON FOLD
H
J
K
L
M
N
G
1
2
3
4
5
6
7
8
9
06
07
08
54
53
52
51
50

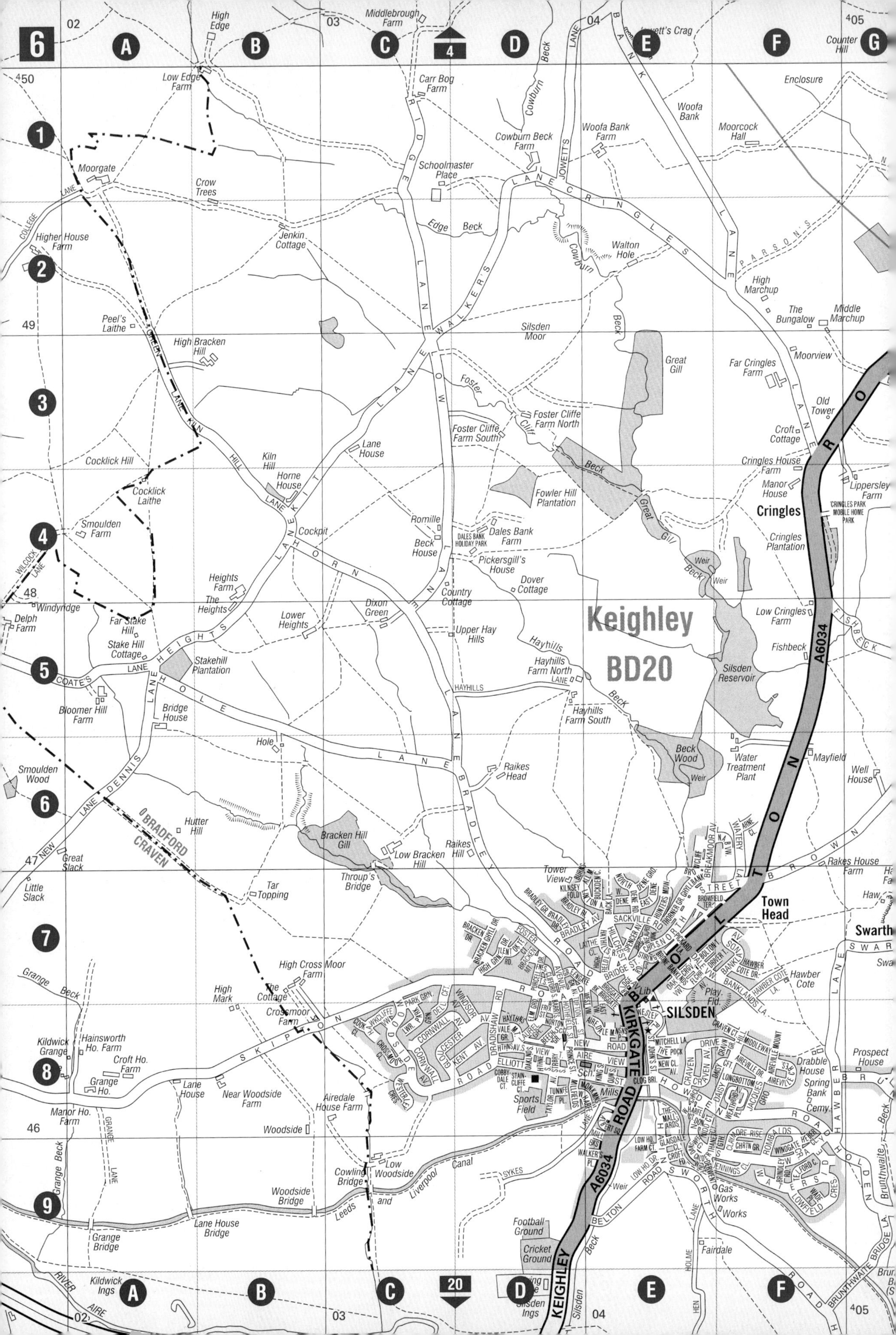
02
03
04
405
A
B
C
D
E
F
G
4
450
49
48
47
46
1
2
3
4
5
6
7
8
9
High Edge
Middlebrough Farm
Jowett's Crag
Counter Hill
Low Edge Farm
Carr Bog Farm
Enclosure
Woofa Bank
Cowburn
Cowburn Beck Farm
Woofa Bank Farm
Moorcock Hall
Moorgate
Crow Trees
Schoolmaster Place
Jowett's Lane
Cringles Lane
College Lane
Higher House Farm
Jenkin Cottage
Edge Beck
Walton Hole
Parson's Lane
High Marchup
The Bungalow
Middle Marchup
Peel's Laithe
High Bracken Hill
Silsden Moor
Walker's Lane
Ridge Lane
Great Gill
Far Cringles Farm
Moorview
Foster Cliff Beck
Foster Cliffe Farm North
Foster Cliffe Farm South
Old Tower
Croft Cottage
Kiln Hill Lane
Cocklick Hill
Kiln Hill
Lane House
Horne House
Fowler Hill Plantation
Cringles House Farm
Manor House
Lippersley Farm
Cringles
Cringles Park Mobile Home Park
Cocklick Laithe
Smoulden Farm
Cockpit
Romille
Beck House
Dales Bank Farm
Dales Bank Holiday Park
Great Gill Beck
Cringles Plantation
Wilcock Lane
Horn Lane
Pickersgill's House
Dover Cottage
Weir
Heights Farm
The Heights
Windyridge
Delph Farm
Far Stake Hill
Lower Heights
Dixon Green
Country Cottage
Upper Hay Hills
Keighley
BD20
Low Cringles Farm
Fishbeck
Fishbeck Lane
Stake Hill Cottage
Heights Lane
Coate's Lane
Stakehill Plantation
Hayhills
Hayhills Farm North
Hayhills Lane
Silsden Reservoir
A6034
Bloomer Hill Farm
Bridge House
Hole Lane
Hole
Hayhills Farm South
Beck
Beck Wood
Water Treatment Plant
Mayfield
Smoulden Wood
Dennis Lane
New Lane
Raikes Head
Well House
Bradley Lane
Bradford
Craven
Hutter Hill
Bracken Hill Gill
Low Bracken Hill
Raikes Hill
Great Slack
Little Slack
Throup's Bridge
Tar Topping
Tower View
Rakes House Farm
Brown Lane
Bolton Road
Town Head
Swartha
Grange Beck
High Cross Moor Farm
High Mark
The Cottage
Crossmoor Farm
Skipton Road
Silsden
Kirkgate
Hawber Cote
Play Fld.
Sports Field
Kildwick Grange
Hainsworth Ho. Farm
Croft Ho. Farm
Grange Ho.
Lane House
Near Woodside Farm
Airedale House Farm
Drabble House
Prospect House
Spring Bank Cemy.
Manor Ho. Farm
Woodside
Mills
Keighley Road
Howden Road
Hawber Lane
Grange Lane
Low Woodside
Cowling Bridge
Leeds and Liverpool Canal
Sykes
Woodside Bridge
Lane House Bridge
Grange Bridge
Gas Works
Works
Brunthwaite
Football Ground
Cricket Ground
Belton Road
Low Ho. Dr.
Holme Lane
Fairdale
Brunthwaite Bridge La.
Kildwick Ings
River Aire
Silsden Ings
20

ADDINGHAM LOW MOOR
Causeway Foot
Prospect House
Esholt Well
Lower Turner Lane Farm
Lower Marchup
Marchup Beck
Marchup Height
SILSDEN ROAD A6034
ADDINGHAM WHARFEDALE RD.
MOOR LANE
Hunterland
Rec. Grd.
Street House Farm
SILSDEN ADDINGHAM
Dark Wood
Addingham First Sch.
ADDINGHAM
MAIN RD.
B6160
ST.
BOLTON RD.
Saw Mill
Mem. Hall
New Town
Pav.
Cricket Ground
Southfield Farm
A65 WHARFEDALE ROAD
Ilkley LS29
Little Round Wood
Street Farm
Addingham Middle Moor
Nudge Hill Farm
Coppy Hill
High House
Gildersber
Hart Rhydding Wood
Throstle Nest
Lumb Gill Wood
Lumb Gill
Briarfield
COCKING LANE
Delf Hill
Middlemoor Farm
Nudge Hill
Addingham Middle Moor
Brocka Bank Farm
Small Banks
Spring Gill Wood
Plumbtree Banks Lathe
Brook's Hill
Valve Chamber
Brook's Crag
Sea Moor Hill
Brocka Bank Hill
High Brocka Bank
Nudge Well
Four Lanes End
Brocka Bank Moor
School Wood
Cuckoo's Nest
Gate Croft
Pentley Hill
Nudge Hill
High House Farm
Caravan Park
Stegg House
Low Lathe
Over Gate Croft
Potters Pits
Sea Moor Farm
STRAIGHT LANE
School Wood Farm
Hodson's Farm
Fell Edge Farm
Ghyll House Farm
Lower Hang Goose Farm
Hang Goose Farm
Slade
Asker Hill
Crag House Farm
BROWN BANK CARAVAN SITE
Scar Gill
MOORSIDE LANE
Sunny Bank Farm
Upper Gatecroft Farm
Addingham Moorside
Cragg House
Hardwick Cottage
ROMBALDS MOOR
Brown Bank
Hugh Teal Spring
Millstone Lumps
Nab End
Windgate Nick
Hugh Teal Hall
Addingham Crag
Noon Stone
Hardwick Holes
Light Bank
Bunthwaite Beck
High Swartha Farm
Black Hill
White Crag Plantation
ADDINGHAM HIGH MOOR
Cote Close
Butts
Long Ridge End
Grouse Butts
North End Farm
Swartha Wood
Aqueduct
Gawk Stones
Madjam Maw
Doubler Stones
Crag Top
White Crag Moor
Brunthwaite Crag
Brunthwaite Crag Wood
LIGHT BANK LANE
Doubler Stones House
Churns
Hutter Hill
JERRY LA.
Black Pots Farm
High Brunthwaite
Townhead House
Club House
Brunthwaite
Cloven Stones
Pump House
GHYLL GRANGE LANE
Ghyll Grange House
Ghyll Grange
Far Ghyll Grange Farm
SILSDEN GOLF COURSE
Tomling Cote Farm
Spinner Beck
Weir
Gill Grange Clough
HIGH MOOR
Holden Beck
Tongue End
Waterfalls
Ford
Lumb Bridge
Scour Valve
Jacob's Wood
RIVOCK EDGE
Holden Bridge
Bucking Hill
Out Laith
5
8
21
06
07
08
49
48
47
46
450

A
B
C
D
E
F
G
09
410
11
450
49
48
47
46
1
2
3
4
5
6
7
8
9
West Hall
Park Wood
Raw Riddings
Nessfield Court
Cat Holes Wood
Lower Dene Farm
Dean
Dean Beck
The Manor Ho.
Owler Wood
The Studio
Nesfield
Fort
Low Holme House
Low Mill Village
Weir
Castleberg Scar
Low Mills
Sewage Works
WHARFEDALE ROAD
A65
SKIPTON ROAD
Austby Wood
High Austby Farm
Sion Hill
North Plantation
Primrose Hill
Windsover Farm
Ing Gills
Old Wives Gill
HARROGATE
BRADFORD
Friars Hill
Tivoli
Austby Gill or Spring Wood
Low Austby
Austby
Laurel Spring
Myddelton Lodge
The Hollies
Pawpots
Terrace Gill
Crabtree Gill
Coppy Wood
Owler Park
Lumb Gill Wood
Lumb Gill
Lumb Ghyll Farm
Hall Gill
Cocking Wood
Wilow Garth
ILKLEY GOLF GOURSE
Hawksworth Island
Spring Bottom
Club Ho.
Plumbtree Banks Lathe
Riddings Lathe
Reynard Ing
Cocking End
Greenwood Wood
Ilkley
Sports Centre
Tennis Cts.
Pav.
Playing Field
Dales Way
The Hollis
Hadfield Farm
LS29
Over Gate Croft
Hollin Hall
Netherwood House Farm
Riverside Gardens
Fish Field
Cragg House
Rams Gill
Briery Wood
Heber's Ghyll
School
Hardwick Cottage
Hardwick House Farm
Briery Wood Farm
Brackenwood
Bracken Wood
Hardwick Holes
Piper's Crag
Rabbit House
Hospice
Parish Ghyll
Bradford & Ilkley Comm. Coll.
Undercrag
Panorama Rocks
Panorama Woods Cup-Marked Rock
Westwood Cottage
Woodhouse Crag
Swastika Stone
Panorama Reservoir
Hill Top Reservoir (covered)
Long Ridge
High Crag
Intake Heads
Intake Beck
Silver Well Cottage
Silver Well (covered)
Barmishaw
Willy Hall's Spout
Long Ridge End
Sluice
Black Beck Hole
Cup & Ring-Marked Rocks
Barmishaw Well (covered)
Grouse Butts
Reservoir (covered)
Weary Hill
Barmishaw Hole
Crawshaw Spring
Coarse Stone Edge
Neb Stone
Cup Marked Rock
Silver Well
Cup & Ring-Marked Rocks
ILKLEY MOOR
Crawshaw Moss
Black Beck Head
Bare Hill
Shepherd's Hill
Waterfall
Grainings Head
Heber Moss
Green Gates
Keighley
HIGH MOOR
BD20
Sike Head
East Buck Stones
West Buck Stones
Cowper's Cross
Bucking Hill
Whetstone Gate
Wireless Station

7
22

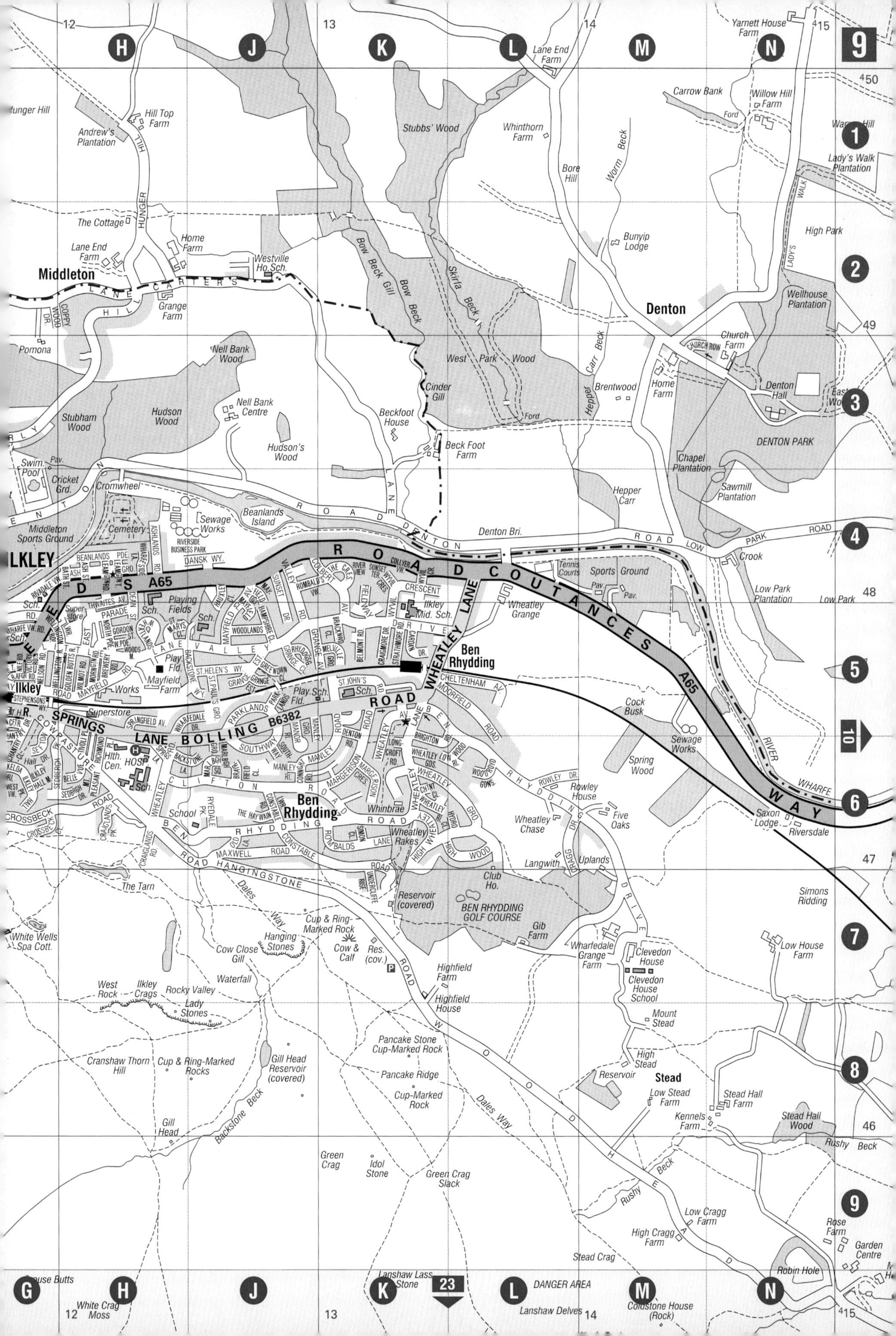

Middleton
Denton
Ilkley
Ben Rhydding
Stead
Yarnett House Farm
Lane End Farm
Carrow Bank
Willow Hill Farm
Hill Top Farm
Andrew's Plantation
Stubbs' Wood
Whinthorn Farm
Lady's Walk Plantation
Bore Hill
Worm Beck
The Cottage
High Park
Home Farm
Lane End Farm
Bunyip Lodge
Westville Ho. Sch.
Bow Beck Gill
Bow Beck
Skirfa Beck
Grange Farm
Wellhouse Plantation
Pomona
Nell Bank Wood
West Park Wood
Church Farm
Hepper Carr Beck
Cinder Gill
Brentwood
Home Farm
Denton Hall
Stubham Wood
Hudson Wood
Nell Bank Centre
Beckfoot House
Hudson's Wood
Beck Foot Farm
DENTON PARK
Chapel Plantation
Sawmill Plantation
Swim. Pool
Cricket Grd.
Cromwheel
Hepper Carr
Middleton Sports Ground
Cemetery
Sewage Works
Beanlands Island
Denton Bri.
DENTON ROAD
LOW PARK ROAD
Crook
Sports Ground
Tennis Courts
Low Park Plantation
Low Park
A65
COUTANCES WAY
Playing Fields
Ilkley Mid. Sch.
Wheatley Grange
WHEATLEY LANE
Play. Fld.
Mayfield Farm
Works
Play. Fld.
Sch.
Cock Busk
Sewage Works
Spring Wood
SPRINGS LANE
BOLLING ROAD B6382
Superstore
Hlth. Cen.
HOSP.
Rowley House
Five Oaks
Wheatley Chase
Saxon Lodge
Riversdale
RIVER WHARFE
School
Whinbrae
Wheatley Rakes
Langwith
Uplands
The Tarn
Club Ho.
Reservoir (covered)
BEN RHYDDING GOLF COURSE
Simons Ridding
Cup & Ring-Marked Rock
Hanging Stones
Cow & Calf
Res. (cov.)
Gib Farm
Wharfedale Grange Farm
Clevedon House
Clevedon House School
Low House Farm
White Wells Spa Cott.
Cow Close Gill
Waterfall
Highfield Farm
Highfield House
West Rock
Ilkley Crags
Rocky Valley
Lady Stones
Mount Stead
Pancake Stone Cup-Marked Rock
High Stead
Cranshaw Thorn Hill
Cup & Ring-Marked Rocks
Gill Head Reservoir (covered)
Pancake Ridge
Reservoir
Cup-Marked Rock
Low Stead Farm
Stead Hall Farm
Kennels Farm
Stead Hall Wood
Rushy Beck
Dales Way
Gill Head
Backstone Beck
Green Crag
Idol Stone
Green Crag Slack
Low Cragg Farm
Rose Farm
High Cragg Farm
Garden Centre
Stead Crag
Robin Hole
Lanshaw Lass Stone
DANGER AREA
Lanshaw Delves
Coldstone House (Rock)
White Crag Moss
WHARFEDALE ROAD
CROSSBECK
HANGINGSTONE ROAD

10

23

Bunker's Hill
Warren Hill
Lady's Walk Plantation
Robins
Scales Gill
Ramsden's Spinny
Top Moorside Farm
Brickhouse Plantation
Brick House
Greystone Plantation
Pickett's Beck
St. Helen's Gill
High Park
Quarry House Farm
Scales House Farm
Moorside Farm
MOORSIDE
Wellhouse Plantation
Ford
Whin Castle Farm
Askwith Gill
Hundwith Gill
White House Farm
East Wood
Town Head
TON PARK
Whitbeck Manor
West Beck
Grassgarth Hill
Grassgarth Farm
Lodge Plantation
Butlers' Wood
Sundial Farm
Hall
Reservoir (covered)
Old Lodges
School Hill Farm
Askwith Prim.Sch.
LOW PARK ROAD
WEST LANE
Carr Wood
West Beck Farm
EAST BECK CT.
Ibbotson Farm
Carr House Farm
Askwith
Lane Top Farm
Pond House
Low Park
Askwith Nurseries
HALLAM
East Beck
Mill Dam Beck
RIVER WHARFE
Stepping Stones
Manor Park
SOUTHWAY
New Bridge
Weston Manor
Jerry Holme
Greystone Manor Farm
Greystone Manor
Wharfeside
Greenholme Farm
Weirs
The Goit
Cock Pit Farm
COUTANCES WAY ILKLEY
Esscroft Cottage
Esscroft
Riversdale
Weston
Black Bull Farm
ROAD
Hall Farm
Far Birka
Simons Ridding
Ilkley
LS29
ILKLEY A65
Greenholme Mills
GREENHOLME TRADING ESTATE
HARROGATE BRADFORD
Grove
Weston Hall
The Lake
WESTON
Near Birka
Low House Farm
SUN LANE
Catton Wood
Sch.
Grange Park
Lib.
Rec. Grd.
Vicarage
Ash Holme
Cricket Grd.
Burley Lodge
Scalebor Gill
BURLEY IN WHARFEDALE
Middle Lodge
Burley Holme
Stead Hall
Scalebor Park Farm
Rushy Beck
Burley Middle School
OTLEY ROAD
A660
Greengate House
Lund Ho. Farm
Goit Stock Farm
Weir
Colston House
Clinic
Sports Grd.
Burley in Wharfedale
Rose Farm
Garden Centre
School
BRADFORD A65 ROAD
Goit Stock Farm
Moor House
Colston Lodge
West Lodge
Maple Grange
Robin Hole
Ashburn
Reservoir (covered)
Coldstone Beck
Woodhead
Hollin Nook
A B C D E F G
1 2 3 4 5 6 7 8 9
16 17 18
415
450
49 48 47
V46d

9
24

Dobpark Wood
Middle Farm
Norwood Bottom
River Washburn
The Rough
Dob Park House Farm
Rough Plantation
LINDLEY WOOD
Weston Moor
Bride Cross Farm
Rose Tree Farm
Weston Moor Cottage
Oxmires Plantation
LINDLEY WOOD RESERVOIR
Moor Plantation
FARNLEY MOOR
Higher Carr Farm
Oxmires Hill
Farnley Crag
Crag Plantation
Crag Farm
Maverick House Farm
Mast
Lane Head Farm
Clifton
Haddockstones Plantation
Haddock Stones
Peartree Farm
Yewtree Farm
Morelane Plantation
Well Farm
Cherry Tree Farm
Sun Dial Farm
Sunnyview Farm
Yew Tree Farm
Carr Side
Middle Wood
Church Plantation
The Old Post Office
Prospect Farm
Tan House Farm
Gragview Farm
Otley
LS21
The Brow
Beckside Cottages
Newall Carr Side
Farnley
Old Smith Cottage
THORNBERRY HILL
Copmanroyd Plantation
Reservoir Plantation
Creamery Farm
Mount Pleasant Farm
Wood Hill
East Wood
Peashills Plantation
Newlands
Copmanroyd Cottages
Copmanroyd Farm
Garden House
Cricket Ground
Eastwood Cottages
Carr Banks Gill
Five Gables
The Whartons Prim. School
HARROGATE
LEEDS
Boots Well
Otley Plantation
Gallows Hill
WHARFEDALE GENERAL HOSPITAL
Thomas Chippendale Prim. School
Newall
Prince Henrys Grammar School
Throstle Nest Farm
Ashfield Inf. School
Newall Hall
The Sandbeds
Playing Field
Tennis Courts
RIVER WHARFE
Ashfield Farm
Playground
Sewage Works
Sports Ground
OTLEY
Ashfield House
Sailing Club
Otley Bri.
Cemetery
Gallows Hill
Rugby Grd.
Cricket Grd.
POOL A659
Caddy Close
Breary Close
Maple Bank Farm
Works
The Bungalow
Guycroft
Rammer's House
BOROUGHGATE
CROSS GRN.
BRIDGE ST.
FARNLEY LA.
B6451
BONDGATE
Mill Ing Br.
Lodge

Otley
LS21
Lindley
Farnley
Fishpool
Leathley
Braythorne
Knotford
LINDLEY WOOD RESERVOIR
Lindley Wood
Lindley Wood Farm
Lindley Wood Cottage
Coppice Wood
Springs Wood
Lindley Hall Farm
Lindley Green
Lindley Bottom
Lindley Warren
Lindley Bridge Lodge
Lindley Bridge
Lindley Farm
Millhill Cottage
Trout Hatchery
Elsingbottom Farm
Oliver Wood
Leathley Grange
Mill Pond
Leathley Mill
Mill Ho.
Brook House
Fishpool Farm
Pear Tree Cottage
Little London
Green Lane Farm
Hartmires
Park Farm Cottage
Park Farm
Manor Ho.
Leathley Hall
Flatts Cottage
Leathley Park or Hartmires
Leathley Bridge
Becklands
Becklands Turn
Becklands Farm
Ellers
Elm Tree Farm
River View Farm
Street Close
Leathley Field
Ashfield Farm
Crosby Close
Hugman Bank
Riffa Cottages
Stream Point
Pool Bridge
The Goit
Cricket Ground
Cartref Cottages
Cartref
Caley Lodge
Midgley Farm
Brick House
Dike
Main
Buttoner House
Moorside Farm
Beck Bottom Farm
Caps Bridge
Hilltop Farm
Mawson's Well
Robins Hill
Braythorne Farm
Gayle Farm
Green Bridge
Braythorne Cottage
Robin's Hill
Upper West End Farm
West End Farm
Smithy Ho.
Low Braythorne Farm
High Wood
West Beck
Stainburn Gill
STAINBURN BANK
LOW BANK
Low Wood
Woodbottom Farm
Fir Tree Farm
Thrispin Beck
Willow Garth
Thrispin
LEATHLEY MOOR
Hilltop Farm
Rooley Well
Scale Hill Farm
Glebe Farm
HOLD GILLS
NORTH FIELD
BARKS HILL
Leafield Bank
Holbeck
Pill White
Hensan's Beck
Guy's Bank
Oxmires Hill
Quarry Hill
Peartree Farm
Farnley Prim. Sch.
The Grove
The Kennels
The Bungalows
The Old Post Office
Gragview Farm
Old Smithy Cotts.
THORNBERRY HILL
Creamery Farm
Home Farm
The Square
Lodge
Wilderness
Farnley Hall
Cricket Ground
Pav.
East Lodge
Mick's Gill
Saw Pit Gill
Whinney Gill
Farnley Lake
Lake Plantation
RIVER WASHBURN
Eland Wood
EAST PARK
Hasling Plantation
FARNLEY PARK
Hasling Hall Farm
RIVER WHARFE
HARROGATE
LEEDS
Weir
Sewage Works
Sandbeds
Sports Ground
Playing Fields
Breary Close
Church Gill
Greystone Beck
LINDLEY WOOD
PILL WHITE LANE
COACH LANE
CINDER LANE
WHITE LANE
LEATHLEY LANE
B6161
GALE LANE
CHURCH LANE
NEW LANE
FARNLEY LA.
B6451
FARNLEY
HALL LANE
LEAFIELD
RIFFA
PARK
POOL ROAD
A659
A658
MOOR DRIVE
EAST BUSK LANE
FOULCAUSEWAY LANE
CASTLE
MILL LA.
WHARFE VW.
MANOR SQ.
CHURCHILL FLATS
WHARFE CRES.
Wks.
11
26
A B C D E F G
1 2 3 4 5 6 7 8 9
22 23 24
450 49 48 47 46

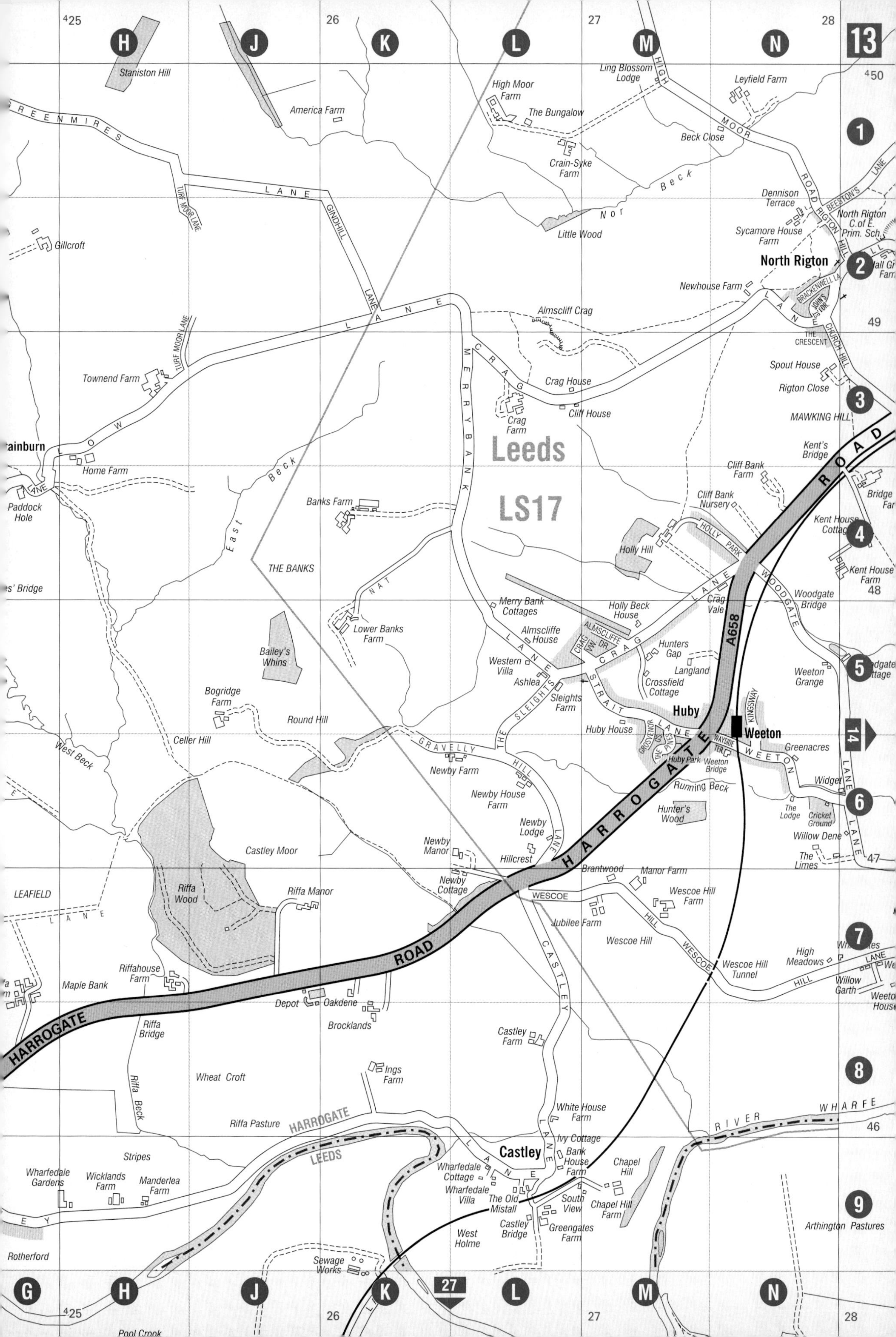
Staniston Hill
America Farm
High Moor Farm
The Bungalow
Ling Blossom Lodge
Leyfield Farm
Beck Close
Crain-Syke Farm
GREENMIRES LANE
TURF MOOR LANE
GINDHILL LANE
Nor Beck
Little Wood
Gillcroft
Dennison Terrace
Sycamore House Farm
North Rigton C.of E. Prim. Sch.
North Rigton
Newhouse Farm
Almscliff Crag
LOW LANE
Townend Farm
CRAG LANE
MERRYBANK LANE
Crag House
Cliff House
Crag Farm
Spout House
Rigton Close
MAWKING HILL
Kent's Bridge
Leeds
LS17
Home Farm
Paddock Hole
East Beck
Banks Farm
THE BANKS
Cliff Bank Farm
Cliff Bank Nursery
HOLLY PARK
Holly Hill
Kent House Cottage
Kent House Farm
Woodgate Bridge
Merry Bank Cottages
Holly Beck House
Crag Vale
Lower Banks Farm
Bailey's Whins
Almscliffe House
Western Villa
Ashlea
Hunters Gap
Langland
Crossfield Cottage
Sleights Farm
Bogridge Farm
Round Hill
Huby
Weeton
Huby House
Weeton Grange
Greenacres
Celler Hill
West Beck
GRAVELLY HILL
Newby Farm
Newby House Farm
Newby Lodge
Huby Park
Weeton Bridge
Running Beck
Hunter's Wood
The Lodge
Cricket Ground
Willow Dene
The Limes
Castley Moor
Newby Manor
Hillcrest
Brantwood
Manor Farm
Newby Cottage
LEAFIELD LANE
Riffa Wood
Riffa Manor
WESCOE
Wescoe Hill Farm
Jubilee Farm
Wescoe Hill
Wescoe Hill Tunnel
High Meadows
Willow Garth
Riffahouse Farm
Maple Bank
HARROGATE ROAD
A658
Depot
Oakdene
Brocklands
Riffa Bridge
Castley Farm
Wheat Croft
Ings Farm
Riffa Beck
White House Farm
Riffa Pasture
HARROGATE
LEEDS
RIVER WHARFE
Castley
Ivy Cottage
Bank House Farm
Chapel Hill
Stripes
Wharfedale Gardens
Wicklands Farm
Manderlea Farm
Wharfedale Cottage
Wharfedale Villa
The Old Mistall
South View
Chapel Hill Farm
Castley Bridge
Greengates Farm
West Holme
Arthington Pastures
Rotherford
Sewage Works
Pool Crook
14
27

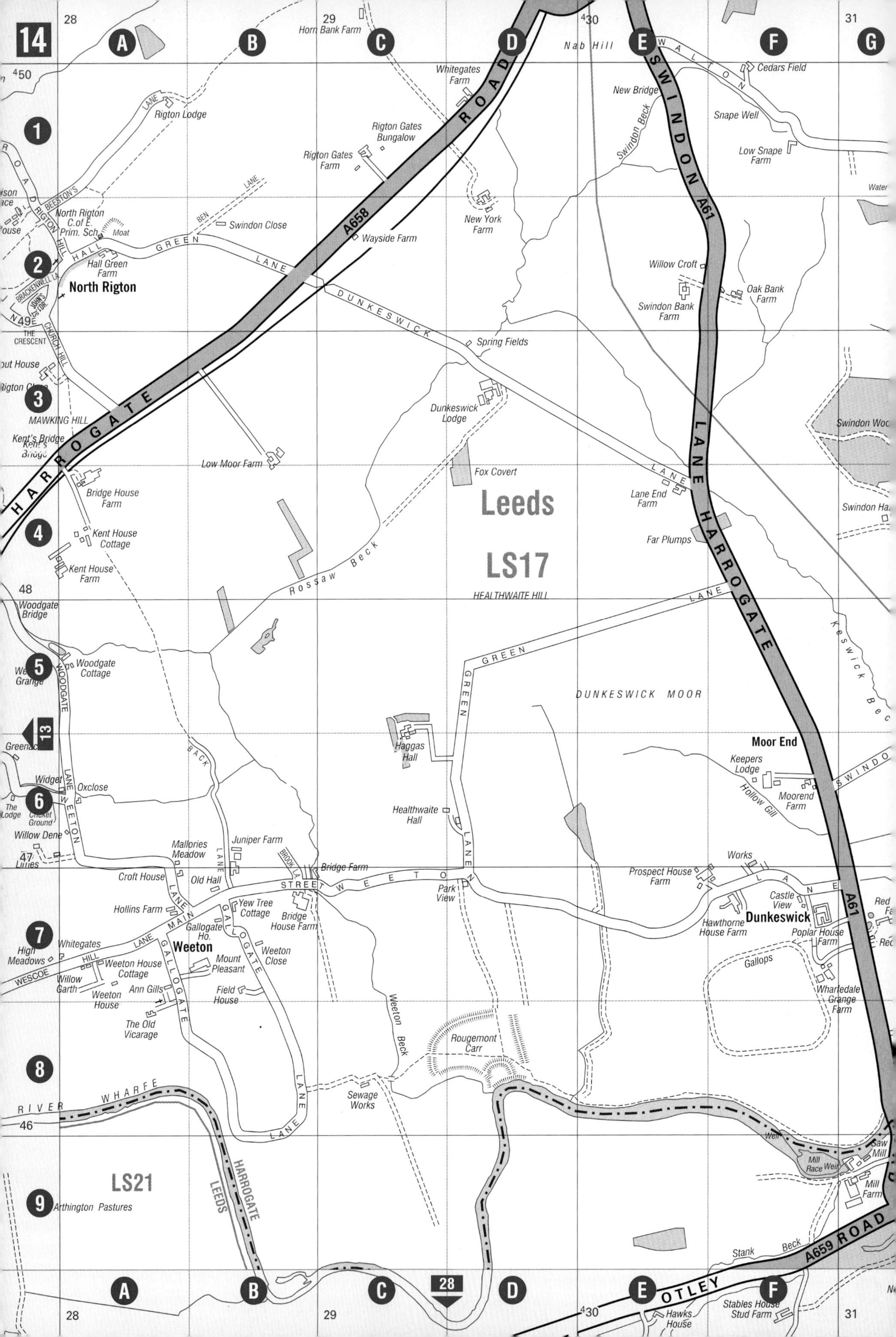
North Rigton
Weeton
Dunkeswick
Moor End
Leeds
LS17
LS21
A658
A61
A659
HARROGATE ROAD
SWINDON LANE
HARROGATE LANE
OTLEY ROAD
DUNKESWICK LANE
GREEN LANE
WEETON STREET
WEETON LANE
WOODGATE
GALLOGATE
MAIN STREET
BACK LANE
RIVER WHARFE
Rigton Lodge
Rigton Gates Farm
Rigton Gates Bungalow
Whitegates Farm
Horn Bank Farm
Nab Hill
Cedars Field
New Bridge
Snape Well
Low Snape Farm
Swindon Close
Wayside Farm
New York Farm
North Rigton C.of E. Prim. Sch.
Moat
Hall Green Farm
Willow Croft
Oak Bank Farm
Swindon Bank Farm
Spring Fields
Dunkeswick Lodge
Low Moor Farm
Fox Covert
Lane End Farm
Far Plumps
Bridge House Farm
Kent House Cottage
Kent House Farm
Kent's Bridge
MAWKING HILL
HEALTHWAITE HILL
DUNKESWICK MOOR
Rossaw Beck
Woodgate Bridge
Woodgate Cottage
Haggas Hall
Healthwaite Hall
Keepers Lodge
Moorend Farm
Hollow Gill
Oxclose
Widget
Willow Dene
Mallories Meadow
Juniper Farm
Bridge Farm
Croft House
Old Hall
Hollins Farm
Park View
Prospect House Farm
Works
Castle View
Hawthorne House Farm
Poplar House Farm
Yew Tree Cottage
Bridge House Farm
Gallogate Ho.
Weeton Close
Mount Pleasant
Whitegates
High Meadows
Weeton House Cottage
Willow Garth
Weeton House
Ann Gills
Field House
The Old Vicarage
Weeton Beck
Rougemont Carr
Sewage Works
Gallops
Wharfedale Grange Farm
Swindon Wood
Swindon Hall
Keswick Beck
Weir
Mill Race
Saw Mill
Mill Farm
Stank Beck
Arthington Pastures
Hawks House
Stables House
Stud Farm
Kent's Bridge
Brackenwell La
Beeston's Road
Church Hill
The Crescent
Rigton Hill
Hall Green
Ben Lane
Brook La
Wescoe Hill

13
28

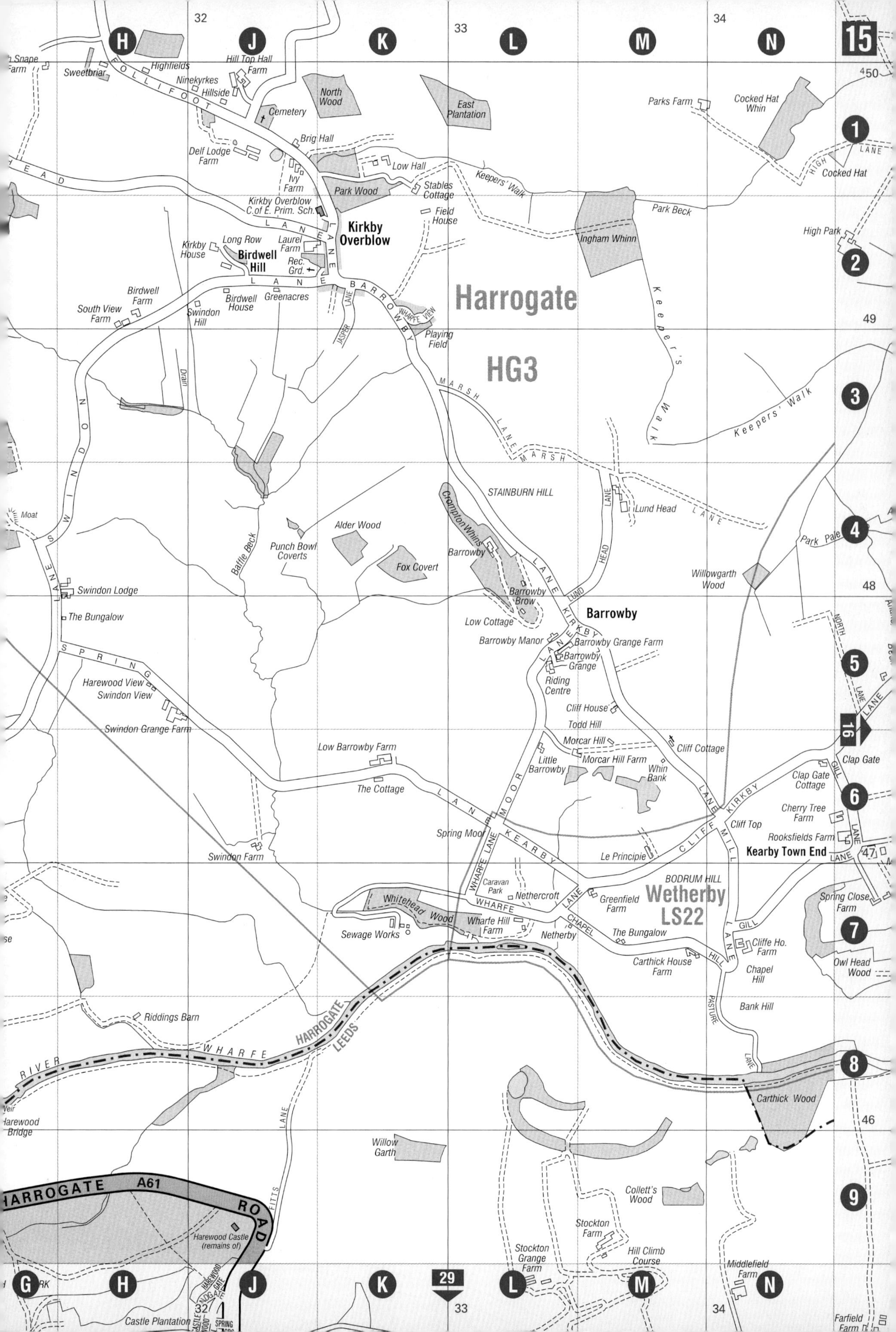
Kirkby Overblow
Birdwell Hill
Harrogate
HG3
Barrowby
Kearby Town End
Wetherby
LS22
Follifoot Lane
Swindon Lane
Spring Lane
Kearby Lane
Cliff Lane
Kirkby Lane
Barrowby Lane
Marsh Lane
Lund Head Lane
Wharfe Lane
Chapel Hill
Mill Lane
Pasture Lane
River Wharfe
Harrogate Road A61
Harrogate Leeds
Keepers' Walk
Keeper's Walk
Park Beck
Park Pale
North Lane
Gill Lane
High Lane
Cocked Hat
Cocked Hat Whin
Parks Farm
High Park
Ingham Whinn
North Wood
East Plantation
Cemetery
Brig Hall
Low Hall
Park Wood
Stables Cottage
Field House
Hill Top Hall Farm
Highfields
Sweetbriar
Ninekyrkes
Hillside
Delf Lodge Farm
Ivy Farm
Kirkby Overblow C.of E. Prim. Sch.
Long Row
Laurel Farm
Kirkby House
Rec. Grd.
Birdwell Farm
Birdwell House
Greenacres
South View Farm
Swindon Hill
Playing Field
Stainburn Hill
Lund Head
Crompton Whins
Alder Wood
Punch Bowl Coverts
Fox Covert
Baffle Beck
Swindon Lodge
The Bungalow
Barrowby Brow
Low Cottage
Barrowby Manor
Barrowby Grange Farm
Barrowby Grange
Riding Centre
Willowgarth Wood
Cliff House
Todd Hill
Morcar Hill
Morcar Hill Farm
Little Barrowby
Cliff Cottage
Whin Bank
Harewood View
Swindon View
Swindon Grange Farm
Low Barrowby Farm
The Cottage
Spring Moor
Swindon Farm
Le Principie
Clap Gate
Clap Gate Cottage
Cherry Tree Farm
Cliff Top
Rooksfields Farm
Bodrum Hill
Caravan Park
Nethercroft
Greenfield Farm
Whitehead Wood
Wharfe Hill Farm
Netherby
The Bungalow
Sewage Works
Carthick House Farm
Cliff Ho. Farm
Chapel Hill
Spring Close Farm
Owl Head Wood
Bank Hill
Riddings Barn
Harewood Bridge
Carthick Wood
Willow Garth
Collett's Wood
Stockton Farm
Stockton Grange Farm
Hill Climb Course
Middlefield Farm
Harewood Castle (remains of)
Castle Plantation
Fitts Lane
Moat
Farfield Farm
H J K L M N G
1 2 3 4 5 6 7 8 9
32 33 34
45 46 47 48 49 450
16
29

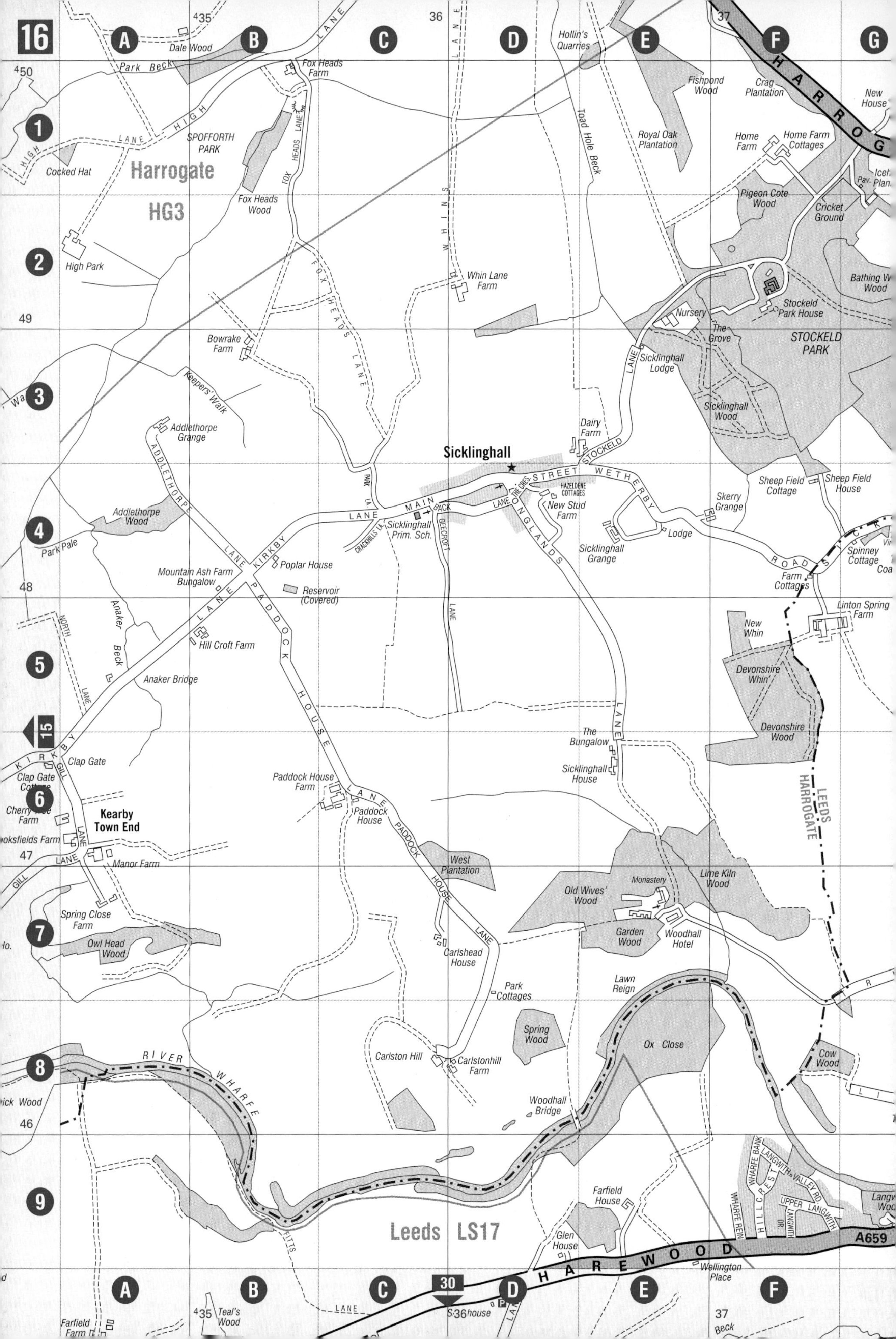

Harrogate
HG3
Leeds LS17
Sicklinghall
Kearby Town End
Dale Wood
Park Beck
Fox Heads Farm
High Lane
Spofforth Park
Cocked Hat
Fox Heads Wood
Fox Heads Lane
High Park
Whins Lane
Whin Lane Farm
Hollin's Quarries
Toad Hole Beck
Fishpond Wood
Royal Oak Plantation
Crag Plantation
Harrogate Road
New House
Home Farm
Home Farm Cottages
Pigeon Cote Wood
Cricket Ground
Pav.
Bathing Wood
Nursery
The Grove
Stockeld Park House
Stockeld Park
Sicklinghall Lodge
Sicklinghall Wood
Bowrake Farm
Keepers Walk
Addlethorpe Grange
Addlethorpe Lane
Addlethorpe Wood
Park Pale
Dairy Farm
Stockeld Lane
Main Street
Wetherby Road
Park La.
Main Lane
Back Lane
The Cres.
Hazeldene Cottages
New Stud Farm
Crackhills La.
Sicklinghall Prim. Sch.
Geecroft Lane
Kirkby Lane
Poplar House
Mountain Ash Farm Bungalow
Reservoir (Covered)
Sicklinghall Grange
Lodge
Skerry Grange
Sheep Field Cottage
Sheep Field House
Spinney Cottage
Farm Cottages
Linton Spring Farm
New Whin
Devonshire Whin
Devonshire Wood
Leeds
Harrogate
North Lane
Anaker Beck
Anaker Bridge
Hill Croft Farm
Paddock House Lane
Longlands Lane
The Bungalow
Sicklinghall House
Clap Gate
Clap Gate Cottage
Kirkby Gill
Cherry Tree Farm
Brooksfields Farm
Gill Lane
Manor Farm
Paddock House Farm
Paddock House
West Plantation
Old Wives' Wood
Monastery
Lime Kiln Wood
Garden Wood
Woodhall Hotel
Spring Close Farm
Owl Head Wood
Carlshead House
Park Cottages
Lawn Reign
Spring Wood
Ox Close
Cow Wood
Carlston Hill
Carlstonhill Farm
River Wharfe
Woodhall Bridge
Farfield House
Glen House
Wharfe Bank
Langwith Valley Rd.
Hillcrest
Upper Langwith
Langwith Dr.
Wharfe Rein
Harewood Road
A659
Wellington Place
Lane
Teal's Wood
Farfield Farm
Beck
15
30

Kirk Deighton
Wetherby
WETHERBY
LS22
LS23
Priest Hill
Deighton Gates
Raby Park
Hallfield
Linton
COLLINGHAM
Collingham Fields
SPOFFORTH HILL
A661 ROAD
A661
WETHERBY ROAD
DEIGHTON ROAD
B6164
NORTH ROAD
YORK ROAD
A661 ROAD
NORTH ST.
HIGH ST.
WEST GATE
MKT. PL.
BOSTON ROAD
BOSTON RD.
WALTON RD.
A58
WETHERBY ROAD
A58 MAIN STREET
LEEDS ROAD
WATTLE SYKE
A659
GREAT NORTH ROAD
A1
LINTON ROAD
LINTON LANE
NORTHGATE LANE
COMMON LANE
LINTON LANE
MAIN STREET
SANDBECK LANE
SANDBECK WAY
SANDBECK INDUSTRIAL ESTATE
HALFIELD LANE
RIVER WHARFE
WETHERBY GOLF COURSE
LINTON INGS
WETHERBY GRANGE PARK
King George's Field Rec. Grd.
Sports Field
Wetherby Leisure Centre
Wetherby Bridge
Magistrates Court
Library
Wetherby High Sch.
Prim. Sch.
Club House
Cricket Ground
Bowling Greens
Crowcroft Bank
Crow Wood
Beilby Wood
Beilby House
Sweep Farm
Gate Plantation
Grange Moor
Collingham Wood
Collingham Wood Ho.
Low Farm
Linton Bridge
Collingham Beck
Nursery
Lilac Farm
Tree Tops
Walk-a-bout
Low Cow Moor Wood
Whinney Cow Moor Wood
Providence House
Collingham Moor
Linton Hills
Westwood
Spring Wood
Linton Spring
Lodge Farm Cottages
Stockfield Lodge Farm
Wetherby Lodge
Lodge Bank Wood
Deer Springs
Ingbarrow Farm
Kingbarrow Farm
Kingbarrow Cottages
Ingbarrow Bridge
Stockeld Beck
Sandbeck Bridge
Greenacres
F'ball Grd.
Quarry Hill
Barleyfields Rd. Bridge
Scaur Bank
HORSEFAIR CENTRE
38
39
440
41
450
49
48
47
46
H
J
K
L
M
N
G
1
2
3
4
5
6
7
8
9
18
31

INGMANTHORPE PARK
Duckpond Plantation
Sandbeck House
Sandbeck Bridge
Sandbeck Wood
Greenacres
Cockshot Wood
Swinnow Hill
SWINNOW PARK
Moss Carrs Farm
Noble Wood
Timber Yard
B1224
Sand Bridge
Champagne Whin
Warehouses
Nova Scotia
Sports Ground
HM Young Offender Institution
Lodge
Sand Beck
Moor Plantation
The Rampart
YORK ROAD
A661
A1
WETHERBY RACE COURSE
Hornshaw Plantation
Grand Stands
Caravan Site
Parade Ring
Stables
Sykes House Farm
LS22
Hallfield
Cemetery
Wetherby High Sch.
Prim. Sch.
Springs Wood
Spring Wood
Jackson Wood
Wetherby
Rose Dene Farm
WALTON RD.
WALTON ROAD
WETHERBY ROAD
Walton Gates
Park Hill Farm
Walton
Snowden Garden
West Field
Flint Mill Farm
The Flint Mill
Weir
Flint Mill Grange
LS23
Horn Bank
Sewage Works
Wray Wood Farm
Wray Wood
The Bank
THORP ARCH GRANGE
WALTON CHASE
Playing Field
Bowling Greens
WETHERBY GRANGE
Hatfield Bank
H.M. Prison Rudgate
WETHERBY GRANGE PARK
Whin Covert
New Springs
Middle Field
H.M. Prison Thorp Arch
Spoilbank Plantation
Long Nursery
Hall Farm
The Leys
Gate Plantation
Jackdaw Crag
Robin Hood's Cave
Hall Wood
RIVER WHARFE
The Firs
Whitegates
Thorp Arch
Gunter Wood
Thorparch Hall
Thorparch Park
Lady Elizabeth Hastings C. of E. Prim. Sch.
Cricket Grnd.
Deepdale Lodge
West Park
Front Wood
Comm. Cen.
Moor End Farm
Cherry Tree Cottages
Grange Moor
BOSTON SPA
A659
Bridge Farm
MOOR END HIGH STREET
Grove Farm
Thorparch Bridge
CHURCH FIELD
Spa Baths
Prim. Sch.
West Oaks
Playing Field
TOWN INGS
32
17
Crowd Bank
Collingham Moor

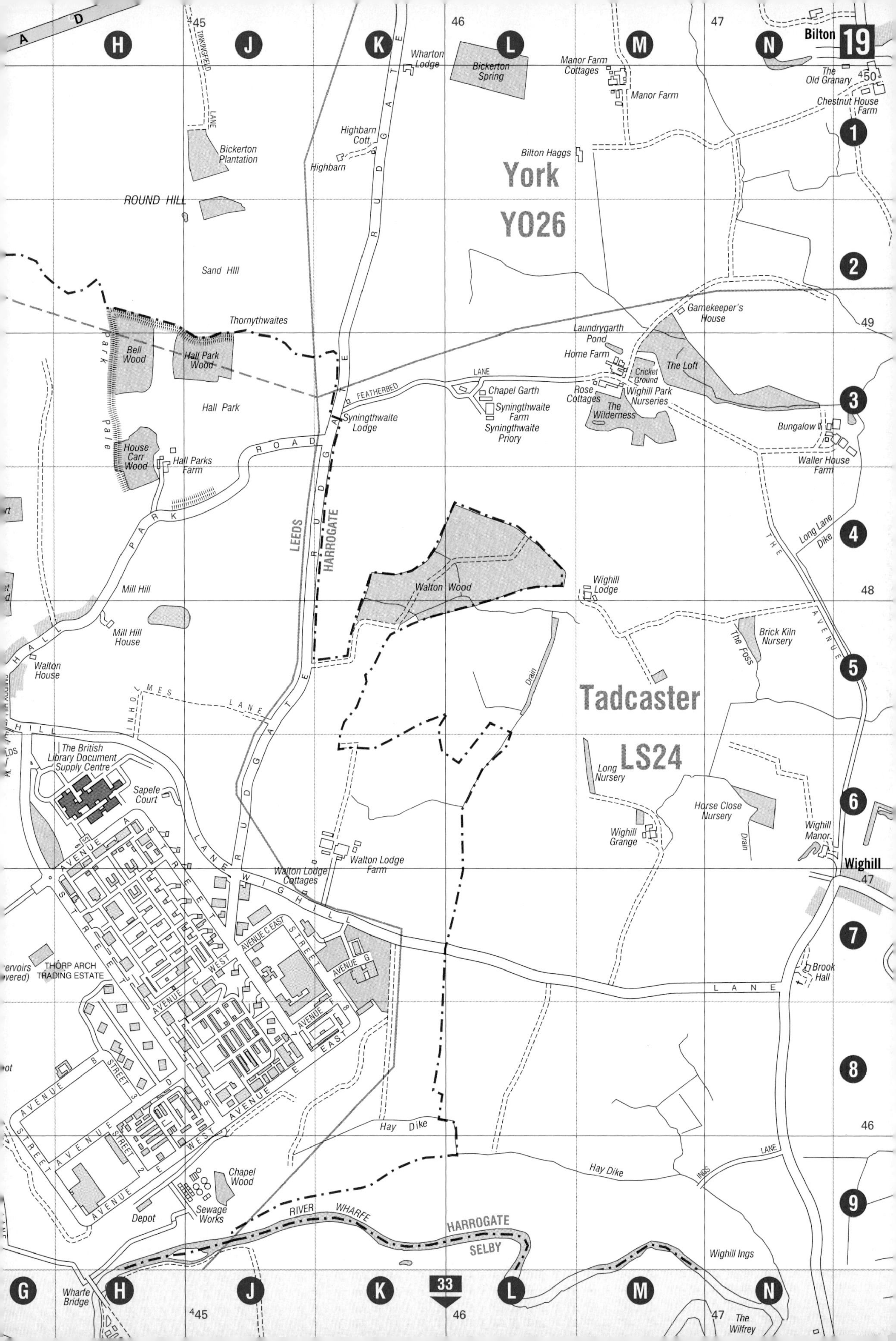

York
YO26
Tadcaster
LS24
Bilton
Wighill
ROUND HILL
Sand Hill
Thornythwaites
Bell Wood
Hall Park Wood
Hall Park
House Carr Wood
Hall Parks Farm
Mill Hill
Mill Hill House
Walton House
Bickerton Plantation
Bickerton Spring
Wharton Lodge
Highbarn Cott.
Highbarn
Bilton Haggs
Manor Farm Cottages
Manor Farm
The Old Granary
Chestnut House Farm
Gamekeeper's House
Laundrygarth Pond
Home Farm
Cricket Ground
The Loft
Rose Cottages
Wighill Park Nurseries
The Wilderness
Chapel Garth
Syningthwaite Farm
Syningthwaite Priory
Syningthwaite Lodge
Bungalow
Waller House Farm
Long Lane Dike
Walton Wood
Wighill Lodge
Brick Kiln Nursery
The Foss
Long Nursery
Horse Close Nursery
Wighill Grange
Wighill Manor
Walton Lodge Farm
Walton Lodge Cottages
Brook Hall
The British Library Document Supply Centre
Sapele Court
THORP ARCH TRADING ESTATE
Chapel Wood
Sewage Works
Depot
Wharfe Bridge
Hay Dike
Wighill Ings
The Wilfrey
RIVER WHARFE
HARROGATE
SELBY
LEEDS
HARROGATE
RUDGATE
FEATHERBED LANE
PARK ROAD
HALL PARK
TINKINGFIELD LANE
HOLMES LANE
WIGHILL LANE
INGS LANE
THE AVENUE
AVENUE A
AVENUE B
AVENUE C EAST
AVENUE C WEST
AVENUE D
AVENUE E EAST
AVENUE E WEST
AVENUE F
AVENUE G
STREET
Drain
H
J
K
L
M
N
G
1
2
3
4
5
6
7
8
9
45
46
47
48
49
50

33

Leeds and Liverpool Canal
Grange Bridge
Lane House Bridge
Football Ground
Cricket Ground
Driving Range
Works
Fairdale
Kildwick Ings
River Aire
Bradford
Craven
A629
KEIGHLEY ROAD
A6034
Silsden Ings
Silsden Bridge
Steeton Ings
Bridge Farm
AIREDALE GENERAL HOSPITAL
Steeton & Silsden
Eastburn
Woollen Mill
Eastburn House
Vehicle Testing Station
Steeton Hall
High Hall
Cemy.
Cricket Ground
SKIPTON ROAD
KEIGHLEY ROAD
Steeton Manor
Currergate
Steeton Prim. Sch.
STEETON
Currer Wood Farm
Coppy Farm
Rec. Ground
Currer Wood
Little Wood
Redding Wood
Hawkcliffe House
Hollings Bank
Hawkcliff Wood
Hawk Cliff
Bank House Farm
Tower Farm
Hawkcliffe Farm
Howden
Howden House
BD20
Silsden Ings
Low Holden Farm
Eastburn Crag
Whitley Head Farm
Whitley Head
Whitley Hill Farm
Anderton Crag
Hollings Bank Farm
Dale View Farm
Little Snowden
INTAKE LANE
Out Moor Farm
Highfield House
Nutt Head Cottages
Nutt Head Farm
Brighton House
Brighton Wood
Great Snowden
Craven Wood
Meadow Field Farm
Rugby Football Ground
Low Hollins Farm
High Hollins Farm
Rose Cottage Farm
STEETON MOOR
White Fields Farm
Hunter's Hill
Lower Redcar Farm
REDCAR LANE
Dam Green Top
Redcar Plantation
Middle Redcar Farm
Whinburn Farm
Whinburn School
Cockshot Dam Green
Tarn Hill
Tarn House Farm
Four Oaks
Cutshaw Moor
Higher Redcar
Redcar Tarn
Keighley
Tarn Laddy
Prospect House
Low Shann Farm
Cutshaw Farm
Higher Shann Farm
Black Hill
Coppy Hill
Daisy Hill Farm
Resr.
Ashfield
Whorls Farm
Edge Farm
Braithwaite
Sutton Stoop
POLE ROAD
Green Syke Farm
Far Laithe Farm
Hill Clough
BD22
Guard House
Schools
BRIGG GARDENS
Laycock
Laycock First Sch.
Works
Butter Clough
Todley Hill
Nettle Hole
Cliffe Green Farm
Longcroft Nurseries
Town End Farm
Burial Ground
Intake Farm
New Town
Glen Bridge
TODLEY HALL RD.
Goose Eye
Lumb
Game Scar
Todley Clough
North Beck
Works
6
36

KEIGHLEY
RIDDLESDEN
ROUGH HOLDEN
RIVOCK EDGE
Bucking Hill
Rivock Well
Rivock Oven (Cave)
Rivock Edge
Rivock
Dirk Hill Sike
Out Laith
Rough Holden Farm
The Crag
Robin Hood Wood
Robin Hood's Stone
Pinfold Hill
Television Relay Station
Holden Gate
Peggy Well
Jaytail Farm
Jay Tail Wood
RIDDLESDEN GOLF COURSE
KEIGHLEY GOLF COURSE
Spring Crag Wood
Alder Carr Wood
Jacob's Wood
Holden Bridge
Howden Park Farm
Holden Bridge (Swing)
Leeds & Liverpool Canal
Lodge Hill Delph
Lodge Hill Wood
Nature Reserve
Low Wood
High Carr
Carr Delph
Rockedge
Club House
Booth's Bridge (Swing)
Wood Head Lodge
High Wood Head
Carr Clough
The Barn
Low Wood Head
Four Winds
Marsh Farm
Larkfield Farm
Larkfield Old Barn
Heights Farm
The Height
South Side Farm
Highfield House
Taylor Lay
Moorcock Farm
High Trees
Rivock Farm
Primrose Farm
Primrose Cottage
Ryding Gate
Moor Side Farm
Elam Grange Cottage
Elam Grange
Howden Field
Aqueduct
Willow Bank Cottage
Leache's Bridge (Swing)
Grange Middle School
Low Banks
Judith Cliff
Bank Top
Hill Top
Overflow
Barley Cote Farm
Barley Cote
Freshwinds
Field Head Farm
Beechcliffe
Refuse Treatment Works
KEIGHLEY INDUSTRIAL PARK
Stockbridge
Cricket Ground
Council Depot
Cougar Park
Leisure Centre
Victoria Park
Eastwood
Aireworth
Worth Village
Miniature Railway
East Riddlesden Hall
Playing Field
Marland Stadium
King George V Playing Fields
Sewage Treatment Works
Strong Close
Foundry
Keighley
Park Wood Bottom
Thwaites
BD21
Clay Hall Farm
Milking Hill
Marley Brow Wood
Royd Field Farm
Jackfields
Swire Smith
High Utley
Greenhead Grammar Sch.
Sports Ground
Moorhouse Wood
Cliffe Castle (Museum)
Devonshire Park
Training Centre
Holy Croft
Education Cen.
Cemetery
Golf Cott.
A629
A650
B6265
A650 VALLEY ROAD
AIRE VALLEY ROAD
BRADFORD ROAD
NORTH ST.
SKIPTON ROAD
CAVENDISH ST.
INGS ROAD
HARD INGS
ELAM WOOD ROAD
WESTERN AVENUE
HOSPITAL ROAD
SILSDEN ROAD
H J K L M N
G H J K L M N
1 2 3 4 5 6 7 8 9
06 07 08
45 44 43 42 41
7
22
37

A
B
C
D
E
F
G
09
410
11
8
21
38
West Buck Stones
Cowper's Cross
Bucking Hill
North Stones
Whetstone Gate
Wireless Station
Masts
Thimble Stone
KEIGHLEY RD.
ROAD
445
Brown Seaves
Kirk Stones
The Two Eggs
Grouse Butts
HIGH MOOR
Black Knoll
Cross (Remains of)
High Bradup
Low Bradup
MORTON
MOOR
Lay Thorn Hill
Bradup Beck
Bradup
Sweet Well
Sweet Well Dike
Grouse Butts
44
Brass Castle
Stone Circle (Remains of)
Bradup Bridge
LOW MOOR
Syon Hill
Upwood Hall Farm
Upwood Hall
Fish Ponds
The Glen
Glen Farm
Reservoir
Reservoir (Covered)
SILSDEN ROAD
Aqueduct
Beck
Sluice
Fenny Shaw
Shaw
Fenny Aqueduct
Richmond's Spa (Chalybeate)
Stanbury Hill
SPA FLAT
Primrose Cottage
ILKLEY ROAD
Upwood Lodge
Weirs
Sunny Dale
Guide Stone
Moor Side Farm
Moor Side Cottages
BENSON'S MOBILE HOME PARK
43
High Ash Farm
Weir
Pond
Spa Dyke
West Morton
BD20
Morton Dam
UPPER MILL ROW
White Flush
SPA FOOT
Barn House Farm
Dimples Farm
Field Head Farm
Glen Esk Farm
Brownhill Farm
Botany Farm
Botany
Ousel Hole
Weirs
Moorlands Farm
UPWOOD LANE
Manor Heath
LAKESIDE ROAD
PROVIDENCE ROW
Todmoor Stones
Aqueduct
Dene Farm
Denehole Farm
Dene Hole
Aqueduct
Cabin Hill
How Beck
SUNNYDALE PK.
BOTANY DR.
ALMA TER.
Keighley
Manor Farm
High Court
STUDLEY
Green End
Sunnybank Nurseries
Fenny Shaw Low Well
Morton Stoop
Great Graincliffe
Little Graincliffe
Valve Well
East Morton
HIGHFIELD M.
HIGHFIELD CL.
Meadowcroft
Belle Vue Farm
SOUTH VW
CARR LANE
BURY
BANK
42
BRADFORD ROAD
The Springs
Cemetery
BEAUVAIS DR.
East Morton C.of E. First Sch.
Carr House
Club Ho.
ST. LUKE'S TER.
MAIN
DIMPLES LA
AMBLERS MEWS
Weirs
Drake Hill Farm
Carr House Farm
Drake Hill
Swing Lane Bridge
FARDEW GOLF COURSE
Recreation Ground
Hebble Bridge
HAWTHORNE
Weirs
PEAS ACRE
CARR LANE
The Riggs
Hill Top Farm
TOP LANE
HILL TOP LANE
Drake Hill Cottages
Cliff Delph
Netherside
SUNNYCLIFFE
THE SPINNEY
B6265
Leeds & Liverpool Canal
Morton Beck
BECK RD.
HIGH FOLD
Micklethwaite Bank
Fairlady Farm
Sewage Treatment Works
BD21
Weirs
Croft House Farm
THE GREEN
Micklethwaite
Cliff Farm
Morton Bri.
Thornfield Farm
Deer Park
AIRE VALLEY ROAD
A650
Airdale Barn
Airedale Farm
MARLEY
Ryshworth Middle Sch.
41
WALSH LANE
HEIGHTS LANE
Marley Brow Wood
Works
KEIGHLEY
MICKLETHWAITE
STY LANE
Lay Thorpe
The Height

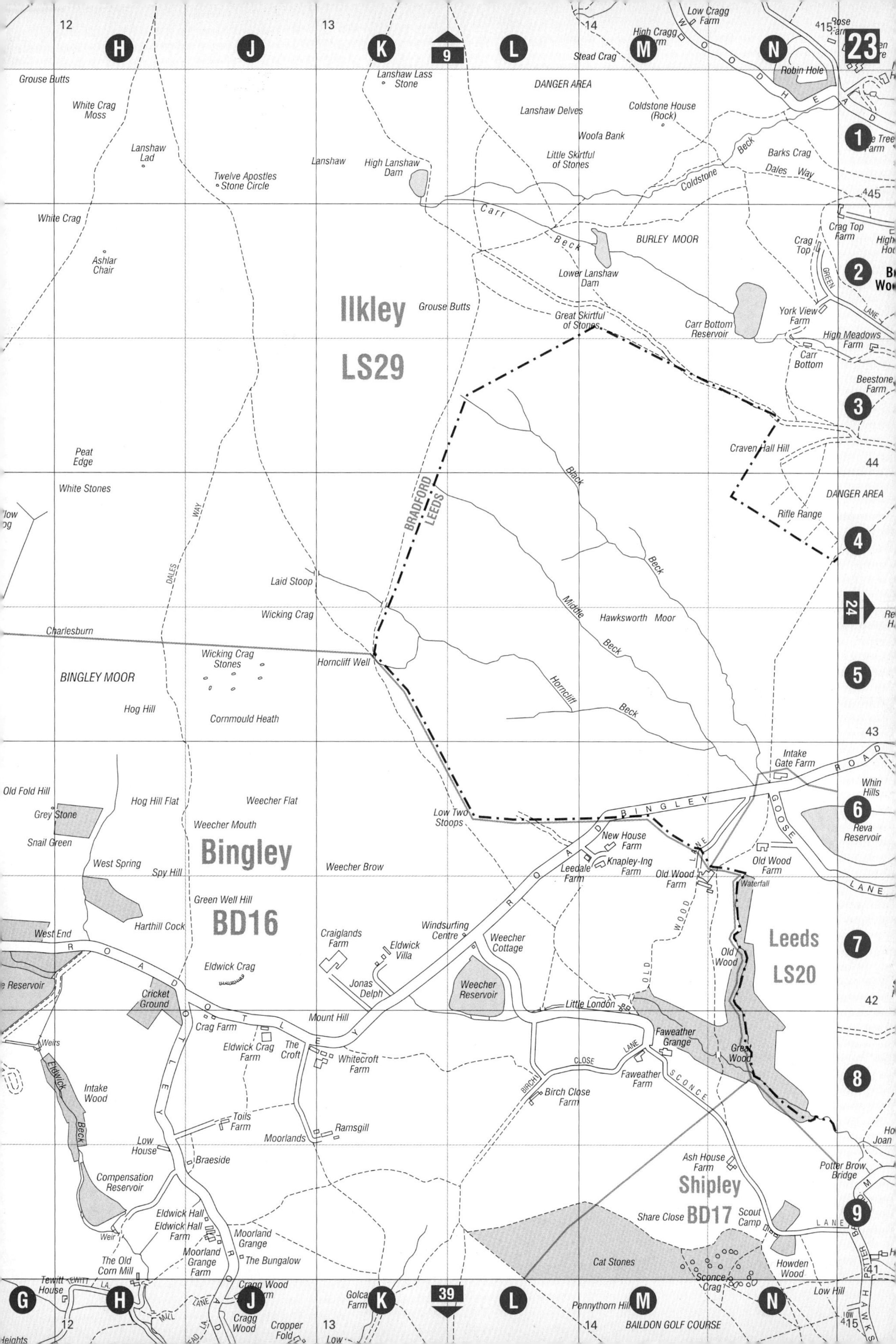

Ilkley
LS29
Bingley
BD16
Leeds
LS20
Shipley
BD17
Grouse Butts
White Crag Moss
Lanshaw Lad
Twelve Apostles Stone Circle
Lanshaw
High Lanshaw Dam
Lanshaw Lass Stone
DANGER AREA
Lanshaw Delves
Coldstone House (Rock)
Woofa Bank
Little Skirtful of Stones
Stead Crag
High Cragg Farm
Low Cragg Farm
Robin Hole
WOODHEAD
Barks Crag
Dales Way
Coldstone Beck
Carr Beck
BURLEY MOOR
Crag Top Farm
Crag Top
White Crag
Ashlar Chair
Lower Lanshaw Dam
Great Skirtful of Stones
Carr Bottom Reservoir
York View Farm
High Meadows Farm
Carr Bottom
Beestone Farm
Craven Hall Hill
Rifle Range
Peat Edge
White Stones
BRADFORD
LEEDS
DALES WAY
Black Beck
Middle Beck
Hawksworth Moor
Horncliff Beck
Laid Stoop
Wicking Crag
Charlesburn
Wicking Crag Stones
Horncliff Well
BINGLEY MOOR
Hog Hill
Cornmould Heath
Intake Gate Farm
BINGLEY ROAD
GOOSE LANE
Whin Hills
Reva Reservoir
Old Fold Hill
Grey Stone
Hog Hill Flat
Weecher Flat
Low Two Stoops
Weecher Mouth
Snail Green
New House Farm
Knapley-Ing Farm
Leedale Farm
Old Wood Farm
Waterfall
West Spring
Spy Hill
Weecher Brow
Green Well Hill
Harthill Cock
West End
OTLEY ROAD
Craiglands Farm
Eldwick Villa
Windsurfing Centre
Weecher Cottage
OLD WOOD LANE
Old Wood
Reservoir
Eldwick Crag
Cricket Ground
Jonas Delph
Weecher Reservoir
Little London
Crag Farm
Mount Hill
Faweather Grange
Great Wood
Weirs
Eldwick Beck
Eldwick Crag Farm
The Croft
Whitecroft Farm
CLOSE LANE
Faweather Farm
Intake Wood
BIRCH CLOSE
Birch Close Farm
SCONCE LANE
Toils Farm
Ramsgill
Moorlands
Low House
Braeside
Ash House Farm
Potter Brow Bridge
Compensation Reservoir
Eldwick Hall
Eldwick Hall Farm
Moorland Grange
Moorland Grange Farm
Share Close
Scout Camp
Weir
The Bungalow
The Old Corn Mill
Cat Stones
Howden Wood
Sconce Crag
Low Hill
Tewitt House
Cragg Wood Farm
Golcar Farm
Pennythorn Hill
Cragg Wood
Cropper Fold
BAILDON GOLF COURSE
G H J K L M N
1 2 3 4 5 6 7 8 9
12 13 14 415
445 44 43 42 41
9
24
39

Burley in Wharfedale
Burley Woodhead
Ilkley
LS29
MENSTON
Menston
BRADFORD
LEEDS
HIGH ROYDS HOSPITAL
White Cross
Tranmere Park
Hawksworth
LS20
BRADFORD GOLF COURSE
Reva Reservoir
Reva Hill
New Dam
DANGER AREA
Rifle Range
OTLEY GOLF COURSE
BRADFORD ROAD BURLEY
A65
A6038
10
23
40
415
16
17
18
445
44
43
42
41

OTLEY
Otley
LS21
Guycroft
Cambridge
THE CHEVIN
Leeds
GUISELEY
Guiseley
Kelcliffe
West Carlton
LS19
YEADON
New Scarborough
Greenbottom
Shaw Lane
Westfield
A660
A659
A6038
A65
B6153
WESTGATE
BOROUGHGATE
CROSS
LEEDS ROAD
BIRDCAGE
YORK GATE
CROSS LANE
CARLTON LANE
MOOR TOP
Mickle Ing Bridge
Grove Hill Park
Chevin Grange
Thornfield
Ashwood Ho.
Woodlands
The Old Vicarage
Beech Grove
Chevin House
Manby House
Cowburn Nursery
Ritchies Plantation
Great Dib
Chevin Hall
Chevin Hall Farm
West Chevin
West Chevin Farm
Dales Way
Beacon Hill
The Bungalow
Beacon House Farm
Woodlands Farm
Danefield Ho.
Springfield Farm
York Gate Farm
Russell Farm
The Old Orchard
Hawes
Sinks
Westfield Farm
Moor View Farm
Chevin Lodge
York Gate Plantation
Bracken Grange
Guiseley Moor
Whale Jaws Hill
Highfield House
Brackencroft
Moor Farm
Upcroft Farm
Old Harrison's Wood
The Grove
Upcroft House Farm
Hopewell Farm
The Grange
Grange Farm
Carlton Moor
Carlton Manor
Mount Pisgah
Calfhole Wood
Greenlaw
Norland Farm
Carlton Lane Nurseries
Lee Garth Plantation
High Cay Birks
Deipkier
Shaw Wood
Wood Plain Plantation
Kelcliffe Farm
Kelcliffe Mount
Cemetery
Bracken End Farm
Cricket Grd.
Guiseley F.C. Grd.
Green Meadows Sch.
Playing Fields
Guiseley School
The Gate Ho.
Park Gate
Park Ghyll House
Esholt Junction
Sodhall Hill
Sodhall Hill Wood
Leisure Cen.
School
Playing Field
Queensway Prim. Sch.
Nunroyd Cottages
Nunroyd Park
Sports Grd.
Kirk Lane Park
Yeadon Banks
Yeadon Haw
Res. (cov.)
Yeadon Cemetery
Maria Regina Convent
Tarnfield
YEADON TARN
Leeds Outdoor Pursuits Centre
Football Grd.
Cricket Grd.
Works
Caddy Close
Breary Close
The Bungalow
Rammer's House
Maple Bank Farm
Windmill Hill
Chevin End Farm
Clarion Camp
26
11
41

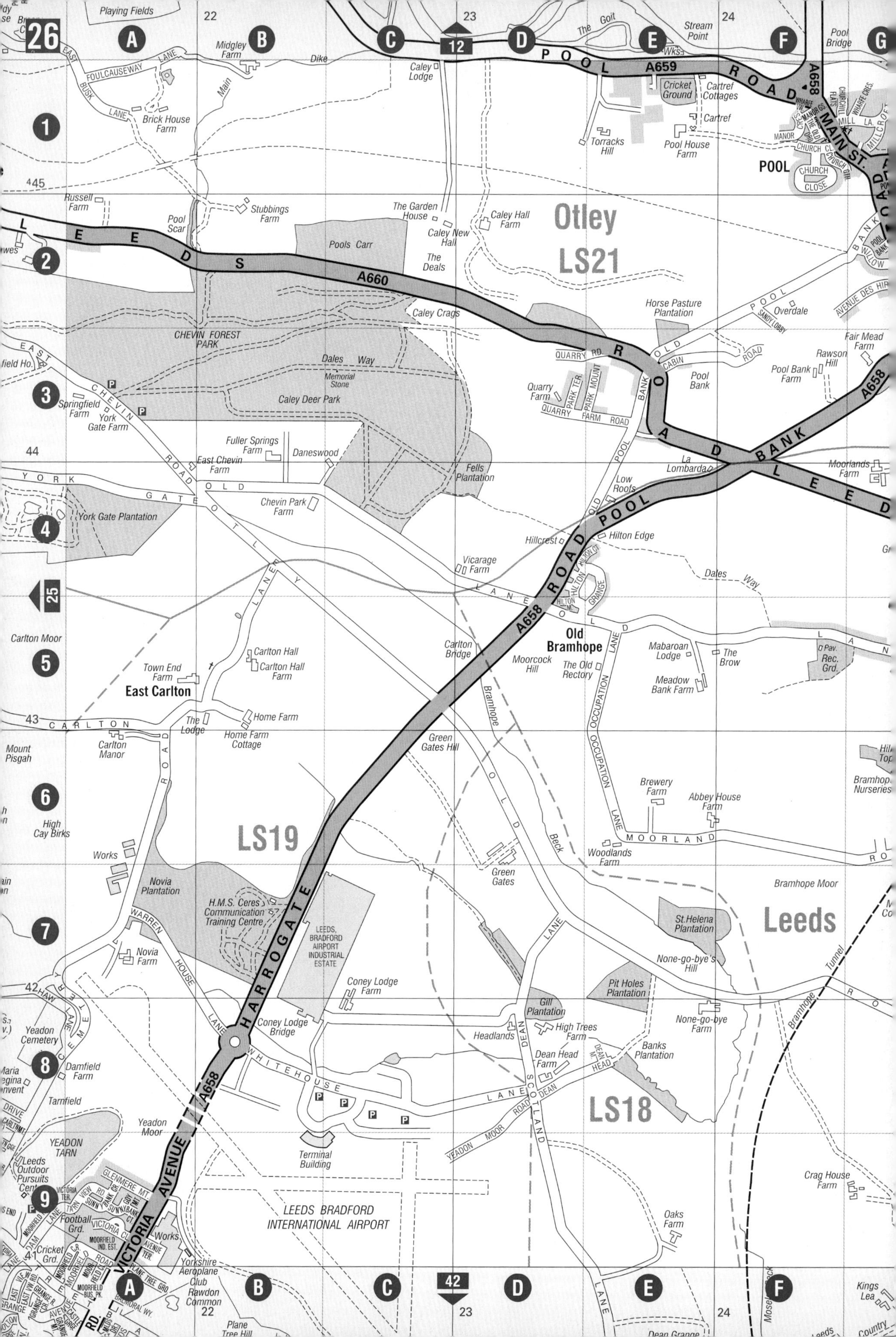

Playing Fields
Midgley Farm
Caley Lodge
Stream Point
Pool Bridge
POOL ROAD
A659
Cricket Ground
Cartref Cottages
Cartref
Torracks Hill
Pool House Farm
Brick House Farm
FOULCAUSEWAY LANE
BUSK LANE
POOL
CHURCH CLOSE
MAIN ST.
Russell Farm
Stubbings Farm
Pool Scar
The Garden House
Caley New Hall
Caley Hall Farm
Otley
LS21
Pools Carr
The Deals
LEEDS ROAD
A660
Caley Crags
Horse Pasture Plantation
Overdale
CHEVIN FOREST PARK
Dales Way
Memorial Stone
Caley Deer Park
Quarry Farm
QUARRY RD.
QUARRY FARM ROAD
Pool Bank
Pool Bank Farm
Rawson Hill
Fair Mead Farm
A658
Springfield Farm
York Gate Farm
EAST CHEVIN ROAD
Fuller Springs Farm
Daneswood
East Chevin Farm
Fells Plantation
La Lombarda
BANK
Moorlands Farm
YORK GATE
OLD
Chevin Park Farm
Low Roofs
York Gate Plantation
POOL ROAD
Hillcrest
Hilton Edge
Vicarage Farm
Dales Way
OLD LANE
Carlton Moor
Carlton Bridge
Old Bramhope
Carlton Hall
Carlton Hall Farm
Town End Farm
East Carlton
Moorcock Hill
The Old Rectory
Mabaroan Lodge
The Brow
Meadow Bank Farm
Rec. Grd.
OCCUPATION LANE
Home Farm
The Lodge
Home Farm Cottage
CARLTON
Carlton Manor
Mount Pisgah
Green Gates Hill
Bramhope
Brewery Farm
Abbey House Farm
Bramhope Nurseries
High Cay Birks
LS19
MOORLAND
Woodlands Farm
Works
Novia Plantation
Green Gates
Beck
Bramhope Moor
H.M.S. Ceres Communication Training Centre
HARROGATE
LEEDS, BRADFORD AIRPORT INDUSTRIAL ESTATE
St.Helena Plantation
Leeds
WARREN HOUSE LANE
Novia Farm
None-go-bye's Hill
Pit Holes Plantation
Coney Lodge Farm
Gill Plantation
None-go-bye Farm
Yeadon Cemetery
Coney Lodge Bridge
Headlands
High Trees Farm
Dean Head Farm
Banks Plantation
Damfield Farm
WHITEHOUSE LANE
Tarnfield
Yeadon Moor
YEADON MOOR ROAD
SCOTLAND
LS18
YEADON TARN
Terminal Building
Leeds Outdoor Pursuits Centre
Crag House Farm
LEEDS BRADFORD INTERNATIONAL AIRPORT
VICTORIA AVENUE
Football Grd.
Works
Oaks Farm
Cricket Grd.
Yorkshire Aeroplane Club
Rawdon Common
Bramhope Tunnel
Kings Lea
Plane Tree Hill
Dean Grange

12
25
42

West Holme
13
28
43
Arthington
West Breary
BRAMHOPE
LS16
ARTHINGTON LANE
A659
A660
LEEDS ROAD
OTLEY ROAD
HARROGATE
LEEDS
Pool in Wharfedale C.of E. Prim.Sch.
Pool Crook Farm
Arthington House
Farfield House
The Woodlands
Whitegates
Sewage Works
Castley Bridge
Greengates Farm
Warren House
Warren Farm
Mill Farm
Arthington Hall
Arthington Park
Cricket Ground
Holt Farm
School
Ash Tree House
Grange Farm
Vicarage
Ingfield Farm
Creskeld Villas
Creskeld Grange Farm
Creskeld Lodge
Creskeld Hall
Springs Wood
Creskeld Ho.
Limekiln Hill
Staircase Wood
Fosterton's Wood
Hunger Hill
Hezicar Wood
Swiss Cottage
Whin Covert
West Hill
Three Corners Wood
Whin Park
Whin Park Cottage
Howgarth Wood
Bank Foot Farm
Fox Covert
Blanket Wood
Staircase House
Broom Bank
Long Balk Wood
Creskeld Wood
Crag Wood
Arthington Bank
Wood Top Farm
Coates's Wood
Bank Side
Bank Top
Dales Way
Spring Wood
East Breary
Lineham Farm
Breary Grange
Bramhope Primary School
Hlth. Cen.
Golden Acre Corner
Cemetery
Camp Plantation
Bramhope Grove
Blackhill Farm
Reefer Plantation
Camp House Farm
Rugby Ground
Blackhill Quarry
Breary Marsh
Black Hill
Bog Plantation
Clonmore Farm
Marsh Beck
Beck Plantation
Cafe
Black Hill Plantation
Sub.
GOLDEN ACRE PARK
Marshes Plantation
Wrinklewood
Wrinkle Hill Wood
Rushes Farm
Leeds Country Way
Five Lane Ends
Parkway Hotel
Lane End Farm
New Rushes Farm
Fish Pond
Fish Pond Plantation
Cocker Hill Farm
Running Sike
Sports Ground
Adel Dam
High Leas
Ridgeside
Adel Mill Farm
Adel Bridge
COOKRIDGE HALL GOLF COURSE
Manor
CRESKELD LANE
BLACK HILL ROAD
ARTHINGTON ROAD
BREARY LANE
BREARY LANE EAST
KINGS ROAD
BLACK HILL LANE
KING LANE
ECCUP LANE
ECCUP MOOR LA.
CAMP ROAD
COOKRIDGE LANE
STAIRCASE LANE
WARREN LANE
STATION ROAD
HALL DRIVE
THE SYCAMORES
BIRCHES
WYNMORE AVENUE
TREDGOLD AVENUE
LONG MEADOW
MEADOW GARTH
THE POPLARS
THE CEDARS
ROWANS
PARKLANDS
EASTGATE
HOLME VIEW
SWAN LANE
BANK TOP LANE

Otley LS21
LS16
OTLEY ROAD A659
ARTHINGTON LANE
The Nunnery
Holt Wood
Holt Farm
Ingfield Farm
Headcroft Wood
Rawden Hill
Low Weardley
Low Lodge
High Lodge
Weardley Farm
High Weardley
Weardley
Hewland House Farm
Tinker Close
Hawks House
Stables House Stud Farm
Nursery Wood
Aviary
The Grove
Home Farm
Terrace Cottage
Harewood House
Kennel Wood
Stank Beck
Stank
The Gardens
Fish Pond
North View
Bog Plantation
Hillside Cottages
Hollins Wood
BEDLAM LANE
ALLUMS LANE
BANK TOP LA.
Bank End
Bank Side
ECCUP LANE
Burden Head
Burden Head Farm
Carr Wood
Carr House
Carr House Park
Carr Plantation
Stub House Plantation
Stub House Farm
Stub House Beck
The Boshaws
Dales Way
Waterhouse Whin
Langley Well
Grove Farm
Woodside Cottage
Swan Bushes
Grey Stone Old Wood
Lineham Farm
Eller Beck
Leeds Country Way
Brookland Farm
Thorn Bush Farm
Mount Pleasant Farm
Bank House Farm
Hazelwood Leys
Weir
Eccup Filtration Works
Herd Farm
Owlet Hall
Eccup
BLACK HILL LANE
BLACKSMITH LA.
VILLAGE
ROAD
Rookery Farm
Eccup Beck
Eccup Whin
Eller-car-nook Beck
Conduit
ECCUP MOOR ROAD
Green Meadows
Merrypoo Kennels
High Wood
ECCUP RESERVOIR
Five Lane Ends
KING LANE
SWAN LANE
Goodrick Plantation
Wigton Knowle
HEADINGLEY GOLF COURSE
Alwoodley Old Hall
Reservoir Lodge
GOODRICK LANE
SAND MOOR GOLF COURSE
Golf Farm
High Leas
Alwoodley
Alwoodley Gates
King Lane Farm
WINDERMERE DR.
LAKELAND CR.
LAKELAND DR.
ALWOODLEY
14
27
44

Harewood
Leeds
LS17
Wike
Blackmoor
Harewood Park
Castle Plantation
Village Farm
Prim. School
Gateways Sch.
Tennis Courts
Cemetery
Sports Ground
Stockton Farm
Stockton Grange Farm
Middlefield Farm
Vicarage Farm
New Laithe Farm
Moor Hill Farm
Vicar's Whin
Cut Whin Wood
Long Ing Pond
Eller Fields
Wall Side Plantation
Rough Bridge
Hollin Hall
Hollin Hall Ponds
Spring Wood
Lofthouse Grange
Jubilee
Lodge Hills Plantation
Lodge Hills
New Bridge
Nan Pie
Wet End Wood
Leeds Country Way
Grey Stone Pasture
Grey Stones
Lofthouse Lodge
Lofthouse Farm
Biggin Farm
Cote Hill
Sugar Hills
Low Green Farm
Fortshot House
Hillcrest Farm
Ginwell Cottage
Ginwell Farm
Grace Beck
Grace Bridge
Camp Site
Manor Farm
Wikefield Farm
School Lane Farm
Leeds Golf Centre
Club House
Hazel Cottage
Ivy Cottage
Hawthorn Cottage
Wike Whin
MOOR ALLERTON GOLF COURSE
Tennis Courts
WIKE RIDGE GOLF COURSE
Sturdy Bridge
Sturdy Beck
Collier Beck
Wike Ridge
Wike Ridge Farm
Millfield Farm
Millfield House
Woodley Lodge
Manor House Farm
Leeds Grammar School
Wigton Heath Farm
Whingate Farm
Wigton Manor
Shaw Hill
One Oak
Brandon Hall
Brandon Cottage
Hall Farm
Brandon Lodge
Brandon Grange Farm
Nursery
Wigton Moor Whin
WIGTON MOOR
HARROGATE ROAD
A61
A659
THE AV.
HAREWOOD AVENUE
HAREWOOD GATE
BOND GATE
CHURCH
CASTLE WOOD CL.
SPRING GDS.
HAREWOOD MEWS
THE SQUARE
SLEIGHTS LA.
WIKE LANE
FORGE LANE
FORTSHOT LANE
SCHOOL LANE
BACKSTONE GILL LANE
COAL ROAD
BRANDON LANE
WIKE RIDGE
MANOR HOUSE LANE
TARN LANE
BRANDON CRES.
Well
Weir
PARK

15
30
45

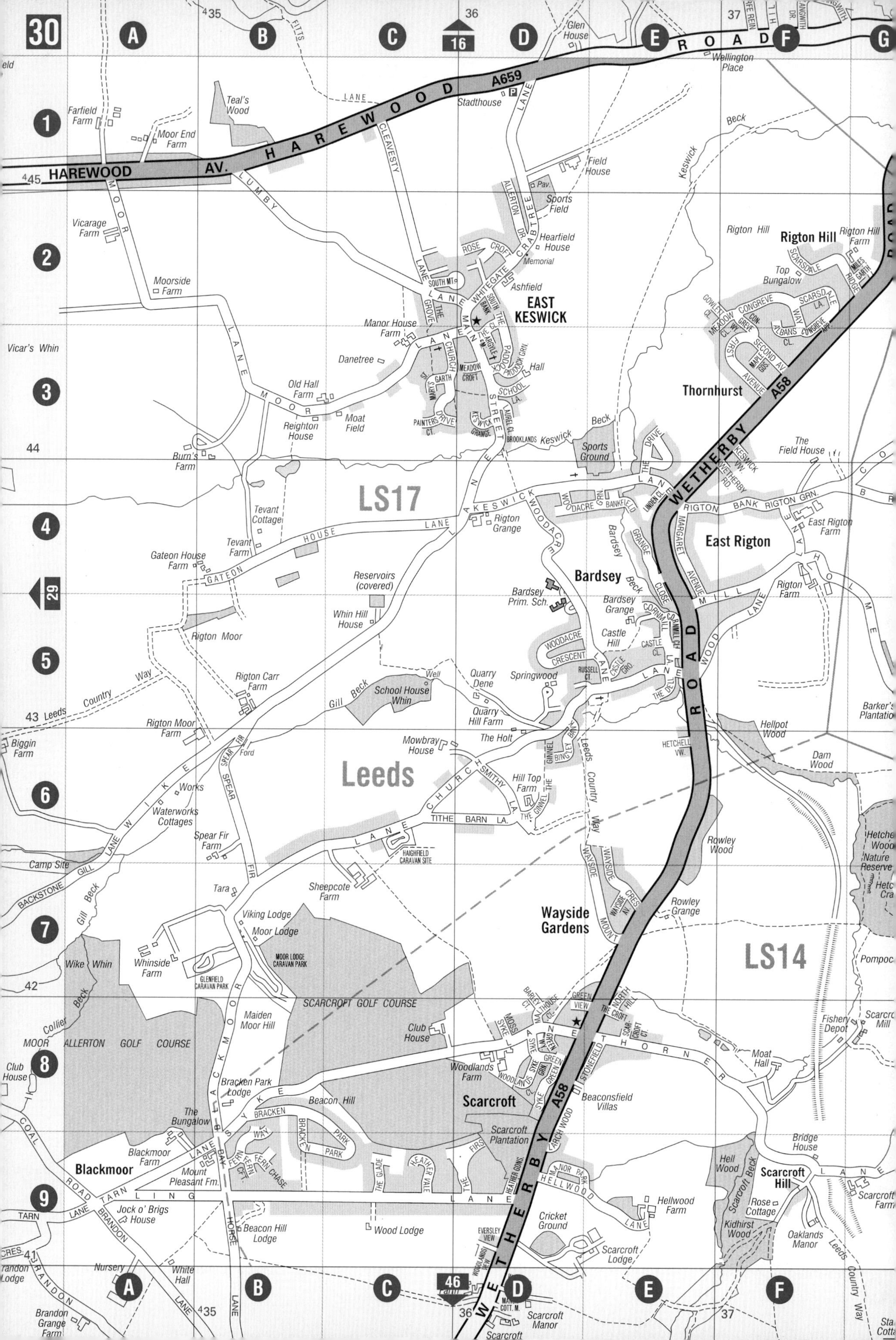

HAREWOOD AV.
HAREWOOD ROAD A659
Farfield Farm
Teal's Wood
Moor End Farm
Stadthouse
Glen House
Wellington Place
Field House
Sports Field
Hearfield House
Vicarage Farm
Moorside Farm
Rigton Hill
Rigton Hill Farm
Top Bungalow
EAST KESWICK
Manor House Farm
Danetree
Ashfield
Hall
Vicar's Whin
Old Hall Farm
Reighton House
Moat Field
Thornhurst
WETHERBY ROAD A58
Sports Ground
The Field House
Burn's Farm
LS17
Tevant Cottage
Tevant Farm
Rigton Grange
East Rigton
East Rigton Farm
Gateon House Farm
Reservoirs (covered)
Bardsey
Bardsey Prim. Sch.
Bardsey Grange
Rigton Farm
Whin Hill House
Rigton Moor
Castle Hill
Rigton Carr Farm
Leeds Country Way
Quarry Dene
Springwood
School House Whin
Quarry Hill Farm
Barker's Plantation
Rigton Moor Farm
Biggin Farm
Mowbray House
The Holt
Hellpot Wood
Dam Wood
Leeds
Works
Hill Top Farm
Waterworks Cottages
Spear Fir Farm
Rowley Wood
Camp Site
Haighfield Caravan Site
Sheepcote Farm
Tara
Viking Lodge
Moor Lodge
Rowley Grange
Wayside Gardens
LS14
Wike Whin
Whinside Farm
Moor Lodge Caravan Park
Glenfield Caravan Park
Scarcroft Golf Course
Maiden Moor Hill
Club House
Moor Allerton Golf Course
Fishery Depot
Moat Hall
Woodlands Farm
Bracken Park Lodge
Beacon Hill
Scarcroft
Beaconsfield Villas
The Bungalow
Scarcroft Plantation
Bridge House
Blackmoor Farm
Blackmoor
Mount Pleasant Fm.
Hell Wood
Scarcroft Hill
Rose Cottage
Hellwood Farm
Scarcroft Farm
Jock o' Brigs House
Beacon Hill Lodge
Wood Lodge
Cricket Ground
Kidhirst Wood
Oaklands Manor
Scarcroft Lodge
Nursery
White Hall
Brandon Grange Farm
Scarcroft Manor

16
29
46

LS22
Wetherby
LS23
Compton
Comb Bank
Compton Cottages
Compton Grove
Waver Spring Pond
Cow Moor
Low Cow Moor Wood
Whinney Cow Moor Wood
Walk-a-bout
Howcroft Wood
Collingham Moor
Quarry Plantation
Dalton Parlours
Parlours Plantation
Rigton Bank
Reservoir (covered)
LADY WOOD
Lund Wood
Lund Wood Close
Dalton Hill
WEST WOODS
Spring Wood
Old Pickhill Rash
Hope Hall
Hope Hall Cottages
Holme Farm Cottages
Holme Farm
Stubbings
Young Pickhill Rash
Wothersome
STUBBING MOOR
Stubbing Moor Plantation
Ragdale Plantation
Lake Plantation
Wothersome Lake
Lendrick Hills
Terry Lug
Terry Lug Plantation
The Shambles
Privet Plantation
Norwood Bottoms
Milner Wood
Milner Beck
Thorner Beck
Bramham Park
THE GARDENS
North Terrace
South Ter.
Thorner Moor Plantation
Norwood House Farm
Nova Scotia
BRAMHAM PARK
COMPTON LANE
JEWITT LANE
MOOR LANE
DALTON LANE
THORNER LANE
THORNER ROAD
FARM LANE
KENNELS LANE
BRAMHAM ROAD
MANGRILL LANE
SOUTH APPROACH
LEEDS ROAD A58
CRABTREE GREEN
CRABTREE HILL
North Lodge Plan
CLIFFO
H J K L M N G
1 2 3 4 5 6 7 8 9
38 39 440 41
445 44 43 42 41
17 32 47

GREAT A1 NORTH ROAD
Grove Farm
Collingham Moor
WINNOW LANE
PRIMROSE LANE
BOSTON SPA
Playing Fields
Boston Spa Comp. Sch.
Helmsley Farm
The Paddocks
St. John's Catholic School for the Deaf
St. John's Farm
ST. JOHN'S RD.
Martin Ho. Hospice
West Oaks Sch.
Jun. & Inf. Sch.
Playing Field
Prim. Sch.
HIGH STREET
A659
Spa Baths
Thorparch Bridge
CHURCH FIELD
TOWN INGS
RIVER WHARFE
CLIFFORD MOOR
RHODES LANE
Clifford Moor Farm Cottage
Clifford Moor Farm
CLIFFORD
Clifford Prim. Sch.
Northways School
The Bungalow
The Orchards
Firs Lodge
Firgreen Beck
Firgreen Bridge
BAR STREET
The Willows
Mills
OLD MILL LANE
Wetherby
LS23
Holly Trees
Victoria Farm
Woodland View
Three Trees Bungalow
Lyncmar
Orchard House
Bramham Croft Farm
Bramham Prim. Sch.
Willowgarth
Carr Beck
Wilks Wood
WEST WOODS
West Woods Farm
31
The Mill House
WINDMILL ROAD
HEYGATE LANE
RHODE'S HILL LANE
THORNER ROAD
TENTER HILL
North Lodge
North Lodge Plantations
BIGGIN PARK
BRAMHAM
TOULSTON LANE
New York Farm
The Bee Farm
Rec. Grd.
Bramham House
Bramham Lodge
HEADLEY LANE
Hume's Plantation
Lendrick Hills
Bramham Beck
College Farm
Bramham Biggin
Oldroad Plantation
East Lodge Cottages
Biggin Wood
Bowcliffe Hall
Bowcliffe Farm
Wellhill Plantation
Well Hill
Wellhill Farm
Playing Field
BRAMHAM MOOR
Headley Plantation
Paradise Farm
Bramham Park
SOUTH APPROACH
RAKES WOOD
Dawsonfield Plantation
Open Rakes
Openrakes Brook
Camp Hill
Spen Common
BRAMHAM PARK
Temple
BLACK FEN
SPEN COMMON
Spen Farm
Lord Bingley's Walk
18
48

Tadcaster
LS24
Newton Kyme
Toulston
BRAMHAM MOOR
A659
A64
RIVER WHARFE
SELBY HARROGATE
SELBY LEEDS
Wharfe Bridge
Ingle Bank Wood
Works
Papyrus Villas
Oglethorpe Bungalows
Oglethorpe Cottage
Oglethorpe Hall Farm
Toulston Hall Farm
Adaman Graves
The Paddocks
Rudgate Bridge
Rudgate Cottages
Lucerne Cotts.
Lucerne Farm
St. Helen's Farm
St. Helen's Cottage
St. Helen's Grange
Tithe Barn Cott.
Newton Kyme Hall
MAIN STREET
CROFT LANE
WATSON'S LANE
RUDGATE
Crow Wood
Bond Ings
Long Plantation
The Wilfrey
Easedike
Wighill Ings
Smaws Ings
New Plantation
Smaws Wood
The Cottages
Smaws Farm
Smaws Bridge
Dog Kennels Wood
Inholmes
Robshaw Hole
Smaws Quarry
Toulston Wood
Oglethorpe Hills
Rose Cottage
Sunflower Cotts.
Ten. Cts.
Running Track
Tadcaster Grammar School
Tadcaster High Moor
Toulston Polo Ground
Manor Farm
Toulston Grange
Lords Plantation
Lordswood Cricket School
High Moor Farm
High Moor Grange Cottages
High Moor Grange Farm
Black Wood
Wise Warren
Headley Hall
WARREN LANE
GARNET LANE
GARNET TERRACE
Roman Ridge
Brick House Farm
MOOR LANE
Jackdaw Crag Quarry
Crag Wood
Hill of Comfort
Gas Valve Compound
Warren Cottages
Warren House Farm
Headley Bar
Wingatehill Farm
Sugar Hill Farm
Wingate Hill
FANNY LANE
BRANT LANE
OLD LONDON RD.
CHANTRY
WILLOW RISE
WOODLANDS
SEDGE RI.
MARLBOROUGH AV.
STUTTON RD.
Depot
Sewage Works
H J K L M N G
1 2 3 4 5 6 7 8 9
19
49
445 46 47
41 42 43 44 445

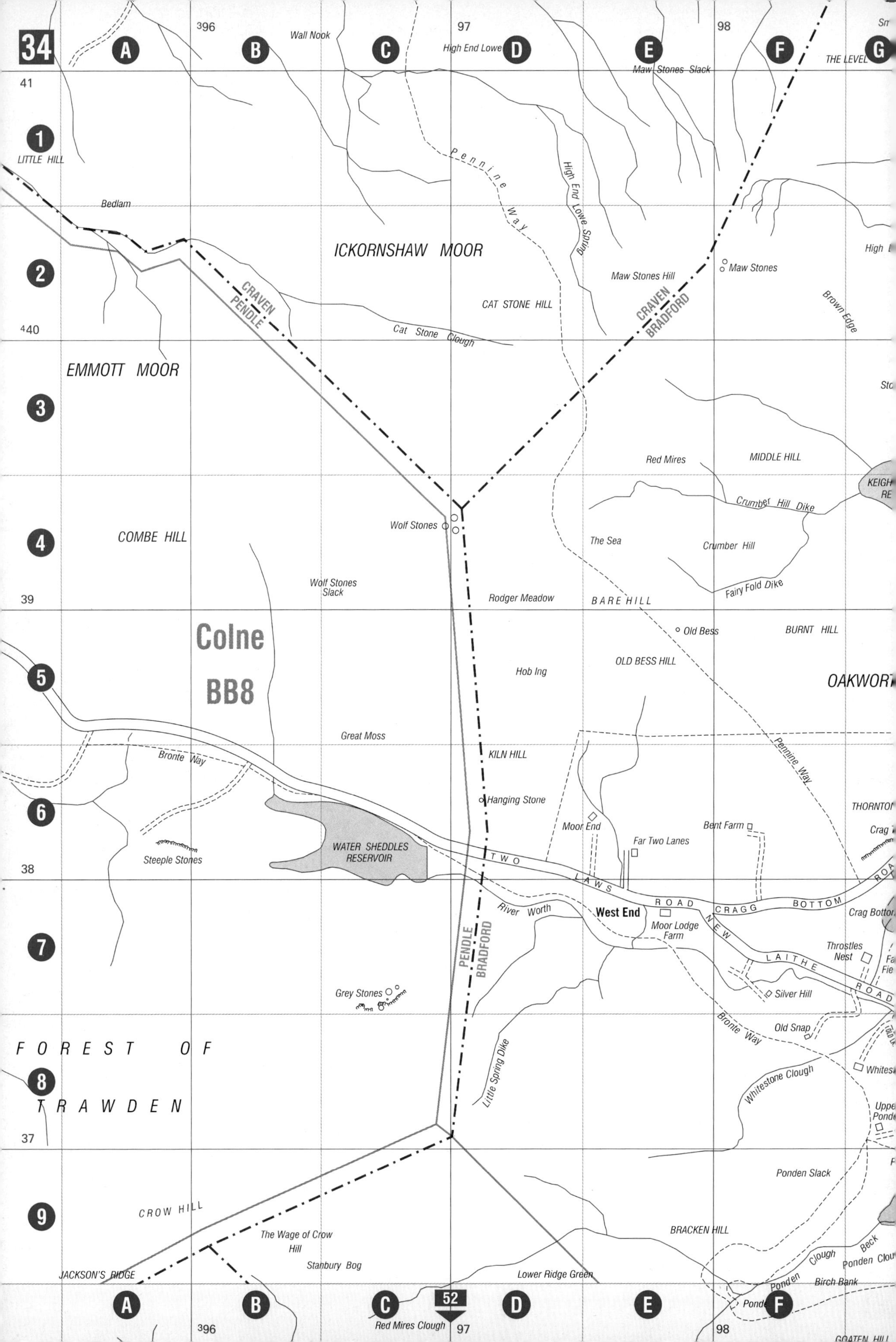
A
B
C
D
E
F
G
396
97
98
41
440
39
38
37
1
2
3
4
5
6
7
8
9
Wall Nook
High End Lowe
Maw Stones Slack
THE LEVEL
LITTLE HILL
Bedlam
Pennine Way
High End Lowe Spring
ICKORNSHAW MOOR
High
Maw Stones
Maw Stones Hill
CRAVEN
PENDLE
CAT STONE HILL
CRAVEN
BRADFORD
Brown Edge
Cat Stone Clough
EMMOTT MOOR
Red Mires
MIDDLE HILL
Crumber Hill Dike
Wolf Stones
COMBE HILL
The Sea
Crumber Hill
Wolf Stones Slack
Fairy Fold Dike
Rodger Meadow
BARE HILL
Old Bess
BURNT HILL
Colne
BB8
Hob Ing
OLD BESS HILL
Great Moss
Bronte Way
KILN HILL
Pennine Way
Hanging Stone
Moor End
Bent Farm
Far Two Lanes
Steeple Stones
WATER SHEDDLES RESERVOIR
TWO LAWS ROAD
CRAGG BOTTOM
River Worth
West End
Moor Lodge Farm
NEW LAITHE ROAD
Throstles Nest
PENDLE
BRADFORD
Silver Hill
Grey Stones
Bronte Way
Old Snap
FOREST OF TRAWDEN
Little Spring Dike
Whitestone Clough
Ponden Slack
CROW HILL
BRACKEN HILL
The Wage of Crow Hill
Ponden Clough
Beck
Stanbury Bog
Birch Bank
JACKSON'S RIDGE
Lower Ridge Green
Red Mires Clough

52

35
Keighley
BD22
KEIGHLEY MOOR
MOOR
The New Allotment
ROUND HILL
LONG GATE
COPPY LA.
GREYSTONES LANE
Grey Stones Hill
Grey Stones
GREYSTONES
Greensykes New Farm
LANE TODLEY HALL ROAD
Todley Hill
Todley Farm
Shooting Box
SLIPPERY FORD
Far Slippery Ford
Middle Slippery Ford
Near Slippery Ford
Bottoms Farm
Sough Hole
Grey Stones Farm
Chamber Hole
Dean Beck
DEAN LANE
Dob Field
DEAN LA.
FALLOW
Newsholme Dean
Newsholme Dean Farm
Dean Br.
Ibber Dike
Ibber Flat
Lower Intake Rough
Black Hill Bottom
MORKIN HILL
Morkin Bridge
Lower White Hill Farm
Higher White Hill Farm
White Hill Farm
Springwood Farm
Crags
Fox Holes
WHITEHILL ROAD
Lower Dean Laithe
Cat Clough
Higher Intake Rough
Higher Intake
Morkin Beck
Wet Head Hill
Denby Ing
Sheep Hills
Hill Top Farm
Cliffe Farm
Newsholme
Church Farm
Green End Farm
High Bobbin Mill
Newsholme Bridge
GREEN LANE
Field Head
Green Lane Bridge
Gutter Beck
Trap Nook Hill
Trap Nook
Blue Scar
Blue Scar Beck
Wet Head Edge
Wet Head
Broad Head
Broad Head Height
Broadhead Dairy Farm
Broadhead Farm
BROAD HEAD LANE
Lumb Head
Clough Hey
Rough Piece
Lime Scar Hole
Nook
Nook Lane
Grange Farm
GRANGE LANE
WHITE LANE
Quake
BROAD ROAD
Clough Hey Allotment
Brook Springs
Lower Turnshaw
Scotland Hill
Moorcock
Tewitt Hall Farm
TURNSHAW ROAD
Turnshaw Farm
Roms Greave Hill
Oakworth Cottage
Higher Turnshaw Farm
KILN HILL
Pine Wood
Sand Pit Hill
Dry Clough Farm
Pickles Hill
Scholes
Middle Hob Cote
Middle Hob Cote Farm
Dean Clough Head
Harehill House
School House Farm
Hare Hill
HAREHILLS LANE
HOB COTE LANE
High Hob Cote Farm
Higher Scholes
Will Clough
Blue Stone Delph
HARE HILL EDGE
DARK LA.
SCHOLES LANE
Near Scholes Farm
Laverock Hall
Lower Scholes Farm
Lower Scholes
Hill Top
Well Head Farm
Works
Oldfield First Sch.
MEAN LANE
Ashcroft Farm
West House Farm
STREET HEAD LANE
Street Head Farm
Daisy Mount
EDGE ROAD
Oldfield
Manor Farm
Bent House Farm
Bronmagnum
Dean Fields
Oldfield House
GRIFFE
Lumb
Higher Pitcher Clough
Dean Field Farm
OLDFIELD LANE
Oldfield House Farm
Oldfield End Farm
Intake Laithe Farm
River Worth
OLDFIELD
Lumb Foot
LUMBFOOT RD.
Hollings Mill Farm
Scar Top Cottages
Cemy.
Milking Hill Farm
Ponden Reservoir
TOP ROAD
Hollings Wood
Sladen Bridge
Hollings
Weir
Ponden Hall
PONDEN LANE
HOB LANE
Stanbury
Dyke Farm
Beck
The Ridge
Bank Cottage
Old Silent Inn
MOOR VW. TER.
Cross Farm
SUN STREET
RESERVOIR ROAD
Sladen
Rush Isles
Royds Hall Farm
Near Coney Garth
MAIN STREET
Far Coney Garth
Stanbury First Sch.
Hob Hill
Works
Hill Top
Clough Hole
Wood
Pennine Way
Lower Laithe Reservoir
Lower Slack
Buckley Farm
Cold Knoll End
CEMETERY ROAD
Penistone Slack
Near Slack
Enfield Side
Intake Farm
Far Slack
Near Enfield Side
Bully Trees Farm
Far Enfield Side
Springs
Beck
Bronte Way
ENFIELD SIDE ROAD
MOOR
The Slack
Picnic Area
Upper Heights
BACK LANE
Stanbury Height
Master Stones
53
36
99
400
01
02
41
440
39
38
37
G
H
J
K
L
M
N
1
2
3
4
5
6
7
8
9

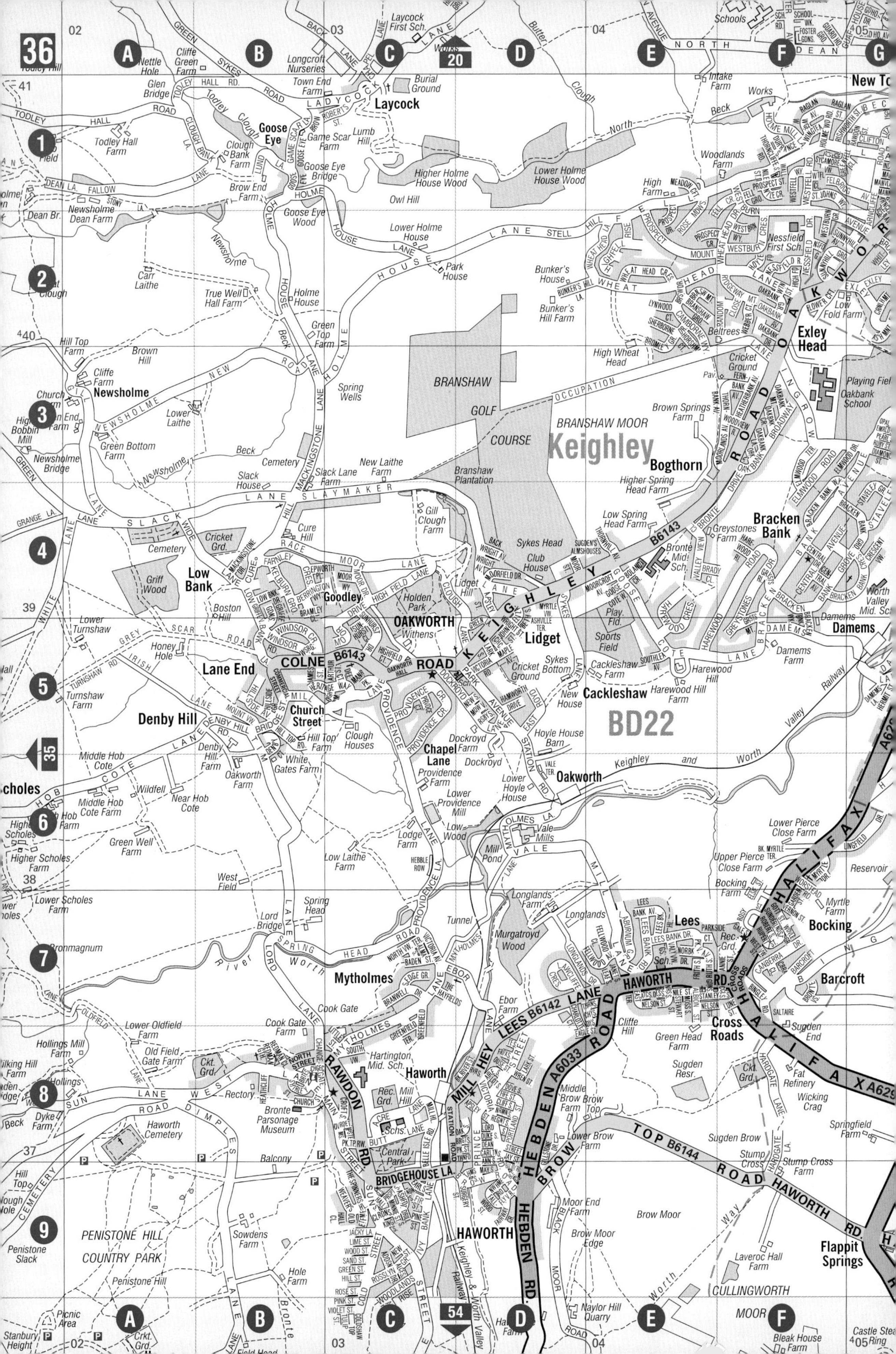
02
03
04
05
A
B
C
D
E
F
G
1
2
3
4
5
6
7
8
9
41
40
39
38
37
20
35
54
Laycock
Laycock First Sch.
Longcroft Nurseries
Town End Farm
Burial Ground
Works
Nettle Hole
Cliffe Green Farm
Glen Bridge
Todley Hall
TODLEY HALL ROAD
GREEN SYKES ROAD
TODLEY HALL RD.
LADYCOCK
Goose Eye
Todley Hall Farm
Todley Clough
Clough Bank Farm
CLOUGH BANK LA.
Game Scar Farm
Lumb Hill
Goose Eye Bridge
Higher Holme House Wood
Lower Holme House Wood
Owl Hill
Brow End Farm
DEAN LA.
FALLOW LANE
Dean Br.
Newsholme Dean Farm
Goose Eye Wood
HOLME HOUSE LANE
Lower Holme House
Park House
Newsholme
Carr Laithe
True Well Hall Farm
Holme House
Green Top Farm
Clough
Hill Top Farm
Brown Hill
Cliffe Farm
Newsholme
Church
NEW ROAD
Lower Laithe
Spring Wells
Green Bottom Farm
Newsholme Bridge
Beck
Cemetery
Slack House
Slack Lane Farm
New Laithe Farm
MACKINGSTONE LANE
SLAYMAKER LANE
SLACK LANE
GRANGE LA.
WHITE LANE
Cricket Grd.
Cemetery
Cure Hill
Gill Clough Farm
RACE MOOR LANE
Griff Wood
Low Bank
Boston Hill
Goodley
HIGH FIELD LANE
Holden Park
OAKWORTH
Withens
Lower Turnshaw
GREY SCAR ROAD
Honey Hole
IRISH
TURNSHAW RD.
Turnshaw Farm
Lane End
COLNE B6143 ROAD
Church Street
Denby Hill
Hill Top Farm
Clough Houses
PROVIDENCE LANE
Middle Hob Cote
Denby Hill Farm
White Gates Farm
Oakworth Farm
Scholes
HOB COTE LANE
Wildfell
Middle Hob Cote Farm
Near Hob Cote
Hob Farm
Higher Scholes
Green Well Farm
Higher Scholes Farm
West Field
Lower Scholes Farm
Lord Bridge
Spring Head
SPRING HEAD ROAD
River Worth
LORD LANE
Bronmagnum
Cook Gate
Cook Gate Farm
Lower Oldfield Farm
OLDFIELD
Hollings Mill Farm
Old Field Gate Farm
Ckt. Grd.
Hollings
Dyke Farm
SUN LANE WEST
Rectory
Bronte Parsonage Museum
Haworth Cemetery
DIMPLES LANE
Balcony
Hill Top
CEMETERY
PENISTONE HILL COUNTRY PARK
Penistone Hill
Penistone Slack
Sowdens Farm
Hole Farm
Picnic Area
Stanbury Height
Crkt. Grd.
Bronte
Mytholmes
MYTHOLMES
Hartington Mid. Sch.
Haworth
Rec. Grd.
Mill Hill
Schs.
Central Park
BRIDGEHOUSE LA.
RAWDON RD.
MAIN STREET
HAWORTH
Keighley & Worth Valley Railway
Tunnel
Low Laithe Farm
Lodge Farm
Low Wood
Lower Providence Mill
Providence Farm
Chapel Lane
Dockroyd Farm
Dockroyd
Mill Pond
Vale Mills
Longlands Farm
Longlands
Murgatroyd Wood
Ebor Farm
MILL HEY
LEES B6142 LANE
HAWORTH ROAD
HEBDEN A6033 ROAD
HEBDEN RD.
BROW
Middle Brow Farm
Brow Top
Lower Brow Farm
Moor End Farm
Brow Moor Edge
BLACK MOOR ROAD
Naylor Hill Quarry
Cliffe Hill
Green Head Farm
Sugden Resr.
Cross Roads
Lees
TOP B6144 ROAD
HAWORTH RD.
Brow Moor
Sugden Brow
Stump Cross
Stump Cross Farm
HARDGATE LANE
Laveroc Hall Farm
CULLINGWORTH MOOR
Bleak House Farm
Castle Stead Ring
Flappit Springs
Springfield Farm
Wicking Crag
Fat Refinery
Sugden End
Barcroft
Bocking
Myrtle Farm
Bocking Farm
Upper Pierce Close Farm
Lower Pierce Close Farm
Reservoir
HALIFAX ROAD
A629
Worth Valley Railway
Keighley and Worth
Oakworth
STATION RD.
Lower Hoyle House
Hoyle House Barn
BD22
New House
Cackleshaw
Harewood Hill Farm
Harewood Hill
Cackleshaw Farm
Sports Field
Play. Fld.
Cricket Ground
Sykes Bottom
Lidget
KEIGHLEY ROAD
B6143
Club House
Sykes Head
Bronte Mid. Sch.
Greystones Farm
Bracken Bank
Damems
Damems Farm
DAMEMS LANE
Worth Valley Mid. Sch.
Keighley
BRANSHAW MOOR
BRANSHAW GOLF COURSE
Branshaw Plantation
Bogthorn
Higher Spring Head Farm
Low Spring Head Farm
Brown Springs Farm
High Wheat Head
OCCUPATION
Cricket Ground
Pav.
OAKWORTH ROAD
INGROW
Playing Field
Oakbank School
Exley Head
Low Fold Farm
Beltrees
Bunker's House
Bunker's Hill Farm
WHEAT HEAD LANE
Nessfield First Sch.
High Farm
Woodlands Farm
STELL HILL
Lower Holme House Wood
North Beck
Intake Farm
Works
Beck
New Town
Schools
NORTH DEAN AVENUE
Butter Clough

KEIGHLEY
BD21
Bingley
BD16
Bradford
BD13
BD15
Thwaites
Thwaites Brow
Park Wood Bottom
Parkwood
Long Lee
Holy Croft
Knowle Park
Spring Bank
Ingrow West
Ingrow
Woodhouse
Hainworth
Hainworth Shaw
Hermit Hole
Moor Edge
HARDEN
CULLINGWORTH
HARDEN MOOR
Midgeham Flat
Spring Head Heights
Grinning Stone
Heather Park
Race Course Hill
Hog Holes Brow
Catstones Hill
Catstones Moor
Hunter Hill Plantation
Rough Plantation
Great Ridge Wood
Goitstock Wood
Goitstock Waterfall
Hallas Lumbs
Sugden Wood
Hunger Hill Plantation
Cullingworth Fields
Swire Smith Middle Sch.
Parkside Middle School
HARDEN & BINGLEY CARAVAN PARK
AIRE VALLEY RD.
SOUTH STREET
A629
HALIFAX RD.
HILL END ROAD B6429
KEIGHLEY ROAD
BINGLEY ROAD
HALIFAX ROAD
LONG LANE
RYECROFT ROAD
B6144
B6143
21
38
55
H
J
K
L
M
N
G
1
2
3
4
5
6
7
8
9
06
07
08
41
440
39
38
37

38
A
B
C
D
E
F
G
1
2
3
4
5
6
7
8
9
09
410
11
41
440
39
38
37
22
37
56
AIRE VALLEY A650 ROAD
Keighley
BD21
Marley Brow Wood
Small Tail Wood
Round Hill Wood
Airdale Barn
Airedale Farm
Ryshworth Middle Sch.
Thornfield Farm
Deer Park
Marley Hall Farm
Round Hill
Marley Brow
Transfield Rock
Transfield Wood
Upper Transfield Farm
Transfield Top
Hutler Hill
Settling Ponds
Morton Beck
Weir
Cop Hirst Wood
Blakey Wood
Mill Race
Works
Castlefields Ind. Est.
Ind. Est.
Sports Ground
Recreation Ground
Playing Field
Offices
Works
KEIGHLEY
Lay Thorpe
Micklethwaite Bridge (Swing)
Green Hill Wood
Greenhill Farm
Greenhill Crag Farm
Higher Heights Farm
Crossflatts
Leeds & Liverpool Canal
Lady Park Nursing Home
PRINCE OF WALES PARK
Altar Farm
Raven Royd Farm
Mill Stream
Bingley Grammar Sch.
Playing Field
Swing Bri.
Five Rise Locks
Five Rise Farm
(Proposed)
Druid's Altar
Altar Wood
Altar Crag
Altar Well
HOLLIN PLANTATION
RIVER AIRE
Bingley Cemetery
A650 ROAD
Three Rise Lock
Priestthorpe
ALTAR LANE
Race Course Plantation
White Cote
Ewe Hills
Square Plantation
Cross Gates
Kettlewell Reservoir
BINGLEY ST.IVES GOLF COURSE
Works
Weir
Ireland Bri.
MILLGATE
MAIN
Crow Nest
Scotch Fir Plantation
Fairfax Entrenchment
Pan Hole
Mon.
Golf Cotts.
The Coppice
Round Plantation
Lady Blantyre's Rock
Club House
Betty's Lodge
Milner Spring
Bingley
Bell Bank Wood
Holme House Wood
Hlth. Cen.
Baths
Arts Cen.
Home Farm
St.Ives
Cuckoo Nest Wood
Goose Wing
Low Park
Resr. (covered)
Clay Gates
Town Hall
BINGLEY
MYRTLE PARK
Paddling Pool
Coppice Pond
Moor Edge
Cuckoo Nest
Lodge
B6429
Carr Wood
Birkey Bank Wood
Harden
Weir
Beckfoot House
Beck
Hesp Hills
Sports Grd.
Cricket Grd.
Tennis Cts.
Works
Beckfoot Grammar School
Play. Fld.
HARDEN
Cricket Grd.
HARDEN
Woodbank Nurseries
Harden Grange Farm
Beck Foot
Beckfoot Farm
Ford
Cock Croft Fold
Woodbank
Harden Grange
Bingley
SHIPLEY GOLF COURSE
BD16
RIVER AIRE
Cottingley Bri.
Club House
Cricket Grd.
Braes Castle
Harden Beck
Weir
Park Rocks
North Wood
Harden Hall
Harden Beck Bridge
Mytholme Beck
Ruin Bank Wood
Black Hills
Park Rocks
Round Hill
Gill Wood
Lamb Hill
Hills Wood
Harden Beck Mill
Weir
Mytholme
Mytholme Bridge
Bank Top
Ridge Holes
COTTINGLEY WOOD ESTATE
Deep Stone
Crag Wood
Bank Top Quarry
LEE LANE
Lee Farm
Bilberry Bank
Wilsden Beck
March Cote Farm
Rec. Grd.
Cottingley First Sch.
Over Bents Farm
BENTS LANE
Bradford
Copy House
CROSS LANE
COPLOWE LANE
BD15
Coplowe Hall
Coplowe Hill
Stock-a-Close Farm
Stockagate
MARCH COTE LANE
COTTINGLEY
Birket Hill
Cottingley Moor
Cottingley Beck Bridge
Pye Bank Farm
Kingscliff
Wilsden Hill
Norr
Claremont Farm
Norr Fold Farm
Norr Hill Farm
Wilsden First School
Norr Farm
Nook House
WILSDEN
Cottingley Moor Bridge
B6146
COTTINGLEY
BRADFORD ROAD

Eldwick Hall Farm
Moorland Grange
Moorland Grange Farm
Bungalow
Tewitt House
Cragg Wood Farm
Cragg Wood
Cropper Fold
Golcar Farm
Low Fold
Raines Farm
Low Gate
Cat Stone
Sconce Crag
Howden Wood
Low Hill
Pennythorn Hill
BAILDON GOLF COURSE
Bracken Hill
Acrehowe Hill
Eldwick Beck
Recreation Ground
Springfield
Spring Farm
Gloversham Farm
Meadowsweet Farm
The Springs
Eldwick First Sch.
Gloversham Beck
Waterfall
Spring Wood
Cup & Ring Marked Rocks
Cup Marked Rocks
Low Plain
Plain Side
Windy Hill
Baildon Hill
Dobrudden Farm
DOBRUDDEN CARAVAN PARK
Eldwick
High Plain
BAILDON MOOR
BD17
Strathmore Farm
Hope Hill
Brandcliffe Hill
Gilstead Middle School
Laurel Bank Farm
Mitton Spring
St. Bees
Gilstead
Sheriff Farm
Hope Farm
CROOK FARM CARAVAN PARK
Crook Farm
Dove Hall
Water Works
Ferncliffe
Lane End Farm
Shipley
Reservoir (covered)
Oakleigh
Belmont Middle School
Clark House
Bracken Hall Green
Bracken Hall (Countryside Centre)
Delph Wood
Shipley Glen
Catten Stones
BAILDON
Trench Wood
Glen Cable Tramway
Walker Wood
Midgeley Wood
Tennis Courts
Trench
Trench Farm
Playing Fields
South Lodge
Milnerfield Farm
Club House
Salt Grammar School
Glenaire First School
Baildon Green
Dowley Gap
Bull Coppy Wood
Scourer Bridge
Locks
Dowley Gap Bridge
Roberts Park
Cricket Grd.
Fairbank Wood
Hirst Wood
Aqueduct
Sewage Works
Hirst Lock
Football Grd.
Cricket Grd.
Swing Bri.
Leeds and Liverpool Canal
Saltaire
Art Gall.
Mill
Dales Way
Govt. Offices
Sports Cen.
Dowley Gap Nursery
Rye Loaf Hill
Nab Wood Cemetery
Works
Chapel Cemetery
Hirst Wood
Rye Loaf Wood
Viaduct
Bankfield Farm
SALTAIRE A657 RD.
COMMERCIAL ST.
BRIGGATE
Crowgill Park
BINGLEY A650 ROAD
Nab Wood
The Yorkshire Clinic
Cottingley Hall Nursing Home
Playing Fields
Nab Wood Middle Sch.
Moorhead
Round Wood
Hlth. Cen.
Superstore
SHIPLEY
BRADFORD ROAD
OTLEY ROAD A6038
VALLEY ROAD
Nab Wood Grammar Sch.
Old Spring Wood
Throstle Nest Farm
New Close
Hollin Hall Farm
Northcliff Playing Fields
Bowling Greens
Putting Green
Shipley Fields
BD18
Stair Foot Farm
Club House
Playing Fields
Stoney Lee Middle School
Dungeon Wood
Northcliff Woods
Dike
COTTINGLEY CLIFFE ROAD B6269
New Brighton
Cliff Farm
Dawson Wood
Bandstand
NORTHCLIFFE GOLF COURSE
Shipley High Moor
Bunkers Hill
Shay Farm
Heaton Shay
Stoney Ridge Plantation
Heaton Royds
23
40
57
12
13
14

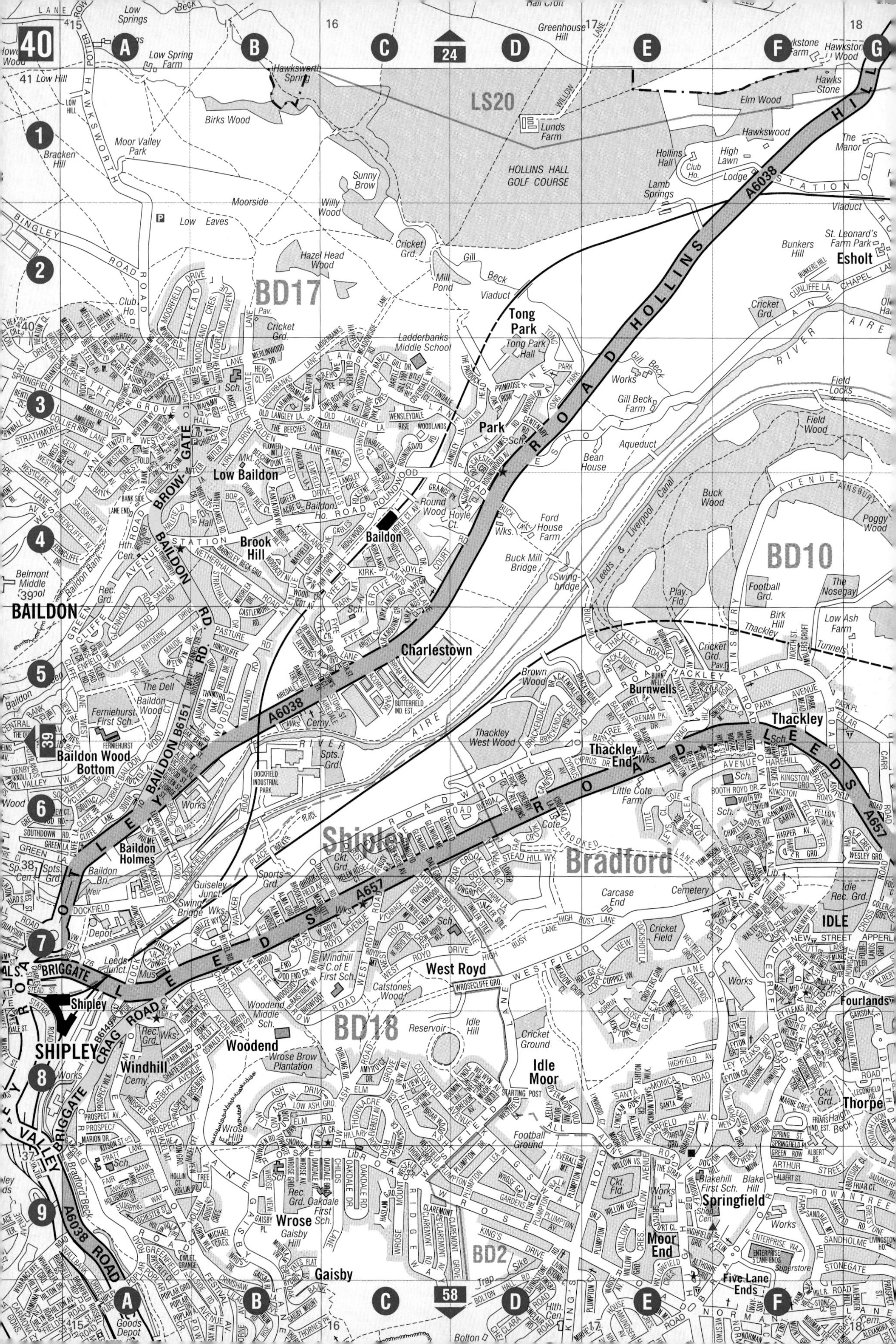

A
B
C
D
E
F
G
16
17
18
15
24
58
39
1
2
3
4
5
6
7
8
9
LS20
BD17
BD10
BD18
BD2
Low Springs
Low Spring Farm
Hawksworth Spring
Greenhouse Hill
Hawkstone Farm
Hawkstone Wood
Hawks Stone
Elm Wood
Hawkswood
Lunds Farm
Birks Wood
Moor Valley Park
Bracken Hill
Low Hill
HOLLINS HALL GOLF COURSE
Hollins Hall
High Lawn
Club Ho.
Lodge
Lamb Springs
The Manor
Sunny Brow
Willy Wood
Moorside
Low Eaves
Cricket Grd.
Hazel Head Wood
Mill Pond
Gill Beck
Viaduct
Bunkers Hill
St. Leonard's Farm Park
Esholt
Tong Park
Tong Park Hall
Ladderbanks Middle School
Park
Works
Gill Beck Farm
Field Locks
Field Wood
Aqueduct
Bean House
Buck Wood
Poggy Wood
Ford House Farm
Buck Mill Bridge
Swing-bridge
Leeds & Liverpool Canal
Low Baildon
Brook Hill
Baildon
Round Wood
Hoyle Ct.
Belmont Middle School
BAILDON
Charlestown
Play. Fld.
Football Grd.
The Nosegay
Birk Hill
Low Ash Farm
Thackley Tunnels
Brown Wood
Burnwells
Thackley
Thackley West Wood
Thackley End
Little Cote Farm
Ferniehurst First Sch.
Baildon Wood Bottom
Baildon Wood
The Dell
Baildon Holmes
Dockfield Industrial Park
Butterfield Ind. Est.
Cemy.
Spts. Grd.
Shipley
Bradford
Ckt. Grd.
Sports Grd.
Guiseley Junct.
Swing Bridge
Leeds Junct.
Cemetery
Carcase End
Cricket Field
IDLE
Idle Rec. Grd.
Fourlands
West Royd
Windhill C.of E First Sch.
Catstones Wood
Woodend Middle Sch.
Woodend
Reservoir
Idle Hill
Cricket Ground
Idle Moor
Wrose Brow Plantation
SHIPLEY
Windhill
Cemy.
Rec. Grd.
Wrose Hill
Rec. Grd. Oakdale First Sch.
Wrose
Gaisby Hill
Gaisby
Football Ground
Ckt. Fld.
Moor End
Blakehill First Sch.
Blake Hill
Springfield
Shop. Cen.
Thorpe
Ckt. Grd.
Haigh Beck
Enterprise Lane Ends
Superstore
Five Lane Ends
Bolton
Goods Depot
Bradford Beck
A6038
A657
A6038 ROAD
B6151
B6149
HOLLINS ROAD
LEEDS ROAD
OTLEY ROAD
BAILDON RD.
BROWGATE
CRAG ROAD
BRIGGATE
VALLEY ROAD
KING'S ROAD
WESTFIELD LANE
HIGH BUSY LANE

New Scarborough
Esholt Junction
Sodhall Hill
Sodhall Hill Wood
Park Ghyll Ho.
Manor Farm
Westfield
Esholt Tunnel
Jerrison Wood
Hollins Hill Bottom
Spring Wood
Belmont Wood
Guiseley Beck
Stone Top Wood
Schools
Henshaw
Symcroft
Low Hall
Greenside Farm
YEADON
Depot
Works
Rufford Park
Cricket Grd.
Football Grd.
Sewage Works
Yeadon Gill
Ghyll Fold Farm
Leeds
Bradford
Nether Yeadon
Benton Park Sch.
Larkfield
Larkfield Dam
RAWDON
Gill Wood
Esholt Hall
Home Farm
Swing-bridge
Storm Water Tanks
Micklefield Park
Playing Fld.
Pease Hill
Little London
Micklefield Grange
Fulford Grange
Beech Cott.
Club House
RAWDON GOLF & LAWN TENNIS CLUB
Crow Trees Farm
Holmehurst
Apperley Grange
Rawdon Hall
Rawdon Hall Farm
Low Green
LS19
Nun Wood
Dawson Wood
Hillcourt
Daisy Hill
Nunwood
Bank Ho.
Summer Hill
Ameni
Cliffe House
Brenaire Park
Buckstone Hall
Cragg Wood
Rawdon Carrs
Suspension Bridge
Acacia Farm
Bronte Ho. Prep. Sch.
Oaklands
Underwood Ho.
Lisieux
Briaden
Swing-bridge
Thackley Canal Bridge
Apperley Viaduct
Walk Hill Farm
Lodge
Cawood
Holly Lodge
Woodlands Farm
Bottom Farm
Walk Hill Bridge
Playing Fields
Woodhouse Bridge
Snaith-rend Wood
Plumpton House
Works
Sch.
Woodhouse Grove School
Tennis Courts
Playing Fields
Dobson Locks
Simpson Green
Sports Grd.
Apperley Junction
Kittycroyd
Leeds Country Way
Leeds and Liverpool Canal
Milman Bri. (Swing)
Elm Tree Farm
Apperley Bri.
Sports Ground
Works
Wood Nook
Woodbottom Farm
Apperley Bridge
Snow Ho.
CALVERLEY WOOD
Pudsey
Lodge Wood
The Knoll
Carr Beck
Parkland First & Mid. Schs.
Play. Fld.
West Wood
Champion House
South Lodge
LS28
Lodge Farm
Lodge Bridge (Swing)
Mudge Bank Wood
Rec. Grd.
Superstore
The Knoll
Calverley Parkside Prim. School
CALVERLEY
Calverley Carr Farm
Calverley House Farm
Thorpe Edge
Greengates
Victoria Park
Swim Pool
Brookfield First Sch.
Carr Hills
Hlth. Cen.
Eccleshill Park
Eccleshill Sch.
Reservoir
Works
Bill Wood
The Grange
Chalybeate Well
Round Hill
Playing Field
Sports Cen.
Recn. Grd.
A65
A658
A657
B6152
B6156
NEW ROAD SIDE
HARROGATE ROAD
GREEN LANE
APPERLEY LANE
CALVERLEY LANE
CARR ROAD
RODLEY LANE
LEEDS ROAD
25
42
59
H J K L M N G
1 2 3 4 5 6 7 8 9
19 420 21
41 40 39 38 37

LEEDS BRADFORD INTERNATIONAL AIRPORT
YEADON
Yorkshire Aeroplane Club
Rawdon Common
Plane Tree Hill
Cold Harbour Farm
HORSFORTH GOLF COURSE
Larkfield
Larkfield Dam
Billing Hill
RAWDON
LS19
Leeds
LS18
LS13
Cookridge
Scotland
Oaks Farm
Dean Grange Farm
Nether Springs Cottage
Moseley Farm
Kings Lea
Dean Grange Bungalow
Rookery Cottage
The Rookery
Moor Grange Farm
Moor Grange
Owlet Farm
Owlet Grange
Scotland Beck
Lantwood House
Moss House
Villanura
Beech House
Ling Bob
Wetstone Plantation
The Bungalow Farm
Leeds Country Way
Whetstone Farm
Bayton House
Club House
Yarnbury Sports Centre
The Croft
Brownberrie Manor
North Ives Farm
Westbrook Farm
Lane Ends
Horsforth
Beechwood
Sports Ground
Trinity & All Saints College
Conv.
Westbrook Lane Prim. School
King George's Field
Football Grds.
Troy
Low Green
Rawdon C.of E. Primary Sch.
Jubilee Hall
Layton Croft
Layton Ghyll
Leyton Hall
Horn Hill
Springfield Cottage
Hill Top Farm
Lee Lane Farm
Rawdon Carrs
Works
Stock Hill
Hunger Hills
Horsforth School
Playing Fields
Training Centre
Springfield Farm
West End Prim. Sch.
West End
Red Beck House
High Knott Wood
Well Royd Wood
Woodleigh Hall
Woodleigh Hall Farm
Crematorium
Wood Nook
Wellroyd
Woodbottom Farm
Woodbottom
Daisybank
The Grange
HORSFORTH
HORSFORTH HALL PARK
Cricket Ground
The Meadow
Low Fold
Low Hall Farm
Low Hall
South Field
Burke Wood
Glenburn
Sough Wood
Horsforth Cemetery
Airedale & Wharfedale College
Lodge Bridge (Swing)
Calverley House Farm
Sports Grd.
Swaine Wood
Rec. Ground
Rec. Grd.
Little Hawksworth Wood
The Outwood
Horsforth Newlaithes Jun. Sch.
Newlay Bri. (Footbridge)
Newlay
Owl Bridge (Swing)
Calverley Bridge
Thornton Wood
Newlay Locks
Rodley Fold Farm
Rodley Bri.
Fallwood Marina & Leisure Cen.
Chalybeate Well
Recn. Grd.
Ckt. Grd.
BRAMLEY FALL
LEEDS ROAD
RAWDON ROAD A65
BROADWAY A6120
NEW ROAD SIDE A65
HORSFORTH NEW RD.
RODLEY A657
HARROGATE A658 RD.
BROWNBERRIE ROAD
SCOTLAND LANE
River Aire
Leeds and Liverpool Canal

COOKRIDGE HALL GOLF COURSE
HEADINGLEY GOLF COURSE
Holt Park
Tinshill Moor
Tinshill
Low Farm
LS16
ADEL
Adel Mill
East Moor
Ireland Wood
Lawnswood
LAWNS WOOD CEMETERY
Crematorium
Government Buildings
Bodington Hall (University of Leeds)
University Athletic Ground
Meanwood Grove
Weetwood
West Park
HORSFORTH RING ROAD
RING ROAD WEST PARK
RING ROAD WEETWOOD
RING ROAD ADEL
A6120
OTLEY ROAD
A660
Hawksworth
LS5
LS6
Carnegie College
Leeds Metropolitan University Beckett Park Campus
Beckett Park
Queen's Wood
HEADINGLEY
Far Headingley
A65
AIRE ROAD

28
A
B
C
D
E
F
G
29
430
31
28
62
43
41
40
39
38
37
1
2
3
4
5
6
7
8
9
High Leas
Golf Farm
Alwoodley Park
Adel Head
SAND MOOR GOLF COURSE
Club House
Wigton Knowle
HEADINGLEY GOLF COURSE
King Lane Farm
Adel Brow
Alwoodley Moss
MOORTOWN GOLF COURSE
LS17
Stair Foot Bridge
Alwoodley Crags
Alwoodley Crags Plantation
Sports Club
Sports Ground
Lib. & Comm. Cen.
Pavilion
ALWOODLEY
George Lyttleton Centre
East Moor
Eastmoor Campus
Black Moor
Camp Town
Allerton High School
Archbishop Cranmer Prim. Sch.
Moor Allerton
Synagogue
Seven Arches
Adel East Moor
Adel Prim. Sch.
Scotland Wood
LS16
Dunstarn Farm
Moortown
Donisthorpe Hall
The Heath
Bywater Farm
Racquet & Fitness Club
Clinic
Hostel
A6120
MEANWOOD RING ROAD
MOORTOWN RING ROAD
HARROGATE ROAD
A61
Valley Farm
Meanwood Grove
Penny Field Sch.
Brandon
Cardinal Heenan High Sch.
Tunnel How Hill
Sports Ground
St. Urbans R.C. Prim. Sch.
Nurseries
Parkside House
Carr Manor
Carr Manor Prim. Sch.
Carr Manor High Sch.
Cricket Ground
Meanwood
Hill Top
LS6
Ridge Plantation
Playing Fields
Stonegate School
Recreation Ground
Hollin House
MEANWOOD
STONEGATE ROAD
Chapel Allerton
Chapeltown
Far Headingley
Miles Hill
LS7
POTTERNEWTON LANE B6159
B6157
SCOTT HALL ROAD
Sports Ground
The Potternewton Cen.
Model Farm
HAREHILLS LA.
Hospice

Alwoodley Gates
Leeds Grammar School
Manor House Farm
Wigton Manor
Wigton Heath Farm
Wigton Moor Whin
WIGTON MOOR
ALWOODLEY GOLF COURSE
Club House
Manor Park
Slaid Hill
Shaw Hill
One Oak
Brandon Cottage
Brandon Hall
Hall Farm
Brandon Lodge
Brandon Grange Farm
Low Brandon Farm
Brandon Drain
Brandon
Brandon Royd
Barn Cottage
BRANDON GOLF COURSE
Brandon House
Brandon Nook
Club House
Cricket Ground
SHADWELL
Library
Hawthorn House
Shadwell Grange
Oakfield House
Oakhill
Wigton Moor Prim. Sch.
Shadwell Centre
Leeds
Pits Wood
Manor Farm
Shadwell Prim. Sch.
Ferndale
Oak Cottage
Woodhouse Farm
A6120 ROAD MOORTOWN RING ROAD
Great Heads Beck
Addyman Wood
Great Heads Wood
Syn. & Comm. Cen.
Rugby Football Ground
Sandfield Nurseries
Red Hall Wood
Red Hall Nurseries
Club House
North Hills Wood
ROUNDHAY GOLF COURSE
The Gorge
A6120 SHADWELL
Ram Wood
Castle Wood
Great Heads Wood
Castle
Upper Lake
Park Villas
Allerton Grange High Sch.
Moor Allerton Hall Prim. Sch.
Playing Fields
Mansion Hotel
Tropical World
Canal Gdns.
The Arboretum Lawn
Braim Wood
Cobble Hall
Cobble Hall Farm
LEEDS GOLF COURSE
ROUNDHAY
ROUNDHAY PARK
Fox Wood
Sports Ground
Barran's Fountain
Club House
Wellington Hill
Roundhay Grange
Lidgett Park
Sports Ground
SOLDIERS FIELD
Cafe
Hammond Hall Hostel
Netherleigh
Gledhow Prim. Sch.
LEEDS BUPA HOSP.
Cricket Grd.
Bowling Green
WATERLOO LAKE
Elmete Wood Sch.
ROUNDHAY CARAVAN & CAMPING PARK
Beechwood
Braimwood High Sch. for Boys
Gledhow
Roundhay School
Kerr Mackie Prim. Sch.
LS8
Lady Wood
School
Low Wood
Gledhow Valley
Gledhow Beck
Weirs
The Lake
Gledhow Valley Woods
Prim. Sch.
Hostel
Weir
A58 ROAD EASTERLY
WETHERBY ROAD
Beechwood
Asket Hill Prim. Sch.
Gipton Wood
Superstore
Oakwood
Football Ground
Sch.
29
63
46

LS17
SHADWELL
LS14
Leeds
Sandhills
Whinmoor
WHINMOOR
Wellington Hill
Beechwood
Seacroft
WETHERBY ROAD A58
A58 WELLINGTON HILL
RING ROAD SHADWELL
RING ROAD SEACROFT A6120
YORK ROAD A64
RED HALL LANE
SKELTONS LANE
CARR LANE
COAL ROAD
THORNER LANE
LOWER SANDHILLS
INTAKE LANE
WHINMOOR LANE
HOBBERLEY LANE
BAY HORSE LANE
BRANDON CRESCENT
STONEY LANE
MAIN STREET
RAMSHEAD APPROACH
BOGGART HILL DRIVE
KENTMERE AVENUE
SCHOLES LANE
STATION ROAD
Jock o' Brigs House
Beacon Hill
Wood Lodge
Cricket Ground
Hellwood Farm
Scarcroft Lodge
Oaklands Manor
Rose Cottage
Wood Farm
Scarcroft Manor
Scarcroft Grange
Brandon Grange Farm
Low Brandon Farm
White Hall
Nursery
Barn Cottage
Beech Grove
Grange Cottages
Bay Horse Farm
Beech View Barn
Eltofts Farm
Eltofts House
Riding School
The Homestead
Tennis Courts
Carr Farm
Shadwell Bridge
Shadwell Prim. Sch.
Manor Farm
Church Farm
Birkby Grange Farm
Birkby Hall Farm
Birkby Hill
Bog Plantation
Bank House
Oak Cottage
South View Cottages
Sandfield Nurseries
Hill Top Farm
Barnaby Cotts.
Hobberley House
Red Hall Wood
Red Hall Nurseries
Red Hall
Red Hall Playing Fields
Red Hall Farm
Sandhills Farm
Sandhills House
Thorner Grange
Hillcrest
Intake Ho.
Intake Dairy Farm
Intake Farm
The Grove
Holly Croft
Miry Carr Farm
Field Head
Thorner Lane Farm
Cricket Ground
Bramley Grange
Bramley Grange Farm
Sports Ground
Thorner Bott Wood
Brookeside
Bridge Ho.
West Field
Whinmoor Grange
Roundhay Grange
Play. Field
Prim. Sch.
Works
Sports Ground
Seacroft Industrial Estate
Oak Tree Business Park
Lime Pits Wood
Low Wood
Ramshead Wood
Training Cen.
Grange Farm Prim. Sch.
Our Lady R.C. Prim. Sch.
Asket Hill Prim. Sch.
White Laith Prim. Sch.
Grimes Dike Farm
Willow Garth Farm
Grimes Dyke Prim. Sch.
Warehouses
Morwick Terrace
Morwick Hall
Morwick Farm
Home Farm
Glebe Farm
Rake Beck
Scholes Prim. Sch.
Scholes Park
Grimes Dike
Cock Beck
30
45
64

THORNER
Thorner Moor Plantation
Norwood House Farm
Nova Scotia
Kellfield Grange
THORNER MOOR
Wetherby
LS23
WHITTLE CAR
Jenny Sober Plantation
Jenny Sober
Lord Bingley's Walk
POTTERTON MOOR
BRAMHAM ROAD
CHURCH HILL
Prim. Sch.
KIRKFIELD LANE
ELLERKER LANE
MILNER LANE
Butts Garth Farm
Leeds Country Way
Park House Farm
Park House Farm Cottages
A64 ROAD
YORK ROAD
Woodlands Farm
Littlemoor Farm
LITTLEMOOR LANE
Redhills Plantation
Kiddal Wood
Kiddal Hall
Kiddal Bridge
Kiddal Lane End
Bar House Farm
KIDDAL LANE
MANGRILL LANE
SAW WOOD
Yorksfield Plantation
Jacob's Well
Old Plantation
Potterton
Brickpond Farm
Potterton Hall
Pavilion
The Rookery
The Cotts.
Morgan Cross
Woodlands
POTTERTON PARK
Manor Garth Farm
Manor Garth
Potterton Grange Farm
POTTERTON LANE
Flying Horse Farm
Potterton Beck
South Plantation
Syke House Farm
LS15
Woodhouse Farm
Whinmoor Nook Farm
Whinmoor Nook Wood
Potterton Bridge
Limekiln Hill
The Ridge
Rake Beck
DARK LANE
Low Laith
Ford
Mill
Arthursdale
Stockheld Grange Farm
Wendel Hill
Hall Tower Hill
BOYLE
The View
The Brae
Ass Bridge
Assbridge Lodge
ABERFORD ROAD
Lowfield Farm
Sewage Works
Rakehill Farm
Rake Hill
RAKEHILL ROAD
Springfield Farm
Rake Bridge
BARWICK IN ELMET
Liby.
Barwick-in-Elmet C. of E. Prim. Sch.
Sports Ground
Playing Fields
CARRFIELD LANE
Leeds Country Way
FLATS ROAD
Cricket Grd.
Pav.
Limekiln Hill
SHAWS LANE
SCHOLES
Green Lodge Farm
LEEDS ROAD
TAYLOR LANE
Longlane Beck
Highfield Farm
Barwick Bank
LONG LANE
PARLINGTON MDW.
GASCOIGNE AV.
WYNCROFT CT.
ELMET DR.
RICHMONDFIELD
H J K L M N G
1 2 3 4 5 6 7 8 9
38 39 440 41 37
31
48
65

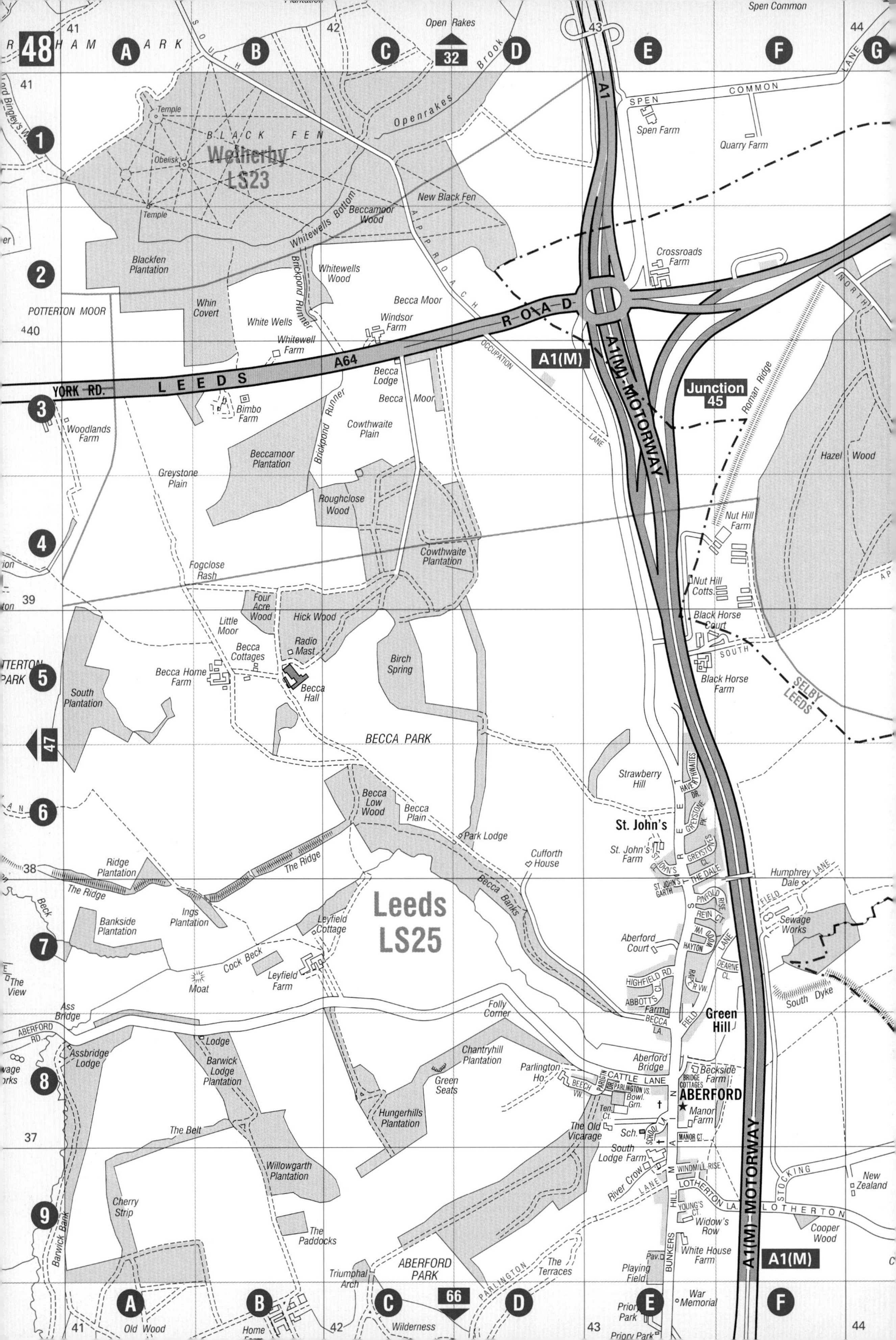

Spen Common
Open Rakes
32
A
B
C
D
E
F
G
Brook
Openrakes
SPEN
COMMON
Spen Farm
Quarry Farm
Temple
Obelisk
Temple
BLACK FEN
Wetherby
LS23
New Black Fen
Beccamoor Wood
Whitewells Bottom
APPROACH
Blackfen Plantation
Whitewells Wood
Crossroads Farm
Becca Moor
Windsor Farm
Whin Covert
White Wells
Brickpond Runner
Whitewell Farm
POTTERTON MOOR
ROAD
A64
LEEDS
YORK RD.
A1(M)
OCCUPATION
LANE
Junction 45
Roman Ridge
Becca Lodge
Becca Moor
Bimbo Farm
Woodlands Farm
Cowthwaite Plain
A1(M) MOTORWAY
A1
Hazel Wood
Beccamoor Plantation
Greystone Plain
Roughclose Wood
Nut Hill Farm
Cowthwaite Plantation
Fogclose Rash
Nut Hill Cotts.
Four Acre Wood
Hick Wood
Little Moor
Radio Mast
Black Horse Court
SOUTH
Becca Cottages
Birch Spring
Becca Home Farm
Becca Hall
Black Horse Farm
SELBY
LEEDS
South Plantation
47
BECCA PARK
Strawberry Hill
HAVERTHWAITES
Becca Low Wood
Becca Plain
DR.
St. John's
GREYSTONE PK.
Park Lodge
Cufforth House
St. John's Farm
GREYSTONES CL.
Ridge Plantation
The Ridge
The Ridge
ST. JOHN'S GARTH
THE DALE
Humphrey Lane
Dale
FIELD
Becca Banks
Leeds
LS25
PINFOLD RISE
REIN CT.
Sewage Works
Beck
Bankside Plantation
Ings Plantation
Leyfield Cottage
Aberford Court
HAYTON
LANE
Cock Beck
Leyfield Farm
DEARNE CL.
The View
Moat
HIGHFIELD RD.
RAPER VW.
ABBOTTS CL.
South Dyke
Abbotts Farm
Green Hill
Ass Bridge
Folly Corner
BECCA LA.
FIELD
ABERFORD RD.
Lodge
Chantryhill Plantation
Aberford Bridge
Assbridge Lodge
Barwick Lodge Plantation
Parlington Ho.
CATTLE LANE
Beckside Farm
BRIDGE COTTAGES
Green Seats
BEECH VW.
PARLINGTON VS.
Bowl. Grn.
ABERFORD
Ten. Ct.
Manor Farm
Hungerhills Plantation
The Old Vicarage
Sch.
SCHOOL LA.
MANOR CT.
MAIN
A1(M) MOTORWAY
The Belt
South Lodge Farm
WINDMILL RISE
Willowgarth Plantation
River Crow
LANE
LOTHERTON LA.
STOCKING
New Zealand
YOUNG'S CT.
LOTHERTON
Cherry Strip
HILL
Widow's Row
Cooper Wood
Barwick Bank
The Paddocks
BUNKERS
White House Farm
A1(M)
ABERFORD PARK
The Terraces
Pav.
Triumphal Arch
PARLINGTON
Playing Field
66
War Memorial
Priory Park
Old Wood
Home
Wilderness
Priory Park
41
42
43
44
40
39
38
37
1
2
3
4
5
6
7
8
9

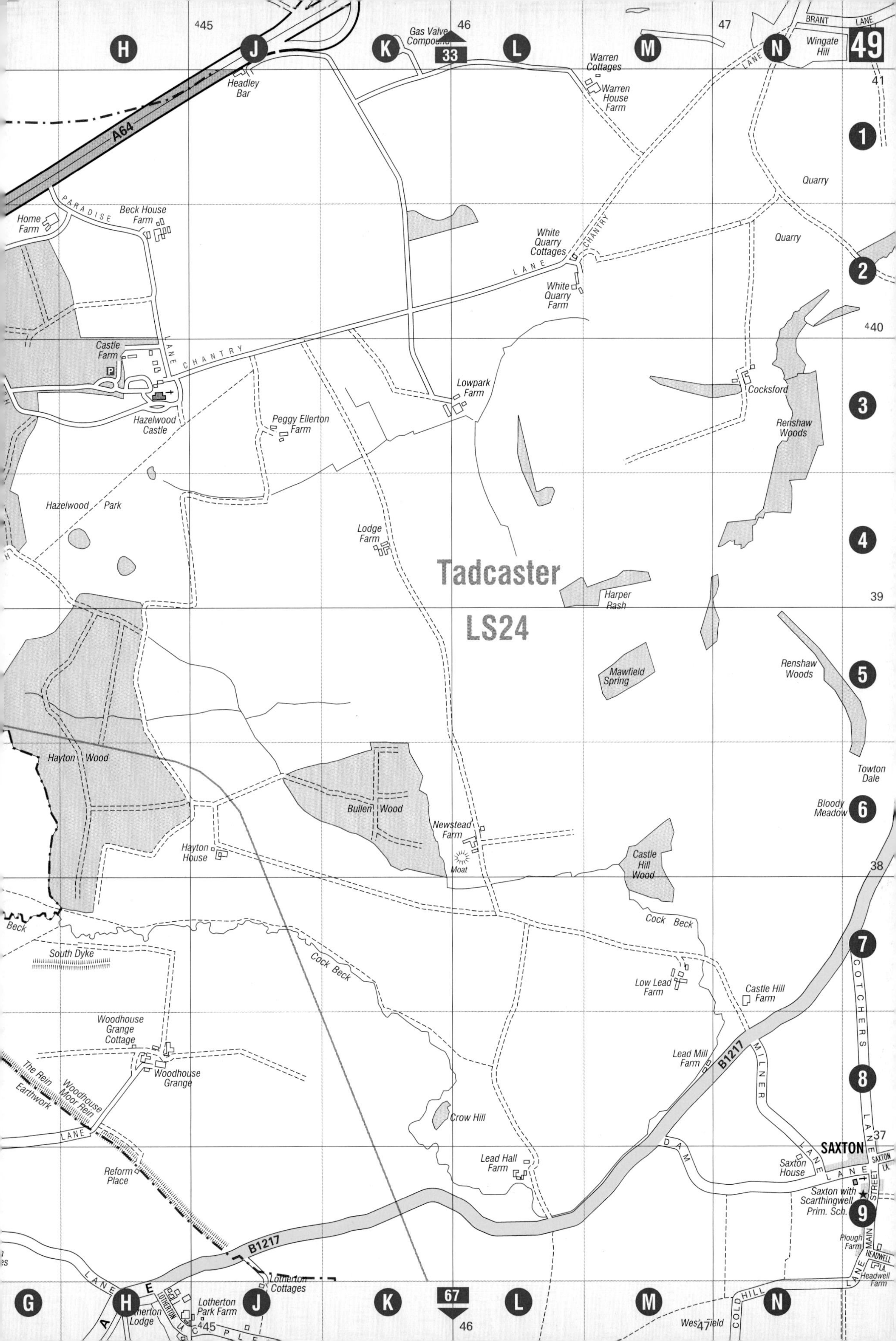

Tadcaster
LS24
A64
B1217
Headley Bar
Gas Valve Compound
Warren Cottages
Warren House Farm
Wingate Hill
Brant Lane
Home Farm
Beck House Farm
Paradise
Castle Farm
Chantry Lane
Hazelwood Castle
White Quarry Cottages
White Quarry Farm
Quarry
Cocksford
Renshaw Woods
Lowpark Farm
Peggy Ellerton Farm
Hazelwood Park
Lodge Farm
Harper Rash
Mawfield Spring
Hayton Wood
Bullen Wood
Newstead Farm
Moat
Hayton House
Castle Hill Wood
Towton Dale
Bloody Meadow
Cock Beck
Beck
South Dyke
Low Lead Farm
Castle Hill Farm
Lead Mill Farm
Woodhouse Grange Cottage
Woodhouse Grange
The Rein Earthwork
Woodhouse Moor Rein
Crow Hill
Lead Hall Farm
Reform Place
Dam Lane
Milner Lane
Cotchers Lane
SAXTON
Saxton House
Saxton Lane
Saxton with Scarthingwell Prim. Sch.
Main Street
Plough Farm
Headwell La.
Headwell Farm
Cold Hill Lane
Lotherton Cottages
Lotherton Park Farm
Lotherton Lodge
West Field
33
67

Ring Stone Hill
Activity Centre
Upper Coldwell Reservoir
DEERSTONE MOOR
Catlow Brook
Pendle Way
Clough
Foulds House Farm
Lower Coldwell Reservoir
WILL MOOR
BEDDIN
Shuttleworth Pasture
Swains Plat Clough
PENDLE
BURNLEY
High Sym
Mere Clark Dike Head
Red Spa
Slack
HALIFAX ROAD
RED SPA MOOR
Long hay Farm
High Ridehalgh
Broad Bank House
Thursden
RIDEHALGH LANE
Braeside
Stephen Hay
MALIFF ROAD
New Bridge
Robin Hood's House
Cockridge Copy
Thursden Valley
New Plantation
Thursden Brook
Park Wood
Black Clough
Tom Groove
Monk Hall
Ell Clough
Rieve Edge
Beadle Hill
Bonfire Hill
Pike Lowe
Elders i' th' Row
Hanson Fold
Rapes Hole
Burnley
BB10
Sweet Well House
Earthwork
Delph Hill
Cairn Circle
Rapes Clough
Western Hills
Twist Castle
Twist Hill
EXTWISTLE MOOR
Birkin Clough
Old Hey Dike
Swinden Reservoirs
Clattering Stones
Swinden Water
BURNLEY
CALDERDALE
Birkin Clough Head
Wasnop Edge
HAMELDON
Standing Stone Height
Ben Edge
Hameldon Pasture
Wether Edge
Gorple Stones
Hurstwood Brook
Smallshaw Clough
Gorple Gate
Antley Gate
Ford

68

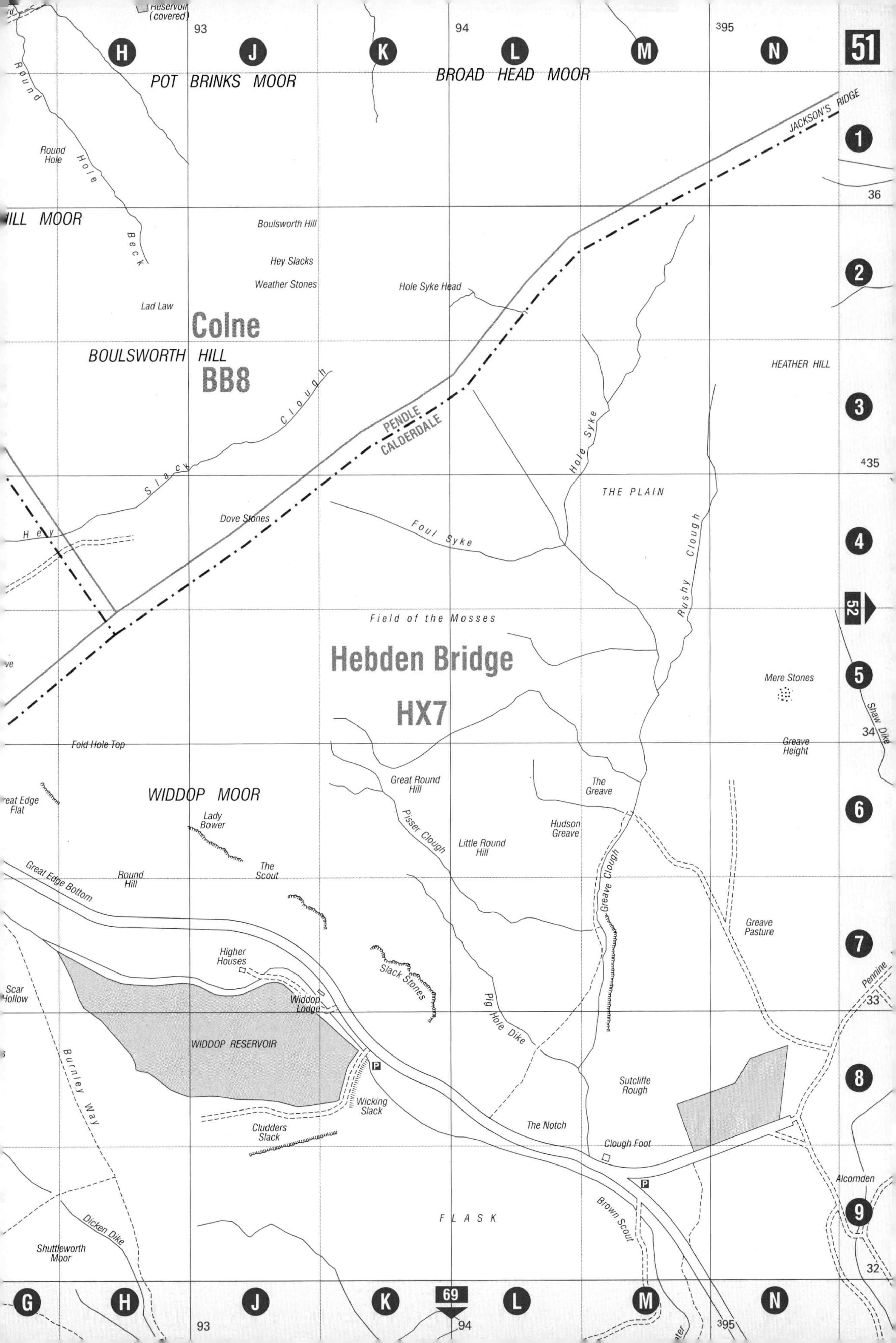

Reservoir (covered)
93
94
395
H
J
K
L
M
N
POT BRINKS MOOR
BROAD HEAD MOOR
JACKSON'S RIDGE
Round Hole Beck
Round Hole
1
36
HILL MOOR
Boulsworth Hill
Hey Slacks
Weather Stones
Hole Syke Head
2
Lad Law
Colne
BB8
BOULSWORTH HILL
HEATHER HILL
Slack Clough
PENDLE
CALDERDALE
Hole Syke
3
435
THE PLAIN
Hey
Dove Stones
Foul Syke
Rushy Clough
4
52
Field of the Mosses
Hebden Bridge
HX7
Mere Stones
5
Shaw Dike
34
Fold Hole Top
Greave Height
WIDDOP MOOR
Great Round Hill
The Greave
Great Edge Flat
Lady Bower
Pisser Clough
Little Round Hill
Hudson Greave
6
Great Edge Bottom
Round Hill
The Scout
Greave Clough
Greave Pasture
7
Higher Houses
Slack Stones
Pennine
Scar Hollow
Widdop Lodge
Pig Hole Dike
33
WIDDOP RESERVOIR
Burnley Way
8
Wicking Slack
Sutcliffe Rough
Cludders Slack
The Notch
Clough Foot
Alcomden
Dicken Dike
FLASK
Brown Scout
9
Shuttleworth Moor
32
G
H
J
K
69
L
M
N
93
94
395

The Wage of Crow Hill
Stanbury Bog
BRACKEN HILL
Lower Ridge Green
Ponden Clough
Beck
Birch Bank
Ponden Kirk
JACKSON'S RIDGE
Red Mires Clough
GOATEN HILL
MIDDLE MOOR HILL
STANBURY MOOR
Low Block Dikes
MIDDLE MOOR
Middle Moor Clough
Withins Slack
Lower Withins
Boft Hole
Alcomden Stones
Walshaw Dean
Blue Scar Clough
Tang Brink Flat
HEATHER HILL
Crumber Red Hill
Crumber Red Dike
Black Sike
Haworth
Withins (Ruin)
Top Withins
Rough Dike
Withins Height
Black Sike Hill
Greave Stone Clough
Burnt Hill Dike
Burnt Hill
Delf Hill
Round Hill
Withins Flat
Green Hole
Burnt Hill Flat
Shoulder Nick
BRADFORD
CALDERDALE
Dick Delf Hill
Grey Fosse Clough
Withins Height End
WALSHAW DEAN UPPER RESERVOIR
Round Hill Moor
Great Hill
Higher Spring Hole
Middle Hill
Pennine Way
Black Dike
MIDDLE
Shaw Dike
Lower Sough
Dean Stones Edge
Greave Height
WALSHAW DEAN MIDDLE RESERVOIR
Hebden Bridge
HX7
Lower Fold Hill
Black Clough
Fenny Lees
Black Clough Hill
White Swamp
The Lodge
Old Dike
Nouch Brink
Old Dike Hill
WADSWORTH MOOR
Back Shaw
WALSHAW DEAN LOWER RESERVOIR
Stony Dike
Clay Dike
WHITE HILL
The Grough
Dean Gate
Black Nursery
Rushy Dike
New Hey
WHITE HILL
Haworth to Hebden Bridge Walk
High Rakes
ROUND HILL
Alcomden
Hare Edge
Shackleton Moor
Delf Brink
Rowshaw Clough
Lower Edge
Higher Edge
Hoar Nib
Navvy
NEW LAITHE MOOR
Knoll Flat
Hardibut

Keighley
BD22
HAWORTH MOOR
ENSHAW KNOLL
HARBOUR HILL
ROUND HILL
Leeshaw Reservoir
Windle House Farm
West Field Farm
Drop Farm
Sand Delf Hill
The Slack
Grove Hill Dike
Stanbury Height
Tom Stell's Seat
New Westfield Farm
New House Farm
Picnic Area
Penistone Slack
Intake Farm
Springs
Enfield Side
Near Enfield Side
Far Enfield Side
Cold Knoll
Bully Trees Farm
Bottoms
Near Slack
Far Slack
Upper Heights
Master Stones
The Heihgt
South Dene
Black Leech
Bronte Bridge
Bronte Waterfalls
The Level
Harbour Lodge
Wether Hill
Wether Hill Clough
Wether Hill Brigstone
Holmes Intake
Spa Hill
Leeshaw Water
Bodkin Rough
Green Holes
Green Holes Hill
Bond Clough Hill
Sheep Cote Swamp
Carr Grough
Stairs Hill
Stairs Hole
Bodkin
Slack Farm
Low Fold
Long Rigging
High Fold
Bodkin Top
Penny Poll
Hardnaze
Stairs Bottom
Lee
Dunkirk Mill
Dike Nook
Grinding Stone Hole
Rushbed Top
Oxenhope Edge
Oxenhope Stoop Hill
Black Edge
MOOR
Middle Moor
Robin Dike
The Waste
Under Hill Flat
Top of Stairs
Stone Heep Stoop
Harry Side Edge
Sun Hill
Mare Greave Slack
Scraping Hill
Under Hill
Stairs Swamp
Yeoman Hill
Stairs Dyke
Stairs Edge
Red Dike Swamp
LORD'S ALLOTMENT
Keepers Lodge
Little Cock Hill
Stake Hill
Thurrish Rough
Stairs Bottom
White Hole Rough
Lower Cock Hill
Cock Hill Swamp
Navigational Aid Station (RAF)
Cock Hill
WILL'S ALLOTMENT
High Greave
Thurrish
Calf Hey Clough
Roms Bottom
Roms Side
ROMS HILL
Roms Greave
Waterfall
White Hole
Lane Head
GRANNY HILL
Shepherd's Lodge Rough
Grain Water Bridge
Roms Clough
Leaning Grooves
Grey Stones
Bedlam Knoll
Grain Slack
Bedlam
Leaning Grooves Flat
The Navvy
Baby House Hill
Grain
Keelam
Spa Clough Head
Haworth to Hebden Bridge Walk
Haworth Moor Bond
Deep Nitch
Deep Dyke
KEIGHLEY HEBDEN BRIDGE ROAD
A6033
Long Dike
H J K L M N
G H J K L M N
1 2 3 4 5 6 7 8 9
35
54
71
99
400
01
02
36
34
33
32

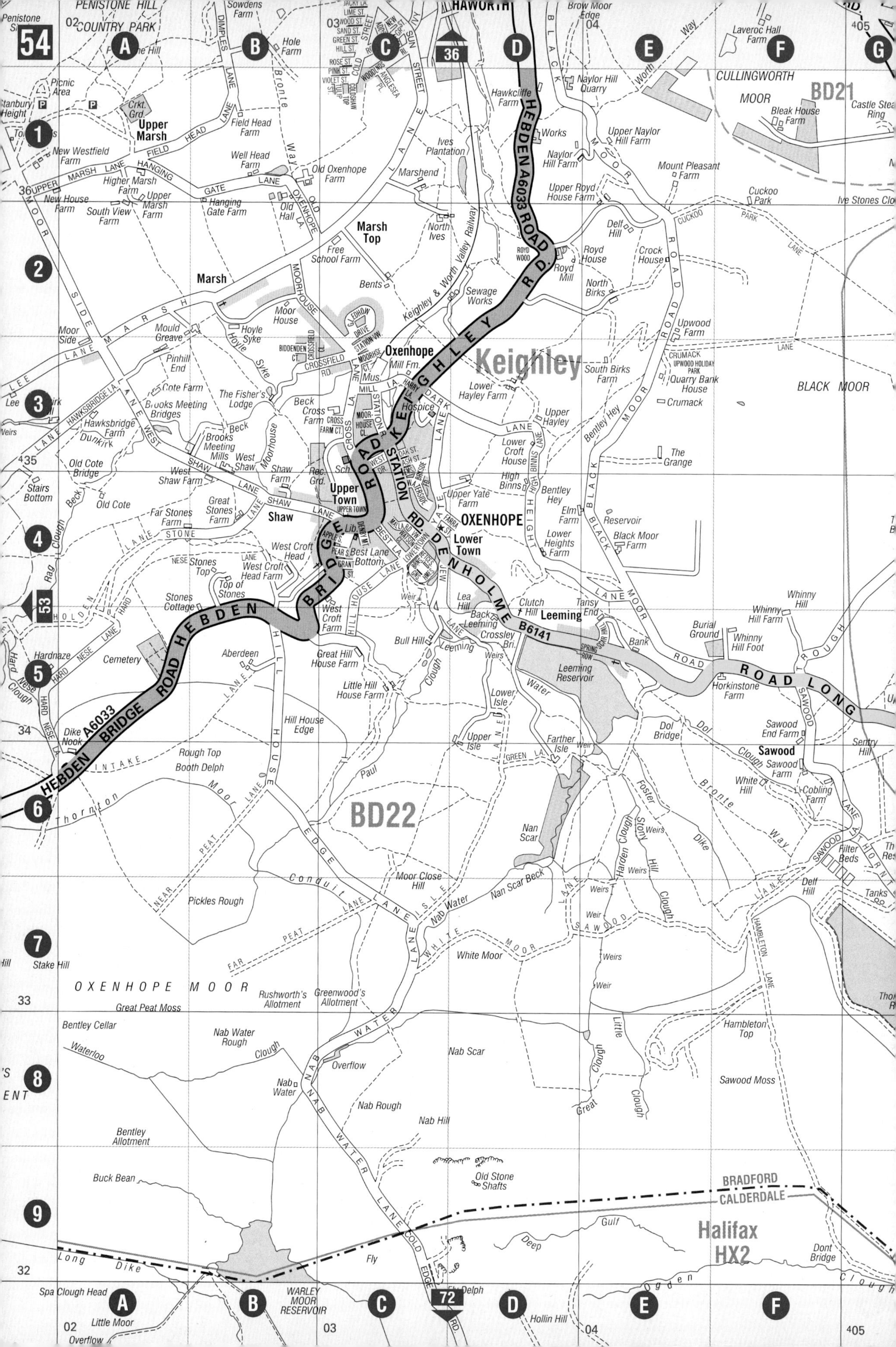
PENISTONE HILL COUNTRY PARK
Haworth
36
53
72
Upper Marsh
Marsh
Marsh Top
Oxenhope
Keighley
OXENHOPE
Upper Town
Lower Town
Shaw
Leeming
Sawood
Cullingworth Moor
BD21
BD22
Black Moor
Oxenhope Moor
Great Peat Moss
White Moor
Nab Scar
Nab Rough
Nab Hill
Sawood Moss
Leeming Reservoir
Warley Moor Reservoir
Bradford
Calderdale
Halifax HX2
Hebden Bridge Road A6033
Keighley Road A6033
Denholme Road B6141
Long Road
Keighley & Worth Valley Railway
Bronte Way
Sewage Works
Hospice
Cemetery
Old Stone Shafts
Farther Isle
Nan Scar
Hambleton Top
Bentley Allotment
Buck Bean
Spa Clough Head
Little Moor
Hollin Hill
Dont Bridge

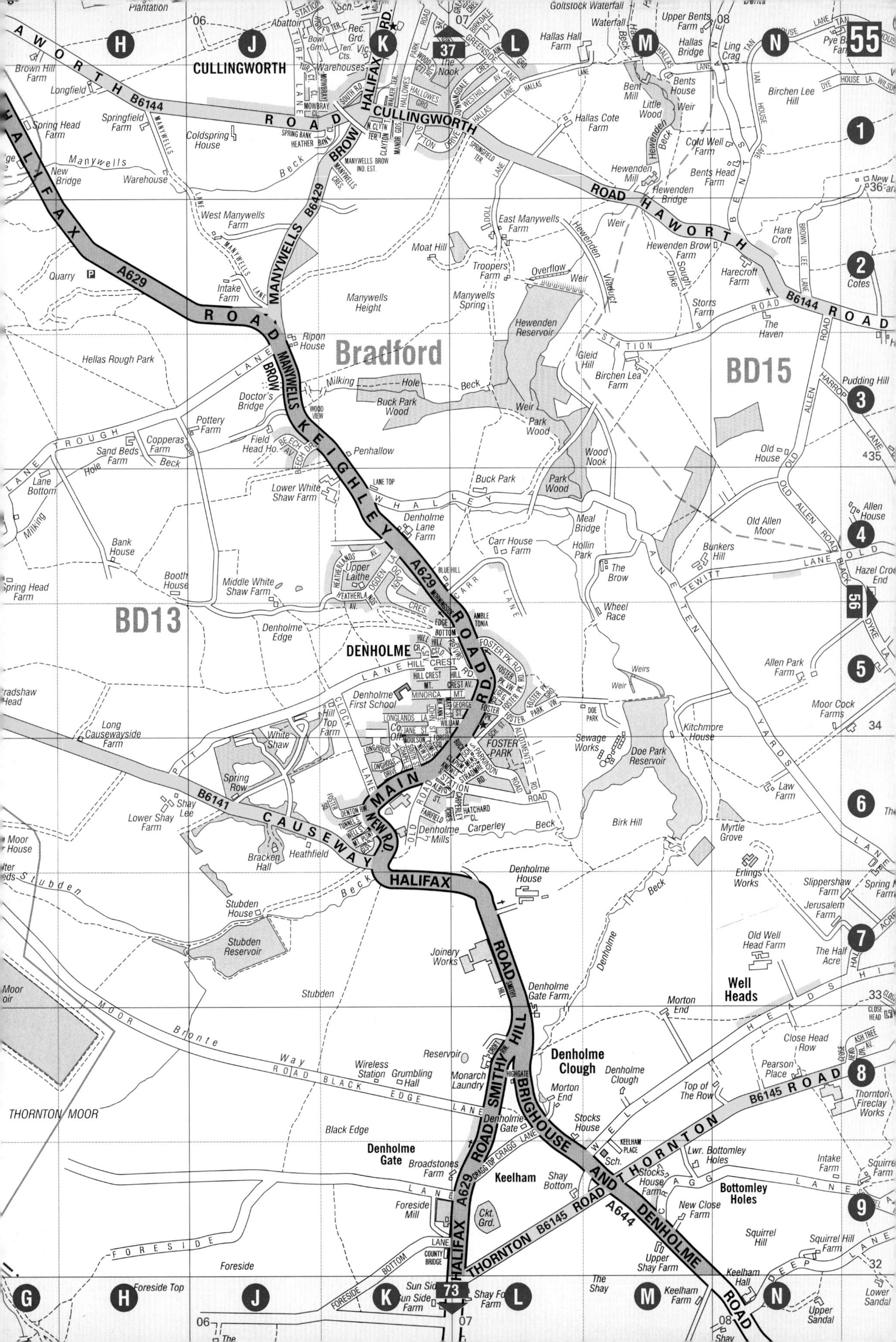
CULLINGWORTH
Bradford
BD15
BD13
DENHOLME
Denholme Clough
Denholme Gate
Keelham
Well Heads
Bottomley Holes
THORNTON MOOR
Hewenden Reservoir
Doe Park Reservoir
Stubden Reservoir
HALIFAX ROAD A629
KEIGHLEY ROAD A629
MANYWELLS BROW B6429
HAWORTH ROAD B6144
CAUSEWAY B6141
THORNTON ROAD B6145
BRIGHOUSE AND DENHOLME ROAD A644
SMITHY HILL
MAIN
Manywells Height
Hellas Rough Park
Buck Park Wood
Park Wood
Foster Park
Denholme First School
Denholme Edge
Denholme Mills
Carperley
Birk Hill
Stubden
Black Edge
Foreside
Foreside Top
Bronte Way
37
56
73

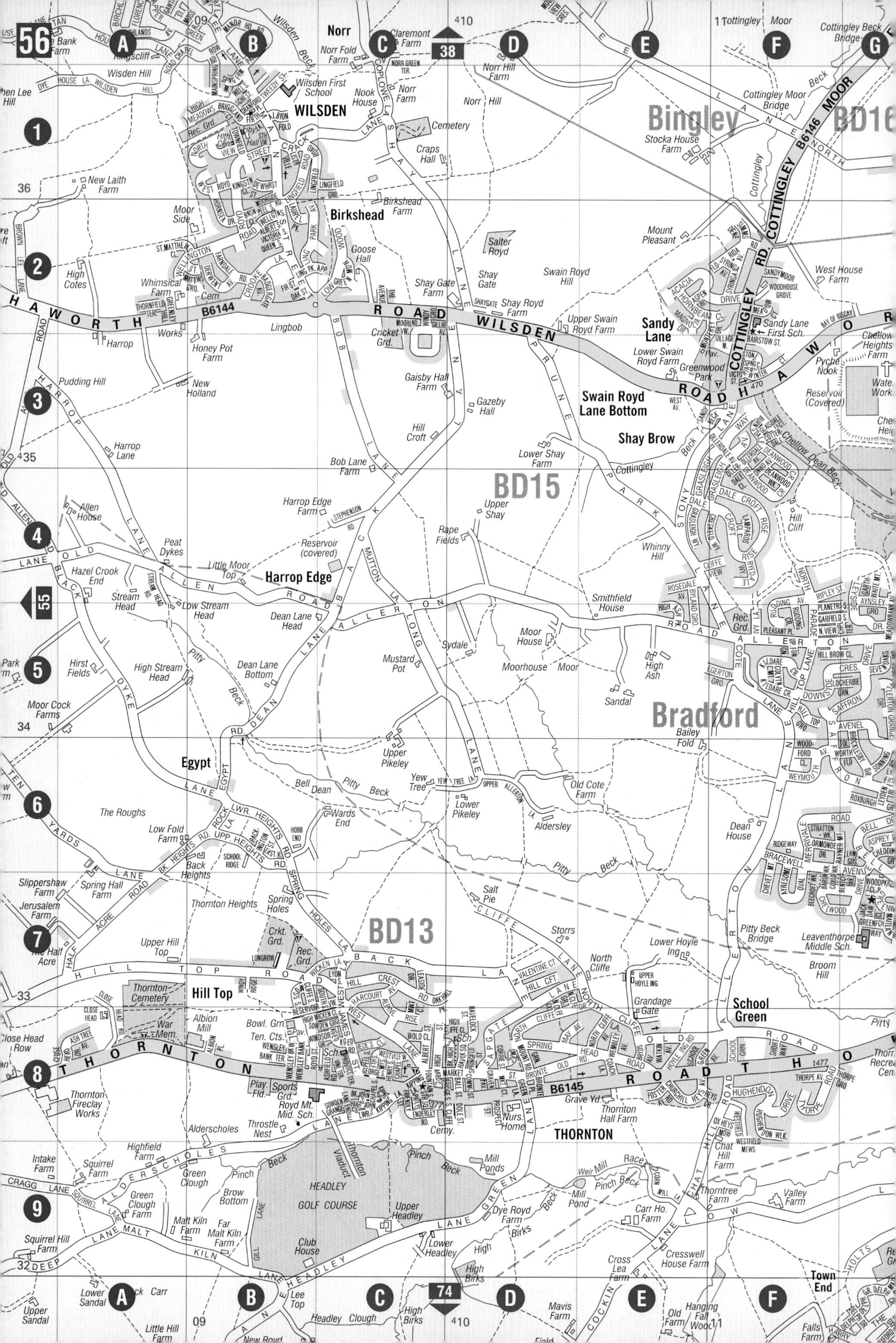

38
410
74
55
A
B
C
D
E
F
G
1
2
3
4
5
6
7
8
9
36
35
34
33
32
09
Norr
Claremont Farm
Norr Fold Farm
Norr Hill Farm
Wilsden Hill
Wilsden First School
WILSDEN
Nook House
Norr Farm
Norr Hill
Cemetery
Craps Hall
New Laith Farm
Birkshead
Birkshead Farm
Moor Side
Goose Hall
Salter Royd
Shay Gate
Shay Gate Farm
Shay Royd Farm
Swain Royd Hill
High Cotes
Whimsical Farm
Cottingley Moor
Cottingley Moor Bridge
Cottingley Beck Bridge
Bingley
BD16
Stocka House Farm
Mount Pleasant
West House Farm
Sandy Lane
Sandy Lane First Sch.
Upper Swain Royd Farm
Lower Swain Royd Farm
Greenwood Park
Chellow Heights Farm
Pyche Nook
Reservoir (Covered)
HAWORTH ROAD
WILSDEN ROAD
B6144
B6146
COTTINGLEY MOOR
Lingbob
Harrop
Works
Honey Pot Farm
Cricket Grd.
Gaisby Hall Farm
Gazeby Hall
New Holland
Pudding Hill
Swain Royd Lane Bottom
Shay Brow
Harrop Lane
Hill Croft
Bob Lane Farm
Lower Shay Farm
Cottingley
BD15
Chellow Dean Beck
Hill Cliff
Allen House
Harrop Edge Farm
Upper Shay
Reservoir (covered)
Rape Fields
Whinny Hill
Peat Dykes
Little Moor Top
Harrop Edge
Hazel Crook End
Stream Head
Low Stream Head
Dean Lane Head
Smithfield House
ALLERTON ROAD
Moor House
Sydale
Mustard Pot
Hirst Fields
High Stream Head
Dean Lane Bottom
Moorhouse
Moor
High Ash
Sandal
Moor Cock Farms
Bradford
Bailey Fold
Egypt
Upper Pikeley
Yew Tree
Bell Dean
Pitty Beck
Old Cote Farm
Lower Pikeley
Aldersley
Dean House
The Roughs
Wards End
Low Fold Farm
Back Heights
Thornton Heights
Slippershaw Farm
Spring Hall Farm
Spring Holes
Salt Pie
Storrs
Pitty Beck Bridge
Leaventhorpe Middle Sch.
Jerusalem Farm
BD13
Lower Hoyle Ing
North Cliffe
Broom Hill
Upper Hill Top
The Half Acre
Crkt. Grd.
Rec. Grd.
HILL TOP ROAD
Thornton Cemetery
Hill Top
Grandage Gate
School Green
Close Head Row
War Mem.
Albion Mill
Bowl. Grn.
Ten. Cts.
THORNTON ROAD
B6145
Thornton Fireclay Works
Play. Fld.
Sports Grd.
Royd Mt. Mid. Sch.
Grave Yd.
Thornton Hall Farm
Nurs. Home
THORNTON
Alderscholes
Throstle Nest
Intake Farm
Highfield Farm
Squirrel Farm
Green Clough
Pinch
Viaduct
Pinch Beck
Mill Ponds
Chat Hill Farm
Thorntree Farm
Valley Farm
Green Clough Farm
Brow Bottom
HEADLEY GOLF COURSE
Upper Headley
Mill Pond
Dye Royd Farm
Birks
Carr Ho. Farm
Malt Kiln Farm
Far Malt Kiln Farm
Club House
Lower Headley
High
Squirrel Hill Farm
High Birks
Cross Lea Farm
Cresswell House Farm
Town End
Lower Sandal
Lee Top
Upper Sandal
Headley Clough
High Birks
Mavis Farm
Little Hill Farm
Old Farm
Hanging Fall Wood
Falls Farm

H
J
K
L
M
N
G
1
2
3
4
5
6
7
8
9
39
58
75
Stoney Lee Middle School
New Brighton
COTTINGLEY
CLIFFE
Cliff Farm
Dungeon Wood
Northcliff Woods
Dawson Wood
NORTHCLIFFE GOLF COURSE
Bandstand
Shipley
BD18
Shipley High Moor
STONEY RIDGE HOSPITAL
Stoney Ridge Plantation
Bunkers Hill
Shay Farm
Heaton Shay
Low Wood
Heaton Royds School
Noon Nick
The Grange
Heaton Moor
Belle Vue Girls Upper Sch.
SHAY GRANGE GOLF COURSE
Shay Grange Farm
Driving Range
Cub House
Royds Hall Farm
Heaton Royds Farm
Heaton Royds
Royds Cliff Wood
Cliff Wood
Cliff Dike
Weirs
Red Beck
BD9
Belle Vue Boys Upper Sch.
Bingley Road Playing Fields
Thorn Park School
High Park Nursery
Heaton Mid. Sch.
Health Cen.
Weather Royds Wood
Boarding Kennels
Bingley Road East Rec. Ground
Sports Grd.
Shay Hall
Heaton Hill
St. Barnabas C. of E. First School
Liby.
Heaton Grove
Botanical Gardens
Met. Sta.
LISTER PARK
Cartwright Hall Gallery Muse
Chellow Grange Quarries
Reservoir
Club House
Heather Grove First School
Recreation Ground
Well Springs
Salem Sports Ground
St. Bedes Grammar School
Heaton Sports Ground
BRADFORD GOLF COURSE
Lake
Wellwood
LYNFIELD MOUNT HOSP.
Daisy Hill
Sunny Bank
Brow Side
Football Ground
Ckt. Grd.
Sports Grd.
MANNINGHAM
HOSP.
Allerton
Temple Bank Spec. Sch.
BRADFORD ROYAL INFIRMARY
Throstle Nest
Daisy Bank
Ladye Royd Hall
Children's Centre
West Royd
Yew Tree Farm
Chellow Dean
Bradford Girls Grammar School
Girlington
BD8
Ladyhill Park
Bowling Green
Tennis Court
Chapel Grange Sch.
Rhodesway Sch.
The Oaks
Cricket Grd.
Health Cen.
Allerton Grange
Chellow Dene Middle Sch.
Playing Field
Fairweather Green
Four Lane Ends
Recreation Ground
Bowl. Grns.
Industrial Estate
VICTORIA SHOPPING CENTRE
Sports Ground
Crossley Hall
Green Side
St. William's R.C. Prim. Sch.
Brown Royd
Lister Hills
BRADFORD
Lower Grange
Blue Weir
Thiefscore Bri.
Bradford Works
Warehouse
Beck
Princeville
Factory
BD7
Depot
Thornton Grammar Sch.
Sports Ground
Leaventhorpe
Crematorium
SCHOLEMOOR CEMETERY
Birks
Lidget Green
Rec. Grd.
Crkt. Gd.
Shearbridge
BD14
Clayton
Cemetery
Bull Greave Wood
Scholemoor
Playing Fields
Football Grd.
St. Anthony's R.C. Prim. Sch.
Crkt. Grd.
Works
Sollars
Clayton C. of E. First School
Brookfields
CLAYTON
Lidget Bridge
Paradise
GREAT
HORTON PARK
Bowling Greens
BINGLEY ROAD B6269
TOLLER LANE
B6144
THORNTON ROAD B6145
WHETLEY LANE A6177
INGLEBY ROAD A6177
HORTON GRANGE RD.
HORTON A647 RD.
KEIGHLEY ROAD A650
ALLERTON ROAD
DUCKWORTH LANE
SMITH LANE
SCOTCHMAN ROAD
CARLISLE
WHETLEY HILL

A
B
C
D
E
F
G
1
2
3
4
5
6
7
8
9
40
57
76
Wrose
Gaisby
Shipley BD18
Moor End
Five Lane Ends
Frizinghall
Owlet
Bolton Wood Quarries
Bolton Old Hall
Bolton Woods
Swain House
ECCLESHILL
BD2
Bolton Outlanes
Bradford Grammar School
BD9
Lister Park
Cartwright Hall Art Gallery & Museum
Bolton
UNDERCLIFFE
Peel Park
Clifton Villas
BRADFORD
Bradford City F.C.
Bradford Cemetery
Bradford Moor Golf Course
Bradford Moor
Bradford Forster Sq.
BD1
Barkerend
BD3
Lister Hills
BD7
Eastbrook
Bradford Interchange
Shearbridge
University of Bradford
Little Horton Green
Dirk Hill
BD5
Broomfields
BOWLING
Horton Park
A6037
A650
A6177
A6176
A658
A6181
A647
A641
B6144
B6145
B6381
MANNINGHAM
CANAL ROAD
QUEEN'S ROAD
LISTER LA.
LEEDS ROAD
WAKEFIELD ROAD
MANCHESTER ROAD
OTLEY ROAD
HARROGATE ROAD
THORNTON ROAD
WHETLEY HILL
WHITE ABBEY RD.
KEIGHLEY ROAD
PULLAN

RODLEY
Carr Hills
Bill Wood
Eccleshill Park
Eccleshill Sch.
Playing Field
Sports Cen.
Round Hill
Stanhope Rein
Low Rein
Round Wood
WOODHALL HILLS GOLF COURSE
Ravenscliffe
Ravenscliffe Wood
Leeds Country Way
Cavendish First Sch.
The Oval
Thorne Dene
Wood Hill
Hazelbrae
Chalybeate Well
CALVERLEY B6156 LANE
FARSLEY
CALVERLEY
Crossfield Farm
Crossfield House
The Rein
Woodlands
Woodlands Hall Farm
Lees Farm
Craven Farm
Brashy Hill
Hawthorn Glen Farm
Priesthorpe
Priesthorpe Farm
The Grange
Greatwood Farm
Club House
Top Farm
Moss House Farm
Woodhall Hills
Woodhall Plantation
Woodhall Quarries
St. Luke's First Sch.
Haigh Fold
Throstles Nest Farm
Lower Fagley
Cherry Tree Farm
Upper Fagley
Industrial Mus.
Pagewood Cottage
CALVERLEY GOLF COURSE
Fagley First Sch.
St. Clare's R.C. Sch.
Fagley Beck
BRADFORD
LEEDS
Woodhall Farm
Play. Fld.
Sports Grd.
Priesthorpe School
Woodhall Park
Farfield Prim. Sch.
Clinic
Offices
Civic Hall
Woodhall Grange
Pond
Woodhall
Fagley
Energy House
Tennis Courts
Sports Ground
Playing Field
Thornbury Barracks
A647
BRADFORD ROAD
RING ROAD
STANNINGLEY
Charity Farm
New Pudsey
Pudsey
A647 BY-PASS
Rec. Grd.
Works
Boating Lake
Bradford Moor Park
LEEDS OLD ROAD
B6381
LEEDS RD.
GIPSY ST.
DICK LA.
Club House
GALLOWAY
Pudsey Bolton Royd Prim. Sch.
Tunnel
Hillfoot
LS28
Owlcotes Hill
High Owlcotes Farm
PHOENIX PARK SPORTS GROUND
Laisterdyke Mid. Sch.
Bus Depot
Thornbury
Engineering Works
Tyersal Beck
PHOENIX PARK GOLF COURSE
Delph End
WATERLOO LA.
B6154
Spring
Ducketts Crossing
Wild Grove
Wild Grove Farm
Reservoirs
Mill
Queen's
UPPERMOOR
Round Hill
Works
Industrial Estate
Wild Grove House
A6177
LAISTERDYKE
Laisterdyke
Community Centre
Bowling Green
Tennis Courts
Sewage Works
Windmill Hill
Rec. Grd.
Tyersal
Tyersal First School
Tyersal Park
Pudsey Tyersal Primary School
Black Hey Farm
Westroyd Hill
Swain Green
STICKER LANE
BD4
Tyersal Hall Farm
Tyersal Hall
The Banks
Bankhouse
Willows Nook
Nesbit Hall
Carr Beck
Black Carr
Depot
Bakery
Tyersal Gate
Harper Gate Farm
Cutler Heights
Bella Vista
Bank House Farm
41
77
60

RODLEY
HORSFORTH
Bridge
Thornton Wood
42
Works
Newlay Locks
Leeds and Liverpool
Chalybeate Well
Rodley Fold Farm
Fallwood Marina & Leisure Cen.
BRAMLEY FALL
Recn. Grd.
A6120 FARSLEY
RING ROAD
CALVERLEY LA.
LANE TOWN
STREET RODLEY
Bagley
Beck
Ckt. Grd.
Sewage Works
RIVER AIRE
Whitecote
LEEDS
Rodley
Rodley Recreation Grd.
Ross Mill Bri. (Swing)
Kirklees Knowl
The Green
Bagley
Coal Hill
A657
B6157 ROAD
WHITECOTE HILL
Intake
Aireview Prim. Sch.
Bramstan Rec. Cen.
Playing Fields
Intake High School
Summerfield Prim. Sch.
FARSLEY
Farsley Beck Bottom
HALF MILE
LEEDS AND BRADFORD
TOWN ST.
Bramley Recreation Ground
Half Mile
Stanningley Park
Stanningley Prim. Sch.
Beecroft Hill
Bramley Prim. Sch.
Bradley Hill
LS13
West Royd Park
Football Grd.
STREET STANNINGLEY RD.
OLD ROAD
Swinnow
Stanningley
Bramley
BRAMLEY
BRADFORD B6157
ROAD TOWN
GRANGEFIELD INDUSTRIAL ESTATE
OWLCOTES SHOPPING CENTRE
RICHARDSHAW
STANNINGLEY BY PASS
A647
Works
Swinnow Moor
Hough End
Park Spring Primary School
St. Joseph's R.C. Sch.
B6155 LANE
Pudsey Cen.
LOWTOWN
HOUGH SIDE ROAD
PUDSEY
Cricket Ground
Council Offices
Playing Fields
RING ROAD BRAMLEY
B6154
Cemetery
QUEEN'S PARK
Cricket Ground
Crimbles
Hough Side
Kent
Pudsey Park
CHURCH
UPPERMOOR
CHAPELTOWN
PUDSEY
Crawshaw School
Sewage Works
Park Spring
Farnley Beck
Post Hill
Mount Pleasant
Acres Hall
Pudsey
Troydale Farm
Troy Dale
Pudsey Beck
Beulah Farm
Oak Tree Farm
Littlemoor Bottom
Southroyd Prim. Sch.
Community Centre
Turkey Hill
Troydale
LS28
Westroyd Hill
Farnley Hall Farm
Parkside Ho.
Cemy.
Woodlands
Bankhouse
Sports Ground
Fulneck
Museum
Nesbit Hall
Hazeldene
East House
FARNLEY PARK
Burial Ground
Hope Farm
78
Low Farm
Club House
Newstead House
Bella Vista
Bank House Farm
Bankhouse
South Park
Weir

HEADINGLEY
Beckett Park
Beckett Park School
Queen's Wood
43
LS6
LS5
LS4
LS12
Leeds
Headingley
Kirkstall
Kirkstall Abbey (rems.)
Kirkstall Lock
Abbey Gardens
Mill Race
Sandford
Moorside
Rugby Football Grd.
Public Park
Recreation Ground
Crooked Acres
Forge Locks
Toads Hole Wood
Yorkshire County Cricket (Headingley)
Leeds R.L & R.U. F.C.
Batcliffe Wood
Burley Pk.
Burley Rec. Ground
Burley
Clarence Field
The Goit
Leeds and Liverpool Canal
GOTTS PARK GOLF COURSE
Ridge Wood
The Mansion (Club House)
GOTTS PARK
Redcote Bridge
Aire Valley Marina
Upper Armley
Armley
Armley Mills Mus.
Armley Park
Armley Cemetery
ST. MARY'S HOSPITAL
Hill Top
Hill End
Far Fold
Moor Top
Armley Moor
Gamble Hill
New Scarborough
Town End
Schools
Houghley Gill
Moor End
Swallow Hill
West Leeds High Sch.
Carr Crofts
Wiring Field
H.M PRISON
New Wortley Cemetery
Castleton Prim. Sch.
Reservoir
Cabbage Hill
Upper Wortley
WORTLEY
Wortley High Sch.
Silver Royd Hill
Low Fold
Ryecroft Prim. Sch.
Bawn
Lower Wortley
Upper & Lower Wortley Cem.
Wortley Recreation Ground
Wortley South Junction
Blue Hill
Recreation Grd.
WESTERN FLATTS PARK
Town End
New Blackpool
Farnley
Lawns Farm
Holly Farm
Playing Fields
Farnley Park High School
Cobden Prim. Sch.
Little Wood
Fish Pond
79
A65
A660
A647
A657
A6110
A58
B6157
B6154
ABBEY ROAD
BRADFORD ROAD
KIRKSTALL ROAD
COMMERCIAL RD.
BRIDGE RD.
STANNINGLEY ROAD
ARMLEY ROAD
TONG ROAD
FARNLEY RING ROAD
LOWER WORTLEY ROAD
WHITEHALL ROAD
GELDERD RD.
OTLEY ROAD
H J K L M N G
1 2 3 4 5 6 7 8 9
62

62
A
B
C
D
E
F
G
1
2
3
4
5
6
7
8
9
44
61
80
28
29
30
31
32
33
34
35
36
HEADINGLEY
Headingley Hill
Miles Hill
Woodhouse Cliff
Model Farm
Meanwood Valley Urban Farm
Scott Hall
Prince Philip Playing Fields
LS7
LS6
Sugarwell Hill Park
Prince Philip Centre
Buslingthorpe
City of Leeds Sch.
Hyde Pk.
Woodhouse Carr
Woodhouse Moor
Reservoir (Covered)
Bagby Flds.
Sheepscar
Thomas Danby Coll.
Little London
Woodhouse
LEEDS UNIVERSITY
Leeds
Little Woodhouse
Yorkshire Television Studio
LS3
LS4
Armley Junc.
Leeds & Liverpool Canal
LEEDS GENERAL INFIRMARY
The Leylands
Mabgate
Quarry Hill
LEEDS
LS1
AIRESIDE CENTRE
Canal Wharf
Crown Point
Royal Armouries Museum
Camp Field
Victoria Bridge
H.M. PRISON
New Wortley
New Wortley Cemetery
Wortley Recreation Ground
Wortley South Junction
LS12
LS11
LS10
Holbeck
Holbeck Moor
Pottery Field
South Leeds Sports Cen.
Junc. 3
Islington
Matthew Murray High Sch.
HEADINGLEY LANE
WOODHOUSE LANE
KIRKSTALL RD.
A65
A660
A58(M)
A64(M)
A61
A62
A643
A653
A647
M621 MOTORWAY
INNER RING ROAD
WELLINGTON ST.
CANAL ST.
ARMLEY RD.
WHITEHALL RD.
DOMESTIC RD.
GREAT WILSON ST.
HUNSLET LA.
CROWN POINT ROAD
VICTORIA RD.
PARKFIELD STREET
SCOTT HALL ROAD
SHEEPSCAR ST. NTH.
BARRACK RD.
REGENT ST.
NEW YORK RD.
RIVER AIRE
POTTERNEWTON LANE
STAINBECK LANE
B6159

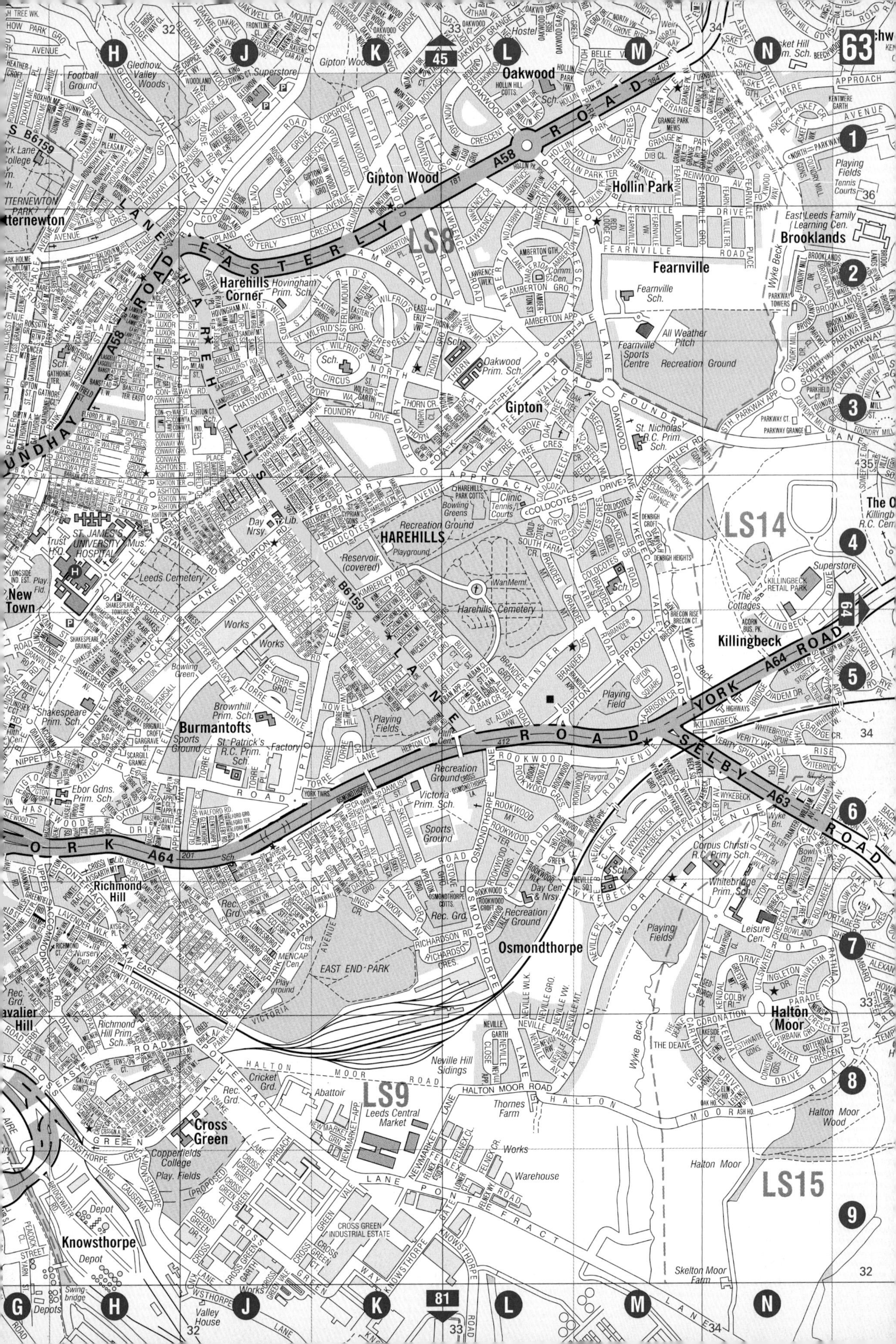
H
J
K
L
M
N
45
Gledhow Valley Woods
Football Ground
Superstore
Gipton Wood
Oakwood
Hostel
Gipton Wood
Hollin Park
EASTERLY ROAD
A58
Playing Fields
Tennis Courts
East Leeds Family Learning Cen.
Brooklands
LS8
Fearnville
Fearnville Sch.
All Weather Pitch
Fearnville Sports Centre
Recreation Ground
Harehills Corner
Hovingham Prim. Sch.
ROUNDHAY ROAD
HAREHILLS LANE
Oakwood Prim. Sch.
Gipton
St. Nicholas R.C. Prim. Sch.
FOUNDRY LANE
LS14
Killingbeck R.C. Cem
ST. JAMES'S UNIVERSITY HOSPITAL
Mus.
Day Nrsy.
Lib.
Clinic
Bowling Greens
Tennis Courts
Recreation Ground
HAREHILLS
Playground
Reservoir (covered)
Superstore
KILLINGBECK RETAIL PARK
The Cottages
New Town
Leeds Cemetery
War Meml.
Harehills Cemetery
Works
B6159
Killingbeck
64
Shakespeare Prim. Sch.
Bowling Green
Brownhill Prim. Sch.
Burmantofts
Sports Ground
St. Patrick's R.C. Prim. Sch.
Factory
Playing Fields
Playing Field
YORK ROAD
A64
SELBY ROAD
A63
Ebor Gdns. Prim. Sch.
Recreation Ground
Victoria Prim. Sch.
Sports Ground
Corpus Christi R.C. Prim. Sch.
Whitebridge Prim. Sch.
Richmond Hill
Rec. Grd.
Day Cen. & Nrsy.
Recreation Ground
Leisure Cen.
EAST END PARK
MENCAP Cen.
Playground
Osmondthorpe
Playing Fields
Halton Moor
Cavalier Hill
Richmond Hill Prim. Sch.
Neville Hill Sidings
Wyke Beck
Cricket Grd.
Abattoir
LS9
Leeds Central Market
HALTON MOOR ROAD
Thornes Farm
Halton Moor Wood
Cross Green
Copperfields College
Play. Fields
Works
Warehouse
Halton Moor
LS15
Depot
CROSS GREEN INDUSTRIAL ESTATE
Knowsthorpe
Depot
Skelton Moor Farm
Swing bridge
Depots
Valley House
81
G
1
2
3
4
5
6
7
8
9
32
33
34
35
36

64
Beechwood
Seacroft
Mill Green
The Green
Stanks
Swarcliffe
Brooklands
LS14
Parklands
Brianside
Manston
The Oval
CROSS GATES
Whitkirk
Graveleythorpe
Halton
LS15
Austhorpe
Whitkirk Lane End
Colton
Halton Moor
TEMPLE NEWSAM GOLF COURSE
TEMPLE NEWSAM COUNTRY PARK
SEACROFT HOSPITAL
YORK ROAD A64
SELBY ROAD A63
RING ROAD A6120
Cross-Gates
46
63
82

SCHOLES
Green Lodge Farm
Scholes Lodge Farm
Sewage Works
Honesty Farm
Carr Head
Barnbow Carr
Upper Barn Bow Farm
Highfield Farm
Throstle Nest Farm
Throstlenest Bridge
Leeds
Barnbow Wood
Leeds Country Way
GARFORTH GOLF COURSE
Club House
Laverack Cottage
The Lake
Parlington
Roundabout
Cock Beck
Weir
Shippen Plantation
Willow Park Farm
Lake Cottage
Manor Farm Cottage
Manor House
Barnbow Common
Manston Ho.
Lazencroft Farm
Shippen House Farm
Sports Ground
Shippen Cottages
Lazencroft
Manston Gate
M1
M1-MOTORWAY
Pear Trees
Lowside Cott.
Rose Cott.
The Elms
White House Farm
Crawshaw Wood
Brown Moor
Barrowby Hall
Leeds Country Way
LS25
GARFORTH
ABERFORD ROAD
Moor Garforth
Garforth
Barrowby Carr
Barrowby
Carr Wood
Clear View Farm
Bradbury Grange
Pond
BARROWBY PARK
Barrowby Cottage
Moorhouse Farm
Warren House
Spring Wood
Ormesby House
Swillington Common Farm
Church Garforth
Junction 46
SELBY ROAD
A63
A642
WAKEFIELD ROAD
Swillington Common
Nurseries
Brookfield Ho.
Brookfield Farm
Waterloo Manor
Lidgett
Playing Fields
Garforth Community College
M1
LS26
Garforth Bridge
West Garforth
Sewage Works
Kippax Lane End
Brayhill
Field Ho.
Southfield Bungalow
Hollinthorpe Farm
Hollinthorpe
47
83
66

Old Wood
Home Farm
Triumphal Arch
ABERFORD PARK
Wilderness
Parlington Gardens
Hangings Plantation
Parlington Hall
Gamekeepers Cottage
Throstlenest Plantation
The Staith Cottage
Bathingwell Plantation
PARLINGTON PARK
Parlington Hollins
Wakefield Lodge
Park House Farm
Lily Pit Cottage
Hook Moor
Hookmoor Lodges
Hookmoor Cottage
Hicklam House
Hicklam Mill
Hicklam Mill Farm
Priory Park
Priory Park Lodge
War Memorial
White House Farm
Widow's Row
Cooper Wood
Dawson's Wood
Junction 44 A1(M)
Junction 48 (M1)
Junction 47
A1(M) MOTORWAY
M1 MOTORWAY
ABERFORD ROAD B1217
COLLIER ROAD
Beech Plantation
Ridge Rd. Bungalow
Ridge Road Farm
Hawk's Nest
Hawk's Nest Wood
Beech Ho. Farm
Weigh House
A656
A642
Leeds LS25
Sturton Dyke
Ash Plantation
Well House Farm
St. Helen's Well
Roman Ridge
Roman Road
Sports Ground
East Garforth
Garforth
Church Garforth
Old Micklefield
Three Acre Plantation
Moat
Sturton Grange Farm
Stub Wood
Roman Ridge Bridge
Ridge Bridge Cott.
The Bungalow
Cliff Villas
Cliffe Bungalows
Warren Farm
Peckfield Quarry (Stone)
Garforth Squash & Leisure Cen.
Recreation Ground
Reservoirs (Covered)
Water Tower
The Mount
Marl Lodge
Gatelands
SELBY ROAD A63
Warren House
Peckfield

48
65
84

Tadcaster
LS24
Lotherton Cottages
Lotherton Park Farm
Lotherton Lodge
Lotherton Cott.
COPLEY LANE
B1217
Bird Garden
Lotherton Hall
Lotherton Hall Estate
Deer Park
Captain Wood
Vevers Bushes
West Field
COLDHILL LANE
Garlic Flats
Rose Cottage
Coldhill Pond
Coldhill Cottage
Lower Cold Hill Farm
Cold Hill
Coldhill Farm
Prospect Hill
The Avenue
Stream Dike
Bragdale
Ringhay Wood
RANGERS WALK
Coburnhill Wood
Scott's Wood
Weet Wood
Near Fox Covert
Far Fox Covert
Middle Fox Covert
SELBY
LEEDS
The Marsh
Longroyd Wood
Daniel Hartly's Wood
LAITH STAID LANE
Huddleston Hall
Riding School
Hartly Wood Cottages
Huddleston Grange
Huddleston Old Wood
Grange Fm.
Manor House Fm.
Hartly Wood
Gunner Hill
Sheep Dike
Sewage Wks.
Keepers Cottage
MICKLEFIELD
GREAT NORTH RD
GARDEN VILLAGE
BAKER PL
Newthorpe Farm
Micklefield
Brookfield House
Newthorpe Barrack
Newthorpe Beck
Newton Fm.
New Micklefield
Highroyds Wood
Newthorpe
Hill House Farm
Newthorpe Grange
Gorse Cottage
Ash Grove
GORSE LANE
HALL LANE
B1222
Beckfield
Woodlands
Castle Hills
Highfield
Newthorpe Quarry
Castle Plains
Micklefield Plantation
A1
HIGHFIELD LANE
Peckfield Plantation
Plough Farm
Headwell Farm
49
85

Hurstwood Reservoir
Pike Stones
Cant Clough Farm
Hindle Banks
Cant Clough Reservoir
BLACK MOOR
Thistleden Dean
Gorple Bottom
GORPLE UPPER RESERVOIR
Hameldon Holes
WORSTHORNE
Burnley
BB10
Sheddon Edge
Sheddon Top
Shedden Clough
Shedden Plantation
Crocker Hill
White Hill
BURNLEY
CALDERDALE
Black Hambeldon
Rush Candle Clough
Hoof Stones Height
STIPERDEN MOOR
Stiperden Slack
Stiperden Bar House
The Lead Mine
THE LONG CAUSEWAY
Warcock Hill
Willingate Wham
COAL CLOUGH WIND FARM
Todmorden
OL14
Stiperden House Farm
Stiperden Bank
Hoppet
STANSFIELD
NEW ROAD
Bent's Pasture
Bank Top Farm
Jack Stones
Riddle Scout
Cartridge Clough
Coal Clough
Burnt Edge Pasture
Cartridge Pasture
Black Scout
Paul Clough
Upper Mount
Cross Hill
Rough Top
Hugeon Croft Farm
Coal Clough Farm
50
86

FLASK
51
87
Hebden Bridge
HX7
HEPTONSTALL MOOR
HOAR SIDE MOOR
MOSS CROP
LORD PIECE
GORPLE LOWER RESERVOIR
Shuttleworth Moor
Dicken Dike
Dicken Rocks
Clegg Foot
Whinberry Flat
Whinberry Clough
Three Nook Bit
Red Carr Clough
Clegg Rough
Tongue
Raistrick Greave
Raistrick Greave Hill
Cabin Hill
Flaight Clough
Rushy Field
Hoar Side Top
North Grain
Hoar Side
Colden Water
Noah Dale
Crabtree Field
Higher Heath
Broad Holme
Pad Laithe
Noah Dale Water
Noon Hill
Cross Clough
Clunters
The Rush Beds
Four Gates End
Moorcocks Hill
Moss Crop Hill
MOOR
Redmires
Earnshaw Hole
Earnshaw Hole Moor
Moss Hall Slades
Earnshaw Water
Well Hill
Great Rough Hey
The Plain
Rushy Sikes
Reaps Level
Reaps Bottom
Reaps Edge
Reaps Cross
Pennine Way
Egypt
Pinion Clough
ROUGH HEY LANE
Rough Hey Clough
MOTH HOLE LA
Workhouse
Workhouse Green
Lower Heath
Golden Water
Higher Ear Lees
Lower Ear Lees
MOOR LANE
LOW LING LANE
Top o' th' Hill
Slade
Greenland
Three Gates End
GREENLAND ROAD
CUT DUKES
MOORCOCK ROAD
Moorhall Farm
Strines Clough
BURNT EDGE LANE
Burnt Edge
Wigg Farm
Mouse Nest
TRIMMER LANE
WARCOCK LANE
Warcock Hill
MOSS HALL LA.
Higher Earnshaw Water
THE LONG CAUSEWAY
KEBS ROAD
Lower Earnshaw Water
Cow Side
Lower Moss Hall
Harleywood Gate
Lane Side
Daisy Bank
Graining Water
Gorple Cottages
Ridge Rough
Ridge Scout
Ridge Nook
Blake Dean
King Common Rough
Ling Hollow
Standing Stone Hill
Popples Close
Lane Side
EDGE LANE
Everhill Shaw
Middle Fold
Lower Fold
PARK LA
Great Clough
New Edge
Salt Pie
Rodmer Clough Farm
DARK LANE
Land Bridge
SCHOOL LAND LA.
Land Farm
Top o' th' Rough
Scotland
NEW ROAD
Field Head Farm
Hill Top Farm
Higher Strines
Waterfall
Strines Clough
Brown Hill Bottom
BROWN HILL LANE
HALIFAX RD.
HIGHER BACK LANE
BROWN HILL
Blackshaw Head
Lane Top
Lane Bottom
PENNINE
H
J
K
L
M
N
G
93
94
395
32
31
430
29
28
1
2
3
4
5
6
7
8
9
70

A
B
C
D
E
F
G
52
88
69
396
97
98
32
31
430
29
28
Delf Brink
Higher Edge
Lower Edge
Rowshaw Clough
Jack Allotment
Knoll Flat
Hardibut
NEW LAITHE MOOR
New Laithe Farm
Rowshaw
Alcomden Water
New Cole
Horodiddle
Ridge Nook
Shackleton Knoll
WALSHAW LANE
Over Wood
Blake Dean
Ridge Scout
HEBDEN DALE
Walshaw
KILN LANE
Coppy
King Common Rough
Stony Edge
Widdop Gate
Hebden Water
COW HEY LANE
Dole
Low Moor
High Laithe
Black Hill
Pennine Camp Site
Ox Holes
Ferny Beds
High Greenwood Farm
High Greenwood House
Abel Cross
Coppy
Lady Royd Edge
Hamlet
Walshaw Wood
Hoar Royd
Kid Stones
Turn Hill
White Mires
Pisser Clough
Ling Hollow
Pennine Way
Clough Head Hill
Lady Royd Farm
Able Cote
Lady Royd
Mould Grain
Hardcastle Craggs
Boothroyd Farm
Clough Head Hill
Higher Mansfield House
Green Hill
Clough House
Clough Head Bullion
Waterfall
Gibson Mill
Hardcastle Crags
Black Mires
Clough Head
Gibson Wood Bridge
Mansfield House
Field Head
Greenwood Lee Clough
Clough Hole Bridge
Greenwood Lee
Bent Head Clough
Shackleton Wood
Raw Hole
Shackleton
Bent Head
Owlers
Laith End
Cock Rock
COW LANE
New Greenwood Lee
Black Scout
Rabbit Hole
Willow Gate
Willow Gate Rock
Cuckoo Rock
Greenwood Gutter
Gibson Wood or Greenwood Lee Wood
New Edge
Pennine Way
Foul Scout Wood
EDGE
LONG TAIL LANE
HOT
Stony Turgate Hill
Acre
Foul Hill
Old Edge
Mould Grain Wood
Bess Barker
HEBDEN DALE
Salt Pie
Mount Pleasant
Hebden Hey
Cragg Side
WIDDOP
Acre Lane Cottage
Land Bridge
Hot Stones Hill
BACK LANE
Tom Bell Cave
Hawden Hole Farm
SCHOOL LAND LANE
HEBDEN WOOD
Stoneshey Gate
Land Farm
Halstead Green Farm
Long High Top
Popples Bottom
BOBBY'S LA.
Hawden Wood
Higher Golden
Ingham Well
Knoll Top
Turf Stone
Top o' th' Rough
Less Colden Farm
Great House Farm
FOLD
High Gate
BROAD LANE
ACRE
ROAD
Slack Top Farm
Burial Ground
Edgehey Green
High Edgehey Green
Knowl Top
Mid Slack
Colden Water
COLDEN
Hudson Fold
Draper Corner
Cklt. Grd.
NEW
Field Head Farm
Lear Ings Hall
SMITHWELL
Popples Side
Slack Top
Slack
DRAPER
Pinfold Top
FAUGH
Black Dyke
SLATER ING
Strines Bridge
MURKING
Slack Bottom
Lower Smithy
Higher Pilling
Goose Hey
Little Lear Ings
Fields Farm
SMITHWELL LANE
Higher Strines
Lower Strines Farm
Great Lear Ings
Pike Stones Bank
Cross Hill
Higher Slater Ing
Lower Slater Ing
LUMB RD.
GREEN
ROAD
Colden Prim. Sch.
SMITHY LANE
South View
Slater Ing Wood
Lumb Cottage
Lumb Bank
Windy Harbour Farm
Heptonstall Primary School
Jack Bridge
Lower Pilling
Hebble Hole
Hudson Mill
Bob Wood Weir
Colden
Foster Wood
Sandal House
Lane Head
Higher Murgatshaw Farm
High Street
HUDSON
MILL
Brown Hill Bottom
NEW SHAW LANE
Dill Scout's Wood
Eaves Wood
BROWN
HILL
LANE
Lower Murgatshaw
Shaw Bottom Cottage
Shaw Bottom Farm
Heptonstall
Grave Yard
Drain
HALIFAX RD.
NEW SHAW LA.
OLD SHAW LA.
BROWN HILL
Pry Hill
Milking Bridge
EAVES
HIGHER BACK LANE
Woodland Hall
Brown Hill
RAWTONSTALL LANE
Rec. Grd.
AVENUE
Hell Hole
West Bar
OLD SHAW LA
BADGER
Bracewell Hall
Cally Hall
Far Rawtonstall
BROOKSIDE
Lane Top
LOWER BACK LA.
THE LONG CAUSEWAY
High Top
BOW LANE
NEW LANE
Works
Mytholm
Lane Bottom
Blackshaw Head
Lane Head
Pry
Higher Rawtonstall
Harleywood Gate
Bullion
High Gate
Scammerton
Green House
Granny Wood
White Windows
Row
MARSH LA.
Rawtonstall House
Works
CHURCH LA.
BANKFOOT

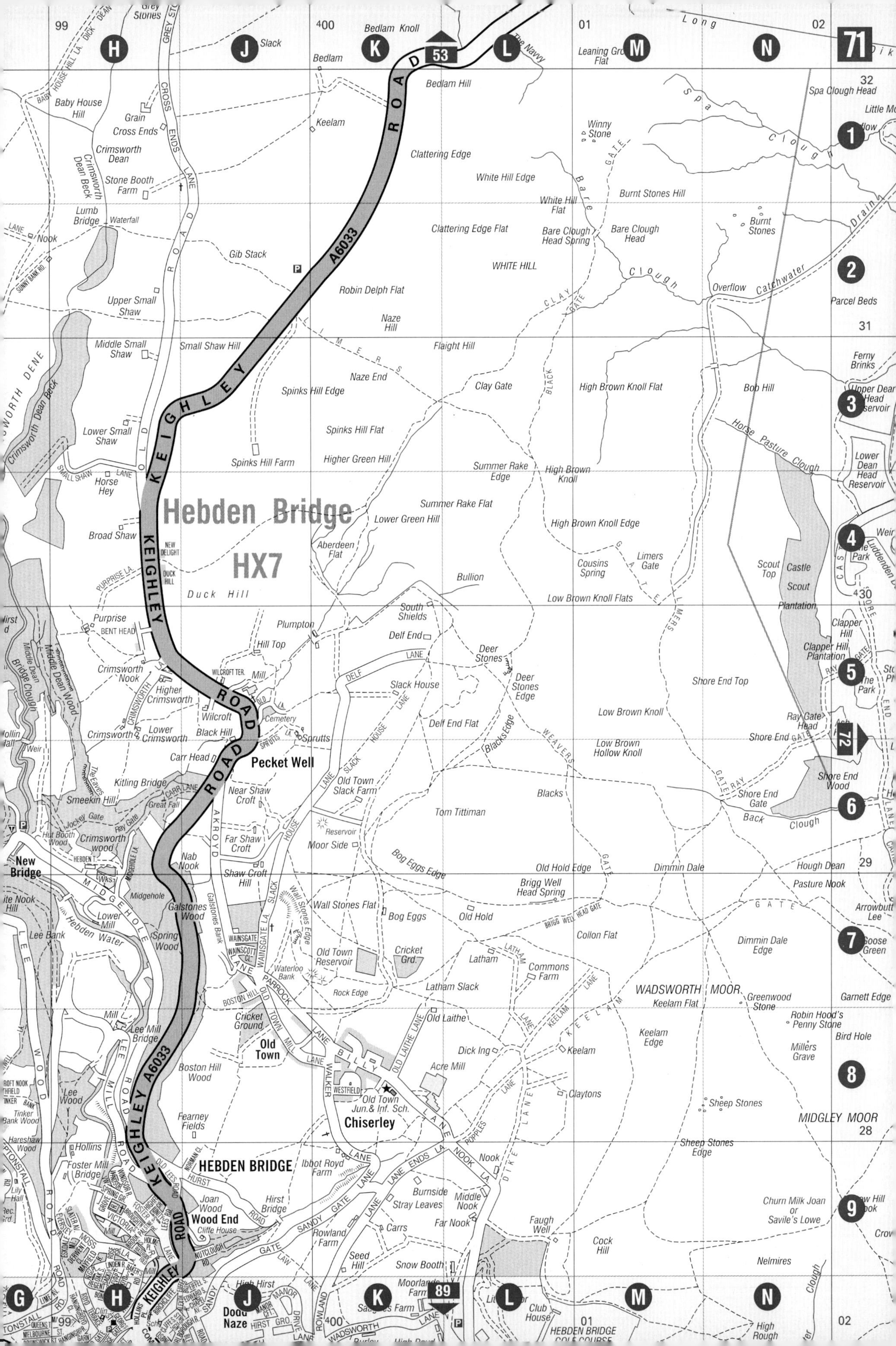
Hebden Bridge
HX7
HEBDEN BRIDGE
Pecket Well
Chiserley
Old Town
Wood End
New Bridge
WADSWORTH MOOR
MIDGLEY MOOR
KEIGHLEY ROAD
A6033
53
72
89
Bedlam Knoll
Bedlam
Bedlam Hill
Keelam
Slack
Grain
Cross Ends
Baby House Hill
Crimsworth Dean
Crimsworth Dean Beck
Stone Booth Farm
Lumb Bridge
Waterfall
Nook
Gib Stack
Upper Small Shaw
Middle Small Shaw
Small Shaw Hill
Lower Small Shaw
Horse Hey
Broad Shaw
Duck Hill
Purpise
Bent Head
Crimsworth Nook
Higher Crimsworth
Lower Crimsworth
Wilcroft
Black Hill
Carr Head
Kitling Bridge
Smeekin Hill
Jockey Gate
Ray Gate
Hud Booth Wood
Crimsworth wood
Great Fall
Near Shaw Croft
Far Shaw Croft
Nab Nook
Shaw Croft Hill
Midgehole
Lower Mill
Hebden Water
Lee Bank
Galstones Wood
Spring Wood
Mill
Lee Mill Bridge
Lee Wood
Tinker Bank Wood
Hareshaw Wood
Hollins
Foster Mill Bridge
Boston Hill Wood
Fearney Fields
Cricket Ground
Joan Wood
Cliffe House
Hirst Bridge
Ibbot Royd Farm
Clattering Edge
White Hill Edge
Clattering Edge Flat
Robin Delph Flat
Naze Hill
Flaight Hill
Naze End
Spinks Hill Edge
Spinks Hill Flat
Spinks Hill Farm
Higher Green Hill
Summer Rake Edge
Summer Rake Flat
Lower Green Hill
Aberdeen Flat
Bullion
Plumpton
Hill Top
South Shields
Delf End
Slack House
Deer Stones
Deer Stones Edge
Delf End Flat
Blacks Edge
Old Town Slack Farm
Reservoir
Moor Side
Bog Eggs Edge
Wall Stones Flat
Wall Stones Edge
Bog Eggs
Old Hold
Old Town Reservoir
Cricket Grd.
Waterloo Bank
Rock Edge
Latham
Latham Slack
Commons Farm
Old Laithe
Dick Ing
Keelam
Acre Mill
Claytons
Old Town Jun.& Inf. Sch.
Burnside
Stray Leaves
Middle Nook
Far Nook
Carrs
Rowland Farm
Seed Hill
Snow Booth
Moorlands Farm
Faugh Well
Cock Hill
Club House
HEBDEN BRIDGE GOLF COURSE
Dodd Naze
High Rough
Tom Tittiman
Blacks
Winny Stone
White Hill Flat
Bare Clough
Bare Clough Head Spring
Bare Clough Head
Burnt Stones Hill
Burnt Stones
WHITE HILL
Clay Gate
High Brown Knoll Flat
High Brown Knoll
High Brown Knoll Edge
Cousins Spring
Limers Gate
Low Brown Knoll Flats
Low Brown Knoll
Low Brown Hollow Knoll
Old Hold Edge
Brigg Well Head Spring
Collon Flat
Dimmin Dale
Dimmin Dale Edge
Keelam Flat
Keelam Edge
Greenwood Stone
Sheep Stones
Sheep Stones Edge
Churn Milk Joan or Savile's Lowe
Nelmires
Leaning Grd Flat
Spa Clough
Spa Clough Head
Overflow
Catchwater Drain
Parcel Beds
Ferny Brinks
Bob Hill
Horse Pasture Clough
Upper Dean Head Reservoir
Lower Dean Head Reservoir
Scout Top
Castle Scout Plantation
Clapper Hill
Clapper Hill Plantation
Shore End Top
Ray Gate Head
Shore End
Shore End Wood
Shore End Gate
Back Clough
Hough Dean
Pasture Nook
Arrowbutt Lee
Goose Green
Garnett Edge
Robin Hood's Penny Stone
Bird Hole
Millers Grave
The Park
Weir
H J K L M N G
1 2 3 4 5 6 7 8 9
99 400 01 02 32 31 30 29 28

Spa Clough Head
Little Moor
Overflow
Spa Clough
Catchwater Drain
Midgley Moor
Tatie Pie Hill
Clunter Clough
Brook
Ferny Brinks
Parcel Beds
Luddenden
Shaw Thorn
WARLEY MOOR RESERVOIR
Slipway
Landing Stage
Overflow
Robin Rock
Weir
Dean Head Stony Edge
Fly Delph
Fly
Old Fly Delph
COLD EDGE
Knoll
Hollin Hill
WIND FARM
OVENDEN MOOR
Skirden Edge
Skirden Head
Skirden
Ogden
Deep
Gulf
Dont Bridge
Fill Belly Flat
Fill Belly
Knoll Hill
ROAD
WITHENS
Cold Edge
Withens Head Farm
Slade
Ferny Brinks
Sheep Cote Brinks
Upper Dean Head Reservoir
Lower Dean Head Reservoir
Pasture Clough
WARLEY MOOR
Withens Gap
Moorlands Farm
Upper Hazelhurst Farm
Lower Hazelhurst Farm
Middle Gra
Warside
The Graining
Wainsley Scar
Castle
Scout Plantation
CASTLE CARR ROAD
The Park
Luddenden Dean
Castle Carr Resr.
Durham
Fulshaw
Fulshaw Clough
Resr.
Deep Clough
Long Pit
Rough Nook
Gauge Basin
Rocking Stone
Stony Edge
Rocking Stone Flat
Haigh Cote
Spring Dam
Spring Farm
Clapper Hill
Clapper Hill Plantation
RAY GATE
SHORE
Stony Spot Plantation
The Park
Deep Clough Edge
Too To Hill
Stony Edge
Sleepy Lowe Flat
Stony Edge Flat
High Cote Dam
Waterloo
Cold Edge Dams
Ray Gate Head
Ash Hole
END
Folds Edge
Folds
Height Edge
WARLEY MOOR
Leadbeater Dam
Plane Trees
Hough Gate Head Farm
Lower Shore End Wood
Shore End Wood
Height Swamp
Clough
Height Lodge
Upper Height
Lower Height Farm
Sleepy Lowe
HX2
Mill Pond
Moor Bottom
Hoyle Bottom Farm
Square Mill
Head House Bridge
Clough
LANE
The Heights
Heys Clough
Height
LOW
Lowe Bri.
The Lowe Farm
Hough Dean
Upper Heys
CATHERINE
Luddenden
Nunnery
LANE HEYS
Pasture Nook
Nunnery Bridge
Upper Heys Wood
CARR ROAD
Moorfield Farm
Lumb Mill
ROPE WALK
WITHENS ROAD
Arrowbutt Lee
HOUSE LANE
Catherine House
Goose Nest
Goose Green
Vicarman Bridge
Lower Heys
Upper Grn. Edge
Stone Farm
Wainstalls Mills
Mill Pond
LUMB LANE
WHITE HA
Dale
WOOD
New Bridge
Throstle Bower
Throstle Bower Farm
Lamb Hill
Lower Green Edge
Garnett Edge
Spa Wood
Frank Wood
LANE
SALTONSTALL
Upper Saltonstall
Field Head
Caty Well
Wainstalls
WAINSTALLS
Wainstalls Mills
Lower Slack Farm
TREE LA
Pav.
COLD EDGE ROAD
Lower Hambleton Hill
Robin Hood's Penny Stone
Bird Hole
Ferney Lee
The Hullet
Caty Well Bridge
ROUGH HALL LANE
Wainstalls Prim. Sch.
Millers Grave
HOLLIN LANE CLOUGH
Brook
Lower Saltonstall
Caty Wood
Ash Tree Farm
Turf Pit Hill
Sload
MOUNT
Hollin Top
Clough Hole
Upper Mytholm
Lower Mytholm
Ridings
HOUSE LANE
Peace Cote
Pav.
Ckt. Grd.
Back Sload Farm
MIDGLEY MOOR
Pasture
Caty Well Brook
Resr.
LANE BALKRAM
Clough Cottage
Dry Carr
DRY
Booth Wood
Well Wood
Resr.
BANK
Reign
Wainstalls Head
Upper Shaw Booth
BOOTH LANE
Sandy Fore Farm
SLACK
Slack
JERUSALEM
Wade Bri.
Jerusalem Farm
Camping Site
Bank House
HOLME HOUSE LA.
Holly Grove
TABOR
Crow Hill Nook
CARR
LANE HIGH
Hawks Clough Farm
Dry Carr
Hoyle Ho.
Peacock House Farm
Sandy Fore
Nell Nook
Reservoir
High House Pasture
Reservoir
LUDDENDEN DEAN
BANK HOUSE LANE
Bullace Trees Farm
Long Riggin
Lower Reap Hurst
Crow Hill
Hoyle Bank
Lower Shaw Booth
SHAW
SPANFIELD
Upp. Reap Hurst
Clough
HOUSE
High House
Booth
Carr House
Height Farm
Laithe
LANE
Kiln House Wood
Mare Hill Farm
LANE STOCKS

54
71
90

Bradford
BD13
BRADFORD
CALDERDALE
Halifax
HX3
OGDEN PLANTATION
OGDEN RESERVOIR
OVENDEN MOOR
HALIFAX GOLF COURSE
Ogden
Causeway Foot
Soil Hill
Bradshaw
Brookhouse
Upper Brockholes
ILLINGWORTH
Holdsworth
Holmfield
Mixenden
Moor End
KEIGHLEY ROAD
A629
CAUSEWAY FOOT
LONG CAUSEWAY
HALIFAX RD.
THORNTON RD.
BRIGHOUSE AND DENHOLME ROAD
A644
QUEENSBURY
Mixenden Reservoir
Mixenden Plantation
Foreside Top
The Allotment
New Moss Farm
Cockhill Hill
Whistle Hole
Windsway
Fireclay Works
Clay Pits
Soil Hill Farm
Pot Ovens
Coal Lane End Farm
Shay Fold Farm
Sun Side
Sun Side Farm
The Shay
Keelham Farm
Keelham Hall
Shay Farm
Far Shay Farm
Upper Sandal
Lower Sandal
Travis House Farm
Small Tail Farm
Hartley Square Farm
Grand View
Sun Farm
Cloth Hall Farm
Black Castle
White Wall End
Great Scar
Spice Cake Hills
Rock Hollow Park
Mount Pleasant
Visitor Cen.
Grey Shaw Syke
Syke Farm
Ash Farm
Stony Hall
Soil Hill End
Delves Farm
Laverock Hall Farm
Jammy Fold Farm
New Fold Farm
Bridle Hall
Rails Cottage
Saddle Hall Farm
Bradshaw Row
Rosemary Hall
Taylor's Farm
Crabtree Hall
Brandy Hall
Bradshaw Hall
Upper Fold
Reservoir Ho.
Black Hill
Mixenden Ings
Rodger Leys
Moorlands
Cow Gate Farm
Cock Hill Gate
Butterclose
Bradshaw House Farm
Harper Bower Farm
Ingham Lane Farm
Woodland Farm
Slack Field
Odd Moor
Cricket Ground
New Grange Farm
Bradshaw Prim. Sch.
Sports Flds.
Club Ho.
Rocks
Moorclose
North Cockhill Farm
Cock Hill
Ash Plant Farm
Upper Schole Croft
Lower Schole Croft Farm
Brookhouse Farm
Lane Head
Park Lane Ends
South Peat Pitts
North Scausby
Middle Schole Croft Farm
Slaughter Gap
Broad Acres
Pundles
West Scausby Farm
Upper West Scausby
The Vicarage
St. John's Cross
Stod Fold
Upper Lane Head
Upper Brockholes Farm
Scausby Hall Farm
Goose Clough
Hunter Hill
Green Lane Farm
Great Scausby Farm
Lower Brockholes
HOLMFIELD INDUSTRIAL ESTATE
Works
Mixenden Crag
Field Head
Spring Clough
White House Farm
Shaking House Farm
Sports Grd.
Reservoir House
Mixenden Green
HEBBLE BROOK BUSINESS PARK
Rec. Grd.
Fold Farm
Schools
Play. Fld.
North Halifax Gram. Sch.
Playing Fields
Holy Trinity Sen. Sch.
Halifax Cath. High Sch.
Youth Centre
Abbey Pk. Prim. Sch.
Ckt. Grd.
Cobble Bank Farm
Springfield Ho.
Heathy Ho.
Netherton Mills
Play. Fld. School
Mixenden Stones
Ashdale
Threap Croft
Edge End Farm
New Laithe Barn
Tar Hill Plantation
Tar Hill
Ovenden Grange
Mason's Green
Adventure Play Area
Ten. Cts.
Bowl. Grn.
Sports Grd.
Sutton
Grindlestone Bank
Scout Edge
North Howcans
South Howcans
Crow Point
Green Royd
Upper Bank
Leighton Farm
Halifax R.U.F.C.
Hollin Hall
Collier Topping
Upper Green Royd
Delf Hill
Upper Brown Hirst
Mount Tabor Quarry
Moor End Quarries
Sunny Bank Quarries
Lower Brown Hirst
Far Royd
Lower Highfield
Gibb Hill
Walt Royd
Deanfield
CALDERDALE BUS. PARK
55
91
74
06
07
08
32
31
30
29
28
1
2
3
4
5
6
7
8
9
G
H
J
K
L
M
N

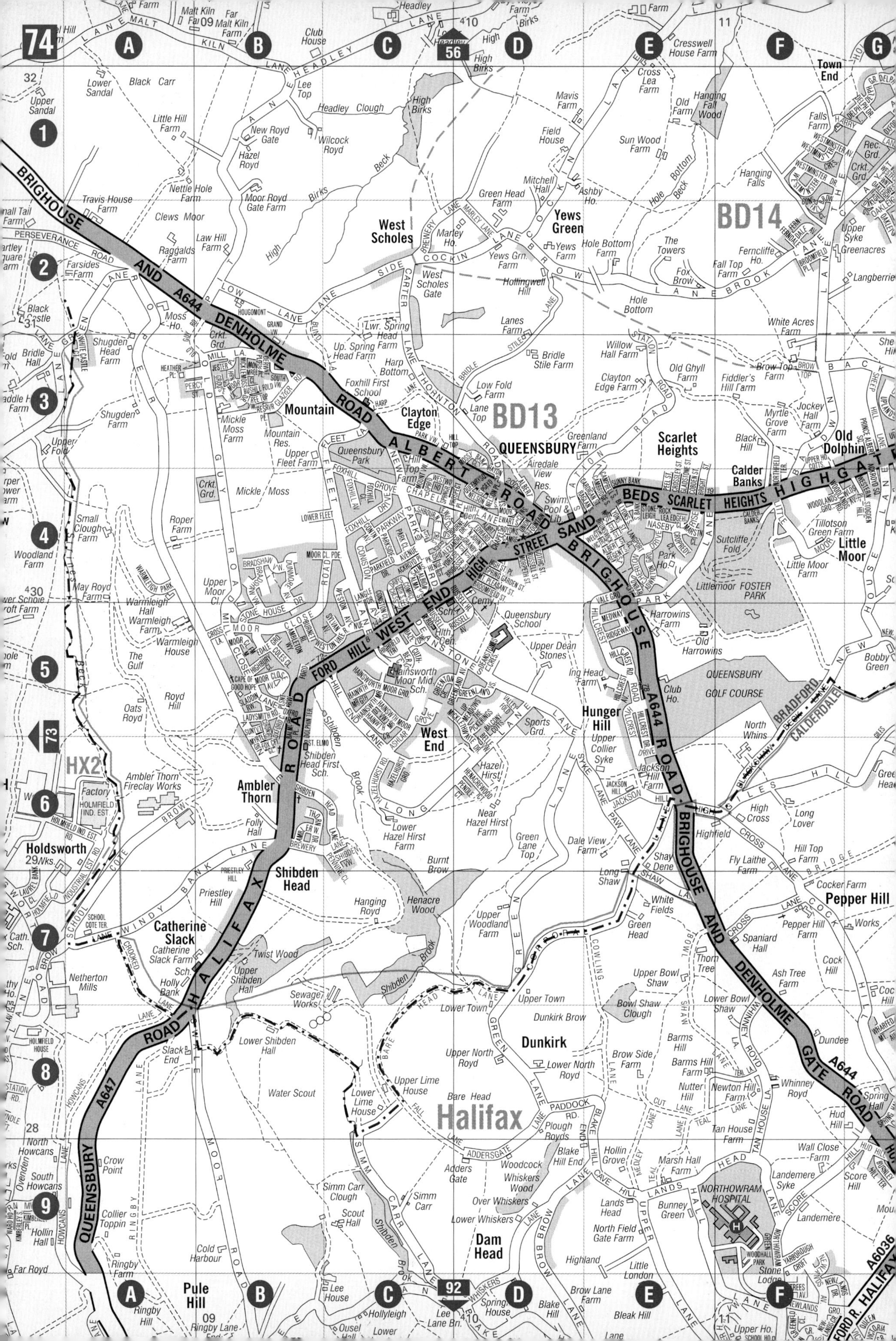
74
A
B
C
D
E
F
G
1
2
3
4
5
6
7
8
9
56
92
73
BD13
BD14
HX2
Halifax
QUEENSBURY
Malt Kiln Farm
Far Malt Kiln Farm
Club House
Headley
Lower Sandal
Upper Sandal
Black Carr
Lee Top
Headley Clough
High Birks
Little Hill Farm
New Royd Gate
Hazel Royd
Wilcock Royd
Cresswell House Farm
Cross Lea Farm
Mavis Farm
Old Farm
Hanging Fall Wood
Town End
Field House
Sun Wood Farm
Falls Farm
Nettle Hole Farm
Moor Royd Gate Farm
Travis House Farm
Clews Moor
Law Hill Farm
Raggalds Farm
Farsides Farm
West Scholes
Marley Ho.
Green Head Farm
Mitchell Hall
Ashby Ho.
Yews Green
Hole Bottom Farm
The Towers
Hanging Falls
Ferncliffe Ho.
Upper Syke
Greenacres
Yews Grn. Farm
West Scholes Gate
Hollingwell Hill
Fall Top Farm
Fox Brow
Hole Bottom
Langberrie
Moss Ho.
Crkt. Grd.
Shugden Head Farm
Lwr. Spring Head Farm
Up. Spring Head Farm
Lanes Farm
Bridle Stile Farm
Willow Hall Farm
White Acres Farm
Old Ghyll Farm
Fiddler's Hill Farm
Brow Top Farm
Harp Bottom
Foxhill First School
Mountain
Clayton Edge
Low Fold Farm
Lane Top
Clayton Edge Farm
Jockey Hall Farm
Myrtle Grove Farm
Shugden Farm
Mickle Moss Farm
Mountain Res.
Upper Fleet Farm
Queensbury Park
Greenland Farm
Airedale View Res.
Scarlet Heights
Black Hill
Calder Banks
Old Dolphin
Mickle Moss
Swim. Pool & Lib.
Small Clough Farm
Roper Farm
Tillotson Green Farm
Little Moor
Woodland Farm
Sutcliffe Fold
Little Moor Farm
Upper Moor Cl.
May Royd Farm
Warmleigh Hall
Warmleigh Farm
Warmleigh House
Littlemoor FOSTER PARK
Park Ho.
Harrowins Farm
Old Harrowins
Queensbury School
The Gulf
Upper Dean Stones
Bobby Green
Ing Head Farm
QUEENSBURY GOLF COURSE
Club Ho.
Hainsworth Moor Mid. Sch.
Oats Royd
Royd Hill
West End
Sports Grd.
Hunger Hill
Upper Collier Syke
North Whins
BRADFORD
CALDERDALE
Shibden Head First Sch.
Ambler Thorn Fireclay Works
Ambler Thorn
Factory
HOLMFIELD IND. EST.
Hazel Hirst
Jackson Hill Farm
High Cross
Long Lover
Holdsworth
Folly Hall
Near Hazel Hirst Farm
Green Lane Top
Dale View Farm
Highfield
Hill Top Farm
Lower Hazel Hirst Farm
Burnt Brow
Shay Dene
Fly Laithe Farm
Shibden Head
Priestley Hill
Long Shaw
Cocker Farm
Pepper Hill
Hanging Royd
Henacre Wood
White Fields
Catherine Slack
Catherine Slack Farm
Upper Woodland Farm
Green Head
Pepper Hill Farm
Spaniard Hall
Works
Cath. Sch.
Netherton Mills
Twist Wood
Thorn Tree
Cock Hill
Upper Shibden Hall
Holly Bank
Ash Tree Farm
Upper Bowl Shaw
Sewage Works
Lower Town
Upper Town
Bowl Shaw Clough
Lower Bowl Shaw
Dunkirk Brow
Lower Shibden Hall
Slack End
Dunkirk
Upper North Royd
Brow Side Farm
Barms Hill
Lower North Royd
Barms Hill Farm
Dundee
Nutter Hill
Newton Hill Farm
Whinney Royd
Water Scout
Upper Lime House
Lower Lime House
Bare Head
Spring Hall
Hud Hill
Tan House Farm
Plough Royds
Wall Close Farm
Crow Point
Blake Hill End
Hollin Grove
Marsh Hall Farm
Score Hill
Landemere Syke
Adders Gate
Woodcock Whiskers Wood
Simm Carr Clough
Simm Carr
Over Whiskers
Lands Head
Bunney Green
NORTHOWRAM HOSPITAL
Landemere
Scout Hall
Lower Whiskers
Collier Toppin
North Field Gate Farm
Cold Harbour
Dam Head
Highland
Little London
Ringby Farm
Stone Lodge
Pule Hill
Lee House
Brow Lane Farm
Ringby Hill
Hollyleigh
Lee Lane Bn.
Spring House
Blake Hill
Bleak Hill
Upper Ho.
Ringby Lane
Ousel Hall
South Howcans
North Howcans
Hollin Hall
Far Royd
BRIGHOUSE AND DENHOLME ROAD
A644
ALBERT ROAD
HIGH STREET
SAND BEDS
SCARLET HEIGHTS
HIGHGATE
WEST END
FORD HILL
HALIFAX ROAD
QUEENSBURY ROAD
A647
BRIGHOUSE AND DENHOLME GATE ROAD
A6036
PERSEVERANCE ROAD
LOW LANE
COCKIN LANE
MALT KILN LANE
HEADLEY LANE
WINDY BANK LANE
SCHOOL COTE BROW
GREEN LANE
CARR LANE
32
31
30
29
28
09
10
11
410

Bradford
BD7
BD6
BD5
BD12
HX3
CLAYTON
Broad Folds
Clayton Heights
Horton Bank
Horton Bank Top
Nab End
Paradise Green
Upper Green
Great Horton
Sellars Fold
Horton Bank Bottom
Pickles Hill
Beldon Hill
Haycliffe Hill
Wibsey
Slack Side
BUTTERSHAW
Witchfield
SHELF
Woodside
Moor Top
Delph Hill
Carr House Gate
Stone Chair
Beck Hill
GREAT HORTON ROAD
A647 ROAD
BEACON ROAD
B6380
COOPER LANE
B6147
HALIFAX ROAD
A6036
FAIR ROAD
HUDSON AV.
SOUTHFIELD LA.
A6177
CLAYTON GOLF COURSE
JAGGER PARK WOOD
WIBSEY PARK
Royds Hall
Gannerthorpe Wood
Horse Close
Royds Hall Great Wood
Old Hanna Wood
North Bierley Cemetery
HAROLD PARK
Park Dam
Sun Wood
Shelf Hall Park
Horsfall Playing Fields
Buttershaw Upper Sch.
Buttershaw First & Mid. Sch.
Reevy Hill First Sch.
St. John the Evangelist R.C. Prim. Sch.
Hollingwood First Sch.
Brackenhill First Sch.
Mandale Middle Sch.
Cooper Lane First Sch.
Haycliffe School
Grange Sch.
Wibsey Mid. Sch.
St. Winefride's R.C. Prim. Sch.
St. Michael's & All Angel Prim. Sch.
St. Michael's First Sch.
Little Horton
High Fernley First School
57
93
76

Dirk Hill
University of Bradford
Horton Green
Broomfield
58
BOWLING
Little Horton
St. Michael's First Sch.
Holme Top
ST. LUKE'S HOSPITAL
Chapel Green
West Bowling
Newby First Sch.
Ryan Mid. Sch.
Bowling Park First Sch.
Bolling Hall (Mus.)
Fairfax Comm. Sch.
Bowling Com. Coll.
Bolling Spec. Sch.
BOWLING PARK
East Bowling
The Roughs
SOUTHFIELD LA.
SOUTHFIELD RD.
SMIDDLES LA.
MANCHESTER ROAD
A641
Marshfields Rec. Grd.
BD5
Staygate
Priestman Middle Sch.
Brownroyd Hill
Carr Wood
Wibsey
Bank Foot
Truncliffe
Richard Dunn Sports Cen.
MAYO AVENUE
A6177
ROOLEY LANE
ROOLEY AVENUE
A6036
Parkside
Goose Hill
Bowling Cemetery
Newhall
Gregory Middle School
Bierley
WEST BOWLING GOLF COURSE
Playing Field
ODSAL ROAD
Odsal
Bradford Bulls R.L.F.C. (Odsal Stadium)
BD6
Odsal Top
Club House
Odsal Wood
M606
Warehouses
Woodhouse Hill
Bierley Hall Wood
HALIFAX ROAD
A6036
75
Horsfall Playing Fields
Coll Place
Playing Fields
Hardy Fold
SOUTH BRADFORD GOLF COURSE
Upper Park House
Park House
Lockwood Farm
Brogden House Farm
Mill Carr Hill
Cheesecake House Farm
Wesley Place
Wire Mills
BD12
Raw Nook
HUDDERSFIELD ROAD
CLECKHEATON ROAD
A638
Mathers Buildings
LOW MOOR
Low Moor Iron Works
Moorside Farm
Works
EUROWAY TRADING ESTATE
Hollowfield
M606 MOTORWAY
Hill Side Cottage
Hagg Hall Farm
Lowroyd
Delph Hill
Moor Side
Depot
Morley Carr
Vehicle Store
New Biggin Bridge
Oakenshaw
VICTORIA PARK
Lower Woodlands
Woodlands C.of E. First Sch.
Chatts Hill
Lower Chatts
Cliff Hollins Farm
WOODSIDE ROAD
A641
B6379
Reservoir
Warehouse
New Road Side
Carr House
Carr House Gate
High Fernley Farm
Fearnley Farm
Mt. of Olives Fm.
Threaklands Farm
Threappleton Farm
BRADFORD RD.
Water Pollution Control Works
Upper Common
Wyke Manor School
Playing Field
High Fernley First School
Wyke Middle Sch.
Croft House
94
OAKENSHAW LANE
A B C D E F G
1 2 3 4 5 6 7 8 9

Bankhouse
59
Tyersal Gate
Harper Gate Farm
Black Carr
Cutler Heights
Holmefield First School
Holme Bank Farm
Holme Wood
Holme Village
Lousy Wood
Maythorne Farm
Scholebrook Farm
Scholebrook
Bank House Farm
Bella Vista
Nesbit Hall
Holme Farm
Holme Wood
Dudley Hill
Warehouses
Recreation Ground
Raikes Farm
Raikes Hall Farm
Calverley Clough Farm
Shackleton Wood
Park Wood
Tong Park
Ryecroft Farm
Kit Wood
Gib Stubbing Farm
Peter's Shrog
Tong Street
Health Centre
BD4
Broomwood Middle Sch.
Factory
Works
Bowling Alley
Training Centre
Westgate Hill Plantation
Shetcliffe Hall Farm
West Yorkshire Industrial Estate
Playing Fields
Yorkshire Martyrs Collegiate School
Tong Upper School
Red Hill
Westgate Hill
Wagon House Farm
New Toftshaw
Toftshaw
Toftshaw Moor
Moorside Farm
Westfield Farm
Booth Holme Farm
Cross Lane End
Lane End Farm
Shawfield Farm
Toftshaw Nurseries
Model Farm
A650 Hill Street
Tong Lane End
78
Bradford & Wakefield Rd.
B6135
East Bierley Golf Course
Tong Moor
Toftshaw Bottom
Bradford Kirklees
East Bierley
Inmoor Dike
Bradford Leeds
Bradford
Whinfield Nurseries
Manor Ho.
Cross Ho.
Crkt. Grd.
Rec. Grd.
Hollbank Farm
Hunsworth Hill
Schools
Swallow Farm
Springfield Farm
Hill Top Farm
Chatts Farm
Football Ground
Birkenshaw
Brown Hill Farm
Hlth. Cen.
Works
Kittle Point Wood
Upper Park House Farm
Copley House Farm
Lower Park House Farm
Copley Springs Farm
Birk Hill Farm
Upper Sunny Bank
Cockleshaw Beck
Cockleshaw Range
Vicarage
Community Centre
Swinroyd
Kittle Point Wood
Wormalds Drain
BD11
Football Ground
Upper Lodge Range
M62
M62 Motorway
Bluehills Farm
Works
Fire Service H.Q.
Rec. Grd.
Birkenshaw Bottoms
Burnt Royd
Birkenshaw Middle Sch.
Play Fld.
Moorfield
Oakwell Wood
Heathfield Farm
Savile Arms Farm
Swincliffe
Hunsworth Great Wood
Hunsworth Lodge Farm
Lodge Farm
Lodge Garage
95
Field Head Farm
Rifle and Pistol Club
Birksland Moor
A58 Road
Whitehall
A651
A650 By-Pass
Drighlington
A6177
Westgate
Bradford Road
Street

Pudsey
LS28
BD4
Bradford
BD11
Batley
WF17
Bankhouse
Bankhouse Bottom
Bank House Farm
Bella Vista
Fulneck Golf Course
Sisters Wood
South Park Villa
Hope Farm
Burial Ground
Hazelden
East House
Low Farm
Roker Lane Bottom
Union Bridge
Park Side Farm
Leeds Country Way
North Wood
Pudsey Beck
Daffels Wood
Acre Wood
Coney Wood
Hollin House
Upland Farm
Whins Wood
Park Wood
Hill Green
The Manor House
Newlands Farm
Helicon Pond
Home Farm
Tong Hall Business Park
Tong
Tong Park
Manor Farm
Corn Mill Farm
Low Moor Side
B.B.C. Transmitting Station
Nurseries
Plane Tree Farm
Moor Top Farm
Upper Moor Side
Cemetery
Poplar Farm
Church Farm
The Pastures
Sewage Works
Cud Hill Farm
Cud Hill
Ings Hall Farm
Crystal Spring Farm
Ringshaw Beck
Thick Thorn Bank
Dale Farm
Cock Beck
Hilly Croft
Barker Hill Farm
Reservoir (covered)
Barron's Wood
Doles Wood
Whiteley Wood
Cockersdale Farm
Cockersdale
Longacre Farm
Moor Head
Carr Hall Farm
Green Acres
Scott Green
Golf Driving Range
The Manor Golf Course
Club House
Manor Farm
Lumb Wood
Lumb Hall Nurseries
Shay Farm
Nethertown
Westfield Farm
Andrew Beck
Andrew Hill
Lumb Bottom
Drighlington Junior School
Spring Gardens
Pitty Close Farm
Birchfield Prim. Sch.
Youth Club
Highfield Farm
Adwalton
Drighlington
Play. Fields
Lib.
Inf. Sch.
Factories
Depot
Wyre Hall Farm
Gildersome Street
Greystone Farm
Greystone House
Cricket Ground
Works
Owlet Hall
Overland Trading Estate
Treefield Industrial Estate
Upper Sunny
Highlands
Adwalton Moor
Moorside
Penfield
Res. (covered)
Reservoir (cov.)
Heightlands Farm
Burnt Hoyd
Warehouse
Moor Fields
M62 Motorway
Junction 27
Cinemas
Centre 27 Business Park
Oakwell Industrial Park
Oakwell Wood
Holly View Farm
Foxhall Farm
Fieldhead Jun., Inf. & Nursy. Sch.
Springwell Farm
Howden Clough Beck
Kirklees
Leeds
Bradford Road
Whitehall Road
Drighlington By-Pass
Gelderd Road
Wakefield Road
King Street
Church St.
Town Street
Tong Lane
Roker Lane
A58
A650
A62
B6125
B6126
B6135
M62

60
77
96

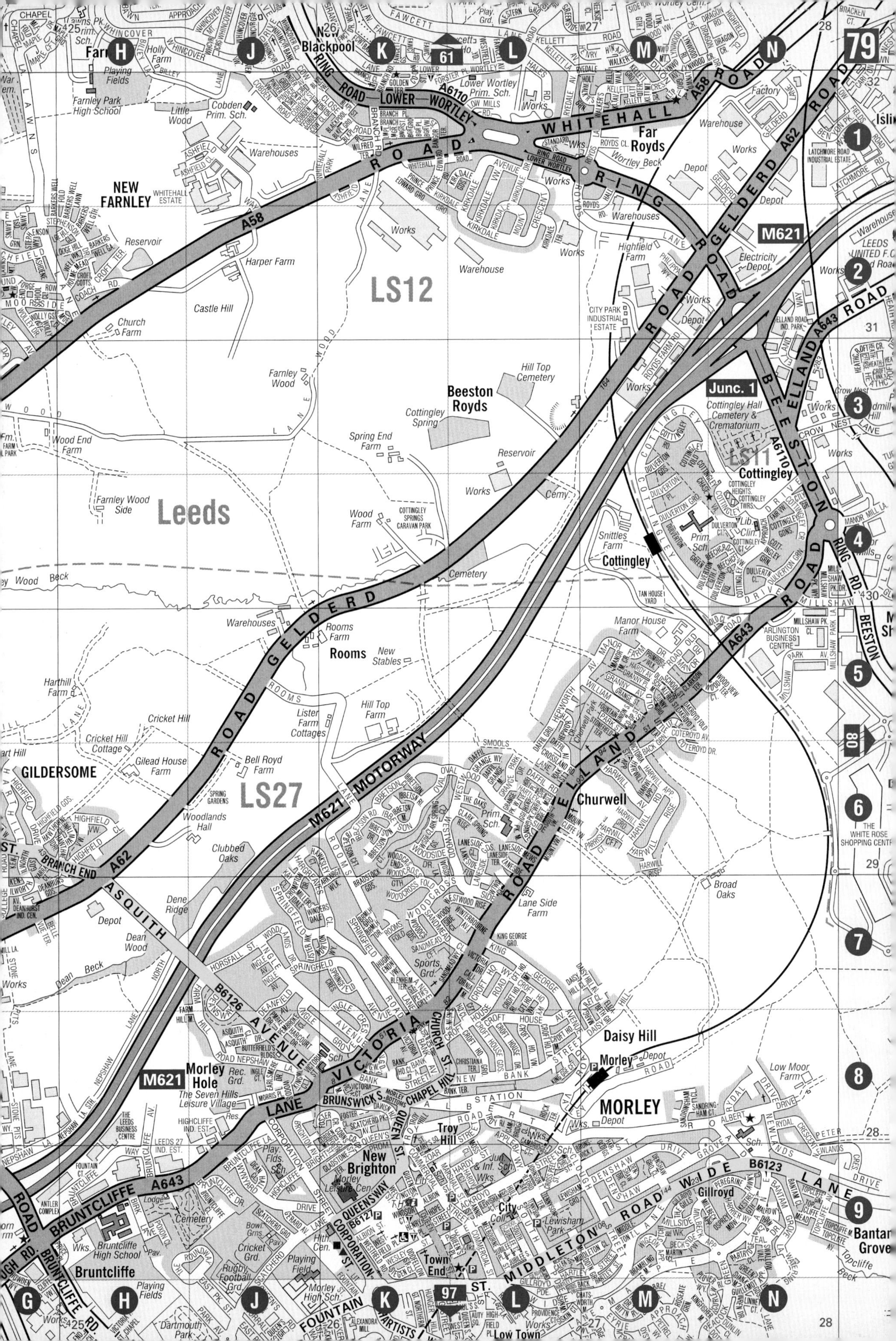
LS12
LS27
LS11
Leeds
NEW FARNLEY
Beeston Royds
Cottingley
Churwell
MORLEY
GILDERSOME
Morley Hole
New Brighton
Bruntcliffe
Far Royds
Rooms
Daisy Hill
Gillroyd
Troy Hill
Town End
Low Town
Junc. 1
M621
A58
A62
A643
A6110
B6126
B6123
RING ROAD LOWER WORTLEY
WHITEHALL ROAD
GELDERD ROAD
ELLAND ROAD
M621 MOTORWAY
ASQUITH AVENUE
VICTORIA ROAD
BRUNTCLIFFE ROAD
WIDE LANE
MIDDLETON ROAD
BEESTON ROAD
RING RD. BEESTON
Cottingley Hall Cemetery & Crematorium
Hill Top Cemetery
Farnley Wood
Castle Hill
Harper Farm
Church Farm
Wood End Farm
Farnley Wood Side
Spring End Farm
Cottingley Spring
Wood Farm
Rooms Farm
New Stables
Hill Top Farm
Lister Farm Cottages
Harthill Farm
Cricket Hill
Cricket Hill Cottage
Gilead House Farm
Bell Royd Farm
Woodlands Hall
Clubbed Oaks
Dene Ridge
Dean Wood
Dean Beck
Wood Beck
Lane Side Farm
Broad Oaks
Manor House Farm
Snittles Farm
Highfield Farm
Low Moor Farm
Bruntcliffe High School
Morley High Sch.
Farnley Park High School
Cobden Prim. Sch.
Lower Wortley Prim. Sch.
Morley Leisure Cen.
The Seven Hills Leisure Village
Dartmouth Park
Lewisham Park
Bantam Grove
Topcliffe Beck
Blackpool
Little Wood
Reservoir
Warehouses
Works
Depot
Cemetery
Electricity Depot
CITY PARK INDUSTRIAL ESTATE
LATCHMORE ROAD INDUSTRIAL ESTATE
ARLINGTON BUSINESS CENTRE
THE LEEDS BUSINESS CENTRE
HIGHCLIFFE IND. EST.
LEEDS 27 IND. EST.
THE WHITE ROSE SHOPPING CENTRE
LEEDS UNITED F.C.
H J K L M N G
1 2 3 4 5 6 7 8 9
61
80
97
25 26 27 28 29 30 31 32

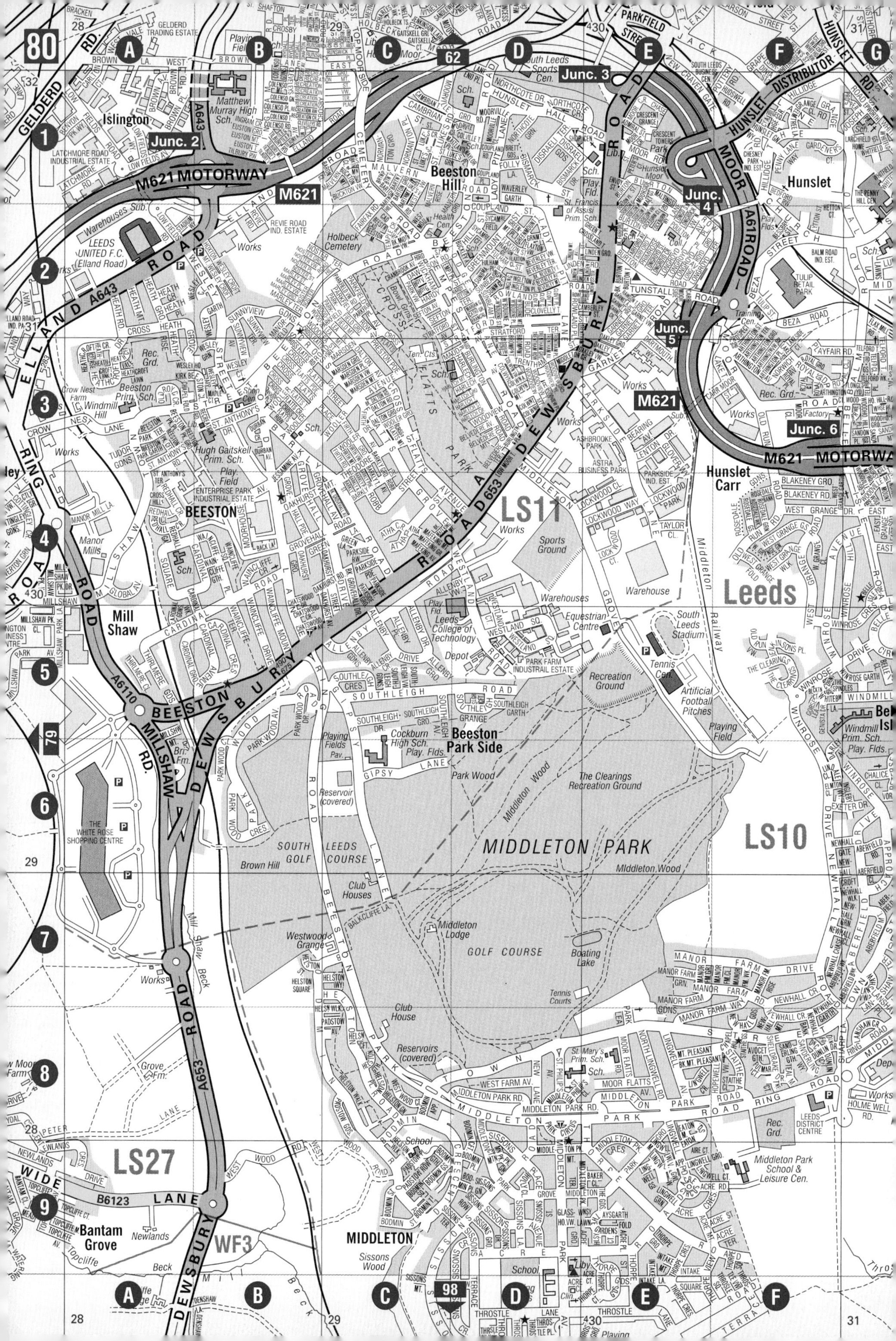

A
B
C
D
E
F
G
1
2
3
4
5
6
7
8
9
28
29
31
Islington
Beeston Hill
Hunslet
Hunslet Carr
Leeds
BEESTON
Mill Shaw
Beeston Park Side
MIDDLETON PARK
MIDDLETON
Bantam Grove
LS11
LS10
LS27
WF3
M621 MOTORWAY
M621
Junc. 2
Junc. 3
Junc. 4
Junc. 5
Junc. 6
ELLAND ROAD A643
DEWSBURY ROAD A653
RING ROAD
A6110
A61 ROAD
HUNSLET DISTRIBUTOR
LEEDS UNITED F.C. (Elland Road)
THE WHITE ROSE SHOPPING CENTRE
South Leeds Stadium
SOUTH LEEDS GOLF COURSE
GOLF COURSE
The Clearings Recreation Ground
Middleton Wood
Boating Lake
Middleton Park School & Leisure Cen.
Cockburn High Sch.
Matthew Murray High Sch.
Holbeck Cemetery
Hugh Gaitskell Prim. Sch.
Leeds College of Technology
Windmill Hill
Manor Mills
Newlands
62
79
98

Knowsthorpe
Cross Green Industrial Estate
Atkinson Hill
Valley House
River Aire
Knostrop Cut
Hunslet Forge
Hunslet Trading Estate
Gibraltar Island Road
Sewage Works
Knostrop Rifle Range
Skelton Grange Cottages
Thwaite Mills Museum
Thwaite Gate
Thwaite Ho.
Aire & Calder Navigation
Skelton Grange Power Station
Skelton Moor Farm
Bell Wood
Wyke Beck
Pontefract Lane
LS9
Recreation Ground
Thwaite Farm Trailer Park
Waterside Ind. Park
Playing Field
Warehouses
Sorting Office
Works
Stourton
Pontefract Road
B6481
Wakefield Road
A61
Freightliner Terminal
Valley Farm Way
Leodis Way
Towpath
Pump Ho.
Junction 7
Junction 44
Junction 43
M1 Motorway
M621
A639
Community Enterprise Resource Centre
Cemetery
Middleton Ring Road
Urn Farm
Bell Hill
Piggery
Rose Cottage Farm
Haigh Cottage Farm
Rothwell Haigh
Mill Pit Lane
John O'Gaunts Trading Estate
Haigh House Farm
Haigh House
Fish Pond
Glebe Farm
Wood Lane
Victoria Jun. Sch.
Haigh Side Fm.
LS26
Recreation Ground
Rothwell C.E. Prim. Sch.
Clapgate Prim. Sch.
Hope's Farm
Football Grd.
Robin Hood
Rothwell Castle (Rems of)
ROTHWELL
Hopefield Farm
Middle Shutts
Carlton Fields
Stone Bridge
Carlton Bri.
Carlton Lane
A654
Leadwell Lane
Howlett Cross
Sports Ground
Rec. Ground
Kiddow Spring
Sharp House
Marsh St.
Commercial St.
Leeds Road
63
82
99

GOLF COURSE
Park Wood
Temple Newsam
Jacob's Well
Mather Wood
64
Little Temple
Stork Pond
Dog Kennel Hill
Wilderness Wood
Hertford Springs
TEMPLE NEWSAM COUNTRY PARK
Charcoal Wood
Avenue Ponds
AVENUE WOOD
Dawson's Wood
Bell Wood
Spring Wood
Dunstan Hills
Pegasus Wood
The Shrogs
Laurel Hill Wood
PONTEFRACT LANE
M1 MOTORWAY
M1
Wyke Beck
Parkinson's Wood
KNOWSTHORPE LANE
Pump Ho.
LS9
LS15
Newsam Green Farm
Lawn Farm
Newsam Green
NEWSAM GREEN ROAD
Leeds
OPENCAST WORKINGS
Gamblethorpe
RIVER AIRE
Lodge
Leventhorpe Hall
Towpath
Fishpond Lock
The Goit
Aire & Calder Navigation
Leventhorpe Cottages
BULLERTHORPE LANE
JINNY MOOR LA.
The Smithy
81
Haigh Farm
Haigh Cottage Farm
John O'Gaunts
Woodlesford Lock
Wood End Farm
Swillington Bridge
South Lodge
Subways
Swillington Bri. Whaff
WOODLESFORD
Woodlesford
Cockpit Round
JOHN O'GAUNTS TRADING ESTATE
Works
Recreation Ground
Football Ground
Warehouses
LEEDS ROAD
A639
A642
Prim. Sch.
Rec. Grd.
Liby.
Cemy.
Springhead Park
Rothwell C.E. Prim. Sch.
Sports Field
Beeston Wood
Playground
Gillett Bri.
Greenland Farm
Gravel Pit Wood
ROTHWELL LANE
OULTON
A654
CALVERLEY RD.
Oulton
Church Plantation
Home Crofts
The Elms
Water Haigh Farm
Football Grd.
Cricket Grd.
OULTON PARK GOLF COURSE
Club Ho.
Oulton Hall
METHLEY
Rothwell Sports Centre
A639
Rifle Range
Golf Driving Range
Rugby League Hall of Fame
ROTHWELL
Robinson's Plantation
Clumpcliffe Wood
Autograss Circuit
Winter Wood
Swithen's Plantation
Waterloo Corner
100
WAKEFIELD A642 RD.

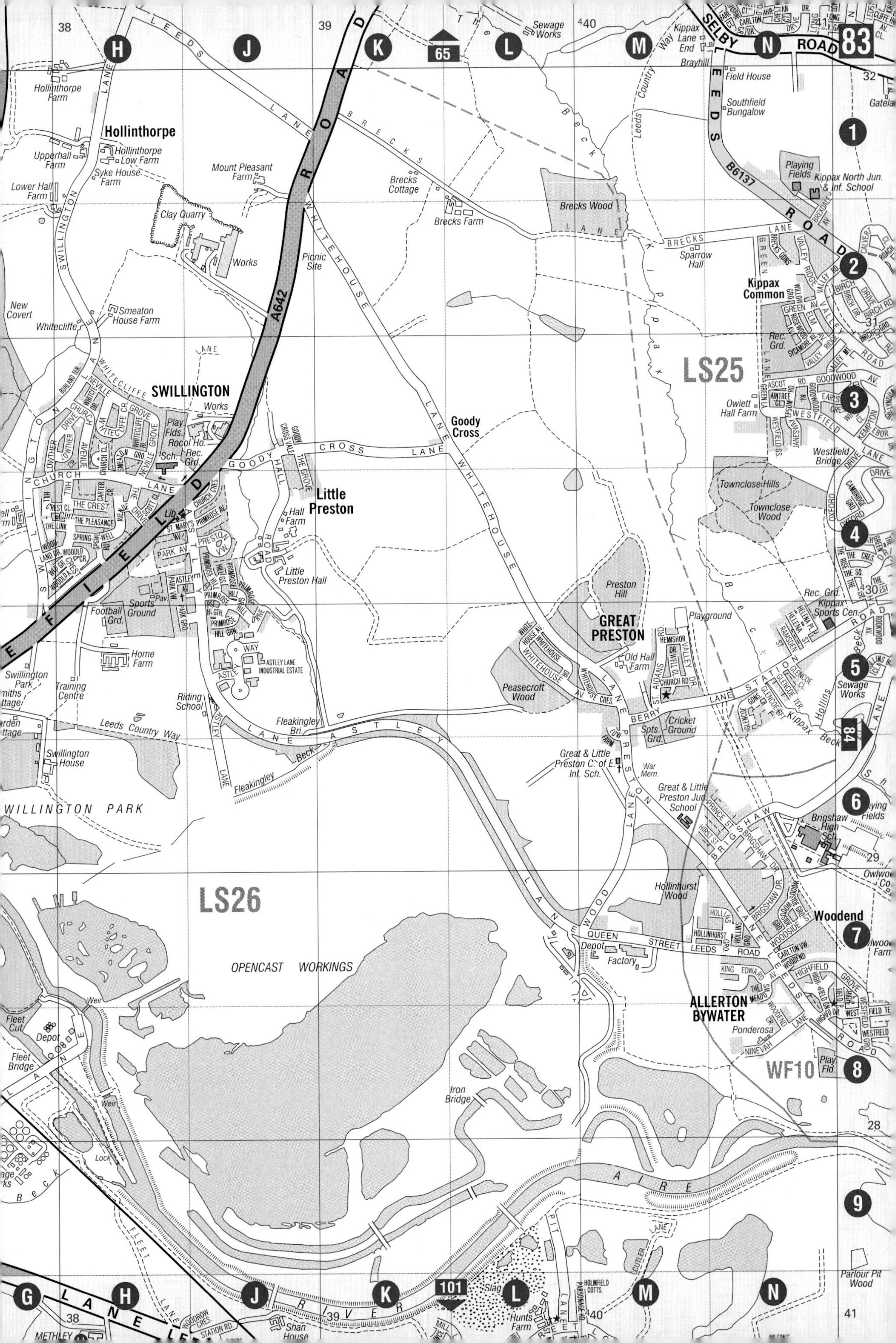

Hollinthorpe
SWILLINGTON
Little Preston
GREAT PRESTON
Kippax Common
Goody Cross
LS25
LS26
WF10
Woodend
ALLERTON BYWATER
OPENCAST WORKINGS
SELBY ROAD
LEEDS ROAD
A642
B6137
WHITEHOUSE LANE
GOODY CROSS LANE
ASTLEY LANE
PRESTON LANE
BRECKS LANE
LEEDS LANE
RIVER AIRE
Kippax Beck
Leeds Country Way
Brecks Wood
Peasecroft Wood
Hollinhurst Wood
Townclose Hills
Townclose Wood
Preston Hill
Clay Quarry
Works
Picnic Site
Mount Pleasant Farm
Brecks Cottage
Brecks Farm
Sparrow Hall
Smeaton House Farm
Whitecliffe
New Covert
Upperhall Farm
Lower Hall Farm
Hollinthorpe Farm
Hollinthorpe Low Farm
Syke House Farm
Little Preston Hall
Hall Farm
Home Farm
Football Grd.
Sports Ground
Training Centre
Riding School
Swillington House
Swillington Park
Fleakingley Bri.
Fleakingley Beck
Old Hall Farm
Owlett Hall Farm
Westfield Bridge
Kippax North Jun. & Inf. School
Kippax Sports Cen.
Great & Little Preston C. of E. Inf. Sch.
Great & Little Preston Jun. School
Brigshaw High Sch.
Sewage Works
Playground
Cricket Ground
Depot
Factory
Iron Bridge
Fleet Bridge
Fleet Cut
Weir
Lock
Slag
Hunts Farm
Shan House
Parlour Pit Wood
Ponderosa
Kippax Lane End
Brayhill
Field House
Southfield Bungalow
Gatela
SWILLINGTON PARK
ASTLEY LANE INDUSTRIAL ESTATE
65
84
101

Castleford
WF10
KIPPAX
Ledston Luck
Ledston
ALLERTON BYWATER
Moor Gate
Mount Pleasant
Woodend
SELBY ROAD A63
ROMAN RIDGE A656
BARNSDALE ROAD
LONGDIKE LANE B6137
HIGH STREET
LEEDS ROAD B6137
Peckfield Common
Warrenhouse Plantation
Quarryfield Plantation
Warren House Cottages
Peckfield Bar
Limekiln Cottages
Roach Grange Farm
Roach Hill
Top Wood
Gatelands
Marl Lodge
Garforth Cliff
Reservoirs (Covered)
Water Tower
The Mount
Kippax North Jun. & Inf. School
Playing Fields
Goodcomb Place
The Fruit Gardens
The Hills
Ledston Luck Enterprise Park
Sheepcote Farm Cottages
Sheepcote Wood
Sheepcote Farm
Works
Ledston Engine
Kippax Mill
Lodge
Sports Ground
Westfield Bridge
Kippax Sports Cen.
Sewage Works
Brigshaw High Sch.
Crispin Plantation
North Park
Park House Farm
Sheldon Hill
Home Farm
Kippax Park
Elm Tree Farm
Ledston Hall
The Grove
Riding Sch.
Lady Elizabeth Hastings C. of E. Prim. Sch.
Manor Farm
Vicarage
Chestnut Farm
Ledston Intake
Owlwood Cotts.
Owl Wood
Owlwood Ho.
Owlwood Farm
Pit Plantation
Whin Covert
Little Plantation
Low Lodge
Allerton Plantation
Park Lane Farm
Allerton Bywater Prim. Sch.
Sewage Wks.
Depot
Sluices
Parlour Pit Wood
Cricket Ground
Spts. Grd.
Peckfield Quarry (Stone)

66
83
102

Castle Hills
Highfield
Newthorpe Quarry
Beckfield
67
46
47
445
H
J
K
L
M
N
Micklefield Plantation
Micklefield Plantation
Peckfield Plantation
A1
HIGHFIELD
A63 ROAD
Milford Lodge
WHITECOTE LANE
Whitecote Plantation
B1222
Beacon Plantation
Hundred Acre Plantation
Pointer Fm.
ROAD
Ledston Lodge
Cattle Grid
Cattle Grid
Peckfield Lodge
WESTFIELD LANE
Scat House Farm
Ledston Park
Hundred Acre Plantation
Long Plantation
Ledsham Beck
NEW ROAD
REDHILL LANE
Hotel
Street Close Plantation
Old Vicarage
Park Lane Farm
PARK LANE
Dale Plantation
Leeds LS25
Forest Plain
Hastings Plantation
St. John's Hosp. (Almshouses)
HOLY ROOD LANE
A63
LUMBY LEYS LANE
Lumby Nursery
Hill Top Farm
Manor Ho.
Ledsham
CHANTREE CL.
MANOR GARTH
NEWFIELD LA.
Plaster Pits
Sewage Works
Capon Hill
Horselock Dale
Newfield Whin
Madbanks
Wormstall Wood
LEEDS SELBY
Mill Hill Plantation
Lambkin Plantation
Lambkin Hill
Newfield Farm
NEWTON
Ledsham Beck
BECKFIELD LANE
Newfield Plantation
Caudle Hill Plantation
Haugh Hill Plantation
Knottingley WF11
Beckfield House
Palmerston Lodge
Caudlehill Wood
Newton Farm
NEWTON LANE
CAUDLE LANE
Priory Cott.
Newton
Fairburn Ings Centre
Fairburn
Low Holland
Spoil Heap
GREAT NORTH ROAD
FAIRFIELD
AWFIELD LANE
ORCHARD DR.
LUNNFIELDS LA.
SILVER STREET
Sch.
Rec. Grd.
Pav.
NEWTON INGS
FAIRBURN INGS
103
G
1
2
3
4
5
6
7
8
9
32
31
430
29
28

Riddle Scout
Cartridge Pasture
Black Scout
Coal Clough
Coal Clough Farm
Ford
Burnt Edge Pasture
Paul Clough
Bank Top Farm
Jack Stone
Lower Mount Farm
Upper Mount Farm
Cross Hill
Rough Top
Hugeon Croft Farm
Hawke Mount
Higher Intake
Lower Intake
Sugar Lane Farm
Raw Hey
Commons
Pudsey Clough
Nant Wood
Dean Farm
Reddish Shore Rocks
Reddish Shaw Wood
Higher Green End
Shaw Law
Dyke
Blue Bell Lane
Sugar Lane
Scarth Rake
River Calder
Chatham Hill Plantation
Whitaker Naze
Brown Birks
Dawk Hole Wood
Weir
Pudsey
Shore
Blue Bell Farm
Hartley Royd
Windy Bank Wood
Mill
Obadiah Wood
Wittonstall
Wittonstall Clough
Heald Moor
Beater Clough
Portsmouth
Cornholme
Vale
HUDSON
Back Wood
Hartley Royd Wood
Clunters
Cat Hole
Burnley Road
A646
Carr Road
Stubley Lane
Tower Wood
Cock Hill Wood
The Old Woman
Robert Mill Stone
Knotts Naze
New Ley Wood
Knotts Wood
Barewise Bridge
Bearnshaw Tower
Height Top
Roundfield
BURNLEY CALDERDALE
Green's Clough
Barewise Wood
Canteen Mill Ind. Est.
Robinwood Terr.
CARR & CRAGGS MOOR
Tower Clough
Falls
Wet Shaw
Eagle's Crag
Fiddlers Bridge
Robin Wood
Lower Moor
New Towneley
Tower Causeway
Flower Scar
Lower Hill
West End
Dyke Green
Flower Scar Road
Flower Scar Hill
Todmorden OL14
Higher Woodfield Farm
Woodfield Top
Ridge Ho.
Lower Woodfield
Sourhall Cottages
Parkin
Slate Pit Hill
TODMORDEN MOOR
Acre Nook Clough
Lower Woodfield Farm
Moor Hey Farm
Little Tooter Hill
Clough Head
Back o' th' Edge
Clinton Farm
Works
Lower Hanging Shaw
Mellings
Holden Gate
North Midgelden
South Midgelden
Middle Midgelden
Clough Foot
Mellings Wood
Astronomy Centre
Hazel Greave Farm
Hollins Grn.
Sourhall Road
A681
Bacup Road
Tooter Hill
Stones Wood
Halshaw Clough
Midgelden Brook
Midgelden Pasture
Trial Holes
Gorpley
Stones Wood House
Bacup OL13
Old Day Hole
Midgelden Bank
Gorpley Clough
Gorpley Wood
CALDERDALE ROSSENDALE
Limers Gate
Maden Pasture
The Bungalow
Works
Gorpley Reservoir
Range Hoyle
Counting Hill
Weirs
Waterfall
Wash Pits Scout
Reaps Moss
Raven Nest
Shaw
68
106

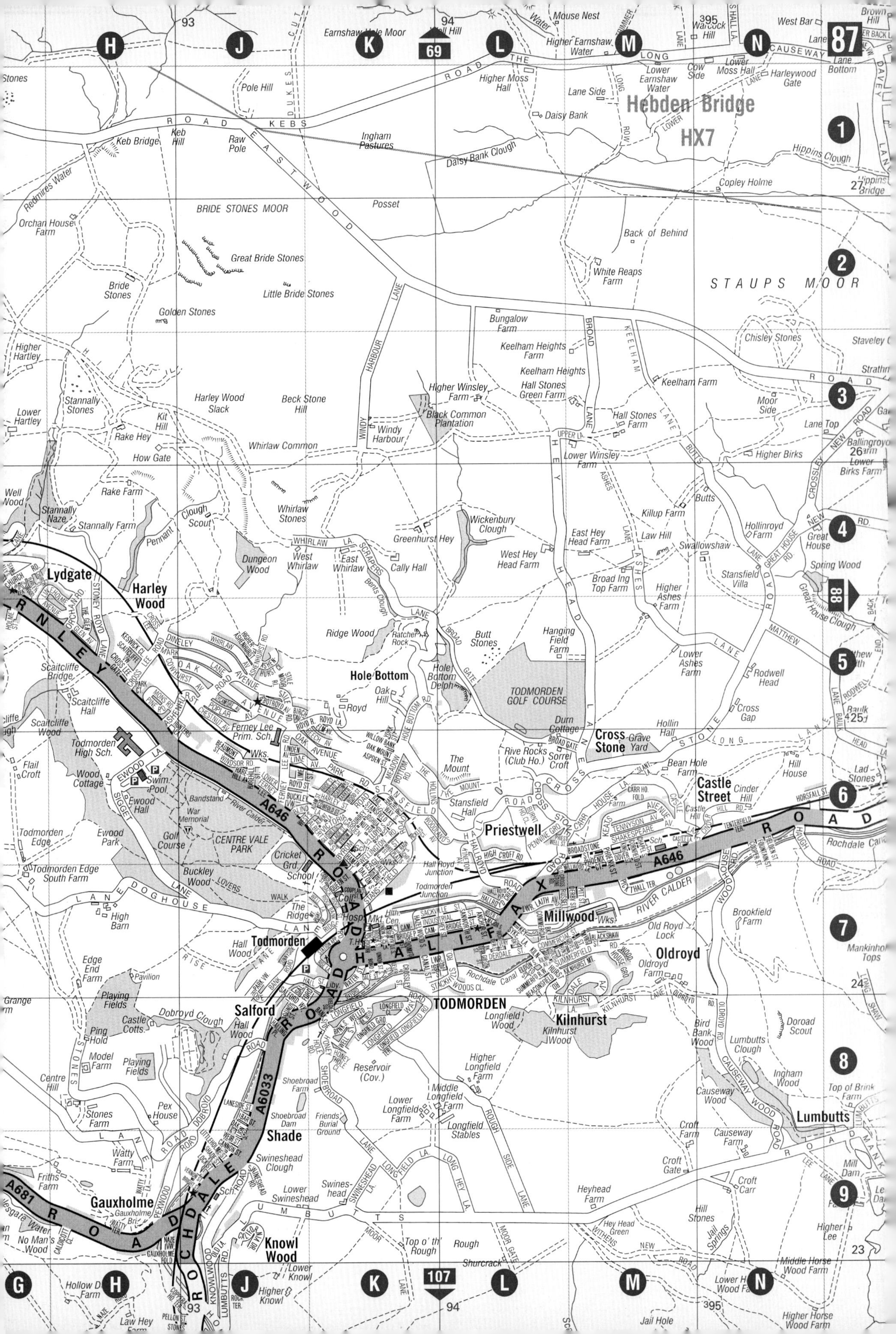

Hebden Bridge
HX7
Earnshaw Hole Moor
Mouse Nest
Higher Earnshaw Water
Warcock Hill
West Bar
Lane Bottom
Lower Earnshaw Water
Cow Side
Lower Moss Hall
Harleywood Gate
Higher Moss Hall
Lane Side
Daisy Bank
Pole Hill
Keb Bridge
Keb Hill
Raw Pole
KEBS ROAD
Ingham Pastures
Daisy Bank Clough
Hippins Clough
Hippins Bridge
Copley Holme
Redmires Water
Orchan House Farm
BRIDE STONES MOOR
Posset
EASTWOOD ROAD
Back of Behind
Great Bride Stones
White Reaps Farm
Bride Stones
Little Bride Stones
STAUPS MOOR
Golden Stones
Bungalow Farm
Keelham Heights Farm
Keelham Heights
Chisley Stones
Staveley
Higher Hartley
Hall Stones Green Farm
Higher Winsley Farm
Keelham Farm
Moor Side
Stannally Stones
Harley Wood Slack
Beck Stone Hill
Black Common Plantation
Windy Harbour
Hall Stones Farm
Lane Top
Lower Hartley
Kit Hill
Rake Hey
Whirlaw Common
Lower Winsley Farm
Higher Birks
Ballingroyd Farm
Lower Birks Farm
How Gate
Rake Farm
Well Wood
Stannally Naze
Stannally Farm
Clough Scout
Pennant
Whirlaw Stones
Wickenbury Clough
Killup Farm
Butts
Greenhurst Hey
East Hey Head Farm
Law Hill
Hollinroyd Farm
Great House
Swallowshaw
Dungeon Wood
West Whirlaw
East Whirlaw
Cally Hall
West Hey Head Farm
Broad Ing Top Farm
Stansfield Villa
Spring Wood
Great House Clough
Higher Ashes Farm
Lydgate
Harley Wood
Ridge Wood
Ratcher Rock
Butt Stones
Hanging Field Farm
Lower Ashes Farm
Rodwell Head
Scaitcliffe Bridge
Hole Bottom
Hole Bottom Delph
TODMORDEN GOLF COURSE
Scaitcliffe Hall
Oak Hill
Royd
Cross Gap
Scaitcliffe Wood
Ferney Lee Prim. Sch.
Durn Cottage
Hollin Hall
Todmorden High Sch.
Wks.
Cross Stone
Grave Yard
Rive Rocks (Club Ho.)
Sorrel Croft
Bean Hole Farm
Hill House
Lad Stones
Flail Croft
Wood Cottage
Swim. Pool
The Mount
Castle Street
Cinder Hill
Ewood Hall
Bandstand
River Calder
Stansfield Hall
Priestwell
War Memorial
A646
Todmorden Edge
Ewood Park
Golf Course
CENTRE VALE PARK
Cricket Grd.
Hall Royd Junction
Rochdale Canal
Todmorden Edge South Farm
School
Todmorden Junction
Buckley Wood
LOVERS WALK
Coll.
Hosp.
Millwood
Brookfield Farm
DOGHOUSE LANE
High Barn
The Ridge
Mkt.
Hlth. Cen.
Old Royd Lock
Hall Wood
Todmorden
Oldroyd
Oldroyd Farm
Mankinholes Tops
Edge End Farm
Pavilion
Liby.
Playing Fields
TODMORDEN
Grange Farm
Salford
Dobroyd Clough
Longfield Wood
Kilnhurst
Kilnhurst Wood
Castle Cotts.
Hall Wood
Bird Bank Wood
Lumbutts Clough
Doroad Scout
Ping Hold
Higher Longfield Farm
A6033
Reservoir (Cov.)
Ingham Wood
Model Farm
Playing Fields
Shoebroad Farm
Middle Longfield Farm
Top of Brink Farm
Centre Hill
Causeway Wood
Lumbutts
Stones Farm
Pex House
Lower Longfield Farm
Shoebroad Dam
Friends' Burial Ground
Longfield Stables
Shade
Croft Farm
Causeway Farm
Watty Farm
Swineshead Clough
Croft Gate
Mill Dam
Friths Farm
Croft Carr
A681 ROAD
Gauxholme
Lower Swineshead
Swineshead
Heyhead Farm
Gauxholme Bri.
LUMBUTTS
Hill Stones
Higher Lee
No Man's Wood
Knowl Wood
Top o' th' Rough
Rough
Hey Head Green
Jail Springs
Middle Horse Wood Farm
Shurcrack
Lower Knowl
Hollow Farm
Higher Knowl
Lower Horse Wood Farm
Law Hey Farm
Jail Hole
Higher Horse Wood Farm
ROCHDALE ROAD
HALIFAX ROAD
BURNLEY ROAD
69
88
107
93
94
395
1
2
3
4
5
6
7
8
9
27
26
25
24
23
G
H
J
K
L
M
N

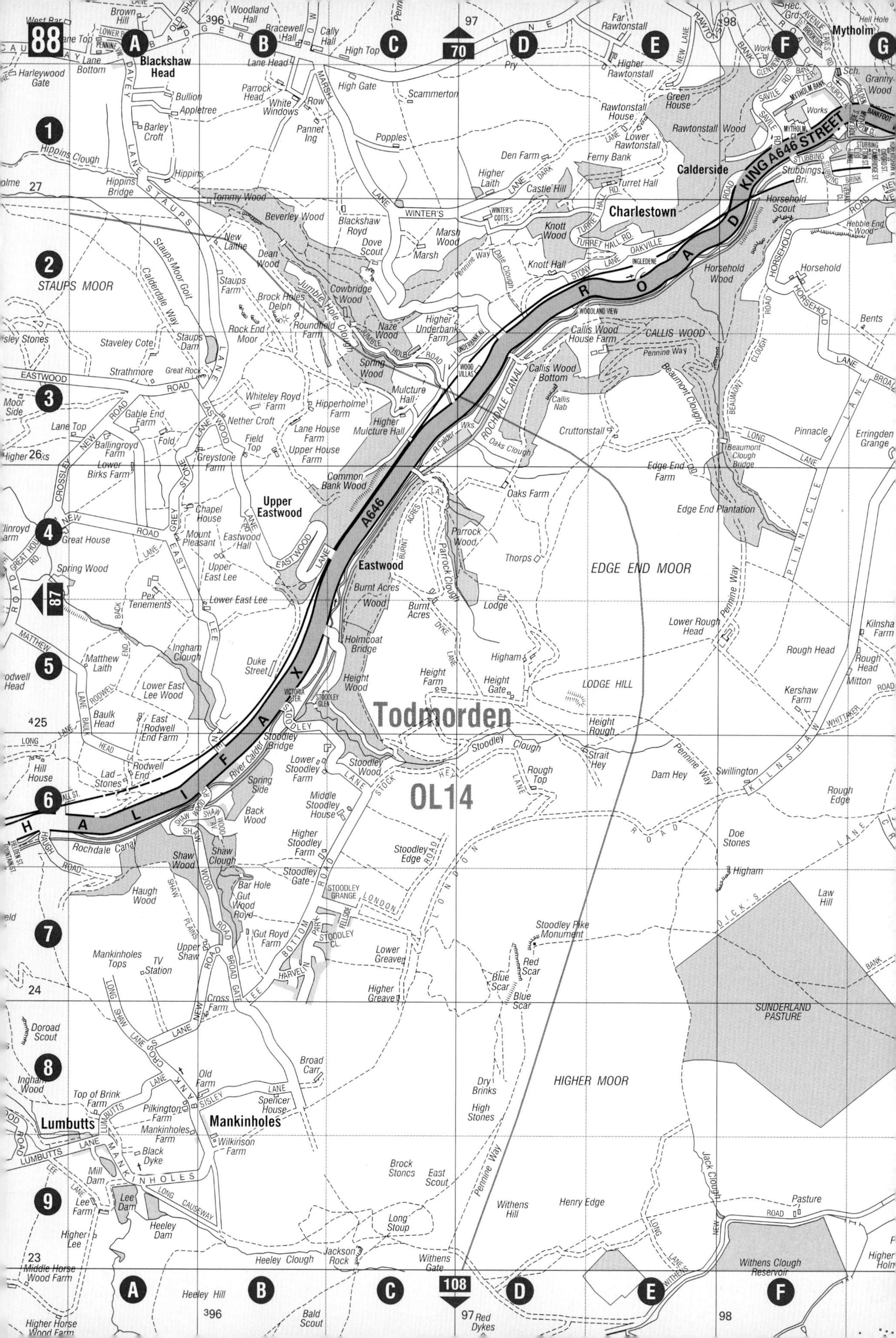
Blackshaw Head
Charlestown
Calderside
Mytholm
Todmorden
OL14
Upper Eastwood
Eastwood
Lumbutts
Mankinholes
STAUPS MOOR
EDGE END MOOR
LODGE HILL
HIGHER MOOR
SUNDERLAND PASTURE
HALIFAX ROAD
KING A646 STREET
A646
Rochdale Canal
River Calder
Pennine Way
Calderdale Way
Stoodley Pike Monument
Withens Clough Reservoir
Callis Wood
Edge End Plantation
Heeley Clough
Jack Clough
Hippins Clough
Jumble Hole Clough
Beverley Wood
Dean Wood
Cowbridge Wood
Spring Wood
Stoodley Wood
Shaw Wood
Haugh Wood
Lee Dam
Heeley Dam
70
87
108
396
97
98
27
26
25
24
23

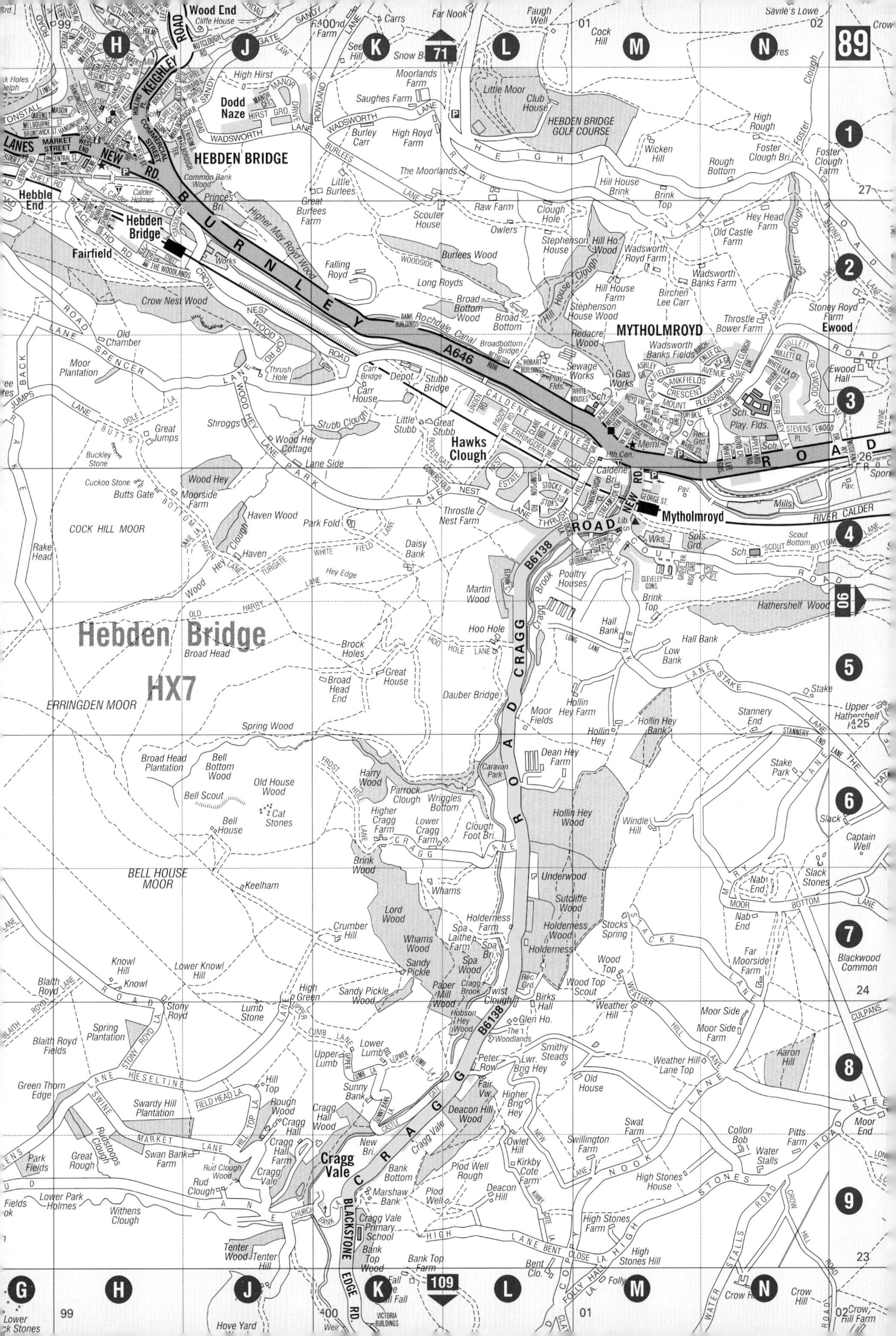
H
J
K
L
M
N
71
Wood End
Cliffe House
Far Nook
Faugh Well
Cock Hill
Savile's Lowe
Carrs
Seeh Hill
Snow B
KEIGHLEY ROAD
High Hirst
Moorlands Farm
Little Moor
Club House
HEBDEN BRIDGE GOLF COURSE
Dodd Naze
Saughes Farm
Burley Carr
High Royd Farm
High Rough
Foster Clough Bri.
Foster Clough Farm
HEBDEN BRIDGE
Wicken Hill
Rough Bottom
The Moorlands
Hebble End
Common Bank Wood
Calder Holmes
Princes Bri.
Little Burlees
Hill House Brink
Brink Top
Great Burlees Farm
Scouter House
Raw Farm
Clough Hole
Hey Head Farm
Owlers
Old Castle Farm
Hebden Bridge
Fairfield
Higher May Royd Wood
BURNLEY
Burlees Wood
Stephenson House
Hill Ho. Wood
Wadsworth Royd Farm
Falling Royd
Long Royds
Hill House Farm
Wadsworth Banks Farm
Birchen Lee Carr
Crow Nest Wood
Broad Bottom Wood
Broad Bottom
Stephenson House Wood
Throstle Bower Farm
Stoney Royd Farm
Ewood
Rochdale Canal
A646
MYTHOLMROYD
Redacre Wood
Wadsworth Banks Fields
Old Chamber
Moor Plantation
Thrush Hole
Carr Bridge
Depot.
Stubb Bridge
Carr House
Sewage Works
Gas Works
Ewood Hall
Play Flds.
Shroggs
Great Jumps
Stubb Clough
Little Stubb
Great Stubb
Hawks Clough
Play. Flds.
Buckley Stone
Wood Hey Cottage
Lane Side
Cuckoo Stone
Butts Gate
Wood Hey
Moorside Farm
Caldene Bri.
Throstle Nest Farm
Mythomroyd
RIVER CALDER
Mills
COCK HILL MOOR
Haven Wood
Park Fold
Haven
Rake Head
Daisy Bank
Hey Edge
Scout Bottom
B6138
Poultry Houses
Martin Wood
90
Hathershelf Wood
Hebden Bridge
Broad Head
Hoo Hole
Brink Top
Hall Bank
Brock Holes
Low Bank
HX7
Broad Head End
Great House
ERRINGDEN MOOR
Dauber Bridge
Stake
Moor Fields
Hollin Hey Farm
Upper Hathershelf
Stannery End
Spring Wood
Hollin Hey
Hollin Hey Bank
Broad Head Plantation
Bell Bottom Wood
Old House Wood
Harry Wood
Dean Hey Farm
Caravan Park
Stake Park
CRAGG ROAD
Bell Scout
Cat Stones
Parrock Clough
Wriggles Bottom
Higher Cragg Farm
Lower Cragg Farm
Bell House
Clough Foot Bri.
Hollin Hey Wood
Windle Hill
Slack
Captain Well
BELL HOUSE MOOR
Brink Wood
Underwood
Keelham
Whams
Sutcliffe Wood
Nab End
Slack Stones
Lord Wood
Holderness Farm
Holderness Wood
Holderness
Stocks Spring
Nab End
Crumber Hill
Spa Laithe Farm
Whams Wood
Spa Bri.
Far Moorside Farm
Blackwood Common
Knowl Hill
Lower Knowl Hill
Sandy Pickle
Spa Wood
Wood Top
Blaith Royd
Knowl
High Green
Sandy Pickle Wood
Paper Mill Wood
Cragg Brook
Twist Clough
Wood Top Scout
Stony Royd
Lumb Stone
Birks Hall
Weather Hill
Moor Side
Hobson Hey Wood
Glen Ho.
Moor Side Farm
Spring Plantation
Blaith Royd Fields
The Woodlands
Upper Lumb
Lower Lumb
Smithy Steads
Peter Row
Lwr. Brig Hey
Aaron Hill
Weather Hill Lane Top
Green Thorn Edge
Hill Top
Old House
Sunny Bank
Fair Vw.
Higher Brig Hey
Swardy Hill Plantation
Rough Wood
Cragg Hall
Cragg Hall Wood
Deacon Hill Wood
Moor End
Swat Farm
Collon Bob
Pitts Farm
Cragg Vale
Owlet Hill
Swillington Farm
Water Stalls
Park Fields
Rudstoops Clough
Great Rough
Swan Bank Farm
Rud Clough Wood
Cragg Hall Farm
Cragg Vale
New Bri.
Kirkby Cote Farm
High Stones House
Plod Well Rough
Bank Bottom
Rud Clough
Marshaw Bank
Plod Well
Deacon Hill
Fields
Lower Park Holmes
Withens Clough
Cragg Vale Primary School
High Stones Farm
Tenter Wood
Tenter Hill
Bank Top Wood
Bank Top Farm
Bent Clo.
High Stones Hill
109
Fall
Folly
Crow Hill
Crow Hill
Crow Hill Farm
Lower Stones
Hove Yard
Weir
VICTORIA BUILDINGS
BLACKSTONE EDGE RD.
G
99
400
01
02
27
26
425
24
23
1
2
3
4
5
6
7
8
9

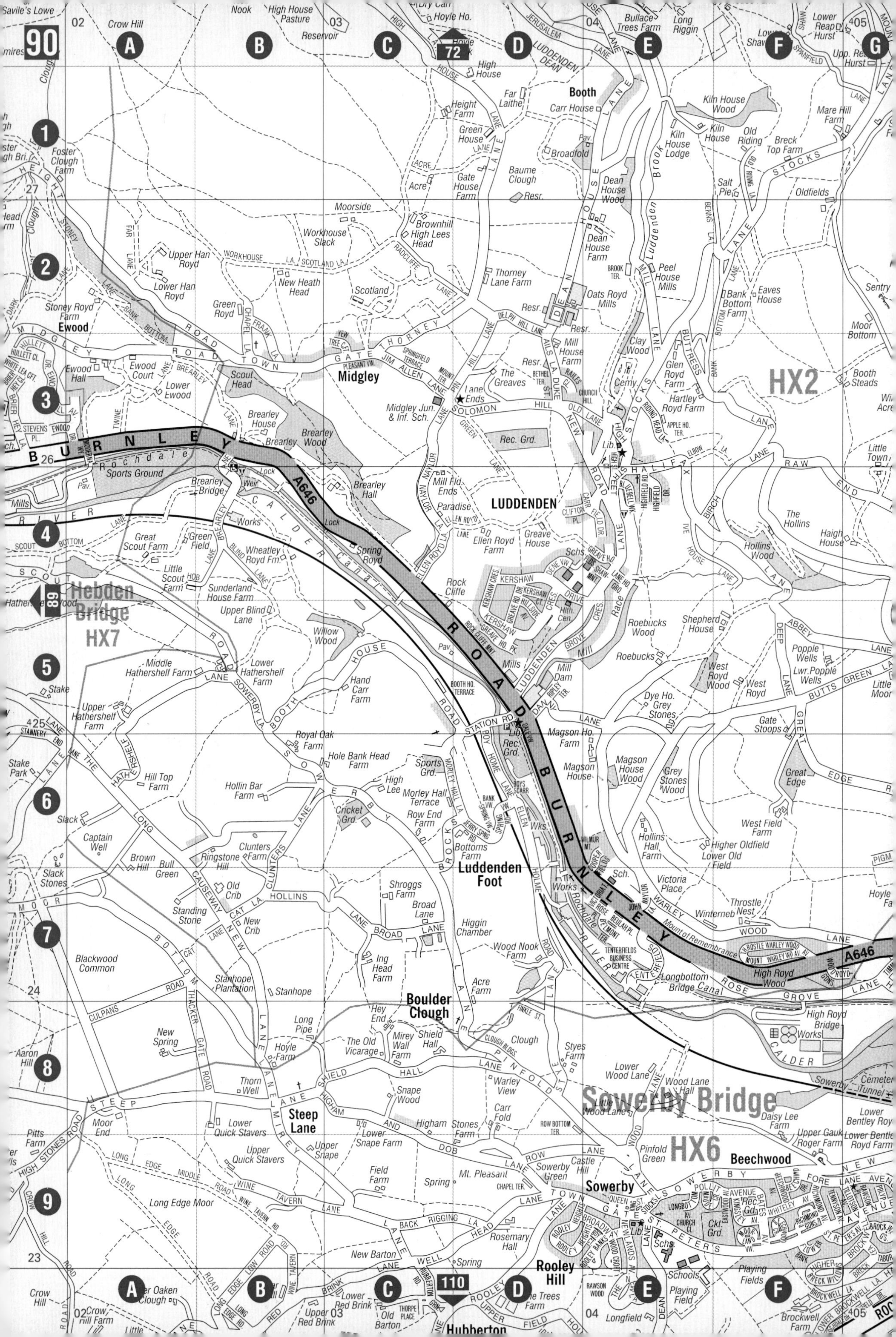

72
Midgley
Luddenden
Booth
Ewood
Luddenden Foot
Boulder Clough
Steep Lane
Sowerby
Sowerby Bridge
HX6
HX2
Hebden Bridge
HX7
89
Beechwood
Rooley Hill
110
Hubberton
BURNLEY ROAD
A646
Rochdale Canal
Calder
Crow Hill

91
H
J
K
L
M
N
G
73
111
1
2
3
4
5
6
7
8
9
92
06
07
08
Halifax
OVENDEN
Ovenden Wood
Wheatley
Boothtown
Lee Mount
Pellon
Highroad Well
Mount Tabor
Norton Tower
Warley Town
Willow Field
King Cross
Pye Nest
Scar Bottom
Delph Hill
SOWERBY BRIDGE
Sowerby Bridge
HX1
HX3
Upper Green Royd
Delf Hill
Mount Tabor Quarry
Leighton Farm
Sunny Bank Quarries
Lower Brown Hirst
Lower Highfield
Gibb Hill
Riding
Ramsden Wood
Resr.
Grove Row
Brown Houses
Park Farm
Ramsden Wood Farm
Spring Lee
Buckley Farm
Brewery
Dodgson Clough
Dodgson Wood
Broadley Hall
Highroad Well Moor
Warley Common
Rushton Hill
Shacks House
Roils Head Playing Fields
Tower Hill
Hatchet Hall
Yew Tree
Grange Farm
Walt Royd Farm
Webster's Maltings
Lane Ends Farm
Riding Bri.
Playing Field
Depot
Works
Playground
St. Malachys Jun.& Inf. Sch.
Deanfield Primary Schools
Playing Fields
Comm. Cen.
Rake Bank
Green Hall
Play. Fld.
The Ridings Sch.
Halifax R.U.F.C.
Hollin Hall
Far Royd
Ringby Farm
Collier Toppin
New Light Buildings
Brackenbed Sports Park
Lee Mount Jun. & Inf. Sch.
Tennis Cts.
SHROGGS PARK
Snake Hill Wood
Works
HALIFAX WEST END GOLF COURSE
North Clough Head
Cricket Grd.
Lane Head
Roils Head Reservoir
Club House
Day Nursery
Ling Bob Junior Infant & Nursery School
Albert Reservoir
Prim. Sch.
Miniature Rifle Range
Football Grd.
Wellesley Park Ten. Cts.
Cricket Ground
Football Grd.
Mkt.
Health Cen.
Prim. Sch.
Camp End
Newlands Farm
Broom Bank
Stock Lane Fm.
Spring Farm
Edge Holme Lodge
Warley House
Warley House Farm
The Hill
Lodge
Warehouse
Football Ground
Cemy.
Hoyle Green
Binns Hill
White Cottage
Ainsworth House
West View Park
Prob. Cen.
Cricket Grnd.
Ten. Cts.
Calderdale College
People's Park
Halifax New College
Play. Fld.
Fieldhouse Farm
Cricket Ground
Playing Field
High Sch.
Jun. Sch.
Rec. Grd.
Crow Wood Park
Fish Pond
Washer Lane Ind. Est.
The Crossley Heath Sch.
SAVILLE PARK
Cricket Grd.
Clinic
Allen Park
Hawks Cliff
Watson Bridge
Weir
Warehouses
Norland Hall
Milner Royd
Lower Wat Ing
Upper Wat Ing
Ashgrove Farm
Upper Old Hall Farm
Sowerby Croft
Green Head
Sewage Works
Sterne Bri.
Hollas Bri.
Calder Dale
Playing Field
The Gleddings Sch.
Long Wood
Spring Wood
RIVER CALDER
Calder & Hebble Navigation
A629
A646
A58
A6139
A6026
KEIGHLEY RD.
OVENDEN RD.
BURNLEY ROAD
ROCHDALE ROAD
KING CROSS ST.
AACHEN WAY
SKIRCOAT MOOR ROAD
WAKEFIELD RD.
PYE NEST ROAD
ST. BOLTON BROW
WHARF ST.
TOWN HALL ST.
TUEL LANE
WEST ST.
HIGHROAD WELL LANE
WARLEY ROAD
NEWLANDS
HOLMES ROAD
HOUSE LANE
MOOR END ROAD
SHROGGS ROAD
HEBBLE LANE
PELLON LANE
SPRING HALL LANE
QUEEN'S ROAD
SCAR BOTTOM

74
112
91
HALIFAX
Halifax
HX1
HX3
Boothtown
Akroydon
Woodlands
Pule Hill
Woodside
Claremount
Stump Cross
Southowram
Bank Top
Caddy Field
Stoney Royd
Siddal
Salterhebble
Savile Park
Delph Hill
Shibden Hall
West Riding Folk Mus.
Shibden Industrial School
Royal Halifax Infirmary
Halifax General Hospital
Halifax Town F.C. & R.L.F.C. (The Shay)
Calderdale College
People's Park
North Bridge Leisure Cen.
Northowram Hospital
Dam Head
Lower Whiskers
Ski Centre
BOOTHTOWN ROAD
HALEY HILL
NEW BANK
GODLEY ROAD
GODLEY LANE
LEEDS BRADFORD ROAD
BACK CLOUGH
BURDOCK WAY
SKIRCOAT ROAD
HUDDERSFIELD ROAD
SKIRCOAT MOOR ROAD
DRYCLOUGH LA.
KING CROSS STREET
OVENDEN
A647
A629
A58
A6036
A646
342232
Peter Colgan

93
415
12
13
14
75
94
113
H
J
K
L
M
N
G
1
2
3
4
5
6
7
8
9
27
26
25
24
23
Bradford
BD12
BRADFORD
CALDERDALE
Windmill Hill
Water House
Stone Leigh Farm
Plane Trees
Stocks
Field Bottom Farm
North Wood
Middle Ox Heys Wood
Madam Wood
Field Head
Birks Close
Old Hanna Wood
High Fernley Farm
High Fernley First School
Woodside Farm
Croft Farm
Lower Ox Heys
Lower Ox Heys Wood
Low Wood
Doctor Wood
Lower Shelf
Coley
Coley Walks
Coley Hall
Cinder Hill
Coley Croft
Coley Chase
Mill Pond
Stockhill Bri.
Treetops
Norwood Green
Green Royd House
Highfield
Coley House
Coley Brow
Wynteredge Hall
Rookes Wood
Upper Rookes
Priestley Green
Holroyd House
Rookes Hall
Holmes Bridge
Wyke Banks
Weir
Shirley Manor
Ingleroyd
Common Wood Head
Throstle Nest
Hole
Lower Winter Edge
Ashfield House Farm
Sewage Works
Lower Rookes
Rookes Bridge
Syke Wells
Rooks Mount
Viaduct
HIPPERHOLME
Helliwell Syke
Bottom Viaduct
LIGHTCLIFFE GOLF COURSE
Playing Fields
Works
Club Ho.
Bottom Hall Farm
Blankney Grange
Lower Wyke
Cockcroft Farm
Fernside
The Stray
The Grange
Cricket Grd.
Till Carr Farm
Light Cliffe
Lightcliffe Prep. Sch.
Lightcliffe
Peartree Farm
Holme Ho.
Bailiff Bri. Prim. Sch.
Bailiff Bridge
Crow Nest Cottages
Upper Park
Hipperholme & Lightcliffe High Sch.
Lydgate
Hill Top
Crow Nest Park
Cliffe Hill
Bowling Grn.
Birkby Hall
Upper Birkby
Birkhouse Farm
Sutcliffe Wood
Upper Lake
CROW NEST PARK GOLF CLUB
Cliffe Hill Prim. Sch.
Playing Field
Harley Head Farm
Lower Park
Hoyle Ho. Fm.
Blakeboroughs Athletic F.C.
Club House
Crowhurst
Oak Gates
Sunny Bank Farm
Pearson Brow
Pinnell Bridge
Giles House
CALDER TRADING ESTATE
Woolrow
Livingstone Works
Comm. Cen.
Cemetery
Hove Edge
St.Joseph's R.C. Primary School
Brighouse High School
Playing Fields
Lower Clay Royd Farm
Sutcliffe Wood Farm
Sutcliffe Wood
Hole Bottom
Upper Clay Royd Farm
Barker Royd
Holly Royd
The Nurseries
Sled Syke Wood
Near Wood Bottom Farm
Brighouse
Thornhills
Cross Platts Farm
Cross Platts
Slead Syke
HD6
Oak Hill Bank
Lodge
Birks Royd
Watson Quarries
Brighouse Wood
Recreation Ground
Lane Head
Cromwell Quarries (Sandstone)
Royd Quarry (Sandstone)
Brookfoot
Squire Hill Quarries (Sandstone)
Waring Green
Art Gallery & Library
BRIGHOUSE
Wellholme Park
Cock Wood Farm
Ashday
Ashday Hall
Cromwell Wood
Brookfoot Works
Cricket Grnd.
Boggart House
Freeman's Wood
Brookfoot Lock
Ganny Lock
The Lillands
DENHOLME GATE ROAD
A644
HALIFAX ROAD
BRIGHOUSE ROAD
WHITEHALL ROAD
A58
LEEDS ROAD
WAKEFIELD ROAD
A649
HUDDERSFIELD ROAD
A641
BRADFORD ROAD
ELLAND ROAD
A6025
ELLAND RIORDAN ROAD
BIRKBY LA.

94
A
B
C
D
E
F
G
1
2
3
4
5
6
7
8
9
76
93
114
Upper Common
Wyke Manor School
Playing Field
High Fernley First School
Worthinghead First School
Chemical Works
Croft House
Fearnley Farm
Mt. of Olives Fm.
Theaklands Farm
Threappleton Farm
Water Pollution Control Works
M606
M606 MOTORWAY
A638
BRADFORD ROAD
Upper Wyke
WYKE
Wyke Common
Bradford
BD12
Elm Cottage
Junction 26
Sugden Beck
CLECKHEATON & DISTRICT GOLF COURSE
Club Ho.
Knowle Farm
Upper Cow Close
Cow Close Farm
The Nurseries
Cricket Ground
Stubs Beck
WESTFIELD
WHITEHALL ROAD
A58
B6379
Fieldhead
Lower Green
Brookfield Farm
Scholes First & Nursery School
Play Fld.
Recn. Grd.
Branch Farm
Cemetery
Chairbarrows Farm
The Royds
WHITECHAPEL ROAD
B6120
Snelsins Bridge
Playing Fields
Whitechapel Middle Sch.
Manor House
Lower Fold Farm
Stancey's Garth Farm
Lower Wyke
Blankney Grange
Ingleroyd
HUDDERSFIELD ROAD
BRADFORD ROAD
BRADFORD
KIRKLEES
Works
Cricket & Athletic Ground
Albert Mills
SCHOLES
Longlands
New Popplewell
Brick Hill Farm
Sports Cen.
Whitcliffe Mount School & Adult Education Centre
West End
TURNSTEADS AV.
Whitwood
Cherry Hall
Birkby Hall
Birkby Lane Top
Birkby La. Head Fm.
Hartshead Moor Top
Oldfieldnook
Moorbottom
BIRKBY LANE
A649
Upper Birk Hey Wood
Birkhouse Farm
Birkhouse
Pond Farm
Whiteacre
Manor Cottage Farm
Manor House
M62 MOTORWAY
MOORSIDE
A643
Broomfield Farm
Works
Whitaker Pits Farm
Whitaker Pits Wood
Whiteacre Farm
WALTON LANE
HALIFAX ROAD
Hartshead Moor Side
Upper Blacup Farm
Woolrow
Livingstone Works
Clough
WILLOW VALLEY GOLF & COUNTRY CLUB
Ckt. Grd.
KIRKLEES
CALDERDALE
Warehouse
Hartsoil
Hightown Heights
Rock Hole
Jay House Farm
JAY HOUSE LANE
Club House
Oakridge Farm
Hartshead Moor Service Area
WINDY BANK
Windy Bank Farm
Hole Bottom
Thorncliffe
Gospel Hall Farm
Brighouse
Thornhills
Oak Hill Bank
HD6
R.M.Grylls Mid. Sch.
Hawthorne Lodge
Thorn Bush Farm
Hare Park Ho.
Triton House
Walton Cross Farm
Walton Cross Cottage
Lodge
Green Farm
Break Head Cottage
Cock Walk Farm
HIGHMOOR LANE
COMMON
Soap House
Nun Brook
M62
Church Farm
B6114
Wellholme
Pav. Cricket Grd.
CLIFTON
Football Grd.
Church Farm
FREAKFIELD LANE
Clifton
Alegar Bank

M62
M62 MOTORWAY
77
115
96
Cleckheaton
CLECKHEATON
BD19
BD11
WF17
WF16
Liversedge
WF15
LIVERSEDGE
HUNSWORTH
Hunsworth Great Wood
Hunsworth Little Wood
Hunsworth Mills Bri.
Savile Arms Farm
Lodge Farm
Lodge Garage
Hunsworth Lodge Farm
Heathfield Farm
Swincliffe
Birkenshaw Middle Sch.
Rifle and Pistol Club
Birksland Moor
Field Head Farm
Canary Hall
Lower Lodge Range
Thorn Hill Knowls
Holme House
West House
Wheatleys Farm
The Wheatleys
Brecks Farm
Oakwell Hall
Oakwell Hall Country Park
Sewage Works
Oakwell House
Drub
Primrose Hill
Owlett Hall Farm
Mazebrook
Merchant Fields
Merchant Fields Farm
Lanes Wood
Latham Farm
Gomersal Hall
Depot
Manor Ho.
Hunsworth Bri.
Upper Brook House
Lands Farm
Round Hill
Nursery
Bawson Cliffe
Gomersal First School
Birdacre
Pollard Hall
Gomersal C. of E. Middle School
Church Wood
Church Farm
MONK INGS
Egypt
Roundhill Mills
Firdene
Moorend
Fusden Wood
Tannery
Gomersal Hill Top
Caledonia Works
Popeley Farm
GOMERSAL
POPELEY FIELDS
Spen Hall
Spen Lower
Football Ground
Rec. Grd.
Royds Hill
Royds Farm
Rec. Ground
Moorgate
Moorfields
St. Peg Bridge
Howard Park
Mount Pleasant Farm
Gomersal House
Walsh Houses
Listing Mill Cottages
Stubley Farm
Marsh
Pyenot Hall
SPEN VALLEY INDUSTRIAL PARK
Royds Park
The Grove
Castle House
Castle Hill
Lower Blacup
Pyenot Hall Bridge
Rawfolds
Primrose Hill Farm
Littletown
Westfield
Primrose Lane Bridge
Rugby Football Grd.
Miniature Golf Course
Swim. Pool
Lawnbank
Hightown
Springfield Farm
Knowler Hill
King George V Play. Fld.
Mill Bridge
Lower Popeley
Millbridge Jun.& Inf. Sch.
Croft Farm
Clough Beck
Upper House Farm
Headlands C.of E. Jun. & Inf. Sch.
Algernon Firth Park
Flush
Triangle Farm
Bullace Trees Farm
Playing Fields
Spen Valley High Sch.
Cemetery
Moorside
Old Hall Farm
Pogg Myres
Smithy Hill
Church Farm
Hartshead Jun.& Inf.
A58 WHITEHALL ROAD
WHITEHALL RD.
A651 BRADFORD RD.
OXFORD ROAD
DEWSBURY ROAD
A652 BRADFORD ROAD
A643 CHURCH LANE
A643 SPEN LANE
MUFFIT LA.
B6121 HUNSWORTH LANE
A638 BRADFORD ROAD
B6120 RD.
WESTGATE
A638 BRADFORD ROAD
A651 GOMERSAL RD.
A62 LEEDS ROAD
B6117 NEW NORTH RD.
A649 HALIFAX ROAD
A638 FLUSH
A62 HUDDERSFIELD ROAD
H J K L M N
G H J K L M N
1 2 3 4 5 6 7 8 9
19 420 21 425 23 24 26 27

97
H
J
K
L
M
N
Bruntcliffe
Playing Fields
Rugby Football Grd.
Dartmouth Park
Playing Field
Morley High Sch.
79
MIDDLETON
STREET
CORPORATION ST.
Lewisham Park
CHARTISTS WAY
Low Town End
MORLEY
Burn Knolls App.
Topcliffe Farm
Depot
Reservoir (Covered)
Street Farm
FOUNTAIN
BRIDGE
Morley Cross Hall Jun. Sch.
A650
B6123
B6127
ROAD
BRITANNIA
ROAD
Birks
Elmfield Inf. Sch.
Tingley Gas Works
Works
Factory
Depot
Topcliffe
TINGLEY
Tingley House Farm
Tingley Common
Junction 28
HOWLEY PARK TRADING ESTATE
America Moor
HOWLEY PARK ROAD EAST
Britannia Quarry
Raynham Ho.
Pewit Nook
COMMON
REIN
A650
M62 MOTORWAY
M62
A6029
Tingley
Woodkirk High School
Morley Spring Wood
Morley Tunnel
Leeds
LS27
WEST ARDSLEY
Briar Knoll Ho.
Rookwood
B6123
HOWLEY HALL GOLF COURSE
Howley Park Quarry
Howley Park Brick Works
Tank
Wakefield
WF3
A653
Howley Hall Farm
Howley Hall (Club House)
Howley Park Quarry Farm
Woodkirk Beck
Westerton Prim. Sch.
Sports Grd.
Woodkirk
Upper Green
Cardigan Farm
Howley Park Farm
LEEDS
KIRKLEES
QUARRY LANE
Depot
Cemetery
Manor House
Dike
Lady Ann
Soothill Wood
DEWSBURY
Baghill
Beggarington Hill
Soothill Wood
Scargill Wood
Woodkirk Mill
Works
Manor Farm
HEY BECK LANE
The Farm
Hill Top Inf. Sch.
Lower Soothill
B6124
Soothill Manor
Lydgate House
Croft House Farm
Hey Beck
Dum Wood
Hey Beck Farm
Hill Top Farm
Highfield House
Lydgate Junior & Infant School
Upper Hey Beck Farm
ROAD
Batley
Warehouses
Lees House Farm
Dewsbury
WF5
GRANGE
B6128
ROAD
CHALLENGE
Grange Farm
Sports Field
Works
Dogloitch Wood
Works
Playing Field
Hanging Heaton
Shaw Cross Infants Sch.
Chidswell
Chidswell House
Windsor Farm
LEEDS
117
Chidswell Farm
Shaw
G
H
J
K
L
M
N
1
2
3
4
5
6
7
8
9
98
24
23
425
26
27
28

MIDDLETON
WEST ARDSLEY
EAST ARDSLEY
Westerton
Tingley
Upper Green
Beggarington Hill
Haigh Moor
Kirkhamgate
Beck Bottom
Brandy Carr
Leeds LS10
WF3
WF2
M62 MOTORWAY
M1 MOTORWAY
ARDSLEY RESERVOIR
Junction 28
Junction 41
DEWSBURY ROAD
BRADFORD ROAD
ROYSTON HILL
LANE MIDDLETON
Thorpe Wood
Jaw Hill
Haigh Hall Spring Wood
Woodhouse Lane Farm
Coglands
Stoney La. Plantation
Police Operations Centre

80
97
118

Robin Hood
Carlton
Ouzlewell Green
Lofthouse
Westgate
Langley
Lingwell Gate
Wakefield
LOFTHOUSE HILL GOLF CLUB
Lofthouse Gate
Lee Moor
Outwood
OUTWOOD
STANLEY
WF1
Lawns
WRENTHORPE
Newton Hill
Snow Hill
Robin Hood Hill
Town End
Thorpe Hall
Thorpe House
Foundry
Robin Hood Quarries
Kiddow Spring
Sports Ground
Warehouse
Carlton Hall
Carlton Carr
Bridge End Farm
Green End Farm
Pymont Farm
Bushey Cliffe Wood
Dungeon Farm
The Grange
Rodillian School
Lofthouse Hall
Church Farm
Castle Head Farm
Langley Farm
Lofthouse Hill
Club House
Depot
Coney Warren
Lee Moor Gate
Springfield Farm
Thorpe Lane Farm
Lingwell Nook
Spring Wood
Sewage Works
WAKEFIELD 41 INDUSTRIAL PARK
Lawns House
Providence Mount
Outwood Grange Sch.
Robin Hood Bridge
The Plump
Council Offices
Hadfield Hall Farm
Hatfield Hall
Boarding Kennels
Ouchthorpe Lane Farm
NORMANTON GOLF COURSE
Stanley Marsh Nature Reserve
Rugby Football Grd.
Canal Hill
Lofthouse Gate Prim. Sch.
Wakefield Road Bridge
Robin Hood Bri.
SHERWOOD INDUSTRIAL ESTATE
Coke Depot
Thorpe La. Bri.
Junc. 29 (M62)
Junction 42 (M1)
M1 MOTORWAY
M62 MOTORWAY
M1
M62
A61
A650
A654
B6135
LEEDS ROAD
THORPE LANE
LONG THORPE LANE
LOWER THORPE LANE
LINGWELL GATE LANE
LEADWELL LANE
CARLTON LANE
CASTLE GATE
PARK DRIVE
CANAL LANE
ABERFORD RD.
LEEDS
WAKEFIELD
81
100
119
H J K L M N G
1 2 3 4 5 6 7 8 9
27 26 425 24 23
32 33 34

A
B
C
D
E
F
G
1
2
3
4
5
6
7
8
9
82
99
120
Rothwell Sports Centre
METHLEY
Rifle Range
Golf Driving Range
Robinson's Plantation
Waterloo Corner
OULTON PARK GOLF COURSE
Swithen's Plantation
Swithen's Farm
Oulton Farm
Recreation Ground
Clumpcliffe Wood
Autograss Circuit
Winter Wood
Royds School
Royds Green Farm
Royds Green
Sugar Hill Plantation
Clumpcliffe
Clumpcliffe Covert
Cheesecake Farm
PENNINGTON LANE
Iveridge Hall
Moss Carr Wood
Dungeon Lane Farm
DUNGEON LANE
SANDERSON LANE
Walsham Cottage
Pindars Screed
The Rookery
Moss Carr
WAKEFIELD ROAD
A642
Junction 30
M62
M62 MOTORWAY
Elm Farm
Hungate
CASTLE GATE
B6135
Patrick Green
Works
Vehicle Testing Station
Royds Hall Riding Sch.
Springs Wood
NEWMARKET
Nelson House
Savile Farm
Playgrd.
Methley Lanes
Coney Warren
Lee Moor
The Bungalow
Newmarket House
West Hall
BOTTOM BOAT RD.
Foxholes Bight
Wakefield WF3
West Farm
Leeds Country Way
Cringlesworth
Cricket Grd.
West Hall Sch.
Roman Station Farm
Bottom Boat
Altofts Ings
Lee Mount
BOTTOM BOAT ROAD
Bottom Boat Reach
Foxholes Reach
Comm. Cen.
THE CHASE
Beechfield House
The Poplars
Factory
King's Rd. Br.
King's Rd. Lock
LAKE LOCK DR.
RIVER CALDER
Lake Lock
AIRE & CALDER NAVIGATION
CALDER CUT
Birkwood Lock
Birkwood Bridge
Glebe Farm
ALTOFTS
Cemetery
STANLEY
Sewage Works
Birkwood Farm
West Garth
Stanley Marsh Nature Reserve
Stanley Gr. Prim. Sch.
Smalley Bight
Birkwood Hill
Top Farm
Hilltop Farm
Play. Fld.
Smalley Bight Farm
Stanley Ferry
BIRKWOOD ROAD
Weir
Boat Repair Yard
Stanley Ferry Br.
Aqueduct
Playing Fields
Birkwood Plantation
ABERFORD ROAD
Aire & Calder Cottages
Works
Newland Park
435
36
37
27
26
425
24
23

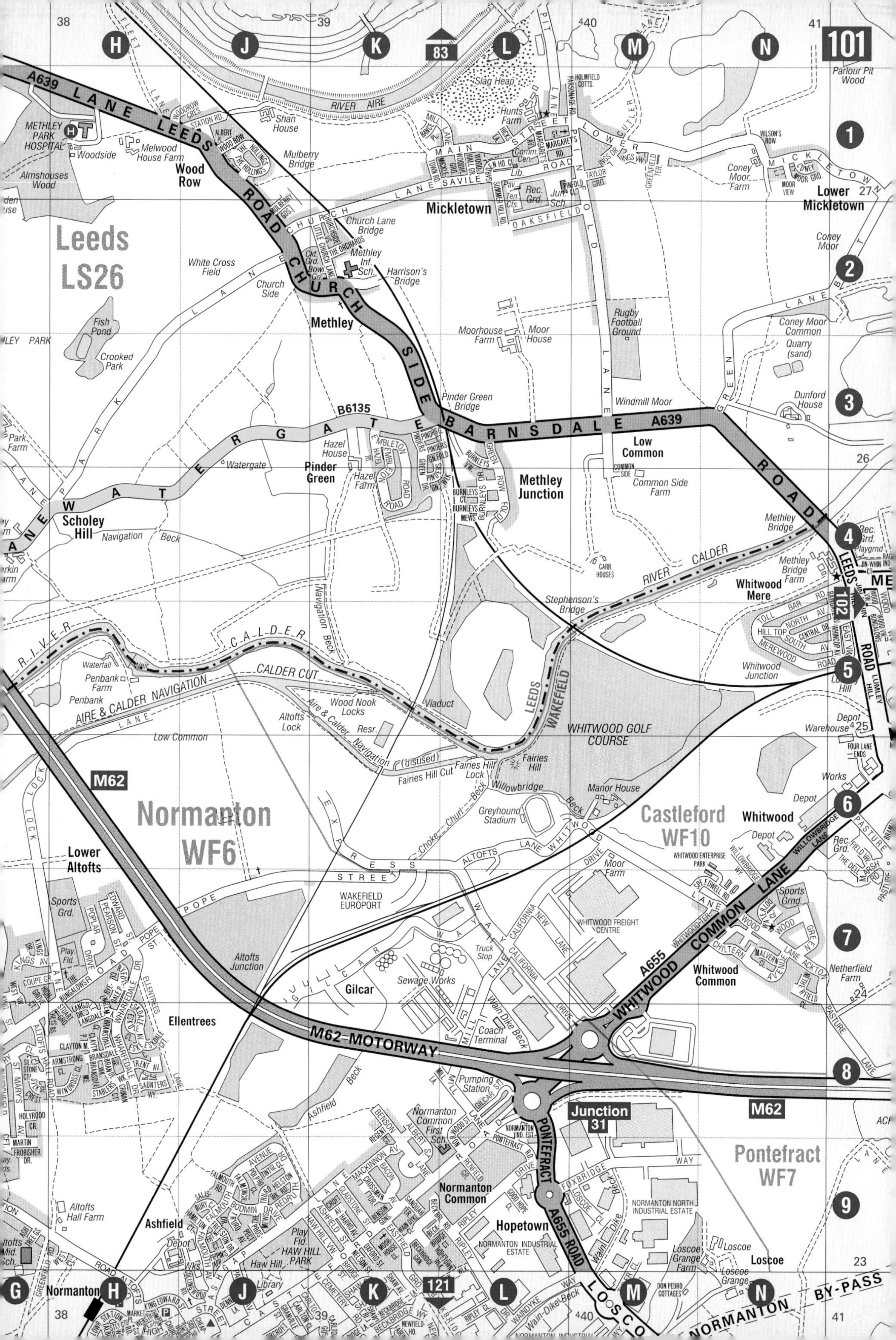
Leeds LS26
Normanton WF6
Castleford WF10
Pontefract WF7
Mickletown
Lower Mickletown
Methley
Methley Junction
Pinder Green
Scholey Hill
Lower Altofts
Ellentrees
Gilcar
Ashfield
Normanton
Normanton Common
Hopetown
Whitwood
Whitwood Common
Whitwood Mere
Loscoe
Wood Row
Low Common
RIVER AIRE
RIVER CALDER
AIRE & CALDER NAVIGATION
CALDER CUT
WHITWOOD GOLF COURSE
M62 MOTORWAY
Junction 31
LEEDS ROAD
CHURCH SIDE
BARNSDALE ROAD
A639
B6135
A655
WHITWOOD COMMON LANE
PONTEFRACT ROAD
WATERGATE
METHLEY PARK HOSPITAL
Wakefield Europort
Whitwood Freight Centre
Normanton Industrial Estate
Normanton North Industrial Estate
Sewage Works
Greyhound Stadium
Rugby Football Ground
Slag Heap
NORMANTON BY-PASS
83
102
121

Leeds
LS26
WF7
CASTLEFORD
Castleford
Castleford Ings
Lower Mickletown
Whitwood Mere
Hightown
Half Acres
Round Hill
Glass Houghton
Cutsyke
Whitwood Common
Methley Bridge
THE OXBOW LAKES
RIVER AIRE
RIVER CALDER
M62 MOTORWAY
NORMANTON BY-PASS
A656
A639
A655
A6032
B6421
FREEPORT CASTLEFORD
PONTEFRACT PARK (RACE COURSE)
84
101
122

Castleford
WF10
Knottingley
WF11
Pontefract
WF8
New Fryston
Wheldale
Water Fryston
Airedale
Red Hill
Townville
Fairy Hill
New Town
Lady Balk
Monkhill
FRYSTON PARK
NEWTON INGS
FAIRBURN INGS NATURE RESERVE
Spoil Heap
WELL WOOD
Whin Covert
Settling Ponds
Brotherton Ings
FERRYBRIDGE POWER STATION
Ferrybridge 'C' Golf Course
HOLYWELL WOOD
Opencast Workings
Slurry Lagoon
RIDGLEY HILL
M62 MOTORWAY
Junction 32
SHEEPWALK LANE
STRANGLANDS LANE
B6136
A639
SELBY
WAKEFIELD
RIVER AIRE
Airedale High School
Redhill Junior Sch.
Oyster Park Jun. Sch.
Townville Infants Sch.
Orchard Head Prim. Sch.
Endless Flat Plantation
Park Plantation
Empire Works
Engineering Works
Prince of Wales Colliery
Park Side Farm
Blind Hardwick Farm
Holmfield House
Holmfields
85
104
123

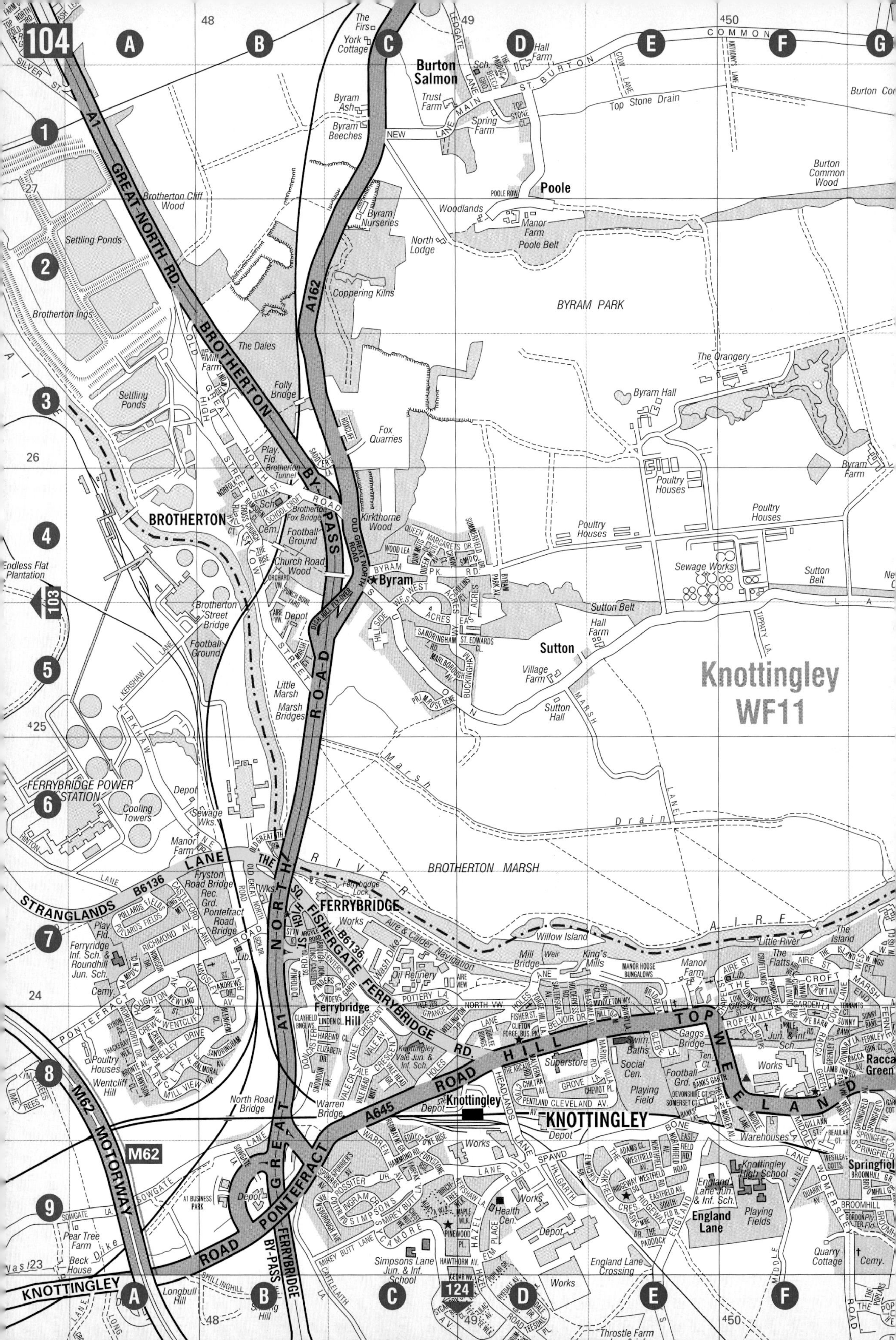

Burton Salmon
Poole
BYRAM PARK
Byram Hall
The Orangery
Burton Common Wood
Byram Farm
Poultry Houses
Sewage Works
Sutton Belt
Sutton
Sutton Hall
Village Farm
Hall Farm
Knottingley WF11
BROTHERTON
Brotherton Ings
Settling Ponds
Brotherton Cliff Wood
The Dales
Mill Farm
Folly Bridge
Fox Quarries
Coppering Kilns
Byram Nurseries
North Lodge
Woodlands
Manor Farm
Poole Belt
Kirkthorne Wood
Byram
Church Road Wood
Football Ground
Brotherton Street Bridge
Little Marsh
Marsh Bridges
Endless Flat Plantation
FERRYBRIDGE POWER STATION
Cooling Towers
Depot
Sewage Wks.
Manor Farm
BROTHERTON MARSH
RIVER AIRE
FERRYBRIDGE
Ferrybridge Lock
Aire & Calder Navigation
Willow Island
Mill Bridge
King's Mills
Oil Refinery
Ferrybridge Hill
Fryston Road Bridge
Pontefract Road Bridge
Ferrybridge Inf. Sch. & Roundhill Jun. Sch.
Poultry Houses
Wentcliff Hill
North Road Bridge
Warren Bridge
Knottingley
KNOTTINGLEY
Superstore
Swim. Baths
Social Cen.
Playing Field
Football Grd.
Gaggs Bridge
Manor Farm
The Island
The Flatts
Little River
Racca Green
Knottingley High School
England Lane Jun. & Inf. Sch.
England Lane
Playing Fields
Springfield
Quarry Cottage
Cemy.
Health Cen.
Pinewood Pl.
Simpsons Lane Jun. & Inf. School
England Lane Crossing
Throstle Farm
Pear Tree Farm
Beck House
Longbull Hill
Stoney Hill
M62 MOTORWAY
A1 GREAT NORTH RD.
BROTHERTON BY-PASS
A162
A645 PONTEFRACT ROAD
FERRYBRIDGE BY-PASS
STRANGLANDS LANE B6136
FISHERGATE FERRYBRIDGE RD. B6136
TOP WEELAND
HILL TOP
KNOTTINGLEY
103
124

Birkin
Beal
Kellingley
Fernley Green
Broomhill
Goole DN14
Burton Common Farm
Barton Common House
Northfield Farm
Burton Common Drain
Swandam Wood
Fleet Drain
Birkin House
Home Farm
Woodhouse Farm
Woodlands
Ashdean
Rose Farm
The Grange
Church Farm
Hall Garth
Park House
Church Hill Houses
Little Ing Clough
Old Eye Bridge
Shillito Old Clough
Old Eye Clough
Shillito Clough
Adam's Nook
Kitson Park
Great Hagg Wood
Old Eye
Beal Short Reach
Ravencroft Belt
Leatherbelly Wood
West Holme
Beal Bridge
Beal Island
Beal Dam
Beal Long Reach
Lock
Wall Close Wood
River Aire
Manor Farm
Wood Holmes
Wood Holmes Clough
Hall Farm
Beal Pig Farm
Smeathalls Wood
Smeathalls Farm
Football Ground
Kellingley Crook
Kellingley Clough
Kellingley Ings
Works
Lunn Hill
Gascoigne Hill Reach
Selby
Wakefield
Maggot Hatchery
Nursery
Sewage Works
Kellingley Farm
Willow Garth
Willow Garths
Brears Farm
Playing Fld.
Trundles Lane Bridge
Bank Dole Cut
Kellingley Colliery
Skew Bridge
Aire & Calder Navigation (Knottingley & Goole Canal)
Calder Grange
Kellingley Bridge
Thornfield House
South Moor
Stubbs Bridge
Slurry Pond
A645 Road
Weeland Road
Haddlesey Road
Main Street
Birkin Lane
Common Lane
Sudforth Lane
Southmoor Lane
Blackburn Lane
Turner's Lane
Lunn Lane
New Lane
Hagg Lane
Barkhouse Wood Lane
Wood Lane
Tinkler's La.
Intake Lane
Green Lane
Marsh La.
Ings Lane
Manor Rd.
Hollygarth Lane
Beal Lane
Gables Cl.
Riverdale
Craven Gth.
Broad La.
Bank Lane
Kemp Lane
Stocking Lane
Glebelands
Turvers La.
The Oval
Trundles La.
Broomhill Avenue
Broomhill Cl.
Broomhill Dr.
Broomhill Av.
125

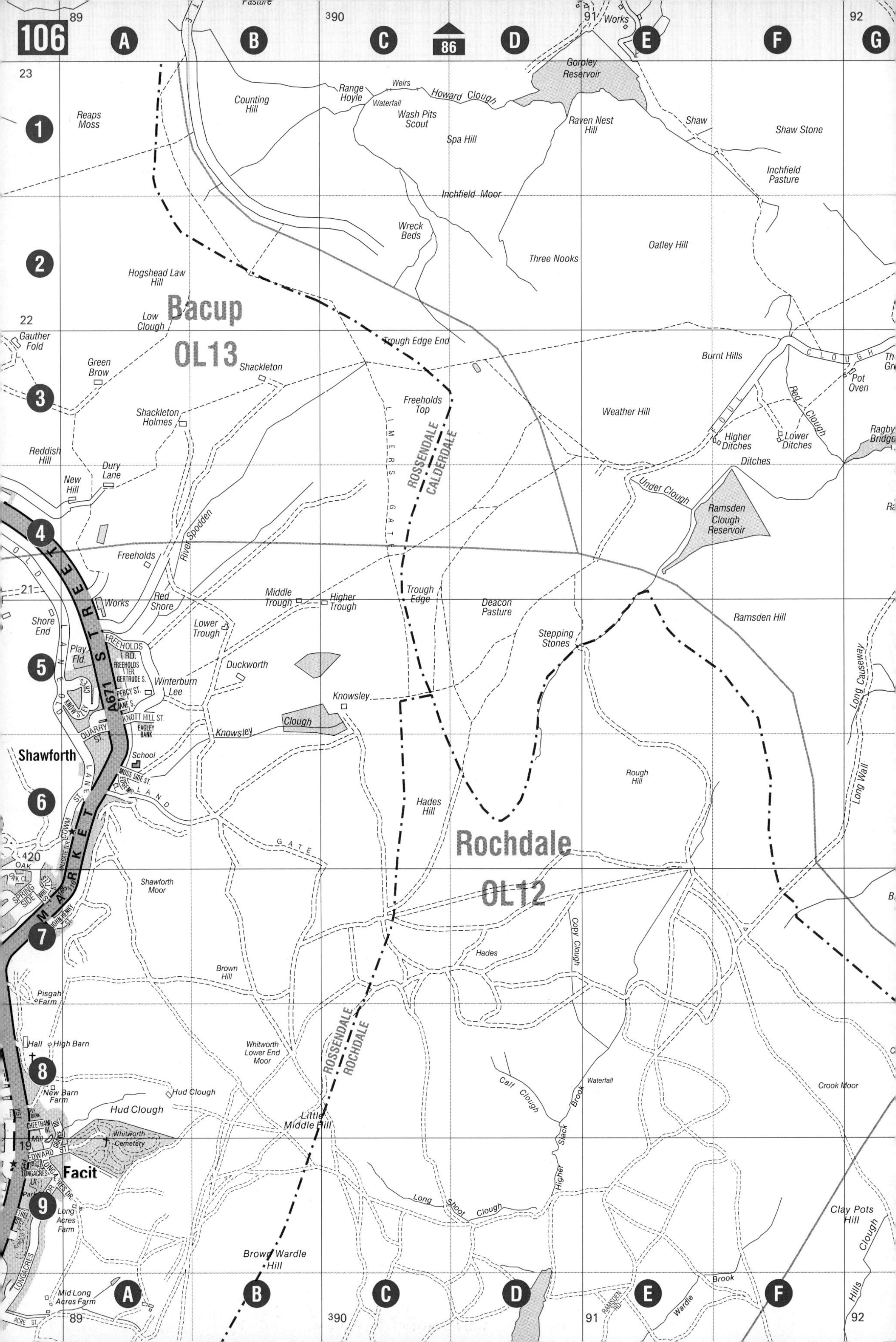
Bacup
OL13
Rochdale
OL12
Shawforth
Facit
Reaps Moss
Counting Hill
Range Hoyle
Weirs
Howard Clough
Waterfall
Wash Pits Scout
Spa Hill
Gorpley Reservoir
Raven Nest Hill
Shaw
Shaw Stone
Inchfield Pasture
Inchfield Moor
Wreck Beds
Three Nooks
Oatley Hill
Hogshead Law Hill
Low Clough
Gauther Fold
Green Brow
Shackleton
Trough Edge End
Burnt Hills
Pot Oven
Freeholds Top
Weather Hill
Shackleton Holmes
ROSSENDALE
CALDERDALE
Higher Ditches
Lower Ditches
Ditches
Ragby Bridge
Reddish Hill
Dury Lane
New Hill
Under Clough
Ramsden Clough Reservoir
River Spodden
Freeholds
Works
Red Shore
Middle Trough
Higher Trough
Trough Edge
Deacon Pasture
Ramsden Hill
Shore End
Lower Trough
Stepping Stones
Play. Fld.
Duckworth
Winterburn Lee
Knowsley
Clough
A671
MARKET STREET
School
Long Causeway
Long Wall
Rough Hill
Hades Hill
Shawforth Moor
Copy Clough
Hades
Brown Hill
Pisgah Farm
Hall
High Barn
Whitworth Lower End Moor
ROSSENDALE
ROCHDALE
Calf Clough
Waterfall
Crook Moor
New Barn Farm
Hud Clough
Little Middle Hill
Whitworth Cemetery
Slack Brook
Higher
Long Shoot Clough
Long Acres Farm
Clay Pots Hill
Brown Wardle Hill
Brook
Wardle
Mid Long Acres Farm
86
89
390
91
92
23
22
21
20
19

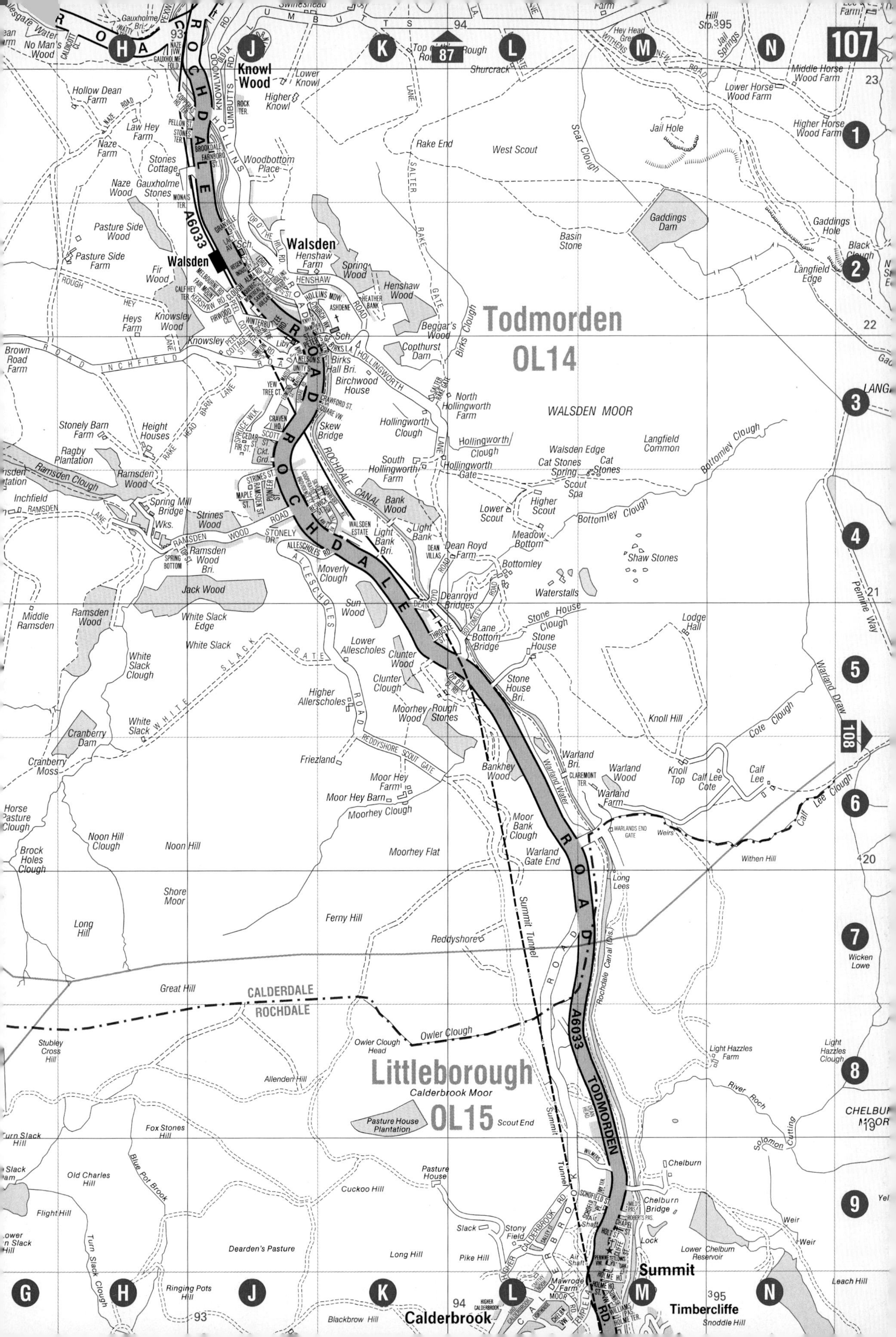

Todmorden
OL14
Walsden
Knowl Wood
WALSDEN MOOR
Littleborough
Calderbrook Moor
OL15
CALDERDALE
ROCHDALE
ROCHDALE ROAD
A6033
TODMORDEN RD.
Rochdale Canal
Summit Tunnel
Summit
Timbercliffe
Calderbrook
Gaddings Dam
Jack Wood
Cranberry Dam
Pasture House Plantation
Hollow Dean Farm
Naze Farm
Law Hey Farm
Stones Cottage
Woodbottom Place
Naze Wood
Gauxholme Stones
Pasture Side Wood
Pasture Side Farm
Fir Wood
Heys Farm
Knowsley Wood
Henshaw Farm
Spring Wood
Henshaw Wood
Beggar's Wood
Copthurst Dam
Birks Hall Bri.
Birchwood House
North Hollingworth Farm
Hollingworth Clough
South Hollingworth Farm
Skew Bridge
Stonely Barn Farm
Height Houses
Ragby Plantation
Ramsden Clough
Ramsden Wood
Inchfield
Spring Mill Bridge
Strines Wood
Ramsden Wood Bri.
Bank Wood
Light Bank Bri.
Dean Royd Farm
Deanroyd Bridges
Moverly Clough
Sun Wood
Lower Allescholes
Clunter Wood
Clunter Clough
Higher Allerscholes
Moorhey Wood
Rough Stones
Friezland
Moor Hey Farm
Moor Hey Barn
Moorhey Clough
Moorhey Flat
Bankhey Wood
Moor Bank Clough
Warland Gate End
Lane Bottom Bridge
Stone House Bri.
Stone House Clough
Stone House
Warland Bri.
Warland Wood
Warland Farm
Knoll Top
Calf Lee Cote
Calf Lee
Knoll Hill
Cote Clough
Lodge Hall
Shaw Stones
Waterstalls
Bottomley
Meadow Bottom
Lower Scout
Higher Scout
Scout Spa
Cat Stones Spring
Cat Stones
Walsden Edge
Langfield Common
Bottomley Clough
Basin Stone
West Scout
Rake End
Jail Hole
Higher Horse Wood Farm
Lower Horse Wood Farm
Middle Horse Wood Farm
Gaddings Hole
Langfield Edge
Black Clough
Pennine Way
Warland Draw
Middle Ramsden
Ramsden Wood
White Slack Edge
White Slack
White Slack Clough
Cranberry Moss
Horse Pasture Clough
Brock Holes Clough
Noon Hill Clough
Noon Hill
Shore Moor
Long Hill
Ferny Hill
Reddyshore
Great Hill
Long Lees
Withen Hill
Weirs
Stubley Cross Hill
Owler Clough Head
Owler Clough
Allenden Hill
Fox Stones Hill
Old Charles Hill
Blue Pot Brook
Flight Hill
Turn Slack Clough
Dearden's Pasture
Cuckoo Hill
Pasture House
Long Hill
Pike Hill
Slack
Stony Field
Scout End
Ringing Pots Hill
Blackbrow Hill
Light Hazzles Farm
Light Hazzles Clough
River Roch
Solomon Cutting
Chelburn
Chelburn Bridge
Lower Chelburn Reservoir
Weir
Leach Hill
Snoddle Hill
Wicken Lowe
Shurcrack
Top o' th' Rough
Lower Knowl
Higher Knowl
Brown Road Farm
Spring Bottom
Air Shaft

Todmorden
OL14
Littleborough
OL15
Heeley Dam
Heeley Clough
Jackson Rock
Long Stoup
Withens Gate
Middle Horse Wood Farm
Heeley Hill
Higher Horse Wood Farm
Bald Scout
Bald Scout Hill
Coldwell Edge
Coldwell Spring
Coldwell Hill
Spittle Clough
Gaddings Hole
Black Clough
Noon Stone
Noon Stone Edge
Jeremy Hill
Pennine Way
Red Dykes Flat
Red Dykes
Withens Clough Reservoir
Withens Clough
Raw Shaw
Moss Crop Hill
Moss Crop Hill Rut
WITHENS MOOR
Great Rut
Deep Slade
Buck Stones Well
Little Buck Stones
Hattering Stones
Fletcher Dyke
Higher Buck Stones
Two Lads (Cairns)
Withens Clough Head
Bird Nest Hill
Cloven Stone
Gaddings Drain
LANGFIELD COMMON
Warland Drain
Holder Stones
TURLEY HOLES AND HIGHER HOUSE MOOR
Middle Moor
Stony Edge
Little Holder Stones
Blake Moor
Wool Pack Stones
Little Dove Low
Warland Reservoir
White Holme Drain
Dry Rut
Warland Drain
Dove Lowe Stones
Round Hills
White Holme Moss
Deep Rut
Calf Lee Clough
Light Hazzles Reservoir
ROCHDALE
CALDERDALE
Closet Stone
Little Moor Clough
Saw Gill Hollow
Clay Roads Clough
White Holme Reservoir
Little Moor
Round Hill
Wicken Lowe
Farther Hill
Light Hazzles Edge
SOYLAND MOOR
Light Hazzles Clough
Middle Hill
Byron Edge Drain
Middle Rut
Great Rut
Nigher Hill
CHELBURN MOOR
Utley Edge
Byron Edge
B6138
BLACKSTONE EDGE ROAD
TURVIN ROAD
Laughton Drain
Cold
Knave Hole Hill
Ford
Head Drain
Yellow Hill
Hassock
Rush Bed Hill
Weir
Black Castle Drain
Leach Hill
Cow Head
BLACKSTONE EDGE
Black Castle Hill
LANE

88
107
126

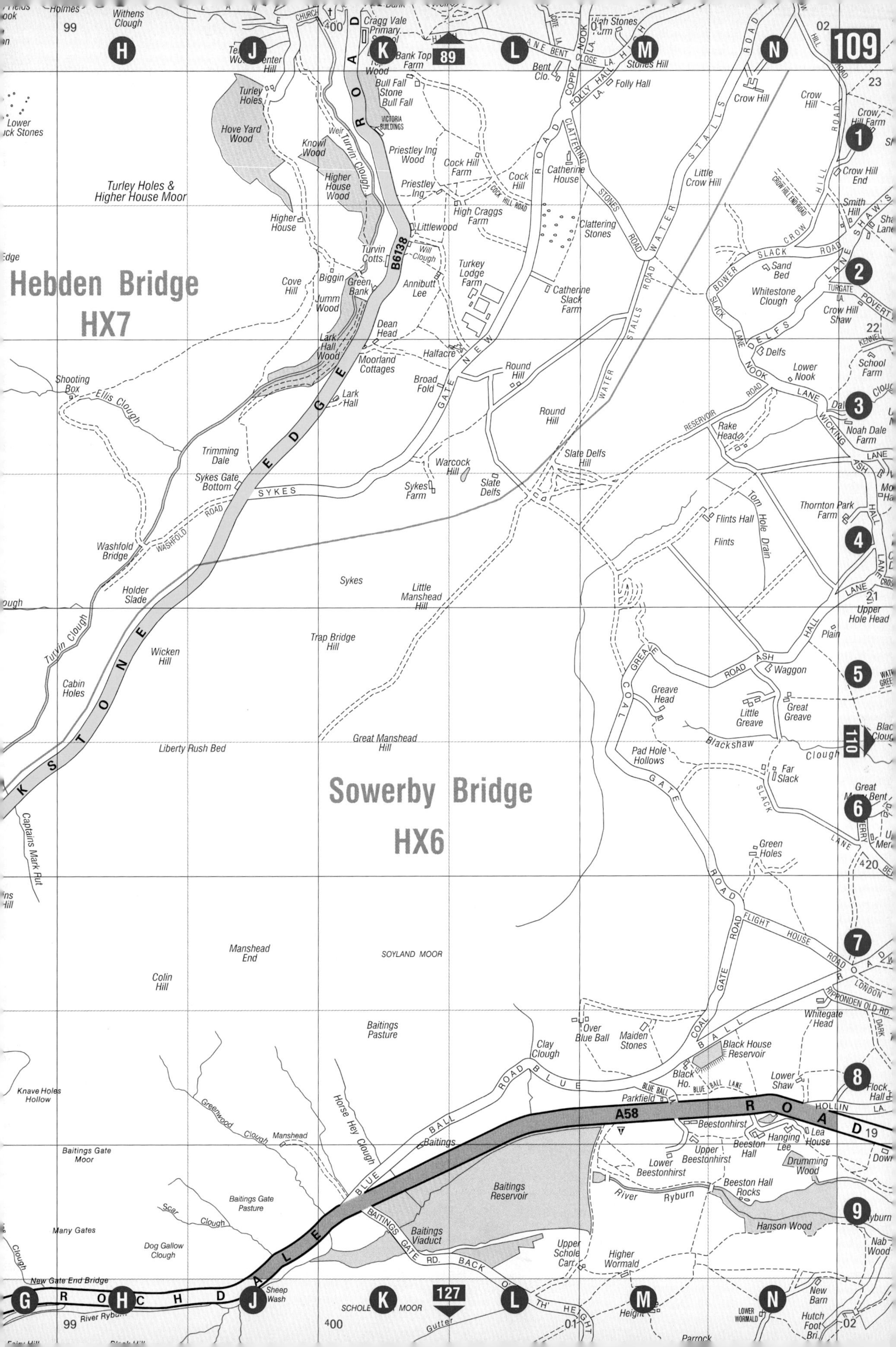
Hebden Bridge
HX7
Sowerby Bridge
HX6
89
127
110
B6138
A58
Cragg Vale Primary School
Turley Holes & Higher House Moor
Hove Yard Wood
Turley Holes
Knowl Wood
Higher House Wood
Priestley Ing Wood
Cock Hill Farm
Priestley Ing
High Craggs Farm
Littlewood
Turvin Cotts.
Turkey Lodge Farm
Catherine House
Clattering Stones
Catherine Slack Farm
Crow Hill
Little Crow Hill
Crow Hill End
Sand Bed
Whitestone Clough
Crow Hill Shaw
Delfs
Lower Nook
School Farm
Noah Dale Farm
Rake Head
Round Hill
Slate Delfs Hill
Warcock Hill
Slate Delfs
Sykes Farm
Trimming Dale
Sykes Gate Bottom
Washfold Bridge
Holder Slade
Sykes
Little Manshead Hill
Flints Hall
Flints
Thornton Park Farm
Upper Hole Head
Waggon
Greave Head
Little Greave
Great Greave
Pad Hole Hollows
Far Slack
Green Holes
Trap Bridge Hill
Wicken Hill
Cabin Holes
Liberty Rush Bed
Great Manshead Hill
Captains Mark Rut
Manshead End
Colin Hill
SOYLAND MOOR
Baitings Pasture
Clay Clough
Over Blue Ball
Maiden Stones
Black House Reservoir
Whitegate Head
Lower Shaw
Parkfield
Beestonhirst
Upper Beestonhirst
Lower Beestonhirst
Beeston Hall
Hanging Lee
Lea House
Drumming Wood
Beeston Hall Rocks
River Ryburn
Hanson Wood
Baitings Reservoir
Baitings Viaduct
Baitings
Upper Schole Carr
Higher Wormald
Knave Holes Hollow
Baitings Gate Moor
Greenwood Clough
Manshead
Horse Hey Clough
Baitings Gate Pasture
Many Gates
Dog Gallow Clough
New Gate End Bridge
Sheep Wash
SCHOLE MOOR
LOWER WORMALD
New Barn
Hutch Foot Bri.
Shooting Box
Ellis Clough
Turvin Clough
Lark Hall
Lark Hall Wood
Moorland Cottages
Dean Head
Halfacre
Broad Fold
Annibutt Lee
Green Bank
Jumm Wood
Biggin
Cove Hill
Higher House
Bank Top Farm
Bull Fall
Stone
Folly Hall
Bent Clo.
Stones Hill
Withens Clough
Lower Rock Stones
Black Ho.
Flock Hall
Nab Wood
KIRKSTONE EDGE ROAD
NEW GATE
SYKES ROAD
WASHFOLD ROAD
COAL GATE ROAD
BLUE BALL ROAD
ROCHDALE ROAD
BAITINGS GATE RD.
BACK O' TH' HEIGHT
FLIGHT HOUSE ROAD
WATER STALLS ROAD
CLATTERING STONES ROAD
COCK HILL ROAD
CROW HILL ROAD
BOWER SLACK ROAD
NOOK LANE
RESERVOIR ROAD
ASH HALL LANE
GREAVE ROAD
SLACK LANE
RIPPONDEN OLD RD.
LONDON ROAD
HOLLIN LA.
CRAGG ROAD
99
400
01
02
23
22
21
20
19
H
J
K
L
M
N
G
1
2
3
4
5
6
7
8
9

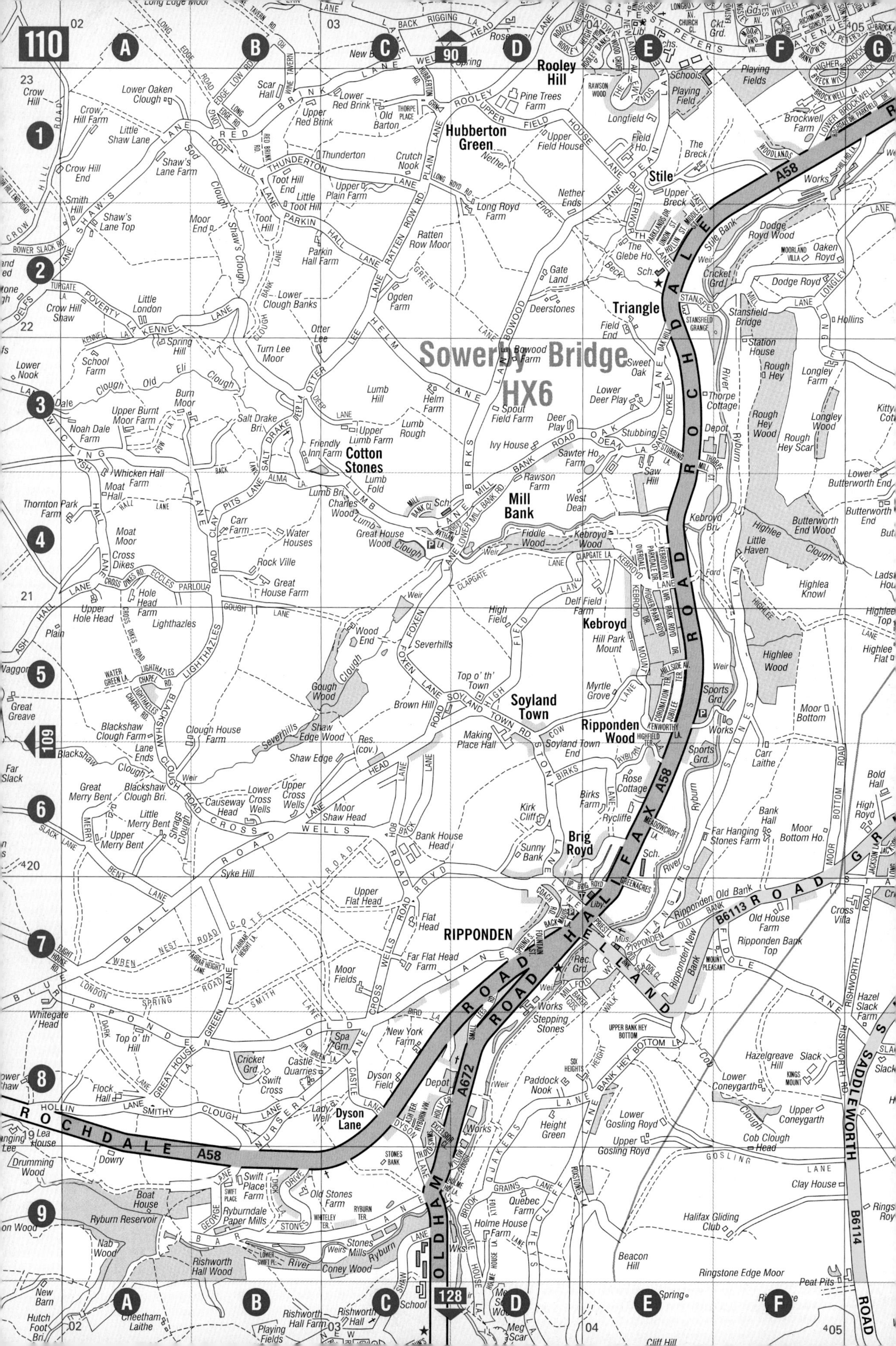
110
Sowerby Bridge
HX6
Rooley Hill
Hubberton Green
Stile
Triangle
Cotton Stones
Mill Bank
Kebroyd
Soyland Town
Ripponden Wood
Brig Royd
RIPPONDEN
Dyson Lane
90
109
128
Crow Hill
Crow Hill Farm
Little Shaw Lane
Crow Hill End
Smith Hill
Shaw's Lane Top
Shaw's Lane Farm
Lower Oaken Clough
Scar Hall
Lower Red Brink
Upper Red Brink
Old Barton
Thunderton
Crutch Nook
Pine Trees Farm
Upper Field House
Toot Hill End
Little Toot Hill
Toot Hill
Moor End
Upper Plain Farm
Long Royd Farm
Ratten Row Moor
Parkin Hall Farm
Nether Ends
Longfield
Field Ho.
The Breck
Upper Breck
The Glebe Ho.
Playing Fields
Playing Field
Schools
Brockwell Farm
Works
Dodge Royd Wood
Oaken Royd
Dodge Royd
Cricket Grd.
Little London
Crow Hill Shaw
Lower Clough Banks
Ogden Farm
Gate Land
Deerstones
Field End
Stansfield Bridge
Hollins
Spring Hill
School Farm
Lower Nook
Turn Lee Moor
Otter Lee
Bowood Farm
Sweet Oak
Station House
Rough Hey
Longley Farm
Dale
Noah Dale Farm
Upper Burnt Moor Farm
Burn Moor
Salt Drake Bri.
Lumb Hill
Helm Farm
Lower Deer Play
Spout Field Farm
Deer Play
Thorpe Cottage
Rough Hey Wood
Longley Wood
Rough Hey Scar
Upper Lumb Farm
Lumb Rough
Friendly Inn Farm
Ivy House
Stubbing
Sawter Ho. Farm
Depot
Saw Hill
Whicken Hall Farm
Moat Hall
Thornton Park Farm
Lumb Fold
Lumb Bri.
Charles Wood
Rawson Farm
West Dean
Lower Butterworth End
Butterworth End
Butterworth End Wood
Carr Farm
Water Houses
Great House Wood
Moat Moor
Cross Dikes
Rock Ville
Fiddle Wood
Kebroyd Wood
Kebroyd Bri.
Highlee
Little Haven
Highlea Knowl
Hole Head Farm
Upper Hole Head
Lighthazles
Great House Farm
Delf Field Farm
High Field
Plain
Wood End
Severhills
Hill Park Mount
Highlee Wood
Gough Wood
Top o' th' Town
Brown Hill
Myrtle Grove
Sports Grd.
Moor Bottom
Great Greave
Blackshaw Clough Farm
Lane Ends
Clough House Farm
Shaw Edge Wood
Res. (cov.)
Making Place Hall
Soyland Town End
Carr Laithe
Bold Hall
Far Slack
Shaw Edge
Rose Cottage
Birks Farm
Rycliffe
Kirk Cliff
Great Merry Bent
Blackshaw Clough Bri.
Causeway Head
Lower Cross Wells
Upper Cross Wells
Moor Shaw Head
Little Merry Bent
Upper Merry Bent
Shrogs Clough
Bank House Head
Sunny Bank
Bank Hall
Moor Bottom Ho.
Far Hanging Stones Farm
High Royd
Syke Hill
Upper Flat Head
Flat Head
Ripponden Old Bank
Old House Farm
Ripponden Bank Top
Cross Villa
Far Flat Head Farm
Rec. Grd.
Mount Pleasant
Ripponden New Bank
Moor Fields
Whitegate Head
Top o' th' Hill
New York Farm
Spa Grn.
Stepping Stones
Upper Bank Hey Bottom
Hazel Slack Farm
Cricket Grd.
Castle Quarries
Swift Cross
Dyson Field
Paddock Nook
Six Heights
Hazelgreave Hill
Slack
Kings Mount
Lower Coneygarth
Flock Hall
Lady Well
Height Green
Lower Gosling Royd
Upper Coneygarth
Upper Gosling Royd
Cob Clough Head
Lea House
Drumming Wood
Dowry
Stones Bank
Clay House
Boat House
Swift Place Farm
Old Stones Farm
Quebec Farm
Ryburn Reservoir
Ryburndale Paper Mills
Holme House Farm
Halifax Gliding Club
Nab Wood
Stones Mills
Coney Wood
Rishworth Hall Wood
Beacon Hill
Ringstone Edge Moor
Peat Pits
New Barn
Hutch Foot Bri.
Cheetham Laithe
Playing Fields
Rishworth Hall Farm
Rishworth Hall
School
Meg Scar
Cliff Hill
Spring
River Ryburn
ROCHDALE ROAD A58
HALIFAX ROAD A58
OLDHAM ROAD A672
SADDLEWORTH ROAD B6114
B6113
A
B
C
D
E
F
G
1
2
3
4
5
6
7
8
9
02
03
04
05
19
20
21
22
23

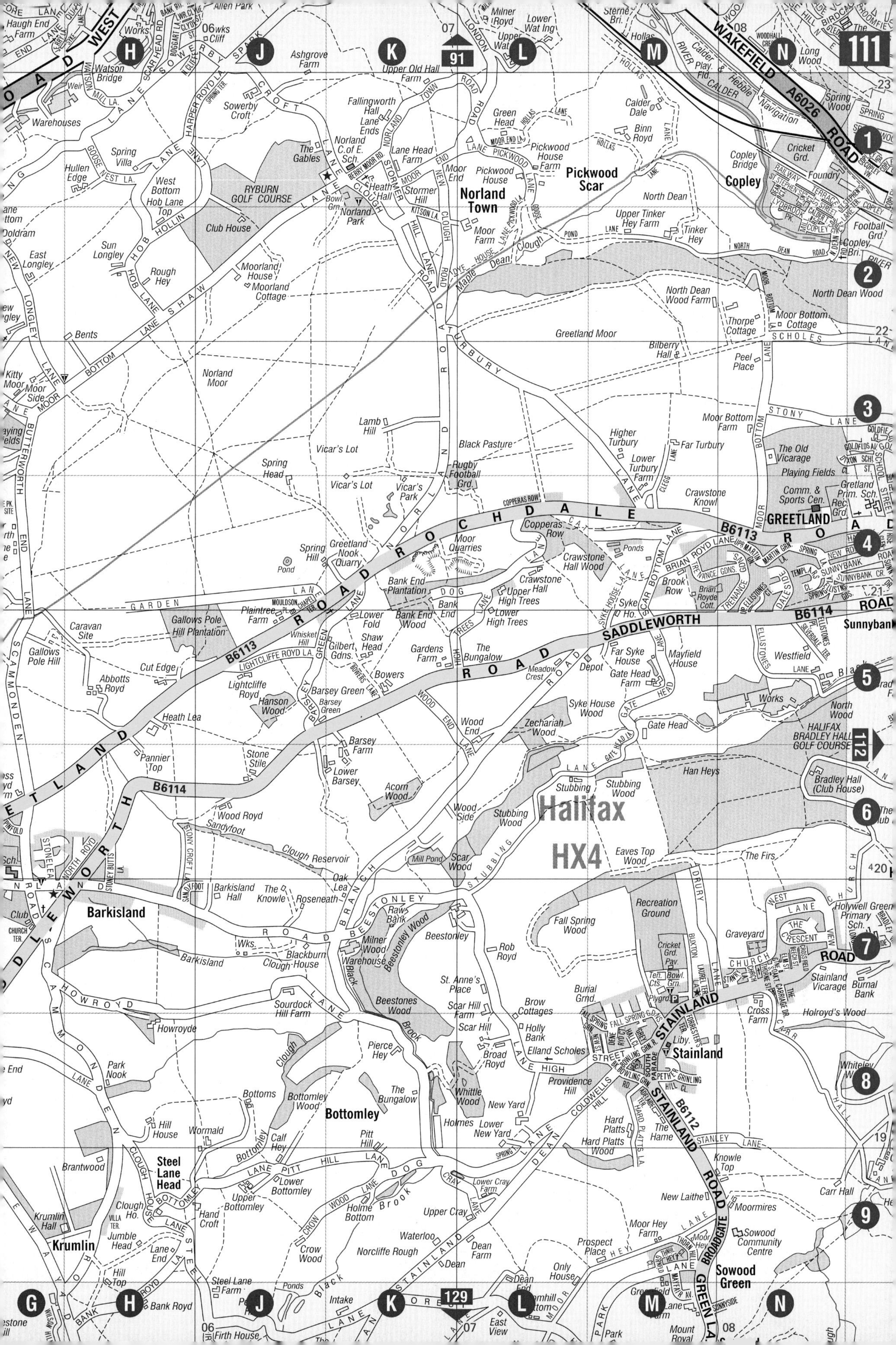
91
129
112
Norland Town
Pickwood Scar
Copley
Ryburn Golf Course
Norland Moor
Greetland Moor
Greetland
Halifax
HX4
Barkisland
Bottomley
Stainland
Sowood Green
Krumlin
Steel Lane Head
Rochdale Road
Saddleworth Road
B6113
B6114
B6112
A6026
Wakefield Road
Stainland Road
Halifax Bradley Hall Golf Course
Recreation Ground
Clough Reservoir
Calder & Hebble Navigation
North Dean Wood
Sunnybank
Heath Lea
Gallows Pole Hill
Sowerby Croft
Norland Park
Moor Bottom Cottage
Stubbing Wood
Scar Wood
Beestonley Wood
Beestones Wood
Rob Royd
Fall Spring Wood
Holywell Green Primary Sch.
Stainland Vicarage
Sowood Community Centre
Moor Hey Farm
Upper Cray
Norcliffe Rough
Crow Wood

A
B
C
D
E
F
G
1
2
3
4
5
6
7
8
9
92
111
130
Skircoat Green
Salterhebble
Halifax General Hospital
Siddal Top
Rosemary Hill
Park Nook Farm
Park Nook
Binns Top
Wood Nook
Park Gate
HX3
Copley
Copley Prim. Sch.
Bankhouse Wood
WAKEFIELD A6026
HUDDERSFIELD A629 RD.
South Halifax High Sch.
Playing Fields
Ash Grove Works
ELLAND PARK WOOD
Park Wood Crematorium
RIVER CALDER
North Dean Wood
North Dean Nature Trail
Sewage Works
Exley
Exley Hall Farm
Upper Exley
Elland Wood
ELLAND WOOD BOTTOM
HALIFAX
STAINLAND ROAD
B6112
Upper Scholes Farm
Scholes Farm
King's Dean
Halifax
GREETLAND
Bank Top Farm
Viaduct Sports Grd.
Lindwell
Cemetery
Elland Tunnel
Elland Wood
Elland Hall Farm
High Croft
ELLAND HALL FARM CARAVAN PARK
CALDERDALE ROAD A6025
Elland Lock
Calder & Hebble Navigation
Oliver Hall Bridge
Elland BUPA Hospital
A629
ROCHDALE ROAD B6113
Cross Hill
Gretland Prim. Sch.
Clayhouse Pk.
Brow Bri.
SADDLEWORTH ROAD B6114
ELLAND
Heathfield
Marshall Hall Cott.
Sunnybank
Greetland Primary Sch. (Annexe)
Woodfield Grange Nursing Home
West Vale
Hospice
Recreation Ground
The Park
DEWSBURY ROAD
Black Brook
Bradley Mill Farm
North Wood
HALIFAX BRADLEY HALL GOLF COURSE
Bradley Hall (Club House)
The Old Club House
Jagger Bridge
Glenholme
Long Heys Farm
Ravenstone Wood
Hullen Edge Hall
Sports Ground
Cricket Ground
ELLAND GOLF COURSE
The Brooksbank School
Playing Fields
Cross Lane Primary School
Rosemount Depot
Ainley Ind. Est.
HX4
Rawroyd Wood
Reservoir (covered)
Ainleys Round Wood
Ainleys Long Wood
Holywell Green
Holywell Green Primary Sch.
Stainland Vicarage
Burnal Bank
Shaw Park
Stainland Works
Greaves Farm
Benroyd Farm
East View
Broad Carr
Blackley End
Clay Pit
Blackley
The Cross
Junction 24
Ainleys
Holroyd's Wood
Whiteley Wood
Jagger Green
Jagger Green Hall
Hollins Hey Farm
Kew Hill
Kew Hill Bottom
Poultry Houses
Middle Haigh House Farm
Middle Haigh Ho.
Haigh House Hill
Thunnerley Wood
Croft House Farm
Copriding Farm
Wappy Spring Farm
Old Lindley
Prospect Place
Old Lindley Farm
Castle Farm
Jagger Green Dean
Dean House Farm
Padanaram
Loltake
Moorside
M62
M62 MOTORWAY
Warren House Farm
Rec. Grd.
Birchencliff
Carr Hall
Helen Hill Farm
Clough Head
Recreation Grd.
Haigh Cross
Peat Ponds Farm
HD3
Mink Farm
Poultry Houses
Turley Cote Farm
Old Lindley Moor
Old Lindley Edge
LINDLEY MOOR A643
Heather Leigh
Peat Ponds
Jericho
Weather Hill
Cowrakes
Lea
Old Lea
Lea Hill Farm
Laund Hill
Hill Grove Farm
Depot

BRIGHOUSE
Brighouse HD6
RASTRICK
Field Lane
Toothill
Elland Lower Edge
Elland HX5
Elland Upper Edge
Lower Edge Bottom
Fixby
Huddersfield
HD2
Top of Cowcliffe
Cowcliffe
Netheroyd Hill
Fartown
Brackenhall
Birds Royd
Prince Royd
M62 MOTORWAY
A6025
A643
A641
A6107
B6114
A629
ELLAND ROAD
HUDDERSFIELD ROAD
BRADFORD ROAD
CROWTREES ROAD
THORNHILL RD.
BRAMSTON ST.
CLOUGH LANE
HEY LANE
FIXBY ROAD
NEW HEY RD.
HALIFAX OLD ROAD
GRIMESCAR ROAD
Calder & Hebble Navigation
HUDDERSFIELD GOLF COURSE
Fixby Hall (Club House)
Huddersfield Crematorium
Gardens of Remembrance
Rastrick High School
Castlefields Inf. Sch.
The William Henry Smith Sch.
Field Lane Prim. Sch.
Highbury Sch.
Carr Green Primary School
Rastrick Cemetery
Fixby Jun. & Inf. Sch.
Ashbrow Jun. Sch.
Ashbrow Infants School
Cromwell Wood
Freeman's Wood
Strangstry Wood
Reins Wood
Gernhill Wood
Grimescar Wood
Cowcliffe Plantation
Ridge Plantation
CALDERDALE KIRKLEES
93
114
131
H J K L M N
G H J K L M N
1 2 3 4 5 6 7 8 9

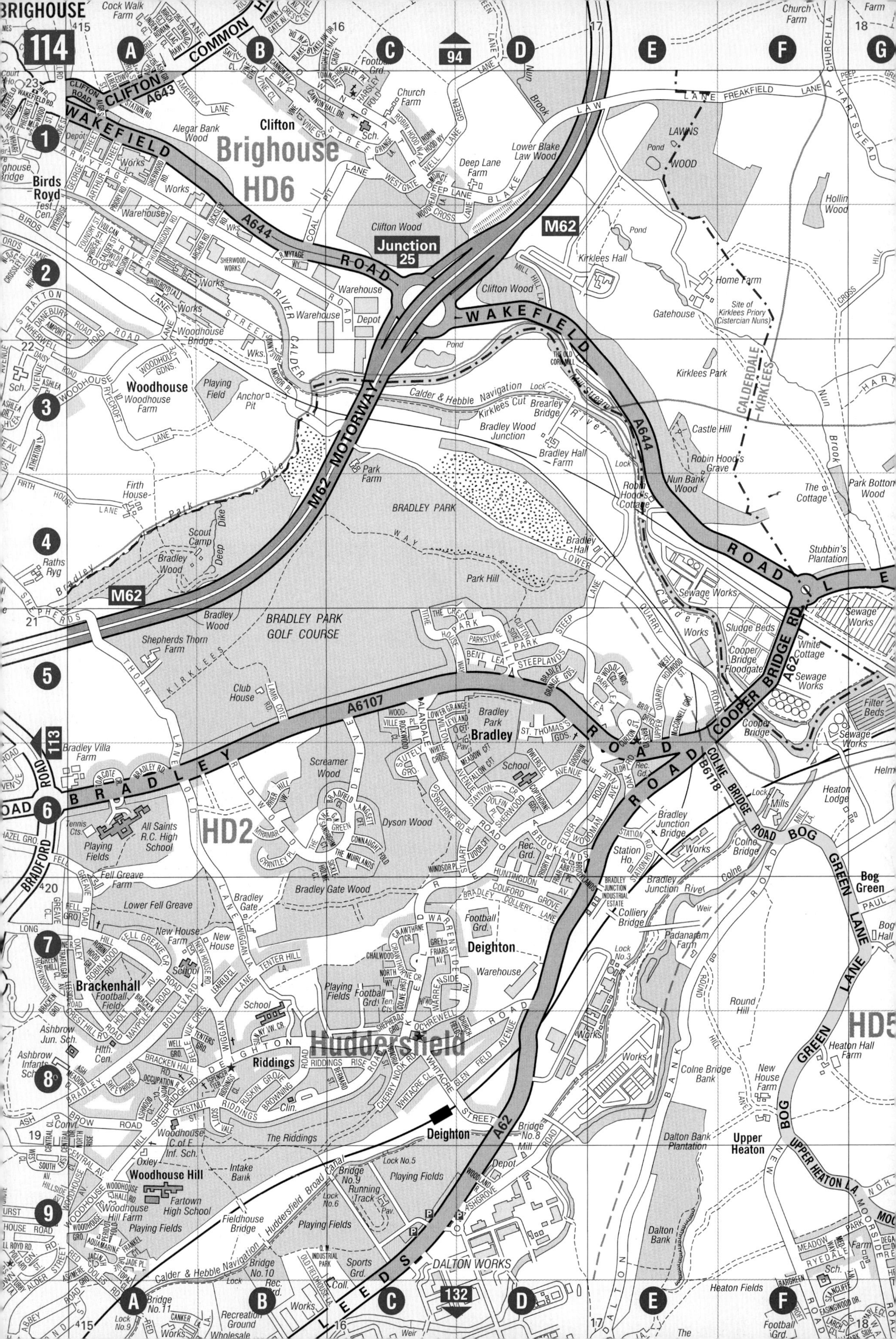

BRIGHOUSE
114
94
113
132
Brighouse
HD6
HD2
HD5
Huddersfield
Clifton
Birds Royd
Woodhouse
Bradley
Deighton
Riddings
Brackenhall
Woodhouse Hill
Upper Heaton
Bog Green
Junction 25
M62
M62 MOTORWAY
A644
A643
A6107
A62
B6118
WAKEFIELD ROAD
CLIFTON COMMON
BRADLEY ROAD
LEEDS ROAD
COOPER BRIDGE RD.
COLNE BRIDGE ROAD
BOG GREEN LANE
UPPER HEATON LA.
BRADFORD ROAD
RIVER CALDER
Calder & Hebble Navigation
Huddersfield Broad Canal
Kirklees Cut
BRADLEY PARK
BRADLEY PARK GOLF COURSE
Bradley Wood
Clifton Wood
Lawns Wood
Kirklees Hall
Kirklees Park
Site of Kirklees Priory (Cistercian Nuns)
Robin Hood's Grave
Nun Bank Wood
Castle Hill
Sewage Works
Dalton Bank Plantation
Colne Bridge Bank
Heaton Hall Farm
All Saints R.C. High School
Fartown High School
Deighton
DALTON WORKS
CALDERDALE
KIRKLEES

95
133
116
Liversedge
WF15
Mirfield
WF14
MIRFIELD
Hartshead
Little Thorpe
Robertown
Norristhorpe
Crossley
Moor Top
Mirfield Moor
Bracken Hill
Kitson Hill
Nab
Battyeford
Stocks Bank
Snake Hill
East Thorpe
Towngate
Northorpe
New Scarbro'
Lower Hopton
Upton Hopton
Kirkheaton
Mirfield
HUDDERSFIELD ROAD
A62
A644
B6119
B6118
Hartshead Jun.& Inf. Sch.
Robertown C.of E. Prim. Sch.
Little Thorpe Wood
Commonside Depot
Grove Cottage
Elm Grove Farm
Taylor Hall
Ashfield
Hartshead Hall
Roe Head Plantation
Hartshead Hall Wood
Holly Bank School
Somerville
Whitegate Farm
Highthorpe
Warren House
Warren Ho. Hill
Mock Hall
Moorlands Farm
Field Head
Coll. of the Resurrection (Theological Coll.)
Football Ground
Calder and Hebble Navigation
Battyeford C.of E. Jun. Mixed & Inf. Sch.
Playing Fields
London Park Estate
Holson
Crossley Hill
Hill Top Farm
Warehouse
Crossley Fields Jun. & Inf. Sch.
Primrose Farm
Croft House Farm
Balderstone Hall
Northorpe Hall
Castle Hall High. Sch.
Castle Hall Hill
Canker Dyke
Gov. Knowl Offs. Park
Knowl Pk. Ho.
Ings Gro. Pk.
Mirfield Mem. Rec. Grnd.
Gill Bridge
Ledgard Br.
Brewery Wharf
Mirfield Cut
Calder and Hebble
River Calder
Hopton Bridge
Heaton Hall Wood
Spring Gro. Gds.
Stancliffe Common
Tib Nether End Farm
Boyfe Hall
Rose Bungalow
Crow Royd
Hopton Jun. & Inf. School
Chadwick Hall Farm
The Waste
North Moor
North Moor House
Hollin Hall
Lower Hand Bank Farm
Hand Bank Farm
Briery Bank
Newhall Wood
Newhall Farm
Tennis Court
Woodlands
Hagg Wood
Broad Oaks
Wheatley's Br.
The Park
Sutcliffe Mem. Grd.
Mount Pleasant Farm
Hopton Hall Farm
Royds House
Whitley Wood Bottom
Whitley Wood
Norris House
Lodge Farm
Low Farm
Owlet Hurst Farm
Woodlands
South Field Farm
Pogg Myres
Smithy Hill
Church Farm
Moorside
Cemetery
Huddersfield Road
Dike
Finching
Valance Beck
H J K L M N G
1 2 3 4 5 6 7 8 9
19 20 21 22
420

116
HECKMONDWIKE
Heckmondwike
WF16
96
Chapel Fold
Dewsbury & District Hospital
Batley Carr
Hyrstlands Park
Mount Pleasant
Knowles Hill
Birkdale High Sch.
Highfield
Wood Hill
Westborough
The Flatts
Dewsbury Moor
St. John Fisher R.C. High Sch.
Boothroyd
Westborough High Sch.
Springfield
Eightlands
Crackenedge
Liversedge Park Farm
Sewage Works
Spring Cottage
Carr Lane House
Norris House
Low Farm
Daw Green
Dewsbury
Crematorium
Crow Nest Park
Dewsbury Museum & Art Gall.
Moor Bottom
WF13
Tattersfield Bridge
Dewsbury Cemetery
West Town
Watergate
Ravens Lodge
Northorpe
Northorpe Hall
Houghton Bridge
Kaye Bridge
RAVENSTHORPE
Scout Hill
Sports Ground
Savile Bridge
Riverside Industrial Estate
Football Grd.
Savile Ckt. Grd.
Canker Dyke Bri.
Ravensthorpe C. of E. Jun. Sch.
Holroyd Park
115
Ravens Wharf
Broad Dam
West Riding Union Bridge
Gleggford Bridge
Sports Grd.
Ravensthorpe
Power Sta.
Lees Hall Bridge
Scholefield Bridge
Thornhill Junction
Goods Yard
Thornhill Lees
Savile Town
Dewsbury
Thornhill Lees Hall
Wallis Farm
Forge Lane Bridge
Ravenshall School
Lees Holm Rec. Grd.
Greenwood Cut
Greenwood Lock
The Lodge
Shepley Br.
Sands House
Mirfield
Lady Wood
Crow Royd
Priest Royd Wood
Moor Farm
Mountain Top
Links Lodge
Club Ho.
Calder Farm
WF14
Lineside Cottages
Priest Royd
Long Plantation
Hagg Wood
Oliver Wood
Jordan Wood
Ouzelwell Hall Farm
Ouzelwell Hall
Shrogg Wood
Foxroyd Shrogg
Foxroyd Wood
Foxroyd Reservoirs (covered)
Fox Royd
Ings Farm
The Ings
Overthorpe C. of E. Jun. & Inf. Sch.
DEWSBURY DISTRICT GOLF COURSE
Whitley Wood Bottom
Whitley Wood
Golgreave
Haley Hill
134
Whitley Grange
A644
A638
A652
B6117
B6409

Hanging Heaton
HANGING HEATON GOLF COURSE
Earlsheaton
Earlsheaton High School
Shaw Cross
Chidswell
Chidswell House
Chidswell Farm
Windsor Farm
Playing Field
Bywell C.of E. Junior Sch.
Resevoir (covered)
Depot
Kennels
Burial Ground
North Ossett High School
Playing Fields
Gawthorpe
Chickenley Heath Farm
Heath Ho.
A638
A653
B6128
B6129
B6117
Recreation Ground
Ossett Street Side
Paleside
Paleside Farm
Warehouses
Earlsheaton Park
DEWSBURY
Goods Sta.
Chickenley
Jilling Ing Mills
Little Royd Mills
Viaduct
Playing Fields
WF12
Works
Ossett Holy Trinity Jun. & Inf. Sch.
Town End
OSSETT
Runtlings
Clough Farm
Hydro Carbon Reforming Works
Mitchell Laithes Farm
Mitchell Laithes Water Pollution Control Centre
Wilcott
Peaseland
Granary Farm
Ossett WF5
Gilbert
The Rookery Farm
Healey Old Mills
Victoria Mills
Ossett School
Lodge Farm
Park House Farm
Combs
Pond
Sports Ground
Mill Bank
Lock
Healey
Healey New Mills
Healey Mills Marshalling Yard
Healey Mills Sidings
Thornhill
The Old Rectory
The Hall (rems. of)
Thornhill Rectory Park
Four Lane Ends
Lodge
The View
Burgoyne Cottage
Hostingley Farm
Calder and Hebble Navigation
River
HOSTINGLEY LANE
KIRKLEES
WAKEFIELD
Thornhill High School
Castle Mount
97
118
135
H J K L M N
G H J K L M N

Spring Wood
98
Kirkham Farm
Beck Bottom Bridge
Beck Bottom
Lower Park Farm
New Park Grange
Bushey Beck Bridge
Kirkhamgate
Engine Fold
Lindale Hill
Lindale Cottage
Cricket Ground
Warren House
Jerry Clay La. Prim. Sch.
Sunrise Farm
GAWTHORPE LANE
Leeds Country Way
Lindale Farm
Highfield Farm
WRENTHORPE
Low Hod
M1
Lofthouse Colliery Memorial
Tufty Farm
Low Laithes Farm
Park Mill Farm
Lodge Hill Farm
Lodge Hill
Ossett WF5
Low Laithes
PARK MILL LANE
Club House
St. Paul's C. of E. Jun. & Inf. Sch.
LOW LAITHES GOLF COURSE
Owlers Farm
Warehouses
A638
WAKEFIELD ROAD
Flushdyke
B6129
Town End
FLANSHAW INDUSTRIAL ESTATE
FLANSHAW WAY
Shepherd Hill
Playing Field
OSSETT
Junction 40
Round Wood
Hotel
Assessment Centre
SPRINGMILL GOLF COURSE
DEWSBURY RD.
Haggs Hill
ROUNDWOOD INDUSTRIAL ESTATE
Low Common
Lupset
117
STATION ROAD
TOWNGATE
Playing Fields
South Ossett
B6128
M1 MOTORWAY
Giggal Hall
Rec. Grd.
Ossett Spa
Depot
Sewage Works
Snapethorpe Prim. & Inf. Schools
Roundwood Hill Sch.
Victoria Mills
Cavewell
Timothy Croft
Spring End Farm
HORBURY
Sowood Farm
SOWOOD
Hall Cliffe
Spring End
WF4
Clifton Infants School
Rock House
Green Park
Healey Mills Sidings
WESTFIELD ROAD
Carr Lodge Park
NORTHFIELD LANE A642
136
QUARRY HILL INDUSTRIAL ESTATE
Horbury Bridge
Horbury Sch.

Newton Hill
Snow Hill
FIELDHEAD HOSPITAL
Stanley Grange
Field Head
Fieldhead Hosp. Sch.
Hospice
Stanley Hall (Nurses Home)
Clark Hall
WF3
A642 ROAD
ABERFORD
Red Hall
Snow Hill Grange
White Hall Farm
Local Gov. Offs.
District Co. Offs.
RENTHORPE
Wakefield
erthorpe
PINDERFIELDS GENERAL HOSPITAL
WF1
Sports Fields
Play. Fld.
Playing Fields
LEEDS ROAD
A61
A650
NORTHGATE
WENTWORTH ST.
MARSH WAY
JACOB'S WELL LA.
STANLEY RD.
East Moor
King George's Field
Heath Vw. Jun. & Inf. School
St. John's
Warehouse Playing Flds.
Playing Flds.
Flanshaw
New Scarborough
Westgate Common
H.M. Prison
Brooks Bank
Westgate
WESTGATE
KIRKGATE
WAKEFIELD
Kirkgate
Borough Corner
St. Michael's C.of E. Primary Sch.
WF2
GREEN ROAD
New Brighton
Trading Estate
Calder Vale
Fall Ings
DONCASTER A638 ROAD
BRIDGE ST.
BARNSLEY ROAD
Belle Isle
Clarence Park
Lowe Hill
Miniature Golf Course
Holmfield House
Thornes Park
Wakefield College
Thornes
THORNES B6475 ROAD
The Cathedral School
The Mount
The Mount Jun. & Inf. School
Empire Buildings
Playing Fields
Club House
DENBY DALE A636 ROAD
RIVER CALDER
Calder Bridge
Boat House Farm
Portobello
Castle Grove Park
Sandal
Castle Grove Inf. Sch.
Sandal Magna Jun.& Inf. Sch.
Agbrigg
B6389
Wakefield Trinity R.L.F.C. (Belle Vue)
Cemy.
St. Thomas a Becket R.C. High Sch.
Sports Ground
Sandal Magna
99
120
137
32
33
34
H
J
K
L
M
N
G
1
2
3
4
5
6
7
8
9

Stanley Ferry Br.
Boat Repair Yard
Playing Fields
Kirkwood Plantation
Aire & Calder Cottages
Ramsdens Br. (swing)
Newland Park
Stanley Lodge
Newland Lodge
St. John's Field
The Old Stables
Newland Hall
Ruddings Wood
Stanley Hall Nurses Home)
WF3
Normanton
WF6
OPENCAST WORKINGS
Old Park
Goosehill Bridge
Goosehill Plantation
Goosehill Common
Goosehill
Goosehill Fold
Wakefield City High Sch.
Play. Fld.
East Moor
King George's Field
Kirkthorpe Weir
Sewage Works
Broadreach Lock
Gravel Ash
Kirkthorpe
Church Field
Cross Hills Fm.
Went Farm
Holly Farm
Cherry Tree Farm
Low Farm
Plump Hill
The Half Moon
Stocks
Grave Yard
Peas Hill
Peashill Plantation
Park Hill
Park Hill Fm.
Low Wood
Boat Ho.
Willow Garth
Kennels
Gled Hill
Wakefield
WF1
Heath Hall Farm
Heath Hall
Heath
Old Hall Wd.
Mount Tarry by it
Long Walk Plantation
Penhill Field
Calder Br. Junc.
Depot
Lock
Beech Lawn
Manor House
The White Ho.
Rose Cottage
Elm Cottage
HEATH COMMON
Belle Vue
Works
Wakefield Trinity R.L.F.C. (Belle Vue)
Agbrigg Farm
Golf House
Heath Farm
Horse Race End
Black Hill
Burcroft Farm
A655
A638
BLACK ROAD
DONCASTER ROAD
WAKEFIELD
B6389
Oakenshaw Junction
Oakenshaw North Junc.
Bracken Hill
Red Beck Bri.
Mount Pleasant
Oakenshaw Wood
Oakenshaw Grange
Crofton East Junction
B6378
Brand Hill
Depot
Sewage Works
Pig & Poultry Farm
Agbrigg
Oakenshaw Farm
Barnsley Canal (disused)
Kennels
Crofton West Junc.
Oakenshaw South Junc.
Crofton Water Pollution Control Centre
Playing Fields
St. Thomas a Becket R.C. High Sch.
Sports Ground
Sandal Magna
Bowling Greens
THE AVENUE
100
119
138
435
36
37

NORMANTON
Pontefract
WF7
WF4
Normanton
Ashfield
Hopetown
Loscoe
Loscoe Grange
Woodhouse
Woodhouse Common
Warmfield
Warmfield Common
Old Snydale
Streethouse
Snydale
Sharlston Common
Sharlston
New Sharlston
Mill Hill
NORMANTON BY-PASS
(Proposed)
LOSCOE BY-PASS
A655
A645
B6133
B6134
B6378
A638
WAKEFIELD ROAD
NORMANTON INDUSTRIAL ESTATE
Sports Ground
Playing Fld.
Beck Bridge
Coalpit Field
Huntwick Whin
Huntwick Grange Farm
Damhead Wood
Colcaring Wood
Obelisk Lodge
OBELISK PARK
Birkwood Farm
Birkwood House
Hall Farm
Low Farm
School Farm
Ings Farm
Hill Top Farm
West End Farm
Grange Farm
Grange Cottage
Snydale Hall
Snydale Hall Cotts.
Council Farm
Cookland House Farm
Manor House Farm
Sunny Dairy Farm
Mill Farm
Greystones
Springfield Farm
Common Side
West End Farm
Garden Centre
Huntwick Lodge
Huntwick Cotts.
Sewage Works

101
122
139

NORMANTON BY-PASS (Proposed)
Frobisher Wood
Cemetery
St. Wilfrid's Catholic High Sch. Playing Field
Reservoir
Quarry Plantation
Aketon Lodge
Ackton
Ackton Hall Farm
West End Farm
Ackton Hall Cottages
LOSCOE LANE
ACKTON
B6134
North Featherstone
Shaw's Farm
Parkfield Farm
Park Farm
Park Grange Farm
PONTEFRACT & DISTRICT GOLF COURSE
Club House
Green Acres
Hill Top Farm
Park Lodge Farm
Bungalow Farm
Pontefract
PONTEFRACT PARK (RACE COURSE)
The Old Vicarage (Nursing Home)
Strawberry Hill
North Featherstone Jun.& Inf. Sch.
Springfield Farm
Warren Plantation
Common Side
NEW ROAD
COMMON SIDE LA.
B6133
Slurry Pond
Reservoir
GREEN LANE
HALFPENNY LANE
FEATHERSTONE
Featherstone Rovers R.L.F.C. (Post Office Road)
Featherstone
Osgoldcross Crematorium
Monkroyd Farm
Monkroyd Cottage
Duchy Farm
Ravensknowle Farm
Ravensknowle Cottages
WF7
Lister Public Baths
Factories
Works
Depot
School
WAKEFIELD ROAD
A645
PONTEFRACT ROAD
ACKWORTH ROAD
Featherstone High School
Tennis Courts
Garden Centre
Huntwick Lodge
Huntwick Whin
Playground
Boating Lake
Purston Park
Lodge
Hawthorne Farm
Purston Jaglin
B6421
B6428
Wakefield WF4
Little Went Bridge
Broomhill Plantation
Lodge Hill Plantation
Long Plantation
Ackworth Park Farm
Brick Villa Farm
Nostell Low Farm
Top Farm (Museum)
West Hardwick
Hilltop Farm
Gamekeepers
102
121
140

Lady Balk
103
Monkhill
Prince of Wales Colliery
Boating Lake
Putting Grn.
Settling Pond
Pontefract West Junction
Pontefract Monkhill
Factory
Park Rd. Retail Park
Football Grd.
Cricket Ground
Pontefract Tanshelf
New College
Cemetery
Leisure Cen.
Swim. Pool
Pontefract Castle
PONTEFRACT
St. John's Priory (site of)
Depots
Depot
Works
Bubwith Bridge
Crow Crowns
KNOTTINGLEY RD.
BONDGATE
STH. BAILEYGATE
SOUTHGATE
A645
A639
B6134
Racing Stables
Halfpenny Lane Jun. & Inf. Sch.
Cen. for Disabled Miners
Pontefract Baghill
Harewood Park
Holy Family & St. Michael's R.C. Prim. Sch.
Cobblers Lane Inf. Sch.
Cobblers Lane Jun. Sch.
Eastbourne
Willow Park
Willow Park Jun. Sch.
Play. Fld.
Baghill Lane Nurseries
Kildare Cottage
Friarwood Valley Gdns.
Pontefract General Infirmary
Priory Wood
Grove Town
Chequerfield
Chequerfield Infant Sch.
Sports Ground
The King's High Sch.
Playing Fields
Fairleigh Farm
Larks Hill Jun. & Inf. Sch.
Carleton Park Prim. Sch.
WF8
The Rookeries
Carleton Jun. & Inf. Sch.
Carleton
Bates Hill
Carleton High School
Playing Fields
Green Leas School
Church Farm
The Grange
Works
Holme Farm
Bennett Ings Farm
A628
ACKWORTH
HARDWICK
Grave Yard
Pontefract Rugby Football Club
Playing Field
Mill House
Mill House Machir
The Old Mill Nursery
Darrington Windmill (Disused)
Roman Ridge
Roman Road (Course Of)
Little Went
Haverlands Farm
Works
Castle Syke Farm
Castle Syke Lodge
Potwells Farm
Plague Stone
SANDY GATE
Hundhill Quarry (Disused)
Reservoir (Covered)
Fox Covert
Moor Bridge
Fletcher's Spring Covert
Ackworth Park
Lodge
Park Croft
Southlands
Burial Field
Hundhill Farm
Hundhill Hall
Cricket Grd.
Hall
East Hardwick
Berrill Farm
Went Hill
141
124
West Fie
Slurry
PONTEFRACT ROAD
CASTLE SYKE HILL

124
KNOTTINGLEY
ROAD
M62 MOTORWAY
M62
Junction 33
A1 (FERRYBRIDGE BY-PASS)
Ferrybridge Services
Longbull Hill
Shilling Hill
SHILLINGHILL LANE
Depot
Crow Crowns
CROWCROWNS LA.
TAYTHES LANE
LOWER
DALES
MIREY BUTT LANE
CATTLELAITH
SYCAMORE
Jun. & Inf. School
104
PINEWOOD
HAZEL
ELM PLACE
POPLAR GR.
Works
England Lane
England Lane Crossing
Playing Fields
Quarry Cottage
WOMERSLEY
THE POPLARS
DOWLAND CR.
Throstle Farm Jun. & inf. Schs.
Ten. Cts.
Doveroyd House
WINDERMERE
AVENUE
THROSTLE ROAD
DRIVE
Bowl. Grn.
Playing Fields
HAWESWATER
CONISTON PL.
Park Balk Farm
LEYS LANE
M62
Cattlelaith
Greavefield Closes
GREAVEFIELD
GROVEHALL LANE
GROVE HALL CARAVAN SITE
HAZEL
Depot
Trinity Farm
Grove Farm
Grove Hall
GREAT NORTH ROAD
Leys Farm
Quarry (Stone)
Baghill Lane Nurseries
EASTBOURNE VW.
Kildare Cottage
Spital Gap
STUBBS LANE
Hodgewood Farm
SPITALGATE
STREET
FURLONG LANE
A1 NORTH
HODGEWOOD LANE
HOLDGATEHILL LANE
Bickering Wood
Millhill Fields
Hunters Wood
MID YORKSHIRE GOLF COURSE
WAKEFIELD
SELBY
MARLPIT LANE
HAVERCROFT
Clump Grange
Church Farm
BACK LANE
LEYS ROAD
Valley Plantation
Wake Wood
123
ASH GR.
BEECH CR.
BEECH CRESCENT
SOTHERON CROFT
DENBY RD.
PARK AV.
PHILIPS LANE
DENBY CREST
HILL
MILL HILL CL.
Darrington C.of E. Prim. Sch.
WENTWORTH PARK RISE
HILL CROFT CL.
CHURCH LA.
Club House
Spring Garden Cottages
Keeper's Cottage
The Willows
CARLETON ROAD
ESTCOURT
ORCHARD VIEW
NEW ROW COTTS.
GREENROYD
THORNTREE
MANOR PK
MANOR PARK RI.
Summerhill
West End Farm
Mill House
Machir
The Old Mill
Nursery
Darrington Windmill
Westfields
WESTFIELD LANE
Greenroyd Farm
ESTCOURT DR.
ROAD
FAIRWAYS CT.
LANE
VALLEY ROAD
BANK
NORTH LODGE LA.
Darrington
MILNERS LA.
Darrington Hall
NORTH ROAD
THE PADDOCKS
Bank Wood
Pontefract WF8
Woodlands
Stapleton Park Cottages
Slurry Ponds
West Field
Long Plantation
Fletcher's Spring Covert
WEST PARK TER.
WEST PARK DR.
WEST PARK CARAVAN SITE
STAPLETON PARK
Thorntree Closes
Round Ash Closes
Went Hill
142
Dale Field
Long Plantation
Kirkdike Plantation
48
49
450
22
21
420
19

Broomhill
South Moor
Goole
DN14
Aire & Calder Navigation
(Knottingley & Goole Canal)
Stubbs Bridge
Slurry Pond
Nearpark Farm
Stubbs Common
M62
M62 MOTORWAY
King's Standard Hill
Cridling Park
Farpark Farm
Sandy Dike
Cobcroft Lane
Knottingley
WF11
Cridling Park Cottages
Northfield House
Gale Common
Works
Cridling Stubbs Crossing
Lowbalk La.
Cridling Stubbs
Shackleton Spring
New Spring
Wrights Lane
Northfield Road
Spring Lodge Cottage
Spring Lodge
Grant Spring
Moat
Wood Hall
Kelseycroft Wood
Springlodge Crossing
North Field
Mill Wood
Quarry (Limestone)
Woodhall Cottages
Bradley Drain
Rows Wood
Dale Hill
Womersley Common
Galecommon Lane
Northside Bungalow
Stapleton
Stapleton Cottages
Doncaster
DN6
Newroad End
Brotherhood Church
Ricketcroft Wood
Sodgel Wood
WOMERSLEY
Manor Farm
Hall
Sch.
Playing Fields
Glebe Farm
Steel Spring
Pontefract Gate
Lodge
Sewage Works
Kingsland Wood
Fish Pond
Fishpond Wood
Rookery Farm
Beck Bridge
Womersley Beck
Low Farm
Cemy.
Icehouse Park
Publichouse Farm
Manor House
Tophouse Farm
Womersley Park
Station Rd.
Highfield Lane
Fulham La.
Grove Wood
Belt Plantation
Birka Drain
The Rookery
Lady Hawke Wood
Home Farm
Churchfield Lane
WOMERSLEY PARK
Castle Farm
Castle Farm Cottage
Castle Hill Wood
Oak Plantation
Beckclose Wood
105
143

108
A
B
C
D
E
F
G
396
97
98
Weir
Pennine Way
Rush Bed
Leach Hill
Cow Head
Higher Chelburn Reservoir
BLACKSTONE EDGE RESERVOIR
TURVIN RD.
B6138
Black Castle Hill
Castle Drain
ROAD ROCHDALE
A58
Black Castle Clough
Slate Pit Hill
Leach
Barrat
18
Ford
White House
Depot
Perkins Bridge
Castle Drain
Spa H
Castle
Broadhead House
Green Halghs
Castle Bungalow
Castle Clough
Weir
Ford
Ford
Rag Sapling Clough
BLACKSTONE EDGE MOOR
Cloise
SWAINROD LANE
OLD PACKHORSE ROAD
Roman Road
Cowberry Hill
Broad Head
HALIFAX
Pennine Way
Fence Nook
BLACKSTONE EDGE OLD ROAD
Ford
17
Blackstone Edge Blue Delf (disused)
Jacob's Well
Roman Road
Dick Slack
Stormer Hill Bar
Stormer Hill
OLD ROAD
Letter Stones
Blackstone Edge Pasture
Blackstone Edge Cote
Red Brook
Broad Head Drain
Blackstone Edge
Rishworth Drain
Littleborough
Oil Mill Bridge
BLACKSTONE EDGE
Lydgate
Weir
Blackstone Edge Fold
Blackstone Edge Holes
Draught Hill
OL15
Green Brows
CALDERDALE
ROCHDALE
Lead Mine Clough
Robin Hood's Bed
16
Salmon Well
Draught Hill Slack
Fern Brakes
Redmires Clough
Red Scars Hill
Lode Nab
Whittaker Spout Gutter
Redmires
Sun End
Whittaker Moor
Turf Hill
Ford
Slippery Moss
Ford
Longden End Clough
CLEGG MOOR
Dry Mere
Hoar Edge
Moss Slack
Pennine Way
Hoar Edge Rakes
Moss Slack Brook
415
Longden End Brook
White Isles
Lads Grave
Syke Moor
Low House Moor
LOW HOUSE MOOR
Little Hoar Edge
Black Moor
Great Hoar Edge
Rook Stones Hill
Castle Shore Clough
Longden End Moor
Castle Shore Hill
M62
A672
T.V. & Radio Station
M62 MOTORWAY
Tag Heys
New Nook
Windy Hill
Longden End Clough
Longden End Brook
Windy Hill
14
Works
Green Meadows
1
2
3
4
5
6
7
8
9

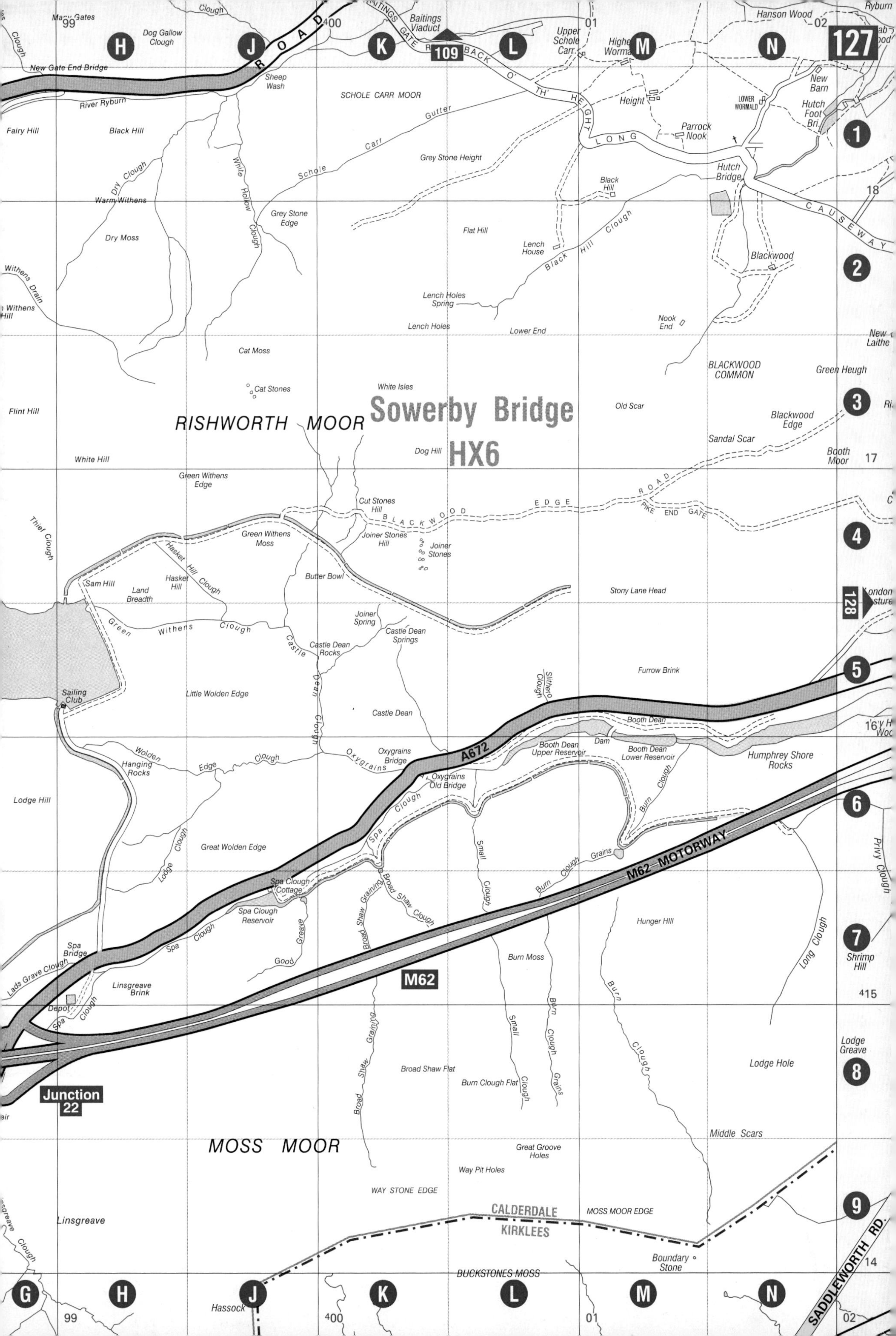
Sowerby Bridge
HX6
RISHWORTH MOOR
MOSS MOOR
SCHOLE CARR MOOR
BLACKWOOD COMMON
Baitings Viaduct
109
128
Junction 22
M62 MOTORWAY
M62
A672
CALDERDALE
KIRKLEES
SADDLEWORTH RD.
Booth Dean Upper Reservoir
Booth Dean Lower Reservoir
Spa Clough Reservoir
Sailing Club
Green Withens Moss
Cat Moss
Dry Moss
Burn Moss
Broad Shaw Flat
Burn Clough Flat
Lodge Hole
Hunger Hill
Middle Scars
Great Groove Holes
Way Pit Holes
WAY STONE EDGE
MOSS MOOR EDGE
BUCKSTONES MOSS
Boundary Stone
Linsgreave
Hassock
Blackwood
Hutch Bridge
Lench Holes
Lower End
Nook End
Old Scar
Sandal Scar
Blackwood Edge
Green Heugh
Booth Moor
Stony Lane Head
Furrow Brink
Humphrey Shore Rocks
Castle Dean
Oxygrains Bridge
Oxygrains Old Bridge
Spa Clough Cottage
Spa Bridge
Depot
Linsgreave Brink
Great Wolden Edge
Little Wolden Edge
Hanging Rocks
Lodge Hill
Flint Hill
White Hill
Fairy Hill
Black Hill
Warm Withens
Cat Stones
White Isles
Dog Hill
Cut Stones Hill
Joiner Stones Hill
Joiner Stones
Butter Bowl
Sam Hill
Land Breadth
Hasket Hill
Joiner Spring
Castle Dean Springs
Castle Dean Rocks
Grey Stone Edge
Grey Stone Height
Flat Hill
Lench House
Lench Holes Spring
Sheep Wash
New Gate End Bridge
River Ryburn
Dog Gallow Clough
Upper Schole Carr
Height
Parrock Nook
LOWER WORMALD
New Barn
Hutch Foot Bri.
Hanson Wood
Shrimp Hill
Lodge Greave
BLACKWOOD EDGE ROAD
PIKE END GATE
LONG CAUSEWAY
BACK O' TH' HEIGHT
Dam

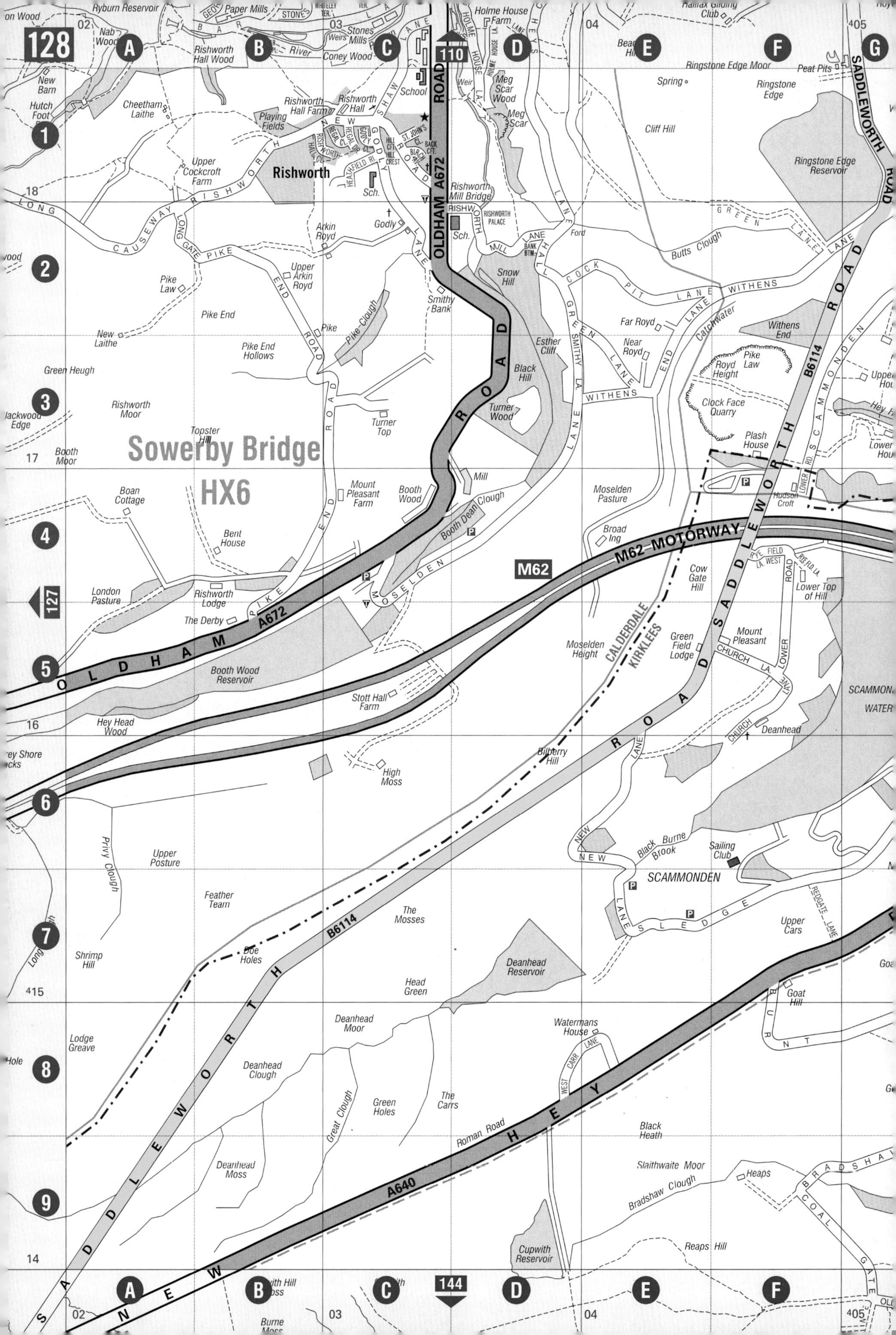
Ryburn Reservoir
Paper Mills
Nab Wood
Rishworth Hall Wood
River
Stones Mills
Weirs
Coney Wood
Holme House Farm
Ringstone Edge Moor
Peat Pits
SADDLEWORTH ROAD
New Barn
Hutch Foot
Cheetham Laithe
Playing Fields
Rishworth Hall Farm
Rishworth Hall
School
Meg Scar Wood
Meg Scar
Spring
Ringstone Edge
Cliff Hill
Ringstone Edge Reservoir
Upper Cockcroft Farm
Rishworth
Sch.
Rishworth Mill Bridge
OLDHAM ROAD A672
LONG CAUSEWAY
RISHWORTH
LONG GATE
PIKE END ROAD
Arkin Royd
Godly
GODLY LANE
RISHWORTH PALACE
MILL LANE
BANK BTM.
HALL LANE
Ford
GREEN LANE
Butts Clough
Upper Arkin Royd
Pike Law
Snow Hill
COCK PIT LANE
WITHENS LANE
Smithy Bank
Pike End
New Laithe
Pike
Pike Clough
Pike End Hollows
Far Royd
Near Royd
Catchwater
Withens End
Esther Cliff
GREEN SMITHY LANE
Black Hill
Royd Height
Pike Law
Green Heugh
Rishworth Moor
Turner Top
Turner Wood
WITHENS
Clock Face Quarry
Blackwood Edge
Topster Hill
Sowerby Bridge
HX6
Plash House
B6114
SCAMMONDEN
Booth Moor
Mount Pleasant Farm
Booth Wood
Mill
Moselden Pasture
Hudson Croft
LOWER RD.
Boan Cottage
Booth Dean Clough
Bent House
Broad Ing
M62
M62 MOTORWAY
Cow Gate Hill
RYE FIELD LA. WEST
RYE FLD. LA.
Lower Top of Hill
London Pasture
Rishworth Lodge
MOSELDEN
CALDERDALE
KIRKLEES
The Derby
OLDHAM ROAD
Booth Wood Reservoir
Moselden Height
Green Field Lodge
Mount Pleasant
CHURCH LA.
LOWER LANE
SCAMMONDEN WATER
Stott Hall Farm
Hey Head Wood
Deanhead
Bilberry Hill
High Moss
Privy Clough
Upper Posture
Black Burne Brook
Sailing Club
NEW LANE
SCAMMONDEN
Feather Team
The Mosses
SLEDGE LANE
REDGATE LANE
Upper Cars
Shrimp Hill
Doe Holes
Deanhead Reservoir
Head Green
Goat Hill
BURNT
Deanhead Moor
Watermans House
Lodge Greave
WEST CARR LANE
Deanhead Clough
Green Holes
The Carrs
Great Clough
NEW HEY ROAD
Roman Road
Black Heath
A640
Deanhead Moss
Slaithwaite Moor
Heaps
Bradshaw Clough
BRADSHAW
COAL GATE
Cupwith Reservoir
Reaps Hill
SADDLEWORTH ROAD
Burne
1 2 3 4 5 6 7 8 9
A B C D E F G
02 03 04 405
18 17 16 415 14
110
127
144

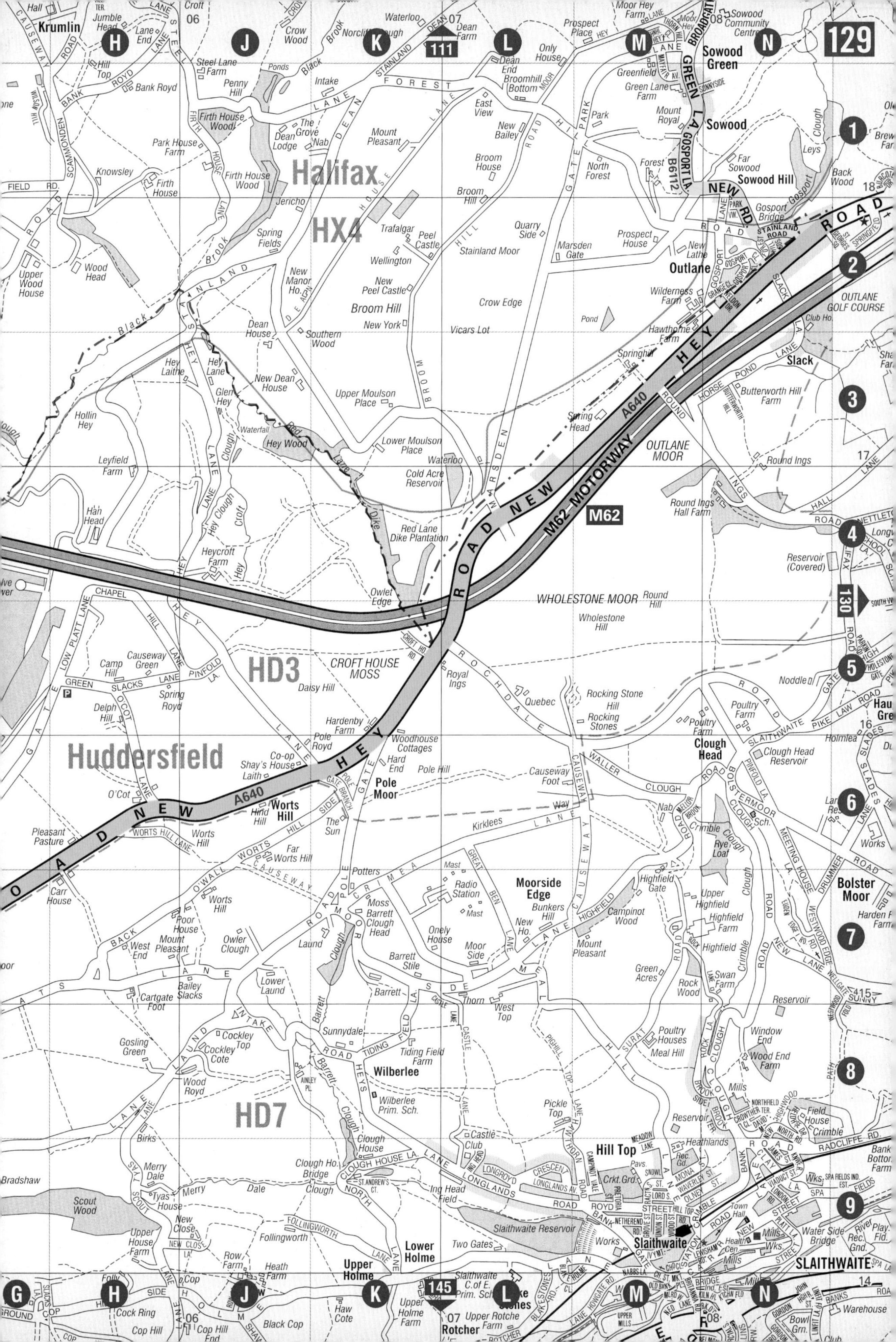
Halifax
HX4
HD3
Huddersfield
HD7
Krumlin
Sowood Green
Sowood
Sowood Hill
Outlane
Slack
OUTLANE GOLF COURSE
OUTLANE MOOR
WHOLESTONE MOOR
CROFT HOUSE MOSS
Broom Hill
Clough Head
Pole Moor
Worts Hill
Moorside Edge
Bolster Moor
Wilberlee
Hill Top
Slaithwaite
SLAITHWAITE
Slaithwaite Reservoir
Lower Holme
Upper Holme
Rotcher
M62 MOTORWAY
A640
B6112
NEW HEY ROAD
Stainland Moor
Crow Edge
Cold Acre Reservoir
Red Lane Dike Plantation
Clough Head Reservoir
Scout Wood
111
130
145

A
B
C
D
E
F
G
1
2
3
4
5
6
7
8
9
09
410
11
112
129
146
HX4
M62
Junction 23
M62 MOTORWAY
A640 HEY
NEW HEY RD.
A643 LINDLEY MOOR ROAD
NEW HEY A640 ROAD NEW
Mink Farm
Poultry Houses
Turley Cote Farm
Old Lindley Moor
Old Lindley Works
Peat Ponds Farm
Peat Ponds
Jericho
Weather Hill
Cowrakes
Laund Hill
Hill Grove Farm
New Lea
Old Lea
Lea Hill Farm
Brewery Farm
Leys
Back Wood
Mount
YMCA Recreation Ground
Sch.
Low Hill
Lindley
Depot
Factory
Wks.
Mills
Leeches Hill
Upper Hirst
Lower Hurst Farm
Snow Lea
Poultry Houses
Shaw Wood
OUTLANE GOLF COURSE
Hirst Wood
Longwood Brook
Club Ho.
Slack
Shaw Farm
Pendle Hill
Pighill Wood
Leys Farm
Compensation Reservoir
Salendine Nook
Sports Ground
Playing Fields
Huddersfield New College
Salendine Nook High School
Tennis Courts
Rec. Grd.
Reservoir
Obsy.
Oakes
Holly Bank Farm
Whin Gate
Poultry Houses
Longwood Edge
Dodlee
Longwood Reservoirs
Nettleton Hill
Mole's Head
Royles Head Farm
Works
Quarmby
Huddersfield
Longwood
Quarmby Cliff
Nab End
Round Ings
Reservoir (Covered)
Green Edge
New Lane Farm
Longwood Common
Scapegoat Hill Prim. Sch.
Greenroyd Farm
Milking Clough
Bonny Clough Wood
Clay Wood Brook
Lockwoods Yard
Scapegoat Hill
Hollin Hall
Whitwam Bank
Hall Ings
Hill Side
Upper Haughs
Upper Fields
Crkt. Grd. Pav.
Moorcroft Farm
Leymoor Sch.
Recreation Ground
Playing Field
Hexham Green
Vicarage
HD3
Noddlear
Haughs Green
Wood Bank
Holmlea
Duke Ings
Clough Head Reservoir
St. John's C. of E. Prim. Sch.
GOLCAR
Golcar Jun. & Inf. Sch.
Cricket Grd.
Town End
Liby.
Tennis Cts.
Rec. Grd.
Playing Field
Wellesley Court
MARKET
LANE
B6111
Scar Wood
SCAR TOP
Britannia Trading Est.
Milnsbridge
Lark's Rest
Heath House Wood
Works
Sharehill
Heath House
Bolster Moor
Harden Road Farm
Bank End
HD7
Headwall Green
Upper Wellhouse
The Gables
Lower Wellhouse
Rob Royd
Scarwood Bridge
Wellhouse
Sunny Bank
Wellhouse Fields
Lock
Guy Edge
Cowlersley
Pymroyd
Cowlersley Jun. & Inf. School
Woodside Cottage
Corona Park
Manor House Farm
Long Wood
Reservoir
Golcar Brook Bridge
Westwood House
Lowestwood
Hazel Grove
Broad Oak
MANCHESTER ROAD
Low Westwood Bridge
Hill Top
Field House
Crimble
Cock's Crossing
Huddersfield Narrow Canal (Disused)
Bank Bottom Farm
Lees Mill Bridge
Bowl. Grn.
Works
Crkt. Grnd.
Play. Fld.
Lees Mill Farm
Colne
River
Water Side Bridge
Rec. Gnd.
Works
Linthwaite
Lane End
Ckt. Grd.
Slaids
Rye Croft Edge
Felks Stile Cottage
CROSSLAND HEATH GOLF COURSE
Club House
Shaw Green
Colne Valley Bus. Park
Clinic
Linthwaite Jun. & Inf. Sch.
Linthwaite Ardron Mem. C. of E. Prim. School
Colne Valley High School
A62
MANCHESTER
SLAITHWAITE
Warehouse
Bowl. Grn.
Lower Clough
Black Rock
Play Fld.
Playing Fields
Hill Tree Park
Bate's Square
BLACKMOORFOOT

HUDDERSFIELD
HD1
HD2
HD4
Birkby
Edgerton
Marsh
Paddock
Gledholt
Royds Hall
Cliff End
Crosland Moor
Barton
Walpole
Lockwood
Salford
Blue Bell Hill
Taylor Hill
Close Hill
Newsome
Stile Common
Primrose Hill
Folly Hall
Shorehead
Aspley
Newtown
Shearing Cross
Fartown
Paddock Foot
Hall Bower
ST. LUKE'S HOSPITAL
HUDDERSFIELD ROYAL INFIRMARY
THE HUDDERSFIELD NUFFIELD HOSPITAL
Greenhead Park
Huddersfield Grammar School
Royds Hall High School
Moor End High Sch.
Newsome High Sch.
University of Huddersfield
A629
A62
A640
A641
A616
B6432
B6108
113
132
147

HD1
HD2
HD4
HD5
A62
A629
B6432
Rawthorpe
Bradley Mills
Dalton Fold
Moldgreen
Dalton
Dalton Green
Waterloo
Tandem
Hill Side
Greenside
Cowmes
Aspley
Almondbury
Benomley
Lower Houses
Ashenhurst
Longley
Almondbury Common
Shorehead
Hall Bower
Lumb
Huddersfield Town F.C. (The Alfred McAlpine Stadium)
LONGLEY PARK GOLF COURSE
WOODSOME HALL GOLF COURSE
Mellor Wood
Calder & Hebble Navigation
Heaton Fields
Cold Royd Wood
King James's School
Almondbury High Sch.
Ravensknowle Park
Castle Hill
Victoria Tower
Fenay Bridge
114
131
148

Kirkheaton
Huddersfield
Mirfield
WF14
HD8
WF4
Gawthorpe
Gawthorpe Green
Stafford Hill
Houses Hill
FENAY BRIDGE
Common Top
Lepton
Lepton Edge
High Green
Rowley Hill
Little Lepton
Falhouse Grn.
Linfit
Dogley Lane
WAKEFIELD ROAD
A642
B6118
B6433
A629
HIGHGATE LANE
BELLSTRING LANE
LILEY LANE
ROWLEY LANE
Hall Wood
Liley Wood
Gregory Spring
Hepworth Wood
Covey Clough Wood
Hutchin Wood
Lepton Great Wood
Highland Sports & Recreation Ground
Cockley Wood
Nineveh Plantation
Low Wood
115
134
149

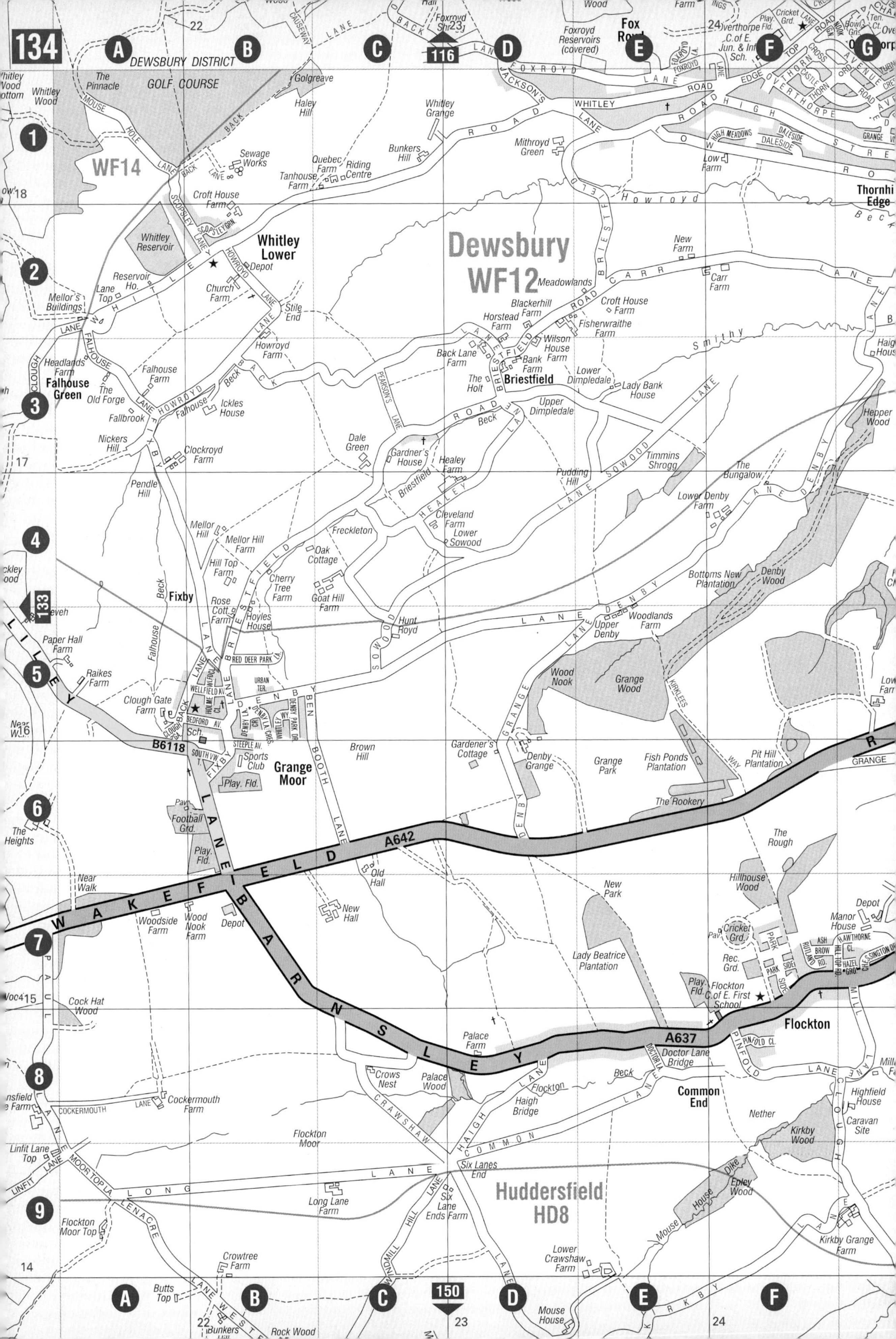

DEWSBURY DISTRICT GOLF COURSE
The Pinnacle
Whitley Wood
WF14
Dewsbury WF12
Whitley Lower
Whitley Reservoir
Falhouse Green
Fixby
Grange Moor
Briestfield
Flockton
Common End
Huddersfield HD8
Thornhill Edge
Fox Royd
Foxroyd Reservoirs (covered)
A642
A637
B6118
WAKEFIELD ROAD
BARNSLEY ROAD
Denby Grange
Grange Wood
Denby Wood
Upper Denby
Woodlands Farm
Lady Beatrice Plantation
Flockton Moor
Six Lanes End
Long Lane Farm
Crowtree Farm
Cockermouth Farm
Linfit Lane Top
Flockton Moor Top
Kirkby Grange Farm
Epley Wood
Kirkby Wood
Lower Crawshaw Farm
Palace Farm
Palace Wood
Crows Nest
Haigh Bridge
New Hall
Old Hall
New Park
Brown Hill
Grange Park
Fish Ponds Plantation
Pit Hill Plantation
The Rookery
The Rough
Hillhouse Wood
Hepper Wood
Timmins Shrogg
Lower Denby Farm
Bottoms New Plantation
Hunt Royd
Healey Farm
Cleveland Farm
Lower Sowood
Dale Green
Gardner's House
Upper Dimpledale
Lower Dimpledale
Lady Bank House
Carr Farm
New Farm
Croft House Farm
Fisherwraithe Farm
Mithroyd Green
Low Farm
Whitley Grange
Bunkers Hill
Quebec Farm
Riding Centre
Tanhouse Farm
Sewage Works
Croft House Farm
Golgreave
Haley Hill
Howroyd Farm
Ickles House
Clockroyd Farm
Nickers Hill
Pendle Hill
Mellor Hill
Mellor Hill Farm
Hill Top Farm
Rose Cott. Farm
Cherry Tree Farm
Oak Cottage
Goat Hill Farm
Freckleton
Paper Hall Farm
Raikes Farm
Clough Gate Farm
Sports Club
Football Grd.
Woodside Farm
Wood Nook Farm
Cock Hat Wood
The Heights
Near Walk
Mellor's Buildings
Reservoir Ho.
Lane Top
Church Farm
Stile End
Headlands Farm
The Old Forge
Fallbrook
Flockton C. of E. First School
Manor House
Highfield House
Caravan Site
Nether
Doctor Lane Bridge
Gardener's Cottage
Wood Nook
116
133
150

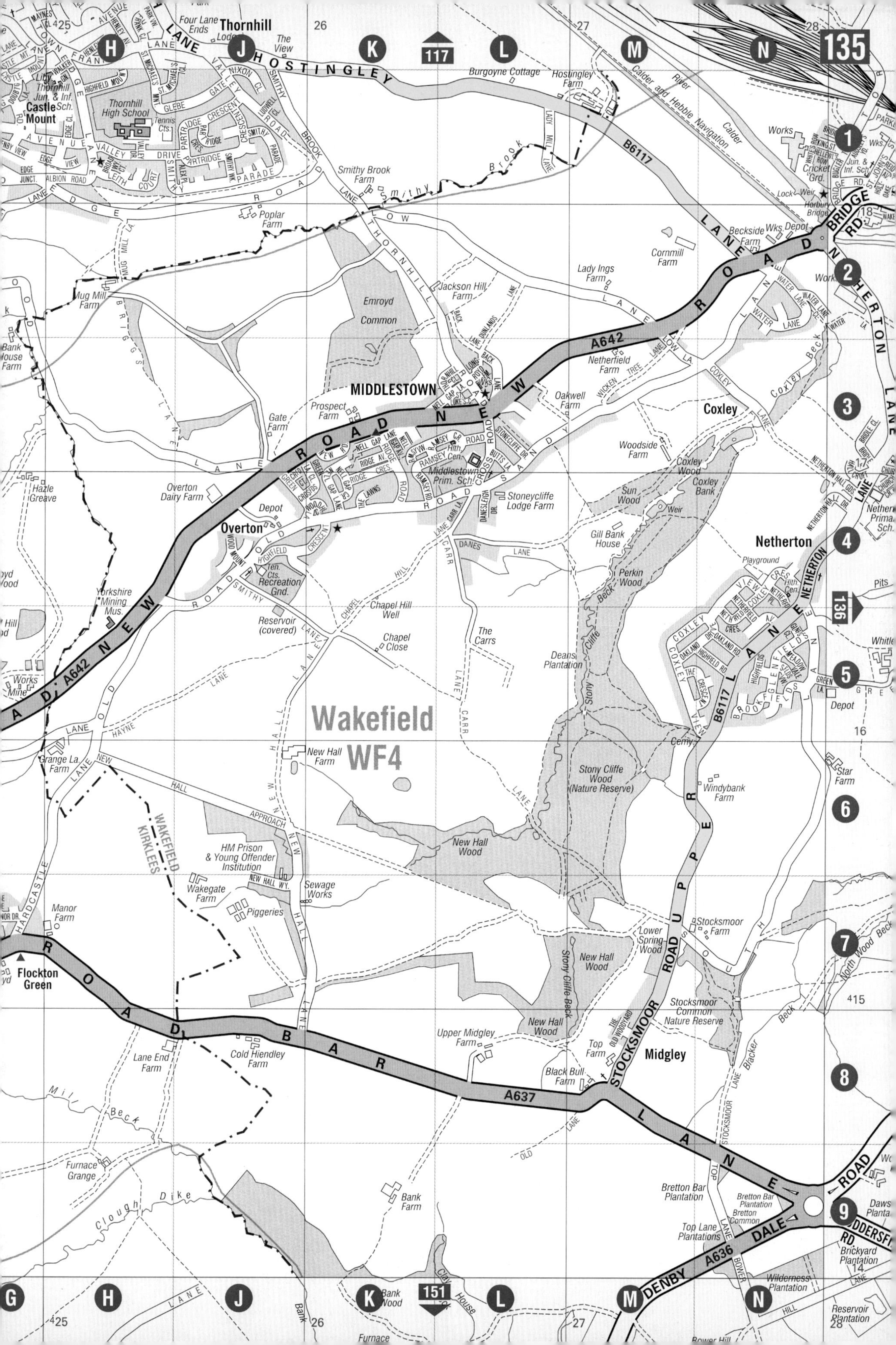
Thornhill
Four Lane Ends
The View
Burgoyne Cottage
Hostingley Farm
HOSTINGLEY LANE
Castle Mount
Thornhill High School
Thornhill Jun. & Inf. Sch.
Calder and Hebble Navigation
River Calder
B6117
Works
Horbury Bridge
Smithy Brook Farm
Smithy Brook
Poplar Farm
EDGE ROAD
LOW LANE
THORNHILL LANE
Beckside Farm
Cornmill Farm
Lady Ings Farm
Jackson Hill Farm
Emroyd Common
Mug Mill Farm
BRIGGS LANE
A642
NEW ROAD
Netherfield Farm
MIDDLESTOWN
Prospect Farm
Gate Farm
Oakwell Farm
Coxley
Woodside Farm
Middlestown Prim. Sch.
Overton Dairy Farm
Stoneycliffe Lodge Farm
Coxley Wood
Coxley Bank
Sun Wood
Hazle Greave
Depot
Overton
Gill Bank House
Netherton
Recreation Gnd.
Perkin Wood
Yorkshire Mining Mus.
Chapel Hill Well
Reservoir (covered)
Chapel Close
The Carrs
Deans Plantation
Works
Mine
Wakefield WF4
New Hall Farm
Grange La. Farm
Stony Cliffe Wood (Nature Reserve)
Windybank Farm
Star Farm
HM Prison & Young Offender Institution
New Hall Wood
WAKEFIELD
KIRKLEES
Wakegate Farm
Piggeries
Sewage Works
Manor Farm
Stocksmoor Farm
Lower Spring Wood
New Hall Wood
Flockton Green
Stocksmoor Common Nature Reserve
New Hall Wood
Upper Midgley Farm
Lane End Farm
Cold Hiendley Farm
Top Farm
Midgley
Black Bull Farm
A637
BAR LANE
STOCKSMOOR ROAD
UPPER ROAD
Mill Beck
Furnace Grange
Clough Dike
Bank Farm
Bretton Bar Plantation
Top Lane Plantations
A636
DENBY DALE ROAD
Brickyard Plantation
Wilderness Plantation
Reservoir Plantation
Bank Wood
Clay House
Furnace
117
136
151
H J K L M N
G H J K L M N
1 2 3 4 5 6 7 8 9
25 26 27 28
415
16
14

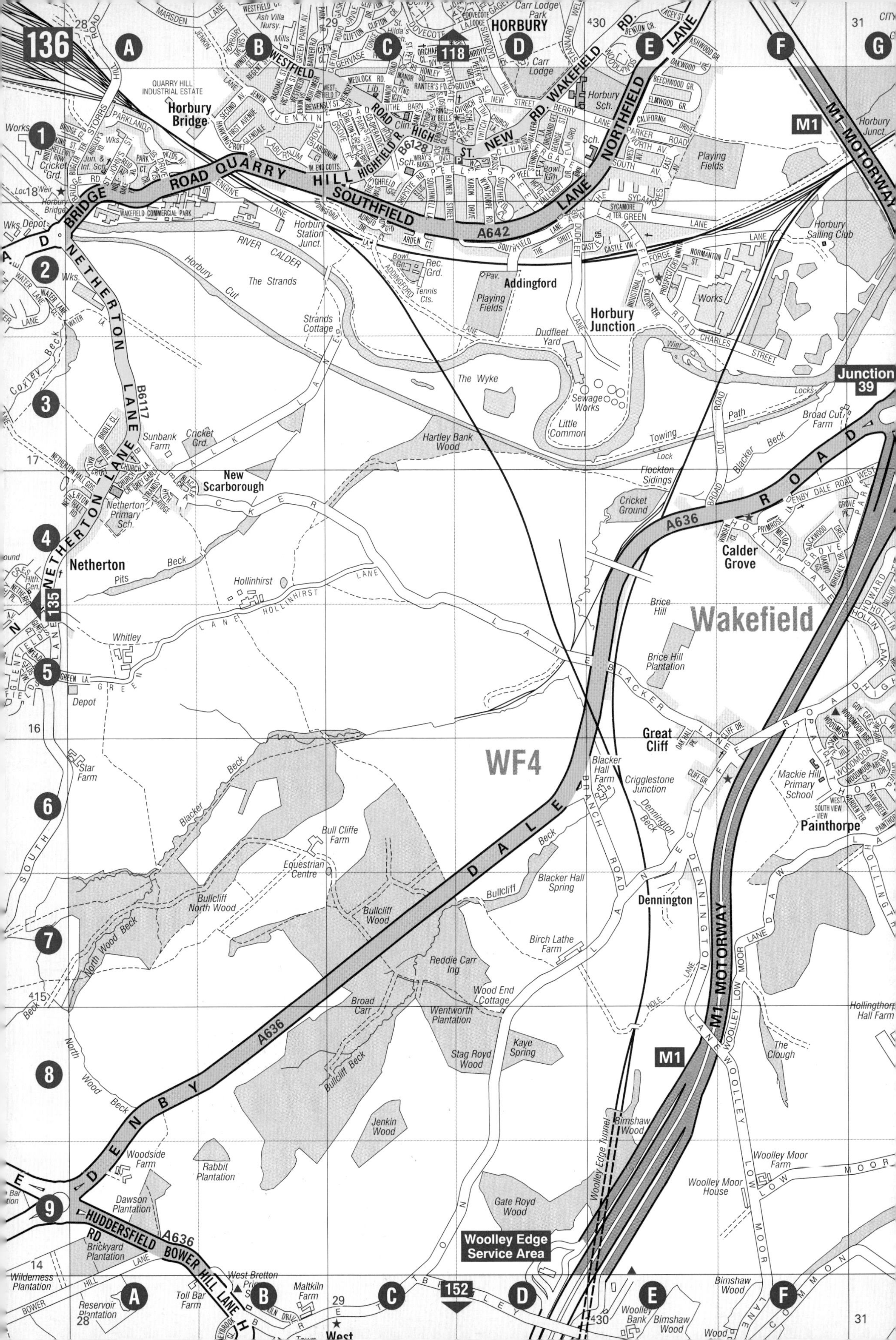

136
118
135
152
A
B
C
D
E
F
G
1
2
3
4
5
6
7
8
9
HORBURY
Horbury Bridge
Quarry Hill Industrial Estate
Westfield
Carr Lodge Park
Carr Lodge
Horbury Sch.
QUARRY HILL ROAD
SOUTHFIELD LANE
NORTHFIELD LANE
WAKEFIELD RD.
NEW RD.
HIGH ST.
B6128
A642
B6117
NETHERTON LANE
BRIDGE RD.
Cricket Grd.
Horbury Bridge
Wakefield Commercial Park
Horbury Station Junct.
River Calder
Horbury Cut
The Strands
Strands Cottage
Addingford
Playing Fields
Horbury Junction
Dudfleet Yard
Sewage Works
Little Common
The Wyke
Towing Path
Hartley Bank Wood
Flockton Sidings
Cricket Ground
Horbury Sailing Club
Horbury Junct.
Broad Cut Farm
Junction 39
M1
M1 MOTORWAY
A636
DENBY DALE ROAD
Calder Grove
Wakefield
Brice Hill
Brice Hill Plantation
Great Cliff
Blacker Hall Farm
Crigglestone Junction
Dennington
Mackie Hill Primary School
Painthorpe
WF4
New Scarborough
Netherton Primary Sch.
Netherton
Sunbank Farm
Cricket Grd.
Hollinhirst
HOLLINHIRST LANE
Whitley
GREEN LA.
Depot
Star Farm
Coxley Beck
Blacker Beck
Bull Cliffe Farm
Equestrian Centre
Bullcliff North Wood
Bullcliff Wood
North Wood Beck
Blacker Hall Spring
Birch Lathe Farm
Reddie Carr Ing
Wood End Cottage
Broad Carr
Wentworth Plantation
Stag Royd Wood
Kaye Spring
Bullcliff Beck
Jenkin Wood
Woodside Farm
Rabbit Plantation
Dawson Plantation
Gate Royd Wood
Woolley Edge Service Area
Woolley Edge Tunnel
Bimshaw Wood
Woolley Moor Farm
Woolley Moor House
WOOLLEY LOW MOOR LANE
The Clough
Hollingthorpe Hall Farm
HUDDERSFIELD RD.
BOWER HILL LANE
Brickyard Plantation
Wilderness Plantation
Reservoir Plantation
Toll Bar Farm
West Bretton
Maltkiln Farm
Woolley Bank
Bimshaw Wood
COMMON LANE
28
29
430
31
18
17
16
415
14

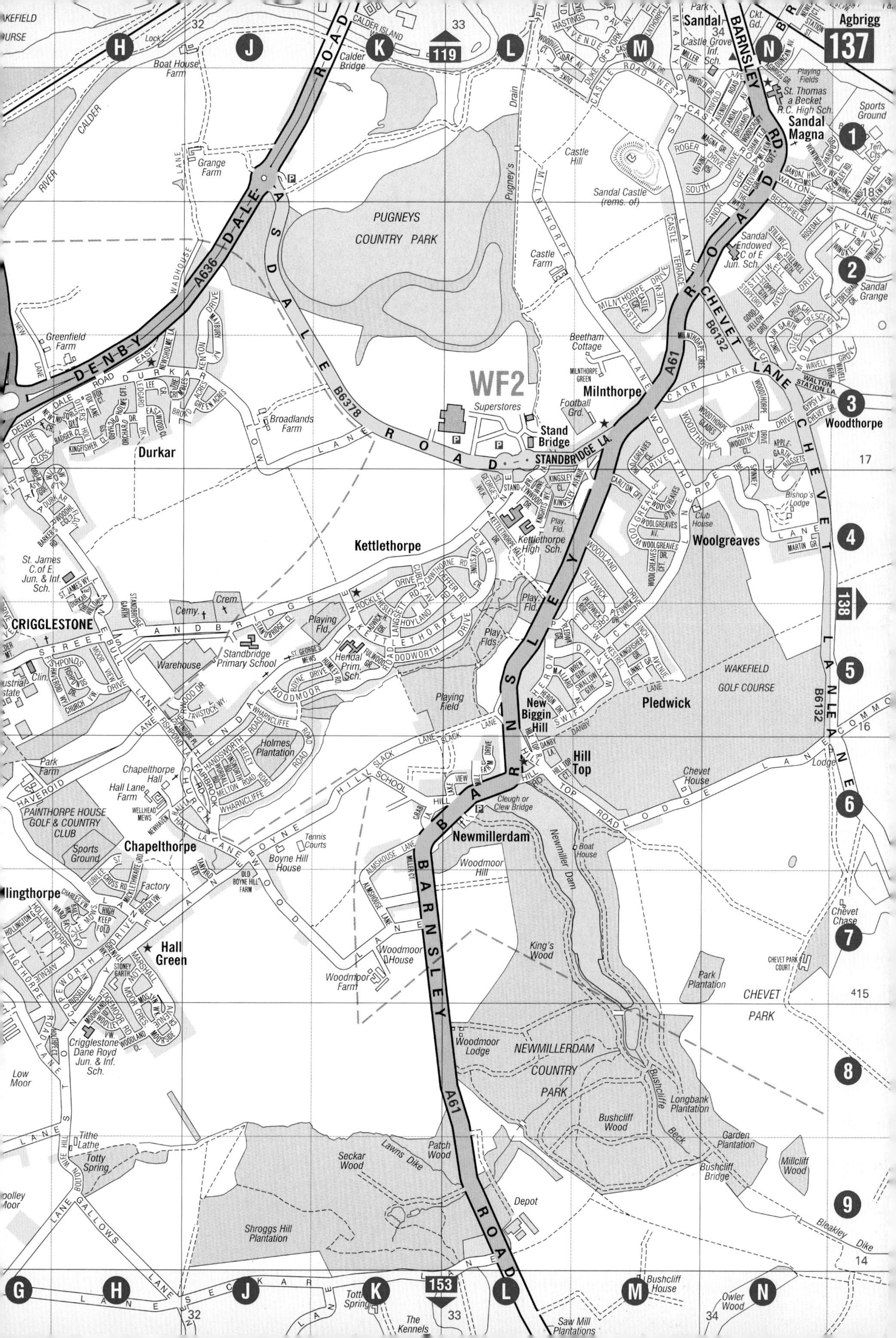

Agbrigg
Sandal
Sandal Magna
St. Thomas a Becket R.C. High Sch.
Castle Grove Inf. Sch.
Sports Ground
Playing Fields
Castle Hill
Sandal Castle (rems. of)
Sandal Endowed C of E Jun. Sch.
Sandal Grange
PUGNEYS COUNTRY PARK
Calder Bridge
Boat House Farm
Grange Farm
RIVER CALDER
Greenfield Farm
Castle Farm
Beetham Cottage
WF2
Milnthorpe
Superstores
Stand Bridge
Football Grd.
Broadlands Farm
Durkar
Woodthorpe
Bishop's Lodge
Club House
Woolgreaves
Kettlethorpe
Kettlethorpe High Sch.
St. James C.of E. Jun. & Inf. Sch.
CRIGGLESTONE
Cemy.
Crem.
Playing Fld.
Standbridge Primary School
Warehouse
Hendal Prim. Sch.
Play. Fld.
Play. Flds.
Playing Field
New Biggin Hill
Pledwick
WAKEFIELD GOLF COURSE
Hill Top
Chevet House
Holmes Plantation
Park Farm
Chapelthorpe Hall
Hall Lane Farm
PAINTHORPE HOUSE GOLF & COUNTRY CLUB
Sports Ground
Chapelthorpe
Factory
Boyne Hill House
Tennis Courts
Cleugh or Clew Bridge
Newmillerdam
Boat House
Newmiller Dam
Woodmoor Hill
Old Boyne Hill Farm
Hall Green
Chevet Chase
King's Wood
Woodmoor House
Woodmoor Farm
Park Plantation
CHEVET PARK
Chevet Park Court
Crigglestone Dane Royd Jun. & Inf. Sch.
Low Moor
Woodmoor Lodge
NEWMILLERDAM COUNTRY PARK
Bushcliff Wood
Longbank Plantation
Bushcliffe Beck
Garden Plantation
Millcliff Wood
Bushcliff Bridge
Tithe Lathe
Totty Spring
Seckar Wood
Lawns Dike
Patch Wood
Depot
Shroggs Hill Plantation
Blackley Dike
Bushcliff House
Owler Wood
The Kennels
Saw Mill Plantations
BARNSLEY ROAD
A61
DENBY DALE ROAD
A636
ASDALE ROAD
B6378
CHEVET LANE
B6132
STANDBRIDGE LA.
119
138
153

Agbrigg
Sandal Magna
WF1
Crofton West Jn.
120
Oakenshaw Farm
Oakenshaw South Junc.
Crofton Water Pollution Control Centre
Brand Hill
CROFTON
Shay Hill
Shay La. Inf. School
Crofton High School
Sandal Grange
Sandal Grange Farm
Elmwood House
Low Lock House
WALTON STATION LA.
Woodthorpe
WALTON
Walton Jun. Sch.
Sports Ground
B6378
Walton Grove Inf. Sch.
Thorntree Farm
Brook Farm
Highwood Farm
Hare Park Junction
Hare Park High Wood
Thorntree Hill
Hare Park Wood
Wakefield
Walton Common Farm
Overtown Grange Farm
The Balk
Overtown
Rose Farm
The Old Barn
WF2
Longacre
Brockswood Court
Water Gate
Hotel (Club Ho.)
WATERTON PARK GOLF COURSE
Walton Park
137
New Park Bridge
Stone Heaps
Stone Heaps Plantation
Stubbs Wood
The Heronry
Green Lane Plantation
Barnsley Canal (disused)
Chevet Chase
Chevet Hill
Clay Royd Bridge
HAW PARK
Sailing Club
Jetty
B6132
Chevet Viaduct
WINTERSETT RESERVOIR
Brickyard Plantation
Rough Bottom Plantation
Blue Bridge
COLD HIENDLEY RESERVOIR
Chevet Grange
Haw Park Bridge
Bleakley Bridge
Millcliff Wood
Sewage Works
Rose Farm
Rose Cottage
Cold Hiendley Bridge
Manor Ho.
Springfield Farm
Cold Hiendley
Ivy Grange Farm
Bleakley Dike
154
Monckton Manor

121
155
140
DONCASTER ROAD
A638
Spring Hill
Windmill Hill
Foulby
Foulby Farm
New Crofton
Crofton Jun. Sch.
Crofton Inf. Sch.
Bedford Farm
Hill Top Farm
Birkwood Farm
School Ho. Farm
West End Farm
Obelisk Lodge
Top Park Wood
OBELISK PARK
Priory Wood
Foulby Park
Lower Lake
Mill Piece
Planetree Hill
Middle Lake
Joiners Shop Plantation
Nostell Priory
The Little House
NOSTELL PARK (Deer Park)
Upper Lake
The Willows
St. Oswald's Plantation
Nursy.
Wragby Lo.
The Cottages
Cricket Grd.
Wakefield Ind. Jun. Sch.
Vicarage
Sewage Works
Wragby Manor Farm
GARMIL LA.
B6273
The Villas
LONG ROW
STATION COTTAGES
Horncastle Wood
Garmil Head
Fishpond Plantation
GARMIL HEAD LANE
Horncastle Farm
Horncastle Hill
Lane Ends Fm.
Hemsworth Lane Ends
Depot
Saltingley Grange
ANGLERS COUNTRY PARK
Wintersett
Rose Cottage
WF4
Reservoir Farm
LONG BACK LANE
MOORHOUSE LANE
SWINE LANE
DAM LANE
Ponds
Laycock Wood
Horncastle View
Rec. Grd.
FITZWILLIAM
Ings Farm
NEWSTEAD LANE
B6428
Horncastle Farm
Common Ing
Newstead Grange
Newstead Hall
Newstead
Pontefract WF9
Kinsley Carr Farm
Moat
RYHILL
HAVERCROFT
Sports Grd.
Cemy.
Mulberry Farm
Play Fld.
Westfield
West Field
RYHILL IND. EST.
Liby.
Havercroft Jun. & Inf. School
Hlth. Cen.
Manor Farm
Green Well
COW LANE
STATION LANE
FERRY TOP LANE

A
B
C
D
E
F
G
41
42
43
44
18
17
16
15
14
1
2
3
4
5
6
7
8
9
122
139
156
Little Went Bridge
Lodge Hill Plantation
Brick Villa Farm
Nostell Low Farm
Top Farm (Museum)
West Hardwick
Hilltop Farm
Gamekeepers Cottage
South Ings Field
Owlett Hall
Manor Farm
Manor Trust Farm
Ackworth Old Hall
Mill Piece
Hardwick
Went Beck
Wakefield
The Bushes
Hessle Cottage
Joiners Shop Plantation
Engine Wood
Roebuck Wood
Ash Wood
Hessle Farm
NOSTELL PARK (Deer Park)
Chestnut Wood
WF4
Hessle Hall
Hessle
Ackworth School
Wragby
Longley Wood
Playing Field
Cricket Grd.
Sewage Works
Wragby Manor Farm
Constitution Hill
Constitution Hill Farm
Ackworth Carr Br.
Longley Edge
Wragby Grange
Hessle Cottage
Brackenhill Common
Brackenhill Farm
Hanging Bank Plantation
Taylor Wood
Brackenhill Quarries
Offley Bridge
Depot
Council Yard
Brackenhill Bridge
Garmil Head
Fishpond Plantation
Hessle Beck
Sewage Works
Brackenhill
Poplar Farm
Kinsley Green Farm
Play. Fld.
Elmcroft Farm
Works
Subway
Cricket Grd.
Lane Ends Fm.
Fitzwilliam First Sch.
Hemsworth Lane Ends
ACKWORTH MOOR TOP
Rhyddings Farm
Moor Top School
Oaktree School
Play. Fld.
Hill Top Farm
Spts. Grd.
FITZWILLIAM
Bowl. Grn.
Kinsley Drift Mine
Poultry Houses
Outgang
Schole Bridge
Spring Wood
Spring Wood Farm
Fitzwilliam
Rec. Grd.
Rose Lane Farm Poultry Houses
Bingley Spring Wood
Railway Farm Poultry Houses
Kinsley Prim. Sch.
Hoyle Mill Farm
Ings Farm
Railway Farm
KINSLEY COMMON
Hemsworth Turkey Farms
Hoyle Mill Dam
Hagg Wood
Mill Road Farm
Stadium
Snipery Farm Poultry Houses
Kinsley Carr Farm
Kinsley
Works
The Hatchery
Anthony's Quarry Wood
Rec. Grd.
Moat
The Snipery
Hagg Wood
Marsh Whin Covert
Works
Hemsworth Water Park
Kinsley Common Farm
Willow Tree Farm
Hemsworth Marsh
Marsh Farm
Marsh Whin Farm
Common Side Farm
VALE HEAD PARK
Golf Course
Studley House Farm
Hollins
DONCASTER ROAD
WAKEFIELD ROAD
A638
B6428
B6421
B6273
A628
CROSS HANDS LA.
WENT LANE
OFFLEY LANE
HEMSWORTH LANE
GARMIL HEAD LANE
ACKWORTH RD.
PURSTON
PONTEFRACT A628
BARNSLEY ROAD
BARNSLEY RD.
PONTEFRACT ROAD
HEMSWORTH A628 BY-PASS
HOYLE MILL ROAD
ROSE LANE
KING ROYD LA.
HESSLE COMMON
HESSLE LANE
TOP ROAD
NEW LANE
ENGINE LANE
ROYD MOOR LANE
STATION ROAD

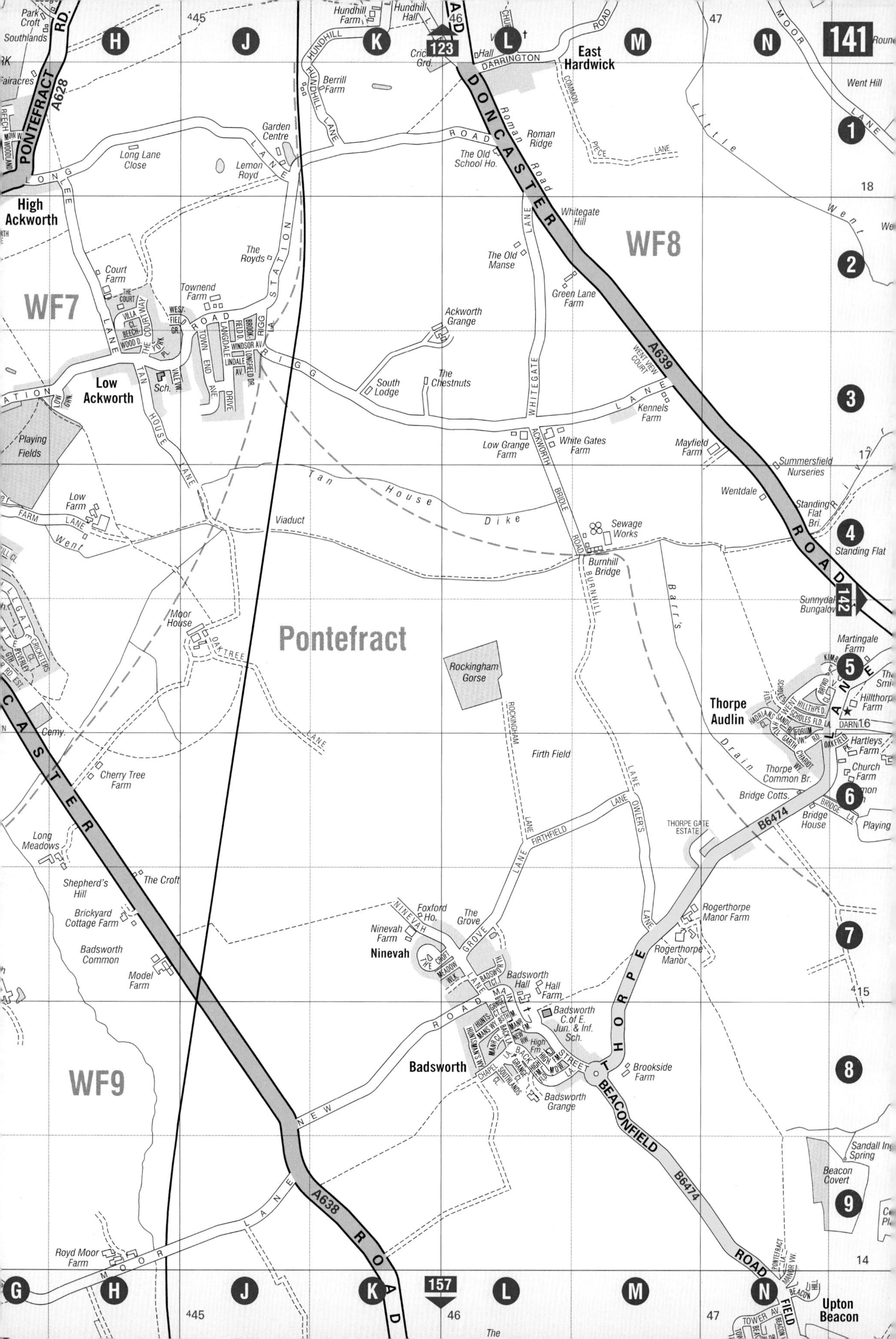
High Ackworth
Low Ackworth
East Hardwick
Pontefract
Thorpe Audlin
Ninevah
Badsworth
Upton Beacon
WF7
WF8
WF9
Park Croft
Southlands
Fairacres
Hundhill Farm
Hundhill Hall
Berrill Farm
Garden Centre
Long Lane Close
Lemon Royd
The Old School Ho.
Roman Ridge
Went Hill
Whitegate Hill
The Royds
Court Farm
Townend Farm
The Old Manse
Green Lane Farm
Ackworth Grange
South Lodge
The Chestnuts
Kennels Farm
Low Grange Farm
White Gates Farm
Mayfield Farm
Summersfield Nurseries
Playing Fields
Low Farm
Viaduct
Tan House Dike
Wentdale
Standing Flat Bri.
Standing Flat
Sewage Works
Burnhill Bridge
Sunnydale Bungalow
Moor House
Rockingham Gorse
Martingale Farm
Hillthorpe Farm
Cemy.
Firth Field
Hartleys Farm
Church Farm
Cherry Tree Farm
Thorpe Common Br.
Bridge Cotts.
Bridge House
Thorpe Gate Estate
Long Meadows
The Croft
Shepherd's Hill
Brickyard Cottage Farm
Foxford Ho.
The Grove
Ninevah Farm
Rogerthorpe Manor Farm
Rogerthorpe Manor
Badsworth Common
Model Farm
Badsworth Hall
Hall Farm
Badsworth C. of E. Jun. & Inf. Sch.
High Fm.
Brookside Farm
Badsworth Grange
Sandall Ings Spring
Beacon Covert
Royd Moor Farm
A628
A639
A638
B6474
Doncaster Road
Pontefract Rd.
Darrington Road
Long Lane
Station Road
Rigg Lane
Tan House Lane
Whitegate Lane
Ackworth Bridle Road
Burnhill Lane
Oaktree Lane
Rockingham Lane
Firthfield Lane
Owler's Lane
Ninevah Lane
Main St.
New Road
Thorpe Lane
Beaconfield Road
Moor Lane
Farm Lane
Hundhill Lane
Common Piece Lane
Roman Road
Little Went
Went
Barr's Drain
123
142
157
H
J
K
L
M
N
G
1
2
3
4
5
6
7
8
9
445
46
47
18
17
16
15
14

124
158
141
Went Hill
Dale Field
Long Plantation
Kirkdike Plantation
Horse Race Closes
Brockadale Plantation
Wenthill Plantation
Wentbridge Ings
Jackson's Hill
Timbertops Equestrian Centre
Swiss Cottage
Jackson's Hill Pantation
Brockadale House
Brockadale Crags
Brockadale Houses
Brockadale Oaks Farm
BROCKADALE PLANTATION
Rectory Farm
Went Bridge
Wentbridge
Castle Hill Enclosure
Brockadale Bridge
Smeaton Crags
Wentbridge Viaduct
Thorp Marsh
Ings Ho.
Little Plantation
Sayle's Plantation
Depot
Summersfield Nurseries
Manor House
WENT EDGE ROAD
GREAT NORTH ROAD
A1
B6474
A639
DONCASTER ROAD
WENTBRIDGE LANE
JACKSON'S LANE
Standing Flat Bridge
Standing Flat
Went Edge
Broom Hill
Thorpe Audlin
Sunnydale Bungalow
Martingale Farm
Thorp Plantation
Peartree Field
WF8
The Smithy
Hillthorpe Farm
Hillthorpe
Hillthorpe Ho.
Pear Tree Farm
PEARTREE FIELD LANE
Hillthorpe Cotts.
Gingerbread Plantation
Hartleys Farm
Went Farm
Church Farm
Thorpe Manor
Manor Farm
Far Thorpe Farm
Common Farm
Hepworth Farm
Pontefract
The Bungalow
Shooters Hill Farm
Upper Wells Lair
Thorpe Common Br.
Bridge House
Playing Fld.
Morning Field Farm
Thorpe Grange Farm
Salliwell Field
Rose Cottage
Poultry Farm
Barnsdale
Mutton Hall Farm
Walton Wood Cottage
Burnshaw
Packsaddle Plantation
Barnsdale Services
Bullcarmires
Walton Wood Ho.
WF9
Walton Wood
Sandall Ing Spring
Glebe Farm
Beacon Covert
Coal Pit Plantation
Tower
Upton Beacon
Barnsdale

WOMERSLEY PARK
Castle Farm
Castle Farm Cottage
Castle Hill Wood
The Bungalow
Oak Plantation
Belt Plantation
Beckclose Wood
Smeaton Leys
Pumping Station
LEYS LANE
Smeaton Bridge
Birka Drain
Grove Farm
Grove Bridge
Forlorn Hope Farm
Long Crag
Smeaton Pasture
River Went
Little Smeaton
Windy Ridge
Mount Pleasant
Stubbs Bridge
Water Mill Farm
Ford
Hodge Bri.
Riverside Farm
Manor House Farm
Playing Field
Sch.
Rectory Farm
Cemy.
Low Farm
Manor House
Kirk Smeaton
Pinfold Cross
Willow Bridge
Doncaster DN6
Little Bottom Plantation
NORTON & KIRK SMEATON ROAD
SPITTLERUSH LANE
River Went
West Field
Westfield House
FLEA LANE
CLIFF HILL ROAD
DONCASTER SELBY
Broomfield Plantation
Highfield Farm
WESTFIELD LANE
Westfield Farm
Southfield Plantation
Cliff Hill
TREE LANE
Barnsdale Bar Quarry
Cusworth Hill
Old Whin Fox Covert
Windmill Cotts.
Windhill Plantation
Black Clump
White Ley Plantation
South Field
Low Pasture Rein
Campsmount School
Playing Fields
School Bungalow
WOODDLE HOLE LA.
Woodlle Hole Plantation
Limestone Quarry
FOX COVERT ROAD OR WHIN COVERT LANE
Middle Pasture Plantation
NORTH PARK
Barnsdale Wood
Campsmount Home Farm
LEY ROAD
Warren Plantation
CAMPSMOUNT PARK
Barnsdale
Barnsdale Warren House
Barnsdale Cottages
Freestone Quarry Plantation
SOUTH PARK
Campsmount Cotts.
Bull Close

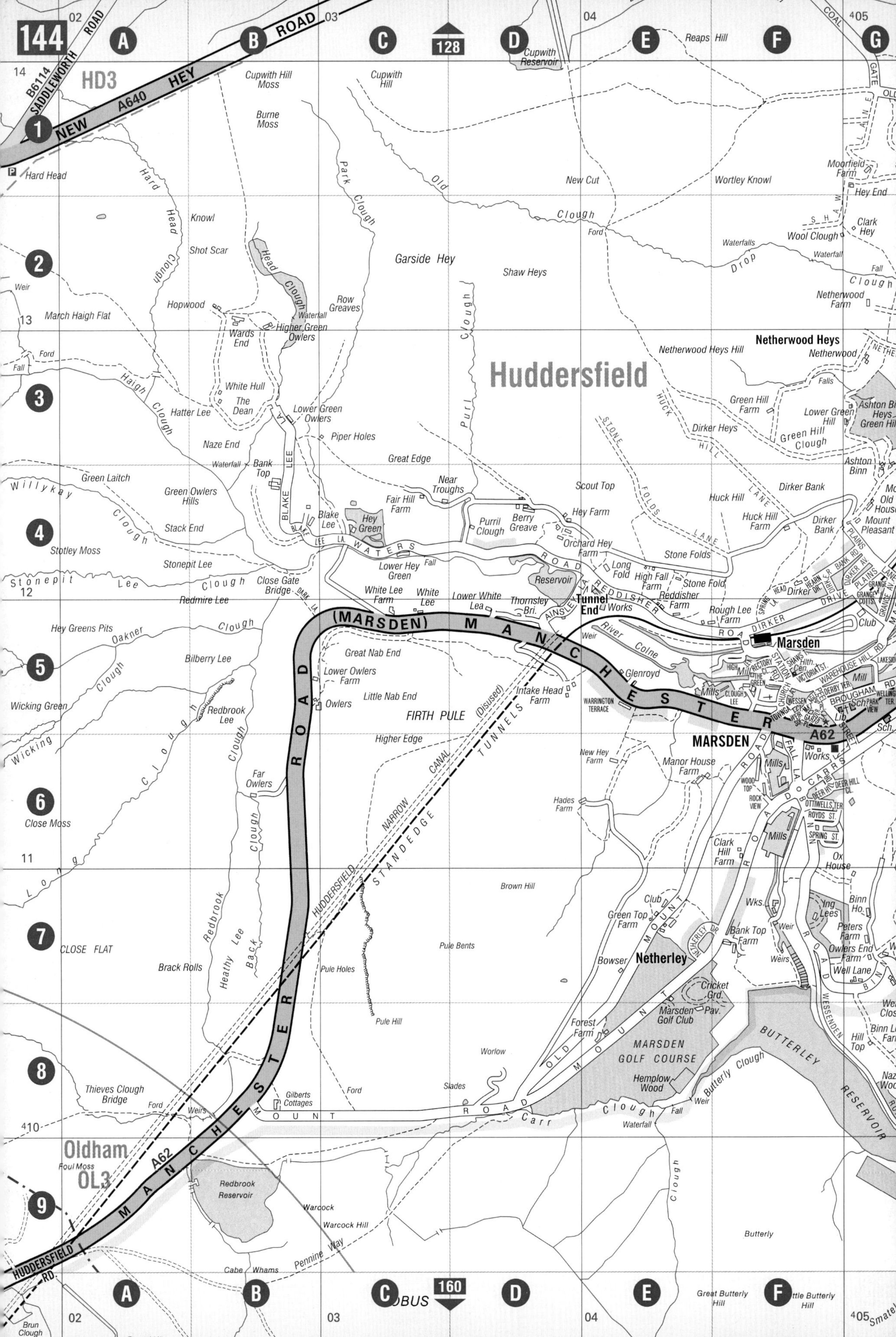
HD3
NEW A640 HEY ROAD
B6114 SADDLEWORTH ROAD
128
Cupwith Reservoir
Reaps Hill
Cupwith Hill Moss
Cupwith Hill
Burne Moss
Hard Head
Knowl
Shot Scar
Park Clough
Old Clough
New Cut
Wortley Knowl
Moorfield Farm
Hey End
Clark Hey
Wool Clough
Garside Hey
Shaw Heys
Waterfalls
Drop
Netherwood Farm
Weir
March Haigh Flat
Hopwood
Row Greaves
Higher Green Owlers
Wards End
Ford
Fall
Netherwood Heys Hill
Netherwood Heys
Netherwood
Huddersfield
White Hull
The Dean
Haigh Clough
Hatter Lee
Lower Green Owlers
Piper Holes
Purl Clough
Green Hill Farm
Lower Green Hill
Ashton Binn Heys
Green Hill Clough
Dirker Heys
Naze End
Bank Top
Great Edge
Near Troughs
Scout Top
Huck Hill Lane
Stone Folds Lane
Green Laitch
Willykay Clough
Green Owlers Hills
Stack End
Blake Lee Lane
Blake Lee
Hey Green
Fair Hill Farm
Purril Clough
Berry Greave
Hey Farm
Orchard Hey Farm
Huck Hill
Huck Hill Farm
Dirker Bank
Mount Pleasant
Stotley Moss
Waters Road
Lower Hey Green
Long Fold
High Fall Farm
Stone Folds
Stonepit Lee
Stonepit Lee Clough
Close Gate Bridge
Dark La.
White Lee Farm
White Lee
Lower White Lea
Thornsley Bri.
Reservoir
Reddisher Road
Reddisher Farm
Tunnel End
Works
Rough Lee Farm
Dirker Drive
Redmire Lee
Hey Greens Pits
Oakner Clough
(MARSDEN) MANCHESTER ROAD
River Colne
Marsden
Bilberry Lee
Great Nab End
Lower Owlers Farm
Glenroyd
Wicking Green
Owlers
Little Nab End
Intake Head Farm
Warrington Terrace
Redbrook Lee
FIRTH PULE
Higher Edge
Canal (Disused)
Tunnels
MARSDEN
A62
Wicking Clough
Long Clough
New Hey Farm
Manor House Farm
Far Owlers
Close Moss
Hades Farm
Narrow Canal
Standedge
Huddersfield
Clark Hill Farm
Mills
Ox House
Brown Hill
Club
Green Top Farm
Wks.
Bank Top Farm
Ing Lees
Peters Farm
Owlers End Farm
Well Lane
Close Flat
Brack Rolls
Redbrook
Heathy Lee Back
Pule Bents
Pule Holes
Bowser
Netherley
Cricket Grd.
Marsden Golf Club
Pav.
Pule Hill
Forest Farm
Old Mount Road
Marsden Golf Course
Hemplow Wood
Butterley Reservoir
Butterly Clough
Worlow
Thieves Clough Bridge
Gilberts Cottages
Slades
Mount Road
Carr Clough
Waterfall
Oldham OL3
Foul Moss
Redbrook Reservoir
Warcock
Warcock Hill
Pennine Way
Butterly
Huddersfield Rd.
Cabe Whams
160
Great Butterly Hill
Little Butterly Hill
Brun Clough

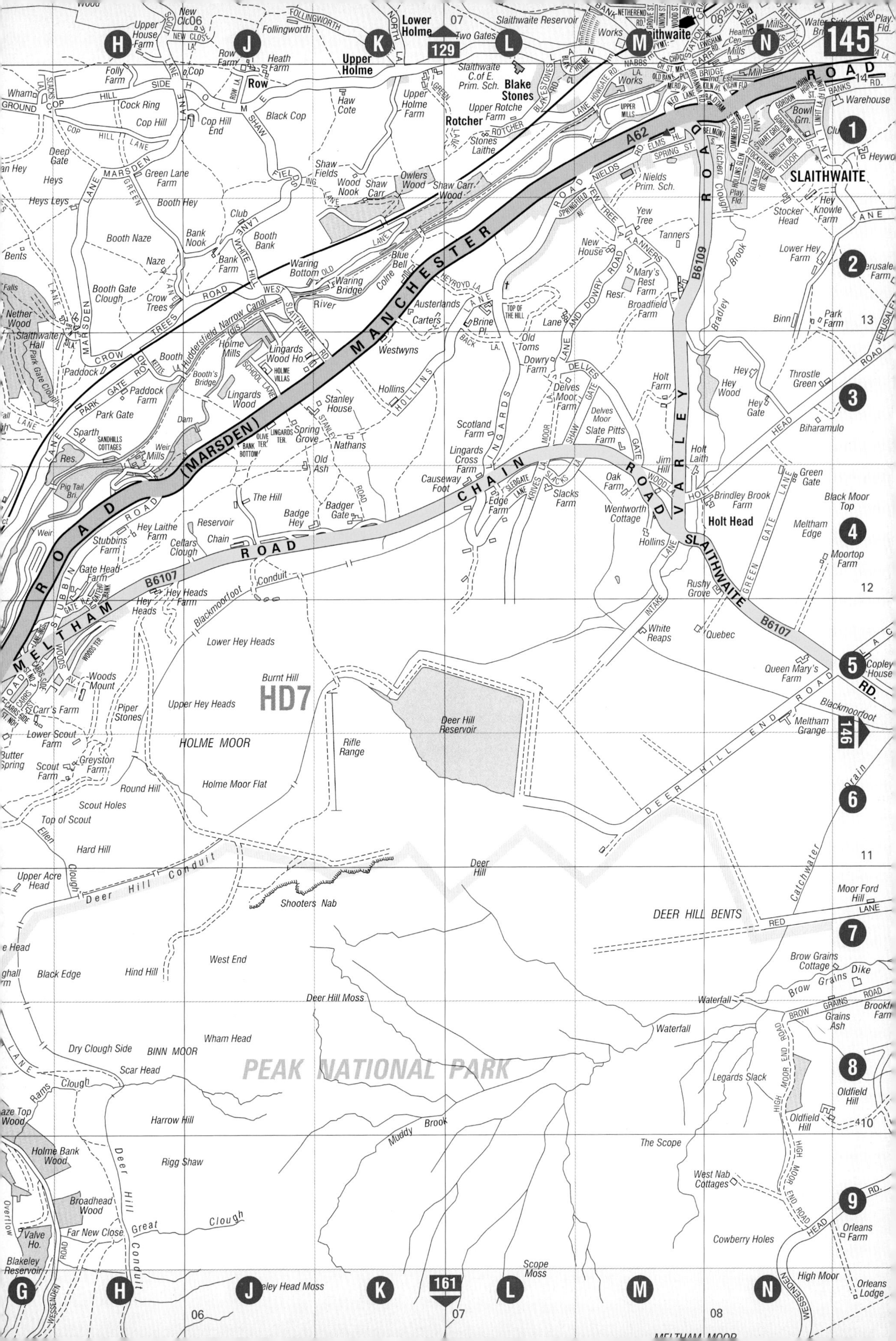

SLAITHWAITE
Slaithwaite Reservoir
Lower Holme
Upper Holme
129
Two Gates
Follingworth
Upper House Farm
Folly Farm
Row
Heath Farm
Cop
Wham
Cock Ring
Cop Hill
Cop Hill End
Black Cop
Haw Cote
Upper Holme Farm
Slaithwaite C.of E. Prim. Sch.
Blake Stones
Upper Rotche Farm
Rotcher
Stones Laithe
Deep Gate
Heys
Heys Leys
Green Lane Farm
Booth Hey
Booth Naze
Naze
Bank Nook
Booth Bank
Club
Bank Farm
Shaw Fields
Wood Nook
Shaw Carr
Owlers Wood
Shaw Carr Wood
Bents
Booth Gate Clough
Crow Trees
Waring Bottom
Waring Bridge
Blue Bell
Colne
River
Huddersfield Narrow Canal (dis.)
Nether Wood
Slaithwaite Hall
Park Gate Clough
Paddock
Booth
Holme Mills
Lingards Wood Ho.
Holme Villas
Booth's Bridge
Paddock Farm
Park Gate
Lingards Wood
Sparth
Sandhills Cottages
Res.
Weir
Mills
Pig Tail Bri.
Dam
Bank Bottom
Olive Ter.
Lingards Ter.
Spring Grove
Stanley House
Nathans
Old Ash
Austerlands
Carters
Westwyns
Brine Pl.
Top of the Hill
Old Toms
Hollins
Dowry Farm
Lane
Delves Moor Farm
Delves Moor
Slate Pitts Farm
Scotland Farm
Lingards Cross Farm
Causeway Foot
Edge Farm
Slacks Farm
Oak Farm
Wentworth Cottage
Hollins
Jim Hill
Holt Farm
Holt Laith
Brindley Brook Farm
Holt Head
Green Gate
Black Moor Top
Meltham Edge
Moortop Farm
Nields
Nields Prim. Sch.
Yew Tree
Tanners
New House
Mary's Rest Farm
Resr.
Broadfield Farm
Stocker Head
Hey Knowle Farm
Lower Hey Farm
Jerusalem Farm
Binn
Park Farm
Hey
Hey Wood
Hey Gate
Throstle Green
Biharamulo
Bradley Brook
Kitchen Clough
Play. Fld.
Bowl Grn.
Warehouse
Heywood
Upper Mills
Works
Ind. Est.
A62
MANCHESTER ROAD (MARSDEN)
B6109 VARLEY ROAD
CHAIN ROAD
SLAITHWAITE ROAD B6107
MELTHAM ROAD B6107
Reservoir
Chain
Cellars Clough
The Hill
Badge Hey
Badger Gate
Hey Laithe Farm
Stubbins Farm
Gate Head Farm
Hey Heads
Hey Heads Farm
Blackmoorfoot Conduit
Lower Hey Heads
Burnt Hill
HD7
Upper Hey Heads
Woods Mount
Carr's Farm
Piper Stones
Lower Scout Farm
Butter Spring
Scout Farm
Greyston Farm
HOLME MOOR
Holme Moor Flat
Round Hill
Scout Holes
Top of Scout
Hard Hill
Ellen Clough
Rifle Range
Deer Hill Reservoir
White Reaps
Rushy Grove
Quebec
Queen Mary's Farm
Copley House
Meltham Grange
Blackmoorfoot
146
DEER HILL END ROAD
Upper Acre Head
Deer Hill Conduit
Deer Hill
Shooters Nab
Catchwater
Drain
Moor Ford Hill
DEER HILL BENTS
RED LANE
West End
Hind Hill
Black Edge
Brow Grains Cottage
Brow Grains Dike
Waterfall
BROW GRAINS ROAD
Grains Ash
Brookfield Farm
Deer Hill Moss
Wham Head
Dry Clough Side
BINN MOOR
Scar Head
Rams Clough
PEAK NATIONAL PARK
Legards Slack
Oldfield Hill
Oldfield Hill
Harrow Hill
Muddy Brook
The Scope
HIGH MOOR END ROAD
Holme Bank Wood
Rigg Shaw
West Nab Cottages
Broadhead Wood
Great Clough
Deer Hill Conduit
Far New Close
Valve Ho.
Overflow
Blakeley Reservoir
Cowberry Holes
Orleans Farm
Orleans Lodge
High Moor
WESSENDEN HEAD RD.
Scope Moss
Blakeley Head Moss
161
MELTHAM MOOR

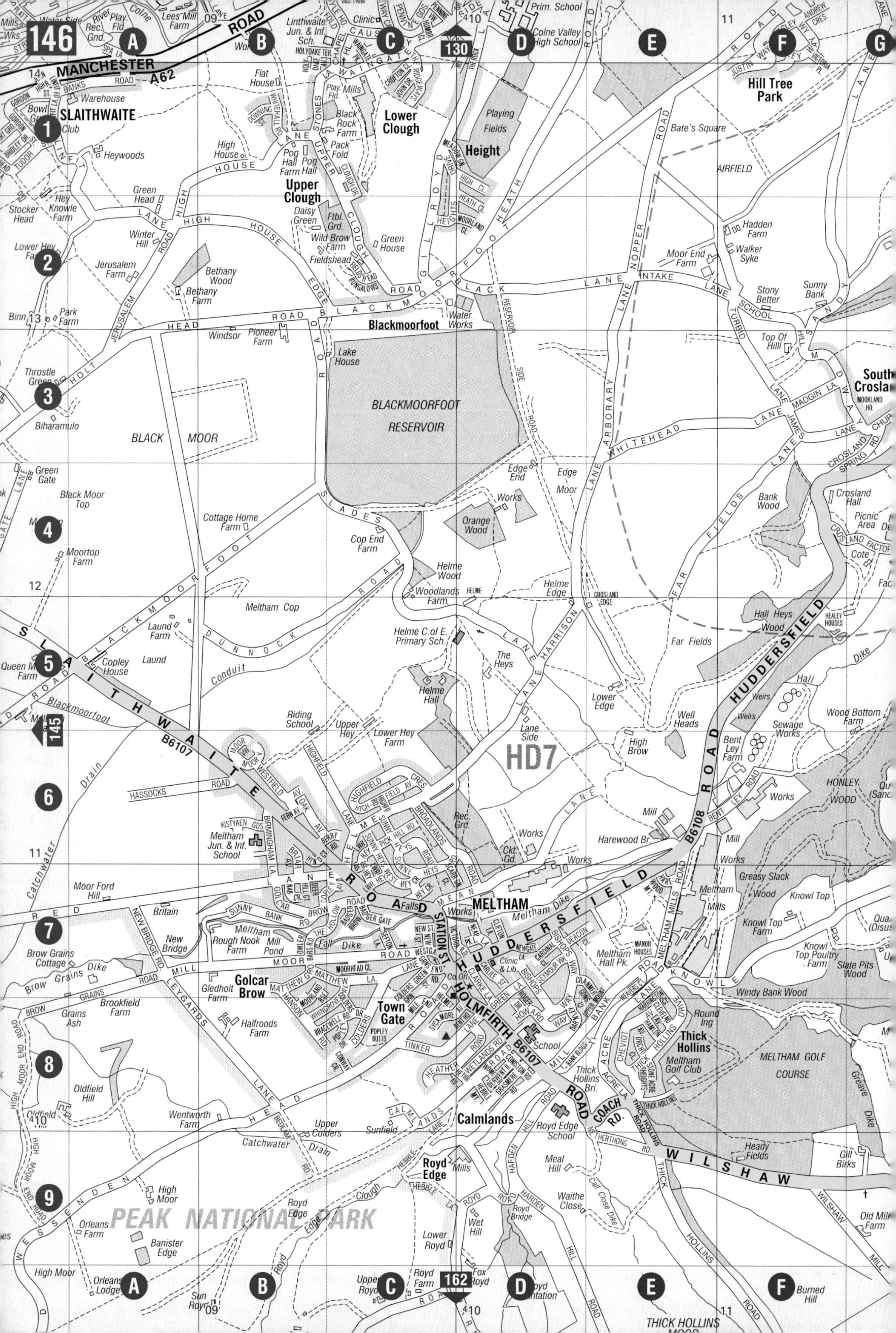

SLAITHWAITE
MANCHESTER ROAD A62
Upper Clough
Lower Clough
Height
Hill Tree Park
Blackmoorfoot
BLACKMOORFOOT RESERVOIR
BLACK MOOR
South Crosland
MELTHAM
HD7
Golcar Brow
Town Gate
Calmlands
Royd Edge
Thick Hollins
MELTHAM GOLF COURSE
PEAK NATIONAL PARK
WILSHAW
HUDDERSFIELD ROAD B6108
SLAITHWAITE ROAD B6107
HOLMFIRTH ROAD B6107
130
145
162

131
163
148
HD4
Huddersfield
NETHERTON
Berry Brow
Armitage Bridge
HONLEY
Honley
NETHERTHONG
Oldfield
Upper Oldfield
Honley Moor
Netherton Moor
Lower Thirstin
Mag Dale
Neiley
Mytholm Bridge
Wilshaw
Hall Bower
Waterholes Quarry (Sandstone)
Beaumont Park
Newsome High Sch.
Butter Nab Spring
Round Wood
Kennels
Delves Wood
Big Valley
Daffy Wood
Delph Farm
Spring Farm
Delves Cotts.
Dean Clough
Dean Wood
Tolson Farm
Crkt. Grd.
Rec. Grd.
Weir
Old Spring Wood
Armitage Bridge Farm
Catterson
Cold Hill
Stirley Farm
Castle Houses
Boggarding
Lower Park
Little Park Wood
Stirley Knoll
Upper Park Wood
Robin Hood Tunnel
Park Wood
Waterfall
Nag Wood
Nan Hob Spring
Mill Steps
Roydland
Scale Hill Farm
The White
Shaw Head Farm
High Royd
Round Wood
Sunnyside Farm
Moor Croft
Stones Wood
Honley High Sch. & Coll.
Northgate House
Northgate Mount
Lodge
Mill Pond
Cemy.
Netherton Bank Bottom
Bridge Row
Scar Top
Netherton Bank
SPRING WOOD
The Stubbings
Mill Ponds
Lower Hall
Lower Crosland
Granby Farm
Mill Pond
Clitheroe Wood
Clitheroe Farm
Wood Royd
Hollin Hall
Hollinhurst
Works
Playing Fields
Quarry (Sandstone)
HONLEY OLD WOOD
The Woodlands
Football Field
Clinic
Honley C.of E. Jun. Sch.
Field End
Marry Carry
Cliff Wood
Sewage Works
Factory
Seventy Acres
Seventy Acres Farm
Bird in the Hand
Wellhouse Farm
Woodfield Cottage
Ponteý Farm
Pontey Cotts.
The Bungalow
Holly Edge
Larkfield
Leather Hall
Middlefield House
Spring Villa
White Gates Farm
Slate Pits Wood
Oak Cottage
Moor Park
Ivy Cott.
Windy Ridge
Gib Cott.
Newfield
Poultry Houses
Oldfield Lane Farm
The Croft
Honey Head
Honey Head Wood
Wood-Nook Farm
Woodville
Wood Nook
Cross La. Farm
Upper Hagg
Moor Croft
Moorfield House
Star House Farm
Hunter House Farm
Mountain Cottage
New Hagg Farm
Lower Hagg Farm
Hagg Wood
Gill Wood
Hag Ho.
Lower Hagg
Pontey Wood
Bank Wood
Deanhouse
Dean Brook Farm
Harroyd Farm
Depot
Knoll Plantation
Holmroyd Wood
Netherthong Prim. Sch.
Cricket Grd.
Longlands Wood
Mills
St. Mary's Court
Holmroyd Nook
Swinny Knoll
Knoll Bridge Farm
New Dam
Sands Farm
Fox House Farm
Newland Wood
Spring Wood
Moor Gate
Lydgett Farm
Wells
Four Ways
Ox Lee Farm
Mill
Berry Bank Wood
HOLME VALLEY MEMORIAL
B6108 ARMITAGE RD.
B6110 RD.
PARKGATE A616
WOODHEAD RD.
WOODHEAD ROAD
HUDDERSFIELD RD.
NEW MILL A616
WOODHEAD ROAD A6024
HUDDERSFIELD ROAD A6024
B6107 LANE
MELTHAM ROAD
MELTHAM MOOR ROAD
WOOD BOTTOM ROAD
SCOTGATE ROAD
OLD MOLL ROAD
HASSOCKS LANE
CHANDLER LANE
NOOK LANE
WOOD NOOK LANE
MIRY LANE
OLDFIELD LANE
CROSS LANE
BRADSHAW LANE
KNOLL LANE
GIB LANE
STATION ROAD
NORTHGATE
WESTGATE
WEST CROFT
JAGGAR LANE
STONY LANE
ROUNDWAY
DEAN BROOK ROAD
THONG LANE
GILES STREET
NEW RD.
ROBIN HOOD HILL
HANGING STONE ROAD
SANDBEDS ROAD
MOOR ROAD
BANK SCAR TOP LA.
BOURNE VIEW ROAD
LANE BANK FOOT
HAWKROYD BANK
NETHERTON MOOR ROAD
NETHER MOOR ROAD
BUTTERNAB ROAD
DELVES ROAD
CALDERCLIFFE RD.
BIRCH ROAD
LADY HOUSE LANE
COLD HILL LANE
PARK LANE
NORTHGATE ROAD
LUDWOOD
HALL ING
MARSH PLATT LA.
GYNN LANE
FAR END LA.
TURNPIKE
UPPER HAGG ROAD
HAGG WOOD RD.
HAGG ROAD
CALF HILL ROAD
ROBINSON LA.
HAGGROYD LA.
SMITHY PLACE LA.
HOLMDALE CRES.
WESLEY AV.
ST. MARY'S RD.
WEST END
12
13
14
415
410
G H J K L M N
1 2 3 4 5 6 7 8 9

132
164
147
Huddersfield
HD4
HD7
Lumb
Netherton
Farnley Tyas
Storthes Hall Student Village
(University of Huddersfield)
Green Side
Brockholes
Thurstonland
Stocksmoor
Thongsbridge
Mytholm Bridge
Castle Hill
Victoria Tower
Lower Castle Hill
Lower Castle Hill Farm
Clay Hall
Fletcher House
Bank Foot Bridge
Bank Foot
Royd House
Shrogg Wood
Low Common
Park Cottage
Carr Wood
Hunter Nab
Stock Dove Wood
Leigh Fields
Farnley Bank
Molly Carr Wood
Lumb Head
Ogley
The Lumb
Roaf Wood
Arthur Wood
Royd House Wood
Farnley Bank Wood
Lower High Fields
Slate Fields
Upper High Fields
Farnley Hey
Cliff Ho.
Bowl. Grn.
Beech Farm
Netherton Farm
Woodview Farm
North Spring Wood
Ray Gate Cottage
York Farm
Croft House Farm
The Range
Scale Hill Farm
The White House
Hey Wood
Shaw Head Farm
Glen Farm
School
Early Crofts
Rec. Grd.
School Wood
Round Wood
West Wood
Lud Hill
Middle Ludhill
Ludhill
Storthes Hall Moor Wood
Moor House
Storthes Hall Moor
Burnt Hill
Far Ludhill
Royd Wood
Farnley Moor
Ivy Farm
Whinny Wood
Hollin Hall
Hall Ing
Royd Farm
Blagdens
Joy Wood
Boothroyd Wood
Runlet End
Longley
Runlet End Wood
Farnley Moor Plump
Wood End
Marry Carry
Cliff Top
Longley Hill
Green Carrs
Colne Bank
Height
Height Green
Farnley Moor End
High Green Side
Low Green Side
Clough Wood
Smith Wood
Black House
Lumb House
Rifle Range
Sewage Works
Colne Bank Wood
Great Plain Wood
Blakehouse Farm
Marsh Hall
Brown's Knoll
Brown's Knoll Wood
Brockholes C.of E. Prim.Sch.
Briery Wood
The Wood
Black Gutters
Thurstonland Tunnel
Shrogg Wood
Moor Bottom
Field Head
Rec. Grd.
Cricket Grd.
Thurstonland First School
Butts Farm
Whitestones
Round Wood
Manor House Farm
Sports Grd.
Ash Cottage
The Old Tannery
Ash Tree Farm
Ingfield Kennels
Ing Head
Stocks
Hagg Wood
Bank End
Bank End Plantation
Bank End Green
Mytholm Bridge
Bank Plantation
Bankside Farm
Haw Cliff
Haw Cliff Top
Hanging Royd Shrogg
Lower Halstead Farm
Upper Halstead
Halstead Wood
Round Wood
Sinking Wood
Spring Wood
Stoney Bank Mill
Thurstonland Bank
Hollingreave Plantation
New Beggin
Beggin
Biggin Shrog
Hunger Hill
Reservoir
Morefield
Holmfirth High Sch.
Playing Fields
Hill Top Bank
Hill Top
Hollin Greave Farm
Croft Bottom Farm
Croft Bottom Cottages
Wood End Wood
Shepley Wood End
Stubs Wood
East Field
Depot
Kaye Wood
Rock Cotts.
Stagwood Hill
Moorlands
West Royd Farm
Moor View Farm
Huddersfield Rd.
A616
A6024
New Mill Road
Woodhead Road

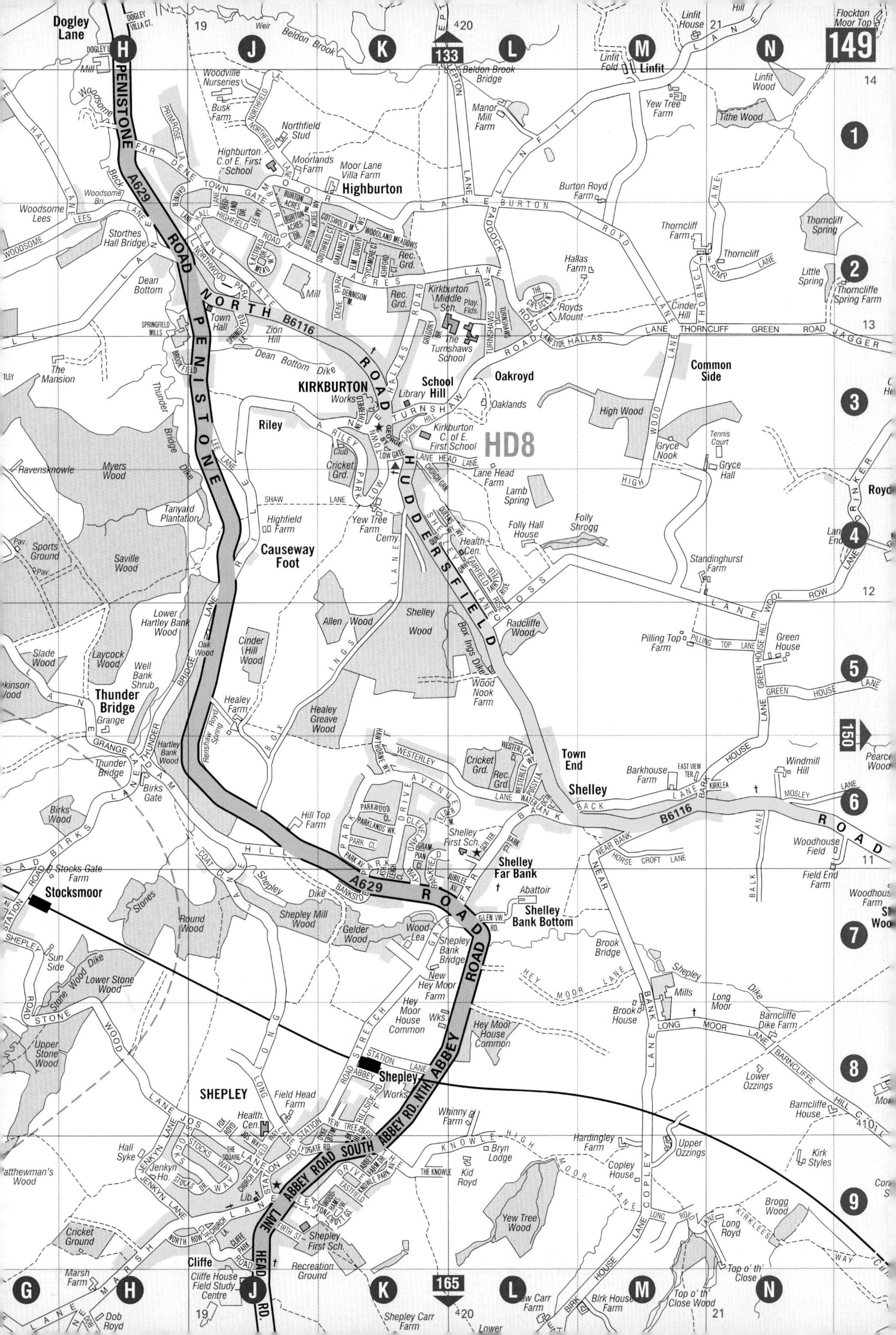
Dogley Lane
Flockton Moor Top
Linfit
Highburton
KIRKBURTON
School Hill
Oakroyd
Common Side
Riley
Causeway Foot
Thunder Bridge
HD8
Town End
Shelley
Shelley Far Bank
Shelley Bank Bottom
Stocksmoor
SHEPLEY
Shepley
Cliffe
PENISTONE ROAD
A629
NORTH ROAD
B6116
HUDDERSFIELD ROAD
ABBEY ROAD
ABBEY ROAD SOUTH
ABBEY RD. NTH.
133
150
165
Highburton C. of E. First School
Kirkburton Middle Sch.
The Turnshaws School
Kirkburton C. of E. First School
Shelley First Sch.
Shepley First Sch.
Cliffe House Field Study Centre
Woodsome Lees
Storthes Hall Bridge
Dean Bottom
Myers Wood
Saville Wood
Allen Wood
Shelley Wood
High Wood
Healey Greave Wood
Shepley Mill Wood
Yew Tree Wood
Hey Moor House Common
Burton Royd Farm
Thorncliff Farm
Cinder Hill
Gryce Hall
Standinghurst Farm
Barkhouse Farm
Green House
Woodhouse Field
Field End Farm
Upper Ozzings
Lower Ozzings
Long Moor
Barncliffe Dike Farm
Barncliffe House
Kirk Styles
Brogg Wood
Long Royd
Top o' th' Close
Top o' th' Close Wood
Birk House Farm
Shepley Carr Farm
Recreation Ground
Marsh Farm
Dob Royd
Cricket Ground
Hall Syke
Jenkyn Ho.
Upper Stone Wood
Lower Stone Wood
Sun Side
Stones
Round Wood
Birks Wood
Birks Gate
Slade Wood
Laycock Wood
Lower Hartley Bank Wood
Tanyard Plantation
Sports Ground
The Mansion
Ravensknowle
19
420
21
14
13
12
11
G H J K L M N
1 2 3 4 5 6 7 8 9

Flockton Moor Top
Ends Farm
134
Lower Crawshaw Farm
Kirkby Grange Farm
Butts Top
Mouse House
Bunkers Hill Farm
Rock Wood Farm
Cross Roads
Sheep Cote
Engine House Farm
Upper Crawshaw
Mouse House Dike
Emley Moor
Cross Lane Farm
Factory Farm
Thorncliff Spring
Holmfield Farm
The Heater
Thorncliffe Spring Farm
Rugby Football Ground
Emley
Highfield House
Caravan Site
Moor Head Plantation
Depot
Hutt Farm
Highlands Court
Phillips House
Television Station
Mast
Emley Moor Business Park
Sports Grd.
Carr House
Moor Head
Tyburn Hill
Leys Farm
Churchill Farm
Kirk Hill
High Chambers
Roydhouse
Taylor Hill
Lane End
Wool Row Farm
Low House Farm Stables
EMLEY
Nineclogs
Upper Owlers Wood
Rough Piece Wood
Lightcliff Wood
Silver Ings
Park Lane House
Huddersfield HD8
Springs Wood
Park Farm
Baildon Place
149
Pearce Wood
Round Wood
Hopstrines Farm
Park Gate
Windmill Hill
Quarry
Blacker Farm
Baildon Dike
Hopstrines Bungalow
Woodlands
Works
Skelmanthorpe
Blacker Wood
Park Gate Dike
Kirklees Light
Woodhouse Field
The Grange
Sycamore Farm
Mill
Field End Farm
Skelmanthorpe Common
School Hill
Cuckoo's Nest Halt
Woodhouse Farm
Shelley Woodhouse
Round Hill
Fair Mount
Common End
Long Royds
HUDDERSFIELD B6116
ROAD COMMERCIAL ROAD
Tennis Courts
Reservoir
Shelley High School
Lib
Hlth Cen.
Skelmanthorpe First School
SKELMANTHORPE
Rec. Grd.
Netherfield Farm
Windmill Farm
BUSKER B6116
Lower Busker
Cliffe Hill Farm
Sch.
Ladyroyd
Nortonthorpe Hall Sch.
Cricket Grd.
Cemetery
Lodge
Mount Pleasant Farm
Barncliffe House
Ponker
Four Winds
Woodlands
Reservoir (covered)
Football Ground
Kirk Styles
Cumberworth Common
Ponker Hill
Thorpe Dike
Common Side
Works
Hob Royd Shrogg
Miry Greaves Shrogg
High Bridge Wood
A636
Bagden Bank Wood
Bagden Hall
Oakcliff Hill
Lower Cumberworth
Kitchenroyd
Little Hackings
Bagden Hall Farm
Top o' th' Hill
Lane Hackings
Perch House Farm
166
BAGDEN PARK
Cricket Grd.
Playground
Gilthwaites Farm
Clay
WAKEFIELD
Lower Clough

135
152
167
Wakefield
WF4
Barnsley
S75
BRETTON PARK
LONG SIDE
CLAYTON WEST
HIGH HOYLAND
Upper Common
Park Mill
Clayton West
Bank Wood
Furnace Hill
Iron Workings
Thorncliffe Cottage
Beancroft Well
Bentley Grange Farm
Emley Woodhouse
Woodhouse Farm
Ash Cottage
Upper Woodhouse
Broom Hall
White Cross
Yew Farm
Woodland View
Owlers Wood
Emley Old Hall Cottages
Emley Old Hall
Gillcar Farm
Lady Oak
Park Mill Colliery
Far Langley
Sewage Works
Upper Langley
Rec. Grd.
Playing Field
Spring Grove
Cliffe Wood Park
Riding Wood
Duke Wood
Ridingwood Lodge
Ridingwood Farm
Lower Common
Wheatley Hill Farm
Round Hill
Wheatley Hill Lodge
Hay Royds Colliery
Lane End
Deffer Nook
Hill Top Farm
Hillside Farm
Earths Plantation
Swallow Hill
Square Spring
Hollin House Farm
Upper Spring
Lower Spring
Horn Wood
Winter Hill
Bank End
Bilham Shrogg
Bilham Spring
Bilham Grange
Bilham Road Farm
Clayton Hall Farm
Factory
Works
Bentley Spring
Abraham Spring
Seven Acre Plantation
Bower Hill
Bower Hill Plantation
Bella Vista Plantation
Wilderness Plantation
Reservoir Plantation
Top Lane Plantations
Sewage Works
Mine
Pikeley Spring
Pikeley Hill
Long Lawn Plantation
Obelisk
Bretton Lakes Nature Reserve
Bridge Royd Wood
Boat Ho.
Upper Lake
Bath Wood
Cascade Bridge
Litherop Spring
Picnic Area
Litherop
Hoyland Lodge
Longsides
Green Acre Pond
Deep Haig
Bretton Hall College of Higher Education
Camellia House
Middle Park
The Hall
Old Rectory
Town Well
Hoyland Hill
Greenland
Friezland
Deffer House
Margery Wood
Upper Stub Nooks Plantation
Lower Stub Nooks Plantation
Emley Lodge
Scisset C of E. First School
KIRKLEES
BARNSLEY
WAKEFIELD
A636
DENBY DALE ROAD
WAKEFIELD ROAD
HOYLAND BANK
RIVER DEARNE
DEARNE WAY
LITHEROP LANE
LITHEROP ROAD
JEBB LANE
HOLLIN HOUSE LANE
UPPER COMMON LANE
WHEATLEY HILL LANE
HIGH STREET
BANK LANE
CHURCH LANE
CHAPEL HILL
BILHAM ROAD
KILN LANE
HAGG HILL LANE
ASH LANE
WOODHOUSE LANE
TIPPING LANE
LEISURE LANE
LANGLEY LANE
Park Gate Dike
Little Dike
Toad Hole Dike
Bentley Brook
Bentley Dike
Clay House Beck
Bank Wood Beck
25
26
27
28
14
12
11
10
H
J
K
L
M
N
G
1
2
3
4
5
6
7
8
9

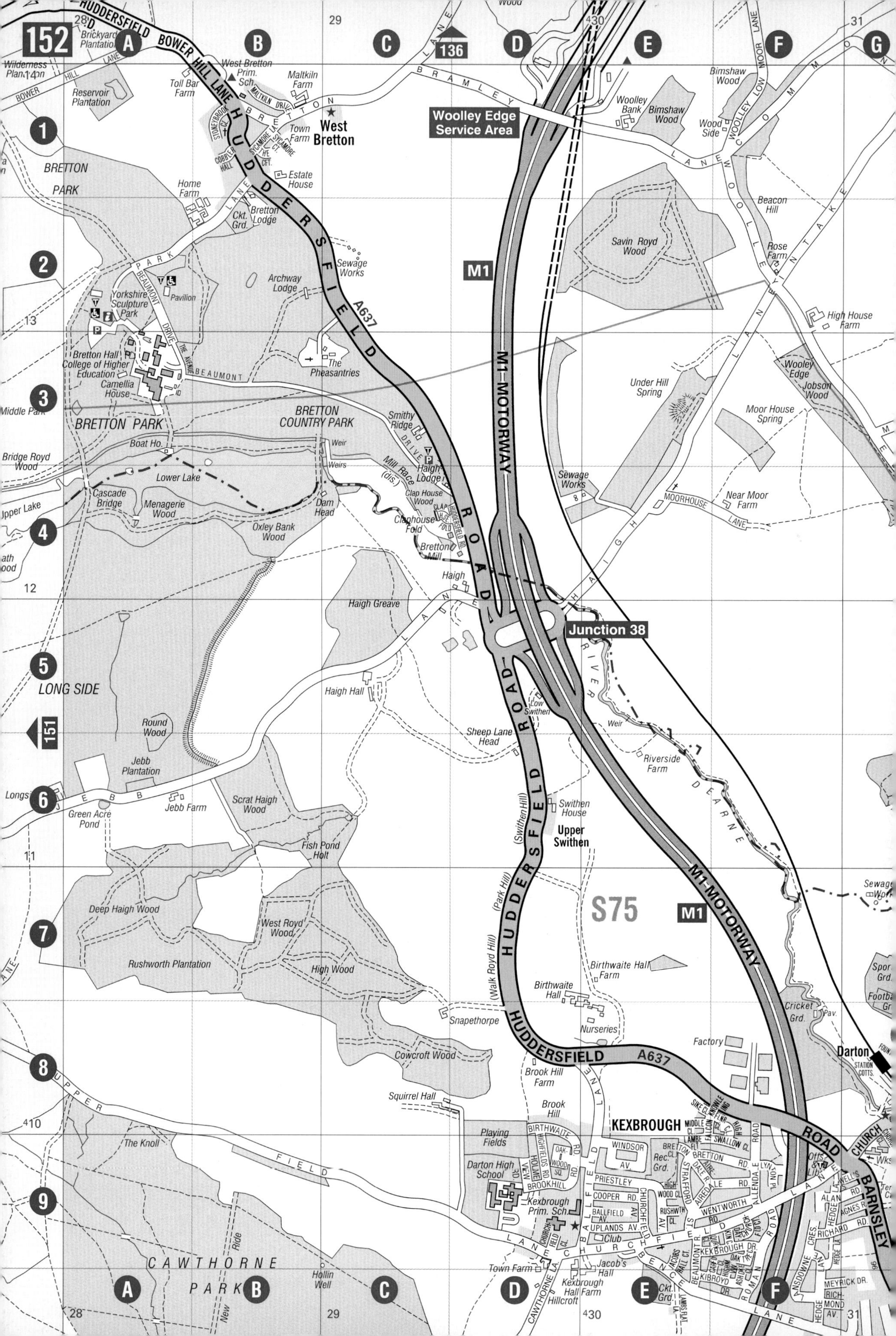

A
B
C
D
E
F
G
28
29
430
31
136
151
1
2
3
4
5
6
7
8
9
14
13
12
11
410
HUDDERSFIELD ROAD
BOWER HILL LANE
Brickyard Plantation
Wilderness Plantation
BOWER HILL LANE
Reservoir Plantation
Toll Bar Farm
West Bretton Prim. Sch.
Maltkiln Farm
MALTKILN DRIVE
BRETTON LANE
BRAMLEY LANE
West Bretton
Town Farm
Estate House
STONEYBROOK CL.
SYCAMORE LA.
SYCAMORE CT.
COBBLER HALL
Woolley Edge Service Area
Woolley Bank
Bimshaw Wood
Wood Side
WOOLLEY LOW MOOR LANE
COMMON
WOOLLEY LANE
BRETTON PARK
Home Farm
Ckt. Grd.
Bretton Lodge
Sewage Works
Archway Lodge
A637
M1
Savin Royd Wood
Beacon Hill
Rose Farm
INTAKE LANE
High House Farm
PARK LANE
BEAUMONT DRIVE
Pavilion
Yorkshire Sculpture Park
THE AVENUE
BEAUMONT
Bretton Hall College of Higher Education
Camellia House
The Pheasantries
M1 MOTORWAY
Under Hill Spring
Woolley Edge
Jobson Wood
Moor House Spring
Middle Park
BRETTON PARK
BRETTON COUNTRY PARK
Smithy Ridge
SMITHY DRIVE
Boat Ho.
Weir
Weirs
Mill Race (dis.)
Haigh Lodge
Bridge Royd Wood
Lower Lake
Upper Lake
Cascade Bridge
Menagerie Wood
Dam Head
Clap House Wood
CLAP HOUSE FOLD
Claphouse Fold
HUDDERSFIELD RD.
Oxley Bank Wood
Bretton Mill
Sewage Works
MOORHOUSE LANE
Near Moor Farm
HAIGH LANE
Haigh
Haigh Greave
HAIGH LANE
Junction 38
RIVER DEARNE
LONG SIDE
Haigh Hall
Low Swithen
Sheep Lane Head
Weir
Riverside Farm
Round Wood
Jebb Plantation
JEBB LANE
Jebb Farm
Green Acre Pond
Scrat Haigh Wood
Fish Pond Holt
Swithen House
Upper Swithen
(Swithen Hill)
Deep Haigh Wood
West Royd Wood
S75
(Park Hill)
(Walk Royd Hill)
Sewage Works
Rushworth Plantation
High Wood
Birthwaite Hall Farm
Birthwaite Hall
Nurseries
Sports Grd.
Football Grd.
Cricket Grd.
Pav.
Snapethorpe
Cowcroft Wood
Factory
Darton
STATION COTTS.
UPPER FIELD LANE
Squirrel Hall
Brook Hill Farm
Brook Hill
KEXBROUGH
The Knoll
Playing Fields
BIRTHWAITE RD.
HIGHFIELDS RD.
OAKWOOD SQ.
WINDSOR AV.
Rec. Grd.
BRETTON RD.
SWALLOW CL.
FALCON KNOWLE LA.
ROAD
BARNSLEY ROAD
CHURCH ST.
Darton High School
HOLME VIEW
BROOKHILL
PRIESTLEY
COOPER RD.
BALLFIELD AV.
UPLANDS AV.
Club
Kexbrough Prim. Sch.
CHURCHFIELD AV.
HIGH WOOD CL.
STRAFFORD
WENTWORTH
RUSHWORTH CL.
ALLENDALE RD.
Offs.
Wks.
ALAN AV.
HEDGE LA.
AGNES RD.
RICHARD RD.
LANSDOWNE CRES.
KEXBROUGH DR.
KIBROYD DR.
ROMAN RD.
CHURCHFIELD LANE
BENCH LANE
Jacob's Hall
JACOBS HALL CT.
BEAUMONT RD.
Ckt. Grd.
Town Farm
CAWTHORNE LA.
Kexbrough Hall Farm
Hillcroft
MEYRICK DR.
RICHMOND AV.
HEDGE LANE
CAWTHORNE PARK
New Ride
Hollin Well

137
154
Wakefield
WF4
High Moor
Shroggs Hill Plantation
Tottie Spring
The Kennels
Sewage Works
Bushcliff House
Owler Wood
Saw Mill Plantations
Seckar Dike
The Willows
Mill Farm
Cricket Gnd.
WOOLLEY PARK
WOOLLEY HALL COLLEGE
Home Farm
Lodge
Waterfall
Eccle Hill
Ash Farm
War Mem.
Church Farm
Woolley
Highfield Farm
Hillside Farm
Flesh Dyke
Lodge Plantation
Brickyard Cottages
Brickyard Plantation
Ridings Wood
Haw Top
Wheatley Wood
Little Spring
Peter Spring
Mine
NOTTON PARK
Windhill Gate
Husband Wood
Woolley Rabbit Warren
Warren Fm.
Owler Well
BARNSLEY (PUBLIC) GOLF COURSE
Club House
Coniston Farm
Barnsley
Lane Head Fm.
Reservoir (covered)
STAINCROSS
Pye Wood Institute
Bloomhouse
DARTON
Oaks Plantation
Greenside
Wellgate Inf. Sch.
Health Cen.
Play Fld.
Rec. Grd.
Mapplewell Prim. Sch.
Woodview Farm
Bleak House Poultry Farm
The Bungalow
S71
ATHERSLEY NORTH
Lawrence Briggs Inf. Sch.
Athersley N. Inf. Sch.
Leisure Cen.
Works
Muscle Hill
MAPPLEWELL
Blacker Hill
Blacker Hill Farm
New Lodge
Factory
BARNSLEY ROAD
WAKEFIELD ROAD
A61
B6131
B6428
B6428
TIPSEY HILL
SECKAR LANE
WATERPARSON LANE
GALLOWS LA.
MILL LANE
GEORGE LANE
GEORGE ROAD
FIELD LANE
BACK LANE
NEW LANE
WOODHOUSE LANE
ABBOT LANE
GIPSY LANE
HAWTOP LANE
KEEPER LANE
WINDHILL LANE
WARREN LANE
SPRING LANE
STAINCROSS COMMON
SHAW LA.
LEE LANE
WOOD LANE
DARTON LANE
STATION RD.
KINGSWAY
TOWNGATE
GREENSIDE
BLACKER RD.
BAR LANE
SPARK LANE
DARTON PYE AV.
CARR GREEN LANE
CARR HILL
RIVER DEARNE
WAKEFIELD
BARNSLEY
H J K L M N G
1 2 3 4 5 6 7 8 9
32 33 34 14 13 12

Wakefield
WF4
Cold Hiendley
Notton
Royston
S71
Carlton
Athersley North
Carlton Green
Carlton Industrial Estate
Cold Hiendley Common
Notton Grange
Applehaigh Wood
Low Common
Royston Welfare Park
Barnsley Canal (disused)
Shaw Viaduct
Sewage Works
Playing Fields
Recreation Ground
Sports Ground
Lund Hill
Cudworth Junct

138
153

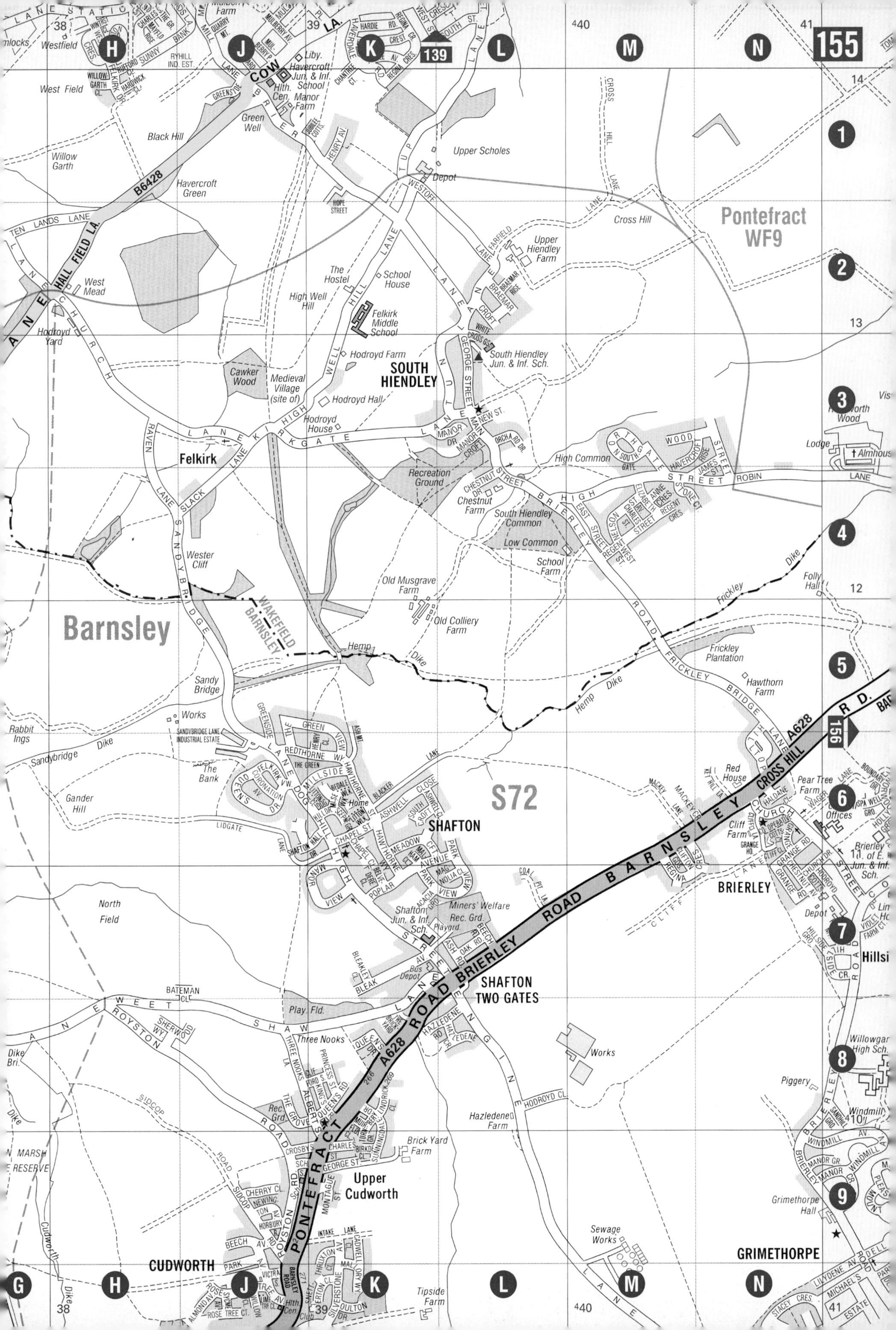

Westfield
West Field
Black Hill
Willow Garth
Havercroft Green
B6428
Green Well
Upper Scholes
Depot
Pontefract WF9
Cross Hill
Upper Hiendley Farm
The Hostel
School House
High Well Hill
Felkirk Middle School
Hodroyd Farm
SOUTH HIENDLEY
South Hiendley Jun. & Inf. Sch.
Cawker Wood
Medieval Village (site of)
Hodroyd Hall
Hodroyd House
West Mead
Hodroyd Yard
Felkirk
Recreation Ground
High Common
Chestnut Farm
South Hiendley Common
Low Common
School Farm
Wester Cliff
Old Musgrave Farm
Old Colliery Farm
Barnsley
WAKEFIELD
BARNSLEY
Hemp Dike
Frickley Dike
Folly Hall
Frickley Plantation
Hawthorn Farm
Sandy Bridge
Works
Rabbit Ings
Sandybridge Dike
The Bank
Gander Hill
S72
SHAFTON
Red House
Pear Tree Farm
Cliff Farm
BRIERLEY
Brierley Jun. & Inf. Sch.
North Field
Miners' Welfare Rec. Grd.
Shafton Jun. & Inf. Sch.
SHAFTON TWO GATES
A628 BARNSLEY ROAD BRIERLEY ROAD
CROSS HILL
Play. Fld.
Three Nooks
Works
Willowgarth High Sch.
Piggery
Windmill
Hazledene Farm
Brick Yard Farm
Upper Cudworth
MARSH RESERVE
Grimethorpe Hall
Sewage Works
GRIMETHORPE
CUDWORTH
Tipside Farm
PONTEFRACT ROAD
139
156

HEMSWORTH
Barnsley
S72
BRIERLEY
GRIMETHORPE
Hillside
Highfield
Cross Hill
Green Hill
Little Hemsworth
Common End
Marsh
South Moor
Church Field
Hemsworth High Sch.
SOUTHMOOR HOSPITAL
Burntwood Sports & Leisure Centre
HOWELL WOOD COUNTRY PARK
Ball Park Wood
Cob Carr Plantation
Hague Plantation
Rushworth Wood
Tom Bank Wood
Spa Well Plantation
Willowgarth High Sch.
Brierley Common
Brierley Gap
Hemsworth Gate
Southgate
Kirkby Common Farm
South Kirkby Common
Avenue Farm
Ringstone Hill
Brierley Manor
Addey Bottoms
Windmill Hill
Grimethorpe Hall
THE PARK
HEMSWORTH BY-PASS
A628
B6273
B6422
BARNSLEY RD.
BAREWELL HILL
SOUTHMOOR ROAD
SOUTHMOOR LANE
KIRKBY ROAD
WAKEFIELD ROAD
MARKET ST.
HOLMSLEY LANE
COMMON ROAD
HAGUE LANE
WAKEFIELD
BARNSLEY
140
155

Pontefract
WF9
Upton Beacon
UPTON
Royd Moor
Minsthorpe
Moorthorpe
SOUTH KIRKBY
SOUTH ELMSALL
South Elmsall
North Elmsall Common
Royd Moor Farm
Royd Moor House
Royd Moor House Farm
Bullinger Wood
Bullenshaw Villas
Aqueduct
Grey Cocks
Paddock Cottage
Elmsall Lodge Farm
The Lawn
The Manor
Lodge
Great Breaks
Moortop Cottage
Nursery
Long Plantation
Recreation Ground
DONCASTER ROAD
A638
MOOR LANE
BEACONFIELD RD.
FIELD LANE
B6474
MINSTHORPE LA.
BACK LA.
INCH LANE
Street Farm
Mile Stone
Elm Farm
Manorcroft Farm
Greystones
Mosley Mires
Minsthorpe High Sch. & Comm. Coll.
Tennis Courts
Playing Field
Kirkby Bri.
Hague Hall Beck
Swimming Baths
Ash Grove Jun. & Inf. Sch.
Depot
Riddings Plantation
South Kirby Junction
Reservoirs
Lower North Field
Gallon Croft Field
Rec. Grd.
Bowl. Plygd. Gn.
Govt. Offs.
Cemy.
Prim. Sch.
R.C. Jun. & Inf Sch.
Hlth. Cen.
Liby.
BARNSLEY STREET
B6422
HIGH ROAD
WHITE APRON LANE
Ball Park Farm
Northfield Jun. & Inf. Sch.
Lib.
LANGTHWAITE GRANGE INDUSTRIAL ESTATE
PARK ESTATE
Burntwood Jun. & Inf.
Playing Field
Westfield Rec. Grd.
Playgrd.
Langthwaite Common
Bowl. Gn.
Ckt. Grd.
Play. Fld.
Sports Ground
Nursing Home
Frickley Athletic F.C. Ground
West Field
Common End
Common Farm
Works
South Elmsall Common
Crkt. Grd.
Football Ground
Jun. Sch.
Langthwaite
Factory
East Farm
West Farm
Stepping Stones
Frickley
Beck
Howell Beck
Hooton Thorn Covert
BROAD LANE
LANGTHWAITE LANE
BROADWAY
WESTFIELD
LIDGATE
CHURCH LANE
H J K L M N G
141
158
445 46 47 410
14 13 12 11
1 2 3 4 5 6 7 8 9

142
157
WF8
WF9
Pontefract
Upton Beacon
UPTON
NORTH ELMSALL
SOUTH ELMSALL
South Elmsall
Hacking Hill
Wrangbrook
Barnsdale
Moorhouse
Moorhouse Common
Frickley
Sleep Hill
Hollins Farm
Coal Pit Field
Cherry Tree Farm
Hollins Plantation
Stubbs Hall
Stubbs Farm
Turnpike Plantation
Hazel Close Plantations
Croft Plantation
Top Ings
Moorhouse Ings
Hampole Field
Lea Farm
Gap Farm
Moorhouse Grange
Station House
Hooton Thorn Covert
The Ashes
Skelbrooke Rein
Stubbs Bridge
Stubbs Ings
Ivy Farm
Quarry Farm
Sludge Beds
Sewage Works
Street Farm
Mile Stone Fm.
Elm Farm
Manorcroft Farm
Greystones
North Elmsall Hall Farm
DALE LANE ENTERPRISE ZONE
The Upton Centre
Upton Jun. & Inf. School
STEED COURT BUSINESS PARK
DONCASTER ROAD
WAKEFIELD ROAD
A638
B6474
B6422
WAKEFIELD
DONCASTER

143
Barnsdale Wood
Campsmount Home Farm
Warren Plantation
Barnsdale
Barnsdale Warren House
Barnsdale Cottages
Freestone Quarry Plantation
CAMPSMOUNT PARK
SOUTH PARK
Campsmount Cotts.
Bull Close
New Fish Pond
CAMPSALL
WOODFIELD ROAD
WHITE LEY ROAD
LONG LA.
NEW ROAD
BONE LANE
WOOD FIELD
GREAT NORTH RD.
A1
Woodfield Cottages
Longland Field
LONGSLAND LA.
Clump Plantation
Summer House Plantation
Summer House Farm
Woodfield House Farm
CLOSE LANE
NEW CLOSE LANE
Primrose Cottage
SIXROOD
Wetflat Plantation
Sutton Field
BURGHWALLIS LANE
Hill Farm
HILL LANE
New Close Farm
Taronga
Quarry Hole
SKELBROOKE PARK
Skelbrooke Hall
Scorcher Hills Wood
SCORCHER HILLS
Cricket Ground
Glebe Cott.
Glebe Fm.
Dower Ho.
The Sycamores
ABBE'S WALK
Quarry Plantation
Skelbrooke
Home Fm.
BANNISTER LANE
STRAIGHT LA.
DONCASTER LANE
Robin Hood's Well
Manor Farm
Depot
Burghwallis
Spindlewood
Convent
Home Farm
Holly Farm
Sewage Works
BURGHWALLIS PARK
The Skell
Doncaster
DN6
GREAT NORTH ROAD
STONY CROFT
SQUIRREL WOOD
Tanks
Quarry (Limestone)
Burghwallis Grange
The Cottages
The Lodge
GRANGE LANE
MILL LANE
GREEN LANE
North Park
Skellow Cross Plantation
Stony Flat Plantation
Playing Fields
Harry Wood
Skellow Mill
Skellow Cross
Owston Skellow Inf. & Jun. Sch.
SKELLOW
LODGE LANE
NORTH LANE
Priory Farm
LEYS LANE
Service Area
Cuckoo Plantation
FIVE LA. ENDS
HAMPOLE BALK
B1220
SKELLOW ROAD
Railway Cotts.
Castle Hill
Hampole Ings
Brookfield
Skellow Bri.
Old Sallow
Skellow Hall
South Farm
Hampole Priory
Manor Farm
Hampole Dike
Hampole
Playing Fields
Park
Playgrd.
Hall
The Lymes
LYMES TER.
Humber Head Ings
Humber Head Bridge
Works
Manor Fm.
CARCROFT
Grange Cott.
A638 ROAD
INGS LANE
Hampole Grange
Size Ing
Red House
Skellow Ings
Adwick Junction
GREAT NTH. RD.
51
52
53
54
48
14
13
12
11
10
H
J
K
L
M
N
G
1
2
3
4
5
6
7
8
9

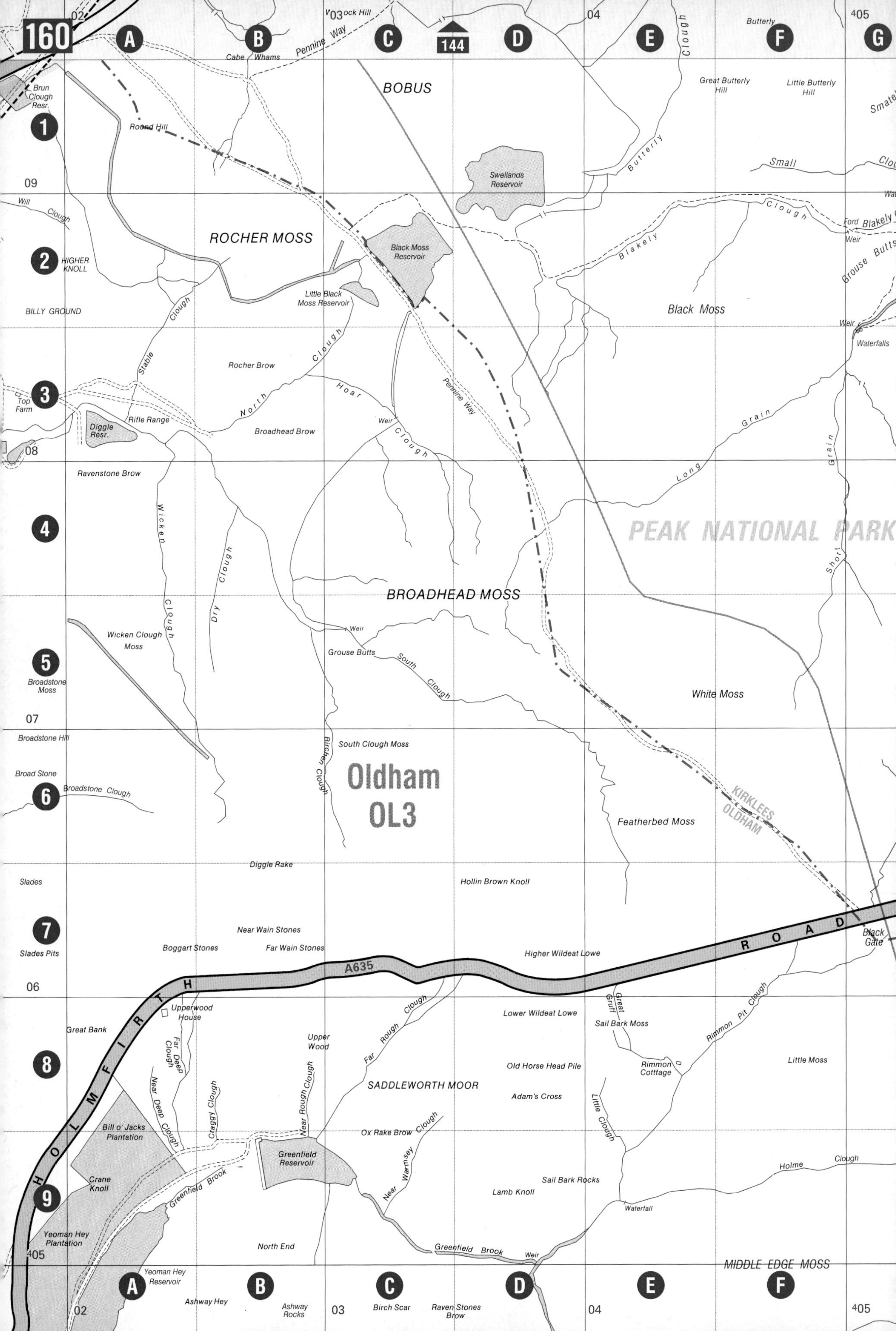

A
B
C
D
E
F
G
1
2
3
4
5
6
7
8
9
02
03
04
405
09
08
07
06
144
Cabe Whams
Pennine Way
Brun Clough Resr.
Round Hill
BOBUS
Great Butterly Hill
Little Butterly Hill
Butterly
Butterly Clough
Swellands Reservoir
Small Clough
ROCHER MOSS
Black Moss Reservoir
Little Black Moss Reservoir
Will Clough
HIGHER KNOLL
BILLY GROUND
Blakely Clough
Ford
Weir
Grouse Butts
Black Moss
Waterfalls
Rocher Brow
Stable Clough
North Hoar Clough
Top Farm
Diggle Resr.
Rifle Range
Broadhead Brow
Long Grain
Short Grain
Ravenstone Brow
Wicken Clough
Dry Clough
PEAK NATIONAL PARK
BROADHEAD MOSS
Wicken Clough Moss
Grouse Butts
South Clough
Broadstone Moss
White Moss
Broadstone Hill
South Clough Moss
Birchen Clough
Broad Stone
Broadstone Clough
Oldham
OL3
KIRKLEES
OLDHAM
Featherbed Moss
Diggle Rake
Slades
Hollin Brown Knoll
Near Wain Stones
Boggart Stones
Far Wain Stones
Slades Pits
A635
Higher Wildeat Lowe
ROAD
Black Gate
HOLMFIRTH
Upperwood House
Great Bank
Far Deep Clough
Near Deep Clough
Upper Wood
Far Rough Clough
Lower Wildeat Lowe
Great Gruff
Sail Bark Moss
Rimmon Pit Clough
Old Horse Head Pile
Rimmon Cotttage
Little Moss
SADDLEWORTH MOOR
Adam's Cross
Craggy Clough
Near Rough Clough
Little Clough
Bill o' Jacks Plantation
Ox Rake Brow
Greenfield Reservoir
Near Warmsey Clough
Holme Clough
Crane Knoll
Greenfield Brook
Sail Bark Rocks
Lamb Knoll
Waterfall
Yeoman Hey Plantation
North End
Greenfield Brook
Weir
MIDDLE EDGE MOSS
Yeoman Hey Reservoir
Ashway Hey
Ashway Rocks
Birch Scar
Raven Stones Brow

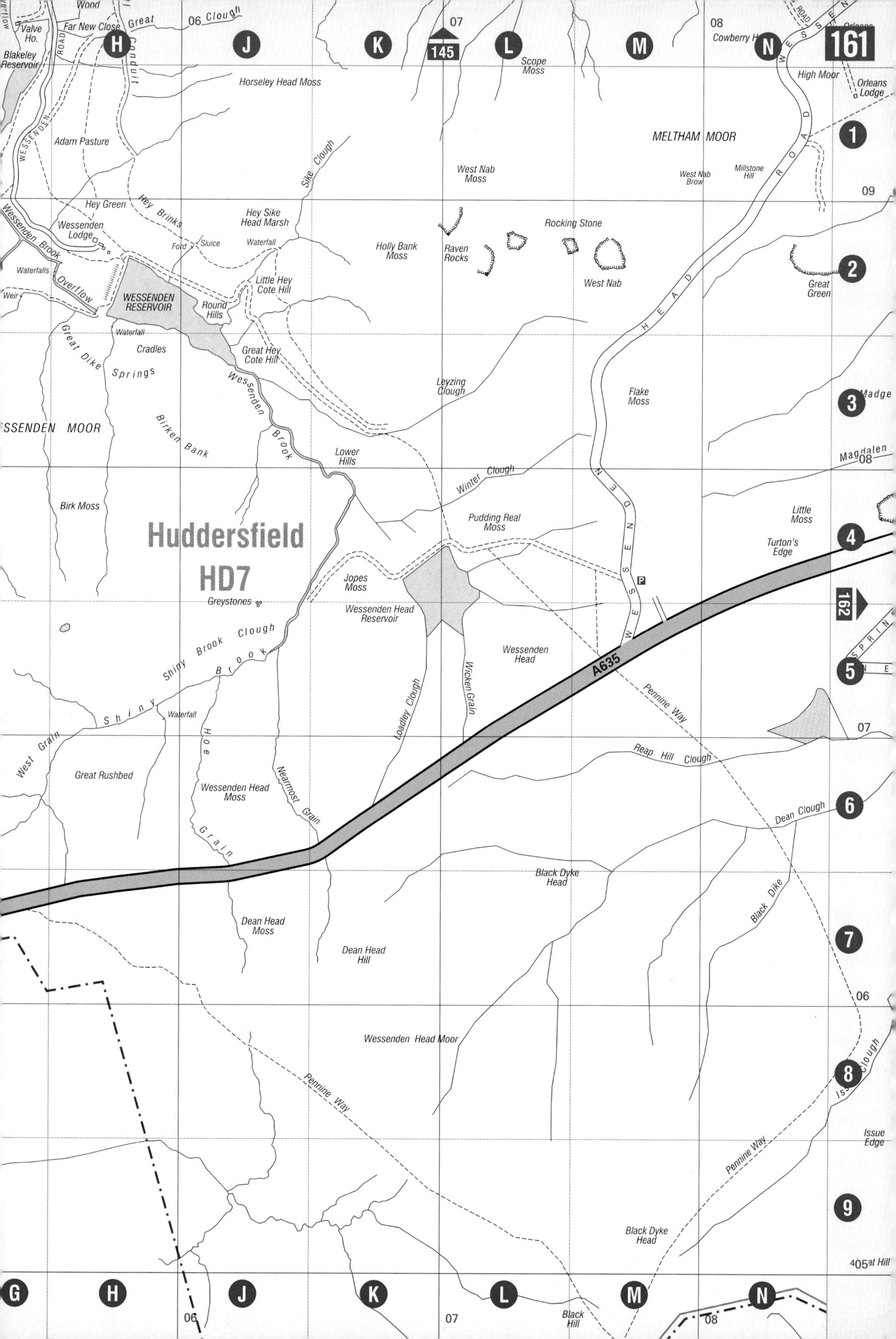

Huddersfield
HD7
Wood
Valve Ho.
Far New Close
Great Conduit
06 Clough
Blakeley Reservoir
Horseley Head Moss
Scope Moss
Cowberry H
High Moor
Orleans Lodge
MELTHAM MOOR
Adam Pasture
Sike Clough
West Nab Moss
West Nab Brow
Millstone Hill
Hey Green
Hey Brinks
Hey Sike Head Marsh
Wessenden Lodge
Ford
Sluice
Waterfall
Holly Bank Moss
Raven Rocks
Rocking Stone
West Nab
Great Green
Wessenden Brook
Waterfalls
Overflow
Weir
WESSENDEN RESERVOIR
Little Hey Cote Hill
Round Hills
Great Hey Cote Hill
Cradles
Great Dike Springs
Leyzing Clough
Flake Moss
Madge
SSENDEN MOOR
Birken Bank
Lower Hills
Magdalen
Winter Clough
Birk Moss
Pudding Real Moss
Little Moss
Turton's Edge
Jopes Moss
Wessenden Head Reservoir
Greystones
Shiny Brook Clough
Shiny Brook
Wessenden Head
A635
Waterfall
Loadley Clough
Wicken Grain
Pennine Way
West Grain
Hoe Grain
Great Rushbed
Wessenden Head Moss
Nearmost Grain
Reap Hill Clough
Dean Clough
Black Dyke Head
Black Dike
Dean Head Moss
Dean Head Hill
Wessenden Head Moor
Issue Clough
Issue Edge
Black Dyke Head
Black Hill
WESSENDEN HEAD ROAD
WESSENDEN ROAD
145
162

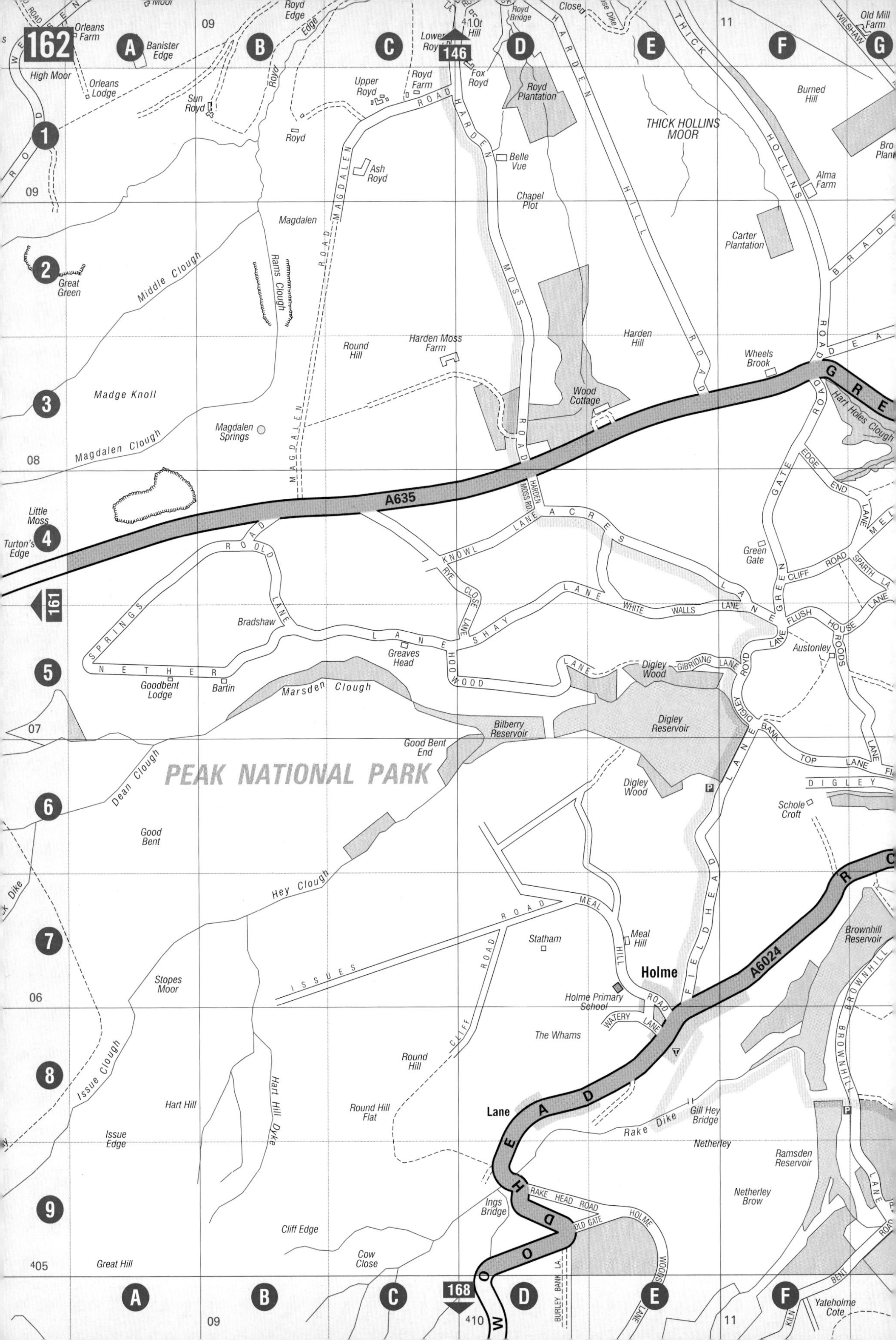
Orleans Farm
Banister Edge
Royd Edge
Lower Royd
410t Hill
Royd Bridge
Old Mill Farm
High Moor
Orleans Lodge
Sun Royd
Upper Royd
Royd Farm
Fox Royd
Royd Plantation
Burned Hill
Royd
Ash Royd
Belle Vue
THICK HOLLINS MOOR
Alma Farm
Chapel Plot
Magdalen
Carter Plantation
Great Green
Middle Clough
Rams Clough
Round Hill
Harden Moss Farm
Harden Hill
Wheels Brook
Madge Knoll
Wood Cottage
Magdalen Springs
Magdalen Clough
Hart Holes Clough
A635
Little Moss
Turton's Edge
Green Gate
Bradshaw
Austonley
Greaves Head
Goodbent Lodge
Bartin
Marsden Clough
Digley Wood
Digley Reservoir
Bilberry Reservoir
Good Bent End
PEAK NATIONAL PARK
Dean Clough
Digley Wood
Schole Croft
Good Bent
Hey Clough
Brownhill Reservoir
Statham
Meal Hill
Holme
A6024
Stopes Moor
Holme Primary School
The Whams
Issue Clough
Round Hill
Hart Hill
Hart Hill Dyke
Round Hill Flat
Lane
Rake Dike
Gill Hey Bridge
Issue Edge
Netherley
Ramsden Reservoir
Netherley Brow
Ings Bridge
Cliff Edge
Cow Close
Great Hill
Yateholme Cote
146
161
168

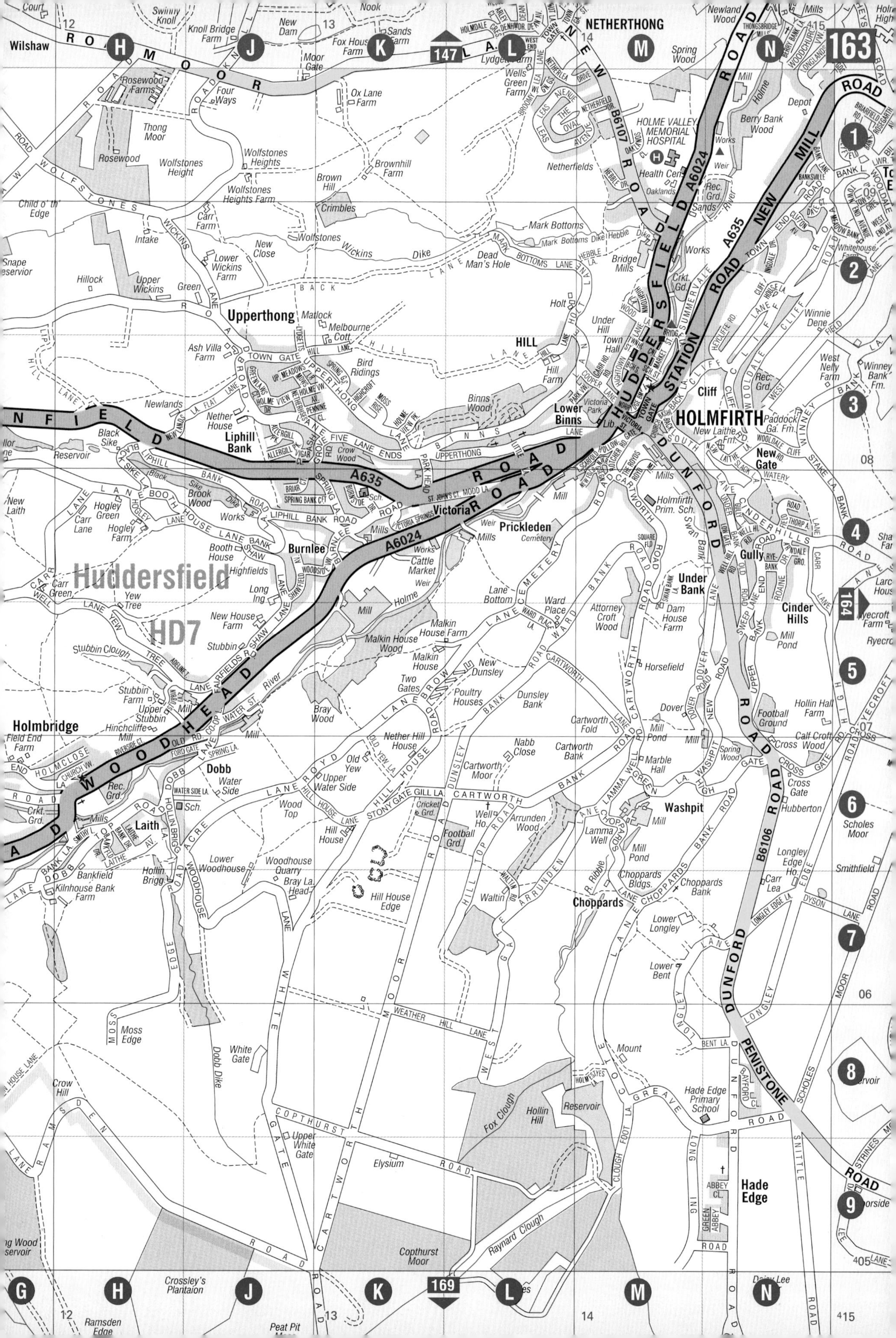
147
169
164
Wilshaw
NETHERTHONG
Upperthong
HOLMFIRTH
Huddersfield
HD7
Holmbridge
Liphill Bank
Burnlee
Victoria
Prickleden
Dobb
Laith
Lower Binns
Cliff
New Gate
Gully
Under Bank
Cinder Hills
Washpit
Choppards
Hade Edge
HILL
MOOR ROAD
WOLFSTONES ROAD
WOODHEAD ROAD
HUDDERSFIELD ROAD
STATION ROAD
NEW MILL ROAD
DUNFORD ROAD
PENISTONE ROAD
A635
A6024
B6107
B6106
HOLME VALLEY MEMORIAL HOSPITAL
Health Cen.
Rosewood Farms
Rosewood
Thong Moor
Four Ways
Wolfstones Heights
Wolfstones Height
Wolfstones Heights Farm
Brownhill Farm
Brown Hill
Crimbles
Ox Lane Farm
Moor Gate
Fox House Farm
New Dam
Sands Farm
Knoll Bridge Farm
Swinny Knoll
Nook
Lydgate Farm
Wells Green Farm
Netherfields
Spring Wood
Newland Wood
Berry Bank Wood
Depot
Works
Weir
Oaklands
Sands
Rec. Grd.
Mark Bottoms
Dead Man's Hole
Bridge Mills
Wolfstones
Wickins Dike
Child o' th' Edge
Intake
Carr Farm
Lower Wickins Farm
New Close
Hillock
Upper Wickins
Green
Matlock
Melbourne Cott.
Ash Villa Farm
Bird Ridings
Holt
Under Hill
Town Hall
Hill Farm
Binns Wood
Victoria Park
Newlands
Nether House
Black Sike
Reservoir
Crow Wood
Brook Wood
Works
Hogley Green
Hogley Farm
Carr Lane
New Laith
Booth House
Highfields
Long Ing
Carr Green
Yew Tree
New House Farm
Stubbin
Stubbin Clough
Stubbin Farm
Upper Stubbin
Hinchcliffe Mill
Field End Farm
Mill
Mills
Cattle Market
Holme
Malkin House Wood
Malkin House Farm
Malkin House
Lane Bottom
Ward Place
Attorney Croft Wood
Dam House Farm
Horsefield
Cemetery
Holmfirth Prim. Sch.
New Laithe Fm.
Paddock Ga. Fm.
Winnie Dene
West Nelly Farm
Winney Bank Fm.
Mill Pond
Hollin Hall Farm
Calf Croft Wood
Cross Gate
Hubberton
Scholes Moor
Smithfield
Longley Edge Ho.
Carr Lea
Lower Longley
Lower Bent
Football Ground
Spring Wood
Dover
Marble Hall
Mill Pond
Lamma Well
Choppards Bldgs.
Choppards Bank
Arrunden Wood
Waltin
Cartworth Fold
Cartworth Bank
Nabb Close
Dunsley Bank
New Dunsley
Poultry Houses
Two Gates
Nether Hill House
Old Yew
Upper Water Side
Cartworth Moor
Well Ho.
Football Grd.
Cricket Grd.
Wood Top
Hill House
Bray Wood
Water Side
Rec. Grd.
Crkt. Grd.
Sch.
Hollin Brigg
Lower Woodhouse
Woodhouse Quarry
Bray La. Head
Hill House Edge
Bankfield
Kilnhouse Bank Farm
Moss Edge
White Gate
Dobb Dike
Crow Hill
Upper White Gate
Elysium
Fox Clough
Hollin Hill
Reservoir
Mount
Raynard Clough
Copthurst Moor
Hade Edge Primary School
Crossley's Plantaion
Ramsden Edge
Peat Pit
Daisy Lee
Snape Reservoir
12
13
14
415
05
06
07
08
09
G
H
J
K
L
M
N
1
2
3
4
5
6
7
8
9

164
148
163
A
B
C
D
E
F
G
1
2
3
4
5
6
7
8
9
415
16
17
18
09
08
07
06
405
Holmfirth High Sch.
Rec. Grd.
Playing Fields
Hill Top Bank
Hollin Green Farm
Hollingreave
Rock Cotts.
Carr Gate
Kaye Wood
Biggin Shrog
Hunger Hill
Stagwood Hill
Croft Bottom Farm
Croft Bottom Cottages
East Field
Wood End Wood Head
Shepley Wood End
Stubs Wood
Moorlands
West Royd Farm
Moor View Farm
Fulstone
Depot
Town End
Schs.
Wooldale Jun. Sch.
WOOLDALE
NEW MILL ROAD
A635
HOLMFIRTH ROAD
HUDDERSFIELD ROAD
A616
New Mill
Carr Wood
Bellgreave
Fulstone Hall
Sude Hill
Horn Cote Wood
Horn Cote
Horn Hill
Drop Down
Ebson Ho.
Brianfield Poultry Farm
Snowgate Head
Lane End
Cemy.
Lib.
Mill
Vic.
Lea Ho.
Carr House
PENISTONE
Whitehouse Farm
Winnie Dene
West Nelly Farm
Winney Bank
Winney Bank Fm.
Res.
West Field
Shaley Wood
Totties
Spring Wood
Oak Lees
Vermont
Bendhill Wood
Butterley
Hole Bottom
Hollin House
Lower Holme House
Holme House Wood
Holme House Dike
Holme Clough
Hirst Brow
Upper Holme House
Short Horns
Fairfield Farm
Downshutts
Wildspur Wood
Mear House
Far High Bank
Near High Bank
Mount Scar
Mount
High Brow
Near Mount
Far Mount
Mount Hill
Brown Hill
Hey Plantation
Jackson Bridge
Stalley Royd
Hullock
Hullock Bank
Shaley Farm
Larch House
Lee Mills Ind. Park
Sandy Gate Farm
Ryecroft Farm
Ryecroft
Cinder Hills
Mill Pond
The Leas (Children's Home)
SCHOLES
Sch.
White Wells
HD7
Dean Bridge Farm
Stubbing Wood
Wood Pit Farm
Rombs Clough
Coal Pit Wood
Scar Hole
Bankhouse Reservoir
High Wood
Bank House
Hill Top
New Field End
Tinker's Tower
Pike Lowe
Hollin Hall Farm
Calf Croft Wood
Cross Gate
Cricket Grd.
Meal Hill
Hall Acre Wood
Brock Holes Nook
Brock Holes
Bank House Wood
Spring Head
Hey Slack Farm
Slack Terrace
Lark's House
HEPWORTH
Dean Bridge
Oak Scar
Scholes Moor
Syke House
Morton Wood
Smithfield
Longley Edge Ho.
Wickleden Wood
Dean Wood
Rec. Grd.
Hepworth Prim. Sch.
How Clough
Rakes Dike
Rakes Wood
Grains Wood
Cheese Gate Nab
Dick Edge
Middle Foster Place
Upper Foster Place
Upper Mill Shaw
Dean Farm
Wickledon
Snug House
SHEFFIELD ROAD
Barnside
Crimes
Strines Moor
Reservoir
Berristal Top
Ox Lee
Cote Hill
Victoria
Berristal Head
Crow Hill
New House
Moorside
Cote
B6106
PENISTONE ROAD
Law
Nab Hill
Upper Nab
Hepshaw Brow
Hepshaw
Wild Boar Clough
Little Law
Bradshaw Edge
Works

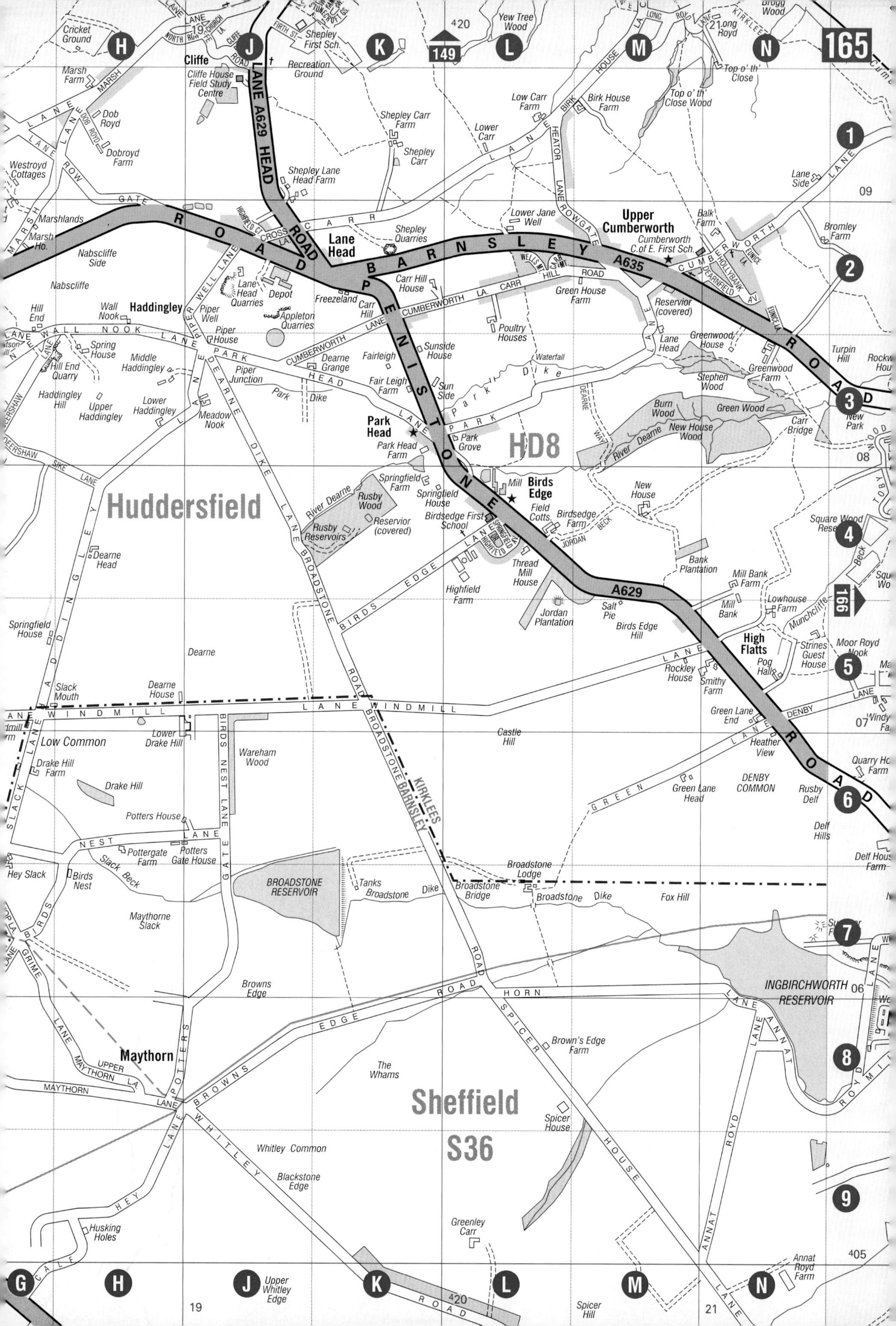
Huddersfield
Sheffield
S36
HD8
Cliffe
Lane Head
Upper Cumberworth
Haddingley
Park Head
Birds Edge
High Flatts
Maythorn
Low Common
DENBY COMMON
BROADSTONE RESERVOIR
INGBIRCHWORTH RESERVOIR
BARNSLEY ROAD
PENISTONE ROAD
A629
A635
KIRKLEES
BARNSLEY
Rusby Wood
Burn Wood
Green Wood
Stephen Wood
Top o' th' Close Wood
Bank Plantation
Jordan Plantation
Wareham Wood
Drake Hill
Whitley Common
Blackstone Edge
The Whams
Browns Edge
Castle Hill
Fox Hill
149
166

Lower Cumberworth
Kitchenroyd
DENBY DALE
Denby Dale
Upper Denby
Lower Denby
Ingbirchworth
Scout Dike
Huddersfield HD8
Sheffield S36
KIRKLEES
BARNSLEY
WAKEFIELD ROAD
BARNSLEY ROAD
A635
A636
A629
B6115
PENISTONE ROAD
HUDDERSFIELD ROAD
INGBIRCHWORTH RESERVOIR
ROYD MOOR RESERVOIR
SCOUT DIKE RESERVOIR
Scout Dike Outdoor Education Centre
Caravan & Camping Site

150
165

Upper Common
Round Hill
Square Spring
Hollin House
151
Horn Wood
Groonland
Friezland
Margery Wood
Wheatley Hill Lodge
Hay Royds Colliery
Lane End Farm
Lower Spring
Upper Spring
Shuff Wood
Upper Stub Nooks Plantation
Lower Stub Nooks Plantation
BAGDEN WOOD
Deffer Nook
Toppitt Farm
Dean Hill Spring
Dean Hill Farm
Hood Wood
Deffer Hill
Ackin Royd
Lodge
Fish Pond
Rookery
Upper Bagden
DEFFER WOOD
Upper Spring
Tower Cottage
Home Farm
Garden Plantation
Cannon Hall
Cannon Hall Museum
Nursery
CANNON HALL
COUNTRY PARK
Weir
Denby Hall Farm
Jowett House Beck
Spring Beck
Jowett House Farm
Lodge
Cascade Bridge
Football Ground
Susannah Spring
Mill
Mill Dam
Killamarsh
Spring House Farm
Daking Brook
Weirs
Flash House Plantation
Barnsley
S75
Beet House
Tivy Dale
Dale House
Royd Wood
Daking Brook Bridge
Raw Green
Somerlees
Bentwood
Cuckold Carr
Ochre Dike
Fryer Royd
Hagg Wood
Daw Walls Farm
Hollin Royd Farm
Daking Brook Farm
Flash House Farm
Clough Green
Woodley
Brookfield
Thimble Hall
ROAD LANE HEAD ROAD A635
Hazel House Farm
Heald Head
Ford
Hill Top Cottages
Rowling Ho.
Works
Bentcliff Hill Plantation
Pease Grove
Ellison Spring
Dixon Wood
Pashley Green Farm
Mount Pleasant
Delph Cottage
Green's Lathe Farm
Upper House
Tanyard Beck
BENTCLIFF HILL
Banks Hall Farm
Banks Hall
Broad Oak
Lane Head Farm
Rons Cliff Wood
Gadding Moor Plantation
Hattersley Wood
Haddon Farmhouse
Hadden Green
Common Side Farm
Tanyard Wood
Ftball. Grd.
Wood Royd
Water Slack
South La.
Grey Cott.
Mill Farm
Rons Cliff Dike
Gunthwaite Bridge
GADDING MOOR
Croft Cottage
Wool Greaves
Small Lanes Farm
Banks Wood
Upper Elmhirst
Clay Pit
Bullhaw Carrs
Bull Haw Hall Farm
Ellhirst Beck
Whin Moor Plantation
Ellhirst Wood
Stud Royd Wood
Roger Royd
Mount Pleasant Farm
Glen Cottage
Whin Moor
Kidfield House Farm
Cat Hill Clough
Cat Hill Clough Wood
Guyder Bottom Farm
Haigh Common
Hill Top
Cat Hill
Prospect House
Hoylandswaine Primary School
Sewage Works
Hill Top House
Pye Flatts
Pye Greave Farm
Vicarage
Renald Lane House
The Cottage
Lower Haigh
Manor House
BARNSLEY RD. NOBLETHORPE A628 LANE
Daw Wells Farm
Cat Hill Firs
Fell Lane Farm
Fell House
Oaks Nook
Hunger Hill
Pinfold Farm
HOYLANDSWAINE
Nook
The Hollies
High Field Plantation
Crab Tree House
Greenside Fm.
New Hall
Green Bottom Farm
Kine Moor Lane
Whin Moor Lane
Cooper Lane
Gadding Moor Road
Gadding Lane
Cross Lane
Renald Lane
North Road
South Road
Haigh Lane
Small Lane
Bark House Lane
High Hoyland Lane
New Road
Bagden Lane
Denby Hall Lane
Hollin House Lane
Wheatley Hill Lane
Upper Lane
Heald Lane
Bentcliff Lane
Woolstocks La.
Dog Kennel Hill
The Park Drive
Back Lane
Tivy Dale
Hill Lane
Green Lane
Whin Lane
Cat Hill Lane
H J K L M N
G H J K L M N
1 2 3 4 5 6 7 8 9
425 26 27 28
09 08 07 06 405

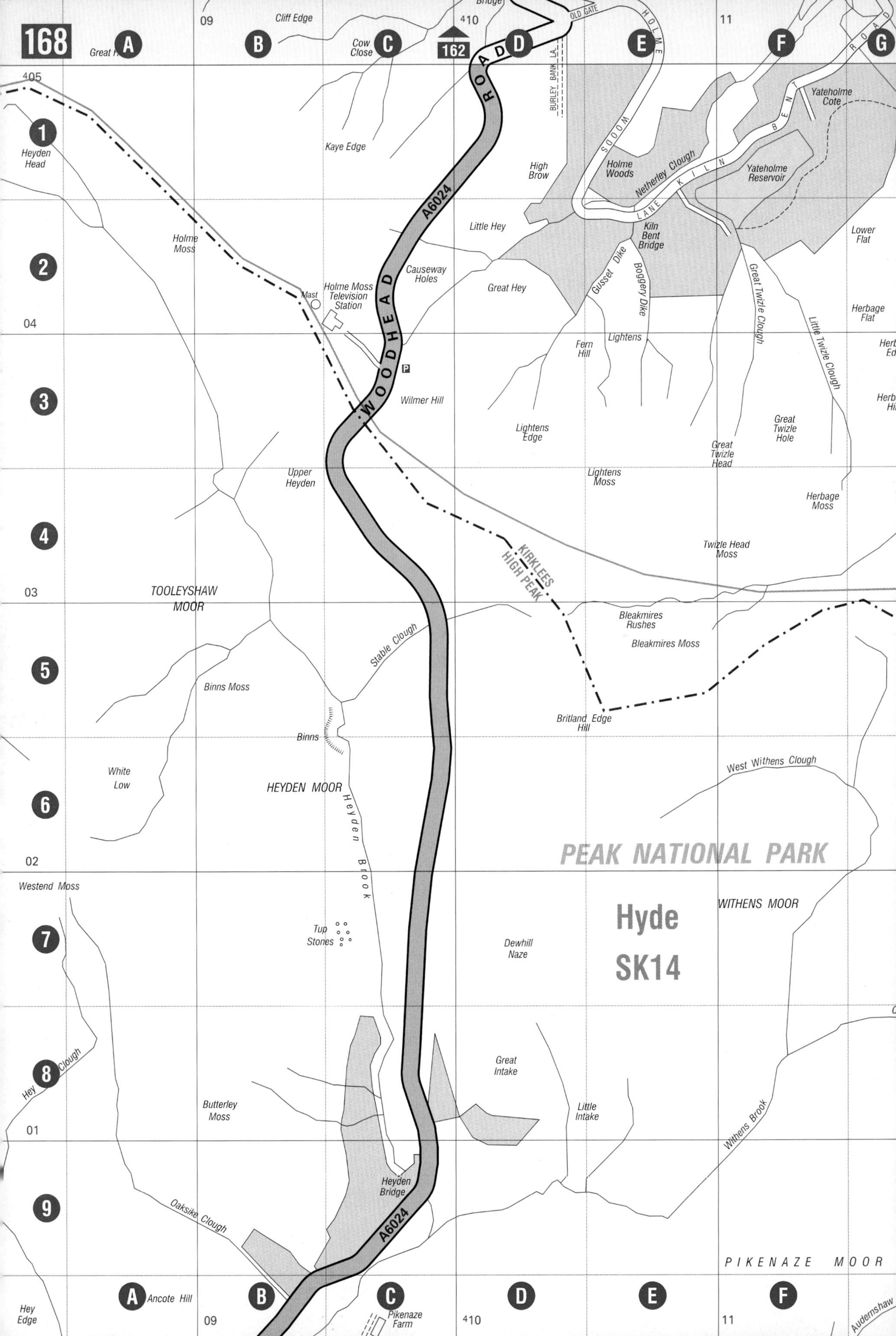

162
Cliff Edge
Cow Close
Kaye Edge
Heyden Head
Holme Moss
Mast
Holme Moss Television Station
WOODHEAD ROAD
A6024
High Brow
Little Hey
Causeway Holes
Great Hey
Holme Woods
Netherley Clough
Yateholme Cote
Yateholme Reservoir
BENT ROAD
KILN BENT LANE
WOODS HOLME
OLD GATE
BURLEY BANK LA.
Kiln Bent Bridge
Gusset Dike
Boggery Dike
Great Twizle Clough
Little Twizle Clough
Lower Flat
Herbage Flat
Lightens
Fern Hill
Wilmer Hill
Lightens Edge
Great Twizle Head
Great Twizle Hole
Upper Heyden
Lightens Moss
Herbage Moss
Twizle Head Moss
KIRKLEES
HIGH PEAK
TOOLEYSHAW MOOR
Bleakmires Rushes
Bleakmires Moss
Stable Clough
Binns Moss
Britland Edge Hill
Binns
White Low
HEYDEN MOOR
Heyden Brook
West Withens Clough
PEAK NATIONAL PARK
Westend Moss
WITHENS MOOR
Hyde
SK14
Tup Stones
Dewhill Naze
Great Intake
Hey Clough
Butterley Moss
Little Intake
Withens Brook
Heyden Bridge
Oaksike Clough
PIKENAZE MOOR
Ancote Hill
Hey Edge
Pikenaze Farm
Audenshaw

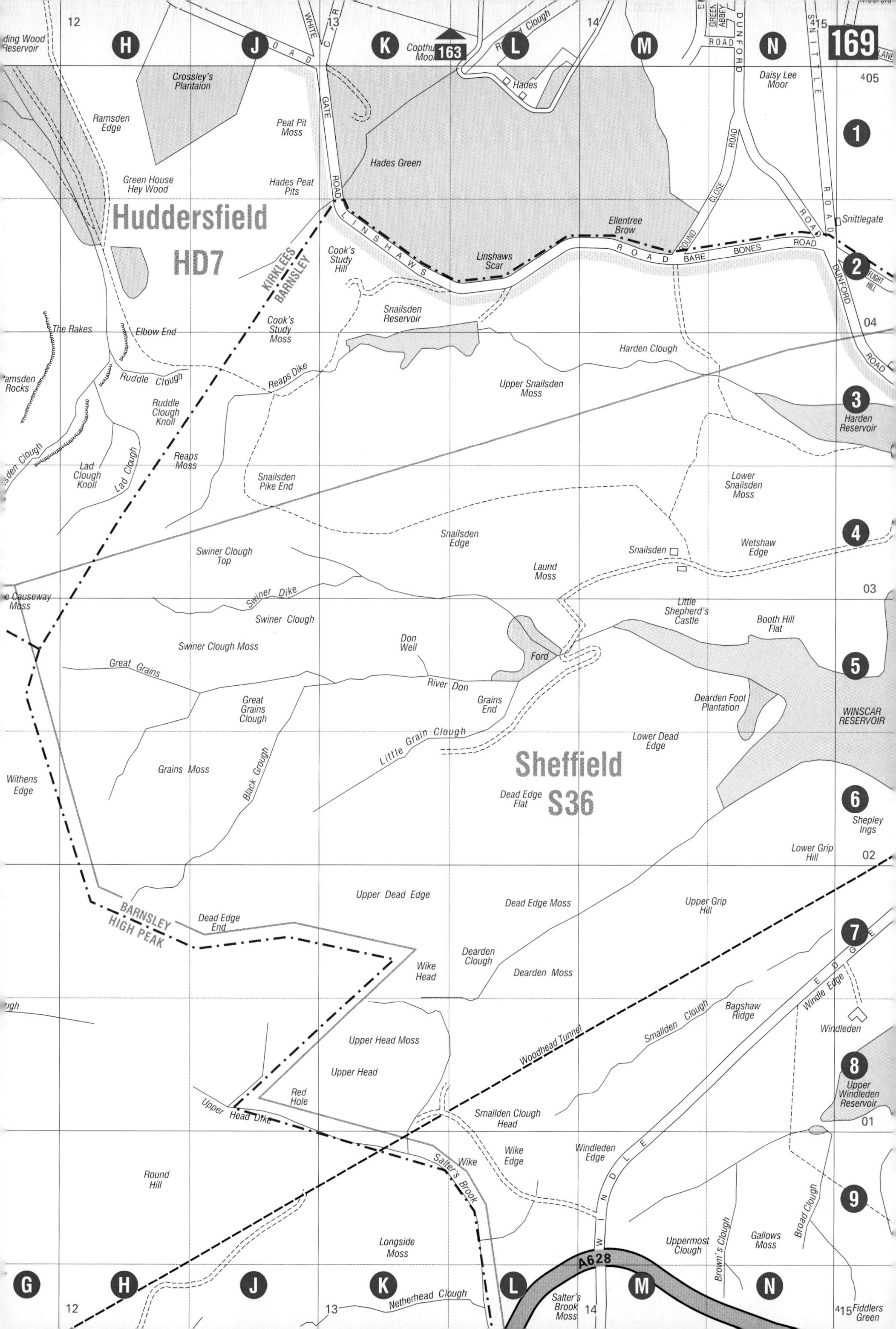
Huddersfield
HD7
Sheffield
S36
KIRKLEES
BARNSLEY
BARNSLEY
HIGH PEAK
Crossley's Plantaion
Ramsden Edge
Green House Hey Wood
Peat Pit Moss
Hades Peat Pits
Hades Green
Hades
Daisy Lee Moor
Snittlegate
Ellentree Brow
Linshaws Scar
Cook's Study Hill
Cook's Study Moss
Snailsden Reservoir
The Rakes
Elbow End
Ruddle Clough
Ruddle Clough Knoll
Reaps Dike
Reaps Moss
Lad Clough Knoll
Lad Clough
Harden Clough
Upper Snailsden Moss
Harden Reservoir
Lower Snailsden Moss
Snailsden Pike End
Snailsden Edge
Snailsden
Wetshaw Edge
Swiner Clough Top
Laund Moss
Swiner Dike
Swiner Clough
Swiner Clough Moss
Little Shepherd's Castle
Booth Hill Flat
Don Well
Ford
River Don
Great Grains
Great Grains Clough
Grains End
Dearden Foot Plantation
WINSCAR RESERVOIR
Little Grain Clough
Lower Dead Edge
Withens Edge
Grains Moss
Black Grough
Dead Edge Flat
Shepley Ings
Lower Grip Hill
Upper Dead Edge
Dead Edge Moss
Upper Grip Hill
Dead Edge End
Dearden Clough
Wike Head
Dearden Moss
Windle Edge
Bagshaw Ridge
Smallden Clough
Windleden
Woodhead Tunnel
Upper Head Moss
Upper Head
Upper Windleden Reservoir
Red Hole
Upper Head Dike
Smallden Clough Head
Wike
Wike Edge
Windleden Edge
Salter's Brook
Round Hill
Broad Clough
Uppermost Clough
Gallows Moss
Brown's Clough
Longside Moss
A628
Netherhead Clough
Salter's Brook Moss
Fiddlers Green
Withens Edge
Causeway Moss
Ramsden Rocks
WHITE GATE ROAD
LINSHAWS ROAD
BARE BONES ROAD
DUNFORD ROAD
SNITTLE ROAD
ROUND CLOSE ROAD
GREEN ABBEY ROAD
WINDLE EDGE
163
H J K L M N G
1 2 3 4 5 6 7 8 9
12 13 14 415
405 04 03 02 01

INDEX

Including Streets, Places & Areas, Industrial Estates, Selected Subsidiary Addresses
and Selected Places of Interest

HOW TO USE THIS INDEX

1. Each street name is followed by its Posttown or Postal Locality and then by its map reference; e.g. Aachen Way. *Hal* —7M **91** is in the Halifax Posttown and is to be found in square 7M on page **91**. The page number being shown in bold type.
A strict alphabetical order is followed in which Av., Rd., St., etc. (though abbreviated) are read in full and as part of the street name; e.g. Alder St. appears after Alderstone Ri. but before Aldersyde.

2. Streets and a selection of Subsidiary names not shown on the Maps, appear in the index in Italics with the thoroughfare to which it is connected shown in brackets; e.g. *Abbey Ct. B'frd —6A **58** (off Stallabrass St.)*

3. Places and areas are shown in the index in bold type, the map reference referring to the actual map square in which the town or area is located and not to the place name; e.g. **Aberford. —8E 48**

4. An example of a selected place of interest is ***Abbey House Museum. —1J 61***

GENERAL ABBREVIATIONS

All : Alley
App : Approach
Arc : Arcade
Av : Avenue
Bk : Back
Boulevd : Boulevard
Bri : Bridge
B'way : Broadway
Bldgs : Buildings
Bus : Business
Cvn : Caravan
Cen : Centre
Chu : Church
Chyd : Churchyard
Circ : Circle
Cir : Circus
Clo : Close
Comn : Common
Cotts : Cottages
Ct : Court
Cres : Crescent
Cft : Croft
Dri : Drive
E : East
Embkmt : Embankment
Est : Estate
Fld : Field
Gdns : Gardens
Gth : Garth
Ga : Gate
Gt : Great
Grn : Green
Gro : Grove
Ho : House
Ind : Industrial
Info : Information
Junct : Junction
La : Lane
Lit : Little
Lwr : Lower
Mc : Mac
Mnr : Manor
Mans : Mansions
Mkt : Market
Mdw : Meadow
M : Mews
Mt : Mount
Mus : Museum
N : North
Pal : Palace
Pde : Parade
Pk : Park
Pas : Passage
Pl : Place
Quad : Quadrant
Res : Residential
Ri : Rise
Rd : Road
Shop : Shopping
S : South
Sq : Square
Sta : Station
St : Street
Ter : Terrace
Trad : Trading
Up : Upper
Va : Vale
Vw : View
Vs : Villas
Vis : Visitors
Wlk : Walk
W : West
Yd : Yard

POSTTOWN AND POSTAL LOCALITY ABBREVIATIONS

Aber : Aberford
Ack : Ackton
Ackw : Ackworth
Add : Addingham
Adel : Adel
Agb : Agbrigg
Ain T : Ainley Top
All : Allerton
All B : Allerton Bywater
Alm : Almondbury
Altft : Altofts
Althpe : Alverthorpe
Alw : Alwoodley
App B : Apperley Bridge
Arm B : Armitage Bridge
A'ley : Armley
Arth : Arthington
Askw : Askwith
Asp : Aspley
Bads : Badsworth
Bail : Baildon
Bail B : Bailiff Bridge
B Top : Bank Top
Bard : Bardsey
Bklnd : Barkisland
Barn : Barnsley
B Grn : Barugh Green
Bar E : Barwick in Elmet
Bat : Batley
Bat C : Batley Carr
Bees : Beeston
Ben R : Ben Rhydding
Ber B : Berry Brow
Bick : Bickerton
Bier : Bierley
Bilt A : Bilton-in-Ainsty
Bgly : Bingley
Birds : Birdsedge
Bkby : Birkby
B'shaw : Birkenshaw
Birk : Birkin
Birs : Birstall
B Mon : Bishop Monkton
B'ley : Blackley
Blkhd : Blackshawhead
B'twn : Boothtown
B Spa : Boston Spa
B'frd : Bradford
Bdly : Bradley
Bshw : Bradshaw
B'ham : Bramham
B'hpe : Bramhope
Bmly : Bramley
Bret : Bretton
Brier : Brierley
Bstfld : Briestfield
Brigh : Brighouse
Broc : Brockholes
B'ton : Brotherton
Brun I : Brunswick Ind. Est.
Burg : Burghwallis
Bur W : Burley in Wharfedale
Bur W : Burton on the Wolds
Bur S : Burton Salmon
Butt : Buttershaw
Byr : Byram
Cald G : Calder Grove
C'ley : Calverley
Cam : Campsall
Carc : Carcroft
C'ton : Carleton
Cltn : Carlton (nr. Nottingham)
Carl : Carlton (nr. Wakefield)
Carr G : Carr Gate
C'frd : Castleford
Caus F : Causeway Foot
Caw : Cawthorne
Chap A : Chapel Allerton
C'thpe : Chapelthorpe
Chap : Chapeltown
C'twn : Charlestown
Chick : Chickenley
Chur : Churwell
Cytn : Clayton (nr. Bradford)
Clay : Clayton (nr. Doncaster)
Clay W : Clayton West
Cleck : Cleckheaton
Cliff : Clifford
Clif : Clifton
Clif C : Clifton Common
C'den : Colden
Coll : Collingham
Colt : Colton
Cnly : Cononley
Cook : Cookridge
Cop : Copley
Corn : Cornholme
Ctly : Cottingley
Cow : Cowlersley
Cowl : Cowling
Crack : Crackenedge
Cra V : Cragg Vale
Crid S : Cridling Stubbs
Crig : Crigglestone
Croft : Crofton
Cros H : Crosland Hill
Cros M : Crosland Moor
C'gts : Crossgates
C Grn : Cross Green
Cro R : Cross Roads
Cud : Cudworth
Cull : Cullingworth
Cumb : Cumberworth
Cut H : Cutler Heights
Cuts : Cutsyke
D Hill : Daisy Hill
Dltn : Dalton
D'ton : Darrington
Dart : Darton
Dean C : Dean Clough Ind. Pk.
D'tn : Deighton
Den D : Denby Dale
Denh : Denholme
Den : Denton
Dew : Dewsbury
Dew M : Dewsbury Moor
Dlgtn : Drighlington
Dunf B : Dunford Bridge
Dur : Durkar
Earl : Earlsheaton
E Ard : East Ardsley
E Bier : East Bierley
Eastb : Eastborough
Ebrn : Eastburn
E Hard : East Hardwick
E Kes : East Keswick
Eastm : Eastmoor
E Mor : East Morton
Eccl : Eccleshill
Eccup : Eccup
Eld : Eldwick
Ell : Elland
Eml : Emley
Eml M : Emley Moor
Err : Erringden
Esh : Esholt
Euro I : Euroway Ind. Est.
Facit : Facit
Fag : Fagley
Fair : Fairburn
F'ley : Farnley
Far T : Farnley Tyas
Fars : Farsley
Far : Fartown
F'stne : Featherstone
Fen B : Fenay Bridge
Fern : Ferncliffe
F'bri : Ferrybridge
Field B : Fieldhead Bus. Cen.
Fitz : Fitzwilliam
Five E : Five Lane Ends
Fix : Fixby
Fla : Flatts, The
Floc : Flockton
Floc M : Flockton Moor
Flush : Flush
Foul : Foulby
Four E : Four Lane Ends
Friz : Frizinghall
Fry : Fryston
Gar : Garforth
Gild : Gildersome
Gil : Gilstead
Glass : Glasshoughton
Gol : Golcar
Gom : Gomersal
Grng M : Grange Moor
Gt Hor : Great Horton
G'fld : Greenfield
Gre : Greengates
G'lnd : Greetland
Grime : Grimethorpe
Guis : Guiseley
Haig : Haigh
Hain : Hainworth
Hal : Halifax
Hall G : Hall Green
Halt : Halton
Hamp : Hampole
Hang H : Hanging Heaton
H'den : Harden
Hare : Harewood
Harts : Hartshead
H'cft : Havercroft
H'clgh : Hawksclough
Haw : Haworth
H'wd : Hazlewood
Head : Headingley
H'th : Heath
H'tn : Heaton
Heb : Hebden
H Bri : Hebden Bridge
Heck : Heckmondwike
Hems : Hemsworth
Hept : Heptonstall
Hep : Hepworth
H Bir : High Birstwith
H Eld : High Eldwick
High : Highfield
H Hoy : High Hoyland
H'town : Hightown
Hill : Hillhouse
Hip : Hipperholme
H'bck : Holbeck
Holmb : Holmbridge
Holme : Holme
H Wd : Holme Wood
H'fld : Holmfield
H'frth : Holmfirth
Holy G : Holywell Green
Hon : Honley
Horb : Horbury
H'fth : Horsforth
Hov E : Hove Edge
Huby : Huby
Hud : Huddersfield
H'let : Hunslet
Hun P : Hunslet Bus. Pk.
Huns : Hunsworth
Hyde P : Hyde Park
Idle : Idle
Idle M : Idle Moor
I'ly : Ilkley
I'wth : Illingworth
Ing : Ingbirchworth
Int : Intake
Jack B : Jackson Bridge
Kear : Kearby
Kei : Keighley
Kild : Kildwick
Kin : Kinsley
Kip : Kippax
Kbtn : Kirkburton
Kirk D : Kirk Deighton
K'gte : Kirkhamgate
Khtn : Kirkheaton
K S'ton : Kirk Smeaton
Kirks : Kirkstall
K'thpe : Kirkthorpe
Knot : Knottingley
Lais : Laisterdyke
Lang G : Langthwaite Grange Ind. Est.
Lay : Laycock
Leat : Leathley
Led : Ledsham
Leds : Ledston
Leeds : Leeds
Lep : Lepton
Light : Lightcliffe
Lind : Lindley
Lint : Linthwaite
Lntn : Linton
List : Listerhills
L'boro : Littleborough
Lit S : Little Smeaton
Lit T : Little Town
Liv : Liversedge
Lock : Lockwood
Loft : Lofthouse
Loft G : Lofthouse Gate
Lgwd : Longwood
Lwr C : Lower Cumberworth
Lwr D : Lower Denby
Lower : Lowerhouses
Lwr W : Lower Wortley
L Wyke : Lower Wyke
Lfds B : Lowfields Bus. Pk.
Low M : Low Moor
Lowt : Lowtown
Low U : Low Utley
Ludd : Luddenden
L'ft : Luddendenfoot
Mann : Manningham
M'well : Mapplewell
Mars : Marsden
Mar : Marsh
Mean : Meanwood
Mel : Meltham
Mel M : Meltham Mills
Men : Menston
Meth : Methley
M'fld : Micklefield
M'wte : Micklethwaite
Mick M : Mickletown Methley
M'twn : Middlestown
Midd : Middleton
Midg : Midgeley
Mill B : Mill Bank
Milns : Milnsbridge
Miln : Milnthorpe
Mir : Mirfield
Mix : Mixenden
Mold : Moldgreen
M'end : Moorend
M'hse : Moorhouse
Msde : Moorside
Moort : Moortown
Morl : Morley
Mnt : Mount
Mt Tab : Mount Tabor
Myth : Mytholmroyd
Nesf : Nesfield
Nthng : Netherthong

Posttown and Postal Locality Abbreviations

Neth : Netherton
N Clift : Newall With Clifton
N Bnk : New Bank
N Brig : New Brighton
New C : New Crofton
N Farn : New Farnley
New M : New Mill
N'dam : Newmillerdam
New S : New Sharlston
New : Newsome
N Hill : Newton Hill
Newt K : Newton Kyme
N Wort : New Wortley
Norl : Norland
Norm : Normanton (nr. Bottesford)
Nor : Normanton (nr. Wakefield)
Nor I : Normanton Ind. Est.
Norr : Norristhorpe
N Elm : North Elmsall
N'wram : Northowram
N Rig : North Rigton
Nort : Norton
Nor G : Norwood Green
Nost : Nostell
Not : Notton
Oaken : Oakenshaw
Oakes : Oakes
Oakw : Oakworth
Ogden : Ogden
Oldf : Oldfield
Old : Oldham
Old Sk : Old Skellow
Old Sn : Old Snydale
Oss : Ossett
Otley : Otley
Oult : Oulton
Outl : Outlane
Out : Outwood
Oven : Ovenden
Oven W : Ovenden Wood
Ove : Overton
Oxe : Oxenhope
Pad : Paddock
Pec W : Pecket Well
Pel : Pellon
Pen : Penistone
Pen I : Penraevon Ind. Est.
Pon : Pontefract
Pool W : Pool in Wharfedale
Pott : Potternewton
Pot : Potterton
Prim H : Primrose Hill
Pud : Pudsey
Quarm : Quarmby
Q'bry : Queensbury
Ragg : Raggalds
Ras : Rastrick
Raven : Ravensthorpe
Rav I : Ravensthorpe Ind. Est.
Rawd : Rawdon
Rawf : Rawfolds
Raw : Rawmarsh
Riddl : Riddlesden
Ripp : Ripponden
Rish : Rishworth
Rbtwn : Roberttown
Rob H : Robin Hood
Rod : Rodley
Rothw : Rothwell
Round : Roundhay
Roys : Royston
Ryh : Ryhill
Ryl : Rylstone
Sal N : Salendine Nook
S'dal : Sandal
Sandb : Sandbeds
Sandt : Sandtoft
Sav T : Savile Town
Saxt : Saxton
Scam : Scammonden
Sca H : Scapegoat Hill
S'cft : Scarcroft
Schol : Scholes (nr. Cleckheaton)
Sch : Scholes (nr. Huddersfield)
Scholes : Scholes (nr. Leeds)
Scis : Scissett
Seac : Seacroft
Shad : Shadwell
Shaf : Shafton
Shar C : Sharlston Common
Shaw B : Shaw Cross Bus. Pk.
S'fth : Shawforth
Sheep : Sheepridge
She : Shelf
Shel : Shelley
Shepl : Shepley
Sher E : Sherburn in Elmet
Shib : Shibden
Shipl : Shipley
Sick : Sicklinghall
Sid : Siddal
Silk : Silkstone
Sils : Silsden
Skelb : Skelbrooke
Skel : Skellow
Skelm : Skelmanthorpe
Ski G : Skircoat Green
Slai : Slaithwaite
S Cro : South Crosland
S Elm : South Elmsall
S Hien : South Hiendley
S Kirk : South Kirkby
S Mil : South Milford
S'wram : Southowram
Sower : Sowerby
Sower B : Sowerby Bridge
Sow : Sowood
Stainb : Stainburn
Stainc : Staincliffe
Slnd : Stainland
Stain : Stainton
Stanb : Stanbury
Stan : Stanley (nr. Ilkeston)
Stanl : Stanley (nr. Wakefield)
S'ley : Stanningley
Stap : Stapleton
Steet : Steeton
Stkmr : Stocksmoor
S'hse : Streethouse
Stum X : Stump Cross
Stut : Stutton
Sum : Summit
Sut : Sutton
Swil : Swillington
Swil C : Swillington Common
Tad : Tadcaster
Tan : Tandem
Tay H : Taylor Hill
Thack : Thackley
Thon : Thongsbridge
Thornb : Thornbury
T'ner : Thorner
Thorn : Thornhill
Thorn L : Thornhill Lees
T'tn : Thornton
Thor L : Thornton Lodge
Thor A : Thorp Arch
Thpe : Thorpe (nr. Ashbourne)
Thor : Thorpe (nr. Wakefield)
Thpe A : Thorpe Audlin
Thur : Thurstonland
T Brow : Thwaites Brow
Ting : Tingley
Todm : Todmorden
Tong : Tong
Tri : Triangle
Tyer : Tyersal
Up Cum : Upper Cumberworth
Up Den : Upper Denby
Uthg : Upperthong
Upt : Upton
Utley : Utley
Wads : Wadshelf
Wadsw : Wadsworth
Wains : Wainstalls
Wake : Wakefield
Wake B : Wakefield 41 Bus. Pk.
Wake I : Wakefield 41 Ind. Est.
Wals : Walsden
Wltn : Walton (nr. Boston Spa)
Walt : Walton (nr. Chesterfield)
W'ton : Walton (nr. Wakefield)
Warley : Warley
Warm : Warmfield
W'loo : Waterloo
Wee : Weeton
Weet : Weetwood
Went : Wentbridge
West I : West 26 Ind. Est.
W Bowl : West Bowling
Wgte : Westgate
W Har : West Hardwick
Weston : Weston
W Park : West Park
Wtwn : Westtown
Weth : Wetherby
Wheat : Wheatley
Whinm : Whinmoor
W'ley : Whitley
W'wood : Whitwood
W'wd M : Whitwood Mere
W'wth : Whitworth
Wibs : Wibsey
Wigh : Wighill
Wigh P : Wighill Park
Wike : Wike
Wilsd : Wilsden
Windh : Windhill
Wome : Womersley
W'ford : Woodlesford
Wool : Woolley
Wort : Wortley
Woth : Wothersome
Wrag : Wragby
Wren : Wrenthorpe
Wrose : Wrose
Wyke : Wyke
Wyth I : Wyther Park Ind. Est.
Yead : Yeadon

INDEX

A1 Bus. Pk. *Knot* —9B **104**
Aachen Way. *Hal* —7M **91**
Aaron Wilkinson Ct. *S Kirk* —7G **156**
Abaseen Clo. *B'frd* —7F **58**
Abbe's Clo., The. *Burg* —4N **159**
Abbe's Wlk., The. *Burg* —4N **159**
Abbey Av. *Leeds* —3J **61**
Abbey Clo. *Add* —1N **7**
Abbey Clo. *H'frth* —9N **163**
Abbey Ct. B'frd —6A ***58***
(off Stallabrass St.)
Abbey Ct. *H'fth* —9E **42**
Abbeydale Gdns. *Leeds* —9H **43**
Abbeydale Gth. *Leeds* —9H **43**
Abbeydale Gro. *Leeds* —9H **43**
Abbeydale Mt. *Leeds* —9H **43**
Abbeydale Oval. *Leeds* —9H **43**
Abbeydale Va. *Leeds* —9H **43**
Abbeydale Way. *Leeds* —9H **43**
Abbey Dri. *Shepl* —8K **149**
Abbey Farm Dri. *Shepl* —9K **149**
Abbey Gth. Yead —1M ***41***
(off Well Hill)
Abbey Gorse. *Leeds* —1K **61**
Abbey House Museum. —1J 61
Abbey La. *Hal* —5F **90**
Abbey Lea. *All* —6H **57**
Abbey Mt. *Leeds* —3J **61**
Abbey Rd. *Bat* —8C **96**
Abbey Rd. *Hud* —1N **131**
Abbey Rd. *Leeds* —9G **42**
Abbey Rd. *Shepl* —9J **149**
Abbey Rd. N. *Shepl* —8K **149**
Abbey Rd. S. *Shepl* —9K **149**
Abbey St. *Leeds* —6B **62**
Abbey Ter. *Kirks* —3J **61**
Abbey Vw. *Kirks* —1K **61**
Abbey Wlk. *Hal* —8B **92**
Abbey Wlk. *Leeds* —1J **61**
Abbey Wlk. S. *Hal* —8C **92**
Abbot La. *Wool* —3K **153**
Abbotside Clo. *B'frd* —9G **40**
Abbots Pl. *Hud* —6D **114**
Abbot St. *Hud* —3K **131**
Abbotsway. *Gar* —8L **65**
Abbots Wood. B'frd —3M ***57***
(off Heaton Rd.)
Abbott Ct. *Leeds* —6N **61**
Abbott Rd. *Leeds* —7N **61**
Abbotts Clo. *Aber* —7E **48**
Abbott Ter. *Wake* —8M **119**
Abbott Vw. *Leeds* —6N **61**
Abb Scott La. *B'frd & Low M* —7N **75**
Abb St. *Hud* —3J **131**
Abelia Mt. *B'frd* —8K **57**
Abel St. *Wyke* —9A **76**
Aberdeen Dri. *Leeds* —7K **61**
Aberdeen Gro. *Leeds* —7K **61**
Aberdeen Pl. *B'frd* —9M **57**
Aberdeen Rd. *Leeds* —7K **61**
Aberdeen Ter. *B'frd* —9M **57**
Aberdeen Ter. *Cytn* —1J **75**
Aberdeen Wlk. *Leeds* —7K **61**
Aberfield Bank. *Leeds* —7G **80**
Aberfield Clo. *Leeds* —6G **80**
Aberfield Crest. *Leeds* —7G **80**
Aberfield Dri. *Crig* —6G **136**
Aberfield Dri. *Leeds* —7G **80**
Aberfield Gdns. *Leeds* —6G **80**
Aberfield Ga. *Leeds* —6G **80**
Aberfield Mt. *Leeds* —7G **80**
Aberfield Ri. *Leeds* —7G **80**
Aberfield Rd. *Leeds* —6G **80**
Aberfield Wlk. *Leeds* —7F **80**
Aberford. —8E 48
Aberford Rd. *Bar E* —8M **47**
Aberford Rd. *B'frd* —5N **57**
Aberford Rd. *B'ham* —7D **32**
Aberford Rd. *Gar* —6N **65**
Aberford Rd. *Oult & W'ford* —8D **82**
Aberford Rd. *Wake & Stan* —3N **119**
Abingdon St. *B'frd* —5N **57**
Abingdon St. *Hud* —1M **131**
Abraham Hill. *Rothw* —8A **82**
Abram St. *B'frd* —1C **76**
Acacia Av. *S Elm* —5N **157**
Acacia Clo. *C'frd* —6K **103**
Acacia Dri. *All* —2E **56**
Acacia Dri. *C'frd* —6J **103**
Acacia Dri. *Hal* —5M **93**
Acacia Grn. *Pon* —2M **123**
Acacia Gro. *H Bri* —3N **89**
Acacia Gro. *Shaf* —7K **155**
Acacia Ho. C'frd —5E ***102***
(off Parklands)
Acacia Pk. Cres. *B'frd* —5K **41**
Acacia Pk. Dri. *B'frd* —5K **41**
Acacia Pk. Ter. *B'frd* —5L **41**
Acacia Rd. *Skel* —7M **159**
Acacia Wlk. *Knot* —9C **104**
Acaster Dri. *Gar* —8A **66**
Acaster Dri. *Low M* —7A **76**
Accommodation Rd. *Leeds* —5G **63**
Acer Way. *Cleck* —4D **94**
Ackroyd Ct. *T'tn* —8C **56**
Ackroyd Pl. *Q'bry* —4C **74**
Ackroyd Sq. *Q'bry* —4G **74**
Ackroyd St. *Morl* —9L **79**
Ackroyd St. *Todm* —3D **86**
Ackton. —3A 122
Ackton Clo. *Ack* —2A **122**
Ackton Hall Cres. *Ack* —3A **122**
Ackton La. *Ack* —3A **122**
Ackton Pasture La. *C'frd* —7N **101**
Ackworth Av. *Yead* —1N **41**
Ackworth Bridle Rd. *E Hard* —3L **141**
Ackworth Cres. *Yead* —1N **41**
Ackworth Dri. *Yead* —1N **41**
Ackworth Ho. Clo. *Ackw* —2G **140**
Ackworth Lodge. *Ackw* —2G **140**
Ackworth Moor Top. —6F 140
Ackworth Rd. *F'stne* —7D **122**
Ackworth Rd. *Pon* —7H **123**
Ackworth St. *B'frd* —1C **76**
Acme Ter. *Wake* —8M **119**
Acomb Ter. *Wyke* —1A **94**
Acorn Bus. Pk. *Leeds* —5N **63**
Acorn Dri. *Leeds* —7D **46**
Acorn Gro. *H'frth* —5B **164**
Acorn Pk. *Bail* —5C **40**
Acorn St. *B'frd* —8E **58**
Acorn St. *Hal* —5N **91**
Acorn St. *Kei* —2H **37**
Acott Av. *Brigh* —3L **113**
Acott Cres. *H Bri* —3M **89**
Acott Ga. *B'frd* —7H **59**
Acre Av. *B'frd* —1F **58**
Acre Cir. *Leeds* —9E **80**
Acre Clo. *B'frd* —1F **58**
Acre Clo. *Leeds* —1D **98**
Acre Ct. *Leeds* —1E **98**
Acre Cres. *B'frd* —1F **58**
Acre Cres. *Leeds* —9E **80**
Acre Dri. *B'frd* —1F **58**
Acre Fold. *Add* —1L **7**
Acre Gro. *B'frd* —1F **58**
Acre Gro. *Leeds* —9E **80**
Acre Ho. Av. *Hud* —2H **131**
Acrehowe Ri. *Bail* —3C **40**
Acre La. *B'frd* —2F **58**
(in two parts)
Acre La. *E Mor* —8D **22**
Acre La. *Haw* —8C **36**
Acre La. *Hept* —7D **70**
Acre La. *H'frth* —6J **163**
Acre La. *L'ft* —1C **90**
Acre La. *Mel* —8E **146**
Acre La. *N Mill* —1E **164**
(nr. Fulstone Hall La.)
Acre La. *N Mill* —2F **164**
(nr. Horn La.)
Acre La. *Pen* —9G **167**
Acre La. *Wibs* —4A **76**
Acre Mt. *Leeds* —9E **80**
Acre Pl. *Midd* —9E **80**
Acre Ri. *Bail* —3A **40**
Acre Rd. *Leeds* —9D **80**
Acres Hall Av. *Pud* —8D **60**
Acres Hall Cres. *Pud* —8D **60**
Acres Hall Dri. *Pud* —8D **60**
Acres La. *Hept* —9G **70**
Acres La. *H'frth* —4D **162**
Acres Rd. *Loft* —4L **99**
Acres St. *Kei* —1H **37**
Acres, The. *Add* —9N **5**
Acre St. *Hud* —2G **131**
Acre St. *Leeds* —9F **80**
Acre St. *W'wth* —9A **106**
Acre Ter. *Leeds* —9F **80**
Acre, The. *Wyke* —8N **75**
Acre Vs. *H Bri* —3M **89**
Acton Flat La. *Hud* —8F **112**
Acton St. *B'frd* —7G **59**
Acute Ter. *Wake* —5G **119**
Adam Ct. *Hud* —1G **130**
Adam Cft. *Cull* —9K **37**
Adam Ga. *Hal* —7M **91**
Adams All. *Rothw* —9K **81**
Adams Gro. *Leeds* —2F **64**
Adams Pk. *Add* —1M **7**
Adam St. *B'frd* —4N **75**
Adam St. *Todm* —6K **87**
Adam's Wlk. Leeds —4B ***62***
(off Moorland Rd.)
Ada's Pl. *S'ley* —4B **60**
Ada St. *Bail* —5C **40**
Ada St. *Hal* —3B **92**
Ada St. *Kei* —9G **21**
Ada St. *Q'bry* —4C **74**
Ada St. *Shipl* —7L **39**
Addersgate La. *Hal* —9D **74**
Addingford. —2D 136
Addingford Clo. *Horb* —2C **136**
Addingford Dri. *Horb* —2C **136**
Addingford La. *Horb* —2C **136**
Addingham. —1L 7
Addingham Gdns. *Leeds* —7K **61**
Addingham Moorside. —5M 7
Addingham Wharfedale Rd. *Add* —7J **5**
Addison Av. *B'frd* —5H **59**
Addison Av. *Nor* —2K **121**
Addison Clo. *Colt* —8E **64**
Addison Ct. *Horb* —9E **118**
Addison Dri. *Haw* —9C **36**
Addi St. *B'frd* —2G **76**
Addle Croft La. *Lep* —5J **133**
Addlethorpe La. *Sick* —3A **16**
Addy Cres. *S Elm* —6M **157**
Adel. —4M 43
Adelaide Ho. *Bgly* —5G **38**
Adelaide Ri. Bail —6A ***40***
(off John St.)
Adelaide St. *B'frd* —9C **58**
Adelaide St. *Hal* —5M **91**
Adelaide St. *H Bri* —1G **88**
Adelaide St. *Todm* —6K **87**
Adelaide Ter. *Holy G* —8M **111**
Adel East Moor. —4A 44
Adel Gth. *Leeds* —2N **43**
Adel Grange Clo. *Leeds* —5M **43**
Adel Grange Cft. *Leeds* —5M **43**
Adel Grange M. *Leeds* —5M **43**
(in two parts)
Adel Grn. *Leeds* —3N **43**
Adeline Ter. *H'frth* —5H **163**
Adel La. *Leeds* —3M **43**
Adel Mead. *Leeds* —3N **43**
Adel Mill. —1M 43
Adel Mill. *Leeds* —1N **43**
Adel Pk. Clo. *Leeds* —4M **43**
Adel Pk. Ct. *Leeds* —4M **43**
Adel Pk. Cft. *Leeds* —4M **43**
Adel Pk. Dri. *Leeds* —4M **43**
Adel Pk. Gdns. *Leeds* —4M **43**
Adel Pasture. *Leeds* —4M **43**
Adelphi Rd. *Hud* —3H **131**
Adel Towers Clo. *Leeds* —4N **43**
Adel Towers Ct. *Leeds* —4N **43**
Adel Va. *Leeds* —3N **43**
Adel Wood Clo. *Leeds* —4N **43**
Adel Wood Dri. *Leeds* —4N **43**
Adel Wood Gdns. *Leeds* —4N **43**
Adel Wood Gro. *Leeds* —4N **43**
Adel Wood Pl. *Leeds* —4N **43**
Adel Wood Rd. *Leeds* —4N **43**
Adgil Cres. *Hal* —8F **92**
Administration Rd. *Leeds* —2L **81**
Admiral St. *Leeds* —1E **80**
Adowsley Clo. *Ackw* —4E **140**
Adwalton. —7D 78
Adwalton Clo. *Dlgtn* —8A **78**
Adwalton Grn. *Dlgtn* —8A **78**
Adwalton Gro. *Q'bry* —4E **74**
Adwick Gro. *Wake* —5K **137**
Adwick Pl. *Leeds* —4M **61**
Agar St. *B'frd* —6L **57**
Agar Ter. *B'frd* —6L **57**
Agbrigg. —9N 119
Agbrigg Gro. *Wake* —1N **137**
Agbrigg Rd. *Wake* —9N **119**
Agincourt Dri. *Nor* —8F **100**
Agnes Rd. *Dart* —9G **152**
Agnes St. *Kei* —7J **21**
Ailsa Ho. B'frd —8G ***40***
(off Fairhaven Grn.)
Ails La. *Hal* —3D **90**
Aimbry Clo. *Hud* —8D **132**
Aimport Clo. *Brigh* —2N **113**
Ainley Bottom. *Ell* —6E **112**
Ainley Clo. *Hud* —9F **112**
Ainley Ind. Est. *Ell* —6F **112**
Ainley Pk. *Gol* —6D **130**
Ainley Pl. *Slai* —8J **129**
Ainley Rd. *Hud* —8F **112**
Ainleys. —7F 112
Ainley St. *Ell* —5E **112**

Ainsbury Av. B'frd —5F 40
(in two parts)
Ainsdale Clo. Roys —4C 154
Ainsdale Gro. Cull —9L 37
Ainsdale Rd. Roys —4C 154
Ainsley La. Mars —5D 144
Ainsty Cres. Weth —2M 17
Ainsty Dri. Weth —2M 17
Ainsty Gth. Weth —2M 17
Ainsty Rd. Weth —2L 17
Ainsty Vw. Weth —2M 17
Aintree Clo. Kip —3N 83
Airdale Ter. Leeds —1C 60
(off Airedale Cft.)
Aireburn Av. Kei —3D 20
Aire Clo. Bail —6N 39
Aire Ct. Leeds —9E 80
Aire Ct. Sils —9E 6
(off Ings Way)
Airedale. —5H 103
Airedale Av. Bgly —8F 38
Airedale Cliff. Leeds —1F 60
Airedale College Mt. B'frd —5E 58
(off Airedale College Rd.)
Airedale College Rd. B'frd —5E 58
Airedale College Ter. B'frd —5E 58
Airedale Ct. Leeds —1A 64
Airedale Cres. B'frd —5E 58
Airedale Cft. Leeds —2C 60
Airedale Dri. C'frd —2J 103
Airedale Dri. Gar —8B 66
Airedale Dri. Hal —8G 74
Airedale Dri. H'fth —7C 42
Airedale Gdns. Leeds —2C 60
Airedale Gro. H'fth —7C 42
Airedale Gro. W'ford —7E 82
Airedale Heights. Wake —7E 118
Airedale Ho. Bat —1F 116
(off Dale Clo.)
Airedale M. Sils —8E 6
Airedale Mt. Leeds —1B 60
Airedale Mt. Sandb —8B 22
Airedale Pl. Bail —5C 40
Airedale Quay. Rod —2D 60
Airedale Rd. B'frd —5D 58
Airedale Rd. C'frd —5H 103
Airedale Rd. Dart —9E 152
Airedale Rd. Kei —8M 21
Airedale Rd. Rothw —7E 82
Airedale Shop. Cen. Kei —9J 21
Airedale St. Bgly —4E 38
Airedale St. B'frd —3F 58
Airedale St. Kei —8L 21
Airedale Ter. Bail —5B 40
Airedale Ter. Morl —9L 79
(off South Pde.)
Airedale Ter. W'ford —7E 82
Airedale Vw. Rawd —4A 42
Airedale Vw. W'ford —7E 82
Airedale Wharf. Rod —1C 60
Aire Gro. Yead —1N 41
Aire Mt. Weth —2L 17
Aire Pl. Leeds —5A 62
Aire Rd. Weth —1L 17
Aireside Cen. Leeds —7C 62
Aire St. Bgly —1D 38
Aire St. B'frd —6E 40
Aire St. Brigh —2N 113
Aire St. C'frd —4D 102
Aire St. Dew —6C 116
Aire St. Haw —8D 36
Aire St. Kei —8K 21
Aire St. Knot —7F 104
(in two parts)
Aire St. Leeds —7D 62
Aire Ter. C'frd —4D 102
Aire Valley Bus. Cen. Kei —9J 21
Aire Valley Marina. Leeds —5L 61
Aire Valley Rd. Kei —8L 21
Aire Vw. B'ton —5B 104
Aire Vw. Knot —7D 104
Aire Vw. Riddl —6M 21
Aire Vw. Sils —8D 6
Aire Vw. Yead —1N 41
Aire Vw. Av. Bgly —7G 38
Aireview Cres. Bail —6M 39
Aire Vw. Dri. Sandb —9B 22
Aire Vw. Gdns. Leeds —9J 43
Aire Vw. N. Shipl —7M 39
Aireview Ter. Leeds —2D 60
Aireview Ter. T Brow —1L 37
Aireville Av. B'frd —1N 57
Aireville Clo. Kei —6G 20
Aireville Clo. Shipl —1N 57
Aireville Cres. B'frd —2N 57
Aireville Cres. Sils —8F 6
Aireville Dri. Shipl —1N 57
Aireville Dri. Sils —8F 6
Aireville Grange. Shipl —1N 57
Aireville Gro. Shipl —1N 57
Aireville Mt. Sandb —8B 22
Aireville Mt. Sils —8F 6
Aireville Ri. B'frd —1N 57
Aireville Rd. B'frd —1N 57
Aireville St. Kei —6G 21
Aireville Ter. Bur W —8C 10
Aire Wlk. Knot —7F 104
Aire Way. Bail —6M 39
Aireworth. —8L 21
Aireworth Clo. Kei —7L 21
Aireworth Gro. Kei —8L 21
Aireworth Rd. Kei —7L 21
Aireworth St. Kei —1H 37
Airey St. Kei —9G 21
Airlie Av. Leeds —2H 63
Airlie Pl. Leeds —2H 63
Air St. Leeds —9G 63
Akam Rd. B'frd —7B 58
Aked's Rd. Hal —6A 92
Aked St. B'frd —7D 58
Aketon Dri. C'frd —6C 102
Aketon Rd. C'frd —7B 102
Akroyd Ct. Hal —4B 92
(off Randolph St.)
Akroyd La. H Bri —6J 71
Akroydon. —3B 92
Akroyd Pl. Hal —4B 92
Akroyd Ter. Hal —7M 91
Alabama St. Hal —5M 91
Alan Cres. Leeds —7B 64
Alandale Cres. Gar —8L 65
Alandale Dri. Gar —8L 65
Alandale Gro. Gar —8L 65
Alandale Rd. Gar —7L 65
Alandale Rd. Hud —5C 114
Alan Rd. Dart —9F 152
Albans Clo. Bard —3F 30
Alban St. B'frd —1F 76
Albany Ct. Kei —8G 21
Albany Ct. Pon —4K 123
Albany Cres. S Elm —7M 157
Albany Dri. Hud —4E 132
Albany Pl. S Elm —7M 157
Albany Rd. Dltn —4E 132
Albany Rd. Rothw —7M 81
Albany St. B'frd —1C 76
Albany St. Hal —7C 92
Albany St. Hud —6L 131
Albany St. Leeds —7K 61
Albany St. S Elm —7M 157
Albany St. Wibs —4A 76
Albany Ter. Hal —7C 92
Albany Ter. Leeds —7K 61
Albany Wlk. I'ly —6G 8
Albert Av. B'frd —7G 40
Albert Av. Hal —4L 91
Albert Av. Shipl —6K 39
Albert Bldgs. B'frd —9F 40
Albert Clo. Bat —1F 116
Albert Ct. Hal —4L 91
Albert Cres. B'shaw —9M 77
Albert Cres. Q'bry —4D 74
Albert Dri. Hal —4K 91
Albert Dri. Morl —8N 79
Albert Edward St. Q'bry —4D 74
Albert Gdns. Hal —4L 91
Albert Gro. Leeds —9N 43
Albert La. Todm —6K 87
Albert Pl. B'frd —6J 59
Albert Pl. H'fth —6F 42
Albert Pl. Meth —1J 101
Albert Promenade. Hal —8N 91
Albert Rd. Clay W —7H 151
Albert Rd. Hal —4K 91
Albert Rd. Morl —8K 79
Albert Rd. Q'bry —3C 74
Albert Rd. Shipl —7G 39
Albert Rd. Sower B —7J 91
Albert Rd. W'ford —7D 82
Albert Sq. Sils —8E 6
Albert Sq. Yead —9N 25
Albert St. Bail —6A 40
Albert St. B'frd —5N 75
Albert St. Brigh —1A 114
Albert St. C'frd —4D 102
Albert St. Cleck —4H 95
(in two parts)
Albert St. Cro R —7F 36
(off Bingley Rd.)
Albert St. Cud —8K 155
Albert St. Ell —5E 112
Albert St. F'stne —6D 122
(in two parts)
Albert St. Hal —5A 92
Albert St. H Bri —1H 89
Albert St. Hud —7L 131
Albert St. Idle —9D 40
Albert St. Kei —9H 21
Albert St. Liv —9N 95
Albert St. Myth —3M 89
Albert St. Nor —8K 101
Albert St. Pud —8A 60
Albert St. Q'bry —4E 74
Albert St. T'tn —8C 56
Albert St. Todm —6K 87
Albert St. Wilsd —2B 56
Albert St. Wyke —2A 94
Albert Ter. Oaken —8D 76
Albert Ter. Shipl —6L 39
Albert Ter. Wyke —2B 94
Albert Ter. Yead —9N 25
(off Rockfield Ter.)
Albert Vw. Hal —4L 91
Albert Wlk. Shipl —7K 39
Albert Way. B'shaw —9M 77
Albert Yd. Hud —4M 131
Albion Av. Leeds —7N 61
Albion Clo. Cliff —3D 32
Albion Ct. B'frd —7C 58
Albion Ct. Hal —5B 92
(off Gt. Albion St.)
Albion Ct. Heck —8A 96
Albion Ct. Wake —5L 119
Albion Cft. Oss —5A 118
Albion Fold. Wilsd —1B 56
Albion Pk. Leeds —6A 62
Albion Pl. Brigh —9M 93
(off Waterloo Rd.)
Albion Pl. Guis —7J 25
Albion Pl. Leeds —6E 62
Albion Pl. S Elm —6N 157
Albion Pl. T'tn —8B 56
Albion Rd. Barn —9D 154
Albion Rd. B'frd —7F 40
Albion Rd. Dew —1H 135
Albion Rd. S'ley —4B 60
Albion Sq. Wake —4G 118
Albion St. Bat —8G 96
(in two parts)
Albion St. B'frd —7C 58
Albion St. Brigh —9M 93
Albion St. Butt —6K 75
Albion St. Carl —1M 99
Albion St. C'frd —5C 102
Albion St. Cleck —5J 95
Albion St. Cliff —3D 32
Albion St. Cro R —7E 36
Albion St. Denh —6K 55
Albion St. Dew —2F 116
Albion St. Ell —5E 112
Albion St. Fitz —7A 140
Albion St. Hal —5B 92
Albion St. Heck —8N 95
Albion St. Hud —5M 131
Albion St. Leeds —6E 62
(in two parts)
Albion St. Liv —8L 95
Albion St. Morl —9K 79
(in two parts)
Albion St. Otley —1M 25
Albion St. Q'bry —4C 74
Albion St. Raven —6C 116
Albion St. Wake —4L 119
Albion Ter. Cliff —3D 32
Albion Ter. H Bri —1G 89
(off Heptonstall Rd.)
Albion Way. Leeds —6A 62
Albion Yd. B'frd —7C 58
Alcester Gth. B'frd —6F 58
Alcester Pl. Leeds —2H 63
Alcester Rd. Leeds —2H 63
Alcester Ter. Leeds —2H 63
Aldams Rd. Dew —4F 116
Alden Av. Morl —2K 97
Alden Clo. Morl —2K 97
Alden Ct. Morl —2K 97
Alden Cres. Pon —4H 123
Alden Fold. Morl —2K 97
Alder Av. H'frth —9A 148
Alder Av. Kei —2L 37
Alder Av. Wake —3J 119
Alder Carr. Bail —4N 39
Alder Clo. M'well —8J 153
Alder Dri. Pud —6L 59
Alder Gth. Pud —6M 59
Alder Gro. Hal —7L 73
Alder Gro. Nor —4J 121
Alder Hill Av. Leeds —8C 44
Alder Hill Gro. Leeds —8C 44
Aldermanbury. B'frd —8C 58
Alderney Rd. Dew —1J 117
Alderscholes Clo. T'tn —8C 56
(off Alderscholes La.)
Alderscholes La. T'tn —9A 56
Aldersgate. Leeds —7M 61
(off Wesley Rd.)
Alderson St. B'frd —6K 75
Alders, The. Leeds —8F 44
Alderstone Ri. Hud —9F 112
Alder St. Hud —2N 131
Aldersyde. Bat —3B 96
Alderton Bank. Leeds —5B 44
Alderton Cres. Leeds —5B 44
Alderton Heights. Leeds —5B 44
Alderton Mt. Leeds —5B 44
Alderton Pl. Leeds —5B 44
Alderton Ri. Leeds —5C 44
Aldonley. Hud —5E 132
Alegar St. Brigh —1A 114
Alexander Av. Leeds —7A 64
Alexander Cres. F'stne —4D 122
Alexander Rd. F'stne —5D 122
Alexander Sq. Cytn —1G 75
Alexander St. B'frd —5N 75
Alexander St. Leeds —6D 62
Alexandra Av. Birs —3C 96
Alexandra Cres. Dew —2D 116
Alexandra Cres. Ell —4G 113
Alexandra Cres. I'ly —5F 8
Alexandra Dri. Nor —3J 121
Alexandra Gro. Leeds —4A 62
Alexandra Gro. Pud —8A 60
Alexandra Mill. Morl —1K 97
Alexandra Rd. Bat —8G 97
Alexandra Rd. Eccl —1G 58
Alexandra Rd. H Bri —1H 89
Alexandra Rd. H'fth —6F 42
Alexandra Rd. Hud —2H 131
Alexandra Rd. Leeds —4A 62
Alexandra Rd. Pud —8N 59
Alexandra Rd. Shipl —8M 39
Alexandra Rd. W. Hud —5H 131
Alexandra Sq. Shipl —7L 39
Alexandra St. B'frd —9A 58
Alexandra St. Hal —5B 92
Alexandra St. Liv —8L 95
Alexandra St. Q'bry —4C 74
Alexandra Ter. B'frd —4G 58
Alexandra Ter. Yead —9N 25
(in two parts)
Alford Ter. B'frd —7M 57
Alfred McAlpine Stadium, The. —2A 132
Alfred St. Bat —8E 96
Alfred St. Brigh —9N 93
Alfred St. Chur —5M 79
Alfred St. Dew —2G 117
Alfred St. G'lnd —4C 112
Alfred St. Hal —5M 91
Alfred St. Heck —9A 96
Alfred St. Hud —5M 131
Alfred St. Liv —8M 95
Alfred St. Roys —5F 154
Alfred St. W'wth —9A 106
Alfred St. E. Hal —5C 92
Alfreds Way. Bat —7F 96
Alhambra Theatre. —8C 58
Alice St. B'frd —6B 58
Alice St. Cleck —4H 95
Alice St. Haw —9C 36
Alice St. Kei —9J 21
Alison Vw. B'frd —1M 75
Alkincote St. Kei —1J 37
All Alone. B'frd —8E 40
All Alone Rd. B'frd —8D 40
Allandale Av. B'frd —6M 75
Allandale Rd. B'frd —6M 75
Allanfield Gro. Weth —2M 17
Allanfield Ter. Weth —1M 17
Allan Haigh Clo. Wake —3F 118
Allan St. B'frd —8F 58
Allan Ter. Sower B —9J 91
Allenby Cres. Leeds —5C 80
Allenby Dri. Leeds —5C 80
Allenby Gdns. Leeds —5C 80
Allenby Gro. Leeds —5C 80
Allenby Pl. Leeds —5C 80
Allenby Rd. Leeds —5C 80
Allenby Vw. Leeds —4D 80
Allen Cft. B'shaw —8L 77
Allendale Rd. Dart —9F 152
Allerby Grn. B'frd —6L 75
Allergill Pk. H'frth —3J 163
Allerton. —5G 57
Allerton Av. Leeds —5F 44
Allerton Bywater. —7N 83
Allerton Clo. All —5G 57
Allerton Ct. Leeds —5F 44
(off Harrogate Rd.)
Allerton Dri. E Kes —1D 30
Allerton Grange Clo. Leeds —7E 44
Allerton Grange Cres. Leeds —7F 44
Allerton Grange Dri. All —5G 56
Allerton Grange Dri. Leeds —7F 44
Allerton Grange Gdns. Leeds —7F 44
Allerton Grange Ri. Leeds —7E 44
Allerton Grange Va. Leeds —7F 44
Allerton Grange Wlk. Leeds —7F 44
Allerton Grange Way. Leeds —7F 44
Allerton Gro. Leeds —5F 44
Allerton Hall. Leeds —8E 44
Allerton Hill. Chap A —8E 44
Allerton La. T'tn & All —7F 56
Allerton M. Leeds —6F 44
Allerton Pk. Leeds —8F 44
Allerton Pl. Hal —5N 91
Allerton Pl. Leeds —5F 44
Allerton Rd. All & B'frd —5C 56
(in two parts)
Allerton St. Leeds —4N 61
Allerton Ter. Leeds —5N 61
Allescholes Rd. Todm —4J 107
Alliance St. Leeds —7K 61
Allinson St. Leeds —8A 62
Allison Dri. Hud —9N 113
Allison La. B'frd —2B 58
Allison St. F'stne —6C 122
Allison Ter. K'gte —1D 118
Alloe Fld. Pl. Hal —7L 73
Alloe Fld. Vw. Hal —7L 73
Allotments Rd. Denh —5L 55
Allott Clo. S Elm —6M 157
All Saint's Circ. W'ford —7E 82
All Saint's Dri. W'ford —7D 82
All Saints Rd. B'frd —9N 57
All Saint's Rd. W'ford —6E 82
All Saint's Vw. Pon —3L 123
(off Baghill La.)
All Saint's Vw. W'ford —6D 82
All Souls' Rd. Hal —3B 92
All Souls' St. Hal —3B 92
All Souls' Ter. Hal —3B 92
Allums La. Arth —4A 28
Alma Clo. Fars —3N 59
Alma Cotts. Leeds —1N 61
Alma Dri. Hud —4B 132
Alma Gro. Shipl —7B 40
Alma La. Heck —6A 96
Alma La. Sower B —4B 110
Alma Pl. Kei —3J 37
Alma Rd. Leeds —1N 61
Alma Rd. Todm —2J 107
Alma St. B'frd —9G 59
Alma St. Cut H —1H 77
Alma St. Haw —7C 36
Alma St. Kei —3J 37
Alma St. Leeds —5G 63
Alma St. Q'bry —4C 74
Alma St. Shipl —7B 40
Alma St. Todm —2J 107
Alma St. W'ford —6D 82
Alma St. Yead —9N 25
Alma Ter. B'frd —6H 59
Alma Ter. E Mor —7D 22
Alma Ter. Kei —3J 37
Alma Ter. Rothw —7M 81
Almcliffe Pl. B'frd —2H 59
Almond Av. Cud —9J 155
Almondbury. —6D 132
Almondbury Bank. Hud —5B 132
Almondbury Clo. Hud —7E 132
Almondbury Common. —8D 132
Almondbury Comn. Hud —9D 132
Almond Clo. S Elm —4N 157
Almondroyd. Heck —7N 95
Almond St. B'frd —8G 59
Almond Way. Bat —3C 96
Almscliffe Av. Dew —3H 117
Almscliffe Dri. Huby —5M 13
Almshouse Hill. B'ham —6D 32
Almshouse La. N'dam —7K 137
Almshouse La. Wake —5L 119
Alpha St. Kei —9K 21
Alpine Clo. Bat —8E 96
Alpine Ct. Hems —1D 156
Alpine Ri. T'tn —7C 56
Alpine Ter. Rothw —7M 81
Alpine Vw. Hems —1D 156
Alston Clo. B'frd —5J 57
Alston La. Leeds —3B 64
Alston Rd. Kei —7K 21
Alston Rd. Retail Pk. Kei —7K 21
Altar Dri. B'frd —3M 57
Altar Dri. Riddl —7N 21
Altar La. Bgly —3M 37
Altar Vw. Bgly —2D 38
(off Sleningford Rd.)
Althorpe Gro. B'frd —9E 40
Altinkool St. Wake —9N 119
Altofts. —9G 100
Altofts Hall Rd. Nor —8G 101
Altofts La. C'frd —6L 101
Altofts Lodge Dri. Nor —9F 100
Altofts Rd. Nor —1H 121
Alton Av. Hud —3D 132
Alton Gro. B'frd —3L 57
Alton Gro. Shipl —1N 57
Alton Way. M'well —8J 153
Alum Ct. B'frd —3M 57
Alum Dri. B'frd —3M 57
Alvanley Ct. B'frd —6J 57
Alva Ter. Shipl —9N 39
Alverthorpe. —3G 119
Alverthorpe Rd. Wake —4H 119
Alwen Av. Hud —9L 113
Alwoodley. —2E 44
Alwoodley Ct. Leeds —2B 44
Alwoodley Ct. Gdns. Leeds —1C 44
Alwoodley Gdns. Leeds —2C 44
Alwoodley Gates. —1G 44
Alwoodley La. Leeds —1B 44
Alwoodley Park. —1C 44
Amberley Ct. B'frd —8G 58
(off Amberley St.)

Amberley Gdns. Leeds —8N 61
Amberley Ri. Skel —7L 159
Amberley Rd. Leeds —8M 61
Amberley St. B'frd —8G 58
(in two parts)
Amberley St. Leeds —8M 61
Amber St. Bat —5D 96
Amberton App. Leeds —2L 63
Amberton Clo. Leeds —1L 63
Amberton Cres. Leeds —2L 63
Amberton Gdns. Leeds —2L 63
Amberton Gth. Leeds —2L 63
Amberton Gro. Leeds —2L 63
Amberton La. Leeds —2L 63
Amberton Mt. Leeds —2L 63
Amberton Pl. Leeds —2K 63
Amberton Rd. Leeds —2K 63
Amberton St. Leeds —2L 63
Amberton Ter. Leeds —2L 63
Ambler Gro. Hal —7M 73
Amblers Bldgs. Pud —8B 60
(off Amblers Ct.)
Amblers Ct. Pud —8B 60
Amblers Cft. B'frd —5F 40
Amblers M. Bail —3A 40
Amblers M. E Mor —8C 22
Amblers Row. Bail —3A 40
Amblers Ter. Hal —3B 92
Ambler St. B'frd —5A 58
Ambler St. C'frd —5D 102
Ambler St. Kei —9K 21
Ambler Thorn. —6B 74
Amblerthorne. B'shaw —8M 77
Ambler Way. Q'bry —6B 74
Ambleside Av. B'frd —4L 57
Ambleside Dri. W'ton —4B 138
Ambleside Gdns. Pud —7N 59
Ambleside Gro. W'ford —7D 82
Ambleside Rd. C'frd —3L 103
Ambleside Wlk. Weth —3J 17
Amble Tonia. Denh —5L 55
Ambleton Way. Q'bry —5B 74
Amelia St. Shipl —6L 39
America La. Brigh —1A 114
America Moor La. Morl —8N 43
Amisfield Rd. Hal —4J 93
Amos St. Hal —5M 91
Amport Clo. Brigh —2N 113
Amundsen Av. B'frd —1E 58
Amyroyce Dri. Shipl —8C 40
Amy St. Bgly —4F 38
Amy St. Hal —2N 91
Anaheim Dri. Out —7M 99
Ancaster Cres. Leeds —8L 43
Ancaster Rd. Leeds —8L 43
Ancaster Vw. Leeds —8L 43
Anchorage, The. Bgly —3E 38
Anchor Bri. Way. Dew —4F 116
Anchor Ct. B'frd —6B 58
(off Jervaulx Cres.)
Anchor Ct. Kbtn —3G 148
Anchor Pl. Brigh —3B 114
Anchor St. Hud —3N 131
Anchor St. Todm —7L 87
Anderson Av. Leeds —4G 63
Anderson Ct. C'frd —7J 103
Anderson Ho. Bail —6N 39
(off Fairview Ct.)
Anderson Mt. Leeds —4G 63
Anderson St. B'frd —5A 58
Anderson St. Pon —2J 123
Anderson St. Wake —8N 119
(WF1)
Anderson St. Wake —5J 119
(WF2)
Anderton Fold. Hal —2F 92
Anderton St. Wake —8N 119
Andover Grn. B'frd —1J 77
Andrew Clo. Hal —8F 92
Andrew Cres. H'frth —9F 130
Andrew Cres. Wake —7K 99
Andrews Gro. Ackw —4F 140
Andrews Mnr. Yead —9M 25
(off Manor Sq.)
Andrew Sq. Far —3A 60
Andrew St. Fars —4A 60
Andrew St. F'stne —7C 122
Andrew St. Wake —3K 119
Anerley St. B'frd —3F 76
Angel Ct. Leeds —5B 62
Angel Pl. Bgly —2F 38
Angel Row. Rothw —8J 81
Angel St. Bail —3B 40
Angel Way. B'frd —7B 58
Angerton Way. B'frd —7M 75
Anglesea Pl. Haw —1C 54
Angus Av. Wyke —3A 94
Anlaby St. B'frd —9H 59
Annat Royd La. Pen —8N 165
Anne Cres. S Hien —4M 155
Anne Ga. B'frd —7D 58
Anne's Ct. Hal —8F 92
Anne St. Bat —5D 96
Anne St. B'frd —2L 75
Annie St. Cro R —7F 36
Annie St. Fitz —6A 140
Annie St. Kei —7J 21
Annie St. Morl —9L 79
Annie St. Shipl —9A 40
Annie St. Sower B —8H 91
Annie St. Wake —8K 99
Anning Fold. Gar —6B 66
Annison St. B'frd —7E 58
Annottes Cft. Hud —3D 132
Ann Pl. B'frd —9C 58
Ann St. Haw —8D 36
Ann St. Kei —1H 37
Anroyd St. Dew —2D 116
Anson Gro. B'frd —3L 75
Anston Dri. S Elm —4N 157
Anthony La. H'den —5A 38
Anthony's La. B'ton —1F 104
Antler Complex. Morl —9G 79
Antony Clo. Hud —1C 130
Anvil Ct. B'frd —5N 57
(off Carlisle St.)
Anvil St. B'frd —5N 57
Anvil St. Brigh —9M 93
Apex Bus. Cen. Leeds —9E 62
Apex Way. Leeds —9E 62
Apperley Bridge. —7J 41
Apperley Gdns. B'frd —7J 41
Apperley La. B'frd & Yead —7J 41
Apperley Rd. B'frd —7G 40
Appleby Clo. Dart —8H 153
Appleby La. Gar —7B 66
Appleby Pl. Leeds —6N 63
Appleby Pl. Skel —7L 159
Appleby Wlk. Leeds —6N 63
Appleby Way. Morl —8L 79
Appleby Way. Weth —2M 17
Apple Clo. Birs —2D 96
Applegarth. Cytn —2H 75
Applegarth. S'dal —3N 137
Applegarth. W'ford —6D 82
Applehaigh Ct. Not —4B 154
Applehaigh Gro. Roys —5B 154
Applehaigh La. Not —3B 154
Applehaigh Vw. Roys —6B 154
Apple Ho. Ter. L'ft —3E 90
Appleshawn Cres. Wren —9H 99
Apple St. Kei —4G 37
Apple St. Oxe —4C 54
Appleton Clo. Bgly —2G 39
Appleton Clo. Leeds —6H 63
Appleton Clo. Oaken —8D 76
Appleton Ct. Leeds —6H 63
Appleton Gro. Leeds —6K 63
Appleton Sq. Leeds —6H 63
Appleton Way. Leeds —6H 63
Apple Tree Clo. B Spa —1D 32
Apple Tree Clo. E Ard —4E 98
Apple Tree Clo. Pon —5H 123
Apple Tree Ct. E Ard —5E 98
Apple Tree Gdns. I'ly —5E 8
Apple Tree Rd. F'stne —7E 122
Appleyard Rd. H Bri —3N 89
Approach, The. Scholes —8G 46
April Ct. Liv —1L 115
Aprilia Ct. Cytn —9J 57
Apsley Cres. B'frd —5A 58
Apsley St. Haw —8D 36
Apsley St. Kei —2H 37
Apsley St. Oakw —4D 36
Apsley Ter. Oakw —4D 36
(off Green La.)
Aquamarine Dri. Far —9A 114
Aquila Way. Liv —7H 95
Arborary La. H'frth —3E 146
Arbour, The. I'ly —3F 8
Arcade, The. Dew —3G 116
(off Market St.)
Arcade, The. Knot —8D 104
Arcadia St. Kei —2H 37
Archbell Av. Brigh —3N 113
Archer Rd. Brigh —2B 114
Archer St. C'frd —6C 102
Archery Pl. Leeds —4D 62
Archery Rd. Leeds —4D 62
Archery St. Leeds —4D 62
Archery Ter. Leeds —4D 62
Arches St. Hal —6A 92
Arches, The. Hal —3B 92
Archibald Ho. Rothw —9N 81
Archibald St. B'frd —7A 58
Arctic Pde. B'frd —1M 75
Arctic St. Cro R —7E 36
Arctic St. Kei —6H 21
Arden Ct. Horb —2C 136
Arden Ct. Hud —3G 132
Arden M. Hal —7A 92
Ardennes Clo. B'frd —2D 58
Arden Rd. B'frd —7H 57
Arden Rd. Hal —6A 92
Ardsley Clo. B'frd —3K 77
(in two parts)
Argent Way. B'frd —3K 77
Argie Av. Leeds —3L 61
Argie Gdns. Leeds —4M 61
Argie Rd. Leeds —4M 61
Argie Ter. Leeds —4M 61
Argyle M. E Kes —3D 30
Argyle Rd. Knot —7B 104
Argyle Rd. Leeds —6F 62
Argyle St. B'frd —2F 76
Argyle St. Kei —9H 21
Argyle St. Mars —5F 144
Argyle St. Wake —7N 119
Argyll Av. Pon —3H 123
Argyll Clo. Bail —5C 40
Argyll Clo. H'fth —3E 42
Arkendale M. B'frd —2K 75
Arkenley La. Hud —8D 132
Arkenmore. Hud —3D 132
Arksey Pl. Leeds —6M 61
Arksey Ter. Leeds —6M 61
Arkwright St. Cytn —1G 75
Arkwright St. Leeds —6A 62
Arkwright St. Tyer —8J 59
Arkwright Wlk. Morl —7K 79
Arlesford Rd. B'frd —3J 77
Arley Clo. H'frth —9L 147
Arley Gro. Leeds —6M 61
Arley Pl. Leeds —6M 61
Arley St. Leeds —6M 61
Arley Ter. Leeds —6M 61
Arlington Bus. Cen. Leeds —5N 79
Arlington Cres. Hal —7K 91
Arlington Gro. C'frd —5F 102
Arlington Gro. Leeds —1K 63
Arlington M. Heck —9B 96
Arlington Rd. Leeds —2K 63
Arlington St. B'frd —8F 58
Arlington St. Wake —3K 119
Armadale Av. B'frd —5F 76
Armgill La. B'frd —2B 58
Armidale Way. B'frd —3D 58
Armitage Av. Brigh —3N 113
Armitage Bridge. —1K 147
Armitage Bri. Mills. Hud —1K 147
Armitage Bldgs. Dew —6L 97
Armitage Rd. Arm B —1K 147
Armitage Rd. Bkby —1L 131
Armitage Rd. Hal —7M 91
Armitage Rd. Milns —5G 130
Armitage Rd. Oaken —9D 76
Armitage Rd. Wake —3F 118
Armitage Sq. Pud —8A 60
Armitage St. C'frd —4C 102
Armitage St. Dew —6A 116
Armitage St. Prim H —6M 131
Armitage St. Rothw —9N 81
Armley Grange Av. Leeds —5J 61
Armley Grange Cres. Leeds —5J 61
Armley Grange Dri. Leeds —6J 61
Armley Grange Mt. Leeds —6J 61
Armley Grange Oval. Leeds —5J 61
Armley Grange Ri. Leeds —6J 61
Armley Grange Vw. Leeds —6K 61
Armley Grange Wlk. Leeds —6K 61
Armley Gro. Pl. Leeds —7N 61
Armley Lodge Rd. Leeds —5M 61
Armley Mills Museum. —5N 61
Armley Pk. Ct. Leeds —6M 61
(off Stanningley Rd.)
Armley Pk. Rd. Leeds —5M 61
Armley Ridge Clo. Leeds —6K 61
Armley Ridge Rd. Leeds —3J 61
(in two parts)
Armley Ridge Ter. Leeds —5K 61
Armley Rd. Leeds —6M 61
(in two parts)
Armouries Dri. Leeds —8F 62
Armoury Av. Mir —6L 115
Armstrong Clo. Nor —8H 101
Armstrong St. B'frd —8H 59
Armstrong St. Fars —4A 60
Armstrong Ter. Pon —4H 123
Army Row. Roys —5E 154
Armytage Cres. Hud —7L 131
Armytage Rd. Brigh —1A 114
Armytage Wlk. S Kirk —6J 157
Armytage Way. Brigh —2B 114
Arncliffe Av. Kei —1G 36
Arncliffe Ct. Hud —3K 131
Arncliffe Cres. Brigh —3K 113
Arncliffe Cres. Morl —8C 44
Arncliffe Dri. Knot —8A 104
Arncliffe Gdns. Bat —7E 96
Arncliffe Gth. S'ley —5A 60
Arncliffe Grange. Leeds —5F 44
Arncliffe Gro. Kei —2G 36
Arncliffe Rd. Bat —7D 96
Arncliffe Rd. Kei —2G 36
Arncliffe Rd. Leeds —7K 43
Arncliffe Rd. Wake —3N 119
Arncliffe St. S'ley —4A 60
Arncliffe Ter. B'frd —8N 57
Arndale Cen. Head —1N 61
Arndale Cen. Leeds —4D 64
Arndale Gro. H'frth —4N 163
Arndale Ho. B'frd —7C 58
(off Charles St.)
Arndale Shop. Cen. Shipl —8N 39
(off Market St.)
Arne Clo. Sils —6F 6
Arnford Clo. B'frd —6D 58
Arnold Av. Barn —9A 154
Arnold Av. Hud —1L 131
Arnold Pl. B'frd —6A 58
Arnold Royd. Brigh —4K 113
Arnold St. B'frd —5A 58
Arnold St. Hal —5N 91
Arnold St. Hud —1L 131
Arnold St. Liv —8L 95
Arnold St. Sower B —8H 91
Arnside Av. Riddl —7L 21
Arnside Clo. C'frd —4K 103
Arnside Cres. C'frd —4K 103
Arnside Rd. B'frd —3C 76
Arran Clo. Gol —5C 130
Arran Ct. Gar —9N 65
Arran Dri. Gar —9N 65
Arran Dri. H'fth —3E 42
Arran Way. Rothw —8A 82
Arrow La. Leds —9E 84
Arrunden La. H'frth —7L 163
Art Gallery (1853) & Salts Mill. —6L 39
Arthington. —2M 27
Arthington Av. Leeds —3F 80
Arthington Clo. Ting —5N 97
Arthington Ct. Leeds —3F 80
Arthington Gth. Arth —2J 27
Arthington Gro. Leeds —3F 80
Arthington La. Pool W —1G 26
Arthington Lawns Pool W —2H 27
Arthington Pl. Leeds —3F 80
Arthington Rd. Leeds —6M 27
Arthington St. B'frd —6A 58
Arthington St. Leeds —3F 80
Arthington Ter. Leeds —3F 80
Arthington Vw. Leeds —3F 80
Arthur Av. B'frd —7H 57
Arthur Gro. Bat —4C 96
Arthursdale. —8G 47
Arthursdale Clo. Scholes —8G 47
Arthursdale Dri. Scholes —8G 47
Arthursdale Grange. Scholes —8G 46
Arthur St. Bgly —3E 38
Arthur St. Brigh —1A 114
Arthur St. Far —4A 60
Arthur St. Gol —6D 130
Arthur St. Idle —9F 40
Arthur St. Oakw —5C 36
Arthur St. S'ley —4B 60
Arthur St. Wake —8N 119
Arthur Ter. Fars —4A 60
(off Arthur St.)
Artillery St. Heck —9A 96
Artist St. A'ley —7B 62
Arum St. B'frd —2A 76
Arundel Clo. Bat —2E 96
Arundel Clo. Wake —8N 119
Arundel St. Gar —6B 66
Arundel St. Hal —5M 91
Arundel St. Wake —4L 119
Arundel Wlk. Bat —3E 96
Ascot Av. B'frd —3K 75
Ascot Dri. B'frd —3K 75
Ascot Gdns. B'frd —3K 75
Ascot Gdns. Leeds —1F 98
Ascot Gro. Brigh —3K 113
Ascot Pde. B'frd —3K 75
Ascot Rd. Kip —3N 83
Ascot Ter. Leeds —7H 63
Asdale Rd. Wake —2J 137
Ash Av. Leeds —1N 61
Ashbourne Av. B'frd —3D 58
Ashbourne Av. Cleck —6H 95
Ashbourne Bank. B'frd —3D 58
Ashbourne Clo. B'frd —3D 58
Ashbourne Cres. B'frd —3D 58
Ashbourne Cres. Gar —9N 65
Ashbourne Cres. Q'bry —4C 74
Ashbourne Cft. Cleck —6H 95
Ashbourne Dri. B'frd —3D 58
Ashbourne Dri. Cleck —6H 95
Ashbourne Dri. Pon —6K 123
Ashbourne Gdns. B'frd —3D 58
Ashbourne Gdns. Cleck —6H 95
Ashbourne Gth. B'frd —2E 58
Ashbourne Gro. B'frd —3D 58
Ashbourne Gro. Hal —5M 91
Ashbourne Haven. B'frd —3D 58
Ashbourne Mt. B'frd —3D 58
Ashbourne Oval. B'frd —3D 58
Ashbourne Ri. B'frd —3D 58
Ashbourne Rd. B'frd —3D 58
Ashbourne Rd. Kei —3G 37
Ashbourne Vw. Cleck —6H 95
Ashbourne Way. B'frd —2D 58
Ashbourne Way. Cleck —6H 95
Ashbrook Clo. Oss —4N 117
Ashbrooke Pk. Leeds —3E 80
Ash Brow. Floc —7F 134
Ash Brow Rd. Hud —8N 113
Ashburn Clo. Weth —2L 17
Ashburn Cft. Weth —2L 17
Ashburn Dri. Weth —2L 17
Ashburn Gro. Bail —3A 40
Ashburn Gro. Weth —2L 17
Ashburnham Gro. B'frd —3N 57
Ashburn Pl. I'ly —6F 8
Ashburn Way. Weth —2L 17
Ashbury Chase. Out —7J 99
Ashby Av. Leeds —4G 60
Ashby Clo. Liv —2K 115
Ashby Cres. Leeds —5G 60
Ashby Mt. Leeds —4G 60
Ashby Sq. Leeds —4G 61
Ashby St. B'frd —1E 76
Ashby Ter. Leeds —4G 60
Ashby Vw. Leeds —4G 60
Ash Clo. Hal —4J 93
Ash Clo. I'ly —5D 8
Ash Clo. Oss —6N 117
Ashcombe Dri. Knot —9E 104
Ash Ct. Schol —4D 94
Ash Cres. Leeds —1N 61
Ash Cres. Stan —8A 100
Ash Cft. B'frd —5M 75
Ashcroft Av. F'stne —7C 122
Ashcroft Clo. Bat —9E 96
Ashcroft Rd. F'stne —7C 122
Ashdale. Wake —1N 137
Ashdale La. Kirk D —1L 17
Ashday La. Hal —9F 92
Ashdene. Leeds —2G 79
Ashdene. Todm —2K 107
Ashdene App. Croft —1G 138
Ashdene Av. Croft —1G 138
Ashdene Clo. Pud —9B 60
Ashdene Ct. Cull —9K 37
Ashdene Cres. Croft —1G 138
Ashdene Cres. Pud —9B 60
Ashdene Dri. Croft —1G 138
Ashdene Gth. Croft —1G 138
Ashdene Gro. Pon —8M 103
Ashdown Clo. B'frd —4N 75
Ashdown Clo. Hal —6K 91
Ashdown Ct. Shipl —8M 39
Ashdown Rd. Wake —8N 119
Ashdown St. Leeds —5F 60
Ash Dyke Clo. Dart —9F 152
Ashenhurst. —7N 131
Ashenhurst Av. Hud —7A 132
Ashenhurst Clo. Hud —7N 131
Ashenhurst Clo. Todm —5J 87
Ashenhurst Ri. Hud —7N 131
Ashenhurst Rd. Hud —7N 131
Ashenhurst Rd. Todm —5H 87
Ashes La. Ber B —1N 147
Ashes La. Todm —4M 87
Ashfield. —9J 101
Ashfield. B'frd —4H 77
Ashfield. Dew —7G 116
Ashfield. Leeds —1K 79
Ashfield. Weth —3N 17
Ashfield Av. B'frd & Shipl —1N 57
Ashfield Av. Morl —2C 62
Ashfield Av. Skelm —8D 150
Ashfield Clo. Hal —2M 91
Ashfield Clo. Leeds —1J 79
(LS12)
Ashfield Clo. Leeds —2E 64
(LS15)
Ashfield Ct. Bgly —5F 38
Ashfield Cres. Bgly —5F 38
Ashfield Cres. S'ley —5A 60
Ashfield Dri. Bail —3B 40
Ashfield Dri. B'frd —1N 57
Ashfield Dri. Hal —2M 91
Ashfield Gro. B'frd —1M 57
Ashfield Gro. S'ley —5A 60
Ashfield Ho. Hems —3D 156
Ashfield Pk. Leeds —1A 62
Ashfield Pl. Fag —4H 59
Ashfield Rd. Birs —2D 96
Ashfield Rd. B'frd —6F 40
Ashfield Rd. G'lnd —4A 112
Ashfield Rd. Hems —4D 156
Ashfield Rd. Hud —1K 131
Ashfield Rd. Morl —2C 62
Ashfield Rd. Shipl —8K 39
Ashfield Rd. S'ley —5A 60
Ashfield Rd. T'tn —8C 56
Ashfield St. Hud —9N 113
Ashfield St. Kei —1H 37
(off Minnie St.)
Ashfield St. Nor —9K 101
Ashfield Ter. Bgly —5F 38
Ashfield Ter. G'lnd —3A 112
Ashfield Ter. Haw —9C 36

Ashfield Ter. Leeds —2E 64
Ashfield Ter. Mar —5J 95
(off Pyenot Hall La.)
Ashfield Ter. Thpe —2H 99
Ashfield Ter. Wyke —9B 76
Ashfield Way. Leeds —1J 79
Ashford Ct. Kbtn —2K 149
Ashford Dri. Pud —8C 60
Ashford Grn. B'frd —4L 75
Ashford Pk. Gol —5C 130
Ashgap La. Nor —1J 121
Ash Gdns. Leeds —1N 61
Ash Ghyll Gdns. Bgly —3E 38
Ash Grn. Pon —2M 123
Ash Gro. Bgly —6F 38
Ash Gro. B'shaw —7L 77
Ashgrove. B'frd —8B 58
Ash Gro. Cleck —6F 94
Ash Gro. Clif C —9A 94
Ash Gro. D'ton —6B 124
Ash Gro. Eccl —3G 58
Ash Gro. Gom —3L 95
Ashgrove. Gre —8J 41
Ash Gro. H'fth —5F 42
Ash Gro. I'ly —4H 9
Ash Gro. Kei —3G 37
Ash Gro. Leeds —3B 62
Ash Gro. Otley —1K 25
Ash Gro. Pud —8B 60
Ash Gro. S Elm —5N 157
Ash Gro. Stan —1A 120
Ash Gro. Steet —3D 20
Ashgrove Av. Hal —9C 92
Ashgrove Cres. Kip —2B 84
Ashgrove Cft. Kip —3B 84
Ash Gro. Ho. S Elm —5N 157
Ashgrove M. Rod —2C 60
Ashgrove Mt. Kip —2A 84
Ashgrove Pl. Hal —9D 92
Ashgrove Rd. Bdly —9D 114
Ash Gro. Rd. H'frth —3K 163
Ashgrove Rd. Kei —6G 20
Ash Gro. Ter. Brigh —2M 113
(off Thomas St.)
Ash Hall La. Ripp —5N 109
Ash Hill. Pon —2L 123
(off Castle Gth.)
Ash Hill Dri. Leeds —3A 46
Ash Hill Gdns. Leeds —3A 46
Ash Hill Gth. Leeds —2A 46
Ash Hill La. Leeds —3A 46
Ash Hill Wlk. B'frd —1F 76
Ash Ho. Leeds —8N 63
Ashington Clo. B'frd —3H 59
Ashlands Rd. I'ly —4H 9
Ash La. Eml —3H 151
Ash La. Gar —6A 66
Ashlar Gro. C'frd —6F 102
Ashlar Gro. Q'bry —6C 74
Ash Lea. Fair —9N 85
Ash Lea. Wake —1A 120
Ashlea Av. Brigh —3N 113
Ashlea Clo. Brigh —3N 113
Ashlea Clo. Gar —9N 65
Ashlea Ct. Leeds —3F 60
(off Ashlea Ga.)
Ashlea Dri. Brigh —3N 113
Ashlea Ga. Leeds —3F 60
Ashlea Grn. Leeds —3F 60
Ashleigh. Brier —6A 156
Ashleigh Av. Pon —4K 123
Ashleigh Av. Wake —6G 118
Ashleigh Clo. Shel —7K 149
Ashleigh Dale. Hud —1J 131
Ashleigh Gdns. Oss —3M 117
Ashleigh Gdns. W'ford —7D 82
Ashleigh Rd. Leeds —7K 43
Ashleigh St. Kei —8J 21
Ashley Av. Leeds —4J 63
Ashley Clo. Gom —2L 95
Ashley Clo. Wren —1H 119
Ashley Ct. S Kirk —8F 156
Ashley Cft. Roys —5C 154
Ashley Gro. H Bri —3M 89
Ashley Ind. Est. Oss —4A 118
Ashley La. Shipl —7N 39
Ashley Pk. M. Gar —5C 66
Ashley Rd. Bgly —5F 38
Ashley Rd. Leeds —4H 63
Ashley Rd. Lwr W —8L 61
Ashley Rd. Wyke —2A 94
Ashley St. Hal —5M 91
Ashley St. Shipl —7N 39
Ashley Ter. Leeds —4J 63
Ashmead. Bat —9D 96
Ashmead. Cliff —3D 32
Ash Mdw. Clo. Hud —8A 114
Ashmere Gro. Hud —9A 114
Ash M. B'frd —8J 41
Ashmore Dri. Oss —2M 117
Ash Mt. B'frd —9N 57
Ashmount. Cytn —1J 75
Ash Mt. Kei —2G 36
Ash Mt. Shaf —5K 155
Ash Rd. Leeds —2M 61
Ash Rd. Shaf —7L 155
Ash Rd. Skel —7N 159
Ashroyd. Rothw —9A 82
Ash St. Cleck —5G 95
Ash St. Hud —2M 131
(in two parts)
Ash St. I'ly —4H 9
Ash St. New C —3H 139
Ash St. Oxe —3C 54
Ash St. Stan —1A 120
Ash Ter. Bgly —5E 38
Ash Ter. Gar —6A 66
Ash Ter. Leeds —1N 61
Ash Ter. Sower B —8C 110
Ashtofts Mt. Guis —7J 25
Ashton Av. B'frd —9K 57
Ashton Av. Leeds —4H 63
Ashton Clough Rd. Liv —8L 95
Ashton Ct. Leeds —3J 63
(nr. Ashton Rd.)
Ashton Ct. Leeds —2H 63
(off Karnac Rd.)
Ashton Cres. Carl —1M 99
Ashton Gro. Leeds —4H 63
Ashton Ho. B'frd —9C 58
(off Crosscombe Wlk.)
Ashton Mt. Leeds —4H 63
Ashton Pl. Leeds —4H 63
Ashton Rd. C'frd —6D 102
Ashton Rd. Leeds —3J 63
Ashton Rd. Ind. Est. Leeds —3J 63
Ashton St. B'frd —7B 58
Ashton St. C'frd —5D 102
Ashton St. Leeds —3H 63
Ashton Ter. Leeds —4H 63
Ashton Ter. Rothw —9K 81
(off Wakefield Rd.)
Ashton Vw. Leeds —4H 63
Ashton Wlk. B'frd —8E 40
Ash Tree App. Leeds —2E 64
Ash Tree Av. T'tn —8A 56
Ash Tree Bank. Leeds —1E 64
Ash Tree Clo. Leeds —1E 64
Ash Tree Ct. Leeds —1E 64
Ash Tree Gdns. Hal —8J 73
Ash Tree Gdns. Leeds —1E 64
Ash Tree Gdns. Nor —9G 101
Ash Tree Grange. Leeds —1E 64
(off Ash Tree Bank)
Ashtree Gro. B'frd —3L 75
Ash Tree Gro. Kip —4B 84
Ash Tree Gro. Leeds —1E 64
Ash Tree Pk. Kip —4B 84
Ash Tree Rd. Hal —8J 73
Ash Tree Vw. Leeds —1E 64
(off Ash Tree Gdns.)
Ash Tree Wlk. Bur W —8C 10
Ash Tree Wlk. Chap —9G 44
Ash Tree Wlk. Leeds —1E 64
(off Ash Tree Clo.)
Ashtree Wlk. Tad —7N 33
Ash Vw. E Ard —5E 98
Ash Vw. Leeds —1N 61
Ash Villa. Hal —6N 91
(off Lister La.)
Ash Vs. Leeds —2E 64
Ashville Av. Leeds —3N 61
Ashville Cft. Hal —4K 91
Ashville Gdns. Hal —4K 91
Ashville Gro. Hal —3K 91
Ashville Gro. Leeds —3N 61
Ashville Rd. Leeds —3N 61
Ashville St. Hal —3N 91
Ashville Ter. Fars —4A 60
(off New St.)
Ashville Ter. Leeds —3N 61
Ashville Ter. Oakw —5D 36
Ashville Vw. Leeds —4A 62
Ash Wlk. Gol —5D 130
Ashwell Clo. Shaf —6K 155
Ashwell La. B'frd —2M 57
Ashwell Rd. H'tn —2M 57
Ashwell Rd. Mann —5N 57
Ashwood. Leeds —6C 46
Ashwood Clo. Hud —8A 114
Ashwood Dri. Gild —6E 78
Ashwood Dri. Riddl —7N 21
Ashwood Gdns. Gild —6E 78
Ashwood Grange. Dur —4G 137
Ashwood Gro. Gild —6F 78
Ashwood Gro. Horb —9E 118
Ashwood Pde. Gild —6E 78
(off Ashwood Gdns.)
Ashwood St. B'frd —4H 77
Ashwood Ter. Leeds —2B 62
Ashwood Vs. Leeds —2B 62
Ashworth Clo. Dew —3F 116
Ashworth Gdns. Dew —3F 116
Ashworth Grn. Dew —3F 116
Ashworth Pl. B'frd —4B 76
Ashworth Rd. Dew —3F 116
Ashworth Rd. Pon —9L 103
Askam Av. Pon —8M 103
Asket Av. Leeds —1N 63
Asket Clo. Leeds —9N 45
Asket Cres. Leeds —1N 63
Asket Dri. Leeds —9N 45
Asket Gdns. Leeds —9M 45
Asket Gth. Leeds —1N 63
Asket Grn. Leeds —9N 45
Asket Hill. Leeds —8M 45
Asket Pl. Leeds —1N 63
Asket Wlk. Leeds —1N 63
Askey Cres. Morl —2L 97
Askham Gro. Upt —2D 158
Askham Rd. C'frd —3K 103
Askrigg Dri. B'frd —3F 58
Askwith. —4D 10
Askwith La. Askw —4D 10
Aspden St. Todm —6K 87
Aspect Gdns. Pud —6N 59
Aspect Ter. Pud —6N 59
Aspen Clo. Kei —2L 37
Aspen Clo. Wake —3J 119
Aspen Ct. Eml —2F 150
Aspen Ct. Ting —3M 97
Aspen Gro. Dew —3E 116
Aspen Mt. Leeds —5H 43
Aspen Ri. All —2E 56
Aspinall St. Hal —6M 91
Aspinall St. H Bri —3M 89
Aspley. —5A 132
Aspley Pl. Hud —4N 131
Asprey Dri. All —6G 56
Asquith Av. Gild —7H 79
Asquith Clo. Morl —8J 79
Asquith Dri. Morl —8J 79
Asquith St. Birs —2E 96
Assembly St. Leeds —7E 62
Assembly St. Nor —1H 121
Astley Av. Swil —4H 83
Astley La. Swil —4J 83
Astley La. Ind. Est. Swil —5J 83
Astley Way. Swil —5J 83
Aston Av. Leeds —4G 61
Aston Clo. Liv —1K 115
Aston Ct. Oss —6C 118
Aston Cres. Leeds —4H 61
Aston Dri. Leeds —4H 61
Aston Gro. Leeds —4H 61
Aston Mt. Leeds —4H 61
Aston Pl. Leeds —4H 61
Aston Rd. B'frd —2C 76
Aston Rd. Leeds —4G 61
Aston St. Leeds —4G 61
Aston Ter. Leeds —4H 61
Aston Vw. Leeds —4G 61
Astor Gro. Leeds —4D 60
Astor St. Leeds —4D 60
Astra Bus. Pk. Leeds —3E 80
Astral Av. Hal —4J 93
Astral Clo. Hal —4J 93
Astral Vw. B'frd —3M 75
Astura Ct. Leeds —1D 62
Atalanta Ter. Hal —8L 91
Atamco Ho. Cleck —5J 95
(off Albion St.)
Atha Clo. Leeds —4C 80
Atha Cres. Leeds —4C 80
Atha St. Leeds —4C 80
Athelstan La. Otley —7L 11
Athene Dri. Hud —7A 132
Athersley North. —9A 154
Atherstone Rd. All —7G 57
Atherton La. Brigh —3N 113
Athlone Dri. Dew —1H 117
Athlone Gro. Leeds —7M 61
Athlone Ri. Gar —7B 66
Athlone St. Leeds —7M 61
Athlone Ter. Leeds —7M 61
Athol Clo. Hal —1N 91
Athol Cres. Hal —1N 91
Athold Dri. Oss —6B 118
Athold St. Oss —6B 118
Athol Gdns. Hal —1N 91
Athol Grn. Hal —1N 91
Athol Rd. B'frd —4N 57
Athol Rd. Hal —1N 91
Athol St. Hal —1N 91
Athol St. Kei —7L 21
Atkinson Ct. Nor —2H 121
Atkinson Hill. —1H 81
Atkinson La. Pon —1M 123
Atkinson's Ct. Hal —4B 92
Atkinson St. H'lct —9G 63
Atkinson St. Shipl —7N 39
Atlanta St. Leeds —4D 60
Atlas Mill Rd. Brigh —1M 113
Atlas St. B'frd —5N 57
Attlee Av. H'cft —9K 139
Attlee Cres. Wake —3N 137
Attlee Gro. Wake —8L 99
Attlee St. Nor —3J 121
Auckland Rd. B'frd —4M 75
Audby Ct. Weth —3N 17
Audby La. Weth —2N 17
Audrey St. Oss —7A 118
Audsley's Yd. Horb —1A 136
Augusta Ct. Wake —6G 119
Augusta Dri. Norm —3L 121
Aurelia Ho. B'frd —4A 58
Austell Ho. B'frd —1B 76
(off Park La.)
Austhorpe. —6F 64
Austhorpe Av. Leeds —7F 64
Austhorpe Ct. Leeds —7F 64
(off Austhorpe Dri.)
Austhorpe Dri. Leeds —7F 64
Austhorpe Gdns. Leeds —6G 64
Austhorpe Gro. Leeds —7F 64
Austhorpe La. Leeds —5E 64
Austhorpe Rd. Leeds —4D 64
Austhorpe Vw. Leeds —6E 64
Austin Av. Brigh —8L 93
Austin Rd. C'frd —4K 103
Austin St. Kei —8K 21
Austwick Clo. M'well —7J 153
Authorpe Rd. Leeds —9B 44
Autumn Av. Leeds —4A 62
Autumn Av. Weth —1M 17
Autumn Cres. H'fth —8G 42
Autumn Gro. Leeds —4A 62
Autumn Pl. Leeds —4A 62
Autumn St. Hal —7M 91
Autumn St. Leeds —4A 62
Autumn Ter. Leeds —4A 62
Auty Cres. Stan —7A 100
Auty M. Stan —7A 100
Auty Sq. Morl —1L 97
Avenel Rd. All —5G 56
Avenel Ter. All —6G 57
Avenham Way. B'frd —6E 58
Avens Clo. Pon —4K 123
Avenue A. Thor A —7H 19
Avenue B. Thor A —8G 19
Avenue C East. Thor A —7J 19
Avenue Cres. Leeds —2H 63
Avenue C West. Thor A —8H 19
Avenue D. Thor A —9H 19
Avenue E East. Thor A —8J 19
Avenue E West. Thor A —9H 19
Avenue F. Thor A —8J 19
Avenue G. Thor A —7K 19
Avenue Gdns. Leeds —2C 44
Avenue Hill. Leeds —2G 63
Avenue Lawns. Leeds —2B 44
Avenue No.1. Brigh —2M 113
Avenue No.2. Brigh —2M 113
Avenue Rd. B'frd —2D 76
Avenue Rd. Wake —1N 137
Avenue St. B'frd —4H 77
Avenue Ter. Pon —3G 123
Avenue Ter. Yead —9A 26
Avenue, The. Alw —2B 44
Avenue, The. Bat —5D 96
Avenue, The. Bgly —7G 38
Avenue, The. Birs —3B 96
(in two parts)
Avenue, The. Bret —3A 152
Avenue, The. Cytn —2F 74
Avenue, The. Coll —8H 17
Avenue, The. Croft —1F 138
Avenue, The. Dew —9C 96
Avenue, The. Haig —3A 152
Avenue, The. Hal —4J 93
Avenue, The. Hare —2J 29
Avenue, The. H'fth —6C 42
Avenue, The. Hud —5B 132
Avenue, The. Idle —4J 41
(in three parts)
Avenue, The. Leeds —7G 62
(nr. Flax Pl.)
Avenue, The. Leeds —3E 82
(nr. Pontefract La.)
Avenue, The. Leeds —3E 64
(nr. Sandbed La.)
Avenue, The. Round —7J 45
Avenue, The. Roys —5F 154
Avenue, The. Scholes —7G 47
Avenue, The. Ting —4C 98
Avenue, The. Wake —8K 99
Avenue, The. Wigh P —4N 19
Avenue, The. Wilsd —2C 56
Avenue Victoria. Leeds —7J 45
Averingcliffe Rd. B'frd —9H 41
Aveue Des Hirondelles. Pool W —2F 26
Aviary Gro. Leeds —6M 61
Aviary Mt. Leeds —6M 61
Aviary Pl. Leeds —6M 61
Aviary Rd. Leeds —6M 61
Aviary Row. Leeds —6M 61
Aviary St. Leeds —6M 61
Aviary Ter. Leeds —6M 61
Aviary Vw. Leeds —6M 61
Avison Rd. Hud —7F 130
Avison Yd. Wake —5M 119
Avocet Clo. B'frd —7H 57
Avocet Gth. Leeds —8F 80
Avon Clo. Leeds —3A 46
Avon Ct. Leeds —2N 45
Avon Ct. Oss —6M 117
Avon Cft. Oss —6M 117
Avondale. Kei —8G 20
Avondale Ct. Leeds —4F 44
Avondale Cres. Shipl —8M 39
Avondale Dri. Barn —8D 154
Avondale Gro. Shipl —8M 39
Avondale Mt. Shipl —8M 39
Avondale Pl. Hal —8A 92
Avondale Rd. Shipl —8K 39
Avondale St. Leeds —5F 60
Avondale St. Wake —7L 119
Avondale Vs. T'ner —4F 46
Avondale Way. Wake —7L 119
Avon Dri. Gar —8N 65
Avon Gth. Weth —4K 17
Avon Wlk. F'stne —4C 122
Aydon Way. She —6K 75
Aygill Av. B'frd —3J 57
Aylesbury St. Kei —3G 37
Aylesford Mt. Leeds —3G 65
Aylesham Ind. Est. Low M —7B 76
Aynholme Clo. Add —1M 7
Aynholme Dri. Add —1M 7
Aynsley Gro. All —4G 56
Ayres Dri. Cow —7F 130
Ayresome Av. Leeds —5J 45
Ayresome Oval. All —7F 56
Ayresome Ter. Leeds —5H 45
Ayreville Dri. Hal —7H 75
Ayrton Cres. Bgly —4F 38
Aysgarth Av. Hal —6M 93
Aysgarth Clo. Leeds —7H 63
Aysgarth Clo. Wake —8F 118
Aysgarth Clo. Wyke —2A 94
Aysgarth Cres. Hal —1G 91
Aysgarth Dri. Leeds —7H 63
Aysgarth Dri. Wake —8F 118
Aysgarth Fold. Midd —9E 80
Aysgarth Pl. Leeds —7H 63
Aysgarth Rd. Bat —7D 96
Aysgarth Rd. Hud —8N 131
Aysgarth Wlk. Leeds —7H 63
Ayton Clo. B'frd —6E 58
Ayton Ho. B'frd —4K 77
Ayton Rd. Hud —4D 130
Azealea Ct. B'frd —6F 58
(in two parts)

Baby Ho. Hill La. Pec W —1G 71
Bachelor La. H'fth —6F 42
Bk. Ada St. Kei —9G 21
(off Devonshire St.)
Bk. Aireview Ter. Kei —1L 37
Bk. Aireville St. Kei —6G 21
Bk. Airlie Av. Leeds —2H 63
(off Airlie Av.)
Bk. Airlie Pl. Leeds —2H 63
(off Airlie Pl.)
Bk. Albert Gro. Leeds —9N 43
Bk. Albert Ter. Leeds —4A 62
(off Burley Lodge Rd.)
Bk. Alcester Pl. Leeds —2H 63
(off Alcester Pl.)
Bk. Alcester Rd. Leeds —2H 63
(off Alcester Rd.)
Bk. Alcester Ter. Leeds —2H 63
(off Alcester Ter.)
Bk. Allerton Ter. Leeds —8F 44
Bk. Alma St. Yead —9N 25
(off Alma St.)
Bk. Anderton St. Wake —8N 119
Bk. Ann St. Denh —5K 55
(off William St.)
Bk. Archery Pl. Leeds —4D 62
(off Archery Pl.)
Bk. Archery Rd. Leeds —4D 62
(off Archery Rd.)
Bk. Archery St. Leeds —4D 62
(off Archery St.)
Bk. Archery Ter. Leeds —4D 62
(off Archery Ter.)
Bk. Armitage Rd. Hud —1K 147
Bk. Ash Gro. Leeds —3B 62
(in two parts)
Bk. Ashgrove W. B'frd —8B 58
Bk. Ashley Av. Leeds —4J 63
(off Ashley Av.)
Bk. Ashley St. Leeds —4J 63
(off Ashley Rd.)
Bk. Ashville Av. Leeds —3A 62
(off Ashville Av.)
Bk. Ashville Gro. Leeds —3N 61
(off Ashville Gro.)
Bk. Ashville Rd. Leeds —3N 61
(off Ashville Rd.)
Bk. Ashville Ter. Leeds —3N 61
(off Ashville Ter.)

Bk. Ashwood Ter. Leeds —2B 62
Bk. Aston Pl. Leeds —4H 61
(off Aston Rd.)
Bk. Aston Rd. Leeds —4G 61
Bk. Aston St. Leeds —4G 61
Bk. Aston Ter. Leeds —4H 61
(off Aston Rd.)
Bk. Aston Vw. Leeds —4G 61
Bk. Athlone Av. Leeds —7M 61
Bk. Athlone Gro. Leeds —7M 61
(off Athlone St.)
Bk. Athlone Ter. Leeds —7M 61
(off Athlone St.)
Bk. Atlanta St. Leeds —4D 60
Bk. Austhorpe Rd. Leeds —4D 64
(off Austhorpe Rd., in two parts)
Bk. Autumn Rd. Leeds —4A 62
(off Autumn Ter.)
Bk. Autumn Ter. Leeds —4A 62
(off Autumn Ter.)
Bk. Aviary Rd. Leeds —6M 61
(off Aviary Gro.)
Bk. Aylesbury St. Kei —3G 37
(off Queen's Rd.)
Bk. Baker St. Shipl —7M 39
Bk. Baldovan Ter. Leeds —2H 63
(off Baldovan Ter.)
Bk. Balfour St. Bgly —5E 38
Bk. Balfour St. Kei —1H 37
Bk. Bank St. C'frd —4D 102
Bk. Bank Ter. Far —4B 60
Bk. Banstead St. Leeds —3H 63
(off Banstead Ter. E.)
Bk. Barden Pl. Leeds —7K 61
(off Whingate Rd.)
Bk. Barkly Gro. Leeds —3C 80
(off Barkly Gro.)
Bk. Barkly Pde. Leeds —4C 80
(off Barkly Pde.)
Bk. Barkly Ter. Leeds —3C 80
(off Barkly Ter.)
Bk. Barrowby Vw. Leeds —7F 64
Bk. Bath Rd. Leeds —4F 60
(off Cross Bath Rd.)
Bk. Beamsley Gro. Leeds —4A 62
(off Beamsley Gro.)
Bk. Beamsley Mt. Leeds —4A 62
(off Beamsley Mt.)
Bk. Beamsley Ter. Leeds —4A 62
(off Beamsley Ter.)
Bk. Beaumont St. Bat —9F 96
Bk. Beck La. Add —9M 5
Bk. Beech St. Bgly —5E 38
Bk. Beech Ter. Hud —1N 131
Bk. Beechwood Gro. Leeds —3N 61
Bk. Beechwood Rd. Leeds —3N 61
(off Beechwood Pl.)
Bk. Bellbrooke Gro. Leeds —4K 63
(off Bellbrooke Gro.)
Bk. Bellbrooke Pl. Leeds —4K 63
(off Bellbrooke Pl.)
Bk. Bellbrooke Ter. Leeds —4K 63
(off Bellbrooke St.)
Bk. Belvedere Av. Leeds —3D 80
(off Belvedere Av.)
Bk. Bentley Av. Leeds —9B 44
(off Bentley Gro.)
Bk. Bentley Gro. Leeds —9B 44
(off Bentley Gro.)
Bk. Berkeley Av. Leeds —3J 63
(off Berkeley Av.)
Bk. Berkeley Ter. Leeds —3J 63
(off Berkeley Ter.)
Bk. Beverley Ter. Leeds —2D 80
Bk. Blackwood Gro. Hal —4M 91
Bk. Blenheim Av. Leeds —4D 62
Bk. Blenheim Mt. B'frd —4A 58
Bk. Blenheim Ter. Leeds —4D 62
Bk. Boundary Ter. Leeds —5A 62
(off Burley Rd.)
Bk. Bower Rd. Ell —4F 112
Bk. Bowling Grn. Rd. Slnd —8M 111
Bk. Bowman St. Wake —8A 120
Bk. Bradshaw Rd. Hon —6L 147
Bk. Branch Pl. Leeds —1K 79
(off Branch Pl.)
Bk. Breary Av. H'fth —6G 43
Bk. Breary Ter. H'fth —6G 43
(off Breary Av.)
Bk. Briggate. Sils —7E 6
Bk. Broad La. Leeds —2G 60
Bk. Broomfield Cres. Leeds —2N 61
Bk. Broomfield Pl. Leeds —3N 61
(off Broomfield Pl.)
Bk. Broomfield Rd. Kei —9H 21
Bk. Broomfield Rd. Leeds —3N 61
(off Newport Rd.)
Bk. Broomfield St. Kei —9H 21
Bk. Broughton Av. Leeds —4J 63
(off Broughton Av.)
Bk. Broughton Ter. Leeds —4J 63
(off Broughton Ter.)
Bk. Brudenell Gro. Leeds —4B 62
(off Brudenell Gro.)
Bk. Brudenell Mt. Leeds —3A 62
(off Brudenell Mt.)
Bk. Brudenell Rd. Leeds —3A 62
(off Brudenell Rd.)
Bk. Brunswick St. Dew —2D 116
Bk. Brunswick St. Leeds —5E 62
Bk. Burchett Gro. Leeds —2C 62
(off Burchett Gro.)
Bk. Burchett Pl. Leeds —2C 62
(off Burchett Pl.)
Bk. Burley Hill. Leeds —4M 61
Bk. Burley Lodge Rd. Leeds —4A 62
(off Burley Lodge Rd.)
Bk. Burley Lodge Ter. Leeds —5A 62
(off Burley Lodge Ter.)
Bk. Burley St. Leeds —6C 62
(off Burley St.)
Bk. Burlington Pl. Leeds —3D 80
(off Burlington Pl.)
Bk. Burlington Rd. Leeds —3D 80
(off Burlington Rd.)
Bk. Burton Cres. Leeds —9N 43
Bk. Burton Ter. Leeds —2E 80
Bk. Buxton St. Kei —9K 21
(off Buxton St.)
Bk. Byrl St. Kei —7J 21
(off Byrl St.)
Bk. Byrom St. Todm —6K 87
Bk. Caister St. Kei —3H 37
(off Oakfield Rd.)
Bk. Caledonia Rd. Kei —8K 21
(off Caledonia Rd.)
Bk. Camberley St. Leeds —2D 80
(off Camberley St.)
Bk. Carberry Pl. Leeds —4A 62
(off Carberry Pl.)
Bk. Carberry Rd. Leeds —4A 62
(off Carberry Rd.)
Bk. Carberry Ter. Leeds —4A 62
(off Carberry Pl.)
Bk. Carlinghow La. Bat —5B 96
Bk. Carter Mt. Leeds —6D 64
(off Carter Mt.)
Bk. Cartmel Rd. Kei —9G 21
(off Devonshire Rd.)
Bk. Castle Rd. Kei —8H 21
Bk. Cavendish Rd. B'frd —8F 40
Bk. Cavendish St. Kei —9J 21
Bk. Cavendish Ter. Hal —5N 91
Bk. Cecil St. Hud —4M 131
Bk. Chapel La. Leeds —2N 61
(off Broomfield Rd.)
Bk. Chapel St. B'frd —7D 58
Bk. Charles St. Brigh —9M 93
(off Charles St.)
Bk. Charlton Rd. Leeds —7J 63
Bk. Chatsworth Rd. Leeds —3J 63
(off Chatsworth Rd.)
Bk. Chestnut Av. Leeds —4E 64
(off Chestnut Av.)
Bk. Chiswick Ter. Leeds —4A 62
(off Burley Lodge Rd.)
Bk. Christ Chu. Vw. Leeds —6L 61
(off Stanningley Rd.)
Bk. Church La. Kirks —2K 61
(off Hesketh Rd.)
Bk. Church La. Leeds —2N 43
Bk. Church Vw. Wake —9A 120
Bk. Claremont Av. Leeds —5C 62
(off Claremont Av.)
Bk. Claremont Gro. Leeds —5C 62
(off Claremont Gro.)
Bk. Claremont St. Rothw —7D 82
Bk. Claremont Ter. Leeds —5C 62
(off Claremont Av.)
Bk. Claremount Ter. Hal —2B 92
Bk. Clarence Rd. H'fth —8E 42
Bk. Clarence St. Hal —5A 92
Bk. Clarendon Pl. Hal —5N 91
Bk. Clarkson Vw. Leeds —2C 62
(off Clarkson Vw.)
Bk. Clayton St. Rothw —8A 82
Bk. Cliff Mt. Leeds —2C 62
(off Cliff Mt.)
Bk. Clifton Rd. Hud —3K 131
Bk. Clifton Ter. Leeds —4K 63
(off Clifton Ter.)
Bk. Clipston Av. Leeds —9B 44
(off Clipston Av.)
Bk. Clough. Hal —2F 92
Bk. Clovelly Pl. Leeds —2D 80
(off Clovelly Pl.)
Bk. Colenso Mt. Leeds —1B 80
(off Colenso Mt.)
Bk. Colenso Rd. Kei —7L 21
(off Aireworth Rd.)
Bk. Colenso Rd. Leeds —1B 80
(off Colenso Rd.)
Bk. Colton Rd. Leeds —7M 61
Bk. Colwyn Vw. Leeds —3D 80
(off Colwyn Vw.)
Bk. Commercial St. Hal —5B 92
(off Commercial St.)
Bk. Commercial St. Todm —7L 87
Bk. Compton St. Kei —8K 21
(off Compton St.)
Bk. Conway St. Leeds —3H 63
(off Conway St.)
Bk. Cowper Gro. Leeds —3J 63
(off Cowper Gro.)
Bk. Cowper St. Leeds —3G 62
(off Cross Cowper St.)
Bk. Craggwood Rd. H'fth —8F 42
Bk. Cranbrook Av. Leeds —2C 80
(off Cranbrook Av.)
Bk. Cranbrook Ter. Leeds —2C 80
(off Cranbrook Av.)
Back Cft. Sower B —1C 128
Bk. Croft Ho. La. Kei —6G 21
Bk. Cromer Av. Kei —2H 37
(off Cromer Rd.)
Bk. Cromer Gro. Kei —3H 37
(off Cromer Rd.)
Bk. Cromer Ter. Leeds —4C 62
Bk. Cromwell Ter. Hal —5A 92
Bk. Cross Flatts Av. Leeds —3C 80
(off Cross Flatts Av.)
Bk. Cross Flatts Cres. Leeds —3B 80
(off Cross Flatts Cres.)
Bk. Cross Flatts Gro. Leeds —3C 80
(off Cross Flatts Gro.)
Bk. Cross Flatts Mt. Leeds —3C 80
(off Cross Flatts Mt.)
Bk. Cross Flatts Pl. Leeds —3B 80
(off Cross Flatts Pl.)
Bk. Cross Flatts Row. Leeds —3B 80
(off Cross Flatts Row)
Bk. Cross Grn. Cres. Leeds —8H 63
(off Cross Grn. Cres.)
Bk. Cross Grn. La. Leeds —8H 63
(off Cross Grn. La.)
Bk. Cross La. Ell —5D 112
(off Linden Rd.)
Bk. Dalton Gro. Leeds —3C 80
(off Dalton Gro.)
Bk. Dalton Rd. Leeds —3C 80
Bk. Dargai St. Leeds —3E 62
Bk. Dawlish Av. Leeds —6K 63
(off Dawlish Av.)
Bk. Dawlish Mt. Leeds —6K 63
(off Dawlish Mt.)
Bk. Dawlish Rd. Leeds —6K 63
(off Dawlish Rd.)
Bk. De Lacy Mt. Leeds —1K 61
(off Abbey Rd.)
Bk. Delph Mt. Leeds —2C 62
(off Delph Mt.)
Bk. Dent St. Leeds —7H 63
(off Dent St.)
Bk. Der St. Todm —7L 87
Bk. Devonshire La. Leeds —5J 45
Bk. Dorset Mt. Leeds —2J 63
(off Dorset Mt.)
Bk. Dorset Rd. Leeds —2J 63
(off Dorset Rd.)
Bk. Dorset Ter. Leeds —3J 63
(off Dorset Ter.)
Bk. Dudley Hill Rd. B'frd —4F 58
Bk. Duke of York St. Wake —4M 119
Bk. Duke St. F'stne —5C 122
Bk. Dunbar St. Wake —7A 120
(off Dunbar St.)
Bk. East Pk. Rd. Leeds —7J 63
(off E. Park Rd.)
Bk. Eaton St. Kei —3G 37
(off Queen's Rd.)
Bk. Ecclesburn Gro. Leeds —7K 63
(off Ecclesburn Gro.)
Bk. Ecclesburn St. Leeds —7J 63
(off Ecclesburn St.)
Bk. Edensor Rd. Kei —9G 21
(off Devonshire Rd.)
Bk. Edinburgh Rd. Leeds —6K 61
(off Town St.)
Bk. Eldon Rd. Hud —3J 131
Bk. Elford Pl. Leeds —3H 63
(off Elford Gro., in two parts)
Bk. Elizabeth St. B'frd —9C 58
Bk. Ellers Gro. Leeds —2H 63
(off Ellers Gro.)
Bk. Ellers Rd. Leeds —2H 63
(off Ellers Rd.)
Bk. Elmfield Ter. Hal —7A 92
Bk. Elsworth St. Leeds —7N 61
Bk. Emily St. Kei —8J 21
(off Cross Emily St.)
Bk. Eric St. Kei —8J 21
(off Eric St.)
Bk. Eric St. Leeds —1F 60
Bk. Eshald Pl. Rothw —7E 82
Bk. Esmond Ter. Leeds —7M 61
Bk. Estcourt Av. Leeds —1M 61
(off Ash Rd.)
Bk. Eversley Mt. Hal —6L 91
Bk. Fairford Pl. Leeds —2E 80
Bk. Ferguson St. Hal —6B 92
Back Fld. T'tn —8D 56
(off Havelock Sq.)
Bk. Field Ct. T'tn —8D 56
(off Bk. High St.)
Bk. Fitzwilliam St. Hud —4L 131
Bk. Florist St. Kei —7L 21
(off Florist St.)
Back Fold. Cytn —9G 57
Bk. Foster Rd. Kei —3H 37
(off Oakfield Rd.)
Bk. Garden St. C'frd —6D 102
Bk. Garden St. Wake —5K 119
Bk. Garton Rd. Leeds —7J 63
(off Garton Rd.)
Bk. Garton Ter. Leeds —7J 63
(off Garton Ter.)
Bk. Gathorne St. Leeds —3G 63
(off Gathorne St.)
Bk. Gerard St. Hal —5A 92
Bk. Giles St. N. B'frd —9B 58
Bk. Giles St. S. B'frd —9B 58
Bk. Gillett La. Rothw —8A 82
Bk. Girlington Rd. B'frd —5L 57
Bk. Gladstone Rd. Hal —5A 92
Bk. Gladstone St. Bgly —5E 38
Bk. Glebe Ter. Leeds —9N 43
(off Glebe Ter.)
Bk. Glen Ter. Hal —7A 92
Bk. Glenthorpe Ter. Leeds —6J 63
(off Glenthorpe Ter.)
Bk. Glossop St. Leeds —2D 62
(off Glossop St.)
Bk. Gooder La. Brigh —2N 113
Bk. Gordon St. Wake —9A 120
Bk. Gordon Ter. Leeds —9B 44
(off Gordon Ter.)
Bk. Graham Gro. Leeds —3N 61
Bk. Granby Gro. Leeds —2N 61
(off Granby Rd.)
Bk. Grange Av. Leeds —2F 62
(off Grange Av.)
Bk. Grange Cres. Leeds —2G 62
(off Grange Cres.)
Bk. Grange Ter. Leeds —2F 62
(off Grange Ter.)
Bk. Grange Vw. Leeds —2G 62
(off Grange Vw.)
Bk. Grantley St. Wake —5M 119
Bk. Grant St. Kei —9G 20
Bk. Grassington Ter. Kei —8J 21
(off Lawkholme La.)
Bk. Gt. Russell St. B'frd —7A 58
Bk. Greaves St. B'frd —2B 76
(off Greaves St.)
Back Grn. Chur —6M 79
Bk. Greenhead Rd. Hud —4L 131
Bk. Greenhow Wlk. Leeds —4N 61
(off Greenhow Rd.)
Bk. Greenmount Ter. Leeds —2D 80
(off Greenmount Ter.)
Bk. Grosvenor Ter. Hal —5N 91
Bk. Grosvenor Ter. Leeds —2B 62
(off Grosvenor Ter.)
Bk. Grouse St. Kei —8K 21
(off Parson St.)
Bk. Grove Gdns. Leeds —9A 44
(off Grove Gdns.)
Bk. Grovehall Av. Leeds —4C 80
Bk. Grovehall Dri. Leeds —4C 80
Bk. Grove Rd. I'ly —5G 8
Bk. Haigh Av. Rothw —6M 81
Bk. Haigh St. Rothw —6L 81
Bk. Haigh Vw. Rothw —6L 81
Bk. Halliday Gro. Leeds —6K 61
Bk. Halliday Pl. Leeds —6K 61
Bk. Hambleton St. Wake —4L 119
(off Tavora St.)
Bk. Hamilton Av. Leeds —2G 62
(off Hamilton Av.)
Bk. Hamilton Vw. Leeds —2G 62
(off Hamilton Vw.)
Bk. Harehills Av. Leeds —2G 62
(off Harehills Av.)
Bk. Harehills Pk. Vw. Leeds —4K 63
(off Harehills Pk. Vw.)
Bk. Harehills Pl. Leeds —3H 63
(off Harehills Pl.)
Bk. Hares Av. Leeds —2H 63
(off Hares Av.)
Bk. Hares Mt. Leeds —2G 63
(off Hares Mt.)
Bk. Hares Ter. Leeds —2H 63
(off Hares Ter.)
Bk. Hares Vw. Leeds —2H 63
(off Hares Vw.)
Bk. Harold Gro. Leeds —4A 62
(off Harold Gro.)
Bk. Hartley Av. Leeds —2D 62
(off Hartley Av.)
Bk. Hartley Gro. Leeds —2C 62
(off Hartley Gro.)
Bk. Hartley St. Morl —1M 97
Bk. Hatfield St. Wake —4L 119
Bk. Hawksworth Gro. Leeds —9G 43
Bk. Headingley Av. Leeds —1M 61
(off Ash Rd.)
Bk. Headingley Mt. Leeds —1M 61
(off Ash Rd.)
Bk. Heathfield Ter. Leeds —9N 43
(off Heathfield Ter.)
Bk. Heddon St. Leeds —9A 44
(off Heddon St.)
Bk. Heights Rd. T'tn —7A 56
Bk. Henrietta St. Bat —7F 96
Bk. Hessle Av. Leeds —3A 62
(off Hessle Av.)
Bk. Hessle Mt. Leeds —3A 62
(off Hessle Mt.)
Bk. Hessle Ter. Leeds —3A 62
(off Hessle Ter.)
Bk. Hessle Vw. Leeds —3A 62
(off Hessle Vw.)
Bk. Highbury Ter. Leeds —9A 44
(off Highbury Ter.)
Bk. Highfield Rd. Leeds —4G 61
Bk. High St. T'tn —8D 56
Bk. Highthorne Gro. Leeds —6K 61
Bk. Hillcrest Av. Leeds —2G 63
(off Hillcrest Av.)
Bk. Hillcrest Vw. Leeds —2G 63
(off Hillcrest Vw.)
Bk. Hilltop Av. Leeds —2H 63
(off Hilltop Av.)
Bk. Hill Top Mt. Leeds —2H 63
(off Hill Top Mt.)
Bk. Hilton Pl. Leeds —2H 63
(off Hilton Pl.)
Bk. Hilton Rd. Leeds —2H 63
(off Hilton Rd.)
Bk. Hird St. Kei —1H 37
Backhold Av. Hal —1D 112
Backhold Dri. Hal —1C 112
Backhold Hall. Hal —9D 92
Backhold La. Hal —1C 112
Backhold Rd. Hal —1D 112
Bk. Hollyshaw Ter. Leeds —6D 64
Bk. Holywell La. Leeds —2M 45
Bk. Honoria St. Hud —1M 131
Bk. Hope Hall Ter. Hal —6B 92
Backhouse La. Wool —2H 153
Bk. Hovingham Gro. Leeds —2J 63
(off Hovingham Gro.)
Bk. Hovingham Mt. Leeds —2J 63
(off Hovingham Mt.)
Bk. Hovingham Ter. Leeds —2J 63
(off Hovingham Ter.)
Bk. Hyde Gro. Kei —8K 21
(off Kirby St.)
Bk. Hyde Ter. Leeds —5C 62
Bk. Ibbetson Pl. Leeds —5D 62
(off Fenton St.)
Bk. Ingledew Cres. Leeds —5K 45
Bk. Ivy Av. Leeds —6J 63
(off Ivy Av.)
Bk. Ivy Gro. Leeds —7K 63
(off Ivy Gro.)
Bk. Ivy Mt. Leeds —6J 63
(off Ivy Mt.)
Bk. Ivy St. Leeds —6J 63
(off Ivy St.)
Bk. John St. T'tn —8C 56
Bk. Karnac Rd. Leeds —2H 63
(off Karnac Rd.)
Bk. Kelso Rd. Leeds —4B 62
Bk. Kendal La. Leeds —5C 62
(off Kendal La.)
Bk. Kennerleigh Wlk. Leeds —5D 64
(off Kennerleigh Wlk.)
Bk. Kensington St. B'frd —5M 57
(off Kensington St.)
Bk. Kensington Ter. Leeds —3B 62
Bk. Kings Av. Leeds —4A 62
(off Kings Av.)
Bk. Kirby St. Kei —8K 21
(off Kirby St.)
Bk. Kirkgate. Shipl —8M 39
Bk. Kitson St. Leeds —7H 63
(off Kitson St.)
Bk. Knowle Mt. Leeds —3N 61
(off Stanmore Hill)
Bk. Knowl Rd. Mir —5K 115
Bk. Laisteridge La. B'frd —8A 58
Bk. Lake St. Leeds —3F 80
Bk. Lambton Gro. Leeds —2H 63
(off Lambton Gro.)
Bk. Landseer Av. Leeds —3H 61
(off Raynville Rd.)
Bk. Landseer Gro. Leeds —3H 61
(off Raynville Rd.)
Bk. Landseer Ter. Leeds —3H 61
(off Raynville Rd.)
Back La. All —4C 56
Back La. All B —1B 102
Back La. Askw —5E 10

Back La. *Bads* —8L **141**
Back La. *Bees* —4B **80**
Back La. *B'ham* —5D **32**
Back La. *Bmly* —5G **60**
Back La. *Brierc* —1C **50**
Back La. *Bstfld* —3B **134**
Back La. *Bur W* —8D **10**
Back La. *Cam* —1N **159**
Back La. *Caw* —4N **167**
Back La. *Cytn* —1H **75**
Back La. *Clay W* —6J **151**
Back La. *C'den* —7C **70**
Back La. *D'ton* —6C **124**
Back La. *Dew* —1B **134**
(in three parts)
Back La. *Dlgtn* —6C **78**
Back La. *E Mor* —7C **22**
Back La. *Eml* —4D **150**
Back La. *Err* —3G **89**
Back La. *Fars* —3A **60**
Back La. *Grng M* —5A **134**
Back La. *Guis* —7G **25**
Back La. *Hal* —8K **73**
Back La. *H'tn* —2M **57**
Back La. *H Bri* —8H **53**
Back La. *Heck* —8A **96**
Back La. *Hept* —8G **70**
Back La. *H'frth* —3M **163**
Back La. *H'fth* —7E **42**
Back La. *Idle* —7F **40**
Back La. *Leeds* —3F **78**
Back La. *Loft* —3L **99**
Back La. *M'twn* —2L **135**
Back La. *Mir* —3M **133**
(nr. Liley La.)
Back La. *Mir* —6J **115**
(nr. Stocks Bank Rd.)
Back La. *N Elm* —3N **157**
Back La. *Nort* —7N **143**
(in two parts)
Back La. *Oakw* —9B **20**
Back La. *Ogden* —2J **73**
Back La. *Oss* —6N **117**
Back La. *Pen* —8B **166**
Back La. *Q'bry* —3F **74**
Back La. *Ripp* —7D **110**
(nr. Halifax Rd.)
Back La. *Ripp* —6C **110**
(nr. Hob La.)
Back La. *Ryh* —6J **139**
(nr. Long Dam La.)
Back La. *Ryh* —9E **138**
(nr. Ryehill Pits La.)
Back La. *Shar C* —9K **121**
Back La. *Shel* —6M **149**
Back La. *Sick* —4C **16**
Back La. *Sils* —7E **6**
Back La. *Slai* —3L **145**
Back La. *Sower B* —3B **110**
Back La. *Stanb* —1J **53**
Back La. *T'tn* —7C **56**
Back La. *Todm* —5A **88**
Back La. *Uthg* —2J **163**
Back La. *Wake* —5K **119**
Back La. *Wee* —6B **14**
Back La. *Wool* —3H **153**
Back La. *Yead* —1L **41**
Back La. W. *Roys* —5B **154**
Bk. Langdale Gdns. Leeds —2M **61**
(off Kirkstall La.)
Bk. Langdale Ter. Leeds —2M **61**
(off Kirkstall La.)
Bk. Laurel Mt. *Leeds* —1F **62**
Bk. Leatham St. *Dew* —2D **116**
Bk. Lime St. Kei —4H **37**
(off Ivy St. S.)
Bk. Linden Gro. Leeds —2E **80**
(off Linden Gro.)
Bk. Lindum St. B'frd —4A **58**
(off Manningham La.)
Bk. Lodge La. Leeds —3D **80**
(off Lodge La.)
Bk. Lombard St. *Yead* —3L **41**
Bk. Longroyd Ter. Leeds —2E **80**
(off Longroyd Ter.)
Bk. Lord St. *Hal* —5A **92**
Bk. Low La. H'fth —6G **43**
(off Springfield Mt.)
Bk. Lucas St. Leeds —2C **62**
(off Lucas St.)
Bk. Lunan Pl. Leeds —2H **63**
(off Lunan Pl.)
Bk. Lunan Ter. Leeds —2H **63**
(off Lunan Ter.)
Bk. Lyons St. *Q'bry* —4E **74**
Bk. Lytton St. *Hal* —3B **92**
Bk. Mafeking Av. Leeds —4C **80**
(off Mafeking Av.)
Bk. Mafeking Mt. *Leeds* —4C **80**
Bk. Malt St. Kei —3G **36**
(off Bracken Rd.)
Bk. Mannville Rd. Kei —1G **37**
(off Malsis Rd.)
Bk. Manor Dri. Leeds —2A **62**
(off Manor Av.)
Bk. Manor Gro. Leeds —9F **44**
(off Manor Gro.)
Bk. Manor St. *B'frd* —3F **58**
Bk. Market St. *B'frd* —4A **76**
Bk. Markham Av. Leeds —2H **63**
(off Markham Av.)
Bk. Marriot St. *Dew* —2G **117**
Bk. Marshall Av. Leeds —4E **64**
(off Marshall Av.)
Bk. Marshall St. Leeds —4D **64**
(off Marshall St.)
Bk. Marshall Ter. Leeds —4D **64**
(off Marshall Ter.)
Bk. Mary St. *Wake* —4G **98**
Bk. Masham St. Leeds —7N **61**
(off Bk. Middle Cross St.)
Bk. Mayville Av. Leeds —3A **62**
(off Mayville Av.)
Bk. Mayville Pl. Leeds —3A **62**
(off Mayville Pl.)
Bk. Mayville St. Leeds —3A **62**
(off Mayville St.)
Bk. Mayville Ter. Leeds —3A **62**
(off Mayville Ter.)
Bk. Meadow Vw. Leeds —3A **62**
(off Meadow Vw.)
Bk. Methley Dri. Leeds —9F **44**
(off Methley Dri.)
Bk. Mexborough Av. Leeds —2F **62**
(off Mexborough Av.)
Bk. Mexborough Dri. Leeds —3F **62**
(off Mexborough Dri.)
Bk. Mexborough Gro. Leeds —2F **62**
(off Mexborough Gro.)
Bk. Mexborough St. Leeds —2F **62**
(off Mexborough St.)
Bk. Meynell Av. *Rothw* —8N **81**
Bk. Middle Cross St. *Leeds* —7N **61**
Bk. Middleton Rd. *I'ly* —5F **8**
Bk. Middleton Vw. *Leeds* —2C **80**
Bk. Midland Rd. Leeds —3B **62**
(off Midland Rd.)
Bk. Milan Av. Leeds —3H **63**
(off Karnac Rd.)
Bk. Milan Rd. Leeds —3H **63**
(off Milan Rd.)
Bk. Milan St. Leeds —3J **63**
(off Milan St.)
Bk. Milton Ter. *Hal* —5A **92**
Bk. Mitchell Ter. *Bgly* —5E **38**
Bk. Mitford Rd. *Leeds* —7N **61**
Bk. Model Rd. *Leeds* —7N **61**
Bk. Model Ter. *Leeds* —7N **61**
Bk. Model Vw. *Leeds* —7N **61**
Bk. Monk Bri. Dri. Leeds —9B **44**
(off Monk Bri. Dri.)
Bk. Monk Bri. St. Leeds —9B **44**
(off Monk Bri. St.)
Bk. Montague St. Wake —8A **120**
(off Montague St.)
Bk. Montpelier Ter. Leeds —2C **62**
(off Montpelier Ter.)
Bk. Moorfield St. *Hal* —7N **91**
Bk. Moorfield Ter. *Leeds* —6K **61**
Bk. Moor La. *Hud* —2J **147**
Bk. Morning St. Kei —3H **37**
(off Morning St.)
Bk. Morritt Dri. *Leeds* —6A **64**
Bk. Mount Av. *Bat* —9G **96**
Bk. Mt. Pleasant. *Leeds* —8E **80**
Bk. Mt. Pleasant. *Wake* —5M **119**
Bk. Mount Vw. Leeds —2B **62**
(off Grosvenor Rd.)
Bk. Muff St. *B'frd* —9F **58**
Bk. Myrtle Av. *Bgly* —5E **38**
Bk. Myrtle Ter. *Cro R* —6F **36**
Bk. Nansen St. *Leeds* —4D **60**
Bk. Nelson St. *Dew* —3F **116**
Bk. Newport Gdns. Leeds —3N **61**
(off Newport Rd.)
Bk. Newport Mt. Leeds —3N **61**
(off Newport Rd.)
Bk. Newport Pl. Leeds —3N **61**
(off Newport Rd.)
Bk. New St. Slnd —8M **111**
(off High St. Stainland.)
Bk. Newton Gro. *Leeds* —2G **62**
Bk. Newton La. *Leds* —5D **84**
Bk. New York St. *Leeds* —7E **62**
Bk. Nice Vw. Leeds —2H **63**
(off Nice Vw.)
Bk. Norman Pl. Leeds —5J **45**
(off Norman Pl.)
Bk. Norman Ter. Leeds —5J **45**
(off Norman Ter.)
Bk. Northbrook St. Leeds —8F **44**
(off Northbrook St.)
Bk. Northgate. *Pon* —2K **123**
Bk. North Pk. Av. *Leeds* —7H **45**
Bk. North St. *Oaken* —9E **76**
Bk. Norwood Gro. Leeds —3A **62**
(off Norwood Gro.)
Bk. Norwood Pl. Leeds —3A **62**
(off Norwood Pl.)
Bk. Norwood Rd. Leeds —3A **62**
(off Norwood Rd.)
Bk. Norwood Ter. *Leeds* —3A **62**
Bk. Nowell Cres. Leeds —5K **63**
(off Nowell Cres.)
Bk. Nowell Mt. Leeds —5K **63**
(off Nowell Mt.)
Bk. Nowell Pl. Leeds —5K **63**
(off Nowell Pl.)
Bk. Nowell Ter. Leeds —5K **63**
(off Nowell Ter.)
Bk. Nunington St. Leeds —6N **61**
(off Armley Pk. Rd.)
Bk. Nunington Vw. Leeds —5M **61**
(off Armley Pk. Rd.)
Bk. Nunroyd Rd. Leeds —6F **44**
(off Nunroyd Rd.)
Bk. Oakfield Ter. Leeds —9A **44**
(off Brookfield Rd.)
Bk. Oakley St. *Wake* —3G **98**
Bk. Oakley Ter. Leeds —3E **80**
(off Oakley Ter.)
Bk. Oak Rd. Leeds —1F **62**
(off Chapel Rd.)
Bk. Oakwood Av. Leeds —9K **45**
(off Oakwood Av.)
Bk. Oakwood Dri. Leeds —9K **45**
(off Oakwood Dri.)
Back O'dam. *Slai* —1N **145**
Bk. of the Mill. *H'den* —6N **37**
Bk. Osmondthorpe La. Leeds
(off Osmondthorpe La.) —6L **63**
Bk. o' th' Height. *Rish* —1L **127**
Bk. Otterburn St. Kei —8J **21**
(off Ashleigh St.)
Bk. Outwood La. *H'fth* —8F **42**
Bk. Overdale Ter. Leeds —6B **64**
(off Overdale Ter.)
Back O'wall. *Slai* —7H **129**
Bk. Oxford Pl. Leeds —6D **62**
(off Oxford Pl.)
Bk. Oxford St. *Wake* —4G **98**
Bk. Paget St. Kei —9G **21**
(off Devonshire St.)
Bk. Parish Ghyll Rd. *I'ly* —6G **8**
Bk. Park Cres. *Leeds* —5K **45**
Bk. Parkfield Pl. Leeds —2C **80**
(off Parkfield Pl.)
Bk. Parkfield Rd. Leeds —2C **80**
(off Parkfield Rd.)
Bk. Park Ter. *Hal* —6N **91**
Bk. Park Vw. Leeds —2C **80**
(off Park Vw.)
Bk. Park Vw. Av. *Leeds* —3N **61**
Bk. Parkville Rd. *Leeds* —3F **60**
Bk. Parnaby Av. Leeds —4H **81**
(off Parnaby Av.)
Bk. Parnaby St. *Leeds* —4H **81**
Bk. Parnaby Ter. Leeds —4H **81**
(off Parnaby Ter.)
Bk. Pasture Gro. Leeds —8F **44**
(off Pasture Gro.)
Bk. Pasture Rd. Leeds —2H **63**
(off Pasture Rd.)
Bk. Pawson St. *Wake* —4G **98**
Bk. Pelham Rd. *B'frd* —3F **58**
Bk. Pleasant St. *Sower B* —8J **91**
Bk. Pollard La. *Leeds* —1F **60**
Bk. Poplar Av. Leeds —4E **64**
(off Poplar Av.)
Bk. Poplar Ter. *Roys* —5F **154**
Bk. Potternewton La. *Leeds* —9E **44**
Bk. Potters St. Leeds —9F **44**
(off Potternewton La.)
Bk. Prospect Pl. *Kei* —1H **37**
Bk. Providence Av. Leeds —2C **62**
(off Delph La.)
Bk. Providence St. *Bat* —7F **96**
Bk. Purlwell Hall Rd. *Bat* —9F **96**
Bk. Purlwell La. *Bat* —8F **96**
Bk. Quarry Mt. Ter. Leeds —2C **62**
(off Quarry Mt. Ter.)
Bk. Queen St. *G'lnd* —5B **112**
Bk. Queen St. *Hud* —5N **131**
Bk. Ravenscar Av. Leeds —9J **45**
(off Ravenscar Av.)
Bk. Ravens St. *Dew* —5D **116**
Bk. Raynville Mt. Leeds —3H **61**
(off Raynville Rd.)
Bk. Regent Pk. Ter. Leeds —2B **62**
(off Regent Pk. Ter.)
Bk. Regent St. *Wake* —8N **119**
Bk. Regent Ter. *Leeds* —4B **62**
Bk. Reginald Mt. Leeds —2F **62**
(off Reginald Mt.)
Bk. Reginald Pl. Leeds —2F **62**
(off Reginald Pl.)
Bk. Reginald Ter. Leeds —2F **62**
(off Reginald St.)
Bk. Rhodes St. *Hal* —5A **92**
Bk. Ribble St. Kei —8M **21**
(off Ribble St.)
Bk. Richardson St. *Oaken* —9E **76**
Bk. Richmond Mt. Leeds —2A **62**
(off Manor Av.)
Bk. Ridge Mt. Ter. Leeds —2C **62**
(off Cliff Rd.)
Bk. Ridge St. *Todm* —7K **87**
Bk. Ridge Vw. *Leeds* —1C **62**
Bk. Rigging La. *Sower B* —9C **90**
Bk. Ripley St. Riddl —7M **21**
(off Ripley St.)
Bk. Ripon St. *Hal* —6L **91**
Bk. Ripon Ter. *Hal* —3A **92**
Bk. River St. *Haw* —8D **36**
Back Rd. *Wyke* —9A **76**
Bk. Roberts St. *Rothw* —7D **82**
Bk. Rochester Ter. Leeds —2N **61**
(off Broomfield Rd.)
Bk. Rokeby Gdns. Leeds —1M **61**
(off Ash Rd.)
Bk. Roman Gro. *Leeds* —5J **45**
Bk. Roman Pl. *Leeds* —5K **45**
Bk. Roman St. *Leeds* —5K **45**
Bk. Rose Av. H'fth —8E **42**
(off Rose St.)
Bk. Rosebank Cres. Leeds —4B **62**
(off Rosebank Cres.)
Bk. Rosemont Wlk. *Leeds* —4F **60**
Bk. Rossall Rd. Leeds —2J **63**
(off Rossall Rd.)
Bk. Rossington Rd. Leeds —2G **63**
(off Spencer Pl.)
Bk. Roundhay Cres. Leeds —1H **63**
(off Roundhay Cres.)
Bk. Roundhay Gro. Leeds —1H **63**
(off Roundhay Gro.)
Bk. Roundhay Pl. Leeds —1H **63**
(off Roundhay Pl.)
Bk. Roundhay Vw. Leeds —1H **63**
(off Roundhay Vw.)
Back Row. *Leeds* —8D **62**
Bk. Rowland Ter. Leeds —2E **80**
(off Rowland Ter.)
Bk. Rowsley St. Kei —9K **21**
(off Rowsley St.)
Bk. Roydwood Ter. *Cull* —9K **37**
Bk. Rupert St. Kei —8J **21**
(off Rupert St.)
Bk. Russell St. *B'frd* —9B **58**
Bk. Ruthven Vw. Leeds —3J **63**
(off Ruthven Vw.)
Bk. Rydal St. *Kei* —1G **37**
Bk. Rylstone St. *Kei* —8L **21**
Bk. St Alban Cres. Leeds —5L **63**
(off St Alban Cres.)
Bk. St Elmo Gro. Leeds —6J **63**
(off St Elmo Gro.)
Bk. St Ives Mt. *Leeds* —6K **61**
Bk. St Mary's Rd. *Leeds* —1F **62**
Bk. St Paul's Rd. *Shipl* —8M **39**
Bk. Salisbury Gro. *Leeds* —6M **61**
Bk. Salisbury Ter. *Hal* —3A **92**
Bk. Salisbury Ter. Leeds —6M **61**
(off Armley Lodge Rd.)
Bk. Saltaire Rd. N. *Shipl* —7M **39**
Bk. Sandhurst Gro. Leeds —3J **63**
(off Sandhurst Gro.)
Bk. Sandhurst Pl. Leeds —3J **63**
(off Sandhurst Pl.)
Bk. Sandhurst Rd. Leeds —3J **63**
(off Sandhurst Rd.)
Bk. Savile Pde. *Hal* —7A **92**
Bk. Savile Pl. Leeds —3F **62**
(off Savile Pl.)
Bk. Savile Rd. Leeds —3F **62**
(off Savile Rd.)
Bk. School St. Morl —9L **79**
(off School St.)
Bk. School Vw. Leeds —3A **62**
(off School Vw.)
Bk. Seaforth Av. Leeds —4K **63**
(off Seaforth Av.)
Bk. Seaforth Pl. Leeds —3J **63**
(off Seaforth Pl.)
Bk. Seaforth Ter. Leeds —3J **63**
(off Seaforth Ter.)
Bk. Sefton Av. Leeds —2C **80**
(off Sefton Av.)
Bk. Sefton Ter. Leeds —2C **80**
(off Sefton Ter.)
Bk. Shaftesbury Av. *Leeds* —6J **45**
Bk. Shaw La. *Kei* —3K **37**
Bk. Shepherds. Leeds —2G **63**
(off Shepherd's La.)
Bk. Shepherd's Pl. Leeds —2H **63**
(off Shepherd's Pl.)
Bk. Sholebroke Av. *Leeds* —1F **62**
Bk. Sholebroke Pl. Leeds —2F **62**
(off Sholebroke Pl.)
Bk. Sholebroke Vw. Leeds —2F **62**
(off Sholebroke Vw.)
Bk. Sidlaw Ter. Leeds —2H **63**
(off Markham Av.)
Bk. Simpson St. *Kei* —9G **21**
Bk. Sladen St. *Kei* —9G **21**
Bk. Slaithwaite Rd. *Dew* —7F **116**
Bk. Smith Row. *B'frd* —2A **76**
Bk. S. End Gro. *Leeds* —4H **61**
Bk. Southfield Sq. B'frd —5A **58**
(off Southfield Sq.)
Bk. South Pde. *Ell* —6D **112**
(in two parts)
Bk. South St. *Pad* —5J **131**
Bk. Spencer Mt. Leeds —2G **63**
(off Spencer Mt.)
Bk. Springfield Mt. *Leeds* —6K **61**
Bk. Springfield Pl. B'frd —5B **58**
(off Springfield Pl.)
Bk. Springfield Rd. *Ell* —4F **112**
Bk. Spring Gro. Wlk. Leeds —4A **62**
(off Spring Gro. Wlk.)
Bk. Spring St. *Hud* —4L **131**
Bk. Stanley St. *Hud* —7K **131**
Bk. Stanley St. Leeds —4H **63**
(off Stanley Av.)
Bk. Stanmore Pl. Leeds —3M **61**
(off St Michaels La.)
Bk. Stanmore St. Leeds —3M **61**
(off St Michaels La.)
Bk. Station Rd. *Bat* —8G **97**
Bk. Station Rd. *Mir* —7L **115**
Bk. Stonegate Rd. *Leeds* —8B **44**
Backstone Gill La. *Wike* —7M **29**
Bk. Stone Hall Rd. *B'frd* —2F **58**
Backstone La. *I'ly* —6H **9**
Backstone Way. *I'ly* —5J **9**
Bk. Storey Pl. *Leeds* —5N **63**
Bk. Stratford Av. Leeds —2C **80**
(off Stratford Av.)
Bk. Stratford St. Leeds —2D **80**
(off Stratford St.)
Bk. Stratford Ter. Leeds —2D **80**
(off Stratford Ter.)
Bk. Strathmore Dri. Leeds —3J **63**
(off Strathmore Dri.)
Back St. *B'ham* —6C **32**
Back St. *Pon* —3J **123**
Bk. Sunnydene. *Leeds* —5A **64**
Bk. Sutton App. *Leeds* —5N **63**
Bk. Sycamore Av. *Bgly* —5E **38**
Bk. Tamworth St. *B'frd* —8J **59**
Bk. Tempest Rd. Leeds —2C **80**
(off Tempest Rd.)
Bk. Temple Vw. *Leeds* —2C **80**
Bk. Thornhill Rd. *Hud* —4F **130**
Bk. Thornhill St. *C'ley* —9M **41**
Bk. Thornville Row. Leeds —3A **62**
(off Thornville Row)
Bk. Tower Gro. *Leeds* —6K **61**
Bk. Trafford Av. Leeds —4K **63**
(off Trafford Av.)
Bk. Trentham Pl. Leeds —3D **80**
(off Trentham Pl.)
Bk. Trinity Ter. *B'frd* —9B **58**
Bk. Union St. *Hud* —3N **131**
Bk. Unity St. N. *Bgly* —5E **38**
Bk. Unity St. S. *Bgly* —5E **38**
Bk. Vicars Rd. Leeds —2H **63**
(off Vicars Rd.)
Bk. Victoria Av. Leeds —6J **63**
(off Victoria Av.)
Bk. Victoria Gro. Leeds —6K **63**
(off Victoria Gro.)
Bk. Victoria St. *Hal* —5B **92**
Bk. Victor Ter. *Hal* —4M **91**
Bk. Violet Ter. Sower B —8J **91**
(off Violet Ter.)
Bk. Wakefield Rd. *Sower B* —8K **91**
Bk. Walmsley Rd. Leeds —3A **62**
(off Walmsley Rd.)
Bk. Walnut St. Kei —3H **37**
(off Walnut St.)
Bk. Warwick Ter. *Bat* —9G **96**
Bk. Waverley Rd. *Ell* —6E **112**
Bk. Webster St. *Dew* —3F **116**
Bk. Welburn Av. *Leeds* —8L **43**
Bk. Wellfield Ter. *Todm* —8K **87**
Bk. Welton Av. Leeds —3A **62**
(off Welton Rd.)
Bk. Welton Gro. Leeds —3A **62**
(off Welton Gro.)
Bk. Welton Mt. Leeds —3A **62**
(off Welton Mt.)
Bk. Welton Pl. Leeds —3A **62**
(off Welton Pl.)
Bk. Wentworth St. *Hud* —3L **131**
Bk. Wesley Rd. *Leeds* —7M **61**
Bk. Wesley St. *C'frd* —4D **102**
Bk. Westbourne Ter. Leeds —4C **62**
(off Cromer Ter.)
Bk. Westbury St. *Leeds* —4H **81**
Bk. Westfield Rd. Leeds —5B **62**
(off Westfield Rd.)

k. Westlock Av. Leeds —5J 63
(off Westlock Av.)
k. Westmorland Mt. Leeds —2G 61
k. Weston Rd. I'ly —5G 9
k. Westover Rd. Leeds —3F 60
k. West St. Sower B —9H 91
k. Wetherby Gro. Leeds —4M 61
(off Argie Av.)
k. Wetherby Rd. Leeds —9K 45
(off Wetherby Rd.)
k. Wharf St. Sower B —8J 91
k. Wheat St. Kei —3G 36
(off Bracken Rd.)
k. Wickham St. Leeds —2C 80
(off Wickham St.)
k. William Av. Leeds —6N 63
(off William Av.)
k. William St. Brigh —2M 113
(off William St.)
k. Wilton Gro. Leeds —9A 44
(off Wilton Gro.)
k. Winfield Gro. Leeds —4D 62
(off Winfield Pl.)
k. Winston Gdns. Leeds —1M 61
(off Ash Rd.)
k. Winterburn St. Kei —8J 21
(off Ashleigh St.)
k. Wolseley Ter. Hal —5M 91
k. Woodbine Ter. Leeds —9A 44
k. Woodland Pk. Rd. Leeds
(off Woodland Pk. Rd.) —1A 62
k. Woodstock St. Leeds —4D 62
(off Bk. Blenheim Ter.)
k. Wood St. Wake —4F 98
k. Wright Av. Oakw —4D 36
k. York Cres. Hal —7M 91
(off Up. Washer La.)
k. York Pl. Leeds —7C 62
(in two parts)
k. York St. Leeds —7F 62
acon Av. Nor —9K 101
acon St. Guis —8K 25
acup Rd. Todm —6A 86
addeley Gdns. B'frd —6E 40
aden Powell Cres. Pon —4K 123
aden St. Haw —7C 36
aden Ter. Cleck —5H 95
(off Tofts Rd.)
aden Ter. Leeds —6F 60
(off Pudsey Rd.)
adger Brow. Mel —7C 146
adger Clo. Dur —3H 137
adger Ga. Mel —7C 146
adgergate Av. Wilsd —2B 56
adger Hill. Brigh —5K 113
adger La. Blkhd —9A 70
adger La. Hal —5G 93
adgers Mt. Leeds —4G 65
adgers Way. B'frd —2C 58
adger Wood Glade. Weth —1M 17
adsworth. —8L 141
adsworth Ct. Bads —7L 141
adsworth Ct. Cytn —9J 57
adsworth M. Bads —8L 141
adsworth Vw. Upt —1N 157
agby Fields. —3D 62
agden La. Clay W —9G 150
(in two parts)
aghill. —6N 97
aghill Ct. Pon —3M 123
aghill Grn. Ting —6N 97
aghill La. Pon —2L 123
aghill Rd. Ting —6N 97
agley. —2B 60
agley La. Fars —2A 60
agley La. Rod —2B 60
agnall Ter. B'frd —4N 75
agshaw Museum &
Art Gallery. —4D 96
aildon. —4A 40
aildon Av. Kip —2B 84
aildon Chase. Leeds —8D 46
aildon Clo. Leeds —9D 46
aildon Dri. Leeds —9D 46
aildon Green. —5N 39
aildon Grn. Leeds —9D 46
aildon Holmes. —6A 40
aildon Holmes. Bail —6A 40
aildon Mills. Bail —3A 40
(off Northgate)
aildon Path. Leeds —9D 46
aildon Pl. Leeds —9D 46
aildon Rd. Bail —4A 40
aildon Rd. Leeds —8D 46
aildon Wlk. Leeds —8D 46
aildon Wood Bottom. —6N 39
aildon Wood Ct. Bail —6A 40
ailes Rd. Leeds —1C 62
ailey Cres. S Elm —4N 157
aileygate Ct. Pon —2K 123
(off Bk. Northgate)
ailey Hall Bank. Hal —5C 92
ailey Hall Rd. Hal —6C 92

Bailey Hills Rd. Bgly —3D 38
Bailey Pl. Leeds —9N 43
Bailey's Clo. Leeds —9B 46
Bailey's Ct. Leeds —1B 64
Bailey's Hill. Leeds —1B 64
Bailey's La. Leeds —1B 64
Bailey's Lawn. Leeds —1B 64
Bailey St. B'frd —9D 58
Bailey Towers. Leeds —1B 64
Bailey Wlk. C'thpe —7H 137
Bailey Wells Av. B'frd —2A 76
Bailiff Bridge. —5N 93
Bainbrigge Rd. Leeds —2N 61
Baines St. Bat —8E 96
Baines St. Hal —4N 91
Baines St. Rothw —9N 81
Baird St. B'frd —1C 76
Bairstow La. Sower B —6J 91
Bairstow Mt. Sower B —7K 91
Bairstow's Bldgs. Hal —1M 91
Bairstow St. All —3F 56
Baitings Ga. Rd. Ripp —9K 109
Baker Av. Leeds —3H 45
Baker Cres. Morl —8F 44
Baker Dri. Leeds —7N 61
Baker Fold. Hal —5N 91
(off Lister's Clo.)
Baker La. Stan —7M 99
Baker M. T'tn —8C 56
Baker Pl. Leeds —1N 61
Baker Rd. Morl —8F 44
Baker Sq. Leeds —4N 43
Baker's St. H Bri —9H 71
Baker St. B'frd —4F 58
Baker St. Hud —2G 131
Baker St. Morl —8F 44
Baker St. Shipl —7M 39
Baker St. N. Hal —8N 73
Baker Vs. All —6G 56
Baker Yd. W'ford —7D 82
Bakes St. B'frd —1M 75
Balbec Av. Leeds —1A 62
Balbec St. Leeds —1A 62
Balcony Cotts. Q'bry —5D 74
Balderstone Hall La. Mir —5N 115
Baldovan Mt. Leeds —2H 63
Baldovan Pl. Leeds —2H 63
Baldovan Ter. Leeds —2H 63
Baldwin La. Q'bry —3F 74
Balfour St. Bgly —5E 38
Balfour St. B'frd —1E 76
Balfour St. Kei —1H 37
Balk Av. Wake —1B 120
Balkcliffe La. Leeds —7C 80
Balk Cres. Stan —2A 120
Balk La. B'frd —1N 75
Balk La. Hud —3F 132
Balk La. Neth —3B 136
Balk La. S Elm —5C 158
Balk La. Up Cum —7N 149
Balk La. Wake —1B 120
Balkram Dri. Hal —8H 73
Balkram Edge. Hal —8F 72
Balkram Rd. Hal —8H 73
Balks. Liv —8K 95
Balk St. Bat —7E 96
Balk, The. Bat —5F 96
Balk, The. M'well —7L 153
Balk, The. W'ton —4B 138
Ballantyne Rd. B'frd —5E 40
Ballater Av. Hud —8H 131
Ballfield Av. Dart —9E 152
Ballfield La. Dart —9E 152
Ballroyd Clough. Hud —3F 130
(in two parts)
Ballroyd La. Hud —4F 130
Ball Royd Rd. Hud —9N 113
Ball St. T'tn —8D 56
Balme La. B'frd —1B 94
Balme Rd. Cleck —4H 95
Balme St. B'frd —7D 58
Balme St. Wyke —1A 94
Balmfield. Liv —1L 115
Balmfield Cres. Liv —1L 115
Balmoral Av. Hud —8H 131
Balmoral Chase. Leeds —2H 81
Balmoral Clo. Pon —6H 123
Balmoral Dri. Knot —8B 104
Balmoral Pl. Hal —6B 92
Balmoral Pl. Q'bry —6B 74
Balmoral St. H Bri —1H 89
(off Osborne St.)
Balmoral Ter. Leeds —9A 44
Balmoral Way. Yead —1A 42
Balm Pl. Leeds —9C 62
Balm Rd. Leeds —3G 80
Balm Rd. Ind. Est. Leeds —2F 80
Balm Wlk. Leeds —9B 62
Balne Av. Wake —4J 119
Balne La. Wake —4H 119
Bamborough St. Wake —8A 120
Bamburgh Clo. Leeds —3F 64
Bamburgh Rd. Leeds —3F 64

Bamford Ho. B'frd —4J 77
(off Tong St.)
Banbury Way. Pon —9L 103
Bance Rd. H'fth —7E 42
Bancroft Av. Hud —5C 132
Bangor Gro. Leeds —1K 79
Bangor Pl. Leeds —1K 79
Bangor St. Leeds —1K 79
Bangor Ter. Leeds —1K 79
Bangor Vw. Leeds —1K 79
Bank. —7G 62
Bank. B'frd —1G 59
Bank Av. H'fth —7E 42
Bank Av. Morl —8K 79
Bank Bottom. Hal —5C 92
Bank Bottom. H Bri —2A 90
Bank Bottom. Mars —3J 145
Bank Bottom. Sower B —2D 128
Bank Bottom La. Hal —3F 90
Bank Bldgs. H Bri —2K 89
Bank Bldgs. Mel —8D 146
Bank Clo. B'frd —1G 59
Bank Crest. Bail —4A 40
Bankcrest Ri. Shipl —8H 39
Bank Dri. B'frd —4B 76
Bank Edge Clo. Hal —8K 73
Bank Edge Gdns. Hal —1L 91
Bank Edge Rd. Hal —9L 73
Bank End. G'lnd —4K 111
Bank End La. H Hoy —8K 151
Bank End La. Hud —6C 132
Bank End Rd. Slai —7A 130
Banker St. Leeds —5N 61
Bankfield. Bard —4E 30
Bankfield. Mars —5G 145
(off Manchester Rd.)
Bankfield. Shel —7K 149
Bankfield Av. Hud —2F 132
Bankfield Av. Shipl —8J 39
Bankfield Clo. Oss —7B 118
Bankfield Ct. Hud —5B 132
Bankfield Ct. Mir —6K 115
Bankfield Ct. Wren —9H 99
Bankfield Dri. H'fth —6H 163
Bankfield Dri. Kei —9E 20
Bankfield Dri. Shipl —8J 39
Bankfield Dri. Wren —9H 99
Bankfield Gdns. Hal —6E 92
Bankfield Gdns. Leeds —4M 61
Bankfield Grange. G'lnd —4B 112
Bankfield Gro. Leeds —3M 61
Bankfield Gro. Shipl —9J 39
Bankfield La. Hud —2F 132
Bankfield Mt. Kei —8E 20
Bankfield Museum & Duke of
Wellington's Regiment
Museum. —3B 92
Bankfield Pk. Av. Hud —9K 131
Bank Fld. Rd. Bat —7F 96
Bankfield Rd. Hud —5L 131
Bankfield Rd. Kei —8E 20
Bankfield Rd. Leeds —4M 61
Bankfield Rd. Shipl —8J 39
Bankfields Av. H Bri —3M 89
Bankfields Cres. H Bri —3M 89
Bankfield St. Kei —8E 20
Bankfield Ter. Arm B —1K 147
Bankfield Ter. Bail —5B 40
Bankfield Ter. Leeds —4M 61
Bankfield Vw. Hal —3A 92
Bankfield Wlk. Kei —8E 20
Bank Foot. —7F 96
(nr. Batley)
Bank Foot. —4A 76
(nr. Truncliffe)
Bankfoot. H Bri —1G 88
Bank Foot La. Hud —2K 147
Bank Foot Pl. Bat —7F 96
Bank Foot Rd. Hud —1D 148
Bank Foot St. Bat —7F 96
Bank Gdns. H'fth —7E 42
Bank Ga. Slai —9M 129
Bank Gro. Dew —4K 117
Bank Hall Gro. Shepl —9K 149
Bank Hey Bottom La. Ripp —8E 110
Bank Holme Ct. B'frd —3K 77
Bank Ho. B'frd —6E 58
(off Barkerend Rd.)
Bankhouse. Pud —9A 60
Bankhouse. —9A 60
Bank Ho. Slnd —7K 111
Bankhouse Bottom. —1A 78
Bank Ho. Clo. Morl —8K 79
Bankhouse La. Hal —1C 112
Bankhouse La. Hud —5H 131
Bank Ho. La. Mt Tab —9D 72
Bankhouse La. Pud —9A 60
Bankhouse Rd. Milns —5G 130
Bank Ho. Ter. Hal —1C 112
Banklands. Sils —7E 6
Banklands Av. Sils —7F 6
Banklands La. Sils —7F 6
Bank La. Den D —3C 166

Bank La. Holmb —6H 163
Bank La. H'frth —1N 163
(nr. New Mill Rd.)
Bank La. H'frth —4J 163
(nr. Shaw La.)
Bank La. Kei —9D 20
Bank La. Oakw —5B 36
Bank La. Oxe —4M 53
Bank La. Sils —9E 4
Bank La. Up Den —4C 166
Bank Pde. Otley —1K 25
Bank Rd. Sower B —9H 91
(in two parts)
Bank Royd La. Bklnd —1H 129
Banks App. Gol —5C 130
Banks Av. Ackw —5E 140
Banks Av. Gol —5B 130
Banks Av. Pon —3J 123
Banks Cres. Gol —5C 130
Banks Dri. Gol —5C 130
Banks End. Ell —5H 113
Banks End Rd. Ell —5H 113
Banksfield Av. Yead —8M 25
Banksfield Clo. Yead —8M 25
Banksfield Cres. Yead —8M 25
Banksfield Gro. Yead —8M 25
Banksfield Mt. Yead —8M 25
Banksfield Ri. Yead —8M 25
Banksfield Rd. H Bri —3M 89
Banksfield Ter. H Bri —3M 89
Banksfield Ter. Yead —9M 25
Banks Garth. Knot —8E 104
Banks Gro. Gol —5C 130
Bank Side. Bail —4A 40
Bankside. Shel —7K 149
Bankside. Todm —8K 87
Bank Side St. Leeds —3H 63
Bankside Ter. Bail —5N 39
Banks La. Knot —8E 104
Banks La. Riddl —5L 21
Banks Mt. Pon —3J 123
Bank Sq. Morl —8K 79
Banks Rd. Gol —5C 130
Banks Rd. Hon —6M 147
Banks Rd. Slai —1A 146
Banks Side. Gol —5C 130
Banks St. Bat —8F 96
Bank St. B'frd —7C 58
(in two parts)
Bank St. Brigh —1M 113
Bank St. C'frd —4D 102
Bank St. Cleck —5G 94
Bank St. Dew —3G 117
Bank St. Hems —2D 156
Bank St. Horb —1C 136
Bank St. Kei —9J 21
(off Airedale Shop. Cen.)
Bank St. Leeds —6E 62
(off Commercial St.)
Bank St. Liv —8M 95
Bank St. Mir —6J 115
Bank St. Morl —8K 79
Bank St. N Mill —4C 164
Bank St. Oss —6N 117
Bank St. Shipl —8N 39
Bank St. Slai —9M 129
Bank St. Todm —8K 87
Bank St. Wake —5L 119
Bank St. Weth —4M 17
Bank St. Wibs —4A 76
Banksville. H'frth —1N 163
Bank Ter. H Bri —1F 88
Bank Ter. Morl —8L 79
Bank Top. —1G 59
(nr. Eccleshill)
Bank Top. —7E 92
(nr. Halifax)
Bank Top. S'wram —6D 92
Bank Top Dri. Riddl —6M 21
Bank Top La. Arth —4N 27
Bank Top La. Cra V —7G 88
Bank Top La. H'frth —5F 162
Bank Top Way. Kei —1M 37
Bank Vw. Bail —5N 39
Bank Vw. Broc —7A 148
Bank Vw. Dew —4K 117
Bank Vw. L'ft —6D 90
Bank Vw. Mill B —4D 110
(off Lumb La.)
Bank Vw. Ho. Bail —5A 40
(off Bank Vw.)
Bank Vw. Ter. Leeds —9D 44
Bank Wlk. Bail —4A 40
Bankwell Fold. B'frd —4B 76
Bankwell Rd. Hud —6G 131
Bank Wood Way. Stap —7E 124
Bankwood Way. Birs —9E 78
Bank Yd. Oss —6N 117
Bannerman St. B'frd —8E 76
Banner St. B'frd —8E 58
Bannister La. Skelb —5G 159
Bannockburn Ct. B'frd —4F 76
Bannockburn Way. Nor —8F 100

Banstead St. E. Leeds —3H 63
Banstead St. W. Leeds —3H 63
Banstead Ter. E. Leeds —3H 63
Banstead Ter. W. Leeds —3H 63
Bantam Clo. Morl —9N 79
Bantam Grove. —9N 79
Bantam Gro. La. Morl —9N 79
Bantree Ct. B'frd —5E 40
Baptist Fold. Q'bry —5C 74
(off Russell Rd.)
Baptist La. Oss —7D 118
Baptist Pl. B'frd —7B 58
Baptist St. Bat —9D 96
Bar Av. M'well —9M 153
Barber Row. Lint —9C 130
Barberry Av. B'frd —6J 59
Barber Sq. Heck —8N 95
Barber St. Brigh —9N 93
Barber Wlk. Dew —3F 116
(off Wellington Wlk.)
Barbor Pk. Leeds —5K 45
Barclay Clo. Cull —9L 37
Barclay St. Leeds —4E 62
(off Meanwood St.)
Barclay St. Leeds —5F 62
(off Sheepscar Gro.)
Barcroft. —7F 36
Barcroft. Cro R —7F 36
Bar Cft. Khtn —1F 132
Barcroft Gro. Yead —1L 41
Barcroft Rd. Hud —8L 131
Barden Av. B'frd —4J 75
Barden Clo. Bat —7E 96
Barden Clo. Leeds —7K 61
Barden Dri. Bgly —3H 39
Barden Grn. Leeds —7K 61
Barden Gro. Leeds —7K 61
Barden Mt. Leeds —7K 61
Barden Pl. Leeds —7K 61
Barden Rd. Eby —1A 4
Barden Rd. Wake —5A 120
Barden St. B'frd —5N 57
Barden Ter. Leeds —7K 61
Bardsey. —4E 30
Bardsey Cres. B'frd —7E 58
Bardsey Ho. B'frd —9H 59
(off Parsonage Rd.)
Bardwell Ct. Stanl —7N 99
Bare Bones Rd. H'frth —2M 169
Bare Head La. Hal —8C 74
Barewell Hill. Brier —5A 156
Barfield Av. Yead —1L 41
Barfield Cres. Leeds —2H 45
Barfield Dri. Yead —1L 41
Barfield Gro. Leeds —2J 45
Barfield Mt. Leeds —2J 45
Barfield Rd. Hal —5H 93
Bargate. Lint —8C 130
Bargess Ter. Kip —4B 84
Barge St. Hud —6L 131
Bargrange Av. Shipl —9N 39
Bargreen. Khtn —1F 132
Barham Gro. C'frd —4D 102
Barham Ter. B'frd —2H 59
Bar Ho. La. Kei —5F 20
Baring Av. B'frd —6H 59
Bark Clo. Shel —6L 149
Barker Clo. Hal —9D 92
Barker Ct. Bkby —1K 131
Barkerend. —7E 58
Barkerend Rd. B'frd —7D 58
Barker Hill. Leeds —4E 78
Barker Ho. Hal —9D 92
Barker Pl. Leeds —5G 60
Barker Rd. Horb —9B 118
Barker's Rd. Dur —4G 137
Barker St. Liv —8M 95
Barker St. Stan —6C 100
Barker St. Todm —6K 87
Barkers Well Fold. Leeds —2G 79
Barkers Well Gth. Leeds —2H 79
Barkers Well Ga. Leeds —2H 79
Barkers Well Lawn. Leeds —2H 79
Bark Ho. La. Caw —4M 167
Bark Ho. La. Shel —6M 149
Barkhouse Wood La. Birk —1N 105
Barkisland. —7H 111
Bark La. Add —9N 5
Bark La. Eby —1A 4
Barkly Av. Leeds —4C 80
Barkly Dri. Leeds —4C 80
Barkly Gro. Leeds —3C 80
Barkly Pde. Leeds —4C 80
Barkly Pl. Leeds —4C 80
Barkly Rd. Bees —3B 80
Barkly St. Leeds —4C 80
Barkly Ter. Leeds —4C 80
Barkston Wlk. All —7F 56
Bar La. B Spa —2F 32
Bar La. Gar —7A 66
Bar La. H'fth —7B 42
Bar La. M'well —9M 153
Bar La. Midg —8K 135

Bar La. Riddl —7M 21
Bar La. Sower B —9B 110
Bar La. Wake —2M 119
Barlbrough Pl. Hud —5F 130
Barlby Way. Leeds —9L 45
Barleycorn Clo. Wake —2N 119
Barleycorn Yd. Leeds —7L 61
Barley Cote Av. Riddl —6M 21
Barley Cote Gro. Riddl —6N 21
Barley Cote Rd. Riddl —6N 21
Barley Cft. Dew —3C 116
Barleyfield Clo. Wake —3N 119
Barley Fld. Ct. Halt —6B 64
Barleyfields Clo. Weth —2M 17
Barleyfields Ct. Weth —3M 17
Barleyfields La. Weth —3M 17
Barleyfields M. Weth —3M 17
Barleyfields Rd. Weth —3M 17
(in two parts)
Barleyfields Ter. Weth —3M 17
Barleyfields Wlk. Weth —4M 17
Barleyhill Cres. Gar —8M 65
Barleyhill La. Gar —7M 65
Barleyhill Rd. Gar —7L 65
Barley M. Rob H —1K 99
Barley St. Kei —3G 37
Barlow Rd. Kei —8H 21
Barlow St. B'frd —7F 58
Barmby Clo. Oss —7B 118
Barmby Cres. Oss —7C 118
Barmby Pl. B'frd —5F 58
Barmby Rd. B'frd —5F 58
Barmby St. Wyke —9B 76
Bar Mt. Gar —7A 66
Barmouth Ter. B'frd —5D 58
Barnaby Rd. Bgly —3H 39
Barnard Clo. Leeds —3F 64
Barnard Rd. B'frd —9E 58
Barnard Ter. B'frd —9E 58
Barnard Way. Leeds —3F 64
Barnbow Carr. —2J 65
Barnbow La. Leeds —2J 65
(in two parts)
Barnbrough St. Leeds —4M 61
Barnby Av. B'frd —7H 57
Barnby Royd. Hud —3C 132
Barncliffe Hill. Shel —8N 149
Barn Clo. Men —4D 24
Barncroft Clo. Leeds —8A 46
Barncroft Ct. Leeds —9N 45
Barncroft Dri. Leeds —9N 45
Barncroft Gdns. Leeds —9A 46
Barncroft Grange. Leeds —9N 45
Barncroft Heights. Leeds —8N 45
Barncroft Mt. Leeds —9N 45
Barncroft Ri. Leeds —9A 46
Barncroft Rd. Leeds —9A 46
Barncroft Towers. Leeds —9N 45
Barnes Av. Wake —9J 99
Barnes Rd. B'frd —6L 57
Barnes Rd. C'frd —6D 102
Barnes St. Todm —2J 107
(off Rochdale Rd.)
Barnet Gro. Morl —2K 97
Barnet Rd. Leeds —7N 61
Barnsdale Bar. —1G 159
Barnsdale Est. C'frd —6B 102
Barnsdale M. Cam —1N 159
Barnsdale Rd. All B —2D 102
Barnsdale Rd. Meth —5H 45
Barnsdale Vw. Nort —7N 143
Barnsdale Way. Upt —2D 158
Barnside. —8E 164
Barnside La. H'frth —7D 164
Barnsley Beck Gro. Bail —4B 40
Barnsley Rd. Ackw —6G 140
Barnsley Rd. Brier & Hems —7M 155
Barnsley Rd. Cud —9J 155
Barnsley Rd. Dart & B Grn —9G 152
Barnsley Rd. Grng M —7B 134
Barnsley Rd. N'dam —6K 137
Barnsley Rd. Scis —8H 151
Barnsley Rd. S Kirk —6K 157
Barnsley Rd. Up Cum —2K 165
Barnsley Rd. Wool —8L 137
Barnstaple Wlk. B'frd —3H 77
Barnstone Va. Wake —3N 119
Barn St. Oxe —4C 54
Barnswick Clo. Pon —5K 123
Barnswick Vw. Leeds —3H 43
Baron Clo. Leeds —1C 80
Baronscourt. Leeds —6E 64
Baronsmead. Leeds —6D 64
Baronsway. Leeds —6D 64
Barrack Rd. Leeds —3F 62
Barracks Fold. H'frth —6C 164
Barracks St. Heck —8N 95
Barrack St. Leeds —4F 62
Barraclough Bldgs. B'frd —8J 41
Barraclough Sq. B'frd —9A 76
Barraclough St. Low M —7N 75
Barran Ct. Leeds —3H 63
Barran St. Bgly —4F 38
Barras Gth. Pl. Leeds —8L 61
Barras Gth. Rd. Leeds —8L 61
Barras Pl. Leeds —8L 61
Barras St. Leeds —8L 61
Barras Ter. Leeds —8L 61
Barratt's Rd. Wake —3L 119
Barrett St. Sils —8D 6
Barrington Clo. Hal —8F 92
Barrington Pde. Gom —4L 95
Barrowby. —6J 65
(nr. Garforth)
Barrowby. —5M 15
(nr. Kirkby Overblow)
Barrowby Av. Leeds —7F 64
Barrowby Clo. Men —4F 24
Barrowby Cres. Leeds —6F 64
Barrowby Dri. Leeds —7G 64
Barrowby La. Gar —6L 65
Barrowby La. Kirk O —2K 15
Barrowby La. Leeds —6F 64
(in two parts)
Barrowby Rd. Leeds —7G 64
Barrowclough La. Hal —5E 92
Barrows La. Steet —4B 20
Barrowstead. Skelm —8E 150
Barr St. Hud —2A 132
Barry St. B'frd —7C 58
Barstow Fall. Pon —9L 103
Barstow Sq. Wake —5L 119
Bar St. Bat —8G 96
Bar St. Todm —8J 87
Barthorpe Av. Leeds —7D 44
Barthorpe Clo. B'frd —3K 77
Barthorpe Cres. Leeds —7E 44
Bartle Clo. B'frd —2L 75
Bartle Fold. B'frd —1M 75
Bartle Gill Dri. Bail —3C 40
Bartle Gill Ri. Bail —3C 40
Bartle Gill Vw. Bail —3C 40
Bartle Gro. B'frd —2L 75
Bartle La. B'frd —2L 75
Bartle Pl. B'frd —2L 75
Bartle Sq. B'frd —1M 75
Bartlett La. Morl —9L 79
Barton. —6H 131
Barton Av. Barn —8A 154
Barton Ct. Leeds —7D 64
Barton Dri. Leeds —3B 80
Barton Gro. Leeds —1C 80
Barton Hill. Leeds —1C 80
Barton Mnr. Clo. Hud —8G 131
Barton Mt. Leeds —1C 80
Barton Pl. Bat —8F 96
Barton Pl. Leeds —1C 80
Barton Rd. Leeds —1C 80
Barton St. B'frd —2N 75
Barton St. Brigh —9M 93
(off Manley St.)
Barton Ter. Leeds —1C 80
Barton Vw. Leeds —1C 80
Barton Way. S Elm —4N 157
Barum Top. Hal —5B 92
Barwick Grn. B'frd —4K 75
Barwick in Elmet. —8L 47
Barwick Rd. Gar —6M 65
Barwick Rd. Leeds —3C 64
Basford Ct. Wake —6J 119
Basford St. Wake —6J 119
Basil St. B'frd —2N 75
Basil St. Hud —6J 131
Baslow Gro. B'frd —4L 57
Bassenthwaite Wlk. Knot —1D 124
Batcliffe Dri. Leeds —9M 43
Batcliffe Mt. Leeds —1M 61
Bateman Clo. Cud —7H 155
Bateman St. B'frd —5B 58
Bates Av. Sower B —9F 90
Bates La. Pon —6M 123
Bateson St. B'frd —8J 41
Bath Clo. Leeds —4F 60
Bath Gro. Leeds —4F 60
Bath La. Leeds —5F 60
Bath Pl. Cleck —5H 95
Bath Pl. Hal —3A 92
Bath Rd. Bmly —5F 60
Bath Rd. Cleck —5H 95
Bath Rd. Hal —8B 92
Bath Rd. Heck —8A 96
Bath Rd. Leeds —8C 62
Bath St. Bat —7G 96
Bath St. B'frd —7E 58
Bath St. Dew —2F 116
Bath St. Ell —5E 112
Bath St. Hal —6C 92
Bath St. Hud —3M 131
Bath St. I'ly —4H 9
Bath St. Kei —9H 21
Bath St. Lock —7L 131
Bath St. Todm —7K 87
(off Dalton St.)
Batley. —8G 97
Batley Art Gallery. —7F 96
Batley Av. Hud —4J 131
Batley Bus. Cen. Bat —6E 96
Batley Carr. —9E 96
Batley Enterprise Cen. Bat —6E 96
Batley Fld. Hill. Bat —6F 96
Batley Rd. Heck —8B 96
Batley Rd. Ting & K'gte —7N 97
Batley Rd. Wren —2E 118
Batley St. Hal —3N 91
Batley St. Hud —4B 132
Batter La. Rawd —3N 41
Battinson Rd. Hal —4M 91
Battinson's St. Hal —7D 92
Battye Av. Hud —7G 131
Battyeford. —6H 115
Battye St. B'frd —8G 59
Battye St. Dew —2G 116
Baulk Head La. Todm —5A 88
Bavaria Pl. B'frd —5N 57
Bawn App. Leeds —9H 61
Bawn Av. Leeds —8H 61
Bawn Chase. Leeds —8H 61
Bawn Dri. Leeds —8H 61
Bawn Gdns. Leeds —8H 61
Bawn La. Leeds —8H 61
Bawn Path. Leeds —8J 61
(off Bawn Gdns.)
Bawn Va. Leeds —8H 61
(off Bawn Gdns.)
Bawn Wlk. Leeds —8J 61
(off Bawn Av.)
Bawson Ct. Gom —3L 95
Baxandall St. B'frd —2B 76
Baxtergate. Pon —3K 123
Baxter La. Hal —1F 92
Bay Clo. Hud —3H 131
Bayford Clo. H'frth —8N 163
Bay Hall Comn. Rd. Hud —2M 131
Bay Horse Ct. Otley —9L 11
(off Courthouse St.)
Bay Horse La. Leeds & S'cft —9B 30
Bay Horse Yd. Fars —3A 60
Bayldons Pl. Bat —7F 96
Baylee St. Hems —3E 156
Bayne Dri. B'frd —5F 76
Bay of Biscay. All —2F 56
Bayswater Cres. Leeds —3H 63
Bayswater Gro. B'frd —4H 59
Bayswater Gro. Leeds —3H 63
Bayswater Mt. Leeds —3H 63
Bayswater Pl. Leeds —3H 63
Bayswater Rd. Leeds —3G 63
Bayswater Row. Leeds —3H 63
Bayswater Ter. Hal —9B 92
Bayswater Ter. Leeds —3H 63
Bayswater Vw. Leeds —4H 63
Bayton La. Yead & H'fth —1A 42
Beacon Av. Morl —2L 97
Beacon Brow. B'frd —3J 75
Beacon Clo. Bgly —4G 39
Beacon Dri. Upt —1N 157
Beaconfield Rd. Pon —8M 141
Beacon Gro. B'frd —4L 75
Beacon Gro. Morl —2L 97
Beacon Hill. Upt —1N 157
Beacon Hill Rd. Hal —4C 92
(in two parts)
Beacon Ho. Upt —1N 157
Beacon Pl. B'frd —4K 75
Beacon Ri. I'ly —5D 8
Beacon Rd. B'frd —3J 75
Beaconsfield Ct. Gar —6N 65
Beaconsfield Rd. Cytn —1H 75
Beaconsfield St. Hal —6D 92
Beaconsfield St. Todm —7L 87
Beacon St. Add —1N 7
Beacon St. B Top —3K 75
Beacon St. Dew —5B 116
Beacon St. Hud —1M 131
Beacon St. Wibs —4M 75
Beacon Vw. S Kirk —6J 157
Beacon Vw. Upt —1N 157
Beaden Dri. Lep —8J 133
Beadon Av. Hud —5F 132
Beagle Av. Hud —9H 131
Beal. —5M 105
Beal La. Beal —5N 105
Beal La. Knot —1L 125
Beamshaw. S Kirk —8H 157
Beamsley. —5M 5
Beamsley Gro. Gil —4G 39
Beamsley Gro. Leeds —4A 62
Beamsley Ho. Shipl —1N 57
(off Bradford Rd.)
Beamsley La. Beam —4M 5
Beamsley Mt. Leeds —4A 62
Beamsley Pl. Leeds —4A 62
Beamsley Rd. B'frd —4N 57
Beamsley Rd. Shipl —1N 57
Beamsley Ter. Leeds —4A 62
Beamsley Vw. I'ly —5D 8
Beamsley Wlk. B'frd —4M 57
Beancroft Rd. C'frd —5D 102
Beancroft St. C'frd —6C 102
Beanlands Pde. I'ly —4H 9
Bean St. Ell —5H 113
Bearing Av. Leeds —3E 80
Bear Pit Gdns. Leeds —3N 61
(off Chapel La.)
Beast Fair. Pon —3J 123
Beast Mkt. Hud —4N 131
Beatrice St. Cleck —4H 95
Beatrice St. Kei —7H 21
Beatrice St. Oxe —4C 54
Beatrice Taylor Ho. Pon —2K 123
(off Horse Fair)
Beaufort Gro. B'frd —3E 58
Beaulah Ct. Knot —8F 104
Beaumont Av. Hud —5B 132
Beaumont Av. Leeds —5J 45
Beaumont Av. S Elm —6M 157
Beaumont Clo. Stan —7A 100
Beaumont Clough Rd. H Bri —3F 88
Beaumont Ct. Bat —8F 96
(off Bank St.)
Beaumont Dri. Bret —2A 152
(in two parts)
Beaumont Dri. Haig —2A 152
Beaumont Pk. Rd. Hud —1J 147
Beaumont Pl. Bat —8C 96
Beaumont Rd. B'frd —5N 57
Beaumont Rd. Dart —9E 152
Beaumont Sq. Pud —8A 60
Beaumont St. Bat —8F 96
Beaumont St. Eml —2F 150
Beaumont St. Hud —3N 131
Beaumont St. Lgwd —5E 130
Beaumont St. Mold —5B 132
Beaumont St. Neth —2H 147
Beaumont St. Stan —7A 100
Beaumont St. Todm —6J 87
Beauvais Dri. Riddl —8A 22
Beaver Dri. Dew —4C 116
Becca Hall. —5B 48
Becca La. Aber —8E 48
Beck Bottom. —9E 98
Beck Bottom. C'ley —3B 60
Beck Bottom. K'gte —9E 98
Beckbridge Ct. Nor —9K 101
Beckbridge Grn. Nor —9K 101
Beckbridge La. Nor —1K 121
(in four parts)
Beckbridge Rd. Nor I —9K 101
Beckbridge Way. Nor —1K 121
Beckbury Clo. Fars —4A 60
Beckbury St. Fars —4A 60
Beckenham Pl. Hal —4L 91
Becket La. Loft —2L 99
Beckett Clo. Horb —9E 118
Beckett Ct. Colt —8E 64
Beckett Cres. Dew —3C 116
Beckett Gro. Dew —4C 116
Beckett La. Dew —4C 116
Beckett Park. —1M 61
Beckett Rd. Dew —1E 116
(in two parts)
Becketts Clo. Hept —9G 70
Beckett's Pk. Cres. Leeds —1M 61
Beckett's Pk. Dri. Leeds —1M 61
Beckett's Pk. Rd. Leeds —1N 61
Beckett Sq. Kbtn —3K 149
Beckett St. Bat —9F 96
Beckett St. Leeds —5G 63
Beckett Wlk. Dew —4C 116
Beckfield La. Leeds —8L 85
Beckfield Rd. Bgly —8E 38
Beckfoot La. Bgly —5D 38
Beck Hill. —7K 75
Beck Hill. B'frd —6K 75
Beckhill App. Leeds —9C 44
Beckhill Av. Leeds —9C 44
Beckhill Chase. Leeds —9C 44
Beckhill Clo. Leeds —9C 44
Beckhill Dri. Leeds —8C 44
Beckhill Fold. Leeds —8C 44
Beckhill Gdns. Leeds —9C 44
Beckhill Gth. Leeds —9C 44
Beckhill Ga. Leeds —9C 44
Beckhill Grn. Leeds —9C 44
Beckhill Gro. Leeds —9C 44
Beckhill Lawn. Leeds —9C 44
Beckhill Pl. Leeds —8C 44
Beckhill Row. Leeds —8C 44
Beckhill Va. Leeds —8C 44
(in two parts)
Beckhill Vw. Leeds —9C 44
Beckhill Wlk. Leeds —8C 44
Beck La. Bgly —2E 38
Beck La. Coll —8J 17
Beck La. Heck —9N 95
Beckley Rd. Wake —5H 119
Beck Mdw. Bar E —9M 47
Beck Ri. Hems —2D 156
Beck Rd. Bgly —8D 22
Beck Rd. Hud —2M 131
Beck Rd. Leeds —2H 63
Becks Ct. Dew —5J 117
Beck Side. Kei —1J 37
Beckside Clo. Add —1M 7
Beckside Clo. Bur W —8C 10
Beckside Gdns. W'loo —6G 132
Beckside La. B'frd —1M 75
Beckside Rd. B'frd —9M 57
Beckside Vw. Morl —9M 79
Becks Rd. Kei —1G 36
Beck St. Kei —1H 37
Beck Vw. Not —3B 154
Beckwith Dri. B'frd —1H 59
Bedale. Ting —4N 97
Bedale Av. Brigh —3K 113
Bedale Av. Skelm —8C 150
Bedale Dri. B'frd —4K 75
Bedale Dri. Knot —1D 124
Bedale Dri. Skelm —8C 150
Bedale Wlk. Shaf —6K 155
Bedding Edge Rd. H'frth —9D 16
Bede Ct. Wake —3L 119
Bede's Clo. T'tn —8C 56
Bedford Av. Grng M —5B 134
Bedford Clo. F'stne —7D 122
Bedford Clo. Leeds —4H 43
Bedford Clo. Lep —7J 133
Bedford Clo. Wake —2H 139
Bedford Ct. F'stne —7D 122
Bedford Ct. Leeds —9L 45
Bedford Dri. Leeds —4H 43
Bedford Gdns. Leeds —4H 43
Bedford Gth. Leeds —4H 43
Bedford Grn. Leeds —4H 43
Bedford Gro. Leeds —5H 43
Bedford Mt. Leeds —5H 43
(in two parts)
Bedford Pl. Guis —8J 25
Bedford Row. Leeds —1F 80
Bedford St. B'frd —8D 58
Bedford St. Cleck —5G 94
(off Westgate)
Bedford St. Ell —5E 112
Bedford St. Hal —5A 92
Bedford St. Kei —9H 21
Bedford St. Leeds —6D 62
Bedford St. N. Hal —5A 92
Bedford Vw. Leeds —4H 43
Bedivere Rd. B'frd —7J 57
Bedlam La. Arth —3B 28
Bedlam Rd. Mel —8B 146
Beech Av. Cud —9J 155
Beech Av. Denh —3J 55
Beech Av. Gol —5D 130
Beech Av. H'frth —8A 148
Beech Av. H'fth —8F 42
Beech Av. Hud —5C 132
Beech Av. Leeds —6M 61
Beech Av. New C —3J 139
Beech Av. Sower B —7H 91
Beech Av. Stan —8A 100
Beech Av. Todm —6K 87
Beech Av. Wake —4H 119
Beechcliffe. —7J 21
Beech Clo. B'frd —5F 40
Beech Clo. Brier —6A 156
Beech Clo. Hal —7J 75
Beech Clo. Leeds —3M 63
Beech Clo. Men —2E 24
Beech Clo. S Kirk —7H 157
Beech Ct. C'frd —6E 102
Beech Ct. Oss —5M 117
Beech Cres. Bail —6L 39
Beech Cres. B'frd —5F 58
Beech Cres. C'frd —6K 103
Beech Cres. D'ton —6B 124
Beech Cres. Leeds —3M 63
Beech Cft. Bail —6N 39
(off Valley Vw.)
Beech Cft. Loft —3M 99
Beech Cft. Pon —9L 103
Beech Cft. W'ton —3B 138
Beechcroft Clo. Leeds —4N 79
Beechcroft Mead. Leeds —3J 45
Beechcroft Vw. Leeds —4N 79
Beechdale Av. Bat —5D 96
Beech Dri. Ackw —1G 141
Beech Dri. Denh —3J 55
Beech Dri. H'fth —8E 42
Beech Dri. Leeds —6M 61
Beecher St. Hal —2A 92
Beecher St. Kei —8L 21
Beeches End. B Spa —1E 32
Beeches Rd. Kei —8L 21
Beeches, The. Bail —3B 40
Beeches, The. Guis —6J 25
Beeches, The. Pud —6M 59
Beeches, The. Schol —4D 94
(off Field Hurst)
Beeches, The. Schol —5D 94
(off Scholes La.)
Beeches, The. Shar C —7J 121
Beeches, The. Weth —3N 17

eechfield. Leeds —2G 78
eechfield. Wake —1N 137
eechfield Av. Skelm —8D 150
eechfield Dri. Shar C —7J 121
eechfield Rd. Hud —1K 131
eechfield Ter. Cleck —5J 95
(off Mayfield Ter.)
eech Gdns. C'frd —6K 103
eech Gro. Bgly —2H 39
eech Gro. B'frd —5F 58
eech Gro. Cytn —1H 75
eech Gro. F'stne —7E 122
eech Gro. Gom —3L 95
eech Gro. Hal —5M 93
eech Gro. Heck —7N 95
eech Gro. Kin —8A 140
eech Gro. Knot —1D 104
eech Gro. Morl —1J 97
eech Gro. Nor —3H 121
eech Gro. Rothw —7A 82
eech Gro. Sils —8D 6
eech Gro. Av. Gar —8M 65
eech Gro. Ter. Gar —8M 65
eech Gro. Ter. Leeds —4D 62
eech Hill. Otley —9L 11
eech Hill. Pon —2L 123
eech La. Leeds —3L 63
eech Lees. Fars —2N 59
eech Mt. Leeds —3M 63
eechmount Clo. Bail —3B 40
eechnut La. Pon —2J 123
eech Rd. B Spa —9C 18
eech Rd. B'frd —6A 76
eech Rd. Shaf —7L 155
eech Rd. Skel —8M 159
eech Rd. Sower B —8J 91
eech Rd. Upt —2A 158
eechroyd. Pud —8B 60
eechroyd Ter. Bgly —5E 38
eech Spinney. Weth —1N 17
eech Sq. Cytn —1H 75
eech St. Bgly —5E 38
eech St. Ell —5E 112
eech St. Hal —5A 92
eech St. H'frth —3M 163
eech St. Holy G —7N 111
eech St. Hud —5H 131
eech St. Kei —8L 21
eech St. Mir —6L 115
eech St. Pon —4K 123
eech St. S Elm —8L 157
eech St. Steet —3C 20
eech St. Ting —3A 98
eech Ter. B'frd —6F 58
eechtree Ct. Bail —5M 39
eech Tree Rd. F'stne —7E 122
eech Vw. Aber —8D 48
eech Vw. Hall G —7H 137
eech Vw. Sower B —7H 91
eech Wlk. Adel —5N 43
eech Wlk. B'shaw —9M 77
eech Wlk. Dew —3F 116
(off Swindon Rd.)
eech Wlk. Leeds —3M 63
eech Way. Birs —2D 96
eechwood. —4E 42
(nr. Horsforth)
eechwood. —9A 46
(nr. Seacroft)
eechwood. —9F 90
(nr. Sowerby Bridge)
eechwood. Pon —4H 123
eechwood. W'ford —6D 82
eechwood Av. B'frd —3M 75
eechwood Av. Dlgtn —6A 78
eechwood Av. Hal —8N 73
eechwood Av. Leeds —3N 61
eechwood Av. Mir —6L 115
(in two parts)
eechwood Av. Pon —3H 123
eechwood Av. Riddl —7M 21
eechwood Av. She —8G 75
eechwood Av. Shipl —8K 39
eechwood Av. Sower B —9F 90
eechwood Av. Wake —5F 118
eechwood Cen. Rothw —6D 82
(off Church St.)
eechwood Clo. Hal —9M 73
eechwood Clo. H'fth —4D 42
eechwood Ct. Leeds —3N 61
(off Bk. Beechwood Gro., LS4)
eechwood Ct. Leeds —2L 43
(LS16)
eechwood Ct. Seac —9N 45
eechwood Cres. Hems —3C 156
eechwood Cres. Leeds —3N 61
eechwood Cres. Pon —4H 123
eechwood Cres. Sower B —9F 90
eechwood Dale. Ackw —3H 141
eechwood Dri. B'frd —3N 75
eechwood Dri. Hal —8M 73
eechwood Dri. Sower B —9F 90
eechwood Gro. B'frd —3N 75
Beechwood Gro. Dlgtn —6A 78
Beechwood Gro. Fix —7M 113
Beechwood Gro. Hal —9M 73
Beechwood Gro. Horb —1E 136
Beechwood Gro. I'ly —5E 8
Beechwood Gro. Leeds —3N 61
Beechwood Gro. Shipl —8K 39
Beechwood Mt. Hems —3D 156
Beechwood Mt. Leeds —3N 61
Beechwood Pl. Leeds —3N 61
Beechwood Ri. Weth —2M 17
Beechwood Rd. B'frd —3M 75
Beechwood Rd. Hal —9M 73
Beechwood Rd. Leeds —3N 61
Beechwood Rd. Mir —5L 115
Beechwood Row. Leeds —3N 61
Beechwood St. Leeds —3N 61
Beechwood St. S'ley —5N 59
Beechwood Ter. Leeds —3N 61
Beechwood Vw. Leeds —3N 61
Beechwood Vs. Hal —9M 73
Beechwood Wlk. Leeds —3N 61
Beecroft Clo. Leeds —3D 60
Beecroft Cres. Leeds —3E 60
Beecroft Gdns. Leeds —3D 60
Beecroft Mt. Leeds —3D 60
Beecroft St. Kei —9K 21
Beecroft St. Leeds —3K 61
Beecroft Wlk. All —7F 56
Beehive St. B'frd —6L 75
Beehive Yd. B'frd —6L 75
Beeston. —3A 80
Beeston Hill. —1C 80
Beestonley La. Slnd —7K 111
Beeston Pk. Cft. Leeds —3A 80
Beeston Pk. Gth. Leeds —3A 80
Beeston Pk. Gro. Leeds —3A 80
Beeston Pk. Pl. Leeds —3A 80
Beeston Park Side. —5D 80
Beeston Pk. Ter. Leeds —3A 80
Beeston Rd. Leeds —3B 80
Beeston Royds. —3L 79
Beeston's La. N Rig —2N 13
Beeston Sq. Barn —9A 154
Beevers Ct. Leeds —5K 43
Beggarington Hill. —6N 97
Bela Av. B'frd —3G 76
Beldon Hill. —3L 75
Beldon La. B'frd —4L 75
Beldon Pk. Av. B'frd —3L 75
Beldon Pk. Clo. B'frd —3L 75
Beldon Pl. B'frd —4F 58
Beldon Rd. B'frd —2M 75
Belfast St. Hal —6M 91
Belford Clo. B'frd —2H 77
Belfry Ct. Wake —7L 99
Belfry, The. Yead —1N 41
Belfry Way. Norm —2L 121
Belgrave Av. Hal —4C 92
Belgrave Av. Oss —7A 118
Belgrave Clo. Hal —4C 92
Belgrave Cres. Hal —4C 92
Belgrave Dri. Hal —3D 92
Belgrave Gro. Hal —3C 92
Belgrave M. Rawd —3L 41
Belgrave Mt. Hal —3C 92
Belgrave Mt. Wake —3M 119
Belgrave Pk. Hal —3C 92
Belgrave Rd. Bgly —3F 38
Belgrave Rd. Kei —8H 21
Belgrave St. Leeds —6E 62
Belgrave St. Oss —6A 118
Belgrave St. Sower B —8H 91
Belgrave Ter. Hud —3L 131
Belgrave Ter. Wake —3M 119
Belgravia Rd. Wake —3K 119
Belinda St. Leeds —1G 81
Belk's Ct. Pon —3J 123
(off Liquorice Way)
Bell Bank Vw. Bgly —3D 38
Bellbank Way. Barn —9A 154
Bellbrooke Av. Leeds —4K 63
Bellbrooke Gro. Leeds —4K 63
Bellbrooke Pl. Leeds —4K 63
Bellbrooke St. Leeds —4J 63
Bellcross Dri. Hal —3C 92
Bell Dean Rd. All & B'frd —6G 56
Belle Green. —9K 155
Belle Isle. —5G 80
Belle Isle Av. Wake —7M 119
Belle Isle Cir. Leeds —5G 80
Belle Isle Clo. Leeds —5G 80
Belle Isle Cres. Wake —7M 119
Belle Isle Dri. Wake —7M 119
Belle Isle Pde. Leeds —4G 80
Belle Isle Rd. Haw —8C 36
Belle Isle Rd. Leeds —3G 80
Bellerby Brow. B'frd —4J 75
Bellerby Pl. Skel —7L 159
Bellerby Rd. Skel —7L 159
Belle Vw. Q'bry —6D 74
Belle Vue. —7A 120
Belle Vue. Eccl —1G 59
Belle Vue. I'ly —6H 9
Belle Vue. Mann —5B 58
Belle Vue Av. B'frd —9M 45
Belle Vue Av. Leeds —9M 45
Belle Vue Av. Scholes —8G 47
Belle Vue Ct. Leeds —5B 62
(off Consort Ter.)
Belle Vue Cres. Hal —8G 75
Belle Vue Cres. Hud —8A 114
Belle Vue Dri. Fars —3N 59
Belle Vue Est. Scholes —9G 47
Bellevue Pl. Hal —5N 91
Belle Vue Ri. Hal —8G 75
Belle Vue Rd. Hal —8G 75
Belle Vue Rd. Leeds —5B 62
Belle Vue Rd. Scholes —9G 47
Belle Vue Rd. Wake —8N 119
Belle Vue Stadium. —8A 120
Belle Vue St. Bat —7C 96
Belle Vue Ter. Gild —7G 79
Belle Vue Ter. Guis —8J 25
Bellevue Ter. Hal —7D 92
Bellgrave Gdns. Hal —3C 92
Bellgreave Av. N Mill —2D 164
Bell Gro. Leeds —3F 60
Bell Hall Mt. Hal —7N 91
Bell Hall Ter. Hal —7N 91
Bell Hall Vw. Hal —7A 92
Bell Ho. Av. B'frd —4F 76
Bellhouse Cres. B'frd —5F 76
Bell La. Ackw —5E 140
Bell La. Leeds —3F 60
Bellmont Cres. Hems —3E 156
Bellmount Clo. Leeds —3G 60
Bellmount Gdns. Leeds —2F 60
Bellmount Grn. Leeds —3G 60
Bellmount Pl. Leeds —2F 60
Bellmount Vw. Leeds —3G 60
Belloe St. B'frd —1B 76
Bell Rd. Leeds —3F 60
Bellshaw St. B'frd —7K 57
Bellspring La. Mir —1J 133
Bell St. Dew —6B 116
Bell St. Hal —3C 92
Bell St. Hud —6N 131
Bell St. Leeds —6F 62
Bell St. Upt —1D 158
Bell St. Wake —4K 119
Bell St. Wyke —9A 76
Bellwood Av. Cliff —2D 32
Belmont. B'ton —3B 104
Belmont Av. Bail —4N 39
Belmont Av. Low M —6C 76
Belmont Av. Otley —8K 11
Belmont Clo. Bail —4N 39
Belmont Clo. Hud —3M 131
(off Belmont St.)
Belmont Ct. Hud —3M 131
(off Belmont St.)
Belmont Cres. Low M —6C 76
Belmont Cres. Shipl —7M 39
Belmont Gdns. Low M —6B 76
Belmont Grange. Liv —1L 115
(off Norristhorpe La.)
Belmont Gro. B'frd —6B 76
Belmont Gro. Leeds —5C 62
Belmont Gro. Rawd —2N 41
Belmont Pl. Hal —6N 91
Belmont Ri. Bail —4N 39
Belmont Ri. Low M —6C 76
Belmont Rd. I'ly —5K 9
Belmont St. B'frd —1G 58
Belmont St. Hal —4D 92
Belmont St. Hud —3M 131
Belmont St. Slai —1N 145
Belmont St. Sower B —8J 91
Belmont St. S'hse —6K 121
Belmont St. Wake —3K 119
Belmont Ter. L'ft —7E 90
Belmont Ter. Shipl —7M 39
Belmont Ter. Thpe —2H 99
Belmont Way. S Elm —6A 158
Belton Clo. B'frd —2M 75
Belton Gro. Hud —9G 112
Belton Rd. Sils —9E 6
Belton St. Hud —5C 132
Belvedere Av. Alw —3F 44
Belvedere Av. Bees —3D 80
Belvedere Clo. Shaf —7K 155
Belvedere Ct. Leeds —1G 62
(off Harehills La.)
Belvedere Gro. Leeds —3F 44
Belvedere Mt. Leeds —3D 80
Belvedere Rd. Bat —9E 96
Belvedere Rd. Leeds —3F 44
Belvedere St. B'frd —6N 57
Belvedere Ter. B'frd —6N 57
Belvedere Ter. Leeds —3D 80
Belvoir Dri. Knot —8D 104
Belvoir Gdns. Hal —9B 92
Bembridge Ct. Wake —6G 119
Bembridge Ho. Wake —6G 119
Bempton Ct. B'frd —1N 75
Bempton Gro. Birs —2C 96
Bempton Ho. B'frd —9G 41
(off Savile Av.)
Bempton Pl. B'frd —1N 75
Ben Booth La. Grng M —5B 134
Benbow Av. B'frd —1J 59
Bence La. Dart —9E 152
Bendigo Rd. Dew —2J 117
Benjamin St. Liv —9M 95
Benjamin St. Wake —4J 119
Benjamin Sykes Way. Wake —7E 118
Ben La. N Rig —2B 14
Benn Av. B'frd —1L 75
Benn Cres. B'frd —1L 75
Bennett Av. Horb —9E 118
Bennett Ct. Leeds —6E 64
Bennett Ct. Otley —8K 11
Bennett La. Dew & Bat —9H 97
Bennett Rd. Leeds —1N 61
Bennett St. Hal —6D 92
Bennett St. Liv —8M 95
Bennetts Yd. Rothw —9N 81
Benn La. Lgwd —4E 130
Benns La. Hal —2E 90
Benny La. Slai —7A 130
Benny Parr Clo. Bat —7H 97
Benomley. —7C 132
Benomley Cres. Hud —7C 132
Benomley Dri. Hud —7C 132
Benomley Rd. Hud —7C 132
Ben Rhydding. —6J 9
Ben Rhydding Dri. I'ly —5K 9
Ben Rhydding Rd. I'ly —6H 9
Benroyd Ter. Holy G —8B 112
(in two parts)
Benson Gdns. Leeds —8L 61
Benson Gdns. Nor —9K 101
Benson La. Nor —8K 101
Benson's Mobile Home Pk. Riddl —5A 22
Benson St. Leeds —4F 62
Bentcliffe Av. Leeds —5F 44
Bentcliffe La. Leeds —6F 44
Bentcliff Hill La. Silk —6N 167
Bentcliff Wlk. All —7G 56
Bent Clo. La. Cra V —9L 89
Bentfield Cotts. Cytn —9H 57
Bentham Way. M'well —7J 153
Bent Head. Pec W —5H 71
Bent Ho. Mel —8D 146
Bent La. H'frth —8N 163
Bent Lea. Hud —5D 114
Bentley Av. Hal —5M 93
Bentley Clo. Bail —3N 39
Bentley Ct. Leeds —9B 44
Bentley Gro. Leeds —9B 44
Bentley La. Leeds —9B 44
Bentley Mt. Leeds —9B 44
Bentley Mt. Sower B —7K 91
Bentley Pde. Leeds —9B 44
Bent Ley Rd. Mel —6F 146
Bentley Rd. Wake —7G 118
Bentley Royd Clo. Sower B —9G 91
Bentley Sq. W'ford —8D 82
Bentley St. Hud —7K 131
Bentley St. Wyke —1B 94
Benton Cres. Horb —9E 118
Benton Pk. Av. Rawd —2N 41
Benton Pk. Cres. Rawd —2N 41
Benton Pk. Dri. Rawd —2N 41
Benton Pk. Rd. Rawd —2N 41
Bent Rd. H'frth —9B 164
Bents La. H'frth —1G 145
(in two parts)
Bents La. Wilsd —2N 55
Bent St. Hud —6N 131
Benyon Pk. Way. Leeds —1N 79
Beresford Rd. B'frd —6N 75
Beresford St. Oaken —8E 76
Berger Bldgs. Ell —4F 112
Berger Ho. B'frd —5A 58
Berkeley Av. Leeds —3J 63
Berkeley Cres. Leeds —3J 63
Berkeley Cft. Roys —5C 154
Berkeley Gro. Leeds —3J 63
Berkeley Ho. B'frd —2J 77
(off Stirling Cres.)
Berkeley Mt. Leeds —3J 63
Berkeley Rd. Leeds —3J 63
Berkeley St. Leeds —3J 63
Berkeley Ter. Leeds —3J 63
Berkeley Vw. Leeds —3J 63
Berking Av. Leeds —6H 63
Berking Row. Leeds —6H 63
Berkley Ct. Leeds —5B 62
Bermondsey St. Otley —1M 25
Bernard St. Hud —8C 114
Bernard St. W'ford —7E 82
Berne Gro. Wake —4L 119
Berners St. Wake —5M 119
Berrington Way. Oakw —4B 36
Berry Bank La. Thon —9N 147
Berry Brow. —1L 147
Berry Cft. Hon —4L 147
Berryfield Gth. Oss —3N 117
Berry La. Hal —5C 92
Berry La. Horb —1D 136
Berry La. Kei —2H 37
Berry La. W'ford —5M 83
Berry Moor Rd. Norl —1K 111
Berry Rd. Mel —6C 146
Berry's Bldgs. Hal —9M 73
Berry St. Kei —9K 21
Berry's Yd. Horb —9D 118
Berry Vw. Hud —9L 131
Bertha St. Fars —4A 60
Bertie St. B'frd —2G 77
Bertram Dri. Bail —6N 39
Bertram Rd. B'frd —4A 58
Bertrand St. Leeds —9C 62
Berwick Av. Heck —6A 96
Berwick St. Hal —5C 92
Beryl Dri. Kei —8K 21
Beryl Mt. Wyke —9A 76
Bescaby Gro. Bail —4C 40
Besha Av. Low M —7B 76
Besha Gro. Low M —7B 76
Bessbrook St. Leeds —2F 80
Bessingham Gdns. B'frd —5L 75
Best La. Hud —3B 148
Best La. Oxe —4C 54
Beswick Clo. B'frd —7H 59
Beswick St. Todm —4J 107
Bethel Rd. Shipl —7B 40
Bethel St. Brigh —1N 113
Bethel St. E Mor —8C 22
Bethel St. Hal —2N 91
Bethel Ter. Ludd —3D 90
Bethesda Row. H'clgh —3L 89
Betula Way. Lep —8J 133
Beulah Gro. Leeds —3D 62
Beulah Mt. Leeds —3D 62
Beulah Pl. L'ft —7E 90
Beulah St. Leeds —3D 62
Beulah Ter. Leeds —4D 64
(off Austhorpe Rd.)
Beulah Ter. Leeds —3D 62
(off Beulah St.)
Beulah Vw. Leeds —3D 62
Bevan Av. Nor —3J 121
Bevan Ct. B'frd —2L 75
Bevan Pl. Wake —7E 118
Beverley Av. Leeds —2D 80
Beverley Av. Wyke —2B 94
Beverley Clo. Ell —4G 113
Beverley Ct. Hud —9N 113
Beverley Ct. Leeds —5F 44
Beverley Dri. Dew —3J 117
Beverley Dri. Wyke —2B 94
Beverley Gdns. Bat —2E 96
Beverley Garth. Ackw —5G 141
Beverley Ho. Far —4A 60
Beverley Mt. Leeds —2D 80
Beverley Pl. Hal —3A 92
Beverley Ri. I'ly —5D 8
Beverley St. B'frd —9H 59
Beverley Ter. Hal —3A 92
(in two parts)
Beverley Ter. Leeds —2D 80
Beverley Vw. Leeds —2D 80
Beverley Wlk. Gar —8N 65
Bevin Clo. Wake —7L 99
Bevin Cres. Wake —7L 99
Bevitt St. Wake —8N 119
Bevor Cres. Heck —6A 96
Bewdley Ct. Roys —5E 154
Bewerley Cres. B'frd —7M 75
Bewick Ct. Q'bry —3G 75
Bewick Gro. Leeds —6H 81
Bexhill Clo. Pon —1M 123
Bexley Av. Leeds —4H 63
Bexley Gro. Leeds —4H 63
Bexley Mt. Leeds —4H 63
Bexley Pl. Leeds —4H 63
Bexley Rd. Leeds —4H 63
Bexley Ter. Leeds —4H 63
Bexley Vw. Leeds —4H 63
Beza Rd. Leeds —2F 80
Beza St. Leeds —2F 80
Bich Ho. C'frd —5E 102
(off Parklands)
Bickerdike Pl. All B —9B 84
(off St Mary's Ct.)
Bickerdike Ter. Kip —4A 84
Bickerton Way. Otley —8J 11
Biddenden Rd. Leeds —4G 64
Bidder Dri. E Ard —3E 98
Bideford Av. Leeds —4H 45
Bideford Mt. B'frd —2J 77
Bierley. —4F 76
Bierley Hall Gro. B'frd —6F 76
Bierley Ho. Av. B'frd —4F 76
Bierley La. B'frd —6F 76
Bierley Vw. B'frd —4G 77
Big Mdw. Dri. Add —1K 7
Bilberry Clo. Cytn —2H 75

Bilberry Ri. Haw —9D 36
Bilham Rd. Clay W —7K 151
Billam's Hill. Otley —8K 11
Billey La. Leeds —9H 61
(in two parts)
Billingbauk Dri. Leeds —5G 60
Billing Ct. Rawd —4A 42
Billing Dri. Rawd —4B 42
Billingham Clo. Wake —3F 118
Billingsley Ter. B'frd —1F 76
Billing Vw. B'frd —8G 40
Billing Vw. Rawd —4A 42
Billingwood Dri. Rawd —4A 42
Bill La. H'frth —1A 164
Billsdale Ho. B'frd —7G 40
(off Thorp Gth.)
Billy La. Wadsw —8K 71
Bilsdale Grange. B'frd —5L 75
Bilsdale Way. Bail —5M 39
Bilton. —1N 19
Bilton Pl. B'frd —6A 58
Bingley. —5E 38
Bingley Bank. Bard —6D 30
Bingley Rd. Bail —1L 39
Bingley Rd. B'frd —1J 57
Bingley Rd. Cro R & Kei —7F 36
Bingley Rd. Cull —9K 37
Bingley Rd. Men —6M 23
(in two parts)
Bingley Rd. Shipl —7J 39
Bingley St. B'frd —7M 57
Bingley St. Leeds —6B 62
Binham Rd. Hud —2J 131
Binks Fold. Wyke —2B 94
Binks St. Wake —8L 99
Binnie St. B'frd —7F 58
Binn La. Mars —7G 144
Binn Rd. Mars —6F 144
Binns Hill La. Sower B —6H 91
Binns La. B'frd —9L 57
Binns La. H'frth —3L 163
Binns St. Bgly —4F 38
Binns Top La. Hal —9F 92
Binswell Fold. Bail —3A 40
Bircham Clo. Bgly —2H 39
Birch Av. B'frd —3D 76
Birch Av. Leeds —6B 64
Birch Av. Lep —8J 133
Birch Av. Skel —8M 159
Birch Av. Sower B —1C 128
Birch Av. Todm —5J 87
Birch Cliff. Bail —5N 39
Birchcliffe. H Bri —1H 89
Birch Clo. B'frd —3D 76
Birch Clo. Brigh —9A 94
Birch Clo. La. Bgly —8L 23
Birch Ct. Morl —2L 97
Birch Cres. Leeds —6B 64
Birchdale. Bgly —1E 38
Birch Dri. Kip —2A 84
Birchen Av. Oss —6M 117
Birchencliffe. —9G 112
Birchencliffe Hill Rd. Hud —9G 112
Birchen Hills. Oss —6M 117
Birchenlee Clo. Myth —3N 89
Birches, The. B'hpe —6J 27
Birches, The. Guis —6J 25
Birchfield Av. Gild —7F 78
Birchfield Gro. Skelm —8D 150
Birchfields Av. Leeds —7D 46
Birchfields Clo. Leeds —8D 46
Birchfields Ct. Leeds —7D 46
Birchfields Cres. Leeds —7D 46
Birchfields Gth. Leeds —7D 46
Birchfields Ri. Leeds —8D 46
Birch Grn. Pon —2M 123
Birch Gro. Bat —4D 96
Birch Gro. B'frd —4C 76
Birch Gro. C'frd —6J 103
Birch Gro. Gol —5D 130
Birch Gro. Kei —3H 37
Birch Gro. Kip —3A 84
Birch Hill Ri. H'fth —7H 43
Birchington Av. Hud —9F 112
Birchington Clo. Hud —9G 112
Birchington Dri. Hud —9F 112
Birchlands Av. Wilsd —9A 38
Birchlands Gro. Wilsd —9A 38
Birch La. B'frd —2C 76
(in five parts)
Birch La. Hal —4E 90
Birch M. Adel —5N 43
Birch Pk. Broc —7B 148
Birch Rd. Hud —9K 131
Birch Rd. Kip —2A 84
Birch Rd. Nor —4J 121
Birchroyd. Rothw —9A 82
Birch St. B'frd —6L 57
Birch St. Morl —2L 97
Birch St. Wake —7N 119
Birchtree Clo. Wake —3A 120
Birch Tree Gdns. Kei —1L 37
Birchtree Wlk. Knot —9C 104
Birchtree Way. Leeds —5H 43
Birch Way. B'frd —3D 76
Birchwood Av. Birs —2C 96
Birchwood Av. Kei —6H 21
Birchwood Av. Leeds —4J 45
Birchwood Clo. Hud —9J 113
Birchwood Ct. I'ly —5F 8
Birchwood Ct. Liv —9M 95
Birchwood Dri. Kei —6G 21
Birchwood Hill. Leeds —3J 45
Birchwood Mt. Leeds —3J 45
Birchwood Rd. Kei —6G 21
Birdacre. —3M 95
Birdale Fld. La. Coll —9L 17
Birdcage. Hal —4C 92
Birdcage Hill. Hal —9N 91
Birdcage La. Hal —9N 91
Birdcage Wlk. Otley —2K 25
Bird Holme La. Hal —3G 93
Bird La. Clay —9H 157
Bird La. Ripp —8C 110
Birds Edge. —4L 165
Birds Edge La. Birds —5K 165
Birds Nest La. Cumb —5J 165
Birds Royd. —2N 113
Birds Royd La. Brigh —2N 113
Birdswell Av. Brigh —9B 94
Birdwalk, The. Q'bry —3H 75
Birdwell Hill. —2J 15
Birfed Cres. Leeds —3L 61
Birkby. —1K 131
Birkby Brow Cres. Bat —2E 96
Birkby Cft. Hud —1L 131
(off Crescent Rd.)
Birkby Fold. Hud —2K 131
Birkby Hall Rd. Hud —1K 131
Birkby Haven. B'frd —5K 75
Birkby La. Bail B —5N 93
Birkby Lodge Rd. Hud —1K 131
Birkby Rd. Hud —9H 113
Birkby St. Wyke —9B 76
Birkdale Av. Hud —2F 130
Birkdale Clo. Cud —9K 155
Birkdale Clo. Cull —9L 37
Birkdale Clo. Leeds —3D 44
Birkdale Ct. Low U —5G 21
Birkdale Dri. Leeds —3C 44
Birkdale Grn. Leeds —3D 44
Birkdale Gro. Dew —1D 116
Birkdale Gro. Hal —6M 73
Birkdale Gro. Leeds —3C 44
Birkdale Mt. Leeds —3D 44
Birkdale Pl. Leeds —3C 44
Birkdale Ri. Leeds —3C 44
Birkdale Rd. Dew —2E 116
Birkdale Rd. Roys —4C 154
Birkdale Wlk. Leeds —3C 44
Birkdale Way. Leeds —3D 44
Birkenshaw. —7L 77
Birkenshaw Bottoms. —9N 77
Birkenshaw La. B'shaw —8M 77
Birkett St. Cleck —4H 95
Birkhead St. Heck —9B 96
Birkhill. C'frd —4J 103
Birkhill Cres. B'shaw —8M 77
Birkhouse La. Brigh —6A 94
Birkhouse La. Mold —5B 132
Birkhouse La. Pad & Hud —5K 131
Birk Ho. La. Up Cum —1L 165
Birkhouse Rd. Brigh —5A 94
Birkin. —2M 105
Birkin La. Birk —5H 105
Birklands Rd. Hud —9L 113
Birklands Rd. Shipl —8N 39
Birklands Ter. Shipl —8N 39
Birk La. Morl —9H 79
Birk Lea St. B'frd —1D 76
Birks. —8L 57
(nr. Bradford)
Birks. —2K 97
(nr. Morley)
Birks Av. B'frd —9L 57
Birks Fold. B'frd —8L 57
Birkshall La. B'frd —8F 58
Birks Hall La. Hal —4N 91
Birks Hall St. Hal —4N 91
Birks Hall Ter. Hal —4N 91
Birkshead. —2C 56
Birksland Ind. Est. B'frd —9F 58
Birksland Moor. B'shaw —1M 95
Birksland St. B'frd —9F 58
Birks La. Fen B —7E 132
Birks La. Hud —6H 149
Birks La. Sower B —4D 110
(nr. Mill Bank Rd.)
Birks La. Sower B —6D 110
(nr. Stony La.)
Birks La. Todm —3K 107
Birks Rd. Lgwd —5F 130
Birkwith Clo. Leeds —7C 46
Birkwood Av. Shar C —9J 121
Birkwood Rd. Nor —9C 100
Birmingham La. Mel —6B 146
Birnam Gro. B'frd —1E 76
Birr Rd. B'frd —3N 57
Birstall. —3B 96
Birstall La. Dlgtn —8B 78
Birstall Smithies. —4C 96
Birthwaite Rd. Dart —8D 152
Bishopdale Dri. Coll —9H 17
Bishopdale Holme. B'frd —5K 75
Bishopgate St. Leeds —7D 62
Bishops Ct. Ber B —2L 147
Bishop St. B'frd —3N 57
Bishops Way. Mel —7D 146
Bishops Way. Mir —4H 115
Bishop Way. Ting —4B 98
Bisley Clo. Roys —6F 154
Bismarck Ct. Leeds —1D 80
(off Bismarck St.)
Bismarck Dri. Leeds —1D 80
Bismarck St. Leeds —1D 80
Bittern Ri. Morl —1M 97
Blackberry Way. Cytn —2G 75
Blackbird Gdns. B'frd —7G 57
Black Brook Way. G'lnd —5B 112
Black Bull St. Leeds —8F 62
Black Bull Yd. Rothw —8A 82
(off Commercial St.)
Blackburn Clo. B'frd —7J 57
Blackburn Clo. Oven —1M 91
Blackburn Ct. Pon —3J 123
Blackburn Ct. Rothw —8A 82
Blackburn Ho. Hal —1N 91
Blackburn La. Knot —9H 105
Blackburn Pl. Bat —7G 96
Blackburn Rd. Birs —3B 96
Blackburn Rd. Brigh —8L 93
Blackburn's Yd. C'frd —4D 102
Black Dyke La. T'tn —4A 56
Blackedge. Hal —5C 92
Black Edge La. Denh —8K 55
Blacker Cres. Neth —4A 136
Blacker La. Horb —4A 136
Blacker La. Shaf —6K 155
Blacker Rd. Hud —3L 131
Blacker Rd. M'well —8L 153
Blacker Rd. N. Hud —2L 131
Blackers Ct. Dew —7E 116
Blackett St. C'ley —8M 41
Black Ga. H Bri —3L 71
Black Gates. —3B 98
Blackgates Ct. Ting —4B 98
Blackgates Cres. Ting —4B 98
Blackgates Dri. Ting —4B 98
Blackgates Fold. Ting —4B 98
Blackgates Ri. Ting —4B 98
Blackgates Rd. Wake —4B 98
Blackheath Rd. Barn —9C 154
Blackheath Wlk. Barn —9C 154
Black Hill. —8F 20
Black Hill La. Kei —7D 20
Black Hill La. Leeds —7M 27
Black Hill Rd. Arth —4L 27
Blackhouse Rd. Hud —9N 113
Black La. Lint —2D 146
Blackley. —7D 112
Blackley Rd. Ell —6C 112
Blackman La. Leeds —4D 62
Blackmires. Hal —8N 73
Black Moor. —3C 44
(nr. Alwoodley)
Blackmoor. —9A 30
(nr. Shadwell)
Blackmoor Ct. Leeds —2B 44
Blackmoorfoot. —2C 146
Blackmoorfoot Rd. Cros H —7H 131
Blackmoorfoot Rd. Mel —5A 146
Blackmoor La. Bard —8B 30
Black Moor Rd. Leeds —4B 44
Black Moor Rd. Oxe —4E 54
Black Moor Top. Haw —9D 36
Blackpool Gro. Leeds —1K 79
Blackpool Pl. Leeds —1K 79
Blackpool St. Leeds —1K 79
Blackpool Ter. Leeds —1K 79
Blackpool Vw. Leeds —1K 79
Black Rd. Wake & Heath —8B 120
Blackshaw Beck La. Q'bry —6F 74
Blackshaw Clough Rd. Sower B —5A 110
Blackshaw Dri. B'frd —5J 75
Blackshaw Head. —9A 70
Blackshaw St. Todm —7M 87
Black Sike La. H'frth —3H 163
Blacksmith Fold. Alm —7D 132
Blacksmith Fold. B'frd —1M 75
Blacksmith La. Leeds —7B 28
Blacksmiths Fold. Alm —8D 132
Blackstone Av. Wyke —2A 94
Blackstone Edge Old Rd. L'boro —5A 126
(in two parts)
Blackstone Edge Rd. Ripp & Cra V —7F 108
Black Swan Ginnell. Hal —5B 92
(off Silver St.)
Black Swan Pas. Hal —5B 92
Blackthorn Ct. Leeds —5F 80
Blackthorn Way. Wake —3J 119
Black Wlk. Pon —1K 123
Blackwall. Hal —6B 92
Blackwall La. Sower B —7G 91
Blackwall Ri. Sower B —7G 91
Blackwood Av. Leeds —4G 42
(in two parts)
Blackwood Edge Rd. Rish —4K 127
Blackwood Gdns. Leeds —4G 42
Blackwood Gro. Hal —4M 91
Blackwood Gro. Leeds —4G 43
Blackwood Mt. Leeds —4G 43
Blackwood Ri. Leeds —4G 43
Blacup Moor Vw. Cleck —5H 95
Blagden La. Hud —9L 131
Blairsville Gdns. Leeds —2E 60
Blairsville Gro. Leeds —2F 60
Blaith Royd La. Cra V —8G 89
Blaithroyd La. Hal —6D 92
Blake Cres. Guis —8K 25
Blake Gro. Leeds —9F 44
Blake Hall Dri. Mir —7M 115
Blake Hall Rd. Mir —7N 115
Blake Hill. Hal —1D 92
Blakehill Av. B'frd —4G 58
Blake Hill End. Hal —8E 74
Blakehill Ter. B'frd —4G 58
Blakeholme Clo. Slai —1L 145
Blakelaw Dri. Clif —9B 94
Blake Law La. Brigh —1D 114
Blake Lee La. Mars —4B 144
Blakeley Clo. Barn —9C 154
Blakeley Gro. Wake —5H 119
Blakeney Gro. Leeds —4F 80
Blakeney Rd. Leeds —4F 80
Blakeridge La. Bat —7E 96
Blake Stones. —1L 145
Blakestones Rd. Slai —1L 145
Blakey Rd. Wake —3H 119
Blamires Pl. B'frd —2L 75
Blamires St. B'frd —2L 75
Blanche St. B'frd —8H 59
Blandford Gdns. Leeds —4D 62
Blandford Gro. Leeds —4D 62
(off Bk. Blenheim Ter.)
Blands Av. All B —8A 84
Bland's Clo. C'frd —5D 102
Blands Cres. All B —8A 84
Blands Gro. All B —8A 84
Blands Ter. All B —8A 84
Bland St. Hal —5A 92
Bland St. Hud —6L 131
Blanket Hall St. Heck —9A 96
Blayds Gth. W'ford —6B 82
Blayd's M. Leeds —7E 62
Blayds St. Leeds —7H 63
Blayd's Yd. Leeds —7E 62
Bleach Mill La. Men —3B 24
Bleak Av. Shaf —7K 155
Bleakley Av. Not —3C 154
Bleakley Clo. Shaf —7K 155
Bleakley La. Not —4C 154
Bleakley Ter. Not —3C 154
Bleak St. Gom —4N 95
Bleak St. Lwr. Gom —4N 95
Bleasdale Av. Hud —1L 131
Bleasdale Av. Knot —7E 104
Blencarn Clo. Leeds —2A 64
Blencarn Gth. Leeds —2A 64
Blencarn Lawn. Leeds —2A 64
Blencarn Path. Leeds —2A 64
Blencarn Rd. Leeds —2A 64
Blencarn Vw. Leeds —2A 64
Blencarn Wlk. Leeds —2A 64
Blenheim Av. Leeds —4D 62
Blenheim Clo. Knot —8B 104
Blenheim Ct. Hal —4A 92
(off Dene Pl.)
Blenheim Ct. Leeds —4D 62
(off Blenheim Wlk.)
Blenheim Cres. Leeds —4D 62
(off Blenheim Av.)
Blenheim Dri. Bat —6F 96
Blenheim Dri. Dew —2D 116
Blenheim Gro. Leeds —4D 62
Blenheim Hill. Bat —5G 96
Blenheim Mt. B'frd —4A 58
Blenheim Pl. B'frd —6F 40
Blenheim Rd. B'frd —5A 58
Blenheim Rd. Wake —3K 119
Blenheim Sq. Bat —6F 96
Blenheim Sq. Leeds —4D 62
Blenheim St. H Bri —1J 89
Blenheim St. Kei —2H 37
(off Victoria Rd.)
Blenheim St. Steet —3C 20
(off Barrows La.)
Blenheim Ter. Bat —6F 96
Blenheim Ter. Leeds —4D 62
(off Bk. Blenheim Ter.)
Blenheim Ter. Morl —7K 79
Blenheim Vw. Leeds —4D 62
Blenheim Wlk. Leeds —4D 62
Blenkinsop Ct. Morl —2L 97
(off Britannia Rd.)
Blind La. Bgly —4C 38
Blind La. Dlgtn —6C 78
Blind La. E Ard —7C 98
Blind La. Hal —5L 73
Blind La. Leeds —3N 45
Blind La. L'ft —4B 90
Blind La. Q'bry —2B 74
Blind La. Ryh —9F 138
Blind La. Todm —6J 87
Bloomfield Ri. Dart —8J 153
Bloomfield Rd. Dart —8H 153
Bloomhouse. —8H 153
Bloomhouse La. Dart —7G 153
Blucher St. B'frd —8H 59
Blue Ball La. Sower B —8M 109
(in two parts)
Blue Ball Rd. Ripp —9K 109
Bluebell Clo. All —6G 57
Bluebell Clo. Pon —4K 123
Bluebell Ct. Birs —2B 96
Blue Bell Hill. —8L 131
Blue Bell Hill. Hud —8L 131
Blue Bell La. Todm —2E 86
Bluebell Rd. Dart —6G 153
Bluebell Wlk. Ludd —4E 90
Bluebell Way. Upt —2M 157
Blue Butts. Oss —6M 117
Blue Hill. Denh —4K 55
Blue Hill Cres. Leeds —8K 61
Blue Hill Grange. Leeds —9K 61
Blue Hill Gro. Leeds —8K 61
Blue Hill La. Leeds —8K 61
Blundell Rd. S Elm —6L 157
Blundell St. Leeds —5D 62
Blythe Av. B'frd —6M 57
Blythe St. B'frd —7A 58
Boardman St. Todm —6K 87
Boar La. Leeds —7E 62
Boathouse La. Mir —8N 115
Boat La. All B —1B 102
Boat La. Meth —2A 102
Bobbin Mill Clo. Steet —3C 20
(off Bobbin Mill Ct.)
Bobbin Mill Clo. Todm —3D 86
Bobbin Mill Ct. Steet —3C 20
Bobbin St. Todm —3E 86
Bobby's La. Hept —7E 70
Bob La. Hal —5K 91
Bob La. Wilsd —3C 56
Bocking. —7F 36
Bodiham Hill. Gar —6B 66
Bodkin La. Oxe —4L 53
(in two parts)
Bodley Ter. Leeds —5N 61
Bodmin App. Leeds —8C 80
Bodmin Av. Shipl —8D 40
Bodmin Cres. Leeds —8C 80
Bodmin Cft. Leeds —8D 80
Bodmin Dri. Nor —9J 101
Bodmin Gdns. Leeds —9C 80
Bodmin Gth. Leeds —9C 80
Bodmin Pl. Leeds —9D 80
(in two parts)
Bodmin Rd. Leeds —7B 80
Bodmin Sq. Leeds —9C 80
Bodmin St. Leeds —9C 80
Bodmin Ter. Leeds —9C 80
Bogart La. Hal —3J 93
Boggart Hill. Leeds —9N 45
Boggart Hill Cres. Leeds —9N 45
Boggart Hill Dri. Leeds —9N 45
Boggart Hill Gdns. Leeds —9N 45
Boggart Hill Rd. Leeds —9N 45
Boggart La. Skelm —6D 150
Bog Green. —7G 114
Bog Grn. La. Hud —6F 114
Bog La. Scholes —1H 65
Bogthorn. —3E 36
Boland Cres. Oakw —4E 36
Boldgrove St. Dew —5K 117
Boldmere Rd. Leeds —7N 63
Boldron Holt. B'frd —5L 75
Boldshay St. B'frd —6F 58
Bold St. B'frd —5A 58
Bolehill Pk. Hov E —6K 93
Bolingbroke Ct. B'frd —9C 58
(off Elsdon Gro.)
Bolingbroke St. B'frd —3B 76
Bolland Bldgs. Low M —8D 76
Bolland St. Low M —8C 76
Bolling Hall Museum. —2E 7
Bolling Rd. B'frd —8D 58
Bolling Rd. I'ly —6J 9
Bolsover Clo. Gar —7B 66
Bolster Moor. —7A 130
Bolstermoor Rd. Gol —6N 129
Boltby La. B'frd —5K 75
Bolton. —3E 58
Bolton Abbey. —1L 5

›lton Bridge. —3K 5
›lton Bri. Rd. I'ly —5F 8
›lton Brow. Sower B —8J 91
›lton Ct. B'frd —4E 58
›lton Ct. I'ly —5F 8
(off Bolton Bri. Rd.)
›lton Cres. B'frd —2F 58
›lton Dri. B'frd —1F 58
›lton Grange. Yead —1N 41
›lton Gro. B'frd —2F 58
›lton Hall Rd. B'frd —2B 58
›lton La. B'frd —4B 58
›lton Outlanes. —2E 58
›olton Priory. —1L 5
›lton Rd. Beam —4L 5
›lton Rd. B'frd —4D 58
›lton Rd. Sils —8E 6
›lton Rd. Yead —1N 41
›lton St. B'frd —7E 58
›lton St. Low M —7A 76
(in two parts)
›lton Ter. Sils —7E 6
›lton Way. B Spa —1C 32
›lton Wife Hill. Wool —9H 137
›lton Woods. —2C 58
›lus Clo. Wake —8L 99
›lus La. Wake —8K 99
›naccord Sq. Bat —8F 96
(off Purlwell La.)
›naccord Ter. Bat —8F 96
(off Greatwood St.)
›nd Ct. Leeds —4A 62
(off Alexandra Rd.)
›nd Ct. Leeds —6D 62
(off Bond St.)
›ndgate. Hare —1J 29
›ndgate. Otley —1L 25
›ndgate. Pon —1M 123
›nd St. Bat —6F 96
›nd St. Birs —3B 96
›nd St. Brigh —9M 93
›nd St. Dew —3F 116
›nd St. H Bri —1H 89
›nd St. Leeds —6D 62
›nd St. Pon —1L 123
›nd St. Todm —7K 87
›nd St. Wake —4K 119
›negate Av. Brigh —9N 93
›negate Rd. Brigh —9M 93
›ne La. Cam —1N 159
›nn Rd. B'frd —4M 57
›nwick Mall. B'frd —6K 75
›okers Fld. Gom —6N 95
›oth. —1E 90
›otham Pk. D Hill —4J 57
›oth Ho. La. H'frth —4H 163
›oth Ho. Rd. L'ft —5B 90
›oth Ho. Ter. L'ft —5D 90
›oth La. Eml —5D 150
›othman Wlk. Kei —2G 37
›othroyd. —3D 116
›oth Royd. B'frd —6F 40
›othroyd Ct. Kbtn —3G 148
›oth Royd Dri. B'frd —6F 40
›othroyd Dri. Hud —7G 131
›othroyd Dri. Leeds —1B 62
›othroyd Grn. Dew —3E 116
›oth Royd La. Brigh —3J 113
›othroyd La. Dew —3D 116
›othroyds Way. F'stne —5A 122
›oth's Bldgs. Brigh —5N 93
(off Wyke Old La.)
›oths, The. Pon —2L 123
›oth St. B'frd —8F 40
›oth St. Bur W —8C 10
›oth St. C'frd —4D 102
›oth St. Cleck —4H 95
›oth St. Q'bry —4C 74
›oth St. Shipl —8B 40
›oth's Yd. Pud —7B 60
›othtown. —3A 92
›othtown Rd. Hal —1A 92
›rder Clo. Hud —1E 130
›rough Corner. —6H 119
›roughgate. Otley —9L 11
›rough Mkt. Hal —5B 92
(off Market St.)
›rough Rd. Wake —4L 119
›rrin's Way. Bail —4B 40
›rrough Av. Leeds —7G 44
›rrough Vw. Leeds —7G 44
›rrowdale Clo. Leeds —4J 61
›rrowdale Cres. Leeds —4J 61
›rrowdale Cft. Yead —9M 25
›rrowdale Dri. C'frd —3K 103
›rrowdale Rd. Dew —1H 117
›rrowdale Rd. Wake —4G 119
›rrowdale Ter. Leeds —3A 64
›ston Av. Leeds —3J 61
›ston Hill. H Bri —7J 71
›ston M. B Spa —1E 32
›ston Rd. B Spa —1D 32
›ston Rd. Weth —5M 17

Boston Spa. —9D 18
Boston St. C'frd —4E 102
Boston St. Hal —5M 91
Boston St. Sower B —9G 91
Boston Towers. Leeds —5G 63
(off Lindsey Gdns.)
Boston Wlk. B'frd —5L 75
Boswell Clo. Roys —5C 154
Bosworth Av. Nor —8F 100
Bosworth Clo. All —4G 57
Botany. —6D 22
Botany Av. B'frd —2D 58
Botany Bay Rd. Leeds —6N 61
Botany Dri. E Mor —6D 22
Botany La. Lep —5J 133
Botham Hall Rd. Hud —4E 130
Bottom Boat. —6C 100
Bottom Boat Rd. Stan —6C 100
(in two parts)
Bottom La. H'frth —1A 164
Bottomley. —8K 111
Bottomley Holes. —9N 55
Bottomley La. Bklnd —9H 111
Bottomley Rd. Todm —5L 107
Bottomley St. B'frd —1B 76
Bottomley St. Brigh —8M 93
Bottomley St. Butt —6L 75
Bottoms. Hal —9C 92
Bottoms La. B'shaw —9M 77
Boulder Bri. Rd. Roys —7F 154
Boulder Clough. —7C 90
Bouldergate. Mars —5H 145
(off Meltham Rd.)
Boulevard Ct. Kbtn —3G 148
(off Storthes Hall la.)
Boulevard, The. Fars —4A 60
Boulevard, The. Hal —6A 92
(off Park Rd.)
Boundary Clo. Colt —7F 64
Boundary Dri. Brier —6A 156
Boundary Farm Rd. Leeds —4C 44
Boundary La. Wake & Nor —4F 120
Boundary Pl. Leeds —4G 62
Boundary Rd. Dew —1C 116
Boundary St. Heck —8N 95
Boundary St. Leeds —4G 62
Boundary Ter. M'end —9C 96
(off Halifax Rd.)
Boundary, The. B'frd —5K 57
Bourbon Clo. B'frd —5N 75
Bourne Ct. M'well —7L 153
Bourne St. Thack —6F 40
Bourne Vw. Clo. Hud —2J 147
Bourne Vw. Rd. Hud —2J 147
Bourne Wlk. M'well —7L 153
Bowater Ct. B'frd —3K 77
Bowbridge Rd. B'frd —1C 76
Bowcliffe Rd. B'ham —6C 32
Bower Grn. B'frd —7G 58
Bower Hill La. Bret —1N 151
Bower La. Dew —9C 96
Bower Rd. Leeds —3F 64
Bower Slack Rd. Sower B —2N 109
Bower St. B'frd —9C 58
Bower, The. Bat —5C 96
Bowes Nook. B'frd —6K 75
Bowfell Clo. Leeds —2B 64
Bow Grn. Cytn —1J 75
Bowland Av. Bail —6K 39
Bowland Clo. Leeds —7N 63
Bowland St. B'frd —6B 58
Bow La. Blkhd —9B 70
Bowler Clo. Low M —7A 76
Bowling. —9F 58
Bowling All. Brigh —3M 113
Bowling All. Ter. Brigh —3M 113
Bowling Av. Wake —1H 119
Bowling Bk. La. B'frd —9E 58
Bowling Ct. Brigh —9L 93
Bowling Ct. Ind. Est. B'frd —8G 58
Bowling Dyke. Hal —4B 92
Bowling Grn. Ct. Holy G —8M 111
(off Bk. Bowling Grn. Rd.)
Bowling Grn. Ct. Hud —3D 130
Bowling Grn. Fold. Wyke —1A 94
Bowling Grn. Rd. Slnd —8M 111
Bowling Grn. Ter. Leeds —9D 62
Bowling Hall Rd. B'frd —1E 76
Bowling La. Wren —1H 119
Bowling Old La. B'frd —3B 76
(in five parts)
Bowling Pk. Clo. B'frd —1D 76
Bowling Pk. Dri. B'frd —2D 76
Bowling St. Hud —6F 130
Bowl Shaw La. Hal —7E 74
Bowman Av. B'frd —6N 75
Bowman Gro. Hal —5N 91
Bowman La. Leeds —7F 62
Bowman Pl. Hal —5N 91
Bowman Rd. B'frd —6N 75
Bowman St. Hal —5N 91
Bowman St. Wake —9A 120
Bowman Ter. Hal —5N 91

Bownas Rd. B Spa —9C 18
Bowness Av. B'frd —2H 59
Bowness Av. C'frd —3L 103
Bowness Dri. Hud —3B 132
Bowood Av. Leeds —8C 44
Bowood Cres. Leeds —8C 44
Bowood Gro. Leeds —8C 44
Bowood La. Sower B —2D 110
Bow St. Hud —5L 131
Bow St. Kei —9J 21
Bow St. Leeds —7G 62
Bowwood Dri. Sandb —8A 22
Box Bldgs. Bat —6C 96
Boxhill Rd. Ell —5E 112
Box Ings La. Kbtn —6J 149
Box La. Pon —1L 123
Box Tree Clo. B'frd —5K 57
Box Trees La. Hal —1K 91
Boxwood Rd. Ell —6E 112
Boycott Way. S Elm —5N 157
Boyd Av. B'frd —5J 59
Boy Home La. Hal —6D 90
Boy La. B'frd —6F 76
Boy La. Hal —2K 91
Boyle, The. Bar E —7L 47
Boyne Dri. Wake —5J 137
Boyne Hill. C'thpe —6J 137
Boyne St. Hal —5A 92
Boynton St. B'frd —2B 76
(in two parts)
Boynton Ter. B'frd —2C 76
Boys La. Hal —7C 92
Boys Scarr. L'ft —6D 90
Bracewell Av. All —6F 56
Bracewell Bank. Hal —2M 91
Bracewell Dri. Hal —2M 91
Bracewell Gro. Hal —3N 91
Bracewell Hill. Hal —2M 91
Bracewell Mt. Hal —2M 91
(off Bracewell Hill)
Bracewell Rd. Mel —8B 146
Bracewell St. Kei —9L 21
Bracken Av. Brigh —7M 93
Bracken Bank. —4F 36
Bracken Bank Av. Kei —5F 36
Bracken Bank Cres. Kei —4F 36
Bracken Bank Gro. Kei —4F 36
Bracken Bank Wlk. Oakw —5F 36
Bracken Bank Way. Kei —4F 36
Brackenbeck Rd. B'frd —1L 75
Brackenbed La. Hal —3M 91
Brackenbed Ter. Hal —3M 91
(off Brackenbed La.)
Bracken Clo. Brigh —7M 93
Bracken Clo. Mir —4H 115
Bracken Ct. Leeds —6E 44
Bracken Ct. Lwr W —9A 62
Brackendale. B'frd —5D 40
Brackendale Av. B'frd —5E 40
Brackendale Dri. B'frd —5D 40
Brackendale Gro. B'frd —5D 40
Brackendale Pde. B'frd —5D 40
Bracken Dri. Sils —7D 6
Bracken Edge. B'frd —8G 41
Bracken Edge. Leeds —1H 63
Bracken Ghyll Dri. Sils —7D 6
Bracken Gro. Hud —7N 113
Bracken Gro. Mir —4H 115
Brackenhall. —7A 114
Bracken Hall Countryside Centre. —4K 39
Brackenhall Ct. B'frd —1L 75
Bracken Hall Rd. Hud —8A 114
Brackenhill. —5D 140
(nr. Ackworth Moor Top)
Bracken Hill. —4H 115
(nr. Mirfield)
Bracken Hill. Ackw —4D 140
Bracken Hill. Hal —3L 91
Bracken Hill. Leeds —6E 44
Bracken Hill. Mir —4H 115
Bracken Hill. S Kirk —5K 157
Brackenhill Dri. B'frd —2L 75
Brackenholme Royd. B'frd —5K 75
Bracken Mt. Sils —7D 6
Bracken Pk. Bgly —4H 39
Bracken Pk. Eld —2G 39
Bracken Pk. S'cft —8B 30
Bracken Rd. Brigh —8M 93
Bracken Rd. Ebrn —3A 20
Bracken Rd. Kei —3G 36
Brackens La. Hal —6G 75
Bracken Sq. Hud —7A 114
Bracken St. Kei —3H 37
Brackenwell La. N Rig —2N 13
Brackenwood Clo. I'ly —5K 9
Brackenwood Clo. Leeds —8G 44
Brackenwood Ct. Out —7M 99
Brackenwood Grn. Leeds —7G 44
Brackenwood Rd. Out —7M 99
Bradbeck Rd. B'frd —7L 57
Bradburn Rd. Rob H —1J 99
Bradbury St. Dew —6A 116

Bradcroft. Hud —1N 131
(off Bradford Rd.)
Bradd Clo. Liv —7M 95
Bradfield Clo. Hud —6C 114
Bradford. —7C 58
Bradford Bulls Rugby League Football Club. —5C 76
Bradford Bus. Pk. B'frd —5C 58
Bradford City Football Club. —5B 58
Bradford Industrial & Horses at Work Museum. —3H 59
Bradford La. B'frd —7H 59
Bradford Moor. —6G 58
Bradford Old Rd. Bgly —8G 39
(in two parts)
Bradford Old Rd. Hal —1B 92
Bradford Rd. Bail B —4N 93
Bradford Rd. Bgly —5F 38
Bradford Rd. Birs & Bat —2N 95
Bradford Rd. B'frd —1E 58
Bradford Rd. Brigh —8N 93
Bradford Rd. Bur W —9E 10
Bradford Rd. Cytn —9H 57
Bradford Rd. Cleck —9E 76
Bradford Rd. Dew —2F 116
Bradford Rd. Dlgtn —8E 78
(nr. Wakefield Rd.)
Bradford Rd. Dlgtn —6A 78
(nr. Whitehall Rd.)
Bradford Rd. Gom —5K 77
Bradford Rd. Hal —1F 92
(nr. Bk. Clough)
Bradford Rd. Hal —3F 92
(nr. Leeds Rd.)
Bradford Rd. Hud & Brigh —3M 131
Bradford Rd. Kei & Riddl —9K 21
Bradford Rd. Men & Guis —4F 24
Bradford Rd. Otley —2F 24
Bradford Rd. Raw & Liv —6K 95
Bradford Rd. Shipl —8M 39
Bradford Rd. Thornb & Pud —5K 59
Bradford Rd. Wake —3N 97
Bradford Rd. Wren & Wake —7G 98
Bradfords Clo. B'ham —5C 32
Bradford St. Dew —2G 116
Bradford St. Kei —8J 21
Bradford & Wakefield Rd. B'frd —6N 77
Bradlaugh Rd. B'frd —4N 75
Bradlaugh Ter. B'frd —4A 76
Bradley. —5D 114
Bradley Av. C'frd —4C 102
Bradley Av. Sils —7D 6
Bradley Boulevd. Hud —8A 114
Bradley Carr Ter. S Elm —9M 157
Bradley Colliery La. Hud —7D 114
Bradley Ct. G'lnd —5A 112
Bradley Dri. Sils —7D 6
Bradley Grange Gdns. Hud —5D 114
Bradley Gro. Sils —7D 6
Bradley Hill. —4D 60
Bradley Junct. Ind. Est. Bdly —7E 114
Bradley La. G'lnd —5A 112
Bradley La. Pud —7M 59
Bradley La. Wome —7N 125
Bradley Mills. —2B 132
Bradley Mills Rd. Hud —2A 132
(in two parts)
Bradley Quarry Clo. Hud —5E 114
Bradley Ri. Sils —7D 6
Bradley Rd. Hud —6A 114
Bradley Rd. Sils —6D 6
Bradley St. Bgly —4E 38
Bradley St. B'frd —2A 58
Bradley St. C'frd —4D 102
Bradley St. Hud —4N 131
Bradley Ter. Leeds —3J 45
Bradley Vw. Holy G —7A 112
Bradshaw. —4M 73
Bradshaw Av. Hon —6K 147
Bradshaw Clo. Hon —6K 147
Bradshaw Cres. Hon —6K 147
Bradshaw Dri. Hon —6K 147
Bradshaw La. Hal —4M 73
Bradshaw La. Slai —9F 128
Bradshaw Rd. Hon —8K 147
Bradshaw Rd. Uthg —2F 162
Bradshaw Row. Hal —3M 73
Bradshaw Vw. Hal —6L 73
(off Moor Top Gdns.)
Bradshaw Vw. Q'bry —4B 74
Bradstock Gdns. Morl —7K 79
Bradwell La. Oss —6A 118
Brady Clo. Oakw —4E 36
Brae Av. B'frd —3D 58
Braemar Cft. S Hien —2L 155
Braemar Dri. Gar —6B 66
Braemar Ri. S Hien —2L 155
Braeside. Hal —5K 91
Brafferton Arbor. B'frd —5K 75

Braine Rd. Weth —3N 17
Braithwaite. —8E 20
Braithwaite Av. Kei —8E 20
Braithwaite Cres. Kei —9F 20
Braithwaite Dri. Kei —9F 20
Braithwaite Edge Rd. Kei —8D 20
Braithwaite Gro. Kei —9F 20
Braithwaite Rd. Kei —9D 20
Braithwaite Row. Leeds —3G 80
Braithwaite St. Leeds —8B 62
Braithwaite St. M'well —8L 153
Braithwaite Wlk. Kei —9F 20
Braithwaite Way. Kei —9F 20
Bramah St. Barn —8D 154
Bramble Av. B Spa —1B 32
Bramble Clo. Cytn —2H 75
Bramble Clo. Haw —9D 36
Bramble Clo. Pon —5H 123
Brambles, The. I'ly —5E 8
Bramble Wlk. Birs —3C 96
Brambling M. Morl —9M 79
Bramby Fold. Oss —7B 118
Bramcote Av. Barn —9N 153
Bramham. —6D 32
Bramham Dri. Bail —3B 40
Bramham La. Woth —4G 30
Bramham Park. —8N 31
Bramham Rd. Bgly —3F 38
Bramham Rd. C'frd —6A 102
Bramham Rd. Cliff —4D 32
Bramham Rd. T'ner —1H 47
Bramhope. —6H 27
Bramhope Rd. Cleck —4G 95
Bramleigh Dri. Morl —7K 79
Bramleigh Gro. Morl —7K 79
Bramley. —4F 60
Bramley Cen. Leeds —3G 60
Bramley Clo. N Mill —1B 164
Bramley Clo. Oakw —4B 36
Bramley Cres. Wake —8K 99
Bramley Fold. Hal —4J 93
Bramley Gdns. Leeds —6D 46
Bramley La. Hal —4H 93
Bramley La. Wool —1C 152
Bramley St. B'frd —9C 58
(in two parts)
Bramley Vw. Hal —4K 93
Brampton Ct. S Elm —4N 157
Bramstan Av. Leeds —3D 60
Bramstan Clo. Leeds —3D 60
Bramstan Gdns. Leeds —3D 60
Bramston Gdns. Ras —3M 113
Bramston St. Brigh —2M 113
Brancepeth Pl. Leeds —7A 62
Branch Clo. Leeds —1K 79
Branch End. Gild —6G 79
Branch La. Hud —8G 112
Branch Pl. Leeds —1K 79
Branch Rd. Ain T —7G 112
Branch Rd. A'ley —6M 61
Branch Rd. Bklnd —7K 111
Branch Rd. Bat —7F 96
Branch Rd. Cald G —6E 136
Branch Rd. Dew —3F 116
Branch Rd. Lwr W —1K 79
Branch Rd. Schol —3D 94
Branch St. Hud —5J 131
Branch St. Leeds —1K 79
Brander App. Leeds —5M 63
Brander Clo. Leeds —5M 63
Brander Dri. Leeds —5L 63
Brander Gro. Leeds —5L 63
Brander Mt. Leeds —4L 63
(in two parts)
Brander Rd. Leeds —4M 63
Brander St. Leeds —4M 63
Brandfort St. B'frd —9M 57
Brand Hill App. Croft —1F 138
Brand Hill Dri. Croft —1F 138
Brandon. —1N 45
Brandon Ct. Leeds —2L 45
Brandon Cres. Leeds —9N 29
Brandon La. Leeds —9A 30
Brandon La. Wike —8M 29
Brandon Rd. Leeds —6C 62
Brandon St. Leeds —7B 62
Brandon Ter. Leeds —2K 45
Brandon Vw. Leeds —2M 45
Brandon Way. Leeds —1F 62
Brandy Carr. —8F 98
Brandy Carr Rd. K'gte —1D 118
Branksome Ct. B'frd —4L 57
Branksome Cres. B'frd —4L 57
Branksome Dri. Shipl —7H 39
Branksome Gro. Shipl —7H 39
Branksome Pl. Leeds —6C 62
(off Brandon Rd., LS3)
Branksome Pl. Leeds —4A 62
(LS6)
Bransby Clo. Fars —4B 60
Bransby Ct. Fars —4B 60
Bransby Ri. Fars —3B 60
Bransdale Av. Guis —8J 25

Bransdale Av. Nor —8H 101
Bransdale Clo. Bail —5M 39
Bransdale Clo. Guis —8J 25
Bransdale Clo. Nor —8H 101
Bransdale Clough. B'frd —4K 75
Bransdale Gdns. Guis —8J 25
Bransdale Gth. Guis —8J 25
Bransdale M. Nor —8H 101
Bransdale Wlk. Nor —8H 101
Branshaw Dri. Kei —2E 36
Branshaw Gro. Kei —2E 36
Branshaw Mt. Kei —2E 36
Branstone Gro. Oss —2M 117
Bran St. Kei —3H 37
Brant Av. Hal —9M 73
Brant Bank La. Nesf —3C 8
Brantcliffe Dri. Bail —3N 39
Brantcliffe Way. Bail —2A 40
Brantdale Clo. B'frd —2H 57
Brantdale Rd. B'frd —2H 57
Brantford St. Leeds —9F 44
Brant La. Tad —9N 33
Brantwood Av. B'frd —2H 57
Brantwood Clo. B'frd —2H 57
Brantwood Cres. B'frd —2G 57
Brantwood Dri. B'frd —2H 57
Brantwood Gro. B'frd —2G 57
Brantwood Oval. B'frd —2H 57
Brantwood Rd. B'frd —2G 57
Brantwood Vs. B'frd —2H 57
Branwell Av. Birs —1B 96
Branwell Dri. Haw —7C 36
Branwell Lodge. B'frd —2M 75
Brassey Rd. B'frd —1E 76
Brassey St. Hal —6A 92
Brassey Ter. B'frd —1E 76
Brathay Gdns. Leeds —3B 64
Braybrook Ct. B'frd —3A 58
Bray Clo. B'frd —3J 75
Brayshaw Dri. B'frd —3J 75
Brayshaw Fold. Low M —7C 76
Brayshaw Rd. E Ard —6E 98
Brayside Av. Hud —9L 113
Braythorne. —2G 12
Braythorne La. Stainb —2G 12
Brayton App. Leeds —1D 64
Brayton Clo. Leeds —1D 64
Brayton Gdns. Cam —9N 143
Brayton Gth. Leeds —1E 64
Brayton Grange. Leeds —1E 64
Brayton Grn. Leeds —1E 64
(in two parts)
Brayton Gro. Leeds —1D 64
Brayton Pl. Leeds —1E 64
Brayton Ter. Leeds —1D 64
Brayton Wlk. Leeds —1D 64
Brazil St. C'frd —4E 102
Bread St. Wake —5L 119
Breakmoor Av. Sils —7E 6
Break Neck. Hal —4F 92
Breaks Fld. Wyke —2B 94
Breaks Rd. Low M —7C 76
Brearcliffe Clo. B'frd —6M 75
Brearcliffe Dri. B'frd —6M 75
Brearcliffe Gro. B'frd —6M 75
Brearcliffe Rd. B'frd —6N 75
Brearcliffe St. B'frd —6M 75
Brearley Gdns. Liv —1L 115
Brearley La. H Bri & L'ft —3A 90
Brearley Pl. Bat —8F 96
(off Gt. Wood St.)
Brearley St. Bat —8E 96
Brearton St. B'frd —6C 58
Breary Av. H'fth —6G 43
(in two parts)
Breary Ct. B'hpe —5H 27
Breary La. B'hpe —5H 27
Breary La. E. B'hpe —5J 27
Breary Ri. B'hpe —5H 27
Breary Ter. H'fth —6G 43
Breary Wlk. H'fth —6G 43
Breck Lea. Sower B —1G 110
Brecks. Cytn —9J 57
Brecks Gdns. Kip —2N 83
Brecks La. Swil & Kip —1K 83
Brecks Rd. Cytn —9J 57
Breck Willows. Sower B —1F 110
Brecon App. Leeds —5M 63
Brecon Av. Hud —1F 130
Brecon Clo. B'frd —8F 40
Brecon Ct. Leeds —5M 63
Brecon Ri. Leeds —5M 63
Bredon Av. Shipl —8D 40
Bredon Clo. Hems —2F 156
Breighton Adown. B'frd —5J 75
Bremit Vs. B'frd —5N 75
Bremit Wlk. B'frd —5N 75
Bremner St. Otley —9M 11
Brendon Ct. B'frd —2H 77
Brendon Ct. Mir —9K 115
Brendon Dri. Hud —1J 131
Brendon Ho. B'frd —3J 77
(off Landscove Av.)
Brendon Wlk. B'frd —3H 77
(in two parts)
Brentford Rd. Low M —6A 76
Brentlea Av. Wake —8N 119
Brentwood Clo. Bat —7H 97
Brentwood Clo. Thpe A —5N 141
Brentwood Ct. Leeds —7K 43
Brentwood Gdns. B'frd —5B 76
Brentwood Gro. Leeds —7M 61
Brentwood St. Leeds —7M 61
Brentwood Ter. Leeds —7M 61
Bretfield Ct. Dew —6G 116
Brettegate. Hems —2C 156
Brett Gdns. Leeds —1D 80
Bretton Clo. Dart —9E 152
Bretton Country Park. —3B 152
Bretton La. Bret —1B 152
Bretton Rd. Dart —9E 152
Bretton St. Dew —7G 116
Brewerton La. Dew —1C 116
Brewery Dri. Hud —8K 131
Brewery La. Cytn —2C 74
Brewery La. Dew —7F 116
Brewery La. Knot —8E 104
Brewery La. Q'bry —6B 74
Brewery Rd. I'ly —5H 9
Brewery Rd. Kei —4G 37
Brewery St. Hal —2B 92
Brewery St. Heck —9A 96
Brewery St. Kei —9K 21
Brewery St. Todm —4G 86
Brewery Wharf. Mir —7L 115
Brexdale Av. Kip —2N 83
Brian Av. Hud —5C 132
Brian Cres. Leeds —4C 64
Brian Pl. Leeds —3C 64
Brian Royd La. G'Ind —4M 111
Brianside. —3C 64
Brian St. Hud —1G 130
Brian Vw. Leeds —3D 64
Briar Av. Mel —6B 146
Briar Bank. Kin —8A 140
Briar Clo. Ell —6D 112
Briar Clo. Fars —4A 60
Briar Clo. Heck —7A 96
Briar Ct. H'frth —4J 163
Briardale Rd. B'frd —2G 57
Briardene. Rothw —9D 82
Briar Dri. Dew —1C 116
Briarfield Av. B'frd —8E 40
Briarfield Clo. B'frd —8E 40
Briarfield Clo. I'ly —6J 9
Briarfield Gdns. Shipl —9N 39
Briarfield Gro. B'frd —8E 40
Briarfield Rd. H'frth —1A 164
Briarfield Rd. Shipl —1A 58
Briar Ga. Weth —2M 17
Briar Gro. Brier —6A 156
Briar Gro. Wake —8N 119
Briar La. Hud —9G 113
Briarlea Clo. Yead —2K 41
Briarlyn Av. Hud —9F 112
Briarlyn Rd. Hud —9F 112
Briarmains Rd. Birs —2C 96
Briar Rhydding. Bail —5C 40
Briar Rd. Skel —8M 159
Briarsdale Ct. Leeds —3L 63
Briarsdale Cft. Leeds —3L 63
Briarsdale Gth. Leeds —3L 63
Briarsdale Heights. Leeds —3L 63
Briar Wood. Shipl —8C 40
Briarwood Av. B'frd —4N 75
Briarwood Av. Riddl —7M 21
Briarwood Clo. Out —7M 99
Briarwood Cres. B'frd —4N 75
Briarwood Dri. B'frd —4N 75
Briarwood Gro. B'frd —3N 75
Brickbank. Hud —7D 132
Brickfield Gro. Hal —8N 73
Brickfield La. Hal —8N 73
Brickfield Ter. Hal —8N 73
Brick Mill Rd. Pud —8C 60
Brick Row. Dew —3C 116
Brick Row. Wyke —1A 94
Brick St. Cleck —5G 94
Brick St. Leeds —7F 62
Brick St. Wake —4F 118
Brick Ter. Brigh —2N 113
Brick & Tile Ter. Brigh —2M 113
Brickyard. Mir —6K 115
Brickyard, The. Shaf —8K 155
Bride St. Todm —6K 87
Bridge Av. Otley —9L 11
Bridge Clo. B Spa —9E 18
Bridge Clo. Horb —1A 136
Bridge Clo. Scis —7H 151
Bridge Cotts. Aber —8E 48
Bridge Ct. Fitz —8A 140
Bridge Ct. Leeds —9C 62
Bridge Ct. Morl —1L 97
Bridge Cft. Hud —6G 130
Bridge End. Brigh —2M 113
Bridge End. Leeds —7E 62
(in two parts)
Bridge End St. Todm —3E 86
Bridge Fold. Kirks —2J 61
Bridge Foot. Thor A —9E 18
Bridge Gth. Cliff —2D 32
Bridge Ga. H Bri —1H 89
Bridgegate Way. B'frd —1H 59
Bridgehouse La. Haw —9C 36
Bridge La. Hal —7F 74
Bridge La. H'frth —2M 163
Bridge La. I'ly —4F 8
Bridge La. Knot —7E 104
Bridge La. Thpe A —6A 142
Bridge Lanes. H Bri —1G 88
Bridge Paddock. Coll —8J 17
Bridge Rd. B Spa —9E 18
Bridge Rd. Brigh —1M 113
Bridge Rd. Horb —2A 136
Bridge Rd. Kirks —2J 61
Bridge Rd. Leeds —9C 62
Bridge Rd. Oxe —7M 53
Bridge Rd. Rod —1B 60
Bridge Rd. Sils —7E 6
Bridge St. Bat —7G 96
Bridge St. Ber B —1L 147
Bridge St. Birs —4B 96
Bridge St. B'frd —8C 58
Bridge St. C'frd —4E 102
Bridge St. Dart —8G 153
Bridge St. Heck —8N 95
Bridge St. Kei —1H 37
Bridge St. Leeds —6F 62
Bridge St. Lock —7L 131
Bridge St. Morl —1L 97
Bridge St. Nor —9K 101
Bridge St. Oakw —5B 36
Bridge St. Otley —9L 11
Bridge St. Pon —2K 123
Bridge St. Sils —7E 6
Bridge St. Slai —1M 145
Bridge St. Sower B —9H 91
Bridge St. T'tn —8D 56
Bridge St. Todm —7K 87
Bridge St. Wake —7M 119
Bridge Ter. Leeds —3B 46
Bridge Vw. Leeds —1B 60
Bridgewater Ct. Leeds —9B 44
Bridgewater Pk. Dri. Skel —7L 159
Bridgewater Rd. Leeds —9H 63
Bridgeway. B'frd —3H 77
Bri. Wood Clo. H'fth —6G 42
Bri. Wood Vw. H'fth —5G 42
Bridgland Av. Men —3E 24
Bridgwater Rd. B'frd —4M 57
Bridle Av. Oss —3M 117
Bridle Clo. Neth —3A 136
Bridle Dene. Hal —8H 75
Bridle La. Neth —3A 136
Bridle La. Oss —3M 117
Bridle Path Rd. Leeds —4B 64
(LS15)
Bridle Path Rd. Leeds —2M 45
(LS17)
Bridle Path Wlk. Leeds —4B 64
Bridle Pl. Oss —3N 117
Bridle Stile. Hal —8H 75
Bridle Stile La. Q'bry —3D 74
Bridle St. Bat —7H 97
Bridley Dri. Slai —1N 145
Bridport Ho. B'frd —6E 58
(off Butler St.)
Brierdene. Sils —7E 6
Brierfield Gdns. Gild —7F 78
Brier Hey Clo. H Bri —3N 89
Brier Hey La. Myth —3N 89
Brier Hill Clo. Cleck —6E 94
Brier Hill Vw. Bdly —6B 114
Brierlands Clo. Gar —6B 66
Brierlands Fold. Gar —6B 66
Brier La. Brigh —1J 113
Brier La. H'cft & S Hien —1J 155
Brierley. —6N 155
Brierley Clo. Shipl —9A 40
Brierley Cres. S Kirk —6J 157
Brierley Rd. Grime —9N 155
Brierley Rd. Shaf —7L 155
Brierley Rd. S Hien —4L 155
Brier St. Hal —2B 92
Brier St. Kei —3H 37
Briery Clo. I'ly —5D 8
Briery Ct. Wake —7B 138
Briery Fld. Shipl —1N 57
Briery Gro. Mir —9L 115
Briery Hall Farm. Wake —7B 138
Briestfield. —3D 134
Briestfield Rd. Grng M & Bstfld —5B 134
Briggate. Brigh —1M 113
(in two parts)
Briggate. Ell —4E 112
Briggate. Hud —3E 132
Briggate. Leeds —7E 62
Briggate. Shipl —7N 39
Briggate. Sils —7E 6
Briggate. Windh —8N 39
Brigg Gdns. Kei —9F 20
Briggland Ct. Wilsd —1B 56
Briggs Av. B'frd —4M 75
Brigg's Av. C'frd —6D 102
Briggs Bldgs. Morl —9L 79
(off Melbourne St.)
Briggs Gro. B'frd —4M 75
Briggs La. Wake —2H 135
Briggs Pl. B'frd —4M 75
Brigg's Row. F'stne —7D 122
Briggs St. Barn —8D 154
Briggs St. Q'bry —4C 74
Briggs Ter. Hud —4B 132
Brigg Well Head Ga. H Bri —7L 71
Brighouse. —9N 93
Brighouse & Denholme Rd. Denh & Q'bry —8L 55
Brighouse & Denholme Rd. Hal —6E 74
Brighouse Rd. Hip —5H 93
Brighouse Rd. Hud —8G 112
Brighouse Rd. Low M —8B 76
Brighouse Rd. Q'bry —4D 74
Brighouse Wood La. Brigh —9L 93
Brighouse Wood Row. Brigh
(off Brighouse Wood La.) —9L 93
Brighton Av. Morl —8J 79
Brighton Cliff. Leeds —4F 60
Brighton Clo. Bat —6B 96
Brighton Gro. Leeds —5G 60
Brighton Rd. I'ly —6K 9
Brighton St. B'frd —6E 40
Brighton St. Hal —3N 91
Brighton St. Heck —7A 96
Brighton St. Shipl —7N 39
Brighton St. Todm —3E 86
Brighton St. Wake —6J 119
Brighton Ter. Schol —4D 94
Bright St. All —5G 57
Bright St. B'frd —3G 77
Bright St. Cytn —1G 75
Bright St. Dew —2F 116
Bright St. E Ard —4F 98
Bright St. Haw —8D 36
Bright St. Mir —3K 115
Bright St. Morl —9J 79
Bright St. Q'bry —4E 74
Bright St. Sower B —7H 91
Bright St. S'ley —4C 60
Bright St. Todm —9J 87
Brignall Cft. Leeds —5H 63
Brignall Gth. Leeds —5H 63
Brignall Way. Leeds —5H 63
Brig Royd. —6D 110
Brigshaw Dri. All B —6N 83
Brigshaw La. All B & Kip —6N 83
Brindle Pk. Dri. C'frd —6G 102
Brindley Gro. B'frd —7H 57
Brindley Rd. Sils —9F 6
Brindley Way. Wake I —8H 99
Brisbane Av. B'frd —3C 58
Briscoe La. G'Ind —4A 112
Bristol Av. Riddl —8A 22
Bristol St. Hal —9C 92
Bristol St. Leeds —5F 62
Britannia Bldgs. Morl —2J 97
Britannia Clo. S'ley —4C 60
Britannia Ct. Leeds —6D 60
Britannia Ho. B'frd —7C 58
(off Broadway)
Britannia Rd. Gol & Hud —7D 130
Britannia Rd. Morl —2J 97
Britannia Rd. Slai —1M 145
Britannia Sq. Morl —2J 97
Britannia St. Bgly —4F 38
Britannia St. B'frd —8D 58
Britannia St. Leeds —7D 62
Britannia St. S'ley —4C 60
Britannia Ter. Cleck —4H 95
Britannia Trad. Est. Milns —6E 130
Britton St. Gom —6K 95
Broadacre Rd. Oss —6A 118
Broad Acres. Dur —3H 137
Broadacres Dri. Weth —4K 17
Broadbent Cft. Hon —5L 147
Broad Carr La. Holy G —7B 112
Broad Carr La. N Mill —5E 164
Broad Carr Ter. Holy G —6C 112
Broadcroft Chase. Ting —5A 98
Broadcroft Dri. Ting —5A 98
Broadcroft Gro. Ting —4A 98
Broadcroft Way. Ting —4A 98
Broad Cut Rd. Cald G —4E 136
Broadfield Clo. B'frd —4J 77
Broadfields. H'fth —6G 42
Broadfield Way. Add —1K 7
Broad Folds. —1H 75
Broadfolds. Cytn —1H 75
Broadgate. Holy G —9M 111
Broadgate. Hud —6B 132
Broadgate. Oss —6A 118
Broad Ga. Todm —5L 87
(nr. Scrapers La., in two parts)
Broad Ga. Todm —7B 88
(nr. Shaw Wood Rd.)
Broadgate Av. H'fth —7G 43
Broadgate Ct. H'fth —7G 43
Broadgate Cres. H'fth —7F 42
Broadgate Cres. Hud —6B 132
Broadgate Dri. H'fth —6G 42
Broadgate La. H'fth —6F 42
Broadgate M. H'fth —7G 43
Broadgate Ri. H'fth —7G 43
Broadgate Wlk. H'fth —7F 42
Broad Head La. Oakw —4K 35
Broad Ings Way. She —8G 75
Broadlands. Kei —8F 20
Broadlands Rd. Mel —6C 146
Broadlands St. B'frd —1H 77
Broad La. Beal —5M 105
Broad La. B'frd —9H 59
Broad La. Err —3G 88
Broad La. Hept —7C 70
Broad La. H'frth —3J 163
Broad La. Hud —4B 132
Broad La. Leeds & S'ley —4D 6
Broad La. L'ft —7C 90
Broad La. Pon —2K 123
Broad La. S Elm —8G 157
Broad La. Todm —2M 87
Broad La. Clo. Leeds —2H 61
Broadlea Av. Leeds —2H 61
Broadlea Clo. Leeds —2H 61
Broadlea Cres. B'frd —2D 76
Broadlea Cres. Leeds —2H 61
Broadlea Gdns. Leeds —2H 61
Broadlea Gro. Leeds —2H 61
Broadlea Hill. Leeds —2H 61
Broadlea Mt. Leeds —3J 61
Broadlea Oval. Leeds —2H 61
Broadlea Pl. Leeds —3H 61
Broadlea Rd. Leeds —2H 61
Broadlea St. Leeds —2H 61
Broadlea Ter. Leeds —2H 61
Broadlea Vw. Leeds —2G 61
Broadley Av. Hal —3H 91
Broadley Clo. Hal —3J 91
Broadley Cres. Hal —3H 91
Broadley Gro. Hal —3J 91
Broadley Laithe. Hal —2J 91
Broadley Rd. Hal —3H 91
Broadmead. C'frd —4F 102
Broadmeadows. Out —7L 99
Broad Oak La. Hal —6J 93
Broad Oak La. Pen —7G 166
Broad Oak Pl. Hal —6J 93
Broadoaks Clo. Dew —4K 117
Broad Oak St. Hal —6J 93
Broad Oak Ter. Hal —6J 93
Broadowler La. Oss —6A 118
Broad Royd. Holy G —8L 111
Broadstone Rd. Cumb —4J 165
Broadstones Pk. Bgly —5J 39
Broadstone St. Todm —6M 87
Broadstone Way. B'frd —4J 77
Broad St. B'frd —7C 58
Broad St. Dew —5D 116
Broad St. Fars —3N 59
Broad St. Hal —5B 92
Broad St. Todm —6K 87
Broad Tree Rd. Hal —2N 91
Broad Vw. Oss —6B 118
Broadwalk, The. Otley —8J 11
Broadwater Ho. B'frd —9C 58
(off Park Rd.)
Broadway. Bgly —4F 38
Broadway. B'frd —8C 58
Broadway. Guis —8G 24
Broadway. Hal —7D 92
Broadway. H'fth —9B 42
Broadway. Hud —3N 131
Broadway. Kirks —8H 43
Broadway. Leeds —8A 64
Broadway. M'well —8K 153
Broadway. Pon —4L 123
Broadway. S Elm —8L 157
Broadway. Sower B —9E 90
Broadway. Wake —6E 118
Broadway Av. B'frd —3B 76
Broadway Av. Leeds —4A 62
Broadway Clo. B'frd —3B 76
Broadway Ct. Sower B —9E 90
Broad Way Ct. Thorn —1H 135
Broadway Dri. H'fth —7E 42
Broadway Ter. S Elm —8L 157
Broadwell Rd. Oss —6B 118
Broadwood Av. Hal —3J 91
Brockadale Av. Pon —6K 123
Brock Bank. Hud —3D 132
Brockholes La. Broc —7A 148
Brocklesby Dri. All —6G 56
Brocks. Hal —7C 90
Brockswood Ct. W'ton —5D 138

rockwell Gdns. Sower B —9G 90
rockwell La. Tri —1F 110
oc-O-Bank. Nort —7N 143
odrick Ct. Leeds —1N 61
roken Cross. Hud —8C 132
roken Way. B'frd —3B 76
(off Manchester Rd.)
romet Pl. B'frd —3F 58
omfield Ct. Roys —5E 154
omford Rd. B'frd —1F 76
omley Av. N Mill —1B 164
omley Gro. Kei —2E 36
omley Mt. Wake —7M 119
omley Rd. Bat —9H 97
omley Rd. Bgly —3E 38
omley Rd. Hud —1L 131
omley Rd. Shipl —7K 39
omley St. Bat —9G 97
ompton Av. B'frd —2E 76
ompton Gro. Leeds —3D 80
ompton Mt. Leeds —3D 80
ompton Rd. B'frd —1E 76
ompton Row. Leeds —3D 80
ompton Ter. B'frd —1E 76
ompton Ter. Leeds —3D 80
ompton Vw. Leeds —3D 80
onshill Gro. All —5H 57
onte Av. Knot —8A 104
onte Clo. B'frd —4K 57
onte Clo. Dew —1C 116
onte Clo. Gom —3M 95
onte Clo. Hud —7J 131
onte Ct. C'frd —7K 103
onte Ct. Pon —1K 123
onte Dri. Oakw —4E 36
onte Gro. Hems —3C 156
onte Gro. Mir —7N 115
onte Ho. B'frd —1J 77
(off Eversley Dri.)
onte Old Rd. T'tn —8D 56
onte Parsonage Museum. —8B 36
onte Pl. T'tn —8D 56
onte Rd. Birs —3B 96
onte St. Haw —8B 36
onte St. Kei —8K 21
onte Vs. Cro R —7F 36
onte Way. Mir —7N 115
ook Clo. Oss —8B 118
ookdale. Todm —1J 107
ookdale Av. Oss —2M 117
ook Dri. Holy G —7B 112
ooke Ct. Pon —6J 123
ooke Fold. Hon —5L 147
ooke St. Brigh —2M 113
ooke St. Cleck —5J 95
ooke St. Heck —9A 96
ookeville Av. Hal —5H 93
ookfield. Kbtn —3H 149
ook Fld. Mir —9K 115
ookfield Av. C'frd —5F 102
ookfield Av. Cleck —3J 95
ookfield Av. Leeds —2H 63
ookfield Av. Rod —9A 42
ookfield Av. Shipl —7B 40
ookfield Ct. Leeds —9A 42
ookfield Ct. Nor —1K 121
ookfield Dri. Ackw —2J 141
ookfield Gdns. Leeds —1A 60
ookfield Pl. Leeds —9A 44
ookfield Rd. B'frd —6E 58
ookfield Rd. Leeds —9A 44
ookfield Rd. Shipl —7B 40
ookfields. Neth —5N 135
ookfields Av. Wyke —3C 94
ookfields Cres. Wake —8L 139
ookfields Rd. Wyke —3C 94
ookfield St. Leeds —9G 62
ookfield St. Todm —3E 86
ookfield Ter. Barn —9D 154
ookfield Ter. Cleck —3J 95
ookfield Ter. Leeds —9A 44
(off Brookfield Rd., LS6)
ookfield Ter. Leeds —9F 62
(LS10)
ookfield Vw. Cleck —3J 95
ookfoot. —9L 93
ookfoot Av. B'shaw —8L 77
ookfoot La. Hal & Brigh —9J 93
ook Gdns. Dew —3E 116
(off Travis Lacey Ter.)
ook Gdns. Mel —7C 146
ook Grain Hill. Brigh —3M 113
ook Grains La. Ripp —9D 110
ook Hill. —4B 40
ook Hill. Bail —4B 40
ookhill Av. Leeds —3G 44
ookhill Clo. Leeds —3G 44
ookhill Cres. Leeds —3G 44
ookhill Dri. Leeds —3G 44
ookhill Gro. Leeds —3G 44
ookhill Rd. Dart —9D 152
ookhouse. —5J 73
Brookhouse Gdns. B'frd —7K 41
Brooklands. —2N 63
Brooklands. E Kes —3D 30
Brooklands. Hal —5J 93
Brooklands. Hud —6D 114
Brooklands Av. Holy G —7A 112
Brooklands Av. Leeds —2A 64
Brooklands Av. T'tn —8E 56
Brooklands Av. W'ton —3C 138
Brooklands Clo. Holy G —7A 112
(off Shaw La.)
Brooklands Clo. Leeds —2N 63
Brooklands Clo. Men —3F 24
Brooklands Ct. Leeds —2A 64
Brooklands Ct. Oss —7C 118
Brooklands Cres. H'cft —9L 139
Brooklands Cres. Leeds —2N 63
Brooklands Cres. Yead —1M 41
Brooklands Dri. Leeds —2N 63
Brooklands Dri. Yead —1M 41
Brooklands Gth. Leeds —2A 64
Brooklands Gro. Men —3F 24
Brooklands La. Leeds —2A 64
Brooklands La. Men —3E 24
Brooklands Rd. W'ton —3C 138
Brooklands Towers. Leeds —1B 64
Brooklands Vw. Leeds —2A 64
(in two parts)
Brooklands Vw. W'ton —3D 138
Brooklands Wlk. Men —3F 24
Brooklands Way. Men —3E 24
Brook La. Cytn —2F 74
Brook La. Gol —6C 130
Brook La. Liv —8G 95
Brook La. Wee —6B 14
Brooklea. Hal —5K 93
Brookleigh. C'ley —9M 41
Brooklyn Av. Hud —4D 132
Brooklyn Av. Leeds —7M 61
Brooklyn Ct. Cleck —4H 95
Brooklyn Dri. Cleck —4H 95
Brooklyn Grange. Cleck —4J 95
Brooklyn Pl. Leeds —7M 61
Brooklyn Rd. Cleck —4H 95
Brooklyn St. Kei —5G 20
Brooklyn St. Leeds —7M 61
Brooklyn Ter. Brigh —7K 93
Brooklyn Ter. Leeds —7M 61
Brook Rd. Dew —4E 116
Brook Row. G'lnd —7B 112
Brookroyd. —4D 96
Brookroyd Av. Brigh —6N 93
Brookroyd Gdns. Bat —4C 96
Brookroyd La. Bat —3C 96
Brooks Bank. —5K 119
Brooksbank. Wake —5K 119
Brooksbank Av. B'frd —9K 57
Brooksbank Dri. Leeds —6B 64
Brooksbank Gdns. Ell —5E 112
Brooksfield. S Kirk —5K 157
Brookside. Coll —9J 17
Brookside. H Bri —9F 70
Brookside. Hems —2E 156
Brook Side. Slai —8M 129
Brookside Fold. Oxe —4C 54
Brookside St. S Elm —6M 157
Brookside Ter. S Elm —6M 157
Brooks Ter. Q'bry —3G 75
Brook St. C'frd —1J 103
Brook St. Dew M —2C 116
Brook St. Ell —5F 112
Brook St. H Bri —9H 71
Brook St. Hud —3M 131
(in two parts)
Brook St. I'ly —5G 8
Brook St. Kei —2H 37
Brook St. Mold —4B 132
Brook St. Nor —9G 100
Brook St. Oss —6N 117
Brook St. Thor L —6K 131
Brook St. Todm —7K 87
Brook St. Wake —5L 119
Brooks Yd. Bdly —5E 114
Brooks Yd. Dew —4E 116
Brook's Yd. Hud —4M 131
Brook Ter. L'ft —2E 90
Brook Ter. Slai —8N 129
Brookway. F'stne —6D 122
Broombank. Den D —3C 166
Broombank. Hud —9J 113
Broom Clo. Brigh —4K 113
Broom Clo. Leeds —6H 81
Broom Ct. Leeds —7H 81
Broom Cres. Leeds —6G 81
Broom Cft. Cytn —1G 75
Broomcroft Rd. Oss —7N 117
Broom Cross. Leeds —6G 81
Broome Av. B'frd —3C 58
Broome Clo. Altft —8H 101
Broomer St. Dew —5B 116
Broomfield. Cleck —6G 94
(off W. End Dri.)
Broomfield. Ell —5C 112
Broomfield. Leeds —3L 43
Broomfield Av. Hal —9A 92
Broomfield Clo. Eml —2F 150
Broomfield Cres. Leeds —2N 61
Broom Fld. La. Eml —1E 150
Broomfield Pl. Cytn —2F 74
Broomfield Pl. Kei —9H 21
Broomfield Pl. Leeds —3N 61
Broomfield Rd. Fix —7M 113
Broomfield Rd. Kei —9H 21
Broomfield Rd. Leeds —2N 61
Broomfield Rd. Mar —4J 131
Broomfields. —9D 58
Broomfield St. Kei —9H 21
Broomfield St. Leeds —3N 61
Broomfield St. Q'bry —4D 74
Broomfield Ter. Cleck —6F 94
Broomfield Ter. Hud —3J 131
Broomfield Ter. Leeds —3N 61
Broomfield Vw. Leeds —3N 61
Broom Gdns. Leeds —6G 81
Broom Gth. Leeds —6H 81
Broom Gro. Leeds —7H 81
Broom Hall Av. Wake —1J 119
Broom Hall Cres. Wake —1J 119
Broomhead Ct. M'well —9K 153
Broomhey Av. Eml —3G 150
Broomhill. —9G 105
Broomhill. C'frd —6G 103
Broomhill Av. Kei —2G 36
Broomhill Av. Knot —9G 104
Broomhill Av. Leeds —5F 44
Broomhill Bottom. Holy G —1L 129
Broomhill Clo. H'frth —5B 164
Broomhill Clo. Knot —9G 105
Broomhill Cres. Knot —9G 104
Broomhill Cres. Leeds —5F 44
Broomhill Dri. Kei —2G 37
Broomhill Dri. Knot —9G 105
Broomhill Dri. Leeds —6E 44
Broomhill Gro. Kei —2G 37
Broomhill Gro. Knot —9G 104
Broomhill Mt. Kei —2G 37
Broomhill Pl. Knot —9G 104
Broom Hill Rd. Leeds —5K 63
Broom Hill Rd. Slnd —3K 129
Broomhill Sq. Knot —9G 104
Broomhill St. Kei —3G 37
Broomhill Ter. Bat —9G 96
Broomhill Wlk. Kei —2G 37
Broomhill Wlk. Knot —9G 104
Broomhill Way. Kei —2G 37
Broomhouse Clo. Den D —3D 166
Broom Lawn. Leeds —6G 81
Broom Mt. Leeds —7H 81
Broom Nook. Leeds —6H 81
Broom Pl. Leeds —6H 81
Broom Rd. Leeds —7G 81
Broom Rd. Tad —6N 33
Broomroyd. Hud —4E 130
Broomsdale Rd. Bat —6H 97
Broom St. B'frd —8D 58
Broom St. Cleck —6F 94
Broom Ter. Leeds —6H 81
Broom Vw. Leeds —6H 81
Broom Wlk. Bat —7H 97
Broom Wlk. Leeds —7H 81
Broomy Lea La. Nthng —1L 163
Broster Av. Kei —9F 20
Brotherton. —4B 104
Brotherton Av. Wake —4N 119
Brotherton By-Pass. Knot —3B 104
Brougham Rd. Hal —3B 92
Brougham Rd. Mars —5F 144
Brougham St. Hal —3B 92
Brougham Ter. Hal —2B 92
Broughton Av. B'frd —4F 76
Broughton Av. Leeds —4J 63
Broughton Ho. B'frd —4K 77
Broughton Rd. Hud —7G 131
Broughton St. H Bri —9H 71
Broughtons Yd. F'bri —7B 104
(off Argyle Rd.)
Broughtons Yd. Knot —7B 104
Broughton Ter. Leeds —4J 63
Broughton Ter. S'ley —6B 60
Brow Bottom. —8H 73
Brow Bottom La. Hal —7G 73
Browcliff. Sils —7E 6
Browfield Ter. Sils —7E 6
Browfoot. Shipl —7B 40
Browfoot Dri. Hal —6K 91
Brow Foot Ga. Hal —6K 91
(off Brow Foot Ga. La.)
Brow Foot Ga. La. Hal —6K 91
Browgate. Bail —4A 40
Brow Grains Rd. Mel —8N 145
Brow La. Cytn —2D 74
Brow La. Den D —2H 167
Brow La. Hal —7N 73
Brow La. H'frth —5K 163
Brow La. She —7J 75
Brow La. Shib —9D 74
Brown Av. Leeds —1A 80
Brown Bank Cvn. Site. Sils —5H 7
Brown Bank La. Sils —7F 6
Brownberrie Av. H'fth —4F 42
Brownberrie Cres. H'fth —4E 42
Brownberrie Dri. H'fth —4F 42
(in two parts)
Brownberrie Gdns. H'fth —4E 42
Brownberrie La. H'fth —4C 42
Brownberrie Wlk. H'fth —4F 42
Brownberry Gro. Hal —6J 75
Brown Birks St. Todm —3D 86
Brown Hill. —4C 96
Brown Hill Av. Leeds —4J 63
Brownhill Clo. Bat —3C 96
Brown Hill Clo. B'shaw —6L 77
Brownhill Cres. Kin —8A 140
Brown Hill Cres. Leeds —4J 63
Brown Hill Dri. B'shaw —7L 77
Brownhill End. —3C 96
Brownhill Gth. Bat —3C 96
Brown Hill La. Blkhd —9N 69
Brownhill La. H'frth —8F 162
Brownhill Rd. Bat —3C 96
Brown Hill Ter. Leeds —4J 63
Browning Av. Hal —9C 92
Browning Rd. Hud —8B 114
Browning St. B'frd —7F 58
Brown La. E. Leeds —9B 62
Brown La. W. Leeds —9A 62
Brownlea Clo. Yead —2K 41
Brown Lee La. Wilsd —2N 55
Brown Pl. Leeds —1A 80
Brown Rd. Leeds —1A 80
Brown Royd. —6N 57
Brown Royd Av. Hud —3B 132
Brownroyd Av. Roys —7D 154
Brownroyd Hill. —4A 76
Brownroyd Hill Rd. B'frd —4N 75
Brownroyd Rd. Hon —5K 147
Brownroyd St. B'frd —6N 57
Brownroyd Wlk. B'frd —3N 75
Browns Edge Rd. Pen —8J 165
Brown's Knoll Rd. Hud —6D 148
Brown's Pl. Bat —8E 96
Brown's St. Bat —8F 96
Brown's Ter. Bat —8E 96
(off Brown's Pl.)
Brown St. Kei —8K 21
Brown St. Mir —6K 115
Brow Quarry Ind. Est. Hal —6J 93
Brow Rd. Haw —9D 36
Browsfield Rd. Add —1K 7
Browsholme St. Kei —1J 37
Brow St. Kei —1K 37
Brow Top. Cytn —3F 74
Brow Top Rd. Cro R —9D 36
Brow Wood Cres. B'frd —3C 58
Brow Wood Ri. Hal —7J 75
Brow Wood Rd. Hal —7J 75
Brow Wood Ter. B'frd —6L 75
Bruce Gdns. Leeds —7A 62
Bruce Lawn. Leeds —7A 62
Bruce St. Hal —6M 91
Brudenell Av. Leeds —3B 62
Brudenell Gro. Leeds —3B 62
Brudenell Mt. Leeds —3A 62
Brudenell Rd. Leeds —3A 62
Brudenell St. Leeds —3B 62
Brudenell Vw. Leeds —3B 62
Brunel Clo. B'frd —4M 57
Brunel Ct. B'frd —4E 58
Brunel Ct. Hal —2A 92
(off See Mill La.)
Brunel Gdns. B'frd —2A 76
(off Ida St.)
Brunel Rd. Wake I —7H 99
Brunswick. Ryh —8J 139
Brunswick Arc. Kei —9J 21
(off Airedale Shop. Cen.)
Brunswick Ct. Leeds —5F 62
Brunswick Dri. Dew —2D 116
Brunswick Gdns. Gar —7N 65
Brunswick Gdns. Hal —5A 92
Brunswick Gro. Wake —5M 119
Brunswick Ho. Bgly —5G 38
Brunswick Pl. B'frd —8H 41
Brunswick Pl. Morl —9L 79
(off Clough St.)
Brunswick Rd. B'frd —8H 41
Brunswick Rd. Pud —6B 60
Brunswick Row. Leeds —5F 62
Brunswick St. Bat —7F 96
Brunswick St. Cull —9L 37
Brunswick St. Dew —2D 116
Brunswick St. Fern —4G 38
Brunswick St. H Bri —1G 89
Brunswick St. Heck —9A 96
Brunswick St. Hud —4M 131
Brunswick St. Morl —8K 79
Brunswick St. Q'bry —4E 74
Brunswick St. Wake —5M 119
Brunswick Ter. Leeds —5E 62
Brunswick Ter. Low M —6A 76
Brunswick Ter. Morl —9M 79
Bruntcliffe. —9H 79
Bruntcliffe Av. Morl —9H 79
Bruntcliffe Clo. Morl —9J 79
Bruntcliffe Dri. Morl —9J 79
Bruntcliffe La. Morl —9H 79
Bruntcliffe Rd. Morl —9G 79
Bruntcliffe Way. Morl —9H 79
Brunthwaite. —8G 6
Brunthwaite Bri. La. Sils —1F 20
Brunthwaite La. Sils —8G 6
Brussels St. Leeds —7F 62
Bryan Clo. C'frd —4A 102
Bryan La. Hud —8H 113
Bryan Rd. Ell —5C 112
Bryan Rd. Hud —2J 131
Bryanstone Rd. B'frd —9H 59
Bryan St. Brigh —2M 113
Bryan St. Fars —2A 60
Bryan St. N. Far —2A 60
Bryan Ter. Hud —4D 130
Bryer St. Dew —3F 116
Bryngate. Oult —7D 82
Bryony Ct. Leeds —8H 81
Bubwith Gro. Hal —6L 91
(off Trimmingham Rd.)
Buchan Towers. B'frd —9C 58
(off Radwell Dri.)
Buckden Ct. Hud —3G 130
(off Chesil Bank)
Buckden Ct. Sils —7E 6
Buckden Rd. Hud —2J 131
Buckfast Ct. B'frd —8F 40
Buckingham Av. Leeds —2A 62
Buckingham Ct. Wake —7A 120
Buckingham Cres. Cytn —9J 57
Buckingham Dri. Leeds —2A 62
Buckingham Dri. Wake —8A 120
Buckingham Gro. Leeds —2A 62
Buckingham Ho. Leeds —2A 62
(off Headingley La.)
Buckingham Mt. Leeds —3A 62
Buckingham Rd. Leeds —3A 62
Buckingham Way. Byr —5D 104
Buckingham Way. Roys —5C 154
Buckland Pl. Hal —6L 91
Buckland Rd. B'frd —6L 57
Buck La. Bail —4D 40
Buckle La. Men —5F 24
Buckle La. Nor —1H 121
Buckley Av. Leeds —2D 80
Buckley La. Hal —2J 91
(in two parts)
Buckley Vw. Todm —6J 87
Buck Mill La. B'frd —5E 40
Buckrose St. Hud —1M 131
Buck Stone Av. Leeds —3B 44
Buck Stone Clo. Leeds —3C 44
Buck Stone Cres. Leeds —3C 44
Buck Stone Dri. Leeds —3B 44
Buckstone Dri. Rawd —4L 41
(in two parts)
Buck Stone Gdns. Leeds —3C 44
Buck Stone Grn. Leeds —3B 44
Buck Stone Gro. Leeds —3B 44
Buck Stone Mt. Leeds —3B 44
Buck Stone Oval. Leeds —3B 44
Buck Stone Ri. Leeds —3B 44
Buck Stone Rd. Leeds —3B 44
Buck Stone Vw. Leeds —3B 44
Buck Stone Way. Leeds —3B 44
Buck St. B'frd —8E 58
Buck St. Denh —6L 55
Buckthorne Clo. E Ard —4F 98
Buckthorne Ct. E Ard —4F 98
Buckthorne Dri. E Ard —4F 98
Buckthorne Fold. E Ard —4F 98
Buckton Clo. Leeds —1C 80
Buckton Mt. Leeds —1C 80
Buckton Vw. Leeds —1C 80
Bude Rd. B'frd —4D 76
Bude Rd. Leeds —2D 80
Bugler Ter. Horb —1A 136
Bula Clo. Kip —3B 84
Bulay Rd. Hud —6L 131
Bullace Trees La. Liv —9J 95
Bull Clo. La. Hal —6A 92
Bullenshaw Rd. Hems —3D 156
Buller Clo. Leeds —5L 63
Buller Ct. Leeds —5L 63
Buller Gro. Leeds —5K 63
Buller St. B'frd —9G 59
Buller St. Rothw —7D 82
Bullerthorpe La. Leeds —8G 64
Bullerthorpe La. W'ford —5F 82
Bullfields Clo. Dew —9H 117
Bullfield, The. H'den —7A 38
Bull Grn. Hal —5B 92
Bull Grn. Rd. Hud —4E 130
Bull Haw La. Silk —8N 167
Bull La. Crig —5H 137
Bull La. S Kirk —7J 157

Bullough La. Rothw —6A 82
Bull Ring. Wake —5L 119
Bullroyd Av. B'frd —6K 57
Bullroyd Cres. B'frd —6K 57
Bullroyd Dri. B'frd —6K 57
Bullroyd La. B'frd —6K 57
Bullstyle Rd. Pon —5J 123
Bungalows, The. Clay W —7H 151
Bungalows, The. F'stne —7D 122
(off Bedford Clo.)
Bungalows, The. Hal —1D 112
(nr. Backhold Av.)
Bungalows, The. Hal —1M 91
(nr. Grove Pk.)
Bungalows, The. Hal —3K 91
(nr. Ryecroft Cres.)
Bungalows, The. Hal —2M 91
(off Ovenden Grn.)
Bungalows, The. Leeds —3E 64
(off Church La.)
Bungalows, The. Nor —7H 101
Bunkers Hill. Aber —9E 48
Bunkers Hill. Esh —2F 40
Bunkers Hill. H'frth —3M 163
Bunkers Hill. Wren —1H 119
Bunker's Hill La. Kei —2D 36
Bunkers La. Bat —8C 96
Bunny Pk. Lock —7J 131
Bunting Dri. Q'bry —4G 75
Burbeary Rd. Hud —7K 131
Burberry Clo. B'frd —5G 77
Burchett Gro. Leeds —2C 62
Burchett Pl. Leeds —2C 62
Burchett Ter. Leeds —2D 62
Burcote Dri. Outl —1A 130
Burdale Pl. B'frd —8N 57
Burdett Ter. Leeds —4M 61
Burdock Way. Hal —6A 92
(in two parts)
Burfitts Rd. Hud —3G 130
Burgh Mill La. Dew —4C 116
Burghwallis. —4N 159
Burghwallis La. Sut —4N 159
Burghwallis Rd. Burg —4N 159
Burhouse Ct. Hon —5L 147
(off Cuckoo La.)
Burkill St. Wake —9M 119
Burking Rd. Dew —3E 116
Burland Ter. Swil —3H 83
Burlees La. H Bri —1K 89
Burleigh St. Hal —7M 91
Burley. —5M 61
Burley Bank La. Holme —1D 168
Burley Ct. Steet —3C 20
Burley Grange Rd. Leeds —4M 61
Burley Hill Cres. Leeds —3L 61
Burley Hill Dri. Leeds —3L 61
Burley in Wharfedale. —8C 10
Burley La. H'fth —8E 42
Burley La. Men —4D 24
Burley Lodge Pl. Leeds —5A 62
(off Burley Lodge Rd.)
Burley Lodge Rd. Leeds —4A 62
Burley Lodge St. Leeds —5A 62
Burley Lodge Ter. Leeds —5A 62
Burley M. Steet —3C 20
Burley Pl. Leeds —5N 61
Burley Rd. Leeds —3M 61
Burley Rd. Men —2E 24
Burley Rd. Trad. Est. Leeds —3M 61
Burley St. B'frd —2B 58
Burley St. Ell —5E 112
Burley St. Leeds —6B 62
Burley Wlk. Bat —7E 96
Burley Wood Cres. Leeds —3L 61
Burley Woodhead. —2A 24
Burley Wood La. Leeds —3M 61
Burley Wood Mt. Leeds —3L 61
Burley Wood Vw. Leeds —3M 61
Burlington Av. B'frd —5J 59
Burlington Pl. Leeds —3D 80
Burlington Rd. Leeds —3D 80
Burlington St. B'frd —5B 58
Burlington St. Hal —5M 91
Burmah St. Hal —5M 91
Burmantofts. —5J 63
Burmantofts St. Leeds —6G 62
Burned Gro. Hal —6H 75
Burned Rd. Hal —6H 75
Burneston Gdns. B'frd —5K 75
Burnett Av. B'frd —2B 76
Burnett Pl. B'frd —2B 76
Burnett Ri. Q'bry —5B 74
Burnett St. B'frd —7D 58
Burnham Av. B'frd —3F 76
Burnham Av. M'well —8K 153
Burnham Ct. Weth —3K 17
Burnham Rd. Gar —9N 65
Burnhill La. Pon —4M 141
Burniston Clo. Wilsd —2B 56
Burniston Dri. Hud —2F 130
Burnlee. —4J 163
Burnlee Rd. H'frth —4K 163
Burnley Hill Ter. Hal —9G 74
Burnley Rd. Hal —6K 91
Burnley Rd. H Bri —3L 89
Burnley Rd. L'ft & Sower B —6D 90
Burnley Rd. Todm —1A 86
Burnleys Ct. Meth —4L 101
Burnleys Dri. Meth —4L 101
Burnleys M. Meth —4L 101
Burnleys Vw. Meth —3L 101
Burnleyville. Gom —3M 95
Burn Rd. Hud —9H 113
Burnsall Av. Bat —7D 96
Burnsall Ct. Hud —4G 131
(off Chesil Bank)
Burnsall Ct. Leeds —6L 61
Burnsall Cft. Leeds —6L 61
Burnsall Gdns. Leeds —6L 61
Burnsall Grange. Leeds —7L 61
(off Gelder Rd.)
Burnsall Ho. B'frd —9G 41
(off Rowantree Dri.)
Burnsall M. Sils —7E 6
Burnsall Rd. Bat —7D 96
Burnsall Rd. B'frd —7F 58
(in two parts)
Burnsall Rd. Brigh —3K 113
Burnsall Rd. Liv —8K 95
Burns Av. S Kirk —8F 156
Burns Ct. Bat —2A 96
Burnsdale. All —3F 56
Burnshaw M. Leeds —1F 98
Burns Hill. Add —1L 7
Burnside Av. Hal —7J 75
Burnside Clo. Bat —3D 96
Burnside Dri. H'frth —4K 163
Burns St. Hal —9M 73
Burns Way. Cliff —2D 32
Burnt Acres La. Todm —4C 88
Burnt Edge La. Blkhd —9M 69
Burnt Ho. Clo. Todm —6L 87
Burnt Plats La. Slai —8F 128
Burnt Side Rd. Leeds —3F 78
Burntwood Av. S Kirk —7J 157
Burntwood Bank. Hems —4D 156
Burntwood Cres. S Kirk —7J 157
Burntwood Dri. S Kirk —7H 157
Burntwood Gro. S Kirk —8J 157
Burnt Wood La. Brier —8E 156
Burnup Gro. Cleck —5G 95
Burnwells. —5E 40
Burnwells. B'frd —5E 40
Burnwells Av. B'frd —5E 40
Burrage St. Bgly —4E 38
Burras Av. Otley —1K 25
Burras Dri. Otley —1K 25
Burras La. Otley —1K 25
Burras Rd. B'frd —3F 76
Burrell Clo. Weth —4A 18
Burrell St. Wake —5M 119
Burrows, The. Bat —5C 96
Burrow St. B'frd —8C 58
Burr Tree Dri. Leeds —7E 64
Burr Tree Gth. Leeds —7E 64
Burr Tree Va. Leeds —7E 64
Burrwood Ter. Holy G —6A 112
Burrwood Way. Holy G —6A 112
Burton Acres Dri. Kbtn —2J 149
Burton Acres La. Kbtn —2J 149
Burton Acres M. Kbtn —2J 149
Burton Acres Way. Kbtn —2J 149
Burton Av. Leeds —2E 80
Burton Comn. La. Knot —1D 104
Burton Cres. Leeds —9N 43
Burton M. Leeds —2F 44
Burton Rd. Leeds —2E 80
Burton Row. Leeds —1E 80
Burton Royd La. Kbtn —2L 149
(in two parts)
Burton Salmon. —1D 104
Burton's Arc. Leeds —7E 62
Burton St. B'frd —1E 76
Burton St. Fars —3A 60
Burton St. Hal —8N 73
Burton St. Kei —6H 21
Burton St. Leeds —1E 80
Burton St. S Elm —7M 157
Burton St. Wake —4K 119
Burton Ter. Leeds —2E 80
Burton Way. Leeds —5J 63
Burwood Rd. Hud —2G 131
Bury La. Sandb —7B 22
Busfield St. Bgly —4E 38
Busfield St. B'frd —2F 76
Bushill Fold. Q'bry —3B 74
Bush St. Hems —3E 156
Busker La. Skelm —8F 150
Buslingthorpe. —2E 62
Buslingthorpe Grn. Leeds —3E 62
Buslingthorpe La. Leeds —2E 62
Buslingthorpe Va. Leeds —2E 62
Bussey Ct. Leeds —3C 62
Busy La. Shipl —6C 40
Butcher Hill. Hems —1E 156
Butcher Hill. Leeds & H'fth —7H 43
Butcher La. Rothw —8N 81
Butchers Gap La. Wake —5H 121
Butchers Row. Leeds —6E 62
(off Kirkgate Mkt.)
Butcher St. B'frd —8B 58
Butcher St. Leeds —8D 62
Bute Av. Brigh —7M 93
Bute St. B'frd —2B 58
Butler La. Bail —4B 40
(in two parts)
Butler St. E. B'frd —6E 58
Butler St. W. B'frd —6E 58
Butterbowl Dri. Leeds —9H 61
Butterbowl Gdns. Leeds —9J 61
Butterbowl Gth. Leeds —9H 61
Butterbowl Gro. Leeds —9H 61
Butterbowl Lawn. Leeds —9H 61
Butterbowl Mt. Leeds —9J 61
Butterbowl Rd. Leeds —9J 61
Buttercross. Old Sk —8M 159
Buttercross Clo. Skel —7M 159
Buttercup Clo. Upt —2M 157
Butterfield Ind. Est. Bail —5C 40
Butterfield's Bldgs. Morl —8J 79
Butterfield St. Leeds —7H 63
Butterley La. N Mill —4C 164
Butterley St. Leeds —9E 62
Buttermere Av. Weth —3K 17
Buttermere Clo. Carc —8N 159
Buttermere Cft. W'ton —4B 138
Buttermere Dri. Hud —4B 132
Buttermere Rd. B'frd —3E 58
Buttermere Wlk. Knot —1D 124
Butternab Ridge. Hud —1J 147
Butternab Rd. Hud —9H 131
Buttershaw. —6L 75
Buttershaw Dri. B'frd —5K 75
Buttershaw La. B'frd —6N 75
Buttershaw La. Liv —7F 94
Butterton Clo. M'well —8L 153
Butterwick Gdns. Weth —4K 17
Butterwood Clo. Hud —1J 147
Butterworth End La. Norl —3G 111
Butterworth Hill. Hud —3N 129
Butterworth La. Sower B —1E 110
Butt Hill. Kip —4A 84
Buttholme Ga. B'frd —5L 75
Butt La. B'frd —7F 40
Butt La. Hamp —9F 158
Butt La. Haw —8C 36
Butt La. H'frth —6C 164
Butt La. Leeds —8G 61
Button Hill. Leeds —2F 62
Button Pk. Pon —4J 123
Buttress La. Ludd —3E 90
Butts Bottom. Err —3H 89
Butts Clo. Far T —3C 148
Butts Ct. Leeds —6E 62
Butts Gth. T'ner —2G 47
Butts Gth. Vw. T'ner —2G 47
Butts Gth. Wlk. T'ner —2G 46
Butts Grn. La. Hal —5F 90
Butts Hill. Gom —4M 95
Butts La. Guis —7J 25
Butts La. M'twn —3L 135
Butts La. Todm —3M 87
Butts Mt. Leeds —7N 61
Butts Rd. Far T —3C 148
Butts Ter. Guis —7J 25
Butts, The. E Mor —8C 22
(off Morton La.)
Butts, The. Pon —2K 123
Butts Way. Far T —3C 148
Butts Yd. Cleck —5H 95
Buxton Av. B'frd —2A 58
Buxton Ho. Hud —5M 131
(off New St.)
Buxton La. B'frd —2A 58
Buxton La. Holy G —7M 111
Buxton Pl. Wake —3K 119
Buxton St. B'frd —4N 57
Buxton St. Hal —3N 91
Buxton St. Kei —9K 21
Byeway. Guis —7G 24
Byland. Hal —6K 73
Byland Clo. B Spa —1C 32
Byland Gro. All —4E 56
Bylands Av. Riddl —6L 21
Byram. —4C 104
Byram Arc. Hud —4M 131
(off Station St.)
Byram Pk. Av. Byr —4D 104
Byram Pk. Rd. Byr —4C 104
Byram St. Hud —4N 131
Byrl St. Kei —8K 21
Byrom St. Todm —6K 87
Byron Av. Sower B —7H 91
Byron Clo. Knot —8A 104
Byron Gro. Dew —1B 116
Byron Gro. Stan —6N 99
Byron M. Bgly —2F 38
Byron St. B'frd —6F 58
Byron St. Hal —5M 91
Byron St. Leeds —5F 62
Byron St. Sower B —7H 91
Bywater Row. B'shaw —8M 77
Byways, The. Pon —5K 123
Bywell Clo. Dew —3K 117
Bywell Rd. Dew —2J 117

Cabbage Hill. Leeds —8L 61
Cabin La. N Mill —3B 164
Cabin Rd. Pool W —3E 26
Cable St. Hud —6M 131
Cackleshaw. —5E 36
Cad Beeston. Leeds —2C 80
Cad Beeston M. Leeds —2C 80
Caddy Field. —6D 92
Cadney Cft. Hal —6B 92
(off Harrison Rd.)
Cadogan Av. Hud —2G 131
Cadwell Clo. Cud —9K 155
Caenarvon Clo. Bat —3D 96
Caernarvon Av. Gar —7B 66
Cain Clo. Leeds —7H 63
Cain La. Hal —8F 92
Cairns Clo. B'frd —3D 58
Caister Clo. Bat —2D 96
Caister Gro. Kei —3H 37
(off Caister Way.)
Caister St. Kei —3H 37
Caister Way. Kei —3H 37
Caistor Gth. B'frd —9G 41
(off Rowantree Dri.)
Calde Ct. Low M —7C 76
Caldene Av. H Bri —3L 89
Caldene Av. Low M —7C 76
Calder Av. Hal —7M 91
Calder Av. Roys —6F 154
Calder Bank Rd. Dew —5E 116
Calder Banks. —4F 74
Calder Banks. Q'bry —4F 74
Calderbrook. —9L 107
Calderbrook Rd. L'boro —9L 107
Caldercliffe Rd. Hud —9L 131
Calder Clo. C'frd —4H 103
Calder Clo. G'lnd —4C 112
(off Calder St.)
Calder Clo. Oss —6M 117
Calder Clo. Weth —1L 17
Caldercroft. Ell —5F 112
Calderdale Bus. Pk. Hal —1M 91
Calderdale Industrial Museum. —5C 92
Calderdale Way. G'lnd & Ell —4D 112
Calder Dri. Hud —1L 147
Calder Grove. —4F 136
Calder Gro. H Bri —3M 89
Calder Ho. Ell —4E 112
(off Southgate)
Calder Island Way. Wake —9K 119
Calder Mt. Crig —5G 137
Calder Rd. Dew —6C 116
Calder Rd. Mir —8L 115
Calderside. —1F 88
Calderstone Av. B'frd —5J 75
Calder St. Brigh —2A 114
Calder St. C'frd —4C 102
Calder St. G'lnd —4C 112
Calder St. Todm —7K 87
Calder St. Wake —7M 119
Calder Ter. Hal —2N 111
Calder Ter. H Bri —1G 89
Calder Ter. Horb —2E 136
Calder Trad. Est. Brigh —6N 93
Calder Vale. —6N 119
Caldervale. Roys —5F 154
Calder Va. Rd. Wake —6M 119
Calder Vw. Crig —5G 136
Calder Vw. Oss —6L 117
Calder Vw. Ras —2L 113
Calder Way. Sils —9E 6
Caldicott Clo. Todm —9H 87
Caledonia Ct. K'gte —1D 118
Caledonian Rd. Dew —5F 116
Caledonia Rd. Bat —7G 96
Caledonia Rd. Kei —8K 21
Caledonia St. B'frd —9C 58
Calf Hey Ter. Todm —2H 107
Calf Hill Rd. Thon —8N 147
Calgary Cres. Wake —5B 98
Calgary Pl. Leeds —9F 44
California Dri. Horb —1E 136
California Dri. Todm —9J 87
California Dri. W'wood —7L 101
California La. Gom —5M 95
California M. Morl —7L 79
California St. Morl —9L 79
Call La. Leeds —7E 62
Calls, The. Leeds —7E 62
Calmlands. —8D 146
Calmlands Rd. Mel —8C 146
Calpin Clo. Idle —7F 40
Calton Gro. Kei —1M 37
Calton Rd. Kei —1M 37
Calton St. Hud —2N 131
Calton St. Kei —2H 37
(in two parts)
Calver Av. Kei —8F 20
Calver Gro. Kei —9G 20
Calverley. —8M 41
Calverley Av. B'frd —6H 59
Calverley Av. Leeds —3E 60
Calverley Bridge. —9B 42
Calverley Ct. Leeds —3E 60
Calverley Ct. W'ford —8C 82
Calverley Cutting. B'frd —7K 41
Calverley Dri. Leeds —3E 60
Calverley Gdns. Leeds —2D 60
Calverley Gth. Leeds —3E 60
Calverley Grn. Rd. Nor —9G 100
Calverley Gro. Leeds —3E 60
Calverley La. C'ley —9N 41
(in two parts)
Calverley La. H'fth —8B 42
Calverley La. Leeds —2C 60
Calverley Moor Av. Pud —5L 59
Calverley Rd. W'ford —8D 82
Calverley St. Leeds —5D 62
Calverley Ter. Leeds —3E 60
Calver Rd. Kei —9G 20
Calversyke St. Kei —9G 20
Calvert Clo. Kip —2A 84
Calverts Wlk. Oss —7B 118
Camargue Fold. B'frd —2D 58
Camberley Clo. Pud —8B 60
Camberley Mt. B'frd —1J 77
Camberley St. Leeds —2E 80
Camberley Way. Pud —8B 60
Camborne Dri. Hud —8L 113
Camborne Rd. Hud —8L 113
Camborne Way. Kei —2E 36
Cambrian Bar. Low M —7N 75
Cambrian St. Leeds —1C 80
Cambrian Ter. Leeds —1C 80
Cambridge. —1M 25
Cambridge Clo. Morl —8L 79
Cambridge Ct. Morl —9L 79
Cambridge Cres. Croft —8D 120
Cambridge Dri. Bmly —3E 60
Cambridge Dri. Otley —1M 25
Cambridge Gdns. Leeds —3E 60
Cambridge Gro. Kip —4A 84
Cambridge Gro. Otley —1M 25
Cambridge Pl. B'frd —6D 58
Cambridge Pl. Q'bry —4D 74
Cambridge Pl. Sid —9D 92
Cambridge Pl. Todm —7K 87
Cambridge Rd. Birs —3A 96
Cambridge Rd. Hud —3M 131
Cambridge Rd. Leeds —3D 62
Cambridge St. Bat —7F 96
Cambridge St. B'frd —1N 75
Cambridge St. C'frd —5D 102
Cambridge St. Cytn —1G 75
Cambridge St. Guis —7J 25
Cambridge St. H Bri —1G 88
Cambridge St. Heck —9B 96
Cambridge St. Nor —2H 121
Cambridge St. Otley —1L 25
Cambridge St. Q'bry —4E 74
Cambridge St. S Elm —6L 157
Cambridge St. Todm —7K 87
Cambridge St. Wake —6J 119
Cambridge Ter. Otley —1L 25
Cambridge Ter. Sid —9D 92
(off Cambridge Pl.)
Cambridge Way. Otley —1M 25
Camden Rd. C'frd —4K 103
Camden St. Sower B —9H 91
Camden Ter. B'frd —5B 58
Camellia Clo. Wake —8F 118
Camellia Mt. B'frd —8K 57
Camelot Ct. Pon —3L 123
Cameron Av. Wyke —3N 93
Camerton Grn. B'frd —3D 76
Camilla Ct. Dew —4J 117
Cam La. Brigh —8B 94
Camm La. Mir —5M 115
Camm St. Brigh —9N 93
Campbell St. Kei —9J 21
Campbell St. Q'bry —4E 74
Campbell St. S'ley —4A 60
Campden Rd. H Bri —9F 70
Camp Field. —8D 62
Campinot Va. Slai —9M 129
Campion Clo. Pon —4K 123
Camp Mt. Pon —3H 123
Camp Ri. Pon —3H 123
Camp Rd. B'hpe —7G 27
Camp Rd. S Kirk —8F 156
Campsmount Dri. Cam —1N 159
Camp Sq. T'ner —2G 46
Camp Town. —3D 44
Campus Rd. B'frd —8A 58
Camroyd St. Dew —2G 117

anada Cres. Rawd —3N 41
anada Dri. Rawd —2N 41
anada Rd. Rawd —2N 41
anada Ter. Rawd —3N 41
anal Ct. Loft —6M 99
anal La. Sils —1G 21
anal La. Stan —6L 99
anal Pl. Leeds —7B 62
anal Rd. A'ley —6M 61
anal Rd. Bgly —1D 38
anal Rd. B'frd —1A 58
anal Rd. Leeds —1B 60
anal Rd. Riddl —7L 21
anal Rd. Sower B —8K 91
anal St. Brigh —1N 113
anal St. Hal —6C 92
anal St. Hud —2A 132
anal St. Leeds —7A 62
anal St. Todm —7K 87
anal Wlk. Stan —6A 100
anal Wharf. Kirks —3J 61
anal Wharf. Leeds —7D 62
anary St. Cleck —4H 95
anberra Clo. Cro R —7F 36
anberra Dri. Cro R —7F 36
anby Gro. Hud —5F 132
anford Dri. All —5G 57
anford Gro. All —5H 57
anford Rd. All —5G 56
anker La. Hal —1N 91
anker La. Hud —1A 132
anning Av. Wake —3F 118
anning St. B'frd —9E 58
annon Gro. Heck —7B 96
annon Hall Clo. Brigh —9B 94
annon Hall Dri. Brigh —1B 114
annon Mill La. B'frd —1M 75
annon St. Bgly —5F 38
annon St. C'frd —7E 102
annon St. Todm —9J 87
annon Way. Dew —4F 116
anon St. Hal —7M 91
anteen Mill Ind. Est. Todm —4F 86
anterbury Av. B'frd —2A 76
anterbury Ct. Pon —9L 103
anterbury Cres. Hal —3A 92
anterbury Dri. Leeds —2M 61
anterbury Rd. Dew —2J 117
anterbury Rd. Leeds —2M 61
apas Heights Way. Heck —9B 96
ape Ind. Est. Far —3B 60
apel Ct. C'ley —9M 41
apel St. Brigh —2M 113
apel St. C'ley —9M 41
ape of Good Hope. Q'bry —5B 74
ape St. B'frd —6C 58
apitol Pde. Leeds —8B 44
aprington Ct. Norm —2L 121
aptain St. B'frd —7D 58
arberry Pl. Leeds —4A 62
arberry Rd. Leeds —4A 62
arberry Ter. Leeds —4A 62 (off Carberry Pl.)
arcroft. —8N 159
ardan Dri. I'ly —5K 9
arden Av. Leeds —7N 63
arden Rd. B'frd —9J 59
ardigan Av. Morl —2K 97
ardigan Clo. Bat —7H 97
ardigan Ct. Leeds —2A 62
ardigan Fields Rd. Leeds —5M 61
ardigan La. Leeds —4N 61 (in three parts)
ardigan La. Oss —8C 118
ardigan Rd. Leeds —2N 61
ardigan St. Q'bry —4E 74
ardigan Ter. E Ard —4G 98
ardigan Ter. Wake —4L 119
ardigan Trad. Est. Leeds —5N 61
ardinal Av. Leeds —5B 80
ardinal Clo. Mel —7D 146
ardinal Cres. Leeds —5B 80
ardinal Gdns. Leeds —5A 80
ardinal Gro. Leeds —5A 80
ardinal Rd. Leeds —5A 80
ardinal Sq. Leeds —4B 80
ardinal Wlk. Leeds —4A 80
ardwell Ter. Dew —5F 116
ardwell Ter. Knot —8G 104 (off Fernley Grn. Rd.)
arforth St. Asp —5A 132
arisbrooke Cres. B'frd —5N 75
arisbrooke La. Gar —6B 66
ark Rd. Kei —8J 21
arlby Gro. Kei —1G 37 (off Carlby St.)
arlby St. Kei —1G 37
arlecotes Ho. B'frd —1J 77 (off Ned La.)
arleton. —6M 123
arleton Clo. B Spa —9B 18
arleton Clo. Pon —4K 123
arleton Crest. Pon —5L 123
Carleton Dri. B Spa —1B 32
Carleton Ga. Pon —5K 123
Carleton Glen. Pon —3K 123
Carleton Grn. Pon —6L 123
Carleton Grn. Clo. Pon —5L 123
Carleton Pk. Av. Pon —5K 123
Carleton Pk. Rd. Pon —5K 123
Carleton Rd. Pon —4K 123
Carleton St. Kei —7H 21
Carleton Vw. Pon —5K 123
Carlile St. Mel —7D 146
Carling Clo. B'frd —2L 75
Carlinghow. —5D 96
Carlinghow Ct. Dew —9C 96 (off Occupation La.)
Carlinghow Hill. Bat —6E 96
Carlinghow La. Bat —5B 96
Carlisle Av. Yead —1N 41
Carlisle Clo. Dew —1F 116
Carlisle Dri. Pud —8A 60
Carlisle Gro. Pud —8A 60
Carlisle Pl. B'frd —5A 58
Carlisle Rd. B'frd —5N 57
Carlisle Rd. Leeds —8F 62
Carlisle Rd. Pud —8A 60
Carlisle St. B'frd —5A 58
Carlisle St. Far —5N 59
Carlisle St. Hal —4L 91
Carlisle St. Kei —9K 21
Carlisle Ter. B'frd —5A 58
Carlrayne La. Men —3E 24
Carlton. —1M 99 (nr. Rothwell)
Carlton. —8D 154 (nr. Royston)
Carlton App. Weth —3K 17
Carlton Av. Bat —9E 96
Carlton Av. C'frd —5F 102
Carlton Av. Pud —7B 60
Carlton Av. Shipl —7K 39
Carlton Carr. Leeds —4E 62
Carlton Clo. Cleck —5H 95
Carlton Clo. Hems —4C 156
Carlton Clo. Leeds —4E 62 (off Carlton Hill)
Carlton Clo. Nor —1J 121
Carlton Ct. Cleck —4H 95
Carlton Ct. Leeds —1A 80
Carlton Ct. Oss —5N 117
Carlton Ct. S Elm —6M 157 (off Carlton Gdns.)
Carlton Cft. Leeds —4E 62 (off Carlton Hill)
Carlton Cft. Wake —4M 137
Carlton Dri. Bail —3A 40
Carlton Dri. B'frd —2N 57
Carlton Dri. Gar —9N 65
Carlton Dri. Guis —6K 25
Carlton Dri. Shipl —1M 57
Carlton Gdns. Leeds —4E 62
Carlton Gdns. Norm —1K 121
Carlton Gdns. S Elm —6M 157
Carlton Gth. Leeds —4E 62 (off Carlton Hill)
Carlton Gth. Shad —2J 45
Carlton Ga. Leeds —4E 62
Carlton Grange. Yead —9N 25 (off Cemetery Rd.)
Carlton Green. —9E 154
Carlton Gro. B'frd —2B 76
Carlton Gro. Ell —4G 113
Carlton Gro. Leeds —4E 62
Carlton Gro. Shipl —1N 57
Carlton Hill. Leeds —4E 62
Carlton Ho. Ter. Hal —7N 91
Carlton Ind. Est. Cltn —9D 154 (in two parts)
Carlton La. Guis & Yead —6K 25
Carlton La. Loft —3L 99
Carlton La. Rothw —9M 81
Carlton Lanes Shop. Cen. C'frd (off Carlton St.) —4D 102
Carlton M. Guis —7K 25
Carlton Mill. Sower B —8K 91
Carlton Moor M. Leeds —8H 81
Carlton Mt. Yead —8N 25
Carlton Pde. Leeds —4E 62
Carlton Pl. Hal —6B 92
Carlton Pl. Leeds —4E 62
Carlton Ri. Leeds —4E 62
Carlton Ri. Pud —7B 60
Carlton Rd. Barn —9C 154
Carlton Rd. Dew —2F 116
Carlton Rd. Heck —6N 95
Carlton Rd. Liv —9L 95
Carlton Rd. Shipl —7K 39
Carlton Rd. S Elm —6M 157
Carlton Row. Leeds —7K 61
Carlton St. B'frd —8B 58
Carlton St. C'frd —4D 102 (in three parts)
Carlton St. F'stne —4D 122
Carlton St. Hal —6B 92
Carlton St. Haw —8D 36
Carlton St. H Bri —1H 89
Carlton St. Horb —1C 136
Carlton St. Nor —1K 121
Carlton St. Otley —1M 25
Carlton St. Wake —6J 119
Carlton Ter. Barn —8F 154
Carlton Ter. Dew —5G 116
Carlton Ter. Hal —6B 92
Carlton Ter. Pud —6B 60
Carlton Ter. Stainc —9D 96
Carlton Ter. Yead —9N 25
Carlton Towers. Leeds —4E 62
Carlton Trad. Est. Leeds —6N 61
Carlton Vw. All B —7N 83
Carlton Vw. Leeds —4E 62
Carlton Wlk. Leeds —4E 62
Carlton Wlk. Shipl —7L 39
Carlton Way. Cleck —5H 95
Carlyle Cres. C'frd —5G 103
Carlyle Rd. C'frd —5G 103
Carmel Rd. Hal —2B 92
Carmine Clo. Hud —4C 132
Carmona Av. Shipl —1N 57
Carmona Gdns. Shipl —1N 57
Carnaby Rd. B'frd —3K 75
Carnation St. B'frd —8G 58
Carnegie Dri. Shipl —8A 40
Carnlea Gro. Wake —8L 119
Carnoustie Gdns. Norm —2L 121
Carnoustie Gro. Bgly —8G 38
Carolan Ct. Gol —6C 130
Caroline St. Cleck —4H 95 (off Carver St.)
Caroline St. Shipl —7L 39
Carperley Cres. Denh —6L 55
Carr Bank. E Mor —7B 22
Carr Bank Otley —7K 11
Carr Bottom Av. B'frd —3N 75
Carrbottom Fold. B'frd —4A 76
Carr Bottom Gro. B'frd —3N 75
Carr Bottom Rd. B'frd —3N 75
Carr Bottom Rd. Gre —8J 41
Carr Bri. Av. Leeds —4G 43
Carr Bri. Clo. Leeds —4G 43
Carr Bri. Dri. Leeds —4G 42
Carr Bri. Vw. Leeds —4G 42
Carr Clo. Rawd —4A 42
Carr Ct. Bat —1F 116 (off Trinity St.)
Carr Crofts. Leeds —7L 61
Carr Crofts Dri. Leeds —7L 61
Carr Croft's Ter. Leeds —7L 61
Carrfield Clo. Dart —9F 152
Carrfield Dri. Bar E —8L 47
Carr Fld. Dri. Ludd —4E 90
Carrfield La. Bar E —8K 47
Carrfield Rd. Bar E —8L 47
Carrfield Vs. Todm —3C 86
Carrgate. Kin —8B 140
Carr Gate. —7G 98
Carr Ga. Cres. Carr G —7F 98
Carr Ga. Dri. Carr G —7F 98
Carr Ga. Mt. Carr G —7F 98
Carr Grn. M'well —9L 153
Carr Grn. Av. Brigh —5L 113
Carr Grn. Clo. Brigh —5L 113
Carr Grn. Dri. Brigh —5L 113
Carr Grn. La. Brigh —4L 113
Carr Grn. La. Hud —3B 132
Carr Grn. La. M'well —9L 153
Carr Gro. Kei —7N 21
Carr Hall La. Holy G —8N 111
Carr Hall Rd. Wyke —1A 94
Carr Head La. Ing —9E 166
Carr Hill Av. C'ley —9L 41
Carr Hill Dri. C'ley —9L 41
Carr Hill Gro. C'ley —9L 41
Carr Hill Nook. C'ley —9L 41
Carr Hill Ri. C'ley —9L 41
Carr Hill Rd. C'ley —9L 41
Carr Hill Rd. Up Cum —2L 165
Carrholm Cres. Leeds —8D 44
Carrholm Dri. Leeds —8D 44
Carrholm Grn. B'frd —7N 75
Carrholm Gro. Leeds —8D 44
Carrholm Mt. Leeds —8D 44
Carrholm Rd. Leeds —8D 44
Carrholm Vw. Leeds —8D 44
Carr Ho. Wake —5L 119 (off George St.)
Carr Ho. Fold. Todm —6M 87
Carr House Gate. —9A 76
Carr Ho. Ga. Wyke —9A 76
Carr Ho. Gro. Wyke —9A 76
Carr Ho. La. Hal —6J 75
Carr Ho. La. Todm —6M 87
Carr Ho. La. Wyke —8N 75 (in three parts)
Carr Ho. Mt. Wyke —9A 76
Carr Ho. Rd. Hal —7J 75
Carr Ho. Rd. H'frth —3M 163
Carr Houses. Meth —4M 101
Carriage Dri. Ber B —1K 147
Carriage Dri., The. G'lnd —3B 112
Carriage Dri., The. Holy G —7N 111
Carriage Dri., The. Leeds —6L 45 (in two parts)
Carricks Clo. Low M —7C 76
Carrier St. Hal —5B 92
Carrington St. B'frd —7G 58 (in two parts)
Carrington Ter. Guis —8H 25
Carr La. Bgly —8D 22
Carr La. Bstfld —2E 134
Carr La. Carl —1N 99
Carr La. C'frd —6E 102
Carr La. Denh —4L 55
Carr La. H'cft & Fitz —7N 139
Carr La. Heck —3A 116
Carr La. H'frth —4N 163 (nr. Cinderhills Rd.)
Carr La. H'frth —4G 163 (nr. Cold Well La.)
Carr La. Ing —8D 166
Carr La. Low M —9B 76
Carr La. M'twn —4L 135
Carr La. Pec W —6H 71
Carr La. Rawd —4A 42
Carr La. Riddl —7N 21
Carr La. Sandb —7B 22
Carr La. Shepl —2K 165
Carr La. Shipl —7A 40
Carr La. Slai —9N 129
Carr La. S Kirk —5J 157
Carr La. T'ner —3B 46
Carr La. Wake —3M 137
Carr La. Weth —2N 17 (in two parts)
Carr La. Av. C'frd —7E 102
Carr Mnr. Av. Leeds —7D 44
Carr Mnr. Cres. Leeds —6D 44
Carr Mnr. Cft. Leeds —8D 44
Carr Mnr. Dri. Leeds —7D 44
Carr Mnr. Gdns. Leeds —7D 44
Carr Mnr. Gth. Leeds —6D 44
Carr Mnr. Gro. Leeds —7D 44
Carr Mnr. Mt. Leeds —7D 44
Carr Mnr. Pde. Leeds —7D 44
Carr Mnr. Pl. Leeds —7D 44
Carr Mnr. Rd. Leeds —8D 44
Carr Mnr. Vw. Leeds —6D 44
Carr Mnr. Wlk. Leeds —8D 44
Carr Moor Side. Leeds —2E 80
Carr Moor St. Leeds —3F 80
Carr Mt. Up Cum —2L 165
Carroll Ct. S Elm —6L 157
Carroll St. B'frd —8E 58
Carr Pit Rd. Hud —5A 132
Carr Rd. C'ley —8K 41
Carr Rd. Todm —3B 86
Carr Rd. Wyke —1A 94
Carr Row. Wyke —1A 94
Carrs Clo. Dew —9C 96
Carr Side Cres. Bat —9F 96
Carrs Rd. Mars —6F 144
Carrs Side St. No.1. Mars —5G 145
Carrs Side St. No.2. Mars —5G 145
Carrs St. Mars —5G 145
Carr St. Birs —3B 96
Carr St. B'frd —3B 76
Carr St. Brigh —8M 93
Carr St. Cleck —5H 95
Carr St. Dew —1F 116
Carr St. Heck —8N 95
Carr St. Hud —3H 131
Carr St. Kei —9J 21
Carr St. Liv —7L 95
Carr Top Clo. Bat —1E 116
Carr Top La. Gol —6C 130
Carr Vw. S Kirk —6J 157
Carr Vw. Rd. N Mill —6D 164
Carr Wood Clo. C'ley —9L 41
Carr Wood Gdns. C'ley —9L 41
Carr Wood Ind. Est. C'frd —7F 102
Carr Wood Rd. C'frd —7F 102
Carr Wood Way. C'ley —8L 41
Carter Av. Leeds —6D 64
Carter La. Leeds —5D 64
Carter La. Q'bry —2C 74
Carter Mt. Leeds —6D 64
Carter's La. Midd —2H 9
Carter Sq. B'frd —8H 41
Carter St. B'frd —8D 58
Carter St. Wake —5K 119
Carter Ter. Leeds —5D 64
Cart Ga. B'frd —4B 76
Cartmell Dri. Leeds —7M 63
Cartmel Rd. Kei —8G 21
Cartworth Bank Rd. H'frth —6L 163
Cartworth La. H'frth —5L 163
Cartworth Moor Rd. H'frth —9K 163
Cartworth Rd. H'frth —4M 163
Cartwright Gdns. Hud —7H 131
Cartwright Hall Art Gallery & Museum. —3A 58
Cartwright St. Rawf —6J 95
Carver St. Cleck —4H 95
Caryl Rd. B'frd —2E 76
Cashmere St. Kei —9G 21
Casson Av. E Ard —3D 98
Casson Dri. E Ard —3D 98
Casson Fold. Hal —2F 92
Casson Gro. E Ard —3D 98
Castle Av. Brigh —3L 113
Castle Av. Hud —9M 131
Castle Av. Wake —9M 119
Castle Carr Rd. Hal —4A 72
Castle Clo. Bard —5E 30
Castle Clo. Birs —3D 96
Castle Cres. Dew —1F 134
Castle Cres. Wake —2M 137
Castle Cft. H'den —6N 37
Castlefield Ct. C'frd —4D 102
Castlefields. Rothw —8K 81
Castlefields Cres. Brigh —3L 113
Castlefields Dri. Brigh —3L 113
Castlefields Ind. Est. Bgly —2C 38
Castlefields La. Bgly —2C 38
Castlefields Rd. Bgly —1C 38
Castlefields Rd. Brigh —3L 113
Castleford. —5D 102
Castleford Ings. —3E 102
Castleford La. Ack —2A 122
Castleford La. Knot —7A 104
Castleford Mkt. Hall. C'frd —4D 102 (off Carlton St.)
Castleford Museum. —4D 102
Castleford Rd. Nor —1J 121
Castleford Tigers Rugby League Football Club. —3F 102
Castle Gth. Pon —2L 123
Castle Ga. Cra V —8K 89
Castlegate. Hud —4M 131
Castle Ga. I'ly —5G 8
Castle Ga. Stan —4B 100
Castle Ga. Weth —4M 17
Castle Ga. W'ford —4A 100
Castlegate Dri. B'frd —9G 41
Castlegate Dri. Pon —6H 123
Castlegate Ho. Ell —4E 112 (off Crown St.)
Castlegate Loop. Hud —3M 131
Castlegate Slip. Hud —3M 131
Castle Grange. Yead —1A 42
Castle Gro. Bard —5E 30
Castle Gro. H'den —6N 37
Castle Gro. Horb —2E 136
Castle Gro. Av. Leeds —8N 43
Castle Gro. Dri. Leeds —9N 43
Castle Head Clo. Loft —4L 99
Castle Head La. Loft —5H 99 (in two parts)
Castle Hill. Brigh —3L 113
Castle Hill. I'ly —5G 8
Castle Hill. Wake —7E 118
Castle Hill Rd. Gom —6M 95
Castle Hill Side. Hud —1A 148
Castle Hill Vw. Heck —9C 96
Castle Ings Clo. Leeds —2G 78
Castle Ings Dri. Leeds —2G 78
Castle Ings Gdns. Leeds —2G 78
Castle La. Ripp —8C 110
Castle La. Slai —8L 129
Castle La. Todm —6M 87
Castle La. Clo. Todm —6M 87
Castle Meadows. Hall G —7H 137
Castle M. Shipl —8N 39
Castlemore Rd. Bail —5B 40
Castle Mount. —1H 135
Castle Mt. Dew —9G 117
Castle Pde. C'frd —6F 102
Castle Pl. Brigh —3M 113 (off Thornhill Rd.)
Castlerigg Grn. B'frd —7L 75
Castle Rd. I'ly —5G 8 (in two parts)
Castle Rd. Kei —8H 21
Castle Rd. Rothw —8M 81
Castle Rd. Shipl —8N 39
Castle Rd. Wake —1M 137
Castle Rd. W. Wake —1M 137
Castle Street. —6M 87
Castle St. B'frd —9C 58
Castle St. Leeds —6C 62
Castle St. Wake —6H 119
Castle Syke Hill. Pon —8H 123
Castle Syke Vw. Pon —5J 123
Castle Ter. Brigh —3L 113 (off Castle Av.)
Castle Ter. Wake —2M 137
Castleton Clo. Leeds —7B 62
Castleton Rd. A'ley —6A 62
Castle Va. Pon —1M 123
Castle Vw. Hon —6L 147
Castle Vw. Horb —2E 136
Castle Vw. Leeds —6D 44
Castle Vw. Mir —6M 115

Castle Vw. *Pon* —2K **123**
Castle Vw. *Wake* —2M **137**
Castle Wood Clo. *Hare* —1J **29**
Castle Wood Clo. *H'fth* —7G **42**
Castley. —9L 13
Castle Yd. *I'ly* —5G **8**
Castley La. *Leat* —9G **12**
Castlfields Dri. *Brigh* —3L **113**
Cater St. *B'frd* —7D **58**
Cathcart St. *Hal* —3A **92**
Cathcart St. *Leeds* —3C **62**
Cathedral Clo. *B'frd* —7D **58**
Cathedral Clo. *Wake* —4K **119**
Cathedral Retail Pk. *Wake* —6K **119**
Cathedral Wlk. *Wake* —5L **119**
Catherine Clo. *Hud* —9F **112**
Catherine Cres. *Ell* —5E **112**
Catherine Gro. *Leeds* —2D **80**
Catherine Ho. La. *Hal* —6A **72**
Catherine Rd. *Hud* —7N **113**
Catherine Slack. —7A 74
Catherine Slack. *Brigh* —6L **93**
Catherine St. *Brigh* —9M **93**
Catherine St. *Ell* —5E **112**
Catherine St. *Fitz* —6A **140**
Catherine St. *Kei* —2H **37**
(in two parts)
Cat Hill. —9G 167
Cat Hill La. *Ing* —9G **167**
Cat La. *Cra V* —7A **90**
(in two parts)
Cat La. *G'lnd* —4L **111**
Catlow St. *C'frd* —5C **102**
Cattlelaith La. *Knot* —1C **124**
Cattle La. *Aber* —8E **48**
Cattle Mkt. St. *Otley* —9L **11**
Caudle Hill. *Fair* —9M **85**
Cauldwell Gdns. *B'frd* —1C **76**
Caulms Wood Rd. *Dew & Earl* —2G **116**
Causeway. *Bklnd* —8G **110**
Causeway. *Hal* —5C **92**
Causeway. *Outl* —6M **129**
Causeway. *Slai* —7J **129**
Causeway Cres. *Lint* —9C **130**
Causeway Foot. *Hal* —2K **73**
Causeway Foot. —2K 73
(nr. Illingworth)
Causeway Foot. —4J 149
(nr. Shepley)
Causeway Garth La. *Thpe A* —6A **142**
Causeway Side. *Lint* —9C **130**
Causeway Wood Rd. *Todm* —8N **87**
Cautley Rd. *Leeds* —8H **63**
Cavalier App. *Leeds* —8H **63**
Cavalier Clo. *Leeds* —8H **63**
Cavalier Ct. *Leeds* —8H **63**
Cavalier Dri. *App B* —8J **41**
Cavalier Gdns. *Leeds* —8H **63**
Cavalier Ga. *Leeds* —8H **63**
Cavalier Hill. —7G 63
Cave Cres. *Wake* —7G **119**
Cave Hill. *N'wram* —9E **74**
Cave La. *E Ard* —4F **98**
Cavendish Av. *Pon* —9L **103**
*Cavendish Ct. B'frd —1G **59***
(off Cavendish Rd.)
Cavendish Ct. Shop. Cen. *Kei* —9J **21**
Cavendish Dri. *Bgly* —3G **38**
Cavendish Dri. *Guis* —8H **25**
Cavendish Gro. *Guis* —8H **25**
Cavendish M. *Leeds* —3F **44**
Cavendish Pl. *S'ley* —5A **60**
Cavendish Ri. *Pud* —7D **60**
Cavendish Rd. *B'frd & Eccl* —1G **59**
Cavendish Rd. *Guis* —8H **25**
Cavendish Rd. *Idle* —8F **40**
Cavendish Rd. *Leeds* —4D **62**
*Cavendish Sq. S'ley —5B **60***
(off Cavendish Pl.)
Cavendish St. *Hal* —5N **91**
Cavendish St. *Kei* —9J **21**
Cavendish St. *Leeds* —6B **62**
Cavendish St. *Pud* —7D **60**
Cavendish St. *Yead* —9N **25**
Cavendish Ter. *Hal* —5N **91**
Cavewell Clo. *Oss* —8B **118**
Cavewell Gdns. *Oss* —8B **118**
Cawcliffe Dri. *Brigh* —7M **93**
Cawcliffe Rd. *Brigh* —8M **93**
Cawley Gth. *Heck* —9B **96**
Cawley La. *Heck* —8B **96**
Cawood Haven. *B'frd* —5K **75**
Cawthorne Av. *Hud* —9M **113**
Cawthorne La. *Dart* —9D **152**
Cawthorne Rd. *Wake* —4K **137**
Caxton Rd. *Otley* —2J **25**
Caxton St. *Weth* —4M **17**
Caycroft Nook. *H Bri* —8G **71**
Caygill Ter. *Hal* —7B **92**
Caythorpe Rd. *Leeds* —8L **43**
Caythorpe Wlk. *B'frd* —1G **59**
Cecil Av. *Bail* —3A **40**
Cecil Av. *B'frd* —1N **75**
Cecil Av. *Hal* —4K **93**
Cecil Gro. *Leeds* —6M **61**
Cecil Mt. *Leeds* —6M **61**
Cecil Rd. *Leeds* —6M **61**
Cecil St. *Cro R* —7F **36**
Cecil St. *Hud* —4M **131**
Cecil St. *Leeds* —6M **61**
Cedar Av. *Hud* —3L **131**
Cedar Av. *Leeds* —7L **61**
Cedar Av. *Oss* —7A **118**
*Cedar Clo. Gol —5E **130***
(off Laburnum Gro.)
Cedar Clo. *Leeds* —7M **61**
Cedar Clo. *Pon* —6J **123**
Cedar Clo. *Roys* —5B **154**
Cedar Ct. *C'frd* —5E **102**
Cedar Ct. *Hud* —3K **131**
*Cedar Ct. Leeds —5F **44***
(off Harrogate Rd.)
Cedar Ct. *Rothw* —7F **82**
Cedar Covert. *Weth* —1M **17**
Cedar Dri. *Dew* —5L **117**
Cedar Dri. *Wyke* —9C **76**
Cedar Gro. *Bail* —6K **39**
Cedar Gro. *Bat* —1F **116**
Cedar Gro. *F'stne* —4D **122**
Cedar Gro. *G'lnd* —4A **112**
Cedar Mt. *Hud* —3L **131**
Cedar Mt. *Leeds* —7L **61**
Cedar Pl. *Leeds* —7L **61**
Cedar Ridge. *Gar* —5B **66**
Cedar Rd. *Dew* —5K **117**
Cedar Rd. *Leeds* —7L **61**
Cedar Rd. *Nor* —4J **121**
Cedars, The. *B'hpe* —6J **27**
Cedar St. *Bgly* —2D **38**
Cedar St. *Hal* —6M **91**
Cedar St. *Hud* —3K **131**
Cedar St. *Kei* —3H **37**
Cedar St. *Leeds* —7L **61**
Cedar St. *Todm* —3J **107**
Cedar Ter. *Leeds* —7L **61**
Cedar Wlk. *Cam* —1N **159**
Cedar Wlk. *F'stne* —5D **122**
Cedar Wlk. *Knot* —1D **124**
Cedar Way. *Gom* —4L **95**
Celandine Av. *Hud* —2D **130**
Celandine Clo. *Pon* —4K **123**
Celandine Dri. *Hud* —2D **130**
Celette Ind. Pk. *Cleck* —5G **95**
Cemetery La. *Carl* —3L **99**
Cemetery La. *Kei* —6H **21**
Cemetery La. *Sower B* —8G **91**
Cemetery Rd. *Bat* —7E **96**
Cemetery Rd. *Bgly* —3D **38**
Cemetery Rd. *Butt* —6N **75**
Cemetery Rd. *Dew* —4D **116**
Cemetery Rd. *Four E & L Grn* —6L **57**
Cemetery Rd. *Heck* —8A **96**
Cemetery Rd. *Hems* —2C **156**
Cemetery Rd. *H'frth* —5L **163**
Cemetery Rd. *Hud* —3L **131**
Cemetery Rd. *Leeds* —1C **80**
Cemetery Rd. *Nor* —1K **121**
Cemetery Rd. *Pud* —6N **59**
Cemetery Rd. *Ryh* —9J **139**
Cemetery Rd. *Stanb* —9N **35**
Cemetery Rd. *Yead* —9N **25**
Centenary Rd. *Bail* —3D **40**
Centenary Sq. *B'frd* —8C **58**
Centenary Sq. *Dew* —7E **116**
Centenary Way. *Bat* —6E **96**
*Central Arc. Cleck —5J **95***
(off Cheapside)
Central Av. *Bail* —5N **39**
Central Av. *B'frd* —1A **76**
Central Av. *Fitz* —6A **140**
Central Av. *Grime* —9A **156**
Central Av. *Hud* —8N **113**
Central Av. *Kei* —4F **36**
Central Av. *Liv* —7F **94**
Central Av. *Shipl* —8N **39**
Central Av. *S Elm* —7M **157**
Central Clo. *Hud* —8N **113**
Central Dri. *C'frd* —5N **101**
Central Dri. *Hud* —9N **113**
Central Dri. *Kei* —4F **36**
Central Dri. *Roys* —6D **154**
*Central Pde. Cleck —5J **95***
(off Market St.)
Central Pde. *Leeds* —2L **81**
Central Pk. *Hal* —7A **92**
Central Rd. *Leeds* —7E **62**
Central St. *Dew* —3E **116**
Central St. *Hal* —5B **92**
Central St. *H Bri* —1H **89**
Central St. *Leeds* —6D **62**
Centre 27 Bus. Pk. *Birs* —1E **96**
Centre St. *B'frd* —2A **76**
Centre St. *Heck* —8N **95**
Centre St. *Hems* —2D **156**
Centre St. *S Elm* —6N **157**
Centre, The. *Pon* —4L **123**
Centuria Wlk. *Hud* —2D **130**
Century Pl. *B'frd* —5A **58**
Century Rd. *Ell* —4E **112**
Century Way. *Leeds* —7G **64**
Ceres Rd. *Weth* —4A **18**
Chaddle Wood Clo. *H'fth* —6F **42**
Chadwell Spring. *Bgly* —8F **38**
Chadwick Cres. *Dew* —2E **116**
Chadwick La. *Mir* —8K **115**
Chadwick St. *Leeds* —8F **62**
(in two parts)
Chadwick St. S. *Leeds* —8F **62**
Chaffinch Rd. *B'frd* —7H **57**
Chaffinch Way. *Neth* —2K **147**
Chain Rd. *Slai* —4L **145**
Chain St. *B'frd* —7B **58**
Chain St. *C'frd* —4C **102**
Chalcroft Clo. *Heck* —7B **96**
Chald La. *Wake* —6K **119**
Chalfont Rd. *Leeds* —1L **43**
Chalice Clo. *Leeds* —6G **80**
Challenge Way. *Bat* —8J **97**
Challenge Way. *Cut H* —1H **77**
Challis Gro. *B'frd* —2C **76**
Chalner Av. *Morl* —2J **97**
Chalner Clo. *Morl* —2J **97**
Chalwood. *Hud* —7C **114**
Chancellor Ct. *Leeds* —7E **62**
Chancellor St. *Leeds* —3D **62**
Chancery La. *Hud* —4M **131**
Chancery La. *Oss* —3L **117**
Chancery La. *Wake* —5L **119**
Chancery Rd. *Oss* —3L **117**
Chancery Ter. *Hal* —1B **112**
Chandler Clo. *Birs* —3B **96**
Chandler La. *Hon* —5J **147**
Chandlers Clo. *Wake* —7K **99**
*Chandlers, The. Leeds —7F **62***
(off Calls, The)
Chandlers Wharf. *Leeds* —9B **42**
Chandos Av. *Leeds* —7G **44**
Chandos Fold. *Leeds* —7G **44**
Chandos Gdns. *Leeds* —7G **44**
Chandos Gth. *Leeds* —7G **44**
Chandos Grn. *Leeds* —7G **44**
Chandos Pl. *Leeds* —7H **45**
Chandos St. *B'frd* —8D **58**
Chandos St. *Kei* —2H **37**
(in two parts)
Chandos Ter. *Leeds* —7H **45**
Chandos Wlk. *Leeds* —7G **44**
Changegate. *Haw* —8B **36**
Changegate Ct. *Haw* —8B **36**
Change La. *Hal* —1D **112**
Channing Way. *B'frd* —8C **58**
Chantree La. *B'frd* —1G **58**
Chantree Mt. *Leeds* —1E **64**
Chantree Vs. *Hal* —8C **92**
Chantrell Ct. *Leeds* —7F **62**
Chantry Bri. Ind. Est. *Wake* —6M **119**
Chantry Clo. *I'ly* —6G **9**
Chantry Clo. *Pon* —4H **123**
Chantry Cft. *Kin* —8A **140**
Chantry Cft. *Leeds* —7E **64**
Chantry Dri. *I'ly* —5G **9**
Chantry Gth. *Leeds* —7E **64**
*Chantry Ho. Hud —4N **131***
(off Oldgate)
Chantry La. *H'wd* —3J **49**
Chantry Rd. *Wake* —7G **118**
Chapel Allerton. —8E 44
Chapel Av. *H Bri* —1J **89**
Chapel Av. *Heck* —7B **96**
Chapel Bank. *N Mill* —5C **164**
Chapel Clo. *Ber B* —1L **147**
Chapel Clo. *Dew* —9G **116**
Chapel Clo. *Gar* —7M **65**
Chapel Clo. *Hal* —7J **75**
Chapel Clo. *Holy G* —7A **112**
Chapel Clo. *Shaf* —6K **155**
Chapel Clo. *Skelm* —7D **150**
Chapel Clo. *Wrag* —3N **139**
Chapel Ct. *Brigh* —7K **93**
Chapel Ct. *Halt* —6B **64**
*Chapel Ct. Q'bry —3G **74***
(off Chapel La.)
Chapel Cft. *Brigh* —4L **113**
Chapel Fld. *S Kirk* —7H **157**
Chapel Fold. —9D 96
*Chapel Fold. A'ley —7M **61***
(off Wesley Rd.)
Chapel Fold. *Bat* —9D **96**
Chapel Fold. *Bees* —3A **80**
Chapel Fold. *B'frd* —4N **75**
Chapel Fold. *Halt* —6B **64**
Chapel Fold. *L Wyke* —4A **94**
*Chapel Fold. Pud —8B **60***
(off Littlemoor Rd.)
Chapel Garth. *Ackw* —4G **140**
Chapel Ga. *Sch* —5B **164**
Chapel Green. —2B 76
Chapel Grn. *Pud* —8A **60**
Chapel Gro. *Bgly* —2D **38**
Chapel Hill. *Clay W* —7H **151**
Chapel Hill. *Hud* —6M **131**
Chapel Hill. *Kear* —7L **15**
Chapel Hill. *Leeds* —8F **80**
Chapel Hill. *Lint* —1C **146**
Chapel Hill. *Mir* —9K **115**
Chapel Hill. *Morl* —8K **79**
Chapel Hill. *Yead* —9M **25**
Chapel Hill La. *Hud* —4H **129**
Chapel Hill La. *Wake* —5K **135**
*Chapel Ho. I'ly —5G **8***
(off Burnside)
Chapel Ho. Rd. *Low M* —6B **76**
Chapel Lane. —5C 36
Chapel La. *All* —6H **57**
Chapel La. *A'ley & N Farn* —7M **61**
Chapel La. *Bads* —8L **141**
Chapel La. *Barn* —9D **154**
Chapel La. *Bar E* —8M **47**
Chapel La. *Bgly* —4E **38**
Chapel La. *Birs* —3B **96**
Chapel La. *Cliff* —2D **32**
Chapel La. *Dew* —9G **116**
Chapel La. *Eml* —2E **150**
Chapel La. *Esh* —2G **40**
Chapel La. *F'ley* —9G **61**
Chapel La. *Gar* —7M **65**
Chapel La. *Gol* —6C **130**
Chapel La. *Hal* —9C **92**
Chapel La. *Heb* —2E **4**
Chapel La. *Heck* —7B **96**
Chapel La. *I'ly* —5F **8**
Chapel La. *Kei* —9H **21**
Chapel La. *Kip* —4B **84**
Chapel La. *Lay* —9C **20**
Chapel La. *Leeds* —2N **61**
(in two parts)
Chapel La. *L'ft* —2B **90**
Chapel La. *Mold* —5B **132**
Chapel La. *Q'bry* —3G **74**
(nr. Highgate Rd.)
Chapel La. *Q'bry* —4C **74**
(nr. New Pk. Rd.)
Chapel La. *S Elm* —6A **158**
Chapel La. *S'wram* —8F **92**
Chapel La. *Sower B* —8K **91**
Chapel La. *Yead* —9M **25**
Chapel Pl. *Leeds* —1N **61**
Chapel Rd. *Bgly* —2D **38**
Chapel Rd. *Leeds* —1F **62**
Chapel Rd. *Low M* —7B **76**
(in two parts)
Chapel Rd. *Steet* —3C **20**
Chapel Row. *Wilsd* —9A **38**
*Chapel Sq. Leeds —1N **61***
(off Chapel St.)
Chapel St. *Add* —1M **7**
Chapel St. *Bgly* —2D **38**
Chapel St. *B'frd* —7D **58**
(BD1)
Chapel St. *B'frd* —1B **76**
(BD5)
Chapel St. *C'ley* —8M **41**
Chapel St. *Carc* —9N **159**
Chapel St. *Cleck* —4J **95**
Chapel St. *Denh* —6K **55**
Chapel St. *Dew* —5F **116**
Chapel St. *E Ard* —5E **98**
Chapel St. *Eccl* —2H **59**
Chapel St. *Halt* —6B **64**
Chapel St. *Head* —1N **61**
Chapel St. *H'town* —7G **95**
Chapel St. *Holy G* —7A **112**
Chapel St. *Hud* —5M **131**
(HD1)
Chapel St. *Hud* —5B **132**
(HD5)
Chapel St. *Knot* —7F **104**
Chapel St. *L'boro* —9M **107**
Chapel St. *Liv* —8N **95**
Chapel St. *L'ft* —4L **91**
Chapel St. *Mir* —6L **115**
Chapel St. *Morl* —1H **97**
Chapel St. *Neth* —2H **147**
Chapel St. *Oss* —7C **118**
Chapel St. *Q'bry* —4D **74**
Chapel St. *Rawd* —3M **41**
Chapel St. *Rod* —1B **60**
Chapel St. *Ryh* —9J **139**
Chapel St. *Sca H* —5A **130**
Chapel St. *Shaf* —6K **155**
Chapel St. *Sils* —7E **6**
Chapel St. *Stan* —7N **99**
Chapel St. *S'ley* —5B **60**
Chapel St. *Tay H* —8K **131**
Chapel St. *T'tn* —8C **56**
Chapel St. *Ting* —3B **98**
Chapel St. *Todm* —6M **87**
Chapel St. *Wibs* —4A **76**
Chapel St. N. *Hal* —1M **91**
Chapel St. S. *Todm* —2J **107**
Chapel Ter. *Hon* —5L **147**
Chapel Ter. *Hud* —6J **131**
*Chapel Ter. Leeds —1N **61***
(off Chapel St.)
Chapel Ter. *Sower B* —9D **90**
Chapel Ter. *T'tn* —8C **56**
Chapelthorpe. —6J 137
Chapeltown. *Hal* —5B **92**
Chapeltown. *Pud* —8A **60**
Chapeltown Rd. *Leeds* —3F **62**
Chapel Wlk. *B'frd* —2H **59**
*Chapel Yd. Colt —8E **64***
(off Meynell Rd.)
Chapel Yd. *W'ford* —8D **82**
Chapman St. *B'frd* —8H **59**
Chappell Rd. *Hoy S* —9J **167**
Charing Cross M. *Leeds* —3D **62**
Chariot Way. *Thpe A* —6N **141**
Charles Av. *Agb* —8A **120**
Charles Av. *B'frd* —7H **59**
Charles Av. *Hal* —8F **92**
Charles Av. *Hud* —2F **130**
Charles Av. *Leeds* —8H **63**
Charles Av. *Out* —7K **99**
Charles Cotton Clo. *Wake* —3F **1**
Charles Gdns. *Leeds* —9C **62**
Charles Gro. *W'ford* —7D **82**
Charles Jones Ct. *Bat* —7E **96**
Charles Sq. Rd. *Hal* —5C **92**
Charles St. *Bat* —8F **96**
Charles St. *Bgly* —4E **38**
Charles St. *B'frd* —7C **58**
Charles St. *Brigh* —9M **93**
Charles St. *C'frd* —5E **102**
Charles St. *Cud* —9K **155**
Charles St. *Dew* —3C **116**
Charles St. *Eastb* —3H **117**
Charles St. *Ell* —5E **112**
Charles St. *Fars* —3A **60**
Charles St. *Gom* —4M **95**
Charles St. *Horb* —3E **136**
Charles St. *H'fth* —7E **42**
Charles St. *Hud* —6J **131**
(in two parts)
Charles St. *Morl* —9L **79**
Charles St. *Oss* —8B **118**
Charles St. *Otley* —1L **25**
Charles St. *Q'bry* —4C **74**
Charles St. *Raven* —6B **116**
Charles St. *Ryh* —9H **139**
Charles St. *Shipl* —7N **39**
Charles St. *Skel* —7N **159**
Charles St. *S Hien* —4M **155**
Charles St. *Sower B* —8H **91**
Charles St. *Wake* —6M **119**
Charlestown. —5C 40
(nr. Baildon)
Charlestown. —2E 88
(nr. Hebden Bridge)
Charlestown. *Ackw* —5G **140**
Charlestown Rd. *Hal* —4C **92**
Charles Vw. *Hall G* —7H **137**
*Charlesworth Bldgs. Horb —1C **1***
(off Manor Rd.)
Charlesworth Ct. *Dew* —9G **117**
Charlesworth Gro. *Hal* —4L **91**
Charlesworth Pl. *Stan* —6C **100**
Charlesworth Sq. *Gom* —4L **95**
Charlesworth St. *Dew* —7F **116**
Charlesworth Ter. *Hal* —4L **91**
Charlesworth Way. *Wake* —6K **1**
Charleville. *S Elm* —5L **157**
Charlotte Clo. *Birs* —1C **96**
Charlotte Ct. *B'frd* —2N **75**
Charlotte Ct. *Haw* —7D **36**
Charlotte Gro. *Leeds* —6C **64**
Charlotte Gro. *Oss* —7B **118**
Charlotte St. *Wake* —6M **119**
Charlton Clo. *B'frd* —2F **58**
Charlton Ct. *Hal* —4L **91**
Charlton Gro. *Leeds* —7J **63**
Charlton Gro. *Sils* —9F **6**
Charlton Pl. *Leeds* —7J **63**
Charlton Rd. *Leeds* —7J **63**
Charlton St. *Leeds* —7J **63**
Charnwood Bank. *Bat* —8B **96**
Charnwood Clo. *B'frd* —4F **58**
Charnwood Gro. *B'frd* —4G **58**
Charnwood Rd. *B'frd* —4G **58**
Chart Clo. *Gar* —7M **65**
Charterhouse Rd. *B'frd* —6F **40**
Charteris Rd. *B'frd* —7H **57**
*Chartist's Ct. Morl —1K **97***
(off Gt. Northern St.)
Chartists Way. *Morl* —1K **97**
Chartwell Ct. *Leeds* —2K **45**
Charville Gdns. *Leeds* —4A **46**
Chase, The. *Bur W* —1D **24**
Chase, The. *Gar* —7B **66**
Chase, The. *Kei* —8F **20**

hase, The. *Rawd* —3L **41**
hase, The. *Stan* —6B **100**
hase, The. *Weth* —3N **17**
hase Way. *B'frd* —3C **76**
hassum Gro. *B'frd* —4M **57**
haster St. *Bat* —6D **96**
(in two parts)
hatham St. *B'frd* —5D **58**
hatham St. *Hal* —5A **92**
hat Hill Rd. *T'tn* —9E **56**
hatswood Av. *Leeds* —5B **80**
hatswood Cres. *Leeds* —5B **80**
hatswood Dri. *Leeds* —4B **80**
hatsworth Av. *Pon* —9L **103**
hatsworth Av. *Pud* —6L **59**
hatsworth Clo. *Hud* —6B **132**
hatsworth Clo. *Leeds* —3J **63**
hatsworth Ct. B'frd —6M ***57***
(off Girlington Rd.)
hatsworth Cres. *Pud* —6L **59**
hatsworth Dri. *Pud* —6L **59**
hatsworth Dri. *Weth* —3K **17**
hatsworth Fall. *Pud* —6L **59**
hatsworth M. *Morl* —1M **97**
hatsworth Pl. *B'frd* —4N **57**
hatsworth Ri. *Pud* —6L **59**
hatsworth Rd. *Barn* —9B **154**
hatsworth Rd. *Leeds* —3J **63**
hatsworth Rd. *Pud* —6L **59**
hatsworth St. *Kei* —9K **21**
hatsworth Ter. *Dew* —4J **117**
hatts Wood Fold. *Oaken* —8F **76**
haucer Av. *Pud* —8C **60**
haucer Av. *Stan* —6N **99**
haucer Clo. *Hon* —6L **147**
haucer Gdns. *Pud* —8C **60**
haucer Gro. *Pud* —8C **60**
heapside. *Bat* —7G **97**
heapside. *B'frd* —7C **58**
heapside. *Cleck* —5J **95**
heapside. *Hal* —5B **92**
heapside. *Nor* —1J **121**
heapside. *She* —7H **75**
heapside. *Wake* —5K **119**
heddington Gro. *All* —6G **56**
heese Ga. Nab Side. *H'frth* —6E **164**
heetham Hill. *Facit* —8A **106**
heetham St. *H Bri* —1H **89**
helburn Vw. *L'boro* —9L **107**
hel Bus. Cen. *Leeds* —4F **62**
hellowfield Ct. *B'frd* —3H **57**
hellow Grange Rd. *B'frd* —3H **57**
hellow La. *B'frd* —4H **57**
hellow St. *B'frd* —3B **76**
hellow Ter. *B'frd* —5J **57**
hellow Way. *Dew* —4F **116**
helmsford Rd. *B'frd* —6G **59**
helmsford Ter. *B'frd* —7G **59**
helsea Clo. *Leeds* —8M **61**
helsea Mans. *Hal* —2F **92**
helsea Rd. *B'frd* —1L **75**
helsea St. *Kei* —1H **37**
helsea Vw. Hal —3F ***92***
(off Bradford Rd.)
helsfield Ct. *Leeds* —3G **65**
helsfield Way. *Leeds* —3G **64**
heltenham Av. *I'ly* —5L **9**
heltenham Ct. *Hal* —8C **92**
heltenham Gdns. *Hal* —8C **92**
heltenham Pl. *Hal* —8C **92**
heltenham Rd. *B'frd* —1D **58**
heltenham St. *Leeds* —8N **61**
helwood Av. *Leeds* —4H **45**
helwood Cres. *Leeds* —5H **45**
helwood Dri. *All* —7F **56**
helwood Dri. *Leeds* —4H **45**
helwood Gro. *Leeds* —4H **45**
helwood Mt. *Leeds* —4H **45**
helwood Pl. *Leeds* —4G **44**
henies Clo. *Leeds* —5N **63**
hepstow Clo. *Gar* —7B **66**
hepstow Gdns. *Leeds* —1F **98**
hequerfield. —4M 123
hequerfield Av. *Pon* —3M **123**
hequerfield Clo. *C'frd* —6A **102**
hequerfield Ct. *Pon* —3M **123**
hequerfield Dri. *Pon* —4L **123**
hequerfield La. *Pon* —3M **123**
hequerfield Mt. *Pon* —4M **123**
hequerfield Rd. *Pon* —4L **123**
hequers Clo. *Pon* —4M **123**
(in four parts)
heriton Dri. *Q'bry* —4E **74**
herry Clo. *Cud* —9J **155**
herry Clo. *Roys* —5B **154**
herry Ct. Leeds —5G ***62***
(off Cherry Pl.)
herry Fields. *B'frd* —2C **58**
herry Gth. *Cam* —1N **159**
herry Gth. *Hems* —3C **156**
herry Gro. *I'ly* —5E **8**
herry Hills. *Dart* —8J **153**
Cherry La. *Clay W* —7J **151**
Cherry Lea Ct. *Rawd* —2M **41**
Cherry Nook Rd. *Hud* —8C **114**
Cherry Pl. *Leeds* —5G **62**
Cherry Ri. *Leeds* —7D **46**
Cherry Row. *Leeds* —5G **62**
Cherry St. *Haw* —7E **36**
Cherry St. *Kei* —8L **21**
Cherry Tree Av. *B'frd* —8H **41**
Cherry Tree Cen. Hud —4M ***131***
(off Half Moon St.)
Cherry Tree Clo. *Gol* —5D **130**
Cherry Tree Clo. *M'well* —8L **153**
Cherry Tree Ct. *E Ard* —5E **98**
Cherry Tree Cres. *Fars* —3A **60**
Cherry Tree Cres. *W'ton* —3C **138**
Cherry Tree Dri. *Fars* —3A **60**
Cherry Tree Dri. *G'lnd* —4A **112**
Cherry Tree Dri. *W'ton* —3C **138**
Cherry Tree Gdns. *Thack* —6D **40**
Cherry Tree Ri. *Kei* —2K **37**
Cherry Tree Rd. *W'ton* —3C **138**
Cherry Tree Row. *H'den* —8A **38**
Cherry Tree Wlk. *E Ard* —5E **98**
Cherry Tree Wlk. *H'frth* —4B **164**
Cherrywood Clo. *Leeds* —6C **46**
Cherrywood Gdns. *Leeds* —6C **46**
Cherwell Cft. *Gar* —9B **66**
Chesham St. *Kei* —9K **21**
Chesil Bank. *Hud* —3G **130**
Chesilton Av. *Hud* —3G **130**
Chesney Av. *Leeds* —1F **80**
Chesney Pk. Ind. Est. *Leeds* —1F **80**
Chessington Dri. *Floc* —7G **134**
Chester Clo. *Hal* —3A **92**
Chester Gro. *Hal* —3A **92**
Chester Pl. *Hal* —3A **92**
Chester Rd. *B'twn* —3A **92**
Chester St. *B'frd* —8C **58**
Chester St. *Hal* —3A **92**
Chester St. *Leeds* —6M **61**
Chester St. *Sower B* —8H **91**
Chester Ter. *Hal* —3A **92**
Chesterton Ct. *Colt* —8E **64**
Chesterton Ct. *Horb* —9E **118**
Chesterton Dri. *Hon* —6L **147**
Chestnut Av. *Bat* —8D **96**
Chestnut Av. *B Spa* —9C **18**
Chestnut Av. *Brier* —7N **155**
Chestnut Av. *Carc* —8N **159**
Chestnut Av. *Head* —3A **62**
Chestnut Av. *Leeds* —4E **64**
Chestnut Av. *Todm* —5J **87**
Chestnut Av. *W'ton* —4B **138**
Chestnut Av. *Weth* —3L **17**
Chestnut Clo. *F'stne* —4D **122**
Chestnut Clo. *G'lnd* —4A **112**
Chestnut Clo. *I'ly* —6K **9**
Chestnut Clo. *Kei* —1F **36**
Chestnut Clo. Leeds —1G ***62***
(off Harehills La.)
Chestnut Clo. *New* —8M **131**
Chestnut Ct. Ripp —7D ***110***
(off Halifax Rd.)
Chestnut Ct. *Shipl* —8L **39**
Chestnut Cres. *Nor* —4H **121**
Chestnut Dri. *Leeds* —2L **43**
Chestnut Dri. *S Hien* —4L **155**
Chestnut End. *B Spa* —1E **32**
Chestnut Gdns. *Leeds* —8M **61**
Chestnut Gth. *Quarm* —3G **130**
Chestnut Grn. *Pon* —2M **123**
Chestnut Gro. *B Spa* —9C **18**
Chestnut Gro. *B'frd* —2C **58**
Chestnut Gro. *C'ley* —9M **41**
Chestnut Gro. *Croft* —1G **138**
Chestnut Gro. *Hems* —3F **156**
Chestnut Gro. *Leeds* —3A **62**
Chestnut Gro. *Pon* —5K **123**
Chestnut Gro. *Rothw* —7F **82**
Chestnut Meadows. *Mir* —4K **115**
(nr. Redlands Clo.)
Chestnut Meadows. *Mir* —4J **115**
(nr. Slipper La.)
Chestnut Pl. *Leeds* —3A **62**
Chestnut Ri. *Leeds* —8L **61**
Chestnut St. *Hal* —6M **91**
Chestnut St. *Hud* —8A **114**
Chestnut St. *Leeds* —3A **62**
Chestnut St. *S Elm* —8L **157**
Chestnut Ter. *Dew* —8F **116**
Chestnut Wlk. *Knot* —9C **104**
Chestnut Wlk. *Wake* —3J **119**
Chestnut Way. *Leeds* —2L **43**
Chevet Cft. *S'dal* —3N **137**
Chevet Gro. *Wake* —3N **137**
Chevet La. *Not* —9B **138**
Chevet La. *Wake & Not* —2N **137**
Chevet Mt. *All* —7F **56**
Chevet Pk. Ct. *Wake* —7N **137**
Chevet Ri. *Roys* —5C **154**
Chevet Ter. *Walt* —1B **138**
Chevet Vw. *Roys* —5B **154**
Chevin Av. *Men* —3E **24**
(in two parts)
Chevin Av. *Men* —3F **24**
(nr. Bradford Rd.)
Chevin Av. *Otley* —2M **25**
Chevin Ct. Otley —9L ***11***
(off Courthouse St.)
Chevinedge Cres. *Hal* —2C **112**
Chevin End. *Men* —5F **24**
Chevin End Rd. *Men & Guis* —5H **25**
Chevin Forest Park. —3B 26
Chevington Ct. *Rawd* —4L **41**
Chevins Clo. *Bat* —4C **96**
Chevin Side *Otley* —2L **25**
Cheviot Av. *Mel* —8E **146**
Cheviot Clo. *Hems* —2F **156**
Cheviot Ct. *Gar* —9N **65**
Cheviot Ga. *Low M* —7N **75**
Cheviot Pl. *Knot* —8E **104**
Cheviot Way. *Mir* —9K **115**
Cheyne Wlk. *Kei* —1G **37**
Chichester St. *Leeds* —6M **61**
Chickenley. —4K 117
Chickenley La. *Dew* —4K **117**
Chidswell. —9L 97
Chidswell Gdns. *Dew* —9L **97**
Chidswell La. *Dew & Oss* —9L **97**
Child La. *Liv* —1K **115**
Childs La. *Shipl* —9C **40**
Childs Rd. *Wake* —3F **118**
Chiltern Av. *C'frd* —7N **101**
Chiltern Av. *Hud* —1F **130**
Chiltern Av. *Knot* —8D **104**
Chiltern Clo. *Gar* —9N **65**
Chiltern Ct. *Gar* —9N **65**
Chiltern Ct. *Hems* —2F **156**
Chiltern Dri. *Ackw* —5F **140**
Chiltern Dri. *Mir* —9K **115**
Chiltern Rd. *Dew* —2J **117**
Chiltern Way. *Liv* —7H **95**
Chilwell Clo. *Barn* —8A **154**
Chilwell Gdns. *Barn* —8A **154**
Chilwell M. *Barn* —8A **154**
Chilwell Rd. *Barn* —8A **154**
Chimney La. *Lep* —6H **133**
Chinewood Av. *Bat* —6E **96**
Chippendale Ct. *Men* —4F **24**
Chippendale Ri. *B'frd* —6J **57**
Chippendale Ri. *Otley* —8L **11**
Chirton Gro. *Leeds* —1J **63**
Chiserley. —8K 71
Chislehurst Pl. *B'frd* —2A **76**
Chiswick St. *Leeds* —5A **62**
Chiswick Ter. Leeds —4A ***62***
(off Chiswick Vw.)
Choppards. —7M 163
Choppards Bank Rd. *H'frth* —7M **163**
Choppards La. *H'frth* —6M **163**
Chorley La. *Leeds* —5C **62**
(in two parts)
Chrisharben Pk. *Cytn* —1H **75**
Chrismoor. *B'frd* —8E **40**
Christ Chu. Av. *Leeds* —6L **61**
Christ Chu. Mt. *Leeds* —6L **61**
Christ Chu. Pde. *Leeds* —6L **61**
Christ Chu. Pl. *Leeds* —6L **61**
Christ Chu. Rd. *Leeds* —6L **61**
Christ Chu. Ter. *Leeds* —6L **61**
Christ Chu. Vw. *Leeds* —6L **61**
Christiana Ter. *Morl* —8L **79**
Christopher Clo. *Sils* —8E **6**
Christopher Rd. *Leeds* —3D **62**
Christopher St. *B'frd* —2A **76**
Christopher Ter. *B'frd* —2A **76**
Church App. *Gar* —7N **65**
Church Av. *Gild* —5F **78**
Church Av. *H'fth* —6E **42**
Church Av. *Hud* —6K **131**
Church Av. *K'thpe* —4D **120**
Church Av. *Leeds* —8B **44**
Church Av. *Lint* —8D **130**
Church Av. *S Kirk* —7J **157**
Church Av. *Swil* —3H **83**
Churchbalk Dri. *Pon* —5L **123**
Church Balk La. *Pon* —4L **123**
Church Bank. *B'frd* —7D **58**
Church Bank. *Hal* —6K **91**
Church Bank. *Sower B* —8J **91**
Chu. Bank La. *Cra V* —9J **89**
Churchbank Way. *Dew* —7F **116**
Church Causeway. *Thor A* —9E **18**
Church Clo. *Dart* —9G **152**
Church Clo. *Hal* —8K **73**
Church Clo. *Hems* —2D **156**
Church Clo. *Leeds* —2C **64**
Church Clo. *M'fld* —6G **66**
Church Clo. *Pool W* —1F **26**
Church Clo. *Shar C* —9J **121**
Church Clo. *Shepl* —9J **149**
Church Clo. *Steet* —3C **20**
Church Clo. *Swil* —3H **83**
Church Ct. *B'frd* —9L **57**
Church Ct. *Nor* —2H **121**
Church Ct. *Oss* —4N **117**
Church Ct. *Riddl* —6M **21**
Church Ct. *Yead* —1M **41**
Church Cres. *H'fth* —6E **42**
Church Cres. *Leeds* —4E **44**
Church Cres. *Neth* —4A **136**
Church Cres. *Swil* —4J **83**
Church Cres. *Yead* —1L **41**
Church Dri. *Brier* —7N **155**
Church Dri. *E Kes* —3C **30**
Church Dri. *S Kirk* —7J **157**
Church Farm. *T'ner* —1G **47**
Chu. Farm Clo. *Loft* —4L **99**
Church Farm Clo. *Nor* —8G **100**
Church Farm Gth. *Leeds* —3A **46**
Church Farm Vw. *Bar E* —8M **47**
Churchfield Av. *Dart* —9E **152**
Churchfield Clo. *Dart* —9D **152**
Churchfield Clo. *Liv* —8L **95**
Churchfield Ct. *Dart* —9F **152**
Churchfield Cft. *Nor* —8G **101**
Churchfield Cft. *Rothw* —8A **82**
Churchfield Gro. *Rothw* —7N **81**
Churchfield La. *C'frd* —6F **102**
Churchfield La. *Dart* —9D **152**
Churchfield La. *Lit S* —4L **143**
Churchfield La. *Rothw* —7N **81**
Churchfield La. *Wome* —2M **143**
Churchfield Rd. *Rothw* —8N **81**
Church Fields. *B'frd* —4H **59**
Churchfields. *Croft* —1G **139**
Churchfields. *Hud* —8D **114**
Church Fields. *Nor* —2H **121**
Churchfields. *Ryh* —8J **139**
Churchfields Rd. *Brigh* —9M **93**
Churchfield St. *Bat* —7F **96**
Chu. Fields Vw. *C'frd* —6F **102**
Churchfield Ter. *Liv* —8L **95**
Church Gdns. *Gar* —7N **65**
Church Gdns. *Gild* —6F **78**
Church Gdns. *Leeds* —4F **44**
Church Garforth. —8N 65
Church Gth. *C'frd* —6F **102**
Church Gth. *Pool W* —1F **26**
Churchgate. *B'hpe* —5G **26**
Churchgate. *Gild* —6F **78**
Church Ga. *H'fth* —6E **42**
Church Grange. Cleck —5J ***95***
(off Church St.)
Church Grn. B'frd —5A ***58***
(off Conduit St.)
Church Grn. *Hal* —3L **91**
Church Grn. *Kbtn* —4K **149**
Church Gro. *H'fth* —6E **42**
Church Gro. *S Kirk* —7J **157**
Church Hill. *Bail* —3B **40**
Church Hill. *B'ham* —6D **32**
Church Hill. *B'hpe* —5G **27**
Church Hill. *Eastb* —2G **117**
Church Hill. *L'ft* —3E **90**
Church Hill. *N Rig* —2N **13**
Church Hill. *Roys* —6E **154**
Church Hill. *T'ner* —1H **47**
Church Hill Gdns. *S'ley* —4C **60**
Church Hill Grn. *S'ley* —4C **60**
Church Hill Mt. *S'ley* —4C **60**
Church Ho. Ell —4E ***112***
(off Church St.)
Churchill Flats. *Pool W* —1F **26**
Churchill Gdns. Leeds —4D ***62***
(off Bk. Blenheim Ter.)
Churchill Gro. *Heck* —9B **96**
Churchill Gro. *Wake* —2N **137**
Churchill Rd. *T'tn* —8E **56**
Churchill St. *Todm* —5G **87**
Church La. *Adel* —3M **43**
Church La. *Bard* —6C **30**
Church La. *B'frd* —5N **75**
Church La. *Brigh* —1M **113**
(nr. Commercial St.)
Church La. *Brigh* —9M **93**
(nr. Elland La.)
Church La. *Chap A* —9F **44**
Church La. *C'thpe* —6J **137**
Church La. *Clay W* —7J **151**
Church La. *Coll* —8J **17**
Church La. *C'gts* —4D **64**
Church La. *D'ton* —6C **124**
Church La. *Dew M* —3C **116**
Church La. *E Ard* —5E **98**
Church La. *E Hard* —9L **123**
Church La. *Ell* —4J **113**
Church La. *Esh* —2G **40**
Church La. *F'stne* —2C **122**
Church La. *Gar* —7N **65**
Church La. *Gom & Birs* —4N **95**
Church La. *Hal* —3L **91**
Church La. *Hare* —1G **29**
Church La. *H Bri* —1F **88**
Church La. *Heck* —9A **96**
Church La. *Hept* —9G **70**
Church La. *H Hoy* —8M **151**
Church La. *H'town* —1F **114**
Church La. *Horb* —1D **136**
Church La. *H'fth* —6E **42**
Church La. *Kip* —4B **84**
Church La. *Khtn* —3F **132**
Church La. *Leeds* —7F **62**
Church La. *Lint* —9D **130**
Church La. *Liv* —7L **95**
Church La. *Mars* —5F **144**
Church La. *Mean* —8B **44**
Church La. *Meth* —2K **101**
Church La. *M'fld* —7E **66**
Church La. *Mir* —6N **115**
Church La. *Mold* —4B **132**
Church La. *Neth* —3A **136**
Church La. *New* —8M **131**
Church La. *Nor* —2H **121**
(in two parts)
Church La. *Old Sn* —3K **121**
Church La. *Otley* —1L **25**
Church La. *Out* —7K **99**
Church La. *Pon* —3K **123**
Church La. *Pud* —7B **60**
Church La. *Ryh* —2F **154**
Church La. *Scam* —5F **128**
Church La. *Shepl* —9J **149**
Church La. *S Cro* —3G **146**
Church La. *S Hien* —2H **155**
Church La. *S'wram* —8G **93**
Church La. *Stainb* —3G **12**
Church La. *Slnd* —7N **111**
Church La. *Swil* —4G **83**
Church La. *Thorn* —9H **117**
Church La. *Ting* —5N **97**
Church La. *Weston* —7F **10**
Church La. Av. *Wake* —7K **99**
Church Meadows. *Birs* —3A **96**
Church Meadows. *B'ham* —5D **32**
Church M. *B Spa* —9D **18**
Church M. B'frd —6K ***75***
(off Church St.)
Church Mt. *H'fth* —6E **42**
Church Mt. *S Kirk* —7J **157**
Church Pk. *Liv* —1J **115**
Church Pl. *Gar* —7N **65**
Church Pl. *Hal* —5A **92**
Church Rd. *Bat* —4C **96**
Church Rd. *B'frd* —5N **75**
Church Rd. *H'fth* —7E **42**
Church Rd. *Leeds* —7M **61**
Church Rd. *Liv* —1H **115**
Church Rd. *Nor* —8F **100**
Church Rd. *Stan* —7A **100**
Church Rd. *Todm* —4G **87**
Church Rd. *W'ford* —5M **83**
Church Row. *Den* —3M **9**
Church Row. *Leeds* —7F **62**
Church Side. *Meth* —2K **101**
Church Side Clo. *Hal* —3B **92**
Church Side Dri. *Hal* —3B **92**
Churchside Vs. *Meth* —2K **101**
Church Sq. *Gar* —7N **65**
Church Street. —5B 36
Church St. *Add* —1N **7**
Church St. *Bgly* —5F **38**
Church St. *Birs* —3B **96**
Church St. *B Spa* —1D **32**
Church St. *Brier* —6N **155**
Church St. *Brigh* —3L **113**
Church St. *B'ton* —4B **104**
Church St. *Butt* —6K **75**
Church St. *Cltn* —8E **154**
Church St. *C'frd* —4D **102**
Church St. *Cleck* —5J **95**
Church St. *Cros M* —6K **131**
Church St. *Cull* —9K **37**
Church St. *Dart* —9G **152**
Church St. *Dew* —3G **116**
Church St. *Ell* —4E **112**
Church St. *Eml* —2F **150**
Church St. *Gild* —6F **78**
Church St. *Gol* —6C **130**
Church St. *G'lnd* —4C **112**
Church St. *Guis* —7J **25**
Church St. *Hal* —6C **92**
Church St. *Haw* —8B **36**
Church St. *Heck* —9A **96**
Church St. *Hept* —8G **70**
Church St. *H'town* —7G **95**
Church St. *Hon* —4L **147**
Church St. *Horb* —1D **136**
Church St. *Hud* —4M **131**
Church St. *I'ly* —5F **8**
Church St. *Kei* —9K **21**
Church St. *Kirks* —2K **61**
Church St. *Leeds* —2F **80**
Church St. *Liv* —7L **95**
Church St. *Lgwd* —4F **130**
Church St. *Mann* —5N **57**
Church St. *M'well* —8L **153**
Church St. *Mold* —5B **132**
Church St. *Morl* —8K **79**
Church St. *N Mill* —2D **164**

Church St. Oss —4N 117
Church St. Pad —5J 131
Church St. Raven —6B 116
Church St. Rothw —8N 81
Church St. Roys —6D 154
Church St. Shipl —7B 40
Church St. Slai —1M 145
Church St. S Elm —7N 157
Church St. Todm —4G 87
Church St. Wake —7L 119
Church St. Weth —4M 17
Church St. W'ford —6D 82
Church St. Wool —2H 153
Church St. Yead —1L 41
Church Ter. Bklnd —7G 111
Church Ter. Hal —8K 73
Church Ter. H'frth —3M 163
Church Ter. Scis —8G 151
Church Top. S Kirk —7J 157
Church Vw. Adel —2M 43
Church Vw. C'frd —5B 102
Church Vw. Cleck —4F 94
Church Vw. Crig —5H 137
Church Vw. F'stne —6C 122
Church Vw. H'frth —6H 163
Church Vw. Kip —3D 84
Church Vw. Leeds —2L 61
Church Vw. S Kirk —7J 157
Church Vw. Sower B —8J 91
Church Vw. T'ner —1G 47
Church Vw. Wake —9N 119
Church Vw. Clo. H'cft —9K 139
Church Vw. Ho. Hud —5K 131
(off Church St.)
Church Vw. M. Cliff —3D 32
Church Vs. S Kirk —7J 157
Churchville. M'fld —7G 66
Churchville Av. M'fld —7F 66
Churchville Dri. M'fld —7G 66
Churchville Ter. M'fld —7G 66
Church Wlk. Bat —9D 96
Church Wlk. Dew —9H 117
Church Wlk. Leeds —7F 62
(off Kirkgate)
Church Wlk. N'wram —2F 92
Church Wlk. Todm —2J 107
Churchway. Croft —1H 139
Church Way. Kei —1J 37
Church Way. Morl —8K 79
Chu. Wood Av. Leeds —9M 43
Churchwood Clo. Slai —9M 129
Chu. Wood Mt. Leeds —8M 43
Chu. Wood Rd. Leeds —9M 43
Churn La. Hal —5K 91
Churn Milk La. Hal —9N 73
Churwell. —6M 79
Churwell Av. Dew —9C 96
Churwell Clo. C'frd —6D 102
Cinder Hill Ct. Kbtn —3G 148
Cinder Hill Rd. Todm —6N 87
Cinder Hills. —5N 163
Cinderhills La. Hal —9D 92
Cinderhills Rd. H'frth —4N 163
Cinder La. C'frd —4C 102
Cinder La. Cliff —2E 32
Cinder La. Lind —4A 12
City. —9L 79
Citygate. Leeds —6B 62
City La. Hal —3L 91
City Mills. Morl —9L 79
(off Peel St.)
City Pk. Ind. Est. Leeds —2M 79
City Rd. B'frd —6A 58
(in two parts)
City Sq. Leeds —7D 62
City Ter. Hal —2M 91
City Varieties. —6E 62
Cityway Ind. Est. B'frd —9F 58
Civic Theatre. —5D 62
Clapgate. Otley —9L 11
Clapgate La. Leeds —8H 81
Clapgate La. Sower B —4D 110
(in two parts)
Clapham Dene Rd. Leeds —5C 64
Clapham St. Denh —6L 55
Clap Ho. Fold. Haig —4C 152
Clapton Av. Hal —6N 91
Clapton Gro. Hal —6N 91
Clapton Mt. Hal —6N 91
(off King Cross St.)
Clara Dri. C'ley —8K 41
Clara Rd. B'frd —1D 58
Clara St. Brigh —2M 113
Clara St. Cow —7F 130
Clara St. Fars —4A 60
Clara St. Hill —2M 131
Clare Cres. Wyke —2A 94
Clare Hall La. Hal —6B 92
Clare Hill. Hud —3M 131
Claremont. B'frd —8B 58
Claremont. Heck —8A 96
Claremont. Pud —7C 60
Claremont. Wyke —2A 94
Claremont Av. Leeds —5C 62
Claremont Av. Shipl —9C 40
Claremont Ct. Leeds —9A 44
Claremont Cres. Croft —2G 139
Claremont Cres. Leeds —1B 62
Claremont Cres. Shipl —9C 40
Claremont Dri. Leeds —9A 44
Claremont Gdns. Bgly —3F 38
Claremont Gdns. Fars —4A 60
Claremont Gro. Leeds —5C 62
Claremont Gro. Pud —7B 60
Claremont Gro. Shipl —9D 40
Claremont Pl. Leeds —7K 61
Claremont Rd. Dew —2E 116
Claremont Rd. Leeds —9A 44
Claremont Rd. Shipl —9C 40
Claremont St. Cleck —4H 95
Claremont St. Hud —3M 131
Claremont St. Leeds —7K 61
Claremont St. Sower B —7J 91
Claremont St. Wake —8N 119
Claremont St. W'ford —7D 82
Claremont Ter. B'frd —8B 58
(off Morley St.)
Claremont Ter. Leeds —7K 61
Claremont Ter. Todm —6M 107
Claremont Ter. Wake —6J 119
Claremont Vw. Leeds —5C 62
Claremont Vw. W'ford —8D 82
Claremount. Leeds —9A 44
Claremount. —3D 92
Claremount Ho. Hal —4C 92
(off Claremount Rd.)
Claremount Rd. Hal —2A 92
Claremount Ter. Hal —2B 92
Clarence Dri. H'fth —8E 42
Clarence Dri. Men —2D 24
Clarence Gdns. H'fth —8E 42
Clarence Gro. H'fth —8E 42
Clarence M. H'fth —8E 42
Clarence Rd. H'fth —8E 42
Clarence Rd. Leeds —7F 62
(in two parts)
Clarence Rd. Shipl —7L 39
Clarence Rd. Wake —8K 119
Clarence St. Bat —7G 96
Clarence St. Cleck —5H 95
Clarence St. Hal —5A 92
Clarence St. Leeds —5F 60
Clarence Ter. Dew —5G 116
Clarence Ter. Pud —6B 60
Clarence Wlk. Wake —6J 119
Clarendon Cotts. Oss —8A 118
(off Horbury Rd.)
Clarendon Ct. Wake —4L 119
Clarendon Pl. Hal —5N 91
Clarendon Pl. Leeds —4C 62
Clarendon Pl. Q'bry —5B 74
Clarendon Rd. Bgly —3G 38
Clarendon Rd. B Spa —1C 32
Clarendon Rd. Leeds —4C 62
Clarendon St. Haw —9C 36
Clarendon St. Kei —2H 37
Clarendon St. Wake —4L 119
(in two parts)
Clarendon Ter. Pud —8B 60
Clarendon Way. Leeds —5C 62
Clare Rd. Cleck —5H 95
Clare Rd. Hal —6B 92
Clare Rd. H Bri —3L 89
Clare Rd. Wyke —2A 94
Clare Rd. Flats. Hal —6B 92
Clare Royd. Light —5M 93
Clare St. Hal —6B 92
Clarges St. B'frd —2A 76
Clarion Camp. Men —3H 25
Clarion Fld. Men —3H 25
Clarion St. Wake —7N 119
Clark Av. Leeds —7H 63
Clark Ct. F'stne —2C 122
Clark Cres. Leeds —7H 63
Clarke Cres. Nor —4H 121
Clarke Gro. Wake —2N 119
Clarke Hall Rd. Stanl —1N 119
Clarke La. Mel —7D 146
Clarke Rd. Wake —7A 98
Clarke St. C'ley —9M 41
Clarke St. Dew —2D 116
Clark Gro. Leeds —8H 63
Clark La. Leeds —7H 63
(in two parts)
Clark Mt. Leeds —7H 63
Clark Rd. Leeds —8H 63
Clark Row. Leeds —8H 63
Clarkson Av. Heck —8B 96
Clarkson Clo. Heck —8B 96
Clarkson Ct. Nor —2K 121
Clarkson St. Dew —5A 116
Clarkson St. Wake —6J 119
Clarkson Ter. Chur —5M 79
Clarkson Vw. Leeds —2C 62
Clark Spring Clo. Morl —6K 79
Clark Spring Ri. Morl —6L 79
Clark Ter. Leeds —7H 63
Clark Vw. Leeds —8H 63
Clattering Stones Rd. Cra V —1L 109
Clayborn Vw. Cleck —6J 95
Clay Butts. Hud —9K 113
Clayfield Bungalows. Knot —8B 104
Clayfield Dri. B'frd —3M 75
Clay Ga. H Bri —2L 71
Clay Hill Dri. Wyke —1B 94
(in two parts)
Clay Ho. La. G'lnd —4B 112
Clay La. Slai —9N 129
Claymore Ri. Sils —9F 6
Clay Pit La. Leeds —5E 62
Claypit La. S Mil —6G 84
Claypit La. T'ner —2G 47
Clay Pits La. Hal —4L 91
Clay Pits La. Sower B —4B 110
Clay Royd La. S'wram —7H 93
Clay St. Hal —5M 91
Clay St. Sower B —8H 91
(in two parts)
Clayton. —1H 75
Clayton Av. Kip —3B 84
Clayton Av. Upt —1D 158
Clayton Clo. Leeds —3H 81
Clayton Ct. F'stne —6C 122
Clayton Ct. H'let —3H 81
Clayton Ct. Leeds —7J 43
Clayton Dri. Leeds —3H 81
Clayton Edge. —3C 74
Clayton Fields. Hud —2L 131
Clayton Grange. Leeds —7J 43
Clayton Gro. Yead —9M 25
Clayton Heights. —3H 75
Clayton Holt. S Kirk —8H 157
Clayton La. B'frd —1C 76
Clayton La. Cytn —2G 74
Clayton M. Nor —8H 101
Clayton Pl. Nor —8H 101
Clayton Ri. Kei —8G 21
Clayton Ri. Wake —7K 99
Clayton Rd. B'frd —1K 75
Clayton Rd. Leeds —3H 81
Claytons Bldgs. F'stne —3D 122
Claytons Cotts. Horb —1C 136
Clayton St. Rothw —8A 82
Clayton St. Wake —6J 119
Clayton Ter. Cull —1K 55
Clayton Vw. S Kirk —8H 157
Clayton Way. Leeds —3H 81
Clayton West. —7J 151
Clayton Wood Bank. Leeds —6J 43
Clayton Wood Clo. Leeds —6J 43
Clayton Wood Ri. Leeds —6J 43
Clayton Wood Rd. Leeds —6H 43
Clay Well. Gol —6C 130
Clearings, The. Leeds —5F 80
Clear Vw. Grime —9A 156
Cleasby Rd. Men —5E 24
Cleavesty La. E Kes —1C 30
Cleckheaton. —5H 95
Cleckheaton Rd. Low M & B'frd —7B 76
Cleeve Hill. Rawd —3M 41
Cleevethorpe Gro. Wake —1N 137
Clegg La. G'lnd —4M 111
Clegg St. Wyke —2A 94
Clement Clo. Norm —2L 121
Clement St. Bkby —2L 131
Clement St. B'frd —6L 57
Clement St. Cros M —6J 131
Clement St. Sower B —8H 91
Clement St. Wake —6H 119
Clement Ter. Dew —5F 116
Clement Ter. Morl —9L 79
(off Ackroyd St.)
Clement Ter. Rothw —9N 81
Clerk Green. —8E 96
Clerk Grn. St. Bat —8E 96
Clervaux Ct. Cytn —9J 57
Cleveden Pl. Hal —2N 91
Clevedon Way. Roys —5C 154
Cleveland Av. Hal —8C 92
Cleveland Av. Knot —8D 104
Cleveland Av. Mel —8E 146
Cleveland Av. Wake —9F 118
Cleveland Gth. Wake —9F 118
Cleveland Gro. Wake —9F 118
Cleveland Pl. H Bri —1H 89
Cleveland Rd. B'frd —3N 57
Cleveland Rd. Hud —3J 131
Cleveland St. Todm —3D 86
Cleveland Way. Shel —6K 149
Cleveley Gdns. H Bri —4M 89
Cleveleys Av. Leeds —1B 80
Cleveleys Ct. Leeds —1B 80
(off Cleveleys Av.)
Cleveleys Mt. Leeds —1B 80
Cleveleys Rd. Leeds —1B 80
Cleveleys St. Leeds —1B 80
(off Cleveleys Rd.)
Cleveleys Ter. Leeds —1B 80
Cliff. —3N 163
Cliff Clo. Brier —6N 155
Cliff Clo. Quarm —4G 130
Cliff Ct. Leeds —2C 62
Cliff Ct. Liv —9L 95
Cliff Cres. Hal —7L 91
Cliff Cres. Kip —4C 84
Cliffdale Rd. Leeds —2D 62
Cliff Dri. Crig —5F 136
Cliffe. —9J 149
Cliffe Ash. Gol —6C 130
Cliffe Av. Bail —5A 40
Cliffe Av. H'den —6N 37
Cliffe Av. Light —5M 93
Cliffe Castle Museum & Gallery. —7H 21
Cliffe Ct. Yead —9N 25
(off Harper La.)
Cliffe Cres. Riddl —8A 22
Cliffe Crest. Horb —9D 118
Cliffe Dri. Rawd —4L 41
(in two parts)
Cliffe End Rd. Hud —4G 130
Cliffe Gdns. Shipl —9N 39
Cliffe Ho. Av. Gar —9A 66
Cliffe La. Bail —6A 40
Cliffe La. Cleck —3J 95
Cliffe La. Hud —3C 148
Cliffe La. Rawd —5N 41
(in two parts)
Cliffe La. T'tn —7D 56
Cliffe La. S. Bail —6A 40
Cliffe La. W. Bail —5A 40
Cliffe Mill Fold. E Mor —8D 22
Cliffe Mt. Gom —3L 95
Cliff End. —4G 131
Cliffe Pk. Shepl —9J 149
Cliffe Pk. Chase. Leeds —8K 61
Cliffe Pk. Clo. Leeds —8K 61
Cliffe Pk. Cres. Leeds —8K 61
Cliffe Pk. Dri. Leeds —8K 61
Cliffe Pk. Mt. Leeds —8K 61
Cliffe Pk. Ri. Leeds —8K 61
Cliffe Rd. B'frd —4D 58
Cliffe Rd. Brigh —1M 113
Cliffe Rd. Kei —3H 37
Cliffe Rd. Shepl —9J 149
Cliffestone Dri. E Mor —8C 22
Cliffe St. Bat —8C 96
Cliffe St. Clay W —7J 151
Cliffe St. Dew —2G 116
Cliffe St. H Bri —1H 89
Cliffe St. Kei —8H 21
Cliffe St. L'boro —9M 107
Cliffe St. T'tn —7B 56
Cliffe Ter. Bail —6A 40
Cliffe Ter. B'frd —5B 58
Cliffe Ter. Denh —6L 55
(off Station Rd.)
Cliffe Ter. Kei —3J 37
Cliffe Ter. Rob H —1J 99
Cliffe Ter. Sower B —7G 91
Cliffe Ter. Weth —4M 17
Cliffe Vw. All —4F 56
Cliffe Vw. Clay W —7J 151
Cliffe Vw. Morl —1G 97
Cliffe Vs. N Brig —1H 57
Cliffe Wood Av. Shipl —9N 39
Cliffe Wood Clo. B'frd —3K 57
Cliffewood Ri. Clay W —7H 151
Cliff Gdns. Hal —7L 91
Cliff Gro. Crig —6E 136
Cliff Hill La. Warley —6H 91
Cliff Hill Rd. Nort —7L 143
Cliff Hollins La. Oaken & E Bier —9F 76
Cliff Ho. La. H'frth —2N 163
Cliff La. Brier —7M 155
Cliff La. H'frth —3M 163
Cliff La. Leeds —2B 62
(in two parts)
Cliff La. Ripp —9D 110
Cliff La. Wake —5K 119
Cliff Mt. Leeds —2C 62
Cliff Mt. Ter. Leeds —2C 62
Clifford. —3D 32
Clifford Av. I'ly —4F 8
Clifford Av. Wake —9M 119
Clifford Clo. B'frd —1B 58
Clifford Ct. Oss —5M 117
(off Pildacre La.)
Clifford Moor Rd. B Spa —9B 18
Clifford Pl. Chur —6L 79
Clifford Rd. Bail —5A 40
Clifford Rd. B Spa —1E 32
Clifford Rd. B'ham —5D 32
Clifford Rd. I'ly —3F 8
Clifford Rd. S Kirk —7H 157
Clifford St. B'frd —9C 58
Clifford St. Cud —8K 155
Clifford St. Sils —7D 6
Clifford St. S Elm —7M 157
Clifford Vw. Wake —9M 119
Cliff Pde. Wake —5K 119
Cliff Pk. Av. Wake —4K 119
Cliff Rd. Crig —6E 136
Cliff Rd. Holme —8D 162
Cliff Rd. H'frth —3N 163
(nr. Cliff La.)
Cliff Rd. H'frth —4F 162
(nr. Green Ga. Rd.)
Cliff Rd. Leeds —2C 62
Cliff Rd. Gdns. Leeds —2C 62
Cliff Side Gdns. Leeds —2C 62
Cliff St. Haw —8D 36
Cliff St. Pon —3J 123
Cliff St. Wake —4H 119
Cliff Ter. Hal —1B 112
Cliff Ter. Leeds —2C 62
Cliff Ter. M'fld —8H 67
Cliff, The. Clay W —7J 151
Cliff Top Pk. Cvn. Site. Gar —1B 8
Cliff Va. Rd. Shipl —1N 57
Cliff Villa Ct. Wake —4K 119
Cliff Vs. Pon —3J 123
(off Cliff St.)
Clifton. —1B 114
(nr. Brighouse)
Clifton. —4J 11
(nr. Newall)
Clifton Av. Barn —9N 153
Clifton Av. Hal —6M 91
Clifton Av. H'frth —2N 163
Clifton Av. Horb —9C 118
Clifton Av. Leeds —5J 63
Clifton Av. Pon —3H 123
Clifton Av. Stan —7N 99
Clifton Clo. Barn —9N 153
Clifton Clo. Horb —9C 118
Clifton Comn. Brigh —1A 114
Clifton Ct. Pud —6B 60
(off Clifton Rd.)
Clifton Cres. Barn —8A 154
Clifton Cres. Horb —9C 118
Clifton Cft. Leeds —2J 43
Clifton Dri. Horb —9C 118
Clifton Dri. Pud —6B 60
Clifton Fld. Cleck —5H 95
Clifton Forge Bus. Pk. Knot —8D 1
Clifton Gdns. Brier —6M 155
Clifton Gth. Pud —7B 60
Clifton Gro. Leeds —5J 63
Clifton Hill. Pud —6B 60
Clifton Ho. H'fth —6G 42
Clifton La. Mel —7D 146
Clifton La. N Clift —5J 11
Clifton Mt. Leeds —5J 63
Clifton Pl. Pud —6B 60
Clifton Pl. Shipl —9N 39
Clifton Pl. Wake —3K 119
Clifton Rd. Brigh —1N 113
Clifton Rd. Grime —9A 156
Clifton Rd. Hal —8B 92
Clifton Rd. Horb —9C 118
Clifton Rd. Hud —3K 131
Clifton Rd. I'ly —6H 9
Clifton Rd. Pud —6B 60
Clifton Rd. Shar C —8J 121
Clifton Side. Hud —5D 114
Clifton St. B'frd —5B 58
Clifton St. Hal —3N 91
Clifton St. Hems —3C 156
Clifton St. Kei —1G 36
Clifton St. Q'bry —4D 74
Clifton St. Sower B —8J 91
Clifton Ter. Bat —7G 97
Clifton Ter. I'ly —5G 9
(off Leeds Rd.)
Clifton Ter. Leeds —5J 63
Clifton Ter. Oss —3M 117
Clifton Vw. Clay W —7J 151
Clifton Vw. Pon —3H 123
Clifton Vs. B'frd —5B 58
Clifton Villas. —5B 58
Clifton Yd. Cro R —7E 36
Clipston Av. Leeds —9B 44
Clipstone Av. Barn —9B 154
Clipstone Mt. Leeds —9B 44
Clipstone St. B'frd —3C 76
Clipstone Ter. Leeds —9B 44
Clipston St. Leeds —9B 44
Clive Pl. B'frd —9N 57
Clive Ter. B'frd —9N 57
Cloberry St. Leeds —4C 62
Clock La. Denh —5K 55
Clock Row Av. S Kirk —6K 157
Clock Row Gro. S Kirk —6K 157
Clock Row Mt. S Kirk —6K 157
Clock Vw. St. Kei —6H 21
Clog Bri. Sils —8E 6
Clog Sole Rd. Brigh —8L 93
Close Head. T'tn —8A 56
Close Head Dri. T'tn —8A 56
Close Head Rd. T'tn —7A 56

ose Hill. —8M 131
ose Hill La. Hud —8L 131
ose Lea. Brigh —2L 113
ose Lea Av. Brigh —2L 113
ose Lea Dri. Brigh —2L 113
ose Lea Way. Brigh —2L 113
ose Rd. C'frd —5F 102
oses Rd. Brigh —2L 113
ose St. Hems —2C 156
ose, The. Alw —2C 44
ose, The. Bar E —9L 47
ose, The. B Spa —9D 18
ose, The. B'frd —9D 40
ose, The. Cltn —8D 154
ose, The. Clay W —7H 151
ose, The. Coll —9J 17
ose, The. Dur —3G 137
ose, The. E Ard —5F 98
ose, The. E Kes —3D 30
ose, The. Guis —8G 25
ose, The. Kip —4A 84
ose, The. Leeds —7G 62
ose, The. Pon —4M 123
ose, The. T'ner —1H 47
oth Hall St. Dew —3G 116
oth Hall St. Hud —4M 131
oth Hall St. Leeds —7E 62
oudberry Way. M'well —9M 153
oudsdale Av. B'frd —1C 76
ough Av. Steet —2C 20
ough Bank. Hal —8H 73
ough Bank La. Oakw —1A 36
ough Bank La. Sower B —2B 110
ough Bldgs. Sower B —8D 90
ough Dri. Birs —2D 96
ough Dri. Fen B —8H 133
ough Dri. Lint —1C 146
ough Foot La. H'frth —9M 163
ough Ga. Grng M —5A 134
ough Ga. Oakw —5D 36
(off Clough La.)
ough Hall La. Hud —8B 132
(in two parts)
ough Head. —6N 129
ough Ho. La. Bklnd —9H 111
ough Ho. La. Den D —3F 166
ough Ho. La. Slai —9K 129
ough La. Brigh —6A 94
(nr. Jay Ho. La.)
ough La. Brigh & Fix —5K 113
(nr. New Hey Rd.)
ough La. Hal —8H 73
ough La. Liv —9H 95
ough La. L'ft —8B 72
ough La. Mir —3N 133
ough La. Oakw —4C 36
ough La. Pad —5H 131
ough Lee. Mars —5F 144
ough Pk. Fen B —8H 133
ough Pl. Hal —8H 73
ough Rd. Floc —8G 134
ough Rd. Hud —9M 113
ough Rd. Norl —1K 111
ough Rd. Slai —6N 129
ough Rd. Todm —2J 107
ough St. B'frd —2C 76
ough St. Morl —9L 79
ough Ter. Sower B —8J 91
ough, The. Fen B —7H 133
ough, The. Mir —5J 115
ough Way. Fen B —8H 133
ovelly Av. Leeds —2D 80
ovelly Gro. Leeds —2D 80
ovelly Pl. Leeds —2D 80
ovelly Row. Leeds —2D 80
ovelly Ter. Leeds —2D 80
over Ct. C'ley —9L 41
over Cres. C'ley —8L 41
overdale. Hal —6J 75
over Hill. Hal —7A 92
over Hill. Liv —7H 95
over Hill Clo. Hal —6A 92
over Hill Rd. Hal —7A 92
over Hill Ter. Hal —7A 92
over Hill Vw. Hal —7A 92
overlands Dri. M'well —9L 153
over St. B'frd —2N 75
overville App. B'frd —6A 76
over Wlk. Upt —2M 157
ub Houses. Arm B —1K 147
ubhouses Cft. Horb —1C 136
ub La. Hal —1L 91
ub La. Leeds —1B 60
ub Row. Leeds —8E 44
ub Row. Wilsd —1B 56
(off Main St.)
ub Row. Yead —9N 25
ub St. B'frd —9L 57
ub St. Todm —3D 86
ub Ter. Fitz —6A 140
umber Dri. Gom —5M 95
untergate. Horb —1D 136
unters La. Hal —7B 90

Clutton St. Bat —7H 97
Clyde App. Leeds —8A 62
Clyde Chase. Leeds —8A 62
(off Clyde Vw.)
Clyde Ct. Leeds —8A 62
Clyde Gdns. Leeds —8A 62
Clyde Grange. Leeds —8A 62
Clydesdale Dri. B'frd —6L 75
Clyde St. Bgly —4E 38
Clyde St. Sower B —9H 91
Clyde St. Wake —7N 119
Clyde Vw. Leeds —8A 62
Clydeville Flats. Otley —1J 25
Clyde Wlk. Leeds —8A 62
Coach Ga. La. Pen —6E 166
Coach Ga. La. Up Den —7G 132
Coach Ho. Dri. Hud —5D 132
Coach La. Cleck —4J 95
Coach La. Lind —3C 12
Coach La. T'tn —8E 56
Coach Rd. Bail —6M 39
Coach Rd. Brigh —7L 93
Coach Rd. Guis —9H 25
Coach Rd. Hal —5K 93
Coach Rd. Hud —9L 113
Coach Rd. Leeds —2H 79
Coach Rd. Mel —8E 146
Coach Rd. Ripp —7D 110
Coach Rd. Wake —7L 99
Coach Row. B'frd —6G 59
Coal Clough Rd. Todm —2D 86
Coal Ga. Slai —9F 128
Coal Ga. Rd. Sower B —5M 109
Coal Hill Dri. Leeds —2C 60
Coal Hill Fold. Leeds —2C 60
Coal Hill Gdns. Leeds —2C 60
Coal Hill Ga. Leeds —2C 60
(off Coal Hill Dri.)
Coal Hill Grn. Leeds —2C 60
Coal Hill La. Fars —2B 60
Coal La. Ogden —2L 73
Coal Pit La. Bat —7C 96
Coal Pit La. Brigh —2B 114
Coalpit La. Hal —8D 92
Coal Pit La. Hud —7L 131
(HD4)
Coal Pit La. Hud —4K 133
(HD5)
Coal Pit La. N Mill —2C 164
Coal Pit La. Shaf —7L 155
Coal Pit La. Shel —8A 150
Coal Pit La. S Elm —5D 158
Coal Pit La. Thpe A —7E 142
Coalpit La. Up Den —5C 166
Coal Rd. Seac —4B 46
Coal Rd. Wike —7M 29
Coat Clo. Shel —6J 149
Coates Clo. Dew —2H 117
Coate's La. Sils —5A 6
Coates St. B'frd —2B 76
Coates Ter. B'frd —1B 76
Cobb Av. Wake —7H 119
Cobbler Hall. Bret —1B 152
Cobbler's La. Pon —1M 123
(in two parts)
Cobbydale Ct. Sils —8D 6
Cobcroft La. Crid S —3K 125
Cobcroft Rd. Hud —1M 131
Cobden Av. Leeds —1J 79
Cobden Clo. Bat —7F 96
Cobden Ct. Hal —4A 92
(off Richmond Rd.)
Cobden Gro. Leeds —1J 79
Cobden M. Morl —8K 79
Cobden Pl. Leeds —1J 79
Cobden Rd. Leeds —1J 79
Cobden St. All —5G 57
Cobden St. Cytn —1G 75
Cobden St. Idle —8F 40
Cobden St. Leeds —1J 79
Cobden St. Morl —8K 79
Cobden St. Q'bry —4E 74
Cobden St. Todm —7K 87
Cobden Ter. Ell —6E 112
(off Savile Rd.)
Cobden Ter. Hal —4H 93
Cobden Ter. Leeds —1J 79
Cobham Pde. Wake —8K 99
Cobham Wlk. Leeds —4G 65
Cockburn Clo. Leeds —2E 80
Cockburn Way. Leeds —2E 80
Cockcroft Gro. B'frd —7E 58
Cockcroft Ho. Leeds —3N 61
(off Chapel La.)
Cockermouth La. Floc M —8A 134
Cockersdale. —5D 78
Cock Hill La. Hal —7F 74
Cock Hill Rd. Cra V —1L 109
Cocking La. Add —4J 7
Cockin La. Cytn —2C 74
Cock La. Croft —9F 120
Cockley Hill La. Hud —1G 132
Cockley M. Khtn —1G 133

Cock Pit La. Rish —2D 128
Cockshot Pit La. M'well —9J 153
Cockshott Clo. Leeds —5J 61
Cockshott Dri. Leeds —5J 61
Cockshott Hill. Pud —3A 60
Cockshott La. Idle —7E 40
Cockshott La. Leeds —5J 61
(in two parts)
Cockshott Pl. Add —1L 7
Coiners Fold. Myth —4K 89
Colbeck Av. Bat —7D 96
(off Nelson St.)
Colbeck Row. Birs —3B 96
Colbeck Ter. Bat —7D 96
(off Nelson St.)
Colbert Av. I'ly —4K 9
Colby Ri. Leeds —7N 63
Coldbeck Dri. B'frd —5K 75
Coldcotes Av. Leeds —4K 63
Coldcotes Cir. Leeds —4L 63
Coldcotes Clo. Leeds —4L 63
Coldcotes Cres. Leeds —4M 63
Coldcotes Dri. Leeds —4L 63
Coldcotes Gth. Leeds —4M 63
Coldcotes Gro. Leeds —4M 63
Coldcotes Vw. Leeds —4M 63
Coldcotes Wlk. Leeds —4M 63
Cold Edge Rd. Hal —8F 72
Cold Edge Rd. Wains —9C 54
Colden. —8B 70
Colden Clo. H Bri —1G 88
Colden La. Hept —7A 70
Colden Rd. H Bri —8E 70
Colders Dri. Mel —8C 146
Colders Grn. Mel —7C 146
Colders La. Mel —8C 146
Cold Hiendley. —9F 138
Cold Hiendley Comn. La. Ryh —8D 138
Coldhill La. Aber —2L 67
Cold Hill La. Ber B —1M 147
Cold Hill La. N Mill —1C 164
Cold Royd La. Hud —3E 132
Coldshaw Top. Haw —1C 54
Cold St. Haw —1C 54
Cold Well La. Holmb —4G 163
Coldwell Rd. Leeds —5C 64
Coldwells Hill. Holy G —8L 111
Coldwell Sq. Leeds —5C 64
Coldwell St. Lint —9C 130
Coleman St. B'frd —5D 58
Coleman St. Leeds —8B 62
Colenso Gdns. Leeds —1B 80
Colenso Grn. Leeds —1B 80
Colenso Gro. Kei —7L 21
(off Aireworth Clo.)
Colenso Mt. Leeds —1B 80
Colenso Pl. Leeds —1B 80
Colenso Rd. Leeds —1B 80
Colenso Ter. Leeds —1B 80
Colenso Wlk. Kei —7L 21
(off Florist St.)
Colenso Way. Kei —7L 21
(off Cornwall Rd.)
Coleridge Clo. Oult —1D 100
Coleridge Cres. Wren —9H 99
Coleridge Gdns. Idle —7G 40
Coleridge La. Pud —9C 60
Coleridge St. Hal —6B 92
Coleridge Way. Pon —1K 123
Coles Way. Riddl —6K 21
Coley. —2J 93
Coley Hall La. Hal —2J 93
Coley Rd. Hal —9H 75
Coley Vw. Hal —1F 92
Coley Vw. Hip —4J 93
Colin Barnaby Ct. Wake —3F 118
Colindale Clo. B'frd —9J 41
Colinsway. Wake —6K 119
Collbrook Av. B'frd —5A 76
Colleen Rd. Dur —5G 136
College Farm La. Lntn —6J 17
College Gro. C'frd —6A 102
College Gro. Wake —3L 119
College Gro. Clo. Wake —3L 119
College Gro. Rd. Wake —4L 119
College Gro. Vw. Wake —3L 119
College La. Sils —2A 6
College Rd. Bgly —1F 38
College Rd. C'frd —5H 103
College Rd. Gild —7G 79
College St. Birs —3B 96
College St. Hud —6J 131
College St. Todm —3E 86
College St. E. Hud —6J 131
College Ter. Ackw —4E 140
College Ter. Hal —7M 91
(off Saville Pk.)
College Vw. Ackw —4E 140
College Wlk. Kei —9J 21
(off Airedale Shop. Cen.)
Collier Clo. Shipl —8K 39
Collier La. Aber —2F 66

Collier La. Bail —3N 39
Colliers La. Leeds —3N 45
Colliers Way. Clay W —5J 151
Colliery App. Loft G —6K 99
Collinfield Ri. B'frd —7L 75
Collingham. —9J 17
Collingham Av. B'frd —5K 75
Collingham Dri. Gar —8N 65
Collingham Fields. —9M 17
Collingwood Ct. B'frd —2C 76
(off Ladywell Clo.)
Collingwood Rd. Nor —1J 121
Collin Moor La. G'lnd —3B 112
Collin Rd. Leeds —5A 64
Collins Ct. Byr —4D 104
Collinson St. Cleck —4H 95
Collins Pl. Ell —4J 113
Collins St. B'frd —1F 76
(BD4)
Collins St. B'frd —2M 75
(BD7)
Collins Yd. Leeds —7E 64
Coll Pl. B'frd —5B 76
Coll Place. —6B 76
Collyer Vw. I'ly —4K 9
Colmore Gro. Leeds —9N 61
Colmore Rd. Leeds —9N 61
Colmore St. Leeds —8N 61
Colne Bri. Rd. Hud —6E 114
Colne Hurst. Hud —7C 114
Colne Rd. Hud —6M 131
Colne Rd. Oakw —5B 36
Colne St. Asp —5A 132
Colne St. Pad —5K 131
Colne Vale Rd. Hud —6F 130
Colne Valley Bus. Pk. Lint —9C 130
Colonel's Wlk. Pon —2J 123
Colour Museum. —7B 58
Colston Clo. B'frd —5K 57
Colton. —8E 64
Colton Ct. Leeds —7E 64
Colton Cft. Leeds —7E 64
Colton Gth. Leeds —7E 64
Colton La. Leeds —7E 64
Colton Retail Pk. Colt —7F 64
Colton Rd. A'ley —7M 61
Colton Rd. Leeds —7D 64
Colton Rd. E. Leeds —8F 64
(in two parts)
Colton St. Leeds —7M 61
Coltsfoot Clo. Pon —4K 123
Columbus St. Hal —3N 91
Colville Ter. Leeds —1D 80
Colville Ter. Thpe —3G 98
Colwyn Av. Leeds —3D 80
Colwyn Mt. Leeds —3D 80
Colwyn Pl. Leeds —3D 80
Colwyn Rd. Leeds —3D 80
Colwyn St. Hud —3J 131
Colwyn Ter. F'stne —5D 122
Colwyn Ter. Leeds —3D 80
Colwyn Vw. Leeds —3D 80
Colyton Mt. All —5F 56
Combs. —8H 117
Combs Rd. Dew —9G 117
Combs, The. Dew —8H 117
Commerce Ct. Cut H —1H 77
Commercial Bldgs. Oaken —9F 76
Commercial Rd. Dew —2F 116
Commercial Rd. Leeds —2K 61
Commercial Rd. Skelm —7D 150
Commercial St. Bat —7F 96
Commercial St. B'frd —7C 58
Commercial St. Brigh —1M 113
Commercial St. C'frd —4D 102
Commercial St. Cleck —5J 95
Commercial St. Denh —6K 55
Commercial St. Earl —4J 117
Commercial St. Hal —5B 92
Commercial St. H Bri —1H 89
Commercial St. Heck —8B 96
Commercial St. Hud —6N 131
Commercial St. Leeds —6E 62
Commercial St. Morl —9K 79
Commercial St. Oakw —5B 36
Commercial St. Q'bry —4C 74
Commercial St. Raven —5C 116
Commercial St. Rothw —8N 81
Commercial St. Shipl —7N 39
Commercial St. Slai —1N 145
Commercial St. T'tn —8D 56
Commercial St. Todm —7L 87
Commercial St. Wake —7M 119
Commercial Vs. Pud —8A 60
Commondale Way. Euro I —7E 76
Common End. —8E 134
(nr. Flockton)
Common End. —3F 156
(nr. Hemsworth)
Common End. —7C 150
(nr. Skelmanthorpe)
Comn. End La. Fen B —7H 133
Common Holme La. I'ly —3C 8

Common Ing La. Ryh —8J 139
(in two parts)
Common La. Beal —7M 105
Common La. Den D —2E 166
Common La. E Ard —4D 98
Common La. Eml —2B 150
Common La. Floc —9D 134
Common La. Hal —7E 92
Common La. Knot —8G 104
Common La. Roys —5D 154
Common La. Thpe A —6A 142
Common La. Upt —2M 157
Common La. Wake —1F 152
Common La. W'ton —5A 138
Common Piece La. E Hard —1L 141
Common Rd. Bat —8C 96
Common Rd. Brier —7A 156
Common Rd. Ell —5H 113
Common Rd. Hud —2M 131
Common Rd. Kin —8A 140
Common Rd. Low M —7N 75
Common Rd. Pon —8D 156
Common Rd. Stan —5A 100
Common Rd. Av. S Kirk —8G 156
Common Rd. Ind. Est. Low M —7B 76
Common Side. —3M 149
Commonside. Bat —1G 116
Commonside. Liv —1J 115
Common Side. Meth —4M 101
Common Side La. Pon —6A 122
Common Ter. Brigh —2M 113
Common, The. Dew —8H 117
Common Top. —7H 133
Como Av. B'frd —5L 57
Como Dri. B'frd —6L 57
Como Gdns. B'frd —5L 57
Como Gro. B'frd —5L 57
Compeigne Av. Riddl —7M 21
Compton. —2K 31
Compton Av. Leeds —4J 63
Compton Cres. Leeds —4J 63
Compton Gro. Leeds —4J 63
Compton La. Coll —2K 31
(in two parts)
Compton La. Woth —3G 30
Compton Mt. Leeds —4J 63
Compton Pl. Leeds —4J 63
Compton Rd. Leeds —4J 63
Compton Row. Leeds —4J 63
Compton St. B'frd —3G 76
Compton St. Kei —8K 21
(off Parson St.)
Compton St. Leeds —4J 63
Compton Ter. Leeds —4J 63
Compton Vw. Leeds —4J 63
Concordia St. Leeds —7E 62
Concord St. Hon —5L 147
Concord St. Leeds —5F 62
Concrete St. Hal —3N 91
Conduit Pl. B'frd —5A 58
Conduit St. B'frd —5A 58
Coney La. Hal —7N 73
Coney La. Kei —9J 21
Coney Moor Gro. Meth —1N 101
Coney Wlk. Dew —3C 116
Coney Warren La. Stan —4N 99
Conference Pl. Leeds —7K 61
Conference Rd. Leeds —7K 61
Conference Ter. Leeds —7K 61
Congress Mt. Leeds —7K 61
Congress St. Leeds —7K 61
Congreve App. Bard —3F 30
Congreve Way. Bard —2F 30
Conisborough La. Gar —7B 66
Coniston Av. Dart —7J 153
Coniston Av. Hud —3B 132
Coniston Av. Leeds —1A 62
Coniston Av. Q'bry —4C 74
Coniston Clo. Ell —4G 112
Coniston Clo. Q'bry —4C 74
Coniston Ct. Loft G —6K 99
Coniston Cres. Wake —3N 119
Coniston Dri. C'frd —5L 103
Coniston Gdns. C'frd —5L 103
Coniston Gdns. Leeds —8N 63
Coniston Gro. Bail —6K 39
Coniston Gro. B'frd —4L 57
Coniston Ho. Ell —4E 112
(off Crown St.)
Coniston Pl. Knot —2D 124
Coniston Rd. B'frd —2K 75
Coniston Rd. Dew —1J 117
Coniston Rd. Mel —8D 146
Coniston Rd. Rothw —6D 82
Coniston Way. Weth —3J 17
Coniston Way. W'ford —7D 82
Connaught Fold. Hud —6C 114
Connaught Rd. I'ly —6J 9
Consort St. Leeds —5B 62
Consort Ter. Leeds —5B 62
Consort Vw. Leeds —5B 62
Consort Wlk. Leeds —5B 62

Constable Gro. *Stan* —6N **99**
Constable Rd. *I'ly* —6J **9**
Constable Rd. *Wake* —4A **98**
Constance Gdns. *Leeds* —4D **62**
Constance St. *Shipl* —7L **39**
Constance Way. *Leeds* —4D **62**
Constitutional St. *Hal* —7N **91**
Convent Av. *S Kirk* —7J **157**
Conway Av. *Leeds* —3H **63**
Conway Cres. *Bat* —1F **116**
Conway Cres. *Mel* —8C **146**
Conway Dri. *Leeds* —3H **63**
Conway Gro. *Leeds* —3H **63**
Conway Mt. *Leeds* —3H **63**
Conway Pl. *Leeds* —3H **63**
Conway Rd. *Leeds* —3H **63**
Conway Rd. *Wake* —4G **119**
Conway St. *B'frd* —9D **58**
Conway St. *Hal* —6N **91**
Conway St. *Leeds* —3H **63**
Conway St. *S'ley* —5A **60**
Conway Ter. *Leeds* —3H **63**
Conway Vw. *Leeds* —3H **63**
Cook Cft. *Dew* —2F **116**
Cooke Cres. *Gom* —4L **95**
Cooke St. *Kei* —9J **21**
Cook Ga. *Cliff* —3D **32**
Cook La. *Heck* —8N **95**
Cook La. *Kei* —9J **21**
Cook Mans. *B'frd* —9C **58**
Cookridge. —1H 43
Cookridge Av. *Leeds* —1H **43**
Cookridge Dri. *Leeds* —1G **43**
Cookridge Gro. *Leeds* —1H **43**
Cookridge La. *Cook* —8G **27**
Cookridge St. *Leeds* —6D **62**
Cooksland La. *Old Sn* —3M **121**
Cookson Clo. *C'frd* —7K **103**
Cookson St. *Brigh* —9L **93**
Cook Sq. *Morl* —6L **79**
Coombe Hill. *Q'bry* —3G **75**
Coombe Rd. *Hud* —5E **130**
Co-op Bldgs. *Bail B* —5N **93**
Co-operation St. *Leeds* —1K **79**
Co-operative Cotts. *Brier* —6N **155**
Co-operative St. *Chur* —5M **79**
Co-operative St. *Dew* —3L **117**
Co-operative St. *Horb* —1C **136**
Co-operative St. *Kei* —4G **37**
Co-operative St. *Loft* —3L **99**
Co-operative St. *Mir* —8L **115**
Co-operative St. *Morl* —8K **79**
Cooperative St. *Todm* —4J **107**
Co-operative St. *Wake* —6J **119**
Co-operative Ter. *H'frth* —1A **164**
Co-operative Ter. *Holy G* —8M **111**
Cooper Bri. Rd. *Mir* —5F **114**
Cooper Clo. *Bgly* —2F **38**
Cooper Fields. *L'ft* —6E **90**
Cooper Gro. *Hal* —6J **75**
Cooper Hill. *Pud* —9C **60**
*Cooper Ho. Hems —3D **156***
(off Lilley St.)
Cooper La. *B'frd & Hal* —3J **75**
Cooper La. *H'frth* —3M **163**
Cooper La. *Hoy S* —8K **167**
Cooper Rd. *Dart* —9E **152**
Cooper Rd. *Weth* —4M **17**
Cooper St. *Todm* —6N **87**
Co-op La. *Holmb* —5J **163**
Copeland St. *B'frd* —9H **59**
Copeworth Dri. *Hall G* —7H **137**
Copgrove Clo. *B'frd* —2J **77**
Copgrove Ct. *B'frd* —2J **77**
Copgrove Rd. *B'frd* —2J **77**
Copgrove Rd. *Leeds* —2J **63**
Cop Hill La. *Slai* —1H **145**
Cop Hill Side. *Slai* —1H **145**
Copley. —2N 111
Copley Av. *Hal* —7M **91**
Copley Av. *Mel* —7B **146**
Copley Bank Rd. *Gol* —7B **130**
Copley Circ. *Hal* —2N **111**
Copley Clo. *Hal* —2A **112**
Copley Glen. *Hal* —1A **112**
Copley Gro. *Hal* —1A **112**
Copley Hall St. *Hal* —2A **112**
Copley Hall Ter. *Hal* —1A **112**
Copley Hill. —2D 96
Copley Hill. *Birs* —3C **96**
Copley Hill. *Leeds* —8A **62**
Copley Hill Trad. Est. *Leeds* —9A **62**
Copley Hill Way. *Leeds* —9A **62**
Copley La. *Aber* —1J **67**
Copley La. *Hal* —2N **111**
Copley La. *Rob H* —9K **81**
Copley La. *Shel* —9M **149**
*Copley Mill Ho. Hal —1N **111***
(off St Stephen's St.)
Copley Mt. *Hal* —1A **112**
Copley St. *Bat* —5D **96**
Copley St. *B'frd* —2N **75**
Copley St. *Leeds* —8A **62**
Copley Ter. *Hal* —1A **112**
Copley Vw. *Hal* —1A **112**
Copley Wood Ter. *Hal* —1A **112**
Copley Yd. *Leeds* —8A **62**
Coplowe La. *Wilsd* —8C **38**
Copmanroyd. *N Clift* —6L **11**
Copperas Ho. Ter. *Todm* —1H **107**
Copperas Row. *G'lnd* —4L **111**
Copper Beech Clo. *Pon* —5L **123**
Copper Beech Ct. *W'ton* —4B **138**
Copperfield Av. *Leeds* —8H **63**
Copperfield Cres. *Leeds* —8H **63**
Copperfield Dri. *Leeds* —8H **63**
Copperfield Gro. *Leeds* —8H **63**
Copperfield Mt. *Leeds* —8J **63**
Copperfield Pl. *Leeds* —8H **63**
Copperfield Row. *Leeds* —8H **63**
Copperfield Ter. *Leeds* —8H **63**
Copperfield Vw. *Leeds* —8H **63**
Copperfield Wlk. *Leeds* —8H **63**
Coppertop M. *Pon* —9L **103**
Coppice Clo. *Wake* —3N **119**
Coppice Dri. *Neth* —3H **147**
Coppice Grange. *Yead* —8M **25**
Coppice, The. *Bar E* —9L **47**
Coppice, The. *Hud* —7N **113**
Coppice, The. *I'ly* —3F **8**
Coppice, The. *Mir* —3K **115**
Coppice, The. *Yead* —2K **41**
Coppice Vw. *B'frd* —7E **40**
Coppice Way. *Leeds* —9J **45**
Coppicewood Av. *B'frd* —8M **57**
Coppice Wood Av. *Guis & Yead* —8L **25**
Coppice Wood Clo. *Guis* —7L **25**
Coppice Wood Cres. *Yead* —8L **25**
Coppicewood Gro. *B'frd* —8M **57**
Coppice Wood Gro. *Guis* —8L **25**
Coppice Wood Ri. *Yead* —8M **25**
Coppies, The. *Wyke* —9N **75**
Coppin Hall Gro. *Mir* —5H **115**
Coppin Hall La. *Mir* —4H **115**
Copplestone Wlk. *B'frd* —3J **77**
Coppy Clo. *Bgly* —9F **38**
Coppy La. *Leeds* —2F **60**
Coppy La. *Oakw* —1K **35**
Coppy La. *Pec W* —2G **70**
Coppy Nook La. *Cra V* —1L **109**
Coppy Rd. *Add* —1L **7**
Coppy Rd. *Steet* —3B **20**
Coppy Wood Dri. *I'ly* —2H **9**
Copse, The. *Bgly* —4J **39**
Copse, The. *Bur W* —9C **10**
Copse, The. *F'stne* —2C **122**
Copse, The. *Schol* —5D **94**
Copthorne Gdns. *Hud* —6D **114**
Copthurst Rd. *H'frth* —8J **163**
Copt Royd Gro. *Yead* —9L **25**
Copy St. *All* —5G **57**
Corban St. *B'frd* —2G **76**
Corby St. *Hud* —1M **131**
Cordingley Clo. *B'frd* —4J **77**
Cordingley St. *B'frd* —4J **77**
Corfe Clo. *Bat* —2E **96**
Corn Bank. *Neth* —3H **147**
*Corn Exchange. Leeds —7E **62***
(off Cloth Hall St.)
Cornfield. *Dew* —2C **116**
Cornfield Av. *Hud* —3F **130**
Cornfield St. *Todm* —6M **87**
Cornholme. —3D 86
*Cornholme Ter. Todm —3D **86***
(off Burnley Rd.)
Corn Mkt. *Hal* —5B **92**
Corn Mkt. *Pon* —3J **123**
Corn Mill. *Men* —4F **24**
Cornmill Av. *Liv* —9N **95**
Cornmill Clo. *Bard* —5E **30**
Cornmill Cres. *Liv* —9M **95**
Cornmill Dri. *Liv* —9M **95**
Corn Mill Fold. *H'fth* —7H **43**
Cornmill La. *Bard* —5E **30**
Corn Mill La. *Bur W* —8E **10**
Corn Mill La. *Cytn* —9E **56**
Cornmill La. *Liv* —9M **95**
Corn Mill Yd. *Leeds* —7G **61**
Cornrace Vw. *Hud* —6N **131**
(in two parts)
Corn Royd. *N Mill* —3B **164**
Cornstone Fold. *Leeds* —7F **60**
Corn St. *Kei* —3G **37**
Cornus Gdns. *Leeds* —5F **80**
Cornwall Av. *Sils* —8C **6**
Cornwall Clo. *Rothw* —7M **81**
Cornwall Cres. *Bail* —3N **39**
Cornwall Cres. *Brigh* —6N **93**
Cornwall Cres. *Rothw* —7M **81**
*Cornwall Ho. Ell —5E **112***
(off Crown St.)
Cornwall Pl. *B'frd* —5B **58**
Cornwall Rd. *Bgly* —5G **38**
Cornwall Rd. *B'frd* —5B **58**
Cornwall Rd. *Kei* —7L **21**
Cornwall Ter. *B'frd* —5B **58**
Coronation Av. *Esh* —3H **41**
Coronation Av. *Kip* —4C **84**
Coronation Av. *Nor* —8G **100**
Coronation Av. *Roys* —5F **154**
Coronation Av. *Shaf* —6J **155**
Coronation Bungalows. *Kip* —4C **84**
Coronation Bungalows. Knot
*(off Ferrybridge Rd.) —8C **104***
Coronation Bus. Cen. *Kei* —7K **21**
Coronation Mt. *Kei* —9F **20**
Coronation Pde. *Leeds* —8N **63**
Coronation Rd. *Hal* —8B **92**
Coronation Rd. *Shar C* —8J **121**
Coronation St. *Carl* —1M **99**
Coronation St. *C'frd* —3F **102**
Coronation St. *Ell* —5E **112**
Coronation St. *G'lnd* —4B **112**
Coronation St. *Oaken* —8E **76**
Coronation St. *Wren* —1H **119**
Coronation Ter. *Birs* —3C **96**
Coronation Ter. *C'frd* —6G **102**
Coronation Ter. *Sower B* —5E **110**
Coronation Wlk. *Kei* —8F **20**
Coronation Way. *Kei* —9E **20**
Corporal La. *Hal* —7D **74**
Corporation St. *B'frd* —3G **58**
Corporation St. *Dew* —3G **116**
Corporation St. *Hal* —4B **92**
Corporation St. *Hud* —5M **131**
Corporation St. *Morl* —8J **79**
Corporation St. *Sower B* —8H **91**
Corrance Rd. *Wyke* —3B **94**
Corrie St. *T'tn* —8D **56**
Cotchers La. *Saxt* —7N **49**
Cote Farm. La. *Thack* —6D **40**
Cotefields Av. *Fars* —3N **59**
Cote Hill Fold. *Hal* —6K **91**
Cote La. *All* —5F **56**
Cote La. *Brigh* —6K **113**
Cote La. *Far* —4N **59**
Cote La. *H'frth* —8M **163**
Cote Rd. *Sower B* —7B **110**
Coteroyd Av. *Chur* —5M **79**
Coteroyd Dri. *Chur* —6M **79**
Cote, The. *Fars* —4N **59**
Cote Wall M. *Mir* —8A **116**
Cotewall Rd. *B'frd* —2B **76**
Cotswold Av. *Shipl* —8C **40**
Cotswold Clo. *Hems* —2F **156**
Cotswold Dri. *Gar* —9N **65**
Cotswold Dri. *Knot* —8D **104**
Cotswold Dri. *Liv* —7H **95**
Cotswold Dri. *Rothw* —7M **81**
Cotswold M. *Kbtn* —2K **149**
Cotswold Rd. *Rothw* —7N **81**
Cotswold Rd. *Wake* —6F **118**
*Cottage Grn. B'frd —6L **57***
(off Lane Ends Clo.)
Cottage Rd. *B'frd* —8H **41**
Cottage Rd. *Leeds* —9N **43**
Cottage, The. *Shepl* —3G **165**
Cottam Av. *B'frd* —8N **57**
Cottam Cft. *Hems* —2E **156**
Cottam Ter. *B'frd* —8N **57**
Cotterdale. *All* —3F **56**
Cotterdale Holt. *Coll* —8H **17**
Cotterdale Vw. *Leeds* —8N **63**
Cotterill Rd. *Knot* —9C **104**
Cottingley. —9G 38
(nr. Bingley)
Cottingley. —4N 79
(nr. Churwell)
Cottingley App. *Leeds* —4N **79**
Cottingley Chase. *Leeds* —4M **79**
Cottingley Cliffe Rd. *Bgly* —9H **39**
Cottingley Ct. *Leeds* —4N **79**
Cottingley Cres. *Leeds* —4N **79**
Cottingley Dri. *Bgly* —7F **38**
Cottingley Dri. *Leeds* —3M **79**
Cottingley Fold. *Leeds* —3M **79**
Cottingley Gdns. *Leeds* —4N **79**
Cottingley Grn. *Leeds* —4N **79**
Cottingley Gro. *Leeds* —4N **79**
Cottingley Heights. *Leeds* —4N **79**
Cottingley Mnr. Pk. *Ctly* —8G **39**
Cottingley Moor Rd. *Bgly* —2F **56**
Cottingley New Rd. *Bgly* —8G **39**
Cottingley Rd. *All* —3F **56**
Cottingley Rd. *Leeds* —3M **79**
Cottingley Springs Cvn. Pk. *Leeds* —4K **79**
Cottingley Ter. *B'frd* —5B **58**
Cottingley Towers. *Leeds* —4N **79**
Cottingley Va. *Leeds* —4N **79**
Cotton Stones. —3C 110
Cotton St. *Wake* —7L **119**
Couford Gro. *Hud* —7D **114**
Coule Royd. *Hud* —3C **132**
*Coulsdon Ho. B'frd —5A **58***
(off Trenton Dri.)
Coultas Clo. *Men* —4F **24**
County Arc. *Leeds* —6E **62**
County Bri. *Denh* —9K **55**
County Clo. *Bat* —6F **96**
Coupe Gro. *Nor* —7G **101**
Coupland Pl. *Leeds* —1D **80**
Coupland Rd. *Gar* —7M **65**
Coupland Rd. *Leeds* —1D **80**
Coupland St. *Leeds* —2D **80**
Coupland St. *Todm* —7K **87**
Courtenay Clo. *B'frd* —7J **59**
Courtenays. *Leeds* —2C **64**
Courthouse St. *Otley* —9L **11**
Court La. *Hal* —5K **91**
*Courtney Ho. B'frd —5B **58***
(off Trenton Dri.)
Court No.6. *Bat* —8F **96**
Courts Leet. *Wyke* —9A **76**
Court, The. *Ackw* —2H **141**
Court, The. *Alw* —2B **44**
Court, The. *Liv* —8J **95**
Courtway, The. *Ackw* —3H **141**
Courtyard M. *Sils* —2F **20**
Courtyard, The. *Birs* —2C **96**
Courtyard, The. *Cros M* —6J **131**
Courtyard, The. *Pon* —9L **103**
Courtyard, The. *Wool* —2J **153**
Cousen Av. *B'frd* —9L **57**
Cousen Rd. *B'frd* —1N **75**
Cousin La. *Hal* —8L **73**
Coutances Way. *Bur W* —4L **9**
Coventry St. *B'frd* —1F **76**
Coventry St. *Hal* —5L **91**
Coverdale Gth. *Coll* —9H **17**
Coverdale Way. *Bail* —3C **40**
Cover Dri. *B'frd* —5M **75**
Coverley Gth. *Yead* —9K **25**
Coverley Ri. *Yead* —9K **25**
Covert, The. *Bat* —5C **96**
Covet, The. *B'frd* —7H **41**
Covey Clough Ct. *Mir* —1K **133**
Cow & Calf. —7K 9
Cowcliffe. —9M 113
Cowcliffe Hill Rd. *Hud* —7L **113**
Cowcliff Hill Rd. *H'frth* —8A **164**
Cow Clo. Cotts. *Wyke* —2D **94**
Cow Clo. Gro. *Leeds* —1K **79**
Cow Clo. La. *Wyke* —2C **94**
Cow Clo. Rd. *Leeds* —1J **79**
Cowdray Dri. *Schol* —4D **94**
Cowdry Clo. *Dew* —9H **117**
Cowfold St. *Todm* —6K **87**
Cow Ga. *Lgwd* —4E **130**
Cowgill St. *B'frd* —5A **58**
Cow Grn. *Hal* —5B **92**
Cow Hey La. *H Bri* —2E **70**
Cow Heys. *Hud* —3C **132**
Cow Hill Ga. La. *Hal* —5L **73**
Cowhurst Av. *Todm* —5H **87**
Cow La. *Bur S* —1E **104**
Cow La. *Hal* —1B **112**
Cow La. *Knot* —8F **104**
Cow La. *Pec W* —5F **70**
Cow La. *Ryh* —1J **155**
Cow La. *Shar C* —7H **121**
Cow La. *S'wram* —8J **93**
Cow La. *Sower B* —5D **110**
(nr. Soyland Town Rd.)
Cow La. *Sower B* —3A **110**
(nr. Wicking La.)
Cow La. *Wome* —8M **125**
Cowlersley La. *Lint & Hud* —9D **130**
Cowlersley. —7F 130
Cowley Cres. *B'frd* —2H **57**
Cowley Rd. *Leeds* —1C **60**
Cowling La. *N'wram* —7E **74**
Cowmes. —5G 132
Cowm St. *S'fth* —6A **106**
Cowpasture Rd. *I'ly* —5G **9**
Cowper Av. *Leeds* —4J **63**
Cowper Cres. *Leeds* —4J **63**
Cowper Gro. *Leeds* —3J **63**
Cowper Mt. *Leeds* —4J **63**
Cowper Rd. *Leeds* —4J **63**
Cowper St. *Dew* —5F **116**
Cowper St. *Leeds* —2F **62**
Cowper Ter. *Leeds* —4J **63**
Cowrakes Clo. *Hud* —1F **130**
Cowrakes Rd. *Hud* —1E **130**
Cowroyd Pl. *Hal* —3C **92**
Cowslip St. *Hud* —5J **131**
Coxley. —3N 135
Coxley Cres. *Neth* —4N **135**
Coxley La. *M'twn* —3N **135**
Coxley Vw. *Neth* —5M **135**
Coxwold Hill. *Weth* —2M **17**
Coxwold Vw. *Weth* —2M **17**
Coxwold Wlk. *All* —7F **56**
Crabby La. *Hud* —1E **132**
Crabgate Dri. *Skel* —7K **159**
Crabgate La. *Skel* —8K **159**
Crab Hill. *Pon* —3J **123**
Crab La. *Leeds* —6M **61**
Crab La. *N'dam* —6K **137**
Crabtree Av. *Heck* —7B **96**
Crabtree Grn. *Coll* —9H **17**
Crabtree Hill. *Coll* —9J **17**
Crabtree La. *E Kes* —2D **30**
Crab Tree La. *S Elm* —6B **158**
Crab Tree La. *Went* —8G **142**
Crabtree St. *B'frd* —1M **75**
Crabtree St. *Hal* —5M **91**
Crabtree Way. *Ting* —5B **98**
Crackenedge. —2G 116
Crackenedge La. *Dew* —1G **116**
(in two parts)
Crackenedge Ter. *Dew* —2G **116**
Crackhills La. *Sick* —4C **16**
Crack La. *Wilsd* —1B **56**
Cracoe Rd. *B'frd* —8F **58**
Crag Clo. *Hal* —9K **73**
Crag Ct. *Hal* —9K **73**
Crag Gdns. *B'ham* —6D **32**
Cragg Av. *H'fth* —7E **42**
Cragg Bottom Rd. *Oldf* —7F **34**
Cragg Dri. *I'ly* —6L **9**
Cragg Hill. *H'fth* —7F **42**
Cragg La. *B'frd* —2M **75**
Cragg La. *Cra V* —6K **89**
Cragg La. *Denh* —9L **55**
Cragg La. *T'tn* —9M **55**
Cragg Rd. *Cra V* —6G **88**
Cragg Rd. *H Bri* —9K **89**
Cragg Rd. *H'fth* —7F **42**
Cragg St. *B'frd* —2M **75**
Cragg Ter. *B'frd* —2M **75**
Cragg Ter. *H'fth* —7E **42**
(in two parts)
Cragg Ter. *Rawd* —5M **41**
Cragg Top. *Denh* —9L **55**
Cragg Vale. —9K 89
Cragg Vw. *Sils* —7E **6**
*Craggwell Ter. H'fth —8F **42***
(off Wood La.)
Craggwood Clo. *H'fth* —8F **42**
Craggwood Rd. *H'fth* —8F **42**
*Craggwood Ter. H'fth —8F **42***
(off Craggwood Rd.)
Crag Hill Av. *Leeds* —9H **27**
Crag Hill Rd. *B'frd* —5E **40**
Crag Hill Vw. *Leeds* —1H **43**
Crag La. *Hal* —9K **73**
Crag La. *Huby* —5M **13**
Crag La. *Leeds* —2A **44**
Crag La. *N Rig* —3L **13**
Crag Mt. *Pon* —3J **123**
Crag Pl. *Kei* —3J **37**
Crag Rd. *Shipl* —8A **40**
Cragside. *B'frd* —6D **40**
Cragside Clo. *Leeds* —8H **43**
Cragside Cres. *Leeds* —8H **43**
Cragside Gdns. *Leeds* —9H **43**
Cragside Gro. *Leeds* —9G **43**
Cragside Mt. *Leeds* —8H **43**
Cragside Pl. *Leeds* —9H **43**
Cragside Wlk. *Leeds* —9G **43**
Crag, The. *B'ham* —6D **32**
*Crag Top. Fair —9N **85***
(off Gauk St.)
Crag Vw. *B'frd* —9G **41**
Crag Vw. *Huby* —5M **13**
Craig Clo. *Bat* —6F **96**
Craiglands. *Hal* —4J **93**
Craiglands Pk. *I'ly* —6H **9**
Craiglands Rd. *I'ly* —6H **9**
Craiglea Dri. *Wyke* —2B **94**
Craigmore Ct. *B'frd* —3K **77**
Craigmore Dri. *I'ly* —5K **9**
Craig-Y-Don. *Dew* —4J **117**
Cranberry Av. *Todm* —4K **107**
Cranborne Dri. *Dart* —8H **153**
Cranbourne Rd. *B'frd* —4J **57**
Cranbrook Av. *B'frd* —5A **76**
Cranbrook Av. *Leeds* —2C **80**
Cranbrook Pl. *B'frd* —2C **76**
Cranbrook St. *B'frd* —2C **76**
Cranbrook St. *Cytn* —1G **74**
Cranbrook Vw. *Pud* —9D **60**
Cranbrook Way. *Pon* —9L **103**
Cranewells Dri. *Leeds* —8E **64**
Cranewells Grn. *Leeds* —8D **64**
Cranewells Ri. *Leeds* —7D **64**
Cranewells Va. *Leeds* —8D **64**
Cranewells Vw. *Leeds* —7D **64**
Cranfield Dri. *Skel* —7M **159**
Cranford Gdns. *Roys* —5C **154**
Cranford Pl. *Wilsd* —1B **56**
Crangle Fields. *Stkmr* —9F **148**
(nr. Far Well La.)
Crangle Fields. *Stkmr* —7G **148**
(nr. Stocks Moor Rd.)
Cranleigh Mt. *Kei* —2G **36**
Cranmer Bank. *Leeds* —4C **44**
Cranmer Clo. *Leeds* —4C **44**
Cranmer Gdns. *Leeds* —4C **44**
Cranmer Gdns. *Mel* —7D **146**
*Cranmer Ho. B'frd —6D **58***
(off Otley Rd.)

ranmer Ri. Leeds —3C 44
ranmer Rd. B'frd —5D 58
ranmer Rd. Leeds —4C 44
(in two parts)
ranmore Cres. Leeds —8H 81
ranmore Dri. Leeds —8H 81
ranmore Gdns. Leeds —8G 81
ranmore Gth. Leeds —8G 81
ranmore Grn. Leeds —8G 81
ranmore Gro. Leeds —8G 81
ranmore La. Leeds —8H 81
ranmore Ri. Leeds —8H 81
ranmore Rd. Leeds —8G 81
ranswick Ho. B'frd —9G 40
(off Summerfield Rd.)
ranwood Dri. Hud —4E 132
raven Av. Sils —8E 6
raven Av. T'tn —8D 56
raven Clo. Gom —4N 95
raven Clo. Roys —5C 154
raven Ct. B'frd —6L 57
(off Lane Ends Clo.)
raven Ct. Hal —5N 91
raven Ct. Sils —8F 6
raven Cres. Add —1L 7
ravendale Rd. Dew —5A 116
raven Dri. Gom —4N 95
raven Dri. Sils —8E 6
raven Gth. Beal —5M 105
raven Gro. Sils —8F 6
raven Ho. Todm —3J 107
raven La. Gom —4N 95
raven Pk. Men —3D 24
raven Pl. Hal —6N 91
raven Rd. Dew —5D 116
raven Rd. Hems —3D 156
raven Rd. Kei —8L 21
raven Rd. Leeds —3D 62
raven St. B'frd —6D 58
raven St. Dew —5A 116
raven St. Hud —6F 130
raven St. Otley —1M 25
raven St. Wake —4L 119
raven Ter. B'frd —3G 58
raven Ter. Hal —6N 91
raven Ter. Otley —1M 25
(off Craven St.)
rawford Av. B'frd —5A 76
rawford Dri. Wake —4H 119
rawford St. B'frd —1E 76
rawford St. Todm —3K 107
rawley Av. S Kirk —6K 157
rawshaw Av. Pud —7C 60
rawshaw Clo. Pud —7B 60
rawshaw Gdns. Pud —7C 60
rawshaw Hill. Pud —7B 60
rawshaw La. Grng M & Eml —8C 134
rawshaw Pk. Pud —7B 60
rawshaw Ri. Pud —8B 60
rawshaw Rd. Pud —7B 60
rawshaw St. Dew —5C 116
rawthorne Cres. Hud —7C 114
rayford Dri. Croft —1G 139
ray La. Holy G —9K 111
rediton Av. All —6G 56
rescent Av. Dew —6A 116
rescent Av. Hud —2J 147
rescent Av. Rothw —6A 82
rescent Bungalows. Thor —2F 98
rescent Ct. Leeds —1B 44
rescent Gdns. Leeds —3F 44
rescent Grange. Leeds —1E 80
rescent Rd. Bkby —1L 131
rescent Rd. H'cft —9L 139
rescent Rd. Neth —2J 147
rescent Royd. Hud —5E 132
rescent St. Todm —7K 87
rescent Ter. I'ly —5G 9
rescent, The. Adel —3K 43
rescent, The. Alw —1B 44
rescent, The. Bail —5A 40
rescent, The. Bgly —1D 38
rescent, The. B'shaw —6L 77
rescent, The. B'frd —5K 75
rescent, The. Bmly —3F 60
rescent, The. Brigh —9N 93
(off Bonegate Rd.)
rescent, The. Bur W —9C 10
rescent, The. C'frd —6F 102
rescent, The. Dew —6A 116
rescent, The. Gar —6A 66
rescent, The. Guis —8G 24
rescent, The. Halt —6C 64
rescent, The. Hip —4J 93
rescent, The. Holy G —7N 111
rescent, The. H'fth —6C 42
rescent, The. I'ly —4K 9
rescent, The. Kip —4A 84
rescent, The. Kbtn —2L 149
rescent, The. Leeds —3C 62
(off Woodhouse La.)
rescent, The. Liv —7H 95
Crescent, The. Men —4F 24
Crescent, The. M'fld —8G 67
Crescent, The. Neth —5M 135
Crescent, The. N Mill —2C 164
Crescent, The. Nor —8G 100
Crescent, The. N Rig —3N 13
Crescent, The. Otley —7L 11
Crescent, The. Pud —6C 60
Crescent, The. Sick —4D 16
Crescent, The. S'wram —6E 92
Crescent, The. S'hse —6L 121
Crescent, The. Ting —4C 98
Crescent Towers. Leeds —1E 80
Crescent Vw. Kei —4G 36
Crescent Vw. Leeds —1B 44
Crescent Wlk. Cytn —9J 57
Crescent Wlk. Dew —6A 116
Creskeld Cres. B'hpe —5J 27
Creskeld Dri. B'hpe —4H 27
Creskeld Gdns. B'hpe —5H 27
Creskeld Gth. B'hpe —5J 27
Creskeld La. B'hpe & Arth —4J 27
(in two parts)
Creskeld Pk. B'hpe —5J 27
Creskeld Way. All —4F 56
Cressfield Rd. Hud —2H 131
Cresswell La. Dew —9C 96
Cresswell Mt. B'frd —3K 75
Cresswell Pl. B'frd —3K 75
Cresswell Ter. B'frd —3K 75
Cresswell Ter. Hal —4K 93
Crest Av. Hud —5C 132
Crest Av. Wyke —3A 94
Crest Dri. Pon —5L 123
Crestfield Av. Ell —5D 112
Crestfield Cres. Ell —6D 112
Crestfield Dri. Ell —6D 112
Crestfield Dri. Hal —7L 91
Crestfield Rd. Ell —6D 112
Crest Hill Rd. Hud —8A 114
Crest Mt. Pon —5L 123
Crest Pl. Brigh —7K 93
(off Halifax Rd.)
Crest Rd. Hud —8F 112
Crest, The. Hud —5C 114
Crest, The. Kip —4A 84
Crest, The. Swil —4H 83
Crest Vw. Brigh —7K 93
Crestville Clo. Cytn —9J 57
Crestville Rd. Cytn —9H 57
Crestville Ter. Cytn —9J 57
Crestwood Clo. B'frd —4F 76
Crewe Av. Knot —8A 104
Crewe Rd. C'frd —5J 103
Crib La. Hal —4B 92
Cricketers App. Wren —9G 99
Cricketers Clo. Ackw —5G 141
Cricketers Clo. Gar —7A 66
Cricketers Grn. Yead —1N 41
Cricketers Ter. Leeds —7M 61
Cricketers Wlk. Colt —7F 64
Cricketers Wlk. Steet —2D 20
Cricketers Way. Kirks —2L 61
Cricklegate. Leeds —6C 64
Cridling Stubbs. —4J 125
Crigglestone. —5G 137
Crimble Bank. Slai —9M 129
Crimble Clo. Hal —5K 93
Crimbles. —7C 60
Crimbles Ct. Pud —7C 60
Crimbles Pl. Pud —7C 60
Crimbles Rd. Pud —7C 60
Crimbles Ter. Pud —7C 60
Crimbles, The. Dur —3H 137
Crimea La. Slai —7K 129
Crimple Grn. Gar —8B 66
Crimshaw La. Shipl —1B 58
Crimsworth La. Pec W —5H 71
Crinan Ct. Nor —8H 101
Cringles. —4F 6
Cringles La. Sils —2E 6
Cringles Pk. Mobile Home Pk. Sils —4F 6
Cripplegate. Hal —5C 92
Critchell Ho. B'frd —9C 58
(off Swan La.)
Croasdale Gdns. Carc —8N 159
(in two parts)
Crodingley. H'frth —9N 147
Crodingley Farm Ct. H'frth —9M 147
Croft Av. Altft —9G 100
Croft Av. Bgly —1C 38
Croft Av. E Ard —5F 98
Croft Av. Fars —3A 60
Croft Av. Knot —7F 104
Croft Av. Nor —9K 101
Croft Av. Otley —7K 11
Croft Av. Roys —6C 154
Croft Bank. W'wth —9A 106
Croft Bri. Oult —8D 82
Croft Clo. Men —4D 24
Cft. Cottage La. Hud —2N 131
Croft Cotts. N Farn —2H 79
Croft Ct. Hon —6L 147
Croft Ct. H'fth —6F 42
Croftdale Gro. Leeds —4E 64
Croft Dri. B'ham —5C 32
Croft Dri. Hon —5K 147
Croft Dri. Men —4E 24
Croft End. Weth —4K 17
Crofters Grn. B'frd —7E 40
Crofters Lea. Yead —1K 41
Croft Fld. Sils —9E 6
Cft. Foulds Ct. Gar —7N 65
Croft Gdns. Hud —1K 131
Croft Head. Guis —7J 25
Croft Head. Skelm —7D 150
Cft. Head La. Wake —4F 120
Croft Ho. Ell —4E 112
(off Southgate)
Croft Ho. H'frth —9M 147
Cft. House Av. Morl —8L 79
Crofthouse Clo. B'frd —5N 75
Cft. House Clo. Morl —7L 79
Cft. House Ct. Pud —6B 60
Cft. House Dri. Morl —8L 79
Cft. House Dri. Otley —8K 11
Cft. House Fold. Add —1N 7
Cft. House Gdns. Morl —8L 79
Cft. House Gro. Morl —8L 79
Cft. House La. Hud —3K 131
Cft. House La. Kei —6G 21
Cft. House La. Morl —8L 79
Cft. House M. Morl —8L 79
Cft. House Mt. Morl —7L 79
Cft. House Ri. Morl —7L 79
Crofthouse Rd. B'frd —5N 75
Croft Ho. Rd. Hud —5K 129
Cft. House Rd. Morl —8L 79
Cft. House Vw. Morl —8L 79
Cft. House Wlk. Morl —7L 79
Cft. House Way. Morl —7L 79
Croftlands. Bat & Dew —9J 97
Croftlands. B'frd —7E 40
Croftlands. Hud —8M 131
Croftlands. Knot —7F 104
Croft La. Newt K —2K 33
Croft La. Wltn —5G 18
Croft Lea. Crid S —4J 125
Crofton. —2H 139
Crofton Clo. Lint —1C 146
Crofton Ri. Leeds —3B 46
Crofton Rd. B'frd —3M 57
Crofton Ter. Leeds —3B 46
Croft Pk. Men —4D 24
Croft Pl. B'frd —4L 75
Croft Pl. Brigh —8N 93
Croft Ri. Men —4E 24
Croft Rd. Bgly —1C 38
Croft Rd. B'ham —5C 32
Croft Rd. E Mor —8C 22
Croft Row. Denh —8L 55
Croft's Ct. Leeds —6D 62
Croftside Clo. Leeds —3C 64
Crofts, The. Eml —2F 150
Crofts, The. Heck —8C 96
(in two parts)
Croft St. B'shaw —8L 77
(in two parts)
Croft St. B'frd —8C 58
(in two parts)
Croft St. Brigh —1M 113
Croft St. Dew —3F 116
Croft St. Fars —3A 60
Croft St. Haw —8C 36
Croft St. H Bri —1H 89
(off Albert St.)
Croft St. Heck —9A 96
Croft St. Hud —5H 131
Croft St. Idle —7G 40
Croft St. Kei —1H 37
Croft St. Otley —1M 25
Croft St. Shipl —8N 39
Croft St. Sower B —8J 91
Croft St. Steet —3C 20
Croft St. Wibs —4A 76
Croft Ter. Leeds —2H 79
Croft, The. Bads —7K 141
Croft, The. Bret —1B 152
Croft, The. C'frd —6F 102
Croft, The. Coll —9H 17
Croft, The. Drau —5D 4
Croft, The. Dlgtn —8B 78
Croft, The. Hoy S —9J 167
Croft, The. Knot —7F 104
Croft, The. Leeds —5C 64
Croft, The. Oaken —9D 76
Croft, The. S'cft —8E 30
Croft, The. Ting —7N 97
Croft, The. W'ford —7D 82
Croftway. Bar E —8M 47
Croft Way. Men —4E 24
Croisdale Clo. Liv —8J 95
Cromack Vw. Pud —7N 59
Cromarty Av. Hud —8H 131
Cromarty Dri. Hud —8H 131
Cromer Av. Kei —2H 37
(off Cromer Rd.)
Cromer Gro. Kei —2H 37
Cromer Pl. Leeds —4C 62
Cromer Rd. Kei —2H 37
Cromer Rd. Leeds —4C 62
Cromer St. Hal —7M 91
Cromer St. Kei —2H 37
Cromer St. Leeds —4C 62
Cromer Ter. Leeds —5C 62
Crompton Dri. Morl —7J 79
Cromwell Clo. B'ton —4C 104
Cromwell Clo. Hal —8F 92
Cromwell Ct. B'frd —1H 57
Cromwell Ct. Dlgtn —8A 78
Cromwell Ct. Skel —8L 159
Cromwell Cres. Pon —3L 123
Cromwell Gro. Skel —7M 159
Cromwell Heights. Leeds —6G 62
(off Cromwell St.)
Cromwell Mt. Leeds —5G 62
Cromwell Pl. Oss —4N 117
Cromwell Ri. Kip —5A 84
Cromwell Rd. C'frd —5K 103
Cromwell Rd. S'wram —8F 92
Cromwell St. Leeds —6G 62
Cromwell Ter. Hal —5A 92
Cromwell Vw. Hal —8G 92
Cromwell Wood La. Brigh —1J 113
Cronkhill La. Barn —8E 154
Crooked La. B'frd —6D 40
(in two parts)
Crooked La. Hal —7A 74
Crooke La. Wilsd —2B 56
Crookes La. Barn —8C 154
(in two parts)
Crook Farm Cvn. Pk. Bail —4L 39
Cropper Ga. Leeds —6C 62
Cropredy Clo. Q'bry —4E 74
Cropstones. B'ham —6D 32
Cropton Rd. Roys —6C 154
Crosby Av. Leeds —1B 80
Crosby Pl. Leeds —9C 62
Crosby Rd. Leeds —1B 80
Crosby St. Cud —9J 155
Crosby St. Kei —8H 21
Crosby St. Leeds —9B 62
Crosby Ter. Leeds —9C 62
Crosby Vw. Leeds —9C 62
Croscombe Wlk. B'frd —9C 58
Crosland Ct. Hud —1E 130
Crosland Edge. Mel —5E 146
Crosland Factory La. Hud —4F 146
Crosland Hill. —8G 130
Crosland Hill Rd. Hud —7G 130
Crosland Moor. —7H 131
Crosland Rd. Hud & Oak —9E 112
Crosland Rd. Thor L —6K 131
Crosland Spring Rd. Hud —3G 146
Crosland St. Hud —6K 131
Crosley Ho. Bgly —5F 38
Crosley Vw. Bgly —5G 39
Crosley Wood Rd. Bgly —5G 38
Cross Albert Pl. Leeds —8N 61
Cross Aston Gro. Leeds —4H 61
Cross Av. Rothw —6A 82
Cross Aysgarth Mt. Leeds —7H 63
Cross Bank. —6D 96
Cross Bank Rd. Add —1J 7
Cross Bank Rd. Bat —6D 96
Cross Banks. Shipl —8N 39
Cross Bank St. Dew —3G 117
Crossbank St. Mir —8L 115
Cross Banstead St. Leeds —3H 63
Cross Barstow St. Leeds —8E 62
Cross Bath Rd. Leeds —4F 60
Crossbeck Clo. I'ly —6G 9
Crossbeck Rd. I'ly —6G 9
Cross Belgrave St. Leeds —6E 62
Cross Bellbrooke Av. Leeds —4K 63
(off Bellbrooke Av.)
Cross Bell St. Leeds —6F 62
(off Bell St.)
Cross Bentley La. Leeds —9B 44
Cross Burley Lodge Rd. Leeds —4A 62
(off Burley Rd.)
Cross Cardigan Ter. Leeds —5M 61
Cross Catherine St. Leeds —7G 63
Cross Chancellor St. Leeds —3D 62
Cross Chapel St. Leeds —1N 61
Cross Chestnut Gro. Leeds —3A 62
(off Chestnut Av.)
Cross Chu. St. Cleck —5J 95
Cross Chu. St. Hud —4N 131
Cross Chu. St. Pad —5J 131
Cross Cliff Rd. Leeds —2B 62
Cross Conway Mt. Leeds —3H 63
Cross Cotts. Mar —3K 131
(off Lawrence Rd.)
Cross Cowper St. Leeds —3F 62
Cross Crown St. Cleck —5H 95
Crossdale Av. B'frd —5K 75
Cross Dawlish Gro. Leeds —6K 63
Cross Dykes Rd. Sower B —4A 110
(in two parts)
Cross Easy Rd. Leeds —8H 63
Cross Emily St. Kei —8J 21
Cross End Fold. Add —1N 7
Cross Ends La. Pec W —1H 71
Cross Farm Ct. Oxe —3C 54
Cross Fld. Holy G —7N 111
Crossfield Clo. Oxe —3B 54
Crossfield Ct. Ove —4J 135
Crossfield Dri. Skel —7M 159
Crossfield Ho. Clo. Skel —7M 159
Crossfield La. Skel —8M 159
Crossfield Rd. Oxe —3B 54
Cross Fields. Hud —3C 132
Crossfields. Ove —4K 135
Crossfield St. Leeds —3C 62
Cross Firs St. Hud —5G 131
Crossflatts. —1E 38
Cross Flatts. Leeds —2C 80
Cross Flatts Av. Leeds —3C 80
Cross Flatts Cres. Leeds —3B 80
Cross Flatts Dri. Leeds —2B 80
Cross Flatts Gro. Leeds —3B 80
Cross Flatts Mt. Leeds —3C 80
Cross Flatts Pde. Leeds —3B 80
Cross Flatts Pl. Leeds —3B 80
Cross Flatts Rd. Leeds —3B 80
Cross Flatts Row. Leeds —3B 80
Cross Flatts St. Leeds —3B 80
Cross Flatts Ter. Leeds —3B 80
Cross Foundry St. Dew —6B 116
Cross Fountaine St. Leeds —6D 62
Cross Francis St. Leeds —3F 62
Crossgate. M'well —8K 153
Crossgate. Otley —1L 25
Cross Ga. Rd. H'frth —6N 163
Cross Gates. —4C 64
Cross Gates Av. Leeds —3D 64
Cross Gates La. Bgly —3B 38
Cross Gates La. Leeds —3C 64
Cross Gates Rd. Leeds —4B 64
(in two parts)
Cross Glen Rd. Leeds —8M 43
Cross Granby Ter. Leeds —1N 61
Cross Grange Av. Leeds —3G 63
Cross Grasmere St. Leeds —7N 61
Cross Green. —9J 63
Cross Grn. B'frd —1J 77
Cross Grn. Otley —9M 11
Cross Grn. App. Leeds —9J 63
Cross Grn. Av. Leeds —8H 63
Cross Grn. Clo. Leeds —9J 63
Cross Grn. Ct. Leeds —9K 63
Cross Grn. Cres. Leeds —8H 63
Cross Grn. Dri. Hud —4E 132
Cross Grn. Dri. Leeds —9J 63
Cross Grn. Gth. Leeds —9J 63
Cross Grn. Gro. Leeds —8H 63
Cross Grn. Ind. Est. Leeds —9K 63
Cross Grn. La. C Grn —8G 63
Cross Grn. La. Halt —6B 64
Cross Grn. Ri. Leeds —9J 63
Cross Grn. Rd. Hud —4E 132
Cross Grn. Rd. Leeds —8H 63
Cross Grn. Row. Leeds —8A 44
Cross Grn. Va. Leeds —1J 81
Cross Grn. Way. Leeds —9J 63
Cross Greenwood Mt. Leeds —8A 44
Cross Gro. St. Hud —5M 131
Cross Hands La. Wake —4B 140
Cross Hartley Av. Leeds —2C 62
(off Delph La.)
Cross Heath Gro. Leeds —2A 80
Cross Henley Rd. Leeds —4F 60
Cross Hill. —4B 112
(nr. Elland)
Cross Hill. —2E 156
(nr. Hemsworth)
Cross Hill. Brier —6N 155
Cross Hill. B'ton —4B 104
Cross Hill. Fair —9N 85
Cross Hill. G'Ind —4B 112
Cross Hill. Hems —2D 156
Cross Hill. Leeds —4A 80
Cross Hill Ct. Skel —7L 159
Cross Hill La. Harts —2G 114
Cross Hill La. Wake —1M 155
Cross Hills. Hal —4B 92
Cross Hills. Kip —4A 84
Cross Hills Ct. Kip —4A 84
Cross Hills Dri. Kip —4A 84
Cross Hills Gdns. Kip —4A 84
Crosshills Mt. G'Ind —4B 112
Cross Hilton Gro. Leeds —2H 63
Cross Ingledew Cres. Leeds —5K 45
Cross Ingram Rd. Leeds —9B 62
Crossings, The. Bat —4C 96
Cross Kelso Rd. Leeds —5B 62
Cross Keys. Oss —4C 118
Cross Keys Ct. Horb —1D 136
Crossland Rd. Chur —6L 79

Crossland St. Leeds —8C 62
Crossland Ter. Leeds —2E 80
Cross La. Bgly —3E 38
Cross La. B'shaw & B'frd —6M 77
Cross La. B'frd —1N 75
(in two parts)
Cross La. Brigh —2C 114
Cross La. Ell —5D 112
Cross La. Eml —1G 151
Cross La. F'ley —9H 61
Cross La. Guis —4K 25
Cross La. Hal —7F 74
(nr. Cock Hill La.)
Cross La. Hal —9G 75
(nr. West St.)
Cross La. H'frth —5A 164
Cross La. Hon —7K 147
Cross La. Hoy S —8J 167
Cross La. Hud —8M 131
Cross La. Kbtn —5L 149
Cross La. Oxe —3C 54
Cross La. Q'bry —5B 74
Cross La. Roys —6F 154
Cross La. Shepl —2J 165
Cross La. Skelm —8D 150
Cross La. Stkmr —7G 148
Cross La. Todm —8A 88
Cross La. Wake —6H 119
Cross La. Wilsd —9B 38
Cross La. Wort —7L 61
Cross Lea Farm Rd. Leeds —8J 43
Cross Lee. Todm —5H 87
Cross Leeds St. Kei —9H 21
(nr. Leeds St.)
Cross Leeds St. Kei —9J 21
(off North St.)
Cross Lee Ga. Todm —5H 87
Cross Lee Rd. Todm —5H 87
Crossley. —3L 115
Crossley Almshouses. Hal —6A 92
Crossley Clo. Hal —5N 91
(off Crossley Gdns.)
Crossley Clo. Mir —3L 115
Crossley Gdns. Hal —5N 91
(in three parts)
Crossley Gro. Mir —3L 115
Crossley Hall. —7K 57
Crossley Hall St. B'frd —7J 57
Crossley Hill. Hal —9C 92
Crossley Hill La. Hal —9C 92
(off Crossley Hill)
Crossley La. Hud —3E 132
Crossley La. Mir —3L 115
Crossley New Rd. Todm —4N 87
Crossley Retail Pk. Hal —4A 92
Crossley St. B'frd —9N 57
Crossley St. Brigh —2N 113
Crossley St. F'stne —6D 122
Crossley St. Hal —5B 92
Crossley St. Liv —1N 115
Crossley St. New S —5G 120
Crossley St. Q'bry —4E 74
Crossley St. Todm —7K 87
Crossley St. Weth —4M 17
Crossley Ter. Bat —9F 96
Crossley Ter. N. Hal —9N 73
Crossley Ter. S. Hal —9N 73
Cross Lidgett Pl. Leeds —7H 45
Cross Louis St. Leeds —3F 62
Crossman Dri. Nor —9K 101
Cross Maude St. Leeds —7F 62
(off Maude St.)
Cross Mitford Rd. Leeds —7N 61
Crossmoor Clo. Sils —8C 6
Crossmount St. Bat —9F 96
Cross Normanton St. Horb —2E 136
Cross Osmondthorpe La. Leeds —6L 63
Cross Pk. Av. C'frd —5F 102
Cross Pk. St. Bat —7G 96
Cross Pk. St. Dew —3J 117
Cross Pk. St. Horb —1C 136
Cross Pk. St. Leeds —6B 64
Cross Peel St. Morl —9L 79
Cross Pipes Rd. Wake —3G 118
Cross Pl. Brigh —8N 93
(off Bradford Rd.)
Cross Quarry St. Leeds —2C 62
Cross Queen St. Nor —1H 121
Cross Reginald Mt. Leeds —2F 62
Cross Rink St. Bat —9G 96
Cross River St. Kei —7L 21
Cross Rd. B'frd —5N 57
Cross Rd. Dew —9F 116
Cross Rd. H'fth —7D 42
Cross Rd. Idle —7G 40
Cross Rd. M'twn —3L 135
Cross Rd. Oaken —8D 76
Cross Rd. Wake —7H 137
Cross Roads. —7F 36
Cross Roads. Kei —7F 36
Cross Rosse St. Shipl —7N 39
Cross Roundhay Av. Leeds —1H 63
Cross Row. Leeds —8H 65
Cross Rydal St. Kei —1G 37
Cross Ryecroft St. Oss —4M 117
Cross St Michaels La. Leeds —2N 61
Cross Speedwell St. Leeds —3D 62
Cross Springwell St. Leeds —8B 62
Cross Sq. Wake —5L 119
Cross Stamford St. Leeds —5F 62
Cross Stone. —6M 87
Cross Stone Rd. Todm —6L 87
Cross St. Bat —7G 96
Cross St. B'frd —6L 75
Cross St. Brigh —8M 93
Cross St. C'frd —4C 102
Cross St. Cytn —1H 75
Cross St. Dew —3G 117
Cross St. E Ard —4G 98
Cross St. G'lnd —4C 112
Cross St. Hal —6C 92
Cross St. Hems —2C 156
Cross St. Holy G —7A 112
Cross St. Hon —5L 147
Cross St. Horb —1D 136
Cross St. Hud —6K 131
Cross St. Leeds —6B 64
Cross St. Liv —1L 115
Cross St. Oaken —9E 76
Cross St. Oss —2M 117
Cross St. Pon —3K 123
Cross St. Rothw —8N 81
Cross St. Sav T —4G 116
Cross St. Upt —1C 158
Cross St. Wake —5L 119
Cross St. W'wd M —4B 102
Cross St. Weth —4M 17
Cross St. W. Hal —4L 91
Cross Sun St. B'frd —6D 58
Cross Ter. Rothw —8N 81
Cross, The. Bar E —8L 47
Cross, The. B'ley —7E 112
Cross, The. B'hpe —5G 27
Cross Valley Dri. Leeds —5B 64
(off Valley Dri.)
Crossway. Bgly —8E 38
Crossways, The. Otley —7L 11
Cross Wells Rd. Ripp —6B 110
Cross Westfield Rd. Leeds —5B 62
(off Westfield Rd.)
Cross Wingham St. Leeds —4F 62
Cross Woodstock St. Leeds —4D 62
(off Blenheim Wlk.)
Cross Woodview St. Leeds —3D 80
(off Woodview St.)
Cross York St. Leeds —7F 62
Crowcrowns La. Pon —1A 124
Crowgill Rd. Shipl —7N 39
Crow Hill End Rd. Sower B —1N 109
Crow Hill Rd. Cra V —9N 89
Crow La. Hud —5F 130
Crow La. Otley —1L 25
Crowlees Clo. Mir —6M 115
Crowlees Gdns. Mir —6M 115
Crowlees Rd. Mir —6L 115
Crown & Anchor Yd. Pon —3J 123
Crown Clo. Dew —4K 117
Crown Ct. Leeds —7E 62
Crown Dri. Wyke —9A 76
Crow Nest. —4F 38
Crownest La. Bgly —3F 38
Crow Nest La. Leeds —3N 79
Crownest Rd. Bgly —4F 38
Crow Nest Rd. H Bri —2J 89
Crow Nest Ter. Dew —4E 116
(off Cemetery Rd.)
Crow Nest Vw. Dew —4D 116
Crown Flatt Way. Dew —2H 117
Crownlands La. Oss —5N 117
Crown La. H'frth —3M 163
Crown Point. —7F 62
Crown Point Clo. Oss —5M 117
Crown Point Dri. Oss —4M 117
Crown Point Retail Pk. Leeds —8E 62
Crown Point Rd. Leeds —8F 62
Crown Point Rd. Oss —5M 117
Crown Rd. Hal —2A 92
Crown St. B'frd —7A 58
Crown St. Brigh —9M 93
Crown St. Bur W —8D 10
Crown St. Cleck —5H 95
Crown St. Ell —4E 112
Crown St. Hal —5B 92
Crown St. H Bri —1H 89
Crown St. Hon —4L 147
Crown St. Leeds —7E 62
Crown St. Oss —8A 118
Crown St. Scis —8G 151
Crown St. Wyke —9A 76
Crown Ter. Clay W —6J 151
Crown Ter. Hal —6M 91
(nr. Hopwood La.)
Crown Ter. Hal —6M 91
(off Queen's Rd.)
Crown Yd. S Kirk —6K 157
Crow's Nest Ct. Mir —6K 115
(off York Rd.)
Crowther Av. C'ley —9K 41
Crowther Clo. Slai —8N 129
Crowther Fold. H'den —6A 38
Crowther Pl. C'frd —5D 102
Crowther Pl. Leeds —3D 62
Crowther Rd. Heck —7B 96
Crowther Rd. Mir —6K 115
Crowthers St. Wyke —9A 76
Crowther St. Bat —7C 96
Crowther St. B'frd —8H 41
Crowther St. C'frd —5C 102
Crowther St. Cleck —4H 95
Crowther St. Hud —5N 131
Crowther St. Lock —7L 131
Crowthers Yd. Pud —8B 60
Crow Tree Clo. Bail —4B 40
Crow Tree La. B'frd —5K 57
Crowtrees Ct. Rawd —4N 41
Crowtrees Cres. Brigh —4L 113
Crowtrees La. Ras —4L 113
Crowtrees Pde. Brigh —4L 113
(off Crowtrees La.)
Crowtrees Pk. Brigh —3L 113
Crow Trees Pk. Rawd —3M 41
Crow Trees Rd. Mars —3H 145
Crow Wood La. Holy G —9J 111
Crow Wood Pk. Hal —7K 91
Croxall Dri. Stan —7N 99
Croydon Rd. B'frd —1L 75
Croydon St. Leeds —8B 62
Croydon St. Q'bry —4D 74
Crumack La. Oxe —3E 54
Crummock Pl. Knot —1D 124
Crystal Ct. Hal —5N 91
(off Hanson La.)
Crystal Pl. Wake —5M 119
Crystal Ter. B'frd —2G 77
Cubley Av. Wake —4K 137
Cuckoo La. Hon —5L 147
Cuckoo Pk. La. Oxe —2E 54
Cuckstool Rd. Den D —2D 166
Cudbear St. Leeds —8F 62
Cullingworth. —1K 55
Cullingworth Rd. Cull —1K 55
Cullingworth St. Dew —9D 96
Culpans Rd. Cra V —8A 90
Culver St. Hal —5B 92
Cumberland Av. Hud —6M 113
Cumberland Clo. Hal —9L 73
Cumberland Ct. Leeds —3N 61
Cumberland Ho. B'frd —6E 58
(off Otley Rd.)
Cumberland Rd. B'frd —9M 57
Cumberland Rd. C'frd —2L 103
Cumberland Rd. Leeds —2B 62
Cumberworth La. Lwr C —1B 166
Cumberworth La. Up Cum —3J 165
Cumberworth Rd. Skelm —8C 150
Cumbrian Way. Wake —8F 118
Cunliffe La. Esh —2F 40
Cunliffe Rd. B'frd —4A 58
Cunliffe Rd. I'ly —5G 8
Cunliffe Ter. B'frd —4B 58
Cunliffe Vs. B'frd —3B 58
Cure Hill. Oakw —4B 36
Curlew Clo. C'frd —6D 102
Curlew Clo. I'ly —5D 8
Curlew Ct. Steet —2B 20
Curlew Ri. Morl —1N 97
Curlew St. B'frd —2A 76
Curly Hill. I'ly —3F 8
Currer Av. B'frd —4F 76
Currer St. B'frd —7D 58
Currer St. Oaken —9E 76
Currer Wlk. Steet —2B 20
Curwen Cres. Heck —7B 96
Curzon Rd. B'frd —7F 58
Curzon St. Hud —5E 114
Cuthberts Clo. Q'bry —5C 74
Cut La. Hal —8E 74
Cutler Heights. —1H 77
Cutler Heights La. B'frd —2G 76
Cutler La. Meth —1M 101
Cutler Pl. B'frd —1H 77
Cut Rd. Fair —9N 85
Cutsyke. —7C 102
Cutsyke Av. C'frd —6B 102
Cutsyke Crest. C'frd —6B 102
Cutsyke Hill. C'frd —6B 102
Cutsyke Rd. C'frd & F'stne —8B 102
Cutsyke Wlk. C'frd —7C 102
Cuttlehurst. Scis —9G 150
Cypress Fold. Lep —7J 133
Cypress Ho. C'frd —5E 102
(off Parklands)
Cypress Rd. Nor —3J 121
Cyprus Av. B'frd —6D 40
Cyprus Av. Wake —3J 119
Cyprus Cres. Mir —4A 116
Cyprus Dri. B'frd —6E 40
Cyprus Gro. Gar —7M 65
Cyprus Gro. Wake —3J 119
Cyprus Mt. Wake —3J 119
Cyprus Rd. Gar —7M 65
Cyprus St. Oss —3M 117
Cyprus St. Wake —3K 119
Cyprus Ter. Gar —7M 65
Czar St. Leeds —9C 62

Dacre Av. Wake —7E 118
Dacre Clo. Liv —7K 95
Dacre St. B'frd —6D 58
Daffels Wood Clo. Bier —5F 76
Daffil Av. Chur —6L 79
Daffil Grange M. Morl —6L 79
Daffil Grange Way. Morl —6L 79
Daffil Gro. Chur —6L 79
Daffil Rd. Chur —6L 79
Daffodil Ct. All —6G 57
Dagenham Rd. B'frd —2G 77
Dahl Dri. C'frd —7J 103
Daily Ct. B'frd —2N 75
Daisy Bank. Hal —7A 92
Daisy Bank St. Todm —3D 86
Daisy Clo. Birs —2B 96
Daisy Cft. Sils —8F 6
Daisyfield Grange. Leeds —5G 60
(off Rossefield App.)
Daisyfield Rd. Leeds —5G 60
Daisy Fold. Upt —2M 157
Daisy Hill. —4K 57
(nr. Allerton)
Daisy Hill. —8M 79
(nr. Morley)
Daisy Hill. Dew —3F 116
Daisy Hill. Morl —8M 79
Daisy Hill. Sils —8F 6
Daisy Hill. Wyke —1A 94
Daisy Hill Av. Morl —7M 79
Daisy Hill Bk. La. B'frd —4K 57
Daisy Hill Clo. Morl —7L 79
Daisy Hill Gro. B'frd —4K 57
Daisy Hill La. B'frd —4K 57
Daisy Lea. Outl —2N 129
Daisy Lea La. Hud —1G 131
Daisy Lee La. H'frth —9A 164
Daisy Mt. Sower B —7G 91
Daisy Pl. Shipl —7L 39
(off Saltaire Rd.)
Daisy Rd. Brigh —2N 113
Daisy Row. Leeds —5G 60
Daisy Royd. Hud —8M 131
Daisy St. B'frd —2M 75
Daisy St. Brigh —1M 113
Daisy St. Hal —6A 92
Daisy St. Haw —8E 36
Daisy Va. Ter. Thor —3G 98
Dalby Av. B'frd —5G 59
Dalby St. B'frd —6G 59
Dalcross Gro. B'frd —1D 76
Dalcross St. B'frd —1C 76
Dale Av. Todm —7M 87
Dale Clo. Bat —1F 116
Dale Clo. Den D —3C 166
Dale Clo. Guis —8F 24
Dale Clo. Oss —5A 118
Dale Ct. H'frth —2N 163
Dale Ct. Oss —5N 117
Dale Ct. Pon —6K 123
Dale Cres. Steet —3C 20
Dale Cft. Gar —6M 65
Dale Cft. I'ly —5D 8
Dale Cft. Skelm —7D 150
Dale Cft. Ri. All —4E 56
Dalecroft Rd. Carc —9N 159
Dalefield Av. Nor —2J 121
Dalefield Rd. Nor —2H 121
Dale Gth. Bail —4N 39
Dale Gro. B'frd —6C 40
Dale La. Heck —7A 96
Dale La. S Elm —4N 157
Dale La. Enterprise Zone. S Elm —5A 158
Dale M. Pon —6K 123
Dale Pk. Av. Leeds —3G 43
Dale Pk. Clo. Leeds —3G 42
Dale Pk. Gdns. Leeds —3G 43
Dale Pk. Ri. Leeds —3G 42
Dale Pk. Vw. Leeds —3G 43
Dale Pk. Wlk. Leeds —3G 42
Dale Rd. Dlgtn —4D 78
Dales Bank Holiday Pk. Sils —4D 6
Dales Dri. Guis —8F 24
Daleside. Dew —1F 134
Daleside. G'lnd —4N 111
Daleside Av. H'frth —1A 164
Daleside Av. Pud —6L 59
Daleside Clo. Pud —5K 59
Daleside Gro. Oaken —9D 76
Daleside Gro. Pud —6L 59
Dale Side Ho. B'frd —4B 58
Daleside Rd. Pud —5K 59
Daleside Rd. Riddl —7N 21
Daleside Rd. Shipl —6B 40
Daleside Wlk. B'frd —3D 76
Daleson Cres. Hal —1F 92
Dale St. B'frd —7C 58
Dale St. Dew —6E 116
Dale St. Hud —5M 131
Dale St. Kei —7L 21
Dale St. Lgwd —4F 130
Dale St. Shipl —8N 39
Dale St. Skelm —7D 150
Dale St. Sower B —8H 91
Dale St. Todm —7K 87
Dalesway. Bgly —2G 39
Dales Way. Guis —8F 24
Dale, The. Aber —6E 48
Dale Vw. Hems —3F 156
Dale Vw. I'ly —5D 8
Dale Vw. L'ft —5D 90
Dale Vw. Pon —6K 123
Dale Vw. Sils —7E 6
Dale Vw. Steet —3C 20
Dale Vw. Clo. Kei —1L 37
Daleview Ct. Bail —5M 39
Dale Vw. Gro. Kei —1L 37
Dale Vw. Rd. Kei —2L 37
Dale Vw. Way. Kei —1L 37
Dale Vs. H'fth —8G 43
Dale Wlk. Pon —7C 122
Dallam Av. Shipl —7K 39
Dallam Gro. Shipl —6K 39
Dallam Rd. Shipl —7K 39
Dallam Wlk. Shipl —7L 39
Dalmeny Av. Hud —8H 131
Dalmeny Clo. Hud —7H 131
Dalton. —3D 132
Dalton Av. Leeds —3C 80
Dalton Bank Rd. Hud —1E 132
Dalton Clowes. Hud —3C 132
Dalton Fold. —3B 132
Dalton Fold Rd. Hud —3B 132
Dalton Green. —3E 132
Dalton Grn. La. Hud —3E 132
Dalton Gro. Hud —3C 132
Dalton Gro. Leeds —3C 80
Dalton La. B'ham —6M 31
(in two parts)
Dalton La. Kei —9K 21
Dalton Rd. Kei —9L 21
Dalton Rd. Leeds —3C 80
Dalton St. Sower B —7H 91
Dalton St. Todm —7K 87
Dalton Ter. B'frd —6N 57
Dalton Ter. C'frd —5D 102
Dalton Ter. Kei —8L 21
(off Surrey St.)
Damask St. Hal —4A 92
Damems La. Oakw —5F 36
Damems Rd. Kei —5G 36
Dam Head. —9D 74
Dam Head La. Lep —4K 133
Dam Head Rd. Sower B —7J 91
Dam Hill. Shel —6H 149
Dam La. Saxt —8M 49
Dam La. Yead —9N 25
Damon Av. B'frd —2J 59
Dampier St. Todm —2J 107
Damside. Kei —1H 37
Damside Rd. Hud —6N 131
Damson Ct. Cytn —2G 75
Danby Av. B'frd —5F 76
Danby La. Wake —6L 137
(in two parts)
Danby Wlk. Leeds —7H 63
Dandy Mill Av. Pon —1M 123
Dandy Mill Cft. Pon —1M 123
Dandy Mill Vw. Pon —1M 123
Danebury Rd. Brigh —2N 113
Dane Ct. Rd. B'frd —2J 77
Danefield Ter. Otley —9M 11
Dane Hill Dri. B'frd —1J 77
Danehurst. Pon —3K 123
Danella Cres. Wren —1H 119
Danella Gro. Wren —1H 119
Danes La. M'twn —4L 135
Danesleigh Dri. M'twn —4L 135
Daniel Ct. B'frd —3K 77
Daniel St. B'frd —7H 59
Danny La. L'ft —5D 90
Dansk Way. I'ly —4J 9
Danum Dri. Bail —5A 40
Darbyfields. Gol —4D 130
Darcey Hey La. Hal —7L 91
Darcy Ct. Leeds —6D 64
Darfield Av. Leeds —3J 63
Darfield Cres. Leeds —3J 63
Darfield Gro. Leeds —3H 63
Darfield Ho. B'frd —9G 40
(off Summerfield Rd.)
Darfield Pl. Leeds —3J 63
Darfield Rd. Leeds —3J 63

ırfield St. B'frd —6B 58
ırfield St. Leeds —3J 63
ırkfield La. Pon —8M 103
ırk La. Bat —8E 96
ırk La. Birs —1C 96
ırk La. Blkhd —1D 88
ırk La. C'den —6N 69
ırk La. Den —2C 166
ırk La. Hal —6H 91
ırk La. H Bri —2N 89
ırk La. Hud —8E 132
ırk La. Mars —4B 144
ırk La. Oxe —3C 54
ırk La. Pon —4J 123
ırk La. Pot —6L 47
ırk La. Schol —7N 35
(in two parts)
ırk La. S'wram —5F 92
(nr. Barrowclough La.)
ırk La. S'wram —8G 93
(nr. Cain La.)
ırk La. Sower B —8A 110
ırk La. Stainb —4G 12
ırkwood Clo. Leeds —3J 45
ırkwood Way. Leeds —3J 45
ırley Av. Leeds —6F 80
ırley Rd. Liv —7K 95
ırley St. B'frd —7C 58
(in two parts)
ırley St. Heck —8A 96
ırley St. Kei —7H 21
ırnay La. B'frd —2C 76
ırnell Ter. Leeds —8E 62
ırnes Av. Hal —7L 91
ırning La. Thpe A —5A 142
ırnley Av. Wake —4J 119
ırnley Clo. Mel —8D 146
ırnley La. Leeds —8D 64
ırnley Rd. Leeds —8L 43
ırren St. B'frd —8J 59
ırrington. —6C 124
ırrington Rd. E Hard —9L 123
ırtmouth Av. Hud —7E 132
ırtmouth Av. Morl —2K 97
ırtmouth Ter. B'frd —4A 58
ırtmouth Ter. Far T —3C 148
ırtmouth Way. Leeds —3E 80
ırton. —8G 152
ırton Hall Clo. Dart —8H 153
ırton Hall Dri. Dart —8H 153
ırton La. Dart —9H 153
ırwin St. B'frd —2A 76
ıvenport Ho. B'frd —6E 58
(off Otley Rd.)
ıvey La. Blkhd —1A 88
ıvid La. Dew —1F 116
ıvid St. C'frd —5B 102
ıvid St. Leeds —8D 62
ıvid St. Wake —7N 119
ıvies Av. Leeds —7H 45
ıvis Av. C'frd —6K 103
ıwes Av. C'frd —6F 102
ıw Green. —3E 116
ıw Grn. Av. Crig —6G 136
ıw La. Horb —2D 136
ıw La. Wake —7F 136
ıwlish Av. Leeds —6K 63
ıwlish Cres. Leeds —6K 63
ıwlish Gro. Leeds —7K 63
ıwlish Mt. Leeds —6K 63
ıwlish Pl. Leeds —6K 63
ıwlish Rd. Leeds —6K 63
ıwlish Row. Leeds —6K 63
ıwlish St. Leeds —6K 63
ıwlish Ter. Leeds —6K 63
ıwlish Wlk. Leeds —7K 63
ıwnay Rd. B'frd —2N 75
ıw Royds. Hud —5E 132
ıwson Av. B'frd —5A 76
ıwson Gdns. Dew —3E 116
(off Halliley St.)
ıwson Hill. Morl —8K 79
ıwson Hill Yd. Horb —1D 136
ıwson La. B'frd —4G 77
ıwson La. Rothw —7N 81
ıwson La. Tong —3B 78
ıwson Mt. B'frd —4G 77
ıwson Pl. B'frd —4H 77
ıwson Pl. Kei —2J 37
ıwson Rd. Hud —7N 131
ıwson Rd. Kei —2J 37
ıwson Rd. Leeds —2C 80
ıwsons Corner. S'ley —4N 59
ıwsons Ct. Leeds —2C 64
ıwsons Mdw. S'ley —4N 59
ıwson St. B'frd —3G 77
ıwson St. S'ley —5A 60
ıwson St. Thack —6F 40
ıwson St. Ting —3N 97
ıwson Ter. B'frd —4H 77
ıwson Way. Kei —2J 37
ıwtrie Clo. C'frd —5K 103
ıwtrie St. C'frd —4K 103
Daykin Clo. Dart —9F 152
Day St. Dew —6B 116
Day St. Hud —5A 132
Deacon Clo. Mel —7D 146
Deaconess Ct. I'ly —6G 8
Deadmanstone. Hud —1L 147
Dealburn Rd. Low M —8B 76
Deal St. Hal —6C 92
Deal St. Kei —8L 21
Dean Av. H'frth —9L 147
Dean Av. Leeds —9J 45
Dean Beck Av. B'frd —4C 76
Dean Beck Ct. B'frd —5D 76
Dean Bri. La. Hep —5B 164
Dean Brook Rd. H'frth —9L 147
Dean Brook Rd. Hud —1K 147
Dean Clo. B'frd —6J 57
Dean Clo. Wren —1H 119
Dean Clough. Hal —4B 92
Dean Ct. Hal —1N 111
Dean Ct. Leeds —9J 45
Dean Edge Rd. Oldf —7G 35
Dean End. G'lnd —3B 112
Deanery Gdns. B'frd —1G 59
Deane, The. Leeds —8M 63
(in two parts)
Deanfield Av. Morl —8J 79
Dean Hall Clo. Morl —9J 79
Dean Head. H'fth —8D 26
Dean Head. L'boro —8M 107
Dean Ho. La. Hal —2D 90
Deanhouse La. H'frth —9M 147
Dean Ho. La. Slnd —2J 129
Deanhurst Gdns. Gild —7G 79
Deanhurst Ind. Cen. Gild —7G 79
Dean La. Guis —8D 24
Dean La. H'frth —7B 164
Dean La. H'fth —8D 26
Dean La. Oakw —1M 35
(in two parts)
Dean La. Sower B —1E 110
(nr. Bowood La.)
Dean La. Sower B —3E 110
(nr. Mill Bank Rd.)
Dean La. T'tn —5B 56
Dean M. H'fth —8E 26
Dean Pk. Av. Dlgtn —6B 78
Dean Pk. Dri. Dlgtn —6B 78
Dean Pastures. Dlgtn —7B 78
Dean Rd. B'frd —5B 76
Dean Rd. H'frth —3F 162
Deanroyd Rd. Todm —4K 107
Deans Ter. Hal —1A 92
Deanstones Cres. Q'bry —5D 74
Deanstones La. Q'bry —5C 74
Dean St. Ell —5E 112
Dean St. G'lnd —5B 112
Dean St. Haw —8D 36
Dean St. Hud —2G 131
Dean St. I'ly —4H 9
Deansway. Morl —7J 79
Deanswood Clo. Leeds —4C 44
Deanswood Dri. Leeds —4B 44
Deanswood Gdns. Leeds —4B 44
Deanswood Gth. Leeds —4C 44
Deanswood Grn. Leeds —4B 44
Deanswood Hill. Leeds —4B 44
Deanswood Pl. Leeds —4C 44
Deanswood Ri. Leeds —4C 44
Deanswood Vw. Leeds —4C 44
Dean Vs. Todm —4K 107
Deanwood Av. All —4F 56
Deanwood Cres. All —3F 56
Deanwood Wlk. All —4F 56
Dearden St. Oss —6N 117
Dearden St. Sower B —7H 91
Dearne Courthouse. Scis —8G 151
(off Wakefield Rd.)
Dearne Cft. Weth —1M 17
Dearne Dike La. Cumb —3J 165
Dearne Fold. Hud —1G 130
Dearne Pk. Clay W —7H 151
Dearne Royd. Scis —7H 151
Dearneside Rd. Den D —3C 166
Dearne St. Dart —8H 153
Dearne St. Scis —8G 151
Dearne St. S Elm —6M 157
Dearne Way. Birds —3M 165
Dearne Way. Clay W —5K 151
Dearnfield. Up Cum —2N 165
Dearnley St. Dew —5B 116
Dee Ct. Oakw —5C 36
Deep Dale. B Spa —8C 18
Deepdale Clo. Bail —5M 39
Deepdale Ho. Bat —1F 116
(off Dale Clo.)
Deepdale La. B Spa —8B 18
Deep La. Brigh —1C 114
Deep La. Cytn —9H 57
Deep La. Hal —5F 90
Deep La. Hud —7G 130
Deep La. Sower B —3B 110
(in two parts)
Deep La. T'tn —1N 73
Deer Cft. Av. Hud —2E 130
Deer Cft. Cres. Hud —2E 130
Deer Cft. Dri. Hud —2E 130
Deer Cft. Rd. Hud —1E 130
Deer Hill Clo. Mars —6F 144
Deer Hill Ct. Mel —7B 146
Deer Hill Cft. Mars —6F 144
(off Deer Hill Dri.)
Deer Hill Dri. Mars —6F 144
Deer Hill End Rd. Mel —6M 145
Deershaw La. Cumb —3G 165
Deershaw Sike La. Cumb —3G 165
Deerstone Ridge. Weth —1M 17
Deerstones. —4N 5
Defarge Ct. B'frd —2C 76
(off Newton St.)
Deffer Rd. Wake —4L 137
Deganwy Dri. Hud —9G 114
Deighton. —7D 114
Deighton Clo. Weth —3N 17
Deighton Gates. —1M 17
Deighton La. Bat —7D 96
Deighton Rd. Hud —8B 114
Deighton Rd. Weth —1M 17
De Lacies Ct. W'ford —6B 82
De Lacies Rd. W'ford —6B 82
De Lacy Av. B'frd —5F 76
De Lacy Av. F'stne —2C 122
De Lacy Av. Hud —6D 132
Delacy Cres. C'frd —3K 103
De Lacy Mt. Leeds —2K 61
De Lacy Ter. Pon —3L 123
Delamere St. B'frd —3B 76
Delf Clo. Hal —6K 75
Delf Hill. Brigh —4K 113
Delf La. Todm —1E 86
Delf La. Wadsw —5K 71
Delf Pl. Brigh —4K 113
Delfs La. Sower B —3N 109
Delius Av. B'frd —1J 59
Dell Av. Grime —9A 156
Dell Cft. Sils —8C 6
Dell, The. Bard —5E 30
Dell, The. C'frd —6A 102
Dell, The. Cull —9K 37
(in two parts)
Dell, The. Hud —7N 113
Delmont Clo. Bat —6B 96
Delph Ct. Leeds —2C 62
Delph Cres. Cytn —1G 74
Delph Dri. Cytn —1G 74
Delph End. —7M 59
Delph End. Pud —7M 59
Delph Gro. Cytn —1G 74
Delph Hill. —8N 91
(nr. Sowerby Bridge)
Delph Hill. —8A 76
(nr. Wyke)
Delph Hill. Bail —3A 40
Delph Hill Fld. Hal —8M 91
Delph Hill La. Hal —2D 90
Delph Hill Rd. Hal —8M 91
Delph Hill Ter. Hal —8M 91
(off Delph Hill Rd.)
Delph Ho. Kei —2J 37
Delph La. Hud —2J 147
Delph La. Leeds —2C 62
Delph Mt. Leeds —2C 62
Delph St. Hal —6A 92
Delph Ter. Cytn —1G 74
Delph, The. F'stne —6F 122
Delph Vw. Leeds —2C 62
Delphwood Clo. Bgly —4H 39
Delverne Gro. B'frd —3G 58
Delves Ga. Slai —3M 145
Delves Wood Rd. Hud —9H 131
Demontfort Ho. B'frd —1J 77
(off Ned La.)
Denbigh App. Leeds —4M 63
Denbigh Cft. Leeds —4M 63
Denbigh Heights. Leeds —4M 63
Denbrook Av. B'frd —4K 77
Denbrook Clo. B'frd —4K 77
Denbrook Cres. B'frd —5K 77
Denbrook Wlk. B'frd —4K 77
Denbrook Way. B'frd —4K 77
Denbury Mt. B'frd —3J 77
Denby Clo. Birs —3A 96
Denby Clo. Liv —7K 95
Denby Ct. Oakw —5B 36
Denby Crest. D'ton —6B 124
Denby Dale. —2C 166
Denby Dale Rd. Clay W & Bret —2M 151
Denby Dale Rd. Wake —1J 137
Denby Dale Rd. E. Dur —3G 137
Denby Dale Rd. W. Cald G —4F 136
Denby Dri. Bail —6N 39
Denby Grange La. Grng M —6D 134
Denby Hall La. Den D —3G 167
Denby Hill. —5A 36
Denby Hill Rd. Oakw —5B 36
Denby Ho. Bail —6A 40
(off Denby Dri.)
Denby Ho. B'frd —4K 77
Denby La. All —5G 57
Denby La. Grng M —5B 134
Denby La. Up Den —5N 165
Denby La. Cres. Grng M —5B 134
Denby Mt. Oxe —4C 54
Denby Pk. Dri. Grng M —5B 134
Denby Rd. D'ton —6B 124
Denby Rd. Kei —2J 37
Denby St. B'frd —6A 58
Denby Vw. Dew —1G 135
Dence Grn. B'frd —9J 59
Dence Pl. Leeds —6N 63
Dene Bank. Bgly —1F 38
Dene Clo. Ell —6D 112
Dene Cres. B'frd —1K 75
Dene Gro. Sils —7E 6
Dene Hill. Bail —4L 39
Denehill. B'frd —5J 57
Dene Ho. Ct. Leeds —4D 62
Dene Mt. All —5H 57
Dene Pk. Kbtn —2K 149
Dene Pl. Hal —4A 92
Dene Rd. B'frd —4J 75
Dene Rd. Skelm —8C 150
Dene Royd Ct. Slnd —8M 111
Deneside. Oss —4M 117
Deneside Mt. B'frd —3B 76
Deneside Ter. B'frd —3B 76
Denesway. Gar —9A 66
Dene Vw. L'ft —4D 90
Deneway. S'ley —4N 59
Denfield Av. Hal —2L 91
Denfield Cres. Hal —2M 91
Denfield Edge. Hal —2M 91
Denfield Gdns. Hal —2M 91
Denfield La. Hal —2L 91
Denfield Sq. Hal —2M 91
Denhale Av. Wake —5G 119
Denham Av. Morl —2K 97
Denham Ct. Bat —5D 96
Denham Dri. H'frth —9L 147
Denham St. Bat —5D 96
Denham St. Brigh —2M 113
Denholme. —5K 55
Denholme Clough. —8L 55
Denholme Dri. Oss —4N 117
Denholme Gate. —9K 55
Denholme Ga. Rd. Hal —9H 75
Denholme Mdw. S Elm —5M 157
Denholme Rd. Oxe —4C 54
Denison Rd. Leeds —6C 62
Denison St. Bat —8F 96
Denison St. Yead —9M 25
Denmark St. Wake —7N 119
Dennil Cres. Leeds —2E 64
Dennil Rd. Leeds —3E 64
Dennington. —7E 136
Dennington La. Crig —6E 136
Dennis La. Sils —6A 6
Dennison Cotts. Leeds —8H 63
Dennison Fold. B'frd —9J 59
Dennison Hill. Otley —9M 11
Dennistead Cres. Leeds —1N 61
Denshaw Dri. Morl —9M 79
Denshaw Dri. Clo. Morl —9M 79
Denshaw Gro. Morl —9M 79
Denshaw Gro. Clo. Morl —9M 79
Denshaw La. Ting —1B 98
Denstone St. Wake —4M 119
Dent Dri. Wake —3A 120
Denton. —2M 9
Denton Av. Leeds —7H 45
Denton Dri. Bgly —3H 39
Denton Gdns. Ackw —5G 140
Denton Gro. Leeds —7H 45
Denton Rd. Ben R —5K 9
Denton Rd. I'ly —4F 8
Denton Row. Denh —6K 55
Denton Row. Holy G —7B 112
Denton Row. Leeds —8K 61
Denton Ter. C'frd —4E 102
Dent St. Leeds —7H 63
Denwell Ter. Pon —2K 123
Derby Pl. B'frd —7H 59
Derby Rd. B'frd —7J 59
Derby Rd. Rawd —3M 41
Derbyshire St. Leeds —2H 81
Derby St. B'frd —1N 75
Derby St. Cytn —1G 74
Derby St. Q'bry —4C 74
Derby St. Sower B —8K 91
Derby St. Todm —7M 87
Derby Ter. B'frd —7J 41
Derby Ter. Mars —5F 144
Derdale St. Todm —7L 87
Derry Hill. Men —5D 24
Derry Hill Gdns. Men —4D 24
Derry La. Men —4D 24
Der St. Todm —7L 87
Derwent Av. Bail —6K 39
Derwent Av. Gar —8N 65
Derwent Av. Wilsd —2B 56
Derwent Av. W'ford —7D 82
Derwent Clo. H Bri —9H 71
Derwent Ct. Sils —9E 6
Derwent Dri. C'frd —3L 103
Derwent Dri. Hud —3B 132
Derwent Dri. Leeds —3N 43
Derwent Gro. Wake —5H 119
Derwent Ho. Hal —3N 91
Derwent Pl. Knot —2D 124
Derwent Pl. Leeds —8C 62
Derwent Pl. Q'bry —3B 74
Derwent Ri. Weth —1L 17
Derwent Rd. B'frd —3E 58
Derwent Rd. Dew —9J 97
Derwent Rd. Hon —6K 147
Derwent Rd. Mel —8D 146
Derwent Rd. Wake —5H 119
Derwent St. Kei —8M 21
Derwentwater Gro. Leeds —1N 61
Derwentwater Ter. Leeds —1N 61
Derwin Av. Stkmr —7G 148
De Trafford St. Hud —6J 131
Detroit Av. Leeds —6E 64
Detroit Dri. Leeds —6F 64
Deveron Gro. Hud —2K 131
Devon Clo. Leeds —4D 62
Devon Gro. Oss —7M 117
Devon Rd. Leeds —4D 62
Devonshire Av. Leeds —6J 45
Devonshire Clo. Round —5J 45
(in two parts)
Devonshire Ct. Knot —8E 104
Devonshire Cres. Leeds —6J 45
Devonshire Gdns. Leeds —3D 62
Devonshire La. Leeds —5J 45
Devonshire Pl. Yead —9M 25
Devonshire St. Hud —7K 131
Devonshire St. Kei —9G 20
Devonshire St. W. Kei —9G 21
Devonshire Ter. B'frd —4A 58
Devon St. Hal —6M 91
Devon Wlk. Dew —3E 116
Devon Way. Brigh —6N 93
Dewar Clo. Coll —8J 17
Dewhirst Clo. Bail —5B 40
Dewhirst Pl. B'frd —9H 59
Dewhirst Rd. Bail —5B 40
Dewhirst Rd. Brigh —8M 93
Dewhurst Rd. Hud —9N 113
Dewhurst St. Wilsd —1B 56
Dewsbury. —4J 117
Dewsbury Ga. Rd. Dew —9C 96
Dewsbury Moor. —2B 116
Dewsbury Museum & Art Gallery. —4D 116
Dewsbury Ring Rd. Dew —3F 116
Dewsbury Rd. Cleck —5J 95
Dewsbury Rd. Dew & Ting —6L 97
Dewsbury Rd. Ell —5F 112
Dewsbury Rd. Gom —1M 95
Dewsbury Rd. Leeds —8E 62
(nr. Meadow La.)
Dewsbury Rd. Leeds —6B 80
(nr. Millshaw Rd.)
Dewsbury Rd. Oss —3M 117
Dewsbury Rd. Ting & Morl —2A 98
Dewsbury Rd. Wake —6E 118
Deyne Rd. Hud —2H 147
Diadem Dri. Leeds —5N 63
Dial St. Leeds —8H 63
Diamond Av. S Elm —6L 157
Diamond St. Bat —6E 96
Diamond St. Hal —4N 91
Diamond St. Hill —2N 131
Diamond St. Kei —3G 36
Diamond St. Mold —5B 132
Diamond Ter. Hal —4N 91
(HX1)
Diamond Ter. Hal —7M 91
(HX2)
Dibb La. Yead —9K 25
Dib Clo. Leeds —1M 63
Dib La. Leeds —1M 63
Dick Dean La. Pec W —9H 53
Dick Edge La. Cumb —6F 164
Dickens Dri. C'frd —7K 103
Dickens St. B'frd —2C 76
Dickens St. Hal —5L 91
Dickinson Ct. Wake —3L 119
Dickinson Gdns. Dew —3E 116
(off Travis Lacey Ter.)
Dickinson St. H'fth —5F 42
Dickinson St. Wake —4L 119
Dickinson Ter. F'stne —5D 122
Dick La. B'frd & Thornb —1H 77
Dick La. Sower B —9B 110
Dick's Gth. Rd. Men —4D 24
Dick's La. Cra V —7F 88
Dickson Fold. Liv —8K 95
Dicky Sykes La. Ackw —5D 140
Digby Rd. Men —4E 24

Digley Rd. H'frth —6F 162
Digley Royd La. H'frth —5F 162
Dike La. Wads —9L 71
Dimple Gdns. Oss —7N 117
Dimples La. E Mor —8C 22
Dimples La. Haw —8B 36
Dimple Wells Clo. Oss —7N 117
Dimple Wells La. Oss —7N 117
Dimple Wells Rd. Oss —7N 117
Dineley Av. Todm —5H 87
Dingle Rd. Hud —4J 131
Dingley Rd. Hud —2H 131
Dinsdale Bldgs. Yead —1L 41
(off Back La.)
Dirker Av. Mars —4G 144
Dirker Bank Rd. Mars —4F 144
Dirker Dri. Mars —5F 144
Dirk Hill. —9A 58
Dirkhill Rd. B'frd —9A 58
Dirkhill St. B'frd —9N 57
Discovery Rd. Hal —6C 92
Dish Hill Fly-Over. Knot —5B 104
Disney Clo. Hud —7J 131
Dispensary Wlk. Hal —5C 92
Disraeli Gdns. Leeds —1D 80
Disraeli Ter. Leeds —1D 80
Dixon Av. B'frd —9L 57
Dixon Clo. G'lnd —3N 111
Dixon Clo. Steet —3C 20
Dixon La. Leeds —9M 61
Dixon La. Rd. Leeds —9M 61
Dixon St. F'stne —4D 122
Dixon's Yd. Wake —5M 119
Dobb. —6J 163
Dobb La. H'frth —6H 163
Dobb Top Rd. Holmb —7G 163
Dob Pk. Rd. Otley —2K 11
Dob Royd. Shepl —1H 165
Dobroyd Rd. Todm —8J 87
Dobrudden Cvn. Pk. Bail —2L 39
Dobson Av. Leeds —2E 80
Dobson Gro. Leeds —2E 80
Dobson Pl. Leeds —2E 80
Dobsons Row. Carl —2M 99
Dobsons Wharfe. Sils —9E 6
Dobson Ter. Leeds —2E 80
Dobson Vw. Leeds —2E 80
Dockery Hud —7L 131
Dockfield Ind. Pk. Bail —6B 40
Dockfield Pl. Shipl —7A 40
Dockfield Rd. Shipl —7A 40
Dockfield Ter. Shipl —7A 40
Dock La. Bail —7A 40
Dock La. Shipl —7A 40
Dockroyd La. Oakw —5C 36
Dock St. Leeds —7E 62
Doctor Fold. Hon —4L 147
Doctor Hill. Hal —3K 91
Doctor Hill. Idle —9E 40
(in two parts)
Doctor La. B'frd —6F 40
Doctor La. Floc —8E 134
Doctor La. Mir —7L 115
Doctor La. Shel —6L 149
Doctors Row. Hud —2G 132
Dodd Naze. —1J 89
Dodds Royd. Hud —1K 147
Dodge Holme Clo. Hal —9K 73
Dodge Holme Ct. Hal —9K 73
(off Dodge Holme Rd.)
Dodge Holme Dri. Hal —9J 73
Dodge Holme Gdns. Hal —9K 73
Dodge Holme Rd. Hal —9K 73
Dodgson Av. Leeds —3G 62
Dodgson St. Ell —6E 112
Dodlee La. Hud —4D 130
Dodsworth Cres. Nor —3J 121
Dodworth Dri. Wake —5K 137
Doe Pk. Denh —5M 55
Dog Hill. Shaf —6J 155
Dog Hill Dri. Shaf —6K 155
Doghouse La. Todm —7H 87
Dog Kennel Bank. Hud —5A 132
Dog Kennel La. Hal —7D 92
Dog La. G'lnd —4K 111
Dog La. Holy G —9K 111
Dogley Lane. —9H 133
Dogley La. Fen B —9H 133
Dogley Villa Ct. Fen B —9H 133
Doldram La. Sower B —2G 110
Dole La. Err —3H 89
Doles Av. Roys —6C 154
Doles Cres. Roys —6C 154
Doles La. Brigh —8C 94
Dole St. T'tn —8D 56
Dolfin Pl. Hud —6D 114
Doll La. Cull —2L 55
Dolly La. Leeds —5G 62
Dolphin Ct. Leeds —7G 63
(nr. Catherine St.)
Dolphin Ct. Leeds —5E 60
(nr. Stanningley Rd.)
Dolphin La. H'den —7L 37
Dolphin La. Thpe —2G 99
Dolphin Rd. Leeds —8G 81
Dolphin St. Leeds —7G 62
Dolphin Ter. Q'bry —5B 74
Dombey St. Hal —5N 91
Domestic Rd. Leeds —9B 62
Domestic St. Leeds —8B 62
Dominion Av. Leeds —9F 44
Dominion Clo. Leeds —9F 44
Donald Av. B'frd —5A 76
Donald St. Fars —4A 60
Don Av. Weth —1L 17
Doncaster La. Hamp —5G 159
Doncaster Rd. Ackw & Bads —5G 140
Doncaster Rd. E Hard —1L 141
Doncaster Rd. Foul & Wrag —2K 139
Doncaster Rd. Knot —8B 104
Doncaster Rd. N Elm —3A 158
Doncaster Rd. S Elm —7N 157
Doncaster Rd. Wake & Croft —7M 119
Doncaster Rd. Est. Ackw —5G 140
Doncaster Sq. Knot —7B 104
Doncaster St. Hal —9C 92
Don Ct. Sils —8E 6
Donisthorpe St. B'frd —2B 76
Donisthorpe St. Leeds —9G 62
Don Pedro Av. Nor I —1L 121
Don Pedro Clo. Nor —2L 121
Don Pedro Cotts. Norm —1M 121
Don St. Kei —8H 21
Dorchester Av. Pon —3H 123
Dorchester Ct. B'frd —2J 77
Dorchester Cres. Bail —3D 40
Dorchester Cres. B'frd —2J 77
Dorchester Dri. Hal —7L 91
Dorchester Dri. Yead —1A 42
Dorchester Rd. Hud —6N 113
Dorian Clo. B'frd —9H 41
Dorman Av. Upt —1C 158
Dorothy St. Kei —4G 37
Dorset Av. Leeds —2J 63
Dorset Clo. B'frd —2A 76
Dorset Clo. Hems —1D 156
Dorset Gro. S'ley —6B 60
Dorset Mt. Leeds —3J 63
Dorset Rd. Leeds —2J 63
Dorset St. B'frd —2A 76
Dorset St. Hud —2L 131
Dorset St. Leeds —2J 63
Dorset Ter. Leeds —3J 63
Dorset Wlk. Dew —3E 116
(off Boothroyd La.)
Dortmund Sq. Leeds —6E 62
(off Wormald Row)
Dotterel Glen. Morl —1N 97
Doubting La. Dew —1G 135
Doubting Rd. Dew —1G 134
Douglas Av. Bat —7J 97
Douglas Av. Mold —5C 132
Douglas Av. Pad —5G 131
Douglas Cres. Shipl —9B 40
Douglas Dri. B'frd —1G 77
Douglas Rd. B'frd —1G 77
Douglas St. Cro R —7E 36
Douglas St. Dew —7F 116
Douglas St. Hal —2A 92
Douglas Towers. B'frd —9C 58
(off Radwell Dri.)
Dove Clo. Weth —1M 17
Dovecote Clo. Horb —9D 118
Dovecote Dri. Leds —7E 84
Dovecote La. Horb —9C 118
Dovecote Lodge. Horb —9D 118
Dovedale Clo. Croft —1H 139
Dovedale Clo. Hal —8G 75
Dovedale Gdns. Leeds —4G 64
Dovedale Gth. Leeds —3G 64
Dove Dri. C'frd —4H 103
Dove Hill. Roys —5E 154
Dover La. H'frth —5M 163
Dover Rd. H'frth —5M 163
Dover St. B'frd —5D 58
Dover St. Gar —7B 66
Dover St. Todm —6M 87
Dovesdale Gro. B'frd —3A 76
Dovesdale Rd. B'frd —3B 76
Dove St. Haw —8D 36
Dove St. Shipl —7L 39
Dowkell La. Thor A —8E 18
Dowker St. Hal —7M 91
Dowker St. Hud —5G 130
Dowland Cres. Knot —1G 124
Dowley Gap. —6H 39
Dowley Gap La. Bgly —6G 38
Downham St. B'frd —8E 58
Downing Clo. B'frd —7E 58
Downing St. Lint —1B 146
Downshutts La. H'frth —3B 164
Downside Cres. All —5F 56
Dracup Av. B'frd —9K 57
Dracup Rd. B'frd —2L 75
Dradishaw Rd. Sils —8D 6
Dragon Cres. Leeds —9N 61
Dragon Dri. Leeds —9M 61
Dragon Rd. Leeds —9N 61
Drake Fold. Wyke —1A 94
Drake La. Dlgtn —8B 78
Drakes Ind. Est. Oven —9N 73
Drake St. B'frd —8D 58
Drake St. Kei —8J 21
Draper La. H Bri —7F 70
Draughton Gro. B'frd —4B 76
Draughton St. B'frd —4B 76
Draycott Wlk. B'frd —3J 77
Draycott Wlk. Carc —9N 159
Drayton Mnr. Yd. Leeds —1E 80
(off Moor Cres.)
Dray Vw. Dew —1C 116
Drewry Rd. Kei —9H 21
Drewton St. B'frd —7B 58
Driffield Ho. B'frd —8G 40
Driftholme Rd. Dlgtn —6C 78
Drighlington. —8B 78
Drighlington By-Pass. B'frd —6N 77
Drill Pde. B'frd —5B 58
Drill St. Haw —9C 36
Drill St. Kei —9J 21
Drinker La. Shel —4A 150
Driver Pl. Leeds —8A 62
Drivers Row. Pon —4H 123
Driver St. Leeds —8B 62
Driver Ter. Leeds —8A 62
Driver Ter. Sils —7E 6
Drive, The. Adel —4K 43
Drive, The. Alw —1B 44
Drive, The. Bard —4E 30
Drive, The. Bat —6D 96
Drive, The. Bgly —1D 38
Drive, The. B'frd —9H 41
Drive, The. Bur W —9C 10
Drive, The. C'gts —4E 64
Drive, The. Hal —4J 93
Drive, The. H Bri —3L 89
Drive, The. Kip —5A 84
Drive, The. Leeds —7G 62
Drive, The. Round —7H 45
Drive, The. Swil —4H 83
Dross St. B'frd —9H 59
Drove Rd. Ho. B'frd —2C 76
(off Bowling Old La.)
Drovers Way. B'frd —3C 58
Drub. —2J 95
Drub La. Cleck —2J 95
Druggist La. Add —1M 7
Druids St. Cytn —1G 75
Druids Vw. Av. Bgly —9C 22
Drummer La. Gol —7N 129
Drummond Av. Leeds —9M 43
Drummond Ct. Leeds —9M 43
Drummond Rd. B'frd —5A 58
Drummond Rd. Leeds —8M 43
Drury Av. H'fth —7E 42
Drury Clo. H'fth —7E 42
Drury La. Holy G —7M 111
Drury La. H'fth —7E 42
(in two parts)
Drury La. Nor —9G 100
Drury La. Wake —5K 119
Dry Carr La. Hal —8C 72
Dryclough Av. Hud —8H 131
Dryclough Clo. Hal —9B 92
Dryclough La. Hal —9B 92
Dryclough Rd. Hud —7H 131
Dryden St. Bgly —4E 38
Dryden St. B'frd —8D 58
Dry Hill La. Den D —3E 166
Dubb La. Bgly —4F 38
Duchy Av. B'frd —3K 57
Duchy Cres. B'frd —3K 57
Duchy Dri. B'frd —4K 57
(in two parts)
Duchy Gro. B'frd —3K 57
Duchy Vs. B'frd —3K 57
Duchywood. B'frd —3K 57
Ducie St. B'frd —6F 40
Duckett Gro. Pud —6K 59
Duck Hill. H Bri —4H 71
Duck La. B'frd —7C 58
Duckworth Gro. B'frd —4L 57
Duckworth La. D Hill —5K 57
Duckworth Ter. B'frd —4L 57
Dudfleet La. Horb —2D 136
Dudley Av. Birs —2D 96
Dudley Av. Hud —4J 131
Dudley Cres. Hal —8K 73
Dudley Gro. B'frd —9J 59
Dudley Hill. —2G 77
Dudley Hill Rd. B'frd —3F 58
Dudley Rd. Hud —4J 131
Dudley St. B'frd —1F 76
(in three parts)
Dudley St. Cut H —9J 59
Dudwell Av. Hal —1C 112
Dudwell Gro. Hal —1B 112
Dudwell La. Hal —1B 112
Dufton App. Leeds —3B 64
Duich Rd. B'frd —7K 75
Duinen St. B'frd —9D 58
Duke of York Av. Wake —1M 137
Duke of York St. Wake —4M 119
Duke of York St. Wren —2H 119
Dukes Cut. Blkhd —1J 87
Duke St. B'frd —7C 58
Duke St. C'frd —4B 102
Duke St. Dew —6B 116
Duke St. Ell —5E 112
Duke St. Fitz —7A 140
Duke St. Haw —8D 36
Duke St. Kei —7H 21
Duke St. Leeds —7F 62
Duke St. L'ft —3D 90
Duke Wood Rd. Clay W —7H 151
Dulverton Clo. Leeds —4N 79
Dulverton Clo. Pon —9M 103
Dulverton Ct. Leeds —4N 79
Dulverton Gdns. Leeds —3M 79
Dulverton Gth. Leeds —4M 79
Dulverton Grn. Ctly —4M 79
Dulverton Grn. Leeds —4N 79
Dulverton Gro. B'frd —2H 77
Dulverton Gro. Leeds —4M 79
Dulverton Pl. Leeds —4M 79
Dulverton Ri. Pon —9M 103
Dulverton Sq. Leeds —4N 79
Dulverton Way. Pon —9M 103
Dunbar Cft. Q'bry —4E 74
Dunbar St. Wake —7A 120
Dunbottle Clo. Mir —6M 115
Dunbottle La. Mir —5M 115
Duncan Av. Otley —2H 25
Duncan Av. Wake —9N 119
Duncan St. B'frd —9C 58
Duncan St. Leeds —7E 62
Dunce Pk. Clo. Ell —6E 112
Duncombe Rd. B'frd —7L 57
Duncombe St. B'frd —7M 57
Duncombe St. Leeds —6C 62
Duncombe Way. B'frd —7M 57
Dundas St. Hal —7M 91
Dundas St. Hud —4M 131
Dundas St. Kei —1K 37
Dundee Rd. Todm —4F 86
Dunderdale Cres. C'frd —3K 103
Dunford Rd. H'frth —3M 163
Dungeon La. Oult —3A 100
Dunham Ct. Hud —3M 131
(off Rook St.)
Dunhill Cres. Leeds —6N 63
Dunhill Ri. Leeds —6N 63
Dunkeswick. —7F 14
Dunkeswick La. Wee —2C 14
Dunkhill Cft. Idle —8F 40
Dunkirk. —8D 74
Dunkirk Cres. Hal —6L 91
Dunkirk Gdns. Hal —7L 91
Dunkirk La. Hal —7L 91
Dunkirk Ri. Riddl —6L 21
Dunkirk St. Hal —6L 91
Dunkirk Ter. Hal —6M 91
Dunlands La. M'twn —2L 135
Dunlin Clo. Morl —1N 97
Dunlin Ct. Leeds —8F 80
Dunlin Cft. Leeds —8F 80
Dunlin Dri. Leeds —8F 80
Dunlin Fold. Leeds —8F 80
Dunlin Way. B'frd —7H 57
Dunmill Fld. Leeds —4F 60
Dunmill Pas. Otley —1K 25
Dunmill Ri. Leeds —3G 80
Dunmill Va. Leeds —6J 61
Dunmore Av. Q'bry —4B 74
Dunn Clo. Wren —9H 99
Dunningley La. Ting —2B 98
Dunnington Wlk. B'frd —7M 75
Dunnock Cft. Morl —1N 97
Dunnock Rd. Mel —5B 146
Dunrobin Av. Gar —7B 66
Dunsford Av. B'frd —5F 76
Dunsil Vs. S Elm —8M 157
Dunsley Bank Rd. H'frth —6L 163
Dunsley La. Pon —7E 156
(in two parts)
Dunsley Ter. S Kirk —7G 156
Dunsmore Dri. Hud —2E 130
Dunstan Clo. Oss —7A 118
Dunstarn Dri. Leeds —4N 43
Dunstarn Gdns. Leeds —4A 44
Dunstarn La. Leeds —5N 43
Durban Av. Leeds —3B 80
Durban Cres. Leeds —3B 80
Durham Ct. Fars —3A 60
Durham Rd. B'frd —5M 57
Durham St. C'frd —7E 102
Durham St. Hal —5L 91
Durham Ter. B'frd —5M 57
Durkar. —3H 137
Durkar Fields. Dur —4G 137
Durkar La. Dur —4G 137
Durkar Low La. Dur —3H 137
Durkar Ri. Crig —4H 137
Durley Av. B'frd —3M 57
Durling Dri. Wrose —8C 40
Durlston Gro. Wyke —9B 76
Durlston Ter. Wyke —9B 76
Durn St. Todm —3C 86
Durrance St. Kei —1F 36
Durrant Clo. Weth —4N 17
Dutton Grn. Leeds —7B 46
Dutton Way. Leeds —8B 46
Duxbury Ri. Leeds —4D 62
Dyas Bldgs. S'hse —6M 121
Dyehouse Dri. West I —2G 95
Dyehouse Fold. Oaken —8E 76
Dyehouse La. Brigh —2N 113
Dye Ho. La. Norl —2L 111
Dyehouse La. Pud —1B 78
(in two parts)
Dye Ho. La. Wilsd —1N 55
Dyehouse Rd. Oaken —8D 76
Dyer La. Hal —3M 91
Dyers Ct. Leeds —2B 62
Dyer St. Leeds —6F 62
Dyke Bottom. Shepl —9K 149
Dyke Clo. Mir —3L 115
Dyke End. Gol —7A 130
Dyke La. Todm —5C 88
Dymond Gro. Liv —9L 95
Dymond Rd. Liv —9M 95
Dymond Vw. Liv —9L 95
Dyson Ho. Leeds —3L 61
Dyson Lane. —8C 110
Dyson La. H'frth —7N 163
Dyson La. Sower B —8C 110
Dyson Pl. Hal —9D 92
(off Ashgrove Av.)
Dyson Rd. Hal —4M 91
Dyson's Hill. Hon —4L 147
Dyson St. B'frd —7B 58
(BD1)
Dyson St. B'frd —2M 57
(BD9)
Dyson St. Brigh —9M 93
Dyson St. Hud —4C 132

Eagle Gro. Wake —5F 118
Eaglesfield Dri. B'frd —7L 75
Eagle St. Haw —8D 36
Eagle St. Kei —9H 21
Eagle St. Todm —7K 87
Eagley Bank. S'fth —5A 106
Ealand Av. Bat —5D 96
Ealand Cres. Bat —5D 96
Ealand Rd. Bat —4C 96
(in two parts)
Ealing Ct. Bat —6D 96
Earles Av. Hud —5C 132
Earle St. F'stne —5C 122
Earlsheaton. —2J 117
Earlsmere Dri. Morl —8J 79
Earl St. Dew —3L 117
Earl St. Fitz —7A 140
Earl St. Haw —9C 36
Earl St. Kei —8H 21
Earl St. Wake —4M 119
Earlswood Av. Leeds —5H 45
Earlswood Chase. Pud —8B 60
Earlswood Cres. Kip —3N 83
Earlswood Mead. Pud —8A 60
Earl Ter. Hal —2N 91
Easby Av. Bat —8C 96
Easby Clo. I'ly —5E 8
Easby Dri. I'ly —5E 8
Easby Rd. B'frd —9B 58
Easdale Clo. Leeds —1A 64
Easdale Cres. Leeds —1B 64
Easdale Mt. Leeds —2A 64
Easdale Rd. Leeds —2A 64
Easingwood Dri. Hud —1F 132
East Acres. Byr —5D 104
East Ardsley. —5C 98
East Av. Horb —1E 136
East Av. Hud —1H 131
East Av. Kei —8J 21
(in two parts)
East Av. Pon —4H 123
East Av. S Elm —5A 158
East Av. Upt —2N 157
E. Bath St. Bat —7G 97
E. Beck Ct. Askw —4D 10
East Bierley. —6K 77
East Bolton. Hal —6L 73
Eastborough. —2G 117
Eastborough Cres. Dew —2G 11
Eastbourne. —3N 123
Eastbourne Av. F'stne —5E 122
Eastbourne Clo. Pon —3N 123
Eastbourne Cres. Pon —3N 123
Eastbourne Dri. Pon —3N 123

stbourne Rd. B'frd —1N 57
stbourne Ter. Pon —3M 123
stbourne Vw. Pon —3M 123
st Bowling. —3E 76
stbrook. —8D 58
stbrook Well. B'frd —7D 58
stburn. —2A 20
stbury Av. B'frd —4J 75
Busk La. Otley —9N 11
stby. —1A 4
stby Bank. Eby —1A 4
st Byland. Hal —7L 73
st Carlton. —5A 26
Causeway. Leeds —2N 43
Causeway Clo. Leeds —2N 43
Causeway Cres. Leeds —3N 43
Causeway Va. Leeds —3A 44
Chevin Rd. Otley —2M 25
Church St. Hal —5C 92
st Clo. Hud —9N 113
st Clo. Pon —6L 123
st Ct. Far —3A 60
off Ebenezer St.)
st Cft. Wyke —2B 94
Dale Clo. Hems —2F 156
stdean Bank. Leeds —9B 46
stdean Dri. Leeds —9B 46
stdean Gdns. Leeds —9C 46
stdean Ga. Leeds —1C 64
stdean Grange. Leeds —1C 64
stdean Gro. Leeds —9C 46
stdean Ri. Leeds —9C 46
stdean Rd. Leeds —9B 46
st Dene. Sils —7E 6
st Down. C'frd —4G 102
st Dri. Gar —1B 84
st Dri. Pon —4M 123
End Cres. Roys —6F 154
sterly Av. Leeds —2J 63
sterly Clo. Leeds —3K 63
sterly Cres. Leeds —2J 63
sterly Cross. Leeds —2K 63
sterly Gth. Leeds —2K 63
sterly Gro. Leeds —2J 63
sterly Mt. Leeds —2K 63
sterly Rd. Leeds —2J 63
sterly Sq. Leeds —2K 63
sterly Vw. Leeds —2K 63
stfield. Shepl —9K 149
stfield Av. Knot —9E 104
stfield Clo. M'well —9M 153
stfield Cres. M'well —9M 153
stfield Cres. W'ford —7C 82
stfield Dri. Kbtn —2J 149
stfield Dri. Pon —2M 123
stfield Dri. W'ford —7C 82
stfield Gdns. B'frd —2J 77
tfield Gro. Nor —9K 101
tfield La. Bur W —9E 10
tfield La. C'frd —4E 102
tfield Rd. Knot —9E 104
tfield Rd. Mir —5A 116
ield St. Leeds —7G 63
t Fold. Skelm —8F 150
t Garforth. —6B 66
tgate. B'hpe —5G 27
tgate. Ell —4E 112
tgate. Hems —3E 156
tgate. Hon —5L 147
tgate. Leeds —6E 62
Grange Clo. Leeds —4G 81
Grange Dri. Leeds —4G 80
Grange Gth. Leeds —4G 81
Grange Ri. Leeds —4G 81
Grange Rd. Leeds —4G 80
Grange Sq. Leeds —4G 80
Grange Vw. Leeds —4G 80
t Gro. Hud —2G 132
t Hardwick. —9M 123
thorpe Ct. B'frd —2H 59
t Keswick. —3D 30
King St. Leeds —7G 62
tlands. Hud —6E 132
tland Wlk. Leeds —5H 61
t Lee La. Todm —4A 88
tleigh. Ting —4C 98
tleigh Ct. Ting —4C 98
tleigh Dri. Ting —4B 98
tleigh Gro. B'frd —2A 76
t Moor. —3A 44
r. Adel)
t Moor. —4N 119
r. Wakefield)
Moor Av. Leeds —6H 45
Moor Clo. Leeds —6H 45
Moor Cres. Leeds —5H 45
Moor Dri. Leeds —6J 45
tmoor Gro. Barn —8D 154
tmoor Ho. B'frd —3K 77
Moor La. Leeds —3N 43
Moor Rd. Leeds —5H 45
tmoor Rd. Wake —3L 119
t Morton. —7C 22

East Mt. Brigh —9M 93
E. Mount Pl. Brigh —9M 93
Easton Pl. Hud —3G 130
East Pde. Bail —3B 40
East Pde. B'frd —7D 58
East Pde. I'ly —5H 9
East Pde. Kei —9J 21
East Pde. Leeds —6D 62
East Pde. Men —4E 24
East Pde. Sower B —8K 91
East Pde. Steet —3D 20
E. Park Dri. Leeds —7H 63
E. Park Gro. Leeds —7J 63
E. Park Mt. Leeds —7J 63
E. Park Pde. Leeds —7J 63
E. Park Pl. Leeds —7J 63
E. Park Rd. Hal —3N 91
E. Park Rd. Leeds —7H 63
E. Park St. Leeds —7J 63
E. Park St. Morl —1J 97
E. Park Ter. Leeds —7J 63
E. Park Vw. Leeds —7J 63
E. Pinfold. Roys —6D 154
East Riddlesden Hall. —7M 21
E. Ridge Vw. Gar —5C 66
East Rigton. —4F 30
East Rd. Low M —7C 76
East Royd. Hal —3H 93
(off Groveville.)
East Royd. Oakw —5D 36
E. Side Ct. Pud —9E 60
E. Squire La. B'frd —5A 58
East St. Bat —7F 96
East St. Brigh —2M 113
East St. Gol —6D 130
East St. Hal —5M 93
East St. H'cft —9L 139
East St. Hud —1G 130
East St. Jack B —5C 164
East St. Leeds —7F 62
(in three parts)
East St. S Elm —5A 158
East St. S Hien —4M 155
East St. Sower B —1E 110
East St. Stan —1B 120
East St. Wake —1L 119
East Ter. Cro R —7E 36
East Thorpe. —7K 115
E. Thorpe Pl. Mir —7M 115
East Vw. C'frd —5A 102
East Vw. Cleck —6E 94
East Vw. Gild —8F 78
East Vw. Kip —3B 84
East Vw. Knot —8F 104
East Vw. Leeds —4D 64
(off Swillington La.)
East Vw. Light —5M 93
East Vw. M'fld —9H 67
East Vw. Mir —5K 115
East Vw. Oss —8A 118
East Vw. Pud —9B 60
East Vw. Sils —8E 6
East Vw. T'tn —6B 56
East Vw. W'ford —8D 82
East Vw. Yead —1N 41
E. View Cotts. Lowt —6C 60
(off Lane End)
E. View Rd. Yead —1N 41
E. View Ter. Otley —1M 25
(off Carlton St.)
E. View Ter. Shel —6M 149
E. View Ter. Wyke —9C 76
E. Ville Rd. Shar C —8J 121
Eastway. Mir —4K 115
Eastway Pk. Mir —4L 115
Eastwood. —4C 88
(nr. Hebden Bridge)
Eastwood. —8K 21
(nr. Keighley)
Eastwood Av. Hal —6L 73
Eastwood Av. Sower B —9F 90
Eastwood Av. Wake —4H 119
Eastwood Clo. Dur —3H 137
Eastwood Clo. Hal —6L 73
Eastwood Cres. Bgly —7G 38
Eastwood Cres. Leeds —2E 64
Eastwood Dri. Leeds —1E 64
Eastwood Gdns. Leeds —2D 64
Eastwood Gth. Leeds —2E 64
Eastwood Gro. Gar —9A 66
Eastwood Gro. Hal —6L 73
Eastwood La. Leeds —2E 64
Eastwood La. Todm —3B 88
Eastwood Nook. Leeds —2E 64
Eastwood Rd. Todm —1J 87
Eastwood's Farm. Hal —6L 73
(off Causeway Foot)
Eastwood St. B'frd —9D 58
Eastwood St. Brigh —9N 93
Eastwood St. Hal —2N 91
Eastwood St. Hud —5B 132
Easy Rd. Leeds —8H 63
Eaton Hill. Leeds —4H 43

Eaton M. Leeds —8E 80
Eaton Pl. Hems —2E 156
Eaton Rd. I'ly —6F 8
Eaton Sq. Leeds —9E 80
Eaton St. Kei —3G 37
Eaton Wlk. S Elm —4N 157
Eaves Av. H Bri —9F 70
Eaves Rd. H Bri —9F 70
Ebberston Gro. Leeds —3B 62
Ebberston Pl. Leeds —3B 62
Ebberston Ter. Leeds —3B 62
Ebenezer Pl. B'frd —1N 75
Ebenezer St. B'frd —8D 58
Ebenezer St. Fars —3A 60
Ebenezer St. Rob H —1K 99
Ebor Gdns. Mir —6K 115
Ebor La. Haw —7C 36
Ebor Mt. Kip —3A 84
Ebor Mt. Leeds —4B 62
Ebor Pl. Leeds —4B 62
Ebor St. Leeds —4B 62
Ebor Ter. Leeds —3G 81
(off Woodhouse Hill Rd.)
Ebor Way. Weth —5K 17
(nr. Linton La.)
Ebor Way. Weth & B Spa —6B 18
(nr. Watersole La.)
Ebridge Ct. Bgly —4F 38
(off Edward St.)
Ebson Ho. La. N Mill —2F 164
Ebury Clo. Bat —6G 96
Ebury St. Bat —6G 96
Ecclesburn Av. Leeds —7J 63
Ecclesburn Rd. Leeds —7J 63
Ecclesburn St. Leeds —7J 63
Ecclesburn Ter. Leeds —7J 63
Eccles Ct. B'frd —2F 58
Eccleshill. —1F 58
Eccles Parlour. Sower B —4A 110
Eccup. —7B 28
Eccup La. Leeds —1N 43
Eccup Moor Rd. Leeds —8A 28
Echo St. Liv —1K 115
Edale Av. New —9L 131
Edale Clo. Kbtn —2F 132
Edale Gro. Q'bry —5B 74
Edale Way. Leeds —4J 43
Eddercliff Cres. Liv —6L 95
Edderthorpe St. B'frd —8E 58
Eddison Clo. Leeds —2N 43
Eddison St. Fars —4A 60
Eddison Wlk. Leeds —2N 43
Eddystone Ri. Knot —8C 104
Edelshain Gro. Wake —2A 138
Eden Av. Oss —5N 117
Eden Av. Wake —6F 118
Eden Clo. Wyke —1B 94
Eden Cres. Leeds —2L 61
Edendale. C'frd —4F 102
Eden Dri. Leeds —3L 61
Eden Gdns. Leeds —3L 61
Eden Gro. Leeds —3L 61
Eden Mt. Leeds —3L 61
Eden Rd. Leeds —2L 61
Edensor Rd. Kei —9G 21
Eden Wlk. Leeds —3L 61
Eden Way. Leeds —3L 61
Ederoyd Av. S'ley —5M 59
Ederoyd Cres. S'ley —5L 59
Ederoyd Dri. S'ley —5M 59
Ederoyd Gro. S'ley —5M 59
Ederoyd Mt. S'ley —5M 59
Ederoyd Ri. S'ley —5L 59
Edgar St. Cytn —1J 75
Edgbaston Clo. Leeds —1C 44
Edgbaston Wlk. Leeds —1C 44
Edge Av. Dew —1G 134
Edgebank Av. B'frd —7L 75
Edge Bottom. Denh —5K 55
Edge Clo. Dew —1H 135
Edge Clo. Gol —6D 130
Edge End. Denh —5L 55
Edge End Gdns. B'frd —6K 75
Edge End La. H'frth —3F 162
Edge End Rd. B'frd —5K 75
Edge Hill Clo. Hud —3B 132
Edgehill Clo. Q'bry —4E 74
Edgehill Rd. M'well —7J 153
Edgeholme La. Hal —5H 91
Edge Junct. Dew —1G 135
Edge La. Dew —9H 117
Edge La. Hept —5M 69
Edgemoor Clo. Hal —8A 92
Edgemoor Clo. S'fth —6A 106
Edgemoor Rd. Hall G —7H 137
Edgemoor Rd. Hon —6K 147
Edge Rd. Dew —1H 135
Edgerton. —3K 131
Edgerton Grn. Hud —3K 131
Edgerton Gro. Rd. Hud —3K 131
Edgerton Ho. Hud —1J 131
Edgerton La. Hud —3K 131
Edgerton Rd. Hud —2K 131

Edgerton Rd. Leeds —7L 43
Edge Ter. Hud —3E 130
Edge Top Rd. Dew —1F 134
Edge Vw. Dew —1H 135
Edge Vw. Gol —6D 130
Edgeware Rd. Hud —4E 132
Edgware Av. Leeds —4H 63
Edgware Gro. Leeds —4H 63
Edgware Mt. Leeds —4H 63
Edgware Pl. Leeds —4H 63
Edgware Rd. Leeds —4H 63
Edgware St. Leeds —4H 63
Edgware Ter. Leeds —4H 63
Edgware Vw. Leeds —4H 63
Edinburgh Av. Leeds —6K 61
Edinburgh Gro. Leeds —6K 61
Edinburgh Pl. Gar —7B 66
Edinburgh Pl. Leeds —6K 61
Edinburgh Rd. Leeds —6K 61
Edinburgh Ter. Leeds —6K 61
Edlington Clo. B'frd —2J 77
Edmonton Pl. Leeds —9F 44
Edmund St. B'frd —8B 58
Edmund St. Todm —3J 107
Edna St. S Elm —6N 157
Edrich Clo. Low M —7C 76
Edroyd Pl. Fars —3A 60
Edroyd St. Fars —3A 60
Education Rd. Leeds —3E 62
Edward Clo. Dew —8E 116
Edward Clo. S'wram —8F 92
Edward Ct. Carr G —7G 98
Edward Dri. Wake —7K 99
Edward Rd. Mir —6K 115
Edward Rd. Skel —7N 159
Edwards Rd. Hal —7L 91
Edward St. Bgly —4F 38
Edward St. B'frd —4J 77
(nr. Tong St.)
Edward St. B'frd —8D 58
(nr. Wakefield Rd.)
Edward St. Brigh —9M 93
Edward St. Clif —1A 114
Edward St. Facit —9A 106
Edward St. H Bri —1J 89
Edward St. Leeds —6E 62
Edward St. Lit T —7L 95
Edward St. Liv —8L 95
Edward St. M'well —9L 153
Edward St. Nor —7H 101
Edward St. Shipl —6L 39
Edward St. Sower B —8H 91
Edward St. Wake —4M 119
Edward Turner Clo. Low M —7A 76
Edwin Rd. Leeds —4A 62
Edwins Clo. Barn —9B 154
Eel Holme Vw. St. Kei —6H 21
Eel Mires Gth. Weth —3N 17
Effingham Rd. H'den —6N 37
Egerton Gro. All —5F 56
Egerton St. Sower B —8H 91
Egerton Ter. Rawd —4A 42
(off Town St.)
Eggleston Dri. B'frd —3K 77
Egglestone Sq. B Spa —1C 32
Eggleston St. Leeds —1C 60
Egham Grn. B'frd —8F 40
(off Ley Fleaks Rd.)
Egmanton Rd. Barn —8A 154
Egremont Cres. B'frd —7L 75
Egremont St. Sower B —9G 91
Egremont Ter. Sower B —9G 91
(off Egremont St.)
Egypt. —6B 56
Egypt Rd. T'tn —6B 56
Eiffel Bldgs. H Bri —1H 89
Eiffel St. H Bri —1J 89
Eighth Av. Leeds —8N 61
Eighth Av. Liv —7F 94
Eighth Av. Rothw —6B 82
Eightlands. —3F 116
Eightlands Av. Leeds —4G 61
Eightlands La. Leeds —4G 61
Eightlands Rd. Dew —3F 116
Ekota Pl. Leeds —2H 63
Elam Wood Rd. Riddl —4J 21
(in two parts)
Eland Ho. Ell —4E 112
(off Southgate)
Elba Ter. Horb —8D 118
Elbow La. B'frd —4F 58
Elbow La. Hal —3E 90
Elder Av. Upt —1B 158
Elder Av. Wake —4J 119
Elder Bank. Cull —9K 37
(off Keighley Rd.)
Elder Clo. Bat —2C 96
Elder Cft. Leeds —5F 60
Elder Dri. Dew —8G 116
Elder Dri. Upt —1B 158
Elder Gth. Gar —8B 66
Elder Grn. Wake —4J 119
Elder Gro. Neth —3J 147

Elder Gro. Wake —4J 119
Elder Gro. M. Neth —3J 147
Elder La. Hud —6E 114
Elder M. Shel —6K 149
Elder Mt. Leeds —5F 60
Elder Pl. Leeds —5F 60
Elder Ri. Rothw —7F 82
Elder Rd. Hud —6D 114
Elder Rd. Leeds —5F 60
Elder St. B'frd —8J 41
Elder St. Kei —6G 21
Elder St. Leeds —5F 60
Eldon Mt. Guis —7J 25
Eldon Pl. B'frd —6B 58
Eldon Pl. Cut H —1H 77
Eldon Rd. Hud —4J 131
Eldon St. Hal —4B 92
Eldon St. Heck —8A 96
Eldon St. Oss —4B 118
Eldon St. Todm —7L 87
Eldon Ter. B'frd —6B 58
Eldon Ter. Leeds —4D 62
Eldroth Mt. Hal —7N 91
Eldroth Rd. Hal —7N 91
Eldwick. —3H 39
Eldwick Beck. —1H 39
Eleanor Dri. C'ley —8K 41
Eleanor St. Brigh —2M 113
Eleanor St. Hud —2M 131
Eleventh Av. Liv —7G 94
Elford Gro. Leeds —3H 63
Elford Pl. E. Leeds —3H 63
Elford Pl. W. Leeds —3H 63
Elford Rd. Leeds —3H 63
Elgar Wlk. Stan —7N 99
Elgin Clo. Hud —8H 131
Elia St. Kei —8K 21
Elim Wlk. Dew —3F 116
(off Willan's Rd.)
Eliot Gro. Guis —8K 25
Eli St. B'frd —2D 76
Elizabethan Ct. Pon —1L 123
Elizabeth Av. S Hien —4M 155
Elizabeth Av. Wyke —9B 76
Elizabeth Clo. Wyke —9B 76
Elizabeth Ct. Coll —9J 17
Elizabeth Ct. Hems —3F 156
Elizabeth Cres. Wyke —9B 76
Elizabeth Dri. C'frd —3J 103
Elizabeth Dri. Knot —8B 104
Elizabeth Dri. Wyke —9B 76
Elizabeth Gdns. Wake —3L 119
Elizabeth Gro. Morl —8M 79
Elizabeth Ho. Hal —1L 91
(off Furness Pl.)
Elizabeth Pl. Leeds —1B 64
Elizabeth St. Bgly —4F 38
Elizabeth St. B'frd —9C 58
Elizabeth St. Ell —5E 112
Elizabeth St. G'lnd —4C 112
Elizabeth St. Hud —7M 131
Elizabeth St. Leeds —3A 62
Elizabeth St. Liv —8J 95
Elizabeth St. Oakw —5D 36
Elizabeth St. Wake —9N 119
Elizabeth St. Wyke —9A 76
Elland. —5E 112
Elland Bri. Ell —4E 112
Elland Hall Farm Cvn. Pk. Ell —4D 112
Elland La. Ell —4F 112
(in two parts)
Elland Lower Edge. —4J 113
Elland Riorges Link. Lfds B —4F 112
Elland Rd. Brigh —1M 113
Elland Rd. Ell —2F 112
Elland Rd. Leeds —3N 79
(nr. Beeston Ring Rd.)
Elland Rd. Leeds —1B 80
(nr. Tilbury Rd.)
Elland Rd. Morl —6L 79
Elland Rd. Sower B —7E 110
Elland Road. —2A 80
Elland Rd. Ind. Pk. Leeds —2N 79
Elland St. C'frd —3E 102
Elland Ter. Leeds —9D 62
Elland Upper Edge. —5H 113
Elland Way. Leeds —3N 79
Elland Wood Bottom. G'lnd —2C 112
Ellar Carr Rd. B'frd —5G 40
Ellar Carr Rd. Cull —8J 37
Ellar Gdns. Men —2E 24
Ella St. Fitz —6A 140
Ella St. Kei —8K 21
Ellen Holme Rd. Hal —6D 90
Ellen Royd La. L'ft —4C 90
(in two parts)
Ellen Royd St. Hal —4B 92
Ellen St. Bgly —4F 38
Ellenthorpe Rd. Bail —5K 39
Ellentrees. —8H 101
Ellentrees La. Nor —7H 101
Ellerby La. Leeds —8G 63

Ellerby Rd. Leeds —7G 62
Eller Ct. Leeds —9L 45
Ellercroft Av. B'frd —8M 57
Ellercroft Rd. B'frd —8M 57
Ellercroft Ter. B'frd —8M 57
Ellerker La. T'ner —2J 47
Ellerker Rd. T'ner —1H 47
Ellers Gro. Leeds —2H 63
Ellerslie Ct. Hud —2J 131
Ellers Rd. Leeds —2H 63
Ellerton St. B'frd —7G 59
Ellicott Ct. Men —4E 24
Ellin's Ter. Nor —3H 121
Ellinthorpe St. B'frd —9F 58
Elliot Ct. Q'bry —4C 74
Elliotts Clo. C'frd —7J 103
Elliott St. Shipl —7M 39
Elliott St. Sils —8D 6
Ellis Ct. Nor G —2L 93
Ellis Ct. Oss —8A 118
Ellis Fold. Leeds —7L 61
Ellis La. Gar —4L 65
Ellison Fold. Bail —3A 40
Ellison St. Hal —3N 91
Ellison St. Hud —6J 131
Ellis St. B'frd —2B 76
Ellis St. Horb —1C 136
Ellis Ter. Leeds —9N 43
Elliston Av. M'well —8L 153
Ellistones Gdns. G'lnd —4N 111
Ellistones La. G'lnd —5N 111
Ellistones Pl. G'lnd —5N 111
Ellmont Av. Eml —3F 150
Ellton Gro. B'frd —4M 75
Ellwood Clo. Mean —8B 44
Elm Av. H'frth —9A 148
Elm Av. Kip —2N 83
Elm Av. Sower B —7H 91
Elm Av. Stan —8A 100
Elm Av. Todm —5K 87
Elm Clo. D'ton —6B 124
Elm Clo. Oss —8A 118
Elm Clo. Pon —1L 123
Elm Ct. B'shaw —9M 77
Elm Ct. Kbtn —2K 149
Elm Cres. E Mor —8C 22
Elm Cft. Leeds —7D 46
Elmet Dri. Bar E —8M 47
Elmete Av. Leeds —8L 45
Elmete Av. Scholes —9G 46
Elmete Clo. Leeds —9M 45
Elmete Ct. Leeds —9L 45
Elmete Cft. Scholes —9G 47
Elmete Dri. Leeds —8M 45
Elmete Grange. Men —4E 24
Elmete Gro. Leeds —8L 45
Elmete Hill. Leeds —9M 45
Elmete La. Leeds —8M 45
Elmete Mt. Leeds —9M 45
Elmete Rd. C'frd —3K 103
Elmete Wlk. Leeds —9L 45
Elmete Way. Leeds —9M 45
Elmet Rd. Bar E —9M 47
Elmet Towers. Leeds —2D 64
Elmfield. Bail —3B 40
Elmfield. Oult —8E 82
Elmfield Av. Hud —5E 130
Elmfield Bus. Pk. Gar —6A 66
Elmfield Ct. Morl —1L 97
Elmfield Dri. B'frd —5A 76
Elmfield Dri. Skelm —8D 150
Elmfield Gro. Leeds —8N 61
Elmfield Pl. Leeds —8N 61
Elmfield Rd. Hud —1K 131
Elmfield Rd. Leeds —8N 61
Elmfield Rd. Morl —2L 97
Elmfield Ter. Hal —7A 92
Elmfield Ter. Hud —5B 132
Elmfield Way. Leeds —5G 61
Elm Gdns. C'frd —7K 103
Elm Gdns. Hal —7B 92
Elm Gro. Bur W —9D 10
Elm Gro. E Mor —8C 22
Elm Gro. Gom —4L 95
Elm Gro. Hal —7J 75
Elm Gro. Heck —7N 95
Elm Gro. Horb —1D 136
Elm Gro. Kei —3G 37
Elm Gro. Shipl —8C 40
Elm Gro. Sils —8D 6
Elm Gro. S Elm —6M 157
Elm Ho. Leeds —8N 63
Elmhurst Clo. Leeds —3J 45
Elmhurst Gdns. Leeds —3J 45
Elmhurst Gro. Knot —9E 104
Elm Pk. Pon —5J 123
Elm Pl. Knot —9D 104
Elm Pl. Sower B —7H 91
Elm Rd. Dew —3C 116
Elm Rd. Hems —2E 156
Elm Rd. Nor —4J 121
Elm Rd. Shipl —8B 40
Elm Rd. Skel —8M 159
Elmroyd. Rothw —9A 82
Elmsall Dri. S Elm —4B 158
Elmsall La. M'hse —9A 158
Elmsall La. S Elm —4A 158
Elmsall St. B'frd —6B 58
Elmsdale Clo. S Elm —7A 158
Elms Hill. Slai —1M 145
Elmsley St. Steet —3C 20
Elms, The. Ackw —5F 140
Elms, The. Guis —7J 25
Elms, The. Leeds —9F 44
Elm St. Holy G —7N 111
Elm St. Hud —6N 131
Elm St. Leeds —2D 62
Elm St. New C —3J 139
Elm St. Oxe —4C 54
Elm St. Skelm —7D 150
Elm Ter. Brigh —7N 93
Elm Ter. Otley —9N 11
Elm Ter. Pon —3J 123
Elmton Clo. Leeds —6F 80
Elm Tree Av. B'frd —5A 76
Elm Tree Clo. B'frd —5B 76
Elm Tree Clo. Kei —1K 37
Elm Tree Clo. Leeds —8F 64
Elm Tree Clo. Liv —1N 115
Elm Tree Clo. Pud —8B 60
Elm Tree Gdns. B'frd —4A 76
Elmtree La. Leeds —1F 80
Elm Tree St. Wake —7N 119
Elm Vw. Steet —2B 20
Elm Wlk., The. Leeds —9C 64
Elm Way. Birs —2D 96
Elmwood Av. Bar E —8L 47
Elmwood Av. Hud —3M 131
Elmwood Av. W'ton —3C 138
Elmwood Chase. Bar E —8L 47
Elmwood Clo. Hud —3M 131
Elmwood Clo. Mir —1K 133
Elmwood Clo. W'ton —3C 138
Elmwood Ct. Bar E —8L 47
Elmwood Dri. Brigh —9L 93
Elmwood Dri. Kei —3F 36
Elmwood Dri. W'ton —3C 138
Elmwood Gth. W'ton —3C 138
Elmwood Gro. Bat —9G 96
Elmwood Gro. Horb —1E 136
Elmwood La. Bar E —8L 47
Elmwood La. Leeds —5E 62
Elmwood Rd. Kei —4F 36
Elmwood Rd. Leeds —5E 62
Elm Wood St. Brigh —8N 93
Elmwood St. Hal —7N 91
Elmwood Ter. Dew —2F 116
Elmwood Ter. Kei —4F 36
Elphanborough Clo. H Bri —4M 89
Elphin Ct. H Bri —4L 89
Elsdon Gro. B'frd —9C 58
Elsham Ter. Leeds —4M 61
Elsicker La. Warm —5G 120
Elsie St. Cro R —7F 36
Elsie St. Kei —6H 21
Elsinore Av. Ell —5D 112
Elsinore Ct. Ell —5D 112
Elstone Vw. Wake —8J 99
Elsworth Av. B'frd —5H 59
Elsworth Ho. Kirks —3J 61
Elsworth St. B'frd —9E 58
Elsworth St. Leeds —7N 61
Eltham Av. Leeds —3D 62
Eltham Clo. Leeds —3D 62
Eltham Ct. Leeds —3D 62
Eltham Dri. Leeds —3D 62
Eltham Gdns. Leeds —3D 62
Eltham Gro. B'frd —5M 75
Eltham Ri. Leeds —3D 62
Elvaston Rd. Morl —1K 97
Elvey Clo. B'frd —2H 59
Elvey St. Wake —4L 119
Elwell Clo. Hal —6J 75
Elwell St. Thpe —3G 98
Elwyn Gro. B'frd —2C 76
Elwyn Rd. B'frd —2D 76
Ely St. G'lnd —5C 112
Ely St. Leeds —6M 61
Emblem Ter. Wake —8M 119
Embleton Rd. Meth —3K 101
Embsay Steam Railway. —3B 4
Emerald St. Bat —6E 96
Emerald St. Hud —2N 131
Emerald St. Kei —3G 36
Emerson Av. B'frd —3J 57
Emily Ct. B'frd —2N 75
(off Oakwell Clo.)
Emily St. Kei —8J 21
Emily St. S Kirk —6K 157
Emley. —2F 150
Emley Moor Bus. Pk. Eml —3E 150
Emmanuel Ter. Hud —8L 131
Emmanuel Trad. Est. Leeds —8B 62
(off Springwell Rd.)
Emmeline Clo. B'frd —7F 40
Emmet Clo. B'shaw —8M 77
Emmfield Dri. B'frd —2M 57
Emm La. B'frd —3M 57
Emmott Dri. Rawd —4A 42
Emmott Farm Fold. Haw —9C 36
Emmott Vw. Leeds —4A 42
Empire Arc. Leeds —6E 62
Empire Ter. Roys —5E 154
Empsall Row. Brigh —9N 93
(off Camm St.)
Emscote Av. Hal —7N 91
Emscote Gdns. Hal —7N 91
Emscote Gro. Hal —7N 91
Emscote Pl. Hal —7N 91
Emscote St. S. Hal —7N 91
Emsley Clo. B'frd —5F 76
Emville Av. Leeds —2L 45
Enderley Rd. T'tn —8C 56
Endor Cres. Bur W —1D 24
Endor Gro. Bur W —1D 24
Endsleigh Pl. Cytn —1G 75
Enfield. Yead —1M 41
Enfield Av. Leeds —4G 62
Enfield Clo. Bat —6C 96
Enfield Dri. Bat —6C 96
Enfield Dri. B'frd —4M 75
Enfield Pde. B'frd —4M 75
Enfield Rd. Bail —5A 40
Enfield Side Rd. Stanb —1L 53
Enfield St. Kei —9H 21
Enfield St. Leeds —4F 62
Enfield Ter. Leeds —4G 62
Enfield Wlk. B'frd —4M 75
Engine La. Horb —1B 136
Engine La. Shaf —8L 155
Engine La. Wrag —1N 139
England Lane. —9E 104
England La. Knot —9E 104
Englefield Cres. B'frd —3J 77
Ennerdale Av. Dew —1H 117
Ennerdale Clo. Weth —3K 17
Ennerdale Cres. Dew —1H 117
Ennerdale Dri. B'frd —3F 58
Ennerdale Dri. Knot —1D 124
Ennerdale Rd. B'frd —3E 58
Ennerdale Rd. Dew —1H 117
Ennerdale Rd. Leeds —3G 78
Ennerdale Rd. Wake —5H 119
Ennerdale Way. Leeds —2G 78
Enoch La. Hud —7L 131
Enterprise 5 La. Ends. B'frd —9F 40
Enterprise Pk. Ind. Est. Leeds —4B 80
Enterprise Way. B'frd —9F 40
Enterprise Way. C'frd —5C 102
Enterprise Way. Leeds —4H 81
Envoy St. Leeds —1E 80
Epsom Rd. Kip —3N 83
Epsom Way. Khtn —1G 133
Epworth Pl. Leeds —1G 80
Epworth Pl. Oakw —4B 36
Equity Chambers. B'frd —7C 58
(off Piccadilly)
Eric St. Kei —8J 21
Eric St. Leeds —1F 60
Eric St. S Elm —6N 157
Erivan Pk. Weth —3A 18
Ernest St. Dew —2G 117
Ernest St. Todm —3E 86
Erringden Rd. H Bri —3L 89
Erringden St. Todm —7L 87
Escroft Clo. Wyke —3B 94
Eshald La. W'ford —8E 82
Eshald Mans. Rothw —7E 82
Eshald Pl. W'ford —7E 82
Eshalt Pl. Dew —2F 116
(off Bradford Rd.)
Esholt. —2G 40
Esholt Av. Guis —9H 25
Esholt La. Bail —3D 40
Eshton Av. Oaken —8D 76
Eshton Ct. M'well —7J 153
Esk Av. C'frd —4H 103
Eskdale Av. Hal —8G 75
Eskdale Av. Nor —8H 101
Eskdale Clo. Dew —9H 97
Eskdale Clo. Guis —8J 25
Eskdale Clo. Nor —8H 101
Eskdale Ct. Nor —8H 101
Eskdale Cft. Guis —8J 25
Eskdale Cft. Nor —8H 101
Eskdale Gro. Gar —8A 66
Eskdale Ho. Sower B —9H 91
(off Quarry Hill)
Eskdale Mt. H Bri —9H 71
Eskdale Ri. All —6G 57
Eskdale Rd. Wake —4G 118
Esk Gdns. Weth —1M 17
Eskine Pde. B'frd —7L 75
Esmond St. B'frd —2L 75
Esmond St. Leeds —7M 61
Esmond Ter. Leeds —7M 61
Essex St. B'frd —8E 58
Essex St. Hal —6M 91
Essex St. H Bri —2H 89
Estcourt Av. Leeds —1M 61
Estcourt Dri. D'ton —7C 124
Estcourt Gro. B'frd —9M 57
Estcourt Rd. B'frd —9M 57
Estcourt Rd. D'ton —6B 124
Estcourt Ter. Leeds —1M 61
Esther Av. Wake —7H 119
Esther Gro. Wake —7H 119
Esthwaite Gdns. Leeds —8N 63
Ethel St. Kei —7H 21
Ethel St. W'wth —9A 106
Etna St. B'frd —2L 75
Eton Av. Hud —4D 132
Eton St. Hal —5M 91
Eton St. H Bri —1G 88
Euden Edge Rd. Slai —7N 129
Eunice La. Up Cum —2N 165
(in two parts)
Eureka. (Museum for Children, The) —6C 92
Eurocam Technology Pk. B'frd —3C 76
Euroway Trad. Est. Euro I —7E 76
Euston Gro. Leeds —1B 80
Euston Mt. Leeds —1B 80
Euston Ter. Leeds —1B 80
Evanston Av. Leeds —5M 61
Evans Towers. B'frd —9C 58
(off Reynor Ho. M.)
Evelyn Av. B'frd —6J 59
Evelyn Pl. Leeds —8M 61
Evens Ter. B'frd —3C 76
Everall Ga. Gar —7B 66
Everall Pas. Kip —4B 84
Everard St. Hud —6J 131
Everdale Mt. Hems —3C 156
Everdale Mt. S Elm —6L 157
Everest Av. Shipl —8C 40
Everleigh St. Leeds —6J 63
Eversley Dri. B'frd —1J 77
Eversley Mt. Hal —6L 91
(off Bk. Eversley Mt.)
Eversley Pl. Hal —6L 91
Eversley Rd. H Bri —9H 71
Eversley Vw. S'cft —9D 30
Everson All. Leeds —6B 64
Every St. Todm —7L 87
Evesham Gro. B'frd —8F 40
Ewart Pl. B'frd —2M 75
Ewart St. B'frd —2M 75
Ewart St. Q'bry —4D 74
Ewood. —3N 89
Ewood Dri. H Bri —3N 89
Ewood Hall Av. H Bri —3N 89
Ewood La. Todm —6H 87
Excell Gdns. Leeds —2G 78
Excell Ter. B'frd —3K 77
Excelsior Clo. Ripp —8C 110
Exchange. Hon —5L 147
Exchange St. Cleck —3H 95
Exchange St. G'lnd —5C 112
Exchange St. Nor —1H 121
Exchange St. S Elm —6M 157
Exe St. B'frd —2A 76
Exeter Dri. Leeds —6F 80
Exeter St. Hal —9C 92
Exeter St. Sower B —8J 91
Exhibition Rd. Shipl —7L 39
Exley. —2C 112
Exley Av. Kei —3G 36
Exley Bank. Hal —1C 112
Exley Bank Top. Hal —2C 112
Exley Cres. Kei —2G 36
Exley Dri. Kei —2G 36
Exley Gdns. Hal —2C 112
Exley Gro. Kei —2G 36
Exley Head. —2F 36
Exley Head Vw. Kei —8E 20
Exley La. Hal & Ell —2C 112
Exley Mt. B'frd —8L 57
Exley Mt. Kei —2G 36
Exley Rd. Kei —2G 36
Exley St. Kei —1G 37
Exley Way. Kei —3G 37
Exmoor St. Hal —6M 91
Exmouth Pl. B'frd —5D 58
Express Way. C'frd —6K 101
Exton Pl. Leeds —7N 63
Eyres Av. Leeds —6M 61
Eyres Gro. Leeds —6M 61
(off Eyres Ter.)
Eyres Mill Side. Leeds —6L 61
Eyres St. Leeds —6M 61
(off Eyres Ter.)
Eyres Ter. Leeds —6M 61
Eyre St. Bat —8G 96
Eyre St. Dew —7E 116
Eyrie App. Morl —1M 97

Facit. —9A 106
Factory La. B'frd —3F 76
Factory La. Eml —1B 150
Factory La. Hud —6H 131
Factory St. B'frd —3F 76
Fagley. —4H 59
Fagley Cres. B'frd —4G 59
Fagley Cft. B'frd —4H 59
Fagley Dri. B'frd —4G 59
Fagley La. B'frd —2H 59
Fagley Pl. B'frd —5G 59
Fagley Rd. B'frd —5G 58
Fagley Ter. B'frd —5G 59
Fair Bank. Shipl —9A 40
Fairbank Rd. B'frd —5M 57
Fairbank Ter. B'frd —5M 57
Fairbrook Rd. Wake —6J 137
Fairburn. —9N 85
Fairburn Dri. Gar —7A 66
Fairburn Gdns. B'frd —2G 58
Fairburn Ho. H'fth —8E 42
(off Regent Cres.)
Fairburn Ings Centre. —9J 8
Fairburn St. C'frd —4C 102
Fairclough Gro. Hal —1M 91
Fairfax Av. B'frd —4G 76
Fairfax Av. Dlgtn —7D 78
Fairfax Av. F'stne —2C 122
Fairfax Av. Knot —9C 104
Fairfax Av. Men —3E 24
Fairfax Clo. Leeds —3C 64
Fairfax Cres. B'frd —4G 76
Fairfax Cres. Hal —7F 92
Fairfax Gdns. Men —3D 24
Fairfax Gro. Yead —9K 25
Fairfax Ho. B'frd —7D 58
(off Barkerend Rd.)
Fairfax Rd. Bgly —2E 38
Fairfax Rd. Cull —8K 37
Fairfax Rd. Leeds —2C 80
Fairfax Rd. Men —3D 24
Fairfax Rd. Pon —3L 123
Fairfax St. B'frd —9D 58
Fairfax St. Haw —8D 36
Fairfax St. Otley —1M 25
Fairfax St. Sils —8D 6
Fairfax Vw. E Bier —6K 77
Fairfax Vw. H'fth —3E 42
Fairfield. —2H 89
Fairfield. Denh —6K 55
Fairfield. Fair —8N 85
Fairfield. H'fth —6F 42
Fairfield Av. Dew —3J 117
Fairfield Av. Heck —7B 96
Fairfield Av. Leeds —4D 60
Fairfield Av. Nor —9F 100
Fairfield Av. Oss —7B 118
Fairfield Av. Pon —3H 123
Fairfield Av. Pud —6B 60
Fairfield Av. Ting —5N 97
Fairfield Clo. C'frd —3L 103
Fairfield Clo. Leeds —4E 60
Fairfield Clo. Oss —7B 118
Fairfield Clo. Rothw —9K 81
Fairfield Ct. Bail —3C 40
Fairfield Ct. C'frd —5G 102
Fairfield Ct. Gar —7L 65
Fairfield Ct. Liv —8K 95
Fairfield Cres. Dew —2D 116
Fairfield Cres. Leeds —4D 60
Fairfield Dri. Bail —3C 40
Fairfield Dri. Heck —7B 96
Fairfield Dri. Oss —7B 118
(in two parts)
Fairfield Dri. Rothw —9K 81
Fairfield Gdns. Oss —6B 118
Fairfield Gdns. Rothw —9K 81
Fairfield Gro. Leeds —4E 60
Fairfield Gro. Rothw —9K 81
Fairfield Hill. Leeds —4E 60
Fairfield La. Rothw —9K 81
Fairfield M. Dew —2D 116
Fairfield Mt. Leeds —4E 60
Fairfield Mt. Oss —7B 118
Fairfield Pde. Heck —7B 96
Fairfield Ri. Kbtn —4L 149
Fairfield Rd. B'frd —5N 57
Fairfield Rd. Heck —7B 96
Fairfield Rd. Leeds —4D 60
Fairfield Rd. Oss —7B 118
Fairfield Rd. Wyke —1B 94
Fairfields. C'frd —5L 103
Fairfields. Up Den —5C 166
Fairfield Sq. Leeds —4E 60
Fairfields Rd. H'frth —5J 163
Fairfield St. B'frd —4H 77
Fairfield St. Leeds —4D 60
Fairfield Ter. Cleck —5J 95
Fairfield Ter. Dew —3J 117
Fairfield Ter. Leeds —4E 60
Fairfield Ter. Oss —7A 118
Fairfield Wlk. Oss —7B 118
Fairford Av. Leeds —2E 80
Fairford Ter. Leeds —2E 80
Fairhaven Grn. B'frd —8G 40

r Hill Flats. Hud —1L 147
r Isle Ct. Kei —9J 21
off Alice St.)
r Lea Av. Hud —9K 131
r Lea Rd. Hud —9K 131
rleigh Cres. Ting —4B 98
rleigh Rd. Ting —4B 98
rless Av. Hal —5M 93
rmoor Way. Heck —7B 96
rmount. B'frd —4A 58
r Mt. Todm —2J 107
rmount Pk. Shipl —8K 39
rmount Ter. Dew —5H 117
rmount Ter. Kei —1M 37
r Rd. B'frd —4N 75
r St. Hud —7L 131
r Vw. Leeds —4N 79
r Vw. Liv —7K 95
r Vw. Pon —6L 123
rview Av. Bat —6C 96
rview Clo. Hal —3A 92
rview Ct. Bail —6N 39
rview Cres. Bat —6D 96
rview Rd. Bat —6D 96
rview Ter. Hal —3N 91
rway. B'frd —4L 75
BD7)
rway. B'frd —6L 41
BD10)
rway. Guis —7F 24
rway. Nor —2K 121
rway. Shipl —8L 39
rway App. Nor —1K 121
way Av. B'frd —4L 75
way Av. M'well —7L 153
way Av. Nor —1K 121
way Clo. B'frd —4L 75
way Clo. Guis —8G 24
way Clo. Nor —1K 121
way Cres. Haw —9D 36
way Dri. B'frd —3L 75
way Dri. Nor —2K 121
way Gdns. Nor —1K 121
way Gro. B'frd —3L 75
way Ind. Pk. Bat —2C 96
way Meadows. Nor —1K 121
Ways. Mir —9K 115
ways Ct. D'ton —7D 124
ways, The. B'frd —1K 57
ways, The. Low U —5G 21
way, The. F'stne —2D 122
way, The. Hal —6M 73
way, The. Hud —7M 113
way, The. Leeds —1D 44
way, The. S'ley —5M 59
way Wlk. B'frd —3L 75
weather Green. —6J 57
weather M. B'frd —7K 57
wood Gro. B'frd —3J 59
y Dell. Bgly —8F 38
y Hill. —7K 103
y Hill La. Pon —7K 103
n two parts)
h St. S Kirk —5K 157
con Cliffe. Steet —3D 20
con Clo. Otley —1L 25
con Dri. C'frd —6C 102
coner Clo. Dart —8F 152
coners Ride. Neth —3K 147
con Knowle Ing. Dart —8E 152
con M. B'frd —6H 57
con M. Morl —1M 97
con Rd. Bgly —2E 38
con Rd. Dew —5G 116
on Sq. Hal —9C 92
con St. B'frd —9N 57
con St. Hal —9C 92
con St. Hud —9L 131
house Green. —3A 134
ouse La. W'ley —3A 134
land Ct. Bgly —4F 38
land Ct. Leeds —6E 44
land Cres. Leeds —6E 44
land Gdns. Leeds —6F 44
land Gro. Leeds —6E 44
land Mt. Leeds —6E 44
land Ri. Leeds —6E 44
land Rd. B'frd —2J 59
land Rd. Leeds —6E 44
Brow Clo. Cytn —2F 74
edge La. Up Den —7B 166
Ings. —6M 119
Ings Rd. Wake —7N 119
La. Dew —5E 116
La. E Ard —4F 98
La. Hal —8C 74
La. Harts —1H 115
La. Mars —6F 144
La. Norl —9K 91
ow Cft. Hud —6D 114
owfield Clo. B'frd —5G 77
owfield Dri. B'frd —4G 77
owfield Gdns. B'frd —4G 76
Fallow La. Oakw —1A 36
Fall Rd. Mir —3J 115
Fall Spring Gdns. Holy G —8M 111
Fall Spring Grn. Slnd —8M 111
Fallswood Gro. Leeds —2G 60
Fall, The. —5F 98
Fallwood St. Haw —9D 36
Falmouth Av. B'frd —5D 58
Falmouth Av. Nor —9J 101
Falmouth Cres. Nor —9J 101
Falmouth Rd. Nor —9J 101
Falsgrave Av. B'frd —4H 59
Faltis Sq. B'frd —9G 41
Fancett Mt. Bgly —3F 38
Fancett Vw. Wilsd —1B 56
Fanny La. Tad —9N 33
Fanny Moor Cres. Hud —8A 132
Fanny Moor La. Hud —8A 132
Fanny St. Kei —1H 37
Fanny St. Shipl —6L 39
Faraday Sq. Hud —6F 130
(off Hoffman St.)
Farah Ct. Leeds —3F 60
Far Bank. Shel —7L 149
Farcliffe Pl. B'frd —5N 57
Farcliffe Rd. B'frd —5N 57
Farcliffe Ter. B'frd —5N 57
Far Comn. Rd. Mir —3J 115
Far Cft. Lep —8L 133
Far Cft. Ter. Leeds —8N 61
Far Crook. Thack —6D 40
Far Dene. Kbtn —1H 149
Fardene St. Sils —7D 6
Fardew Ct. Bgly —3E 38
Fare Hill Flats. Ber B —9L 131
Far End La. Hon —5M 147
Farfield Av. Bat —6C 96
Farfield Av. B'frd —6K 75
Farfield Av. Fars —3N 59
Far Fld. Av. H'frth —7C 164
Farfield Ct. S Elm —5N 157
Farfield Cres. B'frd —6L 75
Farfield Dri. Fars —4N 59
Far Fld. Dri. H'frth —7C 164
Farfield Gro. B'frd —6L 75
Farfield Gro. Fars —3N 59
Farfield La. S Hien —2L 155
Farfield Ri. Fars —3N 59
Farfield Rd. Bail —5B 40
Farfield Rd. B'frd —6M 75
Farfield Rd. Hud —7D 132
Farfield Rd. Shipl —8L 39
Far Fields La. Hud —4E 146
Farfield St. B'frd —4M 57
Farfield St. Cleck —3H 95
Farfield Ter. B'frd —4M 57
Far Headingley. —8A 44
Far La. Hal —2A 90
Far La. H'frth —8B 164
Farlea Dri. B'frd —3G 59
Farleton Dri. B'frd —4H 59
Farm Ct. Leeds —4C 64
Farm Cft. S'hse —6M 121
Farm Mead Cft. Bur W —7C 10
Farmfield Dri. Fitz —7A 140
Farm Gdns. S'hse —6M 121
Farm Hill Ct. B'frd —1F 58
Farm Hill Cres. Leeds —1C 62
Farm Hill M. Morl —7H 79
Farm Hill N. Leeds —9C 44
Farm Hill Ri. Leeds —1C 62
Farm Hill Rd. B'frd —9F 40
Farm Hill Rd. Morl —7J 79
Farm Hill S. Leeds —1C 62
Farm Hill Way. Leeds —1C 62
Farm La. Fitz —8A 140
Farm Mt. Leeds —4D 64
Far Moss. Leeds —2C 44
Farm Pond Dri. Hov E —7K 93
Farm Rd. F'stne —6D 122
Farm Rd. Leeds —4C 64
Farmstead Rd. B'frd —9G 41
Farnboro St. Todm —1J 107
Farndale App. Leeds —1D 64
Farndale Clo. Leeds —1D 64
Farndale Clo. Weth —3J 17
Farndale Ct. Gar —9N 65
Farndale Ct. Leeds —1D 64
Farndale Gdns. Leeds —9D 46
Farndale Gth. Leeds —9D 46
Farndale Pl. Leeds —9D 46
Farndale Rd. Bail —5M 39
Farndale Rd. Wilsd —2B 56
Farndale Sq. Leeds —1D 64
Farndale Ter. Leeds —1D 64
Farndale Vw. Leeds —9D 46
(off Farndale Gdns.)
Farne Av. Wake —5H 119
Farnham Clo. Bail —3B 40
Farnham Clo. Leeds —6C 46
Farnham Cft. Leeds —6C 46
Farnham Rd. B'frd —9N 57
Farnham Way. Croft —1G 139
Farnlee. Lind —1G 130
Farnley. —5A 12
Farnley Clo. Men —4F 24
Farnley Cres. Leeds —8H 61
Farnley Cres. Oakw —4B 36
Farnley La. Otley —8L 11
Farnley Pk. F'ley —6A 12
Farnley Rd. Far T —3D 148
Farnley Rd. Men —4E 24
Farnley Tyas. —3D 148
Farnley Vw. Dlgtn —8D 78
Far Peat La. Oxe —7B 54
Farrar Av. Mir —5K 115
Farrar Cft. Leeds —3K 43
Farrar Dri. Mir —5J 115
Farrar Gro. Leeds —3K 43
Farrar Height La. Sower B —7B 110
Farrar La. Leeds —3J 43
(in two parts)
Farrar Mill La. Hal —8C 92
Farra St. Oxe —4C 54
Far Reef Clo. H'fth —5F 42
Farrer La. Oult —8D 82
Far Richard Clo. Oss —4N 117
Farriers Cft. B'frd —2D 58
Farriers Pl. C'frd —6H 103
Farringdon Clo. B'frd —1H 77
Farringdon Dri. B'frd —2J 77
Farringdon Gro. B'frd —6M 75
Farringdon Sq. B'frd —1J 77
Farrow Bank. Leeds —7H 61
Farrow Grn. Leeds —7J 61
Farrow Hill. Leeds —7J 61
Farrow Rd. Leeds —7H 61
Farrow Va. Leeds —7H 61
Farr Royd. Bur W —7C 10
Farside Grn. B'frd —2A 76
Farsley. —3A 60
Farsley Beck Bottom. —3B 60
Fartown. —9M 113
Fartown. Pud —8A 60
Fartown Clo. Pud —9B 60
Fartown Grn. Rd. Hud —1N 131
Far Vw. Hal —7L 73
Far Vw. Bank. Hud —5C 132
Far Vw. Cres. Hud —5C 132
Farway. B'frd —1J 77
Far Well. Rawd —4A 42
Far Well Fold. Rawd —4A 42
Far Well La. N Mill —9F 148
Far Well Rd. Rawd —4A 42
Fascination Pl. Q'bry —3B 74
(off Mill La.)
Faugh La. Hept —7D 70
Faulkland Ho. B'frd —5A 58
(off Green La.)
Favell Av. Nor —2J 121
Faversham Wlk. B'frd —1J 77
Fawcett Av. Leeds —9L 61
Fawcett Bank. Leeds —9K 61
Fawcett Clo. Leeds —9K 61
Fawcett Dri. Leeds —9K 61
Fawcett Gdns. Leeds —9K 61
Fawcett La. Leeds —9K 61
Fawcett Pl. B'frd —5G 76
Fawcett Pl. Leeds —9K 61
Fawcett Rd. Leeds —9K 61
Fawcett St. Wake —7L 119
Fawcett Va. Leeds —9K 61
(off Fawcett Bank)
Fawcett Vw. Leeds —9K 61
(off Fawcett Dri.)
Fawcett Way. Leeds —9K 61
Fawkes Dri. Otley —2H 25
Faxfleet St. B'frd —4B 76
Faye Gdns. B'frd —4H 77
Fearnley Av. Oss —4M 117
Fearnley Clo. Leeds —7N 61
Fearnley Ct. H'frth —3B 164
Fearnley Dri. Oss —4M 117
Fearnley La. H'frth —3A 164
Fearnley Pl. Leeds —7N 61
Fearnley St. Dew —4E 116
Fearnley St. F'stne —6C 122
Fearnside's Clo. Wake —1C 136
Fearnsides St. B'frd —6N 57
Fearnsides Ter. B'frd —6N 57
Fearn's Island. —8G 62
Fearnville. —2M 63
Fearnville Av. Leeds —2M 63
Fearnville Clo. Leeds —1M 63
Fearnville Dri. B'frd —9H 59
Fearnville Dri. Leeds —2M 63
Fearnville Gro. Leeds —1M 63
Fearnville Gro. Roys —6D 154
Fearnville Mt. Leeds —1M 63
Fearnville Pl. Leeds —1N 63
Fearnville Rd. Leeds —2M 63
Fearnville Ter. Leeds —1N 63
Fearnville Vw. Leeds —2M 63
Feast Fld. H'fth —6E 42
Featherbank Av. H'fth —8E 42
Featherbank Gro. H'fth —7E 42
Featherbank La. H'fth —7E 42
Featherbank Mt. H'fth —7E 42
Featherbank Ter. H'fth —8E 42
Featherbank Wlk. H'fth —8E 42
Featherbed Clo. G'lnd —5C 112
Featherbed La. G'lnd —5C 112
Featherbed La. Wigh P —3K 19
Feather Rd. B'frd —7F 58
Featherstone. —5C 122
Featherstone La. F'stne —3C 122
Featherstone Rovers R.L.F.C. —6D 122
Feather St. Kei —1K 37
Federation St. B'frd —3D 76
Felbrigg Av. Kei —1F 36
Felcote Av. Hud —5C 132
Felcourt Dri. B'frd —3J 77
Felkirk. —3J 155
Felkirk Dri. Ryh —9H 139
Felkirk Vw. Shaf —6J 155
Felks Stile Rd. Hud —8E 130
Fell Cres. Kei —2F 36
Fell Greave Cres. Hud —7A 114
Fell Greave Rd. Hud —6N 113
Fell Gro. Hud —7A 114
Fell Gro. Kei —1F 36
Fell La. Kei —2E 36
Fellowsides La. Oss —6A 118
Fellows, The. Neth —2H 147
Fellside. Todm —7C 88
Fellside Clo. W Bowl —3D 76
Fellwood Av. Haw —7E 36
Fellwood Clo. Haw —7E 36
Felnex Clo. Leeds —9L 63
Felnex Cres. Leeds —9L 63
Felnex Rd. Leeds —9K 63
Felnex Sq. Leeds —9K 63
Felnex Way. Leeds —9L 63
Fenay Bankside. Fen B —7H 133
Fenay Bridge. —7J 133
Fenay Bri. Rd. Fen B —5G 132
Fenay Cres. Alm —7E 132
Fenay Dri. Fen B —7G 133
Fenay La. Alm —8D 132
Fenay Lea Dri. W'loo —6F 132
Fenby Av. B'frd —1F 76
(in two parts)
Fenby Clo. B'frd —2G 76
Fenby Gdns. B'frd —2G 76
Fenby Gro. B'frd —2G 76
Fencote Cres. B'frd —3H 59
Fencote Ho. B'frd —9G 41
(off Rowantree Dri.)
Fender Rd. B'frd —4L 75
Fenned Rd. Bail —3C 40
Fenton Av. W'ford —6C 82
Fenton Clo. S Kirk —8H 157
Fenton Clo. W'ford —6C 82
Fenton Fold. Oaken —9D 76
Fenton Rd. Hal —7M 91
Fenton Rd. Hud —7L 131
Fenton Rd. Stan —5A 100
Fentonsgate. Loft —3L 99
Fenton Sq. Hud —5L 131
Fenton St. Bur W —8D 10
Fenton St. Leeds —5D 62
Fenton St. Mir —7L 115
Fenton St. Ting —3B 98
Fenwick Dri. B'frd —6L 75
Fenwick Ho. B'frd —4D 76
(off Parkway)
Ferguson St. Hal —6B 92
Fern Av. Mel —6B 146
Fern Bank. Otley —9M 11
Fernbank Av. Bgly —4G 38
Fernbank Av. Leeds —3C 60
Fernbank Av. Oakw —3F 36
Fernbank Clo. Leeds —3C 60
Fernbank Dri. Bail —6M 39
Fernbank Dri. Bgly —4F 38
Fernbank Dri. Leeds —3C 60
Fernbank Gdns. Leeds —3C 60
Fernbank Pl. Leeds —3C 60
Fernbank Rd. B'frd —5F 58
Fernbank Rd. Leeds —3C 60
Fernbank St. Bgly —4F 38
Fernbank Ter. Bgly —4F 38
Fern Bank Ter. Yead —9L 25
(off Park Av.)
Fernbank Wlk. Leeds —3C 60
Fern Chase. Leeds —9B 30
Ferncliffe. —4G 38
Ferncliffe Ct. Shipl —7L 39
Ferncliffe Dri. Bail —4N 39
Ferncliffe Dri. Kei —6F 20
Ferncliffe Rd. Bgly —4E 38
Ferncliffe Rd. Leeds —4F 60
Ferncliffe Rd. Shipl —7L 39
Ferncliffe Ter. Leeds —4E 60
Fern Clo. Bat —7J 97
Fern Ct. Kei —6G 20
Fern Cft. Leeds —9B 30
Fern Cft. Liv —8G 94
Fern Cft. Wren —9G 99
Ferndale. Cytn —2F 74
Ferndale. F'stne —7D 122
Ferndale Av. Cytn —2F 74
Ferndale Ct. I'ly —6F 8
Ferndale Gro. B'frd —2A 58
Ferndale Pl. Hems —3D 156
Ferndene. Bgly —4G 38
Ferndene Av. Birs —1C 96
Ferndown Grn. B'frd —2B 76
Ferney Lee Rd. Todm —6J 87
Fernfield Ter. Hal —2B 92
Fern Gdns. I'ly —6F 8
Fernhill. Bgly —2F 38
Fern Hill Av. Shipl —8L 39
Fern Hill Gro. Shipl —8L 39
Fern Hill Mt. Shipl —8L 39
Fern Hill Rd. Shipl —8L 39
Fernhurst Clo. Mir —5L 115
Fernhurst Cres. Mir —5M 115
Fernhurst Lea. Mir —5M 115
Fernhurst Rd. Mir —5L 115
Fernhurst Way. Mir —5L 115
Ferniehurst. Bail —6A 40
Fern Lea. Q'bry —4E 74
(off Scarlet Heights)
Fernlea. Rothw —7A 82
Fernlea Clo. Croft —1H 139
Fernlea Clo. Heck —9B 96
Fern Lea Flats. Lind —1F 130
Fernlea Gro. Gol —7C 130
Fern Lea Rd. Hud —1F 130
Fern Lea St. Sower B —7H 91
Fern Lea Vw. S'ley —4B 60
Fernleigh Ct. Wake —6H 119
Fernley Gdns. Wyke —9A 76
Fernley Green. —8G 105
Fernley Grn. Clo. Knot —8G 104
Fernley Grn. Ct. Knot —8G 104
(off Fernley Grn. Rd.)
Fernley Grn. Ind. Est. Knot —8G 104
Fernley Grn. Rd. Knot —8G 104
Fernley Hill Dri. Nor —7G 100
Fern Pl. Shipl —7L 39
(off George St.)
Fernside. Shar C —8K 121
Fernside Av. Hud —6C 132
Fernside Clo. Hud —5E 132
Fernside Ct. Hud —5E 132
Fernside Cres. Hud —5D 132
Fern St. B'frd —2H 77
Fern St. Hal —2A 92
(in two parts)
Fern St. Hud —2M 131
Fern St. Kei —8J 21
Fern Ter. Far —4B 60
Fern Way. Leeds —9B 30
Fernwood. Leeds —6J 45
Fernwood Ct. Leeds —6J 45
Ferrand Av. B'frd —5G 76
Ferrand La. Bgly —4E 38
Ferrand La. Gom —3L 95
Ferrand Rd. Shipl —7L 39
Ferrands Clo. H'den —6A 38
Ferrands Pk. Way. H'den —6A 38
Ferrand St. Bgly —4F 38
Ferriby Clo. B'frd —3H 59
Ferriby Towers. Leeds —5G 63
(off Granville Rd.)
Ferrybridge. —7B 104
Ferrybridge By-Pass. Knot —9B 104
Ferrybridge Hill. —8C 104
Ferrybridge Rd. C'frd —4E 102
Ferrybridge Rd. Knot —7C 104
Ferrybridge Rd. Pon —1L 123
Ferry La. Stan —9A 100
Ferry Top La. Ryh —9H 139
Festival Av. Shipl —1B 58
Feversham St. B'frd —8E 58
Fewston Av. Leeds —8H 63
Fewston Av. Wake —3A 120
Fewston Ct. Leeds —8H 63
Fiddle La. Ripp —7F 110
Fiddler Hill. Dew —7E 116
Fidler Clo. Gar —7M 65
Fidler La. Gar —7M 65
Field Clo. Heck —6A 96
Field Cres. S Elm —7M 157
Fieldcroft Ct. Mir —6K 115
Fieldedge La. Riddl —6N 21
Field End. Leeds —7B 64
Fld. End Clo. Leeds —7B 64
Fld. End Ct. Leeds —7B 64
Fld. End Cres. Leeds —7B 64
Fld. End Gdns. Leeds —7B 64
Fld. End Gth. Leeds —7B 64
Fld. End Gro. Leeds —7B 64
(nr. Fld. End Gdns.)
Fld. End Gro. Leeds —6C 64
(nr. Selby Rd.)
Fld. End La. Holmb —6G 162
Fld. End La. Hon —5M 147

Fld. End Mt. Leeds —7B 64
Fld. End Rd. Leeds —7B 64
Fieldens Pl. Bat —6D 96
Fielden Sq. Todm —8K 87
Fielden St. Todm —6N 87
Fieldgate Rd. B'frd —8H 41
Field Head. Gol —5C 130
Fieldhead Clo. Pon —2M 123
Fieldhead Ct. B Spa —1C 32
Fieldhead Cres. Birs —1B 96
Fieldhead Dri. Bar E —8N 47
Fieldhead Dri. Guis —8G 25
Fieldhead Gdns. Dew —9L 97
Fieldhead Gro. Guis —8G 25
Fld. Head La. Birs —2B 96
Fld. Head La. Cra V —8J 89
Fld. Head La. Dlgtn —9B 78
Fieldhead La. Holme —7E 162
Fld. Head La. Oxe —1A 54
Fieldhead Paddock. B Spa —9C 18
Fieldhead Rd. Guis —8G 25
Fieldhead St. Field B —8N 57
Fld. Head Way. Hal —6K 73
Fieldhead Way. Heck —7N 95
Fieldhouse Clo. Leeds —5E 44
Fld. House Clo. Weth —4K 17
Fieldhouse Cotts. Hal —7N 91
(off Carlton Ho. Ter.)
Fieldhouse Dri. Leeds —5E 44
Fieldhouse Dri. Slai —8N 129
Fieldhouse Gro. Fars —4N 59
Fieldhouse Lawn. Leeds —5E 44
Fieldhouse Rd. Hud —2A 132
Fieldhouse St. B'frd —7H 59
Fieldhouse St. Wake —8A 120
Fieldhouse Wlk. Leeds —5E 44
(in two parts)
Field Hurst. Schol —5D 94
Fieldhurst Ct. Bier —5G 76
Fielding Ga. Leeds —6N 61
Fielding Ga. M. Leeds —6N 61
Fielding St. H Bri —1H 89
Field Lane. —3L 113
Field La. Aber —8E 48
Field La. Bat —8F 96
Field La. Brigh —3L 113
Field La. Dew —5A 116
Field La. Far T —3D 148
Field La. Oss —5N 117
Field La. S Elm —5A 158
Field La. Upt —1N 157
Field La. Wake —8L 119
Field Pl. Wake —6J 119
Field Rd. H'frth —4N 163
Fieldsend Ct. Upt —2N 157
Fieldshead Bungalows. Lint —2C 146
Field Side. Pel —4M 91
Fieldside Rd. Kin —8B 140
Fields Ri. Hud —1F 132
Fields Rd. Lep —7H 133
Fields Rd. Low M —8C 76
Fields, The. Loft —3M 99
Field St. B'frd —7D 58
Field St. Dew —5B 116
Fields Way. Hud —1F 132
Field Ter. Leeds —6B 64
(nr. Cross St.)
Field Ter. Leeds —5C 64
(nr. Hermon Rd.)
Fld. Top Rd. Brigh —3L 113
Field Tops. Hud —1G 130
Field Vw. C'frd —6A 102
Field Vw. Hal —8L 73
Fld. View Cotts. F'stne —7D 122
(off Katrina Gro.)
Fieldway. Cytn —9G 57
Fieldway. I'ly —4K 9
Field Way. Shepl —9J 149
Fieldway Av. Leeds —2D 60
Fieldway Chase. Oult —8E 82
Fieldway Clo. Leeds —2D 60
Fieldway Ri. Leeds —2D 60
Fife St. Haw —8D 36
Fifth Av. B'frd —5G 59
Fifth Av. Rothw —6B 82
Fifth Av. E. Liv —7F 94
Fifth Av. W. Liv —8F 94
Fifth St. Low M —7C 76
Filbert St. Hud —1M 131
Filey Av. Roys —5E 154
Filey St. B'frd —8D 58
Filley Royd. Cleck —6H 95
Fillingfir Dri. Leeds —7J 43
Fillingfir Rd. Leeds —7J 43
Fillingfir Wlk. Leeds —7J 43
Finch Av. Wake —5M 137
Finching Gro. Mir —3L 115
Finchley St. B'frd —2B 76
Finchley Way. Morl —1K 97
Finch St. B'frd —1B 76
Findon Ter. B'frd —2J 59
Fine Gth. Clo. B'ham —5D 32
Finghall Rd. Skel —7L 159
Fink Hill. H'fth —7D 42
Finkil St. Brigh —7K 93
Finkin Av. Stan —1N 119
Finkin Cft. Stan —1N 119
Finkin La. Stan —1N 119
Finkle Clo. Wool —2H 153
Finkle La. Gild —7F 78
Finkle St. Pon —2K 123
Finkle St. Sower B —8D 90
Finkle St. Wool —2H 153
Finsbury Dri. B'frd —1D 58
Finsbury Rd. Leeds —5D 62
Finthorpe La. Hud —7E 132
Fir Av. Dew —6A 116
Fir Bank. Dew —2D 116
Firbank Grn. B'frd —3H 59
Firbank Gro. Leeds —8N 63
Firbeck. H'den —7A 38
Firbeck Rd. B'ham —5D 32
Firethorn Clo. B'frd —6M 57
Fir Gro. Dew —6A 116
Firham Clo. Roys —5B 154
Fir Pde. Dew —6A 116
Fir Rd. Hud —4H 131
Firs La. Hoy S —9G 167
First Av. Bard —3F 30
First Av. B'frd —5G 59
First Av. Fitz —6A 140
First Av. Gol —6C 130
First Av. Hal —8A 92
First Av. Horb —1B 136
First Av. Hud —3D 132
First Av. Kei —1H 37
First Av. Leeds —7N 61
First Av. Liv —7G 94
First Av. Pon —8F 156
First Av. Rawd —2N 41
First Av. Rothw —6A 82
First Av. Roys —5E 154
First Av. S'ley —5B 60
First Av. Upt —2N 157
First Av. Wake —1K 119
First Av. Weth —4N 17
Firs, The. Roys —5B 154
Firs, The. S'cft —9D 30
Fir St. Haw —9C 36
Fir St. Kei —3H 37
Fir St. Todm —3J 107
Fir St. Wilsd —2B 56
First St. Low M —7C 76
Firth Av. Brigh —9M 93
Firth Av. Leeds —3C 80
Firth Carr. Shipl —1N 57
Firthcliffe Dri. Liv —7M 95
Firthcliffe Gro. Liv —7M 95
Firthcliffe La. Liv —7M 95
Firthcliffe Mt. Liv —6M 95
Firthcliffe Pde. Liv —7M 95
Firthcliffe Pl. Liv —7N 95
Firthcliffe Rd. Liv —7M 95
Firthcliffe Ter. Liv —7M 95
Firthcliffe Vw. Liv —7M 95
Firthcliffe Wlk. Liv —7M 95
Firth Clo. Stan —7N 99
Firthfield La. Pon —6L 141
Firthfields. Gar —7A 66
Firth Gro. Leeds —3C 80
Firth Ho. Wake —5L 119
(off George St.)
Firth Ho. La. Bklnd —1J 129
Firth Ho. La. Brigh —4N 113
Firth La. Wilsd —1B 56
Firth Mt. Leeds —3C 80
Firth Rd. B'frd —3M 57
Firth Rd. Leeds —3C 80
Firths Ter. Hal —2M 91
(off Ramsden St.)
Firth St. Brigh —2M 113
Firth St. Hud —6N 131
Firth St. Leeds —5F 62
Firth St. Shepl —9J 149
Firth St. T'tn —8C 56
Firth Ter. Leeds —5G 62
Firth Vw. Leeds —3C 80
Fir Tree App. Leeds —3D 44
Firtree Av. Gar —8B 66
Fir Tree Clo. Leeds —3E 44
Fir Tree Gdns. B'frd —9H 41
Fir Tree Gdns. Leeds —3D 44
Fir Tree Grn. Leeds —3E 44
Fir Tree Gro. Leeds —4E 44
Fir Tree La. Leeds —4F 44
Fir Tree Ri. Leeds —4E 44
Fir Tree Va. Leeds —4E 44
Firville Av. Nor —2J 121
Firville Cres. Nor —3J 121
Fir Wlk. Dew —6A 116
Firwood Clo. Todm —2J 107
Fishbeck La. Sils —5G 6
(in two parts)
Fish Dam La. Barn —9E 154
Fishergate. Knot —7B 104
Fisher Grn. Hon —5K 147
Fisher Gro. Oss —7B 118
Fisher St. Knot —8D 104
Fishpond La. C'thpe —5H 137
Fishponds Dri. Crig —5G 137
Fishpool. —6D 12
Fish St. Leeds —6E 62
Fitts La. E Kes —9B 16
Fitts La. Hare —9J 15
Fitzgerald Clo. C'frd —7K 103
Fitzgerald St. B'frd —9B 58
Fitzroy Dri. Leeds —9J 45
Fitzroy Rd. B'frd —7F 58
Fitzwilliam. —6A 140
Fitzwilliam St. B'frd —9D 58
Fitzwilliam St. Hud —4L 131
Fitzwilliam St. Kin —9B 140
Five Lane Ends. —9F 40
Five La. Ends. H'frth —3K 163
Five La. Ends. Skel —8K 159
Five Oaks. Bail —5M 39
Five Rise Locks. —3E 38
Fixby. —4B 134
(nr. Grange Moor)
Fixby. —6M 113
(nr. Rastrick)
Fixby Av. Hal —7L 91
Fixby Fold. Ell —5H 113
Fixby La. W'ley —3A 134
Fixby Pk. Dri. Hud —9L 113
Fixby Rd. Hud —6L 113
Flanshaw. —5G 119
Flanshaw Av. Wake —5G 118
Flanshaw Cres. Wake —5G 118
Flanshaw Gro. Wake —5G 118
Flanshaw Ind. Est. Wake —4F 118
Flanshaw La. Wake —4F 118
Flanshaw Rd. Wake —5G 118
Flanshaw St. Wake —5G 118
Flanshaw Vw. Wake —5G 118
Flanshaw Way. Wake —4E 118
Flappit Springs. —9G 36
Flasby St. Kei —8J 21
Flash La. Mir —5M 115
Flass La. C'frd —8C 102
Flat La. H'frth —3J 163
Flat Nook. Bgly —4G 38
Flats La. Bar E —9L 47
Flatts, The. —2E 116
Flavell Clo. S Kirk —8H 157
Flawith Dri. B'frd —4H 59
Flaxen Ct. B'frd —4B 76
Flaxman Rd. B'frd —2G 58
Flax Mdw. Lind —9F 112
Flax Mill Rd. Leeds —2G 80
Flax Pl. Leeds —7G 62
Flaxton Clo. Leeds —2D 80
Flaxton Gdns. Leeds —2D 80
Flaxton Grn. B'frd —4H 59
Flaxton Pl. B'frd —8N 57
Flaxton St. Leeds —2D 80
Flaxton Vw. Leeds —2D 80
Flea La. K S'ton —6J 143
Fledborough Rd. Weth —4K 17
Fleece St. B'frd —6L 75
Fleece St. Kei —9J 21
Fleet La. Q'bry —3C 74
Fleet La. W'ford & Oult —8E 82
(in two parts)
Fleet St. Scis —8G 151
Fleet Thro' Rd. H'fth —9E 42
Fleming Ct. Hud —5E 132
Fleminghouse La. Hud —5E 132
Fleming St. Bat —7F 96
Fletcher Av. Sils —7E 6
Fletcher Cres. Brigh —5K 113
Fletcher La. B'frd —2B 58
Fletcher Rd. B'frd —4N 75
Fletton Ter. B'frd —4F 58
Flexbury Av. Morl —1K 97
Flight Hill. H'frth —2N 169
Flight Ho. Rd. Sower B —7N 109
Flintmill La. B Spa —6C 18
Flinton Gro. B'frd —3H 59
Flint St. Hud —1N 131
Flockton. —8F 134
Flockton Av. B'frd —1E 76
Flockton Clo. B'frd —1E 76
Flockton Cres. B'frd —1E 76
Flockton Dri. B'frd —1E 76
Flockton Green. —7G 135
Flockton Gro. B'frd —1E 76
Flockton Rd. B'frd —1E 76
Flockton Ter. B'frd —1E 76
Floral Av. Leeds —9E 44
Floreat Clo. Bat —4D 96
Florence Av. Leeds —4J 63
Florence Av. Wilsd —9A 38
Florence Gro. Leeds —4J 63
Florence Mt. Leeds —4J 63
Florence Pl. Leeds —4J 63
Florence St. B'frd —8G 58
Florence St. C'frd —4D 102
Florence St. Hal —5N 91
Florence St. Leeds —4J 63
Florence Ter. Morl —1L 97
(off South Pde.)
Florida Rd. All —2F 56
Florist St. Kei —7L 21
Flounders Hill. Ackw —4F 140
Flower Acre. Ell —5E 112
(off Elizabeth St.)
Flower Bank. B'frd —2D 58
Flower Bank. Sower B —9F 90
Flower Clo. Yead —9L 25
Flower Ct. H'fth —8E 42
Flower Cft. Kei —2F 36
Flowerfields. Hip —3K 93
Flower Gth. B'frd —9H 41
Flower Gth. H'fth —8E 42
(off Regent Rd.)
Flower Haven. B'frd —2J 57
Flower Hill. B'frd —2L 57
Flower Mt. Bail —3B 40
Flower Mt. Yead —9N 25
(off Alexandra Ter.)
Flower Scar Rd. Todm —6A 86
Floyd St. B'frd —2N 75
Flush. —8N 95
Flush. Liv —8N 95
Flushdyke. —4B 118
Flush Ho. La. H'frth —5F 162
Flynn Ho. Wake —5G 118
Foldings Av. Schol —4D 94
Foldings Clo. Schol —4C 94
Foldings Ct. Schol —4C 94
Foldings Gro. Schol —4C 94
Foldings Pde. Schol —4C 94
Foldings Rd. Schol —4C 94
Foldings, The. Skelm —7D 150
Fold La. Hept —7B 70
Fold, The. Haw —8B 36
Fold, The. Leeds —2F 64
Foljambe St. Wake —7L 119
Folkestone St. B'frd —7F 58
(in two parts)
Folkton Holme. B'frd —4H 59
Follett Av. Hud —8H 131
Follifoot La. Kirk O —1H 15
Follingworth La. Slai —9J 129
Follingworth Rd. Bat —7J 97
Folly Hall. —5M 131
Folly Hall. Hud —6M 131
Folly Hall Av. B'frd —5N 75
Folly Hall Clo. B'frd —5N 75
Folly Hall Gdns., The. B'frd —5N 75
Folly Hall La. Cra V —1M 109
Folly Hall Mt. Ting —4A 98
Folly Hall Rd. B'frd —5N 75
Folly Hall Rd. Ting —4A 98
Folly Hall Wlk. B'frd —5N 75
Folly La. B'ham —6D 32
Folly La. Leeds —1D 80
Folly La. Ripp —9D 110
Folly Rd. Hud —8M 113
Folly Vw. B'ham —6D 32
Folly Vw. Rd. Haw —9D 36
Fontmell Clo. B'frd —3J 77
Football. Yead —9N 25
Forber Gro. B'frd —9J 59
Forber Pl. Leeds —7N 63
Forbes Ho. B'frd —2J 77
(off Stirling Cres.)
Ford. Q'bry —5B 74
Ford Dri. Mir —5J 115
Ford Ga. H'frth —6H 163
Ford Hill. Q'bry —5B 74
Ford St. Kei —7L 21
Ford St. Kin —9B 140
Fore La. Sower B —9G 91
Fore La. Av. Sower B —9F 90
Foreside Bottom La. Denh —1K 73
Foreside La. Denh —9H 55
Forest Av. Hal —9L 73
Forest Bank. Gild —6F 78
Forest Clo. Wake —2N 119
Forest Cres. Hal —9L 73
Forester Ct. Denh —6K 55
(off Main Rd.)
Forester Sq. Denh —6K 55
Forest Ga. Otley —1L 25
Forest Grn. Hal —1L 91
Forest Gro. Hal —1M 91
Forest Hill Gdns. Outl —2N 129
Forest Hill Rd. Holy G & Outl —1K 129
Forest Ridge. E Ard —3E 98
Forest Rd. Barn —9A 154
Forest Rd. Hud —5C 132
Forest Way. Hon —5K 147
Forge Hill La. Knot —7D 104
Forge La. Dew —7E 116
Forge La. Horb —2E 136
Forge La. Leeds —6N 61
Forge La. Liv —9M 95
(in two parts)
Forge La. Wike —7M 29
Forge Row. Leeds —2G 79
Forge Vw. Steet —3C 20
Forman's Dri. Rob H —1J 99
Formby Av. Hud —8L 113
Forrest Av. Hud —3J 131
Forrester Clo. Fitz —7A 140
Forrester's Ter. Holy G —8M 111
Forrest Ter. Dew —5J 117
Forster Ct. B'frd —7C 58
Forster Dri. Heck —9B 96
Forster Pl. Leeds —1K 79
Forster Sq. B'frd —7D 58
Forster St. Leeds —9G 62
Forsythia Av. E Ard —4E 98
Fort Ann Rd. Bat —8J 97
Forth Ct. Leeds —8C 62
Fortis Way. Hud —2D 130
Fortshot La. Leeds —7J 29
Forum Vw. Thpe A —5N 141
Foss Av. Weth —2L 17
Fosse Way. Gar —8B 66
Foss Wlk. C'frd —4H 103
Foster Av. Hud —8H 131
Foster Av. Nor —2H 121
Foster Av. Sils —7D 6
Foster Av. T'tn —8E 56
Foster Clo. Bur W —8D 10
Foster Clo. Morl —8K 79
Foster Cres. Morl —8K 79
Foster Gdns. Kei —9F 20
Foster La. H Bri —9H 71
Foster Pk. Denh —5L 55
Foster Pk. Gro. Denh —5L 55
Foster Pk. Rd. Denh —5L 55
Foster Pk. Vw. Denh —5L 55
(in two parts)
Foster Pl. La. H'frth —6D 164
Foster Rd. Kei —3H 37
Foster's Ct. Hal —5B 92
(off Union St.)
Foster Sq. Denh —6K 55
Foster St. Morl —8K 79
Foster St. Q'bry —4D 74
Foster Ter. Leeds —3G 61
Foston Clo. B'frd —4J 59
Foston La. B'frd —4H 59
Fothergill Av. Ackw —4E 140
Foulby. —2M 139
Foulcauseway La. Otley —1A 26
Foul Clough Rd. Todm —3F 106
Foulds Ter. Bgly —3F 38
Foundry App. Leeds —4K 63
Foundry Av. Leeds —3K 63
Foundry Dri. Leeds —3K 63
Foundry Hill. Bgly —4E 38
Foundry Ho. C'frd —5B 102
Foundry La. B'frd —1F 76
Foundry La. Knot —8F 104
Foundry La. Leeds & Seac —3M
Foundry Mill Cres. Leeds —3A 6
Foundry Mill Dri. Leeds —3N 63
(in two parts)
Foundry Mill Gdns. Leeds —1N
Foundry Mill Mt. Leeds —3A 64
Foundry Mill St. Leeds —3A 64
Foundry Mill Ter. Leeds —3A 64
Foundry Mill Vw. Leeds —3A 64
Foundry Mill Wlk. Leeds —3A 6
Foundry Pl. Leeds —3K 63
Foundry Rd. S'ley —5B 60
Foundry St. Brigh —2A 114
Foundry St. Cleck —4J 95
Foundry St. Dew —3G 116
Foundry St. Hal —5B 92
Foundry St. Leeds —7G 62
(nr. Saxton La.)
Foundry St. Leeds —8D 62
(nr. Water La.)
Foundry St. Raven —6B 116
Foundry St. Sower B —9H 91
Foundry St. Todm —8J 87
Foundry St. N. Hal —1M 91
Foundry Ter. Cleck —5J 95
Foundry Wlk. Leeds —3J 63
Fountain Clo. Dart —8G 153
Fountain Clo. Liv —2K 115
Fountain Ct. Barn —8N 153
Fountain Ct. Gild —9H 79
Fountain Dri. Liv —2K 115
Fountain Gro. Hud —6H 131
Fountains Av. Bat —8C 96
Fountains Av. B Spa —1C 32
Fountain Sq. Dart —8G 152
Fountain St. B'frd —7C 58
Fountain St. Chur —5M 79
Fountain St. Hal —5B 92
Fountain St. H Bri —1H 89
(off Shelf Rd.)
Fountain St. Heck —7A 96
Fountain St. Leeds —6C 62
Fountain St. Liv —2K 115

›untain St. Low M —7A 76
›untain St. Morl —2J 97
›untain St. Q'bry —4D 74
›untain St. Sower B —7D 110
›untain St. T'tn —8C 56
›untain St. Todm —6N 87
›untains Way. Wake —2A 120
›untain Ter. Wyke —1B 94
›untain Way. Shipl —8A 40
›ur Acres. Mir —8L 115
›urlands. —7G 40
›urlands Ct. B'frd —7G 40
›urlands Cres. B'frd —7G 40
›urlands Dri. B'frd —7G 40
›urlands Gdns. B'frd —7G 40
›urlands Gro. B'frd —7G 40
›urlands Rd. B'frd —7G 41
›ur Lane Ends. —6L 57
›ur La. Ends. C'frd —6A 102
›urteenth Av. Leeds —8N 61
›urth Av. B'frd —5G 59
›urth Av. Kei —1G 37
›urth Av. Liv —7F 94
urth Av. Rothw —6B 82
urth Av. Wake —1K 119
urth Av. Weth —4N 17
urth St. Low M —7C 76
›wler's Pl. S'ley —4B 60
›wler St. B'frd —9F 58
›xbridge Way. Nor I —9M 101
›xcliff. Knot —3C 104
x Clo. Eml —3G 151
x Ct. Dur —3H 137
x Ct. G'lnd —4C 112
x Covert Rd. K S'ton —8K 143
xcroft Clo. Leeds —1L 61
x Cft. Clo. Q'bry —6B 74
xcroft Dri. Brigh —3L 113
xcroft Grn. Leeds —1L 61
xcroft Mt. Leeds —1L 61
xcroft Rd. Leeds —1L 61
xcroft Wlk. Leeds —1L 61
xcroft Way. Leeds —1L 61
xen La. Sower B —5C 110
xglove Av. Leeds —9L 45
xglove Folly. Wake —3G 119
xglove Rd. Birs —2B 96
xglove Rd. Hud —6C 132
x Heads La. Spof —1B 16
xhill. Bail —4M 39
xhill. Weth —3M 17
xhill Av. Leeds —6M 43
xhill Av. Q'bry —4C 74
xhill Clo. Q'bry —4C 74
xhill Ct. Leeds —6M 43
xhill Cres. Leeds —6N 43
xhill Dri. Leeds —6M 43
xhill Dri. Q'bry —4C 74
xhill Grn. Leeds —6N 43
xhill Gro. Leeds —6N 43
xhill Gro. Q'bry —4C 74
xhills, The. Leeds —3G 43
xholes Cres. C'ley —9M 41
xholes La. C'ley —9M 41
xholes La. Nor —7G 100
x La. Dur —3H 137
x La. Wake —2J 119
xlow Av. Hud —2C 132
x Royd. —1E 134
x Royd. Shepl —8J 149
x Royd Av. Mir —5K 115
x Royd Dri. Mir —5K 115
xroyd La. Dew —9D 116
x Royd La. Mir —4K 115
n two parts)
x Royd Vw. Mir —5K 115
xstone Ri. Bail —4C 40
xstones La. Ripp —9D 110
x St. Bat —8G 96
x St. Bgly —4E 38
x St. Cleck —5F 94
x St. Hud —4M 131
x Ter. Pon —2L 123
xton Gdns. Morl —1J 97
x Vw. Stainc —9D 96
xwood Av. Leeds —1N 63
xwood Clo. Leeds —1N 63
xwood Farm Way. Leeds —1N 63
xwood Gro. Leeds —1N 63
xwood Ho. B'frd —9H 59
off Westbury St.)
xwood Ri. Leeds —1N 63
xwood Wlk. Leeds —1N 63
xwood Wlk. Weth —2N 17
n Clo. Pon —3L 123
nce Fold. Hon —4L 147
nces Av. Hud —7G 131
nces Rd. Dew —4J 117
nces St. Brigh —9M 93
nces St. Ell —5E 112
nces St. Fars —4A 60
nces St. Kei —8G 21
nce St. Bat —8H 97
Francis Av. Milns —6F 130
Francis Clo. Hal —5N 91
Francis Ct. Leeds —3F 62
(off Francis St.)
Francis Gro. Leeds —2D 80
Francis Ho. B'frd —4F 58
(off Hatfield Rd.)
Francis La. Ho. Pon —2K 123
(off Horse Fair)
Francis Rd. Shar C —8J 121
Francis Sq. Cull —9K 37
(off Station Rd.)
Francis St. Ackw —5D 140
Francis St. B'frd —9E 58
Francis St. C'frd —4E 102
Francis St. Hal —5N 91
Francis St. Heck —9B 96
Francis St. Leeds —3F 62
Francis St. Milns —6F 130
Francis St. Mir —6J 115
Francis Ter. Ackw —5D 140
Francis Vw. Mir —6K 115
Frank Clo. Dew —9H 117
Frank Clo. Steet —2B 20
Frankel Gdns. Brigh —9M 93
Frankland Gro. Leeds —3G 62
Frankland Pl. Leeds —3G 63
Frank La. Dew —9H 117
Frank La. Eml —3E 150
Frank La. Hal —2B 90
Franklin Ho. B'frd —6D 58
(off Otley Rd.)
Franklin St. Hal —5M 91
Frank Parkinson Ct. Guis —7J 25
(off Kelcliffe Av.)
Frank Parkinson Homes. Guis —7J 25
(off Oxford St.)
Frank Peel Clo. Heck —8A 96
Frank Pl. B'frd —1N 75
Frank St. B'frd —1N 75
Frank St. Hal —6N 91
Fraser Av. H'fth —7C 42
Fraser Rd. C'ley —9K 41
Fraser St. B'frd —6A 58
Fraser St. Leeds —5H 63
Freakfield La. Brigh —1F 114
Frederick Av. Leeds —8J 63
Frederick Av. Wake —8A 120
Frederick Clo. B'frd —6D 40
Frederick St. Fars —3N 59
Frederick St. Hud —6H 131
Frederick St. Kei —9K 21
Frederick St. Liv —9M 95
Frederick St. Wake —5L 119
Frederick Walker Gdns. Bat —8G 96
Fred's Pl. B'frd —2G 77
Fred St. Kei —1H 37
Freeholds Rd. S'fth —5A 106
Freeholds Ter. S'fth —5A 106
Freely La. B'ham —6D 32
Freeman Rd. Hal —7F 92
Freemans Way. Weth —3N 17
Freemantle Pl. Leeds —7N 63
Freemont St. Leeds —4D 60
Freeport Castleford. C'frd —7F 102
Free School La. Hal —7N 91
Freeston Av. K'thpe —4E 120
Freeston Ct. Nor —9J 101
Freeston Dri. K'thpe —5D 120
Freeston Dri. Nor —9J 101
Freestone M. Leeds —7F 60
Freestone Way. Altft —8F 100
Fremantle Gro. B'frd —9J 59
French St. Skel —8M 159
Frensham Av. Morl —1J 97
Frensham Dri. B'frd —2J 75
Frensham Dri. C'frd —6K 103
Frensham Gro. B'frd —2J 75
Frensham Way. B'frd —2J 75
Freshfield Gdns. All —5G 57
Friar Ct. B'frd —9G 40
Friar Pl. Hud —7D 114
Friar's Clo. F'stne —7D 122
Friars Ind. Est. B'frd —8F 40
Friars Nook. Pon —4L 123
Friarwood La. Pon —3K 123
Friar Wood Steps. Pon —3K 123
Friar Wood Ter. Pon —3K 123
Frickley Bri. La. Brier —5M 155
Frieldhurst Rd. Todm —3E 86
Friendly. —7G 90
Friendly Av. Sower B —7G 91
Friendly Fold. Hal —2N 91
Friendly Fold Ho. Hal —2N 91
(off Lentilfield St.)
Friendly Fold Rd. Hal —2N 91
Friendly St. Hal —2N 91
Friendly St. Hud —4N 131
Friendly St. T'tn —8C 56
Frimley Dri. B'frd —3A 76
Frith St. Cro R —7E 36
Frizinghall. —1A 58
Frizinghall Rd. B'frd —3A 58
Frizley Gdns. B'frd —2A 58
Frobisher Gro. Wake —6G 118
Frodingham Vs. B'frd —4H 59
Frogmere Ter. Oaken —8D 76
Frogmore Av. Oaken —8D 76
Frontline Clo. Leeds —9J 45
Front Row. Leeds —8D 62
(in two parts)
Front St. B'ham —6C 32
Front St. C'frd —6F 102
Front St. Leeds —8D 62
Front St. Pon —3J 123
Frost Hill. Liv —8M 95
Frost Hole La. Cra V —6K 89
Fruit St. Kei —8L 21
Fryergate. Wake —4H 119
Fryston La. Knot —6M 103
Fryston Rd. C'frd —5H 103
Fuchsia Cft. Rothw —7F 82
Fulford Av. Hud —9M 113
Fulford Clo. Dart —8J 153
Fulford St. C'frd —5C 102
Fulford Wlk. B'frd —4H 59
Fulham La. Wome —9N 125
Fulham Pl. Leeds —2D 80
Fulham Sq. Leeds —2D 80
(off Fulham St.)
Fulham St. Leeds —2D 80
Fullerton Clo. Skel —7L 159
Fullerton St. B'frd —8E 58
Fullwood Dri. Gol —6C 130
Fulmar Ct. Leeds —8F 80
Fulmar M. B'frd —7H 57
Fulmar Rd. C'frd —6C 102
Fulneck. Pud —1A 78
Fulneck. —9B 60
Fulneck Clo. Hud —8L 113
Fulstone. —1F 164
Fulstone Hall La. N Mill —2D 164
Fulstone Rd. Stkmr —9F 148
Fulton St. B'frd —7B 58
Fulwood Gro. Wake —5K 137
Furever Feline Museum. —7A 40
Furlong La. Pon —7L 123
Furnace Gro. B'frd —8D 76
Furnace Inn St. B'frd —9H 59
Furnace La. B'shaw —7L 77
Furnace Rd. Oaken —8D 76
(in three parts)
Furnbrook Gdns. Hud —3F 132
Furness Av. Hal —8K 73
Furness Av. Wren —1G 118
Furness Cres. Hal —8K 73
Furness Dri. Hal —8K 73
Furness Dri. Wren —1G 118
Furness Gdns. Hal —9L 73
Furness Gro. Hal —9K 73
Furness Pl. Hal —9L 73
Fusden La. Gom —3L 95
Futures Way. B'frd —9D 58
Fyfe Cres. Bail —5B 40
Fyfe Gro. Bail —5C 40
Fyfe La. Bail —4C 40

Gable End Ter. Pud —7C 60
Gables Clo. Beal —5N 105
Gables, The. Bail —4C 40
(nr. Kirklands Rd.)
Gables, The. Bail —5C 40
(off Dewhirst Rd.)
Gables, The. H'fth —5F 42
Gabriel's Corner. Ackw —5F 140
Gadding Moor Rd. Hoy S —8H 167
Gagewell Dri. Horb —9D 118
Gagewell La. Horb —9D 118
Gagewell Vw. Horb —9D 118
Gainest. Hal —7M 91
Gainford Dri. Gar —8N 65
Gain La. B'frd & Fag —5H 59
Gainsborough Clo. B'frd —4E 58
Gainsborough Pl. Leeds —2H 79
(off Well Holme Mead)
Gainsborough Way. Stan —7N 99
Gainsbro' Av. Leeds —2L 43
Gainsbro' Dri. Leeds —2L 43
Gaisby. —9B 40
Gaisby La. B'frd & Shipl —2A 58
Gaisby Mt. Shipl —1B 58
Gaisby Pl. Shipl —9B 40
Gaisby Ri. Shipl —9B 40
Gaitskell Ct. Leeds —9C 62
Gaitskell Grange. Leeds —9C 62
Gaitskell Wlk. Leeds —9C 62
Galecommon La. Wome —7M 125
Galefield Grn. B'frd —7L 75
Gale La. Stainb —2E 12
Gale St. Cro R —7F 36
Gale St. Kei —8J 21
Gallery & Studio Theatre. —5D 62
Gall La. Todm —2E 86
Gallogate La. Wee —7A 14
Gallon Cft. S Elm —6L 157
Galloway Ct. Pud —6L 59
Galloway La. Pud —5L 59
Galloway Rd. B'frd —8H 41
Galloway St. Hud —2N 131
Gallows Hill. C'frd —5J 103
Gallows La. Wool —9H 137
Galsworthy Av. B'frd —3H 57
Gamble Hill. Leeds —6G 61
Gamble Hill Chase. Leeds —6G 60
Gamble Hill Clo. Leeds —6G 61
Gamble Hill Cft. Leeds —6G 61
(off Gamble Hill Vw.)
Gamble Hill Cross. Leeds —6G 61
(off Gamble Hill Lawn)
Gamble Hill Dri. Leeds —6G 61
Gamble Hill Fold. Leeds —6G 61
(off Gamble Hill Dri.)
Gamble Hill Grange. Leeds —6G 61
(off Gamble Hill Lawn)
Gamble Hill Grn. Leeds —6G 60
Gamble Hill Lawn. Leeds —6G 61
Gamble Hill Path. Leeds —6G 60
(off Gamble Hill Grn.)
Gamble Hill Pl. Leeds —6G 61
Gamble Hill Ri. Leeds —6G 60
Gamble Hill Rd. Leeds —6G 60
Gamble Hill Va. Leeds —6G 60
Gamble Hill Vw. Leeds —6G 61
Gamble Hill Wlk. Leeds —6G 60
(off Gamble Hill Ri.)
Gamble La. Leeds —8F 60
Gambles Hill. Fars —3A 60
Gamel Vw. Steet —2B 20
Game Scar La. Oakw —1B 36
Ganners Clo. Leeds —2F 60
Ganners Gth. Leeds —2G 60
Ganners Grn. Leeds —2F 60
Ganners Gro. Leeds —2G 60
Ganners Hill. Leeds —2G 60
Ganners La. Leeds —2F 60
Ganners Mt. Leeds —2F 60
Ganners Ri. Leeds —2G 60
Ganners Rd. Leeds —2F 60
Ganners Wlk. Leeds —2F 60
Ganners Way. Leeds —2F 60
Gannerthorpe Clo. Wyke —1A 94
Gannet Clo. C'frd —6C 102
Ganny Rd. Brigh —1N 113
Ganton Clo. Leeds —2D 62
Ganton Way. Hud —8L 113
Gaol La. Hal —5B 92
(in two parts)
Garden Av. Liv —6L 95
Garden Clo. Liv —7L 95
Garden Clo. Oss —8A 118
Garden Clo. Wyke —9A 76
Garden Ct. Hud —6L 131
(off St Stephen's Rd.)
Garden Cres. Dew —5B 116
Garden Dri. Dew —5B 116
Gardeners Ct. Leeds —1F 80
Gardener's Sq. Hal —4H 93
Garden Fld. Wyke —1A 94
Garden Fold. Hip —4H 93
Garden Ho. Clo. Meth —1L 101
Garden Ho. La. Ting —4C 98
Garden La. B'frd —3L 57
Garden La. Knot —7F 104
Garden Pde. Liv —6L 95
Garden Pl. Dew —2C 116
Garden Rd. Brigh —8L 93
Garden Row. Croft —1G 139
Gardens Rd. Dew —5B 116
Gardens, The. Bgly —4J 39
Gardens, The. Fars —3N 59
Gardens, The. Hal —7B 92
Gardens, The. Midd —9E 80
Gardens, The. Morl —2J 97
Gardens, The. Pon —4H 123
Garden St. Ackw —5D 140
Garden St. Altfts —9F 100
Garden St. B'frd —2L 57
Garden St. C'frd —6D 102
Garden St. Cro R —7F 36
Garden St. Dew —5A 116
Garden St. Glass —6G 102
Garden St. Heck —9A 96
Garden St. Hud —6L 131
Garden St. Nor —1J 121
Garden St. Todm —6K 87
Garden St. Wake —5K 119
Garden St. N. Hal —4C 92
Garden Ter. B'frd —3M 57
Garden Ter. Crig —6G 136
Garden Ter. Den D —3C 166
Garden Ter. Dew —5B 116
Garden Ter. H Bri —1H 89
Garden Vw. Bgly —4H 39
Garden Vw. Liv —6L 95
Garden Vw. Ct. Leeds —6K 45
Garden Village. M'fld —8G 67
Garden Wlk. Liv —7L 95
Gardiner Row. B'frd —3F 76
Garfield Av. B'frd —4N 57
Garfield Ho. B'frd —1B 76
(off Hutson St.)
Garfield Pl. Mars —5F 144
Garfield St. All —5F 56
Garfield St. Hal —3N 91
Garfield St. Todm —3E 86
Garfit Hill. Gom & Birs —4A 96
Garforth. —7M 65
Garforth Av. Steet —2C 20
Garforth Bridge. —9K 65
Garforth Clo. Nor —9F 100
Garforth Ct. Mir —4L 115
Garforth Dri. Nor —9F 100
Garforth Rd. Kei —8L 21
Garforth St. All —5G 57
Garforth St. Neth —2H 147
Gargrave App. Leeds —6H 63
Gargrave Clo. Brigh —3J 113
Gargrave Ct. Leeds —5H 63
Gargrave Cres. Hems —3C 156
Gargrave Ho. B'frd —6E 58
(off Otley Rd.)
Gargrave Pl. Hems —3C 156
Gargrave Pl. Leeds —5H 63
Gargrave Pl. Wake —6E 118
Garibaldi St. B'frd —7J 59
(in two parts)
Garland Dri. Leeds —7E 64
Garlick St. Brigh —5K 113
Garmil Head La. Fitz —5N 139
Garmil La. Wrag —4N 139
Garmont M. Leeds —9F 44
Garmont Rd. Leeds —9F 44
Garner La. Hon —5J 147
Garner La. Kbtn —1H 149
Garnet Av. Leeds —2E 80
Garnet Cres. Leeds —2E 80
Garnet Gro. Leeds —2E 80
Garnet La. Tad —8M 33
Garnet Pde. Leeds —2E 80
Garnet Pl. Leeds —2E 80
Garnet Rd. Leeds —3E 80
Garnet Ter. Leeds —2E 80
Garnet Ter. Tad —7N 33
Garnett St. B'frd —7E 58
Garnett St. Dew —9C 96
Garnett St. H Bri —1H 89
Garnett St. Otley —9L 11
Garnet Vw. Leeds —2E 80
Garrett Clo. Skelm —7C 150
Garros La. Eby —1A 4
Garrowby Ho. B'frd —7F 40
(off Thorp Gth.)
Garsdale Av. B'frd —8G 40
Garsdale Cres. Bail —3C 40
Garsdale Fold. Coll —8H 17
Garsdale Gro. Wake —3A 120
Garsdale Rd. Hud —8N 131
Garsdale Wlk. Knot —1D 124
Garside Ct. Leeds —3D 62
Garside Gro. Altft —8G 100
Garth Av. Coll —9J 17
Garth Av. Leeds —6D 44
Garth Av. Nor —3H 121
Gth. Barn Clo. B'frd —3M 57
Garth Cotts. Knot —8G 104
Garth Dri. Leeds —6D 44
Garth End. Coll —9J 17
Garth Fold. B'frd —7F 40
Garth Gro. Men —4E 24
Gth. Land Way. B'frd —2G 77
Garth Rd. Leeds —6D 44
Garth St. C'frd —6C 102
Garth St. Kei —9H 21
Garth, The. Coll —9J 17
Garth, The. Gar —7A 66
Garth, The. Leeds —7G 62
Garthwaite Mt. All —4G 56
Garth Wlk. Leeds —6D 44
Garton Av. Leeds —7J 63
Garton Dri. B'frd —1H 59
Garton Gro. Leeds —7J 63
Garton Rd. Leeds —7J 63
Garton Ter. Leeds —7J 63
Garton Vw. Leeds —7J 63
Garvey Vw. B'frd —1C 76
Garwick Ter. G'lnd —4C 112
Gascoigne Av. Bar E —9L 47
Gascoigne Ct. Bar E —9M 47
Gascoigne Rd. Bar E —9L 47
Gascoigne Rd. Wake —3G 99
Gascoigne Vw. Bar E —9L 47
Gas Ho. Yd. Oaken —8C 76
Gaskell Dri. Horb —9C 118
Gaskell St. Wake —6J 119
Gasson St. Hud —6F 130
Gas Works La. Ell —4E 112
Gas Works Rd. Kei —8M 21
(in two parts)
Gas Works Rd. Sower B —8K 91

Gasworks St. *Hud* —3N **131**
Gasworks St. *Liv* —8M **95**
*Gas Works Yd. Rothw —8A **82***
(off Commercial St.)
Gatefield Mt. *B'frd* —7M **75**
Gate Foot La. *Shepl* —2G **164**
Gate Head. *Mars* —5H **145**
Gatehead Bank. *Mars* —4H **145**
Ga. Head La. *G'lnd* —6M **111**
Ga. Head La. *H'frth* —8E **164**
*Gatehouse Cen. Hud —7L **131***
(off Albert St.)
Ga. House Ct. *Rothw* —6F **82**
Gateland Dri. *Leeds* —3N **45**
Gateland La. *Leeds* —4N **45**
Gateon Ho. La. *E Kes* —4B **30**
Gatesgarth Cres. *Hud* —1F **130**
Gate Way Dri. *Yead* —9L **25**
Gateways. *Wake* —7L **99**
Gathorne Clo. *Leeds* —3G **63**
Gathorne St. *B'frd* —1N **75**
Gathorne St. *Brigh* —9N **93**
Gathorne St. *Leeds* —3G **63**
(in two parts)
Gathorne Ter. *Leeds* —3G **63**
Gaukroger La. *Hal* —7C **92**
Gauk St. *Fair* —9N **85**
Gauk St. *Knot* —4B **104**
Gauxholme. —9H 87
Gauxholme Fold. *Todm* —9H **87**
Gavin Clo. *B'frd* —7J **59**
Gawcliffe Rd. *Shipl* —8A **40**
Gaw La. *Halt E* —2F **4**
Gawthorpe. —4H 133
(nr. Fenay Bridge)
Gawthorpe. —2M 117
(nr. Ossett)
Gawthorpe Av. *Bgly* —2F **38**
Gawthorpe Dri. *Bgly* —2F **38**
Gawthorpe Green. —4J 133
Gawthorpe Grn. La. *Hud & Lep* —4J **133**
Gawthorpe La. *Bgly* —3F **38**
Gawthorpe La. *Hud* —5H **133**
Gawthorpe La. *Oss & K'gte* —2N **117**
Gawthorpe St. *Wilsd* —9A **38**
Gay La. *Otley* —1L **25**
Gayle Clo. *Wyke* —2A **94**
Gaynor St. *B'frd* —7B **58**
Gaythorne Rd. *B'frd* —2C **76**
Gaythorne Rd. *Fag* —3G **59**
Gaythorne Ter. *Cytn* —1H **75**
Gaythorn Ter. *Hal* —3H **93**
Geary Clo. *Wake* —3F **118**
Geary Dri. *Wake* —3F **118**
Geecroft La. *Sick* —4C **16**
Geelong Clo. *B'frd* —3D **58**
Gelder Ct. *Wake* —3F **118**
Gelder Cft. *Wake* —3F **118**
Gelderd Clo. *Leeds* —1N **79**
Gelderd La. *Leeds* —1N **79**
Gelderd Pl. *Leeds* —3C **62**
Gelderd Rd. *Birs* —3A **96**
Gelderd Rd. *Gild* —8F **78**
Gelderd Rd. *Leeds* —2N **79**
Gelderd Trad. Est. *Leeds* —9A **62**
Gelder Rd. *Leeds* —7L **61**
Gelder Ter. *Hud* —5A **132**
Gemini Ct. *Pon* —9K **103**
Geneva Gro. *Wake* —4M **119**
Genista Dri. *Leeds* —5F **80**
Gentian Ct. *Wake* —4G **119**
George-A-Green Rd. *Wake* —6G **118**
George and Crown Yd. *Wake* —5L **119**
George Av. *Hud* —2K **131**
George Buckley Ct. *S Kirk* —7G **156**
George Cres. *Leeds* —6E **62**
George La. *Not* —3M **153**
George La. *Sower B* —9B **110**
George M. *Weth* —4M **17**
George Pl. *Morl* —1K **97**
George's Pl. *B'frd* —9C **58**
George Sq. *Hal* —5B **92**
George's Sq. *Cull* —9K **37**
George's Sq. *Kei* —1H **37**
George's St. *Hal* —1M **91**
George St. *Add* —1M **7**
George St. *Bail* —6A **40**
George St. *Bat* —8F **96**
George St. *B'frd* —8D **58**
George St. *Brigh* —1A **114**
George St. *Cleck* —4H **95**
George St. *Cros M* —6K **131**
George St. *Cud* —9K **155**
George St. *Denh* —5L **55**
George St. *Dew M* —3C **116**
George St. *Ell* —5E **112**
George St. *F'stne* —6C **122**
George St. *Fla* —3F **116**
George St. *G'lnd* —4C **112**
George St. *Hal* —5B **92**
George St. *H Bri* —4M **89**
George St. *Heck* —8A **96**
George St. *Hems* —3E **156**
George St. *Hip* —5J **93**
George St. *Horb* —1D **136**
George St. *Hud* —4M **131**
George St. *Kbtn* —3K **149**
George St. *Leeds* —6E **62**
George St. *Lind* —1G **131**
George St. *Liv* —8L **95**
George St. *M'well* —8K **153**
George St. *Milns* —5G **130**
George St. *Nor* —9G **100**
George St. *Oss* —4M **117**
George St. *Out* —7K **99**
George St. *Ras* —2M **113**
George St. *Raven* —6B **116**
George St. *Rawd* —3M **41**
George St. *Ryh* —8J **139**
George St. *Shipl* —7L **39**
George St. *Skel* —7N **159**
George St. *S Hien* —3L **155**
George St. *Sower B* —9H **91**
George St. *S'hse* —6L **121**
George St. *T'tn* —8C **56**
*George St. Todm —7K **87***
(off Union St.)
George St. *Wake* —5L **119**
*George Wright Ho. Pon —3K **123***
(off Horse Fair)
Georgia M. *Oss* —7B **118**
Geraldton Av. *B'frd* —3C **58**
Gerard Av. *Morl* —9J **79**
*Gerard Ho. B'frd —8G **41***
(off Fairhaven Grn.)
Gerard St. *Hal* —5A **92**
Germaine Ter. *T'ner* —4F **46**
Gernhill Av. *Hud* —6L **113**
Gertrude St. *S'fth* —5A **106**
Gervase Rd. *Horb* —9C **118**
Ghyllbank. *Sils* —7E **6**
Ghyll Beck Dri. *Otley* —2H **25**
Ghyll Beck Dri. *Rawd* —4B **42**
Ghyll Clo. *Steet* —3C **20**
Ghyll Grange La. *Sils* —8J **7**
Ghyll Lodge. *Bgly* —7F **38**
Ghyll M. *I'ly* —6F **8**
Ghyll Mt. *Yead* —1K **41**
Ghyll Rd. *Leeds* —9K **43**
Ghyll Rd. *Yead* —2L **41**
Ghyll Royd. *Guis* —8J **25**
(in two parts)
Ghyllroyd Av. *B'shaw* —8M **77**
Ghyllroyd Dri. *B'shaw* —8M **77**
Ghyll, The. *Bgly* —7F **38**
Ghyll, The. *Hud* —7M **113**
Ghyll Wood. *I'ly* —6D **8**
Ghyll Wood Dri. *Bgly* —7F **38**
Gibbet St. *Hal* —5K **91**
Gibb La. *Hal* —1H **91**
Gib La. *Hon* —7M **147**
Gib La. *Skelm* —7D **150**
Gibraltar Av. *Hal* —6L **91**
Gibraltar Island Rd. *Leeds* —1H **81**
Gibraltar Rd. *Hal* —5L **91**
Gibraltar Rd. *Pud* —7M **59**
Gibriding La. *H'frth* —5E **162**
Gibson Av. *Wake* —4H **119**
Gibson Clo. *Wake* —4J **119**
Gibson Dri. *Leeds* —7D **64**
Gibson La. *Kip* —3B **84**
Gibson St. *B'frd* —8F **58**
Gibson St. *Hud* —3H **131**
Gibson St. *Todm* —7L **87**
Gilbert Chase. *Leeds* —3K **61**
Gilbert Clo. *Leeds* —3L **61**
Gilbert Gdns. *Bklnd* —5K **111**
Gilbert Gro. *Hud* —8J **131**
Gilbert Mt. *Leeds* —3L **61**
Gilbert St. *Fars* —4A **60**
*Gilbert Wilkinson Ho. Pon —2K **123***
(off Horse Fair)
Gilcar. —7K 101
Gilcar St. *Nor* —8L **101**
Gilcar Way. *Norm* —7K **101**
Gildersome. —6F 78
Gildersome La. *Gild & Leeds* —5E **78**
Gildersome Spur. *Gild* —8G **78**
Gildersome Street. —7E 78
Gilead Rd. *Hud* —3D **130**
Giles Hill La. *Hal* —6F **74**
(in two parts)
Giles St. *B'frd* —9B **58**
Giles St. *H'frth* —9L **147**
Giles St. *Wibs* —4M **75**
Gillann St. *Knot* —8F **104**
Gill Bank Rd. *I'ly* —3F **8**
Gill Beck Clo. *Bail* —3C **40**
Gill Clo. *Add* —1K **7**
Gillett Dri. *Rothw* —8A **82**
Gillett La. *Rothw* —8A **82**
Gilling Av. *Gar* —6B **66**
Gillingham Grn. *B'frd* —2J **77**
Gillion Cres. *Dur* —4G **136**
Gill La. *Cowl* —3A **36**
Gill La. *H'frth* —6K **163**
Gill La. *Kear* —6A **16**
Gill La. *Nesf* —2B **8**
Gill La. *T'tn* —9B **56**
Gill La. *Yead* —3J **41**
Gillrene Av. *Wilsd* —2C **56**
Gillroyd. —9M 79
Gillroyd La. *Lint* —2C **146**
Gillroyd Pde. *Morl* —1L **97**
Gillroyd Pl. *Morl* —1L **97**
Gillroyd Ri. *B'frd* —7N **57**
Gillroyd Ter. *Morl* —9M **79**
Gill's Ct. *Hal* —5B **92**
Gill Sike Av. *Wake* —7H **119**
Gill Sike Bldgs. *Wake* —7H **119**
Gill Sike Gro. *Wake* —7H **119**
Gill Sike Ho. *Wake* —7H **119**
Gill Sike Rd. *Wake* —7H **119**
Gills, The. *Morl* —9M **79**
Gills, The. *Otley* —7L **11**
Gillstone Dri. *Haw* —8D **36**
Gill St. *Wake* —5L **119**
Gill's Yd. *Wake* —4L **119**
Gillygate. *Pon* —3K **123**
Gilmour St. *Hal* —3N **91**
Gilpin Pl. *Leeds* —8N **61**
Gilpin St. *B'frd* —6F **58**
Gilpin St. *Leeds* —8N **61**
Gilpin Ter. *Leeds* —8N **61**
Gilpin Vw. *Leeds* —8N **61**
Gilstead. —4H 39
Gilstead Ct. *Bgly* —4H **39**
Gilstead Dri. *Bgly* —4H **39**
Gilstead La. *Bgly* —4G **39**
Gilstead Way. *I'ly* —4F **8**
Gilthwaites Cres. *Den D* —1D **166**
Gilthwaites Gro. *Den D* —2D **166**
Gilthwaites La. *Den D* —1D **166**
Gilthwaites Top. *Den D* —1D **166**
Gilynda Clo. *B'frd* —7K **57**
Gindhill La. *Stainb* —2K **13**
Gin La. *S'hse* —6K **121**
Ginnel, The. *Bard* —6D **30**
(in two parts)
Ginnel, The. *Weth* —4M **17**
Gipsy Hill. *W'ford* —7C **82**
Gipsy La. *Leeds* —5C **80**
Gipsy La. *W'ford* —7C **82**
Gipsy La. *Wool* —4G **153**
Gipsy Mead. *W'ford* —7C **82**
Gipsy St. *B'frd* —6J **59**
Gipton. —3L 63
Gipton App. *Leeds* —5L **63**
Gipton Av. *Leeds* —3G **63**
Gipton Ga. E. *Leeds* —3L **63**
Gipton Ga. W. *Leeds* —3K **63**
Gipton Sq. *Leeds* —5M **63**
Gipton St. *Leeds* —3G **63**
Gipton Wood. —1K 63
Gipton Wood Av. *Leeds* —1K **63**
Gipton Wood Cres. *Leeds* —1K **63**
Gipton Wood Gro. *Leeds* —1K **63**
Gipton Wood Pl. *Leeds* —1K **63**
Gipton Wood Rd. *Leeds* —1K **63**
Girlington. —5M 57
Girlington Rd. *B'frd* —5L **57**
Girnhill La. *F'stne* —7C **122**
Gisbourne Rd. *Hud* —6C **114**
Gisburn Rd. *Wake* —3A **120**
Gisburn St. *Kei* —8H **21**
Gissing Rd. *Wake* —7F **118**
Glade, The. *S'cft* —9C **30**
Glade, The. *S'ley* —4L **59**
*Gladstone Ct. Dew —2D **116***
(off School La.)
*Gladstone Ct. S'ley —4C **60***
(off Gladstone Ter.)
Gladstone Cres. *Rawd* —2M **41**
Gladstone Pl. *Denh* —6K **55**
Gladstone Rd. *Hal* —5N **91**
Gladstone Rd. *Rawd* —3M **41**
*Gladstone Sq. Morl —9L **79***
(off Middleton Rd.)
Gladstone St. *All* —5G **57**
Gladstone St. *Bgly* —5E **38**
Gladstone St. *B'frd* —8G **58**
Gladstone St. *Cleck* —5H **95**
Gladstone St. *Fars* —3A **60**
Gladstone St. *F'stne* —4D **122**
Gladstone St. *Holy G* —7N **111**
Gladstone St. *Kei* —1H **37**
Gladstone St. *Nor* —9K **101**
Gladstone St. *Q'bry* —4E **74**
Gladstone St. *Todm* —3D **86**
Gladstone Ter. *C'frd* —4E **102**
Gladstone Ter. *Morl* —9K **79**
Gladstone Ter. *S'ley* —4C **60**
Gladstone Vw. *Hal* —9D **92**
Gladstone Vs. *Leeds* —4N **45**
Gladwin St. *Bat* —8E **96**
Glaisdale Clo. *Sils* —9E **6**
Glaisdale Ct. *All* —3F **56**
Glaisdale Gro. *Hal* —5J **93**
*Glaisdale Ho. B'frd —8G **40***
(off Garsdale Av.)
Glamis Clo. *Gar* —6B **66**
Glanville Ter. *Rothw* —8N **81**
Glass Houghton. —7F 102
Glasshouse St. *Leeds* —9F **62**
Glasshouse Vw. *Leeds* —9D **80**
Glastonbury Av. *Wake* —2A **120**
Glastonbury Dri. *Hud* —5E **130**
Glazier Rd. *Q'bry* —3B **74**
Gleanings Av. *Hal* —5J **91**
Gleanings Dri. *Hal* —5H **91**
Glebe Av. *Leeds* —2L **61**
Glebe Clo. *Eml* —2G **151**
Glebe Fld. Chase. *Weth* —3L **17**
Glebe Fld. Clo. *Weth* —3L **17**
Glebe Fld. Cft. *Weth* —3L **17**
Glebe Fld. Dri. *Weth* —3L **17**
Glebe Fld. Gth. *Weth* —3L **17**
Glebe Fld. Holt. *Weth* —3L **17**
Glebe Fold. *Riddl* —6M **21**
Glebe Ga. *Dew* —1H **135**
Glebelands. *Knot* —8L **105**
Glebelands Clo. *Gar* —8N **65**
Glebelands Dri. *Leeds* —9N **43**
Glebe La. *Knot* —8E **104**
Glebe Mt. *Pud* —8B **60**
Glebe Pl. *Leeds* —2L **61**
Glebe St. *C'frd* —5D **102**
(in two parts)
Glebe St. *Hud* —3K **131**
Glebe St. *Nor* —3K **121**
Glebe St. *Pud* —8B **60**
Glebe Ter. *Leeds* —8N **43**
*Gledcliffe. Hal —4C **92***
(off Charlestown Rd.)
Gleddings Clo. *Hal* —9N **91**
Gledhill Rd. *B'frd* —8F **58**
Gledhill St. *Todm* —6K **87**
*Gledhills Yd. Hal —7M **91***
(off King Cross Rd.)
Gledhill Ter. *Dew* —3C **116**
Gledholt. —3K 131
Gledholt Bank. *Hud* —4K **131**
Gledholt Rd. *Hud* —3K **131**
Gledhow. —8H 45
Gledhow Av. *Leeds* —7H **45**
Gledhow Dri. *Oxe* —2C **54**
Gledhow Grange Vw. *Leeds* —8H **45**
Gledhow Grange Wlk. *Leeds* —8H **45**
Gledhow La. *Leeds* —8F **44**
Gledhow La. End. *Leeds* —8F **44**
Gledhow Mt. *Leeds* —4G **63**
Gledhow Pk. *Leeds* —8G **44**
Gledhow Pk. Dri. *Leeds* —9F **44**
Gledhow Pk. Gro. *Leeds* —9G **44**
Gledhow Pl. *Leeds* —4G **63**
Gledhow Ri. *Leeds* —9K **45**
Gledhow Rd. *Leeds* —4G **63**
Gledhow Ter. *Leeds* —4G **63**
Gledhow Towers. *Leeds* —8G **44**
Gledhow Valley Rd. *Leeds* —7F **44**
Gledhow Wood Av. *Leeds* —8H **45**
Gledhow Wood Clo. *Leeds* —8H **45**
Gledhow Wood Ct. *Leeds* —1J **63**
Gledhow Wood Gro. *Leeds* —8H **45**
Gledhow Wood Rd. *Leeds* —9H **45**
Glenaire. *Shipl* —6C **40**
Glenaire Dri. *Bail* —6M **39**
Glen Av. *Bat* —6F **96**
Glen Av. *Todm* —5H **87**
Glenbrook Dri. *B'frd* —7K **57**
Glencoe Clo. *Kip* —5N **83**
Glencoe Cft. *Kip* —5N **83**
Glencoe Gdns. *Kip* —5N **83**
Glencoe Ter. *Kip* —5N **83**
Glencoe Ter. *Liv* —9M **95**
Glencoe Vw. *Leeds* —8H **63**
Glen Ct. *C'frd* —6A **102**
Glendale. *Bgly* —8E **38**
Glendale. *Horb* —1B **136**
Glendale Av. *Gar* —8N **65**
Glendale Clo. *B'frd* —6M **75**
Glendale Dri. *B'frd* —6M **75**
Glendale Ho. *Morl* —1L **97**
Glendare Av. *B'frd* —8L **57**
Glendare Rd. *B'frd* —8L **57**
Glendare Ter. *B'frd* —8L **57**
Glendene. *Bgly* —8E **38**
Glen Dene. *Men* —5F **24**
Glendorne Dri. *Khtn* —1G **133**
Glendower Pk. *Leeds* —5N **43**
Gleneagles Rd. *F'stne* —2D **122**
Gleneagles Rd. *Leeds* —3D **44**
Gleneagles Way. *Hud* —8L **113**
Glenfield. *Shipl* —6C **40**
Glenfield Av. *B'frd* —5B **76**
Glen Fld. Av. *Hud* —8D **114**
Glenfield Av. *Weth* —5N **17**
Glenfield Cvn. Pk. *Leeds* —7B **30**
Glenfield Mt. *B'frd* —5B **76**
Glenfields. *Neth* —5N **135**
Glenfields Clo. *Neth* —5N **135**
Glen Gth. *Kei* —2K **37**
Glen Gro. *Morl* —1L **97**
Glenholme. *Shipl* —6C **40**
Glenholme Heath. *Hal* —5L **91**
Glenholme Rd. *B'frd* —5N **57**
Glenholme Rd. *Fars* —4N **59**
Glenholme Ter. *Oss* —2M **117**
Glenholm Rd. *Bail* —5A **40**
Glenhurst. *B'frd* —4H **77**
Glenhurst Av. *Kei* —2J **37**
Glenhurst Dri. *Kei* —2K **37**
Glenhurst Gro. *Kei* —2K **37**
Glenhurst Rd. *Shipl* —7K **39**
Glenlea Clo. *S'ley* —3D **60**
Glenlea Gdns. *S'ley* —3D **60**
Glen Lee La. *Kei* —3K **37**
Glenlee Rd. *B'frd* —7L **57**
Glenlow Rd. *Dew* —9J **97**
Glenlyon Av. *Kei* —7G **20**
Glenlyon Dri. *Kei* —7G **21**
Glenmere Mt. *Yead* —9A **26**
Glenmore Clo. *B'frd* —5G **58**
Glenmore Ct. *B'hpe* —5H **27**
Glenmount. *Bgly* —8E **38**
Glen Mt. *Men* —5F **24**
Glen Mt. *Morl* —1L **97**
Glen Mt. Clo. *Hal* —2L **91**
Glenn Way. *Croft* —2H **139**
Glen Ri. *Bail* —5L **39**
Glen Rd. *Bail* —3J **39**
Glen Rd. *Bgly* —2H **39**
Glen Rd. *Leeds* —8M **43**
Glen Rd. *Morl* —1M **97**
Glenrose Dri. *B'frd* —8K **57**
Glenroyd. *Shipl* —6C **40**
Glenroyd Av. *B'frd* —5B **76**
Glenroyd Clo. *Pud* —7N **59**
Glensdale Gro. *Leeds* —7H **63**
Glensdale Mt. *Leeds* —7H **63**
Glensdale Rd. *Leeds* —7H **63**
Glensdale St. *Leeds* —7H **63**
Glensdale Ter. *Leeds* —7H **63**
Glenside Av. *Shipl* —6C **40**
Glenside Clo. *Hud* —2J **131**
Glenside Rd. *Shipl* —6C **40**
Glen Side Rd. *Slai* —1N **145**
Glenstone Gro. *B'frd* —7L **57**
Glen Ter. *Hal* —7A **92**
Glen Ter. *Hip* —5H **93**
Glenthorpe Av. *Leeds* —6J **63**
Glenthorpe Cres. *Leeds* —6J **63**
Glenthorpe Ter. *Leeds* —6J **63**
Glenton Sq. *B'frd* —4N **57**
Glen Vw. *Hal* —7A **92**
Glen Vw. *H'den* —6A **38**
Glenview Av. *B'frd* —3K **57**
Glenview Clo. *Shipl* —8H **39**
Glenview Dri. *Shipl* —9H **39**
(in two parts)
Glenview Gro. *Shipl* —8J **39**
Glen Vw. Rd. *Bgly* —2H **39**
Glenview Rd. *H Bri* —1F **88**
Glen Vw. Rd. *Shel* —7L **149**
Glenview Rd. *Shipl* —9H **39**
Glen Vw. St. *Todm* —3E **86**
Glenview Ter. *Shipl* —7L **39**
Glen Way. *Eld* —2J **39**
(nr. Glen Rd.)
Glen Way. *Eld* —1H **39**
(nr. Otley Rd.)
Glenwood Av. *Bail* —5K **39**
Global Av. *Leeds* —4A **80**
Globe Ct. *Liv* —8M **95**
Globe Fold. *B'frd* —6A **58**
Globe Rd. *Leeds* —7C **62**
*Glossop Gro. Leeds —2D **62***
(off Glossop Vw.)
Glossop Mt. *Leeds* —2D **62**
Glossop St. *Leeds* —2D **62**
Glossop Vw. *Leeds* —2D **62**
Gloucester Av. *B'frd* —5H **59**
Gloucester Av. *Sils* —8C **6**
Gloucester Ct. *Wren* —9H **99**
Gloucester Gro. *Wake* —6F **118**
Gloucester Pl. *Wake* —6F **118**
Gloucester Rd. *Bgly* —5G **38**
Gloucester Rd. *Wake* —6F **118**
Gloucester Ter. *Leeds* —7A **62**
Glover Ct. *B'frd* —1C **76**
Glovershaw La. *Bgly* —1K **39**
Glover Way. *Leeds* —3E **80**
Glydegate. *B'frd* —8C **58**
Glyndon Ct. *Brigh* —3N **113**
Glynn Ter. *B'frd* —6N **57**
Gobind Marg. *B'frd* —7E **58**
Godfrey Rd. *Hal* —1B **112**
Godfrey St. *B'frd* —7J **57**
Godley Branch Rd. *Hal* —4D **92**
Godley Clo. *Roys* —5E **154**

odley Gdns. Hal —3E 92
odley La. Hal —4D 92
odley Rd. Hal —4C 92
odley St. Roys —5E 154
odly Clo. Rish —1C 128
odwin St. B'frd —7C 58
off Well La. Kei —4J 37
og Hill. Ell —4E 112
oit Side. B'frd —7B 58
(in two parts)
oit Stock La. H'den —7A 38
oit Stock Ter. H'den —7A 38
olcar. —6C 130
olcar Brow. —7B 146
olcar Brow Rd. Mel —7B 146
oldcrest Av. B'frd —7G 57
oldcrest Ct. Neth —2K 147
olden Acre Park. —8L 27
olden Bank. H'fth —6F 42
olden Butts Rd. I'ly —5H 9
olden Sq. Horb —1D 136
olden Ter. Leeds —1K 79
olden Vw. Dri. Kei —1M 37
oldfields Av. G'ind —3A 112
oldfields Clo. G'ind —3A 112
oldfields Vw. G'ind —3A 112
oldfields Way. G'ind —3A 112
oldington Av. Hud —1E 130
oldington Dri. Hud —2F 130
olf Av. Hal —5J 91
olf Cres. Hal —5J 91
olf La. Morl —3H 97
omersal. —4N 95
omersal Hill Top. —4M 95
omersal La. Cleck —5K 95
omersal Rd. Heck —6N 95
ondal Ct. B'frd —2A 76
ooder Av. Roys —6D 154
ooder La. Brigh —2M 113
ooder St. Brigh —1M 113
ood Hope Clo. Nor I —9L 101
oodley. —5B 36
oodman St. Leeds —9G 62
oodrick La. Leeds —1D 44
oods La. Dew —4G 117
oodwin Ho. Q'bry —4D 74
(off Minstrel Dri.)
oodwin Pl. Hud —6D 114
oodwin Rd. Leeds —8M 61
oodwood. I'ly —3E 8
oodwood Av. Kip —3N 83
oody Cross. —3L 83
oody Cross La. Swil —3J 83
oody Cross Va. Swil —3J 83
oose Cote La. Oakw —4E 36
oose Eye. —1B 36
oose Eye. Oakw —1B 36
oose Eye Brow. Oakw —1B 36
oosefield Ri. Gar —9L 65
oose Grn. H'rth —4M 163
oose Hill. —3F 76
(nr. East Bowling)
oosehill. —3F 120
(nr. Normanton)
oose Hill. Heck —8A 96
oosehill La. Warm —3F 120
oosehill Rd. Nor —3H 121
oosehole La. S Elm —8A 158
oose La. Guis —6N 23
oose Nest La. Norl —1H 111
oose Pond La. Norl —2L 111
ordale Clo. Bat —7E 96
ordale Clo. B'frd —2K 77
ordon Av. Oss —5N 117
ordon Dri. Leeds —9A 44
ordon Larkin Ct. Otley —1J 25
ordon Pl. Leeds —9B 44
ordon Pl. S Elm —7M 157
(in four parts)
ordonsfield. Ackw —5F 140
ordon St. B'twn —2A 92
ordon St. B'frd —9D 58
ordon St. Cytn —1G 75
ordon St. Cro R —7E 36
ordon St. E Ard —4G 98
ordon St. Ell —5E 112
ordon St. F'stne —4D 122
ordon St. I'ly —5H 9
ordon St. Kei —9H 21
ordon St. Slai —1N 145
ordon St. Sower B —9G 91
ordon St. Todm —7L 87
ordon St. Wake —9A 120
ordon Ter. B'frd —6F 40
ordon Ter. Knot —9G 104
ordon Ter. Leeds —9B 44
ordon Ter. Lint —8C 130
ordon Vw. Leeds —9B 44
oring Pk. Av. Oss —7C 118
orse Av. Bail —6K 39
orse La. S Mil —9N 67
orse Lea. Leeds —5F 80
orse Rd. Hud —4H 131
Gorton St. Kin —9B 140
Gosling La. Bklnd —9F 110
Gosport Clo. Hud —2N 129
Gosport La. Outl —2N 129
Gosport La. Sow —1M 129
Gosside Gro. Norm —2L 121
Gothic Mt. Ack —3A 122
Gothic St. Q'bry —4D 74
Gotts Pk. Av. Leeds —5J 61
Gotts Pk. Cres. Leeds —5J 61
Gotts Pk. Vw. Leeds —4J 61
Gotts Rd. Leeds —7B 62
Gotts Ter. Kei —6G 21
Gott St. Cro R —7F 36
Gough La. Sower B —4B 110
Goulbourne St. Kei —1H 37
Governor's Yd. Wake —4M 119
Gower St. B'frd —1C 76
Gower St. Leeds —6F 62
Goy Cres. Slnd —8M 111
Goy Fld. Lwr W —1K 79
Goy Gth. B Spa —9C 18
Goy La. Steet —3C 20
Goy Rd. Ell —5E 112
Goy Ter. Leeds —9A 44
Gracechurch St. B'frd —6B 58
Grace Leather La. Bat —7H 97
Grace St. Kei —9K 21
Grace St. Leeds —6C 62
Gracey La. B'frd —4L 75
Grafton Clo. Bail —3B 40
Grafton Clo. Knot —7E 104
Grafton Pl. Hal —1N 91
Grafton Rd. Kei —2G 36
Grafton St. Bat —9G 96
Grafton St. B'frd —9C 58
Grafton St. C'frd —7E 102
Grafton St. Kei —2H 37
Grafton St. Leeds —5E 62
Grafton Vs. Leeds —2E 64
Graham Av. Leeds —3N 61
Graham Av. Upt —1C 158
Graham Dri. C'frd —5H 103
Graham Gro. Leeds —3N 61
Graham Ho. Leeds —3J 61
(off Broad La.)
Graham Mt. Leeds —3N 61
Graham St. B'frd —4M 57
Graham St. Leeds —3N 61
Graham Ter. Leeds —3N 61
Graham Vw. Leeds —3N 61
Graham Wlk. Gild —6G 78
Grain St. B'frd —3N 75
Gramfield Rd. Hud —7G 131
Grammar School Pl. Brigh —3L 113
(off Church St.)
Grammar School St. B'frd —6C 58
Grampian Av. Wake —8G 118
Grampian Clo. Shel —6K 149
Granary Ct. B'frd —1G 59
Granary Wharf. Leeds —7D 62
Granby Av. Leeds —1N 61
Granby Clo. Leeds —2N 61
(off St Michael's Rd.)
Granby Ct. S Elm —4N 157
Granby Dri. Riddl —7M 21
Granby Gro. Leeds —2N 61
Granby La. Kei —7M 21
Granby Mt. Leeds —1N 61
Granby Pl. Leeds —1N 61
Granby Rd. Leeds —2N 61
Granby St. B'frd —9D 58
(in two parts)
Granby St. Leeds —1N 61
Granby St. Q'bry —4D 74
Granby Ter. Leeds —1N 61
Granby Vw. Leeds —1N 61
Grandage Ter. B'frd —6N 57
Grand Arc. Leeds —6E 62
(off New Briggate)
Grand Cross Rd. Hud —4C 132
Grandsmere Pl. Hal —8A 92
Grand Stand. Gol —5A 130
Grandstand Rd. Wren & Loft —7G 99
Grand Theatre. —6E 62
Grand Vw. Hal —3N 91
(off Ovenden Av.)
Grand Vw. Q'bry —2B 74
Grand Vw. Sower B —9H 91
(off Clyde St.)
Grand Vw. Sower B —4D 110
(off Lumb La.)
Grange Av. All —6H 57
Grange Av. Bat —9E 96
Grange Av. B'frd —6K 59
(BD3)
Grange Av. B'frd —5L 77
(BD4)
Grange Av. Gar —7N 65
Grange Av. Hal —8M 73
Grange Av. Hud —1L 131
Grange Av. I'ly —5J 9
Grange Av. Leeds —2G 62
Grange Av. Mars —5G 144
Grange Av. Men —3D 24
Grange Av. Shipl —7K 39
Grange Av. S Elm —6N 157
Grange Av. Thor A —6G 18
Grange Av. Yead —1N 41
Grange Bank. She —7G 75
Grange Bank Clo. Hud —3B 132
Grange Clo. Bads —8L 141
Grange Clo. Bard —4E 30
Grange Clo. Brier —6N 155
Grange Clo. H'fth —7C 42
Grange Clo. H'let —1F 80
Grange Clo. I'ly —5J 9
Grange Clo. Knot —8C 104
Grange Clo. Outl —2N 129
Grange Cotts. Mars —5G 144
Grange Ct. Bads —8L 141
Grange Ct. Bgly —8F 38
Grange Ct. Hal —9F 92
Grange Ct. Leeds —1B 62
(nr. N. Grange Mt.)
Grange Ct. Leeds —2E 44
(nr. Primley Pk. Rd.)
Grange Ct. Scholes —9G 47
Grange Cres. Leeds —2G 62
Grange Cres. Riddl —7L 21
Grange Cres. Yead —1N 41
Grange Cft. Leeds —2E 44
Grange Dri. All —6H 57
Grange Dri. Eml —1G 150
Grange Dri. H'fth —7C 42
Grange Dri. Oss —8B 118
Grange Est. I'ly —5J 9
Grangefield Av. Bat —8E 96
Grangefield Av. Bur W —8D 10
Grangefield Ct. Gar —7N 65
Grangefield Ind. Est. S'ley —5B 60
Grangefield Rd. S'ley —4B 60
(in three parts)
Grange Fields Mt. Leeds —6H 81
Grange Fields Rd. Leeds —7H 81
Grange Fields Way. Leeds —7H 81
Grange Fold. All —6G 57
Grange Gro. B'frd —6K 59
Grange Gro. Riddl —7L 21
Grange Heights. Hal —9F 92
Grange Holt. Leeds —2E 44
Grange Ho. Brier —6N 155
Grange La. Brigh —1C 114
Grange La. Burg —6L 159
Grange La. Floc —6G 134
Grange La. Kild —8A 6
Grange La. Kip —3B 84
Grange La. Kbtn —6H 149
Grange La. Oakw —4M 35
Grange Moor. —5B 134
Grange Mt. Yead —1N 41
Grange Pk. Bail —4C 40
Grange Pk. Hal —9A 92
Grange Pk. Av. Leeds —1M 63
Grange Pk. Clo. All B —8A 84
Grange Pk. Clo. Leeds —1N 63
Grange Pk. Clo. Morl —6L 79
Grange Pk. Cres. Leeds —1M 63
Grange Pk. Dri. Bgly —7F 38
Grange Pk. Dri. Morl —6L 79
Grange Pk. Gro. Leeds —1M 63
Grange Pk. M. Leeds —1M 63
Grange Pk. M. Morl —6L 79
Grange Pk. Pl. Leeds —1M 63
Grange Pk. Ri. Leeds —1M 63
Grange Pk. Rd. Bgly —7F 38
Grange Pk. Rd. Leeds —1M 63
Grange Pk. Ter. Leeds —1N 63
Grange Pk. Wlk. Leeds —1M 63
Grange Pk. Way. Morl —6L 79
Granger Ct. Hal —4L 91
Granger Gdns. Kei —1G 36
Grange Ri. Hems —2D 156
Grange Rd. All —6H 57
Grange Rd. Bat & Dew —8H 97
(in two parts)
Grange Rd. Bgly —3G 38
Grange Rd. Brier —6N 155
Grange Rd. Bur W —8D 10
Grange Rd. C'frd —3L 103
Grange Rd. Cleck —4G 95
Grange Rd. Ebrn —3A 20
Grange Rd. Gol —4D 130
Grange Rd. H'let —1F 80
Grange Rd. Riddl —7L 21
Grange Rd. Roys —6B 154
Grange Rd. Stainc —9D 96
Grange Rd. W'wth —9A 106
Grange Rd. Yead —1N 41
Grange Rd., The. Leeds —6L 43
Grange St. Chur —5M 79
Grange St. Hal —3N 91
Grange St. Kei —8J 21
Grange St. Wake —6J 119
Grange Ter. All —6H 57
Grange Ter. Ebrn —3A 20
Grange Ter. Leeds —2F 62
Grange Ter. Mars —4G 144
Grange Ter. Morl —6L 79
Grange Ter. Pud —6B 60
Grange Ter. Shipl —9N 39
Grange Ter. Yead —1N 41
(off Grange Rd.)
Grange, The. Gar —7B 66
Grange, The. Hal —9A 92
Grange Vw. B'frd —6K 59
Grange Vw. Colt —8E 64
Grange Vw. Dew —1G 134
Grange Vw. Ebrn —3A 20
Grange Vw. Hems —3D 156
Grange Vw. Leeds —2G 62
Grange Vw. Otley —8K 11
Grange Vw. Pud —6B 60
Grange Vw. Weth —5M 17
Grange Vw. Gdns. Leeds —6A 46
Grange Way. All —6H 57
Grangeway. Hems —2D 156
Grangewood Ct. Leeds —6L 43
Grangewood Ct. Out —7M 99
Grangewood Gdns. Leeds —6L 43
Grange Yd. Sower B —8J 91
(off Wharf St.)
Granhamthorpe. Leeds —4F 60
Granny Av. Chur —5M 79
Granny Hall Gro. Brigh —8L 93
Granny Hall La. Brigh —8L 93
Granny Hall Pk. Brigh —8L 93
Granny Hill. Hal —7L 91
Granny La. Leeds —9K 61
Granny La. Mir —8L 115
Granny Pl. Chur —5M 79
Grant Av. Leeds —4G 62
Grantham Pl. B'frd —9A 58
Grantham Pl. Hal —2A 92
Grantham Rd. B'frd —9A 58
Grantham Rd. Hal —2A 92
Grantham Ter. B'frd —9A 58
Grantham Towers. Leeds —5G 63
(off Lindsey Gdns.)
Grantley Pl. Hud —6B 114
Grantley St. Wake —4M 119
Grantley Way. Wake —4M 119
Granton Rd. Leeds —1F 62
Granton St. B'frd —7G 59
Grant St. B'frd —7E 58
Grant St. Kei —9G 20
Grant St. Oxe —4C 54
Granville Av. Pon —3J 123
Granville Mt. Otley —1K 25
Granville Pl. All —5G 57
Granville Pl. Otley —1K 25
Granville Rd. Leeds —5G 63
Granville Rd. Shipl & B'frd —1N 57
Granville St. C'frd —7C 102
Granville St. Cytn —9H 57
Granville St. Dew —3F 116
Granville St. Ell —5E 112
Granville St. F'stne —7C 122
Granville St. Kei —9H 21
(off Drewery Rd.)
Granville St. Liv —9M 95
Granville St. Nor —1J 121
Granville St. Pud —6N 59
Granville St. S'ley —4C 60
Granville St. Todm —2J 107
Granville Ter. Bgly —4F 38
Granville Ter. Guis —6K 25
(off Moor La.)
Granville Ter. Hud —5K 131
Granville Ter. Otley —1K 25
Granville Ter. Shipl —1N 57
Granville Ter. Yead —9N 25
Grape St. All —5H 57
Grape St. Hal —5A 92
Grape St. Kei —8L 21
Grape St. Leeds —9F 62
Grasleigh Av. All —4F 56
Grasleigh Way. All —4E 56
Grasmere Av. Weth —4K 17
Grasmere Clo. C'frd —3L 103
Grasmere Clo. Leeds —8N 61
Grasmere Ct. Leeds —7N 61
Grasmere Cres. Dart —7J 153
Grasmere Dri. Ell —4G 112
Grasmere Dri. Weth —4K 17
Grasmere Pl. Hal —9N 73
Grasmere Rd. B'frd —3E 58
Grasmere Rd. Carc —8N 159
Grasmere Rd. Dew —1H 117
Grasmere Rd. Hud —3K 131
Grasmere Rd. Knot —1D 124
Grasmere Rd. Leeds —8N 61
Grasmere Rd. Mel —8D 146
Grasmere Rd. Wake —4G 118
Grasmere Rd. Wyke —3C 94
Grasscroft. Hud —8D 132
Grasscroft Av. Hon —5K 147
Grasscroft Rd. Hon —5K 147
Grasscroft Rd. Hud —3K 131
Grassmoor Fold. Hon —6M 147
Grass Rd. Riddl —5B 22
Gratrix La. Sower B —7J 91
Grattan Rd. B'frd —7B 58
Graveleythorpe. —5B 64
Graveleythorpe Ri. Leeds —5C 64
Graveleythorpe Rd. Leeds —5C 64
Gravelly Hill La. Wee —6K 13
Gray Av. Shipl —1B 58
Gray Ct. Leeds —6E 64
Grayrigg Clo. Leeds —7N 63
Grayshon Dri. Wibs —4A 76
Grayshon St. Dlgtn —8C 78
Grayson Crest. Leeds —3L 61
Grayson Heights. Leeds —3L 61
Gray's Rd. Barn —8D 154
Gray St. Liv —8J 95
Grayswood Cres. B'frd —2H 77
Grayswood Dri. B'frd —1H 77
Gt. Albion St. Hal —5B 92
Great Ben La. Slai —6L 129
Great Cliff. —6E 136
Gt. Cross St. B'frd —8D 58
Gt. Edge Rd. Hal —5F 90
Greatfield Clo. Oss —5A 118
Greatfield Dri. Oss —5A 118
Greatfield Gdns. Oss —6A 118
Greatfield Rd. Oss —6A 118
Gt. George St. Leeds —6D 62
Great Horton. —1M 75
Gt. Horton Rd. B'frd —3J 75
Gt. House La. Sower B —8A 110
Gt. House Rd. Todm —4N 87
Gt. Northern Rd. Kei —1J 37
Gt. Northern St. Hud —3N 131
Gt. Northern St. Morl —1K 97
Gt. North Rd. B Spa —8N 17
Gt. North Rd. D'ton —7C 124
Gt. North Rd. Fair —8N 85
Gt. North Rd. Knot —9B 104
Gt. North Rd. M'fld —5F 66
Gt. North Rd. Skel —3J 159
(in two parts)
Gt. North Rd. Went —1C 142
Gt. Pasture. Bur W —7D 10
Gt. Pond St. Dew —6C 116
Great Preston. —5M 83
Gt. Russell Ct. Field B —7A 58
Gt. Russell St. B'frd —7N 57
Gt. Wilson St. Leeds —8E 62
Gt. Wood St. Bat —8F 96
Greave Clo. Hud —7N 113
Greavefield La. Pon —3N 123
Greave Ho. Dri. L'ft —5D 90
Greave Ho. Fields. L'ft —4E 90
Greave Ho. La. Lep —7H 133
Greave Ho. Pk. L'ft —5D 90
Greave Ho. Ter. Lep —7H 133
Greave Rd. H'rth —8M 163
Greave Rd. Sower B —5M 109
Greaves Av. Wake —6E 118
Greaves Cft. Lep —7H 133
Greaves Fold. Holy G —7B 112
Greaves Rd. Dew —2F 116
Greaves St. B'frd —2B 76
Greaves St. C'frd —4D 102
Greave St. Todm —7M 87
Greaves Yd. Pud —9B 60
Greek St. C'frd —4E 102
Greek St. Leeds —6D 62
Green Abbey. H'rth —9N 163
Greenacre Av. Wyke —2B 94
Grn. Acre Clo. Bail —4B 40
Greenacre Clo. Wyke —2B 94
Greenacre Ct. Gar —7A 66
Greenacre Dri. Up Den —5B 166
Greenacre Dri. Wyke —2B 94
Greenacre Pk. Rawd —2M 41
Greenacre Pk. Av. Rawd —2M 41
Greenacre Pk. M. Rawd —2N 41
Greenacre Pk. Ri. Rawd —2M 41
Greenacre Rd. Upt —1B 158
Green Acres. Dur —3J 137
Green Acres. F'stne —8E 122
Greenacres. Oss —2N 117
Greenacres. She —7J 75
Greenacres. Sower B —7E 110
Greenacres Av. Hal —7J 75
Grn. Acres Clo. Eml —3F 150
Greenacres Clo. Oss —2N 117
Greenacres Ct. C'frd —4G 102
Greenacres Dri. Birs —2D 96
Greenacres Dri. C'frd —4G 102
Greenacres Dri. Hal —7J 75
Greenacres Dri. Kei —7G 20
Greenacres Gro. Hal —7J 75
Greenacre Wlk. H'cft —8L 139
Greenacre Way. Wyke —2B 94
Greenaire Pl. B'frd —7B 58
Green Av. Heck —8B 96
Green Av. Kip —2N 83
Green Av. Sils —7D 6

Grn. Balk La. Lep —7K 133
Greenbank. Bail —6N 39
Green Bank. Barn —8A 154
Green Bank. Cleck —6K 95
Green Bank. Loft —3M 99
Greenbank Clo. C'frd —7A 102
Greenbank Gro. Nor —9G 100
Greenbank Rd. All —6H 57
Greenbank Rd. Nor —9G 100
Greenbanks Av. H'fth —5F 42
Greenbanks Clo. H'fth —5F 42
Greenbanks Dri. H'fth —5E 42
Greenbank Wlk. Grime —9N 155
Greenbottom. —8J 25
Green Chase. Leeds —8A 44
Green Cliff. Hon —4L 147
Greencliffe Av. Bail —4N 39
Green Clo. Bat —7H 97
Green Clo. B'frd —6K 57
Green Clo. Dew —1D 116
Green Clo. Ebrn —2A 20
Green Clo. Leeds —8B 44
Green Ct. B'frd —9L 57
Green Ct. Leeds —5F 44
Green Ct. Schol —4D 94
Green Ct. Scholes —8G 46
Green Cres. Gol —5D 130
Green Cres. Leeds —8A 44
Greencroft. Kin —8B 140
Greencroft Av. Hal —1G 92
Greendale Ct. Hon —4L 147
Greendown Clo. I'ly —5J 9
Green End. —7D 22
Green End. Brigh —2M 113
Green End. Cytn —1G 75
Grn. End La. Wake —8K 119
Grn. End Rd. B'frd —5N 75
Grn. End Rd. E Mor —7D 22
Greenfell Clo. Kei —1F 36
Green Fld. Bail —5N 39
Greenfield. Haw —8C 36
Greenfield Av. Gild —6E 78
Greenfield Av. Guis —9F 24
Greenfield Av. Hal —5M 93
Greenfield Av. Hud —2F 130
Greenfield Av. Kip —3A 84
Greenfield Av. Oss —7C 118
Greenfield Av. Shipl —9A 40
Greenfield Clo. Kip —3A 84
Greenfield Clo. N'wram —1F 92
Greenfield Clo. Oss —7C 118
Greenfield Clo. Sow —9M 111
Greenfield Clo. Up Den —5C 166
Greenfield Clo. Wren —1H 119
Greenfield Cotts. Barn —9D 154
Greenfield Ct. Kei —9G 21
Greenfield Cres. Cull —9L 37
Greenfield Dri. Gild —6E 78
Greenfield Dri. Schol —4D 94
(off New Rd. E.)
Greenfield Gdns. Barn —8N 153
Greenfield Gth. Kip —3A 84
Greenfield La. Bier —7F 76
Greenfield La. Gt Hor —1L 75
Greenfield La. Guis —9E 24
Greenfield La. Idle —6F 40
Greenfield Mt. Wren —1H 119
Greenfield Pl. B'frd —5A 58
Greenfield Pl. Hal —5M 93
Greenfield Ri. Kip —3A 84
Greenfield Rd. Hems —4D 156
Greenfield Rd. H'frth —3F 162
Greenfield Rd. Leeds —7G 63
Greenfield Rd. Nor —1G 121
Greenfield Rd. Oss —7C 118
Greenfields. Heck —7N 95
Greenfields Way. Bur W —1D 24
Greenfield Ter. Haw —8C 36
Greenfield Ter. Meth —1M 101
Greenfield Ter. Todm —3C 86
Greenfield Va. Kip —3A 84
Greenfield Vw. Kip —3A 84
Greenfield Way. Wren —1H 119
Greenfinch Gro. Neth —3K 147
Greenfinch Way. All —7G 56
Greenfold La. Weth —4N 17
Green Gdns. Gol —5D 130
Greengate. Oult —7D 82
Greengate. Sils —7D 6
Green Ga. La. Slai —4N 145
Grn. Gate Rd. H'frth —4F 162
Greengate Rd. Kei —1J 37
Greengate Rd. K S'ton —8L 143
Greengates. —9H 41
Greengates Av. Wyke —3A 94
Green Hall Pk. She —8J 75
Greenhead Av. Hud —5D 132
Green Head Av. Kei —6G 20
Greenhead Ct. Hud —3K 131
Green Head Dri. Kei —6G 20
Greenhead La. Brigh —5K 113
Greenhead La. Hud —5D 132
Grn. Head La. Kei —6G 20
Greenhead Rd. Hud —4K 131
Grn. Head Rd. Kei —6G 21
Greenhead Rd. Leeds —7L 43
Green Hill. —7E 48
(nr. Aberford)
Green Hill. —2D 156
(nr. Hemsworth)
Green Hill. Hud —7N 113
Green Hill. Warley —6H 91
Greenhill Av. Pon —5L 123
Greenhill Bank Rd. N Mill —3B 164
Grn. Hill Chase. Leeds —8L 61
Grn. Hill Clo. Leeds —5J 61
Grn. Hill Cres. Leeds —8L 61
Grn. Hill Cft. Leeds —8L 61
Greenhill Dri. Bgly —9D 22
Grn. Hill Dri. Leeds —5H 61
Grn. Hill Gdns. Leeds —8L 61
Grn. Hill Holt. Leeds —8L 61
Greenhill La. Bgly —1E 38
Greenhill La. B'frd —7G 59
Grn. Hill La. Leeds —9K 61
Grn. Hill Mt. Leeds —5H 61
Greenhill Mt. Pon —5L 123
Grn. Hill Pk. Hal —5J 75
Grn. Hill Pl. Leeds —5H 61
Greenhill Rd. Hud —3D 130
Grn. Hill Rd. Leeds —5H 61
Greenhill Rd. Wake —4M 119
Greenhills. Rawd —4N 41
Greenhill St. B'frd —7G 59
Grn. Hill Way. Leeds —5H 61
Greenholme Clo. Bur W —7D 10
Greenholme Ct. B'frd —3K 77
Greenholme Trad. Est. Bur W —7D 10
Green Ho. Hill. Shel —5N 149
Green Ho. La. H'frth —8G 163
Green Ho. La. Shel —5N 149
Greenhouse Rd. Hud —9M 113
Greenhow Clo. Leeds —4N 61
Greenhow Gdns. Leeds —4N 61
Greenhow Pk. Bur W —8B 10
Greenhow Rd. Leeds —4N 61
Greenhow Wlk. Leeds —4N 61
Greenland Av. Q'bry —5D 74
Greenland Rd. C'den —7K 69
Greenland Vs. Q'bry —5D 74
Green La. Ackw —4D 140
Green La. Add —9L 5
Green La. Bail —6M 39
(in two parts)
Green La. B Top —6D 92
Green La. Bklnd —2F 128
Green La. Bees —4B 80
Green La. Birk —4L 105
Green La. B Spa —1E 32
Green La. B'frd —9M 57
(BD7)
Green La. B'frd —5A 58
(BD8)
Green La. Bshw —5L 73
Green La. Brigh —7K 93
Green La. Bur W —6C 10
(nr. Leather Bank)
Green La. Bur W —2N 23
(nr. Moor Rd.)
Green La. C'ton —6L 123
(in two parts)
Green La. C'frd —3F 102
Green La. Clif —1C 114
Green La. Coll —9H 17
Green La. Cook —3G 42
Green La. Cuts —7C 102
Green La. Den D —6M 165
Green La. Dew —2D 116
Green La. Ebrn —2A 20
Green La. Fag —3H 59
Green La. F'ley —9F 60
Green La. F'stne —5C 122
Green La. Gar —7A 66
(nr. Ninelands La.)
Green La. Gar —8B 66
(nr. Severn Dri.)
Green La. G'lnd —5B 112
Green La. Hal —7L 91
(HX2)
Green La. Hal —6J 75
(HX3)
Green La. H'frth —6M 163
Green La. Horb —2E 136
Green La. H'fth —8E 42
Green La. Huns —2H 95
Green La. Idle —7G 41
(nr. Apperley St.)
Green La. Idle —8E 40
(nr. Highfield Rd.)
Green La. Kip —2N 83
(in two parts)
Green La. K'thpe —5D 120
Green La. Leds —7D 84
Green La. Leeds —5C 64
Green La. Liv —9H 95
Green La. Loft —3L 99
Green La. L'ft —3D 90
Green La. Mars —1H 145
Green La. Mel —8D 146
Green La. Meth —3N 101
Green La. Neth —5A 136
Green La. N Wort —8A 62
Green La. N'wram —8D 74
Green La. Not —4B 154
Green La. Oaken —9D 76
Green La. Oakw —5D 36
(nr. Keighley Rd.)
Green La. Oakw —3N 35
(nr. Whithill Rd.)
Green La. Old Sn —5A 122
Green La. Otley —8K 11
Green La. Ove —4J 135
Green La. Oxe —4M 53
(nr. Bodkin La.)
Green La. Oxe —6D 54
(nr. Isle La.)
Green La. Pon —4K 123
Green La. Pud —8A 60
Green La. Q'bry —7D 74
Green La. Ragg —3A 74
Green La. Ryl —1E 4
Green La. She —7J 75
(in two parts)
Green La. Shipl —3M 39
Green La. Silk —9M 167
Green La. Sils —3A 6
Green La. Skel —6K 159
Green La. Slai —1K 145
Green La. S Kirk —7H 157
Green La. Sower B —2C 110
(nr. Bowood La.)
Green La. Sower B —8B 110
(nr. Ripponden Old La.)
Green La. Sow —1M 129
Green La. T'tn —9D 56
Green La. Thpe A —5B 142
Green La. Upt —9B 142
Green La. Wake —3G 118
Green La. Wee —5D 14
Green La. Whinm —7B 46
Green La. Wyke —2N 93
Green La. Yead —2M 41
Green La. Bus. Pk. F'stne —5C 122
Green La. Clo. Ove —3K 135
Green La. Ter. Gol —4B 130
Greenlaws Clo. H'frth —3J 163
Greenlay Dri. K'gte —1D 118
Green Lea. Oult —7C 82
Greenlea Av. Yead —1K 41
Green Lea Clo. B Spa —1E 32
Greenlea Clo. Yead —2K 41
Greenlea Fold. Yead —2K 41
Greenlea Mt. Yead —1K 41
Grn. Lea Rd. Hud —4D 132
Greenlea Rd. Yead —1K 41
Greenley Hill. Wilsd —2A 56
Green Mdw. Wilsd —2C 56
Greenmires La. Stainb —1G 13
Greenmoor Av. Leeds —7G 60
Greenmoor Av. Loft —3L 99
Greenmoor Clo. Loft —3L 99
Greenmoor Cres. Loft —3M 99
Green Mt. Bail —5M 39
Green Mt. Cut H —2H 77
Green Mt. Hud —5B 132
Greenmount Ct. Leeds —2D 80
(off Fulham St.)
Greenmount La. Leeds —2D 80
Greenmount Pl. Leeds —2D 80
Greenmount Retail Pk. Hal —5A 92
Green Mt. Rd. T'tn —8D 56
Greenmount St. Leeds —2D 80
Greenmount Ter. Leeds —2D 80
Greenock Pl. Leeds —6K 61
Greenock Rd. Leeds —6K 61
Greenock St. Leeds —6K 61
Greenock Ter. Leeds —6K 61
Green Pk. Wake —5N 119
Green Pk. Av. Hal —1B 112
Green Pk. Av. Horb —9B 118
Green Pk. Av. Oss —7A 118
Green Pk. Dri. Hal —1B 112
Green Pk. Ga. Hal —1B 112
Green Pk. Rd. Hal —1B 112
Green Pk. St. Hal —9B 92
Green Pl. B'frd —4F 58
Green Rd. Bail —5M 39
Green Rd. Hept —8F 70
Green Rd. Leeds —7A 44
Green Rd. Liv —7L 95
Green Row. B'frd —9F 40
Green Row. Meth —3L 101
Green Row Fold. Meth —3L 101
Green Royd. G'lnd —5B 112
(in two parts)
Green Royd. Nor G —2M 93
Greenroyd Av. Cleck —2H 95
Greenroyd Av. Hal —9A 92
Greenroyd Clo. Hal —1A 112
Greenroyd Ct. D'ton —6B 124
Greenroyd Cres. Hal —3M 91
Greenroyd Cft. Hud —1K 131
Greenroyd La. Hal —3L 91
Greens End Rd. Mel —7C 146
Greenset Vw. Barn —8N 153
Greenshank M. Morl —9N 79
Greenshaw Ter. Guis —7H 25
Green Side. —7L 57
(nr. Bradford)
Green Side. —5E 148
(nr. Brockholes)
Greenside. —5E 132
(nr. Fenay Bridge)
Greenside. —8K 153
(nr. Staincross)
Greenside. Bail —5N 39
Greenside. Cleck —5J 95
Greenside. Den D —2D 166
Greenside. F'stne —5D 122
Greenside. H'cft —1J 155
Greenside. Heck —8N 95
Greenside. Hoy S —9K 167
Greenside. Lwr C —9B 150
Greenside. M'well —8L 153
Greenside. Oaken —9E 76
Greenside. Pud —8A 60
Greenside. Shaf —5J 155
Greenside. W'ton —3B 138
Greenside Av. Hud —5E 132
Grn. Side Av. Leeds —9L 61
Greenside Av. M'well —8L 153
Greenside Clo. Leeds —9M 61
Greenside Ct. Gild —6G 78
Greenside Ct. New C —3J 139
Greenside Cres. Hud —5E 132
Greenside Dri. Hud —5E 132
Greenside Dri. Leeds —9M 61
Green Side Est. Mir —4L 115
Greenside Gro. Pud —8A 60
Greenside Ho. Dart —8L 153
Greenside La. B'frd —7L 57
Greenside La. Cull —9K 37
Greenside Mt. Mir —4M 115
Greenside Pk. New C —3J 139
Greenside Pl. M'well —8L 153
Green Side Rd. Hud —6D 148
Greenside Rd. Leeds —9M 61
Greenside Rd. Mir —4M 115
Greenside Ter. Dew —1B 116
Grn. Side Ter. Leeds —9L 61
Greenside Wlk. Leeds —9L 61
Grn. Slacks La. Hud —5H 129
Green's Sq. Hal —4L 91
Green's Sq. Kip —4A 84
Green's Ter. Oaken —9D 76
Green St. B'frd —7D 58
Green St. C'frd —3D 102
Green St. Haw —9C 36
Green St. Holy G —7B 112
Green St. Hud —3M 131
Green St. Mel —7C 146
Green St. Oxe —4C 54
Greensway. Gar —7M 65
Grn. Sykes Rd. Lay —8A 20
Green Ter. B'frd —4F 58
Green Ter. Dew —2D 116
Green Ter. Guis —8J 25
Green Ter. Leeds —2E 80
Green Ter. Mir —5K 115
Green Ter. Sq. Hal —8N 91
Green, The. —2A 60
(nr. Farsley)
Green, The. —1C 64
(nr. Seacroft)
Green, The. Bgly —1F 38
(nr. College Rd.)
Green, The. Bgly —4J 39
(nr. Sheriff La.)
Green, The. Birs —2C 96
Green, The. B'frd —7F 40
Green, The. C'frd —4K 103
(in two parts)
Green, The. E Bier —6K 77
Green, The. Eld —1H 39
Green, The. Fars —2A 60
Green, The. F'stne —7E 122
Green, The. Gar —8A 66
Green, The. Gild —6G 78
Green, The. Guis —8J 25
Green, The. H'fth —7E 42
Green, The. Hud —6B 114
Green, The. Kip —4A 84
Green, The. Leeds —2B 64
(in two parts)
Green, The. Mars —5F 144
Green, The. M'wte —9D 22
Green, The. Mir —5J 115
Green, The. Oss —7N 117
Green, The. Otley —8K 11
Green, The. Roys —6D 154
Green, The. Shaf —6J 155
Green, The. Shar C —9K 121
Green, The. S Kirk —6J 157
Green, The. Thur —7D 148
Green, The. Wool —2J 153
Green, The. Wren —9H 99
Greenthorpe Hill. Leeds —7H 61
Greenthorpe Mt. Leeds —6H 61
Greenthorpe Rd. Leeds —6H 61
Greenthorpe St. Leeds —7H 61
Greenthorpe Wlk. Leeds —6H 61
Greenton Av. Schol —3C 94
Greenton Cres. Q'bry —5C 74
Green Top. Leeds —9L 61
Greentop. New C —3J 139
Greentop. Pud —8A 60
Grn. Top Gdns. Leeds —9L 61
Green Top St. B'frd —7K 57
Greentrees. B'frd —7N 75
Greenups Ter. Sower B —8H 91
Green Vw. Leeds —8A 44
Greenview. New C —3J 139
Green Vw. S'cft —8D 30
Greenview Ct. Leeds —7J 45
Green Vw., The. Shaf —5J 155
Greenville Av. Leeds —9L 61
Greenville Dri. Low M —6C 76
Greenville Gdns. Leeds —9L 61
Greenway. B'frd —6E 58
Greenway. Guis —9G 24
Green Way. Hal —5L 73
Greenway. Hon —4L 147
Greenway. Hud —5E 130
Greenway. Leeds —5D 64
Green Way. S'cft —8D 30
Greenway Clo. Leeds —5D 64
Greenway Dri. All —7G 56
Greenway Rd. B'frd —3C 76
Greenwell Ct. Leeds —6L 63
Greenwell Row. Cytn —1G 75
Greenwood Av. B'frd —1E 58
Greenwood Av. Dew —4J 117
Greenwood Av. Upt —1B 158
Greenwood Bldgs. Hud —2H 133
Greenwood Bldgs. Khtn —1G 133
Greenwood Clo. Nor —4J 121
Greenwood Clo. Upt —1B 158
Greenwood Ct. B'frd —8C 58
Greenwood Ct. Leeds —7A 44
Greenwood Cres. Roys —5C 154
Greenwood Dri. B'frd —2E 58
Greenwood Ho. Wake —5L 119
(off George St.)
Greenwood Mt. B'frd —2E 58
Greenwood Mt. Leeds —8A 44
Greenwood Pk. Leeds —8A 44
Greenwood Rd. Bail —6N 39
Greenwood Rd. Ting —4B 98
Greenwood Rd. Wake —4M 119
Greenwood Row. Morl —9L 79
(off Commercial St.)
Greenwood Row. Pud —7C 60
Greenwood's Ter. Hal —3M 91
Greenwood St. Fla —3E 116
Greenwood St. H Bri —1H 89
(off Valley Rd.)
Greenwood St. Hud —6M 131
Greenwood St. Sav T —5F 116
Greetland. —4N 111
Gregory Ct. Cytn —1H 75
Gregory Cres. B'frd —3K 75
Gregory Dri. Kbtn —2K 149
Gregory La. Mir —3L 133
Gregory Rd. C'frd —7E 102
Gregory Springs La. Mir —9L 115
Gregory Springs Mt. Mir —9M 11
Gregory Springs Rd. Mir —9M 1
Gregory St. Bat —7H 97
Grenfell Dri. B'frd —6H 59
Grenfell Rd. B'frd —6H 59
Grenfell Ter. B'frd —6H 59
Grenley St. Knot —8F 104
Grenville Wlk. Hall G —7H 137
Gresham Av. B'frd —2D 58
Gresley Ho. H'fth —4F 42
(off Sussex Av.)
Gresley Rd. Kei —9J 21
Grey Clo. Wake —9K 99
Grey Ct. Wake —9K 99
Greycourt Clo. B'frd —9E 40
Greycourt Clo. Hal —6N 91
Greycourt Ho. Hal —6N 91
(off King Cross Rd.)
Greyfriars Av. Hud —7C 114
Greyfriar Wlk. B'frd —2K 75
Grey Gables. Neth —4A 136
Grey Hall Clo. Slnd —8M 111
Greyhound Dri. B'frd —8N 57
Grey Scar Rd. Oakw —5A 36
Greyshiels Av. Leeds —2M 61
Greyshiels Clo. Leeds —2M 61
Greystone Av. Ell —6D 112
Greystone Clo. B Spa —1E 32
Greystone Clo. Bur W —7C 10

Greystone Ct. *Brigh* —4M **113**
Greystone Cres. *B'frd* —9G **40**
Grey Stone La. *Todm* —4A **88**
Greystone Mt. *Leeds* —7N **63**
Greystone Pk. *Aber* —6E **48**
Greystones Clo. *Aber* —6E **48**
Greystones Ct. *Leeds* —3E **44**
Greystones Dri. *Kei* —5F **36**
Greystones Dri. *Oss* —8A **118**
Greystones La. *Lay* —1K **35**
Grey Stones La. *Pec W* —9H **53**
Greystones Mt. *Kei* —5F **36**
Greystones Ri. *Kei* —4F **36**
Grey St. *Wake* —9K **99**
Griffe Dri. *Wyke* —3A **94**
Griffe Gdns. *Oakw* —4B **36**
Griffe Head Cres. *Wyke* —2A **94**
Griffe Head Rd. *Wyke* —2A **94**
Griffe Rd. *Oldf* —7L **35**
Griffe Rd. *Wyke* —2A **94**
Griffe Ter. *Wyke* —3A **94**
Griffe Vw. *Oakw* —4B **36**
Griff Ho. La. *Wake* —4D **98**
Griffin Av. *Leeds* —9D **80**
Griffin Gro. *Otley* —9L **11**
Griffin Mt. *Leeds* —7E **62**
Grime La. *H'frth* —7G **165**
Grime La. *Shar C* —8J **121**
Grimescar Rd. *Hud* —7G **112**
Grimescar Mdw. *Hud* —9J **113**
Grimethorpe. —9A 156
Grimethorpe St. *S Elm* —6M **157**
Grimscar Av. *Hud* —9L **113**
Grimthorpe Av. *Leeds* —1M **61**
Grimthorpe Pl. *Leeds* —1N **61**
Grimthorpe St. *Leeds* —1M **61**
Grimthorpe Ter. *Leeds* —1N **61**
Grisedale Av. *Hud* —1L **131**
Grizedale Clo. *Weth* —3J **17**
Grosmont Pl. *Leeds* —3F **60**
Grosmont Rd. *Leeds* —4F **60**
Grosmont Ter. *Leeds* —3F **60**
Grosvenor Av. *Lep* —7J **133**
Grosvenor Av. *Pon* —2G **123**
Grosvenor Av. *Shipl* —7L **39**
Grosvenor Av. *Upt* —2N **157**
Grosvenor Ct. Leeds —3G ***43***
(off Tinshill Rd.)
Grosvenor Gdns. *Huby* —6M **13**
Grosvenor Hill. *Leeds* —4E **62**
Grosvenor M. *Rawd* —3L **41**
Grosvenor Mt. *Leeds* —2B **62**
Grosvenor Pk. *Leeds* —8E **44**
Grosvenor Pk. Gdns. *Leeds* —2B **62**
Grosvenor Rd. *Bat* —6G **96**
Grosvenor Rd. *B'frd* —5B **58**
Grosvenor Rd. *Hud* —4C **132**
Grosvenor Rd. *Leeds* —2B **62**
Grosvenor Rd. *Shipl* —8L **39**
Grosvenor St. *B'frd* —5B **58**
Grosvenor St. *Dew* —4F **116**
Grosvenor St. *Ell* —5E **112**
Grosvenor St. *Heck* —7A **96**
Grosvenor St. *Wake* —8A **120**
Grosvenor Ter. *B'frd* —5B **58**
Grosvenor Ter. *Hal* —5N **91**
Grosvenor Ter. *Heck* —8A **96**
Grosvenor Ter. *Leeds* —2B **62**
Grosvenor Ter. *Otley* —9M **11**
Grosvenor Ter. *Weth* —3M **17**
Grosvenor Way. *Lep* —7J **133**
Grouse Moor La. *Q'bry* —3B **74**
Grouse St. *Kei* —8K **21**
Grove Av. *Hal* —2M **91**
Grove Av. *Hems* —3E **156**
Grove Av. *I'ly* —6E **8**
Grove Av. *Leeds* —9A **44**
Grove Av. *Pon* —3L **123**
Grove Av. *Pud* —7A **60**
Grove Av. *Shipl* —1N **57**
Grove Av. *S Kirk* —7J **157**
Grove Clo. *B'frd* —2E **58**
Grove Clo. *Gom* —3M **95**
Grove Cotts. *Brigh* —1K **113**
Grove Ct. *Hal* —1N **91**
Grove Ct. *Leeds* —9A **44**
Grove Ct. *Pud* —7A **60**
Grove Cres. *B Spa* —1F **32**
Grove Cres. *L'ft* —5D **90**
Grove Cres. *W'ton* —3C **138**
Grove Cres. S. *B Spa* —1F **32**
Grove Cft. *Hal* —2M **91**
Grove Dri. *Hal* —2M **91**
Grove Dri. *S Kirk* —7H **157**
Grove Edge. *Hal* —2M **91**
Gro. Farm Clo. *Leeds* —3J **43**
Gro. Farm Cres. *Leeds* —4H **43**
Gro. Farm Cft. *Leeds* —3H **43**
Gro. Farm Dri. *Leeds* —3H **43**
Grove Gdns. *B Spa* —1F **32**
Grove Gdns. *Dew* —5K **117**
Grove Gdns. *Hal* —2N **91**
Grove Gdns. *Leeds* —9A **44**
Grovehall Av. *Leeds* —4B **80**
Grove Hall Cvn. Site. *Knot* —2C **124**
Grovehall Dri. *Leeds* —4B **80**
Grovehall La. *Pon & Knot* —3A **124**
Grovehall Pde. *Leeds* —4B **80**
Grovehall Rd. *Leeds* —4B **80**
Grove Head. *S Kirk* —7H **157**
Grove Ho. *Hems* —3E **156**
Grove Ho. Leeds —2G ***62***
(off Woodland Gro.)
Grove Ho. Ct. Leeds —9M ***45***
(off N. Grove Clo.)
Grove Ho. Cres. *B'frd* —2E **58**
Grove Ho. Dri. *B'frd* —3E **58**
Grove Ho. Rd. *B'frd* —2E **58**
Grovelands. *B'frd* —2E **58**
Grove La. *Bads* —7L **141**
Grove La. *Gom* —3M **95**
Grove La. *Hems* —3E **156**
Grove La. *Knot* —8D **104**
Grove La. *Leeds* —9N **43**
Grove La. *S Kirk* —7H **157**
Grove Lea Clo. *Hems* —3E **156**
Grove Lea Cres. *Pon* —4L **123**
Grovelea Wlk. *Pon* —4L **123**
Grove Mill La. *Hal* —2N **91**
Grove Mt. *Pon* —3L **123**
Grove Mt. *S Kirk* —7H **157**
Grove Pk. *Cald G* —4F **136**
Grove Pk. *Hal* —1N **91**
Grove Pl. *B Spa* —1E **32**
Grove Pl. *Hems* —3E **156**
Grove Promenade, The. I'ly —5G ***8***
(off Bk. Grove Rd.)
Grove Ri. *Leeds* —2B **44**
Grove Ri. *Pon* —3L **123**
Grove Rd. *Bgly* —5E **38**
Grove Rd. *B Spa* —1E **32**
Grove Rd. *Head* —1A **62**
Grove Rd. *H Bri* —9H **71**
Grove Rd. *Heck* —8B **96**
Grove Rd. *Horb* —1C **136**
Grove Rd. *H'fth* —7E **42**
Grove Rd. *Hud* —3N **131**
Grove Rd. *H'let* —2G **80**
Grove Rd. *I'ly* —5D **8**
Grove Rd. *Leeds* —7B **64**
Grove Rd. *M'well* —8J **153**
Grove Rd. *Men* —4E **24**
Grove Rd. *Pon* —3K **123**
Grove Rd. *Pud* —7A **60**
Grove Rd. *Shipl* —1N **57**
Grove Rd. *Wake* —6L **119**
Grove Royd. *Hal* —2N **91**
Groves Hall Rd. *Dew* —3C **116**
Grove Sq. *Gom* —3M **95**
Grove Sq. *Hal* —2M **91**
Grove St. *Brigh* —1N **113**
Grove St. *Dew* —3F **116**
Grove St. *Hal* —1M **91**
Grove St. *Heck* —8B **96**
Grove St. *Hud* —5L **131**
Grove St. Leeds —6C ***62***
(off Wellington St.)
Grove St. *Liv* —1N **115**
Grove St. *Lgwd* —4D **130**
Grove St. *Mir* —5M **115**
Grove St. *Oss* —7N **117**
Grove St. *Slai* —9M **129**
Grove St. *S Kirk* —7H **157**
Grove St. *Sower B* —8K **91**
Grove St. *S'ley* —4B **60**
Grove St. *Wake* —6M **119**
Grove St. S. *Hal* —5M **91**
Grove Ter. *B'shaw* —9L **77**
Grove Ter. *B Spa* —1E **32**
Grove Ter. *B'frd* —8B **58**
Grove Ter. *Brigh* —1K **113**
Grove Ter. *H Bri* —4M **89**
Grove Ter. *Hems* —3E **156**
Grove Ter. *Pud* —7A **60**
Grove, The. *Bail* —3A **40**
Grove, The. *Bat* —5D **96**
Grove, The. *Bgly* —1D **38**
Grove, The. *Cud* —8J **155**
Grove, The. *E Ard* —4D **98**
Grove, The. *E Kes* —2C **30**
Grove, The. *Gild* —6G **78**
Grove, The. *Gre* —8H **41**
Grove, The. *Heck* —6N **95**
Grove, The. *Hip* —4J **93**
Grove, The. *H'fth* —7E **42**
Grove, The. *Hud* —9N **113**
Grove, The. *Idle* —8F **40**
Grove, The. *I'ly* —5F **8**
Grove, The. *Kip* —4A **84**
Grove, The. *Leeds* —2B **44**
Grove, The. *Nor* —1J **121**
Grove, The. *Pud* —7A **60**
Grove, The. Q'bry —4C ***74***
(off New Pk. Rd.)
Grove, The. *Ryh* —9H **139**
Grove, The. *Shipl* —8K **39**
Grove, The. *S Elm* —5M **157**
Grove, The. *S Kirk* —7J **157**
Grove, The. *Swil* —3J **83**
Grove, The. *W'ton* —3C **138**
Grove, The. *Yead* —1M **41**
Grove Town. —3L 123
Groveville. *Hal* —3H **93**
Groveway. *B'frd* —2E **58**
Grove Way. *S Kirk* —7H **157**
Grovewood. *Leeds* —9N **43**
Grunberg Pl. *Leeds* —1N **61**
Grunberg St. *Leeds* —1N **61**
Guard House. —9E 20
Guard Ho. Av. *Kei* —9G **20**
Guard Ho. Dri. *Kei* —9G **20**
Guard Ho. Gro. *Kei* —9F **20**
Guard Ho. Rd. *Kei* —9G **20**
Guardian Ct. I'ly —5G ***8***
(off Wells Promenade, in two parts)
Guardian M. Leeds —9M ***61***
(off Lynwood Vw.)
Guernsey Rd. *Dew* —1J **117**
Guide Post Farm. Hal —6L ***73***
(off Keighley Rd.)
Guildford Rd. *Roys* —4C **154**
Guildford St. *H Bri* —2H **89**
Guildford St. *Oss* —7N **117**
Guild Way. *Hal* —6H **91**
Guillemot App. *Morl* —1N **97**
Guisborough Ho. B'frd —8G ***40***
(off Idlethorp Way)
Guiseley. —7J 25
Guiseley Dri. *Men* —6F **24**
Guiseley Retail Pk. *Guis* —8J **25**
Gulley Rd. *Leeds* —2M **81**
Gully. —4N 163
Gully Ter. *H'frth* —4N **163**
Gully, The. *Shepl* —3G **164**
Gunson Cres. *Oss* —5N **117**
Gunter Rd. *Weth* —4A **18**
Gunthwaite La. *Up Den & Pen* —5C **166**
Gurbax Ct. *B'frd* —7J **59**
Gurney Clo. *B'frd* —2B **76**
Guycroft. *Otley* —1K **25**
Guycroft. —1K 25
Guys Cft. *Wake* —7E **118**
Guy St. *B'frd* —8D **58**
Gwynne Av. *B'frd* —5J **59**
Gynn La. *Hon* —5M **147**
Gypsy Ct. *C'frd* —6J **103**
Gypsy La. *C'frd* —6J **103**
Gypsy La. *Wake* —3N **137**
Gypsy Wood Clo. *Leeds* —7E **64**
Gypsy Wood Crest. *Leeds* —7E **64**

Hacking Hill. —6A 158
Hacking La. *S Elm* —6A **158**
Hadassah St. *Hal* —8C **92**
Haddingley. —2H 165
Haddingley La. *Cumb* —5G **165**
Haddlesey Rd. *Birk* —2M **105**
Haddon Av. *Hal* —9B **92**
Haddon Av. *Leeds* —4M **61**
Haddon Clo. *Gom* —4M **95**
Haddon Clo. *S Elm* —4N **157**
Haddon Pl. *Leeds* —4M **61**
Haddon Rd. *Leeds* —4N **61**
Hade Edge. —9N 163
Hadfield Rd. *Heck* —7A **96**
Hadleigh Ct. *Leeds* —5F **44**
Hadleigh Ri. *Pon* —6H **123**
Hadrian Clo. *C'frd* —3J **103**
Hadrian's Clo. *Sal N* —2D **130**
Hadrians Clo. *Thpe A* —5N **141**
Hag Farm Rd. *Bur W* —2B **24**
Hagg Hill. *Eml* —3H **151**
Hagg La. *Birk* —1N **105**
Hagg La. *Mir* —8M **115**
Haggroyd La. *Broc* —7N **147**
Haggs Hill. —6C 118
Haggs Hill Rd. *Oss* —6C **118**
(in two parts)
Haggs La. *Wake* —6E **118**
Hagg Wood Rd. *Hon* —7N **147**
Hag Hill La. *Eml* —3H **151**
Hag La. *Hal* —1B **92**
Hague Cres. *Hems* —4E **156**
Hague La. *S Kirk* —5F **156**
Hague Pk. Clo. *S Kirk* —6H **157**
Hague Pk. Coppice. *S Kirk* —6H **157**
Hague Pk. Dri. *S Kirk* —6H **157**
Hague Pk. Gdns. *S Kirk* —6H **157**
Hague Pk. La. *S Kirk* —6H **157**
Hague Pk. Wlk. *S Kirk* —6H **157**
Hague Ter. *Hems* —3E **156**
Haigh Av. *Rothw* —6L **81**
Haigh Beck Vw. *B'frd* —8G **41**
Haigh Clo. *Hoy S* —9J **167**
Haigh Corner. *B'frd* —8H **41**
Haigh Cft. *Roys* —5C **154**
Haighfield Cvn. Site. *Leeds* —6C **30**
Haigh Fold. —3G 59
Haigh Fold. *B'frd* —3G **59**
Haigh Gdns. *Rothw* —6L **81**
Haigh Hall. *B'frd* —8H **41**
Haigh Hall Rd. *B'frd* —8H **41**
Haigh House Hill. —8D 112
Haigh Ho. Hill. *Hud* —8D **112**
Haigh Ho. Rd. *Hud* —8D **112**
Haigh La. *Floc* —9D **134**
Haigh La. *Haig* —4E **152**
Haigh La. *Hal* —8C **92**
Haigh La. *H'frth* —1N **147**
Haigh La. *Hoy S* —9K **167**
Haigh Moor. —6A 98
Haigh Moor Av. *Ting* —6A **98**
Haigh Moor Cres. *Ting* —6A **98**
Haigh Moor Rd. *Ting* —7A **98**
Haigh Moor St. *Wake* —3M **119**
Haigh Moor Vw. *Ting* —6A **98**
Haigh Moor Way. *Roys* —4D **154**
Haigh Pk. Rd. *Leeds* —3K **81**
Haigh Rd. *Rothw* —7N **81**
Haighside. *Rothw* —7L **81**
Haighside Clo. *Rothw* —7L **81**
Haighside Dri. *Rothw* —7L **81**
Haighside Way. *Rothw* —7L **81**
Haighs Sq. *Hud* —3B **132**
Haigh St. *B'frd* —2F **76**
Haigh St. *Brigh* —9M **93**
Haigh St. *G'lnd* —4A **112**
Haigh St. *Hal* —4M **91**
Haigh St. *Hud* —7L **131**
Haigh Ter. *Rothw* —6L **81**
Haigh Vw. *Rothw* —6L **81**
Haigh Wood Cres. *Leeds* —4G **42**
Haigh Wood Grn. *Leeds* —5G **42**
Haigh Wood Rd. *Leeds* —4F **42**
Hailhead Dri. *Pon* —2M **123**
Haincliffe Pl. *Kei* —3H **37**
Haincliffe Rd. *Kei* —3H **37**
Haines Pk. *Leeds* —4G **62**
Hainsworth Moor Cres. *Q'bry* —5C **74**
Hainsworth Moor Dri. *Q'bry* —5C **74**
Hainsworth Moor Gth. *Q'bry* —5C **74**
Hainsworth Moor Gro. *Q'bry* —5C **74**
Hainsworth Moor Vw. *Q'bry* —5C **74**
Hainsworth Rd. *Sils* —9E **6**
Hainsworth Sq. *Far* —3A **60**
Hainsworth St. *Leeds* —8A **62**
Hainsworth St. *Rothw* —9N **81**
Hainworth. —4H 37
Hainworth Crag Rd. *Kei* —5G **37**
Hainworth La. *Kei* —4H **37**
Hainworth Rd. *Kei* —4H **37**
Hainworth Shaw. —4K 37
Hainworth Wood Rd. *Kei* —4H **37**
Hainworth Wood Rd. N. *Kei* —2J **37**
Haisemount. *Dart* —8J **153**
Halberg Ho. *Pon* —3L **123**
Halcyon Hill. *Leeds* —7E **44**
Halcyon Way. *B'frd* —2A **76**
Haldane Clo. *Brier* —6N **155**
Haldane Cres. *Wake* —3N **119**
Hales Rd. *Leeds* —9L **61**
Halesworth Cres. *B'frd* —3J **77**
Haley Hill. *Hal* —3B **92**
Haley's Yd. *Leeds* —3F **60**
Half Acre Rd. *T'tn* —7A **56**
Half Acres. —6C 102
Half Ho. La. *Brigh* —7J **93**
Half Mile. —3C 60
Half Mile. *Leeds* —4C **60**
Half Mile Clo. *S'ley* —4C **60**
Half Mile Ct. *S'ley* —4C **60**
Half Mile Gdns. *Leeds* —4C **60**
Half Mile Grn. *S'ley* —4C **60**
Half Mile La. *S'ley & Leeds* —3C **60**
Half Moon La. *K'thpe* —5C **120**
Half Moon St. *Hud* —4M **131**
Halfpenny La. *F'stne & Pon* —5D **122**
Half St. *Kei* —8H **21**
Halifax. —5B 92
Halifax Blue Sox Rugby League Football Club. —7B 92
Halifax Ho. *Dew* —9D **96**
Halifax Ind. Cen., The. *Hal* —4N **91**
Halifax La. *L'ft* —4E **90**
Halifax Old Rd. *Hal* —4G **92**
Halifax Old Rd. *Hud* —9K **113**
Halifax Rd. *Blkhd* —9N **69**
Halifax Rd. *Brierc* —3A **50**
Halifax Rd. *Butt* —6K **75**
Halifax Rd. *Cleck & Liv* —5C **94**
Halifax Rd. *Cro R & Kei* —6F **36**
(nr. Cross Roads., in two parts)
Halifax Rd. *Cro R & Cull* —7F **36**
(nr. Hardgate La.)
Halifax Rd. *Denh* —7K **55**
(in two parts)
Halifax Rd. *Dew* —9D **96**
Halifax Rd. *Gol* —4A **130**
Halifax Rd. *G'lnd & Ell* —3C **112**
Halifax Rd. *Hal* —1G **92**
Halifax Rd. *Heck & Stainc* —8C **96**
Halifax Rd. *Hip & Brigh* —6J **93**
(nr. Broad Oak La.)
Halifax Rd. *Hip* —4G **92**
(nr. Leeds Rd.)
Halifax Rd. *Hud* —8G **112**
Halifax Rd. *L'boro* —3A **126**
Halifax Rd. *Q'bry* —7B **74**
Halifax Rd. *Ripp* —7D **110**
Halifax Rd. *Todm* —7K **87**
Halifax Town Football Club. —7B 92
Hallamfield. *Guis* —8J **25**
Hallam La. *Askw* —4E **10**
Hallamshire M. *Wake* —7E **118**
Hallam St. *Guis* —8H **25**
Hallas Gro. *Hud* —5C **132**
Hallas La. *Cull* —1L **55**
(in two parts)
Hallas La. *Kbtn* —3M **149**
Hallas Rd. *Kbtn* —3K **149**
Hall Av. *B'frd* —1H **59**
Hall Av. *Hud* —5L **131**
Hallbank Clo. *B'frd* —4B **76**
Hall Bank Dri. *Bgly* —3F **38**
Hallbank Dri. *B'frd* —4B **76**
Hall Bank La. *H Bri* —4M **89**
Hall Bower. —9N 131
Hall Bower La. *Hud* —1N **147**
Hall Cliffe. —9C 118
Hall Cliffe. *Bail* —3B **40**
Hall Cliffe Ct. *Horb* —9C **118**
Hall Cliffe Cres. *Horb* —9C **118**
Hall Cliffe Gro. *Horb* —9C **118**
Hall Cliffe Ri. *Horb* —9D **118**
Hall Cliffe Rd. *Horb* —9C **118**
Hall Clo. *B Spa* —1E **32**
Hall Clo. *B'hpe* —4H **27**
Hall Clo. *Bur W* —8B **10**
Hall Clo. *Hems* —2D **156**
Hall Clo. *Liv* —9L **95**
Hall Clo. *Oss* —2L **117**
Hall Ct. *B'ton* —4B **104**
Hall Ct. *Leeds* —2F **62**
Hallcroft. *Bgly* —2E **38**
Hall Cft. *Neth* —4A **136**
Hallcroft Clo. *Horb* —1D **136**
Hallcroft Dri. *Add* —2A **8**
Hallcroft Dri. *Horb* —1D **136**
Hall Cft. Ri. *Roys* —6C **154**
Hall Cross Gro. *Hud* —7A **132**
Hall Cross Rd. *Hud* —7A **132**
Hall Dri. *B'hpe* —4G **27**
Hall Dri. *Bur W* —8B **10**
Hall Dri. *Liv* —1M **115**
Hall Farm Gro. *Hoy S* —9K **167**
Hall Farm Pk. *M'fld* —6F **66**
Hallfield. —4N 17
Hallfield Av. *M'fld* —7F **66**
Hallfield Cres. *Weth* —4N **17**
Hallfield Dri. *Bail* —4A **40**
Hall Fld. La. *Ryh* —2H **155**
Hallfield La. *Weth* —3N **17**
Hallfield Pl. *B'frd* —6C **58**
Hallfield Rd. *B'frd* —6B **58**
Hallfield St. *B'frd* —6C **58**
Hallfield Ter. *M'fld* —7F **66**
Hall Garth Rd. *Thpe A* —5N **141**
Hallgate. *B'frd* —6C **58**
Hall Green. —7H 137
Hall Grn. La. *N Rig* —2A **14**
Hall Grn. La. *Rish* —2D **128**
Hall Gro. *Leeds* —4B **62**
Hall Gro. *M'well* —8L **153**
Halliday Av. *Leeds* —6K **61**
Halliday Ct. *Gar* —7M **65**
Halliday Dri. *Leeds* —6K **61**
Halliday Gro. *Leeds* —6K **61**
Halliday Mt. *Leeds* —6K **61**
Halliday Pl. *Leeds* —6K **61**
Halliday Rd. *Gar* —7M **65**
Halliday Rd. *Leeds* —6K **61**
Halliday St. *Pud* —6B **60**
Halliley Gdns. Dew —3F ***116***
(off Halliley St.)
Halliley St. *Dew* —3E **116**
Hall Ing La. *Hon* —4N **147**
Halling Pl. *Todm* —8J **87**
Hall Ings. —5B 130
Hall Ings. *B'frd* —8C **58**
Hall Ings. *Hal* —9F **92**
Hall La. *A'ley* —7M **61**
Hall La. *Askw* —2C **10**
Hall La. *B'frd* —9D **58**
Hall La. *C'thpe* —6H **137**
Hall La. *Cook* —1H **43**
Hall La. *Dew* —9H **117**
Hall La. *F'ley* —8F **60**
Hall La. *Gol* —4N **129**

Hall La. Hal —9E 74
Hall La. H'fth —7C 42
Hall La. Kbtn —2J 149
Hall La. Leat —7D 12
Hall La. Leds —7E 84
Hall La. Leeds —1F 62
Hall La. Pon —3A 158
Hall La. Shipl —7A 40
Hall La. S Mil —9M 67
Hall La. Sower B —4A 110
Hall Lee Rd. Hud —1H 131
Hall M. B Spa —1E 32
Hall Orchards Av. Weth —3N 17
Hallowes Gro. Cull —1K 55
Hallowes Pk. Rd. Cull —1K 55
Hallows Rd. Kei —7L 21
Hallows, The. Kei —8G 20
Hall Pk. Av. Croft —9G 120
Hall Pk. Av. H'fth —6D 42
Hall Pk. Av. Liv —1L 115
Hall Pk. Clo. H'fth —6D 42
Hall Pk. Ct. Kip —4B 84
Hall Pk. Cft. Kip —5B 84
Hall Pk. Gth. H'fth —6D 42
Hall Pk. Meadows. Kip —5B 84
Hall Pk. Mt. H'fth —6D 42
Hall Pk. Orchard. Kip —5B 84
Hall Pk. Ri. H'fth —6E 42
Hall Pk. Ri. Kip —4B 84
Hall Pk. Rd. Wltn —5G 19
Hall Pl. Leeds —7H 63
Hall Ri. B'hpe —5H 27
Hall Ri. Bur W —8B 10
Hall Ri. Clo. B'hpe —5H 27
Hall Ri. Cft. B'hpe —5H 27
Hall Rd. B'frd —1G 59
Hall Rd. Leeds —7M 61
Hall Rd. Swil —4J 83
Hall Rd. Wake —7F 118
Hall Royd. Shipl —8M 39
Hallroyd Cres. Todm —7L 87
Hallroyd Pl. Todm —7L 87
Hallroyd Rd. Todm —6L 87
Hall's Ct. Ackw —2F 140
Hall Sq. C'ley —8M 41
Hall Stone Ct. She —8H 75
Hall St. B'frd —4A 76
Hall St. Brigh —1N 113
Hall St. F'stne —7D 122
Hall St. Hal —5A 92
Hall St. Haw —9C 36
Hall St. Hud —3E 130
Hall St. Oakw —5D 36 (off Clough La.)
Hall St. Todm —7K 87
Hall St. N. Hal —2A 92
Hallwood Grn. B'frd —1J 59
Halstead Dri. Men —3E 24
Halstead Gro. M'well —7J 153
Halstead La. N Mill & Thur —9D 148
Halstead Pl. B'frd —2N 75
Halsteads Way. Steet —2B 20
Halton. —6A 64
Halton Clo. Hud —6D 132
Halton Dri. Leeds —6B 64
Halton East. —1E 4
Halton Green. —1D 4
Halton Hill. Leeds —6A 64
Halton Moor. —8N 63
Halton Moor Av. Leeds —8M 63
Halton Moor Rd. Leeds —8J 63 (in two parts)
Halton Pl. B'frd —2N 75
Halton Rd. Wake —3A 120
Halton St. F'stne —4D 122
Hamble Ct. M'well —9L 153
Hambledon Av. B'frd —4F 76
Hambledon Av. Mel —8E 146
Hambleton Bank. Hal —7H 73
Hambleton Cres. Hal —8H 73
Hambleton Dri. Hal —8G 73
Hambleton La. Oxe —7F 54
Hambleton St. Wake —4L 119
Hamel Ri. Hems —3D 156
Hame, The. Holy G —8M 111
Hamilton Av. Leeds —2G 62
Hamilton Ct. Nor —9J 101
Hamilton Gdns. Leeds —3F 62
Hamilton Pl. Leeds —3G 62
Hamilton St. B'frd —6B 58
Hamilton Ter. Leeds —3G 62
Hamilton Ter. Otley —9M 11 (off North Av.)
Hamilton Vw. Leeds —2G 62
Hammer La. Shar C —7J 121
Hammerstone Leach La. Holy G & Ell —6C 112
Hammerstones Rd. Ell —5C 112
Hammerton Clo. Ell —4E 112
Hammerton Dri. Gar —9A 66
Hammerton Gro. Pud —7C 60
Hammerton Rd. Hud —9M 113
Hammerton St. B'frd —8E 58
Hammerton St. Pud —7B 60
Hammerton Ter. Todm —6K 87
Hammond Cres. Dlgtn —6A 78
Hammond Pl. B'frd —3M 57
Hammond Rd. Knot —9C 104
Hammond St. Hal —6M 91
Hammond St. Hud —1N 131
Hamm Strasse. B'frd —6C 58
Hampden Clo. Knot —7A 104
Hampden Pl. B'frd —1B 76
Hampden Pl. Hal —5A 92
Hampden St. B'frd —1B 76
Hampole. —8G 158
Hampole Balk. Skel —8K 159
Hampole Fld. La. Hamp —8E 158
Hampshire Clo. I'ly —5J 9
Hampshire Clo. Pon —9L 103
Hampshire St. Hud —4B 132
Hampson St. Bat —5D 96
Hampton Ct. I'ly —5F 8 (off Grove Rd.)
Hampton Pl. B'frd —7F 40
Hampton Pl. Leeds —7H 63
Hampton St. Hal —7M 91
Hampton St. Leeds —7G 63
Hampton Ter. Leeds —7H 63
Hamworth Dri. Oakw —5D 36
Hanby Av. Nor —9G 100
Hand Bank La. Mir —9L 115
Handel St. Gol —6C 130
Handel St. List —7A 58
Handel Ter. Hud —5B 132 (off Avenue, The)
Handsworth Rd. Wake —6J 137
Hanging Ga. La. Oxe —1A 54
Hanging Heaton. —9H 97
Hanging Royd. Gol —7C 130
Hangingroyd Clo. H Bri —1H 89
Hangingroyd La. H Bri —1H 89
Hangingroyd Rd. H Bri —1H 89
Hanging Stone Rd. Hud —2L 147
Hangingstone Rd. I'ly —6J 9
Hanging Stones La. Ripp —7E 110
Hanging Wood Way. West I —2G 95
Hangram St. Brigh —1N 113
Hanley Rd. Morl —1K 97
Hanmore Ri. Hud —9N 113
Hannah Ct. Wyke —1A 94
Hanover Av. Leeds —6C 62
Hanover Clo. B'frd —5M 57
Hanover Ct. Dew —2D 116 (off Staincliffe Rd.)
Hanover Cres. Pon —6J 123
Hanover Gdns. Bur W —9C 10
Hanover Gdns. Dew —3E 116
Hanover Ho. Yead —9N 25 (off Harper La.)
Hanover La. Leeds —6C 62
Hanover Mt. Leeds —5B 62
Hanover Pl. Bat —7G 96
Hanover Sq. B'frd —6B 58
Hanover Sq. Leeds —5C 62
Hanover Sq. Wyke —1A 94
Hanover St. Bat —7F 96
Hanover St. Dew —3E 116
Hanover St. Hal —6A 92
Hanover St. Kei —9J 21
Hanover St. Sower B —8K 91
Hanover St. Wake —6J 119
Hanover Wlk. Leeds —6C 62
Hanover Way. Bur W —9C 10
Hansby Av. Leeds —1C 64
Hansby Bank. Leeds —1C 64
Hansby Clo. Leeds —2C 64
Hansby Dri. Leeds —1C 64
Hansby Gdns. Leeds —2C 64
Hansby Ga. Leeds —1C 64
Hansby Grange. Leeds —1C 64
Hansby Pl. Leeds —2C 64
Hanson Av. Nor —2J 121
Hanson Ct. Wyke —2A 94
Hanson Fold. Wyke —1A 94
Hanson La. Hal —5L 91
Hanson La. Hud —8K 131
Hanson Mt. Wyke —2A 94
Hanson Pl. Wyke —1A 94
Hanson Rd. Brigh —3K 113
Hanson Rd. Mel —8B 146
Hanworth Rd. Low M —7B 76
Hapsburg Ct. B'frd —9C 58 (off Elsdon Gro.)
Harbeck Dri. H'den —7A 38
Harborough Grn. App B —7J 41 (off Leavens, The)
Harbour Cres. B'frd —5M 75
Harbour Pk. B'frd —5L 75
Harbour Rd. Wibs —5L 75
Harclo Rd. Kei —8L 21
Harcourt Av. T'tn —7C 56
Harcourt Dri. Add —9M 5
Harcourt Dri. Morl —8J 79
Harcourt Pl. Leeds —6B 62
Harcourt St. B'frd —2F 76
Harcourt St. Wake —6H 119
Hardaker La. Bail —5M 39
Hardaker's App. Ackw —5F 140
Hardaker's La. Ackw —4E 140
Hardaker St. B'frd —6B 58
Hardcastle Av. Pon —2J 123
Hardcastle La. Floc —7G 135
Harden. —6A 38
Harden & Bingley Cvn. Pk. H'den —8N 37
Harden Brow La. H'den —6N 37
Harden Gro. Idle —3J 59
Harden Gro. Kei —2L 37
Harden Hill Rd. Mel —8D 146
Harden La. Wilsd —8A 38
Harden Moss Rd. Mel —1D 162
Harden Rd. H'den —6A 38
Harden Rd. Kei —2L 37
Hardgate La. Cro R —8F 36 (in two parts)
Hardhill Ho. H'den —6A 38 (off Ferrands Pk. Way)
Hardie Rd. H'cft —9K 139
Hardings La. I'ly —3E 8
Hardings La. Midd —1E 8
Hard Ings Rd. Kei —7J 21
Hardistry Dri. Pon —3H 123
Hardknot Clo. B'frd —2K 75
Hard Nese La. Oxe —5N 53 (in two parts)
Hard Platts La. Holy G —8M 111
Hardrow Grn. Leeds —9N 61
Hardrow Gro. Leeds —9N 61
Hardrow Rd. Leeds —9M 61
Hardrow Ter. Leeds —9N 61
Hardwick Clo. Ryh —1H 155
Hardwick Ct. Pon —4J 123
Hardwick Cres. Pon —6K 123
Hardwick Cft. Leeds —9F 44
Hardwick La. W Har —1B 140
Hardwick Rd. E Hard —8M 123
Hardwick Rd. F'stne —7C 122
Hardwick Rd. Pon —5K 123
Hardwick St. Kei —1G 37
Hardy Av. B'frd —5A 76
Hardy Av. Chur —5M 79
Hardy Ct. Morl —9L 79
Hardy Cft. Wake —5M 119
Hardy Gro. Leeds —2C 80
Hardy Pl. Hov E —7K 93
Hardy St. B'frd —8D 58
Hardy St. Brigh —9N 93
Hardy St. Leeds —2C 80
Hardy St. Morl —9L 79
Hardy St. Wibs —4A 76
Hardy Ter. Leeds —2D 80
Hardy Vw. Leeds —2C 80
Harebell Av. Wake —4G 119
Harecroft Rd. Otley —8L 11
Haredon Clo. M'well —7J 153
Hare Farm Av. Leeds —7G 61
Hare Farm Clo. Leeds —7G 61
Harefield Clo. Ebrn —3A 20
Harefield Dri. Bat —3D 96
Harefield E. Leeds —7N 63
Harefield Rd. Pon —3M 123
Harefield W. Leeds —7N 63
Harehill Av. Todm —6J 87
Harehill Clo. B'frd —6F 40
Hare Hill Edge. Oldf —6J 35
Harehill Rd. B'frd —6F 40
Harehills. —4K 63
Harehills Av. Leeds —2G 62
Harehills Corner. —2J 63
Harehills La. Leeds —1G 62
Harehills La. Oldf —6M 35
Harehills Pk. Av. Leeds —4K 63
Harehills Pk. Cotts. Leeds —4L 63
Harehills Pk. Rd. Leeds —4K 63
Harehills Pk. Ter. Leeds —4K 63
Harehills Pk. Vw. Leeds —4K 63
Harehills Pl. Leeds —3H 63
Harehills Rd. Leeds —2H 63
Harehill St. Todm —6J 87
Hare La. Pud —9B 60
Hare Pk. Av. Liv —8G 94
Hare Pk. Clo. Liv —8G 94
Hare Pk. Dri. Liv —8G 95
Hare Pk. Grange. Liv —8G 95 (off Hare Pk. La.)
Hare Pk. La. Croft —3G 138
Hare Pk. La. Liv —9G 94
Hare Pk. Mt. Leeds —7F 60
Hare Pk. Vw. Croft —2G 139
Hares Av. Leeds —2H 63
Hares Mt. Leeds —2G 63
Hares Rd. Leeds —2G 63
Hares Ter. Leeds —2H 63
Hare St. Hal —5M 91
Hares Vw. Leeds —2H 63
Harewood. —1J 29
Harewood Av. Ebrn —3A 20
Harewood Av. Hal —4K 91
Harewood Av. Hare —2K 29
Harewood Av. Heck —9B 96
Harewood Av. Nor —9K 101
Harewood Av. Pon —4L 123
Harewood Clo. Knot —8B 104
Harewood Ct. Leeds —2B 64 (LS14)
Harewood Ct. Leeds —6F 44 (LS17)
Harewood Cres. Oakw —4E 36
Harewood Dri. Wren —2F 118
Harewood Ga. Hare —1J 29
Harewood Gro. Heck —9B 96
Harewood House. —2G 28
Harewood La. Upt & Thpe A —1B 158 (in two parts)
Harewood M. Hare —1J 29
Harewood Mt. Mel —7E 146
Harewood Mt. Pon —3L 123
Harewood Park. —3L 123
Harewood Pl. Hal —6L 91
Harewood Ri. Oakw —4F 36
Harewood Rd. Coll —9F 16
Harewood Rd. E Kes —1B 30
Harewood Rd. Oakw —5E 36
Harewood Rd. Wake —3A 120
Harewood St. B'frd —7F 58 (in two parts)
Harewood St. Leeds —6E 62
Harewood Vw. Pon —3L 123
Harewood Way. Leeds —6E 60
Hargrave Cres. Men —4D 24
Hargreaves Av. Stan —7N 99
Hargreaves Clo. Morl —2L 97
Harker Rd. Low M —6A 76
Harker St. Knot —8G 104
Harker Ter. S'ley —5A 60
Harland Clo. B'frd —4C 58
Harland Sq. Leeds —3C 62 (off Moorfield St.)
Harlech Av. Leeds —3D 80
Harlech Cres. Leeds —3D 80
Harlech Gro. Leeds —3D 80
Harlech Mt. Leeds —3D 80
Harlech Rd. Leeds —3D 80
Harlech St. Leeds —3D 80
Harlech Ter. Leeds —3D 80
Harlech Way. Gar —7B 66
Harley Clo. Leeds —6D 60
Harley Ct. Leeds —6D 60
Harley Dri. Leeds —6D 60
Harley Gdns. Leeds —6D 60
Harley Grn. Leeds —6D 60
Harley Pl. Brigh —2M 113 (off Harley St.)
Harley Ri. Leeds —6D 60
Harley Rd. Leeds —6D 60
Harley St. Brigh —2M 113
Harley St. Todm —6K 87
Harley Ter. Leeds —6D 60
Harley Vw. Leeds —6D 60
Harley Wlk. Leeds —6D 60
Harley Wood. —5H 87
Harley Wood. Todm —4G 87
Harlington Ct. Morl —2K 97
Harlington Rd. Morl —2K 97
Harlock St. Wake —9N 119
Harlow Ct. Leeds —8L 45
Harlow Rd. B'frd —9M 57
Harmby Clo. Skel —7L 159
Harmon Clo. B'frd —5G 76
Harold Av. Leeds —4A 62
Harold Gdns. Morl —9M 79
Harold Gro. Leeds —4A 62
Harold Mt. Leeds —4A 62
Harold Pl. Leeds —4A 62
Harold Pl. Shipl —7L 39
Harold Rd. Leeds —4A 62
Harold Sq. Leeds —4A 62
Harold St. Bgly —3D 38
Harold St. Leeds —4A 62
Harold Ter. Leeds —4A 62
Harold Vw. Leeds —4A 62
Harold Wlk. Leeds —4A 62
Harold Wilson Ho. Nor —2H 121
Harpe Inge. Hud —3C 132
Harper Av. Idle —6F 40
Harper Cres. Idle —6G 40
Harper Gro. B'frd —6F 40
Harper La. Yead —1M 41
Harper Rock. Yead —1M 41 (off Harper La.)
Harper Royd La. Sower B —1H 111
Harper St. Leeds —7F 62
Harper Ter. Yead —1M 41 (off Harper La.)
Harp La. Q'bry —3C 74
Harp Rd. Hud —5G 131
Harrap St. Wake —4F 118
Harrier Clo. B'frd —7G 57
Harrier Way. Morl —9N 79
Harriet St. B'frd —6N 57
Harriet St. Brigh —8M 93
Harriet St. Leeds —3F 62
Harrington Ct. Mel —8E 146
Harris Ct. B'frd —2M 75
Harrison Cres. Leeds —5M 63
Harrison La. Mel —5D 146
Harrison Rd. Croft —1F 138
Harrison Rd. Hal —6B 92
Harrison's Av. S'ley —4C 60
Harrison St. Bgly —5F 38
Harrison St. Leeds —6E 62
Harrison St. Todm —3D 86
Harrison Va. Bgly —4F 38
Harris St. Bgly —5F 38
Harris St. B'frd —7E 58
Harrogate Av. B'frd —4E 58
Harrogate Pde. Leeds —5F 44
Harrogate Pl. B'frd —4E 58
Harrogate Rd. B'frd —4F 58
Harrogate Rd. B'hpe —8B 26
Harrogate Rd. Hare —4F 14
Harrogate Rd. Leat —8G 13
Harrogate Rd. Leeds —7E 44
Harrogate Rd. N Rig —2B 14
Harrogate Rd. Rawd & Leeds (in two parts) —3M 41
Harrogate Rd. Weth —1F 16
Harrogate St. B'frd —4E 58
Harrogate Ter. B'frd —4E 58
Harrogate Vw. Leeds —2L 45
Harrop Av. Morl —2L 97
Harrop Edge. —4B 56
Harrop Gro. Morl —2L 97
Harrop La. Wilsd —3N 55
Harrop Ter. Morl —2L 97
Harrop Well La. Pon —2K 123
Harrowby Cres. Leeds —8L 43
Harrowby Rd. Leeds —8L 43
Harrow St. Hal —5M 91
Harrow St. S Elm —6L 157
Harry Clo. Add —1K 7
Harry La. Cytn —1F 74
Harry La. Oxe —3C 54
Harry St. B'frd —2G 76
Harsley Fold. Brigh —1C 114
Harthill. Gild —6G 79
Harthill Av. Gild —6G 78
Harthill Clo. Gild —6G 78
Harthill La. Gild —6G 78
Harthill Pde. Gild —6G 79 (off Town St.)
Harthill Ri. Gild —6G 78
Hartington St. Bat —9F 96
Hartington St. Kei —8J 21
Hartington Ter. B'frd —9M 57
Hartland Rd. B'frd —1J 77
Hartley Av. Leeds —2C 62
Hartley Bank La. Hal —2H 93
Hartley Clo. S Elm —5N 157
Hartley Cres. Leeds —2C 62
Hartley Gdns. Leeds —2D 62
Hartley Gro. Dew —1F 116
Hartley Gro. Leeds —2C 62
Hartley Hill. Leeds —5E 62
Hartley Pk. Av. Pon —3H 123
Hartley Pk. Vw. Pon —3H 123
Hartley Pl. Morl —1L 97
Hartley's Bldgs. Morl —1L 97
Hartley's Sq. E Mor —7C 22
Hartley St. B'frd —9E 58
Hartley St. C'frd —5C 102
Hartley St. Chur —6L 79
Hartley St. Dew —2F 116
Hartley St. Hal —4N 91
Hartley St. Morl —9L 79
Hartley's Yd. Leeds —7L 61
Hartley Ter. F'stne —7C 122
Hartlington Ct. Bail —4C 40
Hartman Pl. B'frd —4L 57
Hartshead. —1G 115
Hartshead Hall La. Harts —3G 114
Hartshead La. Harts —1F 114
Hartshead Moor Side. —6F 94
Hartshead Moor Top. —5C 94
Hart St. B'frd —1M 75
Hart St. New —8M 131
Hartwell Rd. Leeds —4A 62
Harvelin Pk. Todm —7B 88
Harvest Clo. Pon —9L 103
Harvest Cft. Bur W —8B 10
Harvey Royd. Hud —6E 132
Harvey St. Wake —8N 119
Harwill App. Chur —6M 79
Harwill Av. Chur —6M 79
Harwill Cft. Chur —6M 79
Harwill Gro. Chur —6M 79
Harwill Ri. Chur —6M 79
Harwill Rd. Morl —6M 79
Harwood Clo. Hud —6C 132 (nr. Almondbury Bank)
Harwood Clo. Hud —5D 132 (nr. Greenhead La.)

Harwood Clo. S'dal —1N 137
Haselbury Ho. B'frd —9C 58
(off Crowther Wlk.)
Haselden Cres. Wake —6G 118
Haselden Rd. Wake —6F 118
Haslam Clo. B'frd —6E 58
Haslam Gro. Shipl —9C 40
Haslemere Clo. B'frd —2H 77
Haslewood Clo. Leeds —6G 63
Haslewood Ct. Leeds —6H 63
Haslewood Dene. Leeds —6H 63
Haslewood Dri. Leeds —6G 63
Haslewood Grn. Leeds —6H 63
Haslewood Lawn. Leeds —6H 63
Haslewood M. Leeds —6H 63
Haslewood Pl. Leeds —6H 63
Haslewood Sq. Leeds —6H 63
Hasley Rd. Bur W —9D 10
Haslingden Dri. B'frd —4L 57
Hassocks La. Hon —5H 147
Hassocks Rd. Mel —6A 146
Haste St. C'frd —4B 102
Hastings Av. B'frd —3B 76
Hastings Av. Wake —9L 119
Hastings Ct. Coll —9J 17
Hastings Ct. Nor —8F 100
Hastings Ct. Shad —3N 45
Hastings Cres. C'frd —5H 103
Hastings Gro. Wake —9M 119
Hastings Pl. B'frd —3B 76
Hastings St. B'frd —3B 76
Hastings Ter. B'frd —3B 76
Hastings Wlk. C'frd —5H 103
Hastings Way. Coll —9G 17
Hatchard Bldgs. Leeds —3F 44
Hatchet La. Oaken —9E 76
Hatfield Clo. Barn —9N 153
Hatfield Ct. Wake —4L 119
(off Howard St.)
Hatfield Gdns. Roys —5C 154
Hatfield Pl. H'cft —8L 139
Hatfield Rd. B'frd —4F 58
Hatfield St. Wake —4L 119
Hatfield Vw. Wake —1L 119
Hathaway Av. B'frd —3J 57
Hathaway Dri. Leeds —6C 46
Hathaway La. Leeds —7C 46
Hathaway M. Leeds —6C 46
Hathaway Wlk. Leeds —7C 46
Hathershelf La. Hal —6A 90
Hatters Fold. Hal —5C 92
Hatton Clo. B'frd —5B 76
Haugh End La. Sower B —1G 110
Haugh Rd. Todm —6N 87
Haughs Green. —5A 130
Haughs Grn. Gol —5A 130
Haugh Shaw Cft. Hal —7N 91
Haugh Shaw Rd. Hal —7N 91
Haughs La. Hud —3E 130
Haughs Rd. Hud —3F 130
Hauxley Ct. I'ly —5J 9
Hauxwell Clo. Skel —7L 159
Hauxwell Dri. Yead —1M 41
Havelock Sq. T'tn —8D 56
Havelock St. B'frd —1L 75
Havelock St. Dew —6B 116
Havelock St. T'tn —8D 56
Haven Chase. Leeds —4H 43
Haven Clo. Leeds —3J 43
Haven Ct. Leeds —4J 43
Haven Ct. Pon —6H 123
Haven Cft. Leeds —4J 43
Haven Gdns. Leeds —4H 43
Haven Gth. Leeds —4H 43
Haven Grn. Leeds —4H 43
Haven La. Err —4J 89
Haven Mt. Leeds —4H 43
Haven Ri. Leeds —4H 43
Haven St. Todm —7L 87
Haven, The. B'frd —9G 41
Haven, The. Leeds —6E 64
Haven Vw. Leeds —4H 43
Havercroft. —9K 139
Havercroft. Bat —7F 96
(off Hanover St.)
Havercroft. Leeds —9H 61
Havercroft. Oss —6A 118
Havercroft La. D'ton —5C 124
Havercroft Ri. S Hien —3M 155
Havercroft Way. Bat —7C 96
Haverdale Rd. H'cft —9K 139
Haverlands, The. Hems —3E 156
Haveroid La. Crig —6G 137
Haveroid Way. Crig —5H 137
Haverthwaites Dri. Aber —6E 48
Havertop La. Pon —1N 121
Haw Av. Yead —8N 25
Hawber Cote Dri. Sils —7F 6
Hawber Cote La. Sils —7F 6
Hawber La. Sils —8F 6
Haw Cliff La. Thur —8D 148
Hawes Av. B'frd —3A 76
Hawes Av. Hud —4G 130
Hawes Clo. C'frd —4H 103
(in two parts)
Hawes Cres. B'frd —3A 76
Hawes Dri. B'frd —3A 76
Hawes Gro. B'frd —3A 76
Hawes Mt. B'frd —3A 76
Hawes Rd. B'frd —3N 75
Hawes Ter. B'frd —3A 76
Haweswater Clo. Weth —4J 17
Haweswater Pl. Knot —2D 124
Haw Hill Vw. Nor —9K 101
Hawkcliffe Vw. Sils —8C 6
Hawke Av. Heck —8B 96
Hawke Way. Low M —7C 76
Hawkhill Av. Guis —8H 25
Hawkhill Av. Leeds —4C 64
Hawkhill Dri. Leeds —3C 64
Hawkhill Gdns. Leeds —3C 64
Hawkhurst Rd. Leeds —8M 61
Hawkingcroft Rd. Horb —1B 136
Hawkins Dri. Leeds —4E 62
Hawkroyd Bank Rd. Hud —2K 147
Hawksbridge La. Oxe —3A 54
Hawkshead Clo. B'frd —9C 58
Hawkshead Cres. Leeds —3A 64
Hawkshead Dri. B'frd —9C 58
Hawkshead Wlk. B'frd —9C 58
Hawkshead Way. B'frd —9C 58
(off Hawkshead Clo.)
Hawksley Ct. Morl —6J 79
Hawk's Nest Gdns. E. Leeds —3F 44
Hawk's Nest Gdns. S. Leeds —3F 44
Hawk's Nest Gdns. W. Leeds —3F 44
Hawk's Nest Ri. Leeds —3F 44
Hawkstone Av. Guis —9G 25
Hawkstone Dri. Kei —7G 20
Hawkstone Vw. Guis —9G 25
Hawk St. Kei —8K 21
(off Pheasant St.)
Hawks Wood Av. B'frd —3L 57
Hawkswood Av. Leeds —8H 43
Hawkswood Cres. Leeds —8H 43
Hawkswood Gro. Leeds —8H 43
Hawkswood Mt. Leeds —8H 43
Hawkswood Pl. Leeds —9H 43
Hawkswood St. Leeds —9J 43
Hawkswood Ter. Leeds —9J 43
Hawkswood Vw. Leeds —8H 43
Hawksworth. —8D 24
(nr. Guisley)
Hawksworth. —8H 43
(nr. Horsforth)
Hawksworth Av. Guis —9H 25
Hawksworth Clo. Men —5E 24
Hawksworth Dri. Guis —9H 25
Hawksworth Dri. Men —4D 24
Hawksworth Gro. Leeds —9G 43
Hawksworth La. Guis —8D 24
Hawksworth Rd. Bail —1A 40
Hawksworth Rd. H'fth —8G 42
(in two parts)
Hawksworth St. I'ly —5G 8
Haw La. Yead —9M 25
Hawley Clo. Morl —2J 97
Hawley Ter. B'frd —2J 59
Hawley Way. Morl —2J 97
Haworth. —9D 36
Haworth Clo. Mir —5K 115
Haworth Ct. Yead —9M 25
(off Chapel La.)
Haworth Gro. B'frd —3K 57
Haworth La. Yead —9M 25
Haworth Rd. All —3F 56
Haworth Rd. Birs —2C 96
Haworth Rd. B'frd —3K 57
Haworth Rd. Cro R —7E 36
Haworth Rd. Cull —9F 36
Haworth Rd. Wilsd —2M 55
Haw Pk. La. Ryh —7F 138
Haw Pk. La. Wake —8C 138
Hawthorn Av. Bat —9D 96
Hawthorn Av. B'frd —6J 59
Hawthorn Av. Croft —1F 138
Hawthorn Av. Knot —9C 104
Hawthorn Av. Yead —9M 25
Hawthorn Clo. Brigh —9A 94
Hawthorn Ct. Croft —1F 138
Hawthorn Cres. Bail —4B 40
Hawthorn Cres. Leeds —8F 44
Hawthorn Cres. Yead —9M 25
Hawthorn Cft. Loft —3L 99
Hawthorn Dri. B'frd —8G 41
Hawthorn Dri. Leeds —1A 60
Hawthorn Dri. Yead —8N 25
Hawthorne Av. C'frd —6H 103
Hawthorne Av. F'stne —7C 122
Hawthorne Av. Hems —3D 156
Hawthorne Av. Shipl —1B 58
Hawthorne Av. Weth —2L 17
Hawthorne Clo. Fen B —7H 133
Hawthorne Clo. Floc —7G 134
Hawthorne Clo. Gild —6G 79
Hawthorne Clo. K'gte —9D 98
Hawthorne Cres. Hems —3C 156
Hawthorne Cres. Skel —8M 159
Hawthorne Dri. Gild —6H 79
Hawthorne Gdns. Leeds —2L 43
Hawthorne Gro. Wake —4G 119
Hawthorne Mills. Leeds —1K 79
(off Cow Clo. Gro.)
Hawthorne Mt. Nor —4J 121
Hawthorne St. Shaf —6K 155
Hawthorne St. Sils —8D 6
Hawthorne Ter. Cros M —6H 131
Hawthorne Ter. Gar —9K 65
Hawthorne Ter. Wake —4G 119
Hawthorne Vw. Gild —6H 79
Hawthorne Way. E Mor —8D 22
Hawthorne Way. Shaf —6K 155
Hawthorne Way. Shel —6K 149
Hawthorn Gro. Ackw —5F 140
Hawthorn Gro. Bur W —9D 10
Hawthorn Gro. Leeds —1A 60
Hawthorn Gro. Rothw —9A 82
Hawthorn La. Leeds —8F 44
Hawthorn Mt. Leeds —8F 44
Hawthorn Pl. Todm —6K 87
Hawthorn Ri. Leeds —7D 46
Hawthorn Rd. Leeds —8F 44
Hawthorn Rd. Slai —8L 129
Hawthorn Rd. Yead —9M 25
Hawthorns, The. Oss —8A 118
Hawthorns, The. Wake —7M 99
Hawthorn St. B'frd —6J 59
Hawthorn St. Hal —7N 91
Hawthorn St. Hip —4J 93
Hawthorn Ter. Oss —8A 118
Hawthorn Va. Leeds —8F 44
Hawthorn Vw. Bail —4C 40
Hawthorn Vw. Leeds —8F 44
Hawtop La. Wool —3H 153
Haw Vw. Yead —8N 25
Hayburn Gdns. Bat —7E 96
Hayburn Rd. Bat —7D 96
Haycliffe Av. B'frd —3M 75
Haycliffe Dri. B'frd —3L 75
Haycliffe Gro. B'frd —3M 75
Haycliffe Hill. —3N 75
Haycliffe Hill Rd. B'frd —3N 75
Haycliffe La. B'frd —3M 75
Haycliffe Rd. B'frd —2N 75
Haycliffe Ter. B'frd —2N 75
Hayclose Mead. B'frd —7M 75
Hayden St. B'frd —8F 58
Haydn Av. Stan —6N 99
Haydn Pl. Q'bry —4D 74
Haydn's Ter. Far —4B 60
Hayfield Av. B Spa —9C 18
Hayfield Av. Hud —3F 130
Hayfield Clo. Bail —3C 40
Hayfield Clo. H'frth —4B 164
Hayfields, The. Haw —7C 36
Hayfield Ter. Leeds —8M 61
Haygill Nook. Sils —8D 4
Hayhills La. Sils —5D 6
Hayhills Rd. Sils —7E 6
Hayleigh Av. Leeds —3F 60
Hayleigh Mt. Leeds —3F 60
Hayleigh St. Leeds —4F 60
Hayleigh Ter. Leeds —4F 60
Hayley Ct. Hal —4B 92
(off Hayley Hill)
Hayne La. Wake —5H 135
Haynes St. Kei —1K 37
Hays La. Hal —6H 73
Hayson Clo. Dew —2J 117
Haythorns Av. Sils —8D 6
Haythorns M. Sils —8D 6
Hayton Dri. Weth —5N 17
Hayton Wood Vw. Aber —7E 48
Haywain, The. I'ly —6J 9
Haywood Av. Hud —3H 131
Hazebrouck Dri. Bail —3N 39
Hazel Av. Dew —4L 117
Hazel Av. Leeds —7D 46
Hazel Bank. Wake —3G 119
Hazel Beck. Bgly —7E 38
Hazel Clo. B'shaw —7L 77
Hazel Clo. Dew —4L 117
Hazel Ct. Rothw —9A 82
Hazel Ct. Wake —3J 119
Hazel Cres. Dew —4L 117
Hazelcroft. B'frd —2H 59
Hazel Cft. Shipl —9A 40
Hazel Dene. Holy G —7A 112
(off Cross St.)
Hazeldene. Q'bry —5C 74
Hazeldene Cotts. Sick —4D 16
Hazel Dri. Dew —4L 117
Hazel Gdns. C'frd —6K 103
Hazel Grove. —8D 130
Hazel Gro. Bat —8D 96
Hazel Gro. Floc —7G 134
Hazel Gro. Hal —5M 93
Hazel Gro. Hud —6N 113
Hazel Gro. Pon —1L 123
Hazelheads. Bail —3A 40
Hazelhurst Av. Bgly —7E 38
Hazelhurst Brow. B'frd —4J 57
Hazelhurst Ct. B'frd —8G 59
(BD3)
Hazelhurst Ct. B'frd —4J 57
(BD9)
Hazelhurst Ct. Pud —7C 60
Hazelhurst Gro. Q'bry —6C 74
Hazelhurst Rd. B'frd —4J 57
Hazelhurst Rd. Q'bry —6C 74
Hazelhurst Ter. B'frd —4J 57
Hazel La. Hamp —7F 158
Hazel La. Knot —3E 124
Hazelmere Av. Bgly —7F 38
Hazel Mt. Shipl —8A 40
Hazel Ri. Meth —3K 101
Hazel Rd. Knot —9D 104
Hazel Wlk. B'frd —4J 57
Hazelwood Av. Gar —9A 66
Hazelwood Av. Riddl —7M 21
Hazelwood Castle. —3H 49
Hazelwood Ct. Out —7M 99
Hazelwood Gdns. Hems —3E 156
Hazelwood Rd. B'frd —3H 57
Hazelwood Rd. Kin —9B 140
Hazelwood Rd. Out —7M 99
Hazelwood St. Todm —7K 87
Hazledene Cres. Shaf —8L 155
Hazledene Rd. Shaf —8K 155
Headfield La. Dew —6F 116
Headfield Rd. Dew —7G 116
(in two parts)
Headfield Rd. Hud —7M 131
Headfield Vw. Dew —7G 116
Headingley. —1N 61
Headingley. —2N 61
Headingley Av. Leeds —1M 61
Headingley Ct. Leeds —2B 62
Headingley Cres. Leeds —2N 61
Headingley Hill. —2A 62
Headingley La. Leeds —2A 62
Headingley Mt. Leeds —1M 61
Headingley Office Pk. Leeds —2B 62
Headingley Ri. Leeds —3B 62
(off Welton Rd.)
Headingley Ter. Leeds —2B 62
Headingley Vw. Leeds —2N 61
Headland Gro. B'frd —4L 75
Headland La. Dew —5J 117
Headlands. Liv —9L 95
Headlands Av. Oss —6M 117
Headlands Clo. Liv —9M 95
Headlands Gro. Oss —6M 117
Headlands La. Knot —8D 104
Headlands La. Pon —2J 123
Headlands Pk. Oss —6M 117
Headlands Rd. Hud —3M 131
Headlands Rd. Liv —8L 95
Headlands Rd. Oss —6M 117
Headlands Rd. Bus. Pk. Liv —8L 95
Headlands St. Liv —9L 95
Headlands Wlk. Oss —6M 117
Headley Cotts. Tad —8G 33
Headley La. B'ham —6D 32
Headley La. T'tn —1B 74
Headrow Cen., The. Leeds —6E 62
Headrow, The. Leeds —6D 62
Headwall Green. —7A 130
Headwell La. Saxt —9N 49
Healdfield Rd. C'frd —4E 102
Heald La. Caw —5J 167
Healds Av. Liv —8M 95
Healds Rd. Dew —1D 116
Heald St. C'frd —4F 102
Healdwood Clo. C'frd —4G 102
Healdwood Rd. C'frd —4G 103
Healey. —7C 96
(nr. Batley)
Healey. —8M 117
(nr. Ossett)
Healey Av. Bgly —5F 38
Healey Clo. Bat —7C 96
Healey Cres. Oss —8N 117
Healey Cft. Wake —5D 98
Healey Cft. La. E Ard —5D 98
Healey Dri. Oss —8N 117
Healey Grn. La. Hud —4K 133
Healey Houses. Hud —5F 146
Healey La. Bat —8C 96
(in two parts)
Healey La. Bgly —5F 38
Healey La. Bstfld —4C 134
Healey Rd. Oss —8N 117
Healey St. Bat —7C 96
Healey Vw. Oss —7N 117
Healey Wood Cres. Brigh —3M 113
Healey Wood Gdns. Brigh —3M 113
Healey Wood Gro. Brigh —3N 113
Healey Wood Rd. Brigh —3M 113
Heap La. B'frd —7E 58
Heap St. B'frd —7E 58
Heap St. Hal —2B 92
Hearn Gth. Hal —5B 92
Heath. —6C 120
Heath Av. Hal —8A 92
Heathcliff. Haw —8B 36
Heathcliffe Clo. Birs —1C 96
Heath Clo. Dew —3L 117
Heath Clo. Lint —2D 146
Heathcote Av. T'ner —2G 47
Heath Cres. Hal —7B 92
Heath Cres. Leeds —2A 80
Heathcroft Bank. Leeds —3A 80
Heathcroft Cres. Leeds —3A 80
Heathcroft Dri. Leeds —3A 80
Heathcroft Lawn. Leeds —3A 80
Heathcroft Ri. Leeds —3A 80
Heathcroft Va. Leeds —3A 80
Heathdale Av. Hud —1L 131
Heath Dri. B Spa —1B 32
Heather Av. Mel —8D 146
Heather Bank. Todm —2K 107
Heatherbank Av. Oakw —3F 36
Heather Bank Clo. Cull —1K 55
Heather Clo. Oss —8B 118
Heather Clo. Out —7M 99
Heather Clo. S Kirk —6K 157
Heather Ct. Bgly —2F 38
Heather Ct. Birs —2B 96
Heather Ct. Out —7N 99
Heather Ct. Sal N —2E 130
Heathercroft. Leeds —9G 44
Heather Cft. Shar C —8K 121
Heatherdale Ct. Wake —4A 98
Heatherdale Dri. Ting —4A 98
Heatherdale Rd. Ting —4N 97
Heather Dri. Mt Tab —1G 91
Heatherfield Cres. Hud —4J 131
Heatherfield Rd. Hud —4J 131
Heather Gdns. Leeds —6H 61
Heather Gdns. S'cft —9D 30
Heather Gro. B'frd —2G 57
Heather Gro. Kei —8F 20
Heather Gro. Leeds —6H 61
Heathergrove Fold. Hud —3B 132
Heatherlands Av. Denh —4K 55
Heather Pl. Q'bry —3A 74
Heather Ri. Bur W —9C 10
Heather Rd. Bail —3B 40
Heather Rd. Mel —8C 146
Heatherside. Bail —3N 39
Heathers, The. Shar C —8K 121
Heatherstones. Hal —8A 92
Heather Va. S'cft —9C 30
Heather Vw. Bgly —2J 39
Heather Vw. Oss —6N 117
Heather Vw. Shar C —8K 121
Heathfield. —4F 112
Heathfield. Leeds —3K 43
Heathfield. Mir —5K 115
Heathfield Av. Ell —4G 112
Heathfield Clo. Bgly —3F 38
Heathfield Clo. Ting —5B 98
Heathfield Cft. Leeds —3N 61
Heathfield Gro. B'frd —1K 75
Heathfield Gro. Hal —8B 92
(off Heath Rd.)
Heathfield Ind. Est. Ell —4F 112
Heathfield La. B Spa —9B 18
Heathfield M. Gol —6D 130
Heathfield Pl. Hal —8B 92
Heathfield Ri. Rish —1C 128
Heathfield Rd. Gol —6D 130
Heathfield Rd. Oss —3M 117
Heathfield St. Ell —5F 112
Heathfield Ter. Hal —8B 92
Heathfield Ter. Leeds —9N 43
Heathfield Vw. B'frd —4K 57
Heathfield Wlk. Leeds —2K 43
Heath Gdns. Hal —8B 92
Heath Gro. Bat —7J 97
Heath Gro. E Mor —8C 22
Heath Gro. Leeds —2A 80
Heath Gro. Pud —8N 59
Heath Hall. Hal —7B 92
Heath Hall Av. B'frd —4F 76
Heath Hill Rd. Hal —4G 91
Heath Ho. La. Slai —6A 130
Heath La. Hal —8B 92
Heath Lea. Hal —7B 92
Heathmoor Clo. Hal —8K 73
Heathmoor Clo. Idle —7E 40
Heathmoor Mt. Hal —7K 73
Heathmoor Pk. Rd. Hal —6K 73
Heathmoor Way. Hal —7K 73
Heath Mt. Hal —8A 92
Heath Mt. Leeds —2A 80
Heath Mt. Rd. Brigh —3M 113
Heathness Rd. Add —9K 5
Heath Pk. I'ly —6E 8
Heath Pk. Av. Hal —7B 92
Heath Pl. Leeds —2A 80
Heath Ri. Leeds —3A 80
Heath Rd. B'frd —5F 58

Heath Rd. Dew —3L 117
Heath Rd. Hal —8B 92
Heath Rd. Leeds —2A 80
Heath Rd. Lint —2D 146
Heath Rd. Pud —8N 59
Heath Royd. Hal —8B 92
Heath St. Bgly —4F 38
Heath St. B'frd —7G 58
Heath St. Hal —8A 92
Heath St. Liv —1M 115
Heath Ter. B'frd —7F 58
Heath Vs. Hal —8B 92
Heath Wlk. Dew —3L 117
Heathwood Dri. Gol —5B 130
Heathy Av. Hal —8N 73
Heathy La. Hal —7M 73
Heaton. —3M 57
Heaton Av. Cleck —5G 95
Heaton Av. Dew —3H 117
Heaton Av. Hud —1G 133
Heaton Av. Leeds —9M 61
Heaton Av. Sandb —9B 22
Heaton Clo. Bail —3N 39
Heaton Clo. Bgly —3G 39
Heaton Cres. Bail —2N 39
Heaton Cres. Bgly —3G 39
Heaton Dri. Bail —2N 39
Heaton Dri. Bgly —3G 38
Heaton Dri. Hud —9G 114
Heaton Fold La. Hud —5J 131
Heaton Gdns. Hud —4J 131
Heaton Grove. —2N 57
Heaton Gro. B'frd —2N 57
Heaton Gro. Cleck —5G 95
Heaton Gro. Shipl —8A 40
Heaton Hill. B'frd —6K 75
Heaton Moor Rd. Hud —1G 132
Heaton Pk. Dri. B'frd —3L 57
Heaton Pk. Rd. B'frd —3L 57
Heaton Rd. Bat —5F 96
Heaton Rd. B'frd —3M 57
Heaton Rd. Hud —5J 131
Heaton Royds. —1L 57
Heaton Royds La. B'frd —1L 57
Heaton's Ct. Leeds —7E 62
Heaton Shay. —1L 57
Heaton St. Ackw —5E 140
Heaton St. B'frd —9E 58
Heaton St. Cleck —4H 95
Heatons Yd. Brigh —2N 113
Heator La. Up Cum —1L 165
Hebble Brook Clo. Mix —9J 73
Hebble Brook Bus. Pk. Hal —6J 73
Hebble Cotts. Hal —3L 91
Hebble Ct. Hal —9K 73
Hebble Dean. Hal —3M 91
Hebble Dri. H'frth —1M 163
Hebble End. —1G 89
Hebble End. H Bri —1G 89
Hebble Gdns. Hal —3L 91
Hebble La. Hal —3M 91
Hebble La. H'frth —2M 163
Hebble La. Mel —9C 146
Hebble Mt. Mel —8D 146
Hebble Row. Oakw —6C 36
(off Providence La.)
Hebble St. Dew —6C 116
Hebble St. Hud —2N 131
Hebble Va. Dri. Hal —2L 91
Hebble Vw. Hal —2L 91
Hebb Vw. B'frd —3K 75
Hebden App. Leeds —9C 46
Hebden Bridge. —1H 89
Hebden Bri. Rd. H Bri & Oxe —9L 53
Hebden Chase. Leeds —9C 46
Hebden Clo. Leeds —9C 46
Hebden Ct. Hud —3G 130
(off Chesil Bank.)
Hebden Grn. Leeds —9C 46
Hebden Path. Leeds —9C 46
Hebden Pl. Leeds —9C 46
Hebden Rd. Haw —9D 36
Hebden Rd. Wake —3N 119
Hebden Ter. H Bri —6H 71
Hebden Wlk. Leeds —9C 46
Heber Clo. Sils —9F 6
Heber's Ghyll Dri. I'ly —6C 8
Heber's Gro. I'ly —6D 8
Heber St. Kei —1H 37
Heckmondwike. —9A 96
Heckmondwike Rd. Dew —1B 116
Hector Clo. B'frd —4A 76
Heddon Clo. B'frd —9C 58
Heddon Gro. B'frd —9C 58
Heddon Pl. Leeds —9A 44
Heddon St. Leeds —9A 44
Heddon Wlk. B'frd —9C 58
(off Heddon Clo.)
Hedge Clo. B'frd —5J 57
Hedge La. Dart —9F 152
Hedge Nook. Wyke —9A 76
Hedge Side. B'frd —6K 57
Hedge Top La. Hal —1F 92
Hedge Way. B'frd —5K 57
Hedley Chase. Leeds —7A 62
Hedley Cres. Wake —9K 99
Hedley Grn. Leeds —7A 62
Heeley Rd. Wake —6J 137
Heidelberg Rd. B'frd —4M 57
Height. —1D 146
Height Grn. Sower B —8H 91
Height La. Drau —8D 4
Height La. Oxe —4D 54
Height Rd. H Bri —1L 89
Heights Bank. Leeds —7J 61
Heights Clo. Leeds —7H 61
Heights Dri. Leeds —6H 61
Heights Dri. Lint —2C 146
Heights E., The. Leeds —7J 61
Heights Gth. Leeds —7H 61
Heights Grn. Leeds —7J 61
Heights La. Bgly —7E 22
Heights La. B'frd —3J 57
Heights La. Heck —9B 96
Heights La. Leeds —7J 61
Heights La. Sils —5A 6
Heights Pde. Leeds —7H 61
Heights, The. H'frth —5A 164
Heights Wlk. Leeds —7J 61
Heights Way. Leeds —7H 61
Heights W., The. Leeds —7H 61
Height Wlk. Ripp —8E 110
Held Head. Ackw —5D 140
Helena Pl. Kip —5N 83
Helena St. Kip —5N 83
Helena Way. B'frd —5G 76
Helene Ct. Hud —2D 130
Helen Rose Ct. Shipl —6C 40
Helen St. Hud —7K 131
Helen St. Shipl —7L 39
Helen Ter. Brigh —9L 93
Hellewell's Row. Horb —1N 135
Hellewell St. B'frd —6L 75
Hell La. Wake & New S —7D 120
Hellwood La. S'cft —9D 30
Helme. Mel —5D 146
Helme La. Mel —6C 146
Helmet La. Mel —8C 146
Helm La. Hud —6G 115
Helm La. Sower B —2C 110
Helmshore Dri. B'frd —6J 57
Helmsley Ct. Midd —9E 80
Helmsley Dri. Leeds —8L 43
Helmsley Rd. B Spa —1C 32
Helmsley Rd. Leeds —8L 43
Helmsley Rd. Wake —1N 137
Helmsley St. B'frd —1E 76
Helston Cft. Leeds —8C 80
Helston Gth. Leeds —8C 80
Helston Grn. Leeds —8C 80
Helston Pl. Leeds —8C 80
Helston Rd. Leeds —7C 80
Helston Rd. Nor —9J 101
Helston Sq. Leeds —7B 80
Helston St. Leeds —7B 80
Helston Wlk. Leeds —8C 80
(in three parts)
Helston Way. Leeds —7C 80
Helted Way. Alm —7E 132
Hembrigg Ter. Morl —2K 97
(off Dartmouth Av.)
Hemingway Clo. C'frd —7K 103
Hemingway Clo. Leeds —1G 81
Hemingway Gth. Leeds —2G 81
Hemingway Grn. Leeds —2G 81
Hemingway Rd. B'frd —7H 41
Hemishor Dri. W'ford —5M 83
Hemsby Gro. Kei —3H 37
(off Hemsby St.)
Hemsby Rd. C'frd —5C 102
Hemsby St. Kei —3H 37
Hemsworth. —6J 157
Hemsworth By-Pass. Brier —5B 156
Hemsworth By-Pass. Hems —8F 140
Hemsworth La. Fitz —6A 140
Hemsworth Marsh. —9F 140
Hemsworth Rd. Hems —4E 156
Henacrewood Ct. Q'bry —6D 74
Henage St. Q'bry —4C 74
Henbury St. Leeds —5F 62
Henconner Av. Leeds —9E 44
Henconner Cres. Leeds —9E 44
Henconner Dri. Leeds —9E 44
Henconner Gdns. Leeds —9E 44
Henconner Gth. Leeds —9E 44
Henconner Gro. Leeds —9E 44
Henconner La. Bmly —5H 61
Henconner La. Chap A —9E 44
Henconner Rd. Leeds —9E 44
Hendal La. Wake —5J 137
Henderson Av. Nor —3J 121
Henderson Glen. Roys —6B 154
Henderson Pl. B'frd —4A 76
Hendford Dri. B'frd —7E 58
Hendy Cotts. G'lnd —4C 112
Hendy Pas. Leeds —5E 44
Henfield Av. B'frd —8E 40
Hen Holme La. Sils —9E 6
Henley Av. B'frd —3C 76
Henley Av. Dew —9G 117
Henley Av. Leeds —4F 60
Henley Av. Rawd —4A 42
Henley Clo. Rawd —4A 42
Henley Ct. B'frd —3D 76
Henley Cres. Leeds —4F 60
Henley Cres. Rawd —4A 42
Henley Cft. Hud —4C 132
Henley Dri. F'stne —8D 122
Henley Dri. Rawd —4N 41
Henley Gro. B'frd —3C 76
Henley Gro. Leeds —4F 60
Henley Hill. Rawd —4N 41
Henley Mt. Rawd —4A 42
Henley Pl. Leeds —4F 60
Henley Rd. B'frd —3D 76
Henley Rd. Dew —9H 117
Henley Rd. Leeds —4F 60
Henley St. Leeds —4F 60
Henley Ter. Leeds —4F 60
Henley Vw. Leeds —4F 60
Henley Vw. Rawd —4N 41
Henrietta St. Bat —7F 96
Henry Av. H'cft —1K 155
Henry Av. Leeds —9M 61
Henry Clo. Shaf —6K 155
Henry Frederick Av. Hud —2H 147
Henry Moore Ct. C'frd —5H 103
Henry Moore Pl. C'frd —6E 102
Henry Pl. Morl —9K 79
Henry Price Bldgs. Leeds —4C 62
Henry Ralph Av. Hud —9H 131
Henry St. Bat —1F 116
Henry St. Brigh —8M 93
Henry St. Cytn —1H 75
Henry St. Hal —6A 92
Henry St. Hud —4M 131
Henry St. Kei —9J 21
Henry St. T'tn —8C 56
Henry St. Wake —5J 119
Henry Ter. Yead —9K 25
Henshaw. —1L 41
Henshaw Av. Yead —1M 41
Henshaw Cres. Yead —1M 41
Henshaw La. Yead —2L 41
Henshaw Oval. Yead —1M 41
Henshaw Rd. Todm —2J 107
Henson Gro. C'frd —5H 103
Hepton Ct. Leeds —6K 63
Hepton Dri. H Bri —9G 70
Heptonstall. —8G 70
Heptonstall Rd. H Bri —9G 71
Hepworth. —6C 164
Hepworth Av. Chur —5L 79
Hepworth Clo. Mir —5M 115
Hepworth Cres. Chur —5L 79
Hepworth Cres. N Mill —6C 164
Hepworth Dri. Mir —5N 115
Hepworth La. Mir —5M 115
Hepworth Rd. N Mill —5C 164
Hepworth St. C'frd —3F 102
Herbalist St. Leeds —8A 62
Herbert Pl. B'frd —6J 59
Herbert St. Bgly —4F 38
Herbert St. B'frd —1B 76
Herbert St. C'frd —5D 102
Herbert St. Cytn —2H 75
Herbert St. Ctly —9G 39
Herbert St. Hal —6M 91
Herbert St. Shipl —6L 39
Herbrigg Gdns. Morl —2L 97
Hereford Clo. Hems —1D 156
Hereford St. Leeds —6M 61
Hereford Way. B'frd —1E 76
Heritage Pk. Bgly —1F 38
Heritage Rd. Bat —8F 96
Heritage Way. Oakw —5B 36
Hermitage Pk. Fen B —8J 133
Hermit Hole. —5G 37
Hermit St. Oakw —5G 36
Hermon Av. Hal —6N 91
Hermon Gro. Hal —6N 91
Hermon Rd. Leeds —5C 64
Hermon St. Leeds —5C 64
Heron Clo. Leeds —3H 45
Heron Clo. Q'bry —3B 74
Heron Clo. Steet —2B 20
Heron Ct. Morl —9N 79
Heron Dri. Wake —5L 137
Heron Gro. Leeds —3H 45
Herriot M. C'frd —7K 103
Herschel Rd. B'frd —7J 57
Hertford Chase. Leeds —8D 64
Hertford Clo. Leeds —8E 64
Hertford Cft. Leeds —8E 64
Hertford Fold. Leeds —8D 64
Hertford Lawn. Leeds —8D 64
Heseltine Clo. Nor —2H 121
Heseltine La. Cra V —8H 89
Heshbon St. B'frd —2G 76
Hesketh Av. Leeds —1K 61
Hesketh Av. Ting —4N 97
Hesketh La. Ting —4N 97
Hesketh Mt. Leeds —1K 61
Hesketh Pl. Hal —5M 93
Hesketh Pl. Leeds —1K 61
Hesketh Rd. Leeds —1K 61
Hesketh Ter. Leeds —2K 61
Hesley Rd. Wake —5K 137
Hessle. —3E 140
Hessle Av. Leeds —3A 62
Hessle Comn. La. Wake —4D 140
Hessle Ct. Pon —3J 123
Hessle Ho. B'frd —8G 40
(off Idlethorp Way)
Hessle La. Wake —1D 140
Hessle Mt. Leeds —3A 62
Hessle Pl. Leeds —3A 62
Hessle Rd. Leeds —3A 62
Hessle St. Leeds —3A 62
Hessle Ter. Leeds —3A 62
Hessle Vw. Leeds —3A 62
Hessle Wlk. Leeds —3A 62
Hetchell Vw. Bard —6E 30
Hetton Ct. H'let —2F 80
Hetton Rd. Leeds —1K 63
Heuthwaite Av. Weth —5N 17
Heuthwaite La. Weth —5A 18
Hew Clews. B'frd —2K 75
Hexham Grn. Hud —5E 130
Hey Beck. —7M 97
Hey Beck La. Dew & Wake —7M 97
(in two parts)
Heybeck Wlk. B'frd —3K 77
Heycliffe Rd. H'frth —3N 163
Hey Cres. Mel —7C 146
Heyford Ct. B'frd —3B 58
Heygate Clo. Bail —3B 40
Heygate La. Bail —3B 40
Heygate La. B'ham —5E 32
Hey Head La. Todm —3L 87
Hey La. Hud —2N 147
Hey La. Lower —7B 132
Hey La. Slnd —3J 129
Hey La. Stanb —7N 35
Hey Moor La. Shel —7L 149
Heyroyd La. Slai —2L 145
Heys Av. T'tn —8E 56
Hey's Bldgs. Nor —8H 101
Heys Clo. Knot —8E 104
Heys Cres. T'tn —8F 56
Heys Gdns. Thon —9N 147
Heysham Dri. B'frd —3J 77
Heys Ho. Hal —4N 91
(off Crossley Gdns.)
Hey Slack La. Cumb —6G 165
Heys La. Hal —7B 72
Heys La. Ripp —9D 110
Heys La. Slai —8K 129
Heys Rd. Thon —9A 148
Hey St. B'frd —7B 58
Hey St. Brigh —8N 93
Hey St. Todm —7L 87
Heywood Clo. Hal —2F 92
Hick La. Bat —7G 96
Hicks La. Meth —1L 101
Hick St. B'frd —7D 58
Higgin La. Hal —7D 92
High Ackworth. —2G 140
Higham and Dob La. Sower B —8C 90
Higham Vw. Dart —9F 152
High Ash. Shipl —8C 40
High Ash Av. Clay W —7K 151
High Ash Av. Leeds —2G 44
High Ash Clo. Not —3A 154
High Ash Cres. Leeds —2G 44
High Ash Dri. Leeds —2G 44
High Ash Mt. Leeds —2G 44
High Ash Pk. All —5E 56
High Bank App. Leeds —7E 64
High Bank Clo. Add —1M 7
High Bank Clo. Leeds —7E 64
High Bank Gdns. Leeds —7F 64
High Bank Ga. Leeds —7E 64
High Bank La. Shipl —9J 39
High Bank Pl. Leeds —7E 64
High Banks Clo. Riddl —6M 21
High Bank Vw. Leeds —7E 64
High Bank Way. Leeds —7F 64
High Binns La. Oxc 4D 54
Highbridge La. Skelm —8F 150
Highbridge Ter. B'frd —4D 76
High Brook Fall. Loft —6L 99
High Brooms. Hud —1K 131
Highburton. —2J 149
Highbury Clo. Leeds —9A 44
Highbury Clo. Q'bry —5B 74
Highbury La. Leeds —9A 44
Highbury Mt. Leeds —9A 44
Highbury Pl. Bmly —6D 60
Highbury Pl. Leeds —9A 44
Highbury Rd. Leeds —9A 44
Highbury St. Leeds —9A 44
Highbury Ter. Dew —3G 117
Highbury Ter. Leeds —9A 44
High Busy La. Shipl & B'frd —7C 4
(in three parts)
Highcliffe Av. Hud —9L 113
High Cliffe Clo. T'tn —8D 56
Highcliffe Dri. Hal —5K 91
Highcliffe Ind. Est. Morl —8J 79
Highcliffe Rd. Bat —9F 96
Highcliffe Rd. Morl —9J 79
High Cliffe Ter. Weth —4M 17
High Clo. Dart —8F 152
High Clo. Guis —8F 24
High Clo. Hud —7C 132
High Clo. Lint —1D 146
High Clo. Oss —2N 117
High Clo. Rawd —4M 41
High Cote. Riddl —6K 21
High Ct. Hept —7E 70
High Ct. Leeds —7F 62
High Ct. La. Leeds —7F 62
High Crest. Lint —8D 130
Highcroft. Bat —9F 96
(off Highcliffe Rd.)
Highcroft. Coll —9H 17
Highcroft. H'frth —3K 163
Highcroft Clo. Pud —6N 59
High Cft. Cres. Hud —7D 132
High Cft. Dri. Barn —9A 154
Highcroft Gdns. Kei —1M 37
High Cft. Rd. Todm —6L 87
High Cross La. Q'bry —6E 74
Highdale. Dew —1H 117
Highdale Cft. B'frd —7F 40
High End. Esh —2G 40
Higher Ashenhurst. Todm —5J 87
Higher Back La. Blkhd —9N 69
Higher Brockwell. Sower B —9F 9
Higher Calderbrook. L'boro —9L 10
Higher Calderbrook Rd. L'boro —9L 10
Higher Coach Rd. Bail —5H 39
(in two parts)
Higher Downs. B'frd —6J 57
Higher Grange Rd. Pud —6B 60
Higher Intake Rd. B'frd —5G 58
Higher Pk. Royd Dri. Sower B —4E 11
Higher School St. Shipl —7L 39
Higherwood Clo. Kei —1L 37
High Farm Fold. Bads —8L 141
High Farm Mdw. Bads —8L 141
Highfell Ri. Kei —2E 36
High Fernley Ct. Wyke —9A 76
High Fernley Rd. Wyke —1M 93
(in two parts)
Highfield. —3D 156
(nr. Hemsworth)
Highfield. —9G 20
(nr. Keighley)
Highfield. B'frd —4H 77
Highfield. S'wram —8G 75
Highfield. Ting —3N 97
Highfield Av. Birds —4L 165
Highfield Av. B'frd —8E 40
Highfield Av. Brigh —4N 93
Highfield Av. G'lnd —4A 112
Highfield Av. Hal —6J 75
Highfield Av. Leeds —8M 61
Highfield Av. Mel —6C 146
Highfield Av. Pon —4J 123
(nr. Mill Hill La.)
Highfield Av. Pon —8N 103
(nr. Pontefract Rd.)
Highfield Cen. Hems —3D 156
Highfield Clo. E Mor —7C 22
Highfield Clo. F'stne —3D 122
Highfield Clo. Gild —6H 79
Highfield Clo. Leeds —9N 61
Highfield Ct. C'frd —6C 102
Highfield Ct. Leeds —9M 61
(off Highfield Av.)
Highfield Ct. Oakw —5C 36
Highfield Ct. Shepl —2J 165
Highfield Cres. All B —8N 83
(off Highfield Dri.)
Highfield Cres. Bail —3A 40
Highfield Cres. B'frd —2J 57
Highfield Cres. H Bri —9H 71
Highfield Cres. Leeds —8N 61
Highfield Cres. Mel —6C 146
Highfield Cres. Ove —4J 135
Highfield Cres. Pon —6A 60
Highfield Cres. W'ford —6D 82
Highfield Dri. All B —8N 83
Highfield Dri. Birs —2B 96
Highfield Dri. B'frd —2J 57
Highfield Dri. Gar —9N 65
Highfield Dri. Gild —6G 79
Highfield Dri. Liv —8J 95
Highfield Dri. L'ft —4E 90

Highfield Dri. *Rawd* —4N **41**
Highfield Dri. *Wake* —4G **118**
Highfield Gdns. *B'frd* —3J **57**
Highfield Gdns. *Dew* —8G **116**
Highfield Gdns. *Gild* —6G **79**
Highfield Gdns. *Leeds* —8M **61**
Highfield Gth. *Leeds* —9N **61**
Highfield Grange. *Horb* —1C **136**
Highfield Grn. *All B* —7N **83**
Highfield Grn. *Pud* —6A **60**
Highfield Gro. *All B* —7N **83**
Highfield Gro. *B'frd* —9E **40**
Highfield Gro. *Ell* —3D **112**
Highfield Gro. *Leeds* —8N **61**
Highfield Ho. B'frd —5A ***58***
(off Church St.)
Highfield La. *Bar E* —1L **65**
Highfield La. *Dew* —9C **96**
Highfield La. *Hems* —4C **156**
Highfield La. *Hud & Lep* —5G **133**
Highfield La. *Kei* —8G **20**
Highfield La. *Mel* —6B **146**
Highfield La. *M'fld* —1J **85**
High Fld. La. *Oakw* —4C **36**
Highfield La. *Sils* —7E **6**
High Fld. La. *Sower B* —5D **110**
Highfield La. *Wome* —9N **125**
Highfield La. *W'ford* —6D **82**
Highfield M. *Bail* —3A **40**
Highfield M. *E Mor* —7C **22**
Highfield Mt. *Dew* —1H **135**
Highfield Mt. *Oult* —7D **82**
Highfield Pl. *All B* —7A **84**
Highfield Pl. B'frd —5A ***58***
(off Church St.)
Highfield Pl. *Hal* —6M **91**
Highfield Pl. *Hems* —3C **156**
Highfield Pl. *Horb* —1C **136**
Highfield Pl. *Morl* —1L **97**
Highfield Ri. *Wake* —3G **118**
Highfield Rd. *Aber* —7E **48**
Highfield Rd. *Brigh* —3K **113**
Highfield Rd. *Cleck* —5G **94**
Highfield Rd. *Ell* —5E **112**
Highfield Rd. *Five E & Idle* —1E **58**
Highfield Rd. *Friz* —1A **58**
Highfield Rd. *Hems* —3C **156**
Highfield Rd. *Horb* —1C **136**
Highfield Rd. *Kei* —9G **20**
Highfield Rd. *Leeds* —4G **61**
Highfield Rd. *L'ft* —4E **90**
Highfield Rd. *Mel* —6C **146**
Highfield Rd. *Neth* —5N **135**
Highfield Rd. *Pon* —5J **123**
Highfield Rd. *Pud* —6N **59**
Highfield Rd. *Slai* —7M **129**
Highfields. *Hoy S* —9J **167**
Highfields. *Hud* —3L **131**
Highfields. *Neth* —5N **135**
High Fields. *Sower B* —8L **91**
Highfields. *Wake* —8L **139**
Highfields Ct. Hud —3L ***131***
(off Highfield Rd.)
Highfields Rd. *Dart* —9D **152**
Highfields Rd. *Hud* —3L **131**
Highfield St. *Kei* —9H **21**
Highfield St. *Leeds* —4G **61**
Highfield St. *Pud* —6N **59**
Highfield Ter. *Bgly* —4F **38**
Highfield Ter. *Cleck* —5G **94**
Highfield Ter. *Cull* —9K **37**
Highfield Ter. *Dew* —8G **116**
Highfield Ter. Hal —6M ***91***
(off Highfield Pl.)
Highfield Ter. *Pud* —7N **59**
Highfield Ter. *Q'bry* —5C **74**
Highfield Ter. *Rawd* —4N **41**
Highfield Ter. *Shipl* —7K **39**
Highfield Ter. *Sower B* —6E **110**
Highfield Vw. *Gild* —6H **79**
High Flatts. —5N 165
High Fold. *Bail* —3A **40**
High Fold. *Bgly* —8D **22**
High Fold. *Kei* —2F **36**
Highfold. *Yead* —2L **41**
High Fold La. *Kei* —6G **21**
Highgate. *B'frd* —2L **57**
Highgate. *Denh* —8L **55**
High Ga. *H'frth* —6N **163**
Highgate Av. *Lep* —7K **133**
Highgate Clo. *Q'bry* —3H **75**
Highgate Cres. *Lep* —7J **133**
Highgate Dri. *Lep* —7K **133**
Highgate Gro. *Q'bry* —3H **75**
Highgate La. *Lep* —7J **133**
Highgate La. *Mir* —9H **115**
Highgate Rd. *Dew* —3G **117**
(in two parts)
Highgate Rd. *Q'bry* —4F **74**
Highgate St. *Bat* —9J **97**
High Ga. St. *Leeds* —1G **80**
Highgate Ter. Dew —3G ***117***
(off Highgate Rd.)
Highgate Ter. Lep —7K ***133***
(off Highgate Av.)
Highgate Wlk. *Lep* —7K **133**
High Green. —7J 133
High Grn. Ct. Kbtn —3G ***148***
(off Storthes Hall La.)
High Grn. Dri. *Sils* —7D **6**
High Grn. Rd. *Nor* —8F **100**
Highgrove Ct. *Norm* —3L **121**
High Gro. La. *Hal* —7D **92**
High Ho. Av. *B'frd* —2E **58**
High Ho. Edge. *Lint* —2B **146**
High Ho. La. *Hal* —9C **72**
High Ho. La. *Slai* —2A **146**
High Ho. M. *Add* —1M **7**
High Ho. Rd. *B'frd* —2E **58**
High Hoyland. —8M 151
High Hoyland La. *H Hoy* —1L **167**
High Keep Fold. *Hall G* —7H **137**
Highland Clo. *Pon* —9M **103**
Highlands Av. *Hud* —7D **132**
Highlands Clo. *B'frd* —2K **75**
Highlands Clo. *Leeds* —5H **81**
Highlands Dri. *Leeds* —5H **81**
Highlands Gro. *B'frd* —2K **75**
Highlands Gro. *Leeds* —5H **81**
Highlands La. *Hal* —7M **73**
Highlands Pk. *Hal* —7M **73**
Highlands, The. *Liv* —7H **95**
Highlands, The. *Oss* —6M **117**
Highlands Wlk. *Leeds* —5H **81**
Highland Ville. *Hal* —5J **93**
High La. *Hal* —4H **91**
High La. *H Bri* —9K **89**
High La. *H Bir* —1N **15**
High La. *H'frth* —5A **164**
High La. *Hud* —8N **131**
High La. *Pen* —9A **166**
High Lea. *Mars* —5F **144**
Highlea Clo. *Yead* —2K **41**
Highlee La. *Sower B* —4F **110**
High Lees Rd. *Hal* —8H **73**
High Level Way. *Hal* —4M **91**
Highley Hall Cft. *Clif* —9B **94**
Highley Pk. *Clif* —1C **114**
High Mdw. *Kei* —7G **20**
High Meadows. *G'lnd* —4B **112**
High Meadows. *Thorn* —1F **134**
High Meadows. *W'ton* —4C **138**
High Meadows. *Wilsd* —1B **56**
High Mill La. *Add* —9N **5**
Highmoor. *Bail* —4M **39**
High Moor Av. *Leeds* —5G **44**
High Moor Ct. *Leeds* —5G **44**
Highmoor Cres. *Brigh* —9B **94**
High Moor Dri. *Leeds* —4G **44**
High Moor End Rd. *Mel* —8N **145**
High Moor Gro. *Leeds* —4G **44**
Highmoor La. *Brigh & Cleck* —9B **94**
(in two parts)
High Moor La. *Shepl* —9L **149**
High Moor Rd. *N Rig* —1M **13**
Highmoor Wlk. *Bail* —5M **39**
High Oxford St. *C'frd* —5C **102**
High Pk. Cres. *B'frd* —3K **57**
High Pk. Dri. *B'frd* —3K **57**
High Pk. Gro. *B'frd* —3K **57**
High Peak. *L'boro* —5A **126**
High Poplars. *B'frd* —2D **58**
High Ridge. *Neth* —4A **136**
High Ridge Av. *Rothw* —6M **81**
High Ridge Ct. *Rothw* —7N **81**
High Ridge Pk. *Rothw* —6M **81**
High Ridge Way. *B'hpe* —6J **27**
High Rd. *Dew* —4H **117**
Highroad Well. —4K 91
Highroad Well. *Hal* —5K **91**
Highroad Well Ct. *Hal* —5K **91**
Highroad Well La. *Hal* —5J **91**
Highroyd. *Lep* —7J **133**
Highroyd Cres. *Hud* —4B **132**
Highroyd La. *Hud* —4B **132**
High Royds Dri. *Men* —5F **24**
High Shaw Rd. W. *Hal* —7M **91**
High Spring Gdns. La. *Kei* —7G **21**
High Spring Rd. *Kei* —1M **37**
High Stones Rd. *Cra V* —9M **89**
High St. *Altft* —9G **100**
High St. *Birs* —3B **96**
High St. *B Spa* —9B **18**
High St. *B'ham* —6D **32**
High St. *Brigh* —9M **93**
High St. *B'ton* —3B **104**
High St. *Cam* —1N **159**
High St. *Carc* —9N **159**
High St. *C'frd* —5C **102**
High St. *Clay W* —7J **151**
High St. *Cleck* —4H **95**
High St. *Cliff* —3D **32**
High St. *Crig* —5G **136**
High St. *Croft* —2G **139**
High St. *Dart* —7J **153**
High St. *Dew* —4J **117**
High St. *Far* —3A **60**
High St. *Gol* —5A **130**
High St. *G'lnd* —5C **112**
High St. *Hal* —6A **92**
High St. *Hang H* —9H **97**
High St. *Heck* —9A **96**
High St. *Hon* —5L **147**
High St. *Horb* —1C **136**
High St. *Hud* —5M **131**
High St. *Idle* —7F **40**
High St. *Kei* —9H **21**
High St. *Kip* —4B **84**
High St. *Knot* —7B **104**
High St. *Ludd* —3E **90**
High St. *Morl* —2K **97**
High St. *New S* —6H **121**
High St. *Nor* —1H **121**
High St. *Oss* —2M **117**
High St. *Pad* —5K **131**
High St. *Q'bry* —4D **74**
High St. *Roys* —6B **154**
High St. *Shaf* —6K **155**
High St. *Shipl* —8A **40**
High St. *S Elm* —6N **157**
High St. *S Hien* —4M **155**
High St. *Slnd* —8L **111**
High St. *Steet* —3C **20**
High St. *Thorn* —1F **134**
High St. *T'tn* —8C **56**
High St. Todm —9J ***87***
(off Cannon St.)
High St. *Upt* —2N **157**
High St. *Wtwn* —4E **116**
High St. *Weth* —5M **17**
High St. *Wibs* —4N **75**
High St. *Wool* —2H **153**
High St. *Yead* —9M **25**
High St. Ct. *Ludd* —3E **90**
High St. Pl. *Idle* —7F **40**
High St. Pl. *Q'bry* —4D **74**
High Sunderland La. *Hal* —3C **92**
Highthorne Av. *B'frd* —5G **59**
Highthorne Ct. *Shad* —3H **45**
Highthorne Dri. *Shad* —3H **45**
Highthorne Gro. *A'ley* —6K **61**
Highthorne Gro. *Shad* —3J **45**
Highthorne Mt. *Leeds* —3H **45**
Highthorne St. *A'ley* —6K **61**
Highthorne Vw. *A'ley* —6K **61**
Hightown. —7H 95
Hightown Heights. —7F 94
Hightown La. *H'frth* —3M **163**
Hightown Rd. *Cleck & Liv* —5H **95**
Hightown Vw. *Liv* —7H **95**
High Trees La. *G'lnd* —5L **111**
High Utley. —7G 21
High Vw. *Crig* —5G **136**
High Vw. *Roys* —6C **154**
Highway. *Guis* —7F **24**
Highways. *Leeds* —5N **63**
High Weardley La. *Arth & Hare* —2C **28**
High Well Hill La. *S Hien* —3J **155**
High Wheatley. *I'ly* —6K **9**
High Wicken Clo. *T'tn* —8C **56**
High Wood. *I'ly* —6L **9**
Highwood Av. *Leeds* —4E **44**
Highwood Clo. *Dart* —9E **152**
High Wood Ct. *Leeds* —1A **62**
Highwood Cres. *Leeds* —4E **44**
Highwood Gro. *Leeds* —5E **44**
High Woodlands. *E Ard* —5E **98**
High Wood La. *Kbtn* —4M **149**
Highwood Path. *Slai* —8N **129**
Hilberoyd Rd. *Bat* —8G **96**
Hilda St. *H'tn* —2M **57**
Hilda St. *Oss* —7A **118**
Hill. —3L 163
Hillam Rd. *B'frd* —3B **58**
Hillam St. *B'frd* —2N **75**
Hillary Pl. *Leeds* —4D **62**
Hillary Rd. *Shipl* —8C **40**
Hillary St. *Dew* —9C **96**
Hillbrook Ri. *I'ly* —6E **8**
Hill Brow Clo. *All* —5F **56**
Hill Clo. *Bail* —5N **39**
Hill Clo. *Hud* —1E **130**
Hill Clo. *Pon* —4K **123**
Hill Clough Gro. *Lay* —9C **20**
Hillcote Dri. *B'frd* —1C **76**
Hill Ct. Av. *Leeds* —2F **60**
Hillcourt Cft. *Leeds* —2F **60**
Hillcourt Dri. *Leeds* —2F **60**
Hill Ct. Fold. *Leeds* —2F **60**
Hillcourt Gro. *Leeds* —2F **60**
Hill Cres. *Birs* —2D **96**
Hill Cres. *Bur W* —1D **24**
Hill Cres. *Hal* —7E **92**
Hill Cres. *Rawd* —2N **41**
Hillcrest. *Coll* —9F **16**
Hillcrest. *Gild* —5E **78**
Hill Crest. *H'cft* —9K **139**
Hillcrest. *Nor* —8F **100**
Hill Crest. *Rish* —1C **128**
Hill Crest. *Skel* —8K **159**
Hill Crest. Sower B —7H ***91***
(off Dalton St.)
Hill Crest. *Swil* —4H **83**
Hillcrest Av. *Bat* —7D **96**
Hillcrest Av. *C'frd* —6K **103**
Hill Crest Av. *Denh* —5L **55**
Hillcrest Av. *F'stne* —6B **122**
Hillcrest Av. *Leeds* —3G **63**
Hillcrest Av. *Oss* —3M **117**
Hillcrest Av. *Q'bry* —5E **74**
Hillcrest Av. *Sils* —7E **6**
Hill Crest Av. Sower B —7H ***91***
(off Dearden St.)
Hillcrest Clo. *C'frd* —6K **103**
Hillcrest Clo. *Swil* —4G **83**
Hillcrest Dri. *C'frd* —6K **103**
Hill Crest Dri. *Denh* —5K **55**
Hillcrest Dri. *Q'bry* —5E **74**
Hillcrest Mt. *C'frd* —6L **103**
Hill Crest Mt. *Denh* —5K **55**
Hillcrest Mt. *Leeds* —3H **43**
Hillcrest Mt. *Schol* —5D **94**
Hillcrest Pl. *Leeds* —2G **63**
Hillcrest Ri. *Leeds* —3G **43**
Hillcrest Rd. *C'frd* —6C **90**
Hill Crest Rd. *Denh* —5K **55**
Hillcrest Rd. *Dew* —6F **116**
Hillcrest Rd. *Q'bry* —5E **74**
Hill Crest Rd. *T'tn* —7C **56**
Hill Crest Vw. *Denh* —5K **55**
Hillcrest Vw. *Leeds* —2G **63**
Hill Cft. *Sower B* —1C **128**
Hill Cft. *T'tn* —7D **56**
Hill Cft. Clo. *D'ton* —6C **124**
Hill Dri. *Ackw* —2G **140**
Hill End. *Dew* —3H **117**
Hill End Clo. *Hip* —5H **93**
Hill End Clo. *Leeds* —6J **61**
Hill End Clo. *Nor G* —2M **93**
Hill End Cres. *Leeds* —6J **61**
Hill End Gro. *B'frd* —2K **75**
Hill End La. *H'den* —8L **37**
Hill End La. *Q'bry* —5C **74**
Hill End Rd. *Leeds* —6J **61**
Hill End Rd. *M'well* —9L **153**
Hillesley Rd. *Dew* —9K **97**
Hill Est. *Upt* —1A **158**
Hillfold. *S Elm* —6A **158**
Hillfoot. —6M 59
Hillfoot. *Shipl* —8K **39**
Hillfoot Av. *Pud* —6M **59**
Hillfoot Cotts. *Pud* —6L **59**
Hillfoot Cres. *Pud* —6M **59**
Hillfoot Dri. *Pud* —6M **59**
Hillfoot Ri. *Pud* —6M **59**
Hillgarth. *Dew* —8G **117**
Hillgarth. *Knot* —9D **104**
Hill Green. —3B 78
Hill Grn. Ct. *B'frd* —3B **78**
Hill Gro. *Hud* —1E **130**
Hill Gro. Lea. *Hud* —1E **130**
Hillhead Dri. *Bat* —3C **96**
Hill Ho. Edge La. *Oxe* —5B **54**
Hill Ho. La. *H'frth* —6J **163**
Hillhouse La. *Hud* —2M **131**
Hill Ho. La. *Oxe* —5C **54**
Hill Ho. La. *Sower B* —1F **110**
Hill Ho. Rd. *H'frth* —6K **163**
Hillidge Rd. *Leeds* —1F **80**
(in three parts)
Hillidge Sq. *Leeds* —1F **80**
Hillingdon Way. *Leeds* —1C **44**
Hillings La. *Men & Guis* —4B **24**
Hill Lands. *Wyke* —8A **76**
Hill La. *H'frth* —3K **163**
(in two parts)
Hill Pk. Av. *Hal* —3M **91**
Hill Ri. Av. *Leeds* —2F **60**
Hill Ri. Gro. *Leeds* —2F **60**
Hill Rd. *C'frd* —5F **102**
Hill Rd. *Hal* —5D **92**
Hill Rd. *N'dam* —6L **137**
Hillside. —7A 156
(nr. Brierley)
Hill Side. —3F 132
(nr. Kirkheaton)
Hillside. *Byr* —5C **104**
Hillside. *Den D* —2C **166**
Hillside. *Gar* —8A **66**
Hillside Av. *Guis* —5H **25**
Hillside Av. *Hud* —9N **113**
Hillside Av. *L'ft* —5D **90**
Hill Side Av. *N Mill* —6C **164**
Hillside Av. *Oakw* —5B **36**
Hillside Av. *Sower B* —5E **110**
Hillside Bldgs. Leeds —2C ***80***
(off Beeston Rd.)
Hillside Clo. *Add* —1L **7**
Hillside Clo. *Hoy S* —9J **167**
Hillside Clo. *Wake* —8F **118**
Hillside Ct. *Men* —4D **24**
Hillside Ct. *S Elm* —5N **157**
Hillside Cres. *Brier* —7A **156**
Hillside Cres. *Hud* —8N **131**
Hillside Gro. *Brier* —7N **155**
Hillside Gro. *Oakw* —5B **36**
Hillside Gro. *Pud* —7C **60**
Hillside Mt. *Brier* —7A **156**
Hill Side Mt. *Far* —4B **60**
Hillside Mt. *Pon* —3L **123**
Hillside Mt. *Pud* —7D **60**
Hillside Ri. *Guis* —5H **25**
Hill Side Ri. *Liv* —9L **95**
Hillside Rd. *Ackw* —4G **140**
Hillside Rd. *Bgly* —3E **38**
Hill Side Rd. *B'frd* —7E **58**
Hillside Rd. *Leeds* —8F **44**
Hillside Rd. *Pon* —3L **123**
Hillside Rd. *Shipl* —9A **40**
Hillside Ter. *Bail* —4A **40**
Hill Side Ter. *B'frd* —7E **58**
Hillside Vw. *Lint* —9C **130**
Hillside Vw. *Pud* —7D **60**
Hillside Vw. *Sower B* —8G **91**
Hillside Works Ind. Est. *Cleck* —2H **95**
Hill St. *B'frd* —9F **58**
(BD4)
Hill St. *B'frd* —4M **75**
(BD6)
Hill St. *Cleck* —5G **95**
Hill St. *Hal* —6A **92**
Hill St. *Haw* —9C **36**
Hill St. *Leeds* —5G **62**
(LS9)
Hill St. *Leeds* —2D **80**
(LS11)
Hill St. *N Mill* —5C **164**
Hillthorpe Ct. *Leeds* —1F **98**
Hillthorpe Dri. *Thpe A* —5N **141**
Hillthorpe Ri. *Pud* —9B **60**
Hillthorpe Rd. *Pud* —9B **60**
Hillthorpe Sq. *Pud* —9B **60**
Hillthorpe St. *Pud* —9B **60**
Hillthorpe Ter. *Pud* —9B **60**
Hill Top. —9M 167
(nr. Hoylandswaine)
Hill Top. —7A 44
(nr. Meanwood)
Hill Top. —6L 137
(nr. Sandal Magna)
Hill Top. —9M 129
(nr. Slaithwaite)
Hill Top. —7B 56
(nr. Thornton)
Hilltop. *Brier* —6N **155**
Hill Top. *Bur W* —8C **10**
Hill Top. *C'frd* —5N **101**
Hill Top. *Fitz* —7A **140**
Hill Top. *Hal* —7L **91**
Hill Top. *I'ly* —7F **8**
Hill Top. *Knot* —8D **104**
Hill Top. *Q'bry* —3C **74**
Hill Top. *Steet* —3C **20**
Hilltop Av. *Barn* —8N **153**
Hilltop Av. *Leeds* —2H **63**
Hilltop Clo. *C'frd* —3G **102**
Hill Top Clo. *Fitz* —7A **140**
Hill Top Clo. *Leeds* —6J **61**
Hill Top Clo. *Ting* —6A **98**
Hill Top Cotts. *B'frd* —4K **57**
Hill Top Ct. *N'dam* —6L **137**
Hill Top Ct. *Ting* —6A **98**
Hill Top Cres. *Mir* —1K **133**
Hill Top Cft. *Neth* —3H **147**
Hill Top Dri. *Hud* —2F **130**
Hill Top Est. *Heck* —9B **96**
Hilltop Est. *S Kirk* —8F **156**
Hill Top Fold. Slai —9M ***129***
(off Meal Hill La.)
Hill Top Gdns. *Ting* —6A **98**
Hill Top Grn. *Ting* —6N **97**
Hill Top Gro. *All* —5F **56**
Hill Top Gro. *Ting* —6A **98**
Hill Top La. *All* —5F **56**
Hill Top La. *Bgly* —8E **22**
(in two parts)
Hill Top La. *Cra V* —9J **89**
Hill Top La. *Ting* —6N **97**
Hill Top La. *Wrag* —1C **140**
Hill Top M. *Knot* —8E **104**
Hill Top Mt. *Leeds* —2H **63**
Hill Top Pl. *Leeds* —4B **62**
(LS6)
Hill Top Pl. *Leeds* —2H **63**
(LS8)
Hill Top Rd. *Floc* —7G **134**
Hill Top Rd. *Hain* —6G **36**
Hill Top Rd. *H'frth* —7L **163**
Hill Top Rd. *Leeds* —4B **62**
(LS6)
Hill Top Rd. *Leeds* —6J **61**
(LS12)
Hill Top Rd. *Mold* —4B **132**

Hill Top Rd. N'dam —6L 137
Hill Top Rd. Oakw —5B 36
Hill Top Rd. Pad —5K 131
Hill Top Rd. Sal N —2E 130
Hill Top Rd. Slai —9M 129
Hill Top Rd. T'tn —7A 56
Hill Top St. Leeds —4B 62
Hill Top Vw. Nor —4H 121
Hill Top Vw. Ting —6N 97
Hill Top Wlk. Kei —9F 20
Hill Top Way. Kei —9F 20
Hill Tree Park. —9F 130
Hill Vw. Hal —6M 73
Hill Vw. Av. Leeds —8F 44
Hillview Gdns. Hal —3F 92
Hill Vw. Mt. Leeds —8F 44
Hill Vw. Pl. Leeds —8F 44
Hill Vw. Ri. B'frd —1J 77
Hill Vw. Ter. Leeds —8F 44
Hillway. Guis —9G 24
Hilmian Way. Hems —4F 156
Hilton Av. Shipl —1N 57
Hilton Ct. B'hpe —4D 26
Hilton Cres. Bail —5A 40
Hilton Dri. Shipl —1N 57
Hilton Grange. B'hpe —4D 26
Hilton Gro. B'frd —8M 57
Hilton Gro. Leeds —1H 63
Hilton Gro. Shipl —1N 57
Hilton M. B'hpe —5D 26
Hilton Pl. Leeds —2H 63
Hilton Rd. B'frd —8M 57
Hilton Rd. Leeds —2H 63
Hilton Rd. Shipl —1N 57
Hilton St. H Bri —1H 89
(off Market St.)
Hilton St. Leeds —2H 63
Hilton Ter. Leeds —2H 63
Hinchcliffe Av. Oss —6B 118
Hinchcliffe St. B'frd —6F 58
Hinchliffe Av. Bail —5B 40
Hind Ct. Mel —6B 146
Hindle Pl. Chur —6L 79
Hindley Rd. Liv —9L 95
Hindley Wlk. B'frd —3J 75
Hinds Cres. S Elm —6M 157
Hind St. B'frd —6A 58
Hind St. Wyke —2A 94
Hinton Clo. Pon —9L 103
Hinton La. Knot —6N 103
Hions Clo. Brigh —3M 113
Hipperholme. —3J 93
Hipswell St. B'frd —6G 59
Hird Av. B'frd —5A 76
Hird Rd. Low M —7B 76
Hird St. Kei —2H 37
Hird St. Leeds —2C 80
Hird St. Shipl —7N 39
Hirst Av. Heck —7A 96
Hirst Gro. H Bri —1J 89
Hirstlands Av. Oss —3M 117
Hirstlands Dri. Oss —3M 117
Hirst La. Cumb —4F 164
Hirst La. Shipl —6K 39
Hirst Lodge Ct. B'frd —1D 58
Hirst Mill Cres. Shipl —6K 39
Hirst Rd. Dew —2F 116
Hirst Rd. Wake —6F 118
Hirst St. All B —6M 83
Hirst St. Mir —8L 115
Hirst St. Todm —3D 86
Hirst's Yd. Leeds —7E 62
(off Duncan St.)
Hirst Wood Cres. Shipl —7K 39
Hirst Wood Rd. Shipl —7J 39
Hive St. Kei —1G 37
Hobart Bldgs. H'clgh —3L 89
Hobart Rd. C'frd —4K 103
Hobart Rd. Dew —2J 117
Hobb End. T'tn —6B 56
Hobberley La. Shad —3A 46
Hobb Nook La. Askw —2E 10
Hob Cote La. Oakw —6N 35
Hobcroft Ter. Skel —8N 159
Hob La. Hal —4A 90
Hob La. Hud —8G 131
Hob La. Ripp —6C 110
Hob La. S Kirk —7G 156
Hob La. Sower B —2H 111
Hob La. Stanb —8K 35
Hobson Fold. Wyke —2B 94
Hockney Rd. B'frd —6N 57
Hodge La. K S'ton —4K 143
Hodgewood La. D'ton —5C 124
Hodgson Av. B'frd —6H 59
Hodgson Av. Leeds —4J 45
Hodgson Cres. Leeds —4J 45
Hodgson Fold. Add —9K 5
Hodgson Fold. B'frd —2D 58
Hodgson La. B'shaw —6M 77
Hodgson La. Dlgtn —7A 78
Hodgson Pl. Morl —6L 79
Hodgson St. Morl —3M 97
Hodgson St. Wake —4K 119
Hodgson Ter. Dew —5G 116
Hodgson Yd. B'frd —1G 59
Hodroyd Clo. Shaf —8L 155
Hodroyd Cotts. Brier —7N 155
Hoffman St. Hud —6F 130
Hog Close La. H'frth —8G 164
Hogley La. H'frth —4H 163
Holays. Hud —3C 132
Holbeck. —9C 62
Holbeck La. Leeds —8B 62
Holbeck Moor Rd. Leeds —9C 62
Holbeck Towers. Leeds —9C 62
Holborn App. Leeds —3C 62
Holborn Ct. Leeds —3D 62
Holborn Ct. Low M —7A 76
Holborn Gdns. Leeds —3C 62
Holborn Grn. Leeds —3C 62
Holborn Gro. Leeds —3C 62
Holborn St. Leeds —3D 62
Holborn Ter. Leeds —3D 62
Holborn Towers. Leeds —3D 62
Holborn Vw. Leeds —3C 62
Holborn Wlk. Leeds —3C 62
Holby Sq. Wake —7E 118
Holden Ing Way. Bat —9D 78
Holden La. Bail —3B 40
(in two parts)
Holden La. Oxe —5N 53
Holden La. Sils —9G 6
Holden Rd. B'frd —4N 75
Holderness Rd. Knot —7D 104
Holderness St. Todm —7L 87
Holdforth Clo. Leeds —7A 62
Holdforth Gdns. Leeds —7A 62
Holdforth Grn. Leeds —7A 62
Holdforth Pl. Leeds —7A 62
Holdgatehill La. D'ton —5E 124
Holdsworth. —6N 73
Holdsworth Av. Heck —5B 96
Holdsworth Ct. Cleck —5H 95
Holdsworth Pl. Leeds —7L 61
Holdsworth Rd. H'fld —6N 73
Holdsworth Sq. B'frd —2H 59
Holdsworth St. B'frd —6D 58
Holdsworth St. Cleck —4H 95
Holdsworth St. Shipl —9A 40
Holdsworth Ter. Hal —7C 92
Hole Bottom. —5K 87
Hole Bottom Rd. Todm —6K 87
Hole La. Sils —5A 6
Hole La. Wake —7E 136
Holes La. Knot —8C 104
Holgate Av. Fitz —7B 140
Holgate Cres. Hems —2C 156
Holgate Gdns. Hems —2C 156
Holgate La. B Spa —9D 18
Holgate Rd. Pon —6J 123
Holgate Ter. Fitz —7B 140
Holgate Vw. Brier —6A 156
Holgate Vw. Fitz —7B 140
(off Wakefield Rd.)
Holker St. Kei —8J 21
Holker St. Mann —6N 57
Holland Rd. Kip —3C 84
Holland St. Bat —7G 96
Holland St. B'frd —8H 59
Hollas La. Norl —1L 111
(in two parts)
Hollerton La. Ting —4B 98
Hollin Av. Hud —3J 131
Hollinbank La. Heck —7B 96
Hollin Brigg La. H'frth —6H 163
Hollin Clo. La. B'frd —3C 58
(in three parts)
Hollin Ct. Leeds —8N 43
Hollin Ct. Shipl —9A 40
Hollin Cres. Leeds —8N 43
Hollin Dri. Dur —4G 136
Hollin Dri. Leeds —8A 44
Hollin Edge. Den D —2D 166
Hollin Gdns. Leeds —8M 43
Hollin Ga. Otley —8H 11
Hollingbourne Rd. Leeds —4G 64
Hollin Greaves La. Hal —3C 92
Hollings Rd. B'frd —5N 57
Hollings Sq. B'frd —5N 57
Hollings St. Bgly —9G 39
Hollings St. B'frd —6N 57
Hollings Ter. B'frd —6N 57
Hollings, The. Meth —1J 101
Hollingthorpe. —7G 137
Hollingthorpe Av. Hall G —7G 137
Hollingthorpe Ct. Hall G —8H 137
Hollingthorpe Gro. Hall G —7G 137
Hollingthorpe La. Hall G —6G 136
Hollingthorpe Rd. Hall G —7G 137
Hollingwood Av. B'frd —1L 75
Hollingwood Ct. B'frd —2K 75
Hollingwood Dri. B'frd —1K 75
Hollingwood Ga. I'ly —6E 8
Hollingwood La. Gt Hor —2J 75
Hollingwood Mt. B'frd —1K 75
Hollingwood Ri. I'ly —6E 8
Hollingworth La. Knot —7F 104
Hollingworth La. Todm —3K 107
Hollin Hall Dri. I'ly —6D 8
Hollin Hall La. Gol —5B 130
Hollin Hall La. Mir —9H 115
Hollin Hall Rd. Shipl —9K 39
Hollin Head. Bail —3D 40
Hollin Hill Av. Leeds —1L 63
Hollin Hill Cotts. Leeds —1L 63
Hollin Hill Dri. Leeds —1L 63
Hollinhirst La. Neth —5B 136
Hollin Ho. La. Clay W —1J 167
Hollin Ho. La. N Mill —3D 164
Hollinhurst. All B —7M 83
Hollin La. Cald G —4F 136
Hollin La. Hal —8A 72
Hollin La. Leeds —8N 43
Hollin La. Ripp —8N 109
Hollin La. Shipl —9B 40
Hollin La. Sower B —2H 111
Hollin M. Leeds —8N 43
Hollin Mt. Leeds —8M 43
Hollin Park. —1M 63
Hollin Pk. Av. Leeds —1M 63
Hollin Pk. Ct. C'ley —9L 41
Hollin Pk. Cres. Leeds —1M 63
Hollin Pk. Dri. C'ley —9L 41
Hollin Pk. Mt. Leeds —9M 45
Hollin Pk. Pde. Leeds —1L 63
Hollin Pk. Pl. Leeds —1L 63
Hollin Pk. Rd. Leeds —1L 63
Hollin Pk. Ter. Leeds —1L 63
Hollin Pk. Vw. Leeds —1L 63
Hollin Pl. Leeds —9N 43
Hollin Ri. Shipl —9A 40
Hollin Rd. Leeds —8N 43
Hollin Rd. Shipl —9A 40
Hollinroyd Rd. Dew —3H 117
Hollins Av. Dew —9C 96
Hollins Bank. Sower B —8H 91
Hollins Bank La. Steet —3D 20
Hollins Beck Clo. Kip —5A 84
Hollins Clo. Kei —6F 20
Hollins Glen. Slai —1N 145
Hollins Grn. Todm —8E 86
Hollins Gro. All B —7N 83
Hollins Hey Rd. Ell —7C 112
Hollins Hill. Bail & Guis —2E 40
Hollins La. Hal —8J 73
Hollins La. Hamp —3E 158
Hollins La. Kei —5F 20
Hollins La. L'ft —7B 90
Hollins La. Slai —3K 145
Hollins La. Sower B —7G 90
Hollins Mdw. Todm —2J 107
Hollins Mill La. Sower B —8G 91
Hollins Mt. Hems —2C 156
Hollins Pk. Kip —4A 84
Hollins Pl. H Bri —1H 89
Hollins Pl. Todm —2J 107
Hollins Rd. Dew —1C 116
Hollins Rd. Todm —1J 107
Hollins Row. Slai —1N 145
Hollins, The. Todm —6K 87
Hollin St. Sower B —2E 110
Hollin Ter. Hud —3H 131
Hollin Ter. Shipl —9A 40
Hollinthorpe. —1H 83
Hollin Vw. Leeds —8N 43
Hollin Wood Clo. Shipl —8K 39
Hollinwood Vw. Bgly —9C 22
Hollis Pl. Leeds —5B 62
Hollowfield Cft. Oaken —8F 76
Hollow Ga. H'frth —3M 163
Hollow, The. Mel —7B 146
Holly App. Oss —3N 117
Holly Av. Leeds —4G 42
Holly Bank. Ackw —4E 140
Holly Bank. Gar —8B 66
Holly Bank. Guis —7H 25
Holly Bank. Leeds —9N 43
Hollybank Av. Bat —5F 96
Hollybank Av. Up Cum —2N 165
Hollybank Ct. Quarm —3F 130
Holly Bank Dri. Hal —4J 93
Hollybank Gdns. B'frd —2K 75
Hollybank Gro. B'frd —2K 75
Holly Bank Ho. Brigh —3L 113
(off Field La.)
Holly Bank Pk. Brigh —3L 113
Hollybank Rd. B'frd —2K 75
Holly Bank Rd. Brigh —3K 113
Holly Bank Rd. Hud —1G 131
Holly Bush Ct. B Spa —1E 32
Hollybush Grn. Coll —9K 17
Holly Clo. Croft —1F 138
Holly Clo. S Elm —7M 157
Holly Ct. Guis —8H 25
Holly Ct. Out —7L 99
Holly Ct. Ting —6A 98
Holly Cres. Croft —1F 138
Holly Cres. Sower B —8C 110
Hollycroft Av. Roys —6C 154
Hollycroft Ct. Leeds —4K 43
Hollycroft St. Kei —1H 37
Holly Dene. Oss —3N 117
Holly Dri. Leeds —4G 42
Hollyfield Av. Hud —3F 130
Hollygarth La. Beal —5M 105
Holly Gro. Bat —8E 96
Holly Gro. Brier —6A 156
Holly Gro. Hal —6N 91
Holly Gro. Lind —1H 131
Holly Hall La. Wyke —9A 76
Holly Ho. C'frd —5E 102
(off Parklands)
Holly Mede. Oss —3N 117
Hollynsmill. G'lnd —4C 112
Hollyns Ter. G'lnd —4C 112
Holly Pk. C'ley —9L 41
Holly Pk. Huby —4N 13
Holly Pk. Dri. B'frd —1K 75
Holly Pk. Gro. B'frd —1K 75
Holly Rd. B Spa —9B 18
Holly Rd. Hud —6K 131
Hollyshaw Cres. Leeds —6D 64
Hollyshaw Gro. Leeds —6D 64
Hollyshaw La. Leeds —5D 64
Hollyshaw St. Leeds —6D 64
Hollyshaw Ter. Leeds —6D 64
Hollyshaw Wlk. Leeds —5D 64
Holly St. B'frd —3J 75
Holly St. Hems —2D 156
Holly St. Wake —4H 119
Holly Tree La. Leeds —8F 64
Hollywell Gro. Leeds —6L 61
Hollywell La. Leeds —7L 61
Holman Av. Gar —9N 65
Holmbridge. —6G 163
Holmcliffe Av. Hud —9L 131
Holmclose. H'frth —6G 163
Holmdale Cres. H'frth —9L 147
Holmdene Dri. Mir —5L 115
Holme. —8E 162
Holme Av. Hud —5C 132
Holmecarr Ct. Bgly —3F 38
Holme Clo. Grng M —5B 134
Holme Ct. N Mill —1C 164
Holme Cft. Dur —3H 137
Holme Dri. Hal —6H 91
Holme Farm Ct. Leeds —2G 78
Holme Farm La. Bard & Woth —4F 30
Holme Fld. Oss —4M 117
Holme Gro. Bur W —1D 24
Holme Ho. L'boro —9M 107
Holme Ho. La. Hal —9E 72
Holme Ho. La. N Mill —3E 164
Holme Ho. La. Oakw —1B 36
(in two parts)
Holme Ho. La. Ripp —9C 110
(in three parts)
Holme Ho. Rd. Todm —3E 86
Holme Ho. St. L'boro —9M 107
Holme Ings. Add —2B 8
Holme La. B'frd —2K 77
Holme La. Halt E —2C 4
Holme La. N Mill —1C 164
Holme La. Slai —1J 145
Holme La. Wake —8K 119
Holme Leas Dri. Oss —4M 117
Holme Mill La. Kei —1F 36
Holme Pk. Bur W —1D 24
Holme Pk. Ct. Hud —1L 147
Holme Pl. H Bri —9H 71
Holme Pl. Mar —3J 131
Holme Ri. S Elm —7N 157
Holme Rd. Hal —6H 91
Holmeside Clo. Hud —1K 147
Holmes Rd. Sower B —8J 91
Holmes St. B'frd —6B 58
Holmes St. Leeds —8E 62
Holme's Ter. Hal —4L 91
Holme St. B'frd —1B 76
Holme St. Hal —5M 93
Holme St. H Bri —1H 89
Holme St. Liv —8M 95
Holme St. Oxe —4C 54
Holme St. Todm —5G 87
Holmestyes La. H'frth —8M 163
Holme Ter. L'boro —9M 107
Holme Top. —1B 76
Holme Top La. B'frd —1B 76
Holme Top St. B'frd —1B 76
Holme Vw. Arth —2M 27
Holme Vw. Av. H'frth —3J 163
Holme Vw. Dri. H'frth —3J 163
Holme Vw. Pk. H'frth —3K 163
Holme Vw. Rd. Dart —9D 152
Holme Village. —2K 77
Holme Vs. Mars —3J 145
Holme Way. Oss —4M 117
Holme Well Rd. Leeds —8G 80
Holme Wood. —2H 77
Holme Wood Rd. B'frd —2H 77
Holme Wood Rd. Kei —1F 36
Holme Woods La. Holme —9E 162
Holmfield. —8M 73
Holmfield. Clay W —7J 151
Holmfield Av. Clay W —7J 151
Holmfield Av. Wake —8K 119
Holmfield Cvn. Site. Knot —5M 103
Holmfield Chase. Stan —6C 100
Holmfield Clo. Clay W —7J 151
Holmfield Clo. Pon —8M 103
Holmfield Cotts. Meth —1M 101
Holmfield Dri. Gol —6E 130
Holmfield Dri. Leeds —6J 45
Holmfield Gdns. Hal —8N 73
Holmfield Gro. Wake —8K 119
Holmfield Ho. Hal —8N 73
Holmfield Ind. Est. H'fld —6N 73
Holmfield Ind. Est. Rd. Hal —7N 73
Holmfield La. Pon & Knot —9M 103
Holmfield La. Wake —8K 119
Holmfield Rd. Clay W —7J 151
Holmfield Rd. Hud —4C 130
Holmfield St. B'frd —7B 58
Holmfield Ter. Clay W —7J 151
(off Holmfield Rd.)
Holmfirth. —3M 163
Holmfirth Rd. G'fld —9A 160
Holmfirth Rd. Mel —8D 146
Holmfirth Rd. N Mill —1B 164
Holmsley Av. S Kirk —7G 156
Holmsley Crest. W'ford —7B 82
Holmsley Fld. Ct. W'ford —7D 82
Holmsley Fld. La. W'ford —7C 82
Holmsley Gth. W'ford —6C 82
Holmsley Gro. S Kirk —7G 157
Holmsley Ho. Rothw —7C 82
Holmsley La. S Kirk —8E 156
Holmsley La. W'ford —7B 82
Holmsley Mt. S Kirk —7G 157
Holmsley Wlk. W'ford —7C 82
Holmwood. Leeds —5J 45
Holmwood Av. Leeds —7A 44
Holmwood Clo. Leeds —7B 44
Holmwood Cres. Leeds —7B 44
Holmwood Dri. Leeds —7A 44
Holmwood Gro. Leeds —7B 44
Holmwood Mt. Leeds —7B 44
Holmwood Vw. Leeds —7A 44
Holroyd Hill. B'frd —4A 76
Holroyd Mill La. Bgly —8D 22
Holroyd Sq. Holy G —7M 111
(off Stainland Rd.)
Holroyd St. Leeds —4F 62
Holsworthy Rd. B'frd —3J 77
Holt Av. Hud —8A 114
Holt Av. Leeds —2M 43
Holtby Gro. Hal —5M 93
Holt Clo. Leeds —3M 43
Holt Cres. Leeds —2J 43
Holtdale App. Leeds —2H 43
Holtdale Av. Leeds —2J 43
Holtdale Clo. Leeds —2J 43
Holtdale Cft. Leeds —2J 43
Holtdale Dri. Leeds —2J 43
Holtdale Fold. Leeds —2J 43
Holtdale Gdns. Leeds —2J 43
Holtdale Gth. Leeds —2J 43
Holtdale Grn. Leeds —2J 43
Holtdale Gro. Leeds —2H 43
Holtdale Lawn. Leeds —2J 43
Holtdale Pl. Leeds —2J 43
Holtdale Rd. Leeds —2J 43
Holtdale Vw. Leeds —2J 43
Holtdale Way. Leeds —2J 43
Holt Dri. Leeds —2K 43
Holt Farm Clo. Leeds —2J 43
Holt Farm Ri. Leeds —2J 43
Holt Gdns. Idle —7E 40
Holt Gdns. Leeds —2M 43
Holt Gth. Leeds —2K 43
Holt Ga. Leeds —2K 43
Holt Grn. Leeds —2K 43
Holt Head. —4M 145
Holt Head Rd. Slai —4N 145
Holt La. H'frth —2M 163
Holt La. Leeds —2H 43
Holt La. Ct. Leeds —3L 43
Holt Park. —2K 43
Holt Pk. App. Leeds —2K 43
Holt Pk. Av. Leeds —2K 43
Holt Pk. Clo. Leeds —2K 43
Holt Pk. Cres. Leeds —2J 43
Holt Pk. Dri. Leeds —2K 43
Holt Pk. Gdns. Leeds —2K 43
Holt Pk. Ga. Leeds —2K 43
Holt Pk. Grange. Leeds —2K 43
Holt Pk. Grn. Leeds —2K 43
Holt Pk. Gro. Leeds —2J 43
Holt Pk. La. Leeds —2K 43

olt Pk. Ri. Leeds —2K 43
olt Pk. Rd. Leeds —2K 43
olt Pk. Va. Leeds —2K 43
olt Pk. Vw. Leeds —2J 43
olt Pk. Way. Leeds —2K 43
olt Ri. Leeds —2K 43
olt Rd. Leeds —2K 43
olts La. Cytn —9G 56
olts Ter. Hal —8C 92
olt St. L'boro —9M 107
olt's Yd. Wake —5K 119
olt, The. Shipl —7A 40
olt Va. Leeds —2K 43
olt Wlk. Leeds —2K 43
olt Way. Leeds —2K 43
olybrook Av. B'frd —9H 41
oly Croft. —1H 37
olyoake Av. Bat —7D 96
olyoake Av. Bgly —6E 38
olyoake Av. Lint —1B 146
olyoake St. Todm —3C 86
olyoake Ter. Horb —1A 136
olyoake Ter. Lint —9B 130
olyrood Cres. Nor —8G 101
oly Rood La. S Mil —5K 85
olywell Ash La. B'frd —5B 58
olywell Dene. C'frd —6G 102
(off Garden St.)
olywell Gdns. C'frd —6G 102
olywell Green. —7A 112
olywell Gro. C'frd —6G 102
(off Rock Hill)
olywell La. C'frd —6G 102
olywell La. Leeds —2M 45
olywell Mt. C'frd —6H 103
olywell Vw. Leeds —2M 45
ome Farm Clo. B'frd —4J 75
ome Farm. (Rare Breeds) —9C 64
omefield Av. Morl —2K 97
ome Lea. Rothw —6M 81
ome Lea Dri. Rothw —7M 81
omepaddock Ho. Weth —3N 17
omestead Dri. Wake —5H 119
omestead, The. Heck —8B 96
ome Vw. Ter. B'frd —5N 57
oney Hole Clo. Todm —8K 87
oney Hole Rd. Todm —8K 87
oneysuckle Clo. Wake —4G 119
onley. —5L 147
onley Ho. Horb —1C 136
(off Honley Sq.)
onley La. Hud —3A 148
onley Moor. —6K 147
onley Sq. Horb —1C 136
onoria St. Hud —1M 131
oods, The. Brigh —4L 113
ood St. Ber B —1L 147
ood St. S Elm —8L 157
oo Hole La. Myth —5K 89
ooton Cres. Ryh —9H 139
oowood La. H'frth —5C 162
opbine Av. B'frd —3C 76
opbine Rd. B'frd —3C 76
ope Av. B'frd —3A 76
ope Av. Shipl —7B 40
ope Bldgs. Todm —7L 87
(off Derdale St.)
opefield Chase. Rothw —9K 81
opefield Clo. Rothw —9K 81
opefield Ct. E Ard —5E 98
opefield Ct. Rothw —9K 81
opefield Cres. Rothw —9K 81
opefield Dri. Rothw —9K 81
opefield Gdns. Rothw —9K 81
opefield Grn. Rothw —9K 81
opefield Gro. Rothw —9K 81
opefield M. Rothw —9K 81
opefield Pl. Rothw —9K 81
opefield Vw. Rothw —9K 81
opefield Wlk. Rothw —9K 81
opefield Way. B'frd —4F 76
opefield Way. Rothw —9K 81
ope Hall St. Hal —6B 92
ope Hill Vw. Bgly —8F 38
ope La. Bail —3N 39
ope Pl. Kei —2J 37
ope Rd. Leeds —6F 62
opes Farm Mt. Leeds —6H 81
opes Farm Rd. Leeds —6H 81
opes Farm Vw. Leeds —6H 81
ope St. C'frd —2J 103
ope St. Dew —2F 116
ope St. Hal —5A 92
ope St. H'cft —2K 155
ope St. H Bri —1H 89
ope St. Hud —6M 131
ope St. M'well —9L 153
ope St. Milns —5G 130
ope St. Morl —9K 79
ope St. Nor —3H 121
ope St. Oss —8B 118
ope St. She —9G 74
Hope St. Sower B —9H 91
Hope St. Wake —4L 119
Hope St. E. C'frd —4D 102
Hope St. W. C'frd —5C 102
Hope Ter. Gol —7C 130
Hopetown. —9L 101
Hopetown Wlk. Nor —9L 101
Hope Vw. Shipl —8B 40
Hopewell Pl. Leeds —4A 62
Hopewell St. Bat —6E 96
Hopewell Ter. H'fth —8E 42
Hopewell Ter. Kip —4B 84
Hopewell Vw. Leeds —8F 80
Hopewell Way. Crig —5G 136
Hopkinson Dri. B'frd —5G 76
Hopkinson Rd. Hud —7N 113
Hopkinson St. Hal —1M 91
Hopkin St. B'frd —4J 77
Hopton Av. B'frd —4F 76
Hopton Av. Mir —9J 115
Hopton Ct. Leeds —7L 61
(off Hopton M.)
Hopton Dri. Mir —9J 115
Hopton Hall La. Mir —2K 133
Hopton La. Mir —9J 115
Hopton M. Leeds —7L 61
Hopton New Rd. Mir —8L 115
Hopwood Bank. H'fth —5F 42
Hopwood Clo. H'fth —5F 42
Hopwood Gro. C'frd —5H 103
Hopwood La. Hal —6L 91
Hopwood Rd. H'fth —5F 42
Horace Waller V.C. Pde. Shaw B —1J 117
Horbury. —1D 136
Horbury Bridge. —1A 136
Horbury Junction. —2E 136
Horbury M. Horb —9B 118
Horbury Rd. Cud —9J 155
Horbury Rd. Oss —8A 118
Horbury Rd. Wake —8F 118
Horley Grn. La. Hal —3D 92
Horley Grn. Rd. Hal —3D 92
Hornbeam Av. Wake —3J 119
Hornbeam Clo. All —2E 56
Hornbeam Grn. Pon —2M 123
Hornbeam Way. Leeds —7D 46
Hornby St. Hal —6M 91
Hornby Ter. Hal —6M 91
Horncastle St. Cleck —5J 95
Horncastle Vw. H'cft —8L 139
Horn Cote Clo. N Mill —1E 164
Horn Cote La. N Mill —2E 164
Horner Av. Bat —6C 96
Horner Cres. Bat —6C 96
Hornes La. M'well —8L 153
Horne St. Hal —5A 92
Horne St. Wake —7L 119
Horn La. N Mill —2D 164
Horn La. Pen —7L 165
Horn La. Sils —4B 6
Hornsea Dri. Wilsd —2B 56
Horse Bank Dri. Lock —8J 131
Horse Cft. La. Shel —6M 149
Horse Fair. Pon —2K 123
Horsefair. Weth —4N 17
Horsefair Cen. Weth —4N 17
Horsehold La. H Bri —2F 88
Horsehold Rd. H Bri —2F 88
Horse Pond La. Hud —3N 129
Horse Race End. —8D 120
Horsfall St. Hal —7N 91
Horsfall St. Morl —7J 79
Horsfall St. Todm —6N 87
Horsforth. —7E 42
Horsforth New Rd. Leeds —9B 42
Horsham Ct. Kei —2E 36
Horsham Rd. B'frd —3J 77
Horsley St. B'frd —4A 76
Horsman St. B'frd —4J 77
Horton Bank. —3J 75
Horton Bank Bottom. —2M 75
Horton Bank Top. —3H 75
Horton Clo. Rod —2C 60
Horton Gth. Rod —2C 60
Horton Grange Rd. B'frd —8N 57
Horton Hall Clo. B'frd —9B 58
Horton Pk. Av. B'frd —9N 57
Horton Ri. Rod —2C 60
Horton St. Hal —6B 92
Horton St. Heck —9A 96
Horton St. Oss —5M 117
Horton Ter. Hal —4G 93
Hospital La. Leeds —5J 43
Hospital Rd. Riddl —7M 21
Hostingley La. Thorn & M'twn —9J 117
Hothfield St. Sils —8D 6
Hot La. H Bri —6A 70
Hough. Hal —3E 92
Hough Clo. Leeds —6E 60
Hough End. —6F 60
Hough End Av. Leeds —5G 60
Hough End Clo. Leeds —5G 60
Hough End Ct. Leeds —5G 60
Hough End Cres. Leeds —5F 60
Hough End Gdns. Leeds —5G 60
Hough End Gth. Leeds —5F 60
Hough End La. Leeds —5F 60
Hough Gro. Leeds —4F 60
Hough La. Leeds —4F 60
Houghley Av. Leeds —4J 61
Houghley Clo. Leeds —4H 61
Houghley Cres. Leeds —4J 61
Houghley La. Leeds —4H 61
Houghley Pl. Leeds —4J 61
Houghley Rd. Leeds —4J 61
Houghley Sq. Leeds —4J 61
Hough Side. —7D 60
Hough Side Clo. Pud —7E 60
Hough Side La. Pud —7D 60
Hough Side Rd. Pud —7C 60
Hough Ter. Leeds —4F 60
Houghton Av. Knot —7A 104
Houghton Bungalows. Hud —7D 132
Houghton Pl. B'frd —6B 58
Houghton St. Brigh —9N 93
Houghton Towers. Sower B —8H 91
Hough Top. Leeds —7D 60
Hough Tree Rd. Leeds —6F 60
Hough Tree Ter. Leeds —6F 60
Hougomont. Q'bry —2B 74
Hoults La. G'lnd —3A 112
Houndhill La. F'stne —6F 122
House Gro. Dri. Clay W —7H 151
Houses Hill. —4K 133
Hove Edge. —7L 93
Hovingham Av. Leeds —2J 63
Hovingham Gro. Leeds —2J 63
Hovingham Mt. Leeds —2J 63
Hovingham Ter. Leeds —2J 63
Howard Av. Hud —2H 131
Howard Av. Leeds —7A 64
Howard Ct. Leeds —7A 64
Howard Cres. Dur —4G 136
Howard Pk. Cleck —5J 95
Howard Pl. Bat —9F 96
Howard Rd. Hud —2H 131
Howard St. Bat —9F 96
Howard St. B'frd —8B 58
Howard St. Hal —4N 91
Howard St. Oss —4N 117
Howard St. Wake —4L 119
Howard Way. Mel —8D 146
Howarth Av. B'frd —1E 58
Howarth Cres. B'frd —1E 58
Howarth La. Hud —7K 131
Howbeck Av. Riddl —7N 21
Howbeck Dri. Riddl —8A 22
Howcans La. B'twn —9N 73
(in two parts)
Howden Av. Kei —6G 20
Howden Av. Skel —8K 159
Howden Brook. Hal —6J 75
Howden Clo. B'frd —4K 77
Howden Clo. Cow —8E 130
Howden Clo. Dart —8H 153
Howden Clough. —1E 96
Howden Clough Ind. Est. Bat —1F 96
Howden Clough Rd. Morl —1F 96
Howden Gdns. Leeds —4A 62
Howden Pl. Leeds —4A 62
Howden Rd. Sils —8E 6
Howden Way. Eastm —5N 119
Howden Way. Morl —1G 97
Howes La. N'wram —1E 92
Howgate. B'frd —7G 40
Howgate Ho. Dew —3F 116
(off Wellington Rd.)
Howgate Rd. Slai —1M 145
Howgill Grn. B'frd —7M 75
Howley Mill La. Bat —5G 96
Howley Pk. Clo. Morl —2J 97
Howley Pk. Rd. Morl —2J 97
Howley Pk. Rd. E. Morl —3J 97
Howley Pk. Ter. Morl —2J 97
Howley Pk. Trad. Est. Morl —2J 97
Howley St. Bat —6G 97
Howley Wlk. Bat —7H 97
Howorth St. Todm —4G 86
Howroyd La. Bklnd —7H 111
Howroyd La. W'ley —2B 134
Howson Clo. Guis —7K 25
Hoxton Mt. Leeds —2B 80
Hoxton St. B'frd —6M 57
Hoylake Av. Hud —8L 113
Hoyland Rd. Wake —5K 137
Hoyland Swaine. —9K 167
Hoyland Ter. S Kirk —7G 157
Hoyle Ct. Av. Bail —4C 40
Hoyle Ct. Dri. Bail —4C 40
Hoyle Ct. Rd. Bail —4C 40
Hoyle Fold. Kei —2F 36
Hoyle Ho. Fold. Lint —9C 130
Hoyle Ing. Lint —9C 130
Hoyle Ing Rd. T'tn —8E 56
Hoyle Mill Rd. Kin —9C 140
(in two parts)
Hubberton Green. —1C 110
Hubberton Grn. Rd. Sower B —1C 110
Hubert St. B'frd —8F 58
Hubert St. Hal —5K 91
Hubert St. Hud —1D 130
Huby. —5M 13
Huck Hill La. Mars —3E 144
Huddersfield. —4M 131
Huddersfield Rd. Bret & Haig —9A 136
Huddersfield Rd. Brigh —4N 113
Huddersfield Rd. Dart —7D 152
Huddersfield Rd. Ell —7F 112
Huddersfield Rd. Hal —7B 92
(in two parts)
Huddersfield Rd. Heck & Bat —5B 96
Huddersfield Rd. H'frth —3M 163
Huddersfield Rd. Hon —4M 147
Huddersfield Rd. Hud —8F 112
Huddersfield Rd. Ing & Pen —8C 166
Huddersfield Rd. Kbtn —4K 149
Huddersfield Rd. Liv —2L 115
Huddersfield Rd. Mel —7D 146
Huddersfield Rd. Mir —4G 115
Huddersfield Rd. N Mill —1B 164
Huddersfield Rd. Old —9A 144
Huddersfield Rd. Raven —6B 116
Huddersfield Rd. Wyke & B'frd
(in three parts) —4N 93
Huddersfield Town F.C. —2A 132
Huddleston Ct. Dew —3J 117
Hud Hill. Hal —9G 74
Hudroyd. Hud —7D 132
Hudson Av. B'frd —1N 75
Hudson Av. Not —3C 154
Hudson Clo. B'frd —2N 75
Hudson Clo. Weth —4M 17
Hudson Cres. B'frd —2N 75
Hudson Gdns. B'frd —2N 75
Hudson Gro. Leeds —5J 63
Hudson M. B Spa —1E 32
Hudson Mill Rd. Blkhd —8B 70
Hudson Pl. Leeds —5J 63
Hudson Rd. Leeds —4J 63
Hudson's Ter. Yead —9N 25
Hudson St. B'frd —7H 59
Hudson St. Fars —5A 60
Hudson St. Leeds —5J 63
Hudson St. Todm —3E 86
Hudson, The. Wyke —1A 94
Hudswell Rd. Leeds —1F 80
Hudswell St. Wake —8N 119
Huffa La. Beam —3K 5
Huggan Row. Pud —7C 60
(off Hammerton Gro.)
Hughenden Vw. Morl —7K 79
Hughendon Dri. T'tn —8F 56
Hughendon Wlk. T'tn —8F 56
Hugh St. C'frd —5D 102
(in two parts)
Hugill St. T'tn —8C 56
Hulbert Cft. Hud —6D 132
Hulbert St. Bgly —5F 38
Hullenedge Gdns. Ell —5C 112
Hullenedge La. G'lnd —5B 112
Hullenedge Rd. Ell —5C 112
Hullen Rd. Ell —5C 112
Hullett Clo. H Bri —3N 89
Hullett Dri. H Bri —3N 89
Hull St. Morl —9L 79
Hulme Sq. C'frd —3K 103
Hulme St. Sower B —9H 91
(off Syke La.)
Humber Clo. C'frd —4H 103
Humber Clo. Lint —9C 130
Humber Clo. Skel —8M 159
Humboldt St. B'frd —7E 58
Hume Crest. Bat —7F 96
Humley Rd. Wake —5K 137
Hundhill. E Hard —9K 123
Hundhill La. E Hard —9K 123
Hungate. —4F 100
Hungate La. Meth —4F 100
Hungerford Rd. Hud —2J 131
Hunger Hill. —5E 74
Hunger Hill. Hal —6B 92
Hunger Hill. Midd —2H 9
Hunger Hill. Morl —1K 97
Hunger Hills Av. H'fth —6D 42
Hunger Hills Dri. H'fth —6D 42
Hunslet. —1F 80
Hunslet Carr. —4F 80
Hunslet Distributor. Leeds —1F 80
Hunslet Grn. Way. Leeds —1F 80
Hunslet Hall Rd. Leeds —1D 80
Hunslet La. Leeds —8E 62
Hunslet Rd. Leeds —7E 62
(in two parts)
Hunslet Trad. Est. Leeds —1H 81
Hunston Av. Hud —3G 130
Hunsworth. —1H 95
Hunsworth La. Cleck & E Bier —3H 95
Hunt Ct. Wake —5G 118
Hunter Hill Rd. Hal —8G 73
Hunters Ct. B'frd —2H 57
Hunters Grn. Cull —8K 37
Hunters La. Todm —5H 87
Hunters Mdw. Sils —7E 6
Hunters Pk. Av. Cytn —9J 57
Hunters Wlk. Weth —1M 17
Huntingdon Av. Hud —6D 114
Huntingdon Rd. Brigh —2A 114
Huntock Pl. Brigh —7L 93
Huntsman Fold. Wake —5F 118
Huntsmans Clo. Bgly —2H 39
Huntsmans Clo. Hud —1J 147
Huntsmans Clo. Kei —8G 21
Huntsman's Way. Bads —8L 141
Hunt St. C'frd —3D 102
(in three parts)
Hunt St. W'wd M —4B 102
Huntwick Av. F'stne —7C 122
Huntwick Cres. F'stne —7B 122
Huntwick Dri. F'stne —7B 122
Huntwick La. S'hse —9N 121
Huntwick Rd. F'stne —7C 122
Huntwick Rd. Old Sn —7N 121
Hunt Yd. B'frd —1M 75
Hurst Knowle. Hud —6E 132
Hurst La. Mir —8M 115
Hurst Rd. H Bri —9J 71
Hurstville Av. B'frd —7K 77
Hurstwood. Hud —7C 114
Husler Gro. Leeds —3F 62
Husler Pl. Leeds —3F 62
Hustings, The. Liv —8K 95
Hustlergate. B'frd —7C 58
Hustler's Row. Leeds —7N 43
Hustler St. B'frd —5E 58
Hutchinson La. Brigh —1N 113
Hutchinson Pl. Leeds —3K 61
Hutson St. B'frd —1B 76
Hutton Dri. Heck —8B 96
Hutton Dri. S Elm —5N 157
Hutton Rd. B'frd —3A 76
Hutton Ter. B'frd —1H 59
Hutton Ter. Pud —7B 60
Hydale Clo. Kei —2L 37
Hydale Ct. Low M —7A 76
Hyde Gro. Kei —8K 21
(off Kirby St.)
Hyde Park. —3B 62
Hyde Pk. Hal —6N 91
Hyde Pk. Wake —5N 119
Hyde Pk. Clo. Leeds —4B 62
Hyde Pk. Corner. Leeds —3B 62
Hyde Pk. Gdns. Hal —7N 91
(off Haugh Shaw Rd.)
Hyde Pk. Pl. Leeds —3B 62
Hyde Pk. Rd. Hal —7N 91
Hyde Pk. Rd. Leeds —4B 62
Hyde Pk. St. Hal —7N 91
Hyde Pk. Ter. Leeds —3B 62
Hyde Pl. Leeds —5C 62
Hyde St. B'frd —6F 40
Hyde St. Leeds —5C 62
Hyde Ter. Leeds —5C 62
Hydro Clo. I'ly —6L 9
Hyman Wlk. S Elm —5N 157
Hyne Av. B'frd —4F 76
Hyrst Gth. Bat —9E 96
Hyrstlands Rd. Bat —9E 96
Hyrst Wlk. Bat —9F 96

Ibberson Av. M'well —9K 153
Ibbetson Clo. Morl —6K 79
Ibbetson Ct. Morl —6K 79
Ibbetson Cft. Morl —6K 79
Ibbetson Dri. Morl —6K 79
Ibbetson M. Morl —6K 79
Ibbetson Oval. Morl —6K 79
Ibbetson Ri. Morl —6K 79
Ibbetson Rd. Morl —6K 79
Ibbotroyd Av. Todm —5J 87
Ibbotson Flats. Hud —4N 131
(off Leeds Rd.)
Ibbottson St. Wake —8A 120
Ida's, The. Leeds —3J 81
Ida St. B'frd —2A 76
Ida St. Leeds —3J 81
Iddesleigh St. B'frd —8H 59
Idle. —7F 40
Idlecroft Rd. B'frd —7F 40
Idle Moor. —8D 40
Idle Rd. Five E —1E 58
Idlethorp Way. B'frd —8G 40

Ilbert Av. *B'frd* —4G **76**
Ilford St. *Morl* —9L **79**
Ilkley. —5G 8
Ilkley Hall M. *I'ly* —6G **9**
Ilkley Hall Pk. *I'ly* —6G **9**
Ilkley Rd. *Add* —2N **7**
Ilkley Rd. *Bur W* —6A **10**
Ilkley Rd. *Otley* —1J **25**
Ilkley Rd. *Riddl* —6M **21**
Illingworth. —6M 73
Illingworth Av. *Hal* —5L **73**
Illingworth Av. *Nor* —8F **100**
Illingworth Bldgs. Oaken —9D ***76***
(off Illingworth Rd.)
Illingworth Clo. *Hal* —6L **73**
Illingworth Clo. *Yead* —2N **41**
Illingworth Cres. *Hal* —6L **73**
Illingworth Dri. *Hal* —6L **73**
Illingworth Gdns. *Hal* —7L **73**
Illingworth Gro. *Hal* —6L **73**
Illingworth La. *Hal* —7L **73**
Illingworth Rd. *Oaken* —9D **76**
Illingworth St. *Oss* —6N **117**
Illingworth Way. *Hal* —6L **73**
Imperial Av. *Wren* —1H **119**
Imperial Rd. *Hud* —3J **131**
Inchfield Rd. *Todm* —3H **107**
Inch La. *Pon* —3M **157**
Incline, The. *Hal* —4D **92**
Independent St. *B'frd* —2A **76**
Indus Clo. *Heck* —8B **96**
Industrial Av. *Birs* —3A **96**
Industrial Rd. *Sower B* —8H **91**
Industrial St. *Bgly* —4E **38**
Industrial St. *Brigh* —9N **93**
Industrial St. *Horb* —2E **136**
Industrial St. *Hud* —7M **131**
Industrial St. *Kei* —1G **36**
Industrial St. *Leeds* —5H **63**
Industrial St. *Liv* —8J **95**
Industrial St. *Schol* —4D **94**
Industrial St. *Todm* —7K **87**
Industrial St. *Wake* —4L **119**
Industrial Ter. *Hal* —7A **92**
Industrial Ter. *Hud* —5E **132**
Industry Rd. *Cltn* —9D **154**
Industry St. *Todm* —2J **107**
Infirmary Rd. *Dew* —2E **116**
Infirmary St. *B'frd* —6B **58**
(in two parts)
Infirmary St. *Leeds* —6D **62**
Ingbirchworth. —7B 166
Ingbirchworth La. *Pen* —8B **166**
(in two parts)
Ingdale Dri. *H'frth* —2N **163**
Ing Fld. *Oaken* —9E **76**
Ingfield Av. *Hud* —4B **132**
Ingfield Av. *Oss* —5A **118**
Ingham Clo. *Hal* —5M **73**
Ingham Clo. *Mir* —6N **115**
Ingham Cft. *Mir* —7N **115**
Ingham Gth. *Mir* —6N **115**
Ingham La. *Hal* —4L **73**
Ingham Rd. *Dew* —8F **116**
Inghams Av. *Pud* —7M **59**
Inghams Ct. *Hal* —3N **91**
Inghams Ter. *Pud* —6M **59**
Inghams Vw. *Pud* —6M **59**
Ing Head. *Lint* —9L **129**
Inghead Gdns. *She* —9G **75**
Ing Head La. *Hud* —7E **148**
Ing Head Ter. *Hal* —9G **75**
(in three parts)
Ing La. *Hud* —8M **131**
(in two parts)
Ing La. *Slai* —1K **145**
Ingle Av. *Morl* —7J **79**
Ingleborough Dri. *Morl* —1M **97**
Ingleby Pl. *B'frd* —8M **57**
Ingleby Rd. *B'frd* —6M **57**
Ingleby St. *B'frd* —7M **57**
Ingleby Way. *Leeds* —6G **80**
Ingle Ct. *Fen B* —6H **133**
Ingle Ct. *Morl* —8J **79**
Ingle Cres. *Morl* —7K **79**
Ingledene. *H Bri* —2E **88**
Ingledew Ct. *Leeds* —3F **44**
Ingledew Cres. *Leeds* —5K **45**
Ingledew Dri. *Leeds* —6K **45**
Ingle Gro. *Morl* —8J **79**
Ingle Row. *Leeds* —9F **44**
Ingleton Clo. *Leeds* —2D **80**
Ingleton Dri. *Leeds* —7N **63**
Ingleton Gro. *Leeds* —2D **80**
Ingleton Ho. B'frd —3J ***77***
(off Arlesford Rd.)
Ingleton Pl. *Leeds* —2D **80**
Ingleton Rd. *Hud* —8N **131**
Ingleton St. *Leeds* —2D **80**
Inglewood. *Dart* —8J **153**
Inglewood App. *Leeds* —3C **64**
Inglewood Av. *Hud* —1H **131**
Inglewood Dri. *Leeds* —3C **64**
Inglewood Dri. *Otley* —1K **25**
Inglewood Pl. *Leeds* —3C **64**
Inglewood Ter. Leeds —2C ***62***
(off Delph La.)
Ingram Clo. *Leeds* —9B **62**
Ingram Ct. *Leeds* —9B **62**
Ingram Cres. *Knot* —9C **104**
Ingram Cres. *Leeds* —1B **80**
Ingram Gdns. *Leeds* —9B **62**
Ingram Pde. *Rothw* —8N **81**
Ingram Rd. *Leeds* —1B **80**
Ingram Row. *Leeds* —8D **62**
Ingram Sq. *Hal* —7N **91**
Ingram St. *Hal* —7N **91**
Ingram St. *Kei* —4H **37**
Ingram St. *Leeds* —8D **62**
Ingram Vw. *Leeds* —9B **62**
Ingrow. —3G 37
Ingrow La. *Kei* —3F **36**
Ingrow Railway Centre Museum. —3H 37
Ings Av. *Guis* —6H **25**
Ings Clo. *H'cft* —9K **139**
Ings Clo. *S Kirk* —6K **157**
Ings Ct. *Guis* —6G **25**
Ings Cres. *Dew* —9F **116**
Ings Cres. *Guis* —7G **25**
Ings Cres. *Leeds* —7K **63**
Ings Cres. *Liv* —8M **95**
Ings Dri. *Meth* —1M **101**
Ings Grange. Liv —7M ***95***
(off Ings Rd.)
Ings Holt. *S Kirk* —5K **157**
Ings La. *Beal* —5M **105**
Ings La. *C'frd* —2F **102**
Ings La. *Dew* —9F **116**
Ings La. *Guis* —7G **25**
Ings La. *Leds* —9D **84**
Ings La. *Otley* —9M **11**
Ings La. *Skel* —9M **159**
Ings La. *Thor A* —9G **18**
Ings La. *Wigh* —9N **19**
Ings Mere Ct. *Fair* —9N **85**
Ings Mill Av. *Clay W* —6J **151**
Ings Mill Dri. *Clay W* —6J **151**
Ings Rd. *Bat* —6D **96**
Ings Rd. *Dew* —2H **117**
Ings Rd. *Heck* —8A **96**
Ings Rd. *Hud* —6E **132**
Ings Rd. *Kin* —9B **140**
Ings Rd. *Leeds* —7K **63**
Ings Rd. *Liv* —7M **95**
Ings Rd. *Steet* —2B **20**
Ings Rd. *Wake* —6K **119**
Ings, The. *Clay W* —7J **151**
Ings, The. *Hal* —6M **93**
Ing St. *B'frd* —7H **59**
Ings Vw. *C'frd* —4H **103**
Ings Vw. *Meth* —1M **101**
Ings Villa. *Liv* —1N **115**
Ings Wlk. *S Kirk* —6K **157**
Ings Way. *B'frd* —6K **57**
Ings Way. *Lep* —7J **133**
Ings Way. *Pen* —7A **166**
Ings Way. *Sils* —8E **6**
Ings Way W. *Lep* —7J **133**
Ingswell Av. *Not* —2A **154**
Ingswell Dri. *Not* —2A **154**
Ingwell Ct. *Wake* —5M **119**
Ingwell St. *Wake* —5M **119**
Ingwell Ter. *Cleck* —5J **95**
Inholmes La. *Wltn* —6H **19**
Inkerman Ct. *Den D* —3D **166**
Inkerman St. *B'frd* —1H **77**
Inkerman St. *Haig* —2H **59**
Inkerman Way. *Den D* —3C **166**
Inner Hey. *Mars* —5G **145**
Inner Ring Rd. *Leeds* —5C **62**
Institute Rd. *B'frd* —1G **58**
Intake. —2C 60
Intake. *Gol* —5D **130**
Intake Clo. *Stan* —7A **100**
Intake Gro. *B'frd* —4G **59**
Intake La. *Bat* —4C **96**
Intake La. *Birk* —3M **105**
Intake La. *Cud* —9K **155**
Intake La. *Cumb* —4F **164**
Intake La. *Hud* —2E **146**
Intake La. *Leeds* —1E **98**
Intake La. *Mel* —5M **145**
Intake La. *Oss* —6A **118**
Intake La. *Oxe* —6A **54**
Intake La. *Rawd* —4A **42**
Intake La. *Rod* —3C **60**
Intake La. *Stan* —7A **100**
(in two parts)
Intake La. *Steet* —4A **20**
Intake La. *T'ner* —4E **46**
Intake La. *Wool* —2F **152**
Intake Mt. *Leeds* —9E **80**
Intake Rd. *B'frd* —4G **58**
Intake Rd. *Pud* —6C **60**
Intake Rd. *Slai* —8J **129**
Intake Sq. *Leeds* —9E **80**
Intake Ter. *B'frd* —5G **59**
Intake, The. *Kip* —4B **84**
Intake Vw. *Int* —3D **60**
Intake Vw. *Leeds* —9E **80**
Intercity Way. *Leeds* —5C **60**
Invargarry Clo. *Gar* —6B **66**
Inverness Rd. *Gar* —7B **66**
Invertrees Av. *Rawd* —3N **41**
Iona Pl. Hal —2B ***92***
(off Iona St.)
Iona St. *Hal* —2B **92**
Ireland Cres. *Leeds* —4J **43**
Ireland St. *Bgly* —4D **38**
Ireland Ter. *Bgly* —4D **38**
Ireland Wood. —5J 43
Ireton St. *B'frd* —8N **57**
Irish La. *Oakw* —5A **36**
Iron Row. *Bur W* —8D **10**
Iron St. *Wgte* —5G **95**
Ironwood App. *Leeds* —3B **64**
Ironwood Cres. *Leeds* —3B **64**
Ironwood Vw. *Leeds* —2B **64**
Irvine St. *Hal* —7M **91**
Irving Ter. *Cytn* —2H **75**
Irvin Ter. *C'frd* —5C **102**
Irwell St. *B'frd* —9E **58**
Irwin App. *Leeds* —7A **64**
Irwin Av. *Wake* —4A **120**
Irwin Cres. *Wake* —4N **119**
Irwin St. *Fars* —4A **60**
(in two parts)
Isaac St. *B'frd* —6N **57**
Island Dri. *Broc* —7A **148**
Island, The. *Knot* —7F **104**
Island Vw. *Dew* —5E **116**
Islay Clo. *Rothw* —8A **82**
Isle La. *Oxe* —7C **54**
Isles St. *B'frd* —6L **57**
Islington. —1A 80
Issues Rd. *Holme* —7B **162**
Ivanhoe Rd. *B'frd* —9N **57**
Ivegate. *B'frd* —7C **58**
Ivegate. *Yead* —9M **25**
Ive Ho. La. *Hal* —4E **90**
Iveson App. *Leeds* —5J **43**
Iveson Clo. *Leeds* —5J **43**
Iveson Cres. *Leeds* —5J **43**
Iveson Dri. *Leeds* —5J **43**
Iveson Gdns. *Leeds* —5J **43**
Iveson Gth. *Leeds* —5K **43**
Iveson Grn. *Leeds* —5J **43**
Iveson Gro. *Leeds* —5J **43**
Iveson Lawn. *Leeds* —5K **43**
Iveson Ri. *Leeds* —5K **43**
Iveson Rd. *Leeds* —5J **43**
Ives St. *Shipl* —7N **39**
(in two parts)
Ivory St. *Leeds* —9E **62**
Ivy Av. *Leeds* —6J **63**
Ivy Bank. *W'wth* —8A **106**
Ivy Bank. *Wyke* —9A **76**
Ivy Bank. *Yead* —9L **25**
Ivy Bank Ct. Bail —5B ***40***
(off Dewhirst Clo.)
Ivy Bank La. *Haw* —9C **36**
Ivy Chase. *Leeds* —6E **60**
Ivy Clo. *S Elm* —8L **157**
Ivy Clo. *Wake* —3N **119**
Ivy Cotts. *Roys* —5E **154**
Ivy Ct. *Leeds* —9F **44**
Ivy Cres. *Hal* —5K **93**
Ivy Cres. *Leeds* —6J **63**
Ivy Farm Clo. *Barn* —8E **154**
Ivy Gdns. *Bmly* —2G **60**
Ivy Gdns. *C'frd* —7K **103**
Ivy Gth. *Leeds* —9F **44**
Ivy Gro. *Leeds* —7K **63**
Ivy Gro. *Shipl* —8K **39**
Ivy Gro. *Wake* —3N **119**
Ivy Ho. Rd. *B'frd* —4C **76**
Ivy La. *All* —5F **56**
Ivy La. *B Spa* —1C **32**
Ivy La. *Hal* —7K **73**
Ivy La. *Wake* —3N **119**
Ivy Mt. *Hal* —1C **112**
Ivy Mt. *Leeds* —6J **63**
Ivy Mt. *Slai* —9M **129**
Ivy Pl. *Leeds* —2G **60**
Ivy Rd. *Kei* —1L **37**
Ivy Rd. *Leeds* —7J **63**
Ivy Rd. *Shipl* —8K **39**
Ivy St. *Brigh* —9L **93**
Ivy St. *Cros M* —6H **131**
Ivy St. *F'stne* —5D **122**
Ivy St. *Hal* —7N **91**
Ivy St. *Kei* —8H **21**
Ivy St. *Leeds* —6J **63**
Ivy St. *Mold* —5A **132**
Ivy St. S. *Hal* —7N **91**
Ivy St. S. *Kei* —4H **37**
Ivy Ter. Brigh —9L ***93***
(off Ivy St.)
Ivy Ter. *Horb* —9C **118**
Ivy Ter. *Kei* —1M **37**
Ivy Ter. *Light* —5K **93**
Ivy Ter. *L'boro* —9M **107**
Ivy Ter. *S Elm* —6N **157**
Ivy Vw. *Leeds* —6J **63**

Jacinth Ct. *Far* —9A **114**
Jack Clo. Orchard. *Roys* —5D **154**
Jackdaw Clo. *All* —7G **56**
Jackdaw La. *B Spa* —9C **18**
Jack Hill. *Hud* —1M **131**
Jackie Smart Ct. *Leeds* —3G **62**
Jackie Smart Rd. *B'frd* —2C **76**
Jack La. *Bat* —1G **116**
Jack La. *Leeds* —9D **62**
(in two parts)
Jackman Dri. *H'fth* —7G **42**
Jackroyd La. *Hud* —8M **131**
Jackroyd La. *Mir* —9J **115**
Jackson Av. *Leeds* —8H **45**
Jackson Bridge. —5C 164
Jackson Hill. *Q'bry* —6E **74**
Jackson Ho. Hems —3D ***156***
(off Lilley St.)
Jackson La. *Bklnd* —6G **110**
Jackson Meadows. *Bklnd* —6G **110**
Jackson Rd. *Leeds* —3E **62**
Jacksons Ct. Pon —3J ***123***
(off Liquorice Way)
Jackson's La. *Dew* —1D **134**
Jackson's La. *Went* —3C **142**
Jackson St. *B'frd* —8E **58**
Jacky La. *Haw* —9C **36**
Jacobs Hall Ct. *Dart* —9E **152**
Jacob's Row. *Hud* —7L **131**
Jacob St. *B'frd* —1B **76**
Jacob St. *Leeds* —5E **62**
Jacobs Well. *B'frd* —8C **58**
Jacob's Well La. *Wake* —4M **119**
Jacques Gro. *Sils* —8F **6**
Jade Pl. *Far* —9A **114**
Jaggar La. *Hon* —5L **147**
Jaggar La. *Hud* —2E **132**
Jagger Green. —8B 112
Jagger Grn. Dean. *Holy G* —8A **112**
Jagger Grn. La. *Holy G* —9A **112**
Jagger La. *Eml* —3A **150**
Jaglin Ct. *F'stne* —7E **122**
Jail Rd. *Bat* —7C **96**
Jail Yd. *Rothw* —8A **82**
Jakeman Clo. *Ting* —4A **98**
Jakeman Ct. *Ting* —4A **98**
Jakeman Dri. *Ting* —4A **98**
James Av. *Ebrn* —3A **20**
James Av. *Leeds* —7H **45**
James Baillie Flats. *Leeds* —1B **62**
James Clo. *Gar* —7A **66**
James Ct. Coll —9J ***17***
(off Station La.)
James Ct. Morl —9M ***79***
(off Harold Gdns.)
James Duggan Av. *F'stne* —5D **122**
James Ga. *B'frd* —7C **58**
James Gibbs Clo. *F'stne* —5D **122**
James La. *Hud* —3F **146**
James St. *All* —5H **57**
James St. *Bat* —8E **96**
James St. *B'shaw* —7L **77**
James St. *B'frd* —7C **58**
James St. *Brigh* —8M **93**
James St. *C'frd* —3D **102**
James St. *Dew* —2E **116**
James St. *Ell* —5E **112**
James St. *Gol* —6C **130**
James St. *Holy G* —7A **112**
James St. *Liv* —8L **95**
(nr. Halifax Rd.)
James St. *Liv* —9M **95**
(nr. Union Rd.)
James St. *Mir* —4L **115**
James St. *Oakw* —5B **36**
James St. *Rawd* —3M **41**
James St. *Slai* —9N **129**
James St. *S Hien* —3N **155**
James St. *T'tn* —8C **56**
Jamie Ct. *B'frd* —9H **41**
Jane Grn. *Hal* —3K **73**
Jane Hills. Shipl —7M ***39***
(off Riverside Est.)
Jane St. *Denh* —5K **55**
Jane St. *S'fth* —5A **106**
Jane St. *Shipl* —7L **39**
Janesway. *Kip* —3N **83**
Janet St. *Haw* —7E **36**
Jaques Clo. *Leeds* —2L **61**
Jardine Av. *F'stne* —5D **122**
Jardine Rd. *Bgly* —4F **38**
Jardine St. *Bgly* —4F **38**
Jarratt St. *B'frd* —5N **57**
Jarratt St. E. *B'frd* —5N **57**
Jarrom Clo. *B'frd* —1H **77**
Jarvis Sq. *Rob H* —1J **99**
Jarvis Wlk. *Rob H* —1J **99**
Jasmin Ter. *B'frd* —6A **58**
Jasper La. *Kirk O* —3K **15**
Jasper St. *B'frd* —7F **40**
Jasper St. *Hal* —5M **91**
Javelin Clo. *B'frd* —9F **40**
Jaw Hill. —9C 98
Jay Ho. La. *Brigh* —7A **94**
Jay St. *Haw* —8D **36**
(in two parts)
Jean Av. *Leeds* —7B **64**
Jebb La. *Haig* —6N **151**
Jenkin Dri. *Horb* —1B **136**
Jenkin La. *Horb* —9B **118**
Jenkin Rd. *Horb* —1B **136**
Jenkinson Clo. *Leeds* —9C **62**
Jenkinson Ct. *Kbtn* —3G **148**
Jenkinson Lawn. *Leeds* —9C **62**
Jenkinsons Pl. *Leeds* —5F **80**
Jenkinson St. *Bat* —1F **116**
Jenkyn La. *Shepl* —9H **149**
Jennetts Cres. *Otley* —1K **25**
Jennings Clo. *Sils* —9F **6**
Jennings Pl. *B'frd* —1M **75**
Jennings St. *B'frd* —1M **75**
Jenny La. *Bail* —3B **40**
Jenny La. *Mir* —4M **115**
Jenson Av. *Dew* —9C **96**
Jepson La. *Ell* —5E **112**
Jeremy La. *Heck* —8N **95**
Jer Gro. *B'frd* —3K **75**
Jer La. *B'frd* —3K **75**
Jermyn St. *B'frd* —7D **58**
Jerry Clay Dri. *Wren* —1G **118**
Jerry Clay La. *Wren* —9F **98**
Jerry La. *Sower B* —9G **91**
Jerry Spring Rd. *Hal* —6D **90**
Jersey Clo. *Dew* —1J **117**
Jerusalem La. *Hal* —9C **72**
Jerusalem Rd. *Slai* —3A **146**
Jervaulx Clo. *B Spa* —1C **32**
Jervaulx Cres. *B'frd* —6A **58**
Jerwood Hill Clo. *Hal* —3C **92**
Jerwood Hill Rd. *Hal* —3C **92**
Jesmond Av. *B'frd* —4L **57**
Jesmond Av. *Roys* —6C **154**
Jesmond Gro. *B'frd* —4L **57**
Jesmond Gro. *Dew* —2E **116**
Jessamine Av. *Leeds* —4B **80**
Jessamine St. *Dew* —6A **116**
Jesse St. *B'frd* —9C **58**
(BD5)
Jesse St. *B'frd* —7J **57**
(BD8)
Jessop Av. *Hud* —7E **132**
Jessop Fold. *Hon* —4L **147**
Jessop Row. *Leeds* —7K **61**
Jessop St. *C'frd* —4D **102**
Jessop St. *Wake* —7L **119**
Jester Pl. *Q'bry* —3B **74**
Jewitt La. *Coll* —2J **31**
Jew La. *Oxe* —4C **54**
Jilley Royd La. *Hud* —7M **113**
(in two parts)
Jill La. *Mir* —4N **115**
Jim Allen La. *Hal* —3C **90**
Jim La. *Hud* —4J **131**
Jinny Moor La. *Rothw* —5F **82**
Jin-Whin Ct. *C'frd* —4A **102**
Jin-Whin Hill. *C'frd* —4A **102**
Jin-Whin Ter. *C'frd* —4A **102**
Joan Royd. *Heck* —6A **96**
Joba Av. *B'frd* —7F **58**
Joffre Av. *C'frd* —6E **102**
Joffre Mt. Yead —1N ***41***
(off Springwell Clo.)
John Baker St. *Todm* —4G **87**
John Booth Clo. *Liv* —1K **115**
John Carr Av. *Horb* —9C **118**
John Escritt Rd. *Bgly* —5F **38**
John Haigh Rd. *Slai* —1N **145**
John Henry St. *W'wth* —7A **106**
John Naylor La. *Hal* —7E **90**
John Nelson Clo. *Bat* —3C **96**
Johnny La. *Otley* —2L **25**
John o'Gaunts. —6B 82
John o'Gaunts Trad. Est. *Rothw* —6N
John o'Gaunts Wlk. *Rothw* —7A
John Ormsby V.C. Way. *Dew* —9K
John Ramsden Ct. Hud —5N ***131***
(off Wakefield Rd.)
Johns Av. *Loft* —6L **99**
John's Cres. *Wren* —1G **119**
Johns La. *Ell* —7E **112**
Johnson St. *Bgly* —3E **38**
Johnson St. *B'frd* —7H **59**
Johnson St. *Mir* —8L **115**
Johnson Ter. *Morl* —9L **79**

ohnston St. Leeds —3D 62
ohnston St. Wake —5M 119
ohn St. Bail —6A 40
ohn St. Birs —3B 96
ohn St. B'frd —7C 58
(BD1)
ohn St. B'frd —4J 77
(BD4)
ohn St. Brigh —9M 93
ohn St. C'frd —6C 102
ohn St. Cytn —1H 75
ohn St. Cull —9K 37
ohn St. Denh —5K 55
ohn St. Dew —1F 116
ohn St. Eastb —2H 117
ohn St. Ell —5E 112
ohn St. G'Ind —4B 112
ohn St. Hal —5B 92
ohn St. Heck —9A 96
ohn St. Hud —6G 130
ohn St. Leeds —3A 62
ohn St. Oakw —5D 36
ohn St. Raven —6B 116
ohn St. Rawd —3M 41
ohn St. Shipl —7M 39
ohn St. S Elm —7M 157
ohn St. T'tn —8C 56
ohn St. Todm —7K 87
(off Dalton St.)
ohn St. Wake —5M 119
ohn St. Mkt. B'frd —7C 58
ohn St. W. Sower B —8H 91
ohn William St. Cleck —4H 95
ohn William St. Ell —5E 112
ohn William St. Flush —8N 95
ohn William St. Hud —3M 131
ohn William St. Liv —9M 95
nathan Gth. Add —1L 7
ns Av. S Kirk —7G 157
rdan Beck. Birds —4L 165
seph Av. Hal —2F 92
sephine Rd. Hud —7F 130
seph Ri. Leeds —8F 44
seph St. B'frd —7E 58
(BD3, in two parts)
seph St. B'frd —4J 77
(BD4)
seph St. Leeds —1G 80
seph's Well. Leeds —6C 62
(off Hanover Wlk.)
seph Vs. Cytn —1G 75
seph Wright Ct. B'frd —6E 40
(off Greenfield La.)
shua St. Todm —6K 87
s La. Shepl —8J 149
s Way. Shepl —9J 149
wett Pk. Cres. B'frd —5E 40
wett's La. Sils —1D 6
wett St. B'frd —7A 58
wett Ter. Morl —2K 97
bilee Av. Nor —3H 121
bilee Av. Shel —7L 149
bilee Av. Wake —8L 99
bilee Bungalows. Knot —8D 104
bilee Clo. Hems —3F 156
bilee Cotts. H'cft —1K 155
bilee Ct. Fitz —6A 140
bilee Ct. Morl —9L 79
(off Marshall St.)
bilee Cres. Dlgtn —6D 78
bilee Cres. Shar C —8J 121
bilee Cres. Wake —8L 99
bilee Cft. Dlgtn —6C 78
bilee Dri. Kei —2G 36
bilee La. Hud —7F 130
bilee Mt. Brigh —1L 113
bilee Pl. Morl —9L 79
bilee Pl. Pon —2K 123
bilee Rd. Hal —1C 112
bilee Rd. Shar C —8J 121
bilee St. B'frd —5B 58
(off Hamilton St.)
bilee St. Hal —6C 92
bilee St. Hall G —7H 137
bilee St. H Bri —3M 89
bilee St. Morl —9L 79
bilee St. N. Hal —1N 91
bilee Ter. Hal —6C 92
(off Jubilee St.)
bilee Ter. Morl —9L 79
bilee Ter. Sower B —5E 110
bilee Trees. Bur W —1A 24
bilee Way. Pon —3J 123
bilee Way. Shipl —7B 40
dy Haigh La. Dew —2G 134
dy La. Fix —8N 113
lian Dri. Q'bry —3H 75
lian St. Hud —5C 132
lie Av. Dur —5G 136
mb Beck Clo. Bur W —9D 10
mble Dyke. Brigh —3L 113
mble Hole Rd. C'twn —3C 88
mbles Ct. Loft —3L 99
Jumbles La. Loft —3L 99
Jumble Wood. Fen B —7H 133
Jumples. Hal —9K 73
Jumples Clo. Hal —9K 73
Jumples Ct. Hal —9J 73
Jumples Crag. Hal —9K 73
Jumps La. Err —3G 89
Jumps La. Todm —4G 87
Jumps Rd. Todm —4G 86
Junction Houses. C'frd —3C 102
Junction La. Oss —7C 118
(in two parts)
Junction Rd. Dew —4E 116
Junction Rd. Shipl —7A 40
Junction Row. B'frd —2F 58
(off Bolton Rd.)
Junction St. Leeds —8E 62
Junction Ter. B'frd —2F 58
(off Bolton Rd.)
June St. Kei —8J 21
Juniper Av. Rothw —6F 82
Juniper Clo. B'frd —6N 57
Juniper Gro. Neth —3J 147
Juniper Gro. M. Neth —3J 147
Juniper Pl. Leeds —5K 63
Justin Way. H'frth —1F 146

Kaffir Rd. Hud —2J 131
Karnac Rd. Leeds —2H 63
Karon Dri. Horb —1D 136
Kashmir Ct. Raven —6B 116
(off Church St.)
Katherine St. Shipl —7L 39
Katrina Gro. F'stne —8D 122
Kaycell St. B'frd —3F 76
Kay Clo. Morl —7J 79
Kaye Hill. Cull —9K 37
Kaye La. Hud —8B 132
Kaye La. Lint —8D 130
Kaye St. Dew —5G 116
Kaye St. Heck —9A 96
Kay St. Shipl —1A 58
Kay St. Wake —5M 119
Kearby Cliff. Kear —6L 15
Kearby Town End. —6N 15
Kearsley Ter. Leeds —3G 80
Keats Av. Todm —6M 87
Keats Clo. Pon —1K 123
Keats Dri. Heck —1B 116
Keats Gro. Stan —6N 99
Keat St. Hud —6K 131
Kebble Ct. Gom —5M 95
Keble Gth. Kip —3C 84
Kebroyd. —4E 110
Kebroyd Av. Sower B —4E 110
Kebroyd La. Tri —4E 110
Kebroyd Mt. Sower B —4E 110
Kebs Rd. Todm —9F 68
Kedleston Rd. Leeds —5H 45
Keeble Ho. B'frd —4H 59
(off St Clare's Av.)
Keelam Ga. H Bri —8L 71
Keelam La. H Bri —8L 71
Keeldar Clo. B'frd —2N 75
Keelham. —9L 55
Keelham La. Kei —6G 21
Keelham La. Todm —3M 87
Keelham Pl. Denh —9M 55
Keel Moorings. Rod —1C 60
Keenan Av. S Elm —8L 157
Keeper La. B'frd —2A 78
Keeper La. Wool —4M 153
Keeton St. Leeds —6H 63
Keighley. —2K 37
Keighley Clo. Hal —7K 73
Keighley Dri. Hal —8L 73
Keighley Ind. Pk. Kei —7K 21
Keighley Pl. S'ley —4B 60
Keighley Retail Pk. Kei —7J 21
Keighley Rd. Bgly —1C 38
Keighley Rd. B'frd —2N 57
Keighley Rd. Cull —8J 37
Keighley Rd. Denh —3J 55
Keighley Rd. H'den —3M 37
Keighley Rd. H Bri —1H 89
Keighley Rd. Oakw —5D 36
Keighley Rd. Ogden —4K 73
(in two parts)
Keighley Rd. Oxe —3C 54
Keighley Rd. Pec W —4H 71
Keighley Rd. Riddl —1D 22
(in two parts)
Keighley Rd. Sils —1D 20
Keighley Rd. Steet —3D 20
Keighley & Worth Valley Railway. —9K 21
Keir Hardie Clo. Liv —8M 95
Kelbrook Ho. B'frd —3J 77
(off Muirhead Dri.)
Kelburn Gro. Oakw —4B 36
Kelcliffe. —6H 25
Kelcliffe Av. Guis —7J 25
Kelcliffe Gro. Guis —7J 25
Kelcliffe La. Guis —6H 25
Keldholme Clo. Leeds —1B 60
Keldholme Rd. Leeds —1B 60
Keldregate. Hud —8C 114
Kell Beck. Otley —7K 11
Kellett Av. Leeds —1M 79
Kellett Bldgs. Low M —8B 76
Kellett Cres. Leeds —1M 79
Kellett Dri. Leeds —1M 79
Kellett Gro. Leeds —1M 79
Kellett La. Leeds —9L 61
Kellett Mt. Leeds —1M 79
Kellett Pl. Leeds —1M 79
Kellett Rd. Leeds —9L 61
Kellett Ter. Leeds —1M 79
Kellett Wlk. Leeds —1M 79
Kellingley. —8L 105
Kell La. Stum X —1E 92
Kelloe St. Cleck —3H 95
Kell St. Bgly —4F 38
Kellymoor Wlk. Idle —8D 40
Kelmore Gro. B'frd —7K 75
Kelmore Ho. B'frd —7G 40
(off Albion Rd.)
Kelmscott Av. Leeds —3E 64
Kelmscott Cres. Leeds —3E 64
Kelmscott Gdns. Leeds —3E 64
Kelmscott Gth. Leeds —2F 64
Kelmscott Grn. Leeds —3E 64
Kelmscott Gro. Leeds —3E 64
Kelmscott La. Leeds —3E 64
Kelsall Av. Leeds —4A 62
Kelsall Gro. Leeds —5A 62
Kelsall Ho. B'frd —6D 58
(off Otley Rd.)
Kelsall Pl. Leeds —4A 62
Kelsall Rd. Leeds —4A 62
Kelsall Ter. Leeds —4A 62
Kelsey St. Hal —4M 91
Kelso Ct. Leeds —5B 62
Kelso Gdns. Leeds —5B 62
Kelso Gro. Hud —4E 132
Kelso Pl. Leeds —4B 62
Kelso Rd. Leeds —4B 62
Kelso St. Leeds —5B 62
Kelton Ho. B'frd —3E 76
(off Spring Wood Gdns.)
Kelvin Av. Hal —5K 91
Kelvin Av. Hud —4C 132
Kelvin Cres. Hal —6K 91
Kelvin Ho. B'frd —2K 77
Kelvin Pl. B'frd —9E 58
Kelvin Rd. Ell —5D 112
Kelvin Way. B'frd —4G 58
Kemp Bank. Knot —8H 105
Kemp's Bri. Wake —5J 119
Kemps Way. N Mill —5C 164
Kempton Rd. Kip —3A 84
Kemsing Wlk. Leeds —4G 64
Ken Churchill Dri. Horb —9C 118
Kendal Bank. Leeds —5B 62
Kendal Carr. Leeds —5B 62
(off Hanover Mt.)
Kendal Clo. C'frd —5L 103
Kendal Clo. Leeds —5B 62
Kendal Cft. C'frd —5L 103
Kendal Dri. C'frd —5K 103
Kendal Dri. Croft —9D 120
Kendal Dri. Leeds —7N 63
Kendal Gdns. C'frd —5L 103
Kendal Gth. C'frd —5L 103
Kendal Gro. Leeds —5C 62
Kendal La. Leeds —5B 62
Kendall Av. Shipl —7K 39
Kendal Mellor Ct. Kei —9H 21
Kendal Ri. Croft —9D 120
Kendal Ri. Leeds —6B 62
(off Park La.)
Kendal Ri. W'ton —4C 138
Kendal Rd. Leeds —5C 62
Kendal St. Kei —1K 37
Kendal Wlk. Leeds —6B 62
(off Kendal Bank)
Kendell St. Leeds —7E 62
Kenilworth Av. Gild —7G 79
Kenilworth Dri. Hal —6M 93
Kenilworth Gdns. Gild —6G 79
Kenilworth Rd. Leeds —9M 61
Kenilworth St. B'frd —1F 76
Kenley Av. B'frd —3M 75
Kenley Mt. B'frd —3M 75
Kenley Pde. B'frd —3L 75
Kenmore Av. Cleck —4G 95
Kenmore Clo. Cleck —4G 94
Kenmore Cres. B'frd —3M 75
Kenmore Cres. Cleck —4G 94
Kenmore Dri. B'frd —3M 75
Kenmore Dri. Cleck —4G 95
Kenmore Gro. B'frd —3M 75
Kenmore Gro. Cleck —4G 94
Kenmore Rd. B'frd —3M 75
Kenmore Rd. Cleck —4G 94
Kenmore Rd. Wake I —8H 99
Kenmore Vw. Cleck —4G 95
Kenmore Wlk. B'frd —3M 75
Kenmore Way. Cleck —4G 95
Kennedy Av. Hud —7M 113
Kennedy Clo. Dew —9J 97
Kennedy Ho. Kei —3H 37
(off Hainworth La.)
Kennel La. Oxe —4M 53
(in two parts)
Kennel La. Sower B —3A 110
(in two parts)
Kennels La. T'ner —9G 31
Kennerleigh Av. Leeds —5D 64
Kennerleigh Cres. Leeds —5E 64
Kennerleigh Dri. Leeds —5D 64
Kennerleigh Gth. Leeds —5E 64
Kennerleigh Glen. Leeds —5D 64
Kennerleigh Gro. Leeds —5E 64
Kennerleigh Ri. Leeds —5E 64
Kennerleigh Wlk. B'frd —3K 77
Kennerleigh Wlk. Leeds —5D 64
Kenneth St. Leeds —9B 62
Kennet La. Gar —8A 66
Kennion St. B'frd —1B 76
Kensington Av. T'ner —1H 47
Kensington Clo. Bat —8E 96
Kensington Clo. Hal —8N 91
Kensington Ct. Leeds —3B 62
Kensington Gdns. Ell —5D 112
Kensington Rd. Hal —8N 91
Kensington Rd. Wake —3K 119
Kensington St. B'frd —5M 57
Kensington St. Kei —1H 37
Kensington Ter. Gar —7M 65
(off Main St.)
Kensington Ter. Leeds —3B 62
Kenstone Cres. B'frd —8E 40
Kent. —7B 60
Kent Av. Pud —7D 60
Kent Av. Sils —8D 6
Kent Clo. Pud —7D 60
Kent Cres. Pud —7D 60
Kent Dri. Pud —7D 60
Kentmere App. Leeds —1N 63
Kentmere Av. Gar —8B 66
Kentmere Av. Leeds —8A 46
Kentmere Av. Wyke —3C 94
Kentmere Clo. Leeds —1B 64
Kentmere Cres. Leeds —9A 46
Kentmere Gdns. Leeds —9A 46
Kentmere Gth. Leeds —1A 64
Kentmere Ga. Leeds —8A 46
Kentmere Grn. Leeds —9A 46
Kentmere Ri. Leeds —1B 64
Kenton Dri. Dur —3J 137
Kenton Way. B'frd —1H 77
Kent Rd. Bgly —5G 38
Kent Rd. Pud —7C 60
Kent St. B'frd —8C 58
Kent St. Hal —6A 92
Kent Wlk. Dew —3E 116
Kenwood M. H'fth —7G 43
Kenworthy Clo. Leeds —2K 43
Kenworthy Gdns. Leeds —2K 43
Kenworthy Gth. Leeds —2K 43
Kenworthy Ga. Leeds —2K 43
Kenworthy La. Ripp —5E 110
Kenworthy Ri. Leeds —2K 43
Kenworthy Va. Leeds —2K 43
Kenya Mt. Kei —8F 20
Kenyon La. Hal —5K 91
Kenyon St. S Elm —6N 157
Kepler Gro. Leeds —4G 63
Kepler Ho. B'frd —3G 77
(off Railway St.)
Kepler Mt. Leeds —4G 63
Kepler Ter. Leeds —4G 63
Kepstorn Clo. Leeds —1K 61
Kepstorn Ri. Leeds —1K 61
Kepstorn Rd. Leeds —8L 43
Keren Gro. Wren —1G 118
Kerry Gth. H'fth —6E 42
Kerry Hill. H'fth —7E 42
(in two parts)
Kerry St. H'fth —6E 42
Kerry Vw. H'fth —6F 42
Kershaw Av. C'frd —5H 103
(in two parts)
Kershaw Ct. L'ft —4D 90
Kershaw Cres. L'ft —5D 90
Kershaw Dri. L'ft —4D 90
Kershaw La. F'bri —5A 104
Kershaw La. Knot —9D 104
Kershaw Rd. Todm —2J 107
Kershaw St. B'frd —7H 59
Kertland St. Dew —4F 116
Kester Rd. Bat —7C 96
Kesteven Clo. B'frd —3K 77
Kesteven Ct. B'frd —3K 77
Kesteven Rd. B'frd —3J 77
Kestrel Bank. Hud —2K 147
Kestrel Clo. Leeds —3H 45
Kestrel Dri. B'frd —2E 58
Kestrel Dri. Wake —5M 137
Kestrel Gth. Morl —9N 79
Kestrel Gro. Leeds —3H 45
Kestrel Mt. B'frd —2E 58
Kestrel Vw. Cleck —3H 95
Keswick Clo. Sid —8D 92
Keswick Clo. Todm —5H 87
Keswick Dri. C'frd —2L 103
Keswick Dri. Wake —4G 118
Keswick Grange. E Kes —3D 30
Keswick La. Wike —4D 30
Keswick Rd. Dart —6J 153
Keswick St. B'frd —9H 59
Keswick Vw. Bard —3F 30
Ket Hill La. Brier —6N 155
Kettle La. Mars —3H 145
Kettlethorpe. —5K 137
Kettlethorpe Hall Dri. Wake —4L 137
Kettlethorpe Rd. Wake —5K 137
Kettleton Chase. Oss —2M 117
Kettlewell Dri. B'frd —2N 75
Keverne Ho. B'frd —1B 76
(off Hutson St.)
Kew Hill. —7E 112
Kew Hill. Hud —8E 112
Kexbrough. —9E 152
Kexbrough Dri. Dart —9F 152
Key Syke La. Todm —7L 87
Kibroyd Dri. Dart —9F 152
Kidacre St. Leeds —8E 62
Kiddal La. Pot —4M 47
Kidroyd. Hud —6B 132
Kilburn Clo. Alm —5A 132
Kilburn Ho. B'frd —9G 41
Kilburn La. Dew —2F 116
Kilburn Rd. Leeds —7M 61
Kilby St. Wake —4K 119
Kildale Ho. B'frd —8G 40
(off Garsdale Av.)
Kildare Cres. All —5F 56
Kildare Ter. Leeds —8A 62
Killingbeck. —5N 63
Killingbeck Bri. Leeds —5N 63
Killingbeck Dri. Leeds —5N 63
Killingbeck Retail Pk. Leeds —4N 63
Killinghall Av. B'frd —5F 58
Killinghall Dri. B'frd —5F 58
Killinghall Gro. B'frd —5F 58
Killinghall Rd. B'frd —4F 58
Kiln Bent Rd. Holme —1E 168
Kiln Brow. Gol —6D 130
Kiln Ct. Hud —1D 130
Kilncroft. Holy G —8M 111
(off Stainland Rd.)
Kilner Bank. Hud —3A 132
Kilner Ho. B'frd —4H 59
(off St Clares Av.)
Kilner Rd. B'frd —4M 75
(in two parts)
Kiln Fold. Brigh —9B 94
Kiln Hill. Slai —1N 145
Kiln Hill Ind. Est. Slai —1N 145
(off Kiln Hill)
Kiln Hill La. Sils —3B 6
Kilnhurst. —8L 87
Kilnhurst Av. Todm —7L 87
Kilnhurst La. Todm —8L 87
Kilnhurst Mt. Todm —7M 87
Kilnhurst Rd. Todm —7L 87
Kiln La. Clay W —4H 151
Kiln La. Dew —3G 117
Kiln La. Wals —2D 70
Kilnsea Mt. B'frd —2J 77
Kilnsey Fold. Sils —7D 6
Kilnsey Gro. Wake —3N 119
Kilnsey Hill. Bat —1G 117
Kilnsey Rd. B'frd —8F 58
Kilnsey Rd. Wake —3N 119
Kilnshaw La. Err —6F 88
Kilpin Hill La. Dew —9C 96
Kilroyd Av. Cleck —2H 95
Kilroyd Dri. Cleck —2J 95
Kimberley Pl. Hal —9N 73
Kimberley Pl. Leeds —4K 63
Kimberley Rd. Leeds —4K 63
Kimberley St. B'frd —8G 59
Kimberley St. Brigh —9N 93
Kimberley St. Dew —7E 116
Kimberley St. F'stne —5C 122
Kimberley St. Hal —9N 73
Kimberley St. Wake —8M 119
Kimberley Vw. Leeds —5K 63
Kimberly Clo. Thpe A —5A 142
Kinder Av. Cow —8E 130
Kineholme Dri. Otley —2H 25
Kine Moor La. Silk —9N 167
Kineton Av. Todm —6L 87
King Alfred's Dri. Leeds —6C 44
King Alfred's Grn. Leeds —6C 44
King Alfred's Wlk. Leeds —6C 44
King Alfred's Way. Leeds —6C 44
King Charles St. Leeds —6E 62

King Cliffe Flats. Hud —2M 131
King Cliff Rd. Hud —1M 131
King Clo. Leeds —3C 44
King Cross. —7L 91
King Cross Rd. Hal —7M 91
King Cross St. Hal —7N 91
King Dri. Leeds —3B 44
King Edward Av. All B —7N 83
King Edward Av. H'fth —7E 42
King Edward Cres. Leeds —6F 42
King Edward Rd. T'tn —8C 56
King Edward St. Dew —8E 116
King Edward St. Hal —5B 92
King Edward St. Hems —3E 156
King Edward St. Leeds —6E 62
King Edward St. Nor —1H 121
King Edward Ter. T'tn —8C 56
King Edwins Ct. Leeds —1J 63
Kingfield. Guis —6K 25
Kingfisher Clo. Dur —3H 137
Kingfisher Clo. Leeds —3H 45
Kingfisher Gro. B'frd —7H 57
Kingfisher Gro. Neth —2K 147
Kingfisher Gro. Wake —5M 137
Kingfisher M. Morl —1M 97
Kingfisher Reach. Coll —8J 17
Kingfisher Way. Leeds —3H 45
King George Av. H'fth —6F 42
King George Av. Leeds —8F 44
King George Av. Morl —7L 79
King George Cft. Morl —8L 79
King George Gdns. Leeds —8F 44
King George Gro. Morl —7L 79
King George Rd. H'fth —6F 42
King George St. Wake —9K 99
King Ho. I'ly —5F 8
(off Kings Rd.)
King La. Leeds —8N 27
King Royd La. Wake —4C 140
Kings App. Leeds —4H 61
Kings Av. Altft —7G 101
Kings Av. C'frd —5G 103
Kings Av. I'ly —5F 8
Kings Av. Leeds —5A 62
King's Bri. Rd. Hud —6N 131
Kingsbury Pl. Hal —6M 91
Kings Chase. Rothw —7A 82
Kings Clo. Ackw —5D 140
Kings Clo. I'ly —5D 8
Kings Clo. Oss —4M 117
Kings Clo. Otley —1N 25
Kings Clo. Pon —4J 123
King's Ct. Bgly —4E 38
Kings Ct. Birs —3B 96
Kings Ct. Hal —6A 92
Kings Ct. Kin —9B 140
Kings Ct. Leeds —6E 44
King's Cres. Pon —4L 123
Kings Cft. Gar —8L 65
Kings Cft. Oss —3M 117
Kings Cft. S Kirk —6H 157
King's Cft. Gdns. Leeds —6F 44
Kingsdale Av. B'frd —3E 58
Kingsdale Av. Dlgtn —7B 78
Kingsdale Ct. Leeds —9N 45
(in two parts)
Kingsdale Cres. B'frd —3E 58
Kingsdale Dri. B'frd —3E 58
Kingsdale Gdns. Dlgtn —7B 78
Kingsdale Gro. B'frd —3D 58
Kings Dri. Altft —7G 101
King's Dri. Birs —2B 96
King's Dri. B'frd —9D 40
Kings Dri. B'hpe —7K 27
Kingsfield. Rothw —8K 81
King's Ga. B'frd —5C 58
Kings Gro. Bail —6K 39
Kings Gro. Bgly —3F 38
Kings Head Dri. Mir —5K 115
Kings Head Rd. Mir —5K 115
Kingsland Ct. Roys —5E 154
Kings Lea. Hal —1A 112
Kings Lea. Liv —1N 115
Kings Lea. Oss —3M 117
Kingsley Av. B'shaw —9M 77
Kingsley Av. B'frd —3C 58
Kingsley Av. Croft —9F 120
Kingsley Av. F'stne —3D 122
Kingsley Av. Hud —6K 131
Kingsley Av. Knot —7B 104
Kingsley Av. Leeds —2L 43
Kingsley Av. Miln —4L 137
Kingsley Av. Out —7K 99
Kingsley Av. Sower B —9F 90
Kingsley Clo. B'shaw —9M 77
Kingsley Clo. Croft —9F 120
Kingsley Clo. Miln —4L 137
Kingsley Clo. Out —7K 99
Kingsley Cres. Bail —5A 40
Kingsley Cres. B'shaw —9M 77
Kingsley Dri. B'shaw —9M 77
Kingsley Dri. C'frd —7K 103
Kingsley Dri. Leeds —2L 43
Kingsley Gth. Wake —7K 99
Kingsley Pl. Hal —6N 91
Kingsley Rd. Leeds —2L 43
Kingsmead. Leeds —7B 46
Kingsmead. Oss —3M 117
Kings Mead. Pon —4H 123
Kings Mead. Rothw —7B 82
Kingsmead Dri. Leeds —6A 46
Kings Mdw. Oss —4M 117
Kings Mdw. Clo. Weth —2L 17
Kings Mdw. Dri. Weth —2L 17
Kings Mdw. Gro. Weth —2L 17
Kings Mdw. M. Weth —2L 17
Kings Mdw. Vw. Weth —2L 17
Kingsmill Clo. Morl —8J 79
King's Mill La. Hud —6N 131
Kings Mt. Bklnd —8F 110
King's Mt. Knot —7A 104
King's Mt. Leeds —7E 44
Kings Paddock. Oss —4M 117
Kings Pl. Leeds —2N 61
King's Rd. Bgly —2D 38
King's Rd. B'frd —4C 58
Kings Rd. B'hpe & Eccup —7K 27
King's Rd. Cud —8K 155
Kings Rd. I'ly —5D 8
King's Rd. Leeds —4A 62
Kings Rd. Nor —6F 100
Kingston Av. Hud —4C 132
Kingston Clo. Hal —6M 91
Kingston Clo. Wilsd —1B 56
Kingston Ct. Hal —6M 91
Kingston Dri. Hal —6M 91
Kingston Dri. Norm —2K 121
Kingston Gdns. Leeds —4C 64
Kingston Gro. Thack —6F 40
Kingston Ho. B'frd —9G 40
(off Rowantree Dri.)
Kingston Rd. B'frd —6F 40
Kingston St. Hal —6M 91
Kingston Ter. Hal —6M 91
Kingston Ter. Leeds —4D 62
King St. Altft —7G 101
King St. B'frd —1G 58
King St. Brigh —1N 113
King St. C'frd —7E 102
King St. Cleck —5J 95
King St. Dlgtn —7B 78
King St. Ell —5F 112
(off Brook St.)
King St. Hal —5C 92
King St. Haw —9C 36
King St. H Bri —4M 89
King St. Heck —8A 96
King St. Horb —1N 135
King St. Hud —4N 131
King St. Kei —1H 37
King St. Kin —9B 140
King St. Leeds —7D 62
King St. Lind —2H 131
King St. Mir —7L 115
King St. Morl —1K 97
King St. Nor —2H 121
King St. Oss —7A 118
King St. Pon —3H 123
King St. Rawd —3L 41
King St. Sils —8E 6
King St. Skelm —7D 150
King St. Sower B —9E 90
King St. S'ley —5A 60
King St. Todm —6M 87
King St. Wake —5L 119
King St. Yead —9N 25
Kings Vw. Hal —8F 92
Kingsway. Bgly —4F 38
Kingsway. Birs —2B 96
Kingsway. B'frd —8D 40
Kingsway. Dlgtn —7B 78
Kingsway. Gar —8L 65
Kingsway. Huby —5N 13
Kingsway. Leeds —6D 64
Kingsway. M'well —8H 153
Kingsway. Nor —3H 121
Kingsway. Oss —3M 117
Kingsway. Pon —9K 103
Kingsway. Riddl —7N 21
Kingsway. Stan —1A 120
Kingsway Arc. Dew —3G 116
(off Northgate)
Kingsway Clo. Oss —4M 117
Kingsway Ct. Leeds —6F 44
Kingsway Ct. Oss —4M 117
Kingsway Dri. I'ly —5F 8
Kingsway Gth. Gar —8L 65
Kingswear Clo. Leeds —5E 64
Kingswear Cres. Leeds —5E 64
Kingswear Gth. Leeds —5E 64
Kingswear Glen. Leeds —5E 64
Kingswear Gro. Leeds —5E 64
Kingswear Pde. Leeds —5E 64
Kingswear Ri. Leeds —5E 64
Kingswear Vw. Leeds —5E 64
Kingswell Av. Wake —8L 99
Kingswood Av. Leeds —4J 45
Kingswood Cres. Leeds —4H 45
Kingswood Dri. Leeds —4H 45
Kingswood Gdns. Leeds —4H 45
Kingswood Gro. Leeds —4J 45
Kingswood Pl. B'frd —1M 75
Kingswood Rd. Leeds —8M 61
Kingswood St. B'frd —1M 75
Kingswood Ter. B'frd —1M 75
Kinnaird Clo. Bat —7J 97
Kinnaird Clo. Ell —3E 112
Kinross Ho. B'frd —3J 77
(off Muirhead Dri.)
Kinroyd La. Hud —6C 132
Kinsey M. Bail —4N 39
(off West La.)
Kinsley. —8B 140
Kinsley Ho. Cres. Fitz —8A 140
Kinsley St. Kin —9B 140
Kipling Clo. Hud —7J 131
Kipling Ct. B'frd —8H 41
Kipling Gro. Pon —9K 103
Kippax. —4B 84
Kippax Common. —2N 83
Kippax Mt. Leeds —7H 63
Kippax Pl. Leeds —7H 63
Kipping La. T'tn —8C 56
Kipping Pl. T'tn —8C 56
Kirby Cote La. Cra V —9L 89
(in two parts)
Kirby Row. Hud —1G 132
Kirby St. Kei —8K 21
Kirk Beeston Clo. Leeds —3B 80
Kirkbourne Gro. Bail —5C 40
Kirk Bri. La. N Mill —1B 164
Kirkbridge Way. S Elm —6M 157
Kirkburn Pl. B'frd —8N 57
Kirkburton. —3K 149
Kirkby Av. Barn —9B 154
Kirkby Av. Gar —9A 66
Kirkby Clo. S Kirk —6J 157
Kirkbygate. Hems —4E 156
Kirkby La. Eml —1E 150
Kirkby La. Kirk O —5L 15
Kirkby Leas. Hal —6B 92
Kirkby Overblow. —2K 15
Kirkby Rd. Hems —3E 156
Kirk Clo. Dew —3L 117
Kirk Cross Cres. Roys —7D 154
Kirkdale. C'frd —4J 103
Kirkdale Av. Leeds —2L 79
Kirkdale Cres. Leeds —2L 79
Kirkdale Dri. Cald G —4F 136
Kirkdale Dri. Leeds —1L 79
Kirkdale Gdns. Leeds —1L 79
Kirkdale Gro. Leeds —1K 79
Kirkdale Ho. B'frd —9G 41
(off Rowantree Dri.)
Kirkdale Mt. Leeds —2L 79
Kirkdale Ter. Leeds —2L 79
Kirkdale Vw. Leeds —2L 79
Kirk Deighton. —1L 17
Kirk Dri. Bail —3B 40
Kirkfield Av. T'ner —1H 47
Kirkfield Cres. T'ner —1H 47
Kirkfield Dri. Leeds —7E 64
Kirkfield Gdns. Leeds —7E 64
Kirkfield La. T'ner —1H 47
(in two parts)
Kirkfields. Bail —3C 40
Kirkfields Ind. Cen. Yead —9L 25
Kirkfield Vw. Leeds —7E 64
Kirkfield Way. Roys —7D 154
Kirkgate. Bat —9H 97
Kirk Ga. B'shaw —6K 77
Kirkgate. Birs —3A 96
Kirkgate. B'frd —7C 58
(in three parts)
Kirkgate. Hud —4N 131
Kirkgate. Leeds —6E 62
(in two parts)
Kirkgate. Otley —9L 11
(in two parts)
Kirkgate. Shipl —8M 39
Kirkgate. Sils —8E 6
Kirkgate. Wake —5L 119
(in three parts)
Kirkgate Bus. Cen. Wake —6M 119
Kirkgate Cen. B'frd —7C 58
Kirkgate La. S Hien —3J 155
Kirkgate Mkt. Leeds —6E 62
Kirkham Av. K'gte —9D 98
Kirkhamgate. —1D 118
Kirkham Ho. B'frd —3D 76
(off Parkway)
Kirkham Rd. B'frd —9N 57
Kirkham St. Leeds —1C 60
Kirkhaw La. Knot —5A 104
Kirkheaton. —1G 132
Kirk Hills. T'ner —2H 47
Kirklands. Liv —8L 95
Kirklands. N Mill —1B 164
Kirklands. T'ner —2G 46
Kirklands Av. Bail —4C 40
Kirklands Clo. Bail —5C 40
Kirklands Clo. Men —4E 24
Kirklands Clo. Yead —9L 25
Kirklands Gdns. Bail —5C 40
Kirklands La. Bail —4C 40
Kirklands Rd. Bail —4B 40
Kirkland Vs. Pud —8B 60
Kirk La. Hal —4H 93
Kirk La. Yead —9K 25
Kirklea. Shel —6N 149
Kirk Lea Cres. Hud —1H 131
Kirklees Clo. Fars —2A 60
Kirklees Cft. Fars —2A 60
Kirklees Dri. Fars —2A 60
Kirklees Gth. Fars —2A 60
Kirklees Ri. Fars —2A 60
Kirklees Rd. All —7G 57
Kirklees Way. Brigh —6K 113
Kirklees Way. Floc —5E 134
Kirklees Way. Hud —9H 113
(nr. Burn Rd.)
Kirklees Way. Hud —7K 113
(nr. Cote La.)
Kirklees Way. Hud —5A 114
(nr. Shepherds Thorn La.)
Kirklees Way. Up Cum —9N 149
Kirkless Light Railway. —6G 150
Kirkley Av. Wyke —3A 94
Kirkroyds La. H'frth —1A 164
Kirk Smeaton. —4K 143
Kirkstall. —2L 61
Kirkstall Abbey. —1J 61
Kirkstall Av. Leeds —3J 61
Kirkstall Cen., The. Leeds —5N 61
Kirkstall Gro. B'frd —7J 57
Kirkstall Hill. Leeds —2L 61
Kirkstall La. Leeds —2K 61
Kirkstall Mt. Leeds —3J 61
Kirkstall Rd. Barn —9N 153
Kirkstall Rd. Leeds —3L 61
Kirkstone Av. Hud —4A 132
Kirkstone Dri. Gom —4M 95
Kirkstone Dri. Hal —4H 91
Kirkthorpe. —5D 120
Kirkthorpe La. K'thpe —8B 120
Kirkwall Av. Leeds —7K 63
Kirkwall Dri. B'frd —2J 77
Kirkwood Av. Leeds —3G 43
Kirkwood Clo. Leeds —2G 43
Kirkwood Cres. Leeds —2H 43
Kirkwood Dri. Hud —2F 130
Kirkwood Dri. Leeds —2G 43
Kirkwood Gdns. Leeds —2H 43
Kirkwood Grn. Hud —2G 130
Kirkwood Gro. Leeds —3G 43
Kirkwood Gro. Ting —4B 98
Kirkwood La. Leeds —2G 43
Kirkwood Ri. Leeds —2H 43
Kirkwood Vw. Leeds —2H 43
Kirkwood Way. Leeds —2H 43
Kismet Gdns. B'frd —6G 59
Kistyaen Gdns. Mel —6B 146
Kitchener Av. Leeds —5K 63
Kitchener Gro. Leeds —4K 63
Kitchener Mt. Leeds —5K 63
Kitchener St. Leeds —5K 63
Kitchener St. Oaken —8E 76
Kitchener St. W'ford —7D 82
Kitchen Fold. Slai —1N 145
Kitchenroyd. —9E 150
Kite M. B'frd —7H 57
Kit La. Sils —4B 6
Kitson Clo. Leeds —8M 61
Kitson Gdns. Leeds —8M 61
Kitson Hill. —4K 115
Kitson Hill Cres. Mir —4K 115
Kitson Hill Rd. Mir —5J 115
Kitson La. Sower B —2K 111
Kitson Rd. Leeds —9F 62
Kitson St. Leeds —7H 63
Kitson St. Shipl —9A 40
Kitson St. Ting —3N 97
Kitson Wood Rd. Todm —4G 86
Kitten Clough. Hal —3L 91
Kitwood Clo. B'frd —3K 77
Kliffen Pl. Hal —8C 92
Knaresborough Dri. Hud —9M 113
Knavesmire. Rothw —8K 81
Knightsbridge Wlk. B'frd —6F 76
Knights Clo. Leeds —6D 64
Knights Cft. Weth —2N 17
Knightscroft Av. Rothw —7N 81
Knightscroft Dri. Rothw —7N 81
Knightscroft Pde. S Elm —7N 157
Knight's Fold. B'frd —1M 75
Knightshill. Leeds —6E 64
Knights St. Hud —3N 131
Knight St. Hal —6M 91
Knightsway. Gar —9L 65
Knightsway. Leeds —5D 64
Knightsway. Rob H —2K 99
Knightsway. Wake —4L 137
Knoll Clo. Oss —4N 117
Knoll Gdns. Bail —6N 39
Knoll La. H'frth —9J 147
Knoll Pk. E Ard —5F 98
Knoll Pk. Dri. Bail —6N 39
Knoll Ter. Bail —6N 39
Knoll, The. B'ham —5C 32
Knoll, The. C'ley —4L 59
Knoll Vw. Bail —5N 39
Knoll Wood Pk. H'fth —7G 43
Knostrop La. Leeds —1K 81
Knotford. —8B 12
Knott Hill St. S'fth —5A 106
Knottingley. —8D 104
Knottingley Rd. Pon & Knot —1N 1
Knott La. Rawd —7B 42
Knotts Rd. Todm —4F 86
Knotty La. Lep —7K 133
Knowle Av. Hud —5C 132
Knowle Av. Leeds —3N 61
Knowle Gro. Leeds —3N 61
Knowle La. Mel —7E 146
Knowle La. Wyke —2B 94
Knowle Mt. Leeds —3N 61
Knowle Park. —2H 37
Knowle Pk. Av. Shepl —9K 149
Knowle Pl. Leeds —3N 61
Knowler Clo. Liv —7L 95
Knowler Hill. —7L 95
Knowler Hill. Liv —8L 95
Knowle Rd. Leeds —3N 61
Knowle Rd. Slai —9N 129
Knowler Way. Liv —7L 95
Knowles Av. B'frd —3H 77
Knowles Cft. Dew —1C 116
(off Staincliffe Rd.)
Knowles Hill. —1D 116
Knowles Hill. Dew —1C 116
Knowles Hill Rd. Dew —2C 116
Knowles La. Bat —8E 96
Knowles La. B'frd —3G 77
Knowles La. Gom —1M 95
Knowle Spring Rd. Kei —3H 37
(nr. Foster Rd.)
Knowle Spring Rd. Kei —2H 37
(nr. Selborne Rd.)
Knowles Rd. Bat —8E 96
Knowles Rd. Brigh —3M 113
Knowles St. B'frd —3G 76
Knowles St. Denh —6K 55
Knowles Vw. B'frd —3H 77
Knowle Ter. Leeds —4M 61
Knowle, The. Shepl —9K 149
Knowle Top. Holy G —9N 111
Knowle Top Dri. Hal —4K 93
Knowle Top Rd. Hal —4K 93
Knowl Grange. Mir —6L 115
Knowl Gro. Mir —6L 115
Knowl La. H'frth —4D 162
Knowl Rd. Gol —6C 130
Knowl Rd. Mir —5K 115
Knowl, The. Mir —6K 115
Knowl Wood. —1J 107
Knowlwood Rd. Todm —1J 107
Knowsley Av. Todm —2J 107
(off Rochdale Rd.)
Knowsley Cres. S'fth —5A 106
Knowsley St. B'frd —7E 58
Knowsthorpe. —9H 63
Knowsthorpe Cres. Leeds —8H 6
Knowsthorpe Ga. Leeds —1K 81
Knowsthorpe La. Leeds —9H 63
(in three parts)
Knowsthorpe Rd. Leeds —9L 63
Knowsthorpe Way. Leeds —1K 8
Knox St. Leeds —1A 60
Knutsford Gro. B'frd —3J 77
Krives La. Slai —4L 145
Krumlin. —9H 111
Kyffin Av. Leeds —7N 63
Kyffin Pl. B'frd —9J 59

Laburnum Clo. E Ard —5E 98
Laburnum Ct. C'frd —6E 102
Laburnum Ct. Horb —1B 136
Laburnum Dri. Bail —3B 40
Laburnum Gro. Cro R —7E 36
Laburnum Gro. Gol —5E 130
Laburnum Gro. Gom —3L 95
Laburnum Gro. Hal —6M 93
Laburnum Gro. Horb —1B 136
Laburnum Gro. Skelm —8D 150
Laburnum Pl. App B —7J 41
Laburnum Pl. Mann —5A 58
Laburnum Rd. Dew —1B 116
Laburnum Rd. Shipl —1B 58
Laburnum Rd. Wake —4K 119
Laburnum St. B'frd —5A 58
Laburnum St. Far —5A 60
Laburnum St. Pud —6N 59

aburnum Ter. Hal —2M 93
(off Village St.)
acey Gro. Weth —5N 17
acey M. B'frd —3G 77
acey St. Dew —3E 116
acey St. Horb —9E 118
acy Av. Todm —2J 107
acy St. Hems —2C 156
acy Way. Lfds B —3F 112
adbroke Gro. B'frd —4J 77
adderbanks La. Bail —3B 40
(in two parts)
adstone Pk. Cvn. Site. Sower B —4G 110
adstone Towers. Sower B —8H 91
(off Greenups Ter.)
dy Ann Bus. Pk. Bat —6G 97
dy Ann Rd. Bat —7G 97
dy Balk. —9K 103
dy Balk La. Pon —1K 123
adybeck Clo. Leeds —6F 62
dybower Av. Cow —8E 130
dy Clo. Oss —3M 117
ady Fld. T'tn —8C 56
(off West La.)
dy Heton Av. Mir —5K 115
dy Heton Clo. Mir —5J 115
dy Heton Dri. Mir —5J 115
dy Heton Gro. Mir —5J 115
dy Ho. La. Hud —1L 147
dy La. Bgly —1F 38
dy La. Leeds —6E 62
dy La. Wake —6K 119
dy Mill La. Dew —1L 135
dy Pk. Av. Bgly —1F 38
dy Pk. Ct. Leeds —3H 45
dy Pit La. Leeds —1D 80
(in two parts)
adyroyd Dri. E Bier —7J 77
adysmith Rd. Q'bry —5B 74
ady's Wlk. Den —2N 9
dywell Clo. B'frd —2C 76
dywell La. Liv —9F 94
dy Wood. —8L 45
dywood Grange. Leeds —9M 45
dywood Mead. Leeds —9M 45
dywood Rd. Dew —5D 116
dywood Rd. Leeds —9K 45
dywood Ter. Hal —4N 91
dywood Way. Rav I —7B 116
fflands La. Ryh —9H 139
irum Ri. Cliff —3D 32
isterdyke. —8H 59
isterdyke. Lais —8H 59
isteridge La. B'frd —8A 58
ith. —6H 163
ith Clo. Leeds —4J 43
ithe Av. H'frth —6H 163
ithe Bank Dri. H'frth —6H 163
ithe Clo. Sils —7E 6
ithecroft Rd. Bat —7H 97
ithe Gro. B'frd —4M 75
ithe Rd. B'frd —4N 75
ithes Chase. Wake —4F 118
ithes Clo. Barn —9C 154
ithes Clo. Wake —4F 118
ithes Ct. Wake —4F 118
ithes Cres. Barn —9A 154
ithes Cres. Wake —4F 118
ithes Cft. Dew —5H 117
ithes Dri. Althpe —4F 118
ithes Fold. Wake —4F 118
ithes La. Barn —9A 154
ithes Vw. Wake —4F 118
ith Gdns. Leeds —4K 43
ith Gth. Leeds —4J 43
ith Grn. Leeds —4J 43
ith Rd. Leeds —4J 43
th Staid La. Leeds —5M 67
th Wlk. Leeds —4J 43
keland Cres. Leeds —1C 44
keland Dri. Leeds —1D 44
keland Way. W'ton —4B 138
ke Lock. —7B 100
ke Lock Dri. Stan —6A 100
ke Lock Gro. Stan —7B 100
ke Lock Rd. Stan —7A 100
ke Row. B'frd —9F 58
keside. E Mor —6D 22
keside. Mars —5G 144
keside Chase. Rawd —3N 41
keside Clo. I'ly —4F 8
keside Ct. Halt —8N 63
keside Ct. Hud —2G 130
keside Ct. Leeds —3F 80
keside Est. Ryh —8J 139
keside Gdns. Rawd —3N 41
keside Ind. Est. Leeds —8J 61
keside Meadows. Pon —9K 103
keside Rd. Leeds —8H 61
keside Ter. Rawd —3N 41
keside Vw. Pon —8D 140
keside Vw. Rawd —3N 41
Lakeside Wlk. Rawd —3N 41
(off Lakeside Ter.)
Lake St. B'frd —9F 58
Lake St. Kei —7L 21
Lake Ter. Leeds —3F 80
Lake Vw. Arm B —1K 147
Lake Vw. Hal —4A 92
Lake Vw. N'dam —6L 137
Lake Vw. Pon —9J 103
Lakeview Ct. Leeds —7L 45
Lake Yd. Stan —7B 100
Lamb Cote Rd. Hud —5B 114
Lambe Flatt. Dart —9E 152
Lambert Av. Leeds —9H 45
Lambert Clo. G'Ind —4C 112
Lambert Dri. Leeds —9H 45
Lambert Pl. B'frd —4F 58
(off Thirlmere Gdns.)
Lambert's Arc. Leeds —7E 62
(off Briggate)
Lambert St. G'Ind —4C 112
Lambert Ter. H'fth —7D 42
(nr. Park Side)
Lambert Ter. H'fth —7H 43
(off Low La.)
Lamb Hall Rd. Hud —2C 130
Lamb Inn Rd. Knot —8F 104
Lambourne Av. B'frd —1H 59
Lambrigg Cres. Leeds —2B 64
Lambs Flat La. Dart —9E 152
Lambton Gro. Leeds —2H 63
Lambton Pl. Leeds —2H 63
Lambton St. Leeds —2H 63
Lambton Ter. Leeds —2H 63
Lambton Vw. Leeds —2H 63
Lamma Well Rd. H'frth —6M 163
Lampards Clo. All —4F 56
Lamplands. —6G 96
Lamplands. Bat —5G 96
Lanark Dri. H'fth —3E 42
Lanark Ri. Croft —2H 139
Lancaster Clo. Pon —5K 123
Lancaster Ct. Kei —2H 37
(off Rutland St.)
Lancaster Cres. Hud —6D 132
Lancaster La. H'frth —8A 148
Lancaster Pl. Rothw —9A 82
(off Springfield St.)
Lancaster St. C'frd —3K 103
Lancastre Av. Leeds —3J 61
(in two parts)
Lancastre Gro. Leeds —3J 61
Lancefield Ho. Out —7K 99
Landford Ho. B'frd —1B 76
(off Park La.)
Land Ga. S'fth —6A 106
Landor St. Kei —8K 21
Lands Beck Way. Liv —8K 95
Landscove Av. B'frd —3J 77
Landsdown Av. S Kirk —8G 156
Landseer Av. Leeds —3H 61
Landseer Av. Ting —4A 98
Landseer Clo. Leeds —3G 61
Landseer Cres. Leeds —3H 61
Landseer Dri. Leeds —3G 61
Landseer Gdns. Leeds —3G 61
Landseer Grn. Leeds —3G 60
Landseer Gro. Leeds —3H 61
Landseer Mt. Leeds —3H 61
Landseer Ri. Leeds —3G 61
Landseer Rd. Leeds —3G 61
Landseer Ter. Leeds —3H 61
Landseer Vw. Leeds —3H 61
Landseer Wlk. Leeds —3G 61
(off Landseer Clo.)
Landseer Way. Leeds —3G 61
Lands Head La. Hal —9E 74
Landsholme Ct. B'frd —3K 77
Lands La. B'frd —1G 58
Lands La. Guis —7J 25
Lands La. Leeds —6E 62
Landsmoor Gro. Bgly —2G 39
Land St. Fars —3A 60
Lane. —8D 162
Lane and Dowry Rd. Slai —3L 145
Lane Cotts. Roys —6D 154
Lane Ct. Brigh —9N 93
(off Old La.)
Lane End. —2G 75
(nr. Horton Bank)
Lane End. —5B 36
(nr. Oakworth)
Lane End. Bail —4A 40
Lane End. H'den —6A 38
(off Spring Row)
Lane End. Pud —6C 60
(in two parts)
Lane End. T'tn —8C 56
Lane End Ct. Leeds —2B 44
Lane End Cft. Leeds —2B 44
Lane End Fold. Pud —6C 60
Lane End Mt. Pud —6C 60
Lane End Pl. Leeds —9D 62
Lane Ends. —4C 42
Lane Ends Clo. B'frd —6L 57
Lane Ends Clo. Fitz —6A 140
Lane Ends Grn. Hal —4G 93
Lane Ends La. Wadsw —9K 71
Lane End Vw. Stan —7N 99
Lane Fox Ct. Yead —1M 41
(off Harper La.)
Lane Hackings. Lwr C —1B 166
Lane Hackings Grn. Lwr C —1B 166
Lane Head. —9M 93
(nr. Brighouse)
Lane Head. —2J 165
(nr. Shepley)
Lane Head Clo. M'well —7J 153
Lane Head La. Caus F —5J 73
Lane Head La. Kbtn —3K 149
Lane Head Ri. M'well —7J 153
Lane Head Rd. Caw —5M 167
La. Head Rd. Shepl —9J 149
Lane Head Rd. Sower B —6B 110
Lane Ho. Gro. L'ft —4E 90
Lane Ings. Mars —5G 145
Laneside. Holy G —7A 112
Lane Side. Hud —3G 132
Laneside. Kbtn —3L 149
Laneside. Morl —6L 79
Lane Side. Q'bry —2B 74
Lane Side. Wyke —9N 75
Laneside Clo. Morl —6L 79
Laneside Fold. Morl —6L 79
Laneside Gdns. Morl —7L 79
Laneside M. Morl —6L 79
Laneside St. Todm —8J 87
Laneside Ter. Morl —6L 79
Lanes, The. Pud —6C 60
(in two parts)
Lane, The. Alw —2B 44
Lane, The. Leeds —7G 62
Lane Top. Denh —4K 55
Lane Top. Lint —9D 130
(off Royd Ho. La.)
Langbar App. Leeds —9E 46
Langbar Av. B'frd —3J 57
Langbar Clo. Leeds —9E 46
Langbar Gdns. Leeds —1E 64
Langbar Gth. Leeds —9E 46
Langbar Grange. Leeds —1E 64
Langbar Grn. Leeds —9E 46
Langbar Gro. Leeds —1E 64
Langbar Pl. Leeds —9E 46
Langbar Rd. I'ly —3F 8
Langbar Rd. Leeds —1E 64
Langbar Sq. Leeds —1E 64
Langbar Towers. Leeds —1E 64
(off Swarcliffe Av.)
Langbar Vw. Leeds —9E 46
Langcliff Clo. M'well —7J 153
Langdale Av. B'frd —6K 57
Langdale Av. Leeds —1M 61
Langdale Av. Nor —8H 101
Langdale Av. Out —7M 99
Langdale Av. Wyke —3C 94
Langdale Clo. C'frd —2L 103
Langdale Clo. Weth —3K 17
Langdale Ct. Bgly —3F 38
Langdale Cres. Hal —3L 91
Langdale Dri. Ackw —3J 141
Langdale Dri. Hud —4A 132
Langdale Dri. Nor —8H 101
Langdale Dri. Q'bry —4C 74
Langdale Dri. Wake —5G 119
Langdale Gdns. Leeds —2M 61
Langdale M. Nor —8H 101
Langdale Mt. W'ton —4B 138
Langdale Rd. B'frd —2J 59
Langdale Rd. Carc —8N 159
Langdale Rd. Dew —1J 117
Langdale Rd. W'ford —7C 82
Langdale Sq. Wake —5H 119
Langdale St. Ell —5E 112
Langdale Ter. Leeds —2M 61
Langela Ter. Hal —4H 93
Langford Clo. Bur W —8C 10
Langford Ct. Bur W —8B 10
Langford La. Bur W —8C 10
Langford M. Bur W —8C 10
Langford Ride. Bur W —8D 10
Langford Rd. Bur W —8C 10
Langlands Rd. Bgly —8F 38
Lang La. B'frd —2B 58
Langley. —4K 99
Langley Av. Bgly —3F 38
Langley Av. B'frd —4F 76
Langley Av. Leeds —2D 60
Langley Clo. Leeds —2D 60
Langley Cres. Bail —4C 40
Langley Cres. Leeds —2E 60
Langley Gth. Leeds —2D 60
Langley Gro. Bgly —3F 38
Langley La. Bail —3C 40
Langley La. Clay W —6H 151
Langley Mt. Leeds —2E 60
Langley Pl. Leeds —2D 60
Langley Rd. Bgly —3F 38
Langley Rd. Leeds —2D 60
Langley Ter. Hud —2F 130
Langley Ter. Leeds —2D 60
Langport Clo. Q'bry —4E 74
Langsett Cft. Hud —6C 114
Langsett Rd. Wake —5K 137
Langthorne Cres. Morl —2M 97
Langthwaite Grange Ind. Est. S Kirk —7K 157
Langthwaite Ho. S Kirk —6J 157
Langthwaite La. S Elm —8L 157
Langthwaite Rd. Lang G —6K 157
Langton Av. B'frd —4F 76
Langton Clo. Gom —2M 95
Langton St. Sower B —7H 91
Langtons Wharf. Leeds —7F 62
(off Calls, The)
Langwith Av. Coll —9H 17
Langwith Dri. Coll —9F 16
Langwith M. Coll —9H 17
Langwith Valley Rd. Coll —9F 16
(in two parts)
Lanrick Ho. B'frd —1J 77
(off Broadstone Way)
Lansdale Ct. B'frd —3K 77
Lansdowne Av. C'frd —5F 102
Lansdowne Clo. Bail —4D 40
Lansdowne Clo. Bat —6E 96
Lansdowne Cres. Dart —9F 152
Lansdowne Ho. B'frd —5A 58
(off Trenton Dri.)
Lansdowne Pl. B'frd —8B 58
Lansdowne St. Leeds —8M 61
Lanshaw Bank. Beam —5M 5
Lanshaw Clo. Leeds —7G 80
Lanshaw Cres. Leeds —8G 80
Lanshaw Pl. Leeds —7G 80
Lanshaw Rd. Leeds —7G 80
Lanshaw Ter. Leeds —8G 80
Lanshaw Vw. Leeds —7G 80
Lanshaw Wlk. Leeds —7G 80
Lapage St. B'frd —7G 59
Lapage Ter. B'frd —8G 58
Lapwing Clo. B'frd —7G 57
Larch Av. H'frth —9A 148
Larch Clo. Birs —2D 96
Larch Clo. Hud —1F 132
Larch Clo. Liv —9N 95
Larch Clo. Nor —3K 121
Larch Clo. Oakw —5D 36
Larch Ct. C'frd —6E 102
Larch Dale. Hud —7M 113
Larch Dri. B'frd —6A 76
Larchfield Home. Leeds —1G 80
Larchfield Rd. Leeds —9G 62
Larch Gro. Bail —6K 39
Larch Gro. Bgly —2F 38
Larch Hill. B'frd —6B 76
Larch Hill Cres. B'frd —5B 76
Larch La. Gar —8B 66
Larchmont. Cytn —1H 75
Larch Rd. Hud —5H 131
Larch St. Kei —3H 37
Larchwood. Rawd —6N 41
Larch Wood. S'cft —9D 30
Larkfield. —3N 41
Larkfield. B'frd —3L 57
Larkfield Av. Rawd —3N 41
Larkfield Cres. Rawd —3N 41
Larkfield Dri. Rawd —3N 41
Larkfield Mt. Rawd —3N 41
Larkfield Rd. Pud —6B 60
Larkfield Rd. Rawd —3N 41
Larkfield Ter. Kei —1L 37
Lark Hill. Bat —3D 96
Lark Hill Av. Cleck —6F 94
Lark Hill Clo. Cleck —6F 94
Larkhill Clo. Leeds —7G 44
Lark Hill Dri. Cleck —6F 94
Larkhill Grn. Leeds —6G 44
Larkhill Vw. Leeds —7G 44
Larkhill Wlk. Leeds —6G 44
Larkhill Way. Leeds —6G 44
Larks Hill. Pon —4H 123
Larkspur Way. Wake —4G 119
Lark St. Bgly —4E 38
Lark St. Haw —8D 36
Lark St. Kei —9H 21
Lark St. Oakw —5D 36
Larne Ho. B'frd —1B 76
(off Roundhill St.)
Larwood Av. B'frd —2J 59
Lascelles Hall Rd. Hud —4G 132
Lascelles Mt. Leeds —3H 63
(off Lascelles Rd. E.)
Lascelles Pl. Leeds —3H 63
Lascelles Rd. Heck —9B 96
Lascelles Rd. E. Leeds —3H 63
Lascelles Rd. W. Leeds —3H 63
Lascelles St. Leeds —3H 63
Lascelles Ter. Leeds —3H 63
Lascelles Vw. Leeds —3H 63
Lastingham Grn. B'frd —4K 75
Lastingham Rd. Leeds —1C 60
Latchmere Av. Leeds —7J 43
Latchmere Clo. Leeds —7K 43
Latchmere Crest. Leeds —7J 43
Latchmere Dri. Leeds —7J 43
Latchmere Gdns. Leeds —6K 43
Latchmere Grn. Leeds —7J 43
Latchmere Rd. Leeds —7J 43
Latchmere Vw. Leeds —7J 43
(in two parts)
Latchmere Wlk. Leeds —6K 43
Latchmore Rd. Leeds —1A 80
Latchmore Rd. Ind. Est. Leeds —1N 79
Latham Ct. Gom —2M 95
Latham La. Gom —1L 95
Latham La. Wads —7L 71
Latham Lea. Gom —2L 95
Latimer Ho. B'frd —1C 76
(off Manchester Rd.)
Launceston Dri. B'frd —3J 77
Laund Rd. Hud —9D 112
Laund Rd. Slai —8J 129
Launton Way. B'frd —1B 76
Laura St. Brigh —2M 113
Laura St. Hal —3B 92
Laura St. Leeds —8B 62
Laurel Bank. Leeds —2E 64
Laurel Bank. Wyke —4A 94
Laurel Bank Clo. H'fld —7N 73
Laurel Bank Ct. Leeds —2M 61
Laurel Clo. E Kes —3D 30
Laurel Clo. Ell —5D 112
Laurel Clo. Hal —6H 75
Laurel Ct. Hud —6M 131
(off Industrial St.)
Laurel Ct. Oss —5M 117
Laurel Cres. Hal —1M 91
Laurel Cres. Kei —8H 21
Laurel Dri. Bat —5D 96
Laurel Fold. Leeds —7M 61
Laurel Gro. Bat —5C 96
Laurel Gro. Bgly —2D 38
Laurel Gro. Kei —8H 21
Laurel Gro. Leeds —7M 61
Laurel Gro. Sils —8D 6
Laurel Hill Av. Leeds —8E 64
Laurel Hill Cft. Leeds —7E 64
Laurel Hill Gdns. Leeds —7E 64
Laurel Hill Gro. Leeds —7E 64
Laurel Hill Vw. Leeds —7E 64
Laurel Hill Way. Leeds —8E 64
Laurel Ho. C'frd —5E 102
(off Parklands)
Laurel Mt. Hal —7N 91
Laurel Mt. Heck —8A 96
Laurel Mt. Leeds —1F 62
Laurel Mt. S'ley —6B 60
Laurel Pk. Wilsd —2B 56
Laurel Pl. Leeds —7M 61
Laurels, The. Dew —4J 117
Laurels, The. Leeds —9H 45
Laurel St. B'frd —8G 58
Laurel St. Hal —7N 91
Laurel St. Leeds —7M 61
Laurel Ter. A'ley —7M 61
Laurel Ter. Holy G —7M 111
Laurel Ter. Leeds —2E 64
(off Laurel Bank)
Laurel Ter. Skel —7M 159
Laurel Ter. S'ley —6B 60
Laurence Ct. W'ford —6E 82
Lavender Ct. Neth —3J 147
Lavender Cft. Heck —8B 96
Lavender Cft. Liv —7L 95
(off Carr St.)
Lavender Hill. B'frd —1G 58
Lavender Wlk. Leeds —7H 63
Lavenham Pl. Skel —7K 159
Laverack Fld. Wyke —1A 94
Laverhills. Liv —7H 95
Laverock Cres. Brigh —7L 93
Laverock La. Brigh —7L 93
Laverock Pl. Brigh —7L 93
(off Huntock Pl.)
Laverton Rd. B'frd —1F 76
Lavinia Ter. Cytn —1J 75
Lawcliffe Cres. Haw —7D 36
Law Clo. Weth —2N 17
Lawefield Av. Rothw —7L 81
Lawefield Gro. Wake —6J 119
Lawefield La. Wake —6J 119
Lawkholme Cres. Kei —9J 21
Lawkholme La. Kei —9J 21
Law La. Brigh —6A 94
Law La. Hal —7E 92
Law La. H Bri —9J 71
Lawler Clo. Oven —1M 91
(off Rugby Ter.)
Lawn Av. Bur W —8D 10
Lawn Dale. Skel —7L 159

Lawndale Fold. *Dart* —8H **153**
Lawn Rd. *Bur W* —8D **10**
Lawns. —6G 99
Lawns. *Wake* —6G **99**
Lawns Av. *Leeds* —2G **78**
Lawns Clo. *Leeds* —2G **78**
Lawns Clo. *Nor* —8F **100**
Lawns Ct. *Carr G* —7G **99**
Lawns Cres. *Leeds* —2G **79**
Lawns Cft. *Leeds* —2G **78**
Lawns Dene. *Leeds* —2G **79**
Lawns Dri. *Leeds* —2G **78**
Lawns Grn. *Leeds* —2G **79**
Lawns Hall Clo. *Leeds* —4L **43**
Lawns La. *Carr G* —7G **98**
Lawns La. *F'ley* —1G **79**
Lawns La. *Leeds* —2G **80**
Lawns Mt. *Leeds* —2G **79**
Lawns Sq. *Leeds* —2G **79**
Lawns Ter. *E Ard* —5F **98**
Lawns Ter. *Leeds* —2G **78**
Lawns, The. *Ove* —4K **135**
Lawns Vw. *Nor* —8F **100**
Lawnswood. —5K 43
Lawnswood Gdns. *Leeds* —5L **43**
Lawnswood Rd. *Kei* —2G **36**
Lawrence Av. *Leeds* —2L **63**
Lawrence Av. *Pon* —3H **123**
Lawrence Batley Theatre. —4N 131
Lawrence Ct. *Pud* —8A **60**
Lawrence Cres. *Heck* —6A **96**
Lawrence Cres. *Leeds* —2L **63**
Lawrence Dri. *B'frd* —3K **75**
Lawrence Gdns. *Leeds* —1L **63**
Lawrence Rd. *Hal* —9A **92**
Lawrence Rd. *Hud* —3K **131**
Lawrence Rd. *Leeds* —2L **63**
Lawrence St. *Hal* —3N **91**
Lawrence Wlk. *Leeds* —2L **63**
Law Slack Rd. *H'frth* —9B **164**
Lawson Rd. *Brigh* —1N **113**
Lawson St. *B'frd* —6D **58**
Lawson St. *Leeds* —7L **61**
Law St. *Bat* —4C **96**
Law St. *B'frd* —3G **76**
Law St. *Cleck* —3H **95**
Law St. *Corn* —3D **86**
Law St. *Wals* —4K **107**
Lawton St. *Hud* —7M **131**
*Laxton Ho. B'frd —1B **76***
(off Launton Wlk.)
Laxton Rd. *Barn* —9A **154**
Laycock. —9C 20
Laycock Ct. *Kbtn* —3G **148**
Laycock La. *Lay* —1B **36**
Laycock Pl. *Leeds* —3F **62**
Lay Gth. *Rothw* —8N **81**
Lay Gth. Clo. *Rothw* —8N **81**
Laygarth Dri. *Hud* —4G **132**
Lay Gth. Fold. *Rothw* —9N **81**
Lay Gth. Gdns. *Rothw* —9N **81**
Lay Gth. Grn. *Rothw* —9N **81**
Lay Gth. Mead. *Rothw* —9N **81**
Lay Gth. Pl. *Rothw* —9N **81**
Lay Gth. Sq. *Rothw* —9N **81**
Laythorpe Ct. *Pon* —4N **123**
Laythorp Ter. *E Mor* —7C **22**
Layton Av. *Rawd* —4A **42**
Layton Clo. *Rawd* —5B **42**
Layton Cres. *Rawd* —4A **42**
Layton Dri. *Rawd* —4B **42**
*Layton Ho. B'frd —1B **76***
(off Newall St.)
Layton La. *Rawd* —5B **42**
Layton Mt. *Rawd* —4A **42**
Layton Pk. Av. *Rawd* —5B **42**
Layton Pk. Clo. *Rawd* —4A **42**
Layton Pk. Cft. *Rawd* —5B **42**
Layton Pk. Dri. *Rawd* —4A **42**
Layton Ri. *H'fth* —4C **42**
Layton Rd. *Rawd & H'fth* —4B **42**
Lazenby Dri. *Weth* —3L **17**
Lazenby Fold. *Weth* —3L **17**
Lea Av. *Hal* —9B **92**
Leabank Av. *Gar* —9A **66**
Leach Cres. *Riddl* —6L **21**
Leach Ri. *Riddl* —6L **21**
Leach Rd. *Riddl* —6K **21**
Leach Way. *Riddl* —6L **21**
Lea Clo. *Brigh* —8M **93**
Lea Ct. *B'frd* —3K **75**
Lea Cft. *Cliff* —3D **32**
Lea Cft. *Otley* —1L **25**
Leadenhall St. *Hal* —7M **91**
Lea Dri. *Shepl* —9J **149**
Leadwell La. *Rob H & Rothw* —1K **99**
Lea Farm Cres. *Leeds* —9J **43**
Lea Farm Dri. *Leeds* —8J **43**
Lea Farm Gro. *Leeds* —9J **43**
Lea Farm Mt. *Leeds* —8H **43**
Lea Farm Pl. *Leeds* —9J **43**
Lea Farm Rd. *Leeds* —8H **43**
Lea Farm Row. *Leeds* —9J **43**
Lea Farm Wlk. *Leeds* —8J **43**
Leafield Av. *B'frd* —2G **58**
Leafield Av. *Hud* —4D **130**
Leafield Bank. *Hud* —4D **130**
Leafield Clo. *Hud* —7B **114**
Leafield Clo. *Leeds* —5D **44**
Leafield Cres. *B'frd* —2F **58**
Leafield Dri. *B'frd* —2G **58**
Leafield Dri. *Leeds* —5D **44**
Leafield Dri. *Pud* —9C **60**
Leafield Grange. *Leeds* —5D **44**
Leafield Gro. *B'frd* —3G **58**
*Leafield Ho. B'frd —1B **76***
(off Newall St.)
Leafield La. *Leat* —7F **12**
Leafield Pl. *Yead* —9K **25**
Leafield Ter. *B'frd* —3G **58**
Leafield Towers. *Leeds* —5D **44**
Leafield Way. *B'frd* —3G **58**
Leafland St. *Hal* —5N **91**
Leaf St. *C'frd* —5C **102**
Leaf St. *Haw* —7E **36**
Lea Gdns. *H'frth* —4C **164**
Leah Pl. *Leeds* —8B **62**
Leah Row. *Leeds* —8B **62**
Leake St. *C'frd* —5E **102**
Leak Hall La. *Den D* —2C **166**
Leak Hall Rd. *Den D* —2C **166**
Lea La. *F'stne* —7E **122**
Lea La. *Hud* —3H **147**
Lea Mill Pk. Clo. *Yead* —9L **25**
Lea Mill Pk. Dri. *Yead* —9L **25**
Leamington Dri. *B'frd* —7G **41**
Leamington Rd. *I'ly* —4H **9**
Leamington St. *B'frd* —4N **57**
Leamington Ter. *Dew* —5G **117**
Leamington Ter. *I'ly* —4H **9**
Leamside Wlk. *B'frd* —3J **77**
Lea Pk. Clo. *Leeds* —6H **81**
Lea Pk. Cft. *Leeds* —6J **81**
Lea Pk. Dri. *Leeds* —6H **81**
Lea Pk. Gdns. *Leeds* —6H **81**
Lea Pk. Gth. *Leeds* —6H **81**
Lea Pk. Gro. *Leeds* —6H **81**
Lea Pk. Va. *Leeds* —6J **81**
Lea Ri. *Hon* —6L **147**
Lea Rd. *Bat* —5C **96**
Learoyd St. *Hud* —3N **131**
Leas Av. *H'frth* —1L **163**
Leaside Dri. *T'tn* —7C **56**
Lea Side Gdns. *Hud* —4D **130**
Leasowe Av. *Leeds* —3G **80**
Leasowe Clo. *Leeds* —3G **80**
*Leasowe Ct. Leeds —3G **81***
(off Woodhouse Hill Rd.)
Leasowe Gdns. *Leeds* —3H **81**
Leasowe Gth. *Leeds* —3G **81**
Leasowe Rd. *Leeds* —3G **81**
Lea St. *Hill* —2M **131**
(in two parts)
Lea St. *Lind* —1H **131**
Lea Ter. *Leeds* —6E **44**
Leatham Av. *F'stne* —7E **122**
Leatham Cres. *F'stne* —7E **122**
Leatham Dri. *F'stne* —7F **122**
Leatham Pk. Rd. *F'stne* —7E **122**
Lea, The. *Gar* —9N **65**
Leather Bank. *Bur W* —6C **10**
Leathley. —6D 12
Leathley Av. *Men* —5F **24**
Leathley Cres. *Men* —5F **24**
*Leathley Ho. B'frd —1B **76***
(off Hutson St.)
Leathley La. *Leat* —5D **12**
Leathley La. *Men* —4F **24**
Leathley Rd. *Leeds* —9E **62**
Leathley Rd. *Men* —4F **24**
Leavens, The. *App B* —7H **41**
Leaventhorpe. —8H 57
Leaventhorpe Av. *B'frd* —7H **57**
Leaventhorpe Clo. *B'frd* —7J **57**
Leaventhorpe Gro. *T'tn* —8H **57**
Leaventhorpe La. *T'tn* —8G **57**
Leaventhorpe Way. *B'frd* —7J **57**
Lea Vw. *Bat* —4C **96**
Lea Vw. *H'fth* —6E **42**
Leavington Clo. *B'frd* —7N **75**
Leconfield Ct. *Weth* —3K **17**
Leconfield Ho. *B'frd* —8G **40**
Ledbury Av. *Leeds* —9H **81**
Ledbury Clo. *Leeds* —9H **81**
Ledbury Cft. *Leeds* —9H **81**
Ledbury Dri. *Leeds* —9H **81**
Ledbury Grn. *Leeds* —9H **81**
Ledbury Gro. *Leeds* —9G **81**
Ledbury Pl. *B'frd* —1F **76**
Leddis Ct. *Leeds* —8D **62**
Ledgard Dri. *Dur* —3H **137**
Ledgard Way. *A'ley* —6M **61**
Ledgate La. *Knot* —1D **104**
Ledger La. *Loft* —3L **99**
Ledger La. *Wake* —7K **99**
Ledger Pl. *Wake* —8K **99**
Ledsham. —5K 85
Ledston. —7E 84
Ledston Av. *Gar* —9A **66**
Ledston Luck. —3D 84
Ledston Luck Cotts. *Kip* —3E **84**
Ledston Luck Enterprise Pk. *Leeds* —3D **84**
Ledston Luck Vs. *Kip* —3D **84**
Ledston Mill La. *Leeds* —6E **84**
Lee Bank. *Hal* —3A **92**
Lee Beck Gro. *Stan* —4N **99**
Lee Bottom Rd. *Todm* —7B **88**
Lee Bri. *Dean C* —4A **92**
Lee Bri. Ind. Est. *Hal* —4A **92**
Lee Brig. *Nor* —9F **100**
Leech La. *H'den* —7M **37**
Lee Clo. *Wilsd* —9B **38**
Lee Clough Dri. *H Bri* —3N **89**
Lee Ct. *Kei* —1M **37**
Lee Ct. *Liv* —7L **95**
Lee Ct. *Oss* —7B **118**
Lee Cres. *Dur* —3H **137**
Leeds. —7E 62
Leeds 27 Ind. Est. *Morl* —9H **79**
Leeds and Bradford Rd. *S'ley & Leeds* —4C **60**
Leeds, Bradford Airport Ind. Est. *Yead* —7B **26**
Leeds Bradford International Airport. —9B 26
Leeds Bus. Cen., The. *Gild* —8H **79**
Leeds City Art Gallery. —6D 62
Leeds City Museum. —6D 62
Leeds City Office Pk. *H'bck* —8E **62**
Leeds District Cen. *Leeds* —8F **80**
Leeds La. *Rothw* —9H **65**
Leeds Old Rd. *B'frd* —6H **59**
Leeds Old Rd. *Heck & Bat* —7N **95**
Leeds Rhinos Rugby League Football Club. —2N 61
Leeds Rd. *All B* —7M **83**
Leeds Rd. *Bar E* —1J **65**
Leeds Rd. *Bat* —3C **96**
Leeds Rd. *B'frd* —7D **58**
(in two parts)
Leeds Rd. *B'hpe* —7K **27**
Leeds Rd. *Coll* —1G **30**
Leeds Rd. *Dew* —3G **117**
Leeds Rd. *Eccl* —2F **58**
Leeds Rd. *Glass* —6E **102**
Leeds Rd. *Guis* —8J **25**
Leeds Rd. *Hal* —3E **92**
(nr. Godley La.)
Leeds Rd. *Hal* —4J **93**
(nr. Halifax Rd., in two parts)
Leeds Rd. *Hud & D'tn* —3N **131**
Leeds Rd. *Idle* —5F **40**
Leeds Rd. *I'ly* —5G **8**
Leeds Rd. *Kip* —1N **83**
Leeds Rd. *Leeds* —2F **64**
Leeds Rd. *Liv & Heck* —8M **95**
Leeds Rd. *Loft & Wake* —2K **99**
Leeds Rd. *Meth* —1J **101**
Leeds Rd. *Mir* —4F **114**
Leeds Rd. *Oss* —2L **117**
(in two parts)
Leeds Rd. *Otley* —1M **25**
(in two parts)
Leeds Rd. *Rawd* —3M **41**
Leeds Rd. *Shipl* —7A **40**
Leeds Rd. *Tad* —3A **48**
Leeds Rd. *W'wood* —4A **102**
Leeds Rd. *W'ford & Oult* —6A **82**
Leeds Shop. Plaza. *Leeds* —7E **62**
Leeds St. *Kei* —9H **21**
Leeds Tykes Rugby Union Club. —2N 61
Leeds United Football Club. —2A 80
Leefield Rd. *Bat* —6B **96**
Leef St. *Hud* —4B **132**
Lee Grn. *Holy G* —9B **112**
Lee Grn. *Mir* —4L **115**
Lee Head. *Hud* —2L **131**
Leeke Av. *Horb* —9C **118**
Lee La. *Ackw* —1H **141**
Lee La. *Bgly* —8B **38**
Lee La. *Hal* —1B **92**
Lee La. *Kbtn* —3J **149**
Lee La. *Oxe* —3N **53**
Lee La. *Roys* —7M **153**
Lee La. *Todm* —9N **87**
Lee La. *Wilsd* —9A **38**
Lee La. E. *H'fth* —5E **42**
Lee La. W. *H'fth* —5C **42**
Lee Mill Rd. *H Bri* —8H **71**
Lee Mills Ind. Pk. *H'frth* —4A **164**
Leeming. —5D 54
Leeming St. *B'frd* —6D **58**
Lee Moor. —6N 99
Lee Moor La. *Stan* —4N **99**
Lee Moor Rd. *Stan* —6N **99**
Lee Mount. —3N 91
Lee Mt. Gdns. *Hal* —3N **91**
Lee Mt. Rd. *Hal* —3N **91**
Lee Orchards. *B Spa* —9E **18**
Lee Rd. *Dew* —6A **116**
Lees. —7E 36
Lees Av. *Dew* —7F **116**
Lees Bank Av. *Cro R* —7E **36**
Lees Bank Dri. *Cro R* —7E **36**
Lees Bank Hill. *Cro R* —7E **36**
Lees Bank Rd. *Cro R* —7E **36**
Lees Bldgs. *Hal* —4H **93**
Lees Clo. *Cull* —9J **37**
Lees Clo. *Hud* —3D **132**
Lees Dri. *Dew* —7F **116**
Lees Hall Rd. *Dew* —7E **116**
Lees Holm. *Dew* —7F **116**
Lees Ho. Rd. *Dew* —6F **116**
Leeside Av. *Hud* —7A **114**
Leeside Rd. *Heck & Bat* —6B **96**
Lees La. *Far* —2A **60**
Lees La. *Hal* —3K **93**
Lees La. *Haw* —8D **36**
Lees Mill La. *Lint* —9B **130**
Lees Moor Rd. *Cull* —9J **37**
Lees Rd. *H Bri* —9H **71**
Lee St. *B'frd* —8C **58**
Lee St. *Brigh* —8M **93**
Lee St. *Dew* —5B **116**
Lee St. *Liv* —7L **95**
Lee St. *Q'bry* —5C **74**
Lee St. *Wake* —5L **119**
Lee Ter. *Oaken* —8D **76**
Lee Way. *Kbtn* —2J **149**
Lee Wood Rd. *H Bri* —7G **71**
Legrams Av. *B'frd* —9L **57**
Legrams La. *B'frd* —9M **57**
Legrams Mill La. *B'frd* —8M **57**
Legrams St. *B'frd* —7N **57**
Legrams Ter. *Field B* —7A **58**
Leicester Clo. *Leeds* —4D **62**
Leicester Gro. *Leeds* —4D **62**
Leicester Pl. *Leeds* —4D **62**
Leicester St. *B'frd* —1E **76**
Leicester Ter. *Hal* —8A **92**
Leigh Av. *Ting* —4C **98**
Leigh Rd. *Ting* —4C **98**
Leigh St. *Ackw* —5D **140**
Leigh St. *Sower B* —7J **91**
*Leighton Pl. Leeds —6D **62***
(off Leighton St.)
Leighton St. *Leeds* —6D **62**
Leigh Vw. *Ting* —4B **98**
Leisure La. *Eml* —2H **151**
Leith Ct. *Dew* —1H **135**
*Leith Ho. B'frd —2J **77***
(off Stirling Cres.)
Leith St. *Kei* —8H **21**
Lemans Dri. *Dew* —9C **96**
Le Marchant Av. *Hud* —2H **131**
Lemington Av. *Hal* —6N **91**
Lemon St. *B'frd* —2A **76**
Lemon St. *Hal* —5M **91**
Lemon Tree Clo. *Pon* —5H **123**
Lenacre La. *Eml* —9A **134**
Lenham Clo. *Morl* —2K **97**
Lenhurst Av. *Leeds* —3J **61**
Lennie St. *Kei* —1H **37**
Lennon Dri. *B'frd* —6N **57**
Lennox Dri. *Wake* —9F **118**
Lennox Rd. *Leeds* —5N **61**
Lennox Rd. *Todm* —3B **86**
(in two parts)
Lenny Balk. *Hamp* —9C **158**
Lens Dri. *Bail* —3A **40**
Lentilfield St. *Hal* —2N **91**
Lentilfield Ter. *Hal* —2N **91**
Lenton Dri. *Leeds* —3E **80**
Lenton Vs. *B'frd* —6F **40**
Leodis Ho. *Leeds* —4L **81**
Leodis Way. *Leeds* —5K **81**
Leonard's Pl. *Bgly* —5F **38**
Leonard St. *Bgly* —5F **38**
Leonard St. *Hud* —1N **131**
Leonard St. *Wyke* —1B **94**
Leopold Gdns. *Leeds* —3G **62**
Leopold Gro. *Leeds* —3F **62**
Leopold St. *Leeds* —3F **62**
Leopold St. *Oss* —7C **118**
Lepton. —7L 133
Lepton Edge. —7N 133
Lepton La. *Lep* —9K **133**
Lepton Pl. *Gild* —6G **78**
Lesley Way. *H'frth* —9F **130**
Leslie Av. *Yead* —8N **25**
Leslie St. *Hud* —1M **131**
Leslie Ter. *Leeds* —3C **62**
Lesmere Gro. *B'frd* —3L **75**
Lessarna Ct. *B'frd* —9G **58**
Leven Gdns. *Weth* —2L **17**
Levens Bank. *Leeds* —8M **63**
Levens Clo. *Leeds* —8N **63**
Levens Gth. *Leeds* —8N **63**
Levens Pl. *Leeds* —8N **63**
Leventhorpe Ct. *W'ford* —8D **82**
Leventhorpe Way. *W'ford* —8D **82**
Lever St. *B'frd* —4M **75**
Lever St. *Todm* —7K **87**
Levita Gro. *B'frd* —1H **77**
Levita Pl. *B'frd* —9J **59**
Levita Pl. *Leeds* —6N **63**
Lewin Gro. *C'frd* —4K **103**
Lewis Clo. *Q'bry* —4C **74**
Lewisham Ct. *Morl* —9L **79**
Lewisham Gro. *Morl* —9L **79**
Lewisham Rd. *Slai* —9M **129**
Lewisham St. *Morl* —1H **97**
Lewis St. *Hal* —5A **92**
*Lewis Walsh Ho. Pon —3K **123***
(off Horse Fair)
Leybrook Cft. *Hems* —2E **156**
Leyburn Av. *Hal* —4K **93**
Leyburn Av. *Heck* —6B **96**
Leyburne St. *B'frd* —5A **58**
Leyburn Gro. *Bgly* —3F **38**
Leyburn Gro. *Shipl* —8M **39**
Leyburn Rd. *Skel* —7K **159**
Leyden Ri. *All* —6G **56**
Leyfield. *Bail* —4M **39**
Leyfield Bank. *H'frth* —1A **164**
Ley Fleaks Rd. *B'frd* —8F **40**
(in two parts)
Leygards La. *Mel* —7A **146**
Leyland Cft. *Hud* —5C **114**
Leyland Rd. *Birs* —3A **96**
Leyland Rd. *C'frd* —4J **103**
Leylands Av. *B'frd* —3L **57**
Leylands Gro. *B'frd* —3L **57**
Leylands Ho. *Kei* —1K **37**
Leylands La. *B'frd* —3L **57**
Leylands La. *Kei* —1K **37**
Leylands Rd. *Leeds* —5F **62**
Leylands Ter. *B'frd* —3L **57**
Leylands, The. —5E 62
Ley La. *Leeds* —6N **61**
Leymoor. —5C 130
Leymoor Rd. *Gol & Hud* —5C **13**
Leys Clo. *Thack* —6E **40**
Leysholme Cres. *Leeds* —8K **61**
Leysholme Dri. *Leeds* —9L **61**
Leysholme Ter. *Leeds* —8L **61**
Leysholme Vw. *Leeds* —8L **61**
Leyside Dri. *All* —4G **56**
Leys La. *B Spa* —9B **18**
Leys La. *Eml* —3E **150**
Leys La. *Hamp* —8G **158**
Leys La. *Knot* —1E **124**
Leys La. *Lit S* —3G **143**
Leys Rd. *D'ton* —6D **124**
Leys, The. *Bail* —3A **40**
Leys, The. *S Kirk* —8G **157**
*Leys Yd. H Bri —1H **89***
(off Bridge Ga.)
Leyton Cres. *B'frd* —8F **40**
Leyton Dri. *B'frd* —8F **40**
Leyton Gro. *B'frd* —8F **40**
Leyton Ter. *B'frd* —8F **40**
Ley Top La. *All* —6H **57**
Leywell Ter. *Leeds* —6K **61**
Lichen Clo. *B'frd* —2M **75**
Lichfield Mt. *B'frd* —2C **58**
Lichfield Rd. *Dew* —3J **117**
Lickless Av. *H'fth* —6G **42**
Lickless Dri. *H'fth* —6G **42**
Lickless Gdns. *H'fth* —6G **42**
Lickless Ter. *H'fth* —6G **42**
Lidgate Clo. *Dew* —1F **116**
Lidgate Cres. *Lang G* —7K **157**
Lidgate Gdns. *Dew* —1F **116**
Lidgate La. *Dew* —1F **116**
Lidgate La. *Shaf* —6J **155**
Lidget. —5D 36
Lidget Av. *B'frd* —9L **57**
Lidget Green. —8M 57
Lidget Hill. *Pud* —7B **60**
Lidget La. *Shar C* —9L **121**
Lidget Pl. *B'frd* —9L **57**
Lidget St. *Hud* —1G **130**
Lidgett. —8M 65
Lidgett Av. *Leeds* —8H **45**
Lidgett Ct. *Gar* —8M **65**
Lidgett Ct. *Leeds* —7H **45**
Lidgett Cres. *Leeds* —7H **45**
Lidget Ter. *B'frd* —9L **57**
Lidget Ter. *Cytn* —1J **75**
Lidgett Gro. *Leeds* —8H **45**
Lidgett Hill. *Leeds* —8H **45**
Lidgett La. *Gar* —9M **65**
Lidgett La. *Leeds* —6F **44**
Lidgett La. *Skelm* —8C **150**
Lidgett Mt. *Leeds* —6H **45**
Lidgett Park. —6H 45
Lidgett Pk. Av. *Leeds* —6H **45**
Lidgett Pk. Ct. *Leeds* —6H **45**
Lidgett Pk. Gdns. *Leeds* —7H **45**

dgett Pk. Gro. Leeds —7H 45
dgett Pk. M. Leeds —6J 45
dgett Pk. Rd. Leeds —6H 45
(in two parts)
dgett Pk. Vw. Leeds —6H 45
dgett Pl. Leeds —7H 45
dgett Ri. Skelm —8C 150
dgett Towers. Leeds —6G 44
dgett Wlk. Leeds —8H 45
(in three parts)
fton Pl. Leeds —4C 62
ght Bank La. Sils —5J 7
ghtcliffe. —4L 93
ghtcliffe Rd. Brigh —7M 93
ghtcliffe Rd. Hud —6J 131
ghtcliffe Royd. Bklnd —5J 111
ghtenfield La. Neth —3H 147
(in two parts)
ghtfoot Av. C'frd —6E 102
ghtfoot Clo. C'frd —6D 102
ghthazles Chapel Rd. Sower B —5A 110
ghthazles Rd. Sower B —5B 110
ghthouse. L'boro —9L 107
ght La. Wake —4G 118
ghtowler Clo. Hal —5N 91
ghtowler Rd. Hal —5N 91
ghtowler St. B'frd —4A 76
ghtridge Clo. Hud —7M 113
ghtridge Rd. Hud —7L 113
ac Av. Knot —1D 124
ac Av. Wake —8L 119
ac Clo. Add —1N 7
ac Clo. Brigh —9A 94
ac Gro. B'frd —8H 59
ac Gro. Gom —3L 95
ac Gro. Shipl —1B 58
acs, The. Guis —7J 25
acs, The. Roys —5F 154
ac St. Hal —3N 91
ac Wlk. Gol —5D 130
ey La. Mir & Grng M —2K 133
ian St. B'frd —2G 77
lands Av. Brigh —1L 113
lands La. Brigh —2L 113
lands Ter. Brigh —1L 113
ley St. Hems —3D 156
ley Ter. S Kirk —7H 157
ly La. Hal —6C 92
ly St. Sower B —9H 91
ycroft. B'frd —5N 57
ycroft Pl. B'frd —4N 57
ycroft Rd. B'frd —5M 57
ycroft Wlk. B'frd —4M 57
in two parts)
ydene Av. Grime —9N 155
y St. B'frd —4N 57
y St. Todm —4G 87
ythorne Av. B'frd —7G 41
ne Av. H Bri —1G 89
ne Av. H'frth —9A 148
ne Av. Todm —6J 87
ne Clo. Kei —7G 20
ne Ct. Bgly —1D 38
'off Aire St.)
ne Cres. S Elm —8L 157
ne Cres. Wake —1A 138
ne Gro. Barn —8D 154
ne Gro. Gol —5D 130
ne Gro. S Elm —8L 157
ne Gro. Yead —3L 41
ne Pit La. Stan —7N 99
ners Ga. H Bri —4M 71
ners Ga. Pec W —2J 71
ners Ga. Todm —7A 86
nes Av. Hal —8B 92
nes Av. M'well —7L 153
nes Clo. M'well —7L 153
ne St. Bgly —4E 38
ne St. B'frd —1M 75
ne St. Haw —9C 36
ne St. Hud —7K 131
ne St. Kei —9H 21
ne St. Oss —7A 118
ne St. Todm —6J 87
ne Tree Av. Bat —8D 96
ne Tree Av. B Spa —9D 18
ne Tree Av. Ell —5F 112
ne Tree Av. Pon —3H 123
ne Tree Clo. Cud —9J 155
ne Tree Clo. Rothw —7E 82
ne Tree Ct. Hems —3C 156
ne Tree Cres. Kip —4C 84
ne Tree Gdns. B Spa —1E 32
netree Gro. B'shaw —6L 77
netrees. Pon —8N 103
ne Tree Sq. Shipl —6J 39
newood App. Leeds —8B 46
newood Ct. Leeds —8B 46
newood Rd. Leeds —9B 46
burn Clo. Roys —5B 154
by Rd. Barn —9A 154
coln Av. Heck —7A 96

Lincoln Av. Liv —1K 115
Lincoln Clo. B'frd —5A 58
Lincoln Ct. Fars —4A 60
(off South Dri.)
Lincoln Cres. S Elm —5N 157
Lincoln Dri. Liv —1L 115
Lincoln Grn. Rd. Leeds —5G 62
Lincoln Gro. Hud —6E 132
Lincoln Gro. Liv —1K 115
Lincoln Mt. Leeds —5G 63
Lincoln Rd. B'frd —6A 58
Lincoln Rd. Dew —3J 117
Lincoln Rd. Leeds —5G 62
Lincoln St. All —6H 57
Lincoln St. C'frd —4E 102
Lincoln St. Hud —4A 132
Lincoln St. Todm —3D 86
Lincoln St. Wake —4H 119
Lincoln Towers. Leeds —5G 63
(off Lincoln Rd.)
Lincoln Wlk. Kip —3C 84
Lincoln Way. B'twn —3A 92
Lincroft Av. Hud —5C 132
Lincroft Cres. Leeds —3G 61
Lincs Wold. Liv —8F 94
Lindale Av. Ackw —3J 141
Lindale Clo. Leeds —6F 80
Lindale Gth. K'gte —1E 118
Lindale Gro. Wake —2F 118
Lindale La. K'gte —1E 118
Lindale Mt. Wake —2E 118
Linden Av. B'frd —6J 59
Linden Av. Leeds —2D 80
Linden Av. Todm —6J 87
Linden Clo. Bard —4E 30
Linden Clo. Brigh —9A 94
Linden Clo. C'frd —6K 103
Linden Clo. Dew —4L 117
Linden Clo. Knot —8B 104
Linden Ct. Leeds —8N 43
Linden Gdns. Leeds —2E 80
Linden Gro. Leeds —2E 80
Linden Mt. Av. Leeds —2D 80
Linden Pl. H Bri —9H 71
(off Linden Rd.)
Linden Pl. Leeds —2E 80
Linden Ri. Kei —2L 37
Linden Rd. Ell —5D 112
Linden Rd. Hal —8B 92
Linden Rd. H Bri —9H 71
Linden Rd. Hud —1L 131
Linden Rd. Leeds —2D 80
Linden Rd. Myth —3L 89
Linden St. Leeds —2D 80
Linden Ter. Ackw —5D 140
Linden Ter. Leeds —2E 80
Linden Ter. Pon —3J 123
Linden Way. Weth —2L 17
Lindholme Gdns. All —6G 56
Lindhurst Lodge. Barn —9A 154
Lindhurst Rd. Barn —9N 153
Lindisfarne Rd. Shipl —8L 39
Lindley. —1G 130
(nr. Huddersfield)
Lindley. —2C 12
(nr. Leathley)
Lindley Av. Hud —8F 112
Lindley Dri. B'frd —3L 75
Lindley Moor Rd. Hud —1C 130
Lindley Rd. B'frd —2B 76
Lindley Rd. Ell —7E 112
Lindley St. Milns —5F 130
Lindon St. Haw —9C 36
Lindrick Clo. Cud —8K 155
Lindrick Clo. Hal —6M 73
Lindrick Clo. Norm —2L 121
Lindrick Gro. Hal —6M 73
Lindrick Way. Hal —6M 73
Lindsay Acre. Ting —4C 98
Lindsay Av. Wake —6E 118
Lindsay Rd. Gar —8N 65
Lindsey Ct. Leeds —5G 63
Lindsey Gdns. Leeds —5G 63
Lindsey Mt. Leeds —5G 63
(off Lindsey Rd.)
Lindsey Rd. Leeds —5G 63
Lindwell. —3C 112
Lindwell Av. G'Ind —4B 112
Lindwell Gro. G'Ind —4B 112
Lindwell Pl. G'Ind —4B 112
(off Wellgate)
Linefield Rd. Bat —7G 96
Lineham Ct. Liv —9L 95
Lineholme Av. Todm —4G 87
Linfit. —9M 133
Linfit Fold. Lint —1N 145
Linfit La. Kbtn —1L 149
Linfit La. Lint —1N 145
Lingards Rd. Slai —4L 145
Lingards Ter. Mars —3J 145
Lingard St. B'frd —6D 58
Ling Bob. Hal —4K 91
Ling Bob Clo. Hal —4K 91

Ling Bob Cft. Hal —3K 91
Ling Cft. B Spa —9B 18
Lingcroft Grn. B'frd —3E 76
(off Tristram Av.)
Lingdale Rd. B'frd —7M 75
Lingfield App. Leeds —4D 44
Lingfield Bank. Leeds —4D 44
Lingfield Clo. Leeds —4E 44
Lingfield Cres. Leeds —4D 44
Lingfield Cres. Q'bry —3H 75
Lingfield Dri. Cro R —6G 36
Lingfield Dri. Leeds —4E 44
Lingfield Gdns. Leeds —4D 44
Lingfield Ga. Leeds —4D 44
Lingfield Grn. Leeds —4D 44
Lingfield Gro. Leeds —4E 44
Lingfield Gro. Wilsd —1C 56
Lingfield Hill. Leeds —3D 44
Lingfield Ho. B'frd —9G 41
(off Savile Av.)
Lingfield Mt. Leeds —4E 44
Lingfield Rd. Leeds —4D 44
Lingfield Rd. Wilsd —2B 56
Lingfield Ter. Q'bry —3H 75
Lingfield Vw. Leeds —4D 44
Lingfield Wlk. Leeds —4D 44
Ling La. Leeds —9A 30
Ling Pk. App. Wilsd —2B 56
Ling Pk. Av. Wilsd —2B 56
Ling Royd Av. Hal —4K 91
Lings La. Upt —1F 158
Lingwell App. Leeds —9E 80
Lingwell Av. Leeds —8E 80
Lingwell Chase. Loft G —6L 99
Lingwell Ct. Leeds —9E 80
Lingwell Ct. Loft —6J 99
Lingwell Cres. Leeds —8E 80
Lingwell Gdns. Leeds —9E 80
Lingwell Gate. —5J 99
Lingwell Ga. Cres. Wake —7K 99
Lingwell Ga. Dri. Wake —7J 99
Lingwell Ga. La. Loft & Out —2H 99
Lingwell Grn. Leeds —9E 80
Lingwell Gro. Leeds —9E 80
Lingwell M. Leeds —9E 80
Lingwell Nook Ct. Loft —6L 99
Lingwell Nook La. Loft G —6L 99
Lingwell Nook La. Loft —4J 99
Lingwell Rd. Leeds —8E 80
Lingwell Vw. Leeds —9E 80
Lingwell Wlk. Leeds —9E 80
Lingwood Av. B'frd —5L 57
Lingwood Clo. N Mill —1B 164
Lingwood Rd. B'frd —6L 57
Lingwood Ter. B'frd —6L 57
Link Rd. Dew —4G 116
Link Rd. Hud —4J 131
Link Rd. Wake —3K 119
Links Av. Cleck —3H 95
Links, The. F'stne —2D 122
Links Vw. M'well —7K 153
Link, The. Pon —5J 123
Link, The. Swil —4G 83
Linkway. Bgly —8F 38
Linnburn M. I'ly —6G 8
Linnet Clo. B'frd —6H 57
Linnet Clo. Mir —3L 115
Linnet Ct. Mir —3L 115
Linnet Ct. Morl —1N 97
Linnet Gro. Wake —5M 137
Linnet St. Kei —8J 21
Linnhe Av. B'frd —7L 75
Linsay Acre. Ting —4C 98
Linshaws Rd. H'frth —2K 169
Linthwaite. —9D 130
Linton. —7J 17
Linton Av. Bat —7D 96
Linton Av. Leeds —3H 45
Linton Av. Sils —7E 6
Linton Av. Weth —3L 17
Linton Clo. Leeds —3G 44
Linton Clo. Liv —7K 95
Linton Clo. Norm —2L 121
Linton Comn. Lntn —8G 16
Linton Cres. Leeds —3H 45
Linton Cft. Leeds —7J 43
Linton Dri. Leeds —3G 44
Linton Gro. Brigh —3K 113
Linton Gro. Heck —9B 96
Linton Gro. Leeds —3G 44
Linton Hills Rd. Lntn —4K 17
Linton La. Lntn —6K 17
Linton La. Sick —2H 17
Linton Meadows. Weth —4K 17
Linton Ri. Leeds —3G 44
Linton Rd. Coll —8H 17
Linton Rd. Leeds —3G 44
Linton Rd. Wake —5A 120
Linton Rd. Weth —4K 17
Linton St. B'frd —1D 76
Linton Vw. Leeds —2G 44
Lion Chambers. Cleck —4H 95
(off Whitcliffe Rd.)

Lionel St. Oss —7A 118
Lion St. Todm —9J 87
Liphill Bank. —3J 163
Liphill Bank Rd. H'frth —3H 163
Lip Hill La. H'frth —3G 163
Lippersley La. Sils —3G 6
(in two parts)
Lipscomb St. Hud —5F 130
Liquorice Way. Pon —3J 123
Lisbon Sq. Leeds —6C 62
(off Lisbon St.)
Lisbon St. Leeds —6C 62
Lisheen Av. C'frd —5E 102
Lisheen Gro. C'frd —5E 102
Lisker Av. Otley —1M 25
Lisker Ct. Otley —1M 25
Lisker Dri. Otley —1M 25
Lismore Clo. Rothw —8A 82
Lismore Rd. Kei —8H 21
Lister Av. B'frd —2F 76
Lister Clo. F'stne —6C 122
Lister Ct. Hal —5B 92
(off Chapeltown)
Listerdale. Liv —7L 95
Lister Hill. H'fth —5F 42
Lister Hills. —7A 58
Listerhills Rd. B'frd —8A 58
Lister La. B'frd —4D 58
Lister La. Hal —5N 91
Lister Rd. F'stne —6C 122
Lister's Clo. Hal —5N 91
Listers Rd. Hal —4D 92
Lister's Rd. Hud —8N 113
Lister St. B'frd —3G 77
Lister St. Brigh —9M 93
Lister St. C'frd —4C 102
Lister St. Hud —4C 132
Lister St. I'ly —5F 8
Lister St. Kei —1G 37
Lister St. Tong —4J 77
Lister Vw. B'frd —5A 58
Lister Ville. Wilsd —1B 56
Lister Wlk. Morl —7J 79
Listing Av. Liv —7M 95
Listing Ct. Liv —7M 95
Listing Dri. Liv —7M 95
Listing La. Liv & Gom —7M 95
Litell Royd. S'hse —6L 121
Litherop La. Clay W —3M 151
Litherop Rd. H Hoy —5N 151
Lit. Baines St. Hal —5N 91
Littlebeck Dri. Bgly —4H 39
Lit. Bradley. G'Ind —5B 112
Lit. Brunswick St. Hud —4M 131
Little Cake. H'frth —6A 164
Lit. Church La. Meth —2K 101
Little Cote. B'frd —6E 40
Lit. Cross St. B'frd —3C 76
Littlefield Gro. Oss —5A 118
Littlefield Rd. Oss —6A 118
Littlefield Wlk. B'frd —5N 75
Lit. Fountain St. Morl —1K 97
Lit. Green. La. Heck —7N 95
Little Hemsworth. —3E 156
Lit. Hemsworth. Hems —3E 156
Littleholme St. Todm —9J 87
Little Horton. —1N 75
Little Horton Green. —9B 58
Lit. Horton Grn. B'frd —9B 58
Lit. Horton La. B'frd —3N 75
(in four parts)
Lit. John Cres. Wake —7G 118
Lit. King St. Leeds —7D 62
Littlelands. Bgly —8F 38
Littlelands Ct. Bgly —8F 38
Little La. B'frd —4L 57
Little La. Carl —1N 99
Little La. E Mor —7D 22
Little La. F'stne —7E 122
Little La. Hal —5F 92
Little La. H Bri —8H 53
Little La. H Hoy —8M 151
Little La. H'frth —3L 163
(nr. Upperthong La.)
Little La. H'frth —2A 164
(nr. Wooldale Rd.)
Little La. I'ly —5G 9
Little La. Morl —5M 79
Little La. S Elm —6A 158
(nr. Chapel La.)
Little La. S Elm —6M 157
(nr. Minstorpe Vale)
Little La. Upt —2A 158
Little La. Wome —3M 143
Lit. Lane Ct. Chur —5M 79
Little Lepton. —8L 133
Little London. —4E 62
Little Moor. —4F 74
Little Moor. Q'bry —4F 74
Littlemoor Bottom. —8B 60
Littlemoor Ct. Pud —8B 60
Littlemoor Cres. Pud —9B 60
Littlemoor Cres. S. Pud —9B 60

Littlemoor Gdns. Hal —7L 73
Littlemoor Gdns. Pud —9B 60
Littlemoor Gro. Mir —6K 115
Littlemoor La. T'ner —2G 47
Lit. Moor Pl. Leeds —7L 61
Littlemoor Rd. Hal —6L 73
Littlemoor Rd. Mir —6K 115
Littlemoor Rd. Pud —8B 60
Littlemoor Vw. Pud —8C 60
Lit. Neville St. Leeds —7D 62
Little Pk. B'frd —6J 41
Lit. Pilling La. Skelm —7E 150
Little Preston. —4J 83
Lit. Queen St. Leeds —7C 62
Little Smeaton. —4K 143
Little St. Haw —8C 36
Little Thorpe. —1H 115
Littlethorpe Hill. Harts —1H 115
Littlethorpe Rd. Harts —2H 115
Littletown. —7M 95
Little Way. Leeds —6E 44
Littlewood Clo. B'frd —6A 76
Lit. Woodhouse. Brigh —2M 113
Little Woodhouse. —5C 62
Lit. Woodhouse St. Leeds —5C 62
Litton Clo. Shaf —6K 155
Litton Cft. Wake —4A 120
Littondale Clo. Bail —3C 40
Litton Rd. Kei —1G 36
Litton Wlk. Shaf —6K 155
Litton Way. Leeds —7C 46
Liversedge. —9L 95
Liversedge Hall La. Liv —9L 95
Liversedge Row. B'frd —2M 75
(off Perseverance La.)
Livingstone Clo. B'frd —9D 40
Livingstone Rd. B'frd —1D 58
(nr. Cheltenham Rd.)
Livingstone Rd. B'frd —2B 58
(nr. Gaisby La.)
Livingstone St. Hal —3N 91
Livingstone St. N. Hal —8N 73
Livingston Ho. B'frd —9G 40
Livinia Gro. Leeds —4E 62
Lloyds Dri. Low M —7C 76
Lloyd St. Todm —6K 87
Lobley St. Heck —8B 96
Locarno Av. B'frd —4K 57
Locherbie Grn. All —5G 56
Lochy Rd. B'frd —7L 75
Lock La. C'frd —3D 102
Lock La. Nor —6G 101
Locksley Rd. Brigh —2B 114
Locks, The. Bgly —3E 38
Lock St. Dew —7G 117
Lock St. Hal —6C 92
Lock St. Todm —9J 87
Lock Vw. Bgly —3D 38
(off Cemetery Rd.)
Lock Way. Dew —7B 116
Lockwood. —6K 131
Lockwood Av. Mir —4M 115
Lockwood Clo. Leeds —4E 80
Lockwood Ct. Leeds —4E 80
Lockwood Pk. Leeds —4E 80
Lockwood Rd. Hud —7L 131
Lockwood Scar. Hud —7L 131
Lockwood St. B'frd —4A 76
Lockwood St. Low M —8C 76
Lockwood St. Shipl —7L 39
Lockwood's Yd. Hud —4M 131
Lockwood Way. Leeds —4E 80
Lode Pit La. Bgly —3J 39
Lodge Av. C'frd —5J 103
Lodge Av. Ell —4H 113
Lodge Clo. Hud —9K 131
Lodge Dri. Ell —4H 113
Lodge Dri. Mir —7N 115
Lodge Farm Clo. Dew —7G 117
Lodge Farm Gdns. Altft —9F 100
Lodge Ga. Clo. Denh —5L 55
Lodge Hill. —3A 118
Lodge Hill. Bail —4L 39
Lodge Hill Clo. Leeds —2H 79
Lodge Hill Rd. Oss —3N 117
Lodge Hill Wlk. Leeds —2H 79
Lodge La. Croft —9F 120
Lodge La. Leeds —2D 80
Lodge La. Liv —1N 115
Lodge La. N'dam —6M 137
Lodge Pl. Ell —4H 113
Lodge Rd. Pud —6A 60
Lodge Rd. Skel —7N 159
Lodge Row. Leeds —4D 64
(off Tranquility Av.)
Lodges Clo. H'cft —8K 139
Lodge St. Cull —9K 37
Lodge St. Hems —1D 156
Lodge St. Leeds —4D 62
(in two parts)
Lodge St. Skelm —7D 150
Lodge Ter. Leeds —3D 80
Lodge, The. Lint —8D 130

Lodore Av. B'frd —3E 58
Lodore Pl. B'frd —3F 58
Lodore Rd. B'frd —3E 58
Lofthouse. —4M 99
Lofthouse Gate. —6K 99
Lofthouse Pl. Leeds —4D 62
Loft St. B'frd —6L 57
Logwood St. Hud —6M 131
Loiner Ct. Leeds —9L 63
Lombardi Ct. Oss —7B 118
Lombard St. Hal —7M 91
Lombard St. Leeds —7A 64
Lombard St. Rawd —3L 41
Lombardy Gth. Wake —3J 119
Lomond Av. H'fth —3E 42
Londesboro Gro. Leeds —7J 63
Londesboro Ter. Leeds —7J 63
London La. Rawd —3L 41
London Pk. Mir —4L 115
London Rd. Norl —9K 91
London Rd. Slai —9N 129
London Rd. Todm —7C 88
(in two parts)
London Spring Rd. Sower B —7A 110
London Sq. Rawd —3L 41
London St. Rawd —3L 41
Longacre. C'frd —6D 102
Longacres Dri. W'wth —9A 106
Longacres La. W'wth —9A 106
Longbottom Av. Sils —8F 6
Longbottom Av. Sower B —9E 90
Longbottom Ter. Hal —8C 92
Longcauseway. Dew —4G 116
(in two parts)
Long Causeway. Dew —8G 116
(nr. Thornhill Lees)
Long Causeway. Drau —3D 4
Long Causeway. Hal —2K 73
Long Causeway. Leeds —9H 63
(LS9)
Long Causeway. Leeds —5N 43
(LS16)
Long Causeway. Mir —9B 116
Long Causeway. Oxe —5F 54
Long Causeway. Rish —1M 127
Long Causeway. Stan —7A 100
Long Causeway. Todm —9A 88
Long Causeway. Wake —3M 119
Long Causeway, The. Blkhd —9L 69
Long Causeway, The. Cliv —6A 68
Long Causeway, The. Hal —6A 90
Long Clo. Shepl —1G 164
Long Clo. Wyke —9N 75
Long Clo. La. Leeds —7H 63
Long Clo. La. N Mill & Shep —2F 164
Long Clo. La. N Elm —2B 158
Long Crest. Pon —5L 123
Longcroft. Hud —7C 132
Longcroft. Kei —1J 37
Long Cft. M'well —8K 153
Longcroft Link. B'frd —7B 58
Longcroft Pl. B'frd —7B 58
Longcroft Rd. I'ly —6K 9
Long Cft. St. Gol —7D 130
Longdale Dri. S Elm —5L 157
Long Dales. Pon —1A 124
Long Dam La. Ryh —6H 139
Longden Av. Hud —8H 131
Longdike Ct. Kip —4B 84
Longdike La. Kip —5C 84
Longdon Av. Lep —7J 133
Longdon Wlk. Lep —7J 133
Long Edge Low Rd. Sower B —1B 110
Long Edge Middle Rd. Sower B —9A 90
Long Edge Rd. Sower B —9A 90
(in two parts)
Long Fallas Cres. Brigh —4N 113
Longfellow Gro. Wake —6N 99
Longfield. H Bri —9G 70
Longfield. Holy G —7A 112
Longfield Av. Gol —5D 130
Longfield Av. Hal —3F 92
Longfield Av. Hud —3B 132
Longfield Av. Pud —7C 60
Longfield Clo. Hud —3B 132
Longfield Clo. Todm —8K 87
Longfield Ct. Heck —8A 96
Longfield Ct. Pud —7C 60
Longfield Dri. Ackw —3J 141
Longfield Dri. B'frd —2G 76
Longfield Dri. Halt —6B 64
Longfield Dri. M'well —8K 153
Longfield Dri. Rod —1C 60
Longfield Gth. Leeds —1C 60
Longfield Gro. Pud —7C 60
Longfield Gro. Todm —8K 87
Longfield La. Todm —9K 87
Longfield Mt. Pud —7C 60
Longfield Rd. Heck —8A 96
Longfield Rd. Pud —7B 60
Longfield Rd. Todm —8K 87
Longfield Ter. Hal —3F 92
(off Longfield Av.)
Longfield Ter. Pud —7B 60
Longfield Ter. Todm —8K 87
Longfield Ter. Wake —4H 119
Longfield Vw. Fars —3A 60
(off Croft St.)
Longfield Way. Todm —8K 87
Longford Ter. B'frd —9L 57
Long Ga. Oakw —1K 35
Long Ga. Rish —2A 128
Long Gro. Av. Hud —4C 132
Long Hey La. Todm —9L 87
Long Heys. G'lnd —5B 112
Long Hill Rd. Hud —7N 113
Longhouse Dri. Denh —6K 55
Longhouse La. Denh —6K 55
Long Ho. Rd. Hal —7J 73
Long Ing. H'frth —9M 163
Longlands Av. Slai —9L 129
Longlands Bank. H'frth —1N 163
Longlands Clo. Oss —5A 118
Longlands Dri. Haw —7D 36
Longlands Dri. M'well —9K 153
Longlands Ind. Est. Oss —5A 118
Longlands La. Denh —5K 55
Longlands La. Sick —4D 16
Longlands Rd. Dew —1D 116
Longlands Rd. Oss —5A 118
Longlands Rd. Slai —9L 129
Longlands St. B'frd —7B 58
(in two parts)
Longlands Vw. Bat —9D 96
Long La. Ackw —1G 141
Long La. All —5C 56
Long La. Bar E & Gar —9M 47
Long La. B'frd —1J 57
Long La. Clay W —6J 151
Long La. Cra V —9E 88
Long La. Dew —5H 117
Long La. Err —3F 88
Long La. Floc —9A 134
Long La. H'den —6N 37
Long La. Hon —6L 147
Long La. Hud —4B 132
Long La. K S'ton —1H 159
Long La. Myth —5M 89
Long La. Pon —5M 123
Long La. Q'bry —6C 74
Long La. Shepl —8J 149
Long La. S'wram —5D 92
Long La. Sower B —2G 110
Long La. Todm —6N 87
Long La. Wheat —2L 91
Long Lee. —1L 37
Long Lee La. Kei —2K 37
Longley. —8A 132
Longley Edge La. H'frth —7N 163
Longley Edge Rd. H'frth —8N 163
Longley La. H'frth —8M 163
Longley La. Hud —8A 132
Longley La. Sower B —2F 110
Longley Rd. Hud —7B 132
Longley's Yd. Leeds —3G 80
Long Lover La. Hal —4L 91
Long Mdw. Bklnd —6G 110
Long Mdw. Ct. Gar —9A 66
Long Mdw. Ga. Gar —9N 65
Long Meadows. B'frd —2C 58
Long Meadows. B'hpe —6H 27
Long Meadows. Bur W —7D 10
Long Meadows. Gar —9N 65
Long Moor La. Shel —8M 149
Long Preston Chase. App B —8H 41
Long Reach. Hal —1G 91
Long Riddings. Add —9M 5
Long Ridge. Brigh —4M 113
Long Row. Blkhd —1M 87
Long Row. H'fth —6F 42
(in two parts)
Long Row. Low M —8B 76
Long Row. New S —6H 121
Long Row. Nost —4M 139
Longrow. T'tn —7B 56
Long Row Ct. B'frd —2C 76
(off Gaythorne Rd.)
Longroyd. Thack —7D 40
Longroyd Av. Leeds —2E 80
Longroyd Cres. Leeds —2E 80
Longroyd Cres. Slai —9L 129
Longroyd Cres. N. Leeds —2E 80
Long Royd Dri. Bail —3C 40
Longroyde Clo. Brigh —3L 113
Longroyde Gro. Brigh —3L 113
Longroyde Rd. Brigh —2L 113
Longroyd Farm. M'twn —3L 135
Longroyd Gro. Leeds —2E 80
Longroyd La. Hud —5K 131
Long Royd La. Up Cum —9M 149
Longroyd Pl. Hud —5K 131
Longroyd Pl. Leeds —2E 80
Long Royd Rd. Sower B —1C 110
Longroyd St. Leeds —2E 80
Longroyd St. N. Leeds —2E 80
Longroyd Ter. Leeds —2E 80
Longroyd Vw. Leeds —2E 80
Long Shaw La. Todm —7A 88
Longside Hall. B'frd —8A 58
Longside Ind. Est. Leeds —4G 63
Longside La. B'frd —8A 58
Longsight Rd. M'well —8J 153
Longsight Ter. Kin —9B 140
Longsland La. Cam —2N 159
Long St. B'frd —9F 58
Long Tail La. H Bri —6A 70
Longthorpe La. Wake —3H 99
Long Tongue Scrog La. Hud (in three parts) —3J 133
Long Wall. G'lnd —4C 112
Longwood. —4E 130
Longwood Av. Bgly —2C 38
Longwood Clo. Leeds —2K 45
Longwood Clo. Ting —4N 97
Longwood Ct. Ting —4A 98
Longwood Cres. Leeds —2K 45
Longwood Edge. —3D 130
Longwood Edge Rd. Hud —2C 130
Longwood Fold. Ting —4A 98
Longwood Gth. Ting —4A 98
Longwood Ga. Hud —3D 130
Longwood Ho. Rd. Hud —8M 113
Longwood Rd. Hud —5G 131
Longwood Rd. Ting —4N 97
Longwoods Wlk. Knot —7F 104
Longwood Va. Ting —4A 98
Longwood Vw. Bgly —2D 38
Longwood Way. Leeds —2K 45
Lonsborough Way. S Elm —5N 157
Lonsbrough Av. Heck —7A 96
Lonsbrough Flats. Hud —4N 131
(off Southgate)
Lonsdale Av. Bat —5C 96
Lonsdale Meadows. B Spa —1D 32
Lonsdale Ri. Ting —4A 98
Lonsdale Rd. Wake —3K 119
Lonsdale St. B'frd —6F 58
Lonsdale Ter. Liv —8L 95
(off Halifax Rd.)
Lord La. Haw —7B 36
Lord's Bldgs. Morl —2K 97
Lordsfield Pl. B'frd —4H 77
Lord's La. Brigh —2N 113
Lord St. Chick —4L 117
Lord St. Hal —5B 92
Lord St. Haw —8D 36
Lord St. Hud —4N 131
Lord St. Kei —9J 21
Lord St. Leeds —8B 62
Lord St. Slai —9M 129
Lord St. Sower B —7J 91
Lord St. Stainc —8C 96
Lord St. Todm —2J 107
Lord St. Wake —8A 120
Lord Ter. Leeds —8B 62
Loris St. B'frd —4H 77
Lorne St. B'frd —2F 76
Lorne St. Cro R —7F 36
(off Bingley Rd.)
Lorne St. Kei —8L 21
Loscoe. —1M 121
Loscoe Clo. Nor I —9M 101
Loscoe La. Nor & Ack —1M 121
(in two parts)
Lotherton Hall. —1H 67
Lotherton La. Aber —9E 48
(in two parts)
Lotherton Way. Gar —6N 65
Lot St. Haw —8D 36
Loughrigg St. B'frd —2C 76
Loughrigg Wlk. Ackw —5E 140
Louisa St. B'frd —7F 40
Louisa St. C'frd —4C 102
Louis Av. B'frd —1A 76
Louis Ct. Leeds —3F 62
Louis Gro. Leeds —3G 62
Louis Le Prince Ct. Leeds —3H 63
(off Bayswater Rd.)
Louis St. Leeds —3F 62
Lovaine Gro. Wake —1M 137
Love La. C'frd —6C 102
Love La. Hal —7A 92
Love La. Oss —5M 117
Love La. Pon —4H 123
Love La. Rothw —8N 81
Love La. Wake —5K 119
Love La. Ter. Pon —3J 123
Lovell Pk. Clo. Leeds —5F 62
Lovell Pk. Ct. Leeds —5E 62
(off Lovell Pk. Rd.)
Lovell Pk. Ga. Leeds —5E 62
Lovell Pk. Grange. Leeds —5F 62
(off Lovell Pk. Vw.)
Lovell Pk. Heights. Leeds —5F 62
(off Lovell Pk. Hill)
Lovell Pk. Hill. Leeds —5E 62
Lovell Pk. Rd. Leeds —5E 62
Lovell Pk. Towers. Leeds —5E 62
(off Lovell Pk. Rd.)
Lovell Pk. Vw. Leeds —5F 62
Lovell Vw. Croft —2H 139
Lovers Wlk. Todm —7J 87
Low Ackworth. —3H 141
Low Ash Av. Shipl —8B 40
Low Ash Cres. Shipl —8B 40
Low Ash Dri. Shipl —8B 40
Low Ash Gro. Shipl —8B 40
Low Ash Rd. Shipl —9C 40
Low Baildon. —4B 40
Lowbalk La. Knot —4J 125
Low Bank. —4B 36
Low Bank Dri. Oakw —4B 36
Low Bank La. Oakw —4B 36
Low Banks. —6M 21
Low Bank St. Fars —3A 60
Low Cliff Wlk. Heck —1B 116
Low Clo. Bgly —5G 39
Low Clo. I'ly —3G 8
Low Clo. St. Leeds —3C 62
Low Common. —3M 101
Lowcroft. Coll —9H 17
Low Cft. Ct. B'hpe —5H 27
Low Cronkhill La. Roys —7F 154
Low Cross Ct. Knot —7F 104
Lowdale. Dew —1H 117
Lowell Av. B'frd —9L 57
Lowell Gro. Leeds —6D 60
Lowell Pl. Leeds —6D 60
Lwr. Ainley. Hal —7M 73
Lower Altofts. —7H 101
Lwr. Ashgrove. B'frd —8B 58
Lwr. Back La. Blkhd —9A 70
Lwr. Balfour St. B'frd —1E 76
Lwr. Bankhouse. Pud —1A 78
Lwr. Bank Houses. Holy G —7K 111
Lwr. Bank St. Far —3A 60
Lwr. Basinghall St. Leeds —6D 62
Lwr. Bentley Royd. Sower B —8G 91
Lower Binns. —3L 163
Lwr. Bower La. Dew —9C 96
Lwr. Brockwell La. Sower B —1F 110
Lwr. Brunswick St. Leeds —5F 62
Lwr. Cambridge St. C'frd —4E 102
Lwr. Clay Pits. Hal —4M 91
Lwr. Clifton St. Sower B —8J 91
Lower Clough. —1C 146
Lwr. Clyde St. Sower B —9H 91
Lwr. Common La. Scis —9G 151
Lwr. Constable Rd. I'ly —6J 9
Lwr. Copy. All —5G 57
Lwr. Cross St. Bat —2F 116
Lwr. Crow Nest Dri. Hal —5N 93
Lower Cumberworth. —1B 166
Lower Denby. —4E 166
Lwr. Denby La. Lwr D —4E 166
Lower Edge Bottom. —4G 113
Lwr. Edge Rd. Ell & Brigh —4G 113
Lwr. Ellistones. G'lnd —4N 111
(off Saddleworth Rd.)
Lower Fagley. —3J 59
Lwr. Ferney Lee. Todm —6J 87
Lwr. Finkil St. Brigh —7K 93
Lwr. Fitzwilliam St. Hud —3N 131
Lwr. Fleet. Q'bry —4B 74
Lwr. Fold. Bklnd —5K 111
Lwr. Fold. Brigh —5L 113
Lwr. Fold. Hon —4L 147
Lower Ga. Milns —5G 130
Lwr. George St. B'frd —4N 75
Lwr. George St. Todm —7K 87
Lwr. Globe St. B'frd —6A 58
Lower Grange. —7G 57
Lwr. Grange. Hud —5C 114
Lwr. Grange Clo. B'frd —7H 57
Lwr. Grattan Rd. B'frd —7B 58
Lwr. Greave Rd. Mel —9G 146
Lower Grn. Bail —5M 39
Lwr. Green Av. Schol —4D 94
Lwr. Hall Clo. Liv —8K 95
Lwr. Hall Cres. Hud —4G 132
Lwr. Hall Dri. Liv —8K 95
Lwr. Hall La. Liv —8K 95
Lwr. Hall Mt. Liv —8K 95
Lwr. Hall Rd. Hud —4G 132
Lwr. Hartley Ct. Kbtn —3G 148
Lwr. Heights Rd. T'tn —6B 56
Lwr. Hey. Mel —7C 146
(in two parts)
Lwr. High Royds. Dart —9J 153
Lwr. Holme. Bail —6A 40
Lower Holme. —9K 129
Lower Hopton. —8L 115
Lwr. House Clo. Thack —6D 40
Lower Ho. La. Lep —8M 133
Lower Houses. —7B 132
Lowerhouses La. Hud —7A 132
Lowerhouses Rd. Hud —4G 130
Lower Ings. Hal —4J 73
Lwr. Kipping La. T'tn —8C 56
Lwr. Kirkgate. Hal —5C 92
Lwr. Laith Av. Todm —7L 87
Lower La. Blkhd —1M 87
Lower La. B'frd —1F 76
Lower La. E Bier —8H 77
Lower La. Gom —5M 95
Lower La. Hon —5K 147
Lwr. Langwith. Coll —9H 17
Lwr. Lark Hill. Cleck —5F 94
Lwr. Lumb La. Cra V —8K 89
Lwr. Maythorn La. H'frth —8G 164
Lwr. Meadows. H'frth —3J 163
Lower Mickletown. —1N 101
Lwr. Mickletown. Meth —1M 101
Lwr. Mill Bank Rd. Sower B —4D 11
Lwr. Newlands. Brigh —2N 113
Lwr. Northcroft. S Elm —6N 157
Lwr. Northfield La. S Kirk —5J 15
Lwr. North St. Bat —8E 96
Lwr. Oxford St. C'frd —5D 102
Lwr. Park Grn. Sils —8C 6
Lwr. Pk. Royd Dri. Sower B —4E 11
Lwr. Peel St. Dew —2F 116
Lower Popeley. —7N 95
Lwr. Putting Mill. Den D —1E 166
Lwr. Quarry Rd. Hud —4D 114
Lwr. Range. Hal —3B 92
Lower Rd. Scam & Bklnd —5F 12
Lwr. Rushton Rd. B'frd —7J 59
Lower Sandhills. T'ner —4F 46
Lwr. School St. B'frd —7A 76
Lwr. School St. Shipl —7L 39
Lower Soothill. —7H 97
Lwr. Station Rd. Nor —1H 121
Lwr. Swift Pl. Sower B —9B 110
Lwr. Taythes La. Pon —2N 123
Lower Thirstin. —4L 147
Lwr. Tofts Rd. Pud —7B 60
Lower Town. —4D 54
Lowertown. Oxe —4C 54
Lwr. Town End Rd. H'frth —1A 16
Lwr. Town St. Leeds —3G 60
Lwr. Viaduct St. Hud —3N 131
(in two parts)
Lwr. Warrengate. Wake —5M 119
Lwr. Wellgate. G'lnd —4B 112
Lwr. Wellington Rd. I'ly —5H 9
Lwr. Westfield Rd. B'frd —5M 57
Lwr. Whitegate Rd. Hud —7N 131
Lower Woodlands. —8E 76
Lwr. Wormald. Sower B —1N 127
Lwr. Wortley Rd. Leeds —1K 79
Lower Wyke. —4A 94
Lwr. Wyke Grn. Wyke —4N 93
Lwr. Wyke La. Wyke —4N 93
Lwr. York St. Wake —4L 119
Lowestwood. —8C 130
Lowestwood La. Lint —7C 130
Loweswater Av. B'frd —7L 75
Loweswater Rd. Knot —1D 124
Low Farm. —3J 43
Low Farm. W'ford —5M 83
Low Farm La. Ackw —4G 140
Lowfield Clo. Low M —8C 76
Lowfield Cres. Hems —2E 156
Lowfield Cres. Sils —9F 6
Lowfield La. Beam —5M 5
Lowfield Rd. Dew —3C 116
Lowfield Rd. Hems —2E 156
Low Fields Av. Leeds —1A 80
Low Fields Rd. Leeds —1A 80
(in two parts)
Low Fields Way. Leeds —1A 80
Lowfields Way. Lfds B —3F 112
Low Fold. —7C 42
Low Fold. B'frd —3D 58
Low Fold. H'fth —8D 42
Low Fold. Leeds —8G 62
Low Fold. Oss —5A 118
Low Fold. Rawd —3M 41
Low Fold. Schol —4D 94
Low Fold. Steet —3C 20
Low Fold Ct. Up Den —5C 166
Low Ga. H'frth —4N 163
Low Ga. Kbtn —3K 149
Low Ga. S Elm —6N 157
Low Gipton Cres. Leeds —3M 63
Low Grange Cres. Leeds —4G 80
Low Grange Vw. Leeds —5G 81
Low Green. —4N 41
Low Grn. Ackw —3H 141
Low Grn. B'frd —2M 75
Low Green. Knot —8G 104
Low Grn. Rawd —4N 41
Low Grn. Ter. B'frd —2N 75
Low Hall Clo. Men —4E 24

ow Hall Pl. Leeds —8C 62
ow Hall Rd. H'fth & Rawd —7B 42
ow Hall Rd. Men —4F 24
ow Hill. Bail —1A 40
ow Hills La. Hud —1F 130
ow Ho. Dri. Sils —9E 6
ow Ho. Farm Ct. Sils —9E 6
ow Ho. Flats. Cleck —5H 95
(off Westgate)
ow Ho. Fold. Liv —8K 95
ow Ings Grn. Clay W —6H 151
ow Laithes. —3D 118
owlands Rd. Mir —7L 115
ow La. Birs —3B 96
ow La. Cytn —9E 56
ow La. Drau —5D 4
ow La. Eby —2A 4
ow La. Hal —6A 72
ow La. H'fth —5F 42
ow La. M'twn —2K 135
ow La. Q'bry —2B 74
ow La. Sils —3C 6
ow La. Stainb —3H 13
ow Ling La. C'den —7L 69
ow Mill La. Add —1A 8
ow Mill La. Kei —9K 21
ow Mill La. Rav I —7A 116
ow Mill Rd. Oss —8M 117
ow Mills Rd. Leeds —1L 79
ow Mill Village. —2B 8
ow Moor. —7B 76
ow Moor Cres. Hall G —7H 137
ow Moor La. Wool —9F 136
ow Moor Side. —3F 78
ow Moor Side. Leeds —2G 78
ow Moorside Clo. Leeds —2H 79
ow Moorside Ct. Leeds —2H 79
(off Low Moorside Clo.)
ow Moor Side La. Leeds —3F 78
ow Moor St. Low M —7B 76
ow Moor Ter. Hal —6K 91
ow Moor Ter. Leeds —3D 80
owood La. Birs —1B 96
ow Pk. Rd. I'ly —4M 9
ow Platt La. Scam —5H 129
ow Rd. Dew M —3C 116
ow Rd. Earl —4H 117
ow Rd. Hud —1L 147
ow Rd. Leeds —1G 80
ow Rd. Thorn —1E 134
ow Row. Dart —6G 153
owry Rd. Ting —4N 97
owry Vw. Kei —1J 37
ow Shops La. Rothw —7L 81
ow Spring Rd. Kei —1L 37
ow St. B'ton —4B 104
ow St. Dew —2F 116
ow St. Kei —9J 21
(in two parts)
ow St. Ting —3A 98
owther Av. Gar —8M 65
owther Cres. Swil —3H 83
owther Dri. Gar —8M 65
owther Dri. Swil —4G 83
owther Gro. Gar —8M 65
owther Rd. Gar —8M 65
owther St. B'frd —4F 58
owther St. Leeds —3H 63
owther Ter. Swil C —8H 65
ow Town. Kbtn —4K 149
owtown. Pud —6C 60
ow Town End. —1L 97
ow Utley. —5G 21
ow Way. B'ham —6D 32
ow Way. Cliff —2D 32
ow Well St. B'frd —2B 76
ow Whitehouse Row. Leeds —9F 62
ow Wood. Wilsd —2C 56
ow Wood Ct. Utley —5H 21
ow Wood Ri. I'ly —6L 9
oxley Gro. Weth —1L 17
oxley Mt. Cam —1N 159
oxley St. Bat —5D 96
ucas Ct. Leeds —3E 62
ucas Pl. Leeds —2C 62
ucas St. Leeds —2C 62
uck La. Hud —4H 131
ucy Av. Leeds —6N 63
ucy Hall Dri. Bail —5K 39
ucy La. Lep —5H 133
ucy St. Hal —4C 92
uddenden. —3E 90
uddenden Foot. —6D 90
uddenden La. L'ft —5D 90
uddendon Pl. Q'bry —3B 74
(off Mill La.)
udgate Hill. Leeds —6E 62
udhill La. Hud —4A 148
udlam St. B'frd —9C 58
udlow Av. Gar —7B 66
udolf Dri. Leeds —3N 45
udwell Clo. Dew —1J 135
Ludwood Clo. Hon —4N 147
Luke La. Thon —9A 148
Luke Rd. B'frd —1A 76
Luke Williams Ho. Pon —2K 123
Lulworth Av. Leeds —5E 64
Lulworth Clo. Leeds —5E 64
Lulworth Cres. Leeds —5E 64
Lulworth Dri. Leeds —6E 64
Lulworth Gth. Leeds —6E 64
Lulworth Gro. B'frd —3H 77
(in two parts)
Lulworth Vw. Leeds —5E 64
Lulworth Wlk. Leeds —5E 64
Lumb. —1A 148
Lumb Bottom. Dlgtn —6C 78
Lumbfoot Rd. Stanb —8M 35
Lumb Gill La. Add —3A 8
Lumb La. B'frd —5A 58
Lumb La. Hal —2A 92
Lumb La. Hud —1A 148
Lumb La. Liv —1K 115
Lumb La. Sower B —4C 110
Lumb La. Wains —7F 72
Lumb Rd. H Bri —8E 70
Lumbrook Clo. Hal —1H 93
Lumbutts. —8A 88
Lumbutts La. Todm —8A 88
Lumbutts Rd. Todm —1J 107
Lumby Clo. Pud —9C 60
Lumby La. E Kes —1B 30
Lumby La. Pud —9C 60
Lumby Leys La. Leeds —5M 85
Lumby St. B'frd —7F 40
Lumley Av. C'frd —5A 102
Lumley Av. Leeds —3N 61
Lumley Gro. Leeds —3N 61
Lumley Hill. C'frd —5A 102
Lumley Mt. C'frd —6A 102
Lumley Mt. Leeds —3N 61
Lumley Mt. Bungalows. C'frd —5A 102
Lumley Pl. Leeds —3N 61
Lumley Rd. Dew —1H 117
Lumley Rd. Leeds —3N 61
Lumley St. H'town —6A 102
Lumley St. Leeds —3N 61
Lumley Ter. Leeds —3N 61
Lumley Vw. Leeds —3N 61
Lumley Wlk. Leeds —3N 61
Lunan Pl. Leeds —2H 63
Lunan Ter. Leeds —2H 63
Lund Dri. Heck —9B 96
Lund Head La. Kirk O —4M 15
Lund Hill La. Roys —5F 154
Lund La. Oakw —1B 36
Lund St. Bgly —4E 38
Lund St. B'frd —7K 57
Lund St. Kei —8J 21
Lundy Ct. B'frd —2C 76
Lune St. Cro R —7F 36
Lunnfields La. Fair —9N 85
Lunn La. Beal —7N 105
Lupset. —7G 118
Lupset Cres. Wake —8G 119
Lupton Av. Leeds —6J 63
Lupton Flats. Leeds —1N 61
Lupton's Bldgs. Leeds —7L 61
Lupton St. B'frd —5C 58
Lupton St. Leeds —2G 80
Lustre St. Kei —9G 21
Luther Pl. Hud —2K 131
Luther St. Leeds —1B 60
Luther Way. B'frd —3D 58
Luton St. Hal —5M 91
Luton St. Hud —7E 130
Luton St. Kei —9H 21
Luttrell Clo. Leeds —5K 43
Luttrell Cres. Leeds —5K 43
Luttrell Gdns. Leeds —5K 43
Luttrell Pl. Leeds —5K 43
Luttrell Rd. Leeds —5K 43
Lutyens, The. I'ly —5E 8
(nr. Grove Rd.)
Lutyens, The. I'ly —5F 8
(off Westville)
Luxor Av. Leeds —2H 63
Luxor Rd. Leeds —2H 63
Luxor St. Leeds —2H 63
Luxor Vw. Leeds —2H 63
Lydbrook Pk. Cop —1N 111
Lyddon Ter. Leeds —4C 62
Lydford Ho. B'frd —9C 58
(off Grafton St.)
Lydgate. —5K 93
(nr. Hipperholme)
Lydgate. —5A 126
(nr. Littleborough)
Lydgate. —5G 87
(nr. Todmorden)
Lydgate. Leeds —5H 63
Lydgate. Lep —7L 133
Lydgate. N'wram —1F 92
Lydgate Clo. N Mill —2C 164
Lydgate Dri. Lep —7L 133
Lydgate Dri. N Mill —1B 164
Lydgate Pk. Light —5K 93
Lydgate Pl. C'ley —8L 41
Lydgate Ri. S Kirk —6K 157
Lydgate Rd. Bat —7J 97
Lydgate Rd. Shepl —9J 149
Lydgate St. C'ley —8L 41
Lydgetts. Uthg —2J 163
Lydia St. Leeds —6F 62
(off Bridge St.)
Lyme Chase. Leeds —4A 64
Lymes Ter. Skel —8K 159
Lymington Dri. B'frd —1J 77
Lynch Av. Gt Hor —2L 75
Lyncroft. B'frd —2D 58
Lynda Gro. Oss —7C 118
Lyndale. Kip —5A 84
Lyndale Cres. Heck —8B 96
Lyndale Dri. Shipl —8D 40
Lyndale Dri. Wren —1G 119
(in two parts)
Lyndale Gro. Nor —2K 121
Lyndale M. Dew —9C 96
Lyndale Rd. Bgly —2H 39
Lyndean Gdns. Idle —8E 40
Lynden Av. Shipl —7C 40
Lynden Ct. B'frd —6M 75
Lyndhurst Av. Brigh —4M 113
Lyndhurst Clo. Scholes —8G 47
Lyndhurst Cres. Scholes —8G 46
Lyndhurst Gro. All —5H 57
Lyndhurst Gro. Rd. Brigh —4M 113
Lyndhurst Rd. Brigh —3M 113
Lyndhurst Rd. Hud —2G 131
Lyndhurst Rd. Scholes —9G 46
Lyndhurst Vw. Scholes —9G 47
Lyndon Av. B'ham —5C 32
Lyndon Av. Gar —7M 65
Lyndon Clo. B'ham —5C 32
Lyndon Cres. B'ham —5C 32
Lyndon Rd. B'ham —5C 32
Lyndon Sq. B'ham —5C 32
Lyndon Ter. Bgly —4F 38
Lyndon Way. B'ham —5C 32
Lyndsay Acre. Ting —4C 98
Lyndum Gro. Kip —3A 84
Lynfield Dri. B'frd —3H 57
Lynfield Dri. Liv —7F 94
Lynfield Mt. Shipl —7C 40
Lynndale Av. Hud —1L 131
Lynnfield Gdns. Scholes —9G 46
Lyn Royd Flats. Lint —8C 130
Lynsey Gdns. B'frd —6F 76
Lynthorne Rd. B'frd —2A 58
Lynton Av. B Spa —9D 18
Lynton Av. B'frd —4L 57
Lynton Av. Hud —4L 131
Lynton Av. Thpe —2G 99
Lynton Dri. B'frd —4K 57
Lynton Dri. Kei —7M 21
Lynton Dri. Shipl —8M 39
Lynton Gro. B'frd —4L 57
Lynton Gro. Bshw —4M 73
Lynton Pl. Dart —9F 152
Lynton Ter. Cleck —4H 95
Lynton Vs. B'frd —4L 57
Lynwood Av. Leeds —9M 61
Lynwood Av. Shipl —7C 40
Lynwood Av. W'ford —7E 82
Lynwood Clo. B'shaw —9M 77
Lynwood Clo. Knot —7F 104
Lynwood Clo. S'hse —7L 121
Lynwood Ct. B'frd —8E 40
Lynwood Ct. Kei —2E 36
Lynwood Cres. Fitz —6A 140
Lynwood Cres. Hal —7M 91
Lynwood Cres. Leeds —9M 61
Lynwood Cres. Pon —5K 123
Lynwood Cres. W'ford —7E 82
Lynwood Dri. Barn —8D 154
Lynwood Dri. Wake —4L 137
Lynwood Gdns. Pud —8N 59
Lynwood Gth. Leeds —9M 61
Lynwood Gro. Leeds —1M 79
Lynwood M. B'frd —3K 77
Lynwood Mt. Leeds —9M 61
Lynwood Ri. Leeds —9M 61
Lynwood Vw. Leeds —9M 61
Lyon Rd. Ebrn —2A 20
Lyon Rd. Pon —5K 123
Lyons St. Q'bry —4E 74
Lyon St. T'tn —7C 56
Lytham Clo. Norm —2L 121
Lytham Dri. Q'bry —3G 75
Lytham Gro. Leeds —1K 79
Lytham Pl. Leeds —1K 79
Lytham St. Hal —5M 91
Lytham Way. Hud —2G 130
Lythe Ho. B'frd —6E 58
(off Avenham Way)
Lytton Rd. B'frd —6L 57
Lytton St. Leeds —2F 80
Mabel Royd. B'frd —9L 57
Mabel St. H Bri —3M 89
Mabgate. Leeds —6F 62
Mabgate. —5F 62
Mabgate Grn. Leeds —6F 62
Macaulay Rd. Hud —1L 131
Macaulay St. Leeds —5G 62
McBride Way. Weth —4N 17
McBurney Clo. Hal —2A 92
McClaren Fields. Leeds —4G 61
Macham St. Hud —6L 131
Mackey Cres. Brier —6M 155
Mackey La. Brier —6M 155
Mackie Hill Clo. Crig —6F 136
Mackingstone Dri. Oakw —4B 36
Mackingstone La. Oakw —3B 36
MacKinnon Av. Nor —9K 101
Mackintosh St. Hal —6M 91
McLaren Av. Upt —1C 158
McMahon Dri. Q'bry —3G 75
Macturk Gro. B'frd —5M 57
Maddocks St. Shipl —7M 39
Madeley Rd. H'cft —9K 139
Madeley Sq. C'frd —3J 103
Madewel Ho. Ell —6F 112
Madgin La. Hud —3F 146
Madison Av. B'frd —4J 77
Madni Clo. Hal —5A 92
Mafeking Av. Leeds —4C 80
Mafeking Gro. Leeds —4C 80
Mafeking Mt. Leeds —4C 80
Mafeking Ter. Shipl —1B 58
Mag Dale. —3L 147
Magdalene Clo. Leeds —4K 43
Magdalene Fields. Norm —3L 121
Magdalene Rd. Wake —6E 118
Magdalen Rd. Mel —3B 162
Magna Gro. Wake —1N 137
Magnolia Clo. Shaf —7L 155
Magnolia Dri. All —2E 56
Magnolia Ho. C'frd —5E 102
(off Parklands)
Magpie La. Morl —1L 97
Magup La. H'frth —7C 164
Maidstone St. B'frd —7G 58
Mail Clo. Leeds —3F 64
Main Av. Hud —7E 130
Main Ga. H'frth —6C 164
Main Rd. Denh —6K 55
Main Rd. Ebrn —2A 20
Main Rd. E Mor —8C 22
Mainspring Rd. Wilsd —1B 56
Main St. Aber —8E 48
Main St. Add —1L 7
Main St. All B —9B 84
Main St. Bads —7L 141
Main St. Bar E —8L 47
Main St. Beal —5M 105
Main St. Bgly —4E 38
Main St. Birk —2M 105
Main St. Bur W —7C 10
Main St. Carl —1M 99
Main St. Coll —9J 17
Main St. Ctly —9G 38
Main St. E Kes —3D 30
Main St. Esh —2G 40
Main St. Gar —7M 65
Main St. Guis —8C 24
Main St. Hamp —8G 158
Main St. Haw —8C 36
Main St. K S'ton —4J 143
Main St. Knot —1D 104
Main St. Leds —8E 84
Main St. Lntn —7J 17
Main St. Low M —7C 76
Main St. Men —3D 24
Main St. Meth —1L 101
Main St. Newt K —1L 33
Main St. Pool W —1F 26
Main St. Saxt —9N 49
Main St. Scholes —9G 46
Main St. Shad —2M 45
Main St. Sick —4C 16
Main St. S Hien —3L 155
Main St. Stanb —9L 35
Main St. T'ner —3G 46
Main St. Upt —1C 158
Main St. Wake —5F 98
Main St. Wltn —5G 18
Main St. Wee —7A 14
Main St. Wilsd —1B 56
Main St. Wyke —9A 76
Maitland Clo. All —7G 56
Maitland Clo. Todm —3J 107
Maitland Pl. Leeds —1C 80
Maitland St. Todm —3J 107
Maizebrook. Dew —2C 116
Maize St. Kei —3G 37
Major St. Todm —7L 87
Major St. Wake —8K 119
Makin St. Wake —6J 119
Malham Av. B'frd —3H 57
Malham Av. Brigh —3K 113
Malham Clo. Leeds —2B 64
Malham Clo. Shaf —6K 155
Malham Ct. Hud —3G 131
(off Willwood Av.)
Malham Ct. Sils —9E 6
(off Ings Way)
Malham Dri. Bat —7D 96
Malham Dri. Liv —2K 115
Malham Rd. Brigh —4K 113
Malham Rd. Wake —4A 120
Malham Sq. Wake —4A 120
Maliff Rd. Brierc —4D 50
Malin Rd. Dew —9J 97
Mallard Av. Wake —5L 137
Mallard Clo. B'frd —1G 59
Mallard Clo. Leeds —6H 81
Mallard Ct. B'frd —7H 57
Mallard Rd. C'frd —6C 102
Mallards, The. Sils —8E 6
Mallard Vw. Oxe —4C 54
Mallard Way. Morl —9N 79
Mallard Way. Slai —1M 145
Mallinson St. Dew —2D 116
Mallory Clo. B'frd —8L 57
Mallory Way. Cud —9K 155
Malmesbury Clo. B'frd —4J 77
Malmesbury Clo. Leeds —8M 61
Malmesbury Gro. Leeds —8M 61
Malmesbury Pl. Leeds —8M 61
Malmesbury Ter. Leeds —8M 61
Malsis Cres. Kei —1G 37
Malsis Rd. Kei —1G 37
Maltby Ct. Leeds —7E 64
Maltby Ho. B'frd —1B 76
(off Park La.)
Malthouse Clo. S'cft —8D 30
Malting Clo. Rob H —1K 99
Malting Ri. Rob H —1K 99
Maltings Ct. Leeds —1E 80
(off Moorside Maltings)
Maltings Rd. Hal —2K 91
Maltings Rd. Leeds —2E 80
Maltings, The. Cleck —4G 95
Maltings, The. Leeds —4A 62
(off Alexandra Rd.)
Maltings, The. Mir —6K 115
Maltings, The. Pon —2K 123
Maltings, The. Rob H —1K 99
Maltins, The. C'frd —4E 102
Malt Kiln Cft. Wake —1N 137
Maltkiln Dri. Bret —1B 152
Maltkiln La. C'frd —4E 102
Malt Kiln La. Kip —4B 84
Malt Kiln La. T'tn —9A 56
Malton Ho. B'frd —9G 40
(off Rowantree Dri.)
Malton Rd. Upt —1C 158
Malton St. Hal —2B 92
Malton St. Sower B —7H 91
Malt St. Kei —3G 36
Malvern Brow. B'frd —4J 57
Malvern Clo. C'frd —7N 101
Malvern Cres. Riddl —5L 21
Malvern Gro. B'frd —5J 57
Malvern Gro. Leeds —1C 80
Malvern Ri. Hud —7M 131
Malvern Ri. Leeds —1C 80
Malvern Rd. B'frd —5J 57
Malvern Rd. Dew —2J 117
Malvern Rd. Hud —6N 131
Malvern Rd. Knot —8D 104
Malvern Rd. Leeds —1C 80
Malvern St. Leeds —1C 80
Malvern Vw. Leeds —1C 80
Manchester Rd. B'frd —3B 76
Manchester Rd. G'fld —9A 144
Manchester Rd. Hud —7E 130
Manchester Rd. Mars —5D 144
Manchester Rd. Slai —3K 145
Manchester Sq. Otley —9L 11
Mancot Ho. B'frd —1C 76
(off Manchester Rd.)
Mandale Gro. B'frd —5J 75
Mandale Rd. B'frd —5J 75
Mandarin Way. Leeds —6H 81
Mandela Ct. Leeds —2F 62
Mandeville Cres. B'frd —5L 75
Mangrill La. Woth —9L 31
Mankinholes. —8B 88
Mankinholes Bank. Todm —9A 88
Manley Ct. Gar —9N 65
Manley Dri. Weth —3J 17
Manley Gro. I'ly —5J 9
Manley Ri. I'ly —6J 9
Manley Rd. I'ly —6J 9
Manley St. Brigh —9M 93
Manley St. Pl. Brigh —9M 93
(off Manley St.)
Mannerley Gro. Cleck —6M 95
Mannheim Rd. B'frd —4M 57
Manningham. —4A 58
Manningham La. B'frd —4A 58
Mann's Bldgs. Bat —2E 96

Mann's Ct. B'frd —7C 58
(off Piece Hall Yd.)
Mannville Gro. Kei —1G 36
Mannville Pl. Kei —1G 36
Mannville Rd. Kei —2G 37
Mannville St. Kei —1G 36
Mannville Ter. B'frd —8B 58
Mannville Wlk. Kei —1G 36
(off Mannville St.)
Mannville Way. Kei —1G 36
Manor Av. Leeds —2A 62
Manor Av. Oss —8B 118
Manor Clo. Bads —8L 141
Manor Clo. B'frd —6J 57
Manor Clo. B'hpe —5G 27
Manor Clo. Hal —8A 92
Manor Clo. Not —2A 154
Manor Clo. Oss —8B 118
Manor Clo. Rothw —7N 81
Manor Clo. Yead —9M 25
Manor Cott. M. S'cft —1D 46
Manor Ct. Aber —8E 48
Manor Ct. Bgly —8F 38
Manor Ct. Leeds —3A 46
Manor Ct. Oss —8B 118
Manor Ct. Otley —9L 11
(off Bridge St.)
Manor Ct. Roys —6B 154
Manor Ct. Schol —5D 94
Manor Cres. Grime —9A 156
Manor Cres. Pool W —1F 26
Manor Cres. Rothw —7M 81
Manor Cres. Wake —7G 118
Manor Cres. W'ton —2B 138
Manor Cft. H Bri —1J 89
Manor Cft. Leeds —7D 64
Manorcroft. Nor —1J 121
Manor Cft. S Hien —3L 155
Manor Dri. Bgly —7F 38
Manor Dri. F'stne —2C 122
Manor Dri. Floc —7G 135
Manor Dri. Hal —8A 92
Manor Dri. H Bri —1J 89
Manor Dri. Leeds —2A 62
Manor Dri. Mir —4H 115
Manor Dri. New C —3H 139
Manor Dri. Oss —8B 118
Manor Dri. Roys —6C 154
Manor Dri. Skelm —8D 150
(in two parts)
Manor Dri. S Hien —3L 155
Manor Farm. Bads —8L 141
Mnr. Farm Clo. Barn —9E 154
Mnr. Farm Clo. Bgly —9G 38
Mnr. Farm Clo. Leeds —7F 80
Mnr. Farm Ct. Crig —6G 136
Mnr. Farm Cres. Chur —5M 79
Mnr. Farm Dri. Bat —6J 97
Mnr. Farm Dri. Chur —5M 79
Mnr. Farm Dri. Leeds —7E 80
Mnr. Farm Est. S Elm —6N 157
Mnr. Farm Gdns. Leeds —7E 80
Mnr. Farm Grn. Leeds —7E 80
Mnr. Farm Gro. Leeds —7E 80
Mnr. Farm Ri. Leeds —7F 80
Mnr. Farm Rd. Crig —6G 136
Mnr. Farm Rd. Leeds —7E 80
Mnr. Farm Wlk. Leeds —7F 80
Mnr. Farm Way. Leeds —8E 80
Manorfield. Leeds —2B 80
Manorfield Dri. Horb —9C 118
Manorfields Av. Croft —2H 139
Manorfields Ct. Croft —2H 139
Manor Gdns. Cull —1K 55
Manor Gdns. Dew —1K 117
Manor Gdns. Pool W —1F 26
Manor Gdns. T'ner —1H 47
Manor Gth. Leeds —7D 64
Manor Gth. S Mil —5K 85
Manor Gth. W'ton —2B 138
Mnr. Garth Rd. Dew —4J 117
Manor Gth. Rd. Kip —3B 84
Manor Gro. C'frd —7E 102
Manor Gro. Grime —9N 155
Manor Gro. Leeds —9F 44
Manor Gro. Oss —8B 118
Manor Gro. Riddl —8N 21
Manor Gro. Roys —6C 154
Manor Gro. S Kirk —8G 156
Manor Haigh Rd. Wake —7G 118
Mnr. Heath Rd. Hal —8A 92
Manor Ho. Otley —9L 11
(off Main St.)
Manor Ho. Wake —5M 119
(off Kirkgate)
Manor House Art Gallery & Museum.—5G 8
Manor Ho. Bungalows. Knot —7E 104
Manor Ho. Cvn. Site. Floc —7G 135
Mnr. House Cft. Leeds —4N 43
Mnr. House La. Leeds —9H 29
Mnr. House Rd. Wilsd —9B 38
Manor Houses. Mel M —7E 146
Mnr. House St. Pud —7B 60
Manor La. Oss —8B 118
Manor La. Shipl —8N 39
(in two parts)
Manorley La. B'frd —7K 75
Mnr. Mill La. Leeds —4A 80
Mnr. Occupation Rd. Roys —5C 154
Manor Park. —6B 10
Manor Pk. B'frd —6J 57
Manor Pk. D'ton —6C 124
Manor Pk. Dew —9L 97
(in two parts)
Manor Pk. Mir —4G 115
Manor Pk. Oakw —5C 36
Manor Pk. S'cft —9D 30
Manor Pk. Av. All B —8A 84
Manor Pk. Av. Pon —9M 103
Manor Pk. Gdns. Gom —1M 95
Manor Pk. Ri. D'ton —6C 124
Manor Pk. Way. Lep —7H 133
Manor Pl. Horb —1C 136
Manor Pl. Kei —6G 21
Manor Ri. Hud —6N 131
Manor Ri. I'ly —5J 9
Manor Ri. Skelm —8D 150
Manor Ri. W'ton —3B 138
Manor Rd. Bat —7J 97
Manor Rd. Beal —5L 105
Manor Rd. Bgly —8F 38
Manor Rd. Chur —5M 79
Manor Rd. Clay W —5K 151
Manor Rd. Dew —4E 116
Manor Rd. Far T —3D 148
Manor Rd. Gol —6C 130
Manor Rd. Horb —1C 136
Manor Rd. H'fth —7D 42
Manor Rd. Kei —6G 21
Manor Rd. Leeds —8D 62
Manor Rd. Oss —7A 118
Manor Rd. Rothw —7M 81
Manor Rd. Wake —6H 119
Manor Row. B'frd —7C 58
Manor Row. Low M —6A 76
Manor Royd. Hal —8B 92
Manor Sq. Otley —9L 11
Manor Sq. Yead —9M 25
Manorstead. Skelm —8D 150
Manor St. Barn —9E 154
Manor St. Dew —3G 116
Manor St. Eccl —3F 58
Manor St. Hud —6N 131
Manor St. Leeds —4F 62
Manor St. Otley —9L 11
Manor St. Schol —6D 94
Manor Ter. B'frd —3F 58
Manor Ter. Kip —4B 84
Manor Ter. Leeds —2A 62
Manor Ter. Yead —9M 25
Manor, The. Leeds —9L 45
(off Ladywood Rd.)
Manor Vw. C'frd —7E 102
Manor Vw. Leeds —2A 62
Manor Vw. Pud —7B 60
Manor Vw. Shaf —7K 155
Manor Vw. Upt —1N 157
Manor Way. Bat —8D 96
Manscombe Rd. All —5H 57
Manse Cres. Bur W —8C 10
Manse Dri. Hud —7F 130
Mansel M. B'frd —4J 77
Manse Rd. Bur W —8C 10
Manse St. B'frd —7G 59
Mansfield Av. Bgly —2H 39
Mansfield Cres. Skel —7N 159
Mansfield Pl. Leeds —9N 43
Mansfield Rd. Barn —9A 154
Mansfield Rd. B'frd —4A 58
Mansfield Rd. Bur W —8B 10
Mansion Gdns. Hud —9L 131
Mansion La. Hal —8B 92
Mansion La. Leeds —6K 45
Manston. —3D 64
Manston App. Leeds —3D 64
Manston Av. Leeds —3D 64
Manston Cres. Leeds —3D 64
Manston Dri. Leeds —3D 64
Manston Gdns. Leeds —3E 64
Manston Gro. Leeds —4D 64
Manston La. Leeds —4E 64
Manston Ri. Leeds —3D 64
Manston Ter. Leeds —3E 64
Manston Towers. Leeds —1E 64
Manston Way. Leeds —3D 64
Manygates Av. Wake —8M 119
Manygates Ct. S'dal —8M 119
Manygates Cres. Wake —8M 119
Manygates La. Wake —9M 119
Manygates Pk. Wake —8M 119
Manywells Brow. Cull —2J 55
(in two parts)
Manywells Brow Ind. Est. Cull —1K 55
Manywells Cres. Cull —1K 55
Manywells La. Cull —1H 55
Maple Av. B'frd —6J 59
Maple Av. Gol —5E 130
Maple Av. Oakw —5D 36
Maple Av. Pon —6J 123
Maple Clo. C'frd —7B 102
Maple Clo. Hud —1G 132
Maple Ct. Bgly —5E 38
(off Ash Ter.)
Maple Ct. Leeds —3B 80
Maple Cft. N Farn —9G 61
Maple Dri. N Farn —9G 61
Maple Dri. Pon —5J 123
Maple Dri. Weth —2M 17
Maple Fold. N Farn —9G 61
Maple Gdns. Bard —3F 30
Maple Gro. Bail —6K 39
Maple Gro. Gom —3L 95
Maple Gro. Hud —6M 113
Maple Gro. Kei —7G 20
Maple Gro. N Farn —9H 61
Maple Gro. Nor —4H 121
Maple Gro. Pon —6J 123
Maple Ri. Rothw —9N 81
Maple Rd. Dew —4L 117
Maple Rd. M'well —8J 153
Maple St. Hal —7M 91
Maple St. Hud —5A 132
Maple St. Todm —4J 107
Maple St. Wake —3H 119
Maple Ter. Yead —9K 25
Maple Wlk. Dew —4L 117
Maple Wlk. Knot —9D 104
Maple Way. Leeds —7D 46
Maplin Av. Hud —1E 130
Maplin Dri. Hud —1E 130
Mapplewell. —9K 153
Mapplewell Cres. Oss —6A 118
Mapplewell Dri. M'well —9L 153
Mapplewell Dri. Oss —6A 118
Marbridge Ct. B'frd —3N 75
Marchant St. C'frd —4C 102
Marchbank Rd. B'frd —6G 59
March Cote La. Bgly —9F 38
March St. Nor —2H 121
Marchwood Gro. Cytn —9J 57
Marcus Way. Hud —1C 130
Mardale Cres. Leeds —3B 64
Mardale Rd. Dew —1H 117
Margaret Av. Bard —4E 30
Margaret Clo. Morl —8M 79
Margaret St. Hal —5A 92
Margaret St. Kei —8G 21
Margaret St. Out —8J 99
Margaret St. Wake —4K 119
Margate. W'ford —7D 82
Margate Rd. B'frd —1E 76
Margate St. Sower B —9G 91
Margerison Cres. I'ly —6K 9
Margerison Rd. I'ly —6K 9
Margetson Rd. Dlgtn —8D 78
Margram Bus. Cen. Hal —4A 92
(off Horne St.)
Marian Gro. Leeds —2D 80
Marian Rd. Leeds —3D 62
Marian Ter. Leeds —3D 62
Maria St. Bur W —7C 10
Marie Clo. Hud —4G 132
Marina Cres. Morl —1J 97
Marina Gdns. Sower B —8K 91
(off Park Rd.)
Marina Ter. Gol —5D 130
Marine Villa Rd. Knot —8E 104
Marion Av. Wake —3F 118
Marion Clo. S Kirk —7G 157
Marion Dri. Shipl —8A 40
Marion Gro. Wake —3F 118
Marion St. Bgly —4F 38
Marion St. B'frd —7A 58
Marion St. Brigh —8M 93
Marizon Gro. Wake —4M 119
Mark Bottoms La. H'frth —2L 163
Mark Clo. B'frd —7G 40
Market Av. Hud —4N 131
(off Victoria La.)
Market Clo. T'tn —8D 56
Market Hall. Morl —9K 79
(off Hope St.)
Market Pl. Bat —7F 96
(off Market Sq.)
Market Pl. Cleck —5J 95
(off Albion St.)
Market Pl. Dew —3G 116
Market Pl. Heck —9A 96
Market Pl. Hems —3E 156
Market Pl. Hud —4N 131
Market Pl. Kei —9J 21
Market Pl. Mars —5F 144
Market Pl. Nor —1H 121
Market Pl. Oss —6N 117
Market Pl. Otley —9L 11
Market Pl. Pon —3K 123
Market Pl. Pud —7B 60
Market Pl. Shipl —7N 39
Market Pl. Slai —1M 145
Market Pl. Weth —4M 17
Market Sq. Bat —7F 96
Market Sq. Morl —9K 79
(off Queen St.)
Market Sq. Shipl —8N 39
Market St. Bgly —4E 38
Market St. Birs —3B 96
Market St. B'frd —8C 58
(in two parts)
Market St. Brigh —1N 113
Market St. Brit, S'fth & W'wth —7A 106
Market St. Cleck —5J 95
Market St. Dew —3G 116
Market St. F'stne —5C 122
Market St. Hal —5B 92
Market St. H Bri —1H 89
Market St. Heck —9A 96
(in two parts)
Market St. Hems —2D 156
Market St. H'frth —3M 163
Market St. Hud —4M 131
Market St. Kei —1J 37
Market St. Milns —5G 130
Market St. Nor —1H 121
Market St. Otley —1L 25
Market St. Pad —5K 131
Market St. Shipl —8N 39
Market St. Steet —3D 20
Market St. T'tn —8D 56
Market St. Todm —9J 87
(off Rochdale Rd.)
Market St. Wake —5L 119
Market St. Wibs —4A 76
Market St. Arc. Leeds —7E 62
Market, The. Norm —1H 121
Market Wlk. Mars —5F 144
(off Market Pl.)
Markfield Av. Low M —8A 76
Markfield Clo. Low M —8A 76
Markfield Cres. Low M —8A 76
Markfield Dri. Low M —8A 76
Markham Av. Leeds —2H 63
Markham Av. Rawd —2N 41
Markham Cres. Rawd —2N 41
Markham Cft. Rawd —2N 41
Markham St. Bat —8E 96
Markham St. Wake —5J 119
Markington M. Leeds —1E 98
Markington Pl. Leeds —1E 98
Mark La. Leeds —6E 62
Mark La. Todm —5H 87
Mark St. B'frd —2C 76
Mark St. Hud —5K 131
Mark St. Liv —8M 95
Mark St. Wake —7L 119
Marland Rd. Kei —8L 21
Marlbeck Clo. Hon —6L 147
Marlborough Av. Byr —5C 104
Marlborough Av. Hal —8A 92
Marlborough Av. Tad —6N 33
Marlborough Ct. Men —4F 24
Marlborough Cft. S Elm —5M 157
Marlborough Dri. Tad —6N 33
Marlborough Gdns. Dew —1E 116
Marlborough Gdns. Leeds —4D 62
(off Bk. Blenheim Ter.)
Marlborough Grange. Leeds —6C 62
(off Marlborough St.)
Marlborough Gro. I'ly —6J 9
Marlborough Gro. Leeds —4D 62
(off Bk. Blenheim Ter.)
Marlborough Ho. Ell —4E 112
(off Southgate)
Marlborough Rd. B'frd —5A 58
Marlborough Rd. H Bri —1H 89
Marlborough Rd. Hud —6N 113
Marlborough Rd. Idle —7G 41
Marlborough Rd. Shipl —8M 39
Marlborough Sq. I'ly —6J 9
Marlborough St. Kei —8K 21
Marlborough St. Leeds —6C 62
Marlborough St. Oss —6M 117
Marlborough St. Wake —5J 119
Marlborough Ter. Dew —1E 116
(off Beckett Rd.)
Marlborough Ter. H Bri —1J 89
Marlborough Towers. Leeds —6C 62
Marlborough Vs. Men —4F 24
Marldon Rd. Hal —3F 92
Marley Clo. B'frd —6K 57
Marley Ct. Bgly —9C 22
Marley Gro. Leeds —2B 80
Marley La. Cytn —2D 74
Marley Pl. Leeds —2B 80
Marley Rd. Kei —8M 21
Marley St. B'frd —7E 58
Marley St. Kei —1H 37
Marley St. Leeds —2B 80
Marley Ter. Leeds —2B 80
Marley Vw. Bgly —9C 22
Marley Vw. Leeds —2B 80
Marling Rd. Hud —8G 112
Marlo Rd. Dew —1K 117
Marlott Rd. Shipl —7B 40
Marlow Clo. Hud —4D 132
Marlowe Clo. Pud —9C 60
Marlowe Ct. Gar —7N 65
Marlowe Ct. Guis —7H 25
(off Renton Dri.)
Marlpit La. D'ton —5A 124
Marmion Av. B'frd —7H 57
Marne Av. Cytn —2H 75
Marne Cres. B'frd —8F 40
Marquis Av. Oaken —8F 76
Marriner Rd. Kei —1J 37
Marriner's Dri. B'frd —2N 57
Marriner Wlk. Kei —2J 37
Marriot Gro. Wake —2A 138
Marsden. —5F 144
Marsden Av. Leeds —3C 80
Marsden Ct. Far —3A 60
(off Water La.)
Marsden Ga. Hud —4L 129
Marsden Gro. Leeds —3C 80
Marsden La. Mars —5G 144
Marsden La. Slai —3H 145
Marsden Mt. Leeds —3C 80
Marsden Pl. Leeds —3C 80
Marsden St. Leeds —8J 61
Marsden St. Skelm —7D 150
Marsden Ter. Guis —7H 25
Marsden Vw. Leeds —3C 80
Marsett Way. Leeds —7C 46
Marsh. —6J 95
(nr. Cleckheaton)
Marsh. —3J 131
(nr. Huddersfield)
Marsh. —2B 54
(nr. Oxenhope)
Marsh. Hon —5L 147
Marsh. Pud —7N 59
Marshall Av. Hall G —7H 137
Marshall Av. Leeds —4E 64
Marshall Clo. Morl —9K 79
(off Commercial St.)
Marshall Cres. Morl —2L 97
Marshall Dri. S Elm —6M 157
Marshall Hill. Wake —4E 120
Marshall Mill. Leeds —8C 62
Marshall Mill Ct. Scis —8H 151
Marshall St. C'gts —4D 64
Marshall St. Kei —7H 21
Marshall St. Leeds —8D 62
Marshall St. Mir —8L 115
Marshall St. Morl —9K 79
Marshall St. Stan —7A 100
Marshall St. Yead —9M 25
Marshall Ter. Leeds —4D 64
Marsham Gro. Hud —3H 131
Marsh Cft. B'ton —5B 104
Marsh Delph La. Hal —6E 92
Marsh Delphs. Hal —6E 92
Marsh End. Knot —7G 104
Marshfield Pl. B'frd —2B 76
Marshfields. —3B 76
Marshfield St. B'frd —2B 76
Marsh Gdns. Hon —5L 147
Marsh Gro. B'frd —2A 76
Marsh Gro. Rd. Hud —2J 131
Marsh Hall La. Thur —6D 148
Marsh La. Beal —5M 105
Marsh La. B'shaw —9L 77
Marsh La. Blkhd —1B 88
Marsh La. Byr —5D 104
Marsh La. Hal —6D 92
Marsh La. Kirk O —3K 15
Marsh La. Knot —7G 104
Marsh La. Leeds —7F 62
(in two parts)
Marsh La. Oxe —3A 54
Marsh La. Shepl —2G 164
Marsh Lea Gro. Hems —2F 156
Marsh Platt La. Hon —4M 147
Marsh Ri. Pud —7N 59
Marsh Rd. C'frd —7A 102
Marsh Rd. H'frth —5B 164
Marsh St. B'frd —3B 76
Marsh St. Cleck —6J 95
Marsh St. Leeds —3C 62
Marsh St. Rothw —9N 81
Marsh Ter. Pud —7N 59
Marsh, The. B'frd —6K 77
Marsh Top. —2C 54
Marsh Va. Leeds —3C 62
Marshway. Hal —4N 91
Marsh Way. Wake —4L 119
Marsland Av. Wake —5M 119
Marsland Ct. Cleck —2H 95
Marsland Pl. B'frd —7H 59
Marsland Pl. Wake —5M 119
Marsland St. Wake —5M 119

Marsland Ter. Wake —5M 119
Marston Av. Morl —1K 97
Marston Clo. Q'bry —4E 74
Marston Ct. C'frd —6A 102
Marston Cres. Barn —9A 154
Marston Mt. Leeds —5G 62
(off Cherry Pl.)
Marston Wlk. Nor —8F 100
Marston Way. Weth —3K 17
Marten Dri. Hud —2J 147
Marten Gro. Hud —2J 147
Marten Rd. B'frd —2A 76
Martin Bank Wood. Alm —5B 132
Martin Clo. Morl —9M 79
Martin Ct. Leeds —6E 64
Martindale Dri. Leeds —5H 61
Martindale Wlk. Carc —9N 159
Martin Frobisher Dri. Nor —9G 101
Martingale Dri. Leeds —1E 98
Martin Grn. La. G'lnd —4N 111
Martin Gro. Wake —4N 137
Martin St. Birs —3B 96
Martin St. Brigh —9N 93
Martin St. Nor —3H 121
Martin Ter. Leeds —4M 61
Martlett Dri. B'frd —3D 76
Marton Av. Hems —3C 156
Marwood Rd. Leeds —7H 61
Maryfield Av. Leeds —4B 64
Maryfield Clo. Leeds —4B 64
Maryfield Ct. Leeds —4C 64
Maryfield Cres. Leeds —4C 64
Maryfield Gdns. Leeds —4B 64
Maryfield Grn. Leeds —4B 64
Maryfield M. Leeds —4B 64
Maryfield Va. Leeds —4B 64
Marygate. Wake —5L 119
Mary Rose Ct. F'stne —7C 122
(off Andrew St.)
Mary St. B'frd —9G 58
Mary St. Brigh —8M 93
Mary St. Denh —5L 55
Mary St. E Ard —4G 98
Mary St. Fars —2B 60
Mary St. Oxe —4C 54
(off Denholme Rd.)
Mary St. Shipl —7L 39
Mary St. T'tn —8C 56
Mary St. Wyke —9A 76
Mary Sunley Ho. Leeds —3H 63
(off Banstead St. W.)
Maryville Av. Brigh —7K 93
Masefield Av. B'frd —3H 57
Masefield St. Guis —8K 25
Masham Ct. Leeds —9N 43
Masham Gro. Leeds —7N 61
Masham Pl. B'frd —4L 57
Masham St. Leeds —7N 61
Masonic St. Hal —6L 91
Mason Sq. Hal —1M 91
(off Keighley Rd.)
Mason St. H Bri —1H 89
Master La. Hal —8M 91
Matherville. Skelm —8D 150
Matlock St. Hal —3N 91
Matlock St. Hud —6H 131
Matron Heights. Sower B —8G 91
Matterdale Clo. Dew —1H 117
Matterdale Rd. Dew —1H 117
Matthew Clo. Kei —7L 21
Matthew Gro. Mel —7B 146
Matthew La. Mel —7B 146
Matthew La. Todm —5N 87
Mattyfields Clo. Hal —6L 73
Matty La. Rothw —9K 81
Matty Marsden La. Horb —9A 118
Maud Av. Leeds —3D 80
Maude Av. Bail —5A 40
Maude Cres. Sower B —9E 90
Maude La. Sower B —7D 110
Maude St. G'lnd —4C 112
Maude St. Hal —1N 91
Maude St. Leeds —7F 62
Maud Pl. Leeds —3D 80
Maudsley St. B'frd —7E 58
Maud St. B'frd —8F 58
Maurice Av. Brigh —8L 93
Mavis Av. Dew —5D 116
Mavis Av. Leeds —1H 43
Mavis Gro. Leeds —2H 43
Mavis La. Leeds —1H 43
Mavis Rd. Dew —9C 96
Mavis St. B'frd —7F 58
Mavis St. Dew —5D 116
Mawcroft Clo. Yead —2L 41
Mawcroft Grange Dri. Yead —2L 41
Mawson St. Shipl —7L 39
Maw St. B'frd —9D 58
Maxwell Av. Bat —1F 116
Maxwell Rd. B'frd —5L 75
Maxwell Rd. I'ly —6J 9
Maxwell St. F'stne —6C 122
Maxwell St. Morl —1J 97
May Av. T'tn —8D 56
Maybrook Ind. Pk. Leeds —6A 62
Maybury Av. Dur —2J 137
May Bush Ct. Wake —8N 119
May Bush Rd. Wake —8N 119
Mayfair. B'frd —1B 76
Mayfair Av. Sow —1M 129
Mayfair Pl. Hems —2D 156
Mayfair Way. B'frd —9H 59
Mayfield. Hip —3H 93
Mayfield Av. Brigh —4N 93
Mayfield Av. Hal —6N 91
Mayfield Av. Hud —4D 132
Mayfield Av. I'ly —5J 9
Mayfield Av. Wyke —1A 94
Mayfield Clo. I'ly —5J 9
Mayfield Ct. Oss —8A 118
Mayfield Dri. Hal —6N 91
Mayfield Dri. Sandb —8B 22
Mayfield Gdns. Hal —6N 91
Mayfield Gdns. I'ly —4J 9
Mayfield Gdns. Oss —3M 117
Mayfield Gdns. Sower B —8K 91
(off Park Rd.)
Mayfield Gro. Bail —4B 40
Mayfield Gro. Brigh —4N 93
Mayfield Gro. Hal —6N 91
Mayfield Gro. Hud —4D 132
Mayfield Gro. Wilsd —9A 38
Mayfield Mt. Hal —6N 91
(nr. Parkinson La.)
Mayfield Mt. Hal —7N 91
(off King Cross Rd.)
Mayfield Pl. Dew —2D 116
Mayfield Pl. Wyke —1A 94
Mayfield Ri. Ryh —9H 139
Mayfield Ri. Wyke —1B 94
Mayfield Rd. H Bri —9H 71
Mayfield Rd. I'ly —5H 9
Mayfield Rd. Kei —8H 21
Mayfield Rd. Leeds —6C 64
Mayfield St. Hal —7N 91
Mayfields Way. S Kirk —8H 157
Mayfield Ter. Cytn —2H 75
Mayfield Ter. Cleck —5J 95
Mayfield Ter. Hal —5M 91
Mayfield Ter. Wyke —1B 94
Mayfield Ter. St. Hal —7N 91
Mayfield Vw. Wyke —1B 94
Mayflower Ho. Leeds —3J 81
Maylea Dri. Otley —2H 25
Mayman Clo. Bat —7F 96
Mayman La. Bat —7E 96
Maynes Clo. Dew —9G 117
Mayo Av. B'frd —3B 76
Mayo Clo. Leeds —9M 45
Mayo Cres. B'frd —4C 76
Mayo Dri. B'frd —4C 76
Mayo Gro. B'frd —4C 76
Mayo Rd. B'frd —4C 76
Mayor's Wlk. C'frd —5L 103
Mayor's Wlk. Pon —4K 123
Mayor's Wlk. Av. Pon —4K 123
Mayors Wlk. Clo. Pon —4K 123
Maypole M. Bar E —7L 47
Maypole Rd. Hud —8A 114
Mayster Gro. Brigh —4K 113
Mayster Rd. Brigh —4L 113
May St. Cleck —4H 95
May St. Hal —3A 92
May St. Haw —9D 36
May St. Hud —6K 131
May St. Kei —8J 21
May Ter. Leeds —8H 63
Maythorn. —8H 165
Maythorn Clo. M'well —9L 153
Maythorne Av. Bat —9D 96
Maythorne Cres. Cytn —1J 75
Maythorne Dri. Cytn —1K 75
May Tree Clo. Cytn —9J 57
Mayville Av. Leeds —3A 62
Mayville Av. Sandb —8A 22
Mayville Pl. Leeds —3A 62
Mayville Rd. Leeds —3A 62
Mayville St. Leeds —3A 62
Mayville Ter. Leeds —3A 62
Mazebrook Av. Cleck —2J 95
Mazebrook Cres. Cleck —2J 95
Mead Clo. Leeds —8F 64
Mead Gro. Leeds —8F 64
Meadow Bank. Ackw —1G 140
Meadow Bank. Dew —3C 116
Meadow Bank. H'cft —9K 139
Meadow Bank. H'frth —2A 164
Meadowbank Av. All —5G 56
Mdw. Bank Cres. Mir —6J 115
Mdw. Bottom Rd. Todm —6K 87
Mdw. Brook Chase. Nor —2K 121
Mdw. Brook Clo. Nor —2K 121
Mdw. Brook Ct. Nor —3K 121
Mdw. Brook Grn. Nor —2K 121
Meadow Clo. Bard —2F 30
Meadow Clo. Bat —3D 96
Meadow Clo. B Spa —9C 18
Meadow Clo. H'den —6A 38
Meadow Clo. Hems —3C 156
Meadow Clo. Liv —2K 115
Meadow Clo. She —7J 75
Meadow Ct. All —2F 56
Meadow Ct. Brigh —1C 114
Meadow Ct. C'frd —6K 103
Meadow Ct. Oss —4M 117
Meadow Ct. Roys —6E 154
Meadow Ct. S Elm —6A 158
Meadow Ct. T'tn —8C 56
(off Chapel St.)
Meadow Cres. Grime —9N 155
Meadow Cres. Hal —2L 91
Meadow Cres. Roys —5E 154
Meadowcroft. B'frd —4D 76
Meadow Cft. Drau —4D 4
Meadow Cft. E Kes —3D 30
Meadow Cft. Hems —4E 156
Meadowcroft. Hon —5K 147
Meadow Cft. Hud —6D 114
Meadow Cft. Kei —1E 36
Meadow Cft. Leeds —9D 62
Meadowcroft. Men —5E 24
Meadow Cft. Out —7L 99
(in two parts)
Meadow Cft. Shaf —6K 155
Mdw. Croft Clo. B'frd —7D 40
Meadowcroft Clo. Out —7M 99
Meadowcroft Ct. Out —7M 99
Meadowcroft Cres. C'frd —4G 102
Meadowcroft La. Ripp —6E 110
Meadowcroft M. C'frd —4G 102
Meadowcroft M. Leeds —7G 63
Meadowcroft Ri. B'frd —5G 76
Meadowcroft Rd. Out —7M 99
Meadow Dri. Hal —2L 91
Meadow Dri. Liv —2K 115
Meadow End. B'hpe —6H 27
Meadowfield Clo. Fitz —8A 140
Meadowfields Clo. Croft —2H 139
Meadowfields Dri. Croft —2H 139
Meadowfields Rd. Croft —2H 139
Meadow Gth. B'hpe —7J 27
Meadow Gth. Wake —7L 99
Meadowgate. Oss —4M 117
Meadowgate Cft. Loft —2K 99
Meadowgate Dri. Loft —2K 99
Meadowgate Va. Loft —3K 99
Meadow Grn. Lint —1C 146
Meadowhurst Gdns. Pud —7A 60
Meadowlands. Schol —3C 94
Meadow La. Cnly —1H 21
Meadow La. Dew —2F 116
Meadow La. Hal —2L 91
Meadow La. Leeds —8E 62
Meadow La. Liv —2K 115
Meadow La. Slai —9M 129
Meadow La. Wake —4H 119
Meadow Pk. Hud —9F 114
Mdw. Park Cres. S'ley —4M 59
Mdw. Park Dri. S'ley —4M 59
Meadow Ri. Hems —3C 156
Meadow Rd. B'frd —7J 41
Meadow Rd. C'frd —7B 102
Meadow Rd. Gar —7A 66
Meadow Rd. Roys —6E 154
Meadowside Rd. Bail —3C 40
Meadows, The. All B —7N 83
Meadows, The. Den D —3C 166
Meadows, The. Leeds —4M 43
Meadows, The. Wibs —4A 76
Meadow St. Mar —3J 131
Meadow, The. Nor —4H 121
Meadow Va. Neth —5N 135
Meadow Va. Out —7L 99
Meadow Valley. Leeds —2D 44
Meadow Vw. Bar E —7M 47
Meadow Vw. Hoy S —9J 167
Meadow Vw. Leeds —3A 62
Meadow Vw. Oakw —5D 36
Meadow Vw. Oss —4M 117
Meadow Vw. Skelm —8E 150
Meadow Vw. Wyke —3A 94
Meadow Wlk. Bads —7L 141
Meadow Wlk. Hal —2L 91
(off Meadow La.)
Meadow Way. Ackw —1G 141
Meadow Way. C'frd —4G 102
Meadow Way. Leeds —2C 44
Meadow Way. Ting —5N 97
Mead Rd. Leeds —8F 64
Meadstead Dri. Roys —6C 154
Mead St. Hud —1M 131
Mead Vw. B'frd —2J 77
Meadway. B'frd —7K 75
Mead Way. Kbtn —2J 149
Mead Way. Leeds —8F 64
Meadway. S'hse —6K 121
Meagill Ri. Otley —7H 11
Meal Hill La. Hep —6D 164
Meal Hill La. Slai —7L 129
Meal Hill Rd. Holme —7E 162
Mean La. Mel —7C 146
Mean La. OLdf —6K 35
Meanwood. —9B 44
Meanwood Clo. Leeds —2D 62
Meanwood Grove. —6N 43
Meanwood Gro. Leeds —6A 44
Meanwood Rd. Leeds —9B 44
Meanwood Towers. Leeds —7C 44
Meanwood Valley Clo. Leeds —9B 44
Meanwood Valley Dri. Leeds —9B 44
Meanwood Valley Grn. Leeds —9B 44
Meanwood Valley Gro. Leeds —9B 44
Meanwood Valley Mt. Leeds —9B 44
Meanwood Valley Urban Farm. —1C 62
Meanwood Valley Wlk. Leeds —9B 44
Mearclough Rd. Sower B —8K 91
Mearhouse Bank. New M —4C 164
Mearhouse Ter. N Mill —4C 164
Medeway. S'ley —4N 59
Medhurst Av. Kip —3B 84
Medley La. Hal —9E 74
Medley St. C'frd —5E 102
Medlock Rd. Horb —1C 136
Medway. Hud —9F 114
Medway. Q'bry —5E 74
Medway Av. Gar —9A 66
Meeting Ho. La. Gol —6N 129
Meggison Gro. B'frd —1A 76
Meg La. Hud —5G 130
Megna Way. B'frd —1C 76
Melba Rd. B'frd —2N 75
Melbourne Av. Wren —9H 99
Melbourne Gro. B'frd —6J 59
Melbourne Gro. Leeds —4F 60
Melbourne M. Wake —8G 98
Melbourne Pl. B'frd —9B 58
Melbourne Pl. S'ley —4B 60
Melbourne Rd. Todm —2J 107
Melbourne Rd. Wake —3J 119
Melbourne St. Bmly —4F 60
Melbourne St. Fars —4A 60
Melbourne St. Hal —3N 91
Melbourne St. H Bri —1G 89
Melbourne St. Leeds —5F 62
Melbourne St. Liv —9M 95
Melbourne St. Morl —9L 79
Melbourne St. Shipl —7M 39
Melbourne Ter. B'frd —9C 58
Melbourne Ter. S'ley —4C 60
Melbury Ho. B'frd —6E 58
(off Butler St. W.)
Melcombe Ho. B'frd —7E 58
(off Barkerend Rd.)
Melcombe Wlk. B'frd —1J 77
Melford Clo. M'well —8K 153
Melford St. B'frd —3G 76
Mellor Brook. Slai —6M 129
Mellor La. H'frth —4G 162
Mellor Mill La. Holy G —7A 112
Mellor St. Brigh —1N 113
Mellor St. Hal —7N 91
Mellor St. Todm —4G 87
Mellor Ter. Hal —7N 91
Mellwood Ho. S Elm —6L 157
(off Little La.)
Mellwood La. S Elm —6L 157
Melrose Clo. Hud —4D 132
Melrose Ct. Ell —5D 112
Melrose Dri. Bur W —7C 10
Melrose Gro. H'fth —7H 43
Melrose Ho. B'frd —1J 77
(off Ned La.)
Melrose Pl. H'fth —7G 43
Melrose Pl. Pud —8A 60
Melrose St. B'frd —1M 75
Melrose St. Hal —3N 91
Melrose Ter. Ell —5E 112
(off Savile Rd.)
Melrose Ter. H'fth —7G 43
Melrose Wlk. H'fth —7G 43
Melsonby Ho. B'frd —8G 40
(off Cavendish Rd.)
Meltham. —7C 146
Meltham Ho. La. H'frth —4D 164
Meltham Mills Rd. Mel —7E 146
Meltham Rd. Hon —6H 147
Meltham Rd. Hud & Lock —3H 147
Meltham Rd. Mars —5G 145
Melton Av. Leeds —9H 81
Melton Clo. Leeds —9H 81
Melton Clo. S Elm —4M 157
Melton Gth. Leeds —9H 81
Melton Rd. Wake —6J 137
Melton St. Bat —6E 96
Melton Ter. B'frd —2J 59
Melton Way. Liv —2K 115
Melville Clo. Leeds —3D 62
Melville Gdns. Leeds —2D 62
Melville Gro. I'ly —5K 9
Melville Ho. B'frd —7A 58
(off Preston St.)
Melville Pl. Leeds —2D 62
Melville Rd. Leeds —3D 62
Melville St. B'frd —7A 58
Memorial Dri. Leeds —8B 44
Mendip Av. Hud —1F 130
Mendip Clo. Gar —9N 65
Mendip Rd. Dew —2J 117
Mendip Way. Low M —7N 75
Menin Dri. Bail —2A 40
Menston. —4D 24
Menston Dri. Men —5E 24
Menstone St. B'frd —6A 58
Menston Hall. Men —4F 24
Menston Old La. Men —2D 24
Mercer Clo. Hud —2H 147
Merchants Ct. B'frd —9E 58
Mercia Way. Leeds —3F 64
Mercury Row. Otley —1L 25
Merewood Rd. C'frd —5N 101
Meriden Av. Gar —9N 65
Merlin Clo. Morl —1M 97
Merlin Ct. Bat —4D 96
Merlin Ct. Hud —2K 147
Merlin Gro. B'frd —7H 57
Merlinwood Dri. Bail —3B 40
Merrion Cen. Leeds —5E 62
Merrion Cres. Hal —7D 92
Merrion Pl. Leeds —6E 62
(in two parts)
Merrion St. Hal —7D 92
Merrion St. Leeds —6E 62
(in two parts)
Merrion Way. Leeds —5E 62
Merrivale Rd. All —6F 56
Merriville. H'fth —8G 42
Merrybank La. Huby —4L 13
Merry Bent La. Sower B —6A 110
Merrybents St. Todm —7M 87
Merrydale Rd. Euro I —7E 76
Merton Av. Fars —4A 60
Merton Clo. Kip —3C 84
Merton Dri. Fars —4N 59
Merton Fold. B'frd —1C 76
Merton Gdns. Fars —4N 59
Merton Rd. B'frd —9B 58
Merton St. Hud —5M 131
Merville Av. Bail —2A 40
Metcalfe St. B'frd —1F 76
Methley. —2K 101
Methley Dri. Leeds —9E 44
Methley Gro. Leeds —9E 44
Methley Junction. —4L 101
Methley La. Leeds —9F 44
Methley La. Meth —9D 82
Methley Lanes. —5F 100
Methley Mt. Leeds —9F 44
Methley Pl. Leeds —9E 44
Methley Rd. C'frd —4A 102
Methley Ter. Leeds —9F 44
Methley Vw. Leeds —9F 44
Methuen Oval. Wyke —3A 94
Mews Ct. F'stne —6D 122
Mews, The. Nor —9J 101
Mexborough Av. Leeds —2F 62
Mexborough Dri. Leeds —2F 62
Mexborough Gro. Leeds —2F 62
Mexborough Ho. Ell —4E 112
(off Gog Hill)
Mexborough Pl. Leeds —3F 62
Mexborough Rd. B'frd —1B 58
Mexborough Rd. Leeds —3F 62
Mexborough St. Leeds —2F 62
Meynell App. Leeds —9C 62
Meynell Av. Rothw —8N 81
Meynell Ct. Leeds —7E 64
Meynell Heights. Leeds —9C 62
Meynell Ho. B'frd —9G 41
Meynell Mt. Rothw —8A 82
Meynell Rd. Leeds —7E 64
Meynell Sq. Leeds —9C 62
Meynell Wlk. Leeds —9C 62
Meyrick Av. Weth —3A 18
Meyrick Dri. Dart —9F 152
Miall St. Hal —4N 91
Michael Av. Stan —7N 99
Michael Gth. B'frd —4N 75
Michael's Est. Grime —9A 156
Mickle Ct. C'frd —5C 102
Mickledore Ridge. B'frd —2K 75
Micklefield. —7G 66
Micklefield Ct. Rawd —3M 41
(off Micklefield La.)
Micklefield La. Rawd —3L 41
Micklefield Rd. Rawd —3M 41
Micklegate. Pon —2K 123
Micklegate Sq. Pon —2K 123
Micklemoss Dri. Q'bry —3B 74
Micklethwaite. —9E 22

Micklethwaite Dri. *Q'bry* —5D **74**
Micklethwaite La. *Bgly* —1D **38**
Micklethwaite Rd. *Hall G* —7H **137**
Micklethwaite Vw. *Weth* —5M **17**
Mickletown. —1L 101
Mickletown Rd. *Meth* —1K **101**
Mickley St. *Leeds* —7N **61**
Middlebrook Clo. *B'frd* —7K **57**
Middlebrook Cres. *B'frd* —8J **57**
Middlebrook Dri. *B'frd* —7J **57**
Middlebrook Hill. *B'frd* —7J **57**
Middlebrook Ri. *B'frd* —7J **57**
Middlebrook Vw. *B'frd* —7K **57**
Middlebrook Wlk. *B'frd* —7K **57**
Middlebrook Way. *B'frd* —8J **57**
Middle Calderbrook. *L'boro* —9L **107**
Middle Clo. *Dart* —8E **152**
Middlecroft Clo. *Leeds* —5H **81**
Middlecroft Rd. *Leeds* —5H **81**
Middle Cross St. *Leeds* —7N **61**
(in two parts)
Middle Dean St. *G'lnd* —5B **112**
*Middle Ellistones. G'lnd —4N **111***
(off Saddleworth Rd.)
Middlefield La. *K S'ton* —6F **142**
Middle Fld. La. *Wool* —3G **152**
Middle Fold. *Leeds* —6F **62**
Middlegate. *Birs* —3B **96**
Middle Hall Clo. *Liv* —8K **95**
Middle La. *Cytn* —9H **57**
Middle La. *Knot* —8F **104**
(in three parts)
Middle La. *Lntn* —7K **17**
Middle La. *New C* —3J **139**
Middlemoor. *Leeds* —7C **46**
Middle Oxford St. *C'frd* —5C **102**
Middle Rd. *Earl* —4H **117**
Middle Rd. *Leeds* —3M **81**
Middle Rd. *Wtwn* —4E **116**
Middlestown. —3K 135
Middle St. *B'frd* —7C **58**
Middle St. *Sower B* —2E **110**
Middlethorne Clo. *Leeds* —2K **45**
Middlethorne Ri. *Leeds* —2K **45**
Middleton. —2H 9
(nr. Ilkley)
Middleton. —9D 80
(nr. Morley)
Middleton Av. *I'ly* —3G **8**
Middleton Av. *Leeds* —5H **63**
Middleton Av. *Rothw* —8J **81**
Middleton Clo. *Morl* —9L **79**
Middleton Ct. *Liv* —8J **95**
Middleton Cres. *Leeds* —3D **80**
Middleton Gro. *Leeds* —4D **80**
Middleton Gro. *Morl* —9M **79**
Middleton La. *Midd & Thor* —1E **98**
Middleton La. *Rothw* —8J **81**
(in two parts)
Middleton Pk. Av. *Leeds* —9D **80**
Middleton Pk. Cir. *Leeds* —8D **80**
Middleton Pk. Ct. *Leeds* —9D **80**
Middleton Pk. Cres. *Leeds* —9E **80**
Middleton Pk. Grn. *Leeds* —9D **80**
Middleton Pk. Gro. *Leeds* —8D **80**
Middleton Pk. Mt. *Leeds* —9D **80**
Middleton Pk. Rd. *Leeds* —8D **80**
Middleton Pk. Ter. *Leeds* —9D **80**
Middleton Railway. —4E 80
Middleton Rd. *I'ly* —5F **8**
Middleton Rd. *Leeds* —6G **81**
Middleton Rd. *Morl* —9L **79**
Middleton St. *B'frd* —5N **57**
Middleton Ter. *Morl* —9M **79**
Middleton Way. *Knot* —7E **104**
Middleton Way. *Leeds* —7H **81**
Middle Wlk. *Leeds* —6L **45**
Middle Way. *Kei* —9L **21**
Middleway. *Sils* —8F **6**
Midge Hall Clo. *Bur W* —8C **10**
Midgeham Gro. *H'den* —6N **37**
Midgehole La. *H Bri* —7H **71**
Midgehole Rd. *H Bri* —7H **71**
Midgeley Rd. *Bail* —6M **39**
Midgley. —3C 90
(nr. Luddenden)
Midgley. —8M 135
(nr. Netherton)
Midgley Gdns. *Leeds* —3C **62**
Midgley Pl. *Leeds* —3D **62**
Midgley Ri. *Pon* —9K **103**
Midgley Rd. *Bur W* —8C **10**
Midgley Rd. *H Bri* —3M **89**
Midgley Row. *B'frd* —4F **76**
Midgley Ter. *Leeds* —3D **62**
Midland Clo. *Leeds* —2H **81**
Midland Gth. *Leeds* —2G **81**
Midland Hill. *Bgly* —4E **38**
*Midland Ho. Rothw —7E **82***
(off Midland St.)
Midland Pas. *Leeds* —3B **62**
Midland Pl. *Leeds* —8C **62**
Midland Rd. *Bail* —5B **40**
Midland Rd. *B'frd* —4B **58**
Midland Rd. *Friz* —1A **58**
Midland Rd. *Leeds* —3B **62**
(LS6)
Midland Rd. *Leeds* —2G **80**
(LS10)
Midland Rd. *Pon* —3L **123**
Midland Rd. *Roys* —5D **154**
Midland St. *Hud* —2N **131**
Midland St. *W'ford* —7D **82**
Midland Ter. *B'frd* —3B **58**
Midland Ter. *Kei* —8J **21**
Midway. *S Cro* —3F **146**
Midway Av. *Bgly* —8F **38**
Milan Rd. *Leeds* —3H **63**
Milan St. *Leeds* —3J **63**
Milbrook Gdns. *Heck* —1D **116**
Mildred St. *B'frd* —5E **58**
Mildred Sylvester Way. *Nor I* —1L **121**
Mile Cross Gdns. *Hal* —6L **91**
Mile Cross Pl. *Hal* —6L **91**
Mile Cross Rd. *Hal* —6L **91**
Mile Cross Ter. *Hal* —6L **91**
Mile End. *Mel* —8C **146**
Miles Gth. *Bard* —2G **30**
Miles Hill. —9D 44
Miles Hill Av. *Leeds* —9D **44**
Miles Hill Cres. *B'frd* —4G **77**
Miles Hill Cres. *Leeds* —9D **44**
Miles Hill Dri. *B'frd* —4G **76**
Miles Hill Gro. *Leeds* —9D **44**
Miles Hill Mt. *Leeds* —8C **44**
Miles Hill Pl. *Leeds* —8D **44**
Miles Hill Rd. *Leeds* —8D **44**
Miles Hill Sq. *Leeds* —9D **44**
Miles Hill St. *Leeds* —9D **44**
Miles Hill Ter. *Leeds* —9D **44**
Miles Hill Vw. *Leeds* —9D **44**
Milestone Ct. *S'ley* —4C **60**
Mile Thorn St. *Hal* —5M **91**
Milford Ct. *Hud* —5M **131**
Milford Gro. *Gom* —1L **95**
Milford Pl. *B'frd* —3M **57**
Milford Pl. *Leeds* —5N **61**
Milford St. *Hud* —5M **131**
Milgate St. *Roys* —5E **154**
Millars Wlk. *S Kirk* —8G **157**
Mill Bank. —4D 110
Mill Bank Clo. *Sower B* —4C **110**
Millbank Ct. *Pud* —8C **60**
Millbank Fold. *Pud* —8C **60**
Mill Bank Rd. *Mel* —8D **146**
Mill Bank Rd. *Mill B* —4D **110**
Mill Banks. *Sils* —8E **6**
Millbank Vw. *Pud* —8C **60**
Millbeck App. *Morl* —9M **79**
Millbeck Clo. *B'frd* —8H **57**
Millbeck Clo. *T'tn* —8H **57**
Millbeck Grn. *Coll* —9H **17**
Mill Bridge. —7M 95
Millbrook Gdns. *Dew* —1D **116**
Mill Carr Hill Rd. *Oaken* —8F **76**
Mill Clo. *Ackw* —4G **141**
Mill Clo. *S Kirk* —7G **156**
Mill Clo. La. *Q'bry* —5B **74**
Mill Cotts. *F'stne* —6B **122**
*Mill Ct. Oxe —4C **54***
(off Yate La.)
Mill Cft. *Gild* —6G **78**
Millcroft. *Loft* —6N **99**
Millcroft. *Pool W* —1G **26**
Millcroft Clo. *Loft* —6N **99**
Millcroft Ri. *Loft* —6N **99**
Mill Dam. *Cliff* —3E **32**
Mill Dam La. *Pon* —1L **123**
Miller Av. *Wake* —9M **119**
Miller Ct. *N'dam* —6K **137**
Miller Garth. *Ackw* —5G **140**
Millergate. *B'frd* —7C **58**
Miller Hill. *Den D* —3D **166**
Miller Hill Bank. *Den D* —3D **166**
Millers Ct. *Liv* —1M **115**
Millers Dale. *Morl* —7J **79**
Millersdale Clo. *Euro I* —6E **76**
Mill Farm Dri. *N'dam* —6L **137**
Millfield Clo. *Hud* —3H **131**
Millfield Cres. *Pon* —5J **123**
Millfield Rd. *Horb* —2E **136**
Millfields. *Oss* —6M **117**
Millfields. *Sils* —8D **6**
Mill Fold. *Gild* —6G **78**
Millford Way. *Ripp* —7D **110**
Mill Forest Way. *Bat* —8J **97**
(nr. Oaklands Dri.)
Mill Forest Way. *Bat* —1F **116**
(nr. Town St.)
Mill Gth. *Gild* —6G **78**
Mill Gth. *Pon* —4J **123**
Millgarth Ct. *Coll* —9J **17**
Millgarth St. *Leeds* —6F **62**
Millgate. *Ackw* —5G **140**
Millgate. *Bgly* —4E **38**
Millgate. *Ell* —4E **112**
Millgate. *Fen B* —8F **132**
Millgate. *Hud* —5K **131**
Millgate Ter. *W'wth* —6A **106**
Mill Green. —1D 64
Mill Grn. *Leeds* —8B **62**
Mill Grn. Clo. *Leeds* —1D **64**
Mill Grn. Gdns. *Leeds* —1D **64**
Mill Grn. Gth. *Leeds* —1D **64**
Mill Grn. Pl. *Leeds* —1D **64**
Mill Grn. Rd. *Leeds* —1D **64**
Mill Grn. Vw. *Leeds* —1D **64**
Mill Gro. *Brigh* —8L **93**
Mill Hey. *Haw* —8D **36**
Mill Hill. —4K 121
Mill Hill. *Ackw* —2G **140**
Mill Hill. *Haw* —8C **36**
Mill Hill. *Leeds* —7E **62**
Mill Hill. *Nor* —2H **121**
Mill Hill. *Pud* —9B **60**
Mill Hill. *Rothw* —8N **81**
Mill Hill Av. *Pon* —4H **123**
Mill Hill Clo. *D'ton* —6C **124**
Mill Hill Grn. *Rothw* —8N **81**
Mill Hill La. *Brigh* —8L **93**
Mill Hill La. *Clif* —2D **114**
Mill Hill La. *Pon* —4H **123**
Mill Hill Rd. *Pon* —4J **123**
Mill Hill Sq. *Rothw* —8N **81**
Mill Hill Top. *H'den* —7A **38**
Mill Ho. Ri. *B'frd* —4F **76**
Milligan Av. *B'frd* —1D **58**
Mill La. *Ackw* —5G **140**
Mill La. *Bard* —4F **30**
Mill La. *Bat* —8G **97**
Mill La. *Bgly* —1H **39**
Mill La. *B'shaw* —7L **77**
Mill La. *Birs* —2E **96**
Mill La. *B'twn* —2A **92**
Mill La. *B'frd* —9C **58**
Mill La. *Brigh* —1N **113**
Mill La. *Butt* —7K **75**
Mill La. *C'frd* —3D **102**
Mill La. *Cleck* —1H **95**
Mill La. *Coll* —9J **17**
Mill La. *Dart* —8G **152**
Mill La. *Dew* —4K **117**
Mill La. *E Ard* —4F **98**
Mill La. *Far T* —3E **148**
Mill La. *Floc* —7G **134**
Mill La. *Gild* —6G **78**
Mill La. *Guis* —9A **24**
Mill La. *Holy G* —7B **112**
Mill La. *Hud* —6F **114**
Mill La. *Kear* —6N **15**
Mill La. *Leeds* —3D **60**
Mill La. *Ludd* —2E **90**
Mill La. *Mick M* —1K **101**
Mill La. *Mir* —4H **115**
Mill La. *Mix* —6J **73**
Mill La. *Nor* —8L **101**
Mill La. *Oakw* —5B **36**
Mill La. *Otley* —9L **11**
Mill La. *Oxe* —3C **54**
Mill La. *Pen* —8A **166**
Mill La. *Pon* —9M **103**
Mill La. *Pool W* —1F **26**
Mill La. *Q'bry* —3B **74**
Mill La. *Ryh* —9J **139**
Mill La. *Skel* —6L **159**
Mill La. *S Elm* —4N **157**
Mill La. *S Kirk* —8G **157**
Mill La. *Steet* —3C **20**
Mill La. *S'hse* —6K **121**
Mill La. *Thor A* —9E **18**
Mill La. *Tong* —2C **78**
Mill La. *Wool* —1M **153**
Millmoor Clo. *D Hill* —4J **57**
Mill Moor Rd. *Mel* —7A **146**
Mill Pk. *Mir* —9K **115**
Mill Pit La. *Rothw* —6M **81**
Mill Pond Clo. *Leeds* —9A **44**
Mill Pond Gro. *Leeds* —9A **44**
Mill Pond La. *Leeds* —8A **44**
Mill Pond Sq. *Leeds* —8A **44**
Mill Race Fold. *Thon* —9A **148**
Mill Rd. *Dew* —1F **116**
Mill Row. *Ebrn* —2A **20**
Mill Royd St. *Brigh* —1N **113**
Mill Shaw. —4A 80
Millshaw. *Leeds* —4N **79**
Mill Shaw La. *H'frth* —6E **164**
Millshaw Mt. *Leeds* —5A **80**
Millshaw Pk. Av. *Leeds* —5N **79**
Millshaw Pk. Clo. *Leeds* —5N **79**
Millshaw Pk. Dri. *Leeds* —4N **79**
Millshaw Pk. La. *Leeds* —5N **79**
Millshaw Pk. Way. *Leeds* —4N **79**
Millshaw Rd. *Leeds* —6A **80**
Millside. *Shaf* —6K **155**
Millside Wlk. *Morl* —9M **79**
Millside Wlk. *Shaf* —6K **155**
Millstone Clo. *Ackw* —5G **140**
Millstone Ri. *Liv* —1M **115**
Mill St. *Birs* —4B **96**
Mill St. *B'frd* —6D **58**
Mill St. *C'frd* —5B **102**
Mill St. *Cros M* —6K **131**
Mill St. *Cull* —9K **37**
Mill St. *Hal* —2N **111**
Mill St. *Leeds* —7G **62**
Mill St. *Morl* —1K **97**
Mill St. *S Kirk* —7G **157**
Mill St. *Wibs* —4M **75**
Mill St. E. *Dew* —4G **116**
Mill St. W. *Dew* —4F **116**
Mill Vw. *Bur W* —7C **10**
Mill Vw. *Hems* —3C **156**
Mill Vw. *Knot* —8A **104**
Millward St. *Ryh* —9H **139**
Millwood. —7L 87
Millwood La. *Todm* —7M **87**
Millwright St. *Leeds* —5F **62**
Milne Ct. *Colt* —8E **64**
Milner Bank. *Otley* —2H **25**
Milner Clo. *G'lnd* —4B **112**
Milner Fold. *Pud* —9A **60**
Milner Gdns. *Leeds* —8H **63**
Milner Ing. *Wyke* —9A **76**
Milner La. *G'lnd* —4B **112**
Milner La. *Rob H* —1J **99**
(in two parts)
Milner La. *Saxt* —8N **49**
Milner La. *T'ner* —9G **30**
Milner Rd. *Bail* —6N **39**
Milner Royd La. *Norl* —9L **91**
Milner's La. *D'ton* —7C **124**
Milner's Rd. *Yead* —9K **25**
Milner St. *Hal* —5A **92**
Milner St. *Hud* —7K **131**
Milner St. *Oss* —2M **117**
Milner Way. *Oss* —5A **118**
Milne's Av. *Wake* —8H **119**
Milnes Gro. *C'frd* —5H **103**
Milnes St. *Leeds* —8A **62**
Milne St. *B'frd* —7A **58**
Miln Rd. *Hud* —2M **131**
Milnsbridge. —6F 130
Milnthorpe. —3M 137
Milnthorpe Clo. *B'ham* —5C **32**
Milnthorpe Cres. *Wake* —2M **137**
Milnthorpe Dri. *Wake* —2M **137**
Milnthorpe Gdns. *B'ham* —5C **32**
Milnthorpe Gth. *B'ham* —5C **32**
Milnthorpe La. *B'ham* —5C **32**
Milnthorpe La. *Miln* —1L **137**
Milnthorpe La. *Wake* —9M **119**
Milnthorpe Way. *B'ham* —5C **32**
Milroyd Cres. *Bat* —2D **96**
Milton Av. *Liv* —9N **95**
Milton Av. *Sower B* —7H **91**
Milton Clo. *Cald G* —4F **136**
Milton Clo. *Liv* —1N **115**
Milton Ct. *Wake* —6A **100**
Milton Cres. *Wake* —7E **118**
Milton Dri. *Kin* —8B **140**
Milton Dri. *Liv* —1N **115**
Milton Dri. *Scholes* —8G **46**
Milton Gdns. *Liv* —9N **95**
Milton Gro. *Dew* —1F **116**
Milton Pl. *Hal* —5A **92**
Milton Pl. *Oss* —4N **117**
Milton Rd. *Carc* —8N **159**
Milton Rd. *Liv* —9N **95**
Milton Rd. *Wake* —7E **118**
Milton Sq. *Heck* —8A **96**
Milton St. *B'frd* —7A **58**
Milton St. *C'frd* —4C **102**
Milton St. *Denh* —6L **55**
Milton St. *Heck* —7A **96**
Milton St. *Sower B* —7H **91**
Milton St. *Wake* —6J **119**
Milton Ter. *Cleck* —4G **95**
Milton Ter. *Fitz* —6A **140**
Milton Ter. *Hal* —5A **92**
Milton Ter. *Leeds* —2K **61**
Milton Ter. *Yead* —9K **25**
*Milton Wlk. Dew —3F **116***
(off Wellington Wlk.)
Minden Clo. *Pon* —4G **123**
Minden Way. *Pon* —3G **123**
Minerva Ind. Est. *Rothw* —6F **82**
Minerva St. *Hud* —7E **130**
Minnie St. *Facit* —9A **106**
Minnie St. *Haw* —9C **36**
Minnie St. *Kei* —1H **37**
Minorca Mt. *Denh* —5K **55**
Minstead Av. *Ell* —4J **113**
Minsthorpe. —4N 157
Minsthorpe La. *S Elm* —5M **157**
Minsthorpe Va. *S Elm* —6L **157**
Mint St. *B'frd* —4F **58**
Mint St. *Hud* —3J **131**
Miramar. *Hud* —6B **114**
Mirey Butt La. *Knot* —9B **104**
(in two parts)
Mirey La. *Sower B* —8B **90**
Mirfield. —6L 115
Mirfield Av. *B'frd* —1E **58**
Mirfield Moor. —4J 115
Mirycarr La. *T'ner* —5F **46**
Miry La. *Cra V* —7N **89**
Miry La. *Liv* —8F **94**
Miry La. *Nthng* —8K **147**
Miry La. *Pot* —5M **47**
Miry La. *Thon* —9N **147**
Miry La. *Yead* —9M **25**
Mission St. *Brigh* —2A **114**
Mistral Clo. *Wyke* —2A **94**
Mistral Gro. *Liv* —7F **94**
Mistress La. *Leeds* —6M **61**
Mitcham Dri. *B'frd* —4M **57**
Mitchell Av. *Dew* —1E **116**
Mitchell Av. *Hud* —5F **132**
Mitchell Clo. *B'frd* —6G **40**
Mitchell La. *B'frd* —6G **40**
Mitchell La. *Sils* —8E **6**
Mitchell Sq. *B'frd* —1C **76**
Mitchell St. *Brigh* —9M **93**
Mitchell St. *H Bri* —2H **89**
Mitchell St. *Kei* —8K **21**
Mitchell St. *Sower B* —8J **91**
Mitchell St. *Todm* —5G **86**
Mitchell Ter. *Bgly* —6E **38**
Mitford Pl. *Leeds* —7N **61**
Mitford Rd. *Leeds* —7N **61**
Mitford Ter. *Leeds* —7N **61**
Mitford Vw. *Leeds* —7N **61**
Mitre Ct. *B'frd* —2H **77**
Mitre St. *Dew* —3D **116**
Mitre St. *Hud* —3K **131**
Mitton St. *Bgly* —9G **38**
Mitton St. *B'frd* —2A **76**
Mixenden. —8J 73
Mixenden Clo. *Hal* —8J **73**
*Mixenden Ct. Hal —9K **73***
(off Mixenden Rd.)
Mixenden La. *Hal* —7K **73**
Mixenden Rd. *Hal* —7J **73**
Moat End. *T'ner* —2G **47**
Moat Hill. *Birs* —2D **96**
Moat Hill Farm Dri. *Bat* —2D **96**
Modder Av. *Leeds* —7L **61**
Modder Pl. *A'ley* —7L **61**
Modd La. *H'frth* —4L **163**
Model Av. *Leeds* —7N **61**
Model Rd. *Leeds* —7N **61**
Model Ter. *Leeds* —7N **61**
Moderna Way. *Myth* —3A **90**
Moffat Clo. *B'frd* —6L **75**
Moffatt Clo. *Hal* —1L **91**
Moldgreen. —5A 132
Moles Head. *Gol* —4B **130**
Molly Hurst La. *Wool* —2H **153**
Mona's Ter. *Todm* —1H **107**
Mona St. *Slai* —9M **129**
Mona St. *Wake* —5G **118**
Monckton Dri. *C'frd* —6J **103**
*Monckton Ho. B'frd —3D **76***
(off Parkway)
Monckton Rd. *Wake* —9J **119**
Monckton Rd. Ind. Est. *Wake* —9J **11**
Mond Av. *B'frd* —5H **59**
Monk Barn Clo. *Bgly* —3F **38**
Monk Bri. Av. *Leeds* —9B **44**
Monk Bri. Dri. *Leeds* —9B **44**
Monk Bri. Gro. *Leeds* —9A **44**
Monk Bri. Mt. *Leeds* —9B **44**
Monk Bri. Pl. *Leeds* —9A **44**
Monk Bri. Rd. *Leeds* —9A **44**
Monk Bri. St. *Leeds* —9B **44**
Monk Bri. Ter. *Leeds* —9A **44**
Monkfield. *Mir* —5J **115**
Monkhill. —1K 123
Monkhill Av. *Pon* —1K **123**
Monkhill Dri. *Pon* —1K **123**
Monkhill La. *Pon* —8K **103**
Monkhill Mt. *Pon* —1K **123**
Monk Ings. *Birs* —3A **96**
Monk Ings Av. *Birs* —3N **95**
Monkmans Wharfe. *Sils* —8E **6**
Monk St. *B'frd* —7A **58**
Monk St. *Wake* —6M **119**
Monkswood. *Leeds* —9J **43**
Monkswood Av. *Leeds* —7A **46**
Monkswood Bank. *Leeds* —7A **46**
Monkswood Clo. *Leeds* —7A **46**
Monkswood Dri. *Leeds* —7A **46**
Monkswood Ga. *Leeds* —7B **46**
Monkswood Grn. *Leeds* —7A **46**
Monkswood Hill. *Leeds* —7A **46**
*Monkswood Ho. Leeds —2J **61***
(off Broad La.)
Monkswood Ri. *Leeds* —7A **46**
Monkswood Wlk. *Leeds* —7B **46**
Monkwood Rd. *Wake* —7K **99**
Monson Av. *C'ley* —9M **41**
Mons Rd. *Todm* —5H **87**

Montagu Av. *Leeds* —1K **63**
Montagu Ct. *Leeds* —9K **45**
Montagu Cres. *Leeds* —1L **63**
Montagu Dri. *Leeds* —9K **45**
Montague Ct. *Leeds* —7K **61**
Montague Cres. *Gar* —6A **66**
Montague Pl. *Gar* —7A **66**
Montague St. *B'frd* —2A **76**
Montague St. *Cud* —9K **155**
Montague St. *Sower B* —9G **91**
Montague St. *Wake* —8A **120**
Montagu Gdns. *Leeds* —1K **63**
Montagu Gro. *Leeds* —1L **63**
Montagu Pl. *Leeds* —1K **63**
Montagu Ri. *Leeds* —1L **63**
Montagu Rd. *Weth* —4A **18**
Montagu Vw. *Leeds* —1K **63**
Montcalm Cres. *Leeds* —3G **81**
Montcalm Cres. *Stan* —9A **100**
Monterey Dri. *All* —3E **56**
Montfort Clo. *H'fth* —4E **42**
Montgomery Ho. B'frd —5A ***58***
(off Trenton Dri.)
Mont Gro. B'frd —2A ***76***
(off Montague St.)
Montpelier Ter. *Leeds* —2C **62**
Montreal Av. *Leeds* —9F **44**
Montreal St. *Todm* —2J **107**
Montreal Ter. *Leeds* —6D **60**
Montrose Av. *Dart* —8H **153**
Montrose Pl. *Q'bry* —3B **74**
Montrose St. *B'frd* —2B **58**
Montserrat Rd. *B'frd* —4K **77**
Monument La. *Pon* —4L **123**
Monument M. *Pon* —4L **123**
Moody St. *B'frd* —9D **58**
Moon Clo. *Birs* —3C **96**
Moor Allerton. —4E 44
Moor Allerton Av. *Leeds* —5G **44**
Moor Allerton Cen. *Leeds* —5D **44**
Moor Allerton Cres. *Leeds* —5G **44**
Moor Allerton Dri. *Leeds* —5G **44**
Moor Allerton Gdns. *Leeds* —5F **44**
Moor Allerton Way. *Leeds* —5G **44**
Moor Av. *Cliff* —2D **32**
Moor Av. *Leeds* —7A **64**
Moor Av. *Stan* —6N **99**
Moor Bank. *B'frd* —6L **77**
Moorbank Ct. *Leeds* —1A **62**
Moorbottom. *Cleck* —6F **94**
Moorbottom. *Hon* —5L **147**
Moor Bottom. —4C 116
(nr. Ravensthorpe)
Moorbottom. —5F 94
(nr. Scholes)
Moor Bottom La. *Bgly* —4F **38**
Moor Bottom La. *Cra V* —7N **89**
Moor Bottom La. *G'lnd* —2N **111**
(in two parts)
Moor Bottom La. *Kei* —5H **37**
Moor Bottom La. *Sower B* —3G **111**
Moor Bottom Rd. *Hal* —7M **73**
Moorbottom Rd. *Hud* —6K **131**
Moor Bottom Rd. *Ripp* —6F **110**
Moorbrow. *H'frth* —6A **164**
Moor Clo. *Hud* —9H **131**
Moor Clo. *Leeds* —3F **80**
Moor Clo. Av. *Q'bry* —5B **74**
Moor Clo. Farm M. *Q'bry* —5B **74**
Moor Clo. Pde. *Q'bry* —4B **74**
Moor Clo. Rd. *Q'bry* —5B **74**
Moorcock Rd. *Blkhd* —7L **69**
Moor Cottage Clo. *Hud* —2J **147**
Moor Cres. *Leeds* —1E **80**
Moor Cres. Chase. *Leeds* —1E **80**
Moorcrest Ri. *M'well* —7K **153**
Moor Crest Rd. *Hud* —7H **131**
Moorcroft. *Bgly* —2G **39**
Moorcroft. *Dew* —2D **116**
Moor Cft. *Leeds* —3N **43**
Moorcroft Av. *B'frd* —5H **59**
Moorcroft Av. *Gol* —5C **130**
Moorcroft Av. *Oakw* —4E **36**
Moorcroft Dri. *Dew* —2C **116**
Moorcroft Dri. *E Bier* —4K **77**
Moorcroft Dri. *N Mill* —1B **164**
Moorcroft Pk. Dri. *N Mill* —1C **164**
Moorcroft Rd. *B'frd* —4K **77**
Moorcroft Rd. *Dew* —2C **116**
Moorcroft Ter. *B'frd* —4K **77**
Moor Dri. *Leeds* —9A **44**
Moor Dri. *Oakw* —4C **36**
Moor Dri. *Otley* —9A **12**
Moor Dri. *Pud* —9C **60**
Moore Av. *B'frd & Wibs* —2L **75**
Moor Edge. —5N 37
Moor Edge High Side. *H'den* —5N **37**
Moor Edge Low Side. *H'den* —5N **37**
Moorend. —4H 95
(nr. Cleckheaton)
Moor End. —6F 14
(nr. Dukeswick)
Moor End. —8H 73
(nr. Mixenden)
Moor End. —9E 40
(nr. Springfield)
Moor End. *B Spa* —9A **18**
Moor End Av. *Hal* —3J **91**
Moor End Gdns. *Hal* —3K **91**
Moor End La. *Dew* —1B **116**
Moor End La. *Norl* —1K **111**
(in two parts)
Moor End Rd. *Hal* —8H **73**
Moor End Rd. *Hud* —7K **131**
Moor End Vw. *Hal* —4L **91**
Moore St. *Kei* —1J **37**
Moore Vw. *B'frd* —2L **75**
Moor Farm Gdns. *Leeds* —8E **44**
Moorfield. *Gild* —6F **78**
Moorfield Av. *B'frd* —5H **59**
Moorfield Av. *Leeds* —6K **61**
Moorfield Av. *Men* —4D **24**
Moorfield Av. *Schol* —5C **94**
Moorfield Bus. Pk. *Yead* —1A **42**
Moorfield Clo. *Yead* —1A **42**
Moorfield Ct. *Yead* —1A **42**
Moorfield Cres. *Hems* —3C **156**
Moorfield Cres. *Leeds* —6K **61**
Moorfield Cres. *Pud* —8A **60**
Moorfield Cres. *Yead* —1N **41**
Moorfield Cft. *Yead* —1A **42**
Moorfield Dri. *Bail* —2A **40**
Moorfield Dri. *Oakw* —4D **36**
Moorfield Dri. *Yead* —1A **42**
Moorfield Gdns. *Pud* —8N **59**
Moorfield Gro. *Leeds* —6K **61**
Moorfield Gro. *Pud* —8N **59**
Moorfield Ind. Est. *Yead* —9A **26**
Moorfield Pl. *B'frd* —7F **40**
(in two parts)
Moorfield Pl. *Hems* —3C **156**
Moor Fld. Rd. *Bklnd* —2G **128**
Moorfield Rd. *Bgly* —8F **38**
Moorfield Rd. *Hud* —1N **131**
Moorfield Rd. *I'ly* —5L **9**
Moorfield Rd. *Leeds* —6K **61**
Moorfield Rd. *Yead* —1A **42**
Moorfields. *Bmly* —3F **60**
Moorfields. *Leeds* —5F **44**
Moorfield St. *A'ley* —6K **61**
Moorfield St. *Hal* —8N **91**
Moorfield St. *Leeds* —3C **62**
Moorfield Ter. *Yead* —9N **25**
Moorfield Vw. *Rbtwn* —2J **115**
Moorfield Way. *Schol* —5C **94**
Moor Flatts Av. *Leeds* —8E **80**
Moor Flatts Rd. *Leeds* —8E **80**
Moor Fold. *N Mill* —1C **164**
Moor Garforth. —7N 65
Moorgarth Av. *B'frd* —5H **59**
Moor Gate. —3A 84
Moorgate. *Bail* —3A **40**
Moor Ga. *Todm* —9L **87**
Moorgate Av. *B'frd* —5G **59**
Moorgate Av. *Kip* —2A **84**
Moorgate Clo. *Kip* —3A **84**
Moorgate Dri. *Kip* —3B **84**
Moorgate Ri. *Kip* —3A **84**
Moorgate Rd. *Kip* —2A **84**
Moorgate St. *Hal* —7M **91**
Moor Grange. Yead —1A ***42***
(off Victoria Av.)
Moor Grange Ct. *Leeds* —7J **43**
Moor Grange Dri. *Leeds* —7K **43**
Moor Grange Ri. *Leeds* —7K **43**
Moor Grange Vw. *Leeds* —7K **43**
Moor Gro. *Hal* —6H **75**
Moor Gro. *Pud* —9C **60**
Moor Gro. *Stan* —6N **99**
Moor Haven. *Leeds* —4C **44**
Moor Haven Ct. *Leeds* —4C **44**
Moor Head. —5E 78
(nr. Gildersome)
Moorhead. —8K 39
(nr. Shipley)
Moorhead Cres. *Shipl* —8K **39**
Moorhead La. *Shipl* —8K **39**
Moorhead Ter. *Shipl* —8K **39**
Moorhead Vs. *Morl* —4E **78**
Moor Hey La. *Ell* —6H **113**
Moor Hey La. *Holy G* —1L **129**
Moor Hey La. *Hud* —3L **129**
Moorhill. Holy G —9M ***111***
(off Thorn Hill Clo.)
Moor Hill Rd. *Hud* —2E **130**
Moorhouse. —8C 158
Moorhouse Av. *B'frd* —1E **58**
Moorhouse Av. *Leeds* —4B **80**
Moorhouse Av. *Stan* —5C **100**
Moorhouse Av. *Wake* —5J **119**
Moorhouse Clo. *Nor* —9K **101**
Moor Ho. Clo. *Oxe* —3C **54**
Moorhouse Clo. *Stan* —5C **100**
Moorhouse Common. —9A 158
Moor Ho. Ct. *Leeds* —3K **45**
Moorhouse Ct. *Oxe* —3C **54**
Moorhouse Ct. *S Elm* —8N **157**
Moorhouse Ct. M. *S Elm* —8N **157**
Moorhouse Cres. *Wake* —5J **119**
Moorhouse Dri. *B'shaw* —6K **77**
Moorhouse Gap. *Hamp* —8D **158**
Moorhouse Gro. *Stan* —5C **100**
Moorhouse La. *B'shaw* —6L **77**
Moorhouse La. *Haig* —4E **152**
Moorhouse La. *Hamp* —9B **158**
Moorhouse La. *Oxe* —2B **54**
Moorhouse La. *Wake* —6K **139**
Moorhouse Ter. *Stan* —6C **100**
Moorhouse Vw. *S Elm* —7A **158**
Moorhouse Vw. *Stan* —5C **100**
Moorings, The. *App B* —7H **41**
Moorings, The. *Leeds* —2K **81**
Moorings, The. *Wake* —6C **100**
Moor Knoll Clo. *E Ard* —4F **98**
Moor Knoll Dri. *E Ard* —4E **98**
Moor Knoll La. *E Ard* —3E **98**
Moorland Av. *Bail* —3B **40**
Moorland Av. *Bgly* —2H **39**
Moorland Av. *Gild* —5E **78**
Moorland Av. *Guis* —7J **25**
Moorland Av. *Leeds* —4B **62**
Moorland Av. *M'well* —7K **153**
Moorland Clo. *Gild* —5F **78**
Moorland Clo. *Hal* —1L **91**
Moorland Clo. *Leeds* —6F **44**
Moorland Clo. *Lint* —2D **146**
Moorland Cres. *Bail* —3B **40**
Moorland Cres. *Gild* —5E **78**
Moorland Cres. *Guis* —6J **25**
Moorland Cres. *Leeds* —6E **44**
Moorland Cres. *M'well* —7K **153**
Moorland Cres. *Men* —6G **24**
(nr. Bradford Rd.)
Moorland Cres. *Men* —3E **24**
(nr. Burley Rd.)
Moorland Cres. *Pud* —6L **59**
Moorland Dri. *B'shaw* —6M **77**
Moorland Dri. *Guis* —6J **25**
Moorland Dri. *Hall G* —8H **137**
Moorland Dri. *Leeds* —6E **44**
Moorland Dri. *Pud* —5L **59**
Moorland Gdns. *Leeds* —6F **44**
Moorland Gth. *Leeds* —6E **44**
Moorland Gro. *Leeds* —5E **44**
Moorland Gro. *Pud* —5L **59**
Moorland Ho. *Hud* —3G **146**
Moorland Ings. *Leeds* —6E **44**
Moorland Leys. *Leeds* —6E **44**
Moorland Mills. *Cleck* —3H **95**
Moorland Pl. *Low M* —8C **76**
Moorland Pl. *Stan* —5N **99**
Moorland Ri. *Leeds* —6E **44**
Moorland Ri. *Mel* —8B **146**
Moorland Rd. *B'hpe* —6E **26**
Moorland Rd. *Dlgtn* —7B **78**
Moorland Rd. *Leeds* —4B **62**
Moorland Rd. *Pud* —5L **59**
Moorlands. *H'frth* —5A **164**
(in two parts)
Moorlands. *I'ly* —7F **8**
Moorlands Av. *B'shaw* —6L **77**
Moorlands Av. *B'frd* —5H **59**
Moorlands Av. *Dew* —2E **116**
Moorlands Av. *Hal* —1L **91**
Moorlands Av. *Mir* —5K **115**
Moorlands Av. *Oakw* —3F **36**
Moorlands Av. *Oss* —3M **117**
Moorlands Av. *Yead* —1A **42**
Moorlands Av. N. *Dew* —2E **116**
Moorlands Av. W. *Dew* —2E **116**
Moorlands Clo. *Dew* —9C **96**
Moorlands Ct. *G'lnd* —3A **112**
Moorlands Ct. *Weth* —4N **17**
Moorlands Cres. *Hal* —1L **91**
Moorlands Cres. *Hud* —1C **130**
Moorlands Dri. *Hal* —2L **91**
Moorlands Dri. *Yead* —1A **42**
Moorlands Ind. Cen. *Cleck* —3H **95**
Moorlands Pl. *Hal* —7A **92**
Moorlands Rd. *B'shaw* —6L **77**
Moorlands Rd. *Dew* —3E **116**
Moorlands Rd. *G'lnd* —3A **112**
Moorlands Rd. *Hud* —1C **130**
Moorlands, The. *B Spa* —9C **18**
Moorlands, The. *Leeds* —3G **44**
Moorlands, The. *Weth* —4N **17**
Moorlands Vw. *Hal* —7A **92**
Moorlands Vw. *Weth* —4N **17**
Moorland Ter. *Gar* —8M **65**
Moorland Ter. *Kei* —1M **37**
Moorland Vw. *Clay W* —7K **151**
Moorland Vw. *Eml* —2D **150**
Moorland Vw. *Leeds* —5E **44**
Moorland Vw. *Low M* —8C **76**
Moorland Vw. *Rod* —2E **60**
Moorland Vw. *Sower B* —9F **90**
Moorland Vw. *Wilsd* —2C **56**
Moorland Villa. *Sower B* —2F **110**
Moorland Wlk. *Leeds* —5E **44**
Moor La. *Add* —9J **5**
Moor La. *Askw* —3E **10**
(in two parts)
Moor La. *B'shaw & Gom* —9N **77**
Moor La. *B Mon* —6L **15**
Moor La. *B Spa* —4D **18**
Moor La. *B'ham* —2N **31**
Moor La. *Brier* —8D **156**
Moor La. *Bur W* —1A **24**
Moor La. *C'ton* —7K **123**
Moor La. *C'den* —6L **69**
(in two parts)
Moor La. *Ebrn* —3A **20**
(in two parts)
Moor La. *E Hard* —7N **123**
Moor La. *E Kes* —2A **30**
Moor La. *Far T* —4C **148**
Moor La. *Guis* —5J **25**
Moor La. *Hal* —9L **73**
Moor La. *H'frth* —9H **147**
Moor La. *Hud* —2H **147**
Moor La. *Kbtn* —1J **149**
Moor La. *Men* —3B **24**
Moor La. *Slai* —3L **145**
Moor La. *Stut* —8M **33**
Moor La. *Todm* —9K **87**
Moor La. *Upt* —2M **157**
Moor La. *Went* —8N **123**
Moorlea Dri. *Bail* —4B **40**
Moorleigh Clo. *Kip* —3B **84**
Moorleigh Dri. *Kip* —3B **84**
Moor Lodge Cvn. Pk. *Leeds* —7B **30**
Moor Pk. Av. *Hud* —9H **131**
Moor Pk. Av. *Leeds* —9N **43**
Moor Pk. Clo. *Add* —1K **7**
Moor Pk. Clo. *B'frd* —6G **59**
Moor Pk. Ct. *Dew* —2H **117**
Moor Pk. Cres. *Add* —1K **7**
Moor Pk. Dri. *Add* —1K **7**
Moor Pk. Dri. *B'frd* —6H **59**
Moor Pk. Dri. *Leeds* —9N **43**
Moor Pk. Gdns. *Dew* —3H **117**
Moor Pk. Gro. *Add* —1L **7**
Moor Pk. La. *Dew* —3H **117**
Moor Pk. Mt. *Leeds* —9N **43**
Moor Pk. Rd. *B'frd* —6G **59**
Moor Pk. Vs. *Leeds* —9A **44**
Moor Pk. Way. *Add* —1L **7**
Moor Rd. *B Spa* —1C **32**
Moor Rd. *B'hpe* —5G **27**
Moor Rd. *F'stne* —6D **122**
Moor Rd. *H'let* —1E **80**
(in two parts)
Moor Rd. *Leeds* —9N **43**
Moor Rd. *L'boro* —9L **107**
Moor Rd. *Stan* —6N **99**
Moor Royd. *Hal* —8N **91**
Moor Royd. *Hon* —6K **147**
Moorroyd St. *Oss* —3M **117**
Moors Cen., The. I'ly —5G ***8***
(off S. Hawksworth St.)
Moorshutt Rd. *Hems* —3C **156**
Moor Side. —4G 58
(nr. Bradford)
Moorside. —2F 60
(nr. Bramley)
Moorside. —8C 78
(nr. Drighlington)
Moor Side. —8A 76
(nr. Wyke)
Moor Side. *B Spa* —9B **18**
Moorside. *Cleck* —6E **94**
(in two parts)
Moorside. *D Hill* —4K **57**
Moorside App. *Dlgtn* —8C **78**
Moorside Av. *B'shaw* —6L **77**
Moorside Av. *B'frd* —4G **59**
Moorside Av. *Dew* —1C **116**
Moorside Av. *Dlgtn* —8C **78**
Moorside Av. *Ebrn* —3A **20**
Moorside Av. *Hud* —6J **131**
Moorside Clo. *B'frd* —3G **58**
Moorside Clo. *Dlgtn* —8C **78**
Moorside Clo. *M'well* —9K **153**
Moorside Cres. *Dew* —1C **116**
Moorside Cres. *Dlgtn* —8B **78**
Moorside Cres. *Hall G* —8H **137**
Moorside Cft. *B'frd* —4G **59**
Moorside Dri. *Dlgtn* —8C **78**
Moorside Dri. *Leeds* —2F **60**
Moorside Edge. —7L 129
Moorside End. *Dew* —1C **116**
Moorside Gdns. *B'frd* —3G **59**
Moorside Gdns. *Dlgtn* —8C **78**
Moorside Gdns. *Hal* —9M **73**
Moorside Grn. *Dlgtn* —8C **78**
Moorside Ho. Wilsd —2B ***56***
(off Crooke La.)
Moorside La. *Add* —5L **7**
Moorside La. *Askw* —2D **10**
Moorside La. *B'frd* —7H **59**
Moor Side La. *Oxe* —1N **53**
Moor Side La. *Slai* —7K **129**
Moorside Maltings. *Leeds* —1E **80**
Moorside M. *B'frd* —3G **59**
Moorside Mt. *Dlgtn* —8B **78**
Moorside Paddock. *Cleck* —6F **94**
Moorside Pde. *Dlgtn* —8C **78**
Moorside Pl. *B'frd* —7H **59**
Moorside Pl. *Dew* —1C **116**
Moorside Ri. *Cleck* —5F **94**
Moorside Rd. *B'frd* —2G **58**
Moorside Rd. *Dew* —1C **116**
Moorside Rd. *Dlgtn* —8B **78**
Moorside Rd. *Hon* —6K **147**
Moorside Rd. *Hud* —9G **114**
Moorside Rd. *Wilsd* —2B **56**
Moorside St. *Leeds* —2F **60**
Moorside St. *Low M* —7N **75**
Moorside Ter. *B'frd* —4H **59**
Moorside Ter. *Dlgtn* —8C **78**
Moorside Ter. *Leeds* —2F **60**
Moorside Va. *Dlgtn* —7C **78**
Moorside Vw. *Dlgtn* —8C **78**
Moorside Wlk. *Dlgtn* —7C **78**
Moor Stone Pl. *She* —8H **75**
Moor St. *Oakw* —4D **36**
Moor St. *Q'bry* —4D **74**
Moor Ter. B'frd —5G ***58***
(off Glenmore Clo.)
Moorthorpe. —6L 157
Moorthorpe Av. *B'frd* —5H **59**
Moor Top. —3J 115
(nr. Liversedge)
Moor Top. —7N 75
(nr. Wyke)
Moor Top. *Dlgtn* —7A **78**
(in two parts)
Moor Top. *Leeds* —4F **78**
Moor Top. *Men & Guis* —3H **25**
Moor Top. *Mir* —5J **115**
Moor Top Av. *Ackw* —5E **140**
Moor Top Av. *Thur* —7D **148**
Moor Top Dri. *Hems* —4D **156**
Moor Top Gdns. *Hal* —5L **73**
Moor Top La. *Floc M* —9A **134**
Moor Top Rd. *Hal* —4H **91**
Moor Top Rd. *Hud* —9G **114**
Moor Top Rd. *Low M* —7N **75**
Moortown. —4F 44
Moortown Corner. *Leeds* —5F **44**
Moor Vw. *A'ley* —7L **61**
Moor Vw. *B'frd* —6L **77**
Moor Vw. *Crig* —5H **137**
Moor Vw. Head —3B ***62***
(off Hyde Pk. Rd.)
Moor Vw. *Heck* —1B **116**
Moor Vw. *Leeds* —9C **62**
Moor Vw. *Mel* —6B **146**
Moor Vw. *Meth* —1N **101**
Moor Vw. *Mir* —2L **115**
Moor Vw. Av. *Shipl* —7M **39**
Moor Vw. Clo. *C'frd* —5F **102**
Moor Vw. Ct. *Sandb* —9B **22**
Moor Vw. Cres. *Bgly* —9D **38**
Moorview Cft. *Men* —3D **24**
Moorview Dri. *Bgly* —9D **38**
Moorview Dri. *Shipl* —8D **40**
Moorview Gro. *Kei* —2K **37**
Moor Vw. Ter. *Stanb* —8L **35**
Moorville Av. *B'frd* —5H **59**
Moorville Clo. *Leeds* —1D **80**
Moorville Ct. *Leeds* —1D **80**
Moorville Dri. *B'shaw* —6L **77**
Moorville Gro. *Leeds* —1C **80**
Moorville Rd. *Leeds* —1D **80**
Moorway. *Guis* —7F **24**
Moor Way. *Oakw* —4C **36**
Moorwell Pl. *B'frd* —2G **58**
Moravian Pl. *B'frd* —1B **76**
Morden Ho. B'frd —7E ***58***
(off Bolton St.)
Morefield Bank. *H'frth* —9A **148**
Moresby Rd. *B'frd* —7K **75**
Moresdale La. *Leeds* —3A **64**
Moreton Ho. B'frd —6E ***58***
(off Avenham Way.)
Morley. —1L 97
Morley Av. *B'frd* —5H **59**
Morley Av. *Knot* —8F **104**
Morley Bottoms. *Morl* —8K **79**
Morley Carr. —8B 76
Morley Carr Rd. *Low M* —8B **76**
Morley Fold. *Den D* —3C **166**
Morley Hall La. *L'ft* —6C **90**
Morley Hole. —8J 79
Morley La. *Hud* —6F **130**
Morley Mkt. Morl —9K ***79***
(off Queen St.)
Morley St. *B'frd* —8B **58**
Morley Vw. *Hal* —9D **92**
Morningside. *B'frd* —5N **57**
Morningside. *Denh* —4K **55**
Morning St. *Kei* —3H **37**
Mornington Rd. *Bgly* —4F **38**

Mornington Rd. I'ly —5H 9
Mornington St. Kei —8H 21
Mornington Vs. B'frd —5B 58
Morpeth Pl. Leeds —7G 62
Morpeth St. B'frd —7A 58
Morpeth St. Q'bry —4D 74
Morrell Cres. Wren —9H 99
Morris Av. Leeds —1K 61
Morris Clo. Kin —8B 140
Morris Gro. Leeds —2K 61
Morris La. Leeds —1K 61
Morris Mt. Kirks —2K 61
Morrison St. C'frd —5E 102
Morris Pl. Morl —8J 79
Morris Vw. Leeds —2K 61
Morritt Av. Leeds —5C 64
Morritt Dri. Leeds —6A 64
Morritt Gro. Leeds —6A 64
Mortimer Av. Bat —7C 96
Mortimer Av. B'frd —5H 59
Mortimer Clo. Gar —8M 65
Mortimer Clo. Oss —5B 118
Mortimer Row. B'frd —7H 59
Mortimer Row. Horb —1B 136
Mortimer St. Bat —7C 96
Mortimer St. B'frd —6L 57
Mortimer St. Cleck —5H 95
Mortimer Ter. Bat —7C 96
Morton Cres. C'frd —5F 102
Morton Grn. Hud —6E 132
Morton Gro. Dew —8E 116
Morton Gro. E Mor —8C 22
Morton La. E Mor —8C 22
Morton Pde. Wake —5J 119
Morton Rd. B'frd —9H 59
Mortons Clo. Sid —9D 92
Morton Ter. Guis —7H 25
Morton Way. Hud —1D 130
Morton Wood Gro. H'frth —5B 164
Morvern Meadows. Hems —2F 156
Morwick Gro. Scholes —9G 46
Moselden La. Rish —5C 128
Moseley Pl. Leeds —3D 62
Moseley Wood App. Leeds —3G 42
Moseley Wood Av. Leeds —1G 43
Moseley Wood Bank. Leeds —2G 42
Moseley Wood Clo. Leeds —3G 42
Moseley Wood Cres. Leeds —3G 42
Moseley Wood Cft. Leeds —3F 42
Moseley Wood Dri. Leeds —2G 42
Moseley Wood Gdns. Leeds —2G 42
Moseley Wood Grn. Leeds —2G 42
Moseley Wood Gro. Leeds —2G 42
Moseley Wood La. Leeds —2H 43
Moseley Wood Ri. Leeds —2G 42
Moseley Wood Vw. Leeds —2H 43
Moseley Wood Wlk. Leeds —3G 42
Moseley Wood Way. Leeds —1G 43
Moser Av. B'frd —1E 58
Moser Cres. B'frd —1E 58
Mosley Ho. B'frd —9H 59
(off Parsonage Rd.)
Mosley La. Shel —6N 149
Moss Bri. Rd. Leeds —1C 60
Moss Bldgs. Cleck —4H 95
Moss Carr Av. Kei —2M 37
Moss Carr Gro. Kei —2M 37
Moss Carr Rd. Kei —2M 37
Mosscar St. B'frd —7E 58
Moss Cotts. Leeds —3N 43
Mossdale Av. B'frd —3H 57
Moss Dri. Hal —7L 73
Moss Edge Rd. H'frth —8H 163
Moss Fld. B'frd —7D 58
Moss Gdns. Leeds —2C 44
Moss Grn. Men —4E 24
Moss Hall La. Blkhd —9N 69
Moss La. Hal —7L 73
Moss La. H Bri —9H 71
Mosslea. Chur —6L 79
Moss Mans. Bat —3C 96
Moss Mt. I'ly —5G 8
Moss Pl. Swil —4H 83
Moss Ri. H'frth —3K 163
Moss Ri. Leeds —2C 44
Moss Ri. Mean —9B 44
Moss Rd. Leeds —1H 63
Moss Row. Wilsd —9B 38
Moss Side. B'frd —4K 57
Moss Side St. S'fth —6A 106
Moss St. C'frd —4B 102
Moss St. Cro R —7E 36
Moss St. Gild —6G 78
Moss St. Hud —6N 131
Moss St. T'tn —7B 56
Moss Syke. S'cft —8D 30
Mosstree Clo. Q'bry —3B 74
Moss Valley. Leeds —2C 44
Mossy Bank Clo. Q'bry —3D 74
Mostyn Gro. B'frd —5M 75
Mostyn M. Hal —1N 91
Mostyn Vs. Bat —6G 96
Mostyn Wlk. Hall G —7H 137
Moth Hole La. Hept —5M 69
Motley La. Guis —6J 25
Motley Row. Guis —6J 25
(off Motley La.)
Mouldson Pl. Bklnd —5J 111
Moule Ri. Gar —5B 66
Moulson Ct. B'frd —2C 76
Moulson Ter. Denh —6K 55
Mount. —1D 130
Mountain. —3B 74
Mountain Cres. Dew —9G 116
Mountain Rd. Dew —9G 116
Mountain Vw. Hal —7N 73
Mountain Vw. Shipl —9B 40
Mountain Way. Hud —3G 133
Mount Av. Bat —9G 96
(off Mount St.)
Mount Av. B'frd —1F 58
Mount Av. Grime —9A 156
Mount Av. Hal —5J 91
Mount Av. Heck —6B 96
Mount Av. Hems —1D 156
Mount Av. Hud —1C 130
Mount Av. Wren —8H 99
Mountbatten Av. Out —7L 99
Mountbatten Av. S'dal —3N 137
Mountbatten Ct. B'frd —3C 76
Mountbatten Cres. Wake —8L 99
Mountbatten Gdns. Oakes —3G 131
Mountbatten Gro. Wake —8M 99
Mt. Cliffe Vw. Morl —6L 79
Mount Cres. Cleck —4H 95
Mount Cres. Hal —5J 91
Mount Cres. Wake —8H 119
Mount Dri. Leeds —1D 44
Mountfield Av. Hud —5F 132
Mountfield Rd. Hud —5F 132
Mountfields. Hal —4K 93
Mountfields. Leeds —5B 62
(off Clarendon Rd.)
Mountfields Wlk. S Kirk —8H 157
Mount Gdns. Cleck —4H 95
Mount Gdns. Leeds —1D 44
Mount Gro. B'frd —1F 58
Mountjoy Rd. Hud —3K 131
Mount La. Brigh —4K 113
Mount La. Todm —1E 86
Mountleigh Clo. Euro I —7E 76
Mt. Pellon. Hal —4M 91
Mt. Pellon Rd. Hal —4L 91
Mt. Pisgah. Otley —1L 25
Mount Pl. Shipl —7M 39
Mount Pleasant. —9F 96
(nr. Batley)
Mount Pleasant. —5B 84
(nr. Kippax)
Mt. Pleasant. Ackw —4F 140
Mt. Pleasant. Add —1M 7
Mt. Pleasant. Bmly —2E 60
Mt. Pleasant. Brigh —5K 113
Mt. Pleasant. Butt —6K 75
Mt. Pleasant. C'frd —6F 102
Mt. Pleasant. Denh —6K 55
Mt. Pleasant. Dew —4H 117
Mt. Pleasant. Eml —2G 150
Mt. Pleasant. Grime —9A 156
Mt. Pleasant. Guis —6J 25
Mt. Pleasant. Hud —7L 131
Mt. Pleasant. I'ly —6H 9
Mt. Pleasant. Kip —5B 84
Mt. Pleasant. Leeds —8E 80
Mt. Pleasant. Ripp —7E 110
Mt. Pleasant. Sandb —9B 22
Mt. Pleasant. Wake —9B 120
Mt. Pleasant Av. Hal —4A 92
Mt. Pleasant Av. Leeds —1H 63
Mt. Pleasant Ct. Pud —6B 60
Mt. Pleasant Dri. Myth —3M 89
Mt. Pleasant Gdns. Kip —5B 84
Mt. Pleasant Gdns. Leeds —1H 63
(off Mt. Pleasant Av.)
Mt. Pleasant La. Fen B —6G 133
Mt. Pleasant Rd. Pud —6B 60
Mt. Pleasant St. F'stne —5D 122
Mt. Pleasant St. Hud —4B 132
Mt. Pleasant St. Pud —6C 60
Mt. Pleasant St. Q'bry —4D 74
Mt. Pleasant St. Todm —3C 86
Mt. Pleasant Vw. Todm —7K 87
Mt. Preston St. Leeds —5C 62
Mount Ri. Leeds —1D 44
Mount Rd. B'frd —1G 58
Mount Rd. Grime —9A 156
Mount Rd. Mars —8B 144
Mount Rd. Mar —4J 131
Mount Rd. Stan —6A 100
Mount Rd. Wibs —4M 75
Mt. Royal. Holy G —1M 129
Mt. Royal. H'fth —7E 42
Mt. Royd. B'frd —4B 58
Mt. Scar Vw. Sch —4B 164
Mount St. Bat —9G 96
Mount St. B'frd —8E 58
Mount St. Cleck —4H 95
Mount St. Cow —6F 130
Mount St. Eccl —1F 58
Mount St. Hal —5B 92
Mount St. Kei —9H 21
Mount St. Lock —7L 131
Mount St. Sower B —8H 91
Mt. Street W. Hal —4L 91
Mount Tabor. —1G 90
Mt. Tabor Rd. Hal —8F 72
Mt. Tabor St. Pud —7N 59
Mount Ter. Bat —9F 96
Mount Ter. B'frd —1F 58
Mount Ter. Hal —3L 91
Mount Ter. L'ft —3C 90
Mount, The. Alw —1D 44
Mount, The. Bar E —9L 47
Mount, The. Birs —2B 96
Mount, The. C'frd —5J 103
Mount, The. Kip —4A 84
Mount, The. Leeds —5C 64
Mount, The. Nor —1J 121
Mount, The. Pon —3J 123
Mount, The. Rothw —6A 82
Mount, The. Todm —6L 87
Mount, The. Wake —8H 119
Mount, The. Wren —2F 118
Mt. Vernon Rd. Rawd —3N 41
Mount Vw. Bgly —4G 38
Mount Vw. Hal —1G 91
Mount Vw. Morl —6L 79
Mount Vw. Oakw —5B 36
Mount Vw. Q'bry —4C 74
Mt. View Rd. N Mill —6C 164
Mount Wlk. C'frd —6D 102
Mt. Zion Rd. Hud —4A 132
Mourning Fld. La. Pon —7C 142
Mouse Hole La. Mir —1A 134
Moverley Flats. Pon —4L 123
Mowat Ct. Liv —7F 94
Mowbray Chase. W'ford —6C 82
Mowbray Clo. Cull —1J 55
Mowbray Ct. Leeds —3B 64
Mowbray Cres. Leeds —3B 64
Moxon Clo. Pon —5K 123
Moxon Gro. Wake —9K 99
Moxon Pl. Wake —6E 118
Moxon Sq. Wake —4M 119
(in two parts)
Moxon St. Wake —8L 99
Moxon Way. Wake —8L 99
Mozeley Dri. Hal —7M 73
Muckey La. Skelb —4G 158
Mucky La. Ell —7C 112
Muddy La. Lntn —7J 17
Muffit La. Gom & Heck —4N 95
Muff St. B'frd —9F 58
Muff Ter. B'frd —4M 75
Mug Mill La. Dew —2H 135
Muir Ct. Leeds —2N 61
(off St Michael's Gro.)
Muirfield Av. F'stne —2C 122
Muirfield Clo. Cud —8K 155
Muirfield Dri. Wake —9J 119
Muirfields, The. Dart —8J 153
Muirhead Dri. B'frd —3J 77
Muirlands, The. Hud —6C 114
Mulberry Av. Leeds —3N 43
Mulberry Av. Ryh —9J 139
Mulberry Gdns. Meth —2J 101
Mulberry Gth. Leeds —4A 44
Mulberry Gth. Thor A —8E 18
Mulberry Ho. C'frd —5E 102
(off Parklands)
Mulberry Pl. Ryh —9J 139
Mulberry Ri. Leeds —3N 43
Mulberry St. Hud —5A 132
Mulberry St. Kei —8K 21
Mulberry St. Pud —7B 60
Mulberry Vw. Leeds —4N 43
Mulcture Hall Rd. Hal —5C 92
Mulehouse La. Hud —1A 130
Mulgrave St. B'frd —8F 58
Mullins Ct. Leeds —7H 63
Mumford St. B'frd —2C 76
Munby St. B'frd —7K 57
Muncaster Rd. Gar —6B 66
Munster St. B'frd —2F 76
Munton Clo. B'frd —7K 75
Murdoch St. Kei —8M 21
Murdstone Clo. B'frd —2C 76
Murgatroyd St. B'frd —3C 76
(in two parts)
Murgatroyd St. Shipl —7N 39
Murking La. Hept —7E 70
Murray Rd. Hud —2L 131
Murray St. B'frd —2A 76
Murton Clo. Leeds —2B 64
Museum Ct. B'frd —4G 58
Museum St. Leeds —5H 63
Musgrave Bank. Leeds —4H 61
Musgrave Bldgs. Pud —6C 60
Musgrave Ct. Wake —6F 118
Musgrave Dri. B'frd —4G 59
Musgrave Gro. B'frd —4G 59
Musgrave Mt. B'frd —4G 59
Musgrave Mt. Leeds —4H 61
Musgrave Ri. Leeds —4H 61
Musgrave Rd. B'frd —4G 58
Musgrave St. Bat —3B 96
Musgrave Vw. Leeds —4H 61
Mushroom St. Leeds —5F 62
Musselburgh St. B'frd —7A 58
Mutton La. All —4C 56
Myers Av. B'frd —2E 58
Myers Ct. Kbtn —3G 148
Myers Cft. Hud —4D 132
Myers Cft. Otley —1L 25
Myers La. B'frd —2E 58
Myrtle Av. Bgly —5E 38
Myrtle Av. Dew —6B 116
Myrtle Av. Hal —9L 73
Myrtle Ct. Bgly —5E 38
Myrtle Dri. Cro R —6F 36
Myrtle Dri. Hal —9L 73
Myrtle Gdns. Hal —9L 73
Myrtle Gro. Bgly —5E 38
Myrtle Gro. Hal —9L 73
Myrtle Gro. Hud —4G 130
Myrtle Gro. Q'bry —6B 74
Myrtle Pl. Bgly —4E 38
Myrtle Pl. Hal —9L 73
Myrtle Pl. Shipl —7L 39
Myrtle Rd. Dew —6B 116
Myrtle Rd. Ell —6E 112
Myrtle Rd. Gol —6C 130
Myrtle St. Bgly —4F 38
Myrtle St. B'frd —8G 58
Myrtle St. Hud —3N 131
Myrtle St. Todm —7K 87
Myrtle Vw. Oakw —4D 36
Myrtle Wlk. Bgly —4E 38
(off Ferncliffe Rd.)
Myson Av. Pon —8M 103
Mytholm. —9F 70
Mytholm Bank. H Bri —1F 88
Mytholm Bridge. —8A 148
Mytholm Clo. H Bri —1G 88
Mytholm Ct. H Bri —1F 88
Mytholmes. —7C 36
Mytholmes La. Haw —8C 36
(in two parts)
Mytholmroyd. —3M 89

Nab. —5J 115
Nabbs La. Slai —1M 145
Nab Cres. Mel —7B 146
Nabcroft La. Hud —6J 131
Nabcroft Ri. Hud —6J 131
Nab End Rd. G'lnd —4C 112
Nab La. Birs —2D 96
(in two parts)
Nab La. Mir —5J 115
Nab La. Shipl —8J 39
Nab, The. Mir —5J 115
Naburn App. Leeds —6C 46
Naburn Chase. Leeds —8D 46
Naburn Clo. Leeds —8D 46
Naburn Ct. Leeds —7C 46
Naburn Dri. Leeds —8C 46
Naburn Fold. Leeds —8D 46
Naburn Gdns. Leeds —8C 46
Naburn Grn. Leeds —8C 46
Naburn Pl. Leeds —7C 46
Naburn Rd. Leeds —8C 46
Naburn Vw. Leeds —8D 46
Naburn Wlk. Leeds —8C 46
Nab Vw. Sils —6F 6
Nab Water La. Oxe —8B 54
Nab Wood. —8J 39
Nab Wood Bank. Shipl —8J 39
Nab Wood Clo. Shipl —8K 39
Nab Wood Cres. Shipl —8J 39
Nab Wood Dri. Shipl —9J 39
Nab Wood Gdns. Shipl —8K 39
Nab Wood Gro. Shipl —8J 39
Nab Wood Mt. Shipl —8J 39
Nab Wood Pl. Shipl —8J 39
Nab Wood Ri. Shipl —8J 39
Nab Wood Rd. Shipl —9J 39
Nab Wood Ter. Shipl —8J 39
Nairn Clo. Hud —8H 131
Nancroft Cres. Leeds —7M 61
Nancroft Mt. Leeds —7M 61
Nancroft Ter. Leeds —7M 61
Nanny Goat La. Gar —6M 65
Nansen Av. Leeds —4E 60
Nansen Gro. Leeds —4E 60
Nansen Mt. Leeds —4E 60
Nansen Pl. Leeds —4E 60
Nansen St. Leeds —4D 60
Nansen Ter. Leeds —4E 60
Nansen Vw. Leeds —4E 60
Naomi Rd. New —8M 131
Napier Ho. Todm —3J 107
(off Scott St.)
Napier Rd. B'frd —7H 59
Napier Rd. Ell —5D 112
Napier St. B'frd —7H 59
Napier St. Kei —1K 37
Napier St. Q'bry —4E 74
Napier Ter. B'frd —7H 59
Naples St. B'frd —5N 57
Nares St. Cro R —7E 36
Nares St. Kei —9H 21
Narrow La. H'den —6A 38
Narrows, The. H'den —6A 38
Naseby Gdns. Leeds —6G 62
Naseby Gth. Leeds —6G 62
Naseby Grange. Leeds —6G 62
(off Naseby Gdns.)
Naseby Ho. B'frd —4K 77
Naseby Pl. Leeds —6G 62
Naseby Ri. Q'bry —4E 74
Naseby Ter. Leeds —6G 63
Naseby Vw. Leeds —6G 62
Naseby Wlk. Leeds —6G 63
Nashville Rd. Kei —1G 37
Nashville St. Kei —1G 37
Nashville Ter. Kei —1G 37
(off Nashville Rd.)
Nassau Pl. Leeds —3G 62
Nathan La. Sower B —4C 110
Nathans Folly. Sower B —4D 110
National Museum of Photography, Film & T.V. —8C 5
National Rd. Hun P —9G 63
National Waterhouse Homes. Hal
(off Harrison Rd.) —6B 9
Nat La. Huby —4K 13
Navigation Gdns. Dew —7E 116
Navigation Rd. C'frd —3D 102
Navigation Rd. Dew —7E 116
Navigation Rd. Hal —6C 92
Navigation Wlk. Leeds —7E 62
Navigation Yd. Wake —6M 119
Navvy La. Ryh —2E 154
Naylor Gth. Leeds —1B 62
Naylor La. Hal —4C 90
Naylor Pl. Leeds —1D 80
Naylor St. Dew —1E 116
Naylor St. Hal —5M 91
Naylor St. Oss —3M 117
Naze Rd. Todm —1H 107
Naze Vw. Todm —9H 87
Neale Rd. Hud —7L 131
Neale St. H Bri —2H 89
Neal Pl. Leeds —8F 62
Neal St. B'frd —8C 58
Neap La. Mel —7D 146
Near Bank. Shel —6M 149
Nearcliffe Rd. B'frd —4M 57
Near Crook. Thack —6D 40
Near Peat La. Oxe —7A 54
Near Royd. Oven —1N 91
Neath Gdns. Leeds —3M 63
Necropolis Rd. B'frd —9L 57
Ned Hill Rd. Hal —3L 73
Ned La. B'frd —1J 77
Ned La. Slai —1M 145
Needless Inn La. W'ford —6D 82
Neiley. —5N 147
Nell Gap Av. M'twn —3K 135
Nell Gap Cres. Ove —4K 135
Nell Gap La. Ove —3K 135
(in three parts)
Nelson Ct. I'ly —5G 9
(off Nelson Rd.)
Nelson Ct. Morl —2J 97
Nelson Cft. Gar —9L 65
Nelson Pl. Morl —8K 79
(off S. Nelson St.)
Nelson Pl. Q'bry —4D 74
Nelson Pl. Sower B —8K 91
Nelson Rd. I'ly —5G 9
Nelson St. All —5H 57
Nelson St. Bat —7D 96
Nelson St. Birs —3C 96
Nelson St. B'frd —8C 58
Nelson St. Cro R —7E 36
(nr. Albion St.)
Nelson St. Cro R —7E 36
(nr. East Ter., in two parts)
Nelson St. Dew —3F 116
Nelson St. Hud —6L 131
Nelson St. Liv —9M 95
Nelson St. Nor —9K 101
Nelson St. Otley —1L 25
Nelson St. Q'bry —4D 74
Nelson St. S Hien —4M 155
Nelson St. Sower B —8J 91
Nelson St. Todm —3J 107
Nene St. B'frd —1A 76
Nepshaw La. Gild —9G 79
Nepshaw La. Morl —8J 79
Nepshaw La. N. Gild —8H 79

epshaw La. S. Gild —8H 79
eptune St. Leeds —7F 62
esfield. —2B 8
esfield Clo. Leeds —7H 81
esfield Cres. Leeds —7H 81
esfield Gdns. Leeds —7G 81
esfield Gth. Leeds —7G 81
esfield Grn. Leeds —7G 81
esfield La. Nesf —1B 8
esfield Rd. I'ly —4E 8
esfield Rd. Leeds —7G 81
esfield St. B'frd —6B 58
esfield Vw. I'ly —5D 8
esfield Vw. Leeds —7G 81
esfield Wlk. Leeds —7G 81
essfield Dri. Kei —2F 36
essfield Gro. Kei —2F 36
essfield Rd. Kei —2F 36
est Est. H Bri —3L 89
estfield Clo. Pon —9K 103
est La. H Bri —4L 89
eston Way. Oss —2N 117
etherby St. B'frd —7F 58
ethercliffe Cres. Guis —6H 25
ethercliffe Rd. Guis —6H 25
ether Clo. Hud —2C 132
ether Cres. Hud —2C 132
etherdale Ct. Weth —3A 18
etherend Rd. Slai —9M 129
etherfield Av. Neth —4N 135
etherfield Clo. C'frd —7N 101
etherfield Clo. Kbtn —3K 149
etherfield Clo. Yead —9M 25
etherfield Ct. Guis —7H 25
(off Netherfield Rd.)
etherfield Cres. Neth —5N 135
etherfield Dri. Guis —6H 25
etherfield Dri. H'frth —1M 163
etherfield Pl. Cleck —5J 95
etherfield Pl. Neth —4N 135
etherfield Ri. Guis —7H 25
etherfield Rd. Dew —6B 116
etherfield Rd. Guis —6H 25
etherfield Ter. Guis —7H 25
(off Netherfield Rd.)
etherfield Ter. Yead —9M 25
ether Hall Av. Hud —2C 132
etherhall Rd. Bail —4B 40
etherhouses. H'frth —3J 163
etherlands Av. B'frd —6A 76
etherlands Sq. Low M —7B 76
ether La. H'frth —5A 162
etherlea Dri. H'frth —9L 147
etherley —7F 144
etherley Brow. Oss —8A 118
etherley Dri. Mars —7E 144
ether Moor Rd. Hud —1G 147
ether Moor Vw. Bgly —4F 38
etheroyd. S'hse —6K 121
etheroyd Ct. Shar C —7J 121
etheroyd Hill. —8M 113
etheroyd Hill Rd. Hud —8M 113
ether St. Fars —3A 60
etherthong. —9L 147
etherthong Rd. Mel —9E 146
etherton. —3E 148
nr. Brockholes)
etherton. —2H 147
nr. Honley)
etherton. —4N 135
nr. Middlestown)
etherton Fold. Hud —3H 147
therton Hall Dri. Neth —4N 135
therton Hall Gdns. Neth —4A 136
therton La. Horb —4N 135
therton Moor. —3K 147
therton Moor Rd. Hud —2J 147
thertown. —6D 78
therwood Clo. Hud —8M 113
therwood Heys. —3G 144
therwood La. Mars —3G 144
ther Yeadon. —3M 41
ttle Gro. Hal —3F 92
ttle La. Wake —4M 119
ttleton Av. Mir —6K 115
ttleton Clo. B'frd —3B 78
ttleton Ct. Leeds —6E 64
ttleton Hill. —4A 130
ttleton Hill Rd. Gol —4A 130
ttleton Ho. Hems —3D 156
off Lilley St.)
ttleton Rd. Hud —2E 132
ttleton Rd. Mir —6K 115
ttleton St. Oss —5M 117
ttleton St. Stan —6C 100
ttleton Ter. Hud —2E 132
ville App. Leeds —8L 63
ville Av. B'frd —4F 76
ville Av. Leeds —8L 63
ville Clo. Leeds —8L 63
ville Clo. S Kirk —6J 157
ville Ct. Shipl —7L 39
ville Cres. Leeds —6M 63
Neville Gth. Leeds —8L 63
Neville Gro. Hud —6D 132
Neville Gro. Leeds —8L 63
Neville Gro. Swil —3H 83
Neville Mt. Leeds —8L 63
Neville Pde. Leeds —8L 63
Neville Pl. Leeds —7M 63
Neville Rd. B'frd —1F 76
Neville Rd. Leeds —6M 63
Neville Rd. Otley —1M 25
Neville Rd. Wake —6E 118
Neville Row. Leeds —8L 63
Neville Sq. Leeds —7M 63
Neville St. Kei —8K 21
Neville St. Leeds —8D 62
Neville St. Mar —6J 95
Neville St. Nor —2J 121
Neville St. Wake —7A 120
Neville Ter. Leeds —8L 63
Neville Vw. Leeds —8L 63
Neville Wlk. Leeds —7L 63
Nevill Gro. B'frd —3J 57
Nevins Rd. Dew —5A 116
Nevison Av. Pon —9L 103
New Adel Av. Leeds —4K 43
New Adel Gdns. Leeds —4K 43
New Adel La. Leeds —5K 43
Newall. —8K 11
Newall Av. Otley —8K 11
Newall Carr Rd. Otley & N Clift —3J 11
Newall Clo. Men —3F 24
Newall Clo. Otley —8K 11
Newall Cres. Fitz —7N 139
Newall Hall Pk. Otley —8L 11
Newall Mt. Otley —9K 11
Newall St. B'frd —1B 76
Newall St. Todm —3J 107
New Arc. S Kirk —7H 157
Newark Clo. M'well —7K 153
Newark Ho. B'frd —1B 76
(off Roundhill St.)
Newark Rd. Bgly —2E 38
Newark St. B'frd —9E 58
New Augustus St. B'frd —8D 58
New Av. Hud —1F 132
New Bank. Hal —4C 92
New Bank St. Morl —8L 79
New Biggin Hill. —5L 137
New Bond St. Hal —5A 92
New Bridge. —6G 71
Newbridge La. Halt E —2D 4
New Bri. Rd. Mel —7A 146
New Briggate. Leeds —6E 62
New Brighton. —9H 39
(nr. Cottingley)
New Brighton. —9K 79
(nr. Morley)
New Brighton. —6K 119
(nr. Wakefield)
New Brighton. Bgly —9H 39
New Brook St. I'ly —5G 8
New Brunswick St. Hal —5A 92
New Brunswick St. Wake —7L 119
Newburn Rd. B'frd —9N 57
Newbury Dri. S Elm —4N 157
Newbury Rd. Brigh —4L 113
Newbury Wlk. Khtn —1G 133
Newby Gth. Leeds —2K 45
Newby Ho. B'frd —4F 58
(off Otley Rd.)
Newby St. B'frd —1C 76
Newcastle Clo. Dlgtn —8A 78
Newcastle Farm Ct. Fair —9N 85
Newcastle Ho. B'frd —7D 58
(off Barkerend Rd.)
New Clayton Ter. Cull —1K 55
New Clo. Av. Sils —8E 6
New Clo. La. Skelb —3J 159
New Clo. La. Slai —9J 129
New Clo. Rd. Shipl —8H 39
New Clough Rd. Norl —1K 111
Newcombe St. Ell —6F 112
New Craven Ga. Leeds —9E 62
New Cres. H'fth —7E 42
New Cft. H'fth —7E 42
New Crofton. —3J 139
New Cross St. B'frd —3C 76
(in two parts)
New Cross St. Oaken —8F 76
New Delight. Hal —6J 73
New Delight. Pec W —4H 71
New England Rd. Kei —2J 37
New Farmers Hill. W'ford —6E 82
New Farnley. —2G 79
Newfield Av. C'frd —5E 102
Newfield Av. Nor —2K 121
Newfield Clo. Nor —2K 121
Newfield Ct. Nor —1K 121
Newfield Cres. Nor —2K 121
Newfield Dri. Gar —1B 84
Newfield Dri. Men —4E 24
Newfield Ho. Nor —1K 121
Newfield La. S Mil —5K 85
New Fold. B'frd —6K 75
New Fold. H'frth —4M 163
Newforth Gro. B'frd —3A 76
New Fryston. —1J 103
New Gate. —3N 163
New Ga. H'frth —7A 164
Newgate. Mir —7L 115
Newgate. Pon —3J 123
Newgate La. Mel —7D 146
Newgate St. Bat —9J 97
New Gro. Dri. Hud —3C 132
New Haithe Hill. Hud —8N 131
Newhall. —4E 76
New Hall App. Wake —6H 135
Newhall Bank. Leeds —8F 80
Newhall Chase. Leeds —7F 80
New Hall Clo. Crig —6G 136
Newhall Clo. Leeds —7F 80
Newhall Cres. Leeds —7F 80
Newhall Cft. Leeds —6G 80
Newhall Dri. B'frd —5D 76
Newhall Gdns. Leeds —8F 80
Newhall Gth. Leeds —8F 80
Newhall Ga. Leeds —6F 80
Newhall Grn. Leeds —7G 80
Newhall La. Mir —9M 115
New Hall La. Ove —6J 135
(in two parts)
Newhall Mt. B'frd —5D 76
Newhall Mt. Leeds —8F 80
Newhall Rd. B'frd —4F 76
Newhall Rd. Leeds —7F 80
New Hall Rd. Pon —9L 103
Newhall Wlk. Leeds —7G 80
New Hall Way. Floc —7J 135
Newhaven. C'thpe —6H 137
New Hey Rd. B'frd —1E 76
New Hey Rd. Fix & Brigh —7G 112
New Hey Rd. Hud —6H 129
New Hey Rd. Scam & Hud —1A 144
Newhill. S Kirk —8H 157
Newhold. Gar —6A 66
New Holme Rd. Haw —9D 36
New Ho. La. Q'bry —5G 74
Newhouse Pl. Hud —3M 131
New Ho. Rd. Hud —7B 114
Newill Clo. B'frd —3E 76
Newington Av. Cud —9J 155
Newington St. B'frd —6A 58
New Inn Ct. Otley —1L 25
New Inn St. Leeds —7K 61
New John St. B'frd —7B 58
New Kirkgate. Shipl —7N 39
New Laithe. Holy G —9M 111
New Laithe Clo. Hud —8A 132
New Laithe Hill. Hud —9N 131
New Laithe La. H'frth —3N 163
New Laithe Rd. B'frd —4M 75
New Laithe Rd. Hud —8A 132
New Laithe Rd. Oldf —7E 34
Newlaithes Cres. Nor —1K 121
Newlaithes Gdns. H'fth —8E 42
Newlaithes Gth. H'fth —9D 42
Newlaithes Rd. H'fth —9D 42
Newland Av. Hud —1L 131
Newland Ct. Bkby —2L 131
Newland Ct. Wake —9N 119
Newland Cres. Dur —3G 137
Newland La. Nor —2F 120
Newland Rd. Hud —2E 132
Newlands. Fars —4A 60
Newlands Av. B'frd —5H 59
Newlands Av. Clay W —7J 151
Newlands Av. Hal —9F 74
Newlands Av. Skel —7K 159
Newlands Av. Sower B —9E 90
Newlands Av. Yead —8L 25
Newlands Clo. Brigh —2N 113
Newlands Cres. Hal —1F 92
Newlands Cres. Morl —9N 79
Newlands Dri. Bgly —1D 38
Newlands Dri. Hal —1F 92
Newlands Dri. Morl —8N 79
Newlands Dri. Stan —7N 99
Newlands Gro. Hal —1F 92
Newlands La. H'frth —3H 163
Newlands Pl. B'frd —6F 58
Newlands Ri. Yead —9L 25
Newlands Rd. Hal —5G 91
Newlands, The. Sower B —1E 110
Newland St. Knot —7A 104
Newland St. Wake —9N 119
Newlands Vw. Hal —1F 92
Newlands Wlk. Stan —7N 99
Newland Vw. Nor —1G 120
New La. Beal —6N 105
New La. Blkhd —9E 70
New La. B'frd —8H 59
New La. C'frd —7L 101
New La. Cleck —6E 94
New La. Cra V —9L 89
New La. Dlgtn —5D 78
New La. Dur —2G 137
New La. E Ard —4D 98
(in two parts)
New La. Gol —3A 130
New La. Hal —8C 92
New La. Knot —1C 104
New La. Leeds —8D 80
(LS10)
New La. Leeds —8D 62
(LS11)
New La. L'ft —7B 90
New La. Pon —2K 123
New La. Scam —6E 128
New La. Sils —6A 6
New La. Skelm —8E 150
New La. Ski G —9N 91
New La. Slai —7N 129
New La. Stainb —1G 12
New La. Tong —3M 77
New La. Upt —3N 157
New La. Cres. Upt —2N 157
Newlay. —9E 42
Newlay Bridle Path. H'fth —8E 42
Newlay Clo. B'frd —8J 41
Newlay Gro. H'fth —9E 42
Newlay La. Bmly —2F 60
Newlay La. H'fth —8E 42
Newlay La. Pl. Leeds —2F 60
Newlay Mt. H'fth —9E 42
Newlay Wood Av. H'fth —8F 42
Newlay Wood Clo. H'fth —8F 42
Newlay Wood Cres. H'fth —8F 42
Newlay Wood Dri. H'fth —8F 42
Newlay Wood Fold. H'fth —8E 42
Newlay Wood Gdns. H'fth —8F 42
Newlay Wood Ri. H'fth —8F 42
Newlay Wood Rd. H'fth —8E 42
New Leeds. Leeds —1E 60
Newley Av. Bat —4C 96
New Line. B'frd —8H 41
New Lodge Cres. Barn —9N 153
New Longley La. Sower B —2G 111
Newlyn Dri. Wake —9M 119
Newlyn Rd. Riddl —7N 21
Newman Av. Barn —8D 154
Newman St. B'frd —3F 76
New Mkt. Otley —1L 25
Newmarket App. Leeds —9K 63
Newmarket Grn. Leeds —8K 63
Newmarket La. Leeds —9K 63
Newmarket La. Stan & Meth —5C 100
New Mkt. St. Leeds —7E 62
New Micklefield. —9G 67
New Mill. —2C 164
Newmillerdam. —6K 137
Newmillerdam Country Park. —8L 137
New Mill La. Cliff —3E 32
New Mill Rd. H'frth —2N 163
New Mill Rd. Hon & Broc —5M 147
New N. Pde. Hud —4M 131
New N. Rd. Heck —7N 95
New N. Rd. Hud —3L 131
New N. Rd. Slai —8N 129
New Occupation La. Pud —8N 59
New Otley Rd. B'frd —6E 58
New Pk. Av. Fars —3B 60
New Pk. Clo. Fars —3B 60
New Pk. Cft. Fars —3B 60
New Pk. Gro. Fars —4A 60
New Pk. La. Oss —3D 118
New Pk. Pl. Fars —3B 60
New Pk. Rd. Q'bry —3C 74
New Pk. St. Morl —1J 97
New Pk. Va. Fars —3B 60
New Pk. Vw. Fars —4B 60
New Pk. Wlk. Fars —4A 60
New Pk. Way. Fars —3B 60
New Pepper Rd. Leeds —2H 81
New Popplewell La. Schol —4D 94
Newport Av. Leeds —4D 60
Newport Cres. Leeds —3N 61
Newport Gdns. Leeds —3N 61
Newport Mt. Leeds —3N 61
Newport Pl. B'frd —5A 58
Newport Rd. B'frd —5A 58
Newport Rd. Leeds —3N 61
Newport St. Pon —2J 123
Newport Vw. Leeds —2N 61
New Princess St. Leeds —9D 62
New Pudsey Sq. Far —5N 59
New Rd. Bads —8J 141
New Rd. Blkhd —7N 69
New Rd. B'ham —5D 32
New Rd. Carl —1M 99
New Rd. Caw —2L 167
New Rd. Corn —8E 68
New Rd. Dart —7J 153
New Rd. Denh —6K 55
New Rd. G'lnd —4N 111
New Rd. Hal —6B 92
New Rd. H Bri —1G 88
(in two parts)
New Rd. H'frth —9L 147
New Rd. Holy G —8B 112
New Rd. Horb —1D 136
New Rd. Hud —8F 114
New Rd. Knot —7N 103
New Rd. L'ft —3D 90
New Rd. Myth —4M 89
New Rd. Nort —1M 159
New Rd. Old Sn —3L 121
New Rd. Ove —5H 135
New Rd. Pen —7G 166
New Rd. Sils —8D 6
New Rd. S Mil —4K 85
New Rd. Sow —1N 129
New Rd. Stap —7H 125
New Rd. Todm —8A 88
(nr. Bank Cross La.)
New Rd. Todm —4N 87
(nr. Gt. House Rd.)
New Rd. W Har —1B 140
New Rd. Wool —2J 153
New Rd. Yead —9K 25
New Rd. E. Schol —4D 94
New Road Side. —9B 76
New Rd. Side. H'fth —7D 42
New Rd. Side Rawd —2M 41
New Rd. Sq. Brigh —5K 113
(off New Hey Rd.)
New Row. Bads —8L 141
New Row. Bgly —7G 38
New Row. C'ley —3K 59
New Row. D Hill —4K 57
New Row. H'frth —3M 163
New Row. Holy G —7B 112
New Row. K'gte —1D 118
New Row. Leeds —8F 64
New Row. Wyke —2B 94
New Row Cotts. D'ton —6B 124
Newroyd Rd. B'frd —3C 76
Newsam Ct. Leeds —7B 64
Newsam Dri. Leeds —7N 63
Newsam Green. —3E 82
Newsam Grn. Rd. Leeds —3E 82
New Scarborough. —5G 61
(nr. Bramley)
New Scarborough. —9J 25
(nr. Guisley)
New Scarborough. —4A 136
(nr. Horbury)
New Scarbro'. —6M 115
New Sharlston. —6G 121
New Shaw La. Blkhd —8A 70
Newsholme. —3A 36
Newsholme La. Dur —3H 137
Newsholme New Rd. Oakw —3A 36
Newsome. —8M 131
Newsome Av. Hud —9M 131
Newsome Rd. Hud —6N 131
Newsome Rd. S. Hud —1M 147
Newsomes Row. Bat —8E 96
(off Brown's Pl.)
Newsomes Row. Gom —3M 95
(off Oxford Rd.)
Newsome St. Dew —2E 116
New Station St. Leeds —7D 62
Newstead. —8L 139
Newstead Av. Fitz —7A 140
Newstead Av. Hal —5L 91
Newstead Av. Wake —7J 99
Newstead Cres. Fitz —6A 140
Newstead Dri. Fitz —7A 140
Newstead Gdns. Hal —5L 91
Newstead Gro. Fitz —7A 140
Newstead Gro. Hal —5L 91
Newstead Heath. Hal —5L 91
Newstead La. H'cft & Fitz —7M 139
Newstead Mt. Fitz —7A 140
(off Newstead Av.)
Newstead Pl. Hal —5L 91
Newstead Rd. Barn —9N 153
Newstead Rd. Otley —1L 25
Newstead Rd. Wake —4K 119
Newstead Ter. Fitz —7A 140
Newstead Ter. Hal —5L 91
Newstead Vw. Fitz —7A 140
Newstead Wlk. B'frd —1B 76
New St. Ackw —5F 140
New St. Bail B —5N 93
New St. Bat —7F 96
New St. Bier —5F 76
New St. Bgly —9D 22
New St. C'frd —3E 102
New St. Clif —9B 94
New St. Denh —6K 55
New St. Earl —4J 117
(in two parts)
New St. Far —5A 60
New St. Gol —6D 130
New St. Hal —4L 91
New St. Hang H —9H 97
New St. Haw —9C 36

New St. *Hon* —5L **147**
New St. *Horb* —1D **136**
New St. *H'fth* —7E **42**
New St. *Hud* —5M **131**
New St. *Idle* —7F **40**
New St. *Kin* —8C **140**
New St. *Kip* —4B **84**
New St. *Khtn* —2G **132**
New St. *M'well* —8K **153**
New St. *Mel* —7C **146**
New St. *Milns* —6F **130**
New St. *Neth* —2H **147**
New St. *Oaken* —8F **76**
New St. *Oakw* —5D **36**
New St. *Oss* —6N **117**
New St. *Pad* —5K **131**
New St. *Pud* —8A **60**
New St. *Rawf* —6K **95**
New St. *Roys* —6D **154**
New St. *Scis* —8G **151**
New St. *Skelm* —8D **150**
New St. *Slai* —9N **129**
New St. *S Elm* —6L **157**
New St. *S Hien* —3L **155**
New St. *S'wram* —8F **92**
New St. *Slnd* —8M **111**
New St. Clo. *Pud* —8B **60**
New St. Gdns. *Pud* —8B **60**
New St. Gro. *Pud* —8B **60**
New Sturton La. *Gar* —6B **66**
New Tanhouse. *Mir* —6K **115**
New Temple Ga. *Leeds* —8B **64**
Newthorpe. —9N 67
Newthorpe Rd. *Nort* —7N **143**
New Tofftshaw. —5H 77
New Tofftshaw. *B'frd* —5H **77**
Newton. —9H 85
Newton Av. *Wake* —1K **119**
Newton Bar. *Wake* —3K **119**
Newton Clo. *Rothw* —9K **81**
Newton Clo. *Wake* —2K **119**
Newton Ct. *Leeds* —9L **45**
Newton Ct. *Rothw* —9K **81**
Newton Ct. *Wake* —8K **99**
Newton Dri. *C'frd* —5H **103**
Newton Dri. *Wake* —9L **99**
Newton Gth. *Leeds* —1G **62**
Newton Grn. *Wake* —2K **119**
Newton Gro. *Leeds* —2G **62**
Newton Hill. —1L 119
Newton Hill Rd. *Leeds* —1F **62**
Newton Kyme. —2L 33
Newton La. *Fair* —9J **85**
Newton La. *Leds* —9D **84**
Newton La. *Wake* —8K **99**
Newton Lodge Clo. *Leeds* —1E **62**
Newton Lodge Dri. *Leeds* —1E **62**
Newton Pde. *Leeds* —1F **62**
Newton Pk. *Brigh* —6L **93**
Newton Pk. Ct. *Leeds* —1G **62**
Newton Pk. Dri. *Leeds* —1G **62**
Newton Pk. Vw. *Leeds* —2G **62**
Newton Pl. *B'frd* —1B **76**
Newton Rd. *Leeds* —2F **62**
Newton Sq. *Leeds* —2G **78**
Newton St. *B'frd* —1C **76**
(in two parts)
Newton St. *Sower B* —8H **91**
Newton Vw. *Leeds* —1F **62**
Newton Vs. *Leeds* —9E **44**
Newton Wlk. *Leeds* —2G **62**
Newton Way. *Bail* —3A **40**
New Town. —1M 7
(nr. Addingham)
Newtown. —3M 131
(nr. Huddersfield)
New Town. —1G 36
(nr. Keighley)
New Town. —4G 63
(nr. Leeds)
New Town. —9K 103
(nr. Pontefract)
Newtown Av. *Roys* —5C **154**
New Town Clo. *Kei* —9H **21**
New Town Ct. *Kei* —9H **21**
New Wlk. *Leeds* —6K **45**
New Way. *Bat* —7F **96**
New Way. *Guis* —7F **24**
New Wellgate. *C'frd* —6F **102**
New Wells. *Wake* —6L **119**
New Windsor Dri. *Rothw* —7A **82**
New Works Rd. *Low M* —8A **76**
New York Cotts. *Rawd* —5A **42**
New York La. *Rawd* —5A **42**
New York Rd. *Leeds* —6F **62**
(in two parts)
New York St. *Leeds* —7F **62**
Nibshaw La. *Gom* —4L **95**
Nibshaw Rd. *Gom* —4L **95**
Nice Av. *Leeds* —2H **63**
Nice St. *Leeds* —2J **63**
Nice Vw. *Leeds* —2H **63**
Nicholas Clo. *B'frd* —7L **57**
Nichol La. *H'frth* —6E **164**
Nichols Clo. *Weth* —4K **17**
Nicholson Clo. *Bgly* —1F **38**
Nicholson St. *C'frd* —5C **102**
Nichols Way. *Weth* —4J **17**
Nickleby Rd. *Leeds* —6J **63**
Nicolsons Pl. *Sils* —8E **6**
Nidd App. *Weth* —1L **17**
Nidd Ct. *Sils* —8E **6**
Nidd Dri. *C'frd* —4H **103**
Nidderdale Clo. *Gar* —9B **66**
Nidderdale Wlk. *Bail* —3C **40**
Nidd St. *B'frd* —8F **58**
Nields Rd. *Slai* —1M **145**
Nightingale Crest. *Wake* —7E **118**
Nightingale St. Kei —8J ***21***
(off Linnet St.)
Nile Cres. *Kei* —1F **36**
Nile Rd. *I'ly* —5G **9**
Nile St. *Cro R* —7E **36**
Nile St. *Hud* —5L **131**
Nile St. *Kei* —1F **36**
Nile St. *Leeds* —5F **62**
Nina Rd. *B'frd* —2L **75**
Ninelands La. *Gar* —9A **66**
Ninelands Spur. *Gar* —8A **66**
Ninelands Vw. *Gar* —7A **66**
Ninevah. —7K 141
Ninevah La. *All B* —8N **83**
Ninevah La. *Bads* —7K **141**
Nineveh Gdns. *Leeds* —9C **62**
Nineveh Pde. *Leeds* —9C **62**
Nineveh Rd. *Leeds* —9C **62**
Ninth Av. *Liv* —7F **94**
Nippet La. *Leeds* —6G **63**
Nixon Av. *Leeds* —7K **63**
Nixon Clo. *Dew* —1J **135**
Noble St. *B'frd* —9N **57**
Noblethorpe La. *Silk* —9M **167**
Nog La. *B'frd* —2M **57**
Nook. —3D 96
Nook Gdns. *Scholes* —7G **47**
Nook Grn. *Dew* —9G **116**
Nooking. *K'gte* —9D **98**
Nooking, The. *K'gte* —9D **98**
Nook La. *H Bri* —9L **71**
Nook La. *Sower B* —3N **109**
Nook Rd. *Scholes* —7G **47**
Nooks, The. *Gild* —6G **78**
Nook, The. *Cleck* —4J **95**
Nook, The. *Hoy S* —9K **167**
Nook, The. *Leeds* —2F **44**
Nook, The. *Sower B* —9H **91**
Nook, The. *Ting* —6A **98**
Nook Vw. *Ting* —6A **98**
Nook Wlk. *Dew* —3C **116**
Noon Clo. *Stan* —7N **99**
Noon Nick. —1G 57
Nopper Rd. *H'frth* —2E **146**
Nora Pl. *Leeds* —3D **60**
Nora Rd. *Leeds* —3D **60**
Nora Ter. *Leeds* —3D **60**
Norbeck Dri. *Cro R* —7E **36**
Norbury Rd. *B'frd* —1J **59**
Norcliffe La. *Hal* —6F **92**
Norcroft Brow. *B'frd* —8B **58**
Norcroft St. *B'frd* —7A **58**
Norcross Av. *Hud* —3F **130**
Norfield. *Fix* —7M **113**
Norfolk Av. *Bat* —9E **96**
Norfolk Clo. *B'ton* —4B **104**
Norfolk Clo. *Leeds* —8F **44**
Norfolk Clo. *Oult* —8E **82**
Norfolk Dri. *Oult* —8E **82**
Norfolk Gdns. *B'frd* —8C **58**
Norfolk Gdns. *Leeds* —8F **44**
Norfolk Grn. *Leeds* —8F **44**
Norfolk Ho. *Wake* —8A **120**
Norfolk Mt. *Leeds* —8F **44**
Norfolk Pl. *Hal* —6N **91**
Norfolk Pl. *Leeds* —8F **44**
Norfolk St. *Bat* —8E **96**
Norfolk St. *Bgly* —4F **38**
Norfolk St. *H Bri* —2H **89**
Norfolk Ter. *Leeds* —8F **44**
Norfolk Vw. *Leeds* —8F **44**
Norfolk Wlk. Dew —3E ***116***
(off Boothroyd La.)
Norfolk Wlk. *Leeds* —8F **44**
Norgarth Clo. *Bat* —7J **97**
Norham Gro. *Wykc* —2B **94**
Norland Rd. *G'lnd* —4K **111**
Norland Rd. *Sower B* —9H **91**
Norland St. *B'frd* —2L **75**
Norland Town. —1L 111
Norland Town Rd. *Norl* —1K **111**
Norland Vw. Hal —8N ***91***
(off Albert Promenade)
Norland Vw. *Sower B* —8K **91**
Norman Av. *B'frd* —1F **58**
Norman Av. *Ell* —5F **112**
Norman Cres. *B'frd* —1F **58**
Norman Dri. *Mir* —5K **115**
Norman Gro. *B'frd* —1F **58**
Norman Gro. *Ell* —5F **112**
Norman Gro. *Leeds* —2K **61**
Norman Ho. *Nor* —3J **121**
Norman La. *B'frd* —1F **58**
Norman Mt. *B'frd* —1F **58**
Norman Mt. *Leeds* —2K **61**
Norman Pl. *Horb* —1D **136**
Norman Pl. *Leeds* —5J **45**
Norman Rd. *Den D* —3C **166**
Norman Rd. *Hud* —1M **131**
Norman Rd. *Mir* —5K **115**
Norman Row. *Leeds* —2K **61**
Norman St. *Bgly* —4F **38**
Norman St. *Ell* —5F **112**
Norman St. *Hal* —7M **91**
Norman St. *Haw* —8D **36**
Norman St. *Leeds* —2K **61**
Normans Way. *Wake* —1A **138**
Norman Ter. *B'frd* —1F **58**
Norman Ter. *Ell* —5F **112**
Norman Ter. *Leeds* —5J **45**
Normanton. —1J 121
Normanton By-Pass. *Norm & Old Sn* —4H **121**
Normanton Common. —9L 101
Normanton Gro. *Leeds* —1C **80**
Normanton Ind. Est. *Nor I* —9L **101**
Normanton N. Ind. Est. *Nor* —9M **101**
Normanton Pl. *Leeds* —1C **80**
Normanton St. *Horb* —2E **136**
Normanton Vw. *Nor* —3J **121**
Norman Towers. *Leeds* —9K **43**
Norman Vw. *Leeds* —2K **61**
No Rd. *Cam* —1N **159**
Norquest Ind. Pk. *Birs* —1D **96**
Norr. —9C 38
Norr Grn. Ter. *Wilsd* —9C **38**
Norridge Bottom. *H'frth* —3M **163**
Norris Clo. *Hud* —6E **132**
Norristhorpe. —1L 115
Norristhorpe Av. *Liv* —1L **115**
Norristhorpe La. *Liv* —1L **115**
Nortech Clo. *Leeds* —4F **62**
Northallerton Rd. *B'frd* —5D **58**
Northampton St. *B'frd* —5D **58**
North App. *H'wd* —2G **48**
North Av. *B'frd* —3B **58**
North Av. *C'frd* —5N **101**
North Av. *Horb* —1E **136**
North Av. *Otley* —9L **11**
North Av. *Pon* —4H **123**
North Av. *S Elm* —7L **157**
North Av. *Wake* —3L **119**
N. Baileygate. *Pon* —2K **123**
N. Bank Rd. *Bat* —7D **96**
N. Bank Rd. *Bgly* —1F **56**
N. Bank Rd. *Hud* —1L **131**
North Bolton. *Hal* —6K **73**
North Bri. *Hal* —4B **92**
N. Bridge St. *Hal* —4B **92**
N. Broadgate La. *H'fth* —6F **42**
Northbrook Pl. *Leeds* —8F **44**
N. Brook St. *B'frd* —6D **58**
Northbrook St. *Leeds* —8F **44**
North Carr. *Hud* —3C **132**
N. Carr Cft. *Hud* —3C **132**
North Cliffe. *Sower B* —1H **111**
N. Cliffe Av. *T'tn* —8E **56**
N. Cliffe Clo. *T'tn* —7D **56**
N. Cliffe Dri. *T'tn* —8D **56**
N. Cliffe Gro. *T'tn* —7D **56**
N. Cliffe La. *T'tn* —7E **56**
Northcliffe Rd. *Shipl* —9M **39**
North Clo. *F'stne* —2C **122**
North Clo. *Leeds* —9M **45**
North Clo. *Roys* —6D **154**
Northcote. *Oss* —2M **117**
Northcote Cres. *Leeds* —1D **80**
Northcote Dri. *Leeds* —1D **80**
Northcote Fold. *Lntn* —7J **17**
Northcote Grn. *Leeds* —1D **80**
Northcote Rd. *B'frd* —4F **58**
Northcote St. *Fars* —4A **60**
North Ct. *Leeds* —6E **62**
North Cres. *S Elm* —5A **158**
Northcroft. *S Elm* —6N **157**
Northcroft Av. *S Elm* —5N **157**
N. Croft Gro. Rd. *I'ly* —5F **8**
Northcroft Ri. *B'frd* —5K **57**
N. Cross Rd. *Hud* —9L **113**
North Cut. *Brigh* —1L **113**
Northdale Av. *B'frd* —3A **76**
Northdale Cres. *B'frd* —3A **76**
Northdale Mt. *B'frd* —3A **76**
Northdale Rd. *B'frd* —2N **57**
N. Dean Av. *Kei* —9E **20**
N. Dean Bus. Pk. *G'lnd* —2B **112**
N. Dean Rd. *G'lnd* —2N **111**
N. Dean Rd. *Kei* —9E **20**
N. Dene Rd. *Sils* —7E **6**
North Dri. *B'hpe* —6J **27**
North Dri. *Gol* —5D **130**
North Dri. *Sher E* —9B **66**
North Edge. Hal —3H ***93***
(off Brighouse and Denholme Ga. Rd.)
Northedge La. *Hal* —3H **93**
Northedge Mdw. *B'frd* —9F **40**
Northedge Pk. *Hal* —3J **93**
North Elmsall. —3A 158
Northern Clo. *B'frd* —3L **75**
Northern St. *Leeds* —7C **62**
N. Farm Rd. *Leeds* —3K **63**
North Featherstone. —2C 122
Northfield Av. *Hud* —6K **131**
Northfield Av. *Knot* —9E **104**
Northfield Av. *Oss* —4N **117**
Northfield Av. *Rothw* —9L **81**
Northfield Av. *S Kirk* —6J **157**
Northfield Av. *Weth* —3M **17**
Northfield Clo. Ell —5E ***112***
(off Victoria Av.)
Northfield Cres. *Bgly* —8F **38**
Northfield Dri. *Pon* —2L **123**
Northfield Gdns. *B'frd* —4A **76**
Northfield Gro. *B'frd* —4A **76**
Northfield Gro. *Hud* —7L **131**
Northfield Gro. *S Kirk* —6J **157**
Northfield Ho. *B'frd* —8G **40**
Northfield La. *Crid S* —4J **125**
Northfield La. *Horb* —1E **136**
Northfield La. *Kbtn* —1J **149**
N. Field La. *Skelm* —7D **150**
Northfield La. *S Kirk* —6H **157**
Northfield M. *Weth* —3N **17**
Northfield Pl. *B'frd* —5A **58**
Northfield Pl. *Dew* —2E **116**
Northfield Pl. *Rothw* —9K **81**
Northfield Pl. *Weth* —3M **17**
Northfield Rd. *B'frd* —4N **75**
Northfield Rd. *Dew* —2E **116**
N. Field Rd. *Hamp* —9C **158**
Northfield Rd. *Knot* —9E **104**
Northfield Rd. *Oss* —5N **117**
Northfield Rd. *Shar C* —8J **121**
Northfields. *Wltn* —6G **18**
Northfield St. *Dew* —2F **116**
Northfield St. *S Kirk* —6H **157**
Northfield Ter. *H Bri* —8G **71**
Northfield Ter. *Q'bry* —4F **74**
Northfield Ter. *Slai* —8N **129**
North Fold. *B'frd* —7F **40**
Northgate. *Alm* —7D **132**
Northgate. *Bail* —3A **40**
Northgate. *B'frd* —7C **58**
Northgate. *Cleck* —5H **95**
Northgate. *Dew* —3G **116**
Northgate. *Ell* —4E **112**
Northgate. *Hal* —5B **92**
Northgate. *Heck* —8N **95**
Northgate. *Hept* —8G **70**
Northgate. *Hon* —3M **147**
(in two parts)
Northgate. *Horb* —9C **118**
Northgate. *Hud* —3N **131**
North Ga. *Mir* —9H **115**
Northgate. *Oult* —7D **82**
Northgate. *Pon* —2K **123**
Northgate. *S Hien* —3M **155**
Northgate. *Wake* —4K **119**
(in two parts)
Northgate Clo. *Pon* —2K **123**
Northgate Ho. Weth —4M ***17***
(off Northgate La.)
Northgate La. *Lntn* —4H **17**
Northgate Lodge. *Pon* —2K **123**
Northgate Ri. *Lntn* —7J **17**
Northgates. *Weth* —4M **17**
N. Grange M. *Leeds* —2B **62**
N. Grange Mt. *Leeds* —1A **62**
N. Grange Rd. *Leeds* —2A **62**
North Gro. App. *Weth* —2M **17**
N. Grove Av. *Weth* —2M **17**
N. Grove Clo. *Leeds* —9M **45**
N. Grove Ct. *Weth* —3M **17**
N. Grove Cres. *Weth* —2M **17**
N. Grove Dri. *Leeds* —9M **45**
N. Grove Dri. *Weth* —2M **17**
N. Grove Mt. *Weth* —3M **17**
N. Grove Ri. *Leeds* —9M **45**
N. Grove Rd. *Weth* —2M **17**
N. Grove Way. *Weth* —3M **17**
N. Hall Av. *B'frd* —5E **40**
North Hill. *S'cft* —8E **30**
N. Hill Clo. *Leeds* —9L **45**
N. Hill Ct. *Leeds* —1B **62**
N. Hill Dri. *Hud* —2G **132**
N. Hill Rd. *Leeds* —2B **62**
N. Holme St. *B'frd* —6C **58**
North Ives. Pon —2K ***123***
(off Northgate)
N. John St. *Q'bry* —4D **74**
N. King St. *Bat* —8G **96**
Northlands. *Roys* —5D **154**
Northland Vw. Pon —2K ***123***
(off Bk. Northgate)
North La. *Caw* —7J **167**
North La. *Eml* —2F **150**
North La. *Head* —1N **61**
North La. *Kear* —5A **16**
North La. *Round* —8L **45**
North La. *Slai* —9K **129**
North La. *W'ford & Oult* —7D **82**
N. Lane Gdns. *Leeds* —9L **45**
Northlea Av. *B'frd* —6E **40**
N. Lingwell Rd. *Leeds* —8E **80**
N. Lodge Fold. *Dew* —9C **96**
N. Lodge La. *D'ton* —7E **124**
N. Mead. *B'hpe* —6J **27**
N. Moor La. *Hud* —9G **114**
(in two parts)
Northolme Av. *Leeds* —8L **43**
Northolme Cres. *Leeds* —8L **43**
Northorpe. —4N 115
Northorpe Ct. *Mir* —5N **115**
Northorpe La. *Mir* —4N **115**
Northowram. —2F 92
Northowram Grn. *Hal* —1F **92**
North Pde. *All* —4F **56**
North Pde. *B'frd* —7C **58**
North Pde. *Bur W* —7C **10**
North Pde. *Hal* —5B **92**
North Pde. *I'ly* —5H **9**
North Pde. *Leeds* —7K **43**
North Pde. Morl —1L ***97***
(off Wide La.)
North Pde. *Otley* —9L **11**
N. Park Av. *Leeds* —7H **45**
N. Park Gro. *Leeds* —7J **45**
N. Park La. *Skel* —7N **159**
(in two parts)
N. Park Pde. *Leeds* —6H **45**
N. Park Rd. *B'frd* —3N **57**
N. Park Rd. *Leeds* —7J **45**
(in two parts)
N. Park St. *Dew* —2D **116**
N. Park Ter. *B'frd* —4A **58**
N. Parkway. *Leeds* —1N **63**
N. Queen St. *Kei* —9J **21**
North Rigton. —2A 14
North Ri. *Hud* —9A **114**
North Rd. *Bklnd* —6H **111**
North Rd. *B'frd* —4N **75**
North Rd. *Dew* —5A **116**
North Rd. *Fair* —9N **85**
North Rd. *H'fth* —4E **42**
North Rd. *Kbtn* —2J **149**
North Rd. *Leeds* —2L **81**
(LS9)
North Rd. *Leeds* —4D **64**
(LS15)
North Rd. *Roys* —4E **154**
N. Road E. *Leeds* —2M **81**
N. Road Ter. *Wake* —4K **119**
Northrop Clo. *B'frd* —5L **57**
Northrop Yd. *Pud* —7B **60**
North Row. *Shepl* —9H **149**
N. Royd. *Hip* —3H **93**
Northside Av. *B'frd* —8M **57**
Northside Bus. Pk. Leeds —4F 6
(off Sheepscar Ct.)
Northside Rd. *B'frd* —8L **57**
Northside Shop. Cen. *Leeds* —8B
Northside Ter. *B'frd* —8L **57**
North's Pl. *Mir* —4L **115**
N. Spring Ct. *Kbtn* —3G **148**
Northstead. *Dew* —5A **116**
North St. *Add* —1N **7**
North St. *Bat* —6E **96**
North St. *B'frd* —7D **58**
North St. *C'frd* —4C **102**
North St. *Dew* —2F **116**
North St. *Fry* —1J **103**
North St. *G'lnd* —4C **112**
North St. *Haw* —8B **36**
North St. *Heck* —9A **96**
North St. *Holy G* —7B **112**
North St. *Idle* —5F **40**
North St. *Kei* —9J **21**
North St. *Leeds* —5F **62**
North St. *Lock* —6K **131**
North St. *Mir* —8K **115**
North St. *Nor* —4H **121**
North St. *Oaken* —9E **76**
North St. *Otley* —9L **11**
North St. *Pad* —5J **131**
North St. *Pud* —6B **60**
North St. *Rawd* —3M **41**
North St. *Sils* —7E **6**
North St. *S Kirk* —6H **157**
North St. *Weth* —4M **17**
North Ter. *Birs* —3C **96**
North Ter. Leeds —4D ***64***
(off Tranquility Av.)
North Ter. *Yead* —9M **25**
Northumberland St. *Hud* —4M **1**
North Vw. *All* —5F **56**

Jorth Vw. Bur W —8D 10
Jorth Vw. Ebrn —2A 20
Jorth Vw. Fitz —6A 140
Jorth Vw. Knot —7D 104
Jorth Vw. Leeds —9M 45
Jorth Vw. Men —4E 24
North Vw. Rothw —9A 82
(off Royds La.)
Jorth Vw. Sav T —5G 116
Jorth Vw. Wilsd —1B 56
J. View Rd. B'frd —4D 58
(nr. Bolton Rd.)
J. View Rd. B'frd —6L 77
(nr. Bradford Rd.)
J. View St. Kei —7H 21
J. View St. S'ley —4B 60
J. View Ter. Dew —1E 116
(off Halifax Rd.)
J. View Ter. Dew —1C 116
(off Staincliffe Rd.)
. View Ter. Haw —7C 36
. View Ter. S'ley —4B 60
Jorth Wlk. H'den —6N 37
Jorth Wlk. Hems —1D 156
orth Way. Hud —7C 114
orth Way. Leeds —9M 45
orthway. Mir —4K 115
orthway Cres. Mir —4K 115
orthway Gdns. Mir —4K 115
orthwell Ga. Otley —8J 11
orthwell La. Hept —8G 71
. West Bus. Pk. Leeds —3D 62
. West Rd. Leeds —3D 62
orth Wing. B'frd —6D 58
orthwood Clo. Pud —9C 60
orthwood Clo. W'ford —6D 82
orthwood Cres. B'frd —8G 40
orthwood Falls. W'ford —6D 82
orthwood Gdns. Colt —7F 64
orthwood Mt. Pud —9C 60
orthwood Pk. Kbtn —2J 149
orthwood Pk. W'ford —6D 82
orthwood Vw. Pud —9C 60
orton Clo. Ell —6E 112
orton Clo. Hal —5H 91
orton Dri. Hal —5H 91
orton & Kirk Smeaton Rd. K S'ton —5J 143
orton Mill La. Nort —6N 143
orton Rd. Leeds —5J 45
orton Rd. Wake —4M 119
orton St. Ell —6E 112
orton St. Sils —8D 6
orton St. Wake —7N 119
orton Ter. Stkmr —7G 148
ortonthorpe Ind. Est. Scis —8G 151
orton Tower. —5H 91
orton Way. Morl —7K 79
orwich Av. Leeds —3F 80
orwood. C'ton —6N 123
orwood Av. B'shaw —9M 77
orwood Av. Bur W —8D 10
orwood Av. Shipl —9N 39
orwood Clo. Bur W —8D 10
orwood Cres. B'shaw —9M 77
orwood Cres. S'ley —4C 60
orwood Cft. S'ley —4C 60
orwood Dri. Bat —4C 96
orwood Dri. B'shaw —9M 77
orwood Dri. Brier —6A 156
orwood Green. —2L 93
orwood Grn. Hill. Hal —2L 93
orwood Gro. B'shaw —9M 77
orwood Gro. Leeds —3A 62
orwood Pk. Hud —1J 131
orwood Pl. Leeds —3A 62
orwood Pl. Shipl —9N 39
orwood Rd. Bkby —9K 113
or Wood Rd. Hems —4D 156
orwood Rd. Leeds —3A 62
orwood Rd. Shipl —9N 39
orwood St. B'frd —3B 76
orwood St. Nor —8L 101
orwood St. Shipl —9N 39
orwood Ter. Bur W —8D 10
orwood Ter. Hal —2M 93
orwood Ter. Leeds —3A 62
orwood Ter. Shipl —9N 39
orwood Vw. Leeds —3A 62
ostell Clo. B'frd —6B 58
ostell La. Ryh —8J 139
ostell Priory. —2M 139
ostell Priory Holiday Home Pk. Nost —1M 139
oster Gro. Leeds —2B 80
oster Hill. Leeds —2B 80
oster Pl. Leeds —2B 80
oster Rd. Leeds —2B 80
oster St. Leeds —2B 80
oster Ter. Leeds —2B 80
oster Vw. Leeds —2B 80
ottingham St. B'frd —7J 59
Notton. —2B 154
Notton La. Not —2B 154
Nova La. Birs —2A 96
Nowell App. Leeds —5K 63
Nowell Av. Leeds —5K 63
Nowell Clo. Leeds —5K 63
Nowell Cres. Leeds —5K 63
Nowell End Row. Leeds —5K 63
Nowell Gdns. Leeds —5K 63
Nowell Gro. Leeds —5K 63
Nowell La. Leeds —5K 63
Nowell Mt. Leeds —5K 63
Nowell Pde. Leeds —5K 63
Nowell Pl. Hud —6D 132
Nowell Pl. Leeds —5K 63
Nowell Sq. Leeds —5K 63
Nowell St. Leeds —5K 63
Nowells Yd. Dew —3E 116
Nowell Ter. Leeds —5K 63
Nowell Vw. Leeds —5K 63
Nowell Wlk. Leeds —5K 63
Nunburnholme Wlk. B'frd —9G 41
Nunington Av. Leeds —6M 61
Nunington St. Leeds —6M 61
Nunington Ter. Leeds —6M 61
Nunington Vw. Leeds —5M 61
Nunlea Royd. Hal —6M 93
Nunnery La. Brigh —4J 113
Nunn's Av. F'stne —8D 122
Nunn's Clo. F'stne —7D 122
Nunn's Ct. F'stne —8C 122
Nunn's Cft. F'stne —7D 122
Nunn's Grn. F'stne —7D 122
Nunn's La. F'stne —7D 122
Nunn's Vw. F'stne —7C 122
Nunroyd. —7A 96
Nunroyd. Heck —7A 96
Nunroyd Av. Guis —8K 25
Nunroyd Av. Leeds —6F 44
Nunroyd Gro. Leeds —6F 44
Nunroyd Ho. B'frd —8H 59
(off Sticker La.)
Nunroyd Lawn. Leeds —6F 44
Nunroyd Rd. Leeds —6F 44
Nunroyd St. Leeds —6F 44
Nunroyd Ter. Leeds —6F 44
Nunthorpe Rd. Leeds —1C 60
Nurser La. B'frd —1A 76
Nurser Pl. B'frd —1A 76
Nursery Av. Hal —1M 91
Nursery Clo. Bail —5L 39
Nursery Clo. Hal —2M 91
Nursery Clo. Kei —6G 21
Nursery Clo. Leeds —3E 44
Nursery Gth. Weth —3N 17
Nursery Gro. Hal —1M 91
Nursery Gro. Leeds —3C 44
Nursery La. Hal —1L 91
Nursery La. Leeds —3C 44
Nursery La. Sower B —8B 110
Nursery Mt. Leeds —4G 80
Nursery Mt. Rd. Leeds —3G 80
Nursery Rd. B'frd —3L 75
Nursery Rd. Cytn —1G 75
Nursery Rd. Guis —5H 25
Nursery St. Dew —7F 116
Nursery St. Hud —1M 131
Nursery Way. B Spa —9B 18
Nursery Way. Cliff —3D 32
Nursery Wood Rd. Bat —9G 97
Nussey Av. Birs —2B 96
Nutclough Rd. H Bri —9J 71
Nutfield St. Todm —6K 87
Nuttall Rd. B'frd —7E 58
Nutter La. Birs —2N 95
Nutter St. Cleck —5G 95
Nutting Gro. Ter. Leeds —9H 61

Oak Av. Bgly —6E 38
Oak Av. B'frd —4A 58
Oak Av. Bur W —9D 10
Oak Av. Gar —7N 65
Oak Av. Gol —5D 130
Oak Av. Hud —5C 132
Oak Av. Mel —6B 146
Oak Av. Morl —1L 97
Oak Av. Nor —3H 121
Oak Av. Sower B —7H 91
Oak Av. Stan —8A 100
Oak Av. Todm —5J 87
Oak Bank. Bail —5A 40
Oak Bank. Bgly —5F 38
Oak Bank. Shipl —1B 58
Oakbank Av. Kei —2F 36
Oakbank B'way. Oakw —3F 36
Oakbank Ct. Oakw —3F 36
Oakbank Cres. Oakw —3F 36
Oakbank Dri. Kei —2F 36
Oakbank Gro. Kei —2F 36
Oakbank La. Oakw —3F 36
Oakbank Mt. Oakw —3F 36
Oakburn Rd. I'ly —6F 8
Oak Clo. Bur W —9D 10
Oak Clo. W'wth —7A 106
Oak Cres. Gar —7N 65
Oak Cres. Leeds —7A 64
Oakdale. Bgly —2F 38
Oakdale Av. B'frd —4N 75
Oakdale Av. Shipl —9B 40
Oakdale Clo. B'frd —3J 59
Oakdale Clo. Hal —2N 91
Oakdale Clo. Loft —6K 99
Oakdale Cres. B'frd —4N 75
Oakdale Cres. Hud —2F 130
Oakdale Dri. B'frd —3J 59
Oakdale Dri. Shipl —9C 40
Oakdale Gth. Leeds —6C 46
Oakdale Gro. Shipl —9C 40
Oakdale Mdw. Leeds —6C 46
Oakdale Pk. Pool W —1G 27
Oakdale Rd. Shipl —9C 40
Oakdale Ter. B'frd —4N 75
Oakdean. Hud —7M 113
Oakdene Clo. Pud —9C 60
Oakdene Ct. Leeds —3J 45
Oakdene Dri. Leeds —3J 45
Oakdene Gdns. Leeds —3J 45
Oakdene Va. Leeds —3J 45
Oakdene Way. Leeds —3J 45
Oak Dri. Gar —7N 65
Oak Dri. Gol —7C 130
Oak Dri. Leeds —5L 43
Oaken Bank Cres. Hud —7A 132
Oakenshaw. —8D 76
Oakenshaw Ct. Wyke —2A 94
Oakenshaw La. Schol —2E 94
Oakenshaw La. W'ton & Croft —2B 138
Oakenshaw St. Wake —8A 120
Oakes. —3G 130
Oakes Av. Broc —7A 148
Oakes Fold. Lep —7L 133
Oakes Gdns. Holy G —7A 112
Oakes La. Broc —7A 148
(in two parts)
Oakes Rd. Hud —2G 130
Oakes Rd. S. Hud —3G 130
Oakes St. Wake —5F 118
Oakfield. Leeds —2A 62
Oakfield Av. Bgly —5H 39
Oakfield Av. Rothw —7N 81
Oakfield Clo. Ell —5D 112
Oakfield Clo. Gar —8N 65
Oakfield Ct. M'well —8J 153
Oakfield Cres. Knot —9E 104
Oakfield Dri. Bail —5B 40
Oakfield Gro. B'frd —4A 58
Oakfield Gro. Skelm —8D 150
Oakfield Pk. Thpe A —6A 142
Oakfield Rd. Hud —1K 131
Oakfield Rd. Kei —3G 37
Oakfield Ter. H'fth —7H 43
(off Low La.)
Oakfield Ter. Shipl —8B 40
Oak Gro. Gar —7A 66
Oak Gro. Kei —4G 37
Oak Gro. Morl —1L 97
Oak Hall Pk. Crig —6E 136
Oakhall Pk. T'tn —7C 56
Oakhampton Ct. Leeds —8L 45
Oakham Wlk. B'frd —1E 76
Oak Hill. Sower B —3E 110
Oakhill Rd. Bat —5D 96
Oak Hill Rd. Brigh —9N 93
Oak Ho. C'frd —5E 102
(off Parklands)
Oak Ho. Leeds —8N 63
Oak Ho. Msde —2J 61
Oakhurst Av. Leeds —4C 80
Oakhurst Ct. B'frd —4B 58
Oakhurst Gro. Leeds —4B 80
Oakhurst Mt. Leeds —4B 80
Oakhurst Rd. Leeds —4B 80
Oakhurst St. Leeds —4C 80
Oakland Ct. Kbtn —2K 149
Oakland Dri. Neth —5M 135
Oakland Rd. Neth —5N 135
Oakland Rd. Wake —8N 119
Oaklands. B'frd —7E 40
Oaklands. Brigh —2L 113
Oaklands. I'ly —6F 8
Oaklands. Rob H —1J 99
Oaklands. Shipl —8J 39
Oaklands Av. Adel —4N 43
Oaklands Av. Hal —1F 92
Oaklands Av. Leeds —1B 60
Oaklands Clo. H'frth —1M 163
Oaklands Cft. W'ton —4C 138
Oaklands Dri. Adel —5N 43
Oaklands Dri. Bat —7J 97
Oaklands Dri. Hud —5D 132
Oaklands Fold. Adel —4N 43
Oaklands Gro. Adel —4N 43
Oaklands Gro. Leeds —1B 60
Oaklands Rd. Rod —1B 60
Oaklands Rd. Trad. Est. Leeds —1B 60
Oakland St. Sils —8D 6
Oak La. B'frd —4N 57
Oak La. Hal —5N 91
Oak La. Sower B —3E 110
Oaklea Clo. M'well —7K 153
Oaklea Gdns. Leeds —5N 43
Oaklea Hall Clo. Leeds —5N 43
Oaklea Rd. Scholes —9G 46
Oakleigh Av. Cytn —2G 74
(in two parts)
Oakleigh Av. Hal —9B 92
Oakleigh Av. Wake —6G 118
Oakleigh Clo. Cytn —1G 75
Oakleigh Clo. Shar C —7J 121
Oakleigh Gdns. Cytn —2G 74
Oakleigh Gro. Cytn —2G 74
(in two parts)
Oakleigh M. Oakw —5C 36
Oakleigh Rd. Cytn —2G 74
Oakleigh Ter. Cytn —1G 74
Oakleigh Ter. Todm —3D 86
Oakleigh Vw. Bail —4N 39
Oakley Gro. Leeds —2E 80
Oakley Ho. B'frd —1B 76
(off Park La.)
Oakley St. Thpe —3G 98
Oakley Ter. Leeds —3E 80
Oakley Vw. Leeds —3E 80
Oak Mt. B'frd —4B 58
Oak Mt. Hal —4K 93
Oak Mt. Todm —6K 87
Oak Pl. Bail —3D 40
Oak Pl. Gar —7M 65
Oak Pl. Hal —5N 91
Oak Pl. Sower B —7H 91
Oak Ridge. Weth —4K 17
Oakridge Av. Men —4F 24
Oakridge Ct. Bgly —3F 38
Oak Ri. Cleck —2H 95
Oak Ri. Pon —1L 123
Oak Rd. A'ley —7A 62
Oak Rd. Gar —7M 65
Oak Rd. Hud —6E 114
Oak Rd. Leeds —7A 64
Oak Rd. Morl —1J 97
Oak Rd. Pott —1F 62
Oak Rd. Shaf —7L 155
Oakroyd. —3L 149
Oak Royd. Gar —7N 65
Oakroyd. Rothw —9A 82
Oakroyd Av. B'frd —4A 76
Oakroyd Clo. B'shaw —8L 77
Oakroyd Clo. Brigh —7N 93
Oak Royd Cotts. Hal —1A 112
Oakroyd Dri. B'shaw —9L 77
Oakroyd Dri. Brigh —7N 93
Oakroyd Fold. Chur —5M 79
Oakroyd Mt. S'ley —6B 60
Oakroyd Rd. B'frd —4N 75
Oakroyd Ter. Bail —5B 40
Oakroyd Ter. B'frd —4B 58
Oakroyd Ter. Chur —5M 79
Oakroyd Ter. S'ley —6B 60
Oakroyd Vs. B'frd —4B 58
Oak Scar La. H'frth —6A 164
Oaks Dri. All —6H 57
Oaks Farm Clo. Dart —8H 153
Oaks Farm Dri. Dart —8H 153
Oaksfield. Meth —2L 101
Oaks Fold. B'frd —2C 76
Oaks Grn. Mt. Brigh —4L 113
Oaks La. All —6H 57
Oaks La. B Spa —9C 18
Oaks La. B'frd —7J 57
Oaks Rd. Bat —8H 97
Oaks, The. Guis —6J 25
Oaks, The. Morl —6L 79
Oaks, The. Shar C —7J 121
Oak St. Chur —6L 79
Oak St. Cytn —1G 75
Oak St. Ell —5E 112
Oak St. Haw —8D 36
Oak St. H Bri —1H 89
Oak St. Heck —8A 96
Oak St. New C —3H 139
Oak St. Oxe —3C 54
Oak St. Pud —6N 59
Oak St. S'fth & W'wth —6A 106
Oak St. S Elm —8M 157
Oak St. Sower B —7H 91
Oak St. Todm —8J 87
Oak St. Wake —8L 99
Oak St. Wilsd —2B 56
Oaks Wood Dri. Dart —9H 153
Oak Ter. Hal —5N 91
(off Acorn St.)
Oak Ter. Holy G —7N 111
Oak Ter. Leeds —3E 64
(off Church La.)
Oak Ter. L'boro —9M 107
Oak Tree Av. Cud —9J 155
Oak Tree Av. Fen B —7H 133
Oak Tree Av. H'frth —5B 164
Oak Tree Bus. Pk. Leeds —8B 46
Oak Tree Clo. Dart —9F 152
Oak Tree Clo. Leeds —3L 63
Oak Tree Ct. Leeds —3L 63
(off Oak Tree Pl.)
Oak Tree Ct. Sils —7D 6
Oak Tree Cres. Leeds —3L 63
Oak Tree Dri. Leeds —3L 63
Oak Tree Gro. Hems —3F 156
Oak Tree Gro. Leeds —3L 63
Oaktree La. Pon —5J 141
Oak Tree Mdw. W'ton —4B 138
Oak Tree Mt. Leeds —3L 63
Oak Tree Pl. Leeds —3L 63
Oak Tree Rd. Fen B —7H 133
Oak Tree Ter. Fen B —7H 133
Oak Tree Wlk. Leeds —3L 63
Oak Vw. Sils —7E 6
Oak Vw. Ter. Bat —4C 96
Oak Vs. B'frd —4B 58
Oakville Rd. C'twn —2E 88
Oakway. B'shaw —9M 77
Oakwell. —1A 96
Oakwell Av. Bat —6B 96
Oakwell Av. Leeds —9J 45
Oakwell Av. Pon —5J 123
Oakwell Clo. B'frd —2N 75
Oakwell Clo. Dlgtn —8D 78
Oakwell Ct. Bat —1D 96
Oakwell Cres. Leeds —9J 45
Oakwell Dri. Leeds —9J 45
Oakwell Gdns. Leeds —9J 45
Oakwell Gro. Leeds —3F 60
Oakwell Hall. —1A 96
Oakwell Ind. Est. Bat —1E 96
Oakwell Ind. Pk. Bat —1D 96
Oakwell Mt. Leeds —9J 45
Oakwell Oval. Leeds —9J 45
Oakwell Rd. Dlgtn —8D 78
Oakwell Rd. Kin —8A 140
Oakwell Ter. Fars —3A 60
Oakwell Way. Birs —1D 96
Oakwood. —9K 45
Oakwood. Wake —8F 118
Oakwood Av. B'shaw —9L 77
Oakwood Av. B'frd —2B 58
Oakwood Av. Leeds —9K 45
Oakwood Av. Roys —5D 154
Oakwood Av. Wake —6F 118
Oakwood Boundary Rd. Leeds —9K 45
Oakwood Clo. Nor —8G 100
Oakwood Ct. B'frd —6A 58
Oakwood Ct. Leeds —9L 45
Oakwood Cres. Roys —5C 154
Oakwood Dri. Bgly —2E 38
Oakwood Dri. Hems —4E 156
Oakwood Dri. Leeds —9K 45
Oakwood Dri. Nor —8G 100
Oakwood Dri. Rothw —6M 81
Oakwood Gdns. Cald G —4F 136
Oakwood Gdns. Leeds —9K 45
Oakwood Gth. Leeds —9L 45
Oakwood Grange. Leeds —9L 45
Oakwood Grange La. Leeds —9L 45
Oakwood Grn. Leeds —9L 45
Oakwood Gro. B'frd —5M 57
Oakwood Gro. Horb —9E 118
Oakwood Gro. Leeds —9K 45
Oakwood La. Leeds —9K 45
Oakwood Mt. Leeds —9K 45
Oakwood Nook. Leeds —9K 45
Oakwood Pk. Leeds —1L 63
Oakwood Pl. Leeds —9K 45
Oakwood Ri. Leeds —9L 45
Oakwood Rd. Bat —7H 97
Oakwood Rd. Roys —5C 154
Oak Wood Rd. Weth —2L 17
Oakwood Sq. Dart —9D 152
Oakwood Ter. Pud —8B 60
Oakwood Vw. Leeds —9L 45
Oakwood Wlk. Leeds —9L 45
Oakworth. —5C 36
Oakworth Hall. Oakw —5C 36
Oakworth Rd. Oakw & Kei —3F 36
Oakworth Ter. Oakw —5C 36
(off Dockroyd La.)
Oasby Cft. B'frd —4J 77
Oast Ho. Cft. Rob H —1K 99
Oastler Av. Hud —5L 131
Oastler Pl. Low M —7B 76
Oastler Rd. C'ley —9M 41
Oastler Rd. Shipl —7L 39
Oastler St. Dew —3E 116
Oates St. Dew —3F 116
Oatland Clo. Leeds —4E 62
Oatland Ct. Leeds —4E 62
Oatland Dri. Leeds —4E 62
Oatland Gdns. Leeds —4E 62
Oatland Grn. Leeds —4E 62
Oatland La. Leeds —4E 62

Oatland Pl. Leeds —3E 62
Oatland Rd. Leeds —4E 62
Oatlands Dri. Otley —8L 11
Oatland Towers. Leeds —4E 62
Oat St. Kei —3G 37
Oban Clo. Ting —3N 97
Oban Pl. Leeds —6K 61
Oban St. Leeds —6L 61
Oban Ter. Leeds —6L 61
Oban Ter. Ting —3N 97
Occupation La. B'hpe —5E 26
Occupation La. Hal —7L 73
Occupation La. H'frth —8B 148
Occupation La. Oakw —3D 36
Occupation La. Pud —8N 59
Occupation La. Stainc —9C 96
Occupation La. Tad —3D 48
Occupation Rd. Lind —2H 131
Occupation Rd. Sheep —8A 114
Ochrewell Av. Hud —8C 114
O'cot La. Hud —5H 129
Octagon Ter. Hal —8L 91
Odda La. Guis —7C 24
Oddfellows Club Houses. Ackw —5D 140
Oddfellows Ct. B'frd —7C 58
Oddfellows St. Brigh —9N 93
Oddfellows St. Mir —6L 115
Oddfellows St. Schol —4D 94
Oddfellow St. Morl —9K 79
Oddy Pl. B'frd —4N 75
Oddy Pl. Leeds —9N 43
Oddy's Fold. Leeds —7A 44
Oddy St. B'frd —4J 77
Odsal. —5C 76
Odsal Rd. B'frd —5B 76
(in two parts)
Odsal Stadium. —5C 76
Odsal Top. —5C 76
Offley La. Wake —4B 140
Ogden. —3K 73
Ogden Cres. Denh —4K 55
Ogden Ho. B'frd —2K 77
Ogden La. Brigh —3L 113
Ogden La. Denh —4K 55
Ogden La. Hal —3K 73
Ogden St. Sower B —9G 91
Ogden Vw. Clo. Hal —6K 73
Ogden Water Countryside Centre. —3K 73
Ogilby Ct. W'ford —6C 82
Ogilby M. W'ford —6C 82
O'Grady Sq. Leeds —7H 63
Old Acre La. Nort —7M 143
Old Allen Rd. T'tn —3N 55
Old Arc., The. Hal —5B 92
(off Old Mkt.)
Old Bank. Hal —5C 92
(in two parts)
Old Bank. Ripp —7E 110
Old Bank. Slai —1M 145
Old Bank Rd. Dew —3H 117
Old Bank Rd. Mir —4L 115
Old Barn Clo. Leeds —2C 44
Old Bell Ct. Hal —6B 92
(off Trinity Pl.)
Old Boyne Hill Farm. C'thpe —7J 137
Old Bramhope. —5D 26
Old Brandon La. Leeds —3N 45
Old Bri. Ri. I'ly —5F 8
Old Brookfoot La. Brigh —9L 93
Old Canal Rd. B'frd —6C 58
Old Causeway. Sower B —8J 91
Old Chu. St. Oss —6N 117
Old Clo. Leeds —5N 79
Old Cock Yd. Hal —5B 92
Old Corn Mill La. B'frd —1L 75
Old Corn Mill, The. Brigh —2H 77
Old Cross Stone Rd. Todm —7L 87
Old Crown Rd. Wake —8F 118
Old Dalton La. Kei —9K 21
Old Dan La. Holy G —6B 112
Old Dolphin. —3F 74
Old Earth. Ell —4G 112
Old Farm App. Leeds —7J 43
Old Farm Clo. Leeds —7K 43
Old Farm Cross. Leeds —7K 43
Old Farm Dri. Leeds —7J 43
Old Farm Gth. Leeds —7K 43
Old Farm Pde. Leeds —7K 43
Old Farm Wlk. Leeds —7J 43
Oldfield. —8L 147
(nr. Netherthong)
Oldfield. —7K 35
(nr. Scholes)
Oldfield Av. Leeds —8M 61
Old Fieldhouse La. Hud —9B 114
Oldfield La. Clay W —7J 151
Oldfield La. Coll —8L 17
Oldfield La. Haw —7A 36
Oldfield La. Heck —9A 96
Oldfield La. Leeds —8M 61
Oldfield La. Oldf —8J 35
Oldfield Rd. Hon —8K 147
Oldfield St. Hal —9N 73
Oldfield St. Hud —6K 131
Oldfield St. Leeds —8M 61
Old Fold. Fars —3A 60
Old Forge M. B'hpe —5G 26
Old Gth. Cft. Fair —9N 85
Old Ga. H Bri —1H 89
Old Ga. Holme —9D 162
Oldgate. Hud —4N 131
Old Godley La. Hal —4D 92
Old Gt. North La. M'fld —6F 66
Old Gt. North Rd. B'ton —3A 104
(in two parts)
Old Ground. Slai —1G 144
Old Guy Rd. Q'bry —3A 74
Old Hall Clo. Haw —9C 36
Old Hall La. Eml —4H 151
Old Hall M. Bat —5F 96
Old Hall Rd. Bat —5F 96
Old Hall Rd. Skel —8M 159
Old Hall Rd. Ting —4B 98
Oldham Rd. Ripp —5A 128
Oldham St. Brigh —2M 113
(off Bridge End)
Old Harry La. Err —5J 89
Old Haworth La. Yead —9M 25
Old Hollins Hill. Esh & Guis —1G 40
Old Laithe La. Wadsw —8K 71
Old La. Add —3B 8
Old La. B'shaw —7L 77
Old La. Brigh —9N 93
Old La. Cull —9K 37
Old La. Dlgtn —6C 78
Old La. Gol —5A 130
(in two parts)
Old La. Guis —8B 24
Old La. Hal —1N 91
Old La. H'frth —4B 162
Old La. Hud —6A 114
Old La. I'ly —6J 9
Old La. Leeds —3B 80
Old La. L'ft —3D 90
Old La. Otley & B'hpe —4B 26
Old La. Pec W —5J 71
Old La. Slai —2K 145
Old La. Stanb —8G 34
Old La. Todm —9J 87
Old La. Wake —9L 135
Old La. Ct. Brigh —9N 93
(off Old La.)
Old Langley La. Bail —3B 40
Old Lee Bank. Hal —3A 92
Old Leeds Rd. Hud —4N 131
Old Lees Rd. H Bri —9H 71
Old Lindley. —8B 112
Old Lindley Rd. Holy G —8B 112
Old Lodge Hill. I'ly —4E 8
Old London Rd. H'wd —1N 49
Old Main St. Bgly —3E 38
Old Mkt. Hal —5B 92
Old Marsh. Pud —7N 59
Old Marsh. Sower B —7H 91
(off Burnley Rd.)
Old Micklefield. —7F 66
Old Mill Clo. Bur W —7D 10
Old Mill Clo. Hems —2C 156
Old Mill La. Cliff —3E 32
Old Mill La. Hun P —1G 81
Old Mill Rd. Shipl —7M 39
Old Mill, The. Weth —4M 17
Old Mill Yd. Oss —8L 117
Old Moll Rd. Hud —4J 147
Old Mt. Farm. Wool —2J 153
Old Mt. Rd. Mars —8D 144
Old Oak Clo. Leeds —8K 43
Old Oak Dri. Leeds —8K 43
Old Oak Gth. Leeds —8J 43
Old Oak Lawn. Leeds —8K 43
Old Orchard, The. Hems —2D 156
Old Orchard, The. Pool W —1F 26
Old Oxenhope La. Oxe —1B 54
Old Packhorse Rd. Rish —3E 126
Old Pk. Rd. B'frd —7G 41
Old Pk. Rd. Leeds —7J 45
(in two parts)
Old Pool Bank. Pool W —4E 26
Old Popplewell La. Schol —4C 94
Old Power Way. Lfds B —3F 112
Old Riding La. Ludd —1F 90
Old Rd. B'frd —3K 75
Old Rd. Chur —5M 79
Old Rd. Denh —6K 55
Old Rd. Far —5N 59
Old Rd. H'frth —6H 163
Old Rd. Ove —5H 135
Old Rd. Pec W —3H 71
Old Rd. T'tn —8E 56
Old Robin. Cleck —5H 95
(off Westgate)
Oldroyd. —7M 87
Oldroyd Cres. Leeds —3A 80
Oldroyd Rd. Todm —7M 87
Oldroyd Way. Dew —3E 116
Old Run Rd. Leeds —3F 80
Old Run Vw. Leeds —5F 80
Old Sallow. —8L 159
Old Sawmills, The. Ripp —9C 110
Old Sch. M. Chur —5M 79
Old School Cft. Cuts —7C 102
Old Shaw La. Blkhd —9A 70
(in two parts)
Old Side Ct. E Mor —7D 22
Old Snydale. —3L 121
Old Souls Way. Bgly —1D 38
Old S. St. Hud —4M 131
Old Sta. Way. Add —1M 7
Old St. Hamp —9E 158
Old Tannery. Bgly —4F 38
(off Clyde St.)
Old Tannery. Bgly —4E 38
(off Industrial St.)
Old Town. —8J 71
Old Town Mill La. Wadsw —7J 71
Old Turnpike. Hon —5M 147
Old Village St. Burg —5M 159
Old Wakefield Rd. Hud —5B 132
Old Warehouse, The. Hud —4M 131
(off Henry St.)
Old Well Head. Hal —6B 92
Old Westgate. Dew —3F 116
Old Whack Ho. La. Yead —1K 41
Old Wood La. Bgly —7M 23
Old Woodyard, The. Midg —8M 135
Old Yew La. H'frth —6K 163
Olicana Pk. I'ly —4F 8
Olive Gro. B'frd —6K 57
Oliver Ct. Dlgtn —8A 78
Oliver Gdns. Mir —4K 115
Oliver Hill. H'fth —8F 42
Oliver La. Mars —5F 144
Oliver Meadows. Ell —4G 112
Oliver Rd. Heck —7B 96
Oliver's Mt. Kirks —2L 61
Olivers Mt. Pon —3L 123
Oliver St. B'frd —9E 58
Olive St. Hud —1N 131
Olive Ter. Bgly —4F 38
Olive Ter. Mars —3J 145
Olivia's Ct. B'frd —4K 57
Ollerdale Av. All —3F 56
(in two parts)
Ollerdale Clo. All —4F 56
Ollerton Rd. Barn —8A 154
Olney St. Slai —9M 129
Olympic Pk. Low M —8C 76
Olympic Way. Low M —8C 76
Omar St. Heck —8N 95
One St. B'frd —7B 58
(off Sunbridge Rd.)
Onslow Cres. B'frd —3F 76
Ontario Pl. Leeds —9F 44
Opal St. Kei —3G 36
Orange St. B'frd —8G 59
Orange St. Hal —5B 92
Orange Tree Gro. E Ard —5E 98
Orchan Rd. Todm —5H 87
Orchard Av. Stan —7A 100
Orchard Clo. Dart —8K 153
Orchard Clo. E Ard —6F 98
Orchard Clo. Hal —6K 91
Orchard Clo. Horb —9C 118
Orchard Clo. Mel —8E 146
Orchard Clo. Wren —9G 99
Orchard Ct. B'ham —6D 32
Orchard Ct. Guis —7J 25
(off Orchard La.)
Orchard Ct. Leeds —9N 43
(off St Chads Rd.)
Orchard Cft. Bat —9D 96
Orchard Cft. Horb —1D 136
Orchard Cft. Leeds —4C 64
Orchard Cft. Wake —1G 119
Orchard Cft. W'ton —3B 138
Orchard Dri. Ackw —5G 140
Orchard Dri. Dur —3H 137
Orchard Dri. Fair —8N 85
Orchard Dri. Lntn —6J 17
Orchard Dri. S Hien —3L 155
Orchard Gdns. Dur —3H 137
Orchard Ga. Otley —1L 25
(off Market St.)
Orchard Gro. B'frd —8H 41
Orchard Gro. Men —4E 24
Orchard Head Clo. Pon —9M 103
Orchard Head Cres. Pon —8M 103
Orchard Head Dri. Pon —9L 103
Orchard Head La. Pon —8K 103
Orchard Ho. B Spa —9D 18
(off Albion St.)
Orchard La. Add —1N 7
Orchard La. Guis —7J 25
Orchard Lees. Hud —2G 133
Orchard Mt. Leeds —4D 64
Orchard Rd. Hud —2G 132
Orchard Rd. Leeds —4C 64
Orchard Rd. Wake —1N 137
Orchard Sq. Leeds —4C 64
Orchards, The. Bgly —2F 38
Orchards, The. Gom —4N 95
Orchards, The. Halt —4C 64
Orchards, The. Meth —2K 101
Orchard St. Dew —5F 116
Orchard St. Hud —6M 131
Orchard St. Otley —1M 25
Orchard St. W. Hud —5F 130
Orchard Ter. Hud —6N 131
Orchard, The. B Spa —9D 18
Orchard, The. Cam —1N 159
Orchard, The. Croft —1H 139
Orchard, The. F'stne —2D 122
Orchard, The. Holy G —8M 111
Orchard, The. Kei —9M 21
Orchard, The. Mir —4M 115
Orchard, The. Nor —1J 121
Orchard, The. Oss —6N 117
Orchard, The. Pon —6M 123
Orchard, The. Wren —9H 99
Orchard Vw. B'ton —4B 104
Orchard Vw. D'ton —6B 124
Orchard Vw. S Kirk —6H 157
Orchard Vw. Weth —1M 17
Orchard Wlk. H Bri —3N 89
Orchard Way. Brigh —8M 93
Orchard Way. Guis —7J 25
Orchard Way. Rothw —7N 81
Orchid Ct. Loft —2K 99
Orchid Crest. Upt —2N 157
Oriental St. Leeds —7M 61
Orion Cres. Leeds —6G 81
Orion Dri. Leeds —6G 81
Orion Gdns. Leeds —6H 81
Orion Vw. Leeds —6H 81
Orion Wlk. Leeds —5H 81
Orlando Clo. Mir —4K 115
Orleans St. B'frd —6L 75
Ormonde Dri. All —6F 56
Ormonde Pl. Leeds —3E 62
Ormond Rd. B'frd —4N 75
Ormondroyd Av. B'frd —5A 76
Ormond St. B'frd —1M 75
Orville Gdns. Leeds —2A 62
Orwell Clo. C'frd —7J 103
Osborne Av. Horb —8E 118
Osborne Gro. Hal —5J 93
Osborne Pl. Todm —7L 87
(off Halifax Rd.)
Osborne Rd. Hud —2L 131
Osborne St. B'frd —9B 58
Osborne St. Hal —4M 91
Osborne St. H Bri —1H 89
Osborne St. Hud —5B 132
Osborne Ter. Bat —6E 96
Osbourne Ct. Leeds —5G 61
Osbourne Dri. Q'bry —4C 74
Osdal Rd. B'frd —5B 76
(off Glenfield Mt.)
Osmond Ho. B'frd —9C 58
(off Crosscombe Wlk.)
Osmondthorpe. —7M 63
Osmondthorpe Cotts. Leeds —7L 63
Osmondthorpe La. Leeds —6L 63
Osmondthorpe Ter. Leeds —6K 63
Osprey Clo. Coll —8J 17
Osprey Clo. Leeds —3H 45
Osprey Ct. B'frd —7H 57
Osprey Dri. Neth —2J 147
Osprey Gro. Leeds —3H 45
Osprey Mdw. Morl —9N 79
Ossett. —6N 117
Ossett La. Dew —4J 117
Ossett Spa. —8C 118
Ossett Street Side. —3L 117
Osterley Gro. B'frd —1J 59
Oswald St. B'frd —6M 57
Oswald St. Shipl —8B 40
Oswaldthorpe Av. B'frd —5H 59
Otley. —9L 11
Otley La. Yead —9M 25
Otley Mills. Otley —1J 25
Otley Mt. E Mor —8D 22
Otley Old Rd. Leeds —2H 43
Otley Old Rd. Otley, Yead, H'fth & Leeds —4B 26
Otley Rd. Bgly —2G 38
Otley Rd. B'frd —7D 58
Otley Rd. Bur W —8E 10
Otley Rd. E Mor —7D 22
Otley Rd. Guis —7G 24
Otley Rd. Leeds & Head —8L 27
Otley Rd. Men —3F 24
Otley Rd. Pool W —1C 28
Otley Rd. Shipl & C'twn —9N 39
Otley St. Hal —5M 91
Otley St. Kei —1H 37
Ottawa Pl. Leeds —9F 44
Otterburn Clo. B'frd —9B 58
Otterburn Gdns. Leeds —4L 43
Otterburn St. Kei —8J 21
Otter Lee La. Sower B —3B 110
Otters Holt. Dur —3H 137
Otterwood Bank. Weth —2N 17
Ottiwells Ter. Mars —6F 144
Ouchthorpe Fold. Out —9L 99
Ouchthorpe La. Wake —9L 99
Oulton. —8D 82
Oulton Dri. Cud —9K 155
Oulton Dri. Oult —1D 100
Oulton La. Oult —6D 82
Oulton La. Rothw —8A 82
Oulton Ter. B'frd —9A 58
Ouse Dri. Weth —1L 17
Ousel Hole. —6D 22
Ouse St. Haw —8D 36
Outcote Bank. Hud —5M 131
Out Gang. Leeds —3G 61
Out Gang La. Leeds —3H 61
Outlands Ri. B'frd —7H 41
Outlane. —2N 129
Out La. Eml —2F 150
Out La. Nthng —9L 147
Outside La. Oxe —4M 53
Outwood. —8K 99
Outwood Av. H'fth —8G 42
Outwood Chase. H'fth —7G 43
Outwood La. H'fth —8F 42
Outwood Pk. Ct. Out —8J 99
Outwood Wlk. H'fth —8F 42
Ouzelwell Cres. Dew —8E 116
Ouzelwell La. Dew —9C 116
Ouzelwell Rd. Dew —7E 116
Ouzlewell Green. —3M 99
Ouzlewell Grn. Loft —2M 99
Oval, The. —4A 64
Oval, The. Bail —6N 39
Oval, The. Beal —7L 105
Oval, The. Bgly —5G 38
Oval, The. B'frd —6K 57
Oval, The. Gar —7A 66
Oval, The. Guis —8G 24
Oval, The. H'frth —1L 163
Oval, The. H'let —1F 80
Oval, The. Leeds —4A 64
Oval, The. Liv —7G 95
Oval, The. Not —3C 154
Oval, The. Otley —8K 11
Oval, The. Rothw —8A 82
Ovenden. —2M 91
Ovenden Av. Hal —3N 91
Ovenden Clo. Hal —3N 91
Ovenden Cres. Hal —2N 91
Ovenden Grn. Hal —2M 91
Ovenden Rd. Ter. Hal —2N 91
Ovenden Ter. Hal —2N 91
Ovenden Way. Hal —2L 91
Ovenden Wood. —2J 91
Ovendon Wood Rd. Hal —2J 91
Overcroft, The. Horb —1C 136
Overdale. Sower B —4E 110
Overdale Av. Leeds —2J 45
Overdale Clo. Weth —3L 17
Overdale Dri. B'frd & Shipl —6D
Overdale Mt. Sower B —7J 91
Overdale Ter. Haw —8C 36
Overdale Ter. Leeds —6B 64
Overend St. B'frd —4M 75
Over Hall Clo. Mir —5M 115
Over Hall Pk. Mir —5M 115
Over Hall Rd. Mir —5M 115
Overland Cres. B'frd —7H 41
Overland Trad. Est. Gild —8F 78
Over La. Rawd —4N 41
Overmoor Fold. Idle —8D 40
Overthorpe. —1G 134
Overthorpe Av. Dew —1F 134
Overthorpe Rd. Dew —9G 117
Overton. —4J 135
Overton Dri. B'frd —3J 75
Overton Ho. B'frd —1B 76
(off Newstead Wlk.)
Overtown. —5C 138
Ovington Dri. B'frd —4J 77
Owen Ct. Bgly —1F 38
Owens Ter. Hon —6K 147
Owlcotes Dri. Pud —6N 59
Owlcotes Gdns. Pud —6N 59
Owlcotes Gth. Pud —6M 59
Owlcotes La. Far —5N 59
(in two parts)
Owlcotes La. Pud —6N 59
Owlcotes Rd. Pud —6M 59
Owlcotes Shop. Cen. S'ley —5A
Owlcotes Ter. Pud —6N 59
Owler Bars Rd. Mel —7B 146
Owler Ings Rd. Brigh —1M 113
Owler La. Birs —1B 96
Owler Meadows. Heck —7N 95
Owler Pk. Rd. I'ly —2D 8
Owlers Clo. Hud —6D 114
Owler's La. Pon —6M 141
Owlet. —1B 58

wlet Grange. Shipl —9A 40
wlet Hurst La. Liv —1M 115
wlet Rd. Shipl —8A 40
wlett Mead. Thpe —3G 98
wlett Mead Clo. Thpe —3G 99
wl La. Dew & Oss —9K 97
(in two parts)
wl M. Hud —4G 132
wl Ridge. Morl —1M 97
xenford Ct. Leeds —4K 43
xenhope. —4C 54
xenhope Station Railway Museum. —3C 54
xfield Ct. Hud —4E 132
xford Av. Guis —6H 25
xford Clo. Gom —4M 95
xford Clo. Q'bry —5B 74
xford Ct. Gdns. C'frd —5C 102
xford Cres. Cytn —1G 74
xford Cres. Hal —8C 92
xford Dri. Gom —4M 95
xford Dri. Kip —4N 83
xford La. Hal —8C 92
xford Pl. Bail —5C 40
xford Pl. B'frd —6D 58
xford Pl. Hud —7K 131
xford Pl. Leeds —6D 62
xford Pl. S'ley —5B 60
xford Rd. Birs —3B 96
xford Rd. B'frd —4E 58
xford Rd. Dew —2D 116
xford Rd. Gom —1M 95
xford Rd. Guis —7H 25
xford Rd. Hal —6B 92
xford Rd. Leeds —3E 62
xford Rd. Q'bry —5B 74
xford Rd. Wake —3K 119
xford Row. Leeds —6D 62
(in two parts)
xford St. Bat —8E 96
xford St. Cytn —1G 74
xford St. E Ard —4G 98
xford St. F'stne —6C 122
xford St. Guis —7J 25
xford St. H Bri —1G 88
xford St. Hud —3M 131
xford St. Kei —1G 37
xford St. Morl —2J 97
xford St. Nor —9K 101
xford St. S Elm —7M 157
xford St. Sower B —8K 91
xford St. Todm —8K 87
xford St. Wake —8N 119
xford Ter. Bail —5C 40
(off Union St.)
xford Ter. Bat —8G 97
ford Vs. Guis —7J 25
ford Wlk. Cleck —4M 95
Heys Mdw. T'tn —8F 56
Lee La. H'frth —8B 164
ley Gdns. Low M —6A 76
ley Rd. Hud —7A 114
leys Sq. Mnt —1C 130
ley St. B'frd —6A 58
ley St. Leeds —7H 63
ton Clo. Leeds —6H 63
ton Gdns. Leeds —6H 63
ton Mt. Leeds —6H 63
ton Pl. Leeds —6H 63
ton Rd. Barn —9A 154
ton Way. Leeds —6H 63
ster Clo. Morl —1M 97
acaholme Rd. Wake —3F 118
ck Horse Clo. Clay W —5K 151
ckington St. T'tn —6B 56
dan St. Hal —8C 92
ddock. —4J 131
ddock. B'frd —2A 58
ddock Clo. Dlgtn —8B 78
ddock Clo. Gar —8A 66
ddock Clo. M'well —8L 153
ddock Clo. Wyke —3A 94
ddock Corner. Leeds —7D 64
off Colton Rd.)
ddock Dri. Dlgtn —8B 78
ddock Foot. —5K 131
ddock Foot. Hud —5K 131
ddock Grn. E Kes —3D 30
ddock Ho. La. Sick —4B 16
ddock La. Eld —1J 39
ddock La. Hal —4J 91
ddock Rd. Hal —8D 74
ddock Rd. Kbtn —2L 149
ddock Rd. M'well —8L 153
ddocks, The. D'ton —7C 124
ddock, The. Bail —3D 40
ddock, The. Bur S —1D 104
ddock, The. C'frd —6J 103
ddock, The. Cull —9K 37
ddock, The. Earl —5J 117
ddock, The. E Kes —2D 30
Paddock, The. Kbtn —3G 132
Paddock, The. Knot —9E 104
Paddock, The. Leeds —8B 44
Paddock, The. Nor —2J 121
Paddock, The. Rothw —8N 81
Paddock, The. Schol —4D 94
Paddock, The. Sils —8E 6
Paddock, The. T'ner —2G 46
Paddock, The. Wake —1J 119
Paddock, The. Wool —2J 153
Paddock Vw. C'frd —6H 103
Paddy Bri. Rd. H Bri —3L 89
Padgate Ho. B'frd —1B 76
(off Park La.)
Padgum. Bail —3A 40
Padma Clo. B'frd —7N 57
Padmans La. B Spa —9D 18
Padstow Av. Leeds —8C 80
Padstow Gdns. Leeds —8C 80
Padstow Pl. Leeds —9C 80
Padstow Row. Leeds —9C 80
Page Hill. Hal —1L 91
Page St. Hud —5N 131
Paget Cres. Hud —1J 131
Paget St. Kei —9G 21
Page Wood Clo. B'frd —6E 40
Paignton Ct. Leeds —5G 60
Painthorpe. —6F 136
Painthorpe La. Crig —6F 136
Painthorpe Ter. Crig —6G 136
Paisley Gro. Leeds —6K 61
Paisley Pl. Leeds —6K 61
Paisley Rd. Leeds —6K 61
Paisley St. Leeds —6K 61
Paisley Ter. Leeds —6K 61
Paisley Vw. Leeds —6K 61
Pakington St. B'frd —1B 76
Palace Ho. Rd. H Bri —2H 89
Paleside. —3N 117
Paleside La. Oss —4N 117
Palesides Av. Oss —3N 117
Palestine Rd. H Bri —9H 71
Paley Pl. B'frd —9E 58
Paley Rd. B'frd —1E 76
Paley Ter. B'frd —1E 76
Palin Av. B'frd —5H 59
Palma St. Todm —3D 86
Palm Clo. B'frd —5N 75
Palmer Bldgs. Leeds —4J 63
Palmer Cres. Guis —7J 25
Palmer Cft. Leeds —6H 81
Palmer Mans. Yead —9M 25
Palmer Rd. B'frd —6F 58
Palmer's Av. S Elm —7A 158
Palmer Sq. Oss —2M 117
Palmerston St. B'frd —4F 58
Palm St. Hal —2A 92
Palm St. Hud —6N 131
Pannal Av. Wake —3N 119
Pannal St. B'frd —2M 75
Pannel Hill. Leds —6D 84
Panorama Dri. I'ly —7D 8
Paper Hall, The. —7D 58
Parade, The. Bat —8D 96
Parade, The. Bgly —8F 38
Parade, The. Head —1N 61
(off North La.)
Parade, The. H Wd —2J 77
Parade, The. Leeds —7G 62
Parade, The. Otley —8J 11
Parade, The. Yead —1K 41
(off Westfield Dri.)
Paradise Fields. Pon —2K 123
Paradise Fold. B'frd —1K 75
Paradise Green. —1L 75
Paradise La. Hal —2H 49
Paradise La. Warley —6H 91
Paradise Pl. H'fth —7H 43
Paradise Rd. B'frd —2L 57
Paradise Row. Hal —7M 91
Paradise St. B'frd —7B 58
Paradise St. Hal —6A 92
Parc Mont. Leeds —7L 45
Parish Ghyll Dri. I'ly —6E 8
Parish Ghyll La. I'ly —6E 8
Parish Ghyll Rd. I'ly —6F 8
Parish Ghyll Wlk. I'ly —6F 8
Paris Rd. Sch —5B 164
Park. —3D 40
Park Av. All B —9C 84
Park Av. A'ley —6L 61
Park Av. Bat —6G 97
Park Av. Bgly —5E 38
Park Av. B'frd —5F 40
Park Av. Brier —6B 156
Park Av. Carc —9N 159
Park Av. C'frd —5F 102
Park Av. Clay W —6J 151
Park Av. C'gts —4E 64
Park Av. Cud —9J 155
Park Av. D'ton —6B 124
Park Av. Dew —4E 116
Park Av. Dlgtn —7B 78
Park Av. Ell —5D 112
Park Av. Grime —9A 156
Park Av. Hud —4L 131
Park Av. Kei —1H 37
Park Av. Kip —4C 84
Park Av. K'thpe —4E 120
Park Av. Liv —1L 115
Park Av. Loft —6L 99
Park Av. Mir —7M 115
Park Av. Morl —1J 97
Park Av. Nor —1J 121
Park Av. Oakw —5D 36
Park Av. Out —8J 99
Park Av. Pon —3H 123
Park Av. Pud —7B 60
Park Av. Rawd —3N 41
Park Av. Round —7L 45
Park Av. Roys —6E 154
Park Av. Shel —6K 149
Park Av. Shipl —7M 39
Park Av. S Kirk —7H 157
Park Av. Swil —4H 83
Park Av. Wake —7K 119
Park Av. Yead —9L 25
Park Bottom. Low M —8A 76
Park Cir. Midd —8D 80
Park Cliffe Rd. B'frd —4E 58
Park Clo. Bat —9E 96
Park Clo. Bgly —3F 38
Park Clo. B'frd —1G 59
Park Clo. D'ton —6B 124
Park Clo. Dlgtn —7B 78
Park Clo. Hal —2H 91
Park Clo. Kei —2J 37
Park Clo. Leeds —3F 60
Park Clo. Light —5K 93
Park Clo. M'well —9L 153
Park Clo. Nor —2H 121
Park Clo. Q'bry —4C 74
Park Clo. Shel —6K 149
Park Copse. H'fth —6D 42
Park Cotts. Leeds —6K 45
Park Ct. B'frd —4A 58
Park Ct. F'stne —2D 122
Park Ct. Oss —7B 118
Park Ct. Pool W —2G 27
Park Ct. Todm —5H 87
Park Cres. Add —1N 7
Park Cres. A'ley —6L 61
Park Cres. B'frd —5E 58
Park Cres. C'frd —5J 103
Park Cres. Gild —7G 78
Park Cres. Guis —9G 25
Park Cres. Hal —3N 91
Park Cres. Leeds —5J 45
Park Cres. Rothw —7B 82
Park Cres. Roys —6E 154
Park Cres. Sower B —8K 91
(off Grove St.)
Park Crest. Hems —3D 156
Park Cft. Bat —8E 96
Park Cft. Dew —3D 116
Parkcroft. Fars —4B 60
Park Cross St. Leeds —6D 62
Park Dale. C'frd —3J 103
(in two parts)
Park Dale. Men —4E 24
Parkdale Dri. Sower B —4E 110
Park Dri. Bat —5D 96
Park Dri. Bgly —2G 38
Park Dri. B'frd —2M 57
Park Dri. Hal —6N 91
(HX1)
Park Dri. Hal —7K 91
(HX2)
Park Dri. H'fth —7C 42
Park Dri. Hud —3K 131
Park Dri. Loft —5L 99
Park Dri. Shel —7K 149
Park Dri. E. Mir —6M 115
Park Dri. N. Mir —6M 115
Park Dri. Rd. Kei —2J 37
Park Dri. S. Hud —4K 131
Park Dri. W. Mir —6M 115
Pk. Edge Clo. Leeds —8L 45
Parker Av. Nor —8F 100
Parker La. Mir —6M 115
Parker Rd. Dew —8F 116
Parker Rd. Horb —1E 136
Parker's La. Kei —5G 21
Parker St. E Ard —5E 98
Parker St. Heck —8A 96
Parker St. Liv —9N 95
Park Est. S Kirk —7J 157
Pk. Farm Ind. Est. Leeds —5D 80
Park Fld. Men —4E 24
Parkfield Av. Ell —5E 112
(off Catherine St.)
Parkfield Av. Leeds —2C 80
Parkfield Av. Mir —7N 115
Parkfield Clo. Kip —3B 84
Parkfield Clo. Pud —7A 60
Parkfield Ct. Leeds —3N 63
Parkfield Cres. Mir —7M 115
Parkfield Cft. Mir —7N 115
Parkfield Dri. B Spa —9C 18
Parkfield Dri. Oss —6C 118
Parkfield Dri. Q'bry —4C 74
Parkfield Dri. Sower B —1G 110
Parkfield Gro. Leeds —2C 80
Parkfield La. F'stne & Pon —2C 122
Parkfield Mt. Leeds —2C 80
Parkfield Mt. Pud —7B 60
Parkfield Pl. Leeds —2C 80
Parkfield Rd. B'frd —4B 58
Parkfield Rd. Leeds —2C 80
Parkfield Rd. Shipl —7K 39
Parkfield Row. Leeds —2C 80
Park Fields. Hal —2H 91
Parkfield St. Leeds —9E 62
Parkfield Ter. Pud —7B 60
Parkfield Ter. S'ley —5B 60
(in two parts)
Parkfield Vw. Leeds —2C 80
Parkfield Vw. Oss —6C 118
Parkfield Way. Leeds —3N 63
Parkfield Way. Mir —7M 115
Park Gdns. Hal —7K 91
Park Gdns. Oss —7B 118
Park Gate. —6D 150
Park Ga. B'frd —7D 58
Parkgate. Hud —1L 147
Parkgate. S Kirk —8H 157
Parkgate Av. Wake —5N 119
Park Ga. Clo. H'fth —7E 42
Park Ga. Cres. Guis —8H 25
Park Ga. Rd. Mars —3H 145
Park Grn. Hal —3E 92
Park Grn. Nor —2H 121
Park Grn. Sils —8C 6
Park Grn. Rd. Nor —2G 121
Park Gro. B'frd —2A 58
Park Gro. Gild —7G 78
Park Gro. Hal —3F 92
Park Gro. Horb —9B 118
Park Gro. H'fth —7C 42
Park Gro. Hud —4L 131
Park Gro. Kei —8J 21
Park Gro. Leeds —9E 80
Park Gro. Midd —9N 43
Park Gro. Mir —7N 115
Park Gro. Q'bry —4C 74
Park Gro. Shipl —7L 39
Park Gro. Swil —5H 83
Park Gro. Yead —9L 25
Park Gro. Ct. B'frd —2A 58
Park Gro. Rd. Wake —6J 119
Park Head. —3K 165
Parkhead Clo. B'frd —7M 75
Parkhead Clo. Roys —5B 154
Pk. Head La. Cumb —3J 165
Park Head La. H'frth —3K 163
Park Hill. Hud —5D 114
Pk. Hill Clo. B'frd —5J 57
Pk. Hill Cres. Wake —5N 119
Pk. Hill Dri. B'frd —5J 57
Pk. Hill Gro. Bgly —3F 38
Pk. Hill Gro. Wake —5A 120
Pk. Hill La. Wake —5N 119
Pk. Hill Wlk. Wake —5M 119
Pk. Holme. Leeds —2G 63
Pk. House Clo. Low M —6C 76
Pk. House Ct. Pen —8B 166
Park Ho. Cres. Low M —6C 76
Park Ho. Dri. Dew —7G 117
Park Ho. Gro. Low M —6C 76
Park Ho. Rd. Low M —7B 76
Park Ho. Wlk. Low M —6C 76
Parkin Hall La. Sower B —2B 110
Parkin La. B'frd —7K 41
Parkin La. Todm —6F 86
Parkinson App. Gar —6N 65
Parkinson Clo. Wake —5N 119
Parkinson La. Hal —6L 91
Parkinson Rd. Denh —6L 55
Parkinson St. B'frd —1B 76
Parkin Sq. Gol —5A 130
Parkin St. Liv —7G 95
Parkland Av. Morl —1H 97
Parkland Cres. Leeds —6C 44
Parkland Dri. B'frd —8G 40
Parkland Dri. Leeds —6C 44
Parkland Gdns. Leeds —7C 44
Parklands. —2B 64
Parklands. Bgly —2G 39
Parklands. B'hpe —5G 27
Parklands. C'frd —5E 102
Parklands. I'ly —5J 9
Parklands. Oss —7B 118
Parklands Av. Horb —1A 136
Parklands Ct. Horb —1A 136
Parklands Cres. B'hpe —5H 27
Parklands Cres. Horb —1A 136
Parklands Dri. Horb —1A 136
Parklands Dri. Sower B —2E 110
Parklands Ga. B'hpe —5H 27
Parklands Wlk. Shel —6K 149
Parkland Ter. Leeds —7C 44
Parkland Vw. Yead —9M 25
(off Town St.)
Park La. All B —9B 84
Park La. Bail —3D 40
Park La. Ber B —2L 147
Park La. Birds —3L 165
Park La. B'frd —1B 76
Park La. Bret —2A 152
Park La. Cytn —1G 75
Park La. F'stne & Pon —2D 122
Park La. Gol —6C 130
Park La. Guis —9G 25
Park La. Haig —2A 152
Park La. Hal —1C 112
Park La. H Bri —6N 69
Park La. Kei —1J 37
Park La. Kip —5C 84
Park La. Led —4J 85
(in two parts)
Park La. Leeds —6B 62
Park La. Mel —7D 146
Park La. Meth —3H 101
Park La. Myth —4J 89
Park La. Q'bry —4E 74
Park La. Rothw —8A 82
Park La. Round —5K 45
Park La. Sick —4C 16
Park La. Skelm —6D 150
Park La. Sow —1M 129
Park La. M. Leeds —3K 45
Park Lea. Hud —5D 114
Park Lea. Leeds —8E 80
Parklee Ct. Kei —1K 37
Park Lodge Ct. Wake —5N 119
Park Lodge Cres. Wake —5N 119
Park Lodge Gro. Wake —5M 119
Park Lodge La. Wake —5M 119
Pk. Lodge Vw. Skelm —8D 150
Park Mead. B'frd —5F 40
Parkmere Clo. B'frd —5F 76
Park M. Pool W —2G 26
Park Mill. —5J 151
Park Mill La. Oss —3B 118
Pk. Mill Way. Clay W —6J 151
Park Mt. A'ley —6K 61
Park Mt. Kirks —2K 61
Park Mt. Pool W —3E 26
Park Mt. Av. Bail —4C 40
Park Pde. Dew —4E 116
Park Pde. Leeds —8J 63
Park Pde. Morl —1J 97
Park Pl. Idle —5F 40
Park Pl. Leeds —6D 62
Park Pl. Pon —3H 123
Park Pl. E. Hal —5K 93
Park Pl. W. Hal —5K 93
Park Ri. C'frd —5F 102
Park Ri. Leeds —2F 60
Park Rd. A'ley —6K 61
Park Rd. Bat —7G 96
Park Rd. Bgly —4E 38
Park Rd. B Spa —9C 18
Park Rd. B'frd —9C 58
Park Rd. Brier —6B 156
Park Rd. C'frd & Pon —7G 102
Park Rd. Clay W —6J 151
Park Rd. Cow —6F 130
Park Rd. Cros M —6J 131
Park Rd. Dew —2D 116
Park Rd. Earl —4J 117
Park Rd. Eccl —1G 59
(in two parts)
Park Rd. Ell —3E 112
Park Rd. Grime —9A 156
Park Rd. Guis —9G 25
Park Rd. Hal —6A 92
Park Rd. Heck —8A 96
Park Rd. Leeds —3F 60
(LS13)
Park Rd. Leeds —8E 64
(LS15)
Park Rd. Low M —6A 76
Park Rd. Men —4E 24
Park Rd. Raven —5C 116
Park Rd. Rawd —3M 41
Park Rd. Sav T —5F 116
Park Rd. Shipl —8A 40
Park Rd. Sower B —7J 91
Park Rd. Thack —5F 40
Park Rd. Todm —6K 87
Park Rd. Yead —9L 25
Park Rd. Retail Pk. Pon —1J 123
Park Rd. W. Hud —6H 131
Park Row. Brigh —1N 113
Park Row. Bur W —7D 10
Park Row. Leeds —6D 62
Park Row. Otley —9M 11
(off Cross Grn.)
Park Row. S'ley —5B 60
Parkside. —3E 76

Parkside. Bgly —3F 38
Park Side. Cytn —1G 75
Parkside. Cleck —5J 95
Park Side. Floc —7F 134
Park Side. Gom —5L 95
Parkside. Hal —8A 92
Park Side. H'fth —7D 42
Park Side. Hud —1G 132
Park Side. Sch —4C 164
Parkside Av. Leeds —8B 44
Parkside Av. Q'bry —4C 74
Parkside Clo. Leeds —7B 44
Parkside Clo. Todm —3D 86
Parkside Ct. Cro R —7E 36
Parkside Cres. Leeds —7B 44
Parkside Dri. B'frd —3M 57
Parkside Gdns. Leeds —8B 44
Parkside Grn. Leeds —8B 44
Parkside Gro. B'frd —3M 57
Parkside Gro. Leeds —4C 80
Parkside Ind. Est. Leeds —4E 80
Parkside La. Leeds —3E 80
Parkside La. Stan —1N 119
Parkside Lawns. Leeds —8B 44
Parkside Mt. Leeds —4C 80
Parkside Pde. Leeds —4C 80
Parkside Pl. Leeds —7B 44
Parkside Rd. B'frd —3B 76
Parkside Rd. Fars —4A 60
Parkside Rd. Leeds —6A 44
Parkside Rd. Todm —3D 86
Parkside Row. Leeds —4C 80
Parkside Ter. Cull —9K 37
Parkside Vw. Leeds —7B 44
Parkside Wlk. Fars —4B 60
Parks La. Midd —1F 8
Park Spring. —7F 60
Pk. Spring Gdns. Leeds —5E 60
Pk. Spring Ri. Leeds —6E 60
Park Sq. B'frd —5L 75
Park Sq. Hal —2F 92
(off Hough)
Park Sq. Loft —6L 99
Park Sq. Oss —7B 118
Park Sq. Pool W —2G 27
Park Sq. Pud —7B 60
Park Sq. E. Leeds —6D 62
Park Sq. N. Leeds —6D 62
Park Sq. S. Leeds —6D 62
Park Sq. W. Leeds —6D 62
Parkstone. Hud —5D 114
Parkstone Av. Leeds —6K 43
Parkstone Dri. B'frd —1G 59
Parkstone Grn. Leeds —6K 43
Parkstone Gro. Leeds —6K 43
Parkstone Mt. Leeds —6K 43
Parkstone Pl. Leeds —6K 43
Pk. Stone Ri. She —7G 75
Park St. A'ley —6K 61
Park St. Bat —7G 96
Park St. Birs —4B 96
Park St. Brigh —1N 113
Park St. Chur —5M 79
Park St. Cleck —6F 94
Park St. Dew —2G 116
Park St. Gol —4B 130
Park St. Gom —4N 95
Park St. Halt —6C 64
Park St. Haw —8D 36
Park St. Heck —8A 96
Park St. Horb —1C 136
Park St. Leeds —6D 62
Park St. Oss —7B 118
Park St. Shipl —7M 39
Park St. Sower B —8K 91
Park St. Wake —6M 119
Park St. Yead —9L 25
Park Ter. Hal —6N 91
(in two parts)
Park Ter. Hip —5J 93
Park Ter. Kei —9K 21
Park Ter. Leeds —9N 43
Park Ter. Low M —7A 76
(off Park Rd.)
Park Ter. Otley —9M 11
(off Cross Grn.)
Park Ter. Pool W —3D 26
Park Ter. Shipl —7M 39
Park Ter. S Elm —7A 158
Park Ter. T Brow —1M 37
(off Bank Top Way)
Park, The. Caw —4N 167
Park, The. Clay W —7K 151
Park, The. S'wram —8F 92
Park Top. S'ley —5B 60
Pk. Top Cotts. Bgly —2G 39
Pk. Top Row. Haw —8C 36
Park Vw. B'shaw —8L 77
Park Vw. Brier —6B 156
Park Vw. C'frd —6H 103
Park Vw. Cleck —4G 94
Park Vw. Hal —6N 91
Park Vw. H'frth —3M 163
Park Vw. Holy G —2N 129
Park Vw. Kin —9B 140
Park Vw. Kip —4B 84
Park Vw. Leeds —2C 80
(LS11)
Park Vw. Leeds —3F 60
(LS13)
Park Vw. Light —5K 93
Park Vw. Loft —6L 99
Park Vw. Mars —5G 144
Park Vw. Mir —7N 115
Park Vw. Pud —7B 60
Park Vw. Q'bry —3C 74
Park Vw. Roys —5E 154
Park Vw. Shaf —7K 155
Park Vw. Swil —4H 83
Park Vw. Thorn —9H 117
Park Vw. Thorn L —6F 116
Park Vw. Wake —5G 118
Park Vw. Yead —9K 25
Park Vw. Av. Cro R —7E 36
Park Vw. Av. Leeds —3N 61
Park Vw. Av. Rawd —3N 41
Parkview Ct. Leeds —5K 45
Parkview Ct. Shipl —8M 39
Park Vw. Cres. Leeds —6K 45
Park Vw. Gro. Leeds —3N 61
Park Vw. Rd. B'frd —4N 57
Park Vw. Rd. Hal —3F 92
Park Vw. Rd. Leeds —4N 61
Park Vw. Rd. M'well —8M 153
Park Vw. Ter. B'frd —3N 57
Park Vw. Ter. Leeds —6B 64
(off Park St.)
Park Vw. Ter. Rawd —3M 41
Pk. Villa Ct. Leeds —6J 45
Park Vs. Leeds —6J 45
Park Villas. —6J 45
Park Vs. Dri. Pon —2H 123
Parkville Pl. Leeds —3F 60
Parkville Rd. Leeds —3F 60
Park Way. Bail —6L 39
Parkway. B'frd —3D 76
Parkway. Croft —9G 120
Parkway. Gild —7F 78
Parkway. Kei —2J 37
Park Way. Men —4E 24
Park Way. Pool W —2G 27
Parkway. Q'bry —4C 74
Parkway. Steet —3B 20
(in two parts)
Parkway Clo. Leeds —2N 63
Parkway Ct. Leeds —3N 63
Parkway Grange. Leeds —3N 63
Parkway M. Leeds —1C 64
Parkways. W'ford —7C 82
Parkways Av. W'ford —8C 82
Parkways Clo. W'ford —7C 82
Parkways Ct. W'ford —7C 82
Parkways Dri. W'ford —7C 82
Parkways Gth. W'ford —8C 82
Parkways Gro. W'ford —7C 82
Parkway Towers. Leeds —2N 63
Parkway Va. Leeds —3N 63
(in two parts)
Park W. Rothw —8N 81
Parkwood. —1J 37
Pk. Wood Av. Leeds —5B 80
Parkwood Av. Round —8J 45
Park Wood Bottom. —1K 37
Pk. Wood Clo. Leeds —6B 80
Parkwood Clo. Shel —6K 149
Parkwood Ct. Round —7J 45
Pk. Wood Cres. Leeds —6B 80
Pk. Wood Dri. Leeds —5B 80
Parkwood Gdns. C'ley —9L 41
Parkwood Gdns. Round —8J 45
Parkwood Ri. Kei —1J 37
Parkwood Rd. C'ley —9M 41
Parkwood Rd. Gol & Hud —4D 130
Pk. Wood Rd. Leeds —6B 80
Parkwood Rd. Shipl —8L 39
Parkwood St. Kei —1J 37
Parkwood Way. Round —8J 45
Parliament Pl. Leeds —6N 61
Parliament Rd. Leeds —7N 61
Parliament St. Wake —5K 119
Parlington Ct. Bar E —8M 47
Parlington Dri. Aber —8E 48
Parlington La. Gar —3N 65
Parlington Mdw. Bar E —9M 47
Parlington Vs. Aber —8E 48
Parma St. B'frd —9C 58
Parnaby Av. Leeds —4H 81
Parnaby Rd. Leeds —4H 81
Parnaby St. Leeds —4H 81
Parnaby Ter. Leeds —4H 81
Parratt Row. B'frd —7H 59
Parrish Pl. Kei —9J 21
Parrish Rd. Leeds —2D 80
Parrish Vw. Hal —8F 92
Parrish Wlk. Q'bry —4D 74
Parrock La. Wadsw —7J 71
Parrott St. B'frd —4H 77
Parry La. B'frd —9G 58
Parsonage La. Brigh —9M 93
Parsonage Rd. Lais —9H 59
Parsonage Rd. Meth —1L 101
Parsonage Rd. W Bowl —2C 76
Parsonage St. Hal —3C 92
Parson La. Wool —1J 153
Parsons Grn. Weth —4N 17
Parson's La. Sils —2F 6
Parsons Rd. B'frd —2M 57
Parson St. Kei —8J 21
Partington Ho. B'frd —8G 40
(off Fairhaven Grn.)
Partons Pl. Loft —6L 99
Partridge Clo. Morl —9N 79
Partridge Cres. Dew —1J 135
Pasture Av. Leeds —8F 44
Pasture Clo. Cytn —1J 75
Pasture Cres. Leeds —8F 44
Pasture Dri. C'frd —6A 102
Pasture Fold. Bur W —7C 10
Pasture Grn. Clo. Leeds —6L 63
Pasture Gro. Leeds —8F 44
Pasture La. Cytn & B'frd —1H 75
Pasture La. Kear —8N 15
Pasture La. Leeds —8F 44
Pasture La. S Elm —6C 158
Pasture Mt. Leeds —6L 61
Pasture Pde. Leeds —8F 44
Pasture Pl. Leeds —8F 44
Pasture Ri. Cytn —1J 75
Pasture Rd. Bail —5B 40
Pasture Rd. Leeds —2G 63
Pastureside Ter. E. Cytn —1J 75
Pastureside Ter. W. Cytn —1H 75
Pasture St. Leeds —8F 44
Pastures Way. Gol —5C 130
Pasture Ter. Leeds —8F 44
Pasture Vw. Leeds —6L 61
Pasture Vw. Rd. Rothw —8N 81
Pasture Wlk. Cytn —1H 75
Pasture Way. C'frd —7A 102
Patchett Sq. Q'bry —4G 74
(off Western Pl.)
Pateley Cres. Hud —9M 113
Patent St. B'frd —4N 57
Paternoster La. B'frd —1M 75
Paterson Av. Wake —5J 119
Patience La. Nor —9F 100
Patterdale App. Weth —4J 17
Patterdale Clo. Carc —8N 159
Patterdale Dri. Hud —4B 132
Patterdale Ho. B'frd —1B 76
(off Hutson St.)
Patterdale Rd. Dew —1H 117
Patterson Ct. Wren —9H 99
Pattie St. Kei —7H 21
Paulena Ter. Morl —2L 97
(off Britannia Rd.)
Pauline Ter. C'frd —5C 102
Paul La. Floc M —7N 133
Paul La. Hud —7G 114
Pavement La. Hal —5L 73
Pavilion Clo. Brier —6A 156
Paw La. Q'bry —6E 74
Pawson St. B'frd —8H 59
Pawson St. Loft —2K 99
Pawson St. Morl —1J 97
Pawson St. Wake —4G 98
Peabody St. Hal —3N 91
Peace Hall Dri. Fen B —5G 132
Peace St. B'frd —9G 59
Peace St. Ind. Est. B'frd —8G 59
Peach Tree Clo. Pon —4H 123
Peach Wlk. B'frd —1F 76
Peacock Av. Wake —3H 119
Peacock Clo. Wake —4H 119
Peacock Grn. Morl —1M 97
Peacock Gro. Wake —4H 119
Peacock Ter. Shipl —8M 39
Peak Vw. Dew —1C 116
Pearl St. Bat —6D 96
Pearl St. Kei —3G 36
Pear Pl. Todm —3D 86
Pearsall Gro. B'frd —7D 58
Pearson Av. Leeds —3A 62
Pearson Fold. Oaken —9D 76
Pearson Gro. Leeds —3A 62
Pearson La. B'frd —5J 57
Pearson Rd. B'frd —5B 76
Pearson Rd. W. B'frd —5B 76
Pearson Row. Wyke —1B 94
Pearsons Bldgs. Otley —1M 25
Pearson's La. Bstfld —3C 134
Pearson St. B'frd —8G 59
Pearson St. C'ley —8M 41
Pearson St. Cleck —6J 95
Pearson St. Leeds —3B 62
Pearson St. Msde —6F 94
Pearson St. Nor —7H 101
Pearson Ter. Leeds —3A 62
Pear St. Hal —6M 91
Pear St. Hud —6K 131
Pear St. Kei —4G 37
Pear St. Oxe —4C 54
Pear St. Todm —3D 86
Pear Tree Acre. Thor A —8E 18
Pear Tree Clo. Pon —5H 123
Pear Tree Ct. Sils —7E 6
Peartree Fld. La. Went —6B 142
Pear Tree La. Hems —2D 156
Pear Tree Wlk. Wake —3J 119
Peas Acre. Bgly —8D 22
Peasborough Vw. Bur W —9D 10
Pease Clo. Pon —5K 123
Peasefold. Kip —4B 84
Peasehill Clo. Rawd —3N 41
Peasehill Pk. Rawd —3N 41
Peaseland Av. Cleck —5G 95
Peaseland Clo. Cleck —5H 95
Peaseland Rd. Cleck —5H 95
Peaselands. Shipl —8M 39
Peat Ponds. Hud —1D 130
Peckett Clo. Hud —3H 131
Pecket Well. —6J 71
Peckover Dri. Pud —5K 59
Peckover St. B'frd —7D 58
Peebles Clo. Hud —1F 130
Peel Av. Bat —7F 96
Peel Clo. Horb —1D 136
Peel Clo. Tyer —9J 59
Peel Cottage Rd. Todm —2J 107
Peel Cottage St. Todm —3J 107
Peel Ct. B'frd —4D 58
Peel Ho. Bgly —5G 38
Peel Pk. Dri. B'frd —4F 58
Peel Pk. Ter. B'frd —4F 58
Peel Pk. Vw. B'frd —5E 58
Peel Pl. Bur W —8C 10
Peel Row. B'frd —1M 75
Peel Sq. B'frd —6B 58
Peel Sq. Leeds —2K 61
Peel St. Bgly —4G 38
Peel St. Heck —8N 95
Peel St. Horb —1C 136
Peel St. Hud —5M 131
Peel St. Mars —5F 144
Peel St. Morl —9L 79
Peel St. Q'bry —4E 74
Peel St. Sower B —8H 91
Peel St. T'tn —8C 56
Peel St. Wilsd —2B 56
Peep Grn. La. Liv —1G 114
Peep Grn. Rd. Liv —1G 115
Pegholme Dri. Otley —2H 25
Pelham Ct. B'frd —3F 58
Pelham Pl. Leeds —8E 44
Pelham Rd. B'frd —3F 58
Pell La. H'frth —2A 164
Pellon. —4L 91
Pellon La. Hal —4M 91
Pellon New Rd. Hal —4L 91
Pellon St. Todm —1H 107
Pellon Ter. B'frd —6F 40
Pellon Wlk. B'frd —6F 40
Pemberton Dri. B'frd —8B 58
Pemberton Rd. C'frd —4G 103
Pembridge Ct. Roys —5D 154
Pembroke Clo. Morl —8J 79
Pembroke Dri. Morl —8J 79
Pembroke Dri. Pud —6B 60
Pembroke Grange. Leeds —4M 63
Pembroke Ho. B'frd —3J 77
(off Launceston Dri.)
Pembroke Ri. Kip —3C 84
Pembroke Rd. Pud —6B 60
Pembroke St. B'frd —1C 76
Pembroke Towers. Leeds —3M 63
Pembury Mt. Leeds —3G 64
Penarth Av. Upt —2N 157
Penarth Rd. Leeds —4C 64
Penarth Ter. Upt —2M 157
Pendas Dri. Leeds —4E 64
Pendas Fields. —3G 64
Pendas Gro. Leeds —3E 64
Pendas Wlk. Leeds —4E 64
Pendas Way. Leeds —4E 64
Pendennis Av. S Elm —5L 157
Pendil Clo. Leeds —6D 64
Pendle Ct. Q'bry —6D 74
Pendle Rd. Bgly —4G 39
(in two parts)
Pendragon. B'frd —3E 58
Pendragon La. B'frd —3F 58
Pendragon Ter. Guis —7H 25
Penfield Gro. Cytn —1H 75
Penfield Rd. Dlgtn —3C 78
Pengarth. Bgly —2G 39
Penistone Hill Country Park. —9A 36
Penistone M. Haw —8C 36
Penistone Rd. H'frth —8N 163
Penistone Rd. N Mill & Shep —2C 164
Penistone Rd. Shel —7L 149
Penistone Rd. W'loo & Kbtn —5F 13
Penlands Cres. Leeds —7E 64
Penlands Lawn. Leeds —7E 64
Penlands Wlk. Leeds —7E 64
Penlington Clo. Hems —4D 156
Pennard Ho. B'frd —1B 76
(off Launton Way)
Penn Clo. B'frd —2F 58
Penn Dri. Liv —6H 95
Penn Gro. Liv —6H 95
Pennine Clo. Dart —7J 153
Pennine Clo. H'frth —3J 163
Pennine Clo. Q'bry —6C 74
Pennine Clo. Wake —8G 118
Pennine Cres. Hud —2D 130
Pennine Dri. Scis —7G 151
Pennine Gdns. Lint —9C 130
Pennine Gro. Todm —6L 87
Pennine Ri. Scis —7G 151
Pennine Rd. Dew —3H 117
Pennine Vw. Birs —1D 96
Pennine Vw. Blkhd —9A 70
Pennine Vw. Dart —7J 153
Pennine Vw. Khtn —9G 115
Pennine Vw. Lint —9C 130
Pennine Vw. L'boro —9M 107
Pennine Vw. Pon —1N 157
Pennine Way. Hems —2F 156
Pennine Way. Scis —7G 151
Pennington Ct. Leeds —3C 62
Pennington Gro. Leeds —2C 62
Pennington La. Oult —2C 100
Pennington Pl. Leeds —3C 62
Pennington St. Leeds —3C 62
Pennington Ter. B'frd —1A 76
Pennington Ter. Leeds —2C 62
Pennistone Rd. N Mill —2C 164
Pennithorne Av. Bail —3A 40
Penn St. Hal —4N 91
Pennwell Cft. Leeds —1E 64
(off Whinmoor Way)
Pennwell Dean. Leeds —1E 64
Pennwell Fld. Leeds —1F 64
Pennwell Gth. Leeds —1E 64
Pennwell Ga. Leeds —1E 64
Pennwell Grn. Leeds —1E 64
Pennwell Lawn. Leeds —1E 64
Pennygate. Bgly —2J 39
Penny Hill Cen., The. Leeds —1G
Penny Hill Dri. Cytn —1J 75
Penny La. W'loo —5F 132
Penny La. Way. Leeds —1F 80
Penny Spring. Hud —7C 132
Penny St. B'frd —7E 58
Penraevon Av. Pen I —3E 62
Penrith Cres. C'frd —2L 103
Penrith Gro. Leeds —8M 61
Penrose Beck Dri. Ackw —5E 14
Penrose Dri. Gt Hor —2L 75
Penrose Pl. Wake —5H 137
Penryn Av. Hud —2G 132
Pentland Av. Cytn —1H 75
Pentland Av. Knot —8D 104
Pentland Clo. Kei —1G 37
Pentland Dri. Gar —9N 65
Pentland Gro. Wake —8G 118
Pentland Rd. Dew —5G 116
Pentland Way. Morl —1K 97
Penuel Pl. Hal —9C 92
Pepper Gdns. Bmly —2H 61
Pepper Hill. —7F 74
Pepper Hills. Leeds —3F 44
Pepper La. Leeds —2H 81
Pepper La. Msde —2G 61
Pepper Rd. Leeds —3H 81
Pepper Royd St. Dew —2G 117
Percival St. B'frd —7E 58
Percival St. Hud —4E 130
Percival St. Leeds —5D 62
Percy St. Bgly —4F 38
Percy St. Hud —1M 131
Percy St. Kei —3H 37
Percy St. Leeds —8N 61
Percy St. Q'bry —3B 74
Percy St. S'fth —5A 106
Percy St. S Kirk —7H 157
Peregrine Av. Morl —9N 79
Peregrine Ct. Neth —2K 147
Peridot Fold. Far —9A 114
Perkin La. B'frd —6D 40
(off Far Crook)
Per La. Hal —6K 73
Permain Ct. New —6N 131
Perry Clo. Kei —4G 37
Perserverence St. Cow —7E 130
Perseverance La. B'frd —2M 75
Perseverance Rd. Hal —2N 73
Perseverance St. Bail —3B 40
Perseverance St. C'frd —4C 102
Perseverance St. Hal —7N 91
Perseverance St. Prim H —7M 1
Perseverance St. Pud —7N 59

erseverance St. Sower B —7H 91
erseverance St. Wyke —9A 76
erseverance Ter. Bat —9F 96
erseverance Ter. Rothw —9N 81
erth Av. B'frd —3C 58
erth Dri. Ting —4B 98
'erth Ho. B'frd —9H 59
(off Parsonage Rd.)
erth Mt. H'fth —3E 42
eterborough Pl. B'frd —3F 58
eterborough Rd. B'frd —4F 58
eterborough Ter. B'frd —3F 58
etergate. B'frd —7D 58
eter Hill. Bat —1G 116
eterhouse Dri. Otley —1N 25
eter La. Hal —5H 91
eter La. Morl —8N 79
etersfield Av. Leeds —6G 80
etersgarth. Shipl —7K 39
eterson Rd. Wake —5M 119
ether Hill. Slnd —8M 111
etrel Way. Morl —1M 97
etrie Cres. Leeds —1A 60
etrie Gro. B'frd —7J 59
etrie Rd. B'frd —7J 59
etrie St. Leeds —1A 60
etworth Cft. Roys —5C 154
everell Clo. B'frd —2J 77
everil Mt. B'frd —3G 58
exwood Rd. Todm —9H 87
heasant Dri. Birs —1D 96
heasant St. Kei —8K 21
hilip Gth. Wake —7K 99
hilip Ho. Leeds —5C 62
hilippa Way. Leeds —2M 79
hilip's Gro. Loft —6L 99
hilip's La. D'ton —6B 124
hillips St. C'frd —4B 102
hil May Ct. Leeds —8A 62
(off Green La.)
hilpotts Pl. Kei —2H 37
hipp Av. Leeds —2H 63
hipp Ho. Sils —8E 6
hoebe La. Hal —8C 92
hoebe La. Ind. Est. Hal —8C 92
hoenix Av. Eml —3G 150
hoenix Bldgs. B'frd —8A 58
hoenix Clo. Leeds —3B 64
hoenix Ct. Todm —6M 87
hoenix Ct. Wake —5J 119
hoenix St. Brigh —1N 113
hoenix St. Todm —6M 87
hoenix Way. B'frd —8J 59
ccadilly. B'frd —7C 58
ccadilly. Wake —5K 119
ckard Bank. Leeds —1B 62
ckard Ct. Leeds —6D 64
ckard La. Sils —7E 6
ckard Way. Dew —2E 116
ckering Av. Gar —6B 66
ckering Dri. Oss —2M 117
ckering La. Oss —2M 117
ckering Mt. Leeds —6N 61
ckerings, The. Q'bry —5D 74
ckering St. Leeds —6N 61
ckersgill St. Oss —3M 117
cker St. Todm —4G 86
ckford St. Hud —6F 130
ck Hill Rd. Mel —6C 146
ckles Ct. Todm —6K 87
cklesfield. Bat —1E 116
ckles Hill. —3L 75
ckles La. B'frd —3L 75
ckles La. Skelm —8E 150
ckles St. Bat —1E 116
ckles St. Kei —2H 37
ckpocket La. Rothw —6B 82
ckthall Ter. Todm —7M 87
ckwood La. Norl —1L 111
ckwood Scar. —1L 111
cton Ho. B'frd —5A 58
off Green La.)
cton St. B'frd —5B 58
ce Hall Yd. B'frd —7C 58
ce Wood Rd. Leeds —4G 42
eon Cote Clo. Leeds —9B 46
eon Cote Rd. Leeds —9B 46
gott St. Brigh —9M 93
hill Top La. Slai —8L 129
man La. Hal —6G 90
e End Ga. Rish —4M 127
e End Rd. Rish —2B 128
e Law La. Gol —5A 130
e Law Rd. Gol —5N 129
e Lowe Dri. M'well —9M 153
dacre Brow. Oss —5M 117
dacre Cft. Oss —5M 117
dacre La. Dew & Oss —5K 117
den La. E Ard —6E 98
grim Av. Dew —4C 116
grim Cres. Dew —4C 116
grim Dri. Dew —4C 116
kington St. Wake —7L 119
Pilling La. Skelm —7E 150
Pilling Top La. Shel —5M 149
Pill White La. Lind —4C 12
Pilmer Ct. Wake —6F 118
Pilot St. Leeds —5G 62
Pincheon St. Wake —5M 119
Pinder Av. Leeds —1J 79
Pinderfields Rd. Wake —4L 119
Pinder Green. —3K 101
Pinder Gro. Leeds —1J 79
Pinders Cres. Knot —7B 104
Pinders Garth. Knot —7B 104
Pinders Grn. Ct. Meth —3K 101
Pinders Grn. Dri. Meth —3K 101
Pinders Grn. Fold. Meth —3K 101
Pinders Grn. Wlk. Meth —4K 101
Pinder's Gro. Wake —3N 119
Pinder St. Leeds —1J 79
Pinder Vw. Leeds —1J 79
Pineapple Cotts. Warm —5F 120
Pine Clo. C'frd —6E 102
Pine Clo. Weth —2M 17
Pine Ct. Leeds —7F 62
Pine Ct. Neth —3J 147
Pine Ct. M. Neth —3J 147
Pine Cft. Kei —7G 20
Pinedale. Bgly —2E 38
Pine Gro. Bat —8E 96
Pinehurst Ct. Lind —1G 131
(off Lidget St.)
Pine Rd. Todm —5H 87
Pines Gdns. I'ly —6E 8
Pines, The. Huby —6M 13
Pine St. B'frd —7D 58
Pine St. Hal —6B 92
Pine St. Haw —9C 36
Pine St. Hud —3N 131
Pine St. S Elm —8L 157
Pine Tree Av. B Spa —9E 18
Pinetree Av. Pon —5H 123
Pinewood Av. Wake —5F 118
Pinewood Clo. I'ly —6F 8
Pinewood Gdns. Holy G —7A 112
Pinewood Pl. Knot —9C 104
Pinfold Clo. Bklnd —6G 111
Pinfold Clo. Floc —8F 134
Pinfold Clo. Knot —7B 104
Pinfold Clo. Mick M —1L 101
Pinfold Clo. Mir —6M 115
Pinfold Clo. Thorn —9H 117
Pinfold Ct. Leeds —6C 64
Pinfold Dri. Croft —1H 139
Pinfold Gro. Leeds —6B 64
Pinfold Gro. Wake —1M 137
Pinfold Hill. Dew —3E 116
Pinfold Hill. Leeds —6C 64
Pinfold La. A'ley —7L 61
Pinfold La. Cook —1H 43
Pinfold La. Ell —5J 113
Pinfold La. Floc —8F 134
Pinfold La. Gar —7N 65
Pinfold La. Gol —6N 129
Pinfold La. Hud —5J 129
Pinfold La. K S'ton —5J 143
Pinfold La. Leeds —6B 64
Pinfold La. Lep —7L 133
Pinfold La. Meth —1M 101
Pinfold La. Mir —6M 115
Pinfold La. Roys —6D 154
Pinfold La. Sower B —8D 90
Pinfold La. Wake —1N 137
Pinfold Mt. Leeds —7C 64
Pinfold Ri. Aber —7E 48
Pinfold Rd. Leeds —7C 64
Pinfold Sq. Leeds —6B 64
Pingle Ri. Den D —1D 166
Pin Hill La. Hal —3D 90
Pink St. Haw —1C 54
Pinnacle La. Err —4F 88
Pinnar Cft. Hal —8F 92
Pinnar La. Hal —7E 92
Pioneer St. Dew —8F 116
Pioneer St. Todm —4J 107
Pipe & Nook La. Leeds —7J 61
Pipercroft. B'frd —7K 75
Piper Hill. Fair —9N 85
Piper La. Otley —1K 25
Piper Well La. Cumb —3J 165
Pipit Mdw. Morl —1M 97
Pippin's App. Norm —9J 101
Pippins Grn. Av. K'gte —1D 118
Pirie Clo. B'frd —3D 58
Pitchstone Ct. Leeds —7G 60
Pitcliffe Way. B'frd —1D 76
Pitfall St. Leeds —7E 62
Pit Fld. Rd. Carl —2M 99
Pit La. Butt —6L 75
Pit La. Dew —1C 116
Pit La. Gom —2M 95
Pit La. Meth —9L 83
Pit La. M'fld —1E 84
(in two parts)
Pit La. Q'bry —2B 74
Pits La. Schol —6C 94
Pitt Hill La. Bklnd —9J 111
Pitt La. M'well —8J 153
Pitt Row. Leeds —7E 62
Pitts St. B'frd —1H 77
Pitt St. Kei —9K 21
Pitt St. Liv —1M 115
Pitt St. Todm —7M 87
Place's Rd. Leeds —7G 63
Plaid Row. Leeds —6G 63
Plain La. Sower B —1C 110
Plains. Mars —4G 144
Plains La. Ell —3E 112
Plains La. Mars —4G 144
Plane Grn. Pon —2M 123
Plane St. Hud —7N 131
Plane St. Todm —5G 87
Plane Tree Av. Leeds —3H 45
Plane Tree Clo. Leeds —3H 45
Plane Tree Cft. Leeds —3H 45
Plane Tree Gdns. Leeds —3H 45
Plane Tree Gro. Yead —1A 42
Plane Tree Nest. Hal —6L 91
Plane Tree Nest La. Hal —6L 91
Plane Tree Ri. Leeds —3H 45
Plane Tree Rd. Sower B —7H 91
Plane Trees Clo. Cleck —1H 95
Planetrees Rd. B'frd —8G 59
Planetrees St. All —5F 56
Plane Tree Vw. Leeds —3H 45
Plantation Av. Leeds —7A 64
Plantation Av. Roys —6E 154
Plantation Av. Shad —2J 45
Plantation Dri. New —9M 131
Plantation Gdns. Leeds —2J 45
Plantation Pl. B'frd —1H 77
Plantation Way. Bail —4B 40
Platt La. Slai —9N 129
Platt Sq. Cleck —5H 95
(off Westgate)
Playfair Rd. Leeds —3F 80
Playground. Leeds —2G 78
Pleasance, The. Swil —4H 83
Pleasant Ct. Leeds —3C 62
(off Rampart Rd.)
Pleasant Mt. Leeds —9C 62
Pleasant Pl. All —5F 56
Pleasant Pl. Leeds —9C 62
Pleasant Row. Q'bry —5B 74
Pleasant St. B'frd —1M 75
Pleasant St. Leeds —9C 62
Pleasant St. Sower B —8J 91
Pleasant Ter. Leeds —9C 62
Pleasant Vw. Loft —5H 99
Pleasant Vw. L'ft —3C 90
Pleasant Views. Denh —5L 55
Pleasant Vw. Ter. Rothw —9K 81
(off Copley La.)
Pledwick. —5M 137
Pledwick Cres. Wake —4M 137
Pledwick Dri. Wake —5M 137
Pledwick Gro. Wake —5L 137
Pledwick La. Wake —5M 137
Pledwick Ri. Wake —5M 137
Plevna St. Leeds —3J 81
Plevna Ter. Bgly —3E 38
Plimsoll St. B'frd —1E 76
Plimsoll St. Hems —2D 156
Ploughcroft La. Hal —2A 92
Ploughman's Cft. B'frd —2C 58
Plover Dri. Bat —7C 96
Plover Rd. Lind —2G 130
Plover St. B'frd —2A 76
Plover St. Kei —8J 21
Plover Way. Morl —1M 97
Plumpton Av. B'frd —9D 40
Plumpton Clo. B'frd —1E 58
Plumpton Dri. B'frd —9D 40
Plumpton End. B'frd —9E 40
Plumpton Gdns. B'frd —9C 40
Plumpton Lea. B'frd —9D 40
Plumpton Mead. B'frd —9D 40
Plumpton Pl. Wake —5J 119
Plumpton Rd. Wake —5J 119
Plumpton St. B'frd —6M 57
Plumpton St. Wake —5J 119
Plumpton Ter. Wake —5J 119
Plumpton Wlk. B'frd —9D 40
Plum St. Hal —6M 91
Plum St. Kei —4G 37
Plum Tree Clo. Pon —5H 123
Plymouth Gro. Hal —4N 91
(off Diamond St.)
Poets Pl. H'fth —5F 42
Pogson's Cotts. Leeds —1C 64
(off York Rd.)
Pohlman St. Hal —7M 91
Pole Ga. Slai —7K 129
Pole Ga. Branch. Hud —6K 129
Pole Moor. —6K 129
Pole Rd. Sut Cr —8A 20
Pollard Av. Bgly —2G 38
Pollard Av. Gom —3M 95
Pollard Clo. Gom —3M 95
Pollard La. B'frd —5F 58
Pollard La. Leeds —9E 42
Pollards Fields. Knot —7A 104
Pollard St. Bgly —9G 38
Pollard St. B'frd —9D 58
Pollard St. Hud —9N 113
Pollard St. Loft —6L 99
Pollard St. Todm —5G 86
Pollard St. N. Hal —4C 92
Pollard Way. Gom —3M 95
Pollars St. S. Hud —6G 131
Pollit Av. Sower B —9E 90
Polperro Clo. Nor —9J 101
Pomfret Ct. Pon —3N 123
Pomfret Pl. Gar —6B 66
Pond Clo. Hud —8L 131
Ponden La. Stanb —8G 35
Ponderosa Clo. Leeds —3H 63
Pondfields Clo. Kip —4B 84
Pondfields Crest. Kip —3B 84
Pondfields Dri. Kip —3B 84
Pondfields Ri. Kip —3B 84
Pond La. Lep —8L 133
Pond St. Kei —9J 21
Pond Ter. Brigh —7K 93
Ponker La. Skelm —9B 150
Ponker Nook La. Skelm —8C 150
Pontefract. —3J 123
Pontefract Av. Leeds —7H 63
Pontefract Baghill. —3L 123
Pontefract La. Leeds —6H 63
Pontefract La. Upt —9N 141
Pontefract La. Clo. Leeds —7H 63
Pontefract Monkhill. —1K 123
Pontefract Museum. —3K 123
Pontefract Race Course. —1G 122
Pontefract Rd. Ackw —2G 140
Pontefract Rd. C'frd —4E 102
Pontefract Rd. Croft —9G 120
Pontefract Rd. Cud —9J 155
Pontefract Rd. F'stne —7D 122
Pontefract Rd. Hems —9F 140
Pontefract Rd. Knot —9B 104
Pontefract Rd. Leeds —3J 81
Pontefract Rd. Nor I —9L 101
(in two parts)
Pontefract Rd. Pon & F'bri —9M 103
Pontefract Rd. Rothw —5M 81
Pontefract St. Leeds —7H 63
Pontefract Tanshelf. —2J 123
Pontefract Ter. Hems —3E 156
Pontey Cvn. Site. Hon —6J 147
Pontey Dri. Hud —5F 132
Pontey Mt. Hud —5F 132
Ponyfield Clo. Bkby —2K 131
Pool. —1F 26
Pool Bank Clo. Pool W —1G 26
Pool Bank Ct. Pool W —2G 26
Pool Bank New Rd. B'hpe & Pool W —4E 26
Pool Ct. B'frd —7E 58
Poole. —1D 104
Poole Cres. Leeds —4C 64
Poole Mt. Leeds —5C 64
Poole Rd. Leeds —4C 64
Poole Row. B'ton —1D 104
Poole Sq. Leeds —5C 64
Pool Hill La. Den D —3F 166
Pool Rd. Otley —9N 11
Pools La. Roys —6F 154
Pool St. Kei —7L 21
Popeley Rd. Heck —6N 95
Pope St. Altft —7H 101
Pope St. Kei —8K 21
Poplar Av. B'frd —3L 75
Poplar Av. C'frd —5J 103
Poplar Av. Gar —7M 65
Poplar Av. H'frth —8A 148
Poplar Av. Leeds —4E 64
Poplar Av. Shaf —7K 155
Poplar Av. Shipl —1A 58
Poplar Av. Sower B —7J 91
Poplar Av. Todm —5J 87
Poplar Av. Wake —6F 118
Poplar Av. Weth —2L 17
Poplar Clo. Bur W —9D 10
Poplar Clo. Leeds —6J 61
Poplar Ct. B'frd —8N 57
Poplar Ct. Leeds —6H 61
Poplar Cres. Hal —6M 73
Poplar Cres. Shipl —9A 40
Poplar Cres. Ting —3M 97
Poplar Cft. Leeds —6H 61
Poplar Dri. H'fth —7C 42
Poplar Dri. Nor —7H 101
Poplar Dri. Sandb —9B 22
Poplar Dri. Shipl —1A 58
Poplar Gdns. Leeds —6H 61
Poplar Gth. Leeds —6H 61
Poplar Ga. Leeds —6H 61
Poplar Grn. Leeds —6H 61
Poplar Grn. Pon —2M 123
Poplar Gro. Bail —6K 39
Poplar Gro. B'frd —3K 75
Poplar Gro. Cleck —6F 94
Poplar Gro. H'den —6N 37
Poplar Gro. Knot —1D 124
Poplar Gro. Pon —3H 123
Poplar Gro. Shipl —1A 58
Poplar Ho. C'frd —5E 102
(off Parklands)
Poplar Mt. Leeds —6H 61
Poplar Pl. Pud —7M 59
Poplar Ri. Leeds —5H 61
Poplar Ri. Skelm —8E 150
Poplar Rd. B'frd —3M 75
Poplar Rd. Shipl —1A 58
Poplar Rd. Skel —8N 159
Poplars Pk. Rd. B'frd —2C 58
Poplar Sq. Fars —4A 60
Poplars, The. B'hpe —6J 27
Poplars, The. Guis —6J 25
Poplars, The. Kin —9B 140
Poplars, The. Knot —1G 124
Poplars, The. Leeds —2A 62
Poplars, The. Loft —4L 99
Poplars, The. Nor G —2M 93
Poplar St. Bkby —1M 131
Poplar St. Hal —4B 92
Poplar St. Loft —6L 99
Poplar St. Mold —5A 132
Poplar Ter. Hud —4B 132
Poplar Ter. Kei —9G 21
(off W. Leeds St.)
Poplar Ter. Roys —5E 154
Poplar Ter. Sandb —9C 22
Poplar Ter. S Elm —7N 157
Poplar Vw. B'frd —3K 75
Poplar Vw. Hal —6M 93
Poplar Vw. Leeds —6H 61
Poplar Way. Leeds —6H 61
Popley Butts. Mel —8C 146
Popley Dri. Mel —8C 146
Popples Dri. Hal —6M 73
Popples La. Wads —8L 71
Poppleton Ct. Ting —3A 98
Poppleton Dri. Ting —3A 98
Poppleton Ri. Ting —4A 98
Poppleton Rd. Ting —3A 98
Poppleton Way. Ting —3A 98
Porritt St. Cleck —3H 95
(off Heaton St.)
Portage Av. Leeds —7A 64
Portage Cres. Leeds —7N 63
Portal Cres. Mir —3L 115
(in two parts)
Portal Dri. Mir —3L 115
Portland Av. Pon —2H 123
Portland Clo. Lind —3H 131
Portland Cres. Leeds —6D 62
Portland Ga. Leeds —5D 62
(in two parts)
Portland Ho. B'frd —8H 59
(off Fearnville Dri.)
Portland Ho. Ell —4E 112
(off Huddersfield Rd.)
Portland Pl. Bgly —5F 38
Portland Pl. Upt —2N 157
Portland Rd. Hal —4C 92
Portland Rd. Leeds —8M 61
Portland St. B'frd —8C 58
Portland St. Hal —6B 92
Portland St. Haw —8D 36
Portland St. Hud —3L 131
Portland St. Leeds —6D 62
Portland St. Pud —6D 60
Portland St. Wake —8A 120
Portland Way. Leeds —5D 62
Portman St. C'ley —9M 41
Portobello. —9M 119
Portobello Gro. Wake —8M 119
Portobello Rd. Wake —8M 119
Portsmouth. —3B 86
Portsmouth Av. B'frd —5E 58
Portwood St. B'frd —4J 57
Post Hill Ct. Leeds —7G 60
Post Office Rd. B'frd —1G 58
Post Office Rd. F'stne —6D 122
Post Office Road Stadium. —6D 122
Post Office St. Rawf —6K 95
Pothill La. Upt —1A 158
Pothouse Rd. B'frd —5N 75
Pot La. Steet —3C 20
Potovens Ct. Loft —6L 99
Potovens La. Loft —7K 99
Potovens La. Wren & Out —9H 99
Potter Av. Wake —7G 119
Potter Brow Rd. Bail —9A 24
Potternewton. —2G 62
Potternewton Av. Leeds —9D 44
Potternewton Ct. Leeds —9E 44
Potternewton Cres. Leeds —1D 62
Potternewton Gro. Leeds —9D 44

Potternewton Heights. Leeds —9E 44
Potternewton La. Leeds —9C 44
Potternewton Mt. Leeds —9D 44
Potternewton Vw. Leeds —9D 44
Potters Cft. Loft —6L 99
Potters Ga. Cumb —8H 165
Potters Wlk. Gol —6D 130
Potterton. —4M 47
Potterton Clo. Bar E —7M 47
Potterton Ct. Bar E —7M 47
(off Potterton Clo.)
Potterton Hall. —4N 47
Potterton La. Pot —5M 47
Pottery Field. —9F 62
Pottery La. F'bri —7C 104
Pottery La. W'ford —6E 82
Pottery Rd. Leeds —1F 80
Pottery St. C'frd —4B 102
Pottery St. Hud —2D 130
Pott's Ter. Nor —3J 121
Poulton Pl. Leeds —2E 80
Poverty La. Sower B —2A 110
Powell Av. B'frd —1A 76
Powell Rd. Bgly —4G 38
Powell Rd. Shipl —1B 58
Powell St. C'frd —4D 102
Powell St. Hal —5B 92
(in two parts)
Powell St. Heck —9B 96
Powell St. S Kirk —6K 157
Poxon Ct. Leeds —2K 43
Poxon Grn. Gar —7M 65
Poxon La. B'frd —7B 58
Poxon Yd. Leeds —7C 46
Poxton Gro. S Elm —8L 157
Prail Clo. Pon —2M 123
Prail La. Pon —2M 123
Pratt La. Mir —5L 115
Pratt La. Shipl —9A 40
Precinct, The. F'stne —6C 122
Premiere Pk. I'ly —6D 8
Prescott St. Hal —6B 92
Prescott Ter. All —5G 56
Preston La. Hal —3J 91
(in two parts)
Preston La. W'ford & All B —6M 83
Preston Pde. Leeds —3C 80
Preston Pl. Hal —5N 91
Preston St. Bat —8F 96
Preston St. B'frd —7A 58
Preston St. Dew —5H 117
Preston Ter. Bgly —2E 38
(off Sleningford Rd.)
Preston Vw. Swil —4J 83
Prestwich Dri. Hud —8L 113
Prestwick Clo. Otley —2H 25
Prestwick Fold. Oss —4N 117
Pretoria Rd. B'frd —7H 59
Pretoria St. C'frd —5E 102
Pretoria St. F'stne —5C 122
Pretoria St. Slai —9M 129
Pretoria St. Wake —8M 119
Pretoria Ter. Hal —4K 91
Prickleden. —4L 163
Priest Hill. —1L 17
Priest Hill Gdns. Weth —2L 17
Priesthorpe. x —2N 59
Priesthorpe Av. S'ley —4M 59
Priesthorpe Ct. Fars —2A 60
Priesthorpe La. Fars —3M 59
Priesthorpe Rd. Fars —2L 59
(in two parts)
Priest La. Ripp —7E 110
Priestley Av. B'frd —5A 76
Priestley Av. Dart —9E 152
Priestley Av. Heck —6A 96
Priestley Clo. Pud —6C 60
Priestley Dri. Pud —5C 60
Priestley Gdns. Heck —7N 95
Priestley Gdns. Pud —6C 60
Priestley Green. —3J 93
Priestley Gro. Hud —9L 131
Priestley Hill. Q'bry —7B 74
Priestley Pl. Sower B —9G 90
Priestley Sq. Birs —2B 96
Priestley St. B'frd —6D 58
Priestley St. T'tn —8C 56
Priestley Ter. B'frd —4A 76
Priestley Theatre, The. —7D 58
(off Chapel St.)
Priestley Vw. Pud —6C 60
Priestley Wlk. Pud —6C 60
Priestman Clo. B'frd —5A 58
Priestman St. B'frd —5A 58
Priestthorpe. —3F 38
Priestthorpe Clo. Bgly —3F 38
Priestthorpe La. Bgly —3F 38
Priestthorpe Rd. Bgly —4F 38
Priestwell. —6L 87
Priestwell St. Todm —6L 87
Primitive St. Carl —1M 99
Primitive St. Hud —4N 131
Primley Gdns. Leeds —3E 44
Primley Pk. Av. Leeds —3E 44
Primley Pk. Clo. Leeds —3F 44
Primley Pk. Ct. Leeds —2E 44
Primley Pk. Cres. Leeds —3E 44
Primley Pk. Dri. Leeds —3E 44
Primley Pk. Gth. Leeds —2F 44
Primley Pk. Grn. Leeds —2F 44
Primley Pk. Gro. Leeds —3E 44
Primley Pk. La. Leeds —3E 44
Primley Pk. Mt. Leeds —3F 44
Primley Pk. Ri. Leeds —3F 44
Primley Pk. Rd. Leeds —3E 44
Primley Pk. Vw. Leeds —2E 44
Primley Pk. Wlk. Leeds —2F 44
Primley Pk. Way. Leeds —2E 44
Primrose Av. Leeds —6B 64
Primrose Av. Swil —4J 83
Primrose Bank. Bgly —5G 39
Primrose Clo. Leeds —6B 64
Primrose Clo. Pon —4K 123
Primrose Ct. Guis —7J 25
(off Orchard Way)
Primrose Ct. Leeds —2F 44
Primrose Cres. Leeds —5B 64
Primrose Dene. Byr —5C 104
Primrose Dri. Bgly —5G 39
Primrose Dri. C'frd —6H 103
Primrose Dri. Leeds —6B 64
Primrose Gdns. Leeds —5B 64
Primrose Gth. Leeds —6A 64
Primrose Gro. Hud —7M 131
Primrose Gro. Kei —9L 21
Primrose Gro. Leeds —5B 64
Primrose Hill. —6M 131
Primrose Hill. Bat —6G 97
Primrose Hill. Bgly —6H 39
Primrose Hill. Knot —7F 104
Primrose Hill. S'ley —5B 60
Primrose Hill Clo. Swil —4J 83
Primrose Hill Dri. Swil —4J 83
Primrose Hill Gdns. Swil —4J 83
Primrose Hill Gth. Swil —5J 83
Primrose Hill Grn. Swil —5J 83
Primrose Hill Gro. Swil —4J 83
Primrose Hill Rd. Hud —6M 131
Primrose Ho. Wake —6M 119
(off William St.)
Primrose La. Bgly —6G 39
Primrose La. B Spa —1C 32
Primrose La. B'frd —2B 58
Primrose La. Cald G —4F 136
Primrose La. Halt —6A 64
(in three parts)
Primrose La. Kbtn —1H 149
Primrose La. Leeds —2E 80
Primrose La. Liv —7K 95
Primrose La. Mir —4N 115
Primrose Rd. Leeds —6B 64
Primrose Row. Bail —3D 40
Primrose St. B'frd —6A 58
Primrose St. Hud —6M 131
Primrose St. Kei —9L 21
Primrose Va. Knot —8F 104
Primrose Wlk. Chur —5M 79
Primrose Way. Hal —6J 75
Primrose Yd. Oult —8D 82
Prince Albert Sq. Q'bry —3G 74
Prince Edward Gro. Leeds —1K 79
Prince Edward Rd. Leeds —1K 79
Prince Henry Rd. Otley —7L 11
Prince Royd. —9H 113
Princeroyd Way. B'frd —7M 57
Princes Av. Leeds —8K 45
Prince's Ct. Leeds —6E 44
Prince's Cres. B'frd —3C 58
Prince's Ga. Hal —8A 92
Prince's Gro. Leeds —1N 61
Princess Alexandra Wlk. Hud —5N 131
(off Princess St.)
Princess Av. Dew —3K 117
Princess Av. S Elm —7M 157
Princess Clo. Dew —3K 117
Princess Ct. Colt —8E 64
Princess Ct. Leeds —4F 44
Princess Ct. Norm —2K 121
Princess Cres. Dew —4K 117
Princess Fields. Colt —8E 64
Princess Gdns. Dew —3E 116
(off Halliley St.)
Princess La. Dew —3K 117
Princess Of Wales Precinct, The.
(off Tithe Barn St.) Dew —3G 116
Princess Rd. Dew —3K 117
Princess Rd. I'ly —6F 8
Princess St. Bat —6F 96
Princess St. C'frd —3E 102
Princess St. Cud —8K 155
Princess St. Dew —3K 117
Princess St. G'lnd —4C 112
Princess St. Hal —5B 92
Princess St. Hud —5M 131
Princess St. M'well —8J 153
Princess St. Mir —7L 115
Princess St. Nor —1J 121
Princess St. Out —8K 99
Princess St. Rawd —3L 41
Princess St. Sandt —9M 119
Princess St. Sower B —8J 91
Prince's St. B'frd —5N 75
(nr. Pothouse Rd.)
Prince's St. B'frd —4A 76
(off Horsley St.)
Prince's St. Butt —6K 75
Princes St. Heck —8B 96
Prince St. All B —6N 83
Prince St. Bat —6F 96
Prince St. B'frd —4G 77
Prince St. Dew —3G 116
Prince St. Haw —9D 36
Prince St. Hud —6N 131
Prince St. Sils —8D 6
Prince's Way. B'frd —8C 58
Princeville. —7M 57
Princeville Rd. B'frd —7M 57
Princeville St. B'frd —7N 57
Prince William Ct. F'stne —7C 122
(off Andrew St.)
Prince Wood La. Hud —9H 113
Priordale Rd. F'stne —7B 122
Prior's La. Drau —3E 4
Prior St. Kei —8L 21
Priory Clo. Bgly —3F 38
Priory Clo. Mir —5J 115
Priory Clo. Nor —8G 101
Priory Clo. Oss —7N 117
Priory Clo. Weth —2N 17
Priory Ct. Bgly —3F 38
Priory Ct. B'frd —6B 58
Priory Cft. Oss —6N 117
Priory Est. S Elm —6A 158
Priory Grange. Pon —2L 123
Priory Gro. Bgly —3F 38
Priory Ho. B'frd —8G 40
(off Cavendish Rd.)
Priory M. Stan —6A 100
Priory Pl. Hud —6D 114
Priory Ridge. Croft —2H 139
Priory Rd. Brigh —2A 114
Priory Rd. F'stne —7B 122
Priory Rd. Oss —6N 117
Priory Sq. W'ton —3B 138
Priory Wlk. Mir —5J 115
Priory Way. Mir —5J 115
Privilege St. Leeds —8L 61
Procter Ter. B'frd —4H 77
Proctor St. B'frd —4H 77
Prod La. Bail —5K 39
Progress Av. H'den —6N 37
Prospect Av. Hal —8L 91
Prospect Av. Leeds —3F 60
Prospect Av. Nor —9J 101
Prospect Av. Pud —6A 60
Prospect Av. Shipl —8A 40
Prospect Bank. B'ham —5D 32
Prospect Clo. Hal —8L 91
Prospect Clo. Shipl —8A 40
Prospect Cotts. S Kirk —6L 157
Prospect Ct. Hal —4H 91
Prospect Ct. T'ner —2G 46
Prospect Cres. Kei —2E 36
Prospect Cres. Leeds —2F 80
Prospect Dri. Kei —2E 36
Prospect Gdns. Leeds —6C 64
Prospect Gro. Pud —6A 60
Prospect Gro. Shipl —8A 40
Prospect Ho. Hud —5M 131
(off Prospect St.)
Prospect La. B'shaw —8M 77
Prospect Mt. Kei —2E 36
Prospect Mt. Shipl —8A 40
Prospect Pl. B'frd —5L 57
Prospect Pl. Brigh —1M 113
Prospect Pl. Eccl —4G 59
Prospect Pl. Hal —1M 91
Prospect Pl. H'fth —7E 42
Prospect Pl. Leeds —3F 60
Prospect Pl. Loft —2K 99
Prospect Pl. Nor G —2M 93
(off Village St.)
Prospect Pl. Outl —2M 129
Prospect Pl. Q'bry —4D 74
Prospect Pl. Rothw —9A 82
Prospect Rd. Bgly —2H 39
Prospect Rd. B'frd —6D 58
(in two parts)
Prospect Rd. Bur W —9C 10
Prospect Rd. Cleck —4H 95
Prospect Rd. Harts —2H 115
Prospect Rd. Heck —6N 95
Prospect Rd. Lgwd —4E 130
Prospect Rd. Oss —6N 117
Prospect Row. Broc —6J 73
Prospect Row. Bur W —2A 24
Prospect Row. Hal —1M 91
Prospect Sq. Fars —4A 60
Prospect St. Bat —6F 96
Prospect St. B'frd —9D 58
Prospect St. Butt —6L 75
Prospect St. Cleck —5H 95
Prospect St. Eccl —1G 58
Prospect St. Far —3A 60
Prospect St. Hal —4C 92
Prospect St. Haw —9C 36
Prospect St. Horb —2E 136
Prospect St. Hud —5M 131
Prospect St. Kei —1F 36
Prospect St. Nort —7N 143
Prospect St. Pud —6N 59
Prospect St. Rawd —4N 41
Prospect St. Shipl —8A 40
Prospect St. T'tn —8D 56
Prospect Ter. All —5H 57
Prospect Ter. Bmly —3F 60
Prospect Ter. Cleck —4H 95
Prospect Ter. Fars —4A 60
Prospect Ter. H'fth —6F 42
Prospect Ter. Leeds —7H 63
Prospect Ter. Liv —8K 95
Prospect Ter. L'ft —4N 73
Prospect Ter. M'fld —8G 67
Prospect Ter. Rod —1B 60
Prospect Ter. Rothw —9A 82
Prospect Ter. S Kirk —7H 157
Prospect Vw. Leeds —3F 60
Prospect Vw. Liv —1H 115
Prospect Vs. Weth —3M 17
Prospect Wlk. Shipl —8A 40
Prosper St. Leeds —1G 80
Providence Av. Bail —3A 40
Providence Av. Leeds —2C 62
Providence Bldgs. Hal —8F 92
(off New St.)
Providence Ct. Morl —8K 79
(nr. Victoria Rd.)
Providence Ct. Morl —1L 97
(nr. Wide La.)
Providence Ct. Morl —8K 79
(off Troy Rd.)
Providence Ct. Oakw —5C 36
Providence Cres. Oakw —5C 36
Providence Grn. Pon —9L 103
Providence Hill. Slnd —8L 111
Providence La. Oakw —5C 36
Providence Pl. All B —1B 102
Providence Pl. Brigh —2A 114
Providence Pl. Gar —7M 65
Providence Pl. Leeds —5E 62
Providence Pl. Morl —9H 79
Providence Pl. S'ley —5B 60
Providence Pl. Swil C —8H 65
Providence Pl. Wyke —9A 76
Providence Rd. Leeds —2C 62
Providence Row. Bail —3A 40
Providence Row. E Mor —6D 22
Providence Row. Hal —6J 73
Providence Row. Oven —1M 91
Providence St. Bat —7F 96
Providence St. B'frd —7B 58
Providence St. Cleck —4J 95
Providence St. Earl —4J 117
Providence St. Ell —4E 112
Providence St. Fars —4A 60
(in two parts)
Providence St. Schol —3C 94
Providence St. Todm —4J 107
Providence St. Wake —4L 119
Providence Ter. Leeds —3C 62
Providence Ter. T'tn —8C 56
Providence Vs. Schol —3C 94
Prune Pk. La. All —3D 56
Pudding La. Todm —2E 86
Pudsey. —3D 86
(nr. Cornholme)
Pudsey. —8A 60
(nr. Leeds)
Pudsey Bus. Cen. Pud —7C 60
Pudsey Rd. Leeds —7E 60
Pudsey Rd. Todm —3D 86
Pugneys Rd. Wake —9L 119
Pule Grn. La. Hal —1A 92
Pule Hill. —1A 92
Pullan Av. B'frd —2F 58
Pullan Dri. B'frd —2G 59
Pullan Gro. B'frd —2G 59
Pullan La. Esh —2G 41
Pullan St. B'frd —9B 58
Pulmans Pl. Hal —1B 112
Pulmans Yd. Hal —1B 112
Pumphouse La. Mir —5M 115
Pump La. Dew —3C 116
Pump La. Hal —4E 92
Pump La. Kbtn —2N 149
Pump La. Wake —7A 98
Pump La. Wrag —2A 140
Pump St. B'frd —9H 59
Punch Bowl Yd. B'ton —4B 104
Purbeck Ct. H Wd —3J 77
(off Dorchester Cres.)
Purbeck Gro. Gar —8N 65
Purcell Dri. Sils —7D 6
Purley Wlk. B'frd —5N 75
Purlwell Av. Bat —9E 96
Purlwell Cres. Bat —9E 96
Purlwell Hall Rd. Bat —9F 96
Purlwell La. Bat —8F 96
Purprise La. Pec W —4H 71
Purston Jaglin. —8D 122
Purston La. Ackw —1F 140
Purston Pk. Ct. F'stne —7D 122
Pussy La. Shel —6L 149
Pye Av. M'well —9J 153
Pye Nest. —7L 91
Pye Nest Av. Hal —7K 91
Pye Nest Dri. Hal —8L 91
Pye Nest Gdns. Hal —7L 91
Pye Nest Gro. Hal —7L 91
Pye Nest Ri. Hal —8L 91
Pye Nest Rd. Sower B —8K 91
Pyenot Av. Cleck —5J 95
Pyenot Dri. Cleck —6J 95
Pyenot Gdns. Cleck —6J 95
Pyenot Hall La. Cleck —5J 95
Pymont Ct. Loft —3L 99
Pymont Dri. W'ford —6B 82
Pymont Gro. W'ford —6C 82
Pymroyd La. Hud —6F 130
(in two parts)
Pym St. Leeds —9F 62
Pynate Rd. Bat —6D 96
Pyrah Fold. Wyke —9A 76
Pyrah Rd. Low M —6B 76
Pyrah St. Dew —2F 116
Pyrah St. Wyke —9B 76

QBM Bus. Pk. Bat —2C 96
Q.M. Ind. Pk. Hud —9B 114
Quail St. Kei —8K 21
Quaker Ga. Skelm —6B 150
Quaker La. B'frd —2N 75
Quaker La. Cleck & Liv —5H 95
Quaker La. Hud —5K 131
Quakers La. Rawd —2M 41
Quakers La. Ripp —9D 110
Quarmby. —3G 130
Quarmby Cft. Hud —3F 130
Quarmby Fold. Hud —3F 130
Quarmby Rd. Hud —3G 130
Quarrie Dene Ct. Leeds —9E 44
Quarry Av. Knot —9F 104
Quarry Bank Ct. Leeds —9J 43
Quarry Clo. Broc —7A 148
Quarry Clo. Dart —9F 152
Quarry Cotts. H'fth —6E 42
Quarry Ct. Brigh —7K 93
(off Spout Ho. La.)
Quarry Ct. C'frd —6D 102
Quarry Ct. Lgwd —3E 130
Quarry Dene. Leeds —7N 43
Quarrydene Dri. C'frd —6H 103
Quarry Dri. Tan —4F 132
Quarry Farm Rd. Pool W —3D 2
Quarryfields. Mir —4M 115
Quarryfield Ter. E Ard —5F 98
Quarry Gdns. Leeds —1C 44
Quarry Hill. —6F 62
Quarry Hill. Far —3A 60
(off Wesley St.)
Quarry Hill. Horb —1B 136
Quarry Hill. Hud —6F 132
Quarry Hill. Sower B —9H 91
Quarry Hill. W'ford —8D 82
Quarry Hill Ind. Est. Horb —1A 1
Quarry Hill La. Weth —2L 17
(in two parts)
Quarry Ho. Leeds —6G 62
Quarry La. Bat —4C 96
Quarry La. Dew —6K 97
Quarry La. Morl —2L 97
Quarry La. Neth —2H 147
Quarry La. Tan —5G 132
Quarry La. Upt —1N 157
Quarry Mt. Leeds —2C 62
Quarry Mt. Ryh —9J 139
Quarry Mt. Yead —9N 25
(off King St.)
Quarry Mt. Pl. Leeds —2C 62
Quarry Mt. St. Leeds —2C 62
Quarry Mt. Ter. Leeds —2C 62
Quarry Pl. B'frd —4F 58
Quarry Pl. Leeds —3C 62
Quarry Rd. Brigh —4M 113
Quarry Rd. Cleck —5H 95
Quarry Rd. Cros M —7G 130
Quarry Rd. Dew —4E 116
Quarry Rd. Gom —5M 95
Quarry Rd. Hal —2L 91
Quarry Rd. Liv —8L 95
Quarry Rd. Mar —4K 131
Quarry Rd. Pool W —3D 26
Quarry Rd. W'ford —7E 82

uarryside Rd. *Mir* —5J **115**
uarry St. *Ackw* —5F **140**
uarry St. *H'tn* —2M **57**
uarry St. *Kei* —9K **21**
uarry St. *Leeds* —3C **62**
uarry St. *S'fth* —6A **106**
uarry Ter. *H'fth* —6E **42**
uarry, The. *Leeds* —1C **44**
uarry Vw. *Ackw* —5E **140**
uarry Vw. *Dew* —2C **116**
uayside. *Shipl* —7N **39**
uayside, The. *App B* —7J **41**
uay St. *Hud* —4N **131**
uebec St. *B'frd* —8C **58**
uebec St. *Ell* —4F **112**
uebec St. *Kei* —1H **37**
uebec St. *Leeds* —7D **62**
uebec St. *Todm* —2J **107**
uebec St. *Wake* —5K **119**
ueen Elizabeth Dri. *Nor* —3H **121**
ueen Elizabeth Gdns. *Hud* —4L **131**
ueen Elizabeth Gro. *Wake* —4N **119**
ueen Elizabeth Ho. *Wake* —4N **119**
ueen Elizabeth Rd. *Wake* —4M **119**
ueen Elizabeth St. *Wake* —8K **99**
ueen Margarets Av. *B'ton* —4C **104**
ueen Margarets Clo. *B'ton* —4C **104**
ueen Margarets Dri. *B'ton* —4C **104**
ueen's Arc. *Leeds* —6E **62**
ueen's Av. *B'frd* —3D **58**
ueen's Av. *Pon* —4G **123**
ueensbury. —4D 74
ueensbury Av. *Out* —7L **99**
ueensbury Ct. *Norm* —2K **121**
ueensbury Rd. *Hal* —9A **74**
ueensbury Sq. *Q'bry* —4D **74**
ueens Clo. *Bgly* —5G **39**
ueen's Clo. *Leeds* —7E **44**
ueens Ct. *Bgly* —4E **38**
ueens Ct. Gom —2M 95
(off Queen St.)
ueen's Ct. Leeds —7E 62
(off Briggate)
ueens Ct. *Moort* —6E **44**
ueens Ct. *Shipl* —8L **39**
ueen's Cres. *Oss* —6N **117**
ueen's Cres. *Shar C* —7K **121**
ueens Dri. *Carl* —1M **99**
ueen's Dri. *Cud* —8K **155**
ueens Dri. *Hal* —8F **92**
ueen's Dri. *I'ly* —6E **8**
ueen's Dri. *Oss* —6B **118**
ueens Dri. *Pud* —6A **60**
ueen's Dri. *Shaf* —6J **155**
ueen's Dri. *Wren* —2G **118**
ueens Dri. Clo. *Oss* —6B **118**
ueen's Dri. La. *I'ly* —6E **8**
ueen's Gdns. *I'ly* —6F **8**
ueen's Gdns. *Oss* —6N **117**
ueensgate. *B'frd* —7C **58**
ueen's Ga. *Hal* —8A **92**
ueensgate. *Hud* —5M **131**
ueen's Gro. *Kei* —2H **37**
ueen's Gro. *Morl* —1J **97**
ueenshill App. *Leeds* —5E **44**
ueenshill Av. *Leeds* —5E **44**
ueenshill Clo. *Leeds* —5E **44**
ueenshill Ct. *Leeds* —5E **44**
ueenshill Cres. *Leeds* —4E **44**
ueenshill Dri. *Leeds* —5D **44**
ueenshill Gdns. *Leeds* —5D **44**
ueenshill Gth. *Leeds* —5E **44**
ueenshill Lawn. Leeds —5E 44
(off Queenshill App.)
ueenshill Rd. *Leeds* —5E **44**
ueenshill Vw. *Leeds* —5E **44**
ueenshill Wlk. *Leeds* —5E **44**
ueenshill Way. *Leeds* —5E **44**
ueens Mead. *N'wram* —1F **92**
ueen's Mill Rd. *Hud* —6M **131**
ueens Pde. *Guis* —7H **25**
ueen's Pk. Clo. *C'frd* —4H **103**
ueen's Pk. Dri. *C'frd* —5G **102**
ueen's Pl. *Otley* —1L **25**
ueen's Pl. *Shipl* —7L **39**
ueen's Promenade. *Morl* —8K **79**
ueen Sq. *Leeds* —5E **62**
ueen's Ri. *B'frd* —3D **58**
ueen's Rd. *Bgly* —1D **38**
ueen's Rd. *B Spa* —9C **18**
ueen's Rd. *B'frd* —4D **58**
(D2)
ueen's Rd. *B'frd* —4B **58**
(D8)
ueen's Rd. *C'frd* —5H **103**
ueen's Rd. *Cud* —8K **155**
ueen's Rd. *Hal* —5M **91**
ueen's Rd. *Hud* —2K **131**
Queen's Rd. *I'ly* —6F **8**
Queen's Rd. *Kei* —3G **37**
Queen's Rd. *Leeds* —4A **62**
Queen's Rd. *Morl* —1J **97**
Queen's Rd. *Nor G* —2L **93**
Queen's Rd. *Pon* —4G **123**
Queen's Rd. *Shipl* —7L **39**
Queens Rd. W. *Cow* —6G **130**
Queens Sq. *Hud* —1B **132**
Queen's Sq. *Pon* —4G **123**
Queens Ter. *H Bri* —1G **89**
Queens Ter. *Oss* —6N **117**
Queens Ter. *Otley* —1L **25**
Queens Ter. *Pon* —3H **123**
Queensthorpe Av. *Leeds* —6G **61**
Queensthorpe Clo. *Leeds* —6H **61**
Queensthorpe Ri. *Leeds* —6G **61**
Queen St. *Bail* —6A **40**
Queen St. *Bgly* —4E **38**
Queen St. *Butt* —6K **75**
Queen St. *Carl* —1M **99**
Queen St. *C'frd* —3E **102**
Queen St. *Chick* —4L **117**
Queen St. *Cull* —9K **37**
Queen St. *E Ard* —4F **98**
Queen St. *Gom* —2M **95**
Queen St. *Gre* —8H **41**
Queen St. *G'lnd* —5B **112**
Queen St. *Haw* —9C **36**
Queen St. *Heck* —9N **95**
Queen St. *Horb* —1C **136**
Queen St. *Hud* —4N **131**
Queen St. *H'let* —3J **81**
Queen St. *Leeds* —7C **62**
Queen St. *Mar* —6J **95**
Queen St. *Mir* —7L **115**
Queen St. *Morl* —8K **79**
(in two parts)
Queen St. *Myth* —4M **89**
Queen St. *Nor* —1H **121**
Queen St. *Oss* —6N **117**
Queen St. *Out* —8K **99**
Queen St. *Pon* —3J **123**
Queen St. *Raven* —5B **116**
Queen St. *Rawd* —3M **41**
Queen St. *Sils* —8E **6**
Queen St. *Skelm* —7D **150**
Queen St. *S Elm* —7M **157**
Queen St. *Sower B* —9E **90**
Queen St. *Steet* —3C **20**
Queen St. *Todm* —7K **87**
Queen St. *Wake* —5L **119**
Queen St. *Wilsd* —2B **56**
Queen St. *W'ford* —7M **83**
Queen St. S. *Hud* —6N **131**
Queensview. *Leeds* —1C **64**
Queen's Wlk. *Leeds* —9K **43**
Queen's Wlk. *Oss* —6B **118**
Queensway. *Bgly* —4G **38**
Queensway. *Gar* —7L **65**
Queensway. *Guis & Yead* —7J **25**
Queensway. *Hal* —4M **91**
Queensway. Kei —9J 21
(off Airedale Shop. Cen.)
Queens Way. *Kbtn* —4K **149**
Queensway. *Leeds* —6D **64**
Queensway. *Morl* —9K **79**
Queensway. *Nor* —4H **121**
Queensway. *Pon* —9M **103**
Queensway. *Rothw* —7N **81**
Queensway. *Roys* —5D **154**
Queenswood Clo. *Leeds* —9K **43**
Queenswood Ct. *Leeds* —2M **61**
Queenswood Dri. *Leeds* —8K **43**
Queenswood Gdns. *Leeds* —2M **61**
Queenswood Grn. *Leeds* —8K **43**
Queenswood Heights. *Leeds* —1M **61**
Queenswood Mt. *Leeds* —1L **61**
Queenswood Ri. *Leeds* —1L **61**
Queenswood Rd. *Leeds* —1L **61**
Queen Victoria Cres. *Hal* —1G **92**
Quincy Clo. *B'frd* —2G **58**
Quinsworth St. *B'frd* —1F **76**

Raby Av. *Leeds* —3F **62**
Raby Park. —3M 17
Raby Pk. *Weth* —4L **17**
Raby St. *Leeds* —3F **62**
Raby Ter. *Leeds* —3F **62**
Racca Av. *Knot* —8G **104**
Racca Green. —8G 104
Racca Grn. *Knot* —8F **104**
Race Moor La. *Oakw* —4B **36**
Rachael St. *Horb* —1B **136**
Rachel Grn. *B'frd* —3D **58**
Racton St. *Slai* —9M **129**
Radcliffe Av. *B'frd* —1E **58**
Radcliffe Gdns. *Pud* —8B **60**
Radcliffe Gro. *Pud* —8B **60**
Radcliffe La. *L'ft* —2C **90**
Radcliffe La. *Pud* —7B **60**
Radcliffe Pl. *Wake* —5L **119**
Radcliffe Rd. *Barn* —9A **154**
Radcliffe Rd. *Hud* —6G **130**
(in two parts)
Radcliffe Rd. *Slai* —9N **129**
Radcliffe Rd. *Wake* —7F **118**
Radcliffe St. *Skelm* —7C **150**
Radcliffe Ter. *Pud* —8B **60**
Radfield Dri. *B'frd* —4C **76**
Radfield Rd. *B'frd* —4C **76**
Radford Pk. Av. *S Kirk* —8H **157**
Radnor St. *B'frd* —7G **59**
Radnor St. *Leeds* —8A **62**
Radwell Dri. *B'frd* —9C **58**
Raeburn Dri. *B'frd* —6M **75**
Rae Ct. *Stan* —7N **99**
Rae Rd. *Shipl* —9N **39**
Rafborn Av. *Hud* —1D **130**
Rafborn Gro. *Hud* —1D **130**
Raglan Av. *Kei* —1F **36**
Raglan Clo. *C'frd* —4A **102**
Raglan Ct. Hal —5N 91
(off Raglan St.)
Ragland Ind. Est. *C'frd* —4A **102**
Raglan Dri. *B'frd* —7H **59**
Raglan Gdns. Hal —5N 91
(off Lister's Clo.)
Raglan Rd. *Leeds* —3C **62**
(in two parts)
Raglan St. *B'frd* —7H **59**
Raglan St. *Hal* —5N **91**
Raglan St. *Kei* —1F **36**
Raglan St. *Q'bry* —4E **74**
Raglan St. *Todm* —7K **87**
Raglan Ter. *B'frd* —7J **59**
Raikes La. *Birs* —2B **96**
Raikes La. *B'frd* —3L **77**
Raikes La. *E Bier* —5J **77**
Raikes Wood Dri. *E Bier* —6J **77**
Rail Balk La. *Weth* —2L **17**
(in two parts)
Railes Clo. *L'ft* —3D **90**
Railsfield Mt. *Leeds* —5F **60**
Railsfield Ri. *Leeds* —5F **60**
Railsfield Way. *Leeds* —4G **60**
Railway Av. *Pon* —2J **123**
Railway Cotts. *M'fld* —8G **66**
Railway Cotts. *S Elm* —6N **157**
Railway Cotts. *Upt* —2D **158**
Railway Rd. *C'gts* —4D **64**
(in two parts)
Railway Rd. *Idle* —7F **40**
Railway Rd. *I'ly* —5G **8**
Railway St. *B'frd* —4G **77**
Railway St. *Brigh* —2N **113**
Railway St. *Cleck* —5H **95**
Railway St. *Dew* —3G **117**
Railway St. *Heck* —9A **96**
Railway St. *Hud* —4M **131**
Railway St. *Kei* —7J **21**
Railway St. *Leeds* —7G **62**
Railway St. *Raven* —5D **116**
Railway St. *Todm* —6K **87**
Railway Ter. Brigh —1A 114
(off Clifton Comn.)
Railway Ter. *E Ard* —3E **98**
Railway Ter. *F'stne* —6D **122**
Railway Ter. *Fitz* —7A **140**
Railway Ter. *Hal* —1N **111**
Railway Ter. *Low M* —8C **76**
Railway Ter. *Nor* —1H **121**
Railway Ter. *Wake* —7J **99**
Railway Vw. *C'frd* —5B **102**
Rainbow M. *B'frd* —7L **75**
Raincliffe Gro. *Leeds* —6J **63**
Raincliffe Mt. *Leeds* —7J **63**
Raincliffe Rd. *Leeds* —6J **63**
Raincliffe St. *Leeds* —6J **63**
Raincliffe Ter. *Leeds* —7J **63**
Rainsborough Av. *Knot* —9B **104**
Rainton Ho. B'frd —1B 76
(off Park La.)
Raistrick Way. *Shipl* —7B **40**
Rake. *Err* —3G **89**
Rake Head Barn La. *Todm* —3H **107**
Rake Head Rd. *Holme* —9D **162**
Rakehill Rd. *Bar E* —8K **47**
Rakehill Rd. *Scholes* —8G **46**
(in three parts)
Raleigh St. *Hal* —7M **91**
Rampart Rd. *Leeds* —3C **62**
Ramsden Av. *B'frd* —9K **57**
Ramsden Clo. *B'ton* —4B **104**
Ramsden Ct. *B'frd* —1M **75**
Ramsden Ct. *Hud* —6M **131**
Ramsden La. *H'frth* —9G **162**
Ramsden La. *Todm* —4G **107**
Ramsden Mill La. *Gol* —7D **130**
(in two parts)
Ramsden Pl. *Cytn* —9G **57**
Ramsden Rd. *H'frth* —9G **163**
Ramsden Rd. *Ward* —9E **106**
Ramsden St. *C'frd* —7C **102**
Ramsden St. *Gol* —6D **130**
Ramsden St. *Hal* —2L **91**
Ramsden St. *Hud* —5M **131**
Ramsden St. *Kip* —5N **83**
Ramsden St. *Todm* —4J **107**
Ramsden Wood Rd. *Todm* —4H **107**
Ramsey Cres. *M'twn* —3L **135**
Ramsey Rd. *M'twn* —3K **135**
Ramsey St. *B'frd* —2B **76**
Ramsey Vw. *M'twn* —3K **135**
Ramsgate. *Loft* —3K **99**
Ramsgate Cres. *Loft* —3K **99**
Ramsgate St. *Hal* —5M **91**
Ramshead App. *Leeds* —9B **46**
Ramshead Clo. *Leeds* —8B **46**
Ramshead Cres. *Leeds* —8A **46**
Ramshead Dri. *Leeds* —8A **46**
Ramshead Gdns. *Leeds* —8A **46**
Ramshead Gro. *Leeds* —9B **46**
Ramshead Heights. *Leeds* —9B **46**
(in two parts)
Ramshead Hill. *Leeds* —9B **46**
Ramshead Pl. *Leeds* —9B **46**
Ramshead Vw. *Leeds* —9B **46**
Randall Pl. *B'frd* —3M **57**
Randall Well St. *B'frd* —8B **58**
Randolph St. *B'frd* —6J **59**
Randolph St. *Hal* —3B **92**
Randolph St. *Leeds* —4D **60**
Random Clo. *Kei* —2F **36**
Rand Pl. *B'frd* —9A **58**
Rand St. *B'frd* —9A **58**
Ranelagh Av. *B'frd* —1J **59**
Range Bank. *Hal* —3B **92**
Range Bank Top. Hal —3B 92
(off Range La.)
Range Ct. Hal —3B 92
(off All Saint's St.)
Range Gdns. *Hal* —3B **92**
Range La. *Hal* —4B **92**
Ranger's Wlk. *M'fld* —4J **67**
Range St. *Hal* —3B **92**
Ransdale Dri. *B'frd* —2B **76**
Ransdale Gro. *B'frd* —2B **76**
Ransdale Rd. *B'frd* —2B **76**
Ranson St. *Dew* —1C **116**
Ranter's Fold. *Horb* —1C **136**
Raper Vw. *Aber* —7E **48**
Rashcliffe Hill Rd. *Hud* —6L **131**
Rastrick. —3L 113
Rastrick Comn. *Brigh* —3M **113**
Rathlin Rd. *Dew* —1J **117**
Rathmell Rd. *Leeds* —7N **63**
Rathmell St. *B'frd* —4B **76**
Ratten Row. *Pon* —2K **123**
Ratten Row Rd. *Sower B* —2C **110**
Raven Clo. *Ack* —2A **122**
Ravenham Wlk. B'frd —3J 77
(off Launceston Dri.)
Raven La. *S Hien* —3H **155**
Raven Rd. *Leeds* —2A **62**
Ravens Av. *Dew* —5D **116**
Ravens Av. *Hud* —5C **132**
Ravenscar Av. *Leeds* —9J **45**
Ravenscar Mt. *Leeds* —9J **45**
Ravenscar Ter. *Leeds* —9J **45**
Ravenscar Vw. *Leeds* —9J **45**
Ravenscar Wlk. *Leeds* —9J **45**
Ravenscliffe. —2J 59
Ravenscliffe Av. *B'frd* —1H **59**
Ravenscliffe Rd. *C'ley* —9K **41**
Ravens Clo. *M'well* —9K **153**
Ravens Cres. *Dew* —5D **116**
Ravens Cft. *Dew* —5D **116**
Ravenscroft Rd. *Hal* —9A **92**
Ravensdene. *Hud* —2J **131**
Ravensfield Rd. *Dew* —5D **116**
Ravens Gro. *Dew* —5D **116**
Ravenshouse Rd. *Dew* —4C **116**
Ravensknowle Rd. *Hud* —5C **132**
Ravens Lodge Ter. *Dew* —5D **116**
Ravensmead. *F'stne* —6F **122**
Ravens Mt. *Pud* —7C **60**
Ravens St. *Dew* —5C **116**
Ravensthorpe. —5B 116
Ravensthorpe Rd. *Raven & Dew* —6C **116**
Ravenstone Dri. *G'lnd* —5B **112**
Raven St. *Bgly* —4E **38**
Raven St. *Hal* —5M **91**
Raven St. *Hud* —5J **131**
Raven St. *Kei* —9H **21**
Ravens Wlk. *Dew* —5D **116**
Ravens Way. *H'frth* —4C **164**
Ravenswharf Rd. *Dew* —5D **116**
Ravensworth Clo. *Leeds* —3G **64**
Ravensworth Way. *Leeds* —3G **64**
Raven Ter. *B'frd* —7H **57**
Rawden Hill. *Arth* —2A **28**
Rawdon. —3N 41
Rawdon Dri. *Rawd* —4M **41**
Rawdon Hall Dri. *Rawd* —4M **41**
Rawdon Rd. *Haw* —8C **36**
Rawdon Rd. *H'fth* —5B **42**
Rawdon St. *Kei* —1G **36**
Raw End Rd. *Hal* —3F **90**
Rawfield La. *Fair* —8N **85**
Rawfolds. —6K 95
Rawfolds Av. *Birs* —2C **96**
Rawfolds Way. *Rawf* —6K **95**
Rawgate Av. *C'frd* —4A **102**
Raw Green. —5M 167
Raw Hill. *Brigh* —3L **113**
Raw La. *Hal* —8K **73**
Raw La. *Wadsw* —1L **89**
Rawling St. *Kei* —2H **37**
Rawling Way. *Leeds* —1C **62**
Raw Nook. —7D 76
Rawnook. *Low M* —8C **76**
Raw Nook Rd. *Hud* —2D **130**
Rawnsley Ho. B'frd —1B 76
(off Manchester Rd.)
Rawroyds. *G'lnd* —6B **112**
Rawson Av. *B'frd* —6H **59**
Rawson Av. *Hal* —9A **92**
Rawson Pl. *B'frd* —7C **58**
Rawson Pl. *Sower B* —9G **90**
Rawson Rd. *B'frd* —7B **58**
Rawson Sq. *B'frd* —7C **58**
Rawson Sq. *Idle* —6F **40**
Rawson St. *Hal* —5B **92**
Rawson St. *Wyke* —9B **76**
Rawson St. N. *Hal* —3A **92**
Rawson Ter. *Leeds* —2E **80**
Rawson Wood. *Sower B* —1E **110**
Rawthorpe. —2C 132
Rawthorpe Cres. *Hud* —2C **132**
Rawthorpe La. *Hud* —3B **132**
Rawthorpe Ter. *Hud* —2C **132**
Rawtonstall Bank. *H Bri* —9E **70**
Rayfield. *Wake* —6H **119**
Ray Ga. *H Bri* —6N **71**
Ray Ga. *Hud* —2C **130**
Ray Ga. *N Mill* —9B **148**
Raygill Clo. *Leeds* —2K **45**
Raylands Clo. *Leeds* —7H **81**
Raylands Ct. *Leeds* —7H **81**
Raylands Fold. *Leeds* —7H **81**
Raylands Gth. *Leeds* —7H **81**
Raylands La. *Leeds* —7H **81**
Raylands Pl. *Leeds* —7H **81**
Raylands Rd. *Leeds* —7H **81**
Raylands Way. *Leeds* —8G **81**
Rayleigh St. *B'frd* —1E **76**
Raymond Dri. *B'frd* —3C **76**
Raymond St. *B'frd* —3C **76**
Raynbron Cres. *B'frd* —3D **76**
Raynel App. *Leeds* —4K **43**
Raynel Clo. *Leeds* —3J **43**
Raynel Dri. *Leeds* —4K **43**
Raynel Gdns. *Leeds* —3K **43**
Raynel Gth. *Leeds* —4K **43**
Raynel Grn. *Leeds* —4K **43**
Raynel Mt. *Leeds* —3K **43**
Raynel Way. *Leeds* —3J **43**
Rayner Av. *B'frd* —5L **57**
Rayner Av. *Heck* —6A **96**
Rayner Dri. *Brigh* —8M **93**
Rayner Mt. *All* —6F **56**
Rayner Rd. *Brigh* —8M **93**
Rayners Av. *Liv* —8G **95**
Rayner St. *Horb* —1C **136**
Raynham Cres. *Kei* —8E **20**
Raynor Clo. *Hud* —3H **131**
Raynville App. *Leeds* —4H **61**
Raynville Av. *Leeds* —3H **61**
Raynville Clo. *Leeds* —3H **61**
Raynville Ct. *Leeds* —4H **61**
Raynville Cres. *Leeds* —4J **61**
Raynville Dene. *Leeds* —3J **61**
Raynville Dri. *Leeds* —3H **61**
Raynville Grange. Leeds —4H 61
(off Raynville Rd.)
Raynville Grn. *Leeds* —4H **61**
Raynville Gro. *Leeds* —3H **61**
Raynville Mt. *Leeds* —3H **61**
Raynville Pl. *Leeds* —4H **61**
Raynville Ri. *Leeds* —4H **61**
Raynville Rd. *Leeds* —3G **61**
Raynville St. *Leeds* —3H **61**
Raynville Ter. *Leeds* —3H **61**
Raynville Wlk. *Leeds* —4H **61**
Ray St. *Hud* —3N **131**
Raywood Clo. *Yead* —8L **25**
Reap Hirst Rd. *Hud* —9J **113**
Rebecca St. *B'frd* —6B **58**
Recreation Cres. *Leeds* —1B **80**
Recreation Gro. *Leeds* —1B **80**
Recreation La. *Ell* —5D **112**
Recreation Mt. *Leeds* —1B **80**
Recreation Pl. *Leeds* —1B **80**
Recreation Rd. *Leeds* —3B **80**
Recreation Rd. *Sower B* —8J **91**
Recreation Row. *Leeds* —1B **80**

Recreation St. Leeds —1B 80
Recreation Ter. Leeds —1B 80
Recreation Vw. Leeds —1B 80
Rectory Av. C'frd —4D 102
Rectory Clo. Cltn —8E 154
Rectory Clo. Gar —7N 65
Rectory Clo. Mars —5F 144
Rectory Dri. Bat —3D 96
Rectory Dri. Hud —3F 132
Rectory Garden. Eml —2G 150
Rectory Garth. Hems —2D 156
Rectory La. Eml —2G 150
Rectory Row. Kei —9H 21
Rectory St. C'frd —4D 102
Rectory St. Leeds —5G 63
Rectory Vw. Dew —8H 117
Redbeck Cotts. H'fth —7B 42
Red Beck Rd. Hal —3E 92
Red Beck Va. Shipl —1M 57
Red Brink La. Sower B —1B 110
Red Brink Rd. Sower B —1B 110
Redburn Av. Shipl —1M 57
Redburn Dri. Shipl —1M 57
Redburn Rd. Shipl —1N 57
Redcar La. Steet —6B 20
Redcar Rd. B'frd —9J 41
Redcar St. Hal —5M 91
Redcliffe Av. Kei —9G 21
Redcliffe Gro. Kei —9G 20
Redcliffe St. Kei —9G 20
Redcote La. Leeds —6L 61
(in two parts)
Red Deer Pk. La. Grng M —5B 134
Reddisher Rd. Mars —4E 144
Red Doles La. Hud —1A 132
Red Doles Rd. Hud —9A 114
Reddyshore Scout Ga. Todm —6K 107
Redesdale Gdns. Leeds —4K 43
Redfearn Av. Heck —7A 96
Redgate La. Scam —7F 128
Red Hall App. Leeds —6B 46
Red Hall Av. Leeds —6A 46
Red Hall Chase. Leeds —6B 46
Redhall Clo. Leeds —4A 80
Red Hall Ct. Leeds —6B 46
Redhall Cres. Leeds —4A 80
Red Hall Cft. Leeds —6B 46
Red Hall Dri. Leeds —6B 46
Red Hall Gdns. Leeds —6A 46
Red Hall Gth. Leeds —6B 46
Redhall Ga. Leeds —4A 80
Red Hall Grn. Leeds —6B 46
Red Hall La. Leeds —6A 46
Red Hall La. Wake —2J 119
(in two parts)
Red Hall Va. Leeds —7B 46
Red Hall Vw. Leeds —6B 46
Red Hall Wlk. Leeds —6B 46
Red Hall Way. Leeds —6B 46
Red Hill. —5G 103
Redhill Av. C'frd —6F 102
Redhill Av. Ting —7A 98
Redhill Clo. Ting —7A 98
Redhill Cres. Ting —7A 98
Redhill Dri. C'frd —5G 103
Redhill Dri. Ting —7A 98
Redhill Gdns. C'frd —6G 103
Redhill La. Leeds —4N 85
Redhill Mt. C'frd —5G 102
Redhill Rd. C'frd —5G 102
Redhill Vw. C'frd —6G 102
Red House Museum. —3M 95
Red Laithes Ct. Dew —5B 116
Red Laithes La. Dew —5B 116
Redland Cres. Kin —8B 140
Redland Dri. Kbtn —2J 149
Redland Gro. M'well —7K 153
Redlands Clo. Mir —4L 115
Red La. Fars —3N 59
Red La. Mel —7N 145
Red La. S'hse —6M 121
Red La. Wake & New S —6F 120
Red Lodge Clo. Leeds —2M 63
Redman Clo. Haw —8B 36
Redman Gth. Haw —8B 36
Redmayne Gro. Knot —8C 104
Redmire Ct. Leeds —2B 64
Redmire Dri. Leeds —2B 64
Redmire St. B'frd —7J 59
Redmire Vw. Leeds —2B 64
Redruth Dri. Nor —9J 101
Redshaw Rd. Leeds —8N 61
Redthorne Way. Shaf —6J 155
Redvers Clo. Leeds —6K 43
Redwood Av. Roys —6D 154
Redwood Av. Ting —4C 98
Redwood Clo. Kei —2L 37
Redwood Clo. Rothw —7F 82
Redwood Clo. Yead —9L 25
Redwood Dri. Hud —6B 114
Redwood Gro. Hud —4B 132
(off Highroyd La.)
Redwood Gro. Shar C —7K 121
Redwood Gro. Yead —9K 25
Redwood Way. Yead —9K 25
Reedling Dri. Morl —1M 97
Reed Rd. Leeds —8N 61
Reedsdale Av. Gild —6F 78
Reedsdale Dri. Gild —6F 78
Reedsdale Gdns. Gild —6F 78
Reed St. Hud —3J 131
Rees Way. B'frd —6D 58
Reeth Rd. Brigh —3K 113
Reevy Av. B'frd —6L 75
Reevy Cres. B'frd —6K 75
Reevy Dri. B'frd —5M 75
Reevylands Dri. B'frd —5M 75
Reevy Rd. B'frd —5L 75
Reevy Rd. W. B'frd —5J 75
Reevy St. B'frd —4M 75
Reevy Yd. B'frd —5N 75
(off Green End Rd.)
Reform St. Gom —3M 95
Regal Clo. Sower B —1C 128
Regal Dri. Sower B —1C 128
Regal Pde. Leeds —4C 64
Regency Ct. B'frd —6N 57
Regency Ct. Leeds —2A 62
Regency Gdns. Ting —4C 98
Regency Pk. Gro. Pud —9B 60
Regency Pk. Rd. Pud —9B 60
Regency Rd. Mir —7L 115
Regency Vw. B'frd —4E 58
Regent Av. H'fth —8F 42
Regent Clo. Brigh —5K 113
Regent Clo. H'fth —8F 42
Regent Ct. H'fth —8F 42
Regent Ct. Leeds —7E 62
(off Briggate)
Regent Cres. H'fth —8E 42
Regent Cres. S Hien —4M 155
Regent Ho. Ell —4E 112
Regent M. Bat —8J 97
Regent Pk. Av. Leeds —2B 62
Regent Pk. Cross Av. Leeds —2B 62
(off Regent Pk. Av.)
Regent Pk. Ter. Leeds —2B 62
Regent Pl. B'frd —6E 40
Regent Pl. H Bri —1H 89
Regent Pl. Sower B —7H 91
Regent Rd. H'fth —8E 42
Regent Rd. Hud —3K 131
Regent Rd. I'ly —5F 8
Regent Rd. Khtn —9G 114
Regents Pk. Wake —5N 119
Regent St. B'frd —6E 40
Regent St. C'frd —5C 102
Regent St. Chap A —8F 44
Regent St. F'stne —6C 122
Regent St. Gre —8H 41
Regent St. Hal —6B 92
Regent St. Haw —8D 36
Regent St. H Bri —1H 89
Regent St. Heck —9N 95
Regent St. Hems —2C 156
Regent St. Horb —1B 136
Regent St. Leeds —6F 62
Regent St. Mir —8L 115
Regent St. Nor —8K 101
Regent St. Q'bry —4E 74
Regent St. S Elm —6L 157
Regent St. S Hien —4M 155
Regent St. Todm —2J 107
Regent St. Wake —7N 119
Regent Ter. Chap A —8F 44
Regent Ter. Leeds —4B 62
Regina Cres. Brier —7M 155
Regina Cres. H'cft —9K 139
Regina Dri. Leeds —9F 44
Regina Ho. Leeds —6G 60
Reginald Mt. Leeds —2F 62
Reginald Pl. Leeds —2F 62
Reginald Row. Leeds —2F 62
Reginald St. B'frd —2B 76
Reginald St. Leeds —2F 62
Reginald Ter. Leeds —2F 62
Reginald Vw. Leeds —2F 62
Reid Pk. Av. Horb —1A 136
Reighton Cft. B'frd —9J 41
Rein Ct. Aber —7E 48
Rein Gdns. Ting —4M 97
Rein M. Ting —4M 97
Rein Rd. H'fth —9E 42
(in two parts)
Rein Rd. Morl & Ting —3L 97
Reins Av. Bail —6N 39
Reins Rd. Brigh —3K 113
Reins Ter. Hon —3M 147
Rein St. Morl —3M 97
Rein, The. Leeds —9A 46
Reinwood Av. Hud —3G 131
Reinwood Av. Leeds —1M 63
Reinwood Rd. Hud —4G 130
Rembrandt Av. Wake —4B 98
Renee Clo. B'frd —5G 76
Renfield Gro. Nor —9L 101
Renshaw St. B'frd —6F 40
Renton Av. Guis —7H 25
Renton Dri. Guis —8H 25
Renton Lea. Guis —8H 25
Repton Rd. Skel —8N 159
Reservoir Pl. Dew —2D 116
Reservoir Pl. Q'bry —3B 74
Reservoir Rd. Bat —8C 96
Reservoir Rd. Hal —4L 91
Reservoir Rd. Sower B —3M 109
Reservoir Rd. Stanb —8M 35
Reservoir Side Rd. Mel —2D 146
Reservoir St. Dew —2D 116
Reservoir Vw. Skelm —7B 150
Reservoir Vw. T'tn —8B 56
Restmore Av. Guis —5H 25
Retford Pl. B'frd —9A 58
Reuben St. Liv —7L 95
Reva Clo. Bgly —3G 39
Reva Syke Rd. Cytn —2G 75
Revel Garth. Den D —3D 166
Revie Rd. Leeds —2B 80
Revie Rd. Ind. Est. Leeds —2B 80
Reydon Wlk. B'frd —4L 75
Reyhill Gro. B'frd —9C 58
Reynald La. Hoy S —9H 167
Reyner Ho. M. B'frd —9C 58
Reynolds Av. B'frd —9K 57
Rhine St. B'frd —9E 58
Rhodes Av. Heck —6A 96
Rhodes Cres. Pon —5K 123
Rhodes Gdns. Loft —6L 99
Rhode's Hill La. B'ham —5E 32
Rhodesia Av. All —6H 57
Rhodesia Av. Hal —9B 92
Rhodes La. B Spa —2B 32
Rhodes Pl. Shipl —7N 39
Rhodes St. C'frd —4C 102
Rhodes St. Hal —5A 92
Rhodes St. H'town —5B 102
Rhodes St. Liv —8N 95
Rhodes St. Shipl —7M 39
Rhodes Ter. B'frd —2F 58
Rhodes Ter. Leeds —8A 62
Rhodesway. B'frd —7J 57
Rhondda Pl. Hal —6L 91
Rhum Clo. B'frd —7L 75
Rhyddings Av. Ackw —5F 140
Rhyddings Dri. Ackw —5F 140
Rhyddings Gdns. I'ly —5J 9
Rhylstone Mt. B'frd —7L 57
Rhyl St. F'stne —5D 122
Ribble Ct. Sils —8E 6
(off Howden Rd.)
Ribblesdale Av. Gar —8B 66
Ribble St. Kei —8L 21
Ribbleton Gro. B'frd —6E 58
Riber Av. Barn —9B 154
Ribstone St. H Bri —3M 89
Riccall Nook. B'frd —9H 41
Rice St. Hud —4N 131
Richard Pl. Brigh —8M 93
(off Richard St.)
Richard Rd. Dart —9F 152
Richardshaw Dri. S'ley —5B 60
Richardshaw La. S'ley —5B 60
Richardshaw Rd. S'ley —5B 60
Richardson Av. B'frd —5A 76
Richardson Cres. Leeds —7K 63
Richardson Rd. Leeds —7K 63
Richardson St. Oaken —9E 76
Richard St. B'frd —7E 58
Richard St. Brigh —8M 93
Richard St. Wake —4L 119
Richard Thorpe Av. Mir —6M 115
Richmond Av. Dart —9F 152
Richmond Av. Hud —9M 113
Richmond Av. Knot —7A 104
Richmond Av. Leeds —2A 62
Richmond Av. Pon —2K 123
(off Richmond Ct.)
Richmond Av. Sower B —9F 90
Richmond Clo. Bmly —4D 60
Richmond Clo. Hal —4B 92
Richmond Clo. Morl —1K 97
Richmond Clo. Rothw —7A 82
Richmond Ct. Croft —2H 139
Richmond Ct. Hud —7E 130
Richmond Ct. Leeds —7H 63
Richmond Ct. Pon —2K 123
Richmond Ct. Rothw —7A 82
Richmond Cft. Leeds —7H 63
Richmondfield Av. Bar E —9M 47
Richmondfield Clo. Bar E —9M 47
Richmondfield Cres. Bar E —9M 47
Richmondfield Cross. Bar E —9M 47
Richmondfield Dri. Bar E —9M 47
Richmondfield Gth. Bar E —8M 47
Richmondfield Gro. Bar E —9M 47
Richmondfield La. Bar E —9M 47
Richmondfield Mt. Bar E —9M 47
Richmondfield Way. Bar E —9M 47
Richmond Flats. Hud —3N 131
(off Leeds Rd.)
Richmond Gdns. Pud —7D 60
Richmond Gdns. Sower B —9F 90
Richmond Gth. Oss —7B 118
Richmond Gro. Gom —2M 95
Richmond Hill. —7H 63
Richmond Hill App. Leeds —7G 63
Richmond Hill Clo. Leeds —7G 63
Richmond Ho. Leeds —5K 45
(off Street La.)
Richmond Lea. Mir —5L 115
Richmond M. Shipl —7L 39
Richmond Mt. Leeds —2A 62
Richmond Pl. I'ly —6H 9
Richmond Pl. Shipl —7L 39
Richmond Rd. Bat —1G 117
Richmond Rd. B'frd —7A 58
Richmond Rd. Fars —4N 59
Richmond Rd. Hal —4A 92
Richmond Rd. Heck —6B 96
Richmond Rd. Leeds —2A 62
Richmond Rd. Shipl —7L 39
Richmond Rd. Upt —2N 157
Richmond Rd. Wake —3K 119
Richmond St. C'frd —5D 102
Richmond St. Cleck —5H 95
Richmond St. Hal —4A 92
Richmond St. Kei —8H 21
Richmond St. Leeds —7G 62
Richmond St. Todm —7L 87
Richmond Ter. Guis —7H 25
Richmond Ter. Otley —1K 25
Richmond Ter. Pon —2K 123
(off Finkle St.)
Richmond Ter. Pud —7D 60
Richmond Way. Gar —9N 65
Rickard St. Leeds —8B 62
Ridding Ga. Otley —8J 11
Riddings. —8B 114
Riddings Clo. Hems —4D 156
Riddings Clo. Hud —8B 114
Riddings Ri. Hud —8B 114
Riddings Rd. Hud —8B 114
Riddings Rd. I'ly —6G 8
Riddlesden. —6N 21
Riddlesden St. Riddl —7M 21
Ridehalgh La. Briercl —3B 50
Rider Rd. Leeds —2D 62
Rider St. Leeds —6G 62
Ridge Av. M'twn —3K 135
Ridge Bank. Todm —7K 87
Ridge Clo. Guis —8G 24
Ridge Clo. Hud —7M 131
Ridge Clo. Skelm —8D 150
Ridge Cres. M'twn —4K 135
Ridgedale Mt. Pon —8K 103
Ridgefield St. C'frd —5C 102
Ridge Gro. Leeds —1C 62
Ridge Hill. Brigh —2K 113
Ridge La. Sils —1C 6
Ridge Lea. Brigh —2L 113
Ridge Mt. Leeds —2C 62
Ridgemount Rd. Riddl —6L 21
Ridge Rd. Kip —5D 84
Ridge Rd. Leeds —2D 62
Ridge Rd. M'twn —3K 135
Ridge Rd. Todm —7K 87
Ridgestone Av. Hems —2E 156
Ridge St. Hud —7M 131
Ridge Ter. Leeds —1A 62
Ridge, The. Lntn —6K 17
Ridgeview. Ell —5H 113
Ridge Vw. Leeds —6F 60
Ridge Vw. Dri. Bkby —9J 113
Ridge Vw. Gdns. B'frd —8G 40
Ridge Vw. Rd. Brigh —2L 113
Ridgeway. All —6F 56
Ridgeway. Guis —8F 24
Ridgeway. Hud —3C 132
Ridge Way. Leeds —9H 45
Ridgeway. Q'bry —5E 74
Ridgeway. Shipl —9C 40
Ridge Way Clo. Leeds —9H 45
Ridgeway Cres. Barn —8D 154
Ridgeway Dri. Bat —3D 96
Ridgeway Gdns. Brigh —7K 93
Ridgeway Mt. Kei —2F 36
Ridgeway Sq. Knot —9E 104
Ridgeways, The. Lint —9C 130
Ridgeway Ter. Leeds —2C 62
(off Delph La.)
Ridgeway, The. Knot —9E 104
Ridgewood Clo. Bail —4C 40
Ridgill Av. Skel —8M 159
Riding Head La. Ludd —3E 90
Riding Hill. Hal —7K 75
Riding La. Hal —1J 91
Ridings Clo. Loft —6K 99
Ridings Ct. Loft —6K 99
Ridings Cft. B'frd —4F 76
Ridings Fields. Broc —6A 148
Ridings Gdns. Loft —6K 99
Ridings La. Gol —6B 130
Ridings La. H'frth —1A 164
Ridings La. Loft —6K 99
Ridings M. Loft —6K 99
Ridings Rd. Dew —3G 117
Ridings Shop. Cen., The. Wake —5L 11
Ridings, The. Utley —5H 21
Riding St. Bat —6B 96
Ridings Way. B'frd —4K 75
Ridings Way. Loft G —6K 99
Ridings Wood. Khtn —4F 132
Ridingwood Ri. Clay W —7H 151
Ridleys Fold. Add —1M 7
Rievaulx Av. B'frd —6A 58
Rievaulx Clo. B Spa —1C 32
Riffa La. Leat —6F 12
Rifle St. Hud —5N 131
Rigg La. Ackw & E Hard —3J 14
Rightox Rd. Broc —6A 148
Riglet La. Wake —9A 122
Rigton App. Leeds —6G 63
Rigton Bank. Bard —4E 30
Rigton Clo. Leeds —6H 63
Rigton Dri. Leeds —6G 63
Rigton Grn. Bard —4F 30
Rigton Grn. Leeds —6G 63
Rigton Hill. —2F 30
Rigton Hill. N Rig —2N 13
Rigton Lawn. Leeds —6G 63
Rigton M. Leeds —6G 63
Rigton St. B'frd —2B 76
Riley La. Hal —5M 73
Riley La. Kbtn —4J 149
Riley Pk. Kbtn —3K 149
Riley St. Hud —6N 131
Rillbank La. Leeds —5B 62
Rillbank St. Leeds —5B 62
(off Rillbank La.)
Rill Ct. Hems —2D 156
Rillington Mead. B'frd —9H 41
Rillside. Shepl —8K 149
Rills Mead. Otley —1L 25
Rilston St. B'frd —8N 57
Rimswell Holt. B'frd —9J 41
Ringby La. Hal —9A 74
Ring O Bells Yd. Horb —1C 136
Ring Rd. Adel. Adel —5N 43
Ring Rd. Beeston. Leeds —1M 7
Ring Rd. Beeston Pk. Leeds —5C
Ring Rd. Bramley. Bmly —6G 60
Ring Rd. Cross Gates. Leeds —3D
Ring Rd. Farnley. Leeds —7G 60
Ring Rd. Farsley. Far —4M 59
Ring Rd. Halton. Leeds —5D 64
Ring Rd. Horsforth. H'fth —7H 4
Ring Rd. Lwr. Wortley. Lwr W —8J
Ring Rd. Meanwood. Mean —5A
Ring Rd. Middleton. Midd —8F 8
Ring Rd. Moortown. Moort —5C
Ring Rd. Seacroft. Leeds —7A 4
Ring Rd. Seacroft. Seac —1C 64
Ring Rd. Shadwell. Shad —4L 4
Ring Rd. Weetwood. Weet —6L
Ring Rd. W. Pk. W Park —6J 43
Ringstone Gro. Brier —6A 156
Ringway. Gar —8L 65
Ringwood Av. Leeds —7A 46
Ringwood Ct. Out —7M 99
Ringwood Cres. Leeds —6B 46
Ringwood Dri. Leeds —7B 46
Ringwood Edge. Ell —5C 112
Ringwood Gdns. Leeds —7B 46
Ringwood Mt. Leeds —7B 46
Ringwood Rd. B'frd —2N 75
Ringwood Way. Hems —2E 156
Rink Pde. Bat —9G 96
(off Rink St.)
Rink St. Bat —9G 96
Rink Ter. Bat —9G 96
Ripley Ct. Nor —3J 121
Ripley Dri. Nor I —9L 101
Ripley La. Guis —5J 25
Ripley Rd. B'frd —1D 76
Ripley Rd. Liv —8K 95
Ripley St. All —4F 56
Ripley St. B'frd —1C 76
(in two parts)
Ripley St. Hal —5M 93
Ripley St. Riddl —7M 21
Ripley Ter. B'frd —1D 76
Ripley Ter. L'ft —5D 90
Ripon Av. Hud —9M 113
Ripon Ho. Ell —4E 112
Ripon Ho. Far —3A 60
Ripon Rd. Dew —3J 117
Ripon St. Hal —6L 91
Ripon Ter. Hal —3A 92

Ripponden. —7D 110
Ripponden Old Bank. Ripp —7E 110
Ripponden Old La. Sower B —7A 110
Ripponden Wood. —5E 110
Risedale Av. Birs —2E 96
Risedale Clo. Birs —2E 96
Rise La. Todm —7J 87
(in two parts)
Rise, The. B'ton —4B 104
Rise, The. Hal —2F 92
Rise, The. Kip —4A 84
Rise, The. Leeds —1K 61
Rise, The. Pon —4L 123
Rishworth. —1C 128
Rishworth Av. Eml —3G 150
Rishworth Clo. Wren —1G 119
Rishworth Hall Clo. Sower B —1B 128
Rishworthian Ct. Hal —2N 111
Rishworth Mill La. Rish —2D 128
Rishworth New Rd. Sower B —1B 128
Rishworth Pal. Rish —2D 128
Rishworth Rd. Bklnd —7G 110
Rishworth Rd. Dew —3G 116
Rishworth St. Dew —3G 117
Rishworth St. Kei —1F 36
Rishworth St. Wake —4L 119
Rivadale Vw. I'ly —4G 9
Rivelin Rd. C'frd —6C 102
Riverdale. Beal —5M 105
Riverdale. Weth —5N 17
Riverdale Av. Stan —1A 120
Riverdale Clo. Stan —1A 120
Riverdale Ct. Otley —9L 11
Riverdale Cres. Stan —1A 120
Riverdale Dri. Stan —1A 120
Riverdale Gdns. B Spa —1F 32
Riverdale Gdns. Otley —9L 11
Riverdale Rd. Otley —9L 11
Riverdale Rd. Stan —1A 120
River Holme Vw. Broc —7A 148
Rivermead. Wake —8M 119
River Pk. Hon —4L 147
Riverside. Clay W —7H 151
Riverside. Kei —9L 21
Riverside Av. Otley —7M 11
Riverside Bus. Pk. I'ly —4H 9
Riverside Clo. Otley —8M 11
Riverside Ct. Bail —6M 39
Riverside Ct. H'frth —6H 163
Riverside Ct. Leeds —7E 62
Riverside Cres. Otley —7M 11
Riverside Dri. Otley —7M 11
Riverside Est. Shipl —7M 39
Riverside Ind. Est. Dew —4F 116
Riverside Pk. Otley —8M 11
Riverside Vs. Wake —8M 119
Riverside Wlk. I'ly —4E 8
Riverside Way. Dew —6B 116
River St. Brigh —2A 114
River St. Haw —8D 36
River St. Todm —7L 87
River Valley Vw. Den D —2D 166
(off Miller Hill)
River Vw. B Spa —1F 32
River Vw. C'frd —4B 102
River Vw. H'fth —6E 42
River Vw. I'ly —4K 9
River Vw. Mir —4L 115
River Wlk. Bgly —4E 38
Riverwood Dri. Hal —1A 112
Riviera Gdns. Leeds —9E 44
Rivock Av. Kei —5F 20
Rivock Av. Steet —2D 20
Rivock Gro. Kei —5F 20
Roach Grange Av. Kip —2A 84
Road End. G'lnd —4B 112
Roaine Dri. H'frth —4N 163
Roans Brae. B'frd —9J 41
Robb Av. Leeds —4C 80
Robbins Ter. F'stne —5D 122
Robb St. Leeds —4C 80
Roberson Ter. Gom —4L 95
Robert Ct. Liv —9L 95
Robert La. H'frth —1A 164
Roberts Av. Leeds —4K 63
Roberts Bldgs. Hal —5K 91
(off Gibbet St.)
Roberts Ct. Leeds —4K 63
Robertsgate. Loft —3K 99
Robertsgate Sq. Loft —3K 99
(off Robertsgate)
Robertshaw Pl. Bgly —5F 38
Robertshaw Rd. H Bri —1G 88
Robertson Av. Brigh —3M 113
Roberts Pas. L'boro —9M 107
Roberts Pl. B'frd —7B 58
Roberts Pl. Leeds —5K 63
Robert's St. Cleck —5G 95
Roberts St. Lay —1C 36
Roberts St. W'ford —7D 82
Roberts St. N. Hal —2B 92
Robert St. B'frd —8E 58
Robert St. Cro R —7F 36
Robert St. Hal —2N 91
Roberts Way. Wake —1A 138
Roberttown. —2J 115
Roberttown Grange. Liv —1J 115
(off School St.)
Roberttown La. Liv —2J 115
Robin Chase. Pud —7C 60
Robin Clo. B'frd —2G 58
Robin Clo. Dew —1E 116
Robin Dri. B'frd —2G 58
Robin Dri. Steet —2B 20
Robin Hill. Bat —4D 96
Robin Hood. —1K 99
Robin Hood Av. Roys —5E 154
Robin Hood Cres. Wake —7F 118
Robin Hood Gro. Hud —7A 114
Robin Hood Hill. Hud —2L 147
Robin Hood Rd. Hud —7A 114
Robin Hood St. C'frd —5E 102
Robin Hood Way. Brigh —1C 114
Robinia Wlk. Wake —3J 119
Robin La. Dew —9C 96
Robin La. Hems —4N 155
Robin La. Pon —9K 103
Robin La. Pud —7B 60
Robin La. Roys —5E 154
Robin Rocks. Broc —7A 148
Robin Royd Av. Mir —3L 115
Robin Royd Cft. Mir —3L 115
Robin Royd Dri. Mir —3L 115
Robin Royd Gth. Mir —3L 115
Robin Royd Gro. Mir —3L 115
Robin Royd La. Mir —4L 115
Robin's Gro. Rothw —8A 82
Robinson Ct. B'frd —8L 57
Robinson La. Kip —4B 84
Robinson St. All B —9B 84
Robinson St. Hud —5N 131
Robinson St. Pon —2K 123
Robins, The. Bur W —9C 10
Robin St. B'frd —1A 76
Robin St. Hud —5J 131
Robin Wlk. Shipl —9B 40
Robinwood Ct. Leeds —6J 45
Robinwood Ter. Todm —4G 86
Robson Clo. Pon —5K 123
Robson's Rd. Wake —5K 119
Rochdale Dri. Sower B —1F 110
Rochdale Rd. G'lnd —4K 111
Rochdale Rd. Hud —5L 129
Rochdale Rd. L'boro & Ripp —1E 126
Rochdale Rd. Ripp —8M 109
Rochdale Rd. Sower B —3E 110
(nr. Halifax Rd.)
Rochdale Rd. Sower B & Hal
(nr. Pye Nest Rd.) —7K 91
Rochdale Rd. Todm & Wals —9J 87
Rocheford Clo. Leeds —2H 81
Rocheford Ct. Leeds —2H 81
Rocheford Gdns. Leeds —2H 81
Rocheford Gro. Leeds —2H 81
Rocheford Wlk. Leeds —2H 81
Rochester Ct. Horb —8E 118
Rochester Dri. Horb —8E 118
Rochester Gdns. Leeds —3C 60
Rochester Pl. Ell —5E 112
(off Savile Rd.)
Rochester Rd. Birs —1B 96
Rochester St. B'frd —7G 58
Rochester St. Shipl —9A 40
Rochester Ter. Leeds —2N 61
Rochester Wynd. Leeds —3J 45
Rockcliffe Av. Bail —6A 40
Rock Cliffe Mt. L'ft —5D 90
Rock Edge. Liv —7L 95
Rockery Cft. H'fth —5F 42
Rockery Rd. H'fth —5F 42
Rockfield. Yead —9N 25
(off Rockfield Ter.)
Rockfield Ter. Yead —9N 25
Rock Fold. Gol —6C 130
Rock Hill. C'frd —6F 102
Rockhill Clo. Bat —3C 96
Rockhill La. B'frd —6E 76
Rock Ho. Dri. Dew —1F 116
Rockingham Clo. Leeds —3G 64
Rockingham La. Pon —5L 141
Rockingham Rd. Leeds —3G 64
Rockingham St. Fitz —7B 140
Rockingham Way. Leeds —3G 64
Rockland Cres. B'frd —9K 57
Rocklands Av. Bail —3A 40
Rocklands Pl. Bail —3A 40
Rock La. Leeds —2E 60
Rock La. Slai —7M 129
Rock La. T'tn —6B 56
Rock Lea. Q'bry —4E 74
Rockley Clo. Hud —6C 132
Rockley Dri. Wake —4K 137
Rockley Grange Gdns. Gar —9L 65
Rockley St. Dew —3G 117
Rockmill Rd. Hon —7A 148
Rock Rd. Hud —9G 113
Rocks La. Hal —5K 73
Rocks Rd. Hal —9N 91
Rock St. Brigh —9M 93
Rock St. Hud —4D 130
Rocks Vw. Hal —8N 91
Rock Ter. C'frd —6G 102
Rock Ter. Hip —4J 93
Rock Ter. Hud —1G 130
Rock Ter. Leeds —6A 64
Rock Ter. Morl —8L 79
Rock Ter. Todm —1J 107
Rock, The. Lint —1D 146
Rock Vw. Holy G —7B 112
Rock Vw. Mars —6F 144
Rockville Ter. Hal —7N 91
Rockville Ter. Yead —1N 41
(off S. View Ter.)
Rockwell La. B'frd —9G 40
Rockwood Clo. Dart —8H 153
Rockwood Clo. Hud —5C 114
Rockwood Cres. Cald G —4F 136
Rockwood Cres. C'ley —4L 59
Rockwood Gro. C'ley —3M 59
Rockwood Hill Ct. C'ley —4L 59
Rockwood Ri. Den D —1D 166
Rockwood Rd. C'ley —4L 59
Roderick St. Leeds —7L 61
Rodger La. Wren —1H 119
Rodin Av. B'frd —7J 57
Rodley. —1B 60
Rodley La. C'ley —9N 41
Rodley La. Eml —2G 150
Rodley La. Rod —2D 60
Rodney Yd. Wake —5L 119
Rods Vw. Morl —1L 97
Rodwell End. Todm —5A 88
Roebuck La. N Clift —5K 11
Roebuck St. Birs —3C 96
Roebuck Ter. N Clift —5K 11
Roeburn Clo. M'well —7J 153
Roe Ho. Bail —6N 39
(off Fairview Ct.)
Roe La. Birk —1L 105
Roger Ct. B'frd —5F 58
Roger Dri. Wake —1M 137
Roger Fold. Kip —4B 84
Roger Ga. Myth —3K 89
Roger La. Hud —7N 131
Rogers Ct. Stan —6A 100
Rogerson Sq. Brigh —9M 93
Rogers Pl. Pud —6C 60
Roils Head Rd. Hal —5H 91
Rokeby Gdns. B'frd —9J 41
Rokeby Gdns. Leeds —1M 61
Roker La. Pud —9C 60
Roker Lane Bottom. —1E 78
Rolleston Rd. Carc —9N 159
Roman Av. Hud —1C 130
Roman Av. Leeds —5J 45
Romanby Shaw. B'frd —9H 41
Roman Clo. Hud —1C 130
Roman Ct. Leeds —5K 45
Roman Cres. Leeds —5K 45
Roman Dri. Hud —1C 130
Roman Dri. Leeds —5K 45
Roman Gdns. Leeds —5J 45
Roman Gro. Leeds —5J 45
Roman Mt. Leeds —5K 45
Roman Pl. Leeds —5K 45
Roman Ri. Pon —6J 123
Roman Rd. Bat —4C 96
Roman Rd. Dart —9F 152
Roman Ter. Leeds —5J 45
Roman Vw. Leeds —5K 45
Rombalds Av. Leeds —6M 61
Rombalds Ct. Men —4D 24
Rombalds Cres. Leeds —5M 61
Rombalds Cres. Sils —9F 6
Rombalds Dri. Bgly —4G 39
Rombalds Gro. Leeds —6M 61
Rombalds La. I'ly —6K 9
Rombalds Pl. Leeds —5M 61
Rombalds St. Leeds —5M 61
Rombalds Ter. Leeds —6M 61
Rombald's Vw. I'ly —4J 9
Rombalds Vw. Leeds —5M 61
Rombalds Vw. Otley —7H 11
Romford Av. Morl —1K 97
Romford Ct. B'frd —7L 75
Romney Mt. Pud —9D 60
Romsey Clo. Hud —1E 130
Romsey Gdns. B'frd —2H 77
Romsey M. B'frd —2H 77
Rona Cft. Rothw —8B 82
Ronald Dri. B'frd —8M 57
Roods La. H'frth —5F 162
Rookery La. Hal —9C 92
Rookery Pl. Brigh —9N 93
Rookery, The. Add —1M 7
Rookes Av. B'frd —5A 76
Rookes La. Hal —3M 93
Rook Hill Dri. Pon —4L 123
Rookhill Mt. Pon —4M 123
Rookhill Rd. Pon —4M 123
Rook La. B'frd —3F 76
Rooks Av. Cleck —4G 94
Rooks Clo. Wyke —3B 94
Rook's Nest Rd. Out & Stan —8L 99
Rook St. Bgly —4E 38
Rook St. Hud —3M 131
Rookwith Pde. B'frd —9H 41
Rookwood Av. Kip —5A 84
Rookwood Av. Leeds —6L 63
Rookwood Cres. Leeds —6L 63
Rookwood Cft. Leeds —7L 63
Rookwood Gdns. Leeds —7L 63
Rookwood Hill. Leeds —6L 63
Rookwood Mt. Leeds —6L 63
Rookwood Pde. Leeds —6M 63
Rookwood Pl. Leeds —6L 63
Rookwood Rd. Leeds —6L 63
Rookwood Sq. Leeds —6M 63
Rookwood St. Leeds —7L 63
Rookwood Ter. Leeds —6L 63
Rookwood Va. Leeds —7L 63
Rookwood Vw. Leeds —6L 63
Rookwood Wlk. Leeds —6L 63
Rooley Av. B'frd —5B 76
Rooley Banks. Sower B —9E 90
Rooley Clo. B'frd —4C 76
Rooley Cres. B'frd —4C 76
Rooley Heights. Sower B —9D 90
Rooley Hill. —9D 90
Rooley La. B'frd —4B 76
Rooley La. Sower B —1D 110
Roomfield Ct. Todm —7K 87
(off Halifax Rd.)
Roomfield St. Todm —7K 87
Rooms. —5J 79
Rooms Fold. Morl —7K 79
Rooms La. Morl —5J 79
Roper Av. Leeds —7H 45
Roper Gdns. Hal —9K 73
Ropergate. Pon —3J 123
Ropergate End. Pon —3J 123
(off Ropergate)
Roper Grn. Hal —9K 73
Roper Gro. Leeds —7H 45
Roper Ho. Hal —9K 73
Roper La. Hal —5M 73
Roper La. Q'bry —2A 74
Roper St. Kei —9H 21
Rope Wlk. Hal —6F 72
Ropewalk. Knot —8F 104
Roscoe St. Leeds —4F 62
Roscoe Ter. Leeds —7L 61
Roseate Grn. Morl —1M 97
Rose Av. Cow —7E 130
Rose Av. H'fth —8E 42
Rose Av. Mar —4H 131
Rose Av. Upt —2M 157
Rose Bank. Bur W —9C 10
Rosebank Cres. Leeds —4B 62
Rosebank Gdns. Leeds —5B 62
Rosebank Ho. Leeds —4B 62
(off Belle Vue Rd.)
Rose Bank Pl. B'frd —7K 57
Rosebank Rd. Leeds —5B 62
Rose Bank Rd. Todm —7J 87
Rosebank Row. Leeds —5B 62
Rosebank St. Bat —6D 96
Roseberry St. Oakw —5D 36
Roseberry St. Todm —3E 86
Rosebery Av. Hal —8C 92
Rosebery Av. Shipl —8A 40
Rosebery Mt. Shipl —8B 40
Rosebery Rd. B'frd —4A 58
Rosebery St. Ell —5E 112
Rosebery St. Hud —1L 131
Rosebery St. Pud —6N 59
Rosebery Ter. Hal —4N 91
Rosebery Ter. S'ley —4C 60
Rosebud Wlk. Leeds —4G 62
Rosechapel Clo. B'frd —7L 75
Rosecliffe Mt. Leeds —3E 60
Rosecliffe Ter. Leeds —4F 60
Rose Clo. Upt —2N 157
Rose Ct. Gar —7A 66
Rose Cft. E Kes —2D 30
Rosedale. Rothw —7A 82
Rosedale Av. All —4E 56
Rosedale Av. Harts —1H 115
Rosedale Av. Hud —5C 132
Rosedale Av. Wake —2N 137
Rosedale Bank. Leeds —4F 80
Rosedale Clo. Bail —5M 39
Rose Dale Clo. Norm —2L 121
Rosedale Clo. Upt —2A 158
Rosedale Gdns. Leeds —4F 80
(in two parts)
Rosedale Grn. Leeds —4F 80
Rosedale Ho. B'frd —9H 41
Rosedale Ho. Sower B —9H 91
(off Sowerby St.)
Rosedale Ri. B Spa —1C 32
Rosedale Wlk. Leeds —4F 80
Rose Farm App. Nor —8G 100
Rose Farm Clo. Nor —7G 100
Rose Farm Fold. Nor —7G 100
Rose Farm Ri. Nor —7G 100
Rose Gth. Bur W —1A 24
Rose Gth. Croft —1G 138
Rosegarth Av. H'frth —1A 164
Rose Gro. H Bri —9H 71
Rose Gro. Myth —4M 89
Rose Gro. Rothw —7M 81
Rose Gro. Upt —2N 157
Rose Gro. La. Hal —7F 90
Rose Heath. I'wth —6K 73
Rosehill Av. Hems —3C 156
Rose Hill Cres. Low M —9A 76
Rose Hill Dri. Hud —1K 131
Rose La. Ackw —5D 140
Roselee Clo. Sid —9D 92
Rosemary Clo. Brigh —2M 113
Rosemary Gro. Hal —9D 92
(in two parts)
Rosemary La. Brigh —3M 113
Rosemary La. Sid —9D 92
Rosemary Ter. Hal —9D 92
Rose Meadows. Kei —2E 36
Rosemont Av. Leeds —4F 60
Rosemont Av. Pud —6C 60
Rosemont Dri. Pud —6C 60
Rosemont Gro. Leeds —4E 60
Rosemont La. Bail —5C 40
Rosemont Pl. Leeds —4F 60
Rosemont Rd. Leeds —4F 60
Rosemont St. Leeds —4F 60
Rosemont St. Pud —6C 60
Rosemont Ter. Leeds —4F 60
Rosemont Ter. Pud —6C 60
Rosemont Vw. Leeds —4E 60
Rosemont Vs. Pud —6C 60
Rosemont Wlk. Leeds —4F 60
Rose Mt. B'frd —3E 58
(BD2)
Rose Mt. B'frd —5L 77
(BD4)
Rose Mt. Hal —8N 91
Rose Mt. Hud —1J 131
Rosemount. —6F 112
Rosemount. Leeds —9E 44
(off Henconner La.)
Rosemount Av. Ell —5F 112
Rosemount Clo. Kei —9H 21
(off Well St.)
Rose Mt. Pl. Leeds —8N 61
Rosemount Ter. Ell —5F 112
Rosemount Wlk. Kei —9H 21
(off Well St.)
Roseneath Pl. Leeds —8N 61
Roseneath St. Leeds —8N 61
Roseneath Ter. Leeds —8N 61
Rose Pl. L'ft —7E 90
Rose St. B'frd —5N 57
Rose St. Hal —6M 91
Rose St. Haw —9C 36
Rose St. H'fth —7E 42
Rose St. Kei —9M 21
Rose St. Todm —7K 87
Rose Ter. Add —1M 7
Rose Ter. Hal —5N 91
(off West St., HX1)
Rose Ter. Hal —8N 91
(HX2)
Rose Ter. H'fth —7D 42
Rose Tree Av. Cud —9J 155
Rose Tree Ct. Cud —9J 155
Rosetta Dri. B'frd —7L 57
Roseville Rd. Leeds —4G 62
Roseville St. Leeds —4G 63
Roseville Ter. Dew —3J 117
Roseville Ter. Leeds —3E 64
(off Church La.)
Roseville Way. Leeds —4G 62
Rosewood Av. Kip —2N 83
Rosewood Av. Riddl —7M 21
Rosewood Ct. Rothw —6A 82
Rosewood Gro. B'frd —9H 59
Rosgill Dri. Leeds —1A 64
Rosgill Grn. Leeds —1B 64
Rosgill Wlk. Leeds —1A 64
Rosley Mt. B'frd —7L 75
Roslyn Av. Hud —2H 147
Roslyn Clo. Ackw —5F 140
Roslyn Pl. B'frd —8N 57
Rossall Rd. Leeds —2H 63
Rossefield App. Leeds —5G 60
Rossefield Av. Hud —1K 131
Rossefield Av. Leeds —4G 60
Rossefield Chase. Leeds —4G 60
Rossefield Clo. Leeds —4G 60

Rossefield Dri. Leeds —4G 60
Rossefield Gdns. Leeds —4G 60
Rossefield Gth. Leeds —4G 60
Rossefield Grn. Leeds —4G 60 (off Rossefield Dri.)
Rossefield Gro. Leeds —4G 60
Rossefield Lawn. Leeds —4G 60
Rossefield Pde. Leeds —4G 60 (off Rossefield Gro.)
Rosse Fld. Pk. B'frd —2N 57
Rossefield Pl. Leeds —4G 60
Rossefield Rd. B'frd —2M 57
Rossefield Ter. Leeds —4G 60
Rossefield Vw. Leeds —4G 60
Rossefield Wlk. Leeds —4G 60
Rossefield Way. Leeds —4G 60
Rossendale Pl. Shipl —8M 39
Rosse St. B'frd —7M 57
Rosse St. Shipl —7N 39
Rossett Ho. B'frd —6D 58 (off Otley Rd.)
Ross Gro. Leeds —2D 60
Rossington Gro. Leeds —2G 63
Rossington Pl. Leeds —2G 63
Rossington Rd. Leeds —1J 63
Rossington St. Leeds —6D 62
Rossiter Dri. Knot —9C 104
Rosslyn Av. Ackw —5F 140
Rosslyn Ct. Ackw —5F 140
Rosslyn Ct. Dew —4J 117
Rosslyn Gro. Ackw —5F 140
Rosslyn Gro. Haw —9C 36
Rossmore Dri. All —5H 57
Ross Ter. Leeds —2D 60
Rosy St. Cro R —7F 36
Rotcher. —1L 145
Rotcher La. Slai —1L 145
Rotcher Rd. H'frth —3M 163
Rothbury Gdns. Leeds —4L 43
Rothesay Ter. B'frd —8A 58
Rothwell. —8N 81
Rothwell Dri. Hal —7A 92
Rothwell Haigh. —6N 81
Rothwell La. Oult —7B 82
Rothwell Mt. Hal —7A 92
Rothwell Rd. Hal —7A 92
Rothwell St. Hud —4C 132
Rough. L'boro —5A 126
Rough Hall La. Hal —8E 72
Rough Hey La. C'den —5L 69
Rough Hey La. Todm —2H 107
Rough Side La. Todm —8L 87
Round Clo. Rd. H'frth —2M 169
Roundell Av. B'frd —5F 76
Roundhay. —6J 45
Roundhay Av. Leeds —1H 63
Roundhay Cvn. & Camping Pk. Leeds —7M 45
Roundhay Cres. Leeds —1H 63
Roundhay Gdns. Leeds —1H 63
Roundhay Gro. Leeds —1H 63
Roundhay Mt. Leeds —2H 63
Roundhay Park. —7L 45
Roundhay Pk. La. Leeds —2K 45
Roundhay Pl. Leeds —1H 63
Roundhay Rd. Leeds —4F 62
Roundhay Vw. Leeds —1H 63
Roundhead Fold. App B —7J 41
Round Hill. —6D 102
Round Hill. Hal —7M 73
Round Hill. M'well —8J 153
Roundhill Av. Bgly —7G 38
Round Hill Clo. Hal —7M 73
Round Hill Clo. Q'bry —3G 75
Round Hill La. Hud —7E 114
Roundhill Mt. Bgly —8G 38
Roundhill Pl. B'frd —7B 58
Round Hill Pl. Q'bry —3G 75
Roundhill Rd. C'frd —5D 102
Roundhill St. B'frd —1B 76
Round Ings Rd. Outl —3M 129
Round St. B'frd —2C 76 (in two parts)
Round St. Wake —7N 119
Round Thorn Pl. B'frd —6M 57
Roundway. Hon —5L 147
Roundway, The. Morl —9H 79
Roundwell Rd. Liv —7G 95
Roundwood. Shipl —8K 39
Roundwood Av. Bail —4D 40
Roundwood Av. B'frd —1J 59
Round Wood Av. Hud —4E 132
Roundwood Crest. Wake —6E 118
Roundwood Glen. B'frd —1J 59
Roundwood Ind. Est. Oss —6D 118
Roundwood Ri. Wake —7F 118
Roundwood Rd. Bail —4C 40
Roundwood Rd. Oss —7C 118
Roundwood Vw. B'frd —9J 41
Rouse Fold. B'frd —9D 58
Rouse Mill La. Bat —8G 97
Rouse St. Liv —8L 95
Row. —1J 145
Rowan Av. B'frd —7J 59
Rowan Av. Neth —3J 147
Rowan Av. Nor —3H 121
Rowan Av. M. Neth —3J 147
Rowanberry Clo. B'frd —2F 58
Rowan Clo. Birs —2D 96
Rowan Clo. Knot —1C 124
Rowan Ct. B'frd —5G 59
Rowan Ct. Rawd —2M 41
Rowan Ct. Rothw —7F 82
Rowan Ct. Wake —3H 119
Rowan Dri. Brigh —9A 94
Rowan Grn. Pon —2M 123
Rowan Pl. Gar —8B 66
Rowans, The. Bail —4L 39
Rowans, The. B'hpe —6J 27
Rowans, The. Leeds —3C 60
Rowans, The. Weth —3A 18
Rowan St. Kei —6G 21
Rowantree Av. Bail —3N 39
Rowantree Dri. B'frd —9F 40
Row Bottom Ter. Sower B —8D 90
Rowe Clo. S Elm —5N 157
Row Ga. Shepl —1H 165
Rowgate. Up Cum —2L 165
Rowland La. Wadsw —1K 89
Rowland Pl. Leeds —2D 80
Rowland Rd. Leeds —2D 80
Rowlands Av. Hud —4D 132
Rowlands Av. Upt —2N 157
Rowland St. Roys —5E 154
Rowland Ter. Leeds —2D 80
Row La. Slai —1J 145
Row La. Sower B —9D 90
Rowlestone Ri. B'frd —9J 41
Rowley Dri. Fen B —7H 133
Rowley Dri. I'ly —6L 9
Rowley Hill. —8J 133
Rowley La. Fen B —8H 133
Rowley La. S Elm —8N 157
Rowsley St. Kei —9K 21
Row St. Hud —6K 131
Row, The. Rawd —3L 41
Rowton Thorpe. B'frd —9J 41
Roxburghe Dale. Norm —2L 121
Roxburgh Gro. All —6G 56
Roxby Clo. Leeds —5G 63
Roxby St. B'frd —2B 76
Roxholme Av. Leeds —1G 63
Roxholme Gro. Leeds —1G 63
Roxholme Ho. B'frd —3G 77 (off Prince St.)
Roxholme Pl. Leeds —1G 63
Roxholme Rd. Leeds —1G 63
Roxholme Ter. Leeds —1G 63
Royal Armouries Museum. —8F 62
Royal Birkdale Way. Norm —2L 121
Royal Clo. Gt Hor —2L 75
Royal Clo. Leeds —3F 80
Royal Ct. Leeds —3F 80
Royal Ct. Pon —6H 123
Royal Dri. Leeds —3F 80
Royal Gdns. Leeds —3F 80
Royal Gro. Leeds —3F 80
Royal Pk. Av. Leeds —4B 62
Royal Pk. Gro. Leeds —3B 62
Royal Pk. Mt. Leeds —3B 62
Royal Pk. Rd. Leeds —4A 62
Royal Pk. Ter. Leeds —4B 62
Royal Pk. Vw. Leeds —3B 62
Royal Pl. Leeds —3F 80
Royal Ter. B Spa —9D 18
Royal Ter. Hud —5F 130
Royd Av. Ain T —8F 112
Royd Av. Bgly —4H 39
Royd Av. Heck —6A 96
Royd Av. Lgwd —5F 130
Royd Av. M'well —8K 153
Royd Cres. Hal —4L 91
Royd Cres. H Bri —3N 89
Royd Cft. Hud —4G 131
Royd Edge. —9C 146
Royden Gro. B'frd —4M 57
Royd Farm. Hal —6L 73 (off Causeway Foot)
Roydfield St. Hud —9N 113
Royd Head Farm. Oss —6M 117
Roydhouse. —4A 150
Royd Ho. Gro. Kei —2L 37
Royd Ho. La. Lint —9C 130
Royd Ho. Rd. Kei —2L 37
Royd Ho. Wlk. Kei —2L 37
Royd Ho. Way. Kei —2L 37
Royd Ings Av. Kei —7J 21
Roydlands St. Hal —5J 93
Roydlands Ter. Hal —5J 93
Royd La. Hal —9N 73
Royd La. Holmb —6J 163
Royd La. I'wth —6L 73
Royd La. Kei —7H 21
Royd La. Ripp —7C 110
Royd La. Todm —5K 87
Royd Moor. —1H 157
Royd Moor La. Hems —9F 140 (in two parts)
Royd Mt. Hal —2B 92
Royd Mt. H'frth —4M 163
Royd Pl. Hal —2B 92
Royd Rd. Mel —9D 146
Royd Rd. Todm —5J 87
Royds Av. B'shaw —8M 77
Royds Av. Brigh —4N 93
Royds Av. C'frd —4J 103
Royds Av. Hud —4H 131
Royds Av. Lint —8C 130
Royds Av. N Mill —2B 164
Royds Av. Oss —3M 117
Roydscliffe Dri. B'frd —2L 57
Roydscliffe Rd. B'frd —3L 57
Royds Clo. Leeds —1M 79
Royds Clo. N Mill —2B 164
Royds Ct. Rothw —8A 82 (off Marsh St.)
Royds Cres. Brigh —5N 93
Roydsdale Way. Euro I —7E 76
Royds Dri. N Mill —2B 164
Royds Farm Rd. Leeds —3M 79
Royds Green. —2B 100
Royds Gro. Wake —7L 99
Royds Hall. —5H 131
Royds Hall Av. B'frd —5A 76
Royds Hall La. B'frd —8M 75
Royds Hall La. Butt —7M 75
Royds Hall Rd. Leeds —2M 79
Royds La. Leeds —1M 79
Royds La. Rothw —9A 82
Royds Pk. Den D —2D 166
Royds Pk. Cres. Wyke —9B 76
Royd Sq. H Bri —1H 89 (off Bond St.)
Royds St. Mars —6F 144
Royds, The. Clay W —6K 151
Royds, The. H'frth —4M 163
Roydstone Rd. B'frd —6H 59
Roydstone Ter. B'frd —6H 59
Royd St. Hud —5E 130
Royd St. Kei —6H 21 (in two parts)
Royd St. Slai —9M 129
Royd St. T'tn —8B 56
Royd St. Todm —6J 87
Royd St. Wilsd —2B 56
Royd St. Wyke —9A 76
Royds Vw. Lint —9C 130
Royd Ter. Arm B —1K 147
Royd Ter. H Bri —1H 89
Royd Vw. Brier —6A 156
Royd Vw. H Bri —3M 89
Royd Vw. Pud —8N 59
Royd Way. Kei —7J 21
Royd Wood. Cleck —6H 95
Royd Wood. Oxe —2D 54
Roydwood Ter. Cull —9K 37
Royle Fold. Heck —8A 96
Royles Clo. S Kirk —7J 157
Royles Head La. Lgwd —4D 130
Roy Rd. B'frd —4J 75
Royston. —6D 154
Royston Clo. E Ard —6F 98
Royston Hill. E Ard —6F 98
Royston La. Roys —7D 154
Royston Rd. Cud —8H 155
Roy St. Todm —3C 86
Ruby St. Bat —6D 96
Ruby St. Kei —3G 36
Ruby St. Leeds —5G 62
Rudding Av. All —5F 56
Rudding Cres. All —5F 56
Rudding Dri. Bat —6C 96
Rudding St. Hud —6J 131
Rudd St. B'frd —1M 75
Rudgate. Bilt A —1K 19
Rudgate. Newt K —2K 33
Rudgate. Thor A —6J 19
Rudgate Pk. Wltn —6G 18 (in two parts)
Rud La. Cra V —9G 89
Ruffield Side. Wyke —8A 76
Rufford Av. Barn —9B 154
Rufford Av. Yead —1M 41
Rufford Bank. Yead —1N 41
Rufford Clo. Ryh —1H 155
Rufford Clo. Yead —1N 41
Rufford Cres. Yead —1N 41
Rufford Dri. Yead —1N 41
Rufford Park. —1N 41
Rufford Pl. Hal —8A 92
Rufford Ridge. Yead —1N 41
Rufford Ri. Yead —1M 41
Rufford Rd. Ell —5E 112
Rufford Rd. Hal —8A 92
Rufford Rd. Hud —5E 130
Rufford St. B'frd —7G 58
Rufford St. Wake —5H 119
Rufford Vs. Hal —8A 92
Rufforth Ho. B'frd —9G 40 (off Rowantree Dri.)
Rufus St. B'frd —2N 75
Rufus St. Kei —8J 21
Rugby Av. Hal —1M 91
Rugby Dri. Hal —1M 91
Rugby Gdns. Hal —1M 91
Rugby League Hall of Fame. —9D 82
Rugby Mt. Hal —1M 91
Rugby Pl. B'frd —8N 57
Rugby Ter. Hal —1M 91
Rumble Rd. Dew —2J 117
Rumbold Rd. Hud —3J 131
Rumple Cft. Otley —7J 11
Runnymeade Ct. B'frd —8F 40 (off Cobden St.)
Runswick Av. Leeds —9B 62
Runswick Gro. B'frd —4B 76
Runswick Pl. Leeds —9B 62
Runswick St. B'frd —4B 76
Runswick St. Leeds —9B 62
Runswick Ter. B'frd —4B 76
Runswick Ter. Leeds —9C 62
Runtlings. —6M 117
Runtlings. Oss —6M 117
Runtlings La. Oss —7M 117
Runtlings Ter. Oss —6M 117
Runtlings, The. Oss —6L 117
Rupert Rd. I'ly —4F 8
Rupert St. Cro R —7F 36
Rupert St. Kei —8J 21
Rushbearers Wlk. Hud —6D 132
Rushcroft Ter. Bail —4A 40
Rushdene Ct. Wyke —3A 94
Rushfield Va. Fen B —6G 133
Rushmoor Rd. B'frd —3H 77
Rusholme Dri. Fars —3N 59
Rusholme St. B'frd —3G 76
Rushton Av. B'frd —6J 59
Rushton Hill Clo. Hal —3J 91
Rushton Rd. B'frd —6H 59
Rushton St. C'ley —9M 41
Rushton St. Hal —4M 91
Rushton Ter. B'frd —7J 59
Rushworth Clo. Dart —9E 152
Rushworth Clo. Stanl —7N 99
Rushworth St. Hal —3N 91
Ruskin Av. B'frd —3J 57
Ruskin Av. Wake —1J 119
Ruskin Clo. C'frd —4H 103
Ruskin Ct. Wake —1H 119
Ruskin Cres. Guis —8K 25
Ruskin Dri. C'frd —4G 103
Ruskin Gro. Hud —8B 114
Ruskin Pl. C'frd —4H 103
Ruskin St. S'ley —5N 59
Rusling M. Schol —4D 94
Russel Ho. B'frd —9G 41 (off Yewdall Way)
Russell Av. Hall G —7H 137
Russell Av. Q'bry —5D 74
Russell Clo. Bat —7F 96
Russell Clo. Heck —9B 96
Russell Ct. Bard —5E 30
Russell Gro. B'shaw —8M 77
Russell Gro. Leeds —2H 63
Russell Hall La. Q'bry —4D 74
Russell Rd. Q'bry —5C 74
Russell St. B'frd —9B 58
Russell St. Dew —2D 116
Russell St. Kei —9H 21
Russell St. Leeds —6D 62
Russell St. Q'bry —4D 74
Russell St. Shipl —1A 58
Russell St. Todm —7L 87
Russell St. Wake —7L 119
Russel St. Hal —5B 92
Russet Fold. Liv —8L 95
Russets, The. S'dal —3N 137
Russett Gro. Hud —7N 131
Rustic Av. Hal —8F 92
Ruswarp Cres. B'frd —9H 41
Ruth Ho. B'frd —7E 58 (off Otley Rd.)
Ruth St. Cro R —7E 36
Ruth St. Hud —8M 131
Ruthven Vw. Leeds —3J 63
Rutland Av. Pon —6K 123
Rutland Av. Wake —9L 119
Rutland Clo. Kip —3B 84
Rutland Clo. W'ford —7E 82
Rutland Ct. Pud —6B 60 (off Richardshaw La.)
Rutland Dri. Croft —9D 120
Rutland Dri. Kip —3B 84
Rutland Ho. Bgly —4F 38 (off Lyndon Ter.)
Rutland Ind. Est. Wake —6M 119
Rutland Mt. Leeds —6B 62
Rutland Rd. Bat —6G 96
Rutland Rd. Floc —7F 134
Rutland Rd. Hud —5F 130
Rutland St. B'frd —1E 76
Rutland St. Kei —2H 37
Rutland St. Leeds —6C 62
Rutland Ter. Leeds —6B 62
Rutland Wlk. Dew —3E 116 (off Boothroyd La.)
Ryan Gro. Kei —8D 20
Ryan Pl. Leeds —2J 63
Ryan St. B'frd —2B 76
Ryburn Ct. Hal —5M 91 (off Hanson La.)
Ryburn Ho. Hal —5M 91 (off Clay St.)
Ryburn La. Sower B —6E 110
Ryburn Pl. Wake —6K 119
Ryburn Rd. Hud —3G 130
Ryburn St. Sower B —9H 91
Ryburn Ter. Hal —5M 91
Ryburn Ter. Ripp —9C 110
Ryburn Vw. Hal —7L 91
Ryburn Vw. Sower B —8C 110
Rycroft Av. Bgly —9F 38
Rycroft Av. Leeds —5D 60
Rycroft Clo. Leeds —5E 60
Rycroft Ct. Leeds —5E 60
Rycroft Dri. Leeds —5E 60
Rycroft Grn. Leeds —5E 60
Rycroft Pl. Leeds —5E 60
Rycroft Sq. Leeds —5E 60
Rycroft St. Shipl —1B 58
Rycroft Towers. Leeds —5D 60
Rydal Av. Bail —6K 39
Rydal Av. B'frd —2A 58
Rydal Av. Gar —8N 65
Rydal Cres. Wake —4G 119
Rydal Dri. Hud —4B 132
Rydal Dri. Morl —8N 79
Rydal Dri. Wake —4G 119
Rydale Ct. Oss —7N 117
Rydal Gro. Liv —2L 115
Rydall Pl. Leeds —9B 62
Rydall St. Leeds —9B 62
Rydall Ter. Leeds —9B 62
Rydal Rd. Carc —8N 159
Rydal St. C'frd —4K 103
Rydal St. Kei —1G 37
Ryder Clo. Pon —3H 123
Ryder Gdns. Leeds —8J 45
Rydings Av. Brigh —9M 93
Rydings Clo. Brigh —9L 93
Rydings Dri. Brigh —9L 93
Rydings, The. Brigh —9M 93 (off Halifax Rd.)
Rydings Wlk. Brigh —9L 93
Rydings Way. Brigh —9L 93
Ryebank. H'frth —4N 163
Ryebread. C'frd —3E 102
Rye Clo. La. H'frth —4C 162
Ryecroft. H'den —6M 37
Rye Cft. I'wth —7M 73
Ryecroft Av. H'cft —8K 139
Ryecroft Av. Nort —7N 143
Ryecroft Clo. Wake —7L 99
Ryecroft Cres. Hal —3K 91
Ryecroft Dri. Hud —1G 130
Ryecroft La. Brigh —3A 114
Ryecroft La. Hal —4K 91
Ryecroft La. H'frth —5A 164
Ryecroft Rd. H'den —5K 37
Ryecroft Rd. Nort —7N 143
Ryecroft St. Oss —4M 117
Ryecroft Ter. Hal —3K 91
Ryedale. Hud —9F 114
Ryedale Av. Knot —1D 124
Ryedale Av. Leeds —1L 79
Ryedale Clo. Nor —7H 101
Ryedale Ct. Leeds —1A 64
Ryedale Holt. Leeds —9M 61
Ryedale M. Oss —5N 117 (off Ryedale Ct.)
Ryedale Pk. I'ly —6J 9
Ryedale Pl. Nor —7H 101
Ryedale Way. All —4F 56
Ryedale Way. Ting —5A 98
Ryefield Av. Cytn —9G 57
Rye Fld. La. Scam —4F 128
Rye Fld. La. W. Scam —4F 128
Ryefields. Sch —4B 164
Ryefields Av. Hud —3F 130
Ryefields Rd. Gol —6D 130
Rye Gth. Weth —1L 17
Ryelands Gro. B'frd —2J 57
Rye La. Hal —3J 91
Rye Pl. Leeds —5A 64
Rye St. Kei —3H 37
Rye Way. C'frd —4H 103
Ryhill. —9J 139
Ryhill Ind. Est. Ryh —9J 139
Ryhill Pits La. Ryh —9E 138
Rylands Av. Bgly —4G 39
Rylstone Gdns. B'frd —4E 58
Rylstone Gro. Wake —3N 119
Rylstone Rd. Bail —5L 39

Rylstone St. Kei —8K 21
Ryndleside. Hud —1F 130
Ryshworth Av. Bgly —9C 22
Ryshworth Bri. Bgly —1C 38
Ryton Dale. B'frd —9J 41

S

Sable Crest. B'frd —2D 58
Sackup La. Dart —8H 153
Sackville App. Leeds —3E 62
Sackville Rd. Sils —7E 6
Sackville St. B'frd —7C 58
Sackville St. H Bri —1H 89
Sackville St. Leeds —4E 62
Sackville St. Raven —5B 116
Sackville St. Todm —7K 87
Sackville Ter. Leeds —4E 62
Saddlers Cft. C'frd —6H 103
Saddlers Cft. I'ly —5F 8
Saddler's La. Knot —3B 104
Saddler St. Wyke —9A 76
Saddleworth Rd. Bklnd & Ell —8G 110
Saddleworth Rd. Scam & Hud —9N 127
Sadler Clo. Leeds —3M 43
Sadler Copse. Leeds —3M 43
Sadlers Wlk. Weth —3N 17
Sadler Way. Leeds —3M 43
Saffron Dri. All —5G 56
Sagar Pl. Leeds —2N 61 (off St Michael's Rd.)
Sagar St. C'frd —4D 102
Sage St. B'frd —1A 76
Sahara Ct. B'frd —4B 58
St Abbs Clo. B'frd —6A 76
St Abbs Dri. B'frd —6A 76
St Abbs Fold. B'frd —6A 76
St Abbs Ga. B'frd —6A 76
St Abbs Wlk. B'frd —6A 76
St Abbs Way. B'frd —6A 76
St Aidan's Rd. Bail —5B 40
St Aidans Rd. W'ford —5M 83
St Aidans Sq. Bgly —1D 38 (off Micklethwaite La.)
St Aiden's Wlk. Oss —7C 118
St Alban App. Leeds —5L 63
St Alban Clo. Leeds —5L 63
St Alban Cres. Leeds —5L 63
St Alban Gro. Leeds —5L 63
St Alban Mt. Leeds —5L 63
St Alban Rd. Leeds —5L 63
St Albans Av. Hal —9B 92
St Alban's Av. Hud —8F 112
St Albans Cft. Hal —8C 92
St Alban's Pl. Leeds —5E 62
St Albans Rd. Hal —9B 92
St Alban Vw. Leeds —5L 63
St Andrews Av. Morl —1H 97
St Andrew's Clo. Hal —8N 73
St Andrew's Clo. Leeds —1B 60
St Andrews Clo. Morl —1H 97
St Andrew's Clo. Yead —8N 25
St Andrew's Ct. Leeds —6B 62 (off Cavendish St.)
St Andrew's Ct. Slai —9K 129
St Andrew's Ct. Yead —8N 25 (off St Andrew's Rd.)
St Andrew's Cres. Oaken —9E 76
St Andrew's Cft. Leeds —3D 44
St Andrews Dri. Brigh —8M 93
St Andrews Dri. Dart —8J 153
St Andrews Dri. F'stne —2D 122
St Andrews Dri. Hud —2G 132
St Andrew's Dri. Knot —7B 104
St Andrew's Dri. Leeds —3E 44
St Andrews Gro. Morl —1J 97
St Andrews Pl. B'frd —8A 58
St Andrew's Pl. Leeds —6B 62
St Andrew's Rd. C'frd —3K 103
St Andrew's Rd. Hud —5A 132
St Andrew's Rd. Yead —8N 25
St Andrew's Sq. Bgly —1D 38 (off Mickelthwaite La.)
St Andrew's St. Leeds —6B 62
St Andrew's Vs. B'frd —7A 58
St Andrew's Wlk. Leeds —3E 44
St Anne's Av. Hud —8F 112
St Anne's Clo. Dew —7G 116
St Anne's Dri. Leeds —2M 61
St Anne's Grn. Leeds —2M 61
St Anne's Pl. Hal —4N 91 (off Pellon La.)
St Anne's Pl. Holy G —7L 111
St Anne's Rd. Hal —1B 112
St Anne's Rd. Leeds —1M 61
St Anne's St. Ryh —9J 139
St Annes Ter. Bail —5B 40
St Annies Vs. Pon —1L 123
St Ann's Av. Leeds —4N 61
St Ann's Clo. Leeds —3M 61
St Ann's Ct. Hal —8K 73
St Ann's Gdns. Leeds —3M 61
St Ann's La. Leeds —2M 61
St Ann's Mt. Leeds —3N 61
St Ann's Ri. Leeds —3L 61
St Ann's Sq. Head —3M 61
St Ann's Sq. Leeds —6G 62 (off Shannon St.)
St Anns Sq. Sower B —8J 91
St Ann St. Leeds —6D 62
St Ann's Way. Leeds —3M 61
St Anthony's Dri. Leeds —3B 80
St Anthonys Gdns. Shipl —9B 40 (off Snowden Rd.)
St Anthony's Rd. Leeds —3A 80
St Anthony's Ter. Leeds —4A 80
St Armands Ct. Gar —7N 65
St Augustines Ct. Leeds —3H 63 (off Harehills Pl.)
St Augustine's Ter. B'frd —5E 58
St Augustine's Ter. Hal —5N 91
St Baise Ct. B'frd —9C 58
St Barnabas Rd. Leeds —8D 62
St Barnabas Rd. Liv —7G 95
St Bartholomews Clo. Leeds —7M 61
St Bartholomews Ct. Wake —7E 118
St Bernard's Av. Pon —3H 123
St Bevan's Rd. Hal —9B 92
St Blaise Sq. B'frd —7C 58
St Botolphs Clo. Knot —8F 104
St Catherines Cres. Leeds —2G 61
St Catherine's Dri. Leeds —2G 60
St Catherines Grn. Leeds —2G 61
St Catherine's Hill. Leeds —2G 60
St Catherine St. Wake —8A 120
St Catherine's Vs. Wake —8A 120
St Catherines Wlk. Leeds —9J 45
St Chad's Av. Brigh —7K 93
St Chad's Av. Leeds —9M 43
St Chad's Dri. Leeds —9M 43
St Chad's Gro. Leeds —9M 43
St Chads Pl. Leeds —9N 43
St Chad's Ri. Leeds —9M 43
St Chad's Rd. B'frd —5N 57
St Chads Rd. Leeds —9N 43
St Chad's Vw. Leeds —1M 61
St Christopher's Av. Rothw —8A 82
St Christophers Dri. Add —2M 7
St Clair Grn. Wake —3F 118
St Clair Rd. Otley —9M 11 (in two parts)
St Clair St. Otley —9M 11
St Clair St. Wake —5M 119
St Clair Ter. Otley —9M 11 (off St Clair Rd.)
St Clare's Av. B'frd —4H 59
St Clements Av. Rothw —9N 81
St Clements Clo. Rothw —9M 81
St Clements Ct. Ackw —5E 140
St Clements Ri. Rothw —8M 81
St Cuthberts Ct. Ackw —1G 140
St Cyprian's Gdns. Leeds —4K 63
St David's Rd. Otley —7J 11
St Edmund's Clo. C'frd —4J 103
St Edwards Clo. Byr —5D 104
St Edward's Ter. Cliff —3D 32
St Elmo. Q'bry —6B 74
St Elmo Gro. Leeds —6J 63
St Eloi Av. Bail —3A 40
St Enoch's Rd. B'frd —4N 75
St Francis Gdns. Fix —6M 113
St Francis Pl. Leeds —8D 62
St George's Av. Hud —8F 112
St George's Av. Rothw —6L 81
St Georges Ct. H'cft —8L 139
St George's Cres. Rothw —6L 81
St Georges M. Wake —5J 137
St George's Pl. B'frd —1F 76
St George's Rd. Hal —3N 91
St George's Rd. Leeds —5D 62
St George's Rd. Sch —4B 164
St George's Rd. Wake —8F 118
St George's Sq. Hal —3A 92
St George's Sq. H Bri —1H 89 (off Crown St.)
St George's Sq. Hud —4M 131
St Georges Sq. Outl —2A 130
St George's St. B'frd —8F 58
St Georges St. H Bri —1H 89
St Georges St. Hud —4M 131
St George's Ter. Hal —3A 92
St George's Wlk. Wake —4L 137
St Giles Av. Pon —3H 123
St Giles Clo. Brigh —7K 93
St Giles Ct. Light —5K 93
St Giles Gth. B'hpe —5H 27
St Giles Rd. Hal —5K 93
St Giles Vw. Pon —4K 123
St Helena Rd. B'frd —4N 75
St Helen's Av. Hems —2C 156
St Helens Av. Leeds —4N 43
St Helens Clo. Leeds —4N 43 (in two parts)
St Helens Cft. Leeds —4M 43
St Helen's Dri. M'fld —6F 66
St Helens Gdns. Leeds —4M 43
St Helens Ga. Hud —8E 132
St Helens Gro. Leeds —4M 43
St Helens Gro. Wake —1A 138
St Helens La. Leeds —4L 43
St Helens Pl. C'frd —5E 102
St Helens Sq. Holy G —7B 112 (off Station Rd.)
St Helen's St. Leeds —9F 62
St Helen's Way. I'ly —5J 9
St Helens Way. Leeds —4N 43
St Helier Gro. Bail —3B 40
St Hilda's Av. Leeds —8H 63
St Hilda's Cres. Leeds —8H 63
St Hilda's Gro. Leeds —8H 63
St Hilda's Mt. Leeds —8H 63
St Hilda's Pl. Leeds —8H 63
St Hilda's Rd. Leeds —8H 63
St Hilda's Ter. B'frd —6J 59
St Ians Clo. Add —2M 7
St Ives Clo. Pon —9K 103
St Ives Gdns. Hal —9B 92
St Ives Gro. H'den —5B 38
St Ives Gro. Leeds —6K 61
St Ives Mt. Leeds —6K 61
St Ives Pl. H'den —5B 38
St Ives Rd. Hal —9B 92
St Ives Rd. H'den —5B 38
St James App. Leeds —2B 64
St James Av. H'fth —6F 42
St James Bus. Pk. B'frd —8E 58
St James Clo. Leeds —6J 61
St James Ct. Brigh —9N 93
St James Ct. Hal —5B 92 (off St James Rd.)
St James Ct. H'cft —9K 139
St James Cres. Pud —7M 59
St James Dri. H'fth —6G 42
St James Mkt. B'frd —8E 58
St James M. Leeds —6J 61
St James Pl. Bail —3D 40 (off Otley Rd.)
St James Ri. Wake —7E 118
St James Rd. Bail —3D 40
St James Rd. Hal —5B 92
St James Rd. I'ly —6F 8
St James's Ct. Leeds —4G 63
St James's Ct. Wake —7K 119
St James's Pk. Wake —5N 119
St James's Rd. Hud —3J 131
St James's Sq. B'frd —9C 58
St James's Sq. Hal —2F 92
St James's St. Weth —4M 17
St James St. Bat —7F 96
St James St. Hal —5B 92
St James St. Heck —9A 96
St James Ter. H'fth —6G 42
St James Wlk. H'fth —6G 42
St James Way. Crig —4H 137
St John Pde. Dew —3E 116
St John's. —6E 48
St Johns. Hoy S —9J 167
St Johns. I'ly —6F 8
St Johns Av. Add —1M 7
St John's Av. Bat —6D 96
St John's Av. Fars —4A 60
St John's Av. Khtn —1G 132
St John's Av. Leeds —4B 62
St John's Av. New —8M 131
St John's Av. Oss —6C 118
St John's Av. T'ner —2G 46
St John's Av. Wake —3K 119
St John's Cen. Leeds —6E 62
St John's Chase. Wake —4K 119
St John's Clo. Aber —6E 48
St John's Clo. Cleck —5J 95 (in two parts)
St Johns Clo. Dew —3E 116
St John's Clo. H Bri —1H 89 (off Birchcliffe)
St John's Clo. Leeds —4B 62
St John's Clo. Oss —6C 118
St John's Clo. Sower B —1C 128
St John's Ct. Bail —5C 40
St John's Ct. H'frth —4K 163
St John's Ct. Leeds —2F 62
St John's Ct. Lep —7K 133
St John's Ct. Low U —6G 21 (off St John's Rd.)
St John's Ct. T'ner —2G 46
St John's Ct. Wake —4K 119
St John's Ct. Yead —1L 41
St Johns Cres. B'frd —6K 57
St John's Cres. Hud —2M 131
St John's Cres. Nor —4H 121
St John's Cres. Oss —6B 118
St John's Cft. Wake —4K 119
St John's Dri. Hud —2M 131
St John's Dri. N Rig —2N 13
St John's Dri. Yead —1L 41
St John's Gth. Aber —7E 48
St John's Gro. Leeds —4B 62
St John's Gro. Wake —3L 119
St John's La. Hal —6B 92
St John's M. Wake —4K 119
St John's Mt. Wake —3K 119
St John's N. Wake —4K 119
St John's Pk. Men —3D 24
St John's Pl. B'shaw —7L 77
St John's Pl. Cleck —5J 95
St John's Rd. B Spa —1D 32
St John's Rd. Hud —2M 131
St John's Rd. I'ly —5K 9
St John's Rd. Khtn —1G 132
St John's Rd. Leeds —5B 62
St John's Rd. Low U —6G 21
St John's Rd. Yead —1L 41
St John's Sq. Wake —4K 119
St John's St. Cnly —8E 6
St John's St. Horb —1A 136
St John's St. Oult —8D 82
St John's Ter. Leeds —4B 62
St John St. Brigh —2M 113
St John St. Dew —3E 116
St John's Vw. Bat —6D 96
St John's Vw. B Spa —1C 32
St John's Wlk. Roys —6E 154
St Johns Way. Kei —1F 36
St John's Way. Yead —1L 41
St John's Yd. Oult —8D 82
St John Wlk. Dew —3E 116
St Josephs Mt. Pon —4H 123
St Jude's Pl. B'frd —6B 58
St Jude's St. B'frd —6B 58
St Judes St. Hal —7A 92
St Julien's Way. Caw —4N 167
St Laurence's Clo. B'frd —1B 58
St Lawrence Clo. Pud —7A 60
St Lawrence St. Leeds —9F 44
St Lawrence Ter. Pud —7B 60
St Leonards Clo. Add —2M 7
St Leonard's Farm Park. —2G 40
St Leonard's Gro. B'frd —5L 57
St Leonard's Rd. B'frd —5L 57
St Leonards Yd. Horb —1C 136
St Lukes Clo. Bat —8H 97
St Luke's Clo. Cleck —5F 94
St Luke's Clo. Cliff —3D 32
St Lukes Clo. Far T —3C 148
St Luke's Clo. M'twn —3L 135
St Luke's Cres. Leeds —1C 80
St Luke's Grn. Leeds —1C 80
St Luke's Rd. Leeds —1C 80
St Luke's St. Leeds —1C 80
St Luke's Ter. Cleck —5F 94 (off St Luke's Clo.)
St Luke's Ter. E Mor —8C 22
St Luke's Vw. Leeds —1C 80
St Margaret's Av. B'frd —3H 77
St Margaret's Av. H'fth —6E 42
St Margaret's Av. Leeds —9J 45
St Margaret's Av. Meth —1L 101
St Margaret's Clo. H'fth —5E 42
St Margaret's Ct. N Elm —3A 158
St Margaret's Dri. H'fth —5E 42
St Margaret's Dri. Leeds —9J 45
St Margaret's Gro. Leeds —9J 45
St Margaret's Pl. B'frd —9N 57
St Margaret's Rd. B'frd —8N 57
St Margaret's Rd. H'fth —5E 42
St Margaret's Rd. Meth —1L 101
St Margaret's Ter. B'frd —9N 57
St Margaret's Ter. I'ly —6G 8
St Margaret's Vw. Leeds —9J 45
St Mark's Av. Leeds —4C 62
St Mark's Av. Low M —8A 76
St Mark's Flats. Leeds —3C 62 (off Low Clo. St.)
St Mark's Pl. B'frd —8A 76
St Mark's Rd. Hud —4F 130
St Mark's Rd. Leeds —3C 62 (in two parts)
St Mark's St. Leeds —4C 62
St Mark's St. Wake —4M 119
St Mark's Ter. Low M —8A 76
St Mark's Vw. Lgwd —4F 130
St Martins Av. Field B —7A 58
St Martin's Av. Leeds —1E 62
St Martin's Av. Otley —7K 11
St Martins Clo. F'stne —7C 122
St Martin's Cres. Leeds —1F 62
St Martin's Dri. Leeds —9F 44
St Martin's Gdns. Leeds —1E 62
St Martin's Gro. C'frd —6B 102
St Martin's Gro. Leeds —1F 62
St Martin's Rd. Leeds —1F 62
St Martin's Ter. Leeds —1F 62
St Martin's Vw. Brigh —9M 93
St Martin's Vw. Leeds —1F 62
St Mary Magdalenes Clo. B'frd —6A 58
St Mary's Av. Bat —9E 96
St Mary's Av. Mir —5N 115
St Mary's Av. Nthng —9L 147
St Mary's Av. Nor —8G 101
St Mary's Av. Swil —4H 83
St Mary's Av. Wyke —2A 94
St Mary's Clo. Gar —8N 65
St Marys Clo. I'ly —5H 9
St Mary's Clo. Leeds —8N 61
St Mary's Clo. Pott —1F 62
St Mary's Clo. S Elm —7N 157
St Mary's Clo. Wyke —2N 93
St Mary's Ct. All B —9B 84
St Mary's Ct. Hal —8K 73
St Mary's Ct. Leeds —1F 62
St Mary's Cres. Nthng —9L 147
St Mary's Cres. Wyke —3N 93
St Mary's Dri. Wyke —2A 94
St Mary's Gdns. Wyke —2A 94
St Mary's Gth. E Kes —3C 30
St Mary's Ga. Ell —4E 112
St Mary's Heights. Hal —8K 73
St Mary's La. Hud —3G 132
St Mary's M. Hon —4L 147
St Mary's Mt. Wyke —2N 93
St Mary's Pk. App. Leeds —6J 61
St Mary's Pk. Ct. Leeds —6J 61
St Mary's Pk. Cres. Leeds —6J 61
St Mary's Pk. Grn. Leeds —6J 61
St Mary's Pl. C'frd —4C 102
St Mary's Pl. Dew —5G 116
St Mary's Ri. Nthng —9L 147
St Mary's Rd. B'frd —9H 59
St Mary's Rd. Hon —4L 147
St Mary's Rd. Leeds —1F 62
St Mary's Rd. Mann & B'frd —4A 58
St Mary's Rd. Nthng —9L 147
St Mary's Rd. Nor —9G 100
St Mary's Rd. Riddl —6M 21
St Mary's Sq. Hon —4L 147
St Mary's Sq. Morl —9K 79
St Mary's Sq. Wyke —2A 94
St Mary's St. B Spa —9D 18
St Mary's St. Leeds —6F 62
St Mary St. Hal —6A 92
St Mary's Wlk. M'fld —7F 66
St Mary's Wlk. Mir —5N 115
St Mary's Way. Nthng —9L 147
St Matthew Rd. Dew —3E 116
St Matthews Clo. Wilsd —2A 56
St Matthew's Dri. N'wram —1F 92
St Matthews Gro. Wilsd —2B 56
St Matthews Rd. B'frd —4B 76
St Matthew's St. Leeds —9C 62
St Matthews Wlk. Leeds —7E 44
St Matthias Ct. Leeds —4N 61
St Matthias Gro. Leeds —4N 61
St Matthias St. Leeds —5N 61 (in two parts)
St Matthias Ter. Leeds —4N 61
St Michael Ct. Leeds —3F 60
St Michael's Av. Pon —3H 123
St Michaels Clo. Bgly —9G 39
St Michael's Clo. C'frd —5D 102
St Michael's Clo. Dew —1H 135
St Michael's Clo. Eml —2G 151
St Michael's Clo. Wake —6J 119
St Michael's Ct. Leeds —1N 61
St Michael's Cres. Leeds —2N 61
St Michael's Gdns. Eml —2G 150
St Michael's Grn. Nor —2H 121
St Michael's Gro. Leeds —2N 61
St Michael's Ho. Wake —6J 119
St Michael's La. Leeds —3M 61
St Michael's Mt. Dew —9H 117
St Michael's Rd. B'frd —6A 58
St Michael's Rd. Leeds —2N 61
St Michael's Ter. Leeds —2N 61
St Michael's Vs. Leeds —2N 61 (off St Michael's Cres.)
St Michaels Way. Add —1M 7
St Michael's Way. Bur W —9D 10
St Nicholas Rd. I'ly —4F 8
St Nicholas St. C'frd —5D 102
St Oswald Av. Pon —3H 123
St Oswald Ct. Hems —3E 156 (off Baylee St.)
St Oswald Rd. Wake —6E 118
St Oswald's Gth. Guis —7K 25
St Oswalds Pl. Oss —4A 118
St Oswald's Ter. Guis —7J 25
St Oswald St. C'frd —4D 102
St Paulinus Clo. Dew —3E 116
St Paul's Av. B'frd —5N 75
St Paul's Clo. Mann —5A 58 (off Church St.)
St Paul's Clo. Upt —1C 158
St Pauls Ct. Pon —9L 103
St Paul's Dri. Wake —3F 118
St Paul's Gro. B'frd —5N 75
St Paul's Gro. I'ly —5J 9
St Paul's Pl. Leeds —6D 62
St Pauls Ri. Add —2M 7
St Paul's Rd. B'shaw —8M 77
St Paul's Rd. Hal —7M 91
St Pauls Rd. Hud —2F 132

St Paul's Rd. *Kei* —1K 37
St Paul's Rd. *Mann* —4A 58
St Paul's Rd. *Mir* —7L 115
St Paul's Rd. *Shipl* —8M 39
St Paul's Rd. *Wibs* —5N 75
St Paul's St. *Hud* —5N 131
St Paul's St. *Leeds* —6C 62
St Paul's St. *Morl* —1L 97
St Paul's Ter. *Mir* —7L 115
St Paul's Wlk. *Wake* —3F 118
St Peg Clo. *Cleck* —5J 95
St Peg La. *Cleck* —5J 95
St Peter's Av. *Rothw* —8A 82
St Peter's Av. *Sower B* —9E 90
St Peter's Clo. *Birs* —3A 96
St Peter's Clo. *Mir* —6K 115
St Peters Ct. *Add* —2M 7
St Peters Ct. *Horb* —9C 118
St Peter's Ct. *Leeds* —1E 80
(LS11)
St Peter's Ct. *Leeds* —3G 60
(LS13)
St Peters Cres. *Hud* —2F 132
St Peter's Cres. *Morl* —7K 79
St Peter's Cres. *Stan* —6C 100
St Peter's Gdns. *Dew* —4J 117
St Peter's Gdns. *Leeds* —3F 60
St Peter's Gth. *T'ner* —1H 47
St Peters Ga. *Oss* —4N 117
St Peter's Ga. *Todm* —3J 107
St Peter's Gro. *Horb* —1D 136
St Peter's Mt. *Leeds* —4G 60
St Peter's Pde. *Dew* —4J 117
St Peter's Pl. *Leeds* —6F 62
St Peter's Sq. *Leeds* —6F 62
St Peters Sq. Sower B —9E 90
(off Dean La.)
St Peter's St. *Hud* —4M 131
St Peter's St. *Leeds* —6F 62
St Peter's Way. *Men* —4D 24
St Philip's Av. *Leeds* —8D 80
St Philip's Clo. *Bur W* —9D 10
St Philip's Clo. *Dew* —2G 117
St Philip's Clo. *Leeds* —8D 80
St Philips Ct. *Hud* —9G 113
St Philip's Dri. *Bur W* —9D 10
St Philip's Way. *Bur W* —8D 10
St Richard's Rd. *Otley* —7J 11
St Rouse Fold. *B'frd* —9D 58
St Stephen's Ct. *Hal* —1N 111
St Stephen's Ct. *Leeds* —6H 63
St Stephen's Ct. *Steet* —2C 20
St Stephen's Rd. *B'frd* —2B 76
St Stephen's Rd. *C'ley* —8L 41
St Stephen's Rd. *Hud* —6L 131
St Stephen's Rd. *Leeds* —6H 63
St Stephen's Rd. *Steet* —3C 20
St Stephen's St. *Hal* —1N 111
St Stephen's Ter. *B'frd* —2C 76
St Stephen's Ter. *Hal* —2A 112
Saint St. *B'frd* —1M 75
St Swithins Dri. *Wake* —1A 120
St Swithins Gro. *Stan* —1A 120
St Thomas Rd. *F'stne* —6D 122
St Thomas Rd. *Hud* —5L 131
St Thomas Row. *Leeds* —5F 62
St Thomas's Gdns. *Bdly* —5D 114
St Thomas's Rd. *B'frd* —7B 58
St Thomas's Ter. *Pon* —9M 103
St Vincent Rd. *Pud* —8B 60
St Wilfred's. *Hal* —8K 73
St Wilfrid's Av. *Leeds* —2J 63
St Wilfrid's Cir. *Leeds* —3K 63
St Wilfrid's Clo. *B'frd* —9L 57
St Wilfrid's Cres. *B'frd* —9L 57
St Wilfrid's Cres. *Leeds* —2K 63
St Wilfrid's Dri. *Leeds* —2J 63
St Wilfrid's Gth. *Leeds* —3K 63
St Wilfrid's Gro. *Leeds* —2J 63
St Wilfrid's Rd. *B'frd* —9L 57
St Wilfrid's St. *C'ley* —8M 41
Salcombe Clo. *M'well* —9L 153
Salcombe Pl. *B'frd* —3J 77
Salem Pl. *Gar* —7M 65
Salem Pl. *Leeds* —8E 62
Salem St. *B'frd* —6C 58
Salem St. *H Bri* —1G 89
Salem St. *Q'bry* —4C 74
Salendine Nook. —2D 130
Salford. *Todm* —7J 87
Salford. —8L 131
(nr. Huddersfield)
Salford. —8J 87
(nr. Todmorden)
Salford Way. *Todm* —7J 87
Salisbury Av. *Bail* —4A 40
Salisbury Av. *Leeds* —6M 61
Salisbury Clo. *Dew* —3J 117
Salisbury Clo. *Nor* —9J 101
Salisbury Ct. *H'fth* —6G 42
Salisbury Gro. *Leeds* —6M 61
Salisbury M. *H'fth* —6G 43
Salisbury Pl. *C'ley* —8L 41
Salisbury Pl. *Hal* —3A 92
Salisbury Rd. *B'frd* —1A 58
Salisbury Rd. *Kei* —1G 36
Salisbury Rd. *Leeds* —6M 61
Salisbury Rd. *Low M* —7A 76
Salisbury Rd. *Schol* —4D 94
Salisbury St. *C'ley* —9L 41
Salisbury St. *Rawd* —3M 41
Salisbury St. *Sower B* —9G 91
Salisbury Ter. *Hal* —3A 92
Salisbury Ter. *Leeds* —6M 61
Salisbury Vw. *H'fth* —6G 43
Salisbury Vw. *Leeds* —6M 61
Salley St. *L'boro* —9L 107
Salmon Cres. *H'fth* —6F 42
Sal Nook Clo. *Low M* —6B 76
Sal Royd Rd. *Low M* —8C 76
Saltaire. —7M 39
Saltaire. *Cro R* —7F 36
Saltaire Rd. *Bgly* —2J 39
Saltaire Rd. *Shipl* —7L 39
Saltburn Pl. *B'frd* —4L 57
Saltburn St. *Hal* —5M 91
Salt Drake. *Sower B* —3B 110
Salterhebble. —9C 92
Salterhebble Hill. *Hal* —9C 92
Salterhebble Ter. Hal —9C 92
(off Huddersfield Rd.)
Salter Rake Ga. *Todm* —1K 107
(in two parts)
Salter Row. *Pon* —3K 123
Saltersgate Av. *Knot* —7D 104
Salter St. *Bat* —1E 116
Salt Horn Clo. *Oaken* —8D 76
Saltonstall La. *Hal* —8D 72
Salt Pie All. *Wake* —6K 119
Salt St. *B'frd* —5A 58
Salt St. *Hal* —4N 91
Sampson St. *Liv* —8M 95
Samuel Dri. *Stan* —7N 99
Samuel St. *Kei* —9H 21
Sandacre Clo. *B'frd* —3J 59
Sandal. —1M 137
Sandal Av. *Wake* —1N 137
Sandal Cliff. *Wake* —2N 137
Sandale Wlk. *B'frd* —6L 75
Sandal Hall Clo. *Wake* —1A 138
Sandal Hall M. *Wake* —1N 137
Sandall Clo. *Kip* —3B 84
Sandal Magna. —1N 137
Sandal Magna. *Hal* —6K 75
Sandal Ri. *Thpe A* —5N 141
Sandals Rd. *Bail* —4A 40
Sandal Way. *Birs* —3C 96
Sandbeck Ind. Est. *Weth* —2N 17
Sandbeck La. *Weth* —2N 17
(in two parts)
Sandbeck Way. *Weth* —2N 17
Sandbed Ct. *Leeds* —3E 64
Sandbed La. *Leeds* —3E 64
Sandbed Lawns. *Leeds* —3E 64
Sandbeds. *Hon* —3L 147
Sand Beds. *Q'bry* —4D 74
Sandbeds Cres. *Hal* —3L 91
Sandbeds Rd. *Hal* —4K 91
Sandbeds Ter. *Hal* —3L 91
Sandbeds Trad. Est. *Oss* —4A 118
Sandene Av. *Hud* —8H 131
Sandene Dri. *Hud* —8H 131
Sanderling Ct. *B'frd* —7H 57
Sanderling Gth. *Leeds* —8F 80
Sanderling Way. *Leeds* —8F 80
Sanderson Av. *B'frd* —4A 76
Sanderson Av. *Nor* —2H 121
Sanderson La. *Oult* —2B 100
Sanderson St. *Wake* —5M 119
Sandfield Av. *Leeds* —9A 44
Sandfield Gth. *Leeds* —9A 44
Sandfield Rd. *B'frd* —9F 40
Sandfield Vw. Leeds —9A 44
(off Sandfield Av.)
Sandford. —1H 61
Sandford Pl. *Kirks* —2K 61
Sandford Rd. *B'frd* —7G 58
Sandford Rd. *Leeds* —3L 61
Sandford Rd. *S Elm* —4N 157
Sandforth Dri. *Hal* —2B 92
Sandgate Dri. *Kip* —2B 84
Sandgate La. *M'fld* —4C 84
(in two parts)
Sandgate Ri. *Kip* —3C 84
Sandgate Ter. *Kip* —4C 84
Sandgate Wlk. *B'frd* —3K 77
Sandhall Av. *Hal* —5K 91
Sandhall Cres. Hal —4K 91
(off Sandhall Grn.)
Sandhall Dri. *Hal* —5K 91
Sandhall Grn. *Hal* —5K 91
(in two parts)
Sandhall La. *Hal* —5K 91
Sandhill Clo. *Pon* —8K 103
Sandhill Ct. *Leeds* —4F 44
Sandhill Dri. *Leeds* —3F 44
Sandhill Gro. *Grime* —8A 156
Sandhill Gro. *Leeds* —2G 44
Sand Hill La. *Leeds* —4F 44
Sandhill Lawn. *Pon* —4J 123
Sandhill Lawns. *Leeds* —4F 44
Sandhill Mt. *B'frd* —9F 40
Sandhill Ri. *Pon* —9K 103
Sandhills. —3F 46
Sandhills Cotts. *Mars* —3H 145
Sandholme Cres. *Hip* —5J 93
Sandholme Dri. *B'frd* —9F 40
Sandholme Dri. *Bur W* —9D 10
Sandholme Dri. *Oss* —6N 117
Sandhurst Av. *Leeds* —3J 63
Sandhurst Gro. *Leeds* —3J 63
Sandhurst Mt. *Leeds* —2J 63
Sandhurst Pl. *Leeds* —3J 63
Sandhurst Rd. *Leeds* —3J 63
Sandhurst St. *C'ley* —9L 41
Sandhurst Ter. *Leeds* —3J 63
Sandiford Clo. *Leeds* —3E 64
Sandiford Ter. *Leeds* —3E 64
Sandiway Bank. *Dew* —8G 117
Sand La. *Upt* —2A 158
Sandleas Way. *Leeds* —4G 64
Sandlewood Clo. *Leeds* —9C 62
Sandlewood Grn. *Leeds* —9D 62
Sandmead Clo. *B'frd* —2J 77
Sandmead Clo. *Morl* —7K 79
Sandmead Cft. *Morl* —7K 79
Sandmead Way. *Morl* —7K 79
Sandmoor Av. *Leeds* —1F 44
Sandmoor Chase. *Leeds* —2F 44
Sandmoor Clo. *Leeds* —2F 44
Sandmoor Clo. *T'tn* —8D 56
Sandmoor Ct. *Leeds* —2F 44
Sandmoor Dri. *Hud* —1G 130
Sandmoor Dri. *Leeds* —1F 44
Sandmoor Gdns. *Hal* —8G 74
Sandmoor Gth. *B'frd* —6F 40
Sandmoor Grn. *Leeds* —1E 44
Sandmoor Ho. B'frd —8G 40
(off Fairhaven Grn.)
Sandmoor La. *Leeds* —1F 44
Sandmoor M. *Leeds* —2F 44
Sandon Gro. *Leeds* —3G 80
Sandon Mt. *Leeds* —3G 80
Sandon Pl. *Leeds* —3G 80
Sandown Av. *Croft* —1G 139
Sandown Av. *Hal* —9L 73
Sandown Rd. *Hal* —9L 73
Sandpiper App. *Morl* —1M 97
Sandpiper M. *B'frd* —7H 57
Sandringham Av. *Knot* —8B 104
Sandringham Av. *Pud* —8B 60
Sandringham Clo. *Cytn* —9J 57
Sandringham Clo. *Morl* —8M 79
Sandringham Clo. *Pon* —6J 123
Sandringham Ct. *Cytn* —9J 57
Sandringham Ct. *Hud* —6C 114
Sandringham Ct. *Morl* —8M 79
Sandringham Cres. *Leeds* —4F 44
Sandringham Dri. *Leeds* —4F 44
Sandringham Gdns. *Leeds* —4F 44
Sandringham Rd. *Cytn* —9J 57
Sandringham Rd. *Knot* —5C 104
Sandringham Rd. *Weth* —3M 17
Sandringham Way. *Leeds* —4F 44
Sandrock Rd. *Pon* —1L 123
Sandsend Clo. *B'frd* —3J 57
Sands Ho. La. *Hud* —9G 130
Sandside Clo. *B'frd* —3D 76
Sands La. *Dew* —4G 117
Sands La. *Lep* —4K 133
Sands La. *Mir* —7A 116
Sands Rd. *Dew* —5H 117
Sandstone Clo. *Hon* —6L 147
Sandstone Dri. *Leeds* —7F 60
Sand St. *Haw* —9C 36
Sand St. *Hud* —5N 131
Sand St. *Kei* —9J 21
Sandway. *Leeds* —4C 64
Sandway Gdns. *Leeds* —4C 64
Sandway Gro. *Leeds* —4C 64
Sandwell St. *Slai* —9M 129
Sandwich Cres. *Hud* —8L 113
Sandyacres. *Rothw* —7A 82
Sandyacres Cres. *Rothw* —7A 82
Sandyacres Dri. *Rothw* —7A 82
Sandy Bank Av. *Rothw* —7A 82
Sandy Banks. *H'den* —7A 38
Sandy Beck. *All* —3F 56
Sandybridge La. *Shaf* —4H 155
Sandybridge La. Ind. Est. *Shaf* —6J 155
Sandy Dyke La. *Sower B* —3E 110
Sandyfields. *Skel* —9N 159
Sandyfields Vw. *Carc* —8N 159
Sandyfield Ter. Bat —6E 96
(off Bradford Rd.)
Sandy Ga. *Hare* —1F 28
Sandy Ga. *H Bri* —1J 89
Sandy Ga. *H'frth* —4A 164
Sandy Ga. *Kei* —8G 20
Sandy Ga. La. *Ackw & E Hard* —8H 123
Sandy Ga. La. *H Bri* —9J 71
Sandygate La. *Hems* —2C 156
Sandygate Ter. *B'frd* —9H 59
Sandy Gro. *Rothw* —7A 82
Sandylands. *Neth* —3J 147
Sandy Lane. —2E 56
Sandy La. *M'twn* —3L 135
Sandy La. *S Cro* —3F 146
Sandy Lobby. *Pool W* —2F 26
Sandymoor. *All* —2F 56
Sandy Wlk. *B'hpe* —6J 27
Sandy Wlk. *Wake* —4K 119
Sandy Way. *Yead* —9M 25
Sandywood Ct. *H'fth* —8F 42
Sandywood St. *Kei* —8J 21
Sangster Way. *B'frd* —4E 76
Sanquah Ter. *Nor* —9K 101
Santa Monica Cres. *B'frd* —8E 40
Santa Monica Gro. *B'frd* —8E 40
Santa Monica Rd. *B'frd* —8E 40
Santingley La. *New C* —3H 139
Santon Ho. B'frd —1C 76
(off Manchester Rd.)
Sanworth St. *Todm* —7L 87
Sapgate La. *T'tn* —8D 56
Sapling Gro. Cotts. *Hal* —8M 91
Saplin St. *B'frd* —5N 57
Sapphire Ct. *Bat* —6D 96
Sarah St. *E Ard* —4F 98
Sardinia St. *Leeds* —9F 62
Saunders Clo. *Hud* —3H 131
Saunters Way. *Altft* —8H 101
Savile Av. *B'frd* —9G 41
Savile Av. *Leeds* —3F 62
Savile Clo. *Brigh* —9B 94
Savile Ct. *Mir* —5L 115
Savile Ct. *Raven* —6B 116
Savile Cres. *Hal* —6A 92
Savile Dri. *Hal* —7A 92
Savile Dri. *Horb* —9C 118
Savile Dri. *Leeds* —2F 62
Savile Glen. *Hal* —6A 92
Savile Grn. *Hal* —6B 92
Savile Gro. *Dew* —4F 116
Savile La. *Brigh* —9B 94
Savile Lea. *Hal* —6A 92
Savile M. *Dew* —6F 116
Savile Mt. *Hal* —7A 92
Savile Mt. *Leeds* —3F 62
Savile Pde. *Hal* —7A 92
Savile Pk. *Hal* —7A 92
(in three parts)
Savile Park. —7A 92
Savile Pk. Gdns. *Hal* —7A 92
Savile Pk. Rd. *Cleck* —1H 95
Savile Pk. Rd. *Hal* —7A 92
Savile Pk. St. *Hal* —7N 91
Savile Pk. Ter. Hal —7N 91
(off Moorfield St.)
Savile Pit La. *Dew* —2K 117
Savile Pl. *Leeds* —3F 62
Savile Pl. *Mir* —4L 115
Savile Precinct. *C'frd* —4C 102
Savile Rd. *C'frd* —4C 102
Savile Rd. *Dew* —6F 116
Savile Rd. *Ell* —5E 112
Savile Rd. *Hal* —6A 92
Savile Rd. *H Bri* —1F 88
Savile Rd. *Hud* —2H 131
Savile Rd. *Leeds* —3F 62
Savile Rd. *Meth* —1L 101
Savile Royd. *Hal* —7A 92
Savile Sq. Mir —6L 115
(off Beech St.)
Savile St. *Cleck* —3H 95
Savile St. *Dew & Bat* —1G 116
Savile St. *Hud* —5F 130
Savile Town. —6F 116
Savile Wlk. *Brier* —6B 156
Savile Way. *Lfds B* —3F 112
Saville Av. *Eml* —2G 150
Saville Clo. *Eml* —2G 150
Saville Clo. *Loft* —3L 99
Saville Ct. *Kbtn* —3G 148
(nr. Storthes Hall La.)
Saville Ct. Kbtn —2K 149
(off Ashford Ct.)
Saville Ct. *Otley* —1K 25
Saville Grn. *Leeds* —6H 63
Saville Pk. *Oss* —7B 118
Saville Rd. *Skelm* —7D 150
Saville's Sq. Morl —9K 79
(off Queen St.)
Saville St. *Eml* —2G 150
Saville St. *Oss* —7B 118
Saville St. *Scis* —8G 151
Saville St. *Wake* —4L 119
Saville Wlk. Dew —3F 116
(off Swindon Rd.)
Sawley Clo. *Wake* —3N 119
Sawley St. *Kei* —1H 37
Saw Mill St. *Leeds* —8D 62
Sawood. —6F 54
Sawood La. *Oxe* —5F 54
(in two parts)
Sawrey Pl. *B'frd* —8B 58
Saw Yd. *Wake* —5L 119
Sawyers Gth. *Add* —1N 7
Saxon Av. *S Kirk* —7F 156
Saxon Clo. *Eml* —3F 150
Saxon Clo. *Upt* —2D 158
Saxon Ct. *Leeds* —4D 44
Saxondale Ct. *Horb* —9D 118
Saxon Ga. *Leeds* —5D 44
Saxon Grn. *Leeds* —5C 44
Saxon Gro. *Leeds* —4C 44
Saxon Gro. *S Kirk* —8G 156
Saxon Mt. *Leeds* —4D 44
Saxon Mt. *S Kirk* —7F 156
Saxon Rd. *Leeds* —5C 44
Saxon St. *B'frd* —6A 58
Saxon St. *Hal* —5M 91
Saxon St. *Todm* —2J 107
Saxon Way. *C'frd* —4G 103
Saxton. —9N 49
Saxton Av. *B'frd* —4K 75
Saxton Ct. *Gar* —6N 65
Saxton Gdns. Leeds —7G 62
(off Drive, The)
Saxton Ho. Yead —1M 41
(off Well La.)
Saxton La. *Leeds* —7G 62
Saxton La. *Saxt* —9N 49
Saxton Pl. *Hud* —6E 132
Saxton St. *Liv* —7N 95
Sayers Clo. *Leeds* —2L 61
Sayle Av. *B'frd* —4F 76
Sayner La. *Leeds* —8F 62
Sayner Rd. *H'let* —8F 62
Scafell Ct. *Dew* —1H 117
Scaitcliffe Vw. *Todm* —5H 87
Scalebor Pk. Clo. *Bur W* —9C 10
Scale Hill. *Hud* —9M 113
Scales La. *B'frd* —5F 76
Scaley St. *B'frd* —7H 59
Scaly Ga. *H'frth* —6E 164
Scaly Ga. *N Mill* —3E 164
Scammonden Rd. *Bkind* —5G 111
Scapegoat Hill. —5A 130
Scape Vw. *Gol* —6D 130
Scarborough Gro. *Shipl* —8M 39
Scarborough Junct. *Leeds* —5F 60
Scarborough La. *Ting* —3N 97
Scarborough Rd. *Otley* —1K 25
Scarborough Rd. *Shipl* —8M 39
Scarborough St. *Dew* —5G 116
Scarborough St. *Ting* —3N 97
Scarborough Ter. *Dew* —5G 117
Scarborough Ter. *Ell* —5E 112
Scar Bottom. —8M 91
Scar Bottom. *Hal* —8M 91
Scar Bottom La. *G'lnd* —4M 111
Scarcroft. —8D 30
Scarcroft Ct. *S'cft* —8E 30
Scarcroft Hill. —9F 30
Scarcroft Ho. B'frd —4D 76
(off Parkway)
Scarcroft Vw. *Leeds* —1A 46
Scar End La. *H'frth* —4E 164
Scarfold. *H'frth* —3M 163
Scargill Clo. *Leeds* —5H 63
Scargill Grange. *Leeds* —6H 63
Scargill Ho. B'frd —6D 58
(off Otley Rd.)
Scar Gro. *Hud* —8L 131
Scar Head Rd. *Sower B* —1H 111
Scar Hill. *Oxe* —5E 54
Scar Hole La. *H'frth* —4D 164
Scarhouse La. *Gol* —6D 130
Scar La. *Gol & Hud* —6D 130
Scarlet Heights. —4E 74
Scarlet Heights. *Q'bry* —4E 74
Scarr End La. *Earl* —6J 117
Scarr End La. *M'end* —1C 116
Scarr End Vw. *Dew* —1C 116
Scarr Grn. Clo. *Mel* —7C 146
Scarsdale La. *Bard* —2F 30
Scarsdale Ridge. *Bard* —2F 30
Scarth Av. *Leeds* —4J 63
Scarth Ter. *Stan* —6C 100
Scar Top. *Gol* —6D 130
Scar Top La. *Hud* —3J 147
Scar Top Rd. *Oldf* —8G 35
Scarwood Clo. *Bgly* —3F 38
Scatcherd La. *Morl* —1J 97
Scawthorpe Clo. *Pon* —2M 123
Sceptone Gro. *Shaf* —6K 155
Schofield Ct. Morl —9K 79
(off Queensway)
Schofield La. *Hud* —4B 132
Schofield Pl. *L'boro* —9M 107
Schofield St. *Sum* —9M 107
Schofield St. *Todm* —6K 87

Scholars Wlk. B'frd —3F 58
Scholebrook. —2N 77
Scholebrooke Ct. B'frd —4J 77
(off Broadfield Clo.)
Scholebrook La. B'frd & Pud —2N 77
Scholemoor. —9K 57
Scholemoor Av. B'frd —1K 75
Scholemoor La. B'frd —9K 57
Scholemoor Rd. B'frd —9L 57
Scholes. —4D 94
(nr. Cleckheaton)
Scholes. —5B 164
(nr. Holmfirth)
Scholes. —6N 35
(nr. Oakworth)
Scholes. —9G 47
(nr. Whinmoor)
Scholes Fld. La. Thpe A —5N 141
Scholes La. G'Ind —2N 111
Scholes La. Oakw —6N 35
Scholes La. Schol —4D 94
Scholes La. Whinm —7F 46
Scholes Moor Rd. H'frth —8N 163
Scholes Rd. C'frd —3K 103
Scholes Rd. Hud —9M 113
Scholes Rd. N Mill —4C 164
Scholes St. B'frd —3B 76
Scholey Av. Brigh —3M 113
Scholey Hill. —4H 101
Scholey Rd. Brigh —3M 113
Schoolaboards La. Pon —3M 123
School Av. Dew —2C 116
School Clo. Hal —7M 73
School Clo. Leeds —2G 79
School Clo. Sower B —7E 110
School Clo. Wake —7J 121
School Cote Brow. H'fld —7A 74
School Cote Ter. Hal —7A 74
School Cres. Dew —2C 116
School Cres. Hal —6M 73
School Cres. Wake —7F 118
School Cft. B'ton —4B 104
School Cft. Rothw —7N 81
School Dri. Knot —7B 104
School Fold. Low M —7N 75
School Green. —8F 56
School Grn. B'hpe —6H 27
School Grn. Brigh —3M 113
School Grn. T'tn —8F 56
School Grn. Av. T'tn —8E 56
School Gro. Dew —2C 116
School Hill. —3K 149
School Hill. Kbtn —3K 149
School Hill. N'dam —6K 137
School Hill. S Cro —2F 146
School Ho. Hal —1F 92
School Land La. H Bri —7N 69
School La. Aber —8E 48
School La. Add —9L 5
School La. Ber B —1L 147
School La. B'frd —3A 76
(BD5)
School La. B'frd —4N 75
(BD6)
School La. C'frd —6F 102
School La. Chap A —9E 44
School La. Coll —9J 17
School La. Colt —8F 64
School La. Den D —2D 166
School La. Dew —2C 116
School La. E Kes —3D 30
School La. Eml —2G 150
School La. Gol —4A 130
School La. Halt —6B 64
School La. Harts —1H 115
School La. Horb —1C 136
School La. I'wth —7M 73
School La. Kei —9K 21
School La. Khtn —3F 132
School La. Leeds —9A 44
School La. Mars —3J 145
School La. Pad —5K 131
School La. Ryh —9J 139
School La. S'wram —9F 92
School La. Todm —7K 87
School La. Wake —1G 119
(in two parts)
School La. Wltn —5F 18
School La. W'ton —3B 138
School La. Wike —8K 29
School Pl. S'ley —4C 60
School Pl. Wyke —9A 76
School Ridge. T'tn —6B 56
School Rd. Gol —4A 130
School Rd. Kei —9F 20
School Rd. Pon —4L 123
School Rd. Wake —7F 118
School Rd. Weth —3N 17
School Sq. B'frd —7H 59
School St. Birs —3C 96
School St. B'frd —7C 58
(BD1, in two parts)
School St. B'frd —5F 76
(BD4)
School St. Butt —6K 75
School St. C'frd —4C 102
(nr. Savile Rd.)
School St. C'frd —3E 102
(nr. Wheldon Rd.)
School St. Chick —3L 117
School St. Chur —5M 79
School St. Cytn —1G 75
School St. Cleck —6F 94
School St. Ctly —8G 38
School St. Cud —9J 155
School St. Cull —9K 37
School St. Cut H —2G 77
School St. Dart —8G 153
School St. Denh —6L 55
School St. Dew —3F 116
School St. Far —3A 60
School St. G'Ind —3A 112
School St. Hal —6C 92
School St. H Bri —1H 89
(off Commercial St.)
School St. H'frth —3M 163
School St. Hon —5L 147
School St. Hud —5B 132
School St. Kei —6G 21
School St. Low M —7A 76
School St. M'well —8L 153
School St. Morl —9L 79
School St. Nthng —9M 147
School St. Norr —1M 115
School St. Oaken —9E 76
School St. Oss —2M 117
School St. Pud —8A 60
(in two parts)
School St. Raven —6B 116
School St. Rbtwn —1J 115
School St. Steet —3C 20
(in two parts)
School St. Ting —7N 97
School St. Upt —9C 142
School St. Wilsd —1B 56
School St. W. Hud —2G 131
School Ter. Fair —9N 85
(off Gt. North Rd.)
School Ter. Shel —6L 149
School Vw. Leeds —3A 62
School Wlk. Kei —9F 20
School Yd. Horb —1D 136
Scissett. —8G 151
Sconce La. H Eld —8M 23
Scopsley Grn. W'ley —2B 134
Scopsley La. W'ley —1A 134
Scorcher Hills La. Burg —4J 159
Score Cft. Skelm —7D 150
Score Hill. Hal —9F 74
Scoresby St. B'frd —7D 58
Scotchman Clo. Morl —2J 97
Scotchman La. Morl —5G 96
Scotchman Rd. B'frd —4L 57
Scotch Pk. Ind. Est. Leeds —6N 61
Scotgate Rd. Hon —4J 147
Scotland. —2E 42
Scotland Clo. H'fth —4E 42
Scotland La. Hal —2B 90
Scotland La. H'fth —8D 26
Scotland Mill La. Leeds —5B 44
Scotland St. Birs —2N 95
Scotland Way. H'fth —3D 42
Scotland Wood Rd. Leeds —5B 44
Scott Av. Heck —6A 96
Scott Bldgs. Leeds —9N 43
(off Oddy Pl.)
Scott Clo. Heck —8B 96
Scott Clo. Swil —4H 83
Scott Dri. Croft —2J 139
Scott Green. —6E 78
Scott Grn. Gild —5E 78
Scott Grn. Cres. Gild —5E 78
Scott Grn. Dri. Gild —5E 78
Scott Grn. Gro. Gild —5F 78
Scott Grn. Mt. Gild —5E 78
Scott Grn. Vw. Gild —5F 78
Scott Hall. —1E 62
Scott Hall Av. Leeds —1E 62
Scott Hall Cres. Leeds —9D 44
Scott Hall Dri. Leeds —2E 62
Scott Hall Grn. Leeds —1E 62
Scott Hall Gro. Leeds —1E 62
Scott Hall Pl. Leeds —1E 62
Scott Hall Rd. Leeds —8D 44
Scott Hall Row. Leeds —2F 62
Scott Hall Sq. Leeds —1E 62
Scott Hall St. Leeds —2E 62
Scott Hall Ter. Leeds —1E 62
Scott Hall Wlk. Leeds —2E 62
Scott Hall Way. Leeds —9E 44
Scott Hill. Clay W —6J 151
Scott Ho. Todm —3J 107
(off Scott St.)
Scott La. Cleck —4J 95
Scott La. Gom —3M 95
Scott La. Leeds —8J 61
Scott La. Morl —2G 96
Scott La. Riddl —6L 21
Scott La. Weth —4M 17
Scott La. W. Riddl —6K 21
Scott M. Weth —4M 17
Scotts Almshouse's. Leeds —4G 81
Scotts Hill Clo. T'ner —2G 46
Scott Sq. Leeds —8J 61
Scott St. Kei —9H 21
Scott St. Pud —8C 60
Scott St. Todm —3J 107
Scott Va. Hud —8B 114
Scott Wood La. Leeds —1D 62
(in three parts)
Scotty Bank. Brigh —1M 113
(off Bridge End)
Scotty Cft. La. Brigh —2M 113
(off Bramston St.)
Scout Bottom La. H Bri —4N 89
Scout Clo. Myth —4N 89
Scout Dike. —9E 166
Scout Hill. —5D 116
Scout Hill Rd. Dew —5D 116
Scout Hill Ter. Dew —5D 116
(off Scout Hill Rd.)
Scout Hill Vw. Dew —5D 116
(off Scout Hill Rd.)
Scout La. H Bri —4M 89
Scout La. Slai —9H 129
Scrapers La. Todm —4K 87
Scratcherd Gro. Morl —9J 79
Sculptor Pl. Brigh —9M 93
(off Waterloo Rd.)
Seacroft. —1C 64
Seacroft Av. Leeds —1C 64
Seacroft Cres. Leeds —1C 64
Seacroft Ga. Leeds —1C 64
(in two parts)
Seacroft Ho. B'frd —9G 41
(off Rowantree Dri.)
Seacroft Ind. Est. Leeds —8C 46
(nr. Coal Rd.)
Seacroft Ind. Est. Leeds —8B 46
(nr. Ramshead App.)
Seaforth Av. Leeds —3J 63
Seaforth Gro. Leeds —3J 63
Seaforth Mt. Leeds —3J 63
Seaforth Pl. Leeds —3J 63
Seaforth Rd. Leeds —3J 63
Seaforth Ter. Leeds —3J 63
Seagrave Rd. Hud —7H 131
Seaton St. B'frd —7F 58
Seckar La. Wool —1J 153
Secker St. Wake —8K 119
Second Av. Bard —3F 30
Second Av. B'frd —5G 59
Second Av. Fitz —6A 140
Second Av. Gol —6C 130
Second Av. Hal —8A 92
Second Av. Horb —1B 136
Second Av. Kei —1H 37
Second Av. Khtn —3D 132
Second Av. Leeds —7A 62
Second Av. Liv —8F 94
Second Av. Pon —8F 156
Second Av. Rawd —2N 41
Second Av. Rothw —6A 82
Second Av. Upt —1N 157
Second Av. Wake —1K 119
Second Av. Weth —4N 17
Second St. Low M —7C 76
Sedan St. Hal —6B 92
(off Trinity Rd.)
Sedbergh Dri. I'ly —6H 9
Sedbergh Pk. I'ly —6G 9
Sedburgh Chambers. I'ly —6G 9
(off Chantry Dri.)
Sedburgh Clo. Leeds —7M 63
Sedburgh Rd. Hal —7C 92
Sedge Gro. Haw —7C 36
Sedge Ri. Tad —6N 33
Sedgewick St. Birs —3B 96
Sedgfield Ter. B'frd —7B 58
Sedgwick Clo. B'frd —6B 58
Seed Hill Ter. Hal —7J 73
Seed Hill Ter. Steet —3C 20
Seed Row. B'frd —5F 76
Seed St. Low M —7B 76
See Mill La. Hal —2A 92
Sefton Av. Brigh —7L 93
Sefton Av. Leeds —2C 80
Sefton Cres. Brigh —7L 93
Sefton Dri. Brigh —7L 93
Sefton Dri. I'ly —6G 9
Sefton Gro. B'frd —3F 58
Sefton La. Mel —7C 146
Sefton Pl. B'frd —3F 58
Sefton Pl. Kei —8J 21
Sefton Ri. Dew —7G 116
Sefton St. Hal —4N 91
Sefton St. Kei —8J 21
Sefton St. Leeds —2D 80
Sefton Ter. Hal —4N 91
Sefton Ter. Leeds —2C 80
Selborne Gro. B'frd —3N 57
Selborne Gro. Kei —2G 37
Selborne Mt. B'frd —4A 58
Selborne Ter. B'frd —4N 57
Selborne Ter. Shipl —9N 39
Selborne Vs. B'frd —4N 57
(off Selborne Gro.)
Selbourne Av. Dew —6F 116
Selbourne Dri. Dew —6F 116
Selbourne Rd. Dew —6F 116
Selbourne Vs. Cytn —2H 75
Selby. Hal —7K 73
Selby Av. Leeds —6N 63
Selby Rd. Leeds —6N 63
Selby Rd. M'fld —9L 65
Selby St. Wake —4M 119
Seldon St. B'frd —2N 75
Selene Clo. Gom —2N 95
Sellars Fold. —1M 75
Sellerdale Av. Wyke —3B 94
Sellerdale Dri. Wyke —2B 94
Sellerdale Ri. Wyke —2B 94
Sellerdale Way. Wyke —3B 94
Sellers Fold. B'frd —1M 75
Selside Ho. B'frd —8G 40
(off Garsdale Av.)
Selso Rd. Dew —2J 117
Seminary St. Leeds —5C 62
Semon Av. B'frd —1D 58
Senior St. Dew —4E 116
Senior St. Hud —5C 132
Senior Way. B'frd —8C 58
(in two parts)
Sentry. Hon —4K 147
Sergeantson St. Hud —4M 131
Serpentine Rd. Cleck —4H 95
Servia Dri. Leeds —3E 62
Servia Gdns. Leeds —3E 62
Servia Hill. Leeds —3D 62
Servia Rd. Leeds —3D 62
Service Rd. Leeds —3L 81
Sessions Ho. Yd. Pon —2J 123
Sevenoaks Mead. All —5G 56
Seventh Av. Liv —7F 94
Seventh Av. Rothw —7B 82
Severn Dri. Gar —9B 66
Severn Rd. B'frd —3E 58
Severn Rd. H'let —2H 81
Severn Way. H'let —1H 81
Sewage Works Rd. Leeds —2L 81
Sewell Rd. B'frd —8F 58
Sewerbridge La. Pon —2N 121
Seymour St. B'frd —8E 58
Seymour St. Wake —7L 119
Seymour Wlk. Mel —7D 146
Shackleton. —5F 70
Shackleton St. Todm —3E 86
Shackleton Ter. H'den —6N 37
(off Hill End La.)
Shade. —9J 87
Shade St. Todm —9J 87
Shadwell. —3A 46
Shadwell La. Leeds —5F 44
Shadwell Pk. Av. Leeds —2L 45
Shadwell Pk. Clo. Leeds —2L 45
Shadwell Pk. Ct. Leeds —3L 45
Shadwell Pk. Dri. Leeds —3L 45
Shadwell Pk. Gdns. Leeds —2L 45
Shadwell Pk. Gro. Leeds —3L 45
Shadwell Wlk. Leeds —4G 44
Shaftesbury Av. Beal —7L 105
Shaftesbury Av. B'frd —4J 57
Shaftesbury Av. Brigh —4N 113
Shaftesbury Av. Leeds —6J 45
Shaftesbury Av. Shipl —8A 40
Shaftesbury Ct. B'frd —5J 57
Shaftesbury Rd. Leeds —5J 45
Shafton. —6K 155
Shafton Hall Dri. Shaf —6J 155
Shafton La. Leeds —9B 62
Shafton Pl. Leeds —9B 62
Shafton St. Leeds —9B 62
Shafton Two Gates. —7L 155
Shafton Vw. Leeds —9B 62
Shakespeare App. Leeds —5H 63
Shakespeare Av. Cam —9N 143
Shakespeare Av. Leeds —5H 63
Shakespeare Av. Nor —4H 121
Shakespeare Av. Todm —6M 87
Shakespeare Bldgs. Mar —4J 131
(off Eldon Rd.)
Shakespeare Clo. Guis —8K 25
Shakespeare Clo. Leeds —5H 63
Shakespeare Ct. Leeds —5H 63
Shakespeare Cres. C'frd —7K 103
Shakespeare Gdns. Leeds —5H 63
Shakespeare Grange. Leeds —5H 63
Shakespeare Lawn. Leeds —5H 63
Shakespeare Rd. Guis —8J 25
Shakespeare St. Hal —6B 92
Shakespeare St. Leeds —4H 63
Shakespeare Towers. Leeds —5H 63
Shakespeare Va. Leeds —5H 63
Shakespeare Wlk. Leeds —5H 63
Shalimar St. Hal —5M 91
Shambles, The. Hud —4N 131
Shambles, The. Weth —4M 17
Shann Av. Kei —8F 20
Shann Cres. Kei —8F 20
Shann La. Kei —8F 20
Shannon Clo. Brigh —4K 113
Shannon Clo. I'ly —6E 8
Shannon Dri. Hud —1C 130
Shannon Rd. Brigh —4K 113
Shannon Rd. Leeds —6G 63
Shannon St. Leeds —6G 62
Shann St. B'frd —2B 58
Shapla Clo. Kei —1G 36
Share Hill. Gol —6B 130
Sharlston. —8K 121
Sharlston Common. —7J 121
Sharnaley Ct. Pon —4N 123
Sharon Cotts. Oss —4N 117
(off Northfield Rd.)
Sharp Av. B'frd —5A 76
Sharpe St. B'frd —8C 58
Sharpe St. Heck —9A 96
Sharp Ho. Rd. Leeds —9G 81
Sharp La. Hud —8D 132
Sharp La. Leeds & Rob H —8G 81
(nr. Throstle Rd.)
Sharp La. Leeds —8F 80
(nr. Town St.)
Sharp M. Leeds —1B 62
Sharp Row. Pud —8B 60
Sharp Royd. Hud —6E 132
Sharp St. B'frd —4A 76
Sharp St. Dew —2G 116
Shaw. —4B 54
Shaw Av. Nor —1K 121
Shaw Barn Cft. Weth —4K 17
Shaw Barn La. Weth —4K 17
Shaw Booth La. Hal —9F 72
Shaw Clo. Gar —9A 66
Shaw Clo. Guis —8K 25
Shaw Clo. Holy G —7B 112
Shaw Clo. Nor —1K 121
Shaw Clo. S Elm —5N 157
Shaw Cross. —1K 117
Shawfield Av. H'frth —4J 163
Shaw Fields La. Slai —1J 145
Shaw Fold. Wake —1N 137
Shawforth. —5A 106
Shaw Ga. Slai —3L 145
Shaw Hill. Hal —7B 92
(in two parts)
Shaw Lane. —8L 25
Shaw La. Cltn —8E 154
Shaw La. Ell —3H 113
Shaw La. Gol —3A 130
Shaw La. Guis —7K 25
Shaw La. Hal —7C 92
Shaw La. H'frth —4J 163
Shaw La. Holy G —7A 112
Shaw La. Hud —1A 130
(nr. New Hey Rd.)
Shaw La. Hud —6G 130
(nr. New St.)
Shaw La. Kei —5K 37
Shaw La. Kbtn —4J 149
Shaw La. Leeds —1N 61
Shaw La. M'well —7L 153
Shaw La. Mars —2F 144
Shaw La. Oxe —4B 54
Shaw La. Q'bry —7E 74
Shaw La. Ripp —1C 128
Shaw La. Sower B —2H 111
Shaw La. Todm —1E 86
Shaw La. Gdns. Guis —7K 25
Shaw Leys. Yead —8L 25
Shaw Lodge. Hal —7C 92
Shaw Mt. L'ft —4E 90
Shaw Plains. Todm —7A 88
Shaw Ri. Nor —1K 121
Shaw Royd. Yead —8L 25
Shaw Royd Ct. Yead —8L 25
(off Shaw Royd)
Shaws La. Bar E —9K 47
Shaw's La. Sower B —2A 110
Shaw's Ter. Mars —5F 144
Shaw St. Cleck —5F 94
Shaw St. Holy G —7B 112
Shaw St. Low M —7N 75
Shaw St. Mir —6L 115
Shaw Vs. Guis —7K 25
(off Queensway)
Shaw Wood Av. Todm —6B 88
Shaw Wood Rd. Todm —6A 88
Shay Brow. —3E 56
Shay Clo. B'frd —2L 57
Shay Ct. Croft —1F 138
Shay Cres. B'frd —2K 57
Shay Dri. B'frd —2K 57
Shayfield La. Carl —1M 99

Shay Fold. B'frd —2K 57
Shaygate. Wilsd —2D 56
Shay Grange. B'frd —1K 57
Shay Gro. B'frd —2L 57
Shay La. B'frd —1K 57
Shay La. H Wd —2K 77
Shay La. H'frth —5D 162
Shay La. Oven —1N 91
Shay La. W'ton & Croft —4B 138
Shay La. Wilsd —1C 56
Shay St. Leeds —3D 62
Shay Syke. Hal —6C 92
Shay, The. —7B 92
Sheaf St. Leeds —8F 62
Shearbridge. —8A 58
Shearbridge Grn. B'frd —8A 58
Shearbridge Pl. B'frd —8A 58
Shearbridge Rd. B'frd —8A 58
Shearbridge Ter. B'frd —9A 58
Sheardale. Hon —5K 147
Shearing Cross. —2M 131
Shearing Cross Gdns. Hud —2N 131
Shear's Yd. Leeds —7F 62
Shed St. Kei —9J 21
Sheep Hill La. Q'bry —3G 74
Sheepridge Gro. Hud —8A 114
Sheepridge Rd. Hud —8A 114
Sheepscar. —4F 62
Sheepscar Ct. Leeds —4F 62
Sheepscar Gro. Leeds —5F 62
Sheepscar Row. Leeds —4F 62
Sheepscar St. N. Leeds —3E 62
(in two parts)
Sheepscar St. S. Leeds —4F 62
Sheepscar Way. Leeds —3F 62
Sheepwalk La. C'frd —6J 103
Sheepwalk La. Upt —9D 142
(in two parts)
Sheerien Clo. Barn —9N 153
Sheffield Rd. N Mill & Jack B —2C 164
Shefield Rd. S Elm & Ham —5D 158
Sheila Ter. Heck —9N 95
Sheldon Ridge. Bier —6F 76
Sheldrake Av. B'frd —7H 57
Sheldrake Rd. C'frd —6D 102
Shelf. —7H 75
Shelf Hall La. Hal —8G 75
Shelf Moor. Hal —6H 75
Shelf Rd. H Bri —1G 89
Shelldrake Dri. Leeds —8F 80
Shelley. —6L 149
Shelley Av. Heck —1B 116
Shelley Bank Bottom. —7L 149
Shelley Clo. W'ford —1D 100
Shelley Ct. Horb —9E 118
Shelley Cres. Oult —1D 100
Shelley Dri. Knot —8A 104
Shelley Far Bank. —6L 149
Shelley Gro. B'frd —6K 57
Shelley La. Kbtn —4K 149
Shelley Wlk. Stan —6N 99
Shelley Woodhouse. —7A 150
Shelley Woodhouse La. Shel —7A 150
Shell La. C'ley —9M 41
(in two parts)
Shepcote Clo. Leeds —4J 43
Shepcote Cres. Leeds —4J 43
Shepherd Hill. —5C 118
Shepherds Fold. Hal —1E 92
Shepherds Gro. Hud —8C 114
Shepherd's Gro. Leeds —2G 63
Shepherd's La. Leeds —2G 63
Shepherd's Pl. Leeds —2H 63
Shepherds Thorn La. Brigh & Hud —4N 113
Shepherd St. B'frd —1M 75
Shepley. —9J 149
Shepley Mt. Mir —4M 115
Shepley Rd. Stkmr —7G 149
Shepley St. Wake —5N 119
Shepstye Rd. Horb —1C 136
Shepton Ho. B'frd —9C 58
(off Park Rd.)
Sherborne Dri. Kei —2E 36
Sherborne Rd. Gt Hor —8B 58
Sherborne Rd. Idle —6F 40
Sherbrooke Av. Leeds —7A 64
Sherburn App. Leeds —9D 46
Sherburn Clo. B'shaw —7M 77
Sherburn Clo. Leeds —9D 46
(off Sherburn Pl.)
Sherburn Clo. Skel —7K 159
Sherburn Ct. Leeds —9D 46
(off York Rd.)
Sherburn Gro. B'shaw —7M 77
Sherburn Pl. Leeds —9D 46
Sherburn Rd. Brigh —3J 113
Sherburn Rd. Leeds —9D 46
Sherburn Rd. N. Leeds —7C 46
Sherburn Row. Leeds —9D 46
(off York Rd.)
Sherburn Sq. Leeds —9D 46
(off Sherburn Pl.)
Sherburn Wlk. Leeds —9D 46
(off York Rd.)
Sheridan Clo. Pud —8C 60
Sheridan Ct. Pud —8C 60
Sheridan St. B'frd —1E 76
Sheridan St. Out —7L 99
Sheridan Way. Pud —8C 60
Sheriff La. Bgly —2H 39
Sherwell Gro. All —5H 57
Sherwell Ri. All —5H 57
Sherwood Av. Gom —4M 95
Sherwood Av. Hud —6D 114
Sherwood Clo. Bgly —2H 39
Sherwood Clo. Cam —9N 143
Sherwood Clo. Dew —9C 96
Sherwood Clo. Gom —4M 95
Sherwood Dri. Hud —3H 147
Sherwood Dri. Skel —7K 159
Sherwood Dri. Wake —5H 137
Sherwood Grn. Rob H —1J 99
Sherwood Gro. Shipl —7K 39
Sherwood Gro. Wake —7G 118
Sherwood Ind. Est. Rob H —1K 99
Sherwood Pl. B'frd —4F 58
Sherwood Rd. Brigh —1A 114
Sherwood Way. Cud —8H 155
Sherwood Works. Brigh —2B 114
Shetcliffe La. B'frd —5F 76
Shetcliffe Rd. B'frd —5F 76
Shetland Clo. B'frd —2D 58
Shibden Dri. Bat —6C 96
Shibden Gth. Shib —5F 92
Shibden Grange Dri. Hal —3E 92
Shibden Hall. —4E 92
Shibden Hall Cft. Hal —5F 92
Shibden Hall Rd. Hal —4D 92
Shibden Head. —7B 74
Shibden Head La. Q'bry —6B 74
Shibden Vw. Q'bry —6C 74
Shield Clo. Leeds —3F 64
Shield Hall La. Sower —8C 90
Shill Bank Av. Mir —5A 116
Shill Bank La. Mir —5N 115
Shill Bank Vw. Mir —5N 115
Shillinghill La. Knot —1B 124
Shilling St. Wake —3M 119
Shinwell Dri. Upt —1C 158
Shipley. —7N 39
Shipley Airedale Rd. B'frd —6D 58
Shipley Fields Rd. Shipl —1N 57
(in two parts)
Shipley Glen Cable Tramway. —5L 39
Ship St. Brigh —1N 113
Shipton M. Morl —1L 97
Ship Yd. Leeds —6E 62
(off Queen's Arc.)
Ship Yd. Wake —6M 119
Shire Clo. B'frd —6L 75
Shire Oak Rd. Leeds —1A 62
Shire Oak St. Leeds —1N 61
Shires Gro. Stan —7A 100
Shires Hill. Hud —5K 131
Shirley Av. Birs —2A 96
Shirley Av. Gom —4M 95
Shirley Av. Wyke —3N 93
Shirley Clo. Otley —1M 25
Shirley Cres. Wyke —3N 93
Shirley Dri. Leeds —2F 60
Shirley Gro. Gom —4M 95
Shirley Gro. Hal —5M 93
Shirley Mnr. Gdns. B'frd —7H 59
(off Moorside La.)
Shirley Mt. Gom —4M 95
Shirley Pde. Gom —4L 95
Shirley Pl. Gom —4M 95
Shirley Pl. Wyke —3A 94
Shirley Rd. B'frd —4H 77
(BD4)
Shirley Rd. B'frd —8N 57
(BD7)
Shirley Rd. Gom —5M 95
Shirley Sq. Gom —4M 95
Shirley St. Haw —8B 36
Shirley St. Shipl —7L 39
Shirley Ter. Gom —4M 95
Shirley Wlk. Gom —4M 95
Shoebridge Av. Ebrn —2A 20
Shoebroad La. Todm —8K 87
Shoe Mkt. Pon —3K 123
Sholebroke Av. Leeds —2F 62
Sholebroke Ct. Leeds —2F 62
Sholebroke Mt. Leeds —2E 62
Sholebroke Pl. Leeds —2F 62
Sholebroke St. Leeds —2E 62
Sholebroke Ter. Leeds —1F 62
Sholebroke Vw. Leeds —2F 62
Shop La. Hud —2G 132
Shop La. Loft —4K 99
Shore. —2E 86
Shore End La. Hal —4A 72
Shore Grn. Todm —2E 86
Shoreham Rd. Leeds —7M 61
Shorehead. —4N 131
Shore New Rd. Todm —3D 86
Short Clo. Wyke —8N 75
Shortfield Ct. Barn —9N 153
Short La. Leeds —8E 44
Short Row. Low M —7B 76
Short St. Dew —4K 117
Short St. F'stne —6C 122
Short St. Todm —7K 87
(off Dalton St.)
Short Way. S'ley —5L 59
Shortway. T'tn —8F 56
Shroggs Rd. Hal —2M 91
Shroggs St. Hal —4N 91
Shroggs, The. Steet —3C 20
Shroggs Va. Ter. Hal —4N 91
Shuttleworth La. B'frd —6K 57
Shuttocks Clo. Kip —2A 84
Shuttocks Fold. Kip —2B 84
Shutts La. Nor G —2K 93
Shutt, The. Horb —2D 136
Sickleholme Ct. Hud —6C 114
Sickle St. Cleck —4J 95
Sicklinghall. —4D 16
Sicklinghall Rd. Weth —4G 16
Sidcop Rd. Cud —8H 155
(in two parts)
Siddal. —9D 92
Siddal Gro. Hal —8C 92
Siddal La. Hal —8D 92
Siddall St. Leeds —8D 62
Siddal New Rd. Hal —7C 92
Siddal Pl. Hal —9D 92
Siddal St. Hal —9D 92
Siddal Top La. Hal —8D 92
Siddal Vw. Hal —8D 92
Siddon Dri. Hud —7E 132
Side Copse. Otley —9M 11
Side La. Lgwd —4E 130
Sides Clo. Pon —5K 123
Sides Rd. Pon —5K 123
Sidings Clo. B'frd —3B 58
Sidings, The. Guis —7H 25
Sidings, The. Shipl —7A 40
Sidney St. Leeds —6E 62
Siegen Clo. Morl —9K 79
Siegen Mnr. Morl —9K 79
(off Wesley St.)
Sigget La. Todm —6H 87
Sigott St. Hud —4E 130
Sike Clo. Dart —8E 152
Sike La. H'frth —4A 164
Sike La. W'ton —5C 138
Sikes Clo. Hud —6D 132
Silcoates Av. Wren —2G 118
Silcoates Ct. Wake —3F 118
Silcoates Dri. Wren —2G 118
Silcoates La. Wren —2F 118
Silcoates St. Wake —3H 119
Silk Mill App. Leeds —5H 43
Silk Mill Av. Leeds —4G 43
Silk Mill Bank. Leeds —5G 43
Silk Mill Clo. Leeds —4G 43
Silk Mill Dri. E Mor —7D 22
Silk Mill Dri. Leeds —5G 42
Silk Mill Gdns. Leeds —5G 42
Silk Mill Grn. Leeds —5H 43
Silk Mill M. Leeds —5J 43
Silk Mill Rd. Leeds —5G 43
Silk Mill Way. Leeds —5H 43
Silkstone Clo. Gar —5B 66
Silkstone Ct. Leeds —5D 64
Silk Stone Ct. Nor —8G 101
Silkstone Cres. Wake —4L 137
Silkstone Crest. Nor —8G 101
Silkstone Ho. Pon —2K 123
Silkstone Way. Leeds —5D 64
Silk St. B'frd —4M 57
Silsbridge St. B'frd —7B 58
(off Sunbridge Rd.)
Silsden. —8E 6
Silsden Rd. Add —2H 7
Silsden Rd. Riddl —4L 21
Silson La. Bail —3C 40
Silver Birch Av. Wyke —2B 94
Silver Birch Clo. Wyke —2B 94
Silver Birch Dri. Wyke —2B 94
Silver Birch Gro. Wyke —2B 94
Silver Ct. Leeds —5C 60
Silverdale Av. Guis —8J 25
Silverdale Av. Leeds —2K 45
Silverdale Av. Riddl —7L 21
Silverdale Clo. Guis —9J 25
Silverdale Cres. Guis —8J 25
Silverdale Dri. Guis —9J 25
Silverdale Grange. Guis —9J 25
Silverdale Gro. Guis —9H 25
Silverdale Mt. Guis —9J 25
Silverdale Rd. B'frd —3C 76
Silverdale Rd. Guis —9H 25
Silverdale Ter. G'lnd —5N 111
Silverhill Av. B'frd —5H 59
Silverhill Dri. B'frd —5H 59
Silverhill Rd. B'frd —5G 59
Silver La. Yead —9M 25
Silver Mill Hill. Otley —2M 25
Silver Royd Av. Leeds —8J 61
Silver Royd Clo. Leeds —8J 61
Silver Royd Dri. Leeds —8J 61
Silver Royd Gth. Leeds —8J 61
Silver Royd Gro. Leeds —8J 61
Silver Royd Hill. Leeds —8J 61
Silver Royd Pl. Leeds —8J 61
Silver Royd Rd. Leeds —8J 61
Silver Royd St. Leeds —8J 61
Silver Royd Ter. Leeds —8J 61
Silver St. Bees —8C 62
Silver St. B'frd —5N 57
Silver St. Fair —9N 85
Silver St. Hal —5B 92
Silver St. Hud —5A 132
Silver St. N Hill —9K 99
Silver St. Todm —4J 107
Silver St. Wake —5L 119
Silver St. E. Hud —5A 132
Silverwood Av. Hal —3J 91
Silverwood Wlk. Hal —3J 91
(in two parts)
Silwood Dri. B'frd —3G 58
Simeon St. Todm —3J 107
Simes St. B'frd —7B 58
Simm Carr La. Shib —9C 74
Simmonds La. Hal —7C 92
Simmons Ct. Leeds —8H 63
Simms Dene. All —2F 56
Simon Clo. B'frd —3K 77
Simon Fld. Wyke —2A 94
Simon Grn. Rd. Slai —7A 130
Simon Marks Ct. Leeds —9M 61
(off Lynwood Gth.)
Simpson Green. —6G 41
Simpson Gro. B'frd —6G 41
Simpson Gro. Leeds —7N 61
Simpson Rd. H Bri —4L 89
Simpson Rd. S Elm —5A 158
Simpsons La. Knot —9C 104
Simpson St. E Ard —4G 98
Simpson St. Hal —2A 92
Simpson St. Kei —9G 21
Sim Royd La. Den D —5G 167
Sinclair Gth. Wake —3N 137
Sinclair Rd. B'frd —1D 58
Sinden M. B'frd —5F 40
Singleton St. B'frd —6C 58
Sion Hill. Sid —9D 92
Sir Francis Crossley's Almshouses.
(off Margaret St.) Hal —5A 92
Sir George Martin Dri. Leeds —3N 43
Sir Isaac Holden Pl. List —7N 57
Sir Karl Cohen Sq. Leeds —7L 61
Sir Wilfred Pl. B'frd —7F 40
Siskin Ct. Morl —1L 97
Sisley La. Todm —8B 88
Sissons Av. Leeds —9D 80
Sissons Cres. Leeds —1D 98
Sissons Dri. Leeds —9D 80
Sissons Grn. Leeds —9D 80
Sissons Gro. Leeds —9D 80
Sissons La. Leeds —9D 80
Sissons Mt. Leeds —1C 98
Sissons Pl. Leeds —8D 80
Sissons Rd. Leeds —9C 80
Sissons Row. Leeds —9D 80
Sissons St. Leeds —9D 80
Sissons Ter. Leeds —9C 80
Sissons Vw. Leeds —1C 98
Sitka Clo. Roys —6C 154
Siward St. Fitz —6A 140
Six Heights. Ripp —8D 110
Sixrood La. Burg —3L 159
Sixth Av. B'frd —5G 58
Sixth Av. Liv —7F 94
Sixth Av. Rothw —6B 82
Sizers Ct. Yead —2L 41
Skelbrooke. —4G 159
Skelbrooke Dri. Pon —6K 123
Skelda Ri. I'ly —6G 9
Skellow. —7L 159
Skellow Rd. Skel —8L 159
Skelmanthorpe. —7D 150
Skelmanthorpe Bus. Pk. Skelm —7D 150
Skelton Av. Leeds —6K 63
Skelton Av. M'well —8K 153
Skelton Cres. Hud —7G 131
Skelton Cres. Leeds —6K 63
Skelton Grange Cotts. Leeds —2L 81
Skelton Grange Rd. Leeds —3K 81
Skelton Mt. Leeds —6K 63
Skelton Pl. Leeds —6K 63
(off Skelton Av.)
Skelton Rd. Leeds —6K 63
Skeltons La. T'ner —6C 46
Skelton St. Leeds —6K 63
Skelton Ter. Leeds —6K 63
Skelton Wlk. B'frd —8H 41
Skelwith App. Leeds —4B 64
Skelwith Wlk. Leeds —4B 64
Skinner La. B'frd —4A 58
Skinner La. Leeds —5F 62
Skinner La. Pon —2K 123
Skinner St. Leeds —6C 62
(off Lisbon St.)
Skinpit La. Hoy S —9K 167
Skippon Ter. T'ner —2G 46
Skipton Av. Hud —9N 113
Skipton Ri. Gar —7B 66
Skipton Rd. Add —8K 5
Skipton Rd. Ebrn —3B 20
Skipton Rd. Kei —8J 21
Skipton Rd. Low U —5F 20
Skipton Rd. Sils —8B 6
Skipton St. Bat —9F 96
Skircoat Green. —9B 92
Skircoat Grn. Hal —1B 112
Skircoat Grn. Rd. Hal —9B 92
Skircoat Moor Clo. Hal —8N 91
Skircoat Moor Rd. Hal —7M 91
Skircoat Rd. Hal —6B 92
Skirrow St. Bgly —9G 38
Skye Cft. Roys —4D 154
Skye Vw. Rothw —8A 82
Slack. —7E 70
(nr. Hebden Bridge)
Slack. —3N 129
(nr. Outlane)
Slack Bottom Rd. B'frd —5M 75
Slack Ho. La. Wadsw —7J 71
(in two parts)
Slack La. Bklnd —8G 110
Slack La. Croft —2G 139
Slack La. Hal —9B 72
Slack La. H'frth —3N 163
Slack La. N'dam —6K 137
(in two parts)
Slack La. Oakw —4A 36
Slack La. Outl —2N 129
Slack La. S Hien —4J 155
Slack La. Sower B —2N 109
(nr. Bower Slack Rd.)
Slack La. Sower B —6N 109
(nr. Merry Bent La.)
Slack Side. —4L 75
Slacks La. Slai —1G 145
(nr. Cop Hill Side)
Slacks La. Slai —4L 145
(nr. Krives La.)
Slack Ter. Cumb —6F 164
Slack Top La. Cumb —7G 165
Sladdin Row. Q'bry —5B 74
Slade Clo. B Spa —1D 32
Slade Ct. Kbtn —3F 148
Slade Ho. B'frd —4H 59
(off St Clares Av.)
Slade La. Brigh —5L 113
Slade La. Riddl —6L 21
Sladen St. Kei —9G 21
Slades La. H'frth —4C 146
Slades Rd. Gol —6A 130
Slade Wlk. Bat —3C 96
Slaid Hill. —2L 45
Slaid Hill Ct. Leeds —2K 45
Slaithwaite. —9N 129
Slaithwaite Av. Dew —7F 116
Slaithwaite Clo. Dew —7F 116
Slaithwaite Ga. Slai —6N 129
Slaithwaite Rd. Dew —7F 116
Slaithwaite Rd. Mel —4M 145
Slant Ga. Kbtn —2J 149
Slant Ga. Lint —8D 130
Slant La. Todm —6M 87
Slater Av. H Bri —9H 71
Slater Ing La. Hept —8D 70
Slaters Rd. S'ley —5B 60
Slates La. I'ly —2F 8
Slaymaker La. Oakw —4B 36
Slead Av. Brigh —8L 93
Slead Ct. Brigh —8L 93
Slead Cres. Brigh —8L 93
Slead Gro. Brigh —8L 93
Slead Royd. Brigh —8L 93
Slead Syke. —8L 93
Slead Vw. Brigh —8L 93
Sledgate La. Slai —4L 145
Sledge Ga. Scam —7E 128
Sledmere Cft. Leeds —9D 46
Sledmere Gth. Leeds —9D 46
Sledmere Grn. Leeds —9D 46
(off Sledmere Pl.)
Sledmere La. Leeds —9D 46
Sledmere Pl. Leeds —9D 46
Sledmere Sq. Leeds —9D 46
(off Sledmere Pl.)
Sleep Hill La. Skelb —3G 158
Sleep Hill La. Upt —2D 158
Sleights La. Hare —2K 29

Sleights, The. Huby —6L 13
Sleningford Gro. Shipl —7K 39
Sleningford Ri. Bgly —2E 38
Sleningford Rd. Bgly —2D 38
Sleningford Rd. Shipl —7K 39
Sleningford Ter. Bgly —2E 38 (off Sleningford Rd.)
Sleningford Vs. Bgly —2D 38
Slicer's Yd. Bgly —4E 38 (off Busfield St.)
Slingsby Clo. App B —7H 41
Slipper La. Mir —3J 115
Slippery Ford La. Oakw —1K 35
Slippy La. Hal —8J 73 (in two parts)
Slutwell La. Pon —3K 123
Smalewell Clo. Pud —8A 60
Smalewell Dri. Pud —8N 59
Smalewell Gdns. Pud —8N 59
Smalewell Grn. Pud —8A 60
Smalewell Rd. Pud —8N 59
Small La. Caw —8L 167
Small La. Gol —6C 130
Small Lees Rd. Sower B —8D 110
Small Page Fold. Q'bry —4D 74
Smallpage Yd. Wake —5L 119
Smallshaw La. Pec W —3H 71
Smallwood Gdns. Dew —9L 97
Smallwood Rd. Dew —9K 97 (in two parts)
Smawell La. Not —2B 154
Smawthorne Av. C'frd —5D 102
Smawthorne Gro. C'frd —5D 102
Smawthorne La. C'frd —5D 102
Smeatley's La. Wome —3K 143
Smeaton App. Leeds —3F 64
Smeaton Gro. Swil —4H 83
Smeaton Rd. Upt —1C 158
Smeeton Gdns. Hud —5M 131
Smiddles La. B'frd —3B 76
Smiddy Hill. Wltn —5G 19
Smirthwaite St. Wake —3L 119
Smirthwaite Vw. Nor —2H 121
Smith Art Gallery. —9M 93
Smith Av. B'frd —4A 76
Smith Cres. Brigh —3K 113
Smitherd's St. Kei —1H 37
Smithfield Av. Hal —4H 93
Smith Ho. Av. Brigh —6M 93
Smith Ho. Cres. Brigh —7M 93
Smith Ho. Gro. Brigh —7M 93
Smith Ho. La. Brigh —7M 93
Smithies La. Birs —3B 96
Smithies La. Heck —1A 116
Smithies Moor Clo. Bat —5C 96
mithies Moor Cres. Bat —4C 96
mithies Moor La. Bat —4B 96
mithies Moor Ri. Bat —4C 96
mith La. B'frd —4K 57
mith La. Sower B —7B 110
mith Rd. B'frd —2M 75
mith Rd. Dew —2C 116
miths Av. Hud —3H 131
mithson Av. C'frd —5H 103
mithson St. Rothw —9A 82
mith's Ter. Hal —1N 91
mith St. Bier —5F 76
mith St. B'frd —7B 58
mith St. C'frd —3F 102 (nr. Green La.)
mith St. C'frd —2J 103 (nr. Wheldon Rd.)
mith St. Ctly —9G 38
mith St. Kei —8G 21
mith St. Liv —9M 95
mith St. Wake —5K 119
mithville. Riddl —7M 21
mith Wlk. S Elm —5N 157
mith Way. Oss —4A 118
mithwell La. H Bri —7E 70
mithy Brook La. Dew —1J 135
mithy Carr La. Brigh —8M 93
mithy Clo. Croft —2G 139
mithy Clo. Skelm —8D 150
mithy Clough La. Ripp —8A 110
mithy Ct. Coll —9J 17
mithy Ct. Schol —3D 94
mithy Fold. Q'bry —3H 75
mithy Greaves. Add —2B 8
mithy Hill. B'frd —4A 76
mithy Hill. Denh —8L 55
mithy Hill. Up Den —5C 166
mithy La. Bard —6D 30
mithy La. Bur W —8C 10
mithy La. C'den —8B 70
mithy La. H'frth —6H 163
mithy La. Hud —5A 132
mithy La. Leeds —1H 43
mithy La. Ove —4J 135
mithy La. Rish —3D 128
mithy La. Skelm —8D 150
mithy La. Ting —4B 98
mithy La. Wilsd —9B 38
Smithy Mills La. Leeds —5N 43 (in two parts)
Smithy Nook. L'boro —9L 107
Smithy Pde. Dew —1H 135
Smithy Pl. La. Broc —7N 147
Smithy St. Hal —5C 92
Smithy Wlk. Dew —1J 135
Smools La. Morl —6L 79
Snail La. Err —4J 89
Snailsden Way. M'well —9M 153
Snaith Wood Dri. Rawd —6N 41
Snaith Wood M. Rawd —6N 41
Snake Hill. —6K 115
Snake Hill. Oaken —8E 76
Snake La. Leeds —8J 63
Snape Dri. B'frd —3J 75
Snape St. Kei —3J 37
Snapethorne Ga. Wake —7E 118
Snapethorpe Cres. Wake —7F 118
Snapethorpe Rd. Wake —7F 118
Snelsins La. Cleck —3G 94
Snelsins Rd. Cleck —3G 94
Snetterton Clo. Cud —9K 155
Snittle Rd. H'frth —9N 163
Snowden App. Leeds —3H 61
Snowden Clo. Leeds —4G 61
Snowden Cres. Leeds —4G 61
Snowden Fold. Leeds —4G 61
Snowden Grn. Leeds —4G 61 (off Aston Rd.)
Snowden Gro. Leeds —4G 61
Snowden Lawn. Leeds —4G 61
Snowden Rd. Shipl —9B 40 (in two parts)
Snowden Royd. Leeds —3G 61
Snowden St. B'frd —6C 58
Snowdens Wlk. Cytn —1J 75
Snowden Va. Leeds —4G 61
Snowden Wlk. Leeds —4G 61
Snowden Way. Leeds —3G 61
Snowdon Av. Knot —8B 104
Snowdon St. Bat —8E 96
Snowdrop M. All —6G 57
Snowgate Head. —2F 164
Snow Hill. —1J 119
Snow Hill Clo. Wake —2J 119
Snow Hill Ri. Wake —2J 119
Snow Hill Vw. Wake —3K 119
Snow Lea. —2C 130
Snug La. H'frth —7E 164
Snydale. —6M 121
Snydale Av. Nor —2K 121
Snydale Clo. Nor —2K 121
Snydale Ct. Nor —2K 121
Snydale Gro. Nor —2K 121
Snydale Rd. Nor —1J 121
Soaper Ho. La. Hal —2H 93
Soaper La. She & B'frd —6H 75
Sod Ho. Grn. Hal —1N 91
Soho Gro. Wake —5J 119
Soho Mills. B'frd —7B 58 (off Thornton Rd.)
Soho St. B'frd —7B 58
Soho St. Hal —5M 91
Soil Hill. —2L 73
Solomon Hill. Hal —3D 90
Solway Rd. Bat —7J 97
Somerdale Clo. Leeds —5G 60
Somerdale Gdns. Leeds —5G 61
Somerdale Gro. Leeds —5G 60
Somerdale Wlk. Leeds —5G 60
Somerset Av. Bail —3N 39
Somerset Av. Brigh —4N 113
Somerset Ct. Knot —8E 104
Somerset Rd. Hud —5A 132
Somerset Rd. Pud —6B 60
Somers Pl. Leeds —6D 62 (off Somers St.)
Somers St. Leeds —6D 62
Somerton Dri. B'frd —3H 77
Somerville Av. B'frd —6N 75
Somerville Av. Leeds —4A 64
Somerville Dri. Leeds —4A 64
Somerville Grn. Leeds —4A 64
Somerville Gro. Leeds —3A 64
Somerville Mt. Leeds —4A 64
Somerville Pk. B'frd —6N 75
Somerville Ter. Otley —9M 11
Somerville Vw. Leeds —4A 64
Sonning Rd. All —6G 56
Soothill La. Bat —8G 97
Sorbus Way. Lep —7J 133
Sorrell Clo. Pon —4K 123
Sorrin Clo. Idle —8E 40
Sotheron Cft. D'ton —6B 124
Soureby Cross Way. E Bier —6K 77 (in two parts)
Sourhall Cotts. Todm —6F 86
Sourhall Rd. Todm —8E 86
S. Accommodation Rd. Leeds —9F 62
Southampton St. B'frd —5D 58
South App. Aber —5F 48
South App. B'ham —7N 31
South Av. C'frd —5N 101
South Av. Cow —7E 130
South Av. Far —9N 113
South Av. Horb —1E 136
South Av. Pon —4H 123
South Av. S Elm —7L 157
S. Baileygate. Pon —2L 123
South Bank. E Kes —2D 30
South Bank. Q'bry —4E 74
S. Bank Rd. Bat —6D 96
South Bolton. Hal —6K 73
Southbrook Ter. B'frd —8B 58
Southcliffe. S'wram —7D 92 (off Bank Top)
South Cliffe. T'tn —8D 56
Southcliffe Dri. Bail —6N 39
Southcliffe Way. Bail —6A 40
South Clo. Guis —8F 24
South Clo. Roys —7D 154
S. Clough Head. Hal —5G 91
Southcote Pl. Idle —7F 40
South Cres. S Elm —5A 158
South Cft. Shaf —6K 155
South Cft. Up Den —5C 166
S. Croft Av. B'shaw —7L 77
S. Croft Dri. B'shaw —6L 77
S. Croft Ga. B'shaw —7L 77
South Crosland. —3G 146
S. Cross Rd. Hud —9L 113
Southdale Gdns. Oss —6A 118
Southdale Rd. Oss —6A 118
Southdene. Hud —5C 132
Southdown Clo. B'frd —4K 57
Southdown Ct. B'frd —4K 57 (off Southdown Clo.)
Southdown Rd. Bail —6N 39
South Dri. Fars —3A 60
South Dri. Guis —8F 24
South Dri. Roys —7D 154
South Dri. Wake —1M 137
South Edge. Kei —8G 20
South Edge. Shipl —8K 39
Southedge Clo. Hip —5H 93
Southedge Ter. Hal —5J 93
South Elmsall. —6N 157
S. End Av. Leeds —5H 61
S. End Ct. Leeds —4H 61
S. End Gro. Leeds —5H 61
S. End Mt. Leeds —5H 61
S. End Ter. Leeds —5H 61
Southern Rd. Hud —7F 130
S. Farm Cres. Leeds —4L 63
S. Farm Rd. Leeds —4L 63
Southfield. B'hpe —6J 27
Southfield. Hept —9G 70
Southfield Av. B'frd —5A 76
Southfield Av. F'stne —7B 122 (in two parts)
Southfield Av. Leeds —5G 44
Southfield Av. Riddl —6M 21
Southfield Clo. Horb —1D 136
Southfield Clo. Wren —2G 119
Southfield Cotts. Barn —8D 154
Southfield Ct. Kbtn —2K 149
Southfield Dri. Leeds —5G 44
Southfield Dri. Riddl —6N 21
Southfield Fold. Horb —2D 136
Southfield La. Add —2L 7
Southfield La. B'frd —1M 75
Southfield La. Horb —1C 136 (in two parts)
Southfield Mt. A'ley —7M 61
Southfield Mt. Leeds —4G 80 (off S. View Rd.)
Southfield Mt. Riddl —6M 21
Southfield Rd. Add —1M 7
Southfield Rd. Bgly —6F 38
Southfield Rd. B'frd —2A 76
Southfield Rd. Bur W —8C 10
Southfield Rd. Hud —7D 132
Southfield Rd. Knot —9E 104
Southfield Rd. Nort —7M 143
Southfield Rd. Shar C —8J 121
Southfield Sq. B'frd —5A 58
Southfield St. Leeds —7M 61
Southfields Vw. Neth —5N 135
Southfield Ter. Add —1M 7
Southfield Ter. B'shaw —7L 77
Southfield Ter. Hal —3H 93
Southfield Way. Riddl —6N 21
Southgate. B'frd —7C 58
Southgate. Ell —4E 112
Southgate. Guis —9F 24
Southgate. Hal —5B 92
Southgate. Holy G —8B 112
Southgate. Hon —5L 147
Southgate. Hud —4N 131
Southgate. Oult —7D 82
Southgate. Pon —3K 123
South Ga. S Hien —3M 155
Southgate. Wake —5L 119
South Gro. Brigh —7K 93
South Gro. Shipl —8J 39
S. Hawksworth St. I'ly —5G 8
South Hiendley. —3L 155
S. Hill Clo. Leeds —6H 81
S. Hill Cft. Leeds —6H 81
S. Hill Dri. Bgly —5H 39
S. Hill Gdns. Leeds —6H 81
S. Hill Gro. Leeds —6H 81
S. Hill Ri. Leeds —6H 81
S. Hill Way. Leeds —6H 81
S. Holme La. Brigh —8K 93
South Kirkby. —6J 157
Southlands. Bail —6N 39
Southlands. Hal —4M 73
Southlands. H'fth —6E 42
Southlands. Khtn —1F 132
Southlands Av. Bgly —6F 38
Southlands Av. Leeds —7E 44
Southlands Av. Rawd —5A 42
Southlands Av. Riddl —7N 21
Southlands Av. T'tn —8H 57
Southlands Clo. Bads —8L 141
Southlands Clo. Leeds —6E 44
Southlands Cres. Leeds —7E 44
Southlands Dri. Hud —8M 113
Southlands Dri. Leeds —7E 44
Southlands Dri. Riddl —7N 21
Southlands Gro. Bgly —6E 38
Southlands Gro. Riddl —7N 21
Southlands Gro. T'tn —8G 57
Southlands Gro. W. Riddl —6N 21
Southlands Mt. Riddl —7N 21
Southlands Rd. Riddl —6N 21
South La. B'ley —7E 112
South La. Caw —8K 167
South La. H'frth —3M 163
South La. Neth —7N 135
South La. She —6G 75
South La. Gdns. Ell —6E 112
Southlea. Oaken —8E 76
Southlea Av. Oakw —5E 36
South Lee. H'fth —6E 42
S. Leeds Bus. Cen. Leeds —1E 80
South Leeds Stadium. —5E 80
Southleigh Av. Leeds —5C 80
Southleigh Cres. Leeds —5C 80
Southleigh Cft. Leeds —5D 80
Southleigh Dri. Leeds —5C 80
Southleigh Gdns. Leeds —5C 80
Southleigh Gth. Leeds —5D 80
Southleigh Grange. Leeds —5D 80
Southleigh Gro. Leeds —5C 80
Southleigh Rd. Leeds —5C 80
Southleigh Vw. Leeds —5C 80
S. Mead. B'hpe —6J 27
Southmere Av. B'frd —2M 75
Southmere Cres. B'frd —2M 75
Southmere Dri. B'frd —2L 75 (in two parts)
Southmere Gro. B'frd —2M 75
Southmere Oval. B'frd —3L 75
Southmere Rd. B'frd —2M 75
Southmere Ter. B'frd —2M 75
Southmoor La. Knot —1H 125
Southmoor Rd. Hems —7D 156
South Mt. E Kes —2C 30
S. Nelson St. Morl —8K 79
Southolme Clo. Leeds —9J 43
South Ossett. —7A 118
Southowram. —8F 92
Southowram Bank. Hal —5C 92
South Pde. B'frd —5B 58
South Pde. Cleck —4G 94
South Pde. Ell —6E 112
South Pde. Hal —6C 92
South Pde. Head —1N 61
South Pde. I'ly —5F 8
South Pde. Leeds —6D 62
South Pde. Morl —9L 79
South Pde. Oss —7C 118
South Pde. Otley —1M 25 (off Albion St.)
South Pde. Pud —8A 60
South Pde. Slnd —8M 111
South Pde. Wake —5L 119
S. Parade Clo. Pud —8B 60
S. Park Ter. Pud —1C 78
S. Parkway. Leeds —3N 63 (in three parts)
S. Park Way. Wake B —8H 99
S. Parkway App. Leeds —3N 63
South Pl. Morl —9L 79 (off South St.)
S. Queen St. Morl —1L 97
S. Ridge. Kip —4A 84
South Rd. B'frd —2A 58
South Rd. Cull —1K 55
South Row. H'fth —6F 42
S. Royd Av. Hal —8B 92
Southroyd Pde. Pud —9B 60 (off Fartown)
Southroyd Pk. Pud —9B 60 (in two parts)
Southroyd Ri. Pud —9B 60
South Selby. Hal —7K 73
South Sq. T'tn —8C 56
South St. B'frd —2A 76
South St. Brigh —9M 93
South St. Brun I —6A 92
South St. Denh —6K 55
South St. Dew —3F 116
South St. E Mor —8C 22
South St. H'cft —9L 139
South St. Hems —3E 156
South St. H'frth —2A 164
South St. Holy G —7A 112
South St. Kei —3H 37
South St. Liv —8M 95
South St. Mir —8K 115
South St. Morl —9L 79
South St. Neth —3J 147
South St. Nor —4H 121
South St. Oaken —9E 76
South St. Oss —7N 117
South St. Pad —5J 131
South St. Rawd —3M 41
South St. Sav T —5F 116
South St. T'tn —7C 56
South St. Wake —6M 119
South Ter. Dew —5J 117
South Ter. N'wram —1F 92
South Ter. Oss —8A 118
South Vw. Birs —3C 96
South Vw. B'frd —7K 75
South Vw. C'frd —7E 102
South Vw. Crig —6F 136
South Vw. Dew —5G 116
South Vw. Far —5N 59
South Vw. F'stne —5D 122
South Vw. Friz —2A 58
South Vw. Fry —2J 103
South Vw. Gol —5A 130
South Vw. Gre —8H 41
South Vw. Guis —7J 25
South Vw. Hal —8D 92
South Vw. Haw —8C 36
South Vw. H'fth —8F 42
South Vw. Hud —5J 131
South Vw. Leeds —4D 64 (off Selby Rd.)
South Vw. L'ft —8N 73 (off Blackmires)
South Vw. Men —5E 24
South Vw. Morl —6L 79
South Vw. N Mill —5D 164
South Vw. Pud —7C 60
South Vw. Q'bry —3B 74
South Vw. Rothw —7N 81
South Vw. Sandb —7A 22
South Vw. Schol —5D 94
South Vw. S'wram —8F 92
South Vw. Ting —7N 97
South Vw. Weth —1M 17
South Vw. Wilsd —1B 56
South Vw. Yead —9K 25
S. View Clo. B'frd —6J 77
S. View Clo. Yead —9K 25
S. View Cres. Yead —9K 25
S. View Dri. B'frd —6K 77
S. View Gdns. Pon —3M 123
S. View Gro. Gom —5M 95
S. View Rd. B'frd —6K 77
S. View Rd. Yead —9M 25
S. View St. Todm —3E 86
S. View Ter. Bail —4A 40
S. View Ter. Dew —1E 116 (off Tate Naylor St.)
S. View Ter. Grng M —6B 134
S. View Ter. Hal —4M 91 (off Queen's Rd.)
S. View Ter. Otley —1M 25 (off Bermondsey St.)
S. View Ter. Sils —8D 6
S. View Ter. Yead —1N 41
Southwaite Clo. Leeds —2A 64
Southwaite Gth. Leeds —2A 64
Southwaite La. Leeds —2A 64
Southwaite Lawn. Leeds —2A 64
Southwaite Pl. Leeds —2A 64
South Wlk. H'den —6N 37
Southway. Bgly —2G 39
South Way. B'frd —6J 77
Southway. Bur W —6A 10
Southway. Guis —8E 24
Southway. H'fth —4D 42
Southway. Hud —1H 131
Southway. I'ly —6J 9
Southway. Mir —4K 115
South Way. Shipl —8J 39
Southwell Av. Hud —3G 130
Southwell La. Horb —1C 136
Southwood Av. Hon —4N 147
Southwood Clo. Leeds —2D 64
Southwood Cres. Leeds —2D 64
Southwood Ga. Leeds —2D 64
Southwood Rd. Leeds —2D 64

Sovereign Clo. Birs —3C 96
Sovereign Gdns. Nor —1H 121
Sovereign St. Hal —5A 92
Sovereign St. Leeds —7E 62
Sovereign's Way. Dew —8E 116
Sowden Bldgs. B'frd —4F 58
Sowden Grange. T'tn —8C 56
Sowden La. Nor G —1L 93
(in two parts)
Sowden La. Wyke —1M 93
Sowden Rd. B'frd —3J 57
Sowden St. B'frd —2N 75
Sowden's Yd. Leeds —9N 43
(off Moor Rd.)
Sowerby. —9E 90
Sowerby Bridge. —9H 91
Sowerby Cft. La. Sower B —9H 91
Sowerby La. L'ft —5B 90
Sowerby New Rd. Sower B —9E 90
Sowerby St. Sower B —9H 91
Sowgate La. Pon & F'bri —1N 123
Sowood. —1N 129
Sowood Av. Oss —8A 118
Sowood Gdns. Oss —8B 118
Sowood Green. —9M 111
Sowood Hill. —1N 129
Sowood La. Grng M & Bstfld —5C 134
Sowood La. Oss —8B 118
Sowood St. Leeds —4M 61
Sowood Vw. Oss —7B 118
Soyland Town. —5D 110
Soyland Town Rd. Sower B —5D 110
Spa Bottom. Fen B —6G 132
Spa Cft. Rd. Oss —7C 118
Spa Fields. Slai —9N 129
Spa Fields Ind. Est. Slai —9A 130
Spa Fold. Stan —8A 100
Spa Grn. La. Sower B —8B 110
Spa Gro. Wake —8G 118
Spa Hill. Bat —7F 96
Spa Ind. Est. Leeds —2E 62
Spaines Rd. Hud —1M 131
Spa La. Bgly —2F 38
Spa La. B Spa —1E 32
Spa La. Oss —7C 118
Spa La. Slai —9A 130
Spalding Towers. Leeds —5G 63
(off Lindsey Gdns.)
Spa M. B Spa —1E 32
Spanfield La. Hal —9F 72
Sparable La. Bgly —4H 39
Sparable La. Wake —8N 119
Sparkfields. M'well —9K 153
Spark Ho. La. Sower B —9J 91
Spark La. B Grn & Map —9J 153
Sparks Rd. Hud —3G 130
Spark St. Hud —4E 130
Spartal La. Leds —5E 84
Spartan Rd. Low M —8B 76
Sparth La. H'frth —4G 162
Spa St. Bat —7F 96
Spa St. Oss —7D 118
Spa Ter. Fen B —5G 132
Spa Ter. Hud —7L 131
Spawd Bone La. Knot —9D 104
Spa Well Gro. Brier —6A 156
Speak Clo. Wake —3A 120
Speakers Ct. Dew —3E 116
Spear Fir. Bard —6B 30
Spearhead Way. Kei —8J 21
Speedwell Mt. Leeds —3D 62
Speedwell Rd. W'wood —7N 101
Speedwell St. Hud —5J 131
Speedwell St. Leeds —3D 62
Speeton Av. B'frd —3K 75
Speeton Gro. B'frd —3J 75
Spen App. Leeds —8J 43
Spen Bank. Cleck —5K 95
Spen Bank. Leeds —8J 43
Spence La. Leeds —8B 62
Spenceley St. Leeds —3C 62
(in two parts)
Spencer Av. B'frd —9M 57
Spencer Av. Morl —2K 97
Spencer Av. Sils —7E 6
Spencer La. Err —3H 89
Spencer Mt. Leeds —3G 63
Spencer Pl. Leeds —3G 63
Spencer Rd. B'frd —1L 75
(in two parts)
Spencer St. Kei —9G 21
(in three parts)
Spencer St. Mir —8L 115
Spencer St. Skelm —7D 150
Spencer Ter. Hud —8B 114
Spen Clo. B'frd —6F 76
Spen Comn. La. Tad —1E 48
Spen Cres. Leeds —8J 43
Spen Dri. Leeds —7K 43
Spenfield Ct. Liv —1L 115
Spen Gdns. Leeds —7L 43
Spen Grn. Leeds —8J 43
Spen La. Gom —4K 95
Spen La. Leeds —6K 43
(in two parts)
Spen Lawn. Leeds —8J 43
Spen Lower. —4K 95
Spen M. Leeds —8K 43
Spennithorne Av. Leeds —5K 43
Spennithorne Dri. Leeds —6K 43
Spennithorn Rd. Skel —7L 159
Spen Rd. Leeds —7K 43
Spenser Ri. Guis —8K 25
Spenser Rd. Guis —8K 25
Spenslea Gro. Morl —2K 97
Spen Va. St. Heck —9A 96
Spen Valley Ind. Pk. Rawf —6K 95
Spen Valley Rd. Dew —5B 116
Spen Vw. Dew M —3C 116
Spen Vw. La. B'frd —6F 76
Spen Wlk. Leeds —8J 43
Spibey Cres. Rothw —6M 81
Spibey La. Rothw —6M 81
Spicer Ho. La. Pen —8L 165
Spicer St. B'frd —2A 76
Spiers Gth. B'frd —4B 76
Spindles, The. Leeds —5F 80
Spindle St. Hal —8N 73
Spiners Way. Schol —4D 94
(off Scholes La.)
Spinkfield Rd. Hud —2L 131
Spink La. Pon —2K 123
Spink Pl. B'frd —6B 58
Spinks Gdns. Leeds —2C 64
Spink St. B'frd —6B 58
Spinkwell Clo. B'frd —5D 58
Spink Well La. Wake —3B 98
Spinkwell Rd. Dew —2F 116
Spinners Chase. Pud —7B 60
Spinners, The. Haw —9C 36
Spinneyfield. Hud —8M 113
Spinneyfield Ct. Leeds —7G 63
Spinney, The. Brigh —7M 93
Spinney, The. Drau —5D 4
Spinney, The. E Mor —8C 22
Spinney, The. H'fth —6G 43
Spinney, The. Leeds —7G 63
Spinney, The. Rawd —5L 41
Spinney, The. Wake —3N 137
Spinney, The. Weth —3L 17
Spinning Mill Ct. Shipl —6K 39
Spion Kop. T'ner —2G 47
Spire Ct. Hud —2K 131
(off Ellerslie Clo.)
Spire Ct. Mar —3K 131
Spire Heights. Bgly —4J 39
Spitalgate La. Pon —4A 124
Spittal Hardwick La. C'frd & Pon —6J 103
Spittlerush La. Nort —6M 143
Spofforth Hill. Weth —3K 17
Spofforth Wlk. Gar —7B 66
Spout Fold Wake —5F 118
Spout Hill. Brigh —5K 113
Spout Ho. La. Brigh —6K 93
Spring Av. Gild —6F 78
Spring Av. Kei —1L 37
Spring Bank. —3J 37
Spring Bank. Cull —1J 55
Springbank. Gar —9K 65
Spring Bank. Kirks —2K 61
Spring Bank. Liv —1N 115
Spring Bank. Pon —4K 123
Springbank Av. Fars —3B 60
Springbank Av. Gild —6F 78
Springbank Clo. Barn —9D 154
Springbank Clo. Fars —3A 60
Springbank Cres. Gar —8K 65
Springbank Cres. Gild —5F 78
Springbank Cres. Hud —1B 132
Spring Bank Cres. Leeds —2A 62
Spring Bank Cft. H'frth —4J 163
Springbank Dri. Fars —3B 60
Spring Bank Dri. Liv —1M 115
Springbank Gro. Fars —3B 60
Springbank M. Loft —5H 99
Spring Bank Pl. B'frd —5B 58
Springbank Ri. Fars —3B 60
Spring Bank Ri. Kei —3J 37
Springbank Rd. Fars —3A 60
Springbank Rd. Gild —5F 78
Springbank Rd. Hud —1B 132
Spring Bank Ter. Guis —7J 25
Spring Bottom. Todm —4H 107
Springcliffe. B'frd —5N 57
Springcliffe St. B'frd —5N 57
Spring Clo. Bgly —5G 39
Spring Clo. Gar —8B 66
(nr. Fairburn Dri.)
Spring Clo. Gar —6A 66
(nr. Newhold)
Spring Clo. Kei —1L 37
Spring Clo. Av. Leeds —8H 63
Spring Clo. Gdns. Leeds —8H 63
Spring Clo. St. Leeds —8G 63
Spring Clo. Wlk. Leeds —8H 63
Spring Ct. All —3F 56
Spring Dale. Hon —4L 147
Springdale Av. Hud —6L 131
Springdale Cres. B'frd —8G 41
Springdale St. Hud —6L 131
Spring Dri. Kei —1L 37
Spring Edge. Hal —8N 91
Spring Edge N. Hal —7N 91
Spring Edge W. Hal —7M 91
Spring End. —9D 118
Spring End Rd. Horb —8D 118
Spring Farm La. H'den —6N 37
Spring Farm M. Wilsd —1B 56
Springfield. —2F 116
(nr. Batley)
Springfield. —9F 40
(nr. Idle)
Springfield. B Spa —9D 18
Springfield. Cliff —3D 32
Springfield. Outl —2A 130
Springfield. Q'bry —4C 74
Springfield. Sower B —9G 91
Springfield Av. Bat —7E 96
Springfield Av. B'frd —9L 57
Springfield Av. Clay W —7H 151
Springfield Av. Hems —3E 156
Springfield Av. Hon —6L 147
Springfield Av. I'ly —5H 9
Springfield Av. Knot —8G 104
Springfield Av. Morl —7J 79
Springfield Av. Pon —2M 123
Springfield Av. Slai —2L 145
Springfield Clo. Clay W —7H 151
Springfield Clo. H'fth —6H 43
Springfield Commercial Cen. Far —2B 60
Springfield Ct. Kei —8G 20
Springfield Ct. Yead —8L 25
Springfield Cres. K S'ton —5K 143
Springfield Cres. Morl —7K 79
Springfield Dri. Birds —4L 165
Springfield Dri. Liv —7G 94
Springfield Gdns. H'fth —6G 43
Springfield Gdns. Kei —8G 21
Springfield Gdns. Pud —8C 60
Springfield Grange. Wake —5F 118
Springfield Grn. Leeds —3G 81
Springfield Gro. Bgly —3E 38
Springfield Gro. Brigh —8M 93
Springfield La. B'frd —3C 78
Springfield La. Kbtn —3J 149
Springfield La. Liv —8J 95
Springfield La. Morl —7K 79
Springfield Mills. Kbtn —2H 149
Springfield Mt. Add —9M 5
Springfield Mt. A'ley —6K 61
Springfield Mt. H'fth —6G 42
Springfield Mt. Leeds —5C 62
Springfield Mt. S Elm —8L 157
Springfield Pk. Mir —6M 115
Springfield Pl. B'frd —6B 58
Springfield Pl. Gar —8K 65
Springfield Pl. Guis —7J 25
Springfield Pl. H'let —3J 81
Springfield Pl. Idle —9F 40
Springfield Pl. Leeds —3G 81
Springfield Pl. Otley —1K 25
Springfield Ri. H'fth —6G 43
Springfield Ri. Rothw —9A 82
Springfield Rd. Bail —3N 39
Springfield Rd. Ell —4G 112
Springfield Rd. Guis —8J 25
Springfield Rd. Kei —8G 20
Springfield Rd. Morl —7J 79
Springfields. —8G 104
Springfields. C'frd —4E 102
Springfields. Knot —8G 104
Springfield St. B'frd —6A 58
Springfield St. Rothw —9A 82
Springfield St. T'tn —8D 56
Springfield Ter. B'frd —6A 58
Springfield Ter. Cull —1L 55
Springfield Ter. Dew —2F 116
Springfield Ter. Eml —2D 150
Springfield Ter. Guis —8J 25
Spring Fld. Ter. Hal —4H 93
Springfield Ter. Leeds —3J 45
Springfield Ter. L'ft —3C 90
Springfield Ter. Schol —3D 94
Springfield Ter. S'ley —5A 60
Springfield Vw. Ack —3A 122
Springfield Vs. Gild —5E 78
Springfield Wlk. H'fth —6G 43
Spring Gardens. —7C 78
Spring Gdns. Bat —7E 96
Spring Gdns. B'frd —6C 58
Spring Gdns. Bur W —8D 10
Spring Gdns. Dlgtn —7C 78
Spring Gdns. Earl —4H 117
Spring Gdns. Hal —1L 91
Spring Gdns. Hare —1J 29
Spring Gdns. H'frth —3K 163
Spring Gdns. Morl —6J 79
Spring Gdns. Nor G —2L 93
Spring Gdns. La. Kei —6G 20
Spring Gdns. Mt. Kei —7H 21
Spring Gdns. Rd. B'frd —3M 57
Spring Garden St. Q'bry —4D 74
Spring Gro. Hal —5L 91
Spring Gro. H Bri —9H 71
Spring Gro. Leeds —4A 62
Spring Gro. Av. Leeds —4A 62
Spring Gro. St. Hud —5M 131
Spring Gro. Vw. Leeds —4A 62
Spring Gro. Wlk. Leeds —4A 62
Spring Hall Clo. Hal —8G 74
Spring Hall Ct. Hal —4L 91
Spring Hall Dri. Hal —6L 91
Spring Hall Gdns. Hal —5L 91
Spring Hall Gro. Hal —5L 91
Spring Hall La. Hal —6L 91
Spring Hall Pl. Hal —5L 91
Spring Head. She —8H 75
Spring Head La. Mars —5F 144
Spring Head Rd. Haw —7B 36
Springhead Rd. Rothw —7B 82
Spring Head Rd. T'tn —8D 56
Spring Hill. —1G 139
Spring Hill. Bail —4L 39
Spring Hill. Leeds —3A 44
Spring Hill. Shipl —8C 40
Springhill Av. Croft —1H 139
Springhill Clo. Out —7J 99
Spring Hill Cotts. Leeds —9A 44
(off Monk Bri. Ter.)
Springhill Dri. Croft —1H 139
Springhill Gro. Croft —1H 139
Springhill Mt. Croft —2H 139
Springhills. Out —7J 99
Spring Hill Ter. Leeds —9A 44
(off Monk Bri. Rd.)
Spring Holes La. T'tn —7B 56
Springhurst Rd. Shipl —8M 39
Spring La. Barn —9D 154
Spring La. Bat —5E 96
Spring La. Bgly —1J 39
Spring La. G'lnd —4N 111
Spring La. Holmb —6J 163
Spring La. H'frth —4K 163
Spring La. Kear —4C 18
Spring La. New C —3J 139
Spring La. N Mill —3C 164
Spring La. Pan —5H 15
Spring La. Wool —5L 153
Springlodge Pl. B'frd —5B 58
Springmead Dri. Gar —8N 65
Spring Mill La. Oss —5B 118
Spring Mill St. B'frd —9C 58
Spring Pk. Rd. Wilsd —9B 38
Spring Pl. B'frd —9A 58
Spring Pl. Kei —2L 37
Spring Ri. Drau —5D 4
Spring Ri. Kei —1L 37
Spring Rd. Leeds —2A 62
Spring Rock. Holy G —7B 112
Spring Row. Hal —6J 73
Spring Row. H'den —6A 38
Spring Row. Kei —1H 37
Spring Row. Oxe —5E 54
Spring Row. Q'bry —4C 74
Springroyd Ter. B'frd —6L 57
Spring Side. W'wth —7A 106
Spring Side Ri. Gol —5C 130
Springs La. I'ly —5H 9
Springs La. Wltn —2F 18
Springs Rd. H'frth —5A 162
Springs Rd. Yead —1J 41
Springs, The. Wake —5L 119
Springstone Av. Hems —2E 156
Springstone Av. Oss —4N 117
Spring St. Brigh —1M 113
Spring St. Cro R —7F 36
(off Bingley Rd.)
Spring St. Dew —2F 116
Spring St. Hud —4M 131
Spring St. Idle —8F 40
Spring St. Kei —8J 21
Spring St. Liv —8M 95
Spring St. Mars —6F 144
Spring St. Ripp —7D 110
Spring St. Slai —1M 145
Spring St. Todm —3E 86
Springswood Av. Shipl —8M 39
Springswood Pl. Shipl —8M 39
Springswood Rd. Shipl —8M 39
Spring Ter. Holy G —9L 111
Spring Ter. Kei —1L 37
Spring Ter. N Bnk —4C 92
Spring Ter. S Elm —7M 157
Spring Ter. Sower B —1J 111
Springvale Clo. Shar C —8J 121
Springvale Ri. Hems —1D 156
Springvale Rd. S Kirk —6J 157
Spring Valley. S'ley —5B 60
Spring Valley Av. Leeds —5F 60
Spring Valley Clo. Leeds —5F 60
Spring Valley Clo. Liv —7L 95
(off Spring Valley St.)
Spring Valley Ct. Leeds —5F 60
Spring Valley Cres. Leeds —5F 60
Spring Valley Cft. Leeds —5F 60
Spring Valley Dri. Leeds —5F 60
Spring Valley Sq. Liv —7L 95
(off Spring Valley St.)
Spring Valley St. Liv —7L 95
Spring Valley Vw. Leeds —5F 60
Spring Valley Wlk. Leeds —5F 60
Spring Vw. Gild —5G 78
Spring Vw. L'ft —6D 90
Spring Vw. Oss —5B 118
Spring Vw. Rd. Hal —6D 90
Spring Vs. Corn —3D 86
Springville Gdns. Upt —2A 158
Springville Ter. B'frd —8F 40
Spring Way. Kei —1L 37
Springwell Av. Swil —4H 83
Springwell Clo. Yead —1N 41
Springwell Ct. Leeds —8B 62
Springwell Ct. Ting —3A 98
Springwell Dri. B'frd —1C 76
Springwell Rd. Leeds —8B 62
Springwell Rd. Oss —6A 118
Springwell Rd. Swil —4H 83
Springwell St. Leeds —8B 62
Springwell Ter. Yead —1N 41
Springwell Vw. Birs —3C 96
Springwell Vw. Leeds —8C 62
Springwood Av. B'frd —2D 76
Spring Wood Av. Hal —1A 112
Springwood Av. Hud —5L 131
Springwood Ct. Leeds —9K 45
(off Bk. Wetherby Rd.)
Spring Wood Dri. Hal —1A 112
Springwood Footpath. Hud —5L 13
Spring Wood Gdns. B'frd —3D 76
Spring Wood Gdns. Hal —2A 112
Springwood Gdns. Leeds —9K 45
Springwood Gro. Leeds —9L 45
Springwood Hall Clo. Hud —5K 13
Springwood Hall Gdns. Hud —4L 13
Springwood Pl. B'frd —4C 58
(off Bolton Rd.)
Springwood Rd. H'frth —9A 148
Springwood Rd. Leeds —9K 45
Springwood Rd. Rawd —4L 41
Springwood St. Hud —5M 131
Springwood Ter. B'frd —4C 58
(off King's Rd.)
Spruce Av. Roys —6C 154
Spruce Dri. Neth —3J 147
Spruce Dri. M. Neth —3J 147
Spruce St. Kei —8K 21
Spruce Wlk. Todm —3J 107
Sprutts La. Pec W —6J 71
Spur Dri. Leeds —3F 64
Spurr Gro. W'ton —4C 138
Spurrier's Av. Knot —9B 104
Spurr St. Bat —8G 97
Square Fld. H'frth —4M 163
Square Rd. Todm —3J 107
Square St. B'frd —9E 58
Square, The. Bat —6C 96
Square, The. B Spa —1E 32
Square, The. B'frd —7H 57
Square, The. C'frd —5J 103
Square, The. Hal —7D 92
Square, The. Hare —1J 29
Square, The. Kip —4A 84
Square, The. Knot —6B 104
Square, The. N'wram —1F 92
Square, The. Shepl —9J 149
Square Vw. Todm —3K 107
Squire Grn. B'frd —5L 57
Squire La. B'frd —5L 57
Squirrel Clo. Dew —1D 116
Squirrel Ditch. Hud —7A 132
Squirrel End. Dew —1C 116
Squirrel Hall Dri. Dew —9C 96
Squirrel La. T'tn —9A 56
Squirrels Drey. Dur —3H 137
Squirrel Wlk. Dew —9D 96
Stable Fold. Wyke —2B 94
Stable La. Hal —3A 92
Stablers Wlk. Altft —8H 101
Stables La. B Spa —1E 32
Stables, The. W'ton —3B 138
Stackhills Rd. Todm —7L 87
Stacks La. Cra V —7M 89
Stadium Rd. B'frd —5B 76
Stadium Way. Hud —3A 132
Stadium Way. Leeds —2A 80
Stadium Way. S Elm —4A 158
Stafford Av. Hal —8B 92
Stafford Hill. —2G 132
Stafford Hill La. Hud —2G 132
Stafford Pde. Hal —9B 92
Stafford Pl. Hal —8B 92

Stafford Rd. Hal —9B 92
Stafford Sq. Hal —9C 92
Stafford St. B'frd —1F 76
Stafford St. C'frd —4C 102
Stafford St. Leeds —1G 80
Stafford St. Morl —2J 97
Stafford Ter. Wake —5H 119
Stainbeck Av. Leeds —9B 44
Stainbeck Gdns. B'frd —5J 75
Stainbeck Gdns. Leeds —9D 44
Stainbeck La. Leeds —8C 44
Stainbeck Rd. Leeds —9B 44
Stainbeck Wlk. Leeds —9D 44
Stainburn. —4G 13
Stainburn Av. C'frd —7G 102
Stainburn Cres. Leeds —6F 44
Stainburn Dri. Leeds —6F 44
Stainburn Pde. Leeds —6F 44
Stainburn Rd. Leeds —7F 44
Stainburn Ter. Leeds —7F 44
Staincliffe. —8E 96
Staincliffe Clo. Dew —3D 116
Staincliffe Ct. Sils —8D 6
Staincliffe Cres. Dew —1C 116
Staincliffe Hall Rd. Bat —9C 96
Staincliffe Rd. Dew —9C 96
Staincross. —7K 153
Staincross Comn. M'well —6K 153
Stainecross Av. Hud —8H 131
Staines Cft. Hud —4C 132
Stainland. —8M 111
Stainland Dean. Holy G —2J 129
Stainland Rd. Bklnd —7G 110
Stainland Rd. G'lnd —2C 112
Stainland Rd. Outl —2N 129
(in two parts)
Stainland Rd. Slnd —8M 111
(in two parts)
Stainmore Clo. Leeds —3B 64
Stainmore Pl. Leeds —3B 64
Stainton Clo. B'frd —5K 75
Stainton La. Carl —9M 81
Staircase La. Pool W & B'hpe —2G 27
Stairfoot Clo. Leeds —2N 43
Stair Foot La. Leeds —2N 43
Stairfoot Vw. Leeds —2N 43
Stairfoot Wlk. Leeds —2N 43
Stairs La. Oxe —6K 53
Staithe Av. Leeds —8F 80
Staithe Clo. Leeds —8F 80
Staithe Gdns. Leeds —8F 80
Staithgate La. B'frd —4D 76
Stake La. Cra V —5N 89
Stake La. Bank. H'frth —3N 163
Stakes Fold. Heck —8B 96
Stallabrass St. B'frd —6A 58
Stalley Royd La. H'frth —4D 164
Stamford Av. C'frd —6A 102
Stamford St. B'frd —9F 58
Stamford Way. M'well —7K 153
Stammergate La. Lntn —8J 17
Stamp Hill Clo. Add —1K 7
Stanacre Pl. B'frd —6D 58
Stanage La. Hal —6H 75
Stanally St. Todm —4G 87
Stanbury. —8L 35
Stancliffe Way. Hud —1F 132
Standale Av. Pud —6A 60
Standale Cres. Pud —6A 60
Standale Ho. B'frd —3G 77
(off Prince St.)
Standale Ri. Pud —6A 60
Standard Dri. Hud —8G 130
Standard Ind. Est. B'frd —3G 59
Standard Vs. Leeds —1L 79
Stand Bridge. —4L 137
Standbridge Clo. Wake —5J 137
Standbridge Garth. Crig —5H 137
Standbridge La. Crig & Wake —5H 137
Standhill Cres. Barn —9N 153
Standiforth La. Hud —3C 132
Standiforth Pl. Hud —4D 132
Standiforth Rd. Hud —4B 132
Standish Cres. S Kirk —5J 157
Stanhall Av. S'ley —5A 60
Stanhope Av. H'fth —5F 42
Stanhope Clo. H'fth —5F 42
Stanhope Dri. H'fth —8E 42
Stanhope Gdns. Wake —3G 99
Stanhope Rd. Thpe —3G 98
Stanhope St. Scis —8G 151
Stank. —2E 28
Stanks. —1E 64
Stanks App. Leeds —2E 64
Stanks Av. Leeds —2E 64
Stanks Clo. Leeds —2F 64
Stanks Cross. Leeds —2F 64
Stanks Dri. Leeds —9D 46
Stanks Gdns. Leeds —1E 64
Stanks Gth. Leeds —2F 64
Stanks Grn. Leeds —2F 64
Stanks Gro. Leeds —2E 64
Stanks La. N. Leeds —9D 46
Stanks La. S. Leeds —2E 64
Stanks Pde. Leeds —2E 64
Stanks Ri. Leeds —2F 64
Stanks Rd. Leeds —2E 64
Stanks Way. Leeds —2E 64
Stanley. —8N 99
Stanley Av. Leeds —4H 63
Stanley Cotts. Nor —1H 121
Stanley Ct. Hal —5M 91
(off Queens Rd.)
Stanley Ct. Hud —3J 131
(off Luck La.)
Stanley Dri. Leeds —5K 45
Stanley Ferry. —9B 100
Stanley Gth. Heck —8B 96
Stanley Gro. Guis —8J 25
Stanley La. Holy G —8M 111
Stanley La. Liv —7L 95
Stanley La. Wake —8M 99
Stanley Pl. Bat —7G 96
Stanley Pl. Gol —6C 130
Stanley Pl. Leeds —4J 63
Stanley Rd. Ain T —8F 112
Stanley Rd. B'frd —2B 58
Stanley Rd. Hal —6M 91
Stanley Rd. Kei —3G 36
Stanley Rd. Leeds —3F 62
(LS7)
Stanley Rd. Leeds —4H 63
(LS9)
Stanley Rd. Lind —1H 131
Stanley Rd. Liv —1L 115
Stanley Rd. Slai —3K 145
Stanley Rd. Wake —5M 119
Stanley St. Bgly —4F 38
Stanley St. Brigh —9N 93
Stanley St. C'frd —4E 102
Stanley St. Cleck —4H 95
Stanley St. Cro R —7E 36
Stanley St. F'stne —4D 122
Stanley St. Gre —8H 41
Stanley St. Hud —7K 131
Stanley St. Idle —7F 40
Stanley St. Kei —8H 21
Stanley St. Shipl —1A 58
Stanley St. Sower B —8J 91
Stanley St. Wake —5M 119
Stanley St. N. Hal —8N 73
(off Shay La.)
Stanley Ter. A'ley —7M 61
Stanley Ter. Leeds —4J 63
(in two parts)
Stanley Vw. Leeds —7M 61
Stanmoor Dri. Stan —6N 99
Stanmore Av. Leeds —3M 61
Stanmore Cres. Leeds —3M 61
Stanmore Gro. Leeds —3M 61
Stanmore Hill. Leeds —3N 61
Stanmore Mt. Leeds —3M 61
Stanmore Pl. B'frd —9M 57
Stanmore Pl. Leeds —3M 61
Stanmore Rd. Leeds —3M 61
Stanmore St. Leeds —3M 61
Stanmore Ter. Leeds —3M 61
Stanmore Vw. Leeds —3M 61
Stannard Well Dri. Horb —9D 118
Stannard Well La. Horb —9D 118
Stannary Pl. Hal —4A 92
Stannery. Slnd —7N 111
Stannery End La. Cra V —5N 89
Stanningley. —4C 60
Stanningley Av. Hal —8H 73
Stanningley By-Pass. S'ley —5M 59
Stanningley Dri. Hal —8H 73
Stanningley Fld. Clo. Leeds —5D 60
Stanningley Gro. Heck —9A 96
Stanningley Ind. Est. S'ley —5A 60
Stanningley Rd. Hal —8H 73
Stanningley Rd. Leeds —5H 61
Stanningley Rd. S'ley —4C 60
Stansfield Clo. C'frd —3H 103
Stansfield Clo. Hal —5N 91
Stansfield Ct. Sower B —9H 91
Stansfield Dri. C'frd —4J 103
Stansfield Grange. Sower B —2E 110
Stansfield Hall Rd. Todm —6K 87
Stansfield Mill La. Sower B —2E 110
Stansfield Pl. B'frd —7F 40
Stansfield Rd. C'frd —3G 103
Stansfield Rd. Todm —7K 87
Stansfield St. Todm —6K 87
Stansfield Ter. Todm —3D 86
Stan Valley Clo. Lit S —4K 143
Stanwell Av. Hud —1J 131
Stanwell La. Hamp —8D 158
(in two parts)
Stanwick Ho. B'frd —2B 58
Staples La. Kei —8G 37
Stapleton. —7H 125
Stapleton Ho. B'frd —2B 58
Stapper Grn. Wilsd —9A 38
Starbeck Rd. Wake —3N 119
Starkie St. Kei —1H 37
Starling Ho. Hems —3D 156
(off Lilley St.)
Starling M. All —7G 56
(off Bell Dean Rd.)
Star St. B'frd —2A 76
Star Ter. Brigh —4K 113
Starting Post. Idle M —8D 40
Starwort Clo. Pon —4K 123
Stathers Cotts. Wyke —2B 94
Stathers Gdns. Fars —4A 60
Station App. Bur W —9C 10
Station App. Hal —6C 92
Station App. Hon —4N 147
Station App. Todm —7K 87
Station Av. Leeds —4E 60
Station Clo. Gar —7N 65
Station Cotts. Dart —8G 152
Station Cotts. Newt K —2J 33
Station Cotts. Nost —5L 139
Station Ct. B'frd —7D 58
Station Ct. Clay W —6J 151
Station Ct. Gar —7N 65
Station Ct. Leeds —5D 64
Station Cres. Leeds —7L 61
Station Fields. Gar —7N 65
Station Gdns. Weth —4L 17
Station La. Ber B —9L 131
Station La. B'shaw —7L 77
Station La. Coll —9J 17
Station La. F'stne —5C 122
Station La. Gol —7C 130
Station La. Heck —1N 115
Station La. Pon —3K 123
Station La. Shepl —8K 149
Station La. T'ner —1G 47
Station La. Thpe —3F 98
Station La. Ting —3A 98
Station La. W'ford —6E 82
Station Mt. Leeds —4E 60
Station Pde. Leeds —2L 61
Station Pde. Todm —3B 86
Station Pas. Wake —6M 119
Station Pl. Leeds —4F 60
Station Plaza. I'ly —5G 9
(off Station Rd.)
Station Rd. Ackw —3G 140
Station Rd. All B —9B 84
Station Rd. A'ley —7L 61
Station Rd. Bail —4A 40
Station Rd. Bat —8G 97
Station Rd. B'frd —4C 58
Station Rd. Bdly —6E 114
Station Rd. Brigh —1A 114
Station Rd. Bur W —9C 10
Station Rd. C'frd —4D 102
Station Rd. Chick —5J 117
(in two parts)
Station Rd. Cytn —1H 75
Station Rd. Cull —9J 37
Station Rd. Dart —8G 153
Station Rd. Denh —6K 55
Station Rd. Dew —6F 116
Station Rd. Dlgtn —8B 78
Station Rd. Esh —1F 40
Station Rd. Fen B —7G 133
Station Rd. F'bri —7B 104
Station Rd. Gar —7N 65
Station Rd. Gol —6C 130
Station Rd. Guis —7H 25
Station Rd. Hal —8N 73
Station Rd. Haw —8C 36
Station Rd. H Bri —2H 89
Station Rd. Heck —9A 96
Station Rd. Hems —2E 156
Station Rd. H'frth —3M 163
Station Rd. Holy G —7A 112
Station Rd. Hon —4M 147
Station Rd. H'fth —5F 42
Station Rd. I'ly —5G 8
Station Rd. Kip —5N 83
Station Rd. Leeds —4D 64
Station Rd. Low M —8C 76
Station Rd. L'ft —5D 90
Station Rd. Mars —5F 144
Station Rd. Men —4F 24
Station Rd. Meth —1J 101
Station Rd. Mir —7L 115
Station Rd. Morl —8L 79
Station Rd. Nor —9G 101
Station Rd. Nor G —2M 93
Station Rd. Oakw —5D 36
Station Rd. Oss —6N 117
(in two parts)
Station Rd. Otley —1L 25
Station Rd. Oxe —3C 54
Station Rd. Pool W —3J 27
Station Rd. Q'bry —4D 74
Station Rd. Roys —4C 154
Station Rd. Ryh —9H 139
Station Rd. Scholes —8G 46
Station Rd. Shepl —9J 149
Station Rd. Shipl —7N 39
Station Rd. Skelm —7D 150
Station Rd. Slai —9M 129
Station Rd. S Elm —6N 157
Station Rd. Sower B —9H 91
Station Rd. Steet —3D 20
Station Rd. Stkmr —7G 149
Station Rd. Todm —3E 86
Station Rd. Wilsd —3M 55
Station Rd. Wome —9N 125
Station St. Hud —4M 131
Station St. Mel —7C 146
Station St. Pud —8A 60
Station St. Wake —9N 119
Station Ter. All B —9C 84
Station Ter. Leeds —5F 60
Station Ter. Roys —5F 154
Station Vw. Leeds —5D 64
Station Vw. Oxe —3C 54
Station Vw. Steet —3D 20
Station Way. Leeds —7L 61
Staups La. Blkhd —1A 88
Staups La. Hal —2E 92
Staveley Ct. Bgly —3F 38
Staveley Dri. Shipl —8J 39
Staveley Gro. Kei —4G 36
Staveley M. Bgly —3F 38
Staveley Rd. Bgly —3F 38
Staveley Rd. B'frd —8N 57
Staveley Rd. Kei —4G 36
Staveley Rd. Shipl —7J 39
Staveley Way. Kei —3G 37
Staverton St. Hal —5L 91
Staybrite Av. Bgly —8F 38
Staygate. —3C 76
Staygate Grn. B'frd —4C 76
Staynton Cres. Hud —6D 114
(in two parts)
Stead. —8M 9
Stead Ga. Shel —7A 150
Stead Hill Way. Thack —6D 40
Stead La. Bgly —1J 39
Stead La. Hud —2F 132
Stead La. T'ner —2G 47
Steadman St. B'frd —8F 58
Steadman Ter. B'frd —8F 58
Stead Rd. B'frd —5J 77
Stead St. Hal —5A 92
Stead St. Shipl —7N 39
Steads Yd. H'fth —5F 42
Steanard La. Mir —8M 115
Steed Ct. Bus. Pk. Upt —1B 158
Steele La. Bklnd —9H 111
Steel Lane Head. —9H 111
Steel Ter. Rothw —8A 82
(off Blackburn Ct.)
Steeplands. Hud —5D 114
Steep Lane. —8B 90
Steep La. Hud —5D 114
Steep La. Sower B —8A 90
Steeple Av. Grng M —6B 134
Steep Riding. Broc —6A 148
Steeton. —3C 20
Steeton Gro. Steet —2C 20
Steeton Hall Gdns. Steet —2C 20
Stella Gdns. Pon —1M 123
Stell Hill. Kei —2D 36
Stephen Clo. Hal —3F 92
Stephen Cres. B'frd —3C 58
Stephen Rd. B'frd —3L 75
Stephen Row. Hal —2F 92
(off Windmill La.)
Stephenson Clo. Dew —2H 117
Stephenson Dri. Leeds —2G 79
Stephenson Rd. All —4C 56
Stephenson St. B'frd —2N 75
Stephensons Way. I'ly —5G 9
Stephenson Way. Leeds —2G 79
Stephenson Way. Wake I —7H 99
Stephen St. H Bri —1H 89
Stepping Stones. E Mor —8D 22
Steps La. Sower B —7J 91
Sterne Hill. Hal —8M 91
Stevenson Av. C'frd —7J 103
Stevens Wlk. Cull —9K 37
Stewart Clo. B'frd —1G 59
Stewart Ho. Hud —4N 131
(off Oldgate)
Stewart Royd. Heck —8B 96
Stewart St. Cro R —7E 36
Sticker La. B'frd —2G 76
Stile. —1E 110
Stile Common. —7N 131
Stile Comn. Rd. Hud —6N 131
Stile Hill Way. Colt —7G 64
Stile Moor Ri. Todm —5J 87
Stile Rd. Todm —5J 87
Stillington Ho. B'frd —2B 58
Stillwell Dri. Wake —2N 137
Stillwell Gth. Wake —2N 137
Stillwell Gro. Wake —2N 137
Stirley Hill. Hud —2N 147
Stirling Cres. B'frd —2J 77
Stirling Cres. H'fth —3D 42
Stirling Ind. Est. C'frd —7F 102
Stirling Rd. Bur W —8B 10
Stirling St. Hal —6A 92
Stirling St. Sils —7E 6
Stirling Way. Gar —7B 66
Stirrup Gro. B'frd —2D 58
Stirton St. B'frd —2B 76
Stithy St. Oss —3M 117
(in two parts)
Stockbridge. —7L 21
Stockeld La. Sick —3E 16
Stockeld Park House. —2F 16
Stockeld Rd. I'ly —5F 8
Stockeld Way. I'ly —4F 8
Stockerhead La. Slai —1N 145
Stockheld La. Scholes —6G 47
Stock Hey La. Todm —6C 88
Stockhill Fold. B'frd —7H 41
(in two parts)
Stockhill Rd. B'frd —8H 41
Stockhill St. Dew —3D 116
Stockingate. S Kirk —8H 157
Stockinger La. Add —1M 7
(in two parts)
Stocking La. Aber —9F 48
Stocking La. Knot —8H 105
Stock La. Hal —6H 91
Stocks App. Leeds —2C 64
Stocks Av. H Bri —4L 89
Stocks Bank. —6J 115
Stocksbank Dri. Mir —5H 115
Stocks Bank Rd. Mir —4H 115
Stocks Dri. Shepl —9H 149
Stocks Gdns. H Bri —4L 89
Stocks Hill. Leeds —9C 62
(LS11)
Stocks Hill. Leeds —6M 61
(LS12)
Stocks Hill. Men —4D 24
Stocks Hill Clo. Barn —8D 154
Stocks Hill Clo. E Mor —7C 22
Stocks La. Bat —7F 96
Stocks La. Ludd & Mt Tab —3E 90
Stocks La. Myth —4L 89
Stocks La. Q'bry —4G 75
Stocks La. Sower B —9E 90
Stocks La. Stkmr —8F 148
Stocksmoor. —7G 148
Stocksmoor La. Wake —8N 135
Stocksmoor Rd. Midg —8M 135
Stocks Moor Rd. Stkmr —7E 148
Stocks Ri. Leeds —2C 64
Stocks Rd. Leeds —2D 64
Stocks St. Leeds —3E 62
Stocks Wlk. Hud —7D 132
Stocks Way. Shepl —9H 149
Stockwell Dri. Bat —6F 96
Stockwell Hill. Ber B —1L 147
Stockwell Va. Arm B —1L 147
Stod Fold. Hal —5J 73
Stogden Hill. Q'bry —4G 74
Stoneacre Ct. B'frd —3C 76
Stone Acre Heights. Mel —8E 146
Stone Battery Rd. Hud —6J 131
Stonebridge. B'frd —7F 40
(off Idlecroft Rd.)
Stonebridge App. Leeds —8H 61
Stonebridge Av. Leeds —8J 61
Stonebridge Gro. Leeds —8H 61
Stonebridge La. Leeds —9H 61
Stone Brig Grn. Rothw —9M 81
Stone Brig La. Rothw —9M 81
Stone Chair. —9H 75
Stonechat Ri. Morl —9M 79
Stone Cliffe. Hal —9N 91
(off Wakefield Ga.)
Stonecliffe Bank. Leeds —8H 61
Stonecliffe Clo. Leeds —8H 61
Stonecliffe Cres. Leeds —8H 61
Stonecliffe Dri. Leeds —8H 61
Stonecliffe Dri. M'twn —3L 135
Stonecliffe Gdns. Leeds —8H 61
Stonecliffe Gth. Leeds —8H 61
Stonecliffe Grn. Leeds —8H 61
Stonecliffe Gro. Leeds —8H 61
Stonecliffe Lawn. Leeds —8H 61
Stonecliffe Mt. Leeds —8H 61
Stonecliffe Pl. Leeds —9H 61
(off Stonecliffe Way)
Stonecliffe Ter. Leeds —8H 61
Stonecliffe Vw. Leeds —8H 61
Stonecliffe Wlk. Leeds —9H 61
Stonecliffe Way. Leeds —8H 61
Stone Ct. E Mor —8C 22
Stone Ct. S Hien —4M 155
Stonecroft. B'frd —2G 58
Stonecroft. Stan —7N 99
Stonecroft Gdns. Shepl —9K 149
Stonedale Clo. Pool W —2H 27
Stone Dene. Weth —3N 17
Stonedene Ct. Heck —7A 96

Stonefield. S'cft —8E 30
Stonefield Av. Hud —7G 131
Stonefield Clo. B'frd —1F 58
Stonefield Pl. Bat —3C 96
Stonefield Rd. Hud —7G 131
Stonefield St. Cleck —6E 94
Stonefield St. Dew —2F 116
Stonefield Ter. Chur —5M 79
Stonefleece Ct. Hon —6L 147
Stone Fold. Bail —5M 39
Stone Fold. Hon —5L 147
Stone Folds La. Mars —3E 144
Stonegate. Bgly —2F 38
Stonegate. Leeds —3E 62
(in two parts)
Stonegate. Oss —8A 118
Stonegate App. Leeds —9B 44
Stonegate Chase. Leeds —8B 44
Stonegate Clo. Leeds —4F 44
Stonegate Cres. Mean —8C 44
Stonegate Dri. Leeds —8C 44
Stonegate Dri. Pon —5J 123
Stonegate Edge. Leeds —8C 44
Stonegate Farm Clo. Leeds —8B 44
Stonegate Gdns. Leeds —8B 44
Stonegate Grn. Leeds —9B 44
Stonegate Gro. Leeds —8B 44
(in two parts)
Stonegate La. Ackw —5E 140
Stonegate La. Mean —8B 44
Stonegate M. Leeds —9B 44
Stonegate Pl. Leeds —9B 44
Stonegate Rd. B'frd —9F 40
Stonegate Rd. Leeds —8B 44
Stonegate Vw. Leeds —8B 44
Stonegate Wlk. Leeds —9C 44
Stone Gro. Steet —3C 20
(in two parts)
Stone Hall M. B'frd —2G 58
Stone Hall Rd. B'frd —2F 58
Stonehaven Ct. Kei —2L 37
Stone Hill. Bgly —3G 39
Stone Ho. Dri. Q'bry —5B 74
Stonehurst. Leeds —2E 64
Stonehurst Rd. Mir —5L 115
Stonehyrst Av. Dew —2G 116
Stone La. Oxe —4A 54
Stonelea. Bklnd —6G 111
Stonelea Ct. Head —1N 61
Stonelea Ct. Mean —8C 44
Stonelea Dri. Brigh —4L 113
Stonelea Gro. S Elm —7N 157
Stoneleigh. Q'bry —4E 74
Stoneleigh Gro. Oss —6N 117
Stonely Dri. Todm —4J 107
Stone Mill App. Leeds —8A 44
Stone Mill Ct. Leeds —8A 44
Stone Mill Way. Leeds —8A 44
Stone Pits La. Gild —7G 79
Stones Bank. Sower B —9C 110
Stones Dri. Sower B —9B 110
Stones La. Gol —7C 130
Stones La. Lint —1B 146
Stones La. Todm —7G 86
Stones Rd. Todm —8H 87
Stones Ter. Todm —1H 107
Stone St. All —3F 56
Stone St. Bail —5C 40
Stone St. B'frd —7C 58
Stone St. Cleck —5G 95
Stone St. Haw —9C 36
(off Sun St.)
Stone St. Q'bry —3B 74
Stone Vs. Leeds —9N 43
Stone Wood La. Hud —8G 149
Stoney Bk. La. Hud —8L 131
Stoney Bank La. Thon —9A 148
Stoney Bank St. Dew —5D 116
Stoneybrook Clo. Bret —1B 152
Stoney Butts La. Bklnd —7H 111
Stoney Cft. Gom —5M 95
Stoneycroft. H'fth —7E 42
Stoneycroft. Rawd —3N 41
(off Batter La.)
Stoneycroft La. Kei —6H 21
Stoney Cross St. Hud —8L 131
Stoney Ford La. Kbtn —1F 132
Stoney Gth. Wake —7H 137
Stoney Hill. Brigh —1M 113
Stoneyhurst Sq. B'frd —2J 77
Stoneyhurst Way. B'frd —2H 77
Stoney La. Bat —6G 96
Stoney La. Bur W —2A 24
Stoney La. E Ard —7E 98
Stoney La. Hal —7M 91
Stoney La. H Bri —2A 90
Stoney La. H'fth —7E 42
Stoney La. Leeds —2B 46
Stoney La. Light —5M 93
Stoney La. Lgwd —4D 130
Stoney La. Meth —4F 100
Stoney La. Oven —1N 91
Stoney La. S'wram —7H 93
Stoney La. Tay H —8L 131
Stoney La. Wake —8H 137
Stoney Ridge Av. B'frd —2G 57
Stoney Ridge Rd. Bgly —2G 57
Stoney Ri. H'fth —7E 42
Stoney Rock Ct. Leeds —5H 63
Stoney Rock Gro. Leeds —5H 63
Stoney Rock La. Leeds —5H 63
Stoney Royd. —7C 92
Stoney Royd La. Todm —4H 87
Stoney Royd Ter. Hal —8C 92
Stoneys Fold. Wilsd —9A 38
Stoney St. Kei —6H 21
Stoneythorpe. H'fth —7E 42
Stony Cft. La. Skel —5M 159
Stony Ga. H'frth —6K 163
Stony Hill. Todm —2G 86
Stony La. All —4E 56
Stony La. B'frd —1G 58
Stony La. C'twn —2D 88
Stony La. Clay W —9G 151
Stony La. G'lnd —3N 111
Stony La. Hon —6L 147
Stony La. Oakw —1A 36
Stony La. Sower B —6D 110
Stony Royd. Fars —3N 59
Stony Royd La. Cra V —8H 89
Stoodley Clo. Todm —7B 88
Stoodley Glen. Todm —5B 88
Stoodley Grange. Todm —7C 88
Stoodley La. Todm —5B 88
Stoodley Ter. Hal —6L 91
Stopford Av. Wake —2N 137
Stopford Gth. Wake —2N 137
Storey Pl. Leeds —5N 63
Storie Cres. Wake —7G 119
Storiths. —1N 5
Storiths Ct. Add —2M 7
Storiths La. Stor —1N 5
Stormer Hill La. Norl —1K 111
Storr Hill. Wyke —9A 76
Storr Hill Ter. Wyke —9A 76
Storrs Hill Rd. Horb & Oss —1A 136
Storth Av. Hud —7E 130
Storthes Hall La. Kbtn —4F 148
Storthes Hall Student Village. —3G 148
Storth Pl. Hud —1L 131
Storths Rd. Hud —1K 131
Stott Hill. B'frd —7D 58
Stott Rd. Leeds —3A 62
Stotts Pl. Hal —6D 92
Stott St. Leeds —7N 61
Stott Ter. B'frd —2H 59
Stourton. —4J 81
Stourton Rd. I'ly —4E 8
Stowe Gro. Leeds —6L 63
Stowell Mill St. B'frd —1B 76
Stradmore Rd. Denh —6L 55
Strafford St. Dart —9E 152
Strafford Way. App B —7J 41
Straight Acres La. B'frd —1H 59
Straight La. Add —4J 7
Straight La. Hal —8K 73
Straight La. Skelb —6F 158
(in two parts)
Strait La. Huby —5M 13
Straits. Bail —3A 40
(off Northgate)
Stralau St. Bat —6F 96
Strands Ct. Neth —4A 136
Strangford Ct. B'frd —7H 41
Stranglands La. Knot —6M 103
Stratford Av. Leeds —2C 80
Stratford Clo. Gol —5D 130
Stratford Ct. Leeds —8E 44
Stratford Rd. B'frd —9N 57
Stratford St. Leeds —3D 80
Stratford Ter. Leeds —2D 80
Strathallan Dri. Bail —4B 40
Stratheden Rd. Wake —4J 119
Strathmore Av. Leeds —4J 63
Strathmore Clo. B'frd —3F 58
Strathmore Dri. Bail —3N 39
Strathmore Dri. Leeds —3J 63
Strathmore Gdns. S Elm —5A 158
Strathmore Rd. I'ly —5K 9
Strathmore St. Leeds —4K 63
Strathmore Ter. Leeds —4J 63
Strathmore Vw. Leeds —4J 63
Stratton Ho. B'frd —7E 58
(off Bolton St.)
Stratton Pk. Ras —3N 113
Stratton Rd. Brigh —2N 113
Stratton Vw. B'frd —1J 77
Stratton Wlk. All —6F 56
Strawberry Av. Gar —8M 65
Strawberry Av. Liv —8L 95
Strawberry Bank. Liv —8L 95
Strawberry Fields. Kei —8J 21
Strawberry Gdns. Roys —5D 154
Strawberry La. Leeds —7M 61
(in two parts)
Strawberry Rd. Leeds —7M 61
Strawberry Sq. Heck —9A 96
(off Church La.)
Strawberry St. Kei —8J 21
Strawberry St. Sils —8D 6
Stray, The. B'frd —9E 40
Stream Head Rd. T'tn —4A 56
Streamside. Leeds —9A 44
Streamside Clo. H Bri —4M 89
Street 1. Thor A —9G 19
Street 2. Thor A —9H 19
Street 3. Thor A —8H 19
Street 5. Thor A —7H 19
Street 6. Thor A —6H 19
Street 7. Thor A —6H 19
Street 8. Thor A —7J 19
Street Furlong La. Pon —4A 124
Street Head La. Oakw —6M 35
Streethouse. —6L 121
Street La. E Mor —5A 22
Street La. Leeds —5J 45
(LS8)
Street La. Leeds —5E 44
(LS17)
Street La. Morl —8F 78
Street, The. Add —1K 7
(in two parts)
Strelley Rd. Barn —9N 153
Strensall Grn. B'frd —5K 75
Stretch Ga. Shepl —8K 149
Stretchgate La. Hal —4L 91
Stretton Clo. Ack —2A 122
Strickland Av. Leeds —3A 46
Strickland Clo. Leeds —3A 46
Strickland Cres. Leeds —3A 46
Strickland Rd. Upt —1C 158
Strike La. Skelm —6C 150
Strines Moor Rd. H'frth —9A 164
Strines St. Todm —4J 107
Stringer Ho. La. Eml —2D 150
Stringer La. Horb —1D 136
Stringer's Yd. Horb —1C 136
Strong Close. —9L 21
Strong Clo. Gro. Kei —9L 21
Strong Clo. Rd. Kei —9L 21
Strong Clo. Way. Kei —9L 21
(off Strong Clo. Rd.)
Stuart Ct. B'frd —1C 76
(off Swarland Gro.)
Stuart Gro. Nor —8H 101
Stuart Gro. Slai —1N 145
Stuart Pl. Hud —6D 114
Stuart Rd. Pon —2J 123
Stuart St. C'frd —4E 102
Stuart St. Pon —2J 123
Stubbing Brink. H Bri —1F 88
Stubbing Dri. H Bri —1F 88
Stubbing Holme Rd. H Bri —1G 88
Stubbing La. Sower B —3E 110
Stubbing La. Slnd —7L 111
Stubbings Clo. H Bri —4M 89
Stubbings Rd. Bail —5L 39
Stubbings St. H Bri —4M 89
Stubbing Way. Shipl —9A 40
(in two parts)
Stubbin La. Den D —2E 166
Stubbin La. H'frth —5H 163
Stubbin Rd. Mars —5H 145
Stubbs La. Knot —4F 124
Stubbs La. Wake —5G 98
Stubham Ri. I'ly —4F 8
Stubley Farm Rd. Heck —6A 96
Stubley Holme. Todm —3C 86
Stubley La. Todm —3C 86
Stubley Rd. Heck —6N 95
Stubley St. Wake —5K 119
Stubs Beck La. West I —2H 95
Stub Thorn La. Hal —6E 92
Studdley Cres. Gil —4G 39
Studfold Vw. Leeds —4B 64
Studio Rd. Leeds —5A 62
Studleigh Ter. Brigh —7K 93
(off Brooklyn Ter.)
Studley Av. B'frd —6N 75
Studley Clo. E Mor —7C 22
Studley Rd. B'frd —4D 58
Studley Ter. Pud —6B 60
Stump Cross. —3E 92
Stumpcross Clo. Pon —9M 103
Stumpcross Ct. Pon —9M 103
Stumpcross La. Pon —9N 103
Stumpcross Way. Pon —9M 103
Stunsteds Rd. Cleck —4H 95
Sturges Gro. B'frd —5F 58
Sturton Av. Gar —6A 66
Sturton Grange La. Gar —7B 66
Sturton Gro. Hal —6L 73
Sturton La. Gar —6A 66
Sturton La. Hal —6L 73
Stutely Gro. Hud —6C 114
Stutton Rd. Tad —8N 33
Styebank La. Rothw —7A 82
Stye La. Sower B —8D 90
Sty La. Bgly —1D 38
Styveton Way. Steet —2B 20
Sude Hill. N Mill —2C 164
Sude Hill Ter. N Mill —2D 164
Sudforth La. Beal —7L 105
Suffolk Av. Bat —9D 96
Suffolk Clo. Oss —7M 117
Suffolk Ct. Yead —9M 25
Suffolk Ho. Wake —8A 120
Suffolk Pl. B'frd —2D 58
Suffolk St. Bat —8E 96
Sufton St. Hud —1L 131
Sugar Hill. —4D 96
Sugar Hill. Add —1M 7
Sugar Hill Clo. Oult —1D 100
Sugar La. Dew —2H 117
Sugar La. Todm —2F 86
Sugar La. Wake —7N 119
Sugar Well App. Leeds —1C 62
Sugar Well Mt. Leeds —1C 62
Sugar Well Rd. Leeds —1C 62
Sugden Bank. Sower B —8J 91
(off Sunny Bank St.)
Sugden Clo. Brigh —3M 113
Sugden's Almshouses. Oakw —4D 36
Sugden St. B'frd —7A 58
Sugden St. Oaken —9D 76
Sulby Gro. B'frd —8J 41
Sullivan Clo. Hud —7J 131
Sullivan Gro. S Kirk —8H 157
Summerbridge Clo. Bat —6D 96
Summerbridge Cres. B'frd —1H 59
Summerbridge Cres. Gom —2N 95
Summerbridge Dri. B'frd —1H 59
Summerdale. Gom —2M 95
Summerfield Av. Brigh —6N 93
Summerfield Av. Leeds —3D 60
Summerfield Clo. Bail —4M 39
Summerfield Clo. B'ton —4D 104
Summerfield Dri. Bail —4N 39
Summerfield Dri. B'ton —4D 104
Summerfield Dri. Leeds —3D 60
Summerfield Gdns. Leeds —3D 60
Summerfield Grn. Bail —4N 39
Summerfield Grn. Leeds —3D 60
Summerfield Gro. Bail —4M 39
Summerfield Gro. Lep —8H 133
Summerfield Pk. Bail —4N 39
Summerfield Pl. Leeds —3D 60
Summerfield Pl. Pud —6B 60
(off Richardshaw La.)
Summerfield Rd. B'frd —9G 40
Summerfield Rd. Leeds —3D 60
Summerfield Rd. Todm —7L 87
Summerfield Rd. W. Todm —7L 87
Summerfield Wlk. Leeds —3D 60
Summergate Pl. Hal —6M 91
Summergate St. Hal —6M 91
Summer Hall Ing. Wyke —9N 75
Summerhill Av. Steet —2D 20
Summerhill Dri. Steet —3D 20
Summerhill Gdns. Leeds —5K 45
Summerhill Gro. Gar —8L 65
Summerhill La. Steet —2D 20
Summerhill Pl. Leeds —5K 45
Summerhill Rd. Gar —7L 65
Summer Hill Rd. Meth —1L 101
Summer Hill St. B'frd —9M 57
Summerlands Gro. B'frd —3E 76
Summerland Ter. Sower B —8K 91
Summer La. Eml —3G 151
Summer La. Roys —5C 154
Summer Mdw. Pon —4J 123
Summer Rd. Roys —5C 154
Summerscale St. Hal —4N 91
Summerseat. Rawd —4A 42
Summerseat Pl. B'frd —9A 58
Summersgill Sq. H'fth —7E 42
Summer St. Hal —7M 91
Summer St. Lock —6L 131
Summer St. Neth —3J 147
Summervale. H'frth —2M 163
Summerville Rd. B'frd —8A 58
Summerville Rd. S'ley —5N 59
Summit. —9M 107
Summit St. Kei —8H 21
Sunbeam Av. Leeds —2D 80
Sunbeam Gro. Leeds —2D 80
Sunbeam Pl. Leeds —2D 80
Sunbeam Ter. Leeds —2D 80
Sunbridge Rd. B'frd —7B 58
Sunbury Gro. Hud —4C 132
Sun Ct. F'stne —3C 122
Sunderland Clo. Brigh —9M 93
(off Thornhill Bri. La.)
Sunderland Rd. B'frd —4N 57
Sunderland St. Cro R —7F 36
Sunderland St. Hal —5A 92
Sunderland St. Kei —1H 37
Sundown Av. B'frd —1K 75
Sun Fld. S'ley —5A 60
Sunfield Clo. S'ley —4A 60
Sunfield Dri. S'ley —4A 60
Sunfield Gdns. S'ley —4A 60
Sunfield Pl. S'ley —5A 60
Sunfield Ter. Mar —5J 95
(off Mayfield Ter.)
Sun Fold. Hal —6C 92
Sunhill Dri. Bail —5K 39
Sunhurst Clo. Oakw —5C 36
Sunhurst Dri. Oakw —5C 36
Sun La. Bur W —7B 10
(in three parts)
Sun La. Wake —5M 119
Sunningdale. B'frd —6J 57
Sunningdale. M'fld —6F 66
Sunningdale Av. Dart —8J 153
Sunningdale Av. Leeds —3C 44
Sunningdale Clo. Leeds —3C 44
Sunningdale Cres. Cull —1L 55
Sunningdale Cft. Hud —8L 113
Sunningdale Dri. Cud —9K 155
Sunningdale Dri. Leeds —3C 44
Sunningdale Grn. Leeds —3C 44
Sunningdale Rd. Hud —7J 131
Sunningdales. Norm —2L 121
Sunningdale Wlk. Leeds —3C 44
Sunningdale Way. Leeds —3C 44
Sunny Av. S Elm —7A 158
Sunny Av. Upt —2N 157
Sunnybank. —4A 112
Sunnybank. Den D —3C 166
Sunny Bank. Fitz —7A 140
Sunny Bank. Gol —8A 130
Sunny Bank. H Bri —3M 89
Sunny Bank. Knot —8F 104
(in two parts)
Sunny Bank. Leeds —1H 63
Sunnybank. M'fld —8H 67
Sunny Bank. Nor —3J 121
Sunny Bank. Nor G —2M 91
Sunny Bank. Q'bry —4E 74
Sunny Bank. Ryh —9H 139
Sunny Bank. Shipl —8N 39
Sunny Bank. Wyke —9C 76
Sunnybank Av. B'frd —4B 76
Sunnybank Av. H'fth —8E 42
Sunny Bank Av. Mir —3L 115
Sunnybank Av. Thornb —5K 59
Sunnybank Clo. Schol —6D 94
Sunnybank Ct. Yead —9A 26
Sunnybank Cres. G'lnd —4A 112
Sunnybank Cres. Yead —9A 26
Sunnybank Dri. G'lnd —4A 112
Sunny Bank Dri. Mir —3K 115
Sunny Bank Dri. Sower B —8J 91
Sunny Bank Grange. Brigh —9M 9
(off Sunny Bank Rd.)
Sunny Bank Gro. Leeds —1H 63
Sunny Bank Gro. Mir —4L 115
Sunnybank Gro. Thornb —5K 59
Sunny Bank La. Bat —5G 96
Sunny Bank La. Cra V —8K 89
Sunnybank La. G'lnd —4A 112
Sunny Bank La. Hal —6G 92
Sunny Bank La. S'wram —6G 92
Sunnybank La. Thornb —5K 59
Sunny Bank Mills. Far —3A 60
Sunny Bank Pde. Mir —3K 115
Sunny Bank Rd. Bat —6G 96
Sunny Bank Rd. B'frd —4B 76
Sunny Bank Rd. Brigh —1M 113
Sunnybank Rd. G'lnd —4N 111
Sunny Bank Rd. Hal —8H 73
Sunnybank Rd. H'fth —8E 42
Sunnybank Rd. Hud —2J 131
Sunny Bank Rd. Mel —7B 146
Sunny Bank Rd. Mir —2K 115
Sunny Bank Rd. Pec W —2G 71
Sunnybank St. H'fth —8E 42
Sunnybank St. Oss —6N 117
Sunny Bank St. Sower B —8J 91
Sunny Bank Ter. Hal —3B 92
Sunnybank Ter. H'fth —8E 42
Sunny Bank Ter. Todm —3D 86
Sunny Bank Vw. Leeds —1H 63
Sunny Bank Wlk. Mir —3L 115
Sunny Brae Cres. Bgly —5G 39
Sunny Brow. Ber B —1L 147
Sunny Brow La. B'frd —4J 57
Sunnycliffe. E Mor —8C 22
Sunnydale Av. Brigh —3M 113
Sunnydale Cres. Otley —2H 25
Sunnydale Cft. Oss —7A 118
Sunnydale Gro. Kei —1M 37
Sunnydale Pk. E Mor —7D 22
Sunnydale Pk. Oss —6A 118
Sunnydale Ridge. Otley —2H 25
Sunnydale Rd. Oss —6B 118
Sunnydale Ter. Oss —6A 118
Sunnydene. Leeds —5A 64
Sunnyfield. E Ard —5E 98
Sunnyfield Dri. Fitz —7A 140
Sunny Gro. Chur —5M 79
Sunny Heys Rd. Mel —6C 146

Sunny Heys W. *Mel* —6C **146**
Sunny Hill. *Wake* —2F **118**
Sunnyhill Av. *Kei* —2F **36**
Sunnyhill Clo. *Wren* —1G **118**
Sunnyhill Cres. *Wren* —2F **118**
Sunnyhill Cft. *Wren* —1G **118**
Sunnyhill Gro. *Kei* —2F **36**
Sunny Mead. *Hud* —4E **132**
Sunnymead. *Scis* —7H **151**
Sunny Mt. *H'den* —6A **38**
Sunny Mt. *High* —8H **21**
Sunny Mt. *Sandb* —9B **22**
*Sunnymount Ter. Birs —3C **96***
(off Springwell Vw.)
Sunnyridge Av. *Pud* —6M **59**
Sunnyside. *Brigh* —3B **114**
Sunny Side. *Hal* —5K **93**
Sunnyside. *Heck* —9A **96**
Sunnyside. *Holy G* —1N **129**
Sunnyside. *Hud* —2K **131**
Sunnyside. *Todm* —7J **87**
Sunnyside Av. *Liv* —1K **115**
Sunnyside Av. *Ting* —4N **97**
Sunnyside La. *B'frd* —5D **58**
Sunnyside Rd. *Leeds* —5E **60**
Sunny Side St. *Hal* —3B **92**
Sunnyvale Mt. *S Elm* —6L **157**
Sunnyview. *E Ard* —5E **98**
Sunnyview Av. *Leeds* —2B **80**
Sunny Vw. Cres. *Hud* —8B **114**
Sunnyview Gdns. *Leeds* —2B **80**
Sunnyview Ter. *Leeds* —2B **80**
Sunny Vw. Ter. *Q'bry* —5B **74**
Sunrise Vw. *L'boro* —9M **107**
Sunroyd Av. *Horb* —9D **118**
Sunroyd Hill. *Horb* —9D **118**
Sunset Av. *Leeds* —7A **44**
Sunset Cres. *Hal* —7D **92**
Sunset Dri. *I'ly* —4J **9**
Sunset Dri. *Leeds* —8A **44**
Sunset Hilltop. *Leeds* —7A **44**
Sunset Mt. *Leeds* —8A **44**
Sunset Ri. *Leeds* —7A **44**
Sunset Rd. *Leeds* —7A **44**
Sunset Ter. *I'ly* —4K **9**
Sunset Vw. *Leeds* —7A **44**
Sunshine Ct. *B'frd* —7L **75**
Sunshine Mills. *Leeds* —7L **61**
Sun St. *B'frd* —6D **58**
Sun St. *Ebrn* —3A **20**
Sun St. *Haw* —9C **36**
Sun St. *Kei* —1J **37**
Sun St. *S'ley* —5B **60**
Sun St. *Yead* —9N **25**
Sun Ter. *Todm* —3D **86**
Sun Vale Av. *Todm* —4K **107**
Sun Way. *Hal* —7E **92**
Sun Wood Av. *Hal* —9G **75**
Sun Wood Ter. *Hal* —9G **75**
Surat Rd. *Slai* —8M **129**
Suresnes Rd. *Kei* —9H **21**
Surgery St. *Haw* —9D **36**
Surrey Gro. *B'frd* —1C **76**
Surrey Gro. *Pud* —6B **60**
Surrey Rd. *Pud* —6B **60**
Surrey St. *Bat* —7G **97**
Surrey St. *Hal* —6L **91**
Surrey St. *Kei* —8L **21**
Surrey St. *Todm* —6K **87**
Sussex App. *Leeds* —2H **81**
Sussex Av. *H'fth* —4F **42**
Sussex Av. *Leeds* —2H **81**
Sussex Clo. *Hems* —1D **156**
Sussex Cres. *C'frd* —4L **103**
Sussex Gdns. *Leeds* —2H **81**
Sussex Grn. *Leeds* —2H **81**
Sussex Pl. *Leeds* —2H **81**
Sussex St. *Bat* —7G **97**
Sussex St. *Kei* —8L **21**
Sussex St. *Leeds* —7G **63**
Sussex Wlk. *Dew* —3E **116**
*Sutcliffe Ct. Hal —7D **92***
(off Bank Top)
Sutcliffe Pl. *B'frd* —5B **76**
Sutcliffe St. *Hal* —4L **91**
*Sutcliffe Ter. Hal —3B **92***
(off Amblers Ter.)
Sutcliffe Wood La. *Hal* —5H **93**
Sutherland Av. *Leeds* —6J **45**
Sutherland Cres. *Leeds* —5J **45**
Sutherland Dri. *Hud* —9H **131**
Sutherland Mt. *Leeds* —4J **63**
Sutherland Rd. *Leeds* —4J **63**
Sutherland St. *Leeds* —8A **62**
Sutherland Ter. *Leeds* —4J **63**
Sutton. —5D 104
Sutton App. *Leeds* —5N **63**
Sutton Av. *Barn* —9A **154**
Sutton Av. *B'frd* —1D **58**
Sutton Av. *Hud* —2E **132**
Sutton Cres. *B'frd* —1J **77**
Sutton Cres. *Leeds* —5N **63**
Sutton Dri. *Cull* —1K **55**
Sutton Dri. *Hud* —2E **132**
Sutton Gro. *B'frd* —9J **59**
Sutton Gro. *Morl* —1K **97**
Sutton Ho. *B'frd* —9J **59**
Sutton La. *Byr* —5C **104**
Sutton Rd. *B'frd* —9J **59**
Sutton Rd. *Cam* —1N **159**
Sutton St. *Leeds* —8B **62**
Suzanne Cres. *S Elm* —6L **157**
Swaindrod La. *L'boro* —3A **126**
Swaine Hill Cres. *Yead* —9L **25**
Swaine Hill St. *Yead* —9L **25**
Swaine Hill Ter. *Yead* —9L **25**
Swain Green. —9G 59
Swain House. —1E 58
Swain Ho. Cres. *B'frd* —1E **58**
Swain Ho. Rd. *B'frd* —1E **58**
Swain Mt. *B'frd* —1E **58**
Swain Royd Lane Bottom. —3E 56
*Swale Ct. Sils —9E **6***
(off Ings Way)
Swale Cres. *Gar* —8B **66**
*Swaledale Ho. Sower B —9H **91***
(off Sowerby St.)
Swale Dri. *C'frd* —4H **103**
Swale Ri. *Weth* —1L **17**
Swales Moor Rd. *Hal* —8B **74**
Swales Yd. *Pon* —3J **123**
Swallow Av. *Leeds* —8K **61**
Swallow Clo. *Dart* —9F **152**
Swallow Clo. *Leeds* —3H **45**
Swallow Clo. *Pool W* —2G **27**
Swallow Cres. *Leeds* —8J **61**
Swallow Dri. *Leeds* —3H **45**
Swallow Dri. *Pool W* —2G **26**
Swallow Fold. *B'frd* —7H **57**
Swallow Gth. *Wake* —5M **137**
Swallow Gro. *Neth* —3K **147**
Swallow Hill. *Bat* —4D **96**
Swallow La. *Gol* —5B **130**
Swallow Mt. *Leeds* —8K **61**
Swallow St. *Heck* —9A **96**
Swallow St. *Kei* —8K **21**
Swallow Va. *Morl* —9N **79**
Swan Bank La. *Hal* —7C **92**
Swan Bank La. *H'frth* —4M **163**
Swan Ct. *Hud* —7K **131**
Swanhill La. *Pon* —4K **123**
Swan La. *Leeds* —7N **27**
Swan La. *Lock* —7K **131**
Swan La. *Outl* —1A **130**
Swan St. *B'frd* —9C **58**
*Swan St. Leeds —7E **62***
(off Thornton's Arc.)
Swarcliffe. —2D 64
Swarcliffe App. *Leeds* —2D **64**
Swarcliffe Av. *Leeds* —2D **64**
Swarcliffe Bank. *Leeds* —1D **64**
Swarcliffe Dri. *Leeds* —1D **64**
Swarcliffe Dri. E. *Leeds* —2E **64**
Swarcliffe Grn. *Leeds* —2E **64**
Swarcliffe Pde. *Leeds* —2D **64**
Swarcliffe Rd. *Leeds* —1D **64**
Swarcliffe Towers. *Leeds* —1E **64**
Swardale Grn. *Leeds* —2D **64**
Swardale Rd. *Leeds* —2D **64**
Swarland Gro. *B'frd* —1C **76**
Swartha. —7G 6
Swartha La. *Sils* —7G **6**
Sweep La. *H'frth* —5N **163**
Sweet St. *Leeds* —8D **62**
Sweet St. W. *Leeds* —8C **62**
(in two parts)
Swift Pl. *Sower B* —9B **110**
Swifts Fold. *Hon* —4L **147**
Swift St. *Hal* —9C **92**
Swift Way. *Wake* —5L **137**
Swillington. —3H 83
Swillington La. *Swil & Leeds* —4G **83**
Swincar Av. *Yead* —9L **25**
Swincliffe. —9L 77
Swincliffe Clo. *Gom* —9L **77**
Swincliffe Cres. *Gom* —1L **95**
Swindon La. *Hare* —6G **14**
Swindon La. *Pan* —1E **14**
Swindon Rd. *Dew* —3F **116**
Swinegate. *Leeds* —7E **62**
Swine La. *Nost* —6K **139**
Swine La. *Sandb* —8A **22**
Swine Mkt. La. *Cra V* —8H **89**
Swineshead La. *Todm* —9K **87**
Swineshead Rd. *Todm* —9J **87**
Swinnow. —5D 60
Swinnow Av. *Leeds* —5D **60**
Swinnow Clo. *Leeds* —5D **60**
Swinnow Cres. *S'ley* —4D **60**
Swinnow Dri. *Leeds* —5D **60**
Swinnow Gdns. *Leeds* —5D **60**
Swinnow Gth. *Leeds* —6D **60**
Swinnow Grn. *Pud* —5C **60**
Swinnow Gro. *Leeds* —5D **60**
Swinnow La. *S'ley & Leeds* —4D **60**
Swinnow Moor. —6D 60
Swinnow Pl. *S'ley* —4D **60**
Swinnow Rd. *Pud & Leeds* —6C **60**
Swinnow Vw. *Leeds* —5D **60**
Swinnow Wlk. *Leeds* —5D **60**
Swinton Pl. *B'frd* —9N **57**
Swinton Ter. *Hal* —7M **91**
Swires Rd. *B'frd* —5G **58**
Swires Rd. *Hal* —6A **92**
Swires Ter. *Hal* —6A **92**
Swiss St. *C'frd* —3E **102**
Swiss Wlk. *Bat* —9E **96**
Swithenbank Av. *Oss* —3M **117**
Swithenbank St. *Oss* —2M **117**
Swithen's Ct. *Rothw* —9A **82**
Swithen's Dri. *Rothw* —9N **81**
Swithen's Gro. *Rothw* —9N **81**
Swithen's La. *Rothw* —9A **82**
Swithen's St. *Rothw* —9A **82**
Sycamore Av. *Bgly* —5E **38**
Sycamore Av. *B'frd* —7L **57**
Sycamore Av. *C'gts* —6B **64**
Sycamore Av. *Cud* —9J **155**
Sycamore Av. *Hud* —5E **130**
Sycamore Av. *Kip* —3N **83**
Sycamore Av. *Knot* —9C **104**
Sycamore Av. *Leeds* —1H **63**
Sycamore Av. *Mel* —8C **146**
Sycamore Av. *Todm* —5J **87**
Sycamore Av. *Wake* —4H **119**
Sycamore Av. *Wren* —9H **99**
Sycamore Chase. *Pud* —7C **60**
Sycamore Clo. *B'frd* —6E **58**
Sycamore Clo. *B'hpe* —7J **27**
Sycamore Clo. *Knot* —1C **124**
Sycamore Clo. *Leeds* —2C **62**
Sycamore Clo. *Lep* —7K **133**
Sycamore Clo. *Mean* —8B **44**
Sycamore Copse. *Wake* —6H **119**
*Sycamore Cottage. H'frth —4C **164***
(off Lea Gdns.)
Sycamore Ct. *B'frd* —6E **58**
Sycamore Ct. *Bret* —1B **152**
Sycamore Ct. *Hud* —5E **130**
Sycamore Ct. *Kbtn* —2K **149**
Sycamore Ct. *Pon* —1L **123**
Sycamore Cft. *Leeds* —2D **80**
Sycamore Dri. *Add* —1N **7**
Sycamore Dri. *Cleck* —5F **94**
Sycamore Dri. *Ell* —5C **112**
Sycamore Dri. *Hal* —6M **93**
Sycamore Dri. *Roys* —6B **154**
Sycamore Fld. *Leeds* —2D **80**
Sycamore Grange. *Hud* —5D **130**
Sycamore Grn. *Lwr C* —1B **166**
Sycamore Grn. *Pon* —2M **123**
Sycamore Gro. *Nor* —3H **121**
Sycamore Gro. *Wake* —4H **119**
*Sycamore Ho. C'frd —5E **102***
(off Parklands)
Sycamore Ind. Est. *Heck* —1A **116**
Sycamore La. *Bret* —1B **152**
Sycamore La. *H'frth* —1A **164**
Sycamore Ri. *H'frth* —1B **164**
Sycamore Rd. *Hems* —3C **156**
Sycamore Row. *Leeds* —2D **60**
Sycamores, The. *B'hpe* —7J **27**
Sycamores, The. *Dew* —1E **116**
Sycamores, The. *Guis* —6J **25**
Sycamores, The. *Horb* —1E **136**
Sycamore St. *Wake* —7N **119**
Sycamore Ter. *Horb* —2E **136**
Sycamore Vw. *Kei* —1F **36**
Sycamore Wlk. *Fars* —4A **60**
Sycamore Way. *Birs* —2C **96**
Sycamore Way. *F'stne* —5D **122**
Sydenham Pl. *B'frd* —4E **58**
Sydenham Rd. *Leeds* —8B **62**
Sydenham St. *Leeds* —8B **62**
Sydney St. *Bgly* —4F **38**
Sydney St. *Fars* —4A **60**
Sydney St. *Liv* —9M **95**
Sydney St. *W'ford* —7E **82**
Syke Av. *Dew* —3J **117**
Syke Av. *Ting* —5N **97**
Syke Clo. *Ting* —5M **97**
Syke Fold Grange. *Cleck* —5H **95**
Syke Gdns. *Ting* —5N **97**
Syke Grn. *S'cft* —8D **30**
Syke Gro. *Dew* —3J **117**
Syke Ho. La. *G'lnd* —5M **111**
Syke Ing Clo. *Dew* —4K **117**
Syke Ing Ter. *Dew* —4K **117**
Syke La. *Caus F* —3L **73**
Syke La. *Dew* —4J **117**
Syke La. *Hal* —3K **93**
Syke La. *Q'bry* —6E **74**
Syke La. *S'cft* —9B **30**
Syke La. *Sower B* —9H **91**
Syke Rd. *B'frd* —3M **57**
Syke Rd. *Dew* —3J **117**
Syke Rd. *Ting* —5N **97**
Syke Rd. *Weth* —4A **18**
Sykes Av. *Heck* —7B **96**
Sykes Av. *Mir* —5N **115**
Sykes Clo. *Ackw* —5D **140**
Sykes Clo. *Bat* —6H **97**
Sykes Ga. *Cra V* —4J **109**
Syke Side. *Kei* —6H **21**
Sykes La. *Bat* —8J **97**
Sykes La. *Oaken* —9E **76**
Sykes La. *Oakw* —4D **36**
Sykes La. *Sils* —9D **6**
Sykes Rd. *Bat* —6H **97**
Sykes St. *C'frd* —4D **102**
Sykes St. *Cleck* —5H **95**
Syke St. *Dew* —4J **117**
*Sykes Yd. Hal —7M **91***
(off King Cross Rd.)
Syke Ter. *Ting* —5M **97**
Syke Vw. *Dew* —3J **117**
Sylmet Clo. *B'frd* —6B **58**
Sylvan Av. *Q'bry* —5C **74**
Sylvan Vw. *H'fth* —6F **42**
Sylvester Av. *Nor* —4M **121**
Symons St. *Wake* —6K **119**
Syrett Gro. *Leeds* —6K **61**
Syrett Pk. *Hal* —3N **91**
Syringa Av. *All* —2F **56**
Syringa St. *Hud* —3J **131**

Tabbs Ct. *Schol* —3D **94**
Tabbs La. *Schol* —3C **94**
Tackgarth. *Brigh* —3M **113**
Tadman St. *Wake* —7L **119**
Talbot and Falcon Yd. *Wake* —4L **119**
Talbot Av. *Hud* —2H **131**
Talbot Av. *Leeds* —3M **61**
Talbot Av. *Moort & Round* —5G **44**
Talbot Ct. *Leeds* —6H **45**
Talbot Cres. *Leeds* —5H **45**
Talbot Fold. *Leeds* —6H **45**
Talbot Gdns. *Leeds* —5H **45**
Talbot Gro. *Leeds* —5H **45**
Talbot Ho. *Ell* —5E **112**
Talbot Mt. *Leeds* —3M **61**
Talbot Ri. *Leeds* —5H **45**
Talbot Rd. *Leeds* —5H **45**
Talbot Row. *Bat* —7G **96**
Talbot St. *Bat* —8F **96**
Talbot St. *B'frd* —7N **57**
Talbot St. *Kei* —9G **21**
Talbot St. *Nor* —1H **121**
Talbot Ter. *Leeds* —3M **61**
Talbot Ter. *Rothw* —9N **81**
Talbot Vw. *Leeds* —3M **61**
Talbot Vw. *Mir* —5L **115**
Tallow M. *Skelm* —8D **150**
Tall Trees Dri. *F'stne* —3D **122**
Tamar St. *B'frd* —1A **76**
*Tammy Hall St. Wake —5L **119***
(off Chancery La.)
Tamworth St. *B'frd* —8J **59**
Tandem. —4F 132
Tandem Way. *Tan* —4F **132**
*Tandy Trad. Est. Leeds —5N **61***
(off Canal Rd.)
Tanfield Clo. *Roys* —5B **154**
Tanfield Dri. *Bur W* —7C **10**
Tanfield Rd. *Hud* —2L **131**
Tanglewood Ct. *B'frd* —4M **75**
Tan Ho. Ct. *B'frd* —6F **76**
Tanhouse Hill. *Hip* —5H **93**
Tanhouse Hill. *H'fth* —7H **43**
Tan Ho. La. *Ackw* —3H **141**
Tan Ho. La. *Hal* —9F **74**
Tanhouse La. *Mir* —3M **133**
Tan Ho. La. *Wilsd* —9N **37**
Tanhouse Pk. *Hal* —5H **93**
Tanhouse St. *Dew* —5C **116**
Tan Ho. Yd. *Morl* —4M **79**
Tan La. *B'frd* —7F **76**
Tannerbrook Clo. *Cytn* —1J **75**
Tanner Hill Rd. *B'frd* —2K **75**
Tanners La. *Slai* —2M **145**
Tanner St. *Liv* —7F **94**
Tannett Grn. *B'frd* —3D **76**
*Tanpitts. H Bri —1H **89***
(off Albert St.)
Tanshelf Dri. *Pon* —3J **123**
Tanshelf Ind. Est. *Pon* —2J **123**
Tanton Cres. *Cytn* —1J **75**
Tanton Wlk. *Cytn* —1J **75**
Tanyard Av. *Hud* —3F **130**
Tanyard Fold. *C'thpe* —6J **137**
Tanyard Ind. Est. *Hud* —6G **131**
Tanyard Rd. *Milns* —6G **131**
Tanyard Rd. *Oakes* —3F **130**
Tarn Clo. *C'frd* —3L **103**
Tarn Ct. *Kei* —8F **20**
Tarn Ct. *Out* —9K **99**
Tarnhill M. *B'frd* —1C **76**
Tarn Hows Wlk. *Ackw* —4E **140**
Tarn La. *Leeds* —1L **45**
Tarn La. *Oakw* —8A **20**
Tarn Rd. *F'stne* —7E **122**
Tarnside Dri. *Leeds* —3A **64**
Tarn Vw. Rd. *Yead* —9A **26**
Tatefield Gro. *Kip* —5A **84**
Tatefield Pl. *Kip* —4A **84**
Tateley Clo. *Oss* —2M **117**
Tateley La. *Oss* —2M **117**
Tate Naylor St. *Dew* —1E **116**
*Tatham's Ct. Hal —7M **91***
(off High Shaw Rd. W.)
Tatham Way. *Leeds* —9L **45**
Tatton St. *Wake* —7A **120**
*Taunton Ho. B'frd —9C **58***
(off Crosscombe Wlk.)
Taunton St. *Shipl* —7M **39**
Taverngate. *Guis* —8C **24**
Tavern St. *Wake* —6M **119**
Tavistock Way. *Wake* —5J **137**
Tavora St. *Wake* —4L **119**
Tawny Clo. *Morl* —9N **79**
Tay Ct. *B'frd* —1H **59**
Taylor Av. *Sils* —8D **6**
Taylor Clo. *Oss* —7B **118**
Taylor Cres. *Oss* —7B **118**
Taylor Dri. *Oss* —7B **118**
Taylor Gro. *Meth* —1M **101**
Taylor Hall La. *Mir* —2J **115**
(in two parts)
Taylor Hill. —9L 131
Taylor Hill Rd. *Hud* —9K **131**
Taylor La. *Bar E* —9J **47**
Taylor La. *Gol* —5A **130**
Taylor La. *Hal* —2M **73**
Taylor Rd. *B'frd* —5B **76**
(in three parts)
Taylors Bldgs. *New* —8M **131**
Taylors Clo. *Leeds* —2C **64**
Taylor St. *Bat* —8F **96**
Taylor St. *Cleck* —5G **95**
Taylor St. *Gol* —6D **130**
Taylor Va. *Brigh* —2M **113**
Taylor Wood Cotts. *Wrag* —4B **140**
Tealbeck App. *Otley* —1M **25**
Tealbeck Ho. *Otley* —1M **25**
Tealby Clo. *Leeds* —5H **43**
Teal Clo. *C'frd* —6D **102**
Teal Ct. *Steet* —2B **20**
Teal Dri. *Morl* —9N **79**
Teal La. *Hal* —9E **74**
(in two parts)
Teall Ct. *Oss* —6C **118**
Teall St. *Oss* —6C **118**
Teall St. *Wake* —5L **119**
Teal M. *Leeds* —8F **80**
Teasdale St. *B'frd* —2F **76**
(in two parts)
Teasel Clo. *Oaken* —9E **76**
Techno Cen. *H'fth* —5F **42**
Technology Dri. *Bat* —8H **97**
Teddington Av. *Hud* —4D **132**
Tees Clo. *C'frd* —4H **103**
Teesdale Pl. *Knot* —1D **124**
Tees St. *B'frd* —2A **76**
Telephone Pl. *Leeds* —5F **62**
Telford Clo. *C'frd* —5B **102**
Telford Clo. *Hud* —6M **131**
Telford Clo. *Leeds* —3G **80**
Telford Clo. *Sils* —9F **6**
Telford Gdns. *Leeds* —3G **80**
Telford Pl. *Leeds* —3G **80**
Telford St. *Leeds* —3G **80**
Telford Ter. *Leeds* —3G **80**
Telford Wlk. *Leeds* —3G **80**
Telford Way. *Wake I* —7H **99**
Telscombe Dri. *B'frd* —3H **77**
Temperance Ct. *H'fth* —7E **42**
Temperance Fld. *Schol* —4D **94**
Temperance Fld. *Wyke* —1A **94**
Temperance St. *S'ley* —5B **60**
Tempest Pl. *Leeds* —2C **80**
Tempest Rd. *Leeds* —2C **80**
Tempest Rd. *S Kirk* —5J **157**
Templar Dri. *Hud* —6B **132**
Templar Gdns. *Weth* —2N **17**
Templar La. *Leeds* —6F **62**
(LS2)
Templar La. *Leeds* —2E **64**
(LS15)
Templar Pl. *Leeds* —6F **62**
Templars Clo. *G'lnd* —4N **111**
Templar St. *Leeds* —6E **62**
Templar St. *Wake* —8A **120**
Templars Way. *B'frd* —6K **57**
Templars Way. *Gar* —8N **65**
Templar Ter. *Morl* —2L **97**
Temple Av. *Leeds* —8B **64**
Temple Av. *Rothw* —6A **82**
Temple Clo. *Hud* —4M **131**
Temple Clo. *Leeds* —8B **64**
Temple Ct. *C'frd* —5C **102**
Temple Ct. *Leeds* —7A **64**
Temple Ct. *Rothw* —6A **82**

Temple Cres. Leeds —2C 80
Temple Gdns. Nor —8G 100
Temple Ga. Leeds —7C 64
Templegate Av. Leeds —8B 64
Templegate Clo. Leeds —7C 64
Templegate Cres. Leeds —8C 64
Temple Ga. Dri. Leeds —7B 64
Templegate Grn. Leeds —7C 64
Templegate Ri. Leeds —8B 64
Templegate Rd. Leeds —8B 64
Templegate Vw. Leeds —8B 64
Templegate Wlk. Leeds —7C 64
Templegate Way. Leeds —8C 64
Temple Grn. Rothw —6B 82
Temple Gro. Leeds —7B 64
Temple La. Leeds —7C 64
Temple La. L'boro —9M 107
Temple Lawn. Rothw —6B 82
Temple Lea. Leeds —7B 64
Temple M. C'frd —5C 102
Temple Newsam Country Park. —9C 64
Templenewsam Rd. Leeds —7A 64
Templenewsam Vw. Leeds —8A 64
Temple Pk. Clo. Leeds —7B 64
Temple Pk. Gdns. Leeds —7B 64
Temple Pk. Grn. Leeds —7B 64
Temple Rhydding. Bail —5A 40
Temple Rhydding Dri. Bail —5A 40
Temple Ri. Leeds —8B 64
Temple Rd. Dew —4D 116
Temple Row. Kei —9J 21 (off Temple St.)
Temple Row. Leeds —8F 64
Temple Row Clo. Leeds —8F 64
Templestowe Cres. Leeds —5D 64
Templestowe Dri. Leeds —6D 64
Templestowe Gdns. Leeds —6C 64
Templestowe Hill. Leeds —5C 64
Temple St. B'frd —4N 57
Temple St. C'frd —5C 102
Temple St. Hud —1G 130
Temple St. Kei —9H 21
Temple Vw. Loft —3L 99
Temple Vw. Gro. Leeds —7J 63 (in two parts)
Temple Vw. Pl. Leeds —7H 63
Temple Vw. Rd. Leeds —6H 63
Temple Vw. Ter. Leeds —7H 63
Temple Wlk. Leeds —6C 64
Tenbury Fold. B'frd —2J 77
Tenby Ter. Hal —4M 91 (off Osborne St.)
Ten Lands La. Ryh —2G 155
Tennants Ct. Knot —8F 104
Tennis Av. B'frd —4J 77
Tennis Way. Bail —6M 39
Tennyson Av. Cam —9N 143
Tennyson Av. Sower B —9F 90
Tennyson Av. Stan —6N 99
Tennyson Av. Todm —6M 87
Tennyson Clo. Knot —8A 104
Tennyson Clo. Pud —8C 60
Tennyson Pl. B'frd —6E 58
Tennyson Pl. Cleck —4H 95
Tennyson Pl. Hal —4H 93
Tennyson Rd. B'frd —5N 75
Tennyson St. Far —4A 60
Tennyson St. Guis —8K 25
Tennyson St. Hal —3N 91
Tennyson St. Kei —2H 37
Tennyson St. Morl —9L 79
Tennyson St. Pud —8C 60
Tennyson Ter. Morl —9L 79
Tennyson Way. Pon —9K 103
Tenter Clo. Birs —6F 96
Tenter Clo. Skelm —7D 150
Tentercroft Pl. Bail —3A 40
Tenterden Way. Leeds —3G 65
Tenterfield Ri. Hal —3F 92
Tenterfield Rd. Oss —6A 118
Tenterfields. App B —7H 41
Tenterfields. Hal —7E 90
Tenterfields Bus. Cen. L'ft —7E 90
Tenterfield Ter. Hal —3F 92 (off Bradford Rd.)
Tenterfield Ter. Todm —6N 87
Tenter Hill. B'ham —6C 32 (in two parts)
Tenter Hill. Cytn —1G 75
Tenter Hill. H'frth —4D 164
Tenter Hill La. Hud —7B 114
Tenter Hill Rd. N Mill —1B 164
Tenter La. Leeds —7E 62 (off Bridge End)
Tenters Clo. Knot —7C 104
Tenters Gro. Hud —8B 114
Tenth Av. Liv —7G 94
Ten Yards La. T'tn —5M 55
Terminus Pde. Leeds —4D 64 (off Farm Rd.)
Ternhill Gro. B'frd —9C 58
Tern Pk. Coll —8J 17
Tern St. B'frd —2N 75
Terrace Gdns. Hal —3A 92
Terrace, The. B Spa —1E 32
Terrace, The. B'frd —4D 58
Terrace, The. Cleck —5J 95
Terrace, The. Hon —6K 147
Terrace, The. Pud —1B 78
Terrington Crest. Cytn —1J 75
Terry Rd. Low M —8C 76
Tetley Dri. B'shaw —9L 77
Tetley La. Hal —2F 92
Tetley Pl. B'frd —4D 58
Tetley's Brewery Wharf. —7F 62
Tetley St. B'frd —7B 58
Tetlows Yd. L'boro —9M 107
Teville Ct. B'frd —1E 76
Tewit Clo. Hal —6M 73
Tewit Gdns. Hal —6M 73
Tewit Grn. Hal —6M 73
Tewit Hall Gdns. Hal —7M 73
Tewit Hall Rd. B'frd —6G 59
Tewit La. Hal —6M 73
Tewitt Clo. Steet —2B 20
Tewitt La. Bgly —1G 39
Tewitt La. T'tn —4M 55
Tew St. Wake —7L 119
Texas St. Morl —2L 97
Thackeray Gro. Hud —7J 131
Thackeray Rd. B'frd —2H 59
Thackeray's Medical Museum. —4H 63
Thackeray Wlk. Knot —8A 104
Thacker Ga. Rd. Cra V —7A 90
Thackley. —6E 40
Thackley Av. B'frd —5E 40
Thackley Ct. Shipl —7A 40
Thackley Old Rd. Shipl —7A 40
Thackley Rd. B'frd —5E 40
Thackley Vw. B'frd —5E 40
Thackray Av. Heck —7B 96
Thackray La. Pon —2L 123
Thackray St. Hal —5K 91
Thackray St. Morl —1K 97
Thames Dri. Gar —8A 66
Thanes Clo. Hud —1K 131
Thanet Gth. Sils —9E 6
Thane Way. Leeds —3F 64
Thatchers Way. Gom —3L 95
Theaker La. Leeds —6L 61
Theakston Mead. Cytn —1H 75
Thealby Clo. Leeds —6G 62
Thealby Lawn. Leeds —5G 62
Thealby Pl. Leeds —6G 62
Thearne Grn. Cytn —1J 75
Theodore St. Leeds —4C 80
Thewlis La. Hud —8G 131
Thick Hollins. —8E 146
Thick Hollins. Mel —8E 146
Thick Hollins Dri. Mel —8E 146
Third Av. B'frd —5G 59
Third Av. Gol —6C 130
Third Av. Hal —8A 92
Third Av. Kei —1H 37
Third Av. Khtn —1G 132
Third Av. Leeds —8N 61
Third Av. Liv —8F 94
Third Av. Rothw —6A 82
Third Av. Upt —1N 157
Third Av. Wake —1L 119
Third Av. Weth —4N 17
Third St. Low M —7C 76
Thirkhill Ct. B'frd —1C 76
Thirkleby Royd. Cytn —1H 75
Thirlmere Av. Ell —4G 113
Thirlmere Av. Wyke —3C 94
Thirlmere Clo. Leeds —5A 80
Thirlmere Dri. C'frd —5K 103
Thirlmere Dri. Ting —4C 98
Thirlmere Dri. Weth —3J 17
Thirlmere Gdns. B'frd —4F 58
Thirlmere Gdns. Leeds —5A 80
Thirlmere Gro. Bail —6K 39
Thirlmere Pl. Knot —1D 124
Thirlmere Rd. Dew —1J 117
Thirlmere Rd. Wake —5G 119
Thirsk Clo. Hud —9N 113
Thirsk Dri. Kip —3A 84
Thirsk Grange. Cytn —1J 75
Thirsk Gro. Leeds —1F 98
Thirsk Row. Leeds —7D 62
Thirstin Rd. Hud & Hon —4K 147
Thirteenth Av. Liv —7F 94
Thistle Clo. Hud —9K 113
Thistle Dri. Upt —2M 157
Thistle Hill Av. Hud —5G 132
Thistle St. Hud —2N 131
Thistle Way. Gild —8G 78
Thistlewood Rd. Out —7M 99
Thomas Ct. B'frd —4A 76
Thomas Duggan Ho. Shipl —8N 39
Thomas Fold. B'frd —4F 58
Thomas Hill Ho. Pon —2K 123
Thomas St. Bat —6E 96
Thomas St. Brigh —2M 113
Thomas St. C'frd —3E 102
Thomas St. Ell —5F 112
Thomas St. Hal —7N 91 (nr. Eldroth Rd.)
Thomas St. Hal —5B 92 (nr. Union St.)
Thomas St. Haw —9D 36
Thomas St. Heck —9A 96
Thomas St. Hems —3E 156
Thomas St. Holy G —7A 112
Thomas St. Leeds —3C 62
Thomas St. Lind —1G 130
Thomas St. Liv —9M 95 (nr. Wormald St.)
Thomas St. Liv —8L 95 (off Valley Rd.)
Thomas St. Thor L —6K 131
Thomas St. Todm —3E 86
Thomas St. S. Hal —6M 91
Thomas Way. S Elm —5N 157
Thompson Av. B'frd —1D 58
Thompson Av. C'frd —6L 103
Thompson Dri. Wren —9H 99
Thompson Grn. Bail —5M 39
Thompson La. Bail —6M 39
Thompson St. Hal —5A 92
Thompson St. Nor —1H 121
Thompson St. Shipl —7M 39
Thompson's Yd. Wake —5L 119
Thong La. H'frth —9M 147
Thongsbridge. —9A 148
Thongsbridge Mills. H'frth —9N 147
Thoresby Dri. Gom —4M 95
Thoresby Gro. B'frd —2K 75
Thoresby Pl. Leeds —6D 62
Thornaby Dri. Cytn —1H 75
Thornacre Cres. Shipl —9C 40
Thornacre Rd. Shipl —8C 40
Thorn Av. B'frd —2H 57
Thorn Av. Dew —1F 134
Thornbank Av. Oakw —7F 36
Thornberry Dri. Liv —7F 94
Thornbridge M. B'frd —2F 58
Thornbury. —6H 59
Thornbury Av. B'frd —6H 59
Thornbury Cres. B'frd —6H 59
Thornbury Dri. B'frd —6H 59
Thornbury Gro. B'frd —6H 59
Thornbury Pk. Wake —7H 119
Thornbury Rd. B'frd —7H 59
Thornbury Rd. Wake —7H 119
Thornbury St. B'frd —7H 59
Thorncliffe Est. Bat —9D 96
Thorncliffe La. Eml —2G 150
Thorncliffe Rd. Bat —9D 96
Thorncliffe Rd. B'frd —5B 58
Thorncliffe Rd. Kei —1F 36
Thorncliffe St. Hud —1G 130
Thorncliff Grn. Rd. Kbtn —2M 149
Thorncliff La. Kbtn —2M 149
Thorn Clo. Leeds —3K 63
Thorn Clo. Shipl —9C 40
Thorn Cres. Leeds —3K 63
Thorncroft Rd. B'frd —4L 75
Thorn Cross. Leeds —2L 63
Thorndale Ri. B'frd —2C 58
Thorndene Way. B'frd —6L 77
Thorn Dri. B'frd —2J 57
Thorn Dri. Leeds —3K 63
Thorn Dri. Q'bry —6B 74
Thorne Clo. Barn —9N 153
Thorne Clo. Nor —2K 121
Thorne Clo. Pud —6D 60
Thorne End Rd. M'well —7K 153
Thornefield Cres. Ting —4N 97
Thorne Gro. Rothw —7A 82
Thorner. —2G 47
Thorner Gro. Sils —7E 6
Thorner La. B'ham —6K 31
Thorner La. S'cft —8E 30
Thorner La. T'ner —5F 46
Thorne Rd. Hud —6K 131
Thorner Rd. Woth —9L 31
Thornes. —8J 119
Thornes Ind. Est. Wake —6L 119
Thornes La. Wake —7L 119
Thornes La. Wharf. Wake —7M 119
Thornes Moor Av. Wake —8J 119
Thornes Moor Clo. Wake —8J 119
Thornes Moor Dri. Wake —8J 119
Thornes Moor Rd. Wake —9J 119
Thornes Pk. Brigh —2M 113
Thornes Pk. Shipl —1B 58
Thornes Pk. Ct. Wake —8K 119
Thornes Rd. Wake —8H 119 (in two parts)
Thorne St. Holy G —7N 111
Thorney La. L'ft —3C 90
Thornfield. Bgly —3D 38
Thornfield. Dew —5G 116
Thornfield. Haw —9D 36
Thornfield Av. B'frd —5B 76
Thornfield Av. Fars —3N 59
Thornfield Av. Hud —7K 131
Thornfield Ct. Leeds —4C 64
Thornfield Dri. Leeds —4C 64
Thornfield Hall. T'tn —8D 56 (off Thornton Rd.)
Thornfield M. Leeds —4C 64
Thornfield M. M'wte —9D 22
Thornfield Mt. Birs —3D 96
Thornfield Pl. B'frd —3G 58
Thornfield Ri. G'lnd —4A 112
Thornfield Rd. Hud —8K 131
Thornfield Rd. Leeds —7L 43
Thornfield Sq. B'frd —3G 58
Thornfield St. G'lnd —4A 112
Thornfield Ter. Wilsd —2A 56
Thornfield Way. Leeds —4C 64
Thorn Gth. Cleck —6G 94
Thorn Gth. Kei —7G 20
Thorn Gro. B'frd —2J 57
Thorn Gro. Leeds —3K 63
Thornhill. —9H 117
Thorn Hill. Holy G —9M 111
Thornhill Av. Hud —3H 131
Thornhill Av. Oakw —4E 36
Thornhill Av. Shipl —1B 58
Thornhill Bri. La. Brigh —9M 93
Thornhill Clo. C'ley —8M 41
Thornhill Clo. M'twn —3L 135
Thornhill Clo. W'ton —4B 138
Thornhill Ct. Leeds —8M 61
Thornhill Cft. Leeds —8L 61
Thornhill Cft. W'ton —3B 138
Thornhill Dri. C'ley —7K 41
Thornhill Dri. Shipl —1B 58
Thornhill Dri. W'ton —4B 138
Thornhill Edge. —1G 135
Thornhill Gro. C'ley —8M 41
Thornhill Gro. Shipl —1B 58
Thornhill Gro. Steet —2B 20
Thorn Hill Hey. Holy G —9M 111 (in two parts)
Thornhill Ho. B'frd —6J 59 (off Thornhill Pl.)
Thornhill Lees. —6F 116
Thornhill Pk. Av. Dew —7G 117
Thornhill Pl. B'frd —6J 59
Thornhill Pl. Brigh —2M 113
Thornhill Pl. Leeds —8L 61
Thornhill Rd. Brigh —3L 113
Thornhill Rd. C'frd —6E 102
Thornhill Rd. Dew —5E 116
Thornhill Rd. Hud —3J 131
Thornhill Rd. Leeds —8L 61
Thornhill Rd. Lgwd —4F 130
Thornhill Rd. M'twn —2K 135
Thornhill Rd. Steet —1B 20
Thornhills. —8A 94
Thornhills Beck La. Brigh —8N 93
Thornhills La. Clif —8A 94
Thornhill St. C'ley —8M 41
Thornhill St. Dew —5G 116
Thornhill St. Leeds —8L 61
Thornhill St. Wake —5L 119
Thornhill St. Bungalows. Wake —6L 119
Thornhill Ter. B'frd —6H 59
Thornhurst. —3F 30
Thornie Vw. Dew —7F 116
Thorn La. B'frd —2J 57 (in two parts)
Thorn La. Leeds —8H 45
Thornlea Clo. Yead —2K 41
Thornleigh. Dew —5G 116
Thornleigh Av. Wake —7L 119
Thornleigh Cres. Wake —7L 119
Thornleigh Cft. Wake —7L 119
Thornleigh Dri. Liv —7M 95
Thornleigh Dri. Wake —7L 119
Thornleigh Gdns. Leeds —8H 63
Thornleigh Gth. Wake —8L 119
Thornleigh Gro. Leeds —8H 63
Thornleigh Gro. Wake —8L 119
Thornleigh Mt. Leeds —8H 63
Thornleigh Rd. Hud —7G 131
Thornleigh Rd. Wake —7L 119
Thornleigh St. Leeds —8H 63
Thornleigh Vw. Leeds —8H 63
Thornmead Rd. Bail —5B 40
Thorn Mt. Leeds —2L 63
Thorn Rd. Dew —1F 134
Thorn Royd Dri. B'frd —3K 77
Thornsgill Av. B'frd —2G 77
Thorn St. Birs —3B 96
Thorn St. B'frd —5L 57
Thorn St. Haw —7E 36
Thorn Ter. Leeds —2K 63
Thornton. —8D 56
Thornton Av. Leeds —7K 61
Thornton Clo. Birs —1C 96
Thornton Clo. Hems —4D 156
Thornton Ct. B'frd —6L 57 (off Lane Ends Clo.)
Thornton Ct. Upt —1C 158
Thornton Gdns. Leeds —7K 61
Thornton Gro. Leeds —7K 61
Thornton La. B'frd —2A 76
Thornton Lodge Rd. Hud —6K 131
Thornton Moor Rd. Oxe —6G 54
Thornton Old Rd. B'frd —7J 57
Thornton Rd. B'frd —6M 57
Thornton Rd. Brigh —3K 113
Thornton Rd. Denh & T'tn —9L 55
Thornton Rd. Dew —7E 116
Thornton Rd. Q'bry —3C 74
Thornton's Arc. Leeds —6E 62
Thornton Sq. B'frd —3B 76 (off Delamere St.)
Thornton Sq. Brigh —1N 113 (off Commercial St.)
Thornton St. B'frd —7A 58
Thornton St. Bur W —7C 10
Thornton St. Cleck —6E 94
Thornton St. Dew —4E 116
Thornton St. Hal —7M 91
Thornton St. Rawf —5K 95
Thornton Ter. Hal —7M 91
Thornton Vw. Cytn —2H 75
Thornton Vw. Rd. Cytn —2H 75
Thorntonville. Rawf —6K 95
Thorntree Av. Croft —1F 138
Thorntree Clo. D'ton —7C 124
Thorntree Ct. Croft —1F 138
Thorntree St. Hal —7M 91
Thorn Vw. Ell —5F 112
Thorn Vw. Hal —2B 92
Thorn Vw. Leeds —3L 63
Thorn Vw. Myth —4M 89
Thornville. Morl —6L 79
Thornville Av. Leeds —4A 62
Thornville Ct. B'frd —4A 58
Thornville Ct. Leeds —4A 62 (off Thornville Rd.)
Thornville Cres. Leeds —3A 62
Thornville Gro. Leeds —4A 62
Thornville Mt. Dew —5D 116
Thornville Mt. Leeds —4A 62
Thornville Pl. Dew —5D 116
Thornville Pl. Leeds —4A 62
Thornville Rd. Leeds —4A 62
Thornville Row. Leeds —4A 62
Thornville St. Dew —5D 116
Thornville St. Leeds —4A 62
Thornville Ter. Dew —5E 116
Thornville Ter. Leeds —4A 62
Thornville Vw. Leeds —4A 62
Thornville Wlk. Dew —5D 116
Thorn Wlk. Leeds —3L 63
Thorold Ho. B'frd —8G 41 (off Fairhaven Grn.)
Thorp Arch. —8E 18
Thorp Arch Grange. B Spa —6F 18
Thorp Arch Trad. Est. Thor A —7H 1
Thorp Av. H'frth —4N 163
Thorpe. —8G 40
Thorpe Arch Pk. Thor A —8E 18
Thorpe Audlin. —5N 141
Thorpe Av. T'tn —8F 56
Thorpe Clo. Guis —8F 24
Thorpe Ct. Leeds —1E 98
Thorpe Cres. Leeds —1E 98
Thorpe Dri. Guis —7G 24
Thorpe Edge. —8G 41
Thorpe Gdns. Leeds —9E 80
Thorpe Gth. Leeds —1D 98
Thorpe Ga. Est. Bads —6M 141
Thorpe Grn. Dri. Gol —4D 130
Thorpe Gro. Leeds —9E 80
Thorpe Gro. T'tn —8G 56
Thorpe La. Bads & Thpe A —8M 14
Thorpe La. Den D —1D 166
Thorpe La. Guis —8E 24
Thorpe La. Hud —7D 132
Thorpe La. Ting —3A 98 (in two parts)
Thorpe Lwr. La. Rob H —2H 99
Thorpe Mill Ct. Sower B —3E 110
Thorpe Mt. Leeds —1D 98
Thorpe on the Hill. —2G 98
Thorpe Pl. Sower B —1C 110
Thorpe Rd. E Ard & Leeds —5E 9
Thorpe Rd. Leeds —9E 80
Thorpe Rd. Pud —6A 60
Thorpe Rd. T'tn —8F 56
Thorpes Av. Den D —1D 166
Thorpes Cres. Skelm —8D 150
Thorpe Sq. Leeds —9F 80
Thorpe St. Hal —2A 92
Thorpe St. Halt —6B 64
Thorpe St. Kei —8J 21
Thorpe St. Leeds —9E 80
Thorpe Vw. Leeds —1E 98
Thorpe Vw. Oss —3N 117

Thorpe Vw. Wake —5H 119
Thorp Gth. B'frd —8F 40
Thorp Pyn Cft. Hud —3C 132
Thorverton Dri. B'frd —5J 77
Thorverton Gro. B'frd —5J 77
Threadneedle St. Hal —7M 91
(off Dundas St.)
Threadneedle St. Hud —4M 131
Threelands Grange. B'shaw —7L 77
Three Nooked M. Idle —8F 40
(off Brecon Clo.)
Three Nooks La. Cud —8J 155
Three Sisters Sq. Hud —2M 131
Threshfield. Bail —4A 40
Threshfield Cres. B'shaw —7L 77
Thrift Way. Bgly —5E 38
Throstle Av. Leeds —1D 98
Throstle Bank. Hal —7M 91
(off Gainest)
Throstle Crest. Ack —3A 122
Throstle Dri. Leeds —1C 98
Throstle Gro. Leeds —1E 98
Throstle Hill. Leeds —1D 98
Throstle La. Leeds —1D 98
Throstle Mt. Leeds —1D 98
Throstle Mt. L'ft —7F 90
Throstle Nest. Bat —8D 96
Throstle Nest Clo. Otley —7H 11
Throstle Nest Rd. Sils —7D 6
Throstle Nest Vw. H'fth —8F 42
Throstle Pde. Leeds —1D 98
Throstle Pl. Leeds —1D 98
Throstle Rd. Leeds —8G 81
(nr. Ring Rd. Middleton)
Throstle Rd. Leeds —1E 98
(nr. Thorpe La.)
Throstle Row. Knot —1D 124
Throstle Row. Leeds —1D 98
Throstle Sq. Leeds —1F 98
Throstle St. Leeds —1D 98
Throstle St. Todm —5K 107
Throstle Ter. Leeds —1E 98
Throstle Vw. Leeds —1F 98
Throstle Wlk. Leeds —1D 98
Throxenby Way. Cytn —1H 75
Thrum Hall Clo. Hal —5M 91
Thrum Hall Dri. Hal —5M 91
Thrum Hall La. Hal —5M 91
Thrumpton Rd. Barn —8A 154
Thrush Hill Rd. H Bri —4L 89
Thrush St. Kei —8K 21
Thruxton Clo. Cud —9K 155
Thryberg St. B'frd —7E 58
Thunder Bridge. —6H 149
Thunder Bri. La. Kbtn —6H 149
Thunderton La. Sower B —1B 110
Thurgory Ga. Lep —7J 133
Thurgory La. Lep —6H 133
Thurley Dri. B'frd —3F 76
Thurley Rd. B'frd —3F 76
Thurnscoe Rd. B'frd —6B 58
Thurrish La. Pec W —8J 53
Thursby St. B'frd —7F 58
Thurston Gdns. All —6G 57
Thurstonland. —8D 148
Thurstonland Bank Rd. H'frth & Thur —8A 148
Thurstonland Rd. Hud —4C 148
Thwaite Ga. Leeds —2H 81
Thwaite Gate. —2J 81
Thwaite La. Leeds —2J 81
Thwaite Mills Museum. —2K 81
Thwaites. —9M 21
Thwaites Av. I'ly —5H 9
Thwaites Bri. Kei —9L 21
Thwaites Brow. —1M 37
Thwaites Brow Rd. Kei —9M 21
Thwaites La. Kei —9L 21
Tibgarth. Lntn —6J 17
Tichborne Rd. B'frd —2C 76
Tichborne St. Liv —8J 95
Tichbourne Rd. W. B'frd —2C 76
Tichbourne St. Bat —8C 96
Tickhill St. B'frd —8F 58
Tiding Fld. La. Slai —8K 129
Tidswell St. Heck —8B 96
Tilbury Av. Leeds —1B 80
Tilbury Gro. Leeds —1B 80
Tilbury Mt. Leeds —1B 80
Tilbury Pde. Leeds —1B 80
Tilbury Rd. Leeds —1B 80
Tilbury Row. Leeds —1B 80
Tilbury Ter. Leeds —1B 80
Tilbury Vw. Leeds —1B 80
Tile La. Leeds —4N 43
(in two parts)
Tile St. B'frd —5N 57
Tile Ter. Brigh —2M 113
Tiley Sq. B'frd —1C 76
Till Carr La. Hal —5M 93
Tillotson Av. Sower B —9G 90
Tillotson St. Sils —7D 6
Timbercliffe. —9M 107
Timber St. Ell —5E 112
Timber St. Kei —8L 21
Timble Dri. Bgly —3G 39
Tim La. Oakw —5B 36
Timmey La. Sower B —7G 90
Timothy La. Bat —5F 96
Tinderley Gro. Hud —6C 132
Tingley. —3A 98
Tingley Av. Ting —3A 98
Tingley Comn. Morl —2L 97
Tingley Cres. Ting —3M 97
Tinker Bank. H Bri —8G 71
Tinker La. Lep —8L 133
Tinker La. Mel —8C 146
Tinkingfield La. Bick —1J 19
Tinkler's La. Birk —1M 105
Tinkler Stile. Thack —7D 40
Tinsel Rd. Dew —2J 117
Tinshill. —3H 43
Tinshill Av. Leeds —4H 43
Tinshill Clo. Leeds —4H 43
Tinshill Cres. Leeds —3H 43
Tinshill Dri. Leeds —2H 43
Tinshill Gth. Leeds —3H 43
Tinshill Gro. Leeds —3H 43
Tinshill La. Leeds —4G 42
Tinshill Moor. —2H 43
Tinshill Mt. Leeds —3H 43
Tinshill Rd. Leeds —4G 42
Tinshill Vw. Leeds —3H 43
Tinshill Wlk. Leeds —2H 43
Tinsworth Rd. Wake —6J 137
Tintagel Ct. Nor —9J 101
Tintern Av. B'frd —7J 57
Tintern Av. Hud —5E 130
Tippaty La. Knot —5F 104
Tipping La. Eml —2G 151
Tipsey Hill. Dart —8M 153
Tisma Dri. B'frd —5G 76
Tithe Barn Fold. Bar E —8L 47
Tithe Barn La. Bard —6C 30
Tithe Barn St. Dew —3G 116
Tithe Barn St. Horb —1C 136
Tithe Ho. Way. Hud —5C 114
Titus La. Shel —3A 150
Titus St. Shipl —7L 39
Tiverton Ho. B'frd —9C 58
(off Earl St.)
Tiverton Wlk. B'frd —3J 77
Tivoli Pl. B'frd —2A 76
Tivoli Pl. I'ly —6H 9
Tivy Dale. —4N 167
Tivy Dale Dri. Caw —4N 167
Tivy Dale Rd. Caw —4N 167
Toad La. L'boro —1C 126
Toby La. B'frd —1M 75
Toby Wood La. Den D —4A 166
Todd Ter. B'frd —1N 75
Todley Hall Rd. Oakw —1M 35
Todmorden. —7K 87
Todmorden Rd. L'boro —8M 107
Todwell La. B'frd —2A 76
Toft La. Far T —3D 148
Tofts Av. Wyke —2A 94
Tofts Gro. Brigh —4L 113
Tofts Gro. Gdns. Brigh —4L 113
Tofts Gro. Pl. Brigh —4L 113
(off Tofts Gro.)
Toftshaw. —5H 77
Toftshaw Fold. B'frd —5H 77
Toftshaw La. B'frd —5J 77
Toftshaw New Rd. B'frd —5H 77
Tofts Ho. Clo. Pud —7B 60
Tofts Rd. Cleck —5H 95
Tofts Rd. Pud —7A 60
Toft St. Leeds —8N 61
Toll Bar La. Wren —2G 118
Toll Bar Rd. C'frd —5N 101
Toller Dri. B'frd —3K 57
Toller Gro. B'frd —3L 57
Toller La. B'frd —3K 57
Toller Pk. B'frd —3L 57
Tollgate Ct. B'frd —5M 57
Tolson Cres. Hud —3D 132
Tolson Museum. —4C 132
Tolson St. Dew —2F 116
Tolson St. Oss —3L 117
Tolsons Yd. Hud —5B 132
Tolworth Fold. All —6G 56
Tombridge Cres. Kin —9A 140
Tom Dando Clo. Nor I —1M 121
Tom La. Hud —7G 130
Tomling Cote La. Sils —9G 7
Tomlinson Bldgs. B'frd —6E 40
Tommy La. Lint —9D 130
Tomroyds La. Mir —3A 116
Tom Wood Ash La. Upt —2C 158
Tonbridge Clo. B'frd —5L 75
Tonbridge St. Leeds —5C 62
Tong. —3B 78
Tong App. Leeds —8G 61
Tong Dri. Leeds —7G 60
Tong Ga. Leeds —7G 61
Tong Grn. Leeds —7G 61
Tong Hall Bus. Pk. B'frd —3A 78
Tong Ho. B'frd —3B 78
Tong La. B'frd —5N 77
Tong Park. —3D 40
Tong Pk. Bail —3D 40
Tong Rd. Leeds —1E 78
Tong Street. —4J 77
Tong St. B'frd —3G 76
Tongue La. Leeds —7B 44
Tong Wlk. Leeds —7G 61
Tong Way. Leeds —7G 60
Tootal St. Wake —6M 119
Toothill. —4M 113
Toothill Av. Brigh —4M 113
Toothill Bank. Brigh —3M 113
Toothill La. Brigh —5M 113
Toot Hill La. Sower B —1B 110
Toothill La. S. Brigh —6L 113
Topaz Clo. Far —9A 114
Topcliffe. —2M 97
Topcliffe Av. Morl —9N 79
Topcliffe Ct. Morl —9N 79
Topcliffe Fold. Morl —2M 97
Topcliffe Grn. Morl —9N 79
Topcliffe Gro. Morl —2M 97
Topcliffe La. Morl —2M 97
Topcliffe La. Ting —1N 97
Topcliffe Mead. Morl —9N 79
Topcliffe M. Morl —9N 79
Top Fold. Fair —9N 85
Top Fold. Leeds —8L 61
Top Headlands. Oss —6M 117
Top Ho. Farm M. Fair —9N 85
Top La. Bret —9N 135
Top Mdw. Mir —9K 115
Top Moor Side. Leeds —9C 62
Top of Carr. Bat —1E 116
(off Upper Rd.)
Top of Cowcliffe. —8L 113
Top of the Hill. Slai —2L 145
Top Orchard. Ryh —9J 139
Top O' Th' Bank. Thur —8C 148
Top o'Th Clo. Rd. Todm —5L 107
Top O' The Hill Rd. Wals —2J 107
Top o' the Moor. Stkmr —7G 148
Top Rd. Lwr C —1B 166
Top Row. Dart —6G 153
Top Stone Clo. B'ton —1D 104
Top St. Hems —2C 156
Top St. Todm —4H 107
Tor Av. Wyke —3A 94
Torcote Cres. Hud —6A 114
Tordoff Av. B'frd —9K 57
Tordoff Grn. B'frd —5N 75
Tordoff Pl. Kirks —2K 61
Tordoff Rd. Low M —7C 76
Tordoff Ter. Leeds —2K 61
Toronto Pl. Leeds —9F 44
Toronto St. Hyde P —4A 62
(off Queen's Rd.)
Toronto St. Leeds —6D 62
Torre Clo. Leeds —6J 63
Torre Cres. B'frd —4J 75
Torre Cres. Leeds —6K 63
Torre Dri. Leeds —5J 63
Torre Gdns. Leeds —6H 63
Torre Grn. Leeds —6H 63
Torre Gro. B'frd —4J 75
Torre Gro. Leeds —5J 63
Torre Hill. Leeds —6K 63
Torre La. Leeds —6K 63
Torre Mt. Leeds —5J 63
Torre Pl. Leeds —6J 63
Torre Rd. B'frd —4J 75
Torre Rd. Leeds —6H 63
Torre Vw. Leeds —5K 63
Torre Wlk. Leeds —5K 63
Torridon Cres. B'frd —7L 75
Torridon Rd. Dew —1H 117
Tor Vw. Broc —7A 148
Totley Clo. Barn —9C 154
Totties. —3B 164
Totties La. N Mill —3B 164
Toulston. —3J 33
Toulston La. B'ham —6E 32
Tower Av. Upt —1N 157
Tower Bldgs. Heck —9A 96
(off Church La.)
Tower Causeway. Todm —4D 86
Tower Ct. Leeds —6N 61
Tower Dri., The. Pool W —2H 27
Tower Gdns. Hal —8M 91
Tower Gro. Leeds —6K 61
Tower Hill. Sower B —8H 91
Tower Ho. St. Leeds —5E 62
Tower La. Leeds —6J 61
(in two parts)
Tower Pl. Leeds —6J 61
Tower Rd. Leeds —1M 81
Tower Rd. Shipl —7K 39
Towers Clo. Croft —2H 139
Towers La. Croft —1J 139
Towers Paddock. C'frd —5G 103
Towers Sq. Leeds —7C 44
Tower St. B'frd —4F 58
Tower St. Todm —3C 86
Towers Way. Leeds —7C 44
Tower Works. Leeds —7D 62
Towlerton La. Wren —1G 119
Town Av. Hud —2A 132
Town Clo. H'fth —6E 42
Town Cres. Hud —2A 132
Town End. —4H 61
(nr. Bramley)
Town End. —6B 130
(nr. Golcar)
Town End. —1A 164
(nr. Holmfirth)
Town End. —9K 79
(nr. Morley)
Town End. —4A 118
(nr. Ossett)
Town End. —1F 74
(nr. Queensbury)
Town End. —3L 99
(nr. Rothwell)
Town End. —6L 149
(nr. Shepley)
Town End. B'frd —1M 75
Town End. Gar —6M 65
Town End. Gild —6G 78
Town End. Gol —6C 130
Town End. Hud —6C 132
Town End. Morl —9L 79
(off Middleton Rd.)
Town End. Oss —6N 117
Town End Av. Ackw —3J 141
Town End Av. H'frth —1A 164
Town End Clo. Leeds —5H 61
Town End Cres. H'frth —1A 164
Town End La. Lep —6L 133
Townend Pl. Pud —6C 60
Town End Rd. Cytn —9G 57
Town End Rd. H'frth —2N 163
Townend Rd. Leeds —9L 61
Town End Yd. Leeds —5G 61
Townfield. Wilsd —1B 56
Townfield La. Hept —8G 70
Town Fields Rd. Ell —5D 112
Townfield Vw. H Bri —8G 70
(off Townfield La.)
Townfold. Oss —5A 118
Town Gate. —8C 146
(nr. Meltham)
Towngate. —5M 115
(nr. Mirfield)
Towngate. Bail —3B 40
(off Northgate)
Town Ga. B'frd —7F 40
Towngate. Brigh —9B 94
Town Ga. C'ley —8M 41
Towngate. Dart —8K 153
Town Ga. Guis —7J 25
Town Ga. Hept —8G 70
Town Ga. Hep —6C 164
Towngate. Hip —4H 93
Town Ga. H'frth —3M 163
Towngate. Hud —8M 131
Towngate. Kei —9J 21
Town Ga. Kbtn —1J 149
Town Ga. Lep —6L 133
Town Ga. L'ft —3B 90
Town Ga. Mars —5F 144
Towngate. Mir —5M 115
Town Ga. Nthng —9L 147
Towngate. N'wram —1F 92
Towngate. Oss —5A 118
Town Ga. Schol —4D 94
Towngate. Shipl —8B 40
Towngate. S'wram —8F 92
Town Ga. Sower B —9D 90
Town Ga. Uthg —3J 163
Town Ga. Wyke —2A 94
Towngate Av. Brigh —9B 94
Town Ga. Clo. Guis —7J 25
Towngate Gro. Mir —5M 115
Towngate Ho. Ell —5E 112
Towngate Rd. Bat —7D 96
Town Grn. Dew —4H 117
Town Hall Sq. Yead —9M 25
Town Hall St. Ell —5E 112
Town Hall St. H'frth —3M 163
Town Hall St. Kei —9J 21
Town Hall St. Mir —7L 115
Town Hall St. Sower B —9H 91
Town Hall St. E. Hal —5B 92
Town Hall Way. Dew —3G 116
Town Head. —7F 6
Town Head. Hon —4L 147
Townhead Fold. Add —1L 7
Town Hill. B'ham —6D 32
Town Hill St. Bgly —9G 39
Town La. B'frd —6F 40
Townley Av. Hal —8F 92
Townley Rd. Wake —6F 118
Town Moor. Thur —7D 148
Town Pl. Hud —2A 132
Town Rd. Hud —1G 132
Town St. Bat C & Dew —1F 116
Town St. Bees —4A 80
Town St. B'shaw —7L 77
Town St. Bmly —3F 60
Town St. C'ley —9M 41
Town St. Carl —1M 99
Town St. Chap A —8F 44
Town St. Earl —4J 117
Town St. Far —3A 60
Town St. Gild —6F 78
Town St. Guis —7J 25
Town St. Hems —2C 156
Town St. H'fth —7E 42
Town St. Leeds —6K 61
Town St. Midd —8D 80
Town St. Rawd —4A 42
Town St. Rod —1B 60
Town St. S'ley —5B 60
Town St. Yead —9M 25
Town St. M. Leeds —8F 44
Town St. Wlk. Leeds —8F 44
Town Ter. Hud —2A 132
Town, The. Dew —9G 117
Town Top. Hud —1G 133
Townville. —7K 103
Town Wells Dri. C'ley —9M 41
Towton Dri. C'frd —6A 102
Track Mt. Bat —1E 116
Track Rd. Bat —1E 116
Trafalgar Clo. Hud —7N 113
Trafalgar Gdns. Morl —1K 97
Trafalgar Rd. Dew —2E 116
Trafalgar Rd. I'ly —5G 9
Trafalgar Sq. Hal —7N 91
Trafalgar St. Bat —8D 96
Trafalgar St. B'frd —6C 58
Trafalgar St. Carc —8N 159
Trafalgar St. Hal —7N 91
Trafalgar St. Leeds —6F 62
Trafalgar Way. Carc —8N 159
Trafford Av. Leeds —4K 63
Trafford Gro. Leeds —3K 63
Trafford Ter. Leeds —4K 63
Traines Ho. Wake —6L 119
Tramways. Oaken —8D 76
Tranbeck Rd. Guis —7F 24
Tranfield Av. Guis —7G 25
Tranfield Clo. Guis —7G 25
Tranfield Ct. Guis —7G 25
Tranfield Gdns. Guis —7G 25
Tranmere Dri. Guis —7G 24
Tranmere Park. —8F 24
Tranquility. Leeds —4D 64
Tranquility Av. Leeds —4D 64
Tranquility Ct. Leeds —4D 64
(off Tranquility Av.)
Tranquility Wlk. Leeds —4D 64
Transvaal Ter. Bat —5E 96
Tranter Gro. B'frd —9J 59
Tranter Pl. Leeds —6N 63
Travis Ho. Todm —4J 107
(off Beswick St.)
Travis Lacey Ter. Dew —3E 116
Tredgold Av. B'hpe —6H 27
Tredgold Clo. Leeds —6H 27
Tredgold Cres. B'hpe —6H 27
Tredgold Gth. B'hpe —6H 27
Treefield Ind. Est. Gild —7G 78
Tree La. Hal —8F 72
Trees St. B'frd —5A 58
Tree Top Vw. Q'bry —3B 74
Trelawn Av. Leeds —1N 61
Trelawn Cres. Leeds —1N 61
Trelawn Pl. Leeds —1N 61
Trelawn St. Leeds —1N 61
Trelawn Ter. Leeds —1N 61
Tremont Gdns. Leeds —3G 81
Trenam Pk. Dri. B'frd —5E 40
Trenance Dri. Shipl —8L 39
Trenance Gdns. G'lnd —4N 111
Trenholme Av. B'frd —7N 75
Trenholme Ho. B'frd —8G 40
(off Garsdale Av.)
Trenic Cres. Leeds —3N 61
Trenic Dri. Leeds —3N 61
Trent Av. Gar —9B 66
Trent Av. Nor —8H 101
Trentham Av. Leeds —2D 80
Trentham Gro. Leeds —2D 80
Trentham Pl. Leeds —2D 80
Trentham Row. Leeds —2D 80
Trentham St. Leeds —3D 80
Trentham Ter. Leeds —2D 80
Trenton Dri. B'frd —5A 58
Trenton Rd. Bat —9J 97
Trent Rd. Leeds —6H 63
Trent St. Leeds —9D 62
Trescoe Av. Leeds —5H 61
Tresham Ct. Dew —1J 117
Trevelyan Sq. Leeds —7E 62

Trevelyan St. Brigh —7M 93
Trevelyan St. Hud —5B 132
Trevor Ter. Carr G —6G 99
Triangle. —2E 110
Triangle, The. Hud —5K 131
Triath Ct. Bat —6B 96
Trigg All. Haw —9C 36
Trigg Ter. Liv —8L 95
Trigot Ct. S Kirk —6J 157
Trilby St. Wake —4M 119
Trimmer La. Blkhd —9M 69
Trimmingham La. Hal —6K 91
Trimmingham Rd. Hal —6K 91
Trimmingham Vs. Hal —6L 91
Trinity Bus. Cen. Wake —6N 119
Trinity Chu. Ga. Wake —5L 119
Trinity Clo. Hal —7N 73
Trinity Ct. Hon —5L 147
Trinity Ct. S Elm —5N 157
Trinity Dri. Den D —3C 166
Trinity Fold. Hal —6B 92
(off Blackwall)
Trinity Ho. Wake —5M 119
(off Kirkgate)
Trinity Pl. Bgly —5F 38
Trinity Pl. Hal —6B 92
Trinity Ri. Otley —1M 25
Trinity Rd. B'frd —9B 58
Trinity Rd. Hal —6B 92
Trinity St. Bat —1F 116
Trinity St. Hal —6B 92
(in two parts)
Trinity St. H Bri —1G 88
Trinity St. Hud —3K 131
Trinity St. Kei —8J 21
(off East Av.)
Trinity St. Leeds —6E 62
Trinity St. Mir —7L 115
Trinity St. Pon —2K 123
Trinity St. Wake —8A 120
Trinity St. Arc. Leeds —7E 62
Trinity Ter. Bat —3A 96
Trinity Vw. Hal —6C 92
Trinity Vw. Low M —6C 76
Trinity Vw. Oss —4N 117
Trinity Wlk. Low M —6C 76
Trinity Way. S Elm —5N 157
Trip Gth. Lntn —7J 17
Trip La. Lntn —7G 16
Tristram Av. B'frd —3E 76
Troon Dri. Hud —8L 113
Troon Way. Wake —9J 119
Trooper La. Hal —7C 92
Trooper Ter. Hal —7C 92
Tropical World. —6K 45
Trough Gate. —4A 106
Trough La. Oxe & Denh —5F 54
Trough La. S Elm —6B 158
Troughton Pl. Pud —9C 60
Troughton St. Pud —9C 60
Trough Well La. Wren —9G 98
Troutbeck Av. Bail —6K 39
Trowell Way. Barn —9A 154
Troy. —5F 42
Troydale. —8E 60
Troydale Gdns. Pud —9E 60
Troydale Gro. Pud —9E 60
Troydale La. Pud —8D 60
Troy Hill. —8K 79
Troy Hill. H'fth —5F 42
Troy Hill. Morl —8K 79
Troy Ri. Morl —8L 79
Troy Rd. H'fth —5F 42
Troy Rd. Morl —9K 79
Trueman Av. Heck —8B 96
Trueman Ct. Low M —7C 76
Trueman Way. S Elm —5N 157
Truncliffe. —4B 76
Truncliffe. B'frd —4B 76
Truncliffe Ho. B'frd —4B 76
(off Truncliffe)
Trundles La. Knot —8G 105
Truro Dri. Nor —9J 101
Truro St. Leeds —6M 61
Truro Wlk. Nor —9J 101
Tubby La. Hud —1N 131
Tucknott Dri. Heck —8A 96
Tudor Barn Ct. Wrose —8B 40
Tudor Clo. Fars —4N 59
Tudor Clo. Pon —6J 123
Tudor Ct. B'frd —9C 58
(off Swarland Gro.)
Tudor Ct. S Elm —6M 157
Tudor Cft. Hud —6D 114
Tudor Gdns. Leeds —3A 80
Tudor Ho. Hud —4N 131
(off Oldgate)
Tudor Ho. Wake —5L 119
Tudor Lawns. Carr G —7G 99
Tudor St. B'frd —1B 76
Tudor St. Lint —1N 145
Tudor Way. C'frd —4H 103
Tudor Way. Dew —8E 116
Tuel La. Sower B —7H 91
Tufton St. Sils —8D 6
Tulip Retail Pk. H'let —2F 80
Tulip St. Haw —1C 54
Tulip St. Leeds —2F 80
Tumbling Clo. Oss —5A 118
Tumbling Hill. C'ton —6N 123
Tumbling Hill St. B'frd —8B 58
Tun La. S Hien —3L 155
Tunnacliffe Rd. Hud —7N 131
Tunnel St. Denh —6K 55
Tunnel St. Hud —2H 147
Tunnicliffe Pl. Sils —8D 6
Tunstall Grn. B'frd —2J 77
Tunstall Rd. Leeds —2E 80
Tunwell La. B'frd —2G 58
Tunwell St. B'frd —2G 59
Tup La. Wake —1K 155
Turbary Av. Fars —4B 60
Turbid La. Hud —2F 146
Turbury La. G'lnd —3L 111
Turf Ct. Cull —1J 55
Turf La. Cull —9J 37
Turf Moor La. Stainb —1H 13
(in two parts)
Turgate. Err —4J 89
Turgate La. Sower B —2N 109
Turkey Hill. Pud —8C 60
(in two parts)
Turks Head Yd. Leeds —6E 62
(off Commercial St.)
Turley Cote La. Holy G —1A 130
Turnberry Av. Leeds —3D 44
Turnberry Clo. Leeds —3D 44
Turnberry Clo. Ting —4N 97
Turnberry Ct. Low U —5G 21
Turnberry Ct. Norm —2L 121
Turnberry Dri. Leeds —3D 44
Turnberry Dri. Ting —4N 97
Turnberry Gdns. Ting —4N 97
Turnberry Gro. Cud —9K 155
Turnberry Gro. Leeds —3D 44
Turnberry Pl. Leeds —3D 44
Turnberry Ri. Leeds —3D 44
Turnberry Vw. Leeds —3D 44
Turnbridge Rd. Hud —4A 132
Turnbull Ct. Leeds —1M 63
Turner Av. Bat —7F 96
Turner Av. B'frd —9L 57
Turner Av. N. Hal —8K 73
Turner Av. S. Hal —8L 73
Turner Clo. Ting —4A 98
Turner Cres. Otley —8M 11
Turner Dri. Ting —4A 98
Turner Farm. Hal —6L 73
(off Causeway Foot)
Turner Ho. Kirks —2J 61
Turner La. Add —3J 7
(in two parts)
Turner La. Hal —3C 92
(in two parts)
Turner Pl. B'frd —9N 57
Turner Pl. Hal —9L 73
Turners Ct. Hal —2A 92
Turner's La. Knot —9L 105
Turner St. Fars —3A 60
Turner's Yd. Fars —3A 60
Turner's Yd. Leeds —4G 60
Turner Vw. Hal —9L 73
(off Bank Edge Rd.)
Turney St. Hal —2N 91
Turnip La. Dew —1G 134
Turn O The Nook. Oss —5M 117
Turnpike St. Ell —4F 112
Turnshaw Rd. Kbtn —3K 149
Turnshaw Rd. Oakw —5N 35
Turnshaws Av. Kbtn —3L 149
Turnshaws Clo. Kbtn —2L 149
Turnsteads Av. Cleck —4F 94
Turnsteads Clo. Cleck —4G 94
Turnsteads Cres. Cleck —4G 94
Turnsteads Dri. Cleck —4G 94
Turnsteads Mt. Cleck —4G 94
Turnstone Ct. Leeds —8F 80
Turnways, The. Leeds —2M 61
Turret Hall Rd. C'twn —2D 88
Turton Grn. Gild —6G 79
Turton St. Wake —5M 119
Turton Va. Gild —7G 78
Turver's La. Knot —8K 105
Turvin Rd. L'boro & Ripp —1E 126
Twain Cres. C'frd —7J 103
Tweedale Gdns. Dew —3E 116
Tweedale St. Dew —3E 116
Tweed Clo. Birs —3D 96
Tweedy St. Wilsd —1B 56
Twelfth Av. Liv —7F 94
Twickenham Ct. B'frd —4B 58
Twine La. H Bri —3A 90
Twinge La. Hal —6E 92
Twitch Hill. Horb —1D 136
Twivey St. C'frd —5C 102
Two Laws Rd. Oldf —6D 34
Tyas Gro. Leeds —7K 63
Tyas La. Slai —9H 129
Tyburn La. Eml —3E 150
Tyersal. —8H 59
Tyersal Av. B'frd —7K 59
Tyersal Clo. B'frd —8K 59
Tyersal Ct. B'frd —8J 59
Tyersal Cres. B'frd —8K 59
Tyersal Dri. B'frd —8K 59
Tyersal Gth. B'frd —8K 59
Tyersal Gate. —1J 77
Tyersal Grn. B'frd —8K 59
Tyersal Gro. B'frd —8K 59
Tyersal La. B'frd —1J 77
(in two parts)
Tyersal Pk. B'frd —8K 59
Tyersal Rd. B'frd —8J 59
Tyersal Ter. B'frd —8J 59
Tyersal Vw. B'frd —8J 59
Tyersal Wlk. B'frd —8K 59
Tyler Clo. Nor I —1M 121
Tyler Ct. B'frd —7G 40
Tyndale Av. Horb —9E 118
Tyndale Wlk. Bat —7B 96
Tynedale Ct. Leeds —9C 44
Tyne St. B'frd —6D 58
Tyne St. Haw —8D 36
Tyne St. Kei —9K 21
Tynwald Clo. Leeds —5C 44
Tynwald Dri. Leeds —4C 44
Tynwald Gdns. Leeds —5C 44
Tynwald Grn. Leeds —4C 44
Tynwald Hill. Leeds —5C 44
Tynwald Mt. Leeds —4C 44
Tynwald Rd. Leeds —5C 44
Tynwald Wlk. Leeds —4C 44
Tyrls, The. B'frd —8C 58
Tyrrell Ct. Wake —4F 118
Tyrrel St. B'frd —7C 58
Tyson St. B'frd —6B 58
Tyson St. Hal —6L 91
Tythe Barn Rd. Knot —8F 104

Ullswater Av. Dew —1H 117
Ullswater Clo. Dew —1H 117
Ullswater Clo. Knot —2D 124
Ullswater Cres. Leeds —7N 63
Ullswater Cres. W'ford —7D 82
Ullswater Dri. B'frd —7L 75
Ullswater Dri. Weth —3K 17
Ullswater Ri. Weth —3K 17
Ullswater Rd. Dew —1H 117
Una Pl. Hud —2K 131
Under Bank. —4N 163
Underbank Av. H Bri —3D 88
Under Bank Old Rd. H'frth —4N 163
Undercliffe. —5F 58
Undercliffe La. B'frd —5E 58
Undercliffe Old Rd. B'frd —5F 58
Undercliffe Ri. I'ly —7K 9
Undercliffe Rd. B'frd —3F 58
Undercliffe St. B'frd —6F 58
Underwood Dri. Rawd —5M 41
Underwood Ho. B'frd —6D 58
(off North Wing)
Union Ct. Otley —1K 25
Union Cross Yd. Hal —5B 92
Union Gro. Liv —9M 95
Union Ho. Q'bry —3H 75
Union Ho. La. Q'bry —3H 75
Union La. Hal —5K 73
Union Pl. Leeds —8D 62
Union Rd. B'frd —9N 57
Union Rd. Liv —9M 95
Union Rd. Low M —6A 76
Union Sq. Wake —5M 119
Union St. Bail —5C 40
Union St. Bgly —9D 22
Union St. Birs —3B 96
Union St. C'frd —5B 102
Union St. Chur —5M 79
Union St. Dew —3G 116
Union St. G'lnd —4C 112
Union St. Hal —5B 92
Union St. Heck —9N 95
Union St. Hems —3E 156
Union St. Hud —3N 131
Union St. Leeds —6E 62
Union St. Lind —2G 131
Union St. Oss —5N 117
Union St. Otley —1K 25
Union St. Q'bry —4D 74
Union St. Slai —9M 129
Union St. Sower B —7J 91
(nr. Albert Rd.)
Union St. Sower B —2E 110
(nr. Butterworth La.)
Union St. Todm —7K 87
Union St. Wake —4L 119
Union St. S. Todm —7K 87
Union Ter. Leeds —9E 44
Union Yd. B'frd —7F 40
Unity Clo. Leeds —2D 62
Unity Ct. Brigh —3L 113
Unity St. Carl —1M 99
Unity St. H Bri —9H 71
Unity St. Riddl —6M 21
Unity St. Todm —3J 107
Unity St. N. Bgly —5E 38
Unity St. S. Bgly —5E 38
Unity Ter. Hal —6L 91
University Rd. Leeds —4C 62
University St. C'frd —5D 102
Unwin Pl. B'frd —4K 57
Upland Cres. Leeds —1J 63
Upland Gdns. Leeds —2J 63
Upland Gro. Leeds —1J 63
Upland Rd. Leeds —2J 63
Uplands. Hud —1K 131
Uplands. Kei —7G 20
Uplands Av. Dart —9E 152
Uplands Av. Q'bry —3G 74
Uplands Clo. Q'bry —3G 75
Uplands Cres. Q'bry —3G 74
Uplands Dri. Mir —5L 115
Uplands Gro. Q'bry —3G 74
Uplands, The. Pon —4J 123
Up. Accommodation Rd. Leeds —6G 63
Up. Ada St. Shipl —7L 39
Up. Addison St. B'frd —9D 58
Up. Allerton La. All —6D 56
Upper Armley. —5K 61
Up. Ash Gro. S Elm —6N 157
Up. Ashley La. Shipl —7N 39
Up. Bank End Rd. H'frth —5N 163
Up. Bank Hey Bottom. Ripp —8E 110
Up. Barker St. Liv —8L 95
Up. Basinghall St. Leeds —6D 62
Upper Batley. —4F 96
Up. Batley La. Bat —3C 96
Up. Batley Low La. Bat —2E 96
Up. Battye St. Heck —7A 96
Up. Bell Hall. Hal —7N 91
Up. Bolton Brow. Sower B —7K 91
Up. Bonegate. Brigh —9N 93
Up. Brig Royd. Sower B —7D 110
Upper Brockholes. —5K 73
Up. Brow Rd. Hud —5J 131
Upper Butts. Cleck —5H 95
Up. Calton St. Kei —2H 37
Up. Camroyd St. Dew —2G 117
Up. Carr La. C'ley —9L 41
Up. Carr St. Liv —7L 95
Up. Castle St. B'frd —1C 76
Up. Chelsea St. Kei —2H 37
Upper Clough. —1B 146
Up. Clough La. Lint —1B 146
Up. Commercial St. Bat —7F 96
Upper Common. —9J 151
(nr. Clayton West)
Upper Common. —1B 94
(nr. Wyke)
Up. Common La. Clay W —9J 151
Up. Croft Rd. Bat —8E 96
Up. Cross St. Dew —2G 116
Upper Cudworth. —9K 155
Upper Cumberworth. —2N 165
Up. Cumberworth La. Up Cum —2M 165
Upper Denby. —5C 166
Upper Eastwood. —4B 88
Up. Ellistones. G'lnd —4N 111
(off Martin Grn. La.)
Up. Ellistones Ct. G'lnd —4N 111
Upper Exley. —2D 112
Upper Fagley. —3J 59
Up. Ferndown Grn. All —5F 56
Upperfield Dri. Gol —6B 130
Up. Field Ho. La. Tri —1D 110
Up. Field La. Dart —8M 151
Up. Forest Rd. Barn —9A 154
Upper Forge. Hal —5B 92
Up. Fountaine St. Leeds —6D 62
Up. Fountain St. Sower B —8H 91
Upper Ga. Hep —6C 164
Up. George St. B'frd —4N 75
Up. George St. Heck —8A 96
Up. George St. Hud —4L 131
Up. Grange Av. All —6G 57
Upper Green. —2L 75
(nr. Bradford)
Upper Green. —5N 97
(nr. East Ardsley)
Upper Grn. Bail —5N 39
Upper Grn. B'frd —2L 75
Up. Green Av. Schol —4D 94
Up. Green Av. Ting —5N 97
Up. Green Clo. Ting —5A 98
Up. Green Dri. Ting —5A 98
Up. Green La. Brigh —7K 93
Up. Green Way. Ting —5N 97
Up. Hagg Rd. Thon —7N 147
Up. Hall Vw. N'wram —1F 92
Up. Hatfield Pl. H'cft —8L 139
Up. Haugh Shaw. Hal —7N 91
Upperhead Row. Hud —4M 131
Upper Heaton. —8F 114
Up. Heaton La. Hud —9F 114
Up. Heights Rd. T'tn —6B 56
Up. High Royds. Dart —9J 153
Up. Hird St. Kei —2G 37
Upper Hirst. Hud —2C 130
Upper Holme. —1K 145
Up. House Cotts. Q'bry —3F 74
Upper Ho. Fold. Up Den —5C 166
Up. House La. Liv —8G 95
Up. House Rd. H'frth —8A 164
Up. House St. B'frd —9F 58
Up. Hoyle Ing. T'tn —7E 56
Up. Kirkgate. Hal —5C 92
Upper La. Eml —2F 150
Upper La. Gom —5M 95
Upper La. Hal —9E 74
Upper La. Neth —7M 135
Upper La. Todm —3L 87
Up. Langwith. Coll —9F 16
Up. Lombard St. Rawd —3L 41
Up. Lumb La. Cra V —8J 89
Upper Marsh. —1A 54
Up. Marsh La. Oxe —1N 53
Up. Martin Grn. G'lnd —4N 111
Up. Mary St. Shipl —7L 39
Up. Maythorn La. H'frth —8H 165
Up. Meadows. H'frth —3J 163
Up. Meadows. Q'bry —5D 74
Up. Millergate. B'frd —7C 58
(off Kirkgate)
Up. Mill Row. E Mor —6D 22
Upper Mills. Slai —1M 145
Uppermoor. Pud —7N 59
Uppermoor Clo. Pud —8A 60
Upper Moor Side. —3F 78
Up. Mosscar St. B'frd —7E 58
Upper Mt. Mel —8E 146
Up. Mount St. Bat —9F 96
Upper Mt. St. Hud —6L 131
Up. Nidd St. B'frd —8F 58
Up. North St. Bat —8E 96
Up. North St. Leeds —5D 62
Upper Oldfield. —8K 147
Up. Parish Ghyll La. I'ly —6E 8
Up. Park Ga. B'frd —7D 58
Up. Peel St. Dew —2G 116
Up. Piccadilly. B'frd —7C 58
Up. Quarry Rd. Hud —5E 114
Up. Raglan St. Todm —6K 87
Up. Range. Hal —3B 92
(off Woodlands Gro.)
Upper Rd. Bat & Dew —1E 116
Up. Rushton Rd. B'frd —5H 59
Up. Seymour St. B'frd —8F 58
Up. South St. Dew —2F 116
Up. Station Rd. Bat —8G 97
Up. Sutherland Rd. Hal —4K 93
Upper Swithen. —6D 152
Upperthong. —3J 163
Upperthong La. H'frth —3J 163
Upper Town. —4C 54
Upper Town. Oxe —4C 54
Up. Town St. Leeds —3F 60
Up. Warrengate. Wake —5M 119
Up. Washer La. Hal —7M 91
Up. Wellhouse Rd. Gol —7B 130
Up. Westlock Av. Leeds —5J 63
Up. West St. Bat —7H 97
Up. Willow Hill. Hal —6K 91
Up. Woodlands Rd. B'frd —5M 57
Up. Woodview Pl. Leeds —3D 80
(off Woodview St.)
Up. Wortley Dri. Leeds —7L 61
Up. Wortley Rd. Leeds —7L 61
Upper Wyke. —1B 94
Up. York St. Wake —4L 119
Upton. —1B 158
Upton Beacon. —1N 157
Upton Hopton. —9J 115
Upton St. Bat —6E 96
Upton Wlk. All —6G 57
Upwood Holiday Pk. Oxe —3E 54
Upwood La. E Mor —6C 22
Urban Ter. Grng M —5B 134
Ure Cres. B'frd —6B 58
Ure Gro. Weth —1L 17
Usher St. B'frd —9E 58
Uttley St. Hal —2A 92

Vale. —3E 86
Vale Av. Knot —8C 104
Vale Av. Leeds —5J 45
Vale Clo. Hud —7D 132
Vale Cres. Knot —8C 104
Vale Gro. Q'bry —4E 74
Vale Gro. Sils —8D 6
Vale Head Gro. Knot —8C 104
Vale Head Mt. Knot —8C 104

Vale Mill La. Haw —6D 36
Valentine Ct. T'tn —7D 56
Valentine M. Loft —4L 99
Vale Rd. Kin —9B 140
Valestone Av. Hems —2E 156
Vale St. Brigh —9M 93
Vale St. Kei —7L 21
Vale St. Todm —7K 87
Vale Ter. Knot —7C 104
Vale Ter. Oakw —6D 36
Vale, The. Coll —9H 17
Vale, The. Leeds —1B 62
Vale Vw. Ackw —3H 141
Valley Av. Hal —4L 93
Valley Av. S Elm —6A 158
Valley Clo. Leeds —2C 44
Valley Ct. B'frd —5C 58
Valley Ct. C'frd —7A 102
Valley Ct. Liv —7M 95
Valley Cres. Wren —1H 119
Valley Dri. Dew —1H 135
Valley Dri. I'ly —5J 9
Valley Dri. Leeds —5B 64
Valley Dri. W'ford —5M 83
Valley Dri. Wren —2H 119
Valley Farm Rd. Leeds —4J 81
alley Farm Way. Leeds —4J 81
alley Fold. Q'bry —5D 74
alley Gdns. Leeds —7E 44
alley Grn. Pud —8C 60
Valley Gro. Hal —6M 73
alley Gro. Pud —8C 60
alley Head. Hud —9H 113
alley Heights. Hud —9H 113
alley Mills. Dlgtn —5E 78
alley Mills Ind. Est. B'frd —7J 41
alley Mt. Kip —3N 83
alley Mt. Leeds —6D 60
alley Pde. B'frd —5B 58
alley Parade. —5B 58
alley Pl. B'frd —5C 58
alley Ridge. Kip —2N 83
(in two parts)
alley Ri. Leeds —1F 60
alley Ri. Sower B —4D 110
(off Lumb La.)
alley Rd. B'frd —4B 58
alley Rd. Cleck —4J 95
alley Rd. D'ton —7D 124
alley Rd. Dew —1J 135
alley Rd. H Bri —1H 89
alley Rd. I'ly —4J 9
alley Rd. Kei —9M 21
alley Rd. Kip —2N 83
alley Rd. Leeds —1F 60
alley Rd. Liv —8L 95
alley Rd. M'well —8J 153
alley Rd. Morl —8L 79
alley Rd. Oss —7N 117
alley Rd. Pon —3K 123
alley Rd. Pud —8B 60
alley Rd. Shipl —8N 39
lley Rd. Retail Pk. B'frd —6C 58
alley Sq. Pud —8C 60
alley St. S Elm —7M 157
lley Ter. Leeds —4H 45
lley, The. Leeds —1C 44
lley Vw. Bail —6N 39
lley Vw. Hal —6M 73
lley Vw. H'den —6N 37
lley Vw. S Elm —6A 158
lley Vw. Clo. Oakw —4E 36
lley Vw. Gdns. Cro R —7E 36
lley Vw. Gro. B'frd —4E 58
lley Vw. Rd. Hept —9G 71
lley Vw. Rd. Oss —7N 117
lley Way. Hal —6M 73
rley Rd. Slai —4M 145
rley St. S'ley —5A 60
in two parts)
rleys Yd. Pud —7C 60
ughan St. B'frd —7B 58
ughan St. Hal —7M 91
gal Cres. Hal —2M 91
tch St. Idle —7F 40
tch Wlk. Sower B —8K 91
nn St. Hud —4N 131
ntnor Clo. Gom —2M 95
ntnor Clo. Oss —6N 117
ntnor Dri. Oss —6N 117
ntnor St. B'frd —7E 58
ntnor Ter. Hal —8A 92
ntnor Way. Oss —6N 117
nto Clo. B'frd —5N 75
rdun Rd. B'frd —5M 75
re Sq. B'frd —1C 76
rity Spur. Leeds —6N 63
rity St. B'frd —6K 77
rity Vw. Leeds —5N 63
rmont St. Leeds —4D 60
rner St. Pon —7C 122
rnon Av. Hud —3L 131
rnon Clo. Hud —3L 131

Vernon Ct. Kei —8H 21
Vernon Pl. B'frd —4F 58
Vernon Pl. S'ley —5B 60
Vernon Pl. Wake —7K 119
Vernon Rd. Leeds —5D 62
Vernon Rd. Liv & Heck —8M 95
Vernon St. Cro R —7F 36
Vernon St. Leeds —5D 62
Vernon St. Todm —9J 87
Vesper Clo. Leeds —9J 43
Vesper Ct. Leeds —9H 43
Vesper Ct. Dri. Leeds —9H 43
Vesper Gdns. Leeds —1J 61
Vesper Ga. Cres. Leeds —1J 61
Vesper Ga. Dri. Leeds —9H 43
Vesper Ga. Mt. Leeds —1J 61
Vesper Gro. Leeds —2K 61
Vesper La. Leeds —1J 61
Vesper Mt. Leeds —2K 61
Vesper Pl. Leeds —2K 61
Vesper Ri. Leeds —9H 43
Vesper Rd. Leeds —9G 43
Vesper Ter. Leeds —2K 61
Vesper Wlk. Leeds —1H 61
Vesper Way. Leeds —9H 43
Vestry St. B'frd —2F 76
Viaduct Rd. Leeds —5N 61
Viaduct St. Hud —3M 131
Viaduct St. Slai —9N 129
Viaduct St. S'ley —5A 60
Vicarage Av. Gild —7F 78
Vicarage Av. Leeds —2L 61
Vicarage Clo. S Kirk —6J 157
Vicarage Clo. Wake —7K 99
Vicarage Clo. Wyke —2A 94
Vicarage Dri. Pud —7A 60
Vicarage Gdns. B'shaw —8L 77
Vicarage Gdns. Brigh —3L 113
Vicarage Gdns. F'stne —3D 122
Vicarage Gdns. Otley —1L 25
Vicarage La. B'ham —6D 32
Vicarage La. F'stne —6D 122
Vicarage La. Roys —6D 154
Vicarage Meadows. Mir —6N 115
Vicarage Pl. Leeds —2L 61
Vicarage Rd. Dew —3G 116
Vicarage Rd. Hud —4G 130
Vicarage Rd. Leeds —4B 62
Vicarage Rd. Sav T —6F 116
Vicarage Rd. Shipl —7C 40
Vicarage St. Leeds —2L 61
Vicarage St. Wake —5M 119
Vicarage St. N. Wake —4M 119
Vicarage Ter. Bat —5D 96
Vicarage Ter. Leeds —2L 61
Vicarage Vw. Leeds —2L 61
Vicar La. B'frd —7D 58
(in two parts)
Vicar La. Leeds —6E 62
Vicar La. Oss —8A 118
Vicar Pk. Dri. Hal —4H 91
Vicar Pk. Rd. Hal —5H 91
Vicars Rd. Leeds —2H 63
Vicars Ter. All B —9B 84
Vicars Ter. Leeds —2H 63
Vicar St. Liv —8L 95
Vickerman Cres. Hud —9L 131
Vickerman St. Hal —6M 91
Vickers Av. Leeds —3J 61
Vickers Av. S Elm —8L 157
Vickersdale. S'ley —4B 60
Vickersdale Gro. S'ley —4B 60
(off Haydn's Ter.)
Vickers Pl. S'ley —4B 60
Vickers St. C'frd —4D 102
Vickers St. Morl —1J 97
Vickers Yd. S'ley —5A 60
Victor Dri. Guis —8J 25
Victoria. —4L 163
Victoria Av. Bat —8F 96
Victoria Av. Brigh —9A 94
Victoria Av. Cleck —5H 95
Victoria Av. Eccl —2H 59
Victoria Av. Ell —5D 112
Victoria Av. Hal —6M 91
Victoria Av. Haw —7C 36
Victoria Av. H'fth —8D 42
Victoria Av. I'ly —5E 8
Victoria Av. Kei —8J 21
Victoria Av. Leeds —6J 63
Victoria Av. Men —3D 24
Victoria Av. Morl —8K 79
Victoria Av. Out —9K 99
Victoria Av. Rothw —9N 81
Victoria Av. Shipl —7L 39
Victoria Av. Sower B —8J 91
Victoria Av. Wake —5J 119
Victoria Av. Yead —1A 42
Victoria Bldgs. Cra V —1K 109
Victoria Bldgs. Dew —2H 117
Victoria Clo. All B —9B 84
Victoria Clo. H'fth —8D 42
Victoria Clo. I'ly —5F 8

Victoria Clo. Yead —9A 26
Victoria Ct. Birs —3B 96
Victoria Ct. C'frd —6D 102
Victoria Ct. Hud —6M 131
Victoria Ct. Kei —9H 21
Victoria Ct. Morl —8K 79
Victoria Ct. Shipl —8L 39
(off Victoria Av.)
Victoria Ct. Upt —2N 157
Victoria Ct. M. Leeds —3A 62
Victoria Cres. Dew —1E 116
Victoria Cres. Ell —5E 112
Victoria Cres. H'fth —8D 42
Victoria Cres. Pud —7N 59
Victoria Dri. B'frd —2H 59
Victoria Dri. Dew —7F 116
Victoria Dri. Hal —1G 92
Victoria Dri. H'fth —8D 42
Victoria Dri. I'ly —5E 8
Victoria Dri. Morl —7L 79
Victoria Gdns. H'fth —8E 42
Victoria Gdns. I'ly —5E 8
Victoria Gdns. Pud —7N 59
Victoria Grange Dri. Morl —8K 79
Victoria Grange Way. Morl —8K 79
Victoria Gro. H'fth —9D 42
Victoria Gro. I'ly —5E 8
Victoria Gro. Leeds —6K 63
Victoria Gro. Pud —7N 59
Victoria Gro. Wake —8F 118
Victoria Ho. Kirks —2K 61
Victoria Ind. Est. B'frd —2G 59
Victoria La. Gol —6B 130
Victoria La. Hud —5N 131
Victoria M. H'fth —8D 42
Victoria M. Kei —9H 21
(off Drewry Rd.)
Victoria M. Morl —8K 79
Victoria Mills. Bat —6E 96
Victoria Mt. H'fth —7D 42
Victoria Pk. Shipl —8L 39
Victoria Pk. Av. Bmly & Kirks —3H 61
Victoria Pk. Gro. Bmly —3H 61
Victoria Pk. Gro. Kirks —3J 61
Victoria Pk. St. Kei —8K 21
Victoria Pk. Vw. Kei —8K 21
Victoria Pl. B'frd —1G 59
Victoria Pl. Brigh —2N 113
Victoria Pl. C'frd —4D 102
Victoria Pl. Cliff —4D 32
Victoria Pl. Hon —9F 130
Victoria Pl. Hud —5B 132
Victoria Pl. Mir —6K 115
Victoria Pl. Yead —9L 25
Victoria Quarter. Leeds —6E 62
(LS1)
Victoria Quarter. Leeds —6J 63
(LS9)
Victoria Ri. Pud —7N 59
Victoria Rd. Brigh —5N 93
Victoria Rd. Bur W —8C 10
Victoria Rd. Dew —2F 116
Victoria Rd. Eccl & B'frd —1G 58
Victoria Rd. Ell —6C 112
Victoria Rd. Gom —4N 95
Victoria Rd. Guis —8H 25
Victoria Rd. Hal —5N 91
Victoria Rd. Haw —8D 36
Victoria Rd. H Bri —9H 71
Victoria Rd. Hip —5J 93
Victoria Rd. Hud —7L 131
Victoria Rd. I'ly —5E 8
Victoria Rd. Kei —1H 37
Victoria Rd. Kirks —2K 61
Victoria Rd. Leeds —3A 62
(LS6)
Victoria Rd. Leeds —8D 62
(LS11)
Victoria Rd. Liv —9L 95
Victoria Rd. Mel —7C 146
Victoria Rd. Morl —8K 79
Victoria Rd. Nort —7N 143
Victoria Rd. Oakw —5D 36
Victoria Rd. Pud —4A 60
(nr. Northcote St.)
Victoria Rd. Pud —7N 59
(nr. Uppermoor)
Victoria Rd. Rothw —7M 81
Victoria Rd. Roys —5E 154
Victoria Rd. Shipl —7L 39
Victoria Rd. Sower B —9H 91
Victoria Rd. Thorn L —7F 116
Victoria Rd. Todm —6K 87
Victoria Rd. Wibs —5M 75
Victoria Shop. Cen. B'frd —6M 57
Victoria Springs. H'frth —4K 163
Victoria Sq. Leeds —6D 62
Victoria St. Ackw —5D 140
Victoria St. All —3F 56
Victoria St. All B —9B 84
Victoria St. Bail —6A 40
Victoria St. Bat —6E 96

Victoria St. Bgly —5E 38
Victoria St. Birs —3C 96
Victoria St. B'frd —6B 58
Victoria St. Brigh —2N 113
Victoria St. C'ley —9L 41
Victoria St. C'frd —4B 102
Victoria St. Chur —6M 79
Victoria St. Cytn —1G 75
Victoria St. Clay W —7H 151
Victoria St. Cleck —4H 95
Victoria St. Clif —9A 94
Victoria St. Cud —9J 155
Victoria St. Cull —9L 37
Victoria St. D'tn —8C 114
Victoria St. Fag —4G 59
Victoria St. F'stne —6D 122
Victoria St. G'lnd —4C 112
Victoria St. Hal —5B 92
Victoria St. Heck —8A 96
Victoria St. Hems —3E 156
Victoria St. H'frth —3M 163
Victoria St. Horb —1B 136
Victoria St. Leeds —5B 62
(LS3)
Victoria St. Leeds —8F 44
(LS7)
Victoria St. Lind —2H 131
Victoria St. Lock —6M 131
Victoria St. Mars —5F 144
Victoria St. M'wte —9D 22
Victoria St. Mold —5B 132
Victoria St. Morl —8J 79
Victoria St. Oakw —5D 36
(off Victoria Rd.)
Victoria St. Out —8K 99
Victoria St. Pon —9K 103
Victoria St. Q'bry —4E 74
Victoria St. Raven —5B 116
Victoria St. Shipl —7N 39
Victoria St. Sower B —9H 91
Victoria St. Thack —5F 40
Victoria St. Todm —3E 86
Victoria St. Wake —4J 119
Victoria St. Weth —4M 17
Victoria St. Wilsd —2B 56
Victoria Ter. Clay W —7J 151
Victoria Ter. Guis —7J 25
(off Lands La.)
Victoria Ter. Hal —6N 91
(off Park Dri., HX1)
Victoria Ter. Hal —8N 91
(HX2)
Victoria Ter. Head —9N 43
Victoria Ter. Hip —5J 93
Victoria Ter. Kei —9K 21
(off Dalton La.)
Victoria Ter. Leeds —5B 62
Victoria Ter. L'ft —7E 90
Victoria Ter. Morl —1H 97
Victoria Ter. Shipl —6L 39
Victoria Ter. S'ley —4C 60
Victoria Ter. Todm —5B 88
Victoria Ter. Yead —9N 25
Victoria Vs. S'ley —5B 60
Victoria Wlk. H'fth —8D 42
Victoria Way. Wake —9K 99
Victor Rd. B'frd —4N 57
Victor Rd. S Kirk —7J 157
Victor St. Bat —7G 96
Victor St. B'frd —7J 59
Victor St. Carc —9N 159
Victor St. C'frd —7C 102
Victor St. Mann —4N 57
Victor St. S Elm —7M 157
Victor Ter. B'frd —4N 57
Victor Ter. Hal —4N 91
Victory Av. Hud —5H 131
Victory Av. Wake —1B 120
Victory Rd. I'ly —5G 9
View Cft. Rd. Shipl —7A 40
Viewlands. Hud —7M 113
Viewlands Cres. Men —3H 25
Viewlands Mt. Men —3H 25
Viewlands Ri. Men —4H 25
View Rd. Kei —8G 20
View Row. All —6H 57
View St. Hud —5B 132
View, The. Alw —1B 44
View, The. Round —7H 45
Vigar Mnr. B'frd —7H 57
Vigar Mans. Weth —2M 17
Vigar M. Haw —8D 36
Vignola Ter. Cytn —9H 57
Viking Av. Eml —3G 150
Viking Rd. Pon —3L 123
Villa Clo. Ackw —2H 141
Village Av. Leeds —4N 61
Village Gdns. Leeds —8E 64
(in two parts)
Village M. Wilsd —3F 56
Village Pl. Leeds —4N 61
Village Rd. Eccup —6B 28
Village St. Nor G —1L 93

Village St., The. Leeds —4N 61
Village Ter. Leeds —4N 61
Village, The. Far T —3D 148
Village, The. Thor A —8E 18
Village, The. Thur —8C 148
Villa Gro. Bgly —3F 38
Villa Mt. Wyke —3A 94
Villa Rd. Bgly —3F 38
Villas, The. Cleck —5J 95
Villa St. Sower B —8J 91
Villa Ter. Bklnd —9H 111
Villier Ct. All —5G 57
Vincent Av. Ebrn —3A 20
Vincent St. B'frd —7B 58
Vincent St. Hal —6M 91
Vine Av. Cleck —4G 95
Vine Clo. Clif —1B 114
Vine Ct. Clif —1B 114
Vine Ct. Guis —8J 25
Vine Cres. Cleck —4H 95
Vine Gth. Clif —9B 94
Vine Gro. Clif —1B 114
Vinery Av. Leeds —6J 63
Vinery Clo. Clay W —7J 151
Vinery Gro. Leeds —6J 63
Vinery Mt. Leeds —7J 63
Vinery Pl. Leeds —7J 63
Vinery Rd. Leeds —4N 61
Vinery St. Leeds —6J 63
Vinery Ter. Leeds —7J 63
Vinery Vw. Leeds —7J 63
Vine St. B'frd —9N 57
Vine St. Cleck —4H 95
Vine St. Hud —2N 131
Vine Ter. Hal —6A 92
Vine Ter. T'tn —8C 56
Vine Ter. E. B'frd —6K 57
Vine Ter. W. B'frd —6K 57
Vineyard. Gol —5C 130
Violet Farm Ct. Brier —7A 156
Violet Pritchard Ho. Pon —2K 123
(off Horse Fair)
Violet St. Hal —5N 91
Violet St. Haw —1C 54
Violet St. N. Hal —4N 91
Violet Ter. Sower B —8J 91
Virginia Clo. Loft —6J 99
Virginia Ct. Loft —6J 99
Virginia Ct. Oss —6A 118
Virginia Dri. Loft —6J 99
Virginia Gdns. Loft —6J 99
Virginia Rd. Hud —3H 131
Virginia St. Cytn —2H 75
Virginia Ter. T'ner —2G 46
Vissitt Clo. Hems —3B 156
Vissitt La. Hems —3A 156
Vivian Pl. B'frd —2M 75
Vivien Rd. B'frd —6H 57
Vulcan Clo. Dew —3F 116
Vulcan Gdns. Dew —3F 116
Vulcan Rd. Dew —3E 116
Vulcan St. B'frd —4H 77
Vulcan St. Brigh —2A 114
Vulcan St. Todm —2J 107

Waddington St. Kei —1J 37
Wade Ho. Av. Hal —7H 75
Wade Ho. Rd. Hal —7H 75
Wade La. Leeds —6E 62
Wade St. B'frd —8C 58
Wade St. Fars —3A 60
Wade St. Hal —5B 92
Wadey Ct. Bat —7F 96
Wadey Fld. Bail —3A 40
Wadhouse La. Dur & Wake —2H 137
Wadlands Clo. Fars —3A 60
Wadlands Dri. Fars —3N 59
Wadlands Gro. Fars —2N 59
Wadlands Ri. Fars —3N 59
Wadman Rd. H'frth —5B 164
Wadsworth Av. Todm —9J 87
(off Lion St.)
Wadsworth Ct. Hal —4N 91
Wadsworth La. H Bri —1J 89
Wadsworth St. Hal —4M 91
(in two parts)
Wager La. Brier —6A 156
Waggon La. Upt —2A 158
Wagon La. Bgly —6F 38
Wain Brow. Hud —1L 147
Waincliffe Cres. Leeds —4B 80
Waincliffe Dri. Leeds —5B 80
Waincliffe Gth. Leeds —4B 80
Waincliffe Ho. B'frd —8H 59
(off Fearnville Dri.)
Waincliffe Mt. Leeds —4B 80
Waincliffe Pl. Leeds —4B 80
Waincliffe Sq. Leeds —4B 80
Waincliffe Ter. Leeds —5B 80
Wain Ct. Ber B —1L 147
Waindale Clo. Hal —1G 91

Waindale Cres. Hal —1G 91
Wain Dyke Clo. Nor —9K 101
Waindyke Way. Nor I —1L 121
Wainfleet Ho. B'frd —6J 59
(off Rushton Rd.)
Waingate. Hud —1L 147
Waingate. Lint —1C 146
Waingate Pk. Lint —9C 130
Wainhouse Rd. Hal —7M 91
Wainman Sq. Wyke —1A 94
Wainman St. Bail —3B 40
Wainman St. Hal —5M 91
Wainman St. Shipl —7N 39
Wainman St. Wyke —1A 94
Wain Pk. Ber B —1L 147
Wainscott Clo. H Bri —7J 71
Wainsgate. H Bri —7J 71
Wainsgate La. H Bri —7J 71
Wainstalls. —7F 72
Wainstalls La. Hal —8E 72
Wainstalls Rd. Hal —7F 72
Waites Cft. K'gte —3D 98
Waites Cft. Out —9K 99
Waites Ter. Otley —1M 25
Waite St. Wake —5G 118
Wakefield. —5L 119
Wakefield 41 Ind. Pk. Wake —6H 99
Wakefield Av. Leeds —5A 64
Wakefield Commercial Pk. Horb —2A 136
Wakefield Cres. Dew —3J 117
Wakefield Europort. C'frd —7K 101
Wakefield Ga. Hal —8M 91
Wakefield Museum. —5L 119
Wakefield Old Rd. Dew —3G 116
Wakefield Rd. Ackw —5D 140
Wakefield Rd. B'frd —8D 58
(in two parts)
Wakefield Rd. Brigh —1N 113
Wakefield Rd. Den D —3B 166
Wakefield Rd. Dew —3G 117
Wakefield Rd. Dlgtn —7C 78
(in two parts)
Wakefield Rd. Fitz —6A 140
Wakefield Rd. Hip & Bail B —5J 93
Wakefield Rd. Horb —1D 136
Wakefield Rd. Hud & Fen B —5N 131
Wakefield Rd. Leeds —3H 81
Wakefield Rd. Liv —8M 95
Wakefield Rd. Morl —8F 78
Wakefield Rd. Oss —4A 118
Wakefield Rd. Oult —3C 100
Wakefield Rd. Pon —5G 122
Wakefield Rd. Rothw —8K 81
Wakefield Rd. Sower B —8K 91
Wakefield Rd. S'hse —6M 121
Wakefield Rd. Warm & Nor —5F 120
(in two parts)
Wakefield Rd. W'ford & Gar —5F 82
Wakefield Rd. Wool & Barn —6L 153
Wakefield Trinity R.L.F.C. —8A 120
Walden Dri. B'frd —3H 57
Walden Howe Clo. F'stne —3C 122
Walden St. C'frd —5D 102
Waldorf Way. Wake —6L 119
Waldron Ho. B'frd —9C 58
(off Elizabeth St.)
Walesby Ct. Leeds —5H 43
Walford Av. Leeds —6J 63
Walford Gro. Leeds —6J 63
Walford Mt. Leeds —6J 63
Walford Rd. Leeds —6J 63
Walford Ter. Leeds —6J 63
Walker Av. B'frd —9K 57
(in two parts)
Walker Av. Wake —4H 119
Walker Dri. B'frd —6M 57
Walkergate. Otley —1L 25
Walkergate. Pon —2L 123
Walker Grn. Dew —9H 117
Walker Ho. Kirks —2J 61
Walker La. H Bri —8K 71
Walker La. Horb —1D 136
Walker La. Sower B —8K 91
Walker Pl. Morl —6L 79
Walker Pl. Shipl —7B 40
(in two parts)
Walker Rd. H'fth —6E 42
Walker Rd. Men —4D 24
Walker Rd. Oaken —9D 76
Walkers Ct. Leeds —1B 62
Walker's Grn. Leeds —1M 79
Walker's La. Leeds —1M 79
(in two parts)
Walker's La. Sils —2D 6
Walkers Mt. Bat —9F 96
Walkers Mt. Leeds —1B 62
Walker's Pl. Sils —9E 6
Walkers Row. Yead —9L 25
Walker's Ter. Wake —5K 119
Walker St. B'frd —5F 76
Walker St. Cleck —4H 95
Walker St. Dew —5J 117
Walker St. Raven —7A 116
Walker St. Schol —4D 94
(off Tabbs La.)
Walker St. Thorn L —7G 116
Walker Ter. B'frd —1F 76
Walker Ter. Cull —1K 55
Walker Wood. Bail —5L 39
Walkley Av. Heck —9A 96
Walkley Gro. Heck —9A 96
Walkley La. Heck —9A 96
Walkley Ter. Heck —1B 116
Walkley Vs. Heck —1B 116
Walk, The. Fars —4N 59
Walk, The. Kei —1J 37
Wallace Gdns. Loft G —6K 99
Wallace St. Hal —6M 91
Wallbank Dri. Shipl —9A 40
Walled Garden, The. Wool —2J 153
Waller Clough Rd. Slai —6M 129
Waller Pas. Sils —7E 6
Wallingford Mt. All —7G 57
Wallis St. B'frd —7L 57
(in two parts)
Wallis St. Sower B —8H 91
Wall Nook La. Cumb —2H 165
Wall Rd. Kei —7L 21
Wallroyds. Den D —3B 166
Wall St. Kei —1F 36
Walmer Gro. Pud —9C 60
Walmer Vs. B'frd —5B 58
Walmsley Dri. Upt —2A 158
Walmsley Rd. Leeds —3A 62
Walnut Av. Dew —4K 117
Walnut Av. Wake —4H 119
Walnut Clo. Dew —5K 117
Walnut Clo. Leeds —7D 46
Walnut Clo. Pon —6J 123
Walnut Cres. Dew —4K 117
Walnut Cres. Wake —4H 119
Walnut Dri. Dew —4L 117
Walnut Dri. Nor —4H 121
Walnut Dri. Pon —6H 123
Walnut Gro. Dew —4L 117
Walnut La. Dew —4K 117
Walnut Pl. Dew —4K 117
Walnut Rd. Dew —4K 117
Walnut St. B'frd —8G 58
Walnut St. Hal —5N 91
Walnut St. Kei —3H 37
Walnut St. S Elm —8M 157
Walpole. —7J 131
Walpole Rd. Hud —7H 131
Walsden. —2J 107
Walsden Est. Todm —4K 107
Walsham Dri. Hud —1D 130
Walshaw La. Walsh —2D 70
Walshaw St. B'frd —1M 75
Walsh La. Bgly —1E 38
Walsh La. Hal —3A 92
Walsh La. Leeds —3F 78
Walsh's Sq. Hal —7N 91
(off Mellor Ter.)
Walsh St. Hal —5M 91
Walter Clough La. S'wram —7G 92
Walter Cres. Leeds —7H 63
Walter Pl. Leeds —8J 61
Walter St. B'frd —2B 58
(BD2)
Walter St. B'frd —7F 40
(BD10)
Walter St. Leeds —5N 61
Waltham Dri. Skel —7K 159
Waltin Rd. H'frth —7L 163
Walton. —5G 18
(nr. Boston Spa)
Walton. —3C 138
(nr. Crofton)
Walton Chase. Wltn —6F 18
Walton Cft. Hud —4C 132
Walton Dri. Dlgtn —7C 78
Walton Fold. Todm —6M 87
(off Millwood La.)
Walton Gth. Dlgtn —8C 78
Walton Head La. Kirk O —1E 14
Walton La. Cleck —7C 94
Walton La. Wake —1N 137
Walton Rd. Thor A —8F 18
Walton Rd. Upt —1C 158
Walton Rd. Weth —4N 17
Walton's Bldgs. Hal —9M 73
Walton Sta. La. Wake —3N 137
Walton St. B'frd —9D 58
Walton St. Leeds —8D 62
Walton St. Sower B —8H 91
Walton Vw. Croft —2G 139
Waltroyd Rd. Cleck —5G 94
Wand La. Hal —4H 93
Wansford Clo. B'frd —3J 77
Wanstead Cres. All —6G 57
Wapping Nick La. Hud —8D 112
Wapping Rd. B'frd —6D 58
Warburton Pl. B'frd —4A 76
Warburton Rd. Eml —3F 150
Warcock La. Blkhd —9M 69
Ward Bank Rd. H'frth —5L 163
Ward Ct. Brigh —4L 113
Ward Fall. Hall G —7H 137
Ward La. Stan —1B 120
Wardle Cres. Kei —8F 20
Wardman St. Kei —8L 21
Ward Pl. La. H'frth —5L 163
Ward's End. Hal —6B 92
Wards Hill. Bat —7F 96
Wards Hill Ct. Bat —7F 96
Wards Pl. Bat —7D 96
Ward St. B'frd —2M 75
Ward St. Crack —2F 116
(in two parts)
Ward St. Kei —1H 37
Wareham Corner. B'frd —3J 77
Warehouse Hill Rd. Mars —5F 144
Warehouse St. Bat —8G 97
Warhurst Rd. Lfds B —3F 112
Waring Green. —9M 93
Waring Way. Dew —2H 117
Warlands End Ga. Todm —6M 107
Warlbeck. I'ly —5E 8
Warley Av. B'frd —6H 59
Warley Dene. Hal —6H 91
Warley Dri. B'frd —7H 59
Warley Edge. Hal —5J 91
Warley Edge La. Hal —5H 91
Warley Gro. B'frd —6H 59
Warley Gro. Hal —5K 91
Warley Rd. Hal —5K 91
Warley St. Hal —6N 91
Warley Town. —6H 91
Warley Town La. Hal —5G 91
Warley Vw. Hal —5K 91
Warley Vw. Leeds —2E 60
Warley Wood Av. L'ft —7F 90
Warley Wood La. L'ft —7E 90
Warmfield. —5G 121
Warmfield La. Warm —4F 120
Warmfield Vw. Wake —4A 120
Warm La. Yead —2L 41
Warmleigh Pk. Q'bry —4A 74
Warneford Av. Oss —4N 117
Warneford Ri. Hud —7F 130
Warneford Rd. Hud —6F 130
Warneford Sq. Hal —7M 91
(off King Cross Rd.)
Warnford Gro. B'frd —2H 77
Warrel's Av. Leeds —3F 60
Warrel's Ct. Leeds —4F 60
Warrel's Gro. Leeds —4F 60
Warrel's Mt. Leeds —4F 60
Warrel's Pl. Leeds —3F 60
Warrel's Rd. Leeds —3F 60
Warrel's Row. Leeds —4F 60
Warrel's St. Leeds —4F 60
Warrel's Ter. Leeds —4F 60
Warren Av. Bgly —2G 38
Warren Av. Knot —8C 104
Warren Av. Wake —9M 119
Warren Clo. Liv —1M 115
Warren Clo. Roys —4E 154
Warren Ct. Wake —5M 119
Warren Dri. Ack —3A 122
Warren Dri. Bgly —3G 39
Warren Ho. Pon —2K 123
(off Horse Fair)
Warren Ho. Wake —5L 119
(off Kirkgate)
Warren Ho. La. Hud —8F 112
Warren Ho. La. Yead —7A 26
Warren La. Arth —2K 27
Warren La. Bgly —2G 39
Warren La. Dart —6K 153
Warren La. Not —5L 153
Warren La. Tad —8G 33
Warren Pk. Brigh —7K 93
Warren Pk. Clo. Brigh —7K 93
Warren Rd. F'stne —5B 122
Warrenside. Hud —7C 114
Warrens La. Bat —1A 96
Warrens La. Dlgtn —8B 78
Warren St. Dew —5F 116
Warren Ter. Bgly —4H 39
Warrenton Pl. B'frd —9M 57
Warren Wlk. Roys —5D 154
(in two parts)
Warrington Ter. Mars —5E 144
Warsop Rd. Barn —8N 153
Warton Av. B'frd —4F 76
Warwick Av. Gol —6D 130
Warwick Clo. B'frd —1F 76
Warwick Clo. Hal —8A 92
(off Free School La.)
Warwick Ct. H'fth —8F 42
Warwick Dri. B'frd —1F 76
Warwick Ho. B'frd —7F 40
(off Thorp Gth.)
Warwick Mt. Bat —8G 96
Warwick Rd. Bat —1F 116
Warwick Rd. B'frd —1F 76
Warwick St. Wake —8A 120
Waryn Ho. B'frd —8G 41
(off Fairhaven Grn.)
Wasdale Cres. Wake —4G 119
Wasdale Rd. Wake —4G 118
Washburn Ct. Sils —8E 6
(off Wharfe Ct.)
Washburn Ct. Weth —1L 17
Washer La. Sower B —8L 91
Washer La. Ind. Est. Hal —8M 91
Washfold Rd. Cra V —4H 109
Washington Pl. Leeds —6D 60
Washington St. B'frd —5L 57
Washington St. Hal —3N 91
Washington St. Leeds —6A 62
(LS3)
Washington St. Leeds —6D 60
(LS13)
Washington Ter. Leeds —6D 60
Washpit. —6M 163
Washpit New Rd. H'frth —6N 163
Wasp Nest Rd. Hud —1M 131
Waste La. Hud —7C 132
Waste La. Mir —8K 115
Waste La. Pec W —9H 53
Wastwater Dri. B'frd —7L 75
Watchit Hole La. Thpe A —6B 142
Watercock St. B'frd —9E 58
Watercroft. Hud —7D 132
Waterfall Fold. Pon —9L 103
Waterfront M. App B —7J 41
Water Fryston. —2L 103
Watergate. —4E 116
Watergate. Hal —5H 93
Watergate. Hud —4N 131
Watergate. Meth —4H 101
Watergate. Pon —2J 123
Watergate Rd. Dew —4E 116
Water Grn. La. Sower B —5A 110
Water Hall Ct. N Mill —2C 164
(off Water Row)
Water Hill La. Sower B —7G 91
Water Ho. Ct. H'fth —8E 42
Waterhouse Ct. Leeds —1F 80
(off Oval, The)
Waterhouse Dri. E Ard —5D 98
Waterhouse Gro. Wake —5J 119
Waterhouse St. Hal —5B 92
Waterhouse St. Kei —9G 21
Watering La. Morl —9N 79
Water La. B'frd —7A 58
(in two parts)
Water La. Dew —5E 116
Water La. Eby —2A 4
Water La. E Hard —9K 123
Water La. Fars —3A 60
Water La. Hal —6C 92
Water La. Hems —5F 156
Water La. H'bck —8C 62
Water La. H'fth —6C 42
Water La. Kei —1J 37
Water La. K S'ton —4K 143
Water La. Leeds —7G 61
(LS12)
Water La. Leeds —7E 62
(off Meadow La., LS11)
Water La. M'twn —2N 135
Water La. Pon —9M 103
Water La. Shel —6L 149
Water La. Stan —8A 100
Water La. Wool —2J 153
Water La. Clo. M'twn —2N 135
Waterloo. —4F 132
Waterloo Clo. C'frd —7N 101
Waterloo Cres. B'frd —7K 41
Waterloo Cres. Leeds —3G 61
Waterloo Fold. Wyke —2B 94
Waterloo Gro. Pud —7M 59
Waterloo La. Leeds —3G 60
Waterloo Mt. Pud —6M 59
Waterloo Ri. Hud —5E 132
Waterloo Rd. Bgly —4E 38
Waterloo Rd. Brigh —9M 93
Waterloo Rd. Hud —3F 132
Waterloo Rd. Leeds —1G 81
Waterloo Rd. Pud —6M 59
Waterloo St. Leeds —7E 62
Waterloo St. Wake —7M 119
Waterloo Ter. Sower B —6J 91
Waterloo Way. Leeds —3G 60
Water Row. N Mill —2C 164
Water Royd Av. Mir —5L 115
Water Royd Cres. Mir —5L 115
Water Royd Dri. Mir —5L 115
Water Royd La. Mir —5L 115
Waterside. Bgly —2C 38
Waterside. Hal —6C 92
Waterside. Hud —5K 131
(HD1)
Waterside. Hud —8L 131
(HD4)
Waterside. Oxe —4C 54
Waterside. Sils —9F 6
Waterside Fold. H Bri —9H 71
Waterside Ind. Pk. Leeds —2K 81
Water Side La. H'frth —6H 163
Waterside Rd. B'frd —6M 57
Waterside Rd. Leeds —3K 81
Waterside Wlk. Mir —6H 115
Watersole La. Weth —5A 18
Waters Rd. Mars —4C 144
Water Stalls Rd. Cra V —3M 109
(in two parts)
Water St. Brigh —9N 93
Water St. Holmb —5J 163
Water St. Hud —5L 131
Water St. Lock —7L 131
Water St. Scis —8G 151
Water St. Sower B —9H 91
Water St. Todm —7K 87
Water St. Wyke —2A 94
Waterton Clo. S Kirk —6K 157
Waterton Clo. W'ton —4B 138
Waterton Gro. Wake —6H 119
Waterton Ho. Wake —6G 119
Waterton Rd. Wake —7F 118
Waterton St. C'frd —5B 102
Waterwheel Ri. Lock —8J 131
Waterwood Clo. Ting —5B 98
Waterworks Rd. Bat —8C 96
Watery La. Holme —8E 162
Watery La. H'frth —4N 163
Watery La. Sils —6F 6
Watford Av. Hal —1L 93
Watkin Av. T'tn —8E 56
Watkinson Av. Hal —8N 73
Watkinson Dri. Hal —9M 73
Watkinson Rd. Hal —9M 73
Watling Rd. C'frd —3K 103
Watmough St. B'frd —2M 75
Watnall Rd. Barn —9A 154
Watroyd La. Slai —8A 130
Watson Av. Dew —3L 117
Watson Clo. Oxe —4C 54
Watson Cres. Wake —4N 119
Watson Mill La. Sower B —1H 11
Watson Rd. Leeds —5A 64
Watsons's La. Newt K —3J 33
Watson St. Morl —1J 97
Watson St. Nor —1H 121
Wattlesyke. Coll —8L 17
Watts St. Cytn —1G 75
Watt St. B'frd —9H 59
Watty Hall Av. B'frd —3M 75
Watty Hall La. B'frd —3N 75
Watty Hall Rd. B'frd —3M 75
Watty La. Todm —9H 87
Watty Ter. Todm —9H 87
Wauchope St. Wake —6K 119
Wauds Gates. Bail —6A 40
(off Baildon Rd.)
Waulkmill Clo. Upt —2N 157
Wavell Gth. Wake —3A 138
Wavell Gro. Wake —3N 137
Waveney Rd. Leeds —8M 61
Waverley Av. B'frd —9N 57
Waverley Av. Sandb —8A 22
Waverley Cres. Hal —5H 93
Waverley Gth. Leeds —1D 80
Waverley Pl. B'frd —9N 57
Waverley Rd. B'frd —9N 57
Waverley Rd. Ell —6E 112
Waverley Rd. Hud —3L 131
Waverley St. Dew —4F 116
Waverley St. Slai —9M 129
Waverley Ter. B'frd —9N 57
Waverley Ter. Hal —5H 93
Waverley Ter. Hud —3J 131
Waverton Grn. B'frd —6L 75
Wavertree Pk. Gdns. Low M —9A
Wayland App. Leeds —3N 43
Wayland Clo. Leeds —3N 43
Wayland Ct. Leeds —3N 43
Wayland Cft. Leeds —3N 43
Wayland Dri. Leeds —3N 43
Wayne Clo. Bat —6F 96
Wayside Av. S'cft —7E 30
Wayside Cres. B'frd —1F 58
Wayside Cres. S'cft —6E 30
Wayside Gardens. —7E 30
Wayside Mt. S'cft —6E 30
Wayside Ter. Huby —6N 13
Weardale Clo. B'frd —4G 77
Weardley. —2C 28
Weardley La. Hare —2D 28
Weatherall Pl. Skel —7L 159
Weatherhead Pl. Sils —8F 6
Weatherhill Cres. Hud —9F 112
Weather Hill La. Cra V —7M 89
Weather Hill La. H'frth —8K 163

Weatherhill Rd. *Hud* —8F 112
Weatherhouse Ter. *Hal* —3K 91
Weaver Ct. B'frd —7F 40
(off Moorfield Pl.)
Weaver Gdns. *Morl* —1N 97
Weaver Grn. *Pud* —7B 60
Weavers Cotts. Oxe —4C 54
(off Waterside)
Weavers Ct. *Leeds* —7L 61
Weavers Ct. *Mel* —7E 146
Weavers Ct. *Pud* —9C 60
Weavers Cft. *B'frd* —5E 40
Weavers Cft. *Pud* —8C 60
Weavers Ga. *H Bri* —5L 71
Weavers Grange. *Guis* —6J 25
Weavers Hill. *Haw* —9C 36
Weavers Rd. *Pon* —2L 123
Weavers Row. *Pud* —8C 60
Weaver St. *Leeds* —5N 61
Weavers Wlk. *Den D* —1E 166
Weavers Wlk. *Sils* —7E 6
Weaverthorpe Rd. *B'frd* —4J 77
Webb Dri. *B'frd* —4E 58
Webber Ga. *Kei* —2F 36
Webb's Ter. *Hal* —4C 92
Weber Ct. B'frd —7G 58
(off Amberley St.)
Webster Hill. *Dew* —4E 116
Webster Pl. *B'frd* —7F 58
Webster Pl. *Nor* —1H 121
Webster Row. *Leeds* —8L 61
Webster St. *B'frd* —7F 58
Webster St. *Dew* —3F 116
Webton Ct. *Leeds* —8F 44
Wedgemoor Clo. *Wyke* —9A 76
Wedgewood Ct. *Leeds* —6J 45
Wedgewood Dri. *Leeds* —7J 45
Wedgewood Gro. *Leeds* —7J 45
Weedling Ga. *Tad* —8N 33
Weeland Av. *Shar C* —8J 121
Weeland Ct. *Knot* —8F 104
Weeland Cres. *Shar C* —7K 121
Weeland Dri. *Shar C* —8K 121
Weeland Rd. *Croft & S'hse* —9G 120
Weeland Rd. *Knot* —8F 104
Weetlands Clo. *Kip* —3B 84
Weeton. —7A 14
Weeton La. *Wee & Huby* —6N 13
(in two parts)
Weet Shaw La. *Shaf* —8H 155
Weetwood. —7M 43
Weetwood Av. *Leeds* —8N 43
Weetwood Ct. *Leeds* —7M 43
Weetwood Cres. *Leeds* —7N 43
Weetwood Grange Gro. *Leeds* —7L 43
Weetwood Ho. Ct. *Leeds* —7L 43
Weetwood La. *Leeds* —6M 43
Weetwood Mnr. *Leeds* —7M 43
Weetwood Mill La. *Leeds* —7N 43
Weetwood Pk. Dri. *Leeds* —7L 43
Weetwood Rd. *B'frd* —6M 57
Weetwood Rd. *Leeds* —7L 43
Weetwood Ter. *Leeds* —7N 43
Weetwood Wlk. *Leeds* —7M 43
Weetworth Av. *C'frd* —6F 102
Weir Side. *Mars* —5F 144
Weir St. *Todm* —9J 87
Welbeck Dri. *B'frd* —1K 75
Welbeck La. *Wake* —3B 120
Welbeck Ri. *B'frd* —1K 75
Welbeck Rd. *Birs* —2C 96
Welbeck Rd. *Leeds* —7J 63
Welbeck St. *C'frd* —4D 102
Welbeck St. *Wake* —8M 119
Welburn Av. *Hal* —5J 93
Welburn Av. *Leeds* —8L 43
Welburn Clo. *S'dal* —1N 137
Welburn Dri. *Leeds* —8L 43
Welburn Gro. *Leeds* —8L 43
Welburn Mt. *B'frd* —5K 75
Welbury Dri. *B'frd* —4A 58
Weldon Dri. *Hud* —2N 129
Welfare Av. *Bar E* —8M 47
Welham Wlk. *B'frd* —6E 58
Welland Dri. *Gar* —8A 66
Wellands Grn. *Cleck* —5F 94
Wellands La. *Schol* —4D 94
(in two parts)
Wellands Ter. *B'frd* —7G 58
Well Clo. *Rawd* —4N 41
Well Clo. *W'ford* —5M 83
Well Clo. Ri. *Leeds* —4E 62
Well Clo. St. *Brigh* —9N 93
Wellcroft. *Otley* —1M 25
Well Cft. *Shipl* —8N 39
Wellcroft Gro. *Ting* —5B 98
Wellesley Ct. *Hud* —5F 130
Wellesley Grn. *Wake* —4G 118
Wellesley Ho. B'frd —8H 59
(off Wellington St.)
Wellesley St. *B'frd* —7D 58
Wellfield Av. *Grng M* —5B 134
Wellfield Clo. *Grng M* —5B 134
Wellfield Clo. *Lint* —8D 130
Wellfield Pl. Leeds —1N 61
(off Chapel St.)
Wellfield Rd. *Hud* —4H 131
Wellfield Ter. *Gild* —6F 78
Wellfield Ter. *Todm* —8K 87
Well Fold. *Idle* —7F 40
Wellgarth. *Hal* —7A 92
Well Gth. *Leeds* —4D 64
Well Gth. Bank. *Leeds* —2E 60
Well Gth. Mt. *Leeds* —4D 64
Wellgarth Rd. *F'stne* —7E 122
Well Gth. Vw. *Leeds* —2F 60
Wellgate. *C'frd* —6F 102
Wellgate. *G'lnd* —3B 112
Wellgate. *M'well* —8K 153
Wellgate. *Slai* —7A 130
Well Grn. Ct. *B'frd* —6J 77
Well Grn. La. *Brigh* —7L 93
Well Gro. *Brigh* —7L 93
Well Gro. *Hud* —8A 114
Wellhead Clo. *B'hpe* —5H 27
Well Head Dri. *Hal* —6B 92
Well Head La. *Hal* —7B 92
Well Head La. *Sower B* —9C 90
Wellhead M. *C'thpe* —6H 137
Well Head Ri. *Hal* —7B 92
Well Heads. —7N 55
Well Heads. *T'tn* —9M 55
Well Hill. *Hon* —5L 147
Well Hill. *Otley* —1K 25
Well Hill. *Yead* —9M 25
Well Hill Ct. Yead —1M 41
(off Well Hill)
Well Hill Gro. *Roys* —5D 154
Well Hill Rd. *H'frth* —4N 163
Wellholme. *Brigh* —9N 93
Well Holme Mead. *Leeds* —2H 79
Wellhouse. —7C 130
Wellhouse. *Mir* —4M 115
Well Ho. Av. *Leeds* —1J 63
Wellhouse Av. *Mir* —4M 115
Wellhouse Clo. *Mir* —4L 115
Wellhouse Ct. M. Mir —5M 115
(off Wellhouse La.)
Well Ho. Cres. *Leeds* —1J 63
Well Ho. Dri. *Leeds* —1J 63
Well Ho. Gdns. *Leeds* —1J 63
Wellhouse La. *Hud* —1E 132
Wellhouse La. *Mir* —4M 115
Well Ho. Rd. *Leeds* —1J 63
Wellhouse Rd. *Lint* —7C 130
Wellington Arc. Brigh —1M 113
(off Briggate)
Wellington Bri. Ind. Est. *Leeds* —7B 62
Wellington Bri. St. *Leeds* —6B 62
Wellington Ct. *B'shaw* —7L 77
Wellington Cres. *Shipl* —8M 39
Wellington Gdns. *Leeds* —3G 61
Wellington Gth. *Leeds* —2G 60
Wellington Gro. *B'frd* —4F 58
Wellington Gro. *Leeds* —2G 60
Wellington Gro. *Pud* —7N 59
Wellington Hill. —7A 46
Wellington Hill. *Leeds* —5B 46
Wellington Mt. *Leeds* —2G 60
Wellington Pl. *B'frd* —3G 58
Wellington Pl. *Hal* —6B 92
Wellington Pl. *Knot* —8C 104
Wellington Rd. *B'frd* —3F 58
Wellington Rd. *Dew* —3F 116
Wellington Rd. *I'ly* —5G 9
Wellington Rd. *Kei* —1J 37
Wellington Rd. *Leeds* —8A 62
Wellington Rd. *Todm* —6K 87
Wellington Rd. *Wilsd* —2A 56
Wellington Rd. E. *Dew* —3F 116
Wellington St. *All* —5H 57
Wellington St. *Althpe* —4G 118
Wellington St. *Bat* —7E 96
Wellington St. *Bgly* —4E 38
Wellington St. *B'frd* —7D 58
Wellington St. *C'frd* —4B 102
Wellington St. *Dew* —3F 116
Wellington St. *Eccl* —4F 58
Wellington St. *Hud* —2G 130
Wellington St. *Idle* —8F 40
Wellington St. *Lais* —8H 59
Wellington St. *Leeds* —6B 62
(in two parts)
Wellington St. *Liv* —9M 95
Wellington St. *Morl* —9K 79
Wellington St. *Q'bry* —4E 74
Wellington St. *Wilsd* —2B 56
Wellington St. S. *Hal* —6C 92
Wellington Ter. *Leeds* —2G 60
Wellington Ter. *Mars* —5G 144
Wellington Wlk. *Dew* —3F 116
Well La. *Bat* —7G 96
Well La. *Brigh* —3L 113
Well La. *Burg* —5M 159
Well La. *Clif* —1C 114
Well La. *Dew* —3C 116
Well La. *Guis* —7J 25
Well La. *Hal* —5C 92
Well La. *Kip* —4A 84
Well La. *Leeds* —8F 44
Well La. *Rawd* —4N 41
Well La. *Schol* —3D 94
Well La. *Todm* —7K 87
Well La. *Yead* —1M 41
Well Royd Av. *Hal* —5J 91
Well Royd Clo. *Hal* —5K 91
(in two parts)
Wells Ct. I'ly —6G 8
(off Wells Promenade)
Wells Ct. *Oss* —6M 117
Wells Ct. Yead —1M 41
(off Well La.)
Wells Cft. *Leeds* —8A 44
Wells Grn. Gdns. *H'frth* —1L 163
Wells Gro. *Guis* —7J 25
Wells Ho. Sower B —8J 91
(off Church Vw.)
Wells M. I'ly —6G 8
(off Wells Wlk.)
Wells Mt. *Guis* —7J 25
Wells Mt. *Up Cum* —2L 165
Wells Promenade. *I'ly* —5G 8
Wells Rd. *Dew* —9H 117
Wells Rd. *Guis* —7J 25
Wells Rd. *I'ly* —7F 8
Well's St. *Dart* —9G 152
Wells St. *Guis* —7J 25
Wells Ter. Hal —2M 93
(off Village St.)
Wells, The. *Hal* —7L 91
(nr. Burnley Rd.)
Wells, The. *Hal* —5J 91
(nr. Stock La.)
Wellstone Av. *Leeds* —5E 60
Wellstone Dri. *Leeds* —5E 60
Wellstone Gdns. *Leeds* —6E 60
Wellstone Gth. *Leeds* —6E 60
Wellstone Grn. *Leeds* —5E 60
Wellstone Ri. *Leeds* —6E 60
Wellstone Rd. *Leeds* —6E 60
Wellstone Way. *Leeds* —6E 60
Well St. *B'frd* —7D 58
Well St. *Denh* —6K 55
Well St. *Dew* —3H 117
Well St. *Fars* —3A 60
Well St. *Holy G* —7A 112
Well St. *Hud* —5L 131
Well St. *Kei* —9H 21
Well St. *Lit T* —7L 95
Well St. *Todm* —8K 87
Well St. *Wilsd* —1B 56
Wells Wlk. *I'ly* —6G 8
Well Ter. Guis —7J 25
(off Well St.)
Wellthorne Av. *Pen* —7B 166
Wellthorne La. *Pen* —7A 166
Well Vw. *Guis* —7J 25
Welton Gro. *Leeds* —3A 62
Welton Mt. *Leeds* —3A 62
Welton Pl. *Leeds* —3A 62
Welton Rd. *Leeds* —3A 62
Welwyn Av. *Bat* —6C 96
Welwyn Av. *Shipl* —8D 40
Welwyn Dri. *Bail* —5A 40
Welwyn Dri. *Shipl* —8D 40
Welwyn Rd. *Dew* —9J 97
Wembley Av. *T'tn* —8E 56
Wenborough La. *B'frd* —2K 77
Wendel Av. *Bar E* —8L 47
Wendover Ct. *Leeds* —4N 43
Wendron Clo. *Liv* —2K 115
Wendron Way. *B'frd* —8F 40
Wenlock St. *B'frd* —8E 58
Wenning St. *Kei* —8L 21
Wensley Av. *Leeds* —8E 44
Wensley Av. *Shipl* —8M 39
Wensley Bank. *T'tn* —8B 56
Wensley Bank Ter. *T'tn* —8B 56
Wensley Bank W. *T'tn* —8B 56
Wensley Cres. *Leeds* —8E 44
Wensleydale Av. *Leeds* —4J 61
Wensleydale Clo. *Leeds* —4J 61
Wensleydale Ct. Leeds —8E 44
(off Stainbeck La.)
Wensleydale Cres. *Leeds* —4J 61
Wensleydale Dri. *Leeds* —4J 61
Wensleydale Ho. Bat —1F 116
(off Dale Clo.)
Wensleydale M. *Leeds* —4J 61
Wensleydale Pde. *Bat* —4C 96
Wensleydale Ri. *Bail* —3C 40
Wensleydale Ri. *Leeds* —4J 61
Wensleydale Rd. *B'frd* —7J 59
Wensley Dri. *Leeds* —7D 44
Wensley Dri. *Pon* —5L 123
Wensley Gdns. *Leeds* —7D 44
Wensley Grn. *Leeds* —8D 44
Wensley Gro. *Brigh* —3K 113
Wensley Gro. *Leeds* —8E 44
Wensley Ho. *B'frd* —9H 41
Wensley Lawn. *Midd* —9E 80
Wensley Rd. *Leeds* —7D 44
Wensley St. *Horb* —1C 136
Wensley St. E. *Horb* —1C 136
Wensley Vw. *Leeds* —8E 44
Went Av. *F'stne* —7C 122
Wentbridge. —3C 142
Wentbridge La. *Went* —5A 142
Wentbridge Rd. *F'stne* —7E 122
Wentcliffe Rd. *Knot* —8A 104
Went Cft. *Pon* —6K 123
Wentdale. *Lit S* —4K 143
Went Dale Rd. *Pon* —6J 123
Went Edge Rd. *K S'ton* —4C 142
Went Fold. *Pon* —6K 123
Went Gth. *Pon* —6J 123
Went Gro. *F'stne* —8C 122
Went Hill Clo. *Ackw* —2G 140
Went La. *Wrag* —3B 140
Went Vw. *Thpe A* —5N 141
Went Vw. Ct. *E Hard* —3M 141
Wentwell Rd. *S'hse* —6L 121
Wentworth Av. *Eml* —3F 150
Wentworth Av. *Leeds* —3D 44
Wentworth Clo. *Men* —4E 24
Wentworth Clo. *Wool* —2H 153
Wentworth Ct. *Brigh* —4L 113
Wentworth Cres. *Leeds* —3E 44
Wentworth Cres. *M'well* —9M 153
Wentworth Dri. *Croft* —2H 139
Wentworth Dri. *Eml* —3F 150
Wentworth Dri. *Hal* —6M 73
Wentworth Dri. *M'well* —9L 153
Wentworth Dri. *S Kirk* —6J 157
Wentworth Farm Res. Pk. *Leeds* —3G 78
Wentworth Ga. *Weth* —3J 17
Wentworth Gro. *Hal* —6M 73
Wentworth Pk. *C'frd* —6E 102
Wentworth Pk. Ri. *D'ton* —6C 124
Wentworth Rd. *Dart* —9F 152
Wentworth Rd. *F'stne* —7B 122
Wentworth Rd. *M'well* —9L 153
Wentworth St. *Hud* —3L 131
Wentworth St. *Wake* —3K 119
Wentworth Ter. *Fitz* —7B 140
Wentworth Ter. Rawd —4A 42
(off Town St.)
Wentworth Ter. *Wake* —4K 119
Wentworth Way. *Leeds* —3E 44
Wentworth Way. *S'dal* —1N 137
Wepener Mt. *Leeds* —5K 63
Wepener Pl. *Leeds* —5K 63
Wescoe Hill. *Wee* —7L 13
Wescoe Hill La. *Wee* —7M 13
Wesleyan St. *B'frd* —2G 76
Wesley App. *Leeds* —3B 80
Wesley Av. *H'frth* —9L 147
Wesley Av. *Leeds* —7M 61
Wesley Av. *Low M* —6C 76
Wesley Av. S. *Low M* —7C 76
Wesley Clo. *Birs* —3B 96
Wesley Clo. *Leeds* —2B 80
Wesley Ct. *Hal* —5B 92
Wesley Ct. Leeds —3C 62
(off Woodhouse St., LS6)
Wesley Ct. *Leeds* —3B 80
(LS11)
Wesley Ct. *Oss* —5M 117
Wesley Cft. *Leeds* —2B 80
Wesley Dri. *Low M* —6C 76
Wesley Gth. *Leeds* —2B 80
Wesley Grn. *Leeds* —3B 80
Wesley Gro. *B'frd* —6G 40
Wesley Hall Ct. *Stan* —1A 120
Wesley Ho. *Leeds* —3B 80
Wesley Place. —7B 76
Wesley Pl. *Dew* —3F 116
Wesley Pl. *F'stne* —7D 122
Wesley Pl. *Kei* —4G 37
Wesley Pl. *Leeds* —7G 63
(LS9)
Wesley Pl. *Leeds* —7M 61
(LS12)
Wesley Pl. Low M —7C 76
(off Main St.)
Wesley Pl. *Sils* —8E 6
Wesley Rd. *Leeds* —7M 61
Wesley Rd. *S'ley* —5N 59
Wesley Row. *Pud* —6B 60
Wesley Sq. *Pud* —7B 60
Wesley St. *C'frd* —4D 102
Wesley St. *Cleck* —4H 95
Wesley St. *Cuts* —7C 102
Wesley St. *Dew* —3F 116
Wesley St. *Far* —3A 60
Wesley St. *Leeds* —2B 80
Wesley St. *Morl* —9K 79
Wesley St. *Oss* —5M 117
(in two parts)
Wesley St. *Otley* —9L 11
Wesley St. *Rod* —1C 60
Wesley St. *S Elm* —7L 157
Wesley St. *S'ley* —5A 60
Wesley St. *Wake* —8N 119
Wesley Ter. *Den D* —2C 166
Wesley Ter. *Gar* —7N 65
Wesley Ter. *Leeds* —3G 60
Wesley Ter. *Pud* —7B 60
Wesley Ter. *Rod* —1C 60
Wesley Vw. *Leeds* —1C 60
Wesley Vw. *Pud* —7B 60
Wessen Ct. *Mars* —5F 144
Wessenden Head Rd. *Mel* —5M 161
Wessenden Rd. *Mars* —7F 144
W. Acre Dri. *Bat* —7H 97
(nr. Lady Ann Rd.)
W. Acre Dri. *Bat* —7G 97
(nr. Soothill La.)
Westacres. *Brigh* —3N 113
West Acres. *Byr* —4C 104
West Ardsley. —4A 98
West Av. *All* —3E 56
West Av. *Bail* —4A 40
West Av. *B Spa* —9C 18
West Av. *Hal* —8A 92
West Av. *Hon* —5K 147
West Av. *Horb* —1E 136
West Av. *Hud* —1H 131
West Av. *Light* —5M 93
West Av. *Pon* —4G 123
West Av. *Round* —7L 45
West Av. *Roys* —5E 154
West Av. *S Elm* —5A 158
West Av. *Upt* —2N 157
West Bank. *Bat* —6E 96
West Bank. *B'frd* —2L 57
West Bank. *Hal* —9K 73
West Bank. Kei —8F 20
(off W. Bank Ri.)
W. Bank Clo. *Kei* —8F 20
W. Bank Gro. *Riddl* —6L 21
W. Bank Ri. *Kei* —8F 20
W. Bank Rd. *Riddl* —6K 21
West Bolton. *Hal* —6K 73
Westborough. —2C 116
Westborough Dri. *Hal* —5K 91
Westbourne Av. *Gar* —8L 65
(in two parts)
Westbourne Av. *Leeds* —2D 80
Westbourne Av. *Pon* —4J 123
Westbourne Clo. *Otley* —2J 25
Westbourne Clo. *Wake* —4L 137
Westbourne Cres. *Gar* —8L 65
Westbourne Cres. *Hal* —9C 92
Westbourne Cres. *Pon* —4H 123
Westbourne Dri. *Gar* —8L 65
Westbourne Dri. *Guis* —7G 25
Westbourne Dri. *Men* —3D 24
Westbourne Gdns. *Gar* —8L 65
Westbourne Gro. *Gar* —8L 65
Westbourne Gro. *Hal* —9C 92
Westbourne Gro. *Otley* —2J 25
Westbourne Mt. *Leeds* —2D 80
Westbourne Mt. *Pon* —4J 123
Westbourne Pl. *Leeds* —2D 80
Westbourne Pl. *S'ley* —5A 60
Westbourne Rd. *B'frd* —4N 57
Westbourne Rd. *Hud* —3J 131
Westbourne Rd. *Pon* —4J 123
Westbourne St. *Leeds* —2D 80
Westbourne Ter. *Gar* —8L 65
Westbourne Ter. *Hal* —9C 92
West Bowling. —2D 76
West Breary. —5K 27
West Bretton. —1B 152
Westbrook Clo. *H'fth* —5E 42
Westbrook Ct. Hal —4A 92
(off Stannary Pl.)
Westbrook Dri. *Hud* —4F 132
Westbrook La. *H'fth* —5E 42
Westbrook Ter. *Bat* —6E 96
Westburn Av. *Kei* —1F 36
Westburn Cres. *Kei* —2F 36
Westburn Gro. *Kei* —2F 36
Westburn Pl. *Cleck* —4G 94
Westburn Way. *Kei* —2F 36
Westbury Clo. *B'frd* —9H 59
Westbury Ct. *Hal* —6L 91
Westbury Gro. *Leeds* —3H 81
Westbury Mt. *Leeds* —4H 81
Westbury Pl. *Hal* —6L 91
Westbury Pl. N. *Leeds* —3H 81
Westbury Pl. S. *Leeds* —4H 81
Westbury Rd. *B'frd* —4J 75
Westbury St. *B'frd* —9H 59
Westbury St. *Ell* —4F 112
Westbury St. *Leeds* —4H 81
Westbury Ter. *Hal* —6L 91
Westbury Ter. *Leeds* —4H 81
W. Busk La. *Otley* —2G 25
West Carlton. —6M 25
W. Carr La. *Scam* —8D 128

W. Chevin Rd. Men & Otley —3H 25
Westcliffe Av. Bail —3N 39
Westcliffe Dri. Hal —5K 91
Westcliffe Ri. Cleck —5G 95
Westcliffe Rd. Cleck —4G 95
Westcliffe Rd. Shipl —8M 39
West Clo. Hud —9N 113
West Clo. Nor —9H 101
West Clo. Pon —6L 123
Westcombe Av. Leeds —5J 45
Westcombe Ct. Wyke —9A 76
Westcott Ho. B'frd —5A 58
(off Green La.)
West Ct. Bmly —5F 60
West Ct. Leeds —7L 45
West Cft. Add —1M 7
Westcroft. Hon —5K 147
West Cft. Wyke —2A 94
Westcroft Av. Hal —9G 75
Westcroft Dri. Oss —2M 117
Westcroft Ho. C'frd —4C 102
(off West St.)
Westcroft Rd. B'frd —1M 75
Westcroft Rd. Hems —2D 156
West Dale. B Spa —8C 18
Westdale Dri. Pud —6A 60
Westdale Gdns. Pud —6A 60
Westdale Gro. Pud —6A 60
Westdale Ri. Pud —6A 60
Westdale Rd. Pud —6A 60
West Dene. Leeds —2H 45
West Dene. Sils —7E 6
West Dri. Oxe —3C 54
West Dri. Pon —4L 123
West End. —6C 42
(nr. Horsforth)
West End. —7E 34
(nr. Oldfield)
West End. —5C 74
(nr. Queensbury)
West End. —5G 94
(nr. Scholes)
West End. B Spa —8C 18
West End. Gild —6F 78
West End. H Bri —1H 89
West End. H'frth —9L 147
West End. Leeds —2G 79
West End. Q'bry —5C 74
W. End App. Morl —1H 97
W. End Av. Ack —3A 122
W. End Av. H'frth —2A 164
W. End Av. Roys —6B 154
W. End Clo. H'fth —6C 42
W. End Cotts. Horb —1B 136
W. End Cres. Roys —6B 154
W. End Dri. Cleck —6G 94
W. End Dri. H'fth —6C 42
W. End Gro. H'fth —6C 42
W. End La. H'fth —6C 42
W. End Ri. H'fth —6C 42
W. End Rd. C'ley —9M 41
W. End Rd. Dew —4E 116
W. End Rd. Gol —6B 130
W. End Rd. Hal —6L 91
W. End Rd. Nort —7N 143
W. End St. B'frd —7B 58
W. End Ter. B'frd —1F 58
W. End Ter. Guis —7G 25
W. End Ter. H Bri —3M 89
W. End Ter. Leeds —2B 62
W. End Ter. Shipl —7M 39
Westercroft La. Hal —1F 92
Westercroft Vw. Hal —1G 92
Westerley Clo. Shel —6L 149
Westerley Cres. Sils —8C 6
Westerley La. Shel —6K 149
Westerley Way. Shel —6L 149
Westerly Cft. Leeds —6M 61
Westerly Ri. Leeds —6M 61
(off Stocks Hill)
Westerman Clo. F'stne —5D 122
Westerman St. Wake —8N 119
Western Av. Birs —3D 96
Western Av. Pon —3M 123
Western Av. Riddl —5J 21
Western Ct. Pon —2M 123
Western Gales Way. Norm —3L 121
Western Gro. Leeds —9L 61
Western Mt. Leeds —9L 61
Western Pl. Hud —5M 131
(off Springwood St.)
Western Pl. Q'bry —4G 74
Western Rd. Hud —6F 130
Western Rd. Leeds —9L 61
Western St. Leeds —9L 61
Western Way. Butt —6M 75
Westerton. —5B 98
Westerton Clo. Ting —4D 98
Westerton Ct. Oaken —8F 76
Westerton Rd. Ting —5N 97
Westerton Wlk. Ting —4D 98
W. Farm Av. Leeds —8D 80
Westfell Clo. Kei —1F 36
Westfell Rd. Kei —1F 36
Westfell Way. Kei —1F 36
Westfield. —7N 95
(nr. Heckmondwike)
Westfield. —1K 41
(nr. Yeadon)
Westfield. H Bri —8K 71
Westfield. Leeds —8E 44
Westfield. Oss —6M 117
Westfield. S'ley —5A 60
Westfield. T'tn —8F 56
Westfield Av. All B —8A 84
Westfield Av. C'frd —7C 102
Westfield Av. Dew —3K 117
Westfield Av. Hal —5J 93
Westfield Av. Hud —3G 130
Westfield Av. Kip —4A 84
Westfield Av. Knot —9E 104
Westfield Av. Leeds —6J 61
Westfield Av. Mel —6B 146
Westfield Av. Pon —5J 123
Westfield Av. Skelm —8C 150
Westfield Av. Yead —1K 41
Westfield Bungalows. S Elm
(in two parts) —7M 157
Westfield Clo. Heck —7N 95
Westfield Clo. Nor —2H 121
Westfield Clo. Rothw —9L 81
Westfield Clo. Yead —1K 41
Westfield Ct. Horb —9B 118
Westfield Ct. Leeds —5B 62
(off Westfield Rd.)
Westfield Ct. Mir —6L 115
Westfield Ct. Rothw —9L 81
Westfield Cres. B'frd —5F 58
Westfield Cres. K'gte —1D 118
Westfield Cres. Leeds —5B 62
(in two parts)
Westfield Cres. Oss —6M 117
Westfield Cres. Riddl —6M 21
Westfield Cres. Ryh —9H 139
Westfield Cres. Shipl —9C 40
Westfield Dri. Hal —5J 93
Westfield Dri. Oss —6M 117
Westfield Dri. Riddl —7M 21
Westfield Dri. Skelm —8C 150
Westfield Dri. Yead —1J 41
Westfield Farm. Oss —5M 117
Westfield Gdns. Hal —5J 93
Westfield Gdns. Kip —3N 83
Westfield Grn. B'frd —1J 77
Westfield Gro. Ackw —2H 141
Westfield Gro. All B —8A 84
Westfield Gro. B'frd —7E 40
Westfield Gro. C'frd —7C 102
(in two parts)
Westfield Gro. Dew —3C 116
Westfield Gro. Pen —7A 166
Westfield Gro. Shipl —9C 40
Westfield Gro. Wake —3L 119
Westfield Gro. Yead —1K 41
Westfield Ho. B'frd —8F 40
(off Buckfast Ct.)
Westfield Ind. Est. Yead —1L 41
Westfield La. D'ton —7B 124
Westfield La. Eml —1B 150
W. Field La. H'frth —3N 163
Westfield La. Kip —3N 83
Westfield La. K S'ton —7K 143
Westfield La. Leeds —3M 85
Westfield La. Shipl & Idle —9C 40
Westfield La. S Elm —8M 157
Westfield La. T'ner —3F 46
Westfield La. Wyke & Schol —2A 94
Westfield M. T'tn —9F 56
Westfield Mt. Yead —2K 41
Westfield Oval. Yead —1J 41
Westfield Pk. Wake —3L 119
Westfield Pl. Hal —6N 91
Westfield Pl. K'gte —9D 98
Westfield Pl. Morl —9K 79
Westfield Pl. Schol —3C 94
Westfield Rd. B'frd —4M 57
Westfield Rd. Cytn —1G 74
Westfield Rd. Heck —7N 95
Westfield Rd. Hems —2C 156
Westfield Rd. Horb —9B 118
Westfield Rd. Knot —9E 104
Westfield Rd. Leeds —5B 62
Westfield Rd. Morl —9K 79
Westfield Rd. Riddl —7M 21
Westfield Rd. Rothw & Carl —1L 99
Westfield Rd. Wake —3L 119
Westfields. C'frd —7C 102
Westfields. Roys —5B 154
Westfields Av. Mir —6L 115
Westfields Rd. Mir —6L 115
Westfield St. Brun I —6A 92
Westfield St. Heck —7N 95
Westfield St. Oss —6M 117
Westfield Ter. All B —8A 84
Westfield Ter. Bail —3A 40
Westfield Ter. B'frd —5F 58
Westfield Ter. Cytn —1G 74
Westfield Ter. Hal —4N 91
Westfield Ter. Horb —1C 136
Westfield Ter. Leeds —5B 62
(LS3)
Westfield Ter. Leeds —8E 44
(LS7)
Westfield Ter. Myth —3M 89
Westfield Ter. Wake —3L 119
Westfield Vw. Wake —2L 119
Westfield Vs. Horb —1B 136
Westfield Yd. Leeds —9L 61
West Fold. Bail —3A 40
West Garforth. —9L 65
Westgarth. Lntn —6J 17
Westgate. —4L 99
Westgate. Alm —8D 132
Westgate. Bail —3A 40
Westgate. B'frd —6B 58
Westgate. Brigh —1C 114
Westgate. Cleck —5G 95
Westgate. Dew —3G 116
Westgate. Eccl —2G 59
Westgate. Ell —4E 112
Westgate. Guis —8E 24
Westgate. Hal —5B 92
Westgate. Heck —8N 95
Westgate. Hems —2C 156
West Ga. H'frth —8L 163
Westgate. Holy G —8M 111
(off Stainland Rd.)
Westgate. Hon —5L 147
Westgate. Hud —4M 131
West Ga. Kei —9H 21
Westgate. Leeds —6C 62
(in two parts)
Westgate. Mel —7C 146
Westgate. Otley —1K 25
Westgate. Shipl —7N 39
Westgate. Wake —5K 119
West Ga. Weth —4M 17
Westgate Clo. Loft —4L 99
Westgate Common. —5J 119
Westgate Ct. Loft —4L 99
Westgate End. Wake —6J 119
Westgate Gro. Loft —4L 99
Westgate Hill. —5L 77
Westgate Hill St. B'frd —5K 77
Westgate La. Loft —4K 99
Westgate Mkt. Hal —5B 92
Westgate Pl. B'frd —5L 77
Westgate Ter. B'frd —5L 77
Westgate Ter. Dew —3F 116
(off Old Westgate)
W. Grange Clo. Leeds —4F 80
W. Grange Dri. Leeds —4F 80
W. Grange Fold. Leeds —4F 80
W. Grange Gdns. Leeds —4F 80
W. Grange Gth. Leeds —4F 80
W. Grange Grn. Leeds —4F 80
W. Grange Rd. Leeds —5F 80
W. Grange Wlk. Leeds —4F 80
West Gro. Bail —3A 40
West Gro. Roys —5B 154
West Gro. Av. Hud —4B 132
Westgrove Ct. Cleck —4G 94
W. Grove St. B'frd —7B 58
W. Grove St. S'ley —5A 60
Westgrove Ter. Hal —5A 92
W. Hall La. Nesf —8N 5
West Hardwick. —1B 140
Westhill Av. Cull —1L 55
W. Hill Av. Leeds —8E 44
W. Hill St. Hal —5N 91
W. Hill Ter. Leeds —8E 44
Westholme Rd. Hal —5M 91
Westholme St. B'frd —8B 58
West Ho. Ell —4E 112
(off Gog Hill)
W. Ings Clo. Knot —7G 104
W. Ings Ct. Knot —7G 104
W. Ings Cres. Knot —7G 104
W. Ings La. Knot —7G 104
W. Ings M. Knot —7G 104
W. Ings Way. Knot —7G 104
Westland Ct. Leeds —5D 80
Westland Rd. Leeds —4D 80
Westlands Dri. All —5G 57
Westlands Gro. All —5H 57
Westland Sq. Leeds —5D 80
West La. Askw —4B 10
West La. Bail —4L 39
(in two parts)
West La. B Spa —8C 18
West La. Gom —3M 95
West La. Hal —9E 92
West La. Haw —8B 36
West La. Kei —8F 20
West La. Shar C —9J 121
West La. T'tn —7C 56
Westlea Av. Riddl —7M 21
W. Lea Clo. Leeds —6D 44
Westlea Cotts. Knot —9F 104
W. Lea Cres. Ting —5N 97
W. Lea Cres. Yead —1K 41
W. Lea Dri. Leeds —6D 44
W. Lea Dri. Ting —5N 97
W. Lea Gdns. Leeds —6D 44
W. Lea Gth. Leeds —6D 44
W. Lea Gro. Yead —1K 41
W. Leeds St. Kei —9G 21
Westleigh. Bgly —3F 38
Westleigh Clo. Bail —5M 39
Westleigh Dri. Bail —5M 39
Westleigh Rd. Bail —4M 39
Westleigh Way. Bail —5L 39
Westlock Av. Leeds —5J 63
W. Lodge Cres. Hud —7G 112
W. Lodge Gdns. Leeds —9E 44
West Mead. C'frd —5G 102
Westmead. S'ley —5L 59
Westminster Av. Cytn —1F 74
Westminster Clo. Rod —2C 60
Westminster Cres. Cytn —1F 74
Westminster Cres. Leeds —7N 63
Westminster Cft. Rod —2C 60
Westminster Dri. Cytn —1F 74
Westminster Dri. Rod —2C 60
Westminster Gdns. Cytn —1F 74
Westminster Pl. B'frd —5D 58
Westminster Rd. B'frd —5D 58
Westminster Ter. B'frd —5D 58
Westmoor Av. Bail —3N 39
Westmoor Clo. Bail —3N 39
Westmoor Pl. Leeds —3E 60
Westmoor Ri. Leeds —3E 60
W. Moor Rd. Kin —8A 140
Westmoor Rd. Leeds —3E 60
Westmoor St. Leeds —3E 60
W. Moor Vw. Hon —5K 147
Westmoreland Mt. Leeds —2G 61
Westmorland St. Wake —5L 119
West Morton. —6B 22
W. Mount St. Hal —4N 91
W. Mount St. Leeds —2C 80
W. Mount St. Pon —3J 123
Westmuir Ho. B'frd —1B 76
(off Launton Way)
Westoff La. S Hien —1K 155
Weston. —6F 10
Weston Av. Q'bry —4C 74
Weston Cres. Otley —8J 11
Weston Dri. Otley —7H 11
Weston Hall. —7F 10
Weston La. Otley —8H 11
Weston Moor Rd. Askw —1F 10
Weston Pk. Vw. Otley —7H 11
Weston Ridge Otley —7J 11
Weston Rd. I'ly —5G 9
Weston St. Kei —2F 36
Weston Va. Rd. Q'bry —5C 74
Westover Av. Leeds —3F 60
Westover Clo. Leeds —3G 60
Westover Gdns. Pud —7N 59
Westover Grn. Leeds —3F 60
Westover Gro. Leeds —3F 60
Westover Mt. Leeds —3F 60
Westover Rd. Leeds —3F 60
Westover St. Leeds —3F 60
Westover Ter. Leeds —3F 60
Westover Vw. Leeds —3F 60
West Pde. Guis —7J 25
West Pde. Hal —6A 92
West Pde. I'ly —5H 9
West Pde. Leeds —7K 43
West Pde. Rothw —8A 82
West Pde. Sower B —8K 91
West Pde. Wake —5L 119
W. Parade Ct. Wake —6L 119
West Pde. Flats. Hal —6A 92
(off West Pde.)
W. Parade St. Wake —6L 119
West Park. —8C 18
(nr. Boston Spa)
West Park. —7K 43
(nr. Lawnswood)
West Pk. Guis —6G 25
West Pk. Pud —7A 60
W. Park Av. Leeds —4K 45
W. Park Cvn. Site. D'ton —9C 124
W. Pk. Chase. Leeds —4J 45
W. Park Clo. Leeds —4J 45
W. Park Ct. Leeds —4K 45
W. Park Cres. Leeds —5K 45
W. Park Dri. D'ton —9C 124
W. Park Dri. Leeds —7K 43
W. Park Dri. E. Leeds —4J 45
W. Park Dri. W. Leeds —4H 45
W. Park Gdns. Leeds —5K 45
W. Park Gro. Bat —7D 96
W. Park Gro. Leeds —4J 45
W. Park Ind. Est. B'frd —1L 75
W. Park Pl. Leeds —5K 45
W. Park Rd. Bat —8C 96
W. Park Rd. B'frd —6L 57
W. Park Rd. Leeds —5K 45
W. Park St. Brigh —1N 113
W. Park St. Dew —2E 116
W. Park Ter. Bat —8D 96
W. Park Ter. B'frd —6L 57
W. Park Ter. D'ton —9C 124
W. Pasture Clo. H'fth —6C 42
W. Pinfold. Roys —6D 154
West Pl. Hud —4B 132
Westridge Dri. Hud —9H 131
West Riding Folk Museum. —4E 92
West Rd. Leeds —2L 81
W. Road N. Leeds —2L 81
West Royd. Hal —4H 93
Westroyd. N Clift —6L 11
Westroyd. Pud —8N 59
West Royd. —7C 40
West Royd. Wilsd —1B 56
W. Royd Av. B'frd —2F 58
Westroyd Av. Cleck —1H 95
W. Royd Av. Hal —6N 91
W. Royd Av. Mir —6L 115
Westroyd Av. Pud —8N 59
W. Royd Av. Shipl —7B 40
W. Royd Clo. Hal —7N 91
W. Royd Clo. Shipl —7B 40
Westroyd Cres. Pud —9N 59
W. Royd Cres. Shipl —7C 40
W. Royd Dri. Mir —5L 115
W. Royd Dri. Shipl —7C 40
Westroyd Gdns. Pud —8N 59
W. Royd Gro. Mir —5L 115
W. Royd Gro. Shipl —7C 40
Westroyd Hill. —8N 59
W. Royd Mt. Shipl —7C 40
W. Royd Pk. Mir —5L 115
W. Royd Rd. Shipl —7C 40
W. Royd Ter. Shipl —7C 40
W. Royd Wlk. Shipl —7C 40
W. Scausby Pk. Hal —6L 73
West Scholes. —2C 74
W. Shaw La. Oxe —3A 54
Westside Ct. B'frd —6M 57
(off Bk. Girlington Rd.)
W. Side Retail Pk. Guis —9K 25
W. Slaithwaite Rd. Hud —2J 145
West St. Bail —3A 40
West St. B'frd —5N 93
West St. Bat —7G 97
(in two parts)
West St. B'frd —8D 58
(BD1)
West St. B'frd —3F 58
(BD2)
West St. Brigh —9M 93
West St. C'frd —4C 102
West St. Cleck —5H 95
West St. Dew —4F 116
West St. Dlgtn —8B 78
West St. Gom —3M 95
West St. Guis —7J 25
West St. Hal —5N 91
West St. H'cft —9K 139
West St. Heck —8N 95
West St. Hems —2C 156
West St. Holy G —7A 112
West St. Hud —1F 130
West St. I'ly —5G 8
West St. Leeds —6B 62
West St. Morl —1L 97
West St. Nor —1H 121
West St. Pon —7F 156
(in two parts)
West St. Roys —5E 154
West St. She —9G 75
West St. S Elm —5A 158
West St. S Hien —4M 155
West St. Sower B —9H 91
West St. Stan —1A 120
West St. S'ley —6B 60
West St. Todm —6J 87
West St. Wake —6H 119
W. Terrace St. S'ley —5A 60
West Town. —4E 116
West Vale. —5C 112
West Va. Dew —5E 116
West Va. Leeds —9A 62
Westvale M. Leeds —5H 61
West Vw. Ackw —5D 140
West Vw. Bat —1E 116
West Vw. Bgly —2H 39
West Vw. B'shaw —9M 77
West Vw. B'twn —2A 92
West Vw. B'frd —1E 76
(off New Hey Rd.)
West Vw. Crig —6F 136
West Vw. Fars —4A 60
(off New St.)
West Vw. Hal —6M 91
(off Hopwood La.)
West Vw. H'th —7D 120
West Vw. Holy G —7N 111
West Vw. I'ly —6G 9

West Vw. Kip —3B 84
West Vw. K'gte —1D 118
West Vw. Leeds —2C 80
West Vw. M'fld —8H 67
West Vw. Nor —7G 101
West Vw. Otley —1M 25
West Vw. Pad —5J 131
West Vw. Pool W —2J 27
West Vw. Schol —3D 94
West Vw. Sils —7E 6
West Vw. Sower B —8J 91
West Vw. W'ford —8D 82
West Vw. Yead —9K 25
W. View Av. Bur W —8C 10
W. View Av. C'frd —5G 103
W. View Av. Hal —5L 91
Westview Av. Kei —8G 21
W. View Av. Shipl —8C 40
W. View Clo. Shipl —8C 40
Westview Ct. Kei —8G 21
W. View Ct. Yead —9K 25
W. View Cres. Hal —5L 91
W. View Dri. Hal —5K 91
Westview Gro. Kei —8G 21
W. View Ri. Hud —5J 131
W. View Rd. Bur W —8C 10
W. View Rd. Hal —2A 92
W. View St. Cro R —7F 36
W. View Ter. Bshw —4M 73
W. View Ter. Pel —4L 91
Westview Way. Kei —8H 21
W. Villa Rd. Guis —7J 25
Westville. I'ly —5F 8
Westville Av. I'ly —5F 8
Westville Clo. I'ly —5F 8
Westville Rd. I'ly —5F 8
Westville Way. T'tn —8C 56
Westward Cft. Hud —9H 113
Westward Ho. Hal —9N 73
Westward Ho. Q'bry —4C 74
Westway. Bat —9J 97
Westway. Bgly —2G 39
Westway. B'frd —4H 57
Westway. Fars —3N 59
Westway. Gar —8L 65
Westway. Guis —8F 24
Westway. Kei —8F 20
Westway. Mir —4K 115
Westway. Shipl —8J 39
Westways. Wren —9H 99
Westways Clo. Wren —1H 119
Westways Dri. Leeds —8L 45
Westways Ri. Wren —1H 119
W. Wells Cres. Oss —6M 117
W. Wells Rd. Oss —6M 117
West Winds. Men —3C 24
Westwinn Gth. Leeds —7D 46
Westwinn Vw. Leeds —6D 46
Westwood. B'frd —2L 57
Westwood Av. B'frd —1F 58
Westwood Av. Hon —5A 148
Westwood Clo. F'stne —4D 122
Westwood Clo. Morl —7L 79
W. Wood Ct. Leeds —8C 80
Westwood Cres. Bgly —7F 38
Westwood Dri. I'ly —7E 8
Westwood Edge Rd. Slai —7N 129
Westwood Fold. Slai —8A 130
Westwood Gro. B'frd —1F 58
Westwood Ri. Morl —7L 79
Westwood Rd. C'frd —7B 102
W. Wood Rd. Morl —9B 80
Westwood Rd. Oss —6B 118
Westwood Side. Morl —6K 79
Westwood St. Hud —5E 114
Westwood Way. B Spa —1D 32
W. Yorkshire Ind. Est. B'frd —5H 77
West Yorkshire Playhouse. —6F 62
Wetherby. —4M 17
Wetherby Bus. Pk. Weth —3N 17
Wetherby Grange. Weth —7A 18
Wetherby Gro. Leeds —4M 61
Wetherby Pl. Leeds —4N 61
Wetherby Racecourse. —3B 18
Wetherby Rd. Bard —4F 30
Wetherby Rd. B'ham —5C 32
Wetherby Rd. Coll —8L 17
Wetherby Rd. Kirk D —1L 17
Wetherby Rd. Leeds —9K 45
Wetherby Rd. S'cft & Leeds —8N 45
Wetherby Rd. Sick —4E 16
Wetherby Rd. Wltn —5E 18
Wetherby Ter. Leeds —4M 61
Wetherhill St. Bat —7F 96
Wetherill Ter. Dew —9C 96
(off Kilpin Hill La.)
Wetlands Rd. Mel —8D 146
Wet Shod La. Brigh —8K 93
Weybridge Ho. B'frd —5A 58
(off Trenton Dri.)
Weydale Av. Hud —2F 130
Weyhill Dri. All —6G 57
Weymouth Av. All —6F 56
Weymouth Av. Hud —3G 130
Weymouth St. Hal —5B 92
Whack Ho. Yead —1K 41
(off Whack Houses)
Whack Ho. Clo. Yead —1L 41
Whack Ho. La. Yead —1L 41
Whalley La. Denh —4K 55
Wharfbank Ho. Otley —1J 25
Wharfe Bank. Coll —9F 16
Wharfe Clo. Leeds —3N 43
Wharfe Ct. Bur W —8D 10
Wharfe Ct. Sils —8E 6
Wharfe Cres. Pool W —1G 26
Wharfedale Av. Leeds —2D 62
Wharfedale Ct. Leeds —1A 64
Wharfedale Ct. Otley —9L 11
Wharfedale Cres. Gar —9N 65
Wharfedale Cres. Skelm —8E 150
Wharfedale Dri. I'ly —5H 9
Wharfedale Dri. Nor —8H 101
Wharfedale Gdns. Bail —3C 40
Wharfedale Gro. Leeds —2D 62
Wharfedale Ho. Sower B —9H 91
(off Quarry Hill)
Wharfedale M. Otley —9L 11
Wharfedale Mt. Hal —8G 74
Wharfedale Mt. Leeds —2D 62
Wharfedale Pl. Leeds —2D 62
Wharfedale Ri. B'frd —4H 57
Wharfedale Ri. Ting —5N 97
Wharfedale Rd. Euro I —6E 76
Wharfedale St. Leeds —2D 62
Wharfedale Vw. Add —1L 7
Wharfedale Vw. Leeds —2D 62
Wharfedale Vw. Men —4E 24
Wharfe Grange. Weth —4L 17
Wharfe Gro. Weth —4L 17
Wharfe La. Kear —7L 15
Wharfe Pk. Add —1N 7
Wharfe Rein. Coll —9F 16
Wharfeside. B Spa —1F 32
Wharfeside La. I'ly —4H 9
Wharfe St. B'frd —6D 58
Wharfe St. Otley —9M 11
Wharfe Vw. Kirk O —2K 15
Wharfe Vw. Pool W —1F 26
Wharfe Vw. Weth —4L 17
Wharfe Vw. Rd. I'ly —5G 9
Wharfe Way. C'frd —4H 103
(in two parts)
Wharf St. Brigh —1N 113
Wharf St. Dew —4G 116
Wharf St. Leeds —7F 62
Wharf St. Shipl —7N 39
Wharf St. Sower B —8J 91
Wharf St. Todm —2J 107
Wharncliffe Cres. B'frd —2H 59
Wharncliffe Dri. B'frd —2H 59
Wharncliffe Gro. B'frd —2H 59
Wharncliffe Gro. Shipl —9N 39
Wharncliffe Rd. Shipl —1N 57
Wharncliffe Rd. Wake —6J 137
Wharncliffe St. Cltn —9E 154
Wharton Sq. Q'bry —4G 74
(off Highgate Rd.)
Whartons, The. Otley —7L 11
Wharton St. Liv —8M 95
Wharton Ter. Heck —9A 96
(off Church La.)
Wheat Clo. Dew —3C 116
Wheatcroft. Bat —7F 96
(off Bayldons Pl.)
Wheatcroft. C'frd —6H 103
Wheatcroft Av. Bat —8F 96
Wheater Ho. Wake —5L 119
(off George St.)
Wheater Rd. B'frd —9M 57
Wheatfield Av. Hud —3F 130
Wheatfield Ct. Pud —8A 60
Wheat Head Cres. Kei —2E 36
Wheat Head Dri. Kei —2F 36
Wheat Head La. Kei —2E 36
Wheathouse Rd. Hud —1L 131
Wheathouse Ter. Hud —1L 131
Wheatings, The. Oss —6B 118
Wheatlands. Fars —3N 59
Wheatlands. I'ly —5H 9
Wheatlands Av. B'frd —4K 57
Wheatlands Cres. B'frd —4K 57
Wheatlands Dri. B'frd —4K 57
Wheatlands Dri. Liv —1K 115
Wheatlands Gro. B'frd —4K 57
Wheatlands Sq. B'frd —4K 57
Wheatley. —2L 91
Wheatley Av. I'ly —6K 9
Wheatley Av. Nor —2J 121
Wheatley Clo. Hal —3N 91
Wheatley Ct. Hal —9K 73
Wheatley Dri. Mir —8L 115
Wheatley Gdns. I'ly —6K 9
Wheatley Gro. I'ly —6K 9
Wheatley Hill La. Clay W —9G 151
Wheatley La. Ben R —6K 9
Wheatley La. Hal —3N 91
Wheatley Ri. I'ly —6K 9
Wheatley Ri. M'well —7K 153
Wheatley Rd. Hal —2L 91
Wheatley Rd. I'ly —6H 9
Wheaton Av. Leeds —6B 64
Wheaton Ct. Leeds —6B 64
(off Wheaton Av.)
Wheatroyd Cres. Oss —8N 117
Wheatroyd La. Hud —8C 132
Wheat St. Kei —3G 36
Wheelwright Av. Leeds —9K 61
Wheelwright Clo. Leeds —9K 61
(in two parts)
Wheelwright Dri. Dew —1D 116
Wheelwright St. Dew —3F 116
Wheldale. —2K 103
Wheldale Ct. C'frd —3H 103
(off Stansfield Clo.)
Wheldale La. C'frd —2K 103
Wheldon Road. —3F 102
Wheldon Rd. C'frd —4E 102
Whernside Mt. B'frd —3K 75
Whernside Way. Mt Tab —1G 91
Wherwell Rd. Brigh —2N 113
Whetley Clo. B'frd —6A 58
Whetley Gro. B'frd —5M 57
Whetley Hill. B'frd —5N 57
Whetley La. B'frd —6M 57
Whetley Ter. B'frd —6A 58
Whewell St. Birs —3B 96
Whimbrel Clo. B'frd —7H 57
Whimbrel M. Morl —1M 97
Whinbeck Av. Norm —2K 121
Whinberry Pl. Birs —1C 96
Whinbrook Ct. Leeds —6E 44
Whinbrook Cres. Leeds —6E 44
Whinbrook Gdns. Leeds —6E 44
Whinbrook Gro. Leeds —6E 44
Whin Clo. Hems —4D 156
Whincop Av. C'frd —5A 102
Whincover Bank. Leeds —9J 61
Whincover Clo. Leeds —9J 61
Whincover Cross. Leeds —9J 61
Whincover Dri. Leeds —9H 61
Whincover Gdns. Leeds —9J 61
Whincover Grange. Leeds —9J 61
Whincover Gro. Leeds —9J 61
Whincover Hill. Leeds —9J 61
Whincover Mt. Leeds —9J 61
Whincover Rd. Leeds —9H 61
Whin Covert La. K S'ton —8K 143
Whincover Vw. Leeds —9J 61
Whincup Gdns. Leeds —3G 80
(off Woodhouse Hill Rd.)
Whiney Hill. Q'bry —4E 74
(off Sand Beds)
Whinfield. Leeds —3L 43
Whinfield Av. Kei —9E 20
Whinfield Clo. Kei —8F 20
Whinfield Dri. Kei —8E 20
Whinfield Pl. Oss —7C 118
Whinfield Ter. Oss —7D 118
Whingate. Leeds —6K 61
Whingate Av. Leeds —7K 61
Whingate Clo. Leeds —7K 61
Whingate Grn. Leeds —7K 61
Whingate Gro. Leeds —7K 61
Whingate Rd. Leeds —7K 61
Whingrove Av. Mel —8B 146
Whin Knoll Av. Kei —8F 20
Whin La. Leeds —3N 85
Whin La. Silk —9N 167
Whinmoor. —7C 46
Whinmoor Ct. Leeds —6B 46
Whinmoor Cres. Leeds —6B 46
Whinmoor Gdns. Leeds —6A 46
Whinmoor La. Leeds —4N 45
Whin Moor La. Silk —8M 167
Whinmoor Way. Leeds —8D 46
(in four parts)
Whinmore Gdns. Gom —5N 95
Whin Mt. Nor —3K 121
Whinney Bank La. H'frth —3N 163
Whinney Clo. S'hse —6L 121
Whinney Fld. Hal —8B 92
Whinney Hill Pk. Brigh —7M 93
Whinney La. S'hse —6K 121
Whinney Moor Av. Wake —8F 118
Whinney Royd La. Hal —8F 74
Whinn Wood Grange. Leeds —7C 46
Whins La. Hept —9G 70
Whins La. Sick —2C 16
Whins La. Thor A —8F 18
Whin St. Kei —9G 20
Whin Vw. Ct. H'cft —9K 139
Whirlaw Av. Todm —5J 87
Whirlaw La. Todm —4K 87
Whiskers La. Hal —1D 92
Whisperwood Clo. Out —7M 99
Whisperwood Rd. Out —7M 99
Whitacre Clo. Hud —8C 114
Whitacre St. Hud —8C 114
Whitaker Av. B'frd —3G 59
Whitaker Clo. B'frd —3G 59
Whitaker St. Bat —8G 96
Whitaker St. Fars —5A 60
Whitburn Way. All —6G 57
Whitby Av. Hud —9M 113
Whitby Cres. Dew —3J 117
Whitby Rd. B'frd —5M 57
Whitby Ter. B'frd —5M 57
Whitcliffe Rd. Cleck —4G 94
Whitcliffe Sq. Cleck —4H 95
(off Whitecliffe Rd.)
White Abbey Rd. B'frd —6A 58
White Apron St. S Kirk —7H 157
Whitebeam Grn. Pon —2M 123
Whitebeam La. Leeds —5F 80
Whitebeam Pk. Hud —1J 131
Whitebeam Wlk. B'frd —1F 58
White Birch Ter. Hal —2L 91
Whitebridge Av. Leeds —6N 63
Whitebridge Cres. Leeds —5N 63
Whitebridge Spur. Leeds —5N 63
Whitebridge Vw. Leeds —5N 63
White Castle Ct. Q'bry —3A 74
Whitechapel Clo. Leeds —9K 45
Whitechapel Gro. Schol —3E 94
Whitechapel Rd. Cleck —3D 94
Whitechapel Way. Leeds —9K 45
Whitecliffe Cres. Swil —3H 83
Whitecliffe Dri. Swil —3H 83
Whitecliffe La. Swil —3H 83
Whitecliffe Ri. Swil —3H 83
White Clo. La. Den D —2D 166
Whitecote. —1F 60
Whitecote Gdns. Leeds —2E 60
Whitecote Hill. Leeds —2E 60
Whitecote Ho. Leeds —1E 60
Whitecote La. Leeds —2E 60
(LS13)
Whitecote La. Leeds —1M 85
(LS25)
Whitecote Ri. Leeds —2E 60
White Ct. Croft —2H 139
White Cross. —7F 24
White Cross. Hud —6C 114
White Cross Gdns. S Hien —2L 155
White Cross Rd. Dew —2H 117
White Fld. La. Myth —4K 89
Whitefield Pl. B'frd —6M 57
Whitegate. E Kes —2D 30
Whitegate. Hal —8C 92
White Ga. Hon —4L 147
White Ga. Ogden —6K 73
Whitegate Dri. Hal —8C 92
Whitegate La. E Hard —3L 141
Whitegate Rd. Hal —7C 92
White Ga. Rd. H'frth —7J 163
Whitegate Rd. Hud —6N 131
Whitegates Clo. Wake —2J 119
Whitegates Gro. Fen B —8H 133
Whitegate Ter. Hal —8C 92
Whitegate Top. Hal —8D 92
White Gro. Leeds —7J 45
Whitehall Av. Mir —4L 115
Whitehall Av. Wake —2J 119
Whitehall Av. Wyke —3A 94
Whitehall Ct. Horb —1D 136
Whitehall Cres. Wake —2J 119
Whitehall Cft. Rothw —8A 82
Whitehall Est. Leeds —1J 79
Whitehall Gro. B'shaw —8M 77
Whitehall Gro. Dlgtn —7A 78
White Hall La. Hal —7G 72
Whitehall Pk. Leeds —1K 79
Whitehall Ri. Wake —3J 119
Whitehall Rd. Cleck & Wyke —2G 95
Whitehall Rd. Dlgtn —7A 78
Whitehall Rd. Hal & Wyke —3L 93
Whitehall Rd. Leeds —1L 79
Whitehall Rd. Lint —1B 146
Whitehall Rd. E. B'shaw —9L 77
Whitehall Rd. W. Cleck & B'shaw —2H 95
Whitehall St. Hal —5J 93
Whitehall St. Wake —6H 119
Whitehall Way. Dew —3G 116
White Hart Dri. New —7M 131
White Hart Fold. N Elm —3A 158
White Hart Fold. Todm —7K 87
(off Station App.)
Whitehaven Clo. B'frd —6L 75
Whitehead Gro. Fag —5G 58
Whitehead La. Hud —7L 131
Whitehead La. S Cro —3E 146
Whitehead Pl. B'frd —4G 58
Whitehead's Ter. Hal —5M 91
Whitehead St. B'frd —8F 58
White Hill. Mars —2J 145
Whitehill Cotts. Hal —8L 73
Whitehill Cres. Hal —7L 73
Whitehill Dri. Hal —7L 73
Whitehill Grn. Hal —7M 73
Whitehill Rd. H'fld —8L 73
Whitehill Rd. Oakw —2L 35
White Horse Clo. Birs —2E 96
White Horse Yd. Wake —5L 119
Whitehouse Av. W'ford —5L 83
White Ho. Bungalows. Wake —8K 119
Whitehouse Cres. W'ford —5M 83
Whitehouse Dri. W'ford —5L 83
Whitehouse La. W'ford —2K 83
Whitehouse La. Yead —8B 26
White Houses. H Bri —3M 89
Whitehouse St. Leeds —9F 62
White Laithe App. Leeds —7C 46
White Laithe Av. Leeds —7C 46
White Laithe Clo. Leeds —7C 46
White Laithe Ct. Leeds —7C 46
White Laithe Cft. Leeds —7C 46
White Laithe Gdns. Leeds —7C 46
White Laithe Gth. Leeds —6C 46
White Laithe Grn. Leeds —7D 46
Whitelaithe Gro. Leeds —7D 46
White Laithe Rd. Leeds —7C 46
White Laithe Wlk. Leeds —7D 46
Whitelands. Pud —6C 60
White Lands. Rawd —3L 41
Whitelands Cres. Bail —4B 40
Whitelands Rd. Bail —4B 40
White La. B'frd —4B 76
White La. Oakw —5N 35
White La. Top. B'frd —4B 76
(off White La.)
White Lea Cft. H Bri —3N 89
White Lee. —5B 96
White Lee Clo. Bat —6B 96
White Lee Gdns. H Bri —3N 89
White Lee Rd. Heck & Bat —5B 96
White Lee Side. Heck —6B 96
Whiteley Av. Sower B —9F 90
White Ley Bank. N Mill —1E 164
Whiteley Cft. Otley —1L 25
Whiteley Cft. Clo. Otley —1L 25
Whiteley Cft. Gth. Otley —1K 25
Whiteley Cft. Ri. Otley —1L 25
Whiteley Cft. Rd. Otley —1K 25
White Ley Rd. Cam —1J 159
Whiteley St. F'stne —6C 122
Whiteley St. Hud —6G 130
Whiteley Ter. Sower B —9B 110
Whitelock St. Leeds —5F 62
White Moor La. Oxe —7C 54
White Moss Clo. Ackw —4F 140
Whiteplatts St. Todm —6K 87
White Rose Av. Gar —7N 65
White Rose Av. Hud —3D 132
White Rose Mead. Gar —7A 66
White Rose Shop. Cen., The. Leeds —6A 80
White Rose Way. Gar —7A 66
Whites Clo. B'frd —3J 57
White Slack Ga. Todm —5H 107
Whites Rd. Wake —5M 119
White's Row. Horb —1N 135
White's Ter. B'frd —5N 57
Whitestone Cres. Yead —9M 25
Whitestone La. Hud —2N 131
White St. W'ford —7E 82
White's Vw. B'frd —6N 57
White Va. B'frd —1E 76
White Walls La. H'frth —5E 162
Whiteways. B'frd —3C 58
White Wells Gdns. H'frth —5B 164
White Wells Rd. H'frth —5B 164
White Wells Spa Cottage. —7G 9
Whitewood Clo. Roys —6C 154
Whitfield Av. Leeds —1G 80
Whitfield Gdns. Leeds —1G 80
Whitfield Pl. Leeds —1G 80
Whitfield Sq. Leeds —1G 80
Whitfield St. Cleck —4H 95
Whitfield St. H'let —1G 80
Whitfield St. Leeds —3H 63
Whitfield Way. Leeds —1G 80
Whitham Clo. B Spa —9D 18
Whitham Rd. Shipl —7K 39
Whitkirk. —5C 64
Whitkirk Clo. Leeds —6F 64
Whitkirk La. Leeds —6E 64
Whitkirk Lane End. —7E 64
Whitlam St. Shipl —7L 39
Whitley Dri. Hal —7M 73
Whitley Gdns. Leeds —3G 63
(off Bayswater Rd.)
Whitley La. S'wram —7F 92
Whitley Lower. —2B 134
Whitley Pl. All B —9B 84
Whitley Rd. Dew —1E 134
Whitley Rd. Kei —2G 36
Whitley Rd. Pen —9J 165
Whitley Rd. W'ley —2A 134
Whitley Spring Cres. Oss —5B 118
Whitley Spring Rd. Oss —5B 118

Whitley St. Bgly —4E 38
Whitley St. B'frd —7E 58
Whitley St. Hal —6A 92
Whitley Way. Grng M —5B 134
Whittaker Rd. Err —5F 88
Whitteron Clo. Hud —1G 131
Whittle Cres. Cytn —9G 57
Whittles St. S'fth —7A 106
Whitton Cft. Rd. I'ly —5G 9
Whitty La. Sower B —6H 91
Whitwell Av. Ell —4G 112
Whitwell Dri. Ell —4G 112
Whitwell Grn. La. Ell —5G 112
Whitwell Gro. Ell —4G 112
Whitwell St. B'frd —9E 58
Whitwood. —6N 101
Whitwood Common. —7N 101
Whitwood Comn. La. C'frd —8M 101
Whitwood Enterprise Pk. W'wood —7N 101
Whitwood Freight Cen. C'frd —7M 101
Whitwood La. Brigh —5A 94
Whitwood La. C'frd —6L 101
Whitwood Mere. —4A 102
Whitwood Ter. C'frd —7M 101
Whitworth Rd. Dew —4E 116
Wholestone Ga. Gol —5A 130
Wholestone Hill. —1G 128
Whytecote End. Wyke —9A 76
Wibsey. —4A 76
Wibsey Bank. B'frd —4B 76
Wibsey Pk. Av. B'frd —5L 75
Wickelden Ga. H'frth —5B 164
Wicken Clo. B'frd —9G 41
Wicken La. T'tn —7C 56
Wicken Tree La. M'twn —3M 135
Wickets Clo. B'frd —5B 76
Wickets, The. Colt —7F 64
Wickets, The. Leeds —8B 44
Wickets, The. Wake —1N 137
Wicket, The. C'ley —8M 41
Wickham Av. B Spa —1C 32
Wickham Av. B'frd —5A 76
Wickham Clo. B Spa —9C 18
Wickham St. Leeds —2C 80
Wickham St. Schol —3D 94
Wicking La. Sower B —3N 109
Wickins La. H'frth —2H 163
Widdop Rd. H Bri —6D 70
Wide La. Morl —1L 97
Wide La. Oakw —4A 36
Wigan St. B'frd —7B 58
(in two parts)
Wigeon App. Morl —9M 79
Wiggan La. Hud —7B 114
Wighill. —6N 19
Wighill La. Wltn —5G 18
Wightman St. B'frd —5E 58
Wignall St. Kei —6H 21
Wigton Chase. Leeds —2J 45
Wigton Grn. Leeds —1H 45
Wigton Pk. Clo. Leeds —1H 45
Wike. —7M 29
Wike La. Bard —6A 30
Wike La. Hare —5K 29
Wike Ridge Av. Leeds —2K 45
Wike Ridge Clo. Leeds —1K 45
Wike Ridge Ct. Leeds —1K 45
Wike Ridge Fold. Leeds —1J 45
Wike Ridge Gdns. Leeds —2K 45
Wike Ridge Gro. Leeds —2K 45
Wike Ridge La. Leeds —2K 45
Wike Ridge M. Leeds —2K 45
Wike Ridge Mt. Leeds —2K 45
Wike Ridge Vw. Leeds —2K 45
Wilberlee. —8K 129
Wilby St. Cleck —5H 95
Wilcock La. Sils —4A 6
Wilcroft Ter. Pec W —5J 71
Wilday Clo. Bgly —1D 38
Wild Gro. Pud —7L 59
Wild's Pas. L'boro —9M 107
Wildspur Gro. N Mill —4C 164
Wild's Yd. Wake —6L 119
Wilford Rd. Barn —8N 153
Wilfred Av. Leeds —6C 64
Wilfred St. Cytn —1J 75
Wilfred St. Leeds —6C 64
Wilfred Ter. Leeds —1K 79
Wilkinson Fold. Wyke —1A 94
Wilkinson Ter. B'frd —9L 57
Wilkinson Way. Otley —8J 11
Wilkin St. Kei —9H 21
Willan's Rd. Dew —3F 116
Willerton Clo. Dew —9L 97
Willgutter La. Oakw —5N 35
William Av. Leeds —6N 63
William Henry St. Brigh —9M 93
William Henry St. Shipl —7L 39
William Hey Ct. Leeds —4K 63
William Horsfall St. Hud —7H 131
William Prince Gro. Wake —7N 119
William Ri. Leeds —6N 63
Williams Ct. Fars —3A 60
Williams Dri. Steet —3B 20
Williamson St. Hal —4N 91
Williams Pas. L'boro —9M 107
Williams Rd. Steet —3B 20
William St. B'frd —8C 58
William St. Brigh —2M 113
William St. Butt —6L 75
William St. C'frd —3D 102
(nr. Lock La., in two parts)
William St. C'frd —3E 102
(nr. Wheldon Rd.)
William St. Chur —5M 79
William St. Cros M —6H 131
William St. Denh —5K 55
William St. Dew —3H 117
William St. Fry —2J 103
William St. G'lnd —5C 112
William St. Hud —3N 131
William St. Leeds —3A 62
William St. Liv —8M 95
William St. Raven —6B 116
William St. Stain —9C 96
William St. S'ley —5A 60
(nr. Sun Fld.)
William St. S'ley —4C 60
(nr. Town St.)
William St. Tong —4H 77
William St. Wake —6M 119
William Vw. Leeds —6N 63
Willians Av. Rothw —6N 81
Willington Rd. Skel —8M 159
Willington St. W. Hal —6A 92
Willis St. Leeds —7G 63
Willoughby Ter. Leeds —9B 62
Willow App. Leeds —5A 62
Willow Av. B'frd —9E 40
Willow Av. Cliff —2D 32
Willow Av. Leeds —5A 62
Willow Bank. Hal —7N 91
Willow Bank. Todm —6K 87
Willow Bank Dri. Pon —1L 123
Willow Beck. Not —3B 154
Willowbridge La. C'frd —6N 101
Willowbridge Rd. Lit S —6L 143
Willowbridge Way. W'wood —6N 101
Willowbrook. Skel —7L 159
Willowbrook Rd. M'well —9J 153
Willow Clo. B'frd —6A 76
Willow Clo. Bur W —8C 10
Willow Clo. Cud —9J 155
Willow Clo. Gom —5M 95
Willow Clo. Guis —7J 25
Willow Clo. Hal —6K 91
Willow Clo. Leeds —5A 62
Willow Clough. Ripp —9D 110
Willow Ct. Althpe —4F 118
Willow Ct. Bat —6F 96
Willow Ct. C'frd —6E 102
Willow Ct. F'stne —2C 122
Willow Ct. Pool W —2G 26
Willow Cres. B'frd —9E 40
Willow Cres. Cliff —2D 32
Willow Cres. Leeds —7A 64
Willow Cres. Nor —3H 121
Willow Cres. Sower B —7J 91
Willowcroft. Cleck —6G 94
Willow Cft. Men —4E 24
Willow Dene Av. Hal —7K 91
Willowdene La. Pon —9K 103
Willow Dene Rd. Grime —9A 156
Willow Dri. B'frd —6A 76
Willow Dri. Hal —6K 91
Willow Dri. Hems —4D 156
Willow Dri. Wake —8N 119
Willow Field. —6K 91
Willowfield Av. Hal —7K 91
Willowfield Clo. Hal —6K 91
Willowfield Cres. B'frd —1E 58
Willowfield Cres. Hal —6K 91
Willowfield Dri. Hal —7K 91
Willowfield Lodge. Brigh —4K 113
Willowfield Rd. Hal —6K 91
Willowfield St. B'frd —7N 57
Willowfield Ter. Hal —7L 91
Willowfield Vw. Hal —6K 91
Willow Fold. Wake —4F 118
Willow Gdns. Althpe —4F 118
Willow Gdns. B'frd —9E 40
Willow Gdns. C'frd —7K 103
Willow Gdns. Guis —7J 25
Willow Gdns. Hal —7L 91
Willow Gth. Dur —4G 137
Willow Gth. F'stne —2C 122
Willow Gth. Leeds —5A 62
Willow Gth. S Elm —7A 158
Willow Gth. Av. Leeds —7C 46
Willow Gth. Clo. Leeds —7C 46
Willowgarth. Clo. Ryh —1H 155
Willow Glade. Cliff —3D 32
Willow Grn. Wake —9K 99
Willow Gro. B'frd —9E 40
Willow Gro. Cliff —3D 32
Willow Gro. Gol —5D 130
Willow Gro. Kei —4G 37
Willow Gro. Kip —2N 83
Willow Gro. Oss —8A 118
Willow Gro. Wake —8N 119
Willow Hall Dri. Sower B —7K 91
Willow Hall Fold. Sower B —7K 91
(off Bairstow La.)
Willow Hall La. Sower B —7K 91
Willow Houses. Sower B —7K 91
(off Rochdale Rd.)
Willow La. Cliff —2D 32
Willow La. F'stne —2C 122
Willow La. Guis —1D 40
Willow La. Hud —2M 131
Willow La. K'thpe —4E 120
Willow La. Wake —4E 118
Willow La. E. F'stne —2C 122
Willow La. E. Hud —2N 131
Willow M. Althpe —4F 118
Willow Mt. Althpe —4F 118
Willow Mt. Hal —7J 75
(off Witchfield Hill)
Willow Mt. Sower B —7J 91
(off Overdale Mt.)
Willow Park. —3M 123
Willow Pk. Pon —3M 123
Willow Pk. Wake —1K 119
Willow Pk. Dri. Hal —7J 75
Willow Ri. Hal —6K 91
Willow Ri. Skelm —8C 150
Willow Ri. Tad —6N 33
Willow Rd. Althpe —4F 118
Willow Rd. Bat —8H 97
Willow Rd. C'frd —6D 102
Willow Rd. Fars —4N 59
Willow Rd. Knot —7F 104
Willow Rd. Leeds —5A 62
(LS4)
Willow Rd. Leeds —7A 62
(LS12)
Willow Sq. Oult —8D 82
Willows, The. Crig —5H 137
Willows, The. H'den —6A 38
Willows, The. Horb —1C 136
Willows, The. I'wth —6L 73
Willows, The. Leeds —5E 44
Willows, The. Lep —7L 133
Willow St. B'frd —6L 57
Willow St. Cleck —3H 95
Willow St. Hal —6N 91
Willow St. Sower B —8K 91
Willow Ter. Bat —8H 97
Willow Ter. Leeds —5C 62
Willow Ter. Sower B —7J 91
Willow Tree Clo. Kei —2K 37
Willow Tree Gdns. Bgly —2H 39
Willow Tree Gdns. Bur W —7D 10
Willow Va. Weth —2L 17
Willow Vw. Sower B —7K 91
(off Bairstow Mt.)
Willow Vw. Wake —4F 118
Willow Vs. B'frd —9E 40
Willow Wlk. Liv —9L 95
Willow Well Clo. Leeds —6A 64
Wills Gill. Guis —7K 25
Will St. B'frd —1H 77
Willwood Av. Hud —3G 130
Wilman Dri. Oss —5M 117
Wilman Hill. B'frd —4N 75
Wilman Post. Oss —5M 117
Wilmar Dri. Hud —2D 130
Wilmer Dri. B'frd —2M 57
Wilmer Dri. Shipl —1M 57
Wilmer Rd. B'frd —3M 57
Wilmers. L'boro —9M 107
Wilmington Gro. Leeds —4E 62
Wilmington St. Leeds —4F 62
Wilmington Ter. Leeds —4E 62
Wilmot Rd. I'ly —5H 9
Wilmur Mt. L'ft —6E 90
Wilsden. —1B 56
Wilsden Hill Rd. Wilsd —1A 56
Wilsden Old Rd. H'den —6A 38
Wilsden Rd. All —2D 56
Wilsden Rd. H'den —6A 38
Wilshaw Mill Rd. Mel —9F 146
Wilshaw Rd. Mel —9E 146
Wilson Av. Mir —6K 115
Wilson Av. Oss —7C 118
Wilson Av. Steet —2B 20
Wilson Ct. Wake —8L 99
Wilson Dri. Wake —8K 99
Wilson Fold. Low M —8B 76
Wilson Grn. Sower B —8H 91
Wilson Hill. Bklnd —1G 129
Wilson Rd. Bgly —3E 38
Wilson Rd. Hal —7M 91
Wilson Rd. Mir —6K 115
Wilson Rd. Wyke —9B 76
Wilson Sq. B'frd —5A 58
Wilson's Row. Meth —1N 101
Wilson St. B'frd —5A 58
Wilson St. C'frd —4C 102
Wilson St. F'stne —6C 122
Wilson St. Pon —2K 123
Wilsons Yd. S'ley —5A 60
Wilson Ter. Mir —6K 115
Wilson Wood St. Bat —1F 116
Wilson Yd. Leeds —6D 60
Wilton Av. Hud —5C 114
Wilton Gro. Leeds —9A 44
Wilton Ind. Ct. Bat —4C 96
Wilton Rd. I'ly —6F 8
Wilton St. B'frd —8B 58
Wilton St. Brigh —9L 93
Wilton St. Dew —4G 116
Wilton Ter. Cleck —5H 95
Wimborne Dri. All —5H 57
Wimborne Dri. Kei —8F 20
Winbrooke Ter. B'frd —4M 75
Winburg Rd. B'frd —9M 57
Winchester Clo. Wren —2F 118
Winchester Ho. Sower B —8J 91
(off Church Vw.)
Winchester St. Leeds —7N 61
Winchester Way. S Elm —5N 157
Winden Clo. Cald G —4F 136
Winden Clo. Loft —7L 99
Winden Gro. Loft —7K 99
Windermere Av. Men —2E 24
Windermere Clo. Mel —8D 146
Windermere Clo. Old Sk —8M 159
Windermere Dri. Gar —8N 65
Windermere Dri. Knot —1D 124
Windermere Dri. Leeds —1B 44
Windermere Rd. Bail —6L 39
Windermere Rd. B'frd —2K 75
Windermere Rd. C'frd —5K 103
Windermere Rd. Dew —9H 97
Windermere Rd. Wake —4H 119
Windermere Ter. B'frd —2K 75
Winders Dale. Morl —7J 79
Windgate. Sils —9F 6
Windhill. —8A 40
Windhill Av. Dart —6J 153
Windhill Ct. Wake —3A 120
Windhill Cres. Dart —6J 153
Windhill Cres. Wake —3N 119
Windhill Dri. Dart —6J 153
Windhill La. Dart —6H 153
Windhill Mt. Dart —6J 153
Windhill Old Rd. B'frd & Shipl —6D 40
Windhill Rd. Wake —3N 119
Windhill Vw. Wake —3N 119
Winding Rd. Hal —5B 92
Winding Way. Leeds —2D 44
Windle Edge. Dunf B —9M 169
Windle Royd La. Hal —5J 91
Windmill App. Leeds —5G 81
Windmill Av. Grime —9N 155
Windmill Chase. Rothw —9N 81
Windmill Clo. Leeds —6G 81
Windmill Cotts. Colt —7E 64
(off Colton La.)
Windmill Ct. Leeds —9C 46
Windmill Cres. Hal —2F 92
Windmill Cres. Skelm —8E 150
Windmill Dri. Hal —2F 92
Windmill Fld. Rd. Rothw —9N 81
Windmill Fold. Yead —9N 25
(off Windmill La.)
Windmill Grn. Rothw —9N 81
Windmill Gro. Cleck —6M 95
Windmill Gro. Tad —6N 33
Windmill Hill. —1H 139
(nr. Crofton)
Windmill Hill. —8N 59
(nr. Pudsey)
Windmill Hill. B'frd —4M 75
Windmill Hill. Hal —3F 92
Windmill Hill. Pud —8N 59
Windmill Hill La. Eml M —1C 150
Windmill La. Bat —6E 96
Windmill La. Birs —3D 96
Windmill La. B'frd —4A 76
Windmill La. Cumb —5F 164
Windmill La. Gild —7G 78
Windmill La. Hal —2F 92
Windmill La. Men —4H 25
Windmill La. Nort —8N 143
Windmill La. Rothw —9N 81
Windmill La. Yead —1N 41
Windmill Pl. Yead —1N 41
(off Windmill La.)
Windmill Ri. Aber —9E 48
Windmill Rd. B'ham —5D 32
Windmill Rd. Leeds —5G 80
Windmill Ter. Roys —4C 154
Windmill Vw. H'frth —6A 164
Windross Clo. Nor —8H 101
Windsor Av. Ackw —3J 141
Windsor Av. Dart —9E 152
Windsor Av. Leeds —6C 64
Windsor Av. Sils —8D 6
Windsor Clo. Dew —9L 97
Windsor Clo. Kip —3A 84
Windsor Clo. Norm —2K 121
Windsor Ct. B'frd —9C 58
(off Swarland Gro.)
Windsor Ct. Morl —9K 79
Windsor Cres. Hal —3L 91
Windsor Cres. Oakw —5B 36
Windsor Cres. Rothw —7N 81
Windsor Cres. Wake —2J 119
Windsor Dri. Hud —4E 132
Windsor Dri. Knot —7A 104
Windsor Dri. Liv —1M 115
Windsor Dri. Skelm —8E 150
Windsor Gdns. Dew —9L 97
Windsor Grn. Gar —7B 66
Windsor Gro. Oakw —5B 36
Windsor Gro. T'tn —8C 56
Windsor Mt. Leeds —6C 64
Windsor Pl. Hud —6C 114
Windsor Ri. Pon —6H 123
Windsor Rd. Bat —3D 96
Windsor Rd. Dew —1K 117
Windsor Rd. H Bri —9H 71
Windsor Rd. Hems —3F 156
Windsor Rd. Hud —7E 130
Windsor Rd. Oakw —5B 36
Windsor Rd. Shipl —8N 39
Windsor Rd. Todm —6J 87
Windsor Rd. Wake —1H 119
Windsor St. B'frd —9E 58
Windsor St. Hal —6B 92
Windsor St. S Elm —7A 158
Windsor Ter. Gild —6G 78
Windsor Vw. Dew —1L 117
Windsor Vw. H Bri —9H 71
Windsor Wlk. Bat —2E 96
Windsor Wlk. Hal —6M 93
Windy Bank La. Liv —7F 94
Windy Bank La. Q'bry —7A 74
Windycroft. Hon —6L 147
Windy Gro. Wilsd —2C 56
Windy Harbour La. Todm —3K 87
Windy Ridge. T'tn —7B 56
Windyridge St. Horb —9B 118
Wine Tavern La. Sower B —9B 90
Wine Tavern Rd. Sower B —9B 90
(in two parts)
Winfield Dri. E Bier —7J 77
Winfield Dri. Hud —2E 130
Winfield Gro. Leeds —4D 62
(off Blenheim Av.)
Winfield Pl. Leeds —4D 62
Winfield Ter. Leeds —4D 62
(off Winfield Pl.)
Wingate Av. Kei —1F 36
Wingate Cft. Wake —2A 138
Wingate Gro. Wake —2A 138
Wingate Way. Kei —1F 36
Winget Av. Hud —7E 130
Wingfield Ct. Bgly —3F 38
Wingfield Mt. B'frd —6F 58
Wingfield Rd. Barn —9B 154
Wingfield St. B'frd —6F 58
Winmarith Ct. Roys —6C 154
Winnipeg Pl. Leeds —9F 44
Winnow La. B Spa —1A 32
Winrose App. Leeds —6G 80
Winrose Av. Leeds —5F 80
Winrose Clo. Wyke —9A 76
Winrose Cres. Leeds —5F 80
Winrose Dri. Leeds —5F 80
Winrose Gth. Leeds —5G 80
Winrose Gro. Leeds —5G 81
Winrose Hill. Leeds —4G 80
Winsford Dri. Hud —3F 132
Winslow Rd. B'frd —2J 59
Winstanley Ter. Leeds —3A 62
(off Victoria Rd.)
Winston Gdns. Leeds —1M 61
Winston Mt. Leeds —1M 61
Winston Ter. B'frd —9M 57
Winter Av. Roys —4D 154
Winterbourne Av. Morl —7L 79
Winterburn La. Warley —5G 90
Winterburn St. Kei —8J 21
Winterbutlee Gro. Todm —2J 107
Winterbutlee Rd. Todm —2J 107
Winter Ct. All —3F 56
Winter's Cotts. Blkhd —2D 88
Wintersett. —6H 139
Wintersett Clo. Ryh —9H 139
Wintersett La. Ryh —6H 139
Winter's La. Blkhd —2C 88
Winter St. Hal —7M 91
Winterton Dri. Low M —8A 76
Winthorpe Av. Thpe —2F 98
Winthorpe Cres. Thpe —2F 98
Winthorpe St. Leeds —9B 44
Winthorpe Vw. Wake —2G 98

Vinton Grn. B'frd —7N 75
Vinton Ho. B'frd —1B 76
(off Hutson St.)
Vinton Mill. Sower B —8J 91
(off Wharf St.)
Vinton St. Hud —7K 131
Vintoun St. Leeds —5F 62
Vira Ho. Leeds —6J 43
Viston Dri. Pon —9L 103
Vistons La. Ell —4F 112
(in two parts)
Vitchfield. —7J 75
Vitchfield Ct. Hal —7J 75
(off Shelf Moor Rd.)
Vitchfield Grange. Hal —7H 75
Vitchfield Hill. Hal —7J 75
Vitham Way. Gar —8A 66
Vithens Ct. M'well —8J 153
Vithens End La. Rish —3E 128
Vithens Hill Cft. Hal —6K 73
Vithens La. Bklnd —2F 128
Vithens La. Cra V —9G 89
Vithens New Rd. Hal —3F 72
(in two parts)
Vithens New Rd. Todm —9M 87
(in two parts)
Vithens Rd. Birs —2B 96
Vithens Rd. Wains —3E 72
Vithin Fields. Hal —8F 92
Vithins Clo. B'frd —3N 75
Vithyside. Den D —2D 166
Vitmore St. S Elm —6N 157
Vitton St. Wake —4L 119
Voburn Dri. Hud —4F 132
Voburn Ho. B'frd —1B 76
(off Park La.)
Voburn Ter. Cytn —1G 74
Vold Clo. T'tn —8C 56
Volfstones Rd. Mel —1G 163
Vollaton Clo. Barn —9N 153
Volley Av. Leeds —2G 78
Volley Ct. Leeds —2G 79
Volley Dri. Leeds —2G 79
Volley Gdns. Leeds —2G 79
Volseley Rd. Leeds —5N 61
(in two parts)
Volseley St. Cytn —9H 57
Volsey Av. Pon —3H 123
Volston Clo. B'frd —3J 77
Vomersley. —8M 125
Vomersley Pl. Pud —8A 60
Vomersley Pl. S'ley —5M 59
Vomersley Rd. Knot —9F 104
Vomersley St. Hal —5M 91
Vonder St. Wake —6M 119
Voodacre Cres. Bard —5D 30
Voodacre Grn. Bard —4D 30
Voodacre La. Bard —4D 30
Voodale Av. B'frd —3J 57
Vood Av. Heck —7A 96
Voodbine Av. Pon —3J 123
Voodbine Gro. B'frd —8F 40
Voodbine Rd. Hud —1N 131
Voodbine St. B'frd —7E 58
Voodbine St. Hal —7N 91
Voodbine St. Oss —4N 117
Voodbine Ter. B'frd —8F 40
Voodbine Ter. Bmly —3F 60
Voodbine Ter. Clay W —6J 151
Voodbine Ter. H'fth —8F 42
(off Wood La.)
Voodbine Ter. Leeds —9A 44
Voodbine Ter. Todm —3D 86
Voodbottom. —7B 42
Vood Bottom La. Brigh —7J 93
Vood Bottom Rd. Neth —4G 147
Voodbourne. Leeds —8L 45
Voodbourne Av. Leeds —6E 44
Voodbridge Av. Gar —5C 66
Voodbridge Clo. Eastm —5N 119
Voodbridge Clo. Leeds —1L 61
Voodbridge Cres. Leeds —9K 43
Voodbridge Fold. Leeds —1K 61
Voodbridge Gdns. Leeds —1K 61
Voodbridge Gth. Leeds —1L 61
Voodbridge Grn. Leeds —1L 61
Voodbridge Lawn. Leeds —1K 61
Voodbridge Pl. Leeds —1K 61
Voodbridge Rd. Leeds —1K 61
Voodbridge Va. Leeds —1K 61
Voodbrook Av. Hal —8J 73
Voodbrook Clo. Hal —8J 73
Voodbrook Pl. Hal —8J 73
Voodbrook Rd. Hal —8J 73
Voodburn Av. Dew —5J 117
Voodchurch Vw. Thon —9N 147
Vood Clo. Bail —5N 39
Vood Clo. Kin —8A 140
Vood Clo. Leeds —8E 44
Vood Clo. Nor —9F 100
Vood Clo. Rothw —7M 81
Voodcock St. Wake —8M 119
Voodcock Way. S Elm —5N 157
Woodcot Av. Bail —5B 40
Wood Ct. Chur —5N 79
Wood Cres. Rothw —7M 81
Wood Cft. Brigh —3L 113
Wood Cft. Sower B —9E 90
Woodcroft. Wake —1N 137
Woodcross. Morl —7K 79
Woodcross End. Morl —6K 79
Woodcross Fold. Morl —7K 79
Woodcross Gdns. Morl —7K 79
Woodcross Gth. Morl —6K 79
Wooddle Hole La. K S'ton —8H 143
Wood Dri. Rothw —7L 81
Woodedge Av. Hud —4E 132
Woodend. —7N 83
(nr. Allerton Bywater)
Wood End. —9J 71
(nr. Hebden Bridge)
Woodend. —8B 40
(nr. Shipley)
Woodend. All B —7N 83
Wood End. Lock —7L 131
Wood End Clo. Hal —9A 92
Woodend Ct. B'frd —3D 76
Woodend Cres. All B —8N 83
Wood End Cres. Shipl —7B 40
Wood End La. Bklnd —5K 111
Wood End La. Shepl —1G 164
Wood End Rd. Hud —1K 147
Woodend Rd. Mir —7K 115
Wood Farm La. Broc —7A 148
Woodfield Av. Bat —8D 96
Woodfield Av. G'lnd —4A 112
Woodfield Ct. Bat —1E 116
Woodfield Ct. Hud —2L 131
Woodfield Dri. G'lnd —5A 112
Woodfield Pk. W'ton —4B 138
Woodfield Rd. Cull —8L 37
Woodfield Rd. Went —1H 159
Woodfield Ter. Pud —8C 60
(off Sheridan Way)
Woodford Av. Hal —8C 92
Woodford Clo. All —6F 56
Woodford Dri. Hud —3E 132
Woodgarth Gdns. B'frd —2K 77
Woodgate La. Wee —4N 13
Wood Grn. C'frd —7N 101
Wood Gro. Leeds —7G 60
Wood Gro. Oss —3N 117
Woodhall. —4L 59
Woodhall Av. B'frd —6J 59
Woodhall Av. Leeds —9H 43
Woodhall Clo. Crig —4H 137
Woodhall Clo. Ove —4K 135
Woodhall Clo. S'ley —4L 59
Woodhall Ct. C'ley —1L 59
Woodhall Ct. Leeds —8E 64
Woodhall Cres. Hal —9N 91
Woodhall Cft. S'ley —4L 59
Woodhall Dri. Ackw —4F 140
Woodhall Dri. Bat —8D 96
Woodhall Dri. Leeds —9H 43
Woodhall Gro. Meth —1L 101
(in two parts)
Woodhall Hills. —3L 59
Woodhall Hills. C'ley —3K 59
Woodhall La. S'ley —3L 59
Woodhall La. Wome —7M 125
Woodhall Park. —4M 59
Woodhall Pk. N'wram —9F 74
Woodhall Pk. Av. S'ley —4L 59
Woodhall Pk. Cres. E. S'ley —5M 59
Woodhall Pk. Cres. W. S'ley —5L 59
Woodhall Pk. Dri. S'ley —5L 59
Woodhall Pk. Gdns. S'ley —5M 59
Woodhall Pk. Gro. S'ley —5L 59
Woodhall Pk. Mt. S'ley —4L 59
Woodhall Pl. B'frd —5J 59
Woodhall Rd. B'frd —6J 59
Woodhall Rd. C'ley —2L 59
Woodhall Ter. B'frd —5J 59
Woodhall Vw. B'frd —5K 59
Woodhams Clo. Yead —1N 41
Woodhead. I'ly —8K 9
Woodhead Clo. Hud —8A 114
Woodhead La. Brigh —2C 114
Woodhead La. Gild —6F 78
Woodhead Rd. Bat —1E 96
Woodhead Rd. B'frd —9N 57
Woodhead Rd. Holmb —6G 163
Woodhead Rd. Holme & H'frth —3C 168
Woodhead Rd. Hon —5M 147
Woodhead Rd. Hud —9K 131
(in two parts)
Woodhead St. Hal —4L 91
Woodhead St. Mar —6J 95
Wood Hey La. Err —3J 89
Wood Hill. —1F 116
Wood Hill. Rothw —7M 81
Wood Hill Ct. Leeds —3G 42
Wood Hill Cres. Leeds —4F 42
Wood Hill Gdns. Leeds —3G 42
Wood Hill Gth. Leeds —3G 42
Wood Hill Gro. Leeds —4F 42
Wood Hill La. N Clift —5J 11
Woodhill Ri. App B —7J 41
Wood Hill Ri. Leeds —3G 42
Wood Hill Rd. Leeds —4G 42
Woodhill Vw. Weth —3M 17
Woodhouse. —2J 37
(nr. Keighley)
Woodhouse. —4C 62
(nr. Leeds)
Woodhouse. —3A 114
(nr. Rastrick)
Woodhouse. Bgly —5F 38
Woodhouse Av. Hud —9N 113
Woodhouse Av. Kei —2J 37
Woodhouse Carr. —3C 62
Woodhouse Cliff. —2C 62
Woodhouse Cliff. Leeds —2C 62
Woodhouse Clo. E Ard —6D 98
Woodhouse Clo. Kei —2J 37
Woodhouse Common. —4H 121
Woodhouse Cres. Nor —3J 121
Woodhouse Dri. Kei —3J 37
Woodhouse Gdns. Brigh —3A 114
Woodhouse Gro. All —2F 56
Woodhouse Gro. Hud —9A 114
Woodhouse Gro. Kei —2J 37
Woodhouse Gro. Todm —7M 87
Woodhouse Hall Rd. Hud —9A 114
Woodhouse Hill. —9A 114
(nr. Brackenhall)
Woodhouse Hill. —3G 81
(nr. Hunslet)
Woodhouse Hill. Hud —9A 114
Woodhouse Hill Av. Leeds —3G 80
Woodhouse Hill Gro. Leeds —3G 80
Woodhouse Hill Pl. Leeds —3G 80
Woodhouse Hill Rd. Leeds —3G 80
(in two parts)
Woodhouse La. Brigh —4N 113
Woodhouse La. Eml —2J 151
Woodhouse La. Hal —9N 91
Woodhouse La. H'frth —7J 163
Woodhouse La. K'gte & E Ard —9C 98
Woodhouse La. Leeds —3C 62
Woodhouse La. Wool —3J 153
Woodhouse Mt. Nor —3H 121
Woodhouse Rd. Kei —2J 37
Woodhouse Rd. Todm —7N 87
Woodhouse Rd. Wake —5N 119
Woodhouse Sq. Leeds —6C 62
Woodhouse St. Leeds —3C 62
Woodhouse Ter. B'frd —5C 76
Woodhouse Wlk. Kei —2J 37
Woodhouse Way. Kei —2J 37
Woodkirk. —5M 97
Woodkirk Av. Ting —4M 97
Woodkirk Gdns. Dew —6L 97
Woodkirk Gro. Wake —4N 97
Woodkirk Gro. Wyke —3A 94
Woodland Av. K'thpe —4D 120
Woodland Av. Swil —4H 83
Woodland Clo. B'frd —2H 57
Woodland Clo. Hall G —8H 137
Woodland Clo. Leeds —6D 64
Woodland Ct. Bgly —2D 38
Woodland Ct. Leeds —1J 63
Woodland Cres. B'frd —2G 57
Woodland Cres. Rothw —7M 81
Woodland Cres. Swil —4H 83
Woodland Cft. H'fth —5F 42
Woodland Dri. Brigh —9L 93
Woodland Dri. Hal —7K 91
Woodland Dri. Leeds —8F 44
Woodland Dri. Skelm —8E 150
Woodland Dri. Swil —4G 83
Woodland Dri. Wake —4M 137
Woodland Gro. Ackw —1G 141
Woodland Gro. B'frd —1H 57
Woodland Gro. Dew —3C 116
Woodland Gro. Leeds —2G 62
Woodland Gro. Swil —4H 83
Woodland Hill. Leeds —6C 64
Woodland Ho. B'frd —8G 40
(off Garsdale Av.)
Woodland La. Leeds —8F 44
Woodland Meadows. Kbtn —2K 149
Woodland Mt. Leeds —2G 63
Woodland Pk. W'frd —9D 82
Woodland Pk. Rd. Leeds —1A 62
Woodland Ri. Leeds —6D 64
Woodland Ri. Wake —5F 118
Woodland Rd. Hud —9D 114
Woodland Rd. Leeds —6C 64
Woodland Rd. Wake —5F 118
Woodlands. —3B 92
Woodlands. Bail —3C 40
Woodlands. Croft —1F 138
Woodlands. E Ard —5E 98
Woodlands. Horb —9E 118
Woodlands. I'ly —5J 9
Woodlands. Oss —4N 117
Woodlands. Sower B —1F 110
Woodlands Av. C'frd —6J 103
Woodlands Av. Gom —3L 95
Woodlands Av. Hal —3B 92
Woodlands Av. H'frth —9A 148
Woodlands Av. Lep —7J 133
Woodlands Av. Q'bry —4G 74
Woodlands Av. S'ley —5N 59
Woodlands Av. Tad —6N 33
Woodlands Av. Todm —6K 87
Woodlands Clo. App B —6K 41
Woodlands Clo. Den D —2D 166
Woodlands Clo. E Ard —5E 98
Woodlands Clo. Hud —5E 114
Woodlands Clo. I'ly —5E 8
Woodlands Clo. Leeds —8D 30
Woodlands Ct. Leeds —6L 43
Woodlands Ct. Pud —9B 60
Woodlands Cres. Gom —3L 95
Woodlands Cres. Hems —1E 156
Woodlands Cft. Kip —5B 84
Woodlands Dri. B'frd & Rawd —6K 41
Woodlands Dri. E Ard —5D 98
Woodlands Dri. Gar —8B 66
Woodlands Dri. Gom —3L 95
Woodlands Dri. Lep —8J 133
Woodlands Dri. Morl —7J 79
Woodlands End. Lep —7J 133
Woodlands Fold. B'shaw —8M 77
Woodlands Gdns. S'cft —1D 46
Woodlands Gro. Bail —5L 39
Woodlands Gro. Bgly —8G 38
Woodlands Gro. Hal —3B 92
Woodlands Gro. I'ly —5E 8
Woodlands Gro. Kip —5C 84
Woodlands Gro. Q'bry —4F 74
Woodlands Gro. S'ley —5N 59
Woodlands La. Dew —3C 116
Woodlands Mt. Hal —2B 92
Woodlands Pk. Gro. Pud —9A 60
Woodlands Pk. Rd. Pud —9A 60
Woodland Sq. Brigh —2A 114
Woodland Sq. Leeds —6J 61
Woodlands Ri. Haw —1C 54
Woodlands Ri. I'ly —5D 8
Woodlands Rd. Bat —4D 96
Woodlands Rd. Bgly —3H 39
Woodlands Rd. B'frd —6M 57
Woodlands Rd. Ell —3E 112
Woodlands Rd. Gom —3L 95
Woodlands Rd. Hal —3B 92
Woodlands Rd. Lep —7J 133
Woodlands Rd. Q'bry —4F 74
Woodlands Rd. E. Fen B —7H 133
Woodlands St. B'frd —6A 58
Woodlands Ter. B'frd —5M 57
Woodlands Ter. Oaken —8F 76
Woodlands Ter. S'ley —5N 59
Woodlands, The. H Bri —2H 89
Woodlands, The. Pon —5L 123
Woodlands Vw. Kip —5C 84
Woodlands Vw. S'cft —9D 30
Woodlands Way. Lep —8J 133
Woodland Ter. Leeds —8C 44
Woodland Vw. C'ley —8L 41
Woodland Vw. H'th —7D 120
Woodland Vw. H Bri —2D 88
Woodland Vw. Leeds —8F 44
Woodland Vw. Pon —5L 123
Woodland Vw. Ting —7N 97
Wood Land Vs. Leeds —2E 64
Woodland Way. Upt —9C 142
Wood La. Bard —5E 30
Wood La. Barn —7N 153
Wood La. Bat —9G 97
Wood La. Bgly —9E 22
Wood La. Birk —1N 105
Wood La. B'frd —2C 58
(in two parts)
Wood La. Bmly —2F 60
Wood La. Cltn —7B 154
(in two parts)
Wood La. C'frd —7N 101
Wood La. Chap A —8E 44
(in two parts)
Wood La. C'thpe & N'dam —7J 137
Wood La. Den D —2B 166
(in two parts)
Wood La. Dew —2F 116
Wood La. Hal —7B 72
Wood La. Head —1N 61
Wood La. Hip —3G 93
Wood La. H'frth —2M 163
Wood La. H'fth —8F 42
Wood La. Hud —7N 131
Wood La. Leeds —6G 60
Wood La. Mir —6H 115
Wood La. N Farn —3G 79
Wood La. Oven W —3K 91
Wood La. Ove —2G 135
Wood La. Pud —8M 41
Wood La. Rothw —6K 81
Wood La. Scholes —1F 64
Wood La. Slai —4M 145
Wood La. S'wram —9G 93
Wood La. Sower B —9E 90
Wood La. Wltn —5E 18
Wood La. W'ford —7M 83
Wood La. Ct. Leeds —1A 62
Woodlea. B Spa —9D 18
Wood Lea. Byr —4C 104
Woodlea. S Elm —7M 157
Wood Lea. Todm —4G 87
Woodlea App. Mean —6B 44
Woodlea App. Yead —1K 41
Woodlea Chase. Mean —7B 44
Woodlea Clo. Yead —2K 41
Woodlea Ct. Leeds —3K 45
Woodlea Ct. Mean —7B 44
Woodlea Cft. Mean —6B 44
Woodlea Dri. Mean —6B 44
Woodlea Dri. Yead —2K 41
Woodlea Gdns. Mean —6B 44
Woodlea Gth. Mean —6B 44
Woodlea Grn. Leeds —6B 44
Woodlea Gro. Leeds —2B 80
(off Woodlea St.)
Woodlea Gro. Mean —6B 44
Woodlea Gro. Yead —1K 41
Woodlea Holt. Leeds —6B 44
Woodlea La. Leeds —6B 44
Woodlea Lawn. Mean —6B 44
Woodlea Mt. Leeds —2B 80
Woodlea Mt. Yead —1K 41
Woodlea Pk. Mean —6B 44
Woodlea Pl. Leeds —2C 80
Woodlea Pl. Mean —6B 44
Woodlea Rd. Yead —1K 41
Woodlea Sq. Mean —7B 44
Woodlea St. Leeds —2B 80
Woodlea Vw. Mean —7B 44
Woodlea Vw. Yead —2K 41
Woodleigh Av. B'frd —4C 76
Woodleigh Av. Gar —7M 65
Woodleigh Cres. Ackw —4F 140
Woodleigh Gro. Hud —9H 131
Woodlesford. —6D 82
Woodlesford Cres. Hal —2H 91
Woodliffe Ct. Leeds —8E 44
Woodliffe Cres. Leeds —8E 44
Woodliffe Dri. Leeds —8E 44
Woodman Av. Ell —6E 112
Woodman Av. Hud —6D 114
Woodman Ct. B'frd —6L 75
(off Pit La.)
Woodman Ct. Butt —7K 75
Woodman St. Leeds —6B 64
Woodman Works. Ell —6E 112
Woodmoor Clo. Crig —6G 136
Woodmoor Dri. Crig —6G 136
Woodmoor Ri. Crig —5F 136
Wood Moor Rd. Hems —2F 156
Woodmoor Rd. Wake —5J 137
Woodmoor St. Barn —9E 154
Wood Mt. Hal —8M 91
Wood Mt. Ove —4J 135
Wood Mt. Rothw —7L 81
Wood Nook. Mel —7H 147
Woodnook Clo. Leeds —5G 42
Woodnook Dri. Leeds —5G 42
Woodnook Gth. Leeds —5G 42
Wood Nook La. Mel —7G 147
Wood Nook La. Sower B —7J 91
Woodnook Rd. Leeds —4G 43
Wood Nook Ter. S'ley —5N 59
Woodpecker Clo. All —7G 56
Wood Pl. B'frd —6A 58
(BD8)
Wood Pl. B'frd —2A 58
(BD9)
Wood Rd. B'frd —1C 76
Wood Rd. Friz —2A 58
Wood Row. —1J 101
Wood Row. Meth —1J 101
Woodrow Cres. Meth —1H 101
Woodrow Dri. Low M —7C 76
Woodroyd. Gol —5B 130
Woodroyd Av. Barn —8D 154
Woodroyd Av. B'frd —3D 76
Woodroyd Av. Hon —4N 147
Woodroyd Clo. Barn —8D 154
Woodroyd Dri. Hal —2M 91
Woodroyd Gdns. I'ly —6L 9
Woodroyd Gdns. L'ft —7F 90
Woodroyd Hill La. H'frth —9F 164
Woodroyd Rd. B'frd —2C 76
(in three parts)
Woodroyd Ter. B'frd —3D 76
Woods Av. Mars —5H 145
Woodside. —4A 92
(nr. Halifax)
Woodside. —6M 75
(nr. Shelf)
Woodside. C'frd —3J 103

Woodside. Den D —2D 166
Woodside. H Bri —2K 89
Woodside. Kei —7G 20
Woodside. Shipl —7B 40
Woodside. Wren —1G 119
Woodside Av. Bgly —8E 38
Woodside Av. Leeds —4M 61
Woodside Av. Mean —8B 44
Woodside Av. Shar C —8K 121
Woodside Av. Shipl —7K 39
Woodside Av. Wren —1G 118
Woodside Clo. Morl —7K 79
Woodside Ct. Cull —9K 37
Woodside Ct. H'fth —7H 43
Woodside Ct. Leeds —6J 43
Woodside Cres. Bat —8D 96
Woodside Cres. Bgly —8E 38
Woodside Cres. Hal —3A 92
Woodside Cres. Shar C —7K 121
Woodside Dri. Bgly —8E 38
Woodside Dri. Morl —6K 79
Woodside Dri. Wren —1G 119
Woodside Gdns. Morl —6K 79
Woodside Gro. All B —7N 83
Woodside Gro. G'lnd —5B 112
Woodside Gro. Hal —3B 92
Woodside Hill Clo. H'fth —7H 43
Woodside La. Hud —7N 113
Woodside La. Morl —6K 79
Woodside M. Mean —8B 44
Woodside Mt. Hal —4A 92
Woodside Pk. Av. H'fth —7G 42
Woodside Pk. Dri. H'fth —7G 42
Woodside Pl. Hal —3A 92
Woodside Pl. Leeds —4M 61
Woodside Rd. B Spa —1B 32
Woodside Rd. Hal —4A 92
Woodside Rd. Hud —9H 131
Woodside Rd. Sils —8C 6
Woodside Rd. Wyke —1A 94
Woodside St. All B —7N 83
Woodside Ter. G'lnd —5C 112
Woodside Ter. Hal —3B 92
Woodside Ter. Leeds —4M 61
Woodside Vw. Bgly —8E 38
Woodside Vw. G'lnd —5C 112
(off Woodside Ter.)
Woodside Vw. Hal —3A 92
Woodside Vw. H'frth —4J 163
Woodside Vw. Hud —7E 130
Woodside Vw. Leeds —3M 61
Woodsley Grn. Leeds —4B 62
Woodsley Rd. B'frd —9E 40
Woodsley Rd. Leeds —5A 62
Woodsley Ter. Leeds —5C 62
Woods M. I'ly —5H 9
Woodsome Av. Mir —5J 115
Woodsome Dri. Fen B —8H 133
Woodsome Dri. Mir —5K 115
Woodsome Est. Bat —8D 96
Woodsome Hall La. Fen B —9G 132
Woodsome Lees La. Kbtn —2G 149
Woodsome Pk. Fen B —8H 133
Woodsome Rd. Far T —3D 148
Woods Rd. Mars —5H 145
Woods Row. S'ley —5B 60
Woods Ter. Mars —5H 145
Woodstock Clo. Leeds —4N 43
Woodstock Cres. Hud —2G 131
Woodstock Wlk. B'frd —9C 58
(off Park Rd.)
Wood St. All —5H 57
Wood St. Bail —6A 40
Wood St. Bat —7F 96
Wood St. Bgly —1D 38
Wood St. B'frd —6A 58
Wood St. Brigh —1N 113
Wood St. C'frd —4C 102
Wood St. Clay W —8G 151
Wood St. Cleck —5G 94
Wood St. Dew —2G 116
Wood St. E Ard —4F 98
Wood St. Ell —5F 112
Wood St. Haw —9C 36
Wood St. H'fth —5F 42
Wood St. Hud —4M 131
Wood St. Lgwd —5F 130
Wood St. Low M —7B 76
Wood St. Mold —4B 132
Wood St. Morl —8J 79
Wood St. Oss —3N 117
Wood St. Shar C —8J 121
Wood St. Skelm —7C 150
Wood St. Slai —9M 129
Wood St. S Hien —3M 155
Wood St. Steet —3C 20
Wood St. Todm —6K 87
Wood St. Wake —5L 119
Wood Ter. Hud —7M 131
Woodthorne Cft. Leeds —3J 45
Woodthorpe. —3A 138
Woodthorpe Clo. Wake —3N 137
Woodthorpe Dri. Wake —3N 137
Woodthorpe Glades. Wake —3N 137
Woodthorpe La. Wake —3M 137
Woodthorpe Pk. Dri. Wake —3M 137
Woodthorpe Ter. Hud —5L 131
Woodtop. Brigh —7K 93
Wood Top. Mars —6F 144
Wood Top Rd. H Bri —2J 89
Woodvale Clo. B'frd —9J 59
Woodvale Cres. Bgly —2F 38
Woodvale Gro. B'frd —9K 57
Woodvale Rd. Brigh —9N 93
Woodvale Ter. H'fth —8G 43
Woodvale Way. B'frd —9K 57
Wood Vw. Bkby —1J 131
Wood Vw. B'frd —3B 58
Wood Vw. C'frd —4A 102
Wood Vw. Cull —3J 55
Woodview. Dlgtn —6A 78
Wood Vw. Oaken —9E 76
Woodview Av. Bail —3D 40
Wood Vw. Av. C'frd —5A 102
Wood Vw. Bungalows. C'frd —5A 102
Wood Vw. Clo. C'frd —5A 102
Woodview Clo. H'fth —5F 42
Wood Vw. Cres. C'frd —4A 102
Wood Vw. Dri. B'frd —4G 59
Wood Vw. Gro. Brigh —8L 93
Woodview Gro. Leeds —3D 80
Woodview Mt. Leeds —3D 80
Woodview Pl. Leeds —3D 80
Woodview Rd. Leeds —3D 80
Woodview Rd. Oakw —3F 36
Woodview St. Leeds —3D 80
Woodview. Ter. B'frd —3B 58
Wood Vw. Ter. Chur —5N 79
Woodview Ter. Kei —3H 37
(off Haincliffe Pl.)
Woodview Ter. Leeds —3D 80
Wood Vs. H Bri —3D 88
Woodville Av. Gol —6D 130
Woodville Av. H'fth —7G 43
Woodville Ct. Leeds —6K 45
Woodville Ct. Wake —9L 119
Woodville Cres. H'fth —7H 43
Woodville Gro. Cro R —7F 36
Woodville Gro. H'fth —6G 43
Woodville Gro. Leeds —4G 80
Woodville Mt. Leeds —4G 80
Woodville Pl. B'frd —2L 57
Woodville Pl. H'fth —7H 43
Woodville Pl. Hud —5C 114
Woodville Rd. Dew —3G 117
Woodville Rd. Kei —8H 21
Woodville Sq. Leeds —4G 80
Woodville St. Hal —3N 91
Woodville St. H'fth —7H 43
Woodville St. Shipl —7B 40
Woodville Ter. B'frd —9B 58
Woodville Ter. Cro R —7F 36
(off Vernon St.)
Woodville Ter. H'fth —7G 43
Wood Vine St. S'ley —5N 59
Woodward Ct. Mir —4M 115
Woodway. Bgly —8E 38
Woodway. H'fth —8F 42
Woodway Dri. H'fth —8F 42
Woodworth Gro. Kei —4H 37
Wood Yd. Cotts. Walt —2C 138
Woolcroft Dri. H'frth —2A 164
Wooldale. —2B 164
Wooldale Cliff Rd. H'frth —3N 163
Wooldale Rd. H'frth —1A 164
Wooler Av. Leeds —3C 80
Wooler Dri. Leeds —3C 80
Wooler Gro. Leeds —3C 80
Wooler Pl. Leeds —3B 80
Wooler Rd. Leeds —3B 80
Wooler St. Leeds —3B 80
Wool Exchange, The. —7C 58
(off Market St.)
Woolford Way. Loft —6M 99
Woolgreaves. —4N 137
Woolgreaves Av. Wake —4M 137
Woolgreaves Clo. Wake —3M 137
Woolgreaves Cft. Wake —4M 137
Woolgreaves Dri. Wake —4M 137
Woolgreaves Gth. Wake —4M 137
Wooller Rd. Low M —8B 76
Woolley. —2J 153
Woolley Colliery Rd. Dart —8G 153
Woolley Edge La. Wool —1F 152
Woolley Low Moor La. Wool —8F 136
Woolley Pk. Gdns. Wool —2J 153
Woolley Vw. Wake —8H 137
Woollin Av. Ting —7A 98
Woollin Cres. Ting —6A 98
Woolmarket. Pon —3K 123
Woolpack. Hal —5B 92
Woolpack's Yd. Wake —5K 119
Woolrow La. Brigh —6A 94
Wool Row La. Shel —5N 149
Woolshops Sq. Hal —5B 92
Woolstocks La. Caw —5N 167
Wool St. Bat —7G 96
Wool St. Heck —9A 96
Wootton St. B'frd —1C 76
Worcester Av. Leeds —9H 81
Worcester Dri. E Ard —3E 98
Worcester Dri. Leeds —9H 81
Worcester Gro. Hud —7N 131
Worcester Pl. B'frd —1E 76
Worden Gro. B'frd —1K 75
Wordsworth App. Pon —1K 123
Wordsworth Ct. W'ford —1D 100
Wordsworth Dri. Knot —8A 104
Wordsworth Dri. Oult —1D 100
Wordsworth Gro. Stan —7N 99
Wordsworth Way. Bgly —2F 38
Workhouse La. G'lnd —5C 112
Workhouse La. Hal —5G 91
Workhouse La. Midg —2B 90
World's End. Yead —9N 25
Wormald Lea. B'frd —2J 77
(off Stirling Cres.)
Wormald Row. Leeds —6E 62
Wormald St. Dew —3F 116
Wormald St. Hud —7D 132
Wormald St. Liv —9N 95
Worrall Rd. Wake —6J 137
Worrall St. Morl —1J 97
Worsley Pl. Skel —7L 159
Worsnop Bldgs. Wyke —9A 76
Worsnop St. Low M —7B 76
Worstead Rd. Cro R —6F 36
Worth Av. Kei —7L 21
Worth Bri. Rd. Kei —9L 21
Worthing Head Clo. Wyke —1B 94
Worthing Head Rd. Wyke —1A 94
Worthing St. Wyke —1B 94
Worthington St. B'frd —6A 58
Worth Village. —8L 21
Worthville Clo. Kei —2J 37
Worth Way. Kei —1J 37
Wortley Heights. Leeds —8N 61
Wortley La. Leeds —8B 62
Wortley Moor La. Leeds —8L 61
Wortley Moor La. Trad. Est. Leeds —8L 61
Wortley Moor Rd. Leeds —7K 61
Wortley Pk. Leeds —8N 61
Wortley Pl. Hems —2C 156
Wortley Rd. Leeds —7K 61
Wortley St. Bgly —4G 38
Wortley Towers. Leeds —8A 62
(off Tong Rd.)
Worts Hill. —6J 129
Worts Hill La. Slai —6H 129
Worts Hill Side. Slai —6J 129
Wragby. —3A 140
Wragby Cotts. Wake —3A 140
Wrangbrook. —2D 158
Wrangbrook La. Upt —3B 158
Wrangbrook Rd. Upt —1C 158
Wrangthorn Av. Leeds —3B 62
Wrangthorn Pl. Leeds —3B 62
Wrangthorn Ter. Leeds —3B 62
Wray's Bldgs. Horb —1C 136
Wrelton Clo. Roys —6C 154
Wren Av. B'frd —9K 57
Wrenbeck Av. Otley —7L 11
Wrenbeck Clo. Otley —7L 11
Wrenbeck Dri. Otley —7L 11
Wrenbury Av. Leeds —2G 43
Wrenbury Cres. Leeds —2G 43
Wrenbury Gro. Leeds —2H 43
Wren Cft. Pon —9K 103
Wren Dri. Morl —1N 97
Wren Gth. Wake —5M 137
Wren Hill. Bat —4D 96
Wren Nest Rd. Sower B —7A 110
Wren St. Haw —8D 36
Wren St. Hud —5J 131
Wren St. Kei —8J 21
Wrenthorpe. —1G 119
Wrenthorpe La. Wren —2E 118
Wrenthorpe Rd. Wren & Wake —1G 119
Wrexhall Rd. Dew —1H 117
Wrexham Rd. Bur W —8B 10
Wright Av. Oakw —4D 36
Wrights La. Crid S —4J 125
Wright St. Oakw —5D 36
Wrigley Av. B'frd —4F 76
Wrigley Hill. Hal —8L 73
Wroe Cres. Wyke —1A 94
Wroe Pl. Wyke —1A 94
Wroe St. Dew —2C 116
Wroe Ter. Wyke —1A 94
Wrose. —9B 40
Wrose Av. B'frd —1E 58
Wrose Av. Shipl —9B 40
Wrose Brow Rd. Shipl —7B 40
Wrosecliffe Gro. B'frd —7D 40
Wrose Dri. Shipl —9B 40
Wrose Gro. B'frd —9D 40
Wrose Gro. Shipl —9B 40
Wrose Hill Pl. B'frd —1B 58
Wrose Mt. Shipl —9C 40
Wrose Rd. Shipl & B'frd —9B 40
Wrose Vw. Bail —3A 40
Wrose Vw. Shipl —9B 40
Wycliffe Clo. Leeds —1A 60
Wycliffe Dri. Leeds —5F 44
Wycliffe Gdns. Shipl —7M 39
Wycliffe Rd. Leeds —1A 60
Wycliffe Rd. Shipl —7M 39
Wycliffe St. Oss —4M 117
Wycoller Rd. Wyke —9A 76
Wycombe Grn. B'frd —2J 77
Wyke. —2A 94
Wykebeck Av. Leeds —7M 63
Wykebeck Cres. Leeds —6M 63
Wykebeck Gdns. Leeds —6M 63
Wykebeck Gro. Leeds —6M 63
Wykebeck Mt. Leeds —7M 63
Wykebeck Pl. Leeds —6N 63
Wykebeck Rd. Leeds —6M 63
Wykebeck Sq. Leeds —6M 63
Wykebeck St. Leeds —6M 63
Wykebeck Ter. Leeds —6M 63
Wykebeck Valley Rd. Leeds —4M 63
Wykebeck Vw. Leeds —6M 63
Wyke Bottoms. Oaken —9D 76
Wyke Common. —2B 94
Wyke Cres. Wyke —2B 94
Wyke La. Wyke —2A 94
Wykelea Clo. Wyke —1B 94
Wyke Old La. Brigh —5N 93
Wyncliffe Ct. Leeds —5E 44
Wyncliffe Gdns. Leeds —5F 44
Wyncroft Ct. Bar E —9M 47
Wyncroft Gro. B'hpe —6J 27
Wyncroft Ri. Shipl —1B 58
Wyndham Av. B'frd —3D 58
Wynford Av. Leeds —6L 43
Wynford Dri. S Elm —6N 157
Wynford Gro. Leeds —6L 43
Wynford Mt. Leeds —6K 43
Wynford Ri. Leeds —6K 43
Wynford Ter. Leeds —6K 43
Wynford Way. Low M —5C 76
Wynmore Av. B'hpe —6H 27
Wynmore Cres. B'hpe —6J 27
Wynmore Dri. B'hpe —6J 27
Wynmore Dri. Hud —1E 130
Wynne St. B'frd —6B 58
Wynthorpe Rd. Horb —1D 136
Wynyard Dri. Morl —9J 79
Wyther Av. Kirks —3J 61
Wyther Dri. Wyth I —3K 61
Wyther Grn. Wyth I —3K 61
Wyther La. Leeds —3J 61
Wyther La. Ind. Est. Kirks —3K 61
Wyther Pk. Av. Leeds —5J 61
Wyther Pk. Clo. Leeds —5J 61
Wyther Pk. Cres. Leeds —5J 61
Wyther Pk. Gro. Leeds —4J 61
Wyther Pk. Hill. Leeds —4J 61
Wyther Pk. Mt. Leeds —5J 61
(in three parts)
Wyther Pk. Pl. Leeds —4J 61
Wyther Pk. Rd. Leeds —5H 61
(in three parts)
Wyther Pk. Sq. Leeds —5H 61
Wyther Pk. St. Leeds —5J 61
Wyther Pk. Ter. Leeds —5J 61
Wyther Pk. Vw. Leeds —4J 61
Wyvern Av. Hud —4H 131
Wyvern Clo. Bat —6F 96
Wyvern Clo. B'frd —9L 57
Wyverne Rd. Gol —6D 130
Wyvern Pl. Hal —4L 91
Wyvern Ter. Hal —4L 91
Wyvil Cres. I'ly —5K 9

Yarborough Cft. N'wram —9F 74
Yardley Way. Low M —7C 76
Yard No.4. Bat —4C 96
Yarn St. Leeds —9G 63
Yarra Ct. Gild —6G 79
Yarwood Gro. B'frd —2K 75
Yate La. Oxe —4C 54
Yates Flat. Shipl —9B 40
Yates La. Hud —6G 130
Yeadon. —9M 25
Yeadon Dri. Hal —8F 92
Yeadon Moor Rd. Yead —1B 42
(in two parts)
Yeadon Row. H'fth —8F 42
(off South Vw.)
Yeadon Stoops. Yead —1A 42
(off Bayton La.)
Ye Farre Clo. Brigh —8M 93
Yewbank Clo. I'ly —5F 8
Yewbank Ter. I'ly —5F 8
Yewdall Rd. Leeds —1A 60
Yewdall Way. B'frd —9G 41
Yew Grn. Av. Hud —7K 131
Yew Grn. Rd. Hud —7K 131
Yew Gro. Hud —7E 130
Yew La. Gar —8B 66
Yew Pk. Brigh —7K 93
Yews Green. —2D 74
Yews Hill Rd. Hud —6K 131
Yews Mt. Hud —6L 131
Yew St. Hud —1M 131
Yew Tree Av. B'frd —5J 57
Yew Tree Clo. Shipl —9B 40
Yew Tree Ct. Liv —7L 95
Yew Tree Ct. Todm —3J 107
Yew Tree Cres. B'frd —5K 57
Yew Tree Cft. L'ft —3C 90
Yew Tree Dri. Rothw —7F 82
Yew Tree Gro. B'frd —5K 57
Yew Tree La. All —6C 56
Yew Tree La. H'frth —5H 163
Yew Tree La. Hud —7E 130
Yew Tree La. Leeds —7F 64
Yew Tree La. Slai —2M 145
Yew Tree Rd. Hud —9F 112
Yew Tree Rd. Shepl —8K 149
Yew Trees. S'wram —8F 92
Yew Trees Av. N'wram —1F 92
Yew Tree St. Wake —7N 119
Yew Tree Wlk. Knot —1D 124
York Av. Hud —9L 113
York Clo. S Elm —5N 157
York Cres. Bgly —5F 38
York Dri. Bat —6G 96
York Dri. Heck —6A 96
York Ga. Otley —4J 25
York Gro. Bat —6G 96
York Gro. Mir —6K 115
York Ho. B'frd —8G 41
(nr. Billing Vw.)
York Ho. B'frd —8G 41
(off Fairhaven Grn.)
York Ho. Ell —4E 112
(off Gog Hill)
York Ho. Far —4A 60
(off South Dri.)
York Ho. Hud —4N 131
(off Oldgate)
York Ho. Sower B —8J 91
(off Beech Rd.)
York Pl. Ackw —3H 141
York Pl. Cleck —4H 95
York Pl. Leeds —6D 62
York Pl. Todm —7K 87
(off Bond St.)
York Pl. Weth —3M 17
York Rd. Bat —6F 96
York Rd. Bur W —8D 10
York Rd. Dew —2J 117
York Rd. Leeds & Pot —6G 63
(in three parts)
York Rd. Mir —6K 115
York Rd. Weth —3N 17
York Rd. Ind. Est. Weth —3N 17
Yorkshire Car Collection Museum. —8J
Yorkshire County Cricket. —2N
Yorkshire Dri. B'frd —4E 76
Yorkshire Mining Museum. —5H 1
Yorkshire Way. B'frd —2N 75
York St. Bgly —5F 38
York St. B'frd —7K 57
York St. Brigh —2M 113
York St. C'frd —4E 102
York St. Hal —6A 92
York St. H Bri —2H 89
York St. Hems —4E 156
York St. Leeds —7F 62
York St. Nor —9G 100
York St. Q'bry —4C 74
York St. Todm —6K 87
York Ter. Hal —3A 92
York Towers. Leeds —6J 63
York Vs. Nor —1J 121
Young's Ct. Aber —4E 48
Young St. B'frd —6L 57

Zealand St. B'frd —1H 77
Zermatt Gro. Leeds —9E 44
Zermatt Mt. Leeds —9E 44
Zermatt St. Leeds —9F 44
Zermatt Ter. Leeds —9F 44
Zetland Pl. Leeds —3H 63
Zetland St. Hud —4N 131
Zetland St. Wake —5L 119
Zion Clo. Hud —1G 130
Zion Dri. M'well —8K 153
Zion St. H Bri —3M 89
Zion St. Oss —2M 117
Zoar St. Morl —9K 79

HOSPITALS, HEALTH CENTRES and HOSPICES covered by this atlas

with their map square reference

N.B. Where Hospitals, Health Centres and Hospices are not named on the map, the reference given is for the road in which they are situated.

AIREDALE GENERAL HOSPITAL — 2B **20**
Skipton Rd., Steeton, KEIGHLEY,
West Yorkshire. BD20 6TD
Tel: 01535 652511

Airedale Health Centre — 5J **103**
The Square, CASTLEFORD,
West Yorkshire. WF10 3JJ
Tel: 01977 465700

Allerton Health Centre — 6G **57**
Wanstead Cres., Allerton,
BRADFORD. West Yorkshire. BD15 7PA
Tel: 01274 548577

Altofts Health Centre — 7H **101**
Lock La., NORMANTON
West Yorkshire. WF6 2QJ
Tel: 01924 327920

Ardenlea Hospice (Marie Curie Centre) — 6F **8**
Queen's Dri., ILKLEY
West Yorkshire. LS29 9QR
Tel: 01943 607505

Ardsley Health Centre — 4D **98**
Bradford Rd., East Ardsley,
WAKEFIELD
West Yorkshire.
WF3 2DN
Tel: 0113 2537627

aildon Health Centre — 4A **40**
Cliffe Av., Baildon,
SHIPLEY
West Yorkshire.
BD17 6NX
Tel: 01274 581086

rkerend Road Health Centre — 6G **59**
Barkerend Rd., BRADFORD
Vest Yorkshire. BD3 8QH
el: 01274 661353

tley Health Centre — 7F **96**
30 Upper Commercial St.,
ATLEY, West Yorkshire.
VF17 5ED
el: 01924 516100

ston Hill Health Centre — 2C **80**
eeston Rd., LEEDS. LS11 8BS
l: 0113 2709721

gley Health Centre — 4E **38**
yrtle Pl., BINGLEY
est Yorkshire. BD16 2TL
: 01274 569131

LEY HOSPITAL — 4G **38**
nbank Dri., BINGLEY
st Yorkshire. BD16 4HD
Tel: 01274 563438

rkenshaw Health Centre — 7L **77**
Town St., Birkenshaw, BRADFORD
West Yorkshire. BD11 2HX
Tel: 01274 682374

RADFORD ROYAL INFIRMARY — 5K **57**
Duckworth La., BRADFORD
West Yorkshire. BD9 6RJ
Tel: 01274 542200

amhope Health Centre — 6H **27**
Tredgold Cres., Bramhope,
LEEDS. LS16 9BR
Tel: 0113 2672664

ighouse Health Centre — 1N **113**
Lawson Rd., BRIGHOUSE
West Yorkshire. HD6 1NY
Tel: 01484 712515

rmantofts Health Centre — 5G **63**
Cromwell Mt.,
LEEDS. LS9 7TA
Tel: 0113 2953330

stleford Health Centre — 4D **102**
Welbeck St., CASTLEFORD
West Yorkshire. WF10 1HB
Tel: 01977 465755

CASTLEFORD NORMANTON & DISTRICT HOSPITAL — 6B **102**
Lumley St., CASTLEFORD
West Yorkshire. WF10 5LT
Tel: 01977 605500

CHAPEL ALLERTON HOSPITAL — 1F **62**
Chapeltown Rd., LEEDS. LS7 4SA
Tel: 0113 262 3404

Chapeltown Health Centre — 3G **63**
Spencer Pl., LEEDS. LS7 4BB
Tel: 0113 2407000

Clayton Health Centre — 1H **75**
Station Rd., Clayton, BRADFORD
West Yorkshire. BD14 6JA
Tel: 01274 882043

CLAYTON HOSPITAL — 4K **119**
Northgate, WAKEFIELD
West Yorkshire, WF1 3JS
Tel: 01924 375217

Cleckheaton Health Centre — 5J **95**
Greenside, CLECKHEATON
West Yorkshire. BD19 5AP
Tel: 01274 242000

COOKRIDGE HOSPITAL — 5H **43**
Hospital La., LEEDS
LS16 6QB
Tel: 0113 267 3411

CORONATION HOSPITAL (ILKLEY) — 6H **9**
Springs La., ILKLEY
West Yorkshire. LS29 8TG
Tel: 01943 609666

Crofton Health Centre — 2G **139**
Slack La., Crofton,
WAKEFIELD, West Yorkshire.
WF4 1ET
Tel: 01924 862612

Denholme Health Centre — 6K **55**
1 Longhouse La., Denholme,
BRADFORD, West Yorkshire
BD13 4NQ
Tel: 01274 832878

DEWSBURY & DISTRICT HOSPITAL — 1D **116**
Healds Rd., DEWSBURY
West Yorkshire. WF13 4HS
Tel: 01924 465105

Drighlington Health Centre — 7B **78**
Station Rd., Drighlington,
BRADFORD, West Yorkshire.
BD11 1JU
Tel: 0113 2852115

Eastmoor Health Centre — 3A **120**
Windhill Rd., WAKEFIELD
West Yorkshire. WF1 4SE
Tel: 01924 327625

Eccleshill Health Centre — 9H **41**
Rillington Mead, BRADFORD
West Yorkshire. BD10 0ED
Tel: 01274 612121

Edmund Street Health Centre — 8B **58**
26 Edmund St., BRADFORD
West Yorkshire. BD5 0BJ
Tel: 01274 728421

ELLAND BUPA HOSPITAL — 4F **112**
Elland La., ELLAND
West Yorkshire. HX5 9EB
Tel: 01422 375577

Ellen Royde Health Centre — 4E **112**
Westgate, ELLAND
West Yorkshire. HX5 0BB
Tel: 01422 373647

Elms Mental Health Resource Centre, The — 5B **76**
55 Odsal Rd., BRADFORD
West Yorkshire. BD6 1PR
Tel: 01274 693161

Elmwood Health Centre — 1M **163**
Huddersfield Rd.,
Holmfirth,
HUDDERSFIELD. HD7 2TT
Tel: 01484 681777

Fartown Health Centre — 1N **131**
Spaines Rd.,
HUDDERSFIELD
HD2 2QA
Tel: 01484 536981

FIELDHEAD HOSPITAL — 2L **119**
Ouchthorpe La., WAKEFIELD
West Yorkshire. WF1 3SP
Tel: 01924 327000

Frank Swire Health Centre — 1M **91**
Nursery La., HALIFAX
West Yorkshire. HX3 5TE
Tel: 01422 355626

Gildersome Health Centre — 7G **78**
Finkle La., Morley,
LEEDS. LS27 7HL
Tel: 0113 2954030

HALIFAX GENERAL HOSPITAL — 9B **92**
Huddersfield Rd., HALIFAX
West Yorkshire. HX3 0PW
Tel: 01422 357171

Havercroft Health Centre — 1J **155**
Cow La., Havercroft,
WAKEFIELD
West Yorkshire. WF4 2AX
Tel: 01226 725555

Haworth Road Health Centre — 2J **57**
130 Haworth Rd., BRADFORD
West Yorkshire. BD9 6LL
Tel: 01274 491181

Hemsworth Health Centre — 3D **156**
Highfield Rd., Hemsworth,
PONTEFRACT
West Yorkshire. WF9 4DS
Tel: 01977 465600

HIGH ROYDS HOSPITAL — 6F **24**
Bradford Rd., Menston, ILKLEY
West Yorkshire. LS29 6AQ
Tel: 01943 876151

HOLME VALLEY MEMORIAL HOSPITAL — 1M **163**
Huddersfield Rd., Holmfirth.
HUDDERSFIELD. HD7 2TS
Tel: 01484 681711

Holmewood Health Centre — 2J **77**
Holme Wood Rd., BRADFORD
West Yorkshire. BD4 9EJ
Tel: 01274 681103

Holt Park Health Centre — 2J **43**
Holt Rd., LEEDS
LS16 7QD
Tel: 0113 2951855

HUDDERSFIELD NUFFIELD HOSPITAL,THE — 1K **131**
Birkby Lodge Rd.,
HUDDERSFIELD.
HD2 2BL
Tel: 01484 533131

HUDDERSFIELD ROYAL INFIRMARY — 2H **131**
Acre St., HUDDERSFIELD
HD3 3EA
Tel: 01484 422191

Hunslet Health Centre — 1G **81**
24 Church St., Hunslet
LEEDS. LS10 2PE
Tel: 0113 2771811

IDA & ROBERT ARTHINGTON HOSPITAL — 5J **43**
Hospital La., LEEDS
LS16 6QA
Tel: 0113 267 3411

Ilkley Health Centre — 6H **9**
Springs La., ILKLEY
West Yorkshire. LS29 8TH
Tel: 01943 608118

Keighley Health Centre — 1H **37**
Oakworth Rd., KEIGHLEY
West Yorkshire. BD21 1SA
Tel: 01535 606111

Kensington Street Health Centre — 6M **57**
Whitefield Pl., BRADFORD
West Yorkshire. BD8 9LB
Tel: 01274 495631

Kippax Health Centre — 3B **84**
Moorgate Dri., Kippax
LEEDS. LS25 7QT
Tel: 0113 2874427

Kirkburton Health Centre — 4L **149**
Shelley La., Kirkburton
HUDDERSFIELD. HD8 0SJ
Tel: 01484 602040

Kirkstall Health Centre — 2K **61**
15 Morris La., LEEDS
LS5 3DB
Tel: 0113 2951160

Kirkwood Hospice — 3E **132**
21 Albany Rd., Dalton,
HUDDERSFIELD. HD5 9UY
Tel: 01484 557900

Knottingley Health Centre — 9D **104**
Hazel Rd., KNOTTINGLEY
West Yorkshire. WF11 0LG
Tel: 01977 465500

Laura Mitchell Health Centre — 5B **92**
Great Albion St., HALIFAX
West Yorkshire. HX1 1YR
Tel: 01422 363541

LEEDS BUPA HOSPITAL — 8J **45**
Roundhay Hall, Jackson Av.,
LEEDS. LS8 1NT
Tel: 0113 2693939

LEEDS CHEST CLINIC — 6E **62**
74 New Briggate,
LEEDS. LS1 6PH
Tel: 0113 2951100

Leeds Dental Institute — 5C **62**
Clarendon Way,
LEEDS. LS2 9LU
Tel: 0113 2440111

LEEDS GENERAL INFIRMARY — 5D **62**
Great George St.,
LEEDS. LS1 3EX
Tel: 0113 243 2799

LEEDS ROAD HOSPITAL — 7F **58**
Leeds Rd., BRADFORD
West Yorkshire. BD3 9LH
Tel: 01274 494194

Liversedge Health Centre — 7M **95**
Valley Rd., LIVERSEDGE
West Yorkshire. WF15 6DF
Tel: 01924 516200

Luddenden Foot Health Centre — 5D **90**
Kershaw Dri., Luddenden Foot,
HALIFAX, West Yorkshire. HX2 6PD
Tel: 01422 882988

LYNFIELD MOUNT HOSPITAL — 4J **57**
Heights La., BRADFORD
West Yorkshire. BD9 6DP
Tel: 01274 494194

MALHAM HOUSE DAY HOSPITAL — 5C **62**
25 Hyde Ter., LEEDS. LS2 9LN
Tel: 0113 2926716

Manningham Health Centre — 5B **58**
Lumb La., BRADFORD
West Yorkshire. BD8 7SY
Tel: 01274 724298

Hospitals, Health Centres and Hospices

Manorlands (Sue Ryder) Hospice — 3C **54**
Keighley Rd., Oxenhope, KEIGHLEY
West Yorkshire. BD22 9HJ
Tel: 01535 642308

Marsden Health Centre — 5F **144**
Victoria St., Marsden
HUDDERSFIELD. HD7 6DF
Tel: 01484 844332

Martin House Hospice — 1E **32**
Grove Rd., Boston Spa,
WETHERBY, West Yorkshire.
LS23 6TX
Tel: 01937 844836

Meanwood Health Centre — 9B **44**
548 Meanwood Rd., LEEDS. LS6 4JN
Tel: 0113 2951350

METHLEY PARK HOSPITAL — 1H **101**
Methley La., Methley,
LEEDS. LS26 9HG
Tel: 01977 518518

Middlestown Health Centre — 3L **135**
Ramsey Cres., Middlestown,
WAKEFIELD, West Yorkshire.
WF4 4QQ
Tel: 01924 327700

MID-YORKSHIRE NUFFIELD HOSPITAL, THE — 7G **43**
Outwood La. Horsforth,
LEEDS. LS18 4HP
Tel: 0113 258 8756

Mill Hill Health Centre — 3E **132**
86 Dalton Grn. La.,
HUDDERSFIELD. HD5 9TS
Tel: 01484 319942

Morley Health Centre — 9K **79**
Corporation St., Morley,
LEEDS. LS27 9NB
Tel: 0113 2522051

Mytholmroyd Health Centre — 3M **89**
Thrush Hill Rd., HEBDEN BRIDGE
West Yorkshire. HX7 5AQ
Tel: 01422 884199

Netherton Health Centre — 4N **135**
Netherfield Place, Netherton,
WAKEFIELD, West Yorkshire. WF4 4LS
Tel: 01924 277716

New Cross Street Health Centre — 2B **76**
New Cross St., BRADFORD
West Yorkshire. BD5 7AW
Tel: 01274 731006

New Wortley Health Centre — 8A **62**
15 Green La., LEEDS. LS12 1JE
Tel: 0113 2310626

Normanton Health Centre — 2H **121**
Church La., NORMANTON
West Yorkshire. WF6 1AZ
Tel: 01924 327900

NORTHOWRAM HOSPITAL — 9F **74**
Hall La., HALIFAX
West Yorkshire. HX3 7SW
Tel: 01422 201101

Odsal Health Centre — 5B **76**
55 Odsal Rd., BRADFORD
West Yorkshire. BD6 1PR
Tel: 01274 674952

Oulton Health Centre — 7D **82**
Quarry Hill, Woodlesford,
LEEDS. LS26 8SZ
Tel: 0113 2821149

Overgate Hospice — 5C **112**
30 Hullen Edge Rd., ELLAND
West Yorkshire. HX5 0QY
Tel: 01422 379151

Oxley Road Health Centre — 8A **114**
68 Oxley Rd.,
HUDDERSFIELD. HD2 1NT
Tel: 01484 300391

Park Road Medical Centre — 9C **58**
Park Rd., BRADFORD
West Yorkshire. BD5 0SG
Tel: 01274 227575

PINDERFIELDS GENERAL HOSPITAL —2M **119**
Aberford Rd., WAKEFIELD
West Yorkshire. WF1 4DG
Tel: 01924 375217

PONTEFRACT GENERAL INFIRMARY — 3K **123**
Friarwood La., PONTEFRACT
West Yorkshire. WF8 1PL
Tel: 01977 600600

Prince of Wales Hospice — 3G **123**
Halfpenny La., PONTEFRACT
West Yorkshire. WF8 4BG
Tel: 01977 708868

Princess Royal Community Health Centre — 4K **131**
Greenhead Rd., HUDDERSFIELD. HD1 4EW
Tel: 01484 545411

Pudsey Health Centre — 7B **60**
18 Mulberry St., PUDSEY
West Yorkshire. LS28 7XP
Tel: 0113 2953200

Queensbury Health Centre — 5C **74**
Russell Rd., Queensbury, BRADFORD
West Yorkshire. BD13 2AG
Tel: 01274 882531

Rastrick Health Centre — 4L **113**
Chapel Cft., BRIGHOUSE
West Yorkshire. HD6 3NA
Tel: 01484 714688

Reevy Hill Health Centre — 5K **75**
50 Reevy Rd. W., BRADFORD
West Yorkshire. BD6 3LX
Tel: 01274 679605

Rothwell Health Centre — 8N **81**
Stone Brig La., Rothwell,
LEEDS. LS26 0UE
Tel: 0113 2820520

ROYAL HALIFAX INFIRMARY — 7A **92**
Free School La., HALIFAX
West Yorkshire. HX1 2YP
Tel: 01422 357222

ST CATHERINES HOSPITAL — 4A **58**
St Mary's Rd., BRADFORD
West Yorkshire. BD8 7QG
Tel: 01274 227599

St Gemma's Hospice — 5F **44**
333 Harrogate Rd.,
LEEDS. LS17 6QD
Tel: 0113 269 3231

ST JAMES'S UNIVERSITY HOSPITAL — 4H **63**
Beckett St., LEEDS. LS9 7TF
Tel: 0113 2433144

St John's Health Centre — 5N **91**
Lightowler Rd., HALIFAX
West Yorkshire. HX1 5NB
Tel: 01422 341611

ST LUKE'S HOSPITAL — 1B **76**
Little Horton La., BRADFORD
West Yorkshire. BD5 0NA
Tel: 01274 734744

ST LUKE'S HOSPITAL — 7J **131**
Blackmoorfoot Rd.,
HUDDERSFIELD. HD4 5RQ
Tel: 01484 654711

ST MARY'S HOSPITAL — 6J **61**
Greenhill Rd., LEEDS. LS12 3QE
Tel: 0113 2790121

Saint Street Health Centre — 1M **75**
Saint St., BRADFORD
West Yorkshire. BD7 4AB
Tel: 01274 521378

SEACROFT HOSPITAL — 5B **64**
York Rd. LEEDS. LS14 6UH
Tel: 0113 2648164

Sharlston Medical Centre — 8J **121**
Clifton Rd., Sharlston Common,
WAKEFIELD, West Yorkshire.
WF4 1AS
Tel: 01924 862738.

Shelf Health Centre — 7H **75**
Shelf Moor Rd., HALIFAX
West Yorkshire. HX3 7PQ
Tel: 01274 691159

Shepley Health Centre — 8J **149**
Fieldhead, Shepley,
HUDDERSFIELD. HD8 8DR
Tel: 01484 604989

Shipley Health Centre — 8M **39**
Alexandra Rd., SHIPLEY
West Yorkshire. BD18 3EG
Tel: 01274 595611

SHIPLEY HOSPITAL — 8M **39**
90 Kirkgate, SHIPLEY
West Yorkshire. BD18 3LT
Tel: 01274 773390

Skelmanthorpe Health Centre — 7D **150**
Commercial Rd., Skelmanthorpe
HUDDERSFIELD. HD8 9DA
Tel: 01484 863 403

Slaithwaite Health Centre — 9N **129**
New St., Slaithwaite,
HUDDERSFIELD. HD7 5AB
Tel: 01484 842479

South Elmsall Health Centre — 6M **157**
Little La., South Elmsall, PONTEFRACT
West Yorkshire. WF9 2NJ
Tel: 01977 465300

SOUTHMOOR HOSPITAL — 3D **156**
Southmoor Rd., Hemsworth,
PONTEFRACT, West Yorkshire.
WF9 4LU
Tel: 01977 465630

Stanley Health Centre — 7A **100**
Lake Lock Rd., Stanley, WAKEFIELD
West Yorkshire. WF3 4HS
Tel: 01924 822328

Steeton Health Centre — 3C **20**
Chapel Rd., Steeton, KEIGHLEY
West Yorkshire. BD20 6NU
Tel: 01535 65244

STONEY RIDGE HOSPITAL — 1H **57**
Stoney Ridge Rd., BINGLEY
West Yorkshire. BD16 1UL
Tel: 01274 495737

Sunny Bank Medical Centre — 2A **94**
Town Ga., Wyke, BRADFORD
West Yorkshire. BD12 9NG
Tel: 01274 424111

Thornton Health Centre — 8D **56**
Market St., Thornton, BRADFORD
West Yorkshire. BD13 3EY
Tel: 01274 833441

Vulcan Street Health Centre — 4H **77**
Vulcan St., BRADFORD
West Yorkshire. BD4 9QU
Tel: 01274 682082

Wakefield Hospice — 2N **119**
Aberford Rd., WAKEFIELD
West Yorkshire. WF4 4TS
Tel: 01924 387260

Westwood House — 4H **75**
Cooper La., BRADFORD
West Yorkshire. BD6 3NL
Tel: 01274 882001

WHARFEDALE GENERAL HOSPITAL — 7K **11**
Newall Carr Rd., OTLEY
West Yorkshire. LS21 2LY
Tel: 01943 465522

Wheatfields Hospice — 1A **62**
Grove Rd., Headingley,
LEEDS. LS6 2AE
Tel: 0113 278 7249

Wilsden Health Centre — 1B **56**
Townfield, Wilsden, BRADFORD
West Yorkshire. BD15 0HT
Tel: 01535 273227

Woodhouse Health Centre — 3D **62**
Woodhouse St., LEEDS. LS6 2SF
Tel: 0113 2951400

Woodside Health Centre — 7M **75**
Eaglesfield Dri., BRADFORD
West Yorkshire, BD6 2PR
Tel: 01274 675113

Woodsley Road Health Centre — 4B **62**
3 Woodsley Rd. LEEDS. LS6 1SG
Tel: 0113 2951240

Wrenthorpe Health Centre — 1G **119**
Wrenthorpe La., Wrenthorpe, WAKEFIELD
West Yorkshire, WF2 0NE
Tel: 01924 327545

Wrose Health Centre — 1D **58**
King's Rd., BRADFORD
West Yorkshire. BD2 1QG
Tel: 01274 633711

Yeadon Health Centre — 9N **25**
17 South Vw. Rd., Yeadon
LEEDS. LS19 7PS
Tel: 0113 2954280

YORKSHIRE CLINIC, THE — 8H **39**
Bradford Rd., BINGLEY
West Yorkshire. BD16 1TW
Tel: 01274 560311